Adolescence

An Introduction

Third Edition

Adolescence

An Introduction

John W. Santrock
University of Texas at Dallas

ⱳcb
Wm. C. Brown Publishers
Dubuque, Iowa

Book Team

Editor James M. McNeil
Developmental Editor Sandra E. Schmidt
Designer Mark D. Hantelmann
Production Editor Barbara Rowe Day
Photo Research Editor Michelle Oberhoffer
Permissions Editor Carla D. Arnold
Product Manager Marcia H. Stout

wcb group

Wm. C. Brown Chairman of the Board
Mark C. Falb President and Chief Executive Officer

wcb

Wm. C. Brown Publishers, College Division

G. Franklin Lewis Executive Vice-President, General Manager
E. F. Jogerst Vice-President, Cost Analyst
George Wm. Bergquist Editor in Chief
Beverly Kolz Director of Production
Chris C. Guzzardo Vice-President, Director of Sales and Marketing
Bob McLaughlin National Sales Manager
Marilyn A. Phelps Manager of Design
Julie A. Kennedy Production Editorial Manager
Faye M. Schilling Photo Research Manager

Cover photo by Keith Lanpher, photographer.

To Tracy and Jennifer, who, as they have matured, have helped me to appreciate the marvels of adolescent development.

Brief Contents

Expanded Contents

7

Peers, Friends, and Group Relations   260

8

Schools   308

12

Moral Development, Values, and Religion   486

13

Achievement, Careers, and Work   522

15

Problems and Disturbances in Adolescence and
the Nature of Abnormality   616

Preface

*T*his book is about you and it is about me. It is the scientific story of the transition from childhood to adulthood. This intriguing and complex story is written in a manner that I think you will find is both informative and enjoyable. You will see yourself as an adolescent and be stimulated to consider how those years influenced the type of person you have become today. You will be motivated to think about how childhood experiences might have influenced your adolescent years. And you will learn a great deal about the developing minds and behaviors of all adolescents, as well as about their unique, individual differences.

In 1981, in the preface to the first edition of this book, I wrote, "Scientific data are presented in an easy-to-read style and are freely applied to the real world of today's adolescent. Although emphasis is placed on scientific data throughout the book, it is my firm belief that science is anything but a dull, dreary affair." This tradition continued in the second edition of *Adolescence,* published in 1984, and it remains a hallmark of the third edition.

To The Instructor

The study of adolescence has come of age. Several days ago, I looked at the 1981 version of this text and compared it with the content in this third edition. When I put together the first edition in 1981, I remember frequently being frustrated by the lack of empirical research about topics I thought were important in understanding adolescent development. In the preface to the second edition in 1984, I wrote that I didn't realize that the first edition would need to be revised so

soon. The 1980s truly has involved an explosion of knowledge about adolescent development. While there still are many unresolved issues and unanswered questions, we are making significant scientific progress in understanding adolescent development. Because of the major advances in research inquiry, it was necessary to revise the second editon in the mid-1980s to an equal or greater degree as was required with the first edition in the early 1980s. As was true in the second edition, at least half of the material in this third edition is new. However, it is rewarding that much of the knowledge explosion we are witnessing in adolescent development fits within the conceptual framework already in place in *Adolescence.* For this reason, it was not necessary to add new sections or chapters in the third edition; the extensive changes occurred within chapters.

What is so new about the third edition of *Adolescence?* First, the text has been completely updated with new scientific information. Second, substantial improvements have been made in the organization and pedagogy within chapters.

Updating of Scientific Information

Adolescence is an exciting field of scientific inquiry. Still a very young science, it is one that has gained considerable respect in recent years. New research is being generated at a rapid pace. To capture the lively enthusiasm of this research inquiry, each chapter of the third edition has been completely rewritten to provide the latest research information. A brief look at each of the chapters clearly reveals some of the highlights of this updating.

Chapter 1: Introduction, History, and Issues

New material on inventionist views of adolescence has been added, and there is a stronger emphasis on historical factors in understanding adolescence.

Chapter 2: The Scientific Study of Adolescent Development: World Views, Theories, and Methods

The strong scientific orientation of the book is highlighted in this chapter. Half of the chapter is now devoted to methods, including ideas about measures, strategies of research design, and time span of inquiry.

Chapter 3: Biological Processes and Physical Development

Fascinating new research on the direct assessment of hormone levels and their association with adolescent adjustment has been added, as has a provocative discussion of the adolescent's brain, brain spurts, cognitive development, and education. New research on early and late maturation and an evaluation of on-time and off-time in pubertal development have been incorporated.

Chapter 4: Cognitive Development and Social Cognition

Substantial material has been added on the nature of adolescent cognition including intriguing ideas about changes in language development. There is much more coverage of the expanding field of social cognition, including recent ideas about egocentrism, perspective taking, and the personal fable.

Chapter 5: Information Processing and Intelligence

This new edition includes more exciting coverage of the information processing perspective. It includes a very provocative discussion of the role information processing plays in the education of adolescents, as well as a discussion of what the adolescent's mind can do that a computer cannot. Sternberg's ideas about how information processing can help us understand intelligence is accompanied by a discussion of the distinction between knowledge and process in cognition. Intriguing new ideas about social intelligence have been added.

Chapter 6: Family Processes and Parent–Adolescent Relationships

This chapter now includes a very contemporary discussion of issues in the study of family processes, including the construction of close relationships, the attachment and connectedness of adolescents to their parents, and the different family environments of adolescent siblings. There is extensive updating of research on latchkey experiences, divorce, and stepfamilies, including Wallerstein's ten-year-follow-up study.

Chapter 7: Peers, Friends, and Group Relations

New information on the coordinated world of family and peers, social knowledge and social information processing, and a discussion of intention cue detection as a factor in social skills have been added. Contemporary studies of adolescent friendships, and the links between clique membership and self-esteem are presented. Other new topics include the construction of dating relationships, and skill-streaming the adolescent with social inadequacies.

Chapter 8: Schools

A provocative discussion of the purpose of schools for adolescents includes Lipsitz's studies of effective schools. Updated scientific information and a discussion of the issues involved in the transition from elementary school to middle or junior high school are presented.

Chapter 9: Culture

The chapter includes more extensive information about the nature of neighborhood settings, the "beeper" research of Csikszentmihalyi and Larson, and Bronfenbrenner's ecological model of culture. We discuss the Jigsaw Classroom, and offer expanded coverage of ethnic and social class effects on adolescent development.

Chapter 10: The Self and Identity

This chapter contains new information about the distinction between "I" and "me" in understanding the self, the role of information processing in self-development, and Selman's views of self-development. We have extensively updated the coverage of identity development, including an overview of the complex aspects of Erikson's theory. There is a new evaluation of the latest research on sex differences and similarities in identity development. This chapter includes new research focused on the role of individuation and connectedness in family relationships in predicting identity development, and recent studies on the nature of intimacy in adolescence.

Chapter 11: Sex Roles and Sexuality

The section on sex roles and androgyny was completely rewritten, with an emphasis on making sense out of the huge volume of research on androgyny that has been generated in the last few years. New information on sexism in language and the use of computers by females is presented, along with comments about the role of personal fables in understanding adolescent pregnancy. Coverage of adolescent attitudes about sexuality has been expanded and updated.

Chapter 12: Moral Development, Values, and Religion

Kohlberg's research is substantially updated, and we have added new ideas about the nature of transactive discussion in peer groups and Gilligan's care perspective on moral development. There is also new material on the nature of social conventional reasoning.

Chapter 13: Achievement, Careers, and Work

Much of the achievement section was rewritten, incorporating an increased emphasis on understanding internal-external aspects of motivation, attribution theory, and delay of gratification, including Mischel's recent research on delay of gratification and adjustment during adolescence. There is a new evaluation of sex differences and similarities in achievement, with an emphasis on self-assertion and integration. New research on career planning and knowledge of educational requirements as well as redirecting the career paths of talented adolescent females has been included.

Chapter 14: Drugs, Alcohol, and Delinquency

This chapter includes very recent updating of data on drug use by adolescents, based on the data collected by the University of Michigan Institute of Social Research, and an intriguing description of agent, environment, and host in substance abuse. It also includes a provocative discussion of the relationship between family processes and delinquency: cause, correlate, or consequence.

Chapter 15: Problems and Disturbances in Adolescence, and the Nature of Abnormality

This chapter includes a new section on the important issue of continuity–discontinuity in disorders and offers expanded coverage of adolescent depression. Very recent research on family processes, and more information about adolescent suicide have been added.

Improved Organization and Pedagogy within Chapters

One of the most important features of the third edition of *Adolescence* is the improved organization and pedagogy within chapters. The learning aids have been carefully designed to enhance student learning and to provide an organized, structured presentation of concepts and information. Each chapter begins with an **Outline** and a **Preview** of major topics. A very special, innovative feature of the third edition of *Adolescence* is called **Concept Table,** which appears two to three times in each chapter. It is an organizational device that activates memory of major topics or key topics discussed, and shows how important concepts are related. The Concept Tables also enhance student comprehension of complex concepts and ideas, allowing a student to "get a handle" on such ideas before reaching the end of the chapter. As the study of adolescence has increased, more information must be put into a book for comprehensive coverage of topics to be accomplished. The Concept Table is the key pedagogical device that allows such comprehensive coverage to be carried out without overwhelming the student like so many other books do. Then, at the end of each chapter, students are provided with a functional **Summary** that stimulates them to put all of the pieces of the chapter together.

The extensive organization just described is a key pedagogical feature of the third edition of the book. However, there are other learning aids as well. Each chapter opens with a **Prologue,** an easy-to-read discussion of an aspect of adolescence related to some chapter topic. For example, Chapter 4 opens with "Sandy's Personal Fable," and Chapter 8 begins with "From No More 'What If' Questions to Author's Week." In addition to the prologues, each chapter has a number of boxes called Perspective on Adolescent Development, which provide the student with other points of view, applications, or detailed research information. In particular, there has been an increase in the number of boxes devoted to showing students how research on adolescence is actually carried out. In this way, students get a feel for how the procedures of a study actually are conducted and discover how we obtain scientific information. **Key Terms** are boldfaced in the text, listed at the end of each chapter, and defined in a page-referenced **Glossary** at the end of the book. **Suggested Readings** also appear at the end of each chapter.

To The Student: How to Profit From the Pedagogy

Adolescence, third edition, contains many pedagogical, or learning, devices that have been carefully designed to make your learning more efficient. Before starting each chapter, read the **Outline,** which organizes the most important ideas of the chapter. By studying the outline

for a few minutes before beginning the chapter, you will get an advanced look at the content of the chapter and an understanding of how major topics and subtopics are related. Then read the chapter **Prologue,** a short essay designed to increase your interest in the subject matter of the chapter and to motivate you to read further. The final introductory part of each chapter is called the **Preview.** Read this useful, brief overview to prepare yourself for the major topics of the chapter.

As you move through the interior of the chapter, two to three times you will come across **Concept Tables.** They serve the dual purpose of reinforcing what you already have read and alerting you to main topics you now should understand. Go through each of these tables to review major features, concepts, and their characteristics and descriptions. If some of these concepts still seem foreign to you, go back and reread those sections of the chapter. A number of times in each chapter you will come across boldfaced **Key Terms,** which should alert you to the fact that you should learn the definition of the term. It also signals you that the term is defined in the page-referenced **Glossary** at the end of the book.

At the end of the chapter, read the **Summary.** The summary provides a review of the major topics and concepts of the entire chapter. By the time you have read the summary, you should have a feel for the overall structure of the chapter and how all of the pieces fit together. You also will find the **Key Terms** listed with page references at the end of the chapter. If a term is not familiar to you, go back to its appearance in the chapter and review the term. Finally, read the section called **Suggested Readings.** You will find a combination of articles and books listed and briefly discussed, some of which are more detailed, scientific reading than this text, others that are lighter, more personal pieces. Both types of articles should further your understanding of the exciting field of adolescence.

Instructional and Learning Aids

A helpful **Instructor's Manual** has been prepared by Jay B. Pozner, Jackson Community College. The Instructor's Manual includes, for each chapter, page-referenced learning objectives, key terms, a detailed chapter summary, discussion questions, classroom activities, and student activities. The Instructor's Manual also includes a comprehensive Test Item File, prepared by Gregory T. Fouts, University of Calgary. The **Test Item File** offers more than 800 high-quality multiple choice and eighty essay questions. Every objective test item is page-referenced, coded by difficulty level, and identified as knowledge, conceptual, or applied.

All test items are available on **wcb TestPak,** the free, computerized testing service available to adopters of *Adolescence*. The call-in/mail-in service offers a test master, a student answer sheet, and an answer key within two working days of receipt of the instructor's request. TestPak is also available for instructors who want to use their Apple IIc, or IBM PC microcomputer system to create their own tests. Upon adoption of *Adolescence* and upon request, the instructor will receive the program diskettes, and user's guide. With these, the instructor will be able to create tests, answer sheets, and answer keys. The program allows for adding, deleting, or modifying test questions. No programming experience is necessary.

Acknowledgments

This text is the product of many hands and minds. The publisher, Wm. C. Brown, has continued to provide excellent support for the book. James McNeil, Editor, and Sandy Schmidt, Senior Developmental Editor, have a contagious enthusiasm about *Adolescence*. I very much have enjoyed working with them on this project and continue to be impressed by their professional judgments of what a book should be. Barbara Rowe Day has spent long hours overseeing the production of *Adolescence*—I appreciate her careful work with the manuscript. Mark Hantelmann, Designer, has provided creative touches that make the book more attractive. Michelle Oberhoffer, Photo Research Editor, made special efforts to track down meaningful and effective photographs. And, Carla Arnold efficiently obtained permissions. Thanks also go to Jay B. Pozner, who prepared the Instructor's Manual and Student Study Guide, to Gregory T. Fouts, who prepared the Test Item File, and to Nancy Martens for putting together the glossary of the text.

The reviewers of the third edition of *Adolescence* were special and provided expertise on what to keep in, what to throw out, and what to add. I am indebted to their constructive criticism:

Fredda Blanchard-Fields, Louisiana State University
James A. Doyle, Roane State Community College
Richard M. Ehlenz, Lakewood Community College
Martin E. Ford, Stanford University
Gregory T. Fouts, University of Calgary
Charles L. Fry, University of Virginia
Beverly Jennings, University of Colorado–Denver
Emmett C. Lampkin, Scott Community College
Royal Louis Lange, Ellsworth Community College
Daniel K. Lapsley, University of Notre Dame
Susan McCammon, East Carolina University
Joseph G. Marrone, Siena College
Vern Tyler, Western Washington University

I would like to also thank the reviewers of the first edition of *Adolescence:* Frances Harnick, University of New Mexico, Indian Children's Program, and Lovelace-Bataan Pediatric Clinic; Robert Bornstein, Miami University; Toni E. Santmire, University of Nebraska; and Lynn F. Katz, Univeristy of Pittsburgh; and of the second edition: Martin E. Ford, Stanford University; B. Jo Hailey, University of Southern Mississippi; June V. Irving, Ball State University; Alfred L. Karlson, University of Massachusetts–Amherst; E. L. McGarry, California State University–Fullerton; John J. Mirich, Metropolitan State College; Anne Robertson, University of Wisconsin–Milwaukee; Douglas Sawin, University of Texas; and Carolyn L. Williams, University of Minnesota.

A final note of special thanks goes to my family, particularly my two daughters, Tracy, 20, and Jennifer, 17. When I wrote the first edition of this book, they were just beginning adolescence and now after two more editions, they are competently making the transition into adulthood. Through the past decade they have helped me to understand the complexities, subtleties, and humaneness of this fascinating period of life.

Adolescence

An Introduction

Part 1

Perspective on Adolescent Development

Brian Jordan is ten years old and in the fifth grade. He is four feet, seven inches tall and weighs seventy pounds. Kim Krane sits next to him at school and has started to show an interest in him. Last week at recess she even grabbed him on the playground and kissed him in front of his two best friends. Was Brian ever embarrassed! His buddies still tease him about it. He told Kim to never try to kiss him again. She just giggled and told him he was cute. What has happened to Kim? Last year when she was in the fourth grade she didn't have very much interest in boys, but now she is starting to look at them in a different light.

Looking at Kim, we can easily tell that she is starting to show some signs of puberty—her breasts are developing noticeably and she has started to wear a training bra, although she has not had her first period yet. Brian has not started puberty yet—he has no pubic or facial hair, his voice hasn't changed, and his height and weight have only shown very gradual increases during the last several years. When Kim kissed him, she even had to bend down because she is four inches taller than Brian and she outweighs him by fifteen pounds. Nonetheless, Brian still feels he is a lot stronger than Kim and he is more physically aggressive than she is—that is, other than when it comes to making passes at somebody.

Cognitively, both Brian and Kim are what psychologists call concrete thinkers—that is, much of their thought is about their actual experiences, and they don't yet think very abstractly. Many of their thoughts are about momentary, concrete experiences. For example, they are incapable of imagining a community or a society radically different from the one they now live in.

When we look at Kim and Brian's relationships with their parents and peers, we find that while they sometimes have differing ideas from those of their parents, there doesn't seem to be much parent-child conflict. Both Kim and Brian have shown an interest in spending more time with their peers in the last several years, and much of that time is spent with same-sex peers, although Kim has already started to show a stronger opposite-sex interest. The culture Brian and Kim live in is suburban, southern, American, and middle-class. Both Brian and Kim are achievement-oriented children and do well in school, although Kim's parents feel she has started to daydream too much lately and Brian's parents sometimes feel he is not serious enough about school.

When we enter the lives of Brian and Kim at the age of thirteen, we find that some significant changes have occurred. Gradually, over the last year, Brian has entered puberty. He now has some pubic hair, his voice is getting deeper, and he is five feet, one inch tall and weighs ninety-five pounds. Last week he woke up somewhat surprised because he had his first wet dream. Also last week, he went to an eighth-grade boy–girl party at one of his best friend's homes. At this time, Brian is showing a very strong interest in the opposite sex. Unfortunately, the girl he likes doesn't seem to like him as much as he likes her. Every time he tries to talk to her she abruptly walks away—he thinks maybe it is because he is so short.

Kim, at the age of thirteen, is much further into puberty than Brian. She had her first period sixteen months ago, and her breasts are almost fully developed. She no longer is interested in Brian—instead she is trying to interest the captain of the junior high football team, a ninth grader, in asking her to the homecoming dance. So far, she hasn't been successful, but she is working on it. Last night, for example, one of her girl friends called the boy on the phone and told him how much Kim likes him.

Cognitively, there are several changes that seem to have just begun for Brian and Kim. They have started to think in more abstract ways, not always relying on concrete experiences for generating thoughts, and they are more organized problem solvers than they were in the fifth grade. Both seem to be somewhat egocentric—for example, they often think that people are looking at them. The other day, Kim walked into a restaurant with her parents and said, "Oh, no, my hair. What can I do?" When her parents asked what was the matter, she replied, "Everybody is looking at me—look

. . . not quite children and certainly not adults, in many ways privileged, wielding unprecedented economic power as consumers of clothing, entertainment, and other amenities, the object of a peculiar blend of tenderness, indulgence, distrust, hostility, moving through a seemingly endless course of "preparation for life". . . , playing furiously at 'adult' games but resolutely confined to a society of their own peers and excluded from serious and responsible participation in the world of their elders . . . a few years ago it occurred to me that when I was a teenager, in the early depression years, there were no teenagers! The teenager has sneaked up on us in our own lifetime, and yet it seems to us that he always has been with us. . . . The teenager had not yet been invented (though, and) there did not yet exist a special class of beings, bounded in a certain way . . . not quite children and certainly not adults.

Source: A. K. Cohen, 1964

at this hair, it just won't stay down." Kim had just walked by a mirror at the entrance of the restaurant and checked her appearance.

Brian and Kim and their parents all agree that parent–adolescent conflict seems to be greater than was the case when Brian and Kim were in the fifth grade. Brian's parents say that he just doesn't seem to want to listen to them anymore, and Kim's mother says that she has a hard time taking the rude comments Kim makes about her. Both Brian and Kim have shown a stronger push for independence from their parents than they did three years ago, and their parents seem to be having a little bit of a tough time accepting it—their parents seem to want them to conform to their adult standards. Nonetheless, the parent–adolescent conflict we find between Brian and Kim and their parents has not even come close to the point of being pathological; it has just increased in the last year or so.

While Brian and Kim had shown some increased interest in peers during the latter part of the elementary school years, now they seem to want to spend just about all of their free time with their peers. Indeed, they spend a lot of time during the week thinking about what they can do with their friends on the weekends.

At the age of seventeen Brian and Kim are seniors, and both have already sent in their applications to several colleges and universities. Brian finally began to grow as much as he wanted to; by the time he was fifteen he was five feet, eleven inches tall and weighed 135 pounds. Since then he hasn't grown any more but he has put on ten more pounds. Brain is now much more muscular than he was in the eighth grade, and girls no longer are taller than he is—to his relief. Kim is still five feet, one inch tall, but she has gained fifteen pounds and now weighs 115 pounds. Both Brian and Kim think a lot about their bodies, but it doesn't preoccupy their thoughts as much as was true when they were in the eighth grade. Both Brian and Kim have come very close to having sexual intercourse with the people they are going steady with, but so far they have not. Kim says that it is getting harder and harder to refrain from having sex with Bob, whom she has been dating for about fourteen months now.

Cognitively, both Brian and Kim, at the age of seventeen, are more advanced thinkers than they were in the junior high school years. Their thoughts have become even more abstract and they engage more frequently in extended speculation about what their lives are going to be like in the future, their ideals and goals, and about what an idealistic world would be like. As part of their concern for the future, they have begun to think much more seriously about the kinds of occupations they are going to pursue. Kim is debating whether she will get married after high school or pursue a college degree. Recently, she has entertained the possibility of doing both. Brian is not sure what he wants to do with his life, but it's not because he hasn't thought about it. He has continued to do well in school and has a job in a brokerage office as a "gopher," running errands for the brokers.

Both Brian and Kim feel their relationships with their parents have cooled down somewhat from earlier adolescence, and both seem to think more independently from both their parents and their peers. Still, they retain close ties to both their parents and their peers, spending more and more time with their friends but still being monitored and influenced by their parents. An overriding concern for both Brian and Kim is the development of an identity, developing a sense of who they are, what they are all about, and what they are going to do with their lives.

You have just been introduced to Brian Jordan and Kim Krane. In some ways they are like all adolescents, and yet in other ways each is like no other adolescent. One of the goals of this book is to point out the communalities, exceptions, and individual variations in adolescent development. Brian and Kim are but two of the more than dozen adolescents you will be introduced to at the beginning of each section of this book. As you read the descriptions of adolescents in the Part openers, keep in mind that there is a great deal of individual variation as well as some common themes among adolescents.

Chapter · 1

Introduction, History, and Issues

Why don't you grow up?

If I said it to them once I said it a million times. Is it my imagination, or have I spent a lifetime shutting refrigerator doors, emptying nose tissue from pants pockets before washing, writing checks for milk, picking up wet towels and finding library books in the clothes hamper?

Mr. Matterling said, "Parenting is loving." (What did he know? He was an old Child Psychology teacher who didn't have any children. He only had twenty-two guppies and two catfish to clean the bowl.) How I wish that for one day I could teach Mr. Matterling's class. How I would like to tell him it's more than loving. More than clean gravel. More than eating the ones you don't like.

Parenting is frustration that you have to see to believe. Would I have ever imagined there would be whole days when I didn't have time to comb my hair? Mornings after a slumber party when I looked like Margaret Mead with a migraine? Could I have ever comprehended that something so simple, so beautiful and so uncomplicated as a[n] [adolescent] could drive you to shout, "We are a family and you're a part of this family and by God, you're going to spend a Friday night with us having a good time if we have to chain you to the bed!"

And a plaintive voice within me sighed, "Why don't you grow up!"

Parenting is fearful, Mr. Matterling. You don't know how fearful until you sit next to your son on his maiden voyage behind the wheel of your car and hear him say, "My Driver's Ed teacher says I've got only one problem and that's every time I meet a car I pass over the center line."

And you worry. I worried when they stayed home. . . . I worried when they dated a lot. ("They're not meditating in the Christian Science reading room until 2 A.M., Ed.") I worried when they didn't date ("Maybe we should try a sixteenth of an inch padding.")

I worried when their grades were bad. ("He won't be able to get into karate school with those marks.") I worried when their grades were good. ("So swing a little. You wanta spend the rest of your life reading William F. Buckley and basting your acne?")

I worried when they got a job. ("She looks so tired, and besides it could bring back her asthma attacks.") I worried when they didn't get a job. ("Mark my word, he'll take after your brother, Wesley, who didn't get a paper route until he was thirty-three.")

And a tired voice within me persisted, "Why don't you grow up?". . .

This half-child, half-adult groping miserably to weigh life's inconsistencies, hypocrisy, instant independence, advice, rules, and responsibilities.

The blind date that never showed. The captaincy that went to the best friend. The college reject, the drill team have-nots, the class office also-rans, the honors that went to someone else. And they turned to me for an answer. . . .

And there were joys. Moments of closeness . . . an awkward hug; a look in the semidarkness as you turned off the test pattern as they slept. The pride of seeing them stand up when older people entered the room and saying, "Yes, sir," and "No, ma'am," without your holding a cue card in front of them. The strange, warm feeling of seeing them pick up a baby and seeing a wistfulness in their faces that I have never seen before. . . .

I shall never forgive Mr. Matterling for not warning me of the times of panic. It's not time yet. It can't be. I'm not finished. I had all the teaching and discipline and the socks to pick up and the buttons to sew on and those lousy meal worms to feed the lizard every day . . . there was no time for loving. That's what it's all about, isn't it? Did they ever know I smiled? Did they ever understand my tears? Did I talk too much? Did I say too little? Did I ever look at them and really see them? Do I know them at all? Or was it all a lifetime of "Why don't you grow up? . . ."

Source: Bombeck, E., and Keane, B. Just wait till you have children of your own. New York: Fawcett/Crest, 1971.

Preview

Adolescent-parent relationships are clearly an important part of every adolescent's development. This chapter will provide an introduction and overview of adolescent development. First, we begin by asking: what are some of the important things that parents, educators, and scientists want to know about adolescence? Then, we survey the rather extensive historical background of adolescence. Next, we consider the major issues that interest scientists who study adolescent development. Finally, we describe the periods and processes of development, and preview the organization of the text.

Parents, Educators, and Scientists: What They Want to Know about Adolescents

What do you think your parents would have liked to know about adolescent development as they reared you? What do your teachers and scientists want to know about you? They all would have liked to know the most effective ways adults can deal with adolescents.

The Interests of Parents

You have lived through adolescence. I once was an adolescent. No one else experienced adolescence in quite the same way you or I did—your thoughts, feelings, and actions during your adolescent years, like mine, were unique. But we also encountered and handled some experiences in the same ways during adolescence. In high school, we learned many of the same skills that other students learned and grew to care about the same things others cared about. Peers were important to us. And, at one time or another, we probably felt that our parents had no idea what we were all about.

Not only did we feel that our parents misunderstood us, but our parents felt that we misunderstood them, as well. Parents want to know why adolescents have such mercurial moods—happy one moment, sad the next. They want to know why their teenagers talk back to them and challenge their rules and values. They want to know what parenting strategies will help them rear a psychologically healthy, competent adolescent who likely will become a mature adult. Should they be authoritarian or permissive in dealing with their adolescents? And what should they do when their adolescents increasingly rely on peers to influence their decisions—sometimes peers who have backgrounds and standards the parents detest? Parents worry that their adolescent will have a drinking problem, a smoking problem, take drugs, have sexual intercourse too early, or do poorly in school. They want to know if the situations they are encountering with their adolescents are unique, or if other parents are experiencing the same difficulties and frustrations with their youth.

The Interests of Educators

Educators, as well as parents, have a strong interest in trying to understand adolescents. Adolescents spend a large part of their day at school. What is the best way to teach English to a thirteen-year-old or biology to a sixteen-year-old? What can educators change about the nature of today's schools that will foster the development of social as well as intellectual competence in adolescents? What can they do in our schools to direct adolescents toward careers that best suit their abilities and desires? And teachers want to know the best strategies for instructing adolescents—for example, should they be more directive or let students be more active in classroom decision making?

The Interests of Scientists

Scientists, as well as parents and educators, are interested in adolescents. They want to know how biological heritage and individual environments influence adolescent behavior. Do the genes the adolescents inherited some fifteen years before still influence how they act, feel, and think? What aspects of family life, peer interaction, school experiences, and cultural standards cause adolescents to become responsible or irresponsible socially?

Source: © 1986, Washington Post Writer's Group, reprinted with permission.

In answer to these and other questions, scientists develop theories about adolescents. These theories help them to explain why adolescents behave in particular ways, whether they will behave the same way in other circumstances, and what their behavior will be like in the future.

Foremost among the interests of scientists who study adolescents is finding out if there is something unique about adolescents that sets them apart from children and adults. Does the fifteen-year-old think differently than the eight-year-old? Does the sixteen-year-old interact differently with her parents than the ten-year-old? Does the seventeen-year-old view himself differently than the twenty-three-year-old? Do adolescents have problems that are not found at other points in development? (For example, consider premarital sex and delinquency.)

Not only are scientists interested in what ways adolescents are different from children and adults, they also are intrigued by how adolescents might be similar to them. Further, in thinking about similarities, scientists are interested in how all adolescents might be similar to each other in some ways yet different in others. Later in this chapter, we will explore the important issue of individual differences.

In their concern for developing a clear demarcation between the child and the adolescent, and between the adolescent and the adult, scientists have debated whether it is appropriate to describe adolescence as a *stage* of development. Does the child's biological, so-

cial, and cognitive functioning undergo dramatic transformations at the onset of adolescence and does something similar occur at the end of adolescence? Or, by contrast, is the child's progress to adolescence smooth (or devoid of abrupt transition) and the adolescent's change to adulthood likewise? Interest in evaluating the unique and stagelike properties of adolescence has led scientists to study youth in a variety of environmental circumstances—adolescents from different historical time periods are compared, as are adolescents who grow up in very different cultures.

Now that we have considered the interests that parents, educators, and scientists have in adolescents, we turn our attention to a historical perspective on adolescence. You will discover that a scientific interest in adolescence developed rather late in history.

Historical Perspective: From Miniature Adults to the Adolescent Generalization Gap

Our journey through history to determine how adolescents were viewed at different times is a long one. We begin by studying how adolescents were viewed by early Greeks, and during the Middle Ages and the Renaissance. Then, we investigate the lives of adolescents in the early years of America and, subsequently, what has been called the period of adolescence. We conclude this historical overview with a discussion of how easy it is to stereotype the adolescents of any era.

The Greeks

An interest in adolescence can be traced to early Greece. Both Plato and Aristotle commented about the nature of youth in their culture.

Plato

In the *Republic* (1921 translation), Plato described three facets of human development (or as he called it, the "soul"): desire, spirit, and reason. According to Plato, reason, the highest of the facets, does not develop in childhood, but rather first appears in most individuals at about the age period we call adolescence today. Plato argued that since reason does not mature in childhood, the education of children should focus on music and sports. But the onset of rational thought in adolescence requires a change in the educational curricula—at that point, sports and music should be replaced by science and mathematics, in Plato's view.

Plato believed that in the early years of childhood, character, not intellect, should be developed. Even though Plato stressed the importance of early experience in the formation of character, he nonetheless pointed out that experiences in later years could modify character. Arguments about the importance of early experience in human development are still prevalent today. Do the first few years of life determine the adolescent's or adult's personality? Are later experiences in adolescence just as important in forming and shaping personality as experiences in the early years?

Aristotle

For Aristotle (1941 translation), the most important aspect of the age period we call adolescence is the development of the ability to choose. This self-determination becomes the hallmark of maturity in Aristotle's view. Aristotle viewed the individual at the onset of youth as unstable and impatient, lacking the self-control to develop into a mature person.

Aristotle was one of the first individuals to provide specific time periods for stages of human development. He defined three stages: infancy, the first seven years of life; boyhood, age seven to puberty; and young manhood, puberty to age twenty-one. According to Aristotle, then, from puberty to age twenty-one, youth need to replace their lack of self-control with self-determination. This view of adolescence is not unlike some of our current views, as we use labels like independence, identity, and career choice.

The Middle Ages and the Renaissance

Society's view of adolescence changed considerably during the Middle Ages. Subsequently, during the Renaissance, Rousseau offered a more enlightened view of adolescent development.

The Middle Ages

From the time of Aristotle and Plato through the sixteenth century, knowledge about human development actually took a step backward. It was during this time period that the view of the child as a miniature adult was dominant. Children and adolescents were believed to entertain the same interests as adults. And, since they were simply miniature adults, they were treated as such, with strict, harsh discipline. In the Middle Ages (or Dark Ages, as they sometimes are referred to), neither the adolescent nor the child was given status apart from the adult (Muuss, 1975).

Rousseau

Jean Jacques Rousseau, a French philosopher who lived in the eighteenth century, did more than any other individual to restore the belief that a child is not the same as an adult. In *Emile* (1911 translation), Rousseau argued that treating the child like a miniature adult is not appropriate and is potentially harmful. Rousseau believed that children up until the age of twelve or so should be free of adult restrictions and allowed to experience their world naturally, rather than having rigid regulations imposed on them.

Rousseau, like Aristotle and Plato, believed that development in childhood and adolescence occurs in a series of stages. From Rousseau's perspective, the four stages of development are:

Infancy (the first four to five years). The infant is much like an animal with strong physical needs, and the child is hedonistic (dominated by pleasure and pain).

Savage (five to twelve years). During this time, sensory development is most important. Sensory experiences such as play, sports, and games should be the focus of education. Like Aristotle, Rousseau argued that reason had not developed by the end of this time period.

Stage 3 (twelve to fifteen years). Reason and self-consciousness develop during this stage, along with an abundance of physical energy. Curiosity should be encouraged in the education of twelve-to-fifteen-year-olds by providing a variety of exploratory activities. According to Rousseau, *Robinson Crusoe* is the book to read during this stage of human development because it includes insightful ideas about curiosity and exploratory behavior.

Stage 4 (fifteen to twenty years). The individual begins to mature emotionally during this time period—interest in others replaces selfishness. Virtues and morals also appear at this point in development.

Rousseau, then, helped to restore the belief that development is stratified, or subject to distinct phases. But his ideas about adolescence were speculative. Other individuals in the nineteenth and twentieth centuries had to bridge the gap between the ideas of philosophers and the empirical approach of scientists (Muuss, 1975).

Adolescence in the Early Years of America

Have adolescents of different eras always had the same interests? Have adolescents always experienced the same kind of academic, work, and family environments as they do today? Today's adolescents spend far more time in school than at work, in structured rather than unstructured environments, and in sessions with their agemates than their counterparts of the 1800s and early 1900s did. Let's look more closely at two time periods in the history of America and discover what adolescence was like in each time as described by Joseph Kett (1977) in his book, *Rites of Passage*.

The Early Republic, 1790–1840

The migration of young people from the farms to urban life began during this time. School opportunities became a reality, and career choices grew more varied. However, increasing disorderliness and violence characterized the society.

Work apprenticeships took up much of the day for many adolescent boys, with some apprentices beginning as early as the age of twelve, others as late as sixteen or seventeen. Some children left home to become servants even at the age of eight or nine. Many adolescents remained dependent on their families while they engaged in apprentice work experiences. Ages twenty to twenty-five were then usually filled with indecision. But as in most eras, there were exceptions to this generalization—for example, the man Francis Lieber wrote about in his diary:

Story from real life. I arrived here in October, 1835.
In January, 1836, W _____ and another student were expelled from college on account of a duel. Since that time W _____ has:
First: Shot at this antagonist in the streets of Charleston.
Second: Studied (?) law with Mr. DeSaussure in Charleston.
Third: Married.
Fourth: Been admitted to the Bar.
Fifth: Imprisoned for two months in the above shooting.

Sixth: Become father of fine girl.
Seventh: Practiced law for some time.
Eighth: Been elected a member of the legislature.
Now he is only twenty-two years old. What a
state of society this requires and must produce
. . . (Perry, 1882, as described in Kett, 1977).

Approaching the Age of Adolescence, 1840–1900

Perhaps the most important period within this time
frame was the era from 1880 to 1900. A tremendous
gap in economic opportunities developed between lower
class and middle-class adolescents. Middle-class parents were pressed into selecting child-rearing orientations that would ensure the successful placement of
their youth in jobs. These child-rearing practices encouraged the adolescent to become passive and conform to societal standards.

To capitalize on the new jobs created by the industrial revolution, youth had to stay in school longer
and even go on to college. Delay of gratification and
self-restraint became behaviors that were encouraged
by parents who saw that going to school longer and
studying harder meant greater returns for their adolescents in the future.

While college was becoming more of a reality for
many youth, it mainly was open to middle-class, but
not to lower-class, adolescents. Similarly, the youth
groups that developed as part of school and church activities were essentially middle-class in nature.

The conformity to adult leadership in most of the
youth groups coincided with the general orientation toward adolescents at this time in America: adults know
what is right; do what they tell you, and you'll get
somewhere someday.

The Period of Adolescence: 1900 to the Present

The end of the nineteenth century and the early part
of the twentieth century represented an important period in the invention of the concept we now call adolescence. And there were subsequent changes
adolescents experienced later in the twentieth century
that influenced their lives in substantial ways.

The Turn of the Century

Between 1890 and 1920 a cadre of psychologists, urban
reformers, educators, youth workers, and counselors
began to mold the concept of adolescence. At this time,
young people, especially boys, no longer were viewed
as decadent problem causers, but instead were seen as
increasingly passive and vulnerable—qualities previously associated only with the adolescent female. When
G. Stanley Hall's book on adolescence was published
in 1904, it played a major role in restructuring thinking
about adolescents. Hall was saying that while many
adolescents appear to be passive, they are experiencing
considerable turmoil within.

Norms of behavior for adolescents began to be developed by educators, counselors, and psychologists.
The storm-and-stress concept that Hall had created influenced these norms considerably. As a result, adults
attempted to impose conformity and passivity on adolescents in the 1900–1920 period. Examples of this
conformity can be observed in the encouragement of
school spirit, loyalty, and hero worship on athletic
teams.

G. Stanley Hall

Most historians label G. Stanley Hall (1844–1924) the
father of the scientific study of adolescence. Hall's ideas
were published in the two-volume set, *Adolescence,* in
1904 (for a sample of what the first academic text on
adolescence was like, read Perspective on Adolescent
Development 1.1).

Charles Darwin, the famous evolutionary theorist,
had a tremendous impact on Hall's thinking. Hall applied the scientific, biological aspects of Darwin's views
to the study of adolescent development. He believed that
all development is controlled by genetically determined physiological factors. Environmental influences
on development were minimized in his view, particularly in infancy and childhood. Hall did acknowledge

*H*all's two-volume set, published in 1904, included the following chapters:

Volume I

Chapter

1 Growth in Height and Weight
2 Growth of Parts and Organs During Adolescence
3 Growth of Motor Power and Function
4 Diseases of Body and Mind
5 Juvenile Faults, Immoralities, and Crimes
6 Sexual Development: Its Dangers and Hygiene in Boys
7 Periodicity
8 Adolescence in Literature, Biography, and History

Volume II

Chapter

9 Changes in the Sense and Voice
10 Evolution and the Feelings and Instincts Characteristic of Normal Adolescence
11 Adolescent Love
12 Adolescent Feelings toward Nature and a New Education in Science
13 Savage Public Initiations, Classical Ideals and Customs, and Church Confirmations
14 The Adolescent Psychology of Conversion
15 Social Instincts and Institutions
16 Intellectual Development and Education
17 Adolescent Girls and their Education
18 Ethnic Psychology and Pedagogy, or Adolescent Races and their Treatment

Hall's strong emphasis on the biological basis of adolescence can be seen in the large number of chapters on physical growth, instincts, evolution, and periodicity. His concern for education also is evident, as is his interest in religion. Further insight into Hall's concept of adolescence can be gleaned from his preface to the volumes:

Development (in adolescence) is less gradual and more saltatory, suggestive of some ancient period of storm and stress when old moorings were broken and a higher level attained. . . . Nature arms youth for conflict with all the resources at her command—speed, power of shoulder, biceps, back, leg, jaw—strengthens and enlarges skull, thorax, hips, makes man aggressive and prepares woman's frame for maternity. . . .

Sex asserts its mastery in field after field, and works its havoc in the form of secret vice, debauch, disease, and enfeebled heredity, cadences the soul to both its normal and abnormal rhythms, and sends many thousand youth a year to quacks, because neither parents, teachers, preachers, or physicians know how to deal with its problems. . . . The social instincts undergo sudden unfoldment and the new life of love awakens. . . . Youth awakes to a new world and understands neither it nor himself. . . .

Never has youth been exposed to such dangers of both perversion and arrest as in our land and day. Urban life has increased temptations, prematurities, sedentary occupations, and passive stimuli, just when an active, objective life is most needed. Adolescents' lives today lack some of the regulations they still have in older lands with more conservative traditions . . . (Volume I, pp. xi, xiii, xv)

Hall's preoccupation with the evils of adolescence are threaded throughout the texts. This is nowhere more clear than in his comments about masturbation:

One of the very saddest of all the aspects of human weakness and sin is [masturbation]. . . Tissot, in 1759, found every pupil guilty. . . Dr. G. Bachin (1895) argued that growth, especially in the moral and intellectual regions, is dwarfed and stunted [by masturbation]. Bachin also felt that masturbation caused gray hairs, and especially baldness, a stooping and enfeebled gait. . . .

Perhaps masturbation is the most perfect type of individual vice and sin . . . it is the acme of selfishness.

Prominent among predisposing causes are often placed erotic reading, pictures, and theatrical presentations. . . Schiller protests against trousers pockets for boys, as do others against feather beds, while even horseback riding and the bicycle have been placed under the ban by a few extremist writers.

. . . The medical cures of masturbation that have been prescribed are almost without number: bromide, ergot, lupin, blistering, clitoridectomy, section of certain nerves, small mechanical appliances, of which the Patent Office at Washington has quite a collection. Regimen rather than special treatment must, however, be chiefly relied on. Work reduces temptation, and so does early rising. . . Good music is a moral tonic . . . (Volume I, pp. 411–471)

Clearly, our current beliefs about masturbation differ substantially from those of Hall's time. As indicated in the overview of chapters in Hall's volumes, he wrote about many other aspects of adolescence in addition to sex and

G. Stanley Hall

masturbation. His books are entertaining as well as informative. You are encouraged to look up his original work in your library and compare his comments with those made about adolescence in this text.

Source: Hall, G. S. *Adolescence* (2 vols.). New York: Appleton, 1904.

that the environment accounts for more change in development during adolescence than in earlier age periods. Thus, Hall believed—as we do today—that at least during adolescence, heredity interacts with environmental influences to determine the individual's development.

Like Rousseau, Hall subscribed to a four-stage approach to development: infancy, childhood, youth, and adolescence. Adolescence is the period of time from about twelve to about twenty-three years of age, or when adulthood is achieved. Hall saw adolescence as the period of *Sturm und Drang,* which means storm and stress. This label was borrowed from the German writings of Goethe and Schiller, who wrote novels full of idealism, commitment to goals, revolution, passion, and feeling. Hall sensed there was a parallel between the themes of the German authors and the psychological development of adolescents.

According to Hall, the adolescent period of storm and stress is full of contradictions and wide swings in mood and emotion. Thoughts, feelings, and actions oscillate between humility and conceit, goodness and temptation, and happiness and sadness. One moment the adolescent may be nasty to a peer, yet in the next moment be extremely nice to her. At one time he may want to be left alone, but shortly thereafter desire to cling to somebody. In sum, G. Stanley Hall views adolescence as a turbulent time charged with conflict (Ross, 1972), a perspective labeled the **storm and stress view** of adolescence.

Hall's view also had implications for social development and education (White, 1985). Hall conceived of development as a biological process directed toward a series of possibilities of social organization. As children moved into adolescence they were thought to be capable of entering progressively more complicated and powerful social arrangements. In the terminology of today, Hall might be called a "sociobiological developmentalist." Hall's analysis of the adolescent years also led him to believe that the time to begin strenuously educating such faculties as civility, scientific thinking, and morality is after the age of fifteen. However, Hall's developmental vision of education rested mainly on highly speculative theory rather than empirical data. While Hall believed systematic methods should be developed to study adolescents, his research efforts usually resorted to the creation of rather weak and unconvincing questionnaires. Even though the quality of his research was suspect, Hall should be considered a giant in the history of understanding adolescent development. It was he who began the theorizing, the systematizing, and the inquiry that went beyond mere speculation and philosophy. Indeed, we owe the scientific beginnings of the study of adolescent development to Hall.

The Inventionist View of Adolescence

In the quote by A. K. Cohen that opened this section, comments were made about the teenager sneaking up on us in our own lifetime. That is, at a point not too long ago in history, the teenager had not yet been invented. Social and historical conditions have led a number of writers to argue that adolescence has been "invented" (Elder, 1975; Field, 1981; Finley, 1985; Hill, 1980; Lapsley, Enright, and Serlin, 1985). So, while adolescence clearly has biological foundations, there are nonetheless many social and historical occurrences that have contributed to acceptance of adolescence as the transitional time between childhood and adulthood. We have discussed many of these circumstances in our overview of the historical background of adolescence. They include the decline in apprenticeship; increased mechanization during the industrial revolution including upgraded skill requirements of labor and specialized divisions of labor; the separation of work and the home; the writings of G. Stanley Hall; the increased use of child guidance tracks; changes in fertility patterns and family structure; urbanization; the appearance of youth groups such as the YMCA and Boy Scouts; and age-segregated schools.

Table 1.1 Percentage of males and females, aged 10–15, who were gainfully employed in selected states 1910–1930[1]

States	1910 M	1910 F	1920 M	1920 F	1930 M	1930 F	% Decline 1910–1930[2] M	% Decline 1910–1930[2] F
New Hampshire	10.2	7.1	4.4	2.3	1.4	1.2	−86	−83
Vermont	10.3	3.2	4.8	1.8	2.6	1.0	−75	−69
Massachusetts	11.3	8.6	10.0	7.1	2.3	2.0	−82	−77
Rhode Island	15.5	13.2	14.3	12.6	3.1	3.0	−81	−77
Connecticut	11.7	8.3	9.0	7.1	3.2	2.8	−76	−66
New York	8.4	5.5	5.5	3.9	1.9	1.3	−77	−76
New Jersey	11.0	8.0	8.3	6.9	2.2	2.4	−80	−70
Pennsylvania	15.1	7.8	6.7	4.5	2.0	2.1	−86	−74
Delaware	23.3	8.6	7.9	3.8	2.6	1.4	−88	−70
Maryland	21.1	10.2	10.0	5.0	4.7	2.5	−77	−75
Virginia	33.2	10.6	12.7	3.6	7.3	2.0	−78	−81
North Carolina	57.5	34.1	21.7	11.5	15.1	7.2	−74	−79
South Carolina	58.2	45.4	28.7	20.1	23.0	13.6	−60	−70

[1]Source: Abstract of the 15th Census of the United States, 1930. (In Lapsley, Enright, and Serlin, 1985).
[2]Calculation of Lapsley, et al. 1985.

The role of schools, work, and economics have figured prominently in the current flourish of interest that has developed in the historical invention of adolescence. Some contributors argue that the institutionalization of adolescence was a by-product of the cultural motivation to create a system of compulsory public education. From this view, secondary schools are seen mainly as vehicles for transmitting intellectual skills to youth (e.g., Callahan, 1962; Cremin, 1961; Stedman and Smith, 1983). However, others argue that the primary purpose of secondary schools has been to deploy youth within the economic sphere and to serve as an important cog in the authority structure of the culture.

Daniel Lapsley, Robert Enright, and Ronald Serlin (1985) adopt the latter stance. They believe that American society "inflicted" the status of adolescence on its youth, and argue that the history of child-saving legislation is actually the history of the origins of adolescence. By developing laws for youth, the adult power structure placed young people in a submissive position in the authority hierarchy of our culture. It is a location that restricts their options, encourages dependency, and makes their move into the world of work more manageable.

The period of 1890–1920 is now considered the age of adolescence—the time when adolescence was invented. It was during this time period that a great deal of compulsory legislation was enacted (Tyack, 1976). In virtually every state there were laws excluding youth from most employment and requiring them to attend secondary school. Extensive enforcement provisions administered by the state characterized most of this legislation.

Two clear changes resulted from such legislation—decreased employment and increased school attendance by youth. From 1910 to 1930 there was a dramatic decrease in the number of ten- to fifteen-year-olds who were gainfully employed, dropping about seventy-five percent in this time frame (table 1.1). Between 1900 and 1930 there also was a tremendous

Table 1.2 Percentage of growth in high school graduation, 1870–1940

Year	% Change
1870	
1880	50
1890	83
1900	116
1910	64
1920	112
1930	101
1940	83

Source: Series H598-681, Historical Statistics of the United States.

increase in the number of high school graduates (table 1.2). Approximately six hundred percent more individuals graduated from high school and there was approximately a four hundred and fifty percent increase in enrollment in high schools during this historical period.

Just as school and work figured prominently in the invention of adolescence, historical changes continued to accompany the lives of adolescents during more recent times.

1920–1950

The lives of adolescents took a turn for the better in the 1920s, but moved through difficult times in the 1930s and 1940s.

During the three decades from 1920 to 1950, adolescents gained a more prominent status in society as they went through a number of complex changes. In the 1920s, the Roaring Twenties atmosphere rubbed off on adolescents. Passivity and conformity to adult leadership was replaced by increased autonomy and conformity to peer values. Adults began to model the styles of youth, rather than vice versa. If a new dance came in vogue, the adolescent girl did it first and her mother learned it from her. Prohibition was the law of the time, but many adolescents drank heavily. More permissive attitudes toward the opposite sex developed,

In the Roaring Twenties, adolescents began to behave more permissively.

and kissing parties were standard fare. Short skirts even led to a campaign by the YWCA against such abnormal behavior (Lee, 1970).

Just when adolescence was getting to be fun, the Great Depression arrived in the 1930s, followed by World War II in the 1940s. Economic and political concerns of a serious nature replaced the hedonistic adolescent values of the 1920s. Radical protest groups that were critical of the government increased in number during the 1930s, and World War II exposed adolescents to another serious, life-threatening event. Military service provided travel and exposure to other youth from different parts of the United States. This experience promoted a broader perspective on life and a greater sense of independence.

1950–Present

By 1950, there was considerable change in the way adolescents were viewed. New experiences continued to confront adolescents in the 1960s as well. Life for today's adolescents is similar to their predecessors in some aspects, and different in others.

By 1950, the developmental period we refer to as adolescence had come of age—not only did it possess physical and social identity, but legal attention was paid to it as well. Every state had developed special laws for youth between the ages of sixteen and eighteen or twenty. Adolescents in the 1950s have been described as the silent generation (Lee, 1970). Life was much better for adolescents in the 1950s than it had been in the 1930s and 1940s. The government was paying for many adolescents' college educations through the GI bill, and television was beginning to invade most homes.

Getting a college degree, the key to a good job, was on the minds of many adolescents during the 1950s—so were getting married, having a family, and settling down to the life of luxury displayed in television commercials.

While the pursuit of higher education persisted among adolescents in the 1960s, it became painfully apparent that many black adolescents not only were being denied a college eduction, but were receiving an inferior secondary education as well. Racial conflicts in the form of riots and "sit-ins" were pervasive, with college-age adolescents among the most vocal participants.

Adolescents today

The political protest of adolescents reached a peak in the late 1960s and early 1970s, when millions of adolescents violently reacted to what they saw as unreasonable American participation in the Vietnam war. As parents watched the 1968 Democratic presidential nominating committee, they not only saw political speeches in support of candidates but also their adolescents fighting with the police, yelling obscenities at adults, and staging sit-ins.

Parents became more concerned in the 1960s about teenage drug use and abuse than in past eras. Sexual permissiveness in the form of premarital sex, cohabitation, and endorsement of previously prohibited sexual conduct also increased.

Adolescents Today

By the mid-1970s, much of the radical protest of adolescents had abated and was replaced by increased concern for an achievement-oriented, upwardly mobile career to be attained through hard work in high school, college, or a vocational training school. Material interests began to dominate adolescent motives again, while ideological challenges to social institutions seemed to become less central. The women's movement has involved the greatest amount of protest in the 1970s. If you carefully read the descriptions of adolescents in America in earlier years, you noticed that much of what was said pertained more to adolescent males than females. The family and career objectives of adolescent

Table 1.3 Adolescents in the 1980s

In a recent class discussion, students commented on how they think the adolescents of the 1980s are different from the adolescents of approximately ten or fifteen years ago. The adolescents of the 1980s are perceived to be:

1. More achievement-, money-, and college-oriented.
2. Growing up earlier, experiencing things earlier, being pushed into adult life-styles sooner.
3. More likely to be working at a job.
4. More financially dependent on parents for a longer period of time.
5. Using alcohol more (particularly females).
6. Showing more interest in equality of the sexes.
7. Growing up in a greater variety of family structures— for example, more adolescents now live in divorced and working-mother families.
8. Reacting to authority differently. In the late 1960s and early 1970s, the rebelliousness of adolescents seemed to be politically motivated and directed at the government, while the rebelliousness now has taken the form of more open, overt confrontation with parents and school authorities. Also, the rebelliousness of the 1960s and 1970s seemed to be directed more toward attaining peace and showing a concern for others.
9. More aware of their rights. School dress codes and physical punishment by school officials are not as common as they were. Adolescents have discovered they have certain rights and that they are no longer completely at the mercy of adults.
10. More interested in physical fitness.
11. More influenced by the media, which expose them to a world beyond their immediate families, schools, and neighborhoods. The media also carry more open messages about sexuality.
12. More sexually permissive.
13. More preoccupied with self.

females in the 1970s would barely be recognized by the adolescent females of the 1890s and early 1900s. Later in the text much more will be said about the increased participation of adolescent females in the work force, including the impact this movement has had on the family and on the female adolescent's relationships with males.

What are adolescents like today? Think back to when you were twelve, thirteen, fourteen, or fifteen years of age. Then think about the adolescents you know today. In what ways are they similar to or different from what you were? I asked this question in a recent class, querying students about how the adolescents of the 1980s might be different from the adolescents of ten to fifteen years earlier. A summary of their responses is presented in table 1.3.

We have described some important sociohistorical circumstances experienced by adolescents, and we have described how society viewed adolescents at different points in history. As we see next, caution needs to be exercised in generalizing about the adolescents of any era.

Stereotyping Adolescents

First we will explore the nature of the stereotyping process and then turn to ideas about how it is easy to generalize too much about a population of adolescents based on information about a minority of adolescents.

The Nature of Stereotypes

It is very easy to stereotype a person, groups of people, or classes of people. A **stereotype** is a broad category that reflects our impressions about people, including ourselves. The world is extremely complex—every day we are confronted with thousands of different configurations of stimuli. The creation of stereotypes is one way we simplify this complexity. We simply assign a label to a group of people (for example, "youth are promiscuous") and we then have much less to consider when we think about this set of people. Once we assign these labels, however, it is very difficult to abandon them—even in the face of contradictory evidence.

Stereotypes about the interests, behaviors, and emotions of adolescents abound: "They say they want a job, but when they get one, they don't want to work"; "They're all lazy"; "They're all sex fiends"; "They're all into drugs, every last one of them"; "Kids today don't have the moral fiber of my generation"; "The problem with adolescents is that they have it too easy"; "They're a bunch of smart-alecks";—and so it goes.

The Adolescent Generalization Gap

A study by Daniel Yankelovich (1974) indicates that many such stereotypes about youth are false. Yankelovich compared the attitudes of adolescents with those of their parents about different values, life-styles, and codes of personal conduct. There was little or no difference in the attitudes of the adolescents and their parents toward self-control, hard work, saving money, competition, compromise, legal authority, and private property. There was a substantial difference between the adolescents and their parents when their attitudes toward religion were sampled (eighty-nine percent of the parents said that religion was important to them, compared to only sixty-six percent of the adolescents). But note that a majority of the adolescents still subscribed to the belief that religion is important.

John Hill (1983) also believes that many of the ideas the layperson has about adolescents are based on stereotypes that develop in a particular culture. For example, he points out that independence from and conflict with parents is likely overestimated in most views of the adolescent's development. In reality, many individuals move through the adolescent period in a reasonably smooth fashion. Similarly, we have gone through an era when adolescents as a group were branded as rebellious and deviant, while in reality, many of them were plugging along efficiently and competently toward mature adulthood.

Hill thinks adolescents would benefit if less dramatization of the adolescent period occurred. Then, the majority of adolescents—who do not follow the pattern of the deviant minority—would not be penalized as heavily.

Joseph Adelson (1979) also stresses that far too many stereotypes about adolescents exist—many of which, he says, are based on the visible, rebellious adolescents of the 1960s. Adelson points out that there is an **adolescent "generalization gap"** rather than a "generation gap," meaning that widespread generalizations have developed based on information about a limited group of adolescents. Adelson points out that one of the reasons such stereotypes have been accepted perhaps more readily than for other developmental periods is the weak research base from which we can make generalizations about adolescence. He mentions, for example, that in searching for information about the psychological impact of a young girl's first menstruation, he could find hardly any research information, even though clinicians and counselors report that such a developmental milestone seems to affect the psychological relationship between mother and daughter.

There has been a tendency to study the abnormalities and deviancies of adolescence more than the normalities. Consider the images and descriptions of adolescents that come to your mind when you think about this group—rebellious, in conflict, impulsive, faddish, and so forth. Adelson (1979) argues, just as Yankelovich (1974) and Hill (1976) do, that the majority of adolescents are not experiencing a generation gap any more than the adolescents of any other era. Most adolescents do not experience intense turmoil or deep emotional disturbances, they are not completely controlled by their immediate impulses, and they do not totally reject parental values.

A summary of main ideas related to a historical perspective on adolescent development is presented in Concept Table 1.1. Now that we have studied at length the historical interest in adolescents, we turn our attention to a number of issues that confront theorists and researchers as they investigate adolescent development.

HISTORICAL PERSPECTIVE ON ADOLESCENCE

Concept	Processes/related ideas	Characteristics/description
The Greeks	Plato	Argued that reason emerges in adolescence and that childhood experiences are important for understanding the time frame we now call adolescence.
	Aristotle	Believed the most important aspect of adolescence is the ability to choose. Self-determination thought to be the hallmark of adolescent maturity. Specified three stages of development.
The Middle Ages and the Renaissance	Middle Ages	Knowledge about adolescents took a step backward; miniature adult view of children emerged; children became adults, not adolescents.
	Renaissance	Rousseau, a French philosopher who lived in the eighteenth century, saw the miniature adult view as harmful and proposed a four-stage developmental timetable. Reason and self-consciousness were thought to develop at twelve to fifteen years and emotional maturity was believed to replace selfishness in the fifteen to twenty year age period.
The period of adolescence: 1900 to the present	The turn of the century	Between 1890 and 1920 a cadre of psychologists, urban reformers, youth workers, and counselors began to mold the concept of adolescence. G. Stanley Hall's book, *Adolescence,* was published in 1904, marking the beginning of the scientific study of adolescence. Hall is known for his storm and stress view of adolescence and the belief that biology plays a prominent role in development. A number of scholars argue for an inventionist view of adolescence. They believe that legislation insured the dependency of youth and made their move into the economic sphere more manageable.
	1920–1950	Adolescents gained a more prominent status in society from 1920 to 1950. During the 1920s, adults even began to model some of their behaviors after adolescents. During the 1930s, major historical events—the Great Depression and World War II—signalled the importance of historical considerations in understanding adolescent development.
	1950–present	By 1950, the developmental period we know as adolescence had come of age. It possessed physical and social identity. During the 1960s and early 1970s, adolescent rebelliousness came to the forefront of American society. Much of the radical protest of adolescents has abated today, yet other confrontations with adult standards still appear in the form of such concerns as women's rights, nuclear protest, and the rights of adolescents.

HISTORICAL PERSPECTIVE ON ADOLESCENCE

Concept	Processes/related ideas	Characteristics/description
Stereotyping adolescents	The nature of stereotypes	A stereotype is a broad category reflecting our impressions about people. Stereotypes are one way we simplify the complexity we experience in our world.
	The adolescent generalization gap	There are many stereotypes about adolescents that are inaccurate. Often widespread generalizations about adolescents have developed based on information about a limited group of adolescents.

Issues in Adolescent Development: Enduring Concerns

A developmental perspective on adolescence raises important questions that often guide research on adolescents. These include defining development and identifying the contributions of heredity and environment to development. Other concerns are the question of qualitative change; the issue of stages of development; the concern about continuity–discontinuity in development; the existence of individual differences; and the extent to which age is an important variable in the study of adolescent development.

Development, Maturation, and the Contribution of Heredity and Environment

A central concept in this text is development. What does it mean when we say a child or adolescent has developed in some respect? We use the term **development** to refer to a pattern of change or movement that begins at conception and continues through the entire life span. The pattern of change involves growth (as in the emergence of increased cognitive skills and sexual maturation in adolescence) and decay (as in death). The pattern is complex because it is often the product of several factors, particularly the manner in which heredity and environment interact.

Maturation, like the term *development,* describes a pattern of change or movement. Historically, both development and maturation have been more closely associated with changes in our genetic blueprint than our environmental experiences. For example, our brain and nervous system grow and become differentiated; our anatomy changes; and there are changes in our chemical and hormonal make-up as we move toward maturity. One example of maturation involves the gradual specialization of the brain, in which one of the hemispheres directs certain psychological activities more so than the other hemisphere. For example, spatial processing is more likely to be directed by the right hemisphere and language by the left hemisphere (Gazzinga, 1983). Prior to adolescence, these functions within the brain are quite flexible. So, an injury to a specific part of the brain during early childhood may temporarily disrupt one of these activities; but, in many instances, other parts of the brain gradually will take over, functioning as backup systems. As the individual approaches and develops through adolescence, however, accidents are more likely to produce permanent damage because the specialized functions have become more rigidly locked into specific locations in the brain.

So far, we have been describing development primarily as genetically determined according to a programmed genetic blueprint. But already we have had to introduce environmental experiences into our equation of children's and adolescent's development because we have seen how accidents at various points in development may have different outcomes for the individual. The issue of whether development is primarily determined by heredity or environment has been a major concern of psychologists and, particularly, developmental psychologists for many years. This argument is referred to as the genetic–environmental, heredity–experience, or nature-nurture controversy. Scientists now agree that development is not determined separately by heredity or environment, but by the interaction of heredity and environment. Even biologists who study lower animals (e.g., Johnson, 1983) agree that it is virtually impossible to tease apart the effects of an animal's genes and the effects of the environment. For example, at the very least, the expression of a given behavior requires a proper environment and the existence of stimulus objects. Similarly, no behavior can be attributed to environmental factors alone. At the very least, the multicellular animal must have sensory receptors, motor nerve cells, and a brain that detects and processes relevant information, as well as muscles that perform the behavior. To capture the importance of heredity–environmental interaction in development, Sandra Scarr and Richard Weinberg (1980) concluded, "No genes, no organism; no environment, no organism." In Chapter 3, we will explore in much greater detail the role of genes and genetic–environmental interaction in adolescent development.

Qualitative Change

Jean Piaget, a great pioneer in developmental psychology, made many important claims about the intellectual functioning of infants, children, and adolescents. Among these claims, perhaps none is more provocative than his claim of **qualitative change** in the development of intelligence. That is, an adolescent's intelligence is qualitatively different than a child's—it is not simply just more than a child's intelligence. For example, Piaget (1952) argued that the adolescent's intelligence is more abstract than the child's. According to Piaget, the abstract nature of intelligence is something that develops during the adolescent years, particularly the early adolescent years. Prior to the adolescent years,

Piaget believed that thought is more concrete. That is, he argued that children need to have objects present to reason and think about them. During adolescence, however, Piaget believed that thought takes wings as the adolescent thinks about objects in abstract ways. The adolescent will often think and reason about objects that are far removed in time and space from the present situation. The development of abstract thought in adolescence represents a prototype of what qualitative change in development can mean.

Does development in adolescence involve the qualitative changes of the sort that Piaget claimed? The answer is not obvious, but a developmental perspective suggests such qualitative changes are possible. For example, there may be qualitative changes in physical development, although not necessarily for all adolescents, and not necessarily in cognitive or personality development. These are empirical issues that must be resolved on the basis of intensive research in specific areas of development. The developmental perspective simply raises the question of qualitative change; it does not answer the question.

Stages of Development

Piaget went further than simply to propose qualitative changes in adolescent intelligence. He also proposed that there are identifiable stages of intellectual development. The notion of stages is a controversial one in psychology; not only do researchers disagree about the existence of stages, they also argue about the characteristics of such stages.

Any conceptualization of developmental **stages** must incorporate the notion of qualitative change. Beyond this, the stages concept implies that qualitative changes must occur in certain sequences (stage two must be preceded by stage one, and not vice versa).

Many developmental psychologists (e.g., Flavell, 1985) go still further to claim that the idea of stages implies (1) a certain degree of abruptness or transition from one stage to another and (2) concurrence about the appearance of behaviors or competencies that characterize a given stage. That is, if an entire set of organized behaviors appeared rather suddenly in the course of development and did so for most, if not all, individuals at a certain point in the life span, we would have clear evidence for a developmental stage of some sort. Unfortunately, evidence for such occurrences is quite rare and unconvincing, leading some investigators to doubt the utility of the stage concept (Flavell, 1985) and others to redefine the concept (Wohlwill, 1973). Despite these problems, the concept of stages has had an enduring appeal in developmental psychology and we return to it repeatedly throughout this text.

What is the nature of some of the stages that theorists have proposed to describe adolescent development? We explore such theories in considerable detail in Chapter 2—Piaget's cognitive stages and the psychoanalytic stages of Freud and Erikson, for example. Stage theorists have labeled their efforts to pinpoint what is unique about adolescence in different ways. Some theorists refer to developmental tasks to be mastered (Havighurst, 1972), others describe conflicts that need to be resolved (Erikson, 1968), and yet others mention cognitive capabilities that unfold (Piaget, 1952). For example, as shown in table 1.4, Robert Havighurst outlined eight developmental tasks that must be mastered during adolescence for optimal development to occur. One such task is achieving emotional independence from parents and other adults. The implication is that unless independence from parents and other adults is achieved during adolescence, the individual risks maladjustment and departure from a normal developmental sequence. Nonstage theorists, by contrast, deemphasize the resolution of particular issues or the mastery of certain tasks at a particular point in development. Instead, they argue that working through most of these issues and tasks is a life-long process, not a series of specific critical stages.

Table 1.4 Developmental tasks to be mastered during adolescence

1. Achieving new and more mature relations with agemates of both sexes.
2. Achieving a masculine or a feminine role.
3. Accepting one's physique and using one's body effectively.
4. Desiring, accepting, and achieving socially responsible behavior.
5. Achieving emotional independence from parents and other adults.
6. Preparing for an economic career.
7. Preparing for marriage and family life.
8. Acquiring a set of values and an ethical system as a guide to behavior—developing an ideology.

Source: From Developmental Tasks and Education, *Third Edition,* by Robert J. Havighurst. Copyright © 1972 by Longman, Inc.

Continuity-Discontinuity in Development

The issue of **continuity–discontinuity** in adolescent development is not simple. We will discuss two important dimensions of this issue. First, stage theorists imply abruptness of change from one stage to the next, suggesting a discontinuity from one stage to the next. For example, Erik Erikson's theory implies that identity is a crisis only in adolescence, not at other points in the life cycle, and that such a crisis appears rather abruptly. At another level, however, stage theories imply that achievement of one stage is dependent on achievement of prior stages; an adolescent cannot achieve stage 5 in Erikson's theory, without having moved through four previous stages of development. Though change from one stage to the next may be abrupt, stage theorists assume a connectivity of the present stage to prior stages (Brim and Kagan, 1980). Such connectivity is a form of continuity; thus, the second and most widely discussed dimension of the continuity–discontinuity issue is the extent later development is dependent on earlier experiences and/or development.

For many years it was believed that early experience, particularly within the family during the first five years of life, is the primary determinant of later development, whether the time period be later childhood, adolescence, or adulthood. This view initially was proposed by Sigmund Freud and the psychoanalytic theorists. The early experience view continued to have a strong impact on developmental thinking for many years. Such a view represents a strong version of the continuity argument. In recent years, psychologists have begun to question whether such early experience is the sole or even primary determinant of later development. While it is agreed that early experiences represent important prototypical models for how later experiences will be handled, many developmental psychologists now argue that early experience may not have irreversible effects. These psychologists take a discontinuity stance in the sense they emphasize an individual's capacity for change throughout the life cycle rather than later development being determined by early experience alone. While early experiences in childhood have important ramifications for adolescent development, experiences during later childhood and adolescence also contribute to the nature of adolescent development.

The issue of early and later experience is an important and enduring aspect of studying adolescents. What are some of the factors that might contribute to discontinuity and continuity in adolescent development?

Factors That Can Promote Discontinuity in Adolescent Development

Four factors that can produce discontinuity in adolescent development are:

1. Changes in broad expectations at different historical points in time. For example, adolescent males may be more nurturant and females more assertive because of changes in sex roles linked to the women's movement. Further, historical changes in an adolescent's lifetime may lead to discontinuous changes in personality, cognition, or even health (due, for example, to exercise).

2. Changes in specific life experiences of the adolescent. Whenever the adolescent's environment changes radically, we would expect changes in the adolescent to occur. Such experiences as the death of a parent, the divorce of parents, a long distance move, or the loss of a boyfriend or girlfriend are experiences that can produce significant changes in the adolescent.

3. Regular changes in life tasks at different ages, consisting of different demands. For example, independence may become a crisis in adolescence, but not in childhood.

4. Biological changes, such as those related to hormones. The hormone alterations related to puberty exemplify this kind of change.

Factors That Can Generate Continuity in Adolescent Development

By contrast, there are reasons why stability, or consistency, in adolescent development could occur:

1. Biological processes. The adolescent may inherit certain tendencies and characteristics. There is some indication, for instance, that some forms of disturbances, such as depression and schizophrenia, are influenced by heredity. And intelligence, as well as some aspects of personality, such as introversion and extraversion, have a genetic component.

2. The continuing influence of early experience. If early experience is more important in development than later experience, then the tendencies and characteristics we develop in childhood are likely to persist through adolescence. Both Freud and Piaget have taken this position. Further information about the importance of childhood characteristics and experiences in predicting adolescent development and adjustment is presented in Perspective on Adolescent Development 1.2.

3. Early experience plus consistent later experience. Many of us choose life courses that are compatible with the way we think about ourselves. Consequently, we may continue to show consistency over our life course, not necessarily because early childhood experiences predominate but because early patterns continue

*T*he issue of continuity–discontinuity raises the possibility that problems and disturbances appearing to surface in adolescence may have their origin in childhood. It may be that adolescence only increases the intensity of problems that have emerged earlier for some individuals. A continuity view of adolescent development argues that we should not only look at what is happening in the adolescent's life for clues to his or her adjustment, but rather should delve into the childhood background of the adolescent as well.

One widely known investigation that addresses the continuity issue in regard to adolescent adjustment is the New York Longitudinal Study (Chess and Thomas, 1977, 1984; Thomas, Chess, and Birch, 1968; Thomas and Chess, 1977). This investigation now has spanned almost 30 years. One recent report from this large scale study (Hertzog, Lerner, and Hooker, 1985) focused on the extent to which information about negative emotional states and behavioral characteristics (such as aggression, anxiety, noncompliance, depression) in childhood is related to adjustment during the adolescent years. One hundred thirty-three white, middle-class children were rated on these negative characteristics from infancy to adolescence. Measures of family, peer, and personal adjustment also were obtained.

The most intriguing results from this investigation revealed how early negative emotional behaviors in the years one through six were highly related to adolescent

Negative emotional states in the years one through six were related to adolescent adjustment in the New York Longitudinal Study.

to be rewarded in the circumstances we choose later in our development. Social learning theory, which will be described in detail in Chapter 2, accepts this scenario as a major reason why individuals show consistency and stability in their lives.

Individual Differences in Development

An important concept in psychology is that in some ways an individual is like everyone else in the world, yet in many other ways the individual is different. Every adolescent has a brain and some way of communicating, but each adolescent's way of thinking and communicating is different from that of others.

Shy, introverted adolescents often have friendship and peer difficulties.

adjustment problems with parents and peers. This pattern was specific to the type of emotional difficulty—aggression predicting poor family adjustment in adolescence and anxiety predicting peer adjustment problems. Subsequent emotional difficulties in the seven through twelve year age range did not provide added accuracy in predicting parent and peer adjustment in adolescence. School adjustment problems in adolescence, however, were best predicted by aggressive behaviors in the seven through twelve year age range. The overall pattern of findings is consistent with the findings of other research suggesting that aggressive adolescents have difficulty adjusting to parents and anxious, shy, or otherwise introverted adolescents often have problems with friendships and peer relationships (Asher, Oden, and Gottman,

1976; Foster and Ritchey, 1979; Gottman, Ganso, and Rasmussen, 1975; Robbins, 1972). What is important about these findings is the long-term prediction of adolescent adjustment by emotional behavior problems in the *early* part of childhood and the lack of additional prediction of adolescent adjustment by later childhood characteristics. This lack of additional predictability of adolescent adjustment by later childhood characteristics and adjustment likely was related to the fact that aggression and anxiety were relatively stable over the one through twelve year age range in the New York Longitudinal Study. One interpretation of these data is that negative emotional behaviors often emerge in the early part of childhood, are carried through the childhood years into adolescence, and influence the nature of adjustment during adolescence. These findings clearly point to the importance of a continuity view of adolescent development, and the attendant theme that experiences and development during the childhood years should not be ignored in our evaluation of the adjustment and social competence of adolescents. We believe, however, that experiences throughout childhood and adolescence are important determinants of adolescent development. The story told by the recent New York Longitudinal Study simply instructs us not to ignore early childhood characteristics and experiences in our attempt to chart the manner in which adolescents construct a vision of reality and social maturity.

Individual differences are simply the consistent, *stable* ways adolescents differ from each other. The entire psychological testing movement was (and still is) concerned with how individuals think, feel, and act in a consistent manner and how they think, feel, and act in relation to others.

Developmental psychologists have added a unique twist to the individual differences idea, however. They often talk about individual differences in **intraindividual change.** Going beyond the idea of consistency in

differences among adolescents, they argue that we also need to study *change* and *stability* within children and adolescents as they develop. For example, development in a given type of functioning (e.g., creative thought) may follow a declining course of development in some adolescents, a stable course of development in others, and an increasing course in others. This possibility is not inconsistent with the impressions we form from everyday experiences. And we may be impressed by someone who was a problem child, but by the end of adolescence had shown signs of maturity. By contrast, we may know someone else who was socially competent as a child, but who made life miserable for everyone involved during adolescence. Such everyday impressions do not constitute scientific evidence; however, a developmental perspective suggests that individual differences in the course of development may be critical for understanding biological, cognitive, and social functioning.

Age as a Variable in the Study of Adolescents

A final issue raised in a developmental perspective on adolescence is how best to conceive of age. What is age? How is it best defined? Can it be considered a cause of adolescent development? These questions are considered by Jack Botwinick, who notes that there is some dissatisfaction with the concept of age. He presents an argument that age per se probably is not the best way to study adolescent development:

> It is not difficult to argue for this extreme position. **Age,** as a concept, is synonymous with time, and time in itself cannot affect living function, behavior or otherwise. Time does not "cause" anything; it does not have physical dimensionality to impinge upon the sensorium, and it does not have psychological meaning independent of related social and biological parameters.
>
> To continue the argument: Time is a crude index of many events and experiences, and it is these indexed events which are "causal." If we study these events and experiences, we need not be concerned with the crude index of time. We need not be concerned with age in order to understand that which has been "caused" by the time-indexed variables. These variables, unlike age itself, can be manipulated experimentally while holding related factors constant.

Although acceptance of age as a purely descriptive variable is one approach to our conceptual problems, another approach is to refine our conceptualization of time since time is the foundation upon which any understanding of the age variable must be based. Some

steps in this direction have been taken by Bernice Neugarten (Neugarten, 1980; Neugarten and Datan, 1973), who has distinguished three perspectives of time as they relate to the life cycle: life time, social time, and historical time.

Life Time, Social Time, and Historical Time

Life time is based heavily on the biological timetable that governs the sequence of changes in the process of growing up. However, as Neugarten (1980) suggests, chronological age is at best only a rough indicator of an individual's position in any one of a number of physical or psychological dimensions because from early infancy on, individual differences are a major factor in development. Also, age is often not a very good index of many forms of social and psychological behavior, unless there is accompanying knowledge of the particular society in which the individual lives as a frame of reference. An obvious example compares a girl in the United States who is a schoolgirl with the same-aged girl in a rural village in the Near East who may be the mother of two children. It is argued that the significance of a given chronological age, or a given marker of life time, when viewed from a sociological or anthropological perspective, is directly a function of the social definition of age, or social time (Neugarten and Datan, 1973).

Social time refers to the dimension that underlies the age-grade system of a particular society. It has been characteristic of preliterate societies to have "rites de passage" marking the transition from one age status to the next, such as the passage from youth to maturity and to marriage (Van Gennep, 1960). According to Neugarten and Datan (1973), however, only a rough parallel exists between social time and life time in most societies. There are different sets of age expectations and age statuses in different societies.

Historical considerations also are encompassed in Neugarten's analysis of time. **Historical time** focuses on the timing of major historical events in the life of the individual. Wars and depressions often act as historical watersheds; that is, major turning points in the social system. Significant historical events affect levels of education, fertility patterns, sexual mores, labor

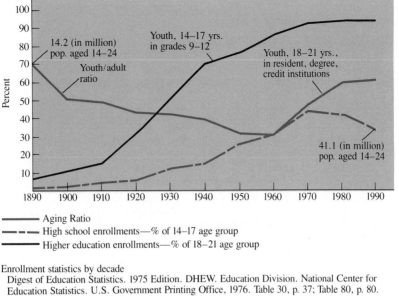

Aging Ratio
High school enrollments—% of 14–17 age group
Higher education enrollments—% of 18–21 age group

Enrollment statistics by decade
Digest of Education Statistics. 1975 Edition. DHEW. Education Division. National Center for Education Statistics. U.S. Government Printing Office, 1976. Table 30, p. 37; Table 80, p. 80. Historical statistics of the United States. Bureau of the Census, 1975, p. 383. Projections of Education Statistics to 1984–85. National Center for Education Statistics. 1976. Table 3, p. 18. Table 5, p. 21. Table B-2, p. 154 and Table B-3, p. 155.

Aging ratio.
Ratio of population, 14–24 to population aged 25–64 from Table 2. Chapter 3 of PSAC report. 1973. Chapter 3 prepared by Norman Ryder.

Figure 1.1 **Secular trends in population aging and enrollment rates for secondary and higher education, United States.**

participation patterns, and so forth. We can also consider historical time in terms of the emergence of the concepts of childhood, adolescence, and life-span development. Childhood as a distinct phase of life did not emerge until the seventeenth and eighteenth centuries, and the concept of adolescence did not emerge until the twentieth century. Similarly, middle age as a stage is a recent concept resulting from our increased longevity. Changes in industrialization, urbanization, and education account for these changing concepts. It is clear, then, that our notion of age as "time by the clock since birth" is but one of several important dimensions of developmental time.

In our outline of the history of adolescence and here in our discussion of historical time, we have seen that adolescents often experience a world that is not always the same as their counterparts from earlier historical times. In studying historical influences on adolescent development, psychologists refer to the importance of **cohort effects.** A cohort refers to a person's time of birth or generation but not actually to his or her age. At points of rapid change, the historical experience of successive cohorts varies through exposure to different events (such as the Great Depression and World War II) and by exposure to the same event at different points in the life cycle. Thus, individuals who were of draft age when World War II occurred experienced this war very differently than children. Cohort effects were quite apparent during the 1960s (Elder, 1980). For the most part, we think of the late 1960s as a time when adolescent deviance was highly visible. An often overlooked factor in this cohort was the sheer numerical size of the cohort relative to adults (figure 1.1). The

COHORT EFFECTS AND ADOLESCENT PREGNANCY

Glenn Elder (1980) has argued strongly that a historical perspective on adolescence illuminates important factors that a nonhistorical view does not. To illustrate this point, Elder describes the research of Frank Furstenberg (1976) pertaining to adolescent pregnancy. Furstenberg points out that it only was in the 1960s that public concern about the problem of adolescent pregnancy appeared. This concern surfaced in the popular press, government clinics, and programs for mothers. Furstenberg argues that this concern about adolescent pregnancy came about through a convergence of developments, including the large adolescent cohort of the 1960s and the general issue of overpopulation. More adolescent girls of childbearing age existed than ever before in history. An increasing proportion of teenagers' babies were born out of wedlock (from fifteen percent in 1960 to thirty percent in 1970), likely due to sexual experience beginning at a younger age and a rising trend toward later marriage. Through the decade of the 1960s, interest in unplanned childbearing and its social disadvantages during adolescence produced more than a hundred programs offering educational and health services.

A more detailed look at Furstenberg's research reveals how a careful analysis of cohort effects sheds light on adolescent development. The research was started in 1966 as a traditional, short-term evaluation of a service program for adolescent (before age 18) mothers in primarily low-income, urban, black neighborhoods. Like most research on this topic, the program emphasized the causes of adolescent parenthood and out-of-wedlock births, paying no attention to historical trends, demographic trends, or developmental changes in adolescents. But events, such as lack of research funds, provided Furstenberg with an opportunity to rethink the investigation in terms of emerging ideas about the life cycle. He recast it as a longitudinal inquiry on adaptation to pregnancy and early parenthood. In terms of the approved timetable for parenting, adolescent parenthood is off schedule for a number of reasons—maturation, schooling, and prospects for economic support. Marital postponement, support systems in the form of relatives (parents, grandparents, and so forth), a rescheduling of work and schooling, and fertility control reflect potential options for successfully coping with the deprivations, stress, and disequilibrium engendered by the birth of an unplanned child.

With this coping and adaptational perspective in mind, Furstenberg set out to obtain a matched sample of adolescents who were former classmates of the teenage mothers, but had not become pregnant in adolescence. Interviews with both the adolescent mothers and the comparison group were conducted between 1970 and 1972. Furstenberg studied these girls during the course of postwar developments when rising levels of teenagers were giving birth, often out of wedlock. By doing so, he placed the analysis in a context that has broad implications. For example, what are the life outcomes and social consequences of the increased trend of illegitimate births? And, a historical importance to the study also was imparted. In this regard, distinctive features of the cohort and its historical setting were noted, such as the availability of birth control devices for adolescents. Also, this investigation revealed the importance of studying the interconnection of different contexts in the adolescent's life, such as family, school, and career/work. The study also produced important information about the adaptation patterns of adolescent mothers, signalling which factors led to better adjustment than others. Rather than stopping at the conclusion that adolescent pregnancy and out-of-wedlock birth inevitably lead to a life of deprivation and stress, by following the adolescent mothers into their early adulthood years, Furstenberg revealed diversity in the life courses of the girls. While most of the women grew up in disadvantaged homes, their life circumstances five years after the birth of their first child in adolescence reflected a wide range of advantage and hardship. While many questions about pregnancy remain unanswered, this investigation of adolescent development suggested the importance of studying historical, social, and developmental aspects of the adolescent's life.

substantial increase of the size of the adolescent cohort in the 1960s has been proposed as one reason responsible for public concern about juvenile delinquency, deprived youth, student radicals, and teenage parenthood. To see further how such cohort effects are related to adolescent development, read Perspective on Adolescent Development 1.3, where information about adolescent pregnancy is discussed.

Now that we have considered a number of issues that characterize a developmental perspective of adolescence, we turn our attention to the periods and processes of adolescent development.

Periods and Processes of Development: Age and Beyond

In the contemporary study of development, we often refer to certain periods. And it is important to investigate the nature of processes that provide change from one period to the next.

Periods of Development

For our purposes of organization and understanding at a general level, we can divide development into the periods of childhood, adolescence, and adulthood. However, the childhood period has been subdivided into periods of infancy (approximately birth to two years), early childhood (three to five years), and middle and late childhood (six to ten or eleven years) by developmental psychologists. Adolescence has been divided into early and late adolescence, and a period called youth sometimes identifies the transition between adolescence and adulthood. Further, developmental psychologists often describe adulthood in terms of early, middle, and late periods. Let's now briefly study a number of these periods to learn some of the major characteristics of them.

The Prenatal Period

The **prenatal period** represents the time from conception to birth. It is a time of tremendous growth—a single cell develops into an organism complete with brain and behavioral capabilities in approximately nine months.

The prenatal period can be described in terms of a detailed biological timetable and there are environmental hazards that can significantly alter the entire course of adolescent development.

Infancy

Infancy is usually recognized as extending from birth to eighteen or twenty-four months. (For the first few days after birth, an infant is referred to as a **neonate.**) Infancy is a time of extreme dependence upon adults, with many physiological and psychological activities just beginning (language, symbolic thought, sensorimotor coordination, social learning). This period usually ends when the child talks in short phrases and finds it easy to walk great distances from the caretaker.

Early Childhood

Early childhood, which extends from the end of infancy to about five or six years, roughly corresponds to the period in which the child prepares for formal schooling. Sometimes this period of development is referred to as the preschool years. Among the tasks mastered are the ability to care for oneself (e.g., personal hygiene, dressing oneself), self-sufficiency (e.g., self-initiated play), and development of school-readiness skills (e.g., following instructions; using writing implements; identifying letters, numbers, and sounds). Peer relationships and play become more pronounced. First grade usually marks the end of this period.

Middle and Late Childhood

Middle and **late childhood** extends from about six to ten or eleven years of age, roughly corresponding to the elementary school years. Sometimes this period of development is called the elementary school years. Such fundamental skills as reading, writing, and arithmetic are mastered, and there is formal exposure to the larger world and its culture through the study of history, civics, business and government, art and music, and contemporary social problems. Thought processes usually are very concrete and less abstract than in the next period.

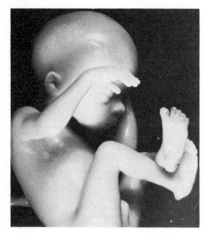

Fetus.

Infancy lasts from birth to twenty-four months.

Early childhood involves increased play and peer activity.

Middle and late childhood requires adaptation to schooling.

Early adolescence roughly corresponds to the middle or junior high school years.

Late adolescence spans the latter half of the second decade of life.

Kenniston described a transition from adolescence to adulthood as youth.

Early adulthood is a time of establishing personal and economic independence.

Adolescence

Our major interest in this text is the development of adolescents; however, a great deal of development and experiences have occurred before the individual enters adolescence. No boy or girl enters adolescence as a blank slate with only a genetic blueprint determining his or her thoughts, feelings, and behaviors. Rather, the combination of a genetic blueprint, adolescent experiences, and childhood experiences determine the course of adolescent development. Keep this point in mind about the continuity between childhood and adolescence as we study adolescent development in this text.

Can we define adolescence? It is not an easy task because, as we already have seen in our discussion of age as a variable, we need to consider life time, social time, and historical time in our conceptualization of adolescence. With this limitation in mind, we define **adolescence** as the period of transition between childhood and adulthood. Keeping in mind that there may be cultural and historical limitations on the age band of adolescence, in America and in most cultures today adolescence begins at roughly ten to thirteen years of age and ends at eighteen to twenty-two years of age. This period consists of biological-physical changes, cognitive changes, and social-emotional-personality changes ranging from the development of sexual functions to abstract thinking capabilities to independence. As we see next, there is a trend toward thinking about adolescence in terms of early and late periods.

Early and Late Adolescence

There is an increasing tendency to talk about early and late periods of adolescent development. **Early adolescence** encompasses the greatest pubertal change and the middle school or junior high school years. **Late adolescence** refers to the latter half of the second decade of life, roughly the ages of sixteen to eighteen or twenty-two years of age. As we discuss various aspects of physical, cognitive, and social development in adolescence, you will discover that investigators are increasingly sensitive to the distinction between early and late adolescence. Researchers now are much more likely to control for or investigate the age of the adolescents than in past years and more care is being taken to specify that the results of an investigation may not generalize to all ages of adolescents.

Youth

Kenneth Kenniston (1970) suggests that adolescents do not abruptly move into the period of adulthood. Rather, he argues that as they have been faced with a complex world of work that involves many highly specialized tasks, many older adolescents and young adults must spend an extended period of time training in technical institutes, colleges, and postgraduate centers. For many of them, this situation creates an extended sense of economic and personal "temporariness." Their earning levels are low and sporadic, and they may change residences frequently. Marriage and a family are put off until later. In many instances, this period lasts for two to four years, although it is not unusual for it to exist for eight to ten years. Kenniston refers to this period as **youth,** which might be entered as early as seventeen or eighteen years of age or as late as twenty-one or twenty-four years, and the period could last even through the late twenties.

Adulthood

Early adulthood usually begins in the late teens or early twenties and lasts through the thirties. It is a time of establishing personal and economic independence, and career development takes on an even more important role than in late adolescence. For many young adults, selecting a mate, learning to live with someone else in an intimate way, and starting a family take up a great deal of time. Probably the most important, widely recognized marker of entry into adulthood is the occasion when the young individual takes a more or less permanent, full-time job. It usually happens when individuals finish school—high school for some, college for others, and postgraduate training for others. Clear-cut patterns of determining when an individual has left adolescence or youth and entered adulthood are not easy to pin down. One of every four adolescents does not finish high school and many students who finish college cannot find a job. Further, only a small percentage of graduates settle into jobs that are permanent through their adult years. Further, if we consider economic independence as a criterion for adulthood, such independence is more often a long, gradual process rather than an abrupt one. Increasingly, we find college graduates who are returning to live with their families as they attempt to get their feet on the ground economically.

As we have just seen, defining when adolescence ends is not an easy task. It has been said that adolescence begins with biology and ends in culture. This means that the marker for entry into adolescence is determined by the onset of pubertal maturation and that entry into adulthood is determined more by cultural standards and experiences. As we will discover in Chapter 3, defining entry into puberty is not easy either. For boys, is it the first whisker or the first wet dream? For girls, is it the enlargement of breasts or the first period? For boys and girls, is it a spurt in height? We usually can tell when a boy or girl is in puberty, but its actual onset likely goes unnoticed.

Keep in mind also that **middle adulthood** is important in understanding adolescence as well. This period of adult development is entered roughly at thirty-five to forty-five years and exited at some point between fifty-five to sixty-five years of age. The reason this period is so salient in the lives of adolescents is that the parents of adolescents either are beginning to enter this adult period or are already in it. Middle adulthood is a time of increased concern about transmitting values to the next generation, enhanced interest in one's physical body, a changing time perspective, and often a changing view of careers. We will discover in Chapter 6, where we discuss parent–adolescent relationships, that in understanding adolescents and their families, it is important to consider both the maturation of the adolescent and the maturation of their parents, many of whom are entering or are in middle adulthood.

A summary of main ideas related to issues raised by a developmental perspective on adolescence and the nature of periods of development is presented in Concept Table 1.2. Now that we have considered a number of periods of development and focused on what constitutes the period of adolescence, we turn our attention to the processes or strands of development.

Processes and Strands of Development

The sections about adolescent development in this text often are organized around different strands or processes of development. The strands or processes of development that will be emphasized are biological processes and physical development; cognitive processes and development; and social, emotional, and personality processes and development.

Biological Processes and Physical Development

In Chapter 3, the role of biological processes and physical development in adolescence is discussed. The focus is on the importance of evolution and heredity in understanding adolescence. We will talk about a contemporary theory called ethology, which places a premium on the importance of biological processes in development. And we will chart the physical changes that characterize adolescence, spending considerable time describing the nature of the pubertal process including the manner in which hormonal changes affect adolescent behavior. We will discuss the heightened concern of adolescents with their body image and the degree to which early and late maturation influence adolescent development. We must keep in mind as we study about biological processes and physical development that they are important in understanding cognitive and social development as well.

Cognitive Processes and Development

We are in the midst of a cognitive revolution in psychology. No longer do we define psychology as the science of behavior, but as the science of mind and behavior (Santrock, 1986). Here we consider the mind synonymous with cognition. **Cognitive development** refers to changes that occur in mental activity, some of which are age-related, such as thought, memory, attention, perception, language, problem solving, intelligence, creativity, and decision making. We study cognitive processes and development in Chapters 4 and 5. In particular, we learn about three different perspectives on the cognitive development of adolescents: one emphasizing the developmental unfolding of cognitive structures, another stressing how the adolescent basically should be viewed as a system of information processing, and yet another focusing on individual differences in adolescent thought and their measurement. While cognitive processes and thought are housed primarily in Chapters 4 and 5, Jean Piaget's theory of cognitive development is described in Chapter 2, and in our discussion of social contexts of development and personality, we will see the impact of the cognitive orientation. For example, when we study family processes, information about cognitive changes in the adolescent will be brought to bear on an understanding of parent–adolescent conflict. And when we study the self and identity development, the importance of cognitive activity will become clear.

Social, Emotional, and Personality Processes and Development

Social, emotional, and personality processes are broad labels that encompass many different aspects of the adolescent's world; aspects that often overlap. The word **social** refers to the adolescent's interactions with other individuals in the environment. Two siblings arguing with each other, adolescents engaged in peer discussion, a teacher smiling at an adolescent, an adolescent attempting to control her mother—all are examples of social processes. In this text, we have devoted an entire section to the social contexts of adolescent development, those environmental settings in which adolescent development primarily unfolds. Chapter 6 describes family processes and parent–adolescent relationships.

Chapter 7 focuses on peer relations, friendships, and group relations; Chapter 8 evaluates the role of schools in adolescent development, and Chapter 9 deals with the influence of culture in adolescents' lives.

Discussions of **emotional processes and development** often contain many of the same components as social development. However, emotional development places more emphasis on the adolescent's feelings and affective responses (the words *affect, emotion,* and *feeling* can be used interchangeably). In Chapter 10, we study the humanistic perspective, a view that argues for the importance of affect in studying adolescents, and in Chapter 2, we evaluate psychoanalytic theory, a view that stresses the significance of such emotions as guilt and shame. As we discuss moral development later in the text, you will discover that it has

an affective component. Further, as we study problems and disturbances in adolescent development in Chapters 14 and 15, we will frequently encounter references to the emotional aspects of the adolescent's development.

Personality processes and development generally refer more to a property of the individual adolescent than to his or her commerce with the social world. Yet, it is often impossible to talk about personality without referencing the individual's interactions with and thoughts about the social world. Indeed, rather than calling Section IV only "Personality Processes and Development," we have chosen to label it "Social, Emotional, and Personality Processes and Development" to emphasize the close interrelation of social, emotional, and personality aspects of the adolescent. In Chapter 10, we study the development of the self and identity, in Chapter 11, the nature of sex role development and sexuality; in Chapter 12, moral development and values; and in Chapter 13, achievement and careers.

The Adolescent as an Integrated Human Being

Keep in mind that while it is helpful to study different strands of adolescent development (such as physical development, cognitive development, and social development) in separate chapters and sections, the adolescent is an integrated human being. The adolescent has only one mind and body. Physical, cognitive, and social development are inextricably woven together to form the total development of the adolescent. Many chapters and sections will describe how social experiences shape cognitive development, how cognitive development restricts or enhances social development, and how cognitive development is tied to biological processes and physical development.

Concept Table 1.2

ISSUES IN THE STUDY OF ADOLESCENT DEVELOPMENT AND PERIODS OF DEVELOPMENT

Concept	Processes/related ideas	Characteristics/description
Issues in a developmental perspective on adolescence	Development, maturation, and genetic-environmental interaction	Development refers to the process of change or movement in the life span, which may involve growth or decay. Historically, maturation has referred more to the genetic blueprint that produces a developmental unfolding of characteristics. However, in discussing the adolescent's development or maturation, it always is important to consider the contribution of hereditary-environmental interaction rather than the importance of either factor alone. The nature-nurture controversy is another label for the issue of heredity-environmental contributions to development.
	Qualitative change in development	This issue focuses on whether development is different from one point to another point, rather than simply being more or less.
	Stages of development	An emphasis on stages implies that qualitative changes must occur and happen in certain sequences.
	Continuity-discontinuity in development	We described two aspects of this issue—the abruptness and discontinuity between stages, as well as the most widely discussed aspect, that of the extent later development is based on or related to earlier experiences and/or development. There are a number of reasons that both continuity and discontinuity can occur in development. It is important to recognize some continuity between childhood and adolescence, however, and also to view the adolescent as capable of change as well.
	Individual differences	The extent to which individuals are the same as or different than others in a stable way. Developmental psychologists study intraindividual change as well.
	Age as a variable	Age merits further study, but undoubtedly has some limitations because of its descriptive rather than explanatory nature. Conceptualizations such as life time, social time, and historical time expand the age concept and may ultimately strengthen its use in understanding adolescent development.

Concept Table 1.2 (Continued)

ISSUES IN THE STUDY OF ADOLESCENT DEVELOPMENT AND PERIODS OF DEVELOPMENT

Concept	Processes/related ideas	Characteristics/description
Periods of development	Prenatal and infancy	Prenatal period lasts from conception to birth, a time of tremendous change and physical growth. Infancy lasts from birth to about two years and is a time of considerable dependence on adults as well as the emergence of many abilities such as language.
	Early, middle, and late childhood	Early childhood lasts from about two to five or six years of age and also is known as the preschool years. Self-sufficiency increases as do school-readiness skills. During middle and late childhood, from about six to ten or eleven years of age, academic skills are mastered and there is formal exposure to the larger world. This period also is referred to as the elementary school years.
	Adolescence	Adolescence is a transition from childhood to adulthood, involving changes in physical, cognitive, and social development. It is entered roughly between the ages of ten and thirteen and exited approximately between the ages of eighteen and twenty-two. There is an increasing tendency to describe adolescence in terms of early and late periods, with early adolescence referring to approximately the ages of ten to fifteen and late adolescence to the latter half of the second decade of life and possibly even into the early twenties. Rapid physical changes, the process of puberty, corresponds more to early than late adolescence. Defining just when adolescence begins and when it ends is difficult. It has been said that adolescence begins in biology and ends in culture.
	Youth	Kenneth Kenniston proposed that a period called youth represents a transition from adolescence to adulthood. This period lasts roughly for two or four up to ten years and consists of a great deal of temporariness.
	Adulthood	The period of early adulthood, which roughly covers the third and fourth decades of life, involves themes of career development and intimacy. Taking a more or less permanent job has been offered as one marker of the beginning of early adulthood, but this criterion does not always hold up on careful scrutiny. Middle adulthood is particularly salient in our study of adolescents because many parents of adolescents are beginning to enter or are in this period.

Summary

I. Parents, educators, and scientists all are interested in the development of adolescents. They all share a concern about the most effective way of socializing adolescents.

II. An interest in the historical background of adolescence focuses on the Greeks, the Middle Ages, the Renaissance, the period of adolescence (1900 to the present), and the stereotyping of adolescents.

   A. Both Plato and Aristotle commented about adolescents. Plato argued that reason emerges in adolescence and that childhood experiences are important in the time frame we now call adolescence. Aristotle believed the most important aspect of adolescence is the ability to choose. He also thought that self-determination is a hallmark of adolescent development. Aristotle specified three stages of development.

   B. During the Middle Ages, knowledge about adolescents took a step backward; this was the time when the miniature adult view of children appeared. Rosseau, a French philosopher during the Renaissance, did much to counter the negative view of the child and adolescent as a miniature adult. He proposed a four-stage developmental timetable. Reason and self-consciousness were thought to develop between twelve and fifteen years of age and emotional maturity was believed to replace selfishness in the fifteen to twenty year age span.

   C. At the turn of the century, approximately 1890–1920, a cadre of psychologists, educators, urban reformers, youth workers, and counselors began to mold the concept of adolescence.

      1. G. Stanley Hall's book, *Adolescence,* was published in 1904, marking the beginning of the scientific study of adolescence. Hall is known for his storm and stress view of adolescence and the belief that biology plays a prominent role in development. A number of scholars argue that adolescence was invented through a combination of social and historical circumstances, particularly those involving school and work. State legislation of youth insured their dependency and made their move into the world of work more manageable.

   D. From 1920–1950, adolescents gained a more prominent status in society. During the 1920s, adults even began to model some of their behaviors after adolescents. During the 1930s and 1940s, major historical events— the Great Depression and World War II— signalled the importance of historical considerations in understanding adolescent development.

   E. By 1950, the developmental period we now call adolescence had come of age. It possessed physical and social identity. During the 1960s and early 1970s, adolescent rebelliousness came to the forefront of American society. Much of the radical protest of adolescents has abated today, yet other confrontations with adult standards still appear in the form of women's rights, nuclear protest, hunger in the third world, and the rights of adolescents.

III. A number of issues come to light when a developmental perspective on adolescence is adopted. Among them are: the nature of development, maturation, and genetic– environmental interaction; qualitative change; stages of development; continuity–discontinuity; individual differences; and age as a variable.

   A. Development refers to the process of change or movement in the life span, which may involve growth or decay. Historically, maturation has referred more to the genetic blueprint that produces a developmental unfolding of characteristics. However, in discussing the adolescent's development or maturation, it always is important to consider the contribution of hereditary–environmental interaction rather than the importance of either factor alone. The nature-nurture controversy is another label for the issue of heredity–environmental contributions to development.

B. Qualitative change focuses on whether development is different from one point to another point rather than simply being more or less.

C. Stages of development refer to qualitative changes that must occur in a particular sequence.

D. Two aspects of the continuity–discontinuity issue were discussed—the abruptness and discontinuity between stages, as well as the most widely debated aspect, that of the extent later development is based on or related to earlier experiences and/or development. There are a number of reasons both continuity and discontinuity can occur in development. It is important to recognize some continuity between childhood and adolescence; however, at the same time, it is equally important to view the adolescent as capable of change.

E. Individual differences refers to the extent individuals are the same as or different than others in some stable manner. Developmental psychologists also are interested in intraindividual change, stability/change within individuals as they develop.

F. Age as a variable in the development of adolescents merits further study, but it is important to recognize its descriptive rather than explanatory nature. Conceptualizations such as life time, social time, and historical time expand the age concept and may ultimately strengthen its utility in understanding adolescent development.

IV. While there is not complete agreement on the exact labels and their age bands, developmental psychologists have proposed a number of periods of development. For purposes of understanding and organization, we described the following developmental periods—prenatal and infancy; early, middle, and late childhood; adolescence; youth; and adulthood.

A. The prenatal period lasts from conception to birth, a time of tremendous change and physical growth. Infancy lasts from birth to about two years and is a time of considerable dependence on adults as well as the emergence of many abilities such as language.

B. Early childhood lasts from about two to five or six years of age and also is known as the preschool years. Self-sufficiency increases as do school-readiness skills. During middle and late childhood, from about six to ten or eleven years of age, academic skills are mastered and there is formal exposure to a larger world. This period also is called the elementary school years.

C. Adolescence is the transition from childhood to adulthood, involving changes in physical, cognitive, and social development. It is entered roughly between the ages of ten and thirteen, and exited approximately between the ages of eighteen and twenty-two. There is an increasing tendency to describe adolescence in terms of early and late periods, with early adolescence referring to approximately the ages of ten to fifteen and late adolescence the latter half of the second decade of life and possibly even into the early twenties. Rapid physical changes, the process of puberty, corresponds more to early than to late adolescence. Defining just when adolescence begins and ends is difficult. It has been said that the end of adolescence is more difficult to mark than the beginning because adolescence might well begin in biology and end in culture.

D. Kenneth Kenniston proposed that a period called youth represents a transition from adolescence to adulthood. This period lasts roughly from two or four up to ten years and consists of a great deal of temporariness.

E. The period of early adulthood, which roughly covers the third and fourth decades of life, involves themes of career development and intimacy. Taking a more or less permanent job has been proposed as one marker of adulthood, but this criterion, under careful scrutiny, does not always hold up. Developmental psychologists who study adolescence also have shown an increased interest in middle adulthood because the majority of adolescents' parents are beginning to enter that period of adulthood or are in it.

V. A strong process orientation characterizes this textbook. The sections and chapters are often organized around strands or processes of adolescent development, such as biological-physical processes; cognitive processes; and social, emotional, and personality processes.

A. Biological processes include information about evolutionary, hereditary, and hormonal influences. Physical development involves the study of bodily changes over time.

B. Cognitive development refers to the unfolding of changes over time in mental activity—thought, attention, memory, perception, language, problem solving, decision making, and the like.

C. Social development focuses on the individual's interactions with the environment and how such commerce with others changes over time. A major emphasis in this book involves the social contexts in which adolescents develop such as families, peer settings, and schools. Personality development tends to refer more to properties of the individual than social development, although it is difficult to talk about personality without referencing social matters. Emotional development focuses on the feelings and affective life of individuals, matters such as guilt, shame, pride, happiness, sadness, self-esteem, and such.

D. While it is helpful to study separate processes and strands of development, it is important to remember the adolescent has only one mind, body, and personality. Therefore, it is necessary to study how these are integrated in the adolescent.

Key Terms

adolescence *33*

adolescent generalization gap *20*

age *28*

cognitive development *34*

cohort effects *29*

continuity–discontinuity *24*

development *22*

early adolescence *33*

early adulthood *33*

early childhood *31*

emotional processes and development *35*

historical time *28*

individual differences *27*

infancy *31*

intraindividual change *27*

late adolescence *33*

life time *28*

maturation *22*

middle adulthood *34*

middle and late childhood *31*

neonate *31*

personality processes and development *35*

prenatal period *31*

qualitative change *23*

social *35*

social time *28*

stages *23*

stereotype *19*

storm and stress view *14*

youth *33*

Suggested Readings

Developmental Psychology, Child Development, Journal of Youth and Adolescence, and *Journal of Early Adolescence.*

The chances are excellent that your library will have one or more of these research journals that either focus exclusively on adolescents or include many articles about adolescents. Take some time to leaf through issues of the journals published within the last several years to obtain a glimpse of the research issues that interest the scientists who study adolescents.

Elder, G. H. (1980). Adolescence in historical perspective. In *Handbook of adolescent psychology,* ed. J. Adelson. New York: John Wiley.
An intriguing portrayal of how historical time influences the nature of adolescent development.

Hill, J. P. (1980). *Understanding early adolescence: A framework.* Chapel Hill, N.C.: University of North Carolina.
This booklet provides an excellent overview of the nature of development in early adolescence. Written by John Hill, one of the leading scholars in adolescent development.

Kett, J. F. (1977). *Rites of passage.* New York: Basic Books.
Kett describes in great detail three major historical phases in the way the adolescent has been dealt with in the United States. The nature of adolescence from 1790 to the present is discussed.

Lee, C. B. T. (1970). *The campus scene: 1900–1970.* New York: McKay.
Lee's book is an excellent, entertaining description of late adolescent development and college life. The author makes many comparisons between peer- and parent-adolescent interaction in different decades of the twentieth century.

Ross, D. (1972). *G. Stanley Hall: The psychologist as prophet.* Chicago: University of Chicago Press.
This is an intriguing biographical sketch of the father of adolescent psychology, G. Stanley Hall.

Chapter 2

The Scientific Study of Adolescent Development: World Views, Theories, and Methods

Prologue

The Youths of Famous Theorists—The Adolescent Years of B. F. Skinner, Jean Piaget, and Erik Erikson

How does someone develop a theory about adolescence? The individual usually goes through a long university training program that culminates in a doctoral degree. As part of the training, the individual is exposed to many ideas about adolescence. But another factor that might help explain how such a person might develop a particular theory is the kind of life experience the theorist had during his or her infant, childhood, and adolescent years. This introduction to various theories that have been proposed to explain adolescent development will describe the youths of three prominent theorists who have helped to shape our views.

B. F. Skinner. B. F. Skinner was born in 1904 in Susquehanna, Pennsylvania, where he lived until he went to college. Skinner describes his home environment as "warm and stable." His younger brother (by 2½ years) was much better at sports and more popular than B. F. was, and he frequently teased B. F. about his literary and artistic interests. When the younger brother died suddenly at the age of sixteen, Skinner felt guilty because his brother's death didn't bother him. B. F. Skinner says about his youth:

> I was always building things. I built roller skates, scooters, steerable wagons, sleds, and rafts to be poled about on shallow ponds. I made seesaws, merry-go-rounds, and slides. I made slingshots, bows and arrows, blowguns and water pistols from lengths of bamboo, and from a discarded water boiler a steam cannon with which I could shoot plugs of potato and carrot over the houses of our neighbors. I made tops, diabolos, model airplanes driven by twisted rubber bands, box kites, and tin propellers which could be sent high into the air with a spool-and-string spinner. I tried again and again to make a glider in which I myself might fly . . .

B. F. Skinner (b. 1904)

> I went through all twelve grades of school in a single building, and there were only eight students in my class when I graduated. *I liked school.* . . . An old maid school teacher, Mary Graves, was an important figure in my life. Her father was the village atheist and an amateur botanist who believed in evolution . . . Miss Graves was a dedicated person with cultural interests far beyond the level of the town . . . She was my teacher in many fields

Erik Erikson (b. 1902)

for many years . . . Miss Graves was probably responsible for the fact that in college I majored in English literature and afterwards embarked upon a career as a writer.

B. F. was never physically punished by his father, and was punished only once by his mother—she washed his mouth out with soap and water because he said a bad word. However, B. F.'s father frequently informed B. F. of the punishment he would get if he turned out to be a delinquent. He took B. F. through the county jail, and once on a summer vacation took him to a color slide show of Sing Sing prison! His mother monitored his behavior closely. If B. F. deviated, she would say, "Tut-tut, what will people think?" (Skinner, 1967)

Erik Erikson. Erik Homberger Erikson was born June 15, 1902, near Frankfurt, Germany to Danish parents. Before Erik was born, his parents separated and his mother left Denmark to live in Germany, where she had some friends. At age three, Erik became ill, and his mother took him to see a pediatrician named Homberger. Young Erik's mother fell in love with the pediatrician, married him, and gave Erik the middle name of his new stepfather.

Erik attended primary school between the ages of six and ten, and then the Gymnasium (high school) from age eleven to eighteen. He studied art and a number of languages rather than scientific courses like biology and chemistry. Erik did not like the formal atmosphere of his school, and this was reflected in his grades. At age eighteen, rather than going to college, the adolescent Erikson wandered through the continent, keeping notes about his experiences in a personal diary. After a year of travel through Europe, he returned to Germany and enrolled in an art school, became dissatisfied, and enrolled in another. Then he began to give up his sketching and eventually traveled to Florence, Italy. Robert Coles vividly describes Erikson at this time:

To the Italians he was not an unfamiliar sight: the young, tall, thin Nordic expatriate with long, blond hair. He wore a corduroy suit and was seen by his family and friends as not odd or "sick" but as a wandering artist who was trying to come to grips with himself, a not unnatural or unusual struggle—particularly in Germany. (Coles, 1970, p. 15)

Prologue (Continued)

Jean Piaget. Jean Piaget was born August 9, 1896, in Neuchâtel, Switzerland. Jean's father was an intellectual type who taught young Jean to think systematically. Jean's mother also was very bright, and strongly religious as well. His father seemed to maintain an air of detachment from his mother, who has been described by Piaget as prone to frequent outbursts of neurotic behavior.

In his autobiography, Piaget detailed why he chose to pursue the study of cognitive rather than emotional development.

> I started to forego playing for serious work very early. Indeed, I have always detested any departure from reality, an attitude which I relate to . . . my mother's poor mental health. It was this disturbing factor which at the beginning of my studies in psychology made me keenly interested in psychoanalytic and pathological psychology. Though this interest helped me to achieve independence and to widen my cultural background, I have never since felt any desire to involve myself deeper in that particular direction, always much preferring the study of normalcy and of the workings of the intellect to that of the tricks of the unconscious. (Piaget, 1952, p. 238)

Jean Piaget (1896–1980)

While his studies took him in the direction of biology and other intellectual pursuits, the deteriorated health of Piaget's mother had an important impact on his first job after he completed his doctorate degree. In 1918, Piaget took a position at Bleuler's psychiatric clinic in Zurich, where he learned about clinical techniques for interviewing children. Then, still at the young age of twenty-two, he went to work in the psychology laboratory at the University of Zurich. There he was exposed to the insights of Alfred Binet, who developed the first intelligence test. By the time Piaget was twenty-five, his experience in varied disciplines had helped him see important linkages between philosophy, psychology, and biology.

After you have read each of these theorist's views in this chapter, come back to this description of their infant, childhood, and adolescent years. Try to detect ways in which their experiences might have led each to develop his own view of adolescence.

*W*hen we say that we need to further our scientific understanding of adolescent development, what do we mean by the label "scientific"? You will discover that the label "scientific" implies the use of theories and/or methods. First, we describe the nature of the scientific basis of adolescent development, then we discuss a number of world views and theories that characterize the study of adolescent development. And, we conclude with an overview of the methods used to investigate adolescent development.

What We Mean When We Refer to the Science of Adolescent Development: Theories and Methods

The **science** of adolescent development is characterized by a systematic body of theories that can be verified or proved false on the basis of actual evidence collected about adolescents. The science of adolescent development includes a variety of methods of collecting information. These theories and methods are at the heart of understanding adolescent development. Without them, adolescent development might as well be classified as an art or a religion. But with them, we are able to describe, predict, understand, and change adolescent development.

World Views: Reactive, Active, and Interactive

World views are grand models that transcend more precise, specific, testable models. World views are highly abstract, containing ideas that cannot be directly proved or disproved scientifically. However, while the world views themselves are not testable, they do serve to stimulate ideas, issues, and questions that can be tested. Three prominent world views have characterized inquiry about adolescent development: mechanistic, organismic, and contextual.

The Mechanistic World View

One way we compare mechanistic, organismic, and contextual world views is in terms of the assumptions they make about the nature of the developing individual. The **mechanistic world view** assumes a vision of the adolescent as a passive machine that reacts to events in the environment but does not actively anticipate events, does not formulate its own goals, and in most instances does not engage in complex internal mental activity of any kind. For the most part, the mechanistic world view also assumes that social, environmental experiences are more important determinants of development than biological foundations. Further, analysis of psychological phenomena is carried out in a very fine-grained, molecular manner.

The Organismic World View

The **organismic world view** assumes the adolescent is active and mindful. From this view, an adolescent has goals and plans, and is a person who uses complex strategies to attain ends. For the most part, the organismic world view assumes a strong biological foundation of development. From this view, experiences with the social world primarily provide the setting for the unfolding of development rather than being the causes of development. This approach typically is more molar and global than the fine-grained analysis of the mechanistic world view. And, while most organismic perspectives stress the maturational unfolding of cognition, this view is not constrained to cognitive theories alone. Both biological and personality views have organismic characteristics as well.

The Contextual World View

The **contextual world view** is neither a purely passive nor a purely active view of the adolescent, but an interactive perspective. The basic conception is that the

"Well, whatever it is we change into, it can't come soon enough for me."

Drawing by D. Reilly; © 1973 The New Yorker Magazine, Inc.

adolescent continuously responds to and acts on the contexts in which he or she lives. There are many contexts in an adolescent's life—environmental contexts, sociohistorical contexts, and biological contexts, for example. Environmental contexts pertain to such settings as family, school, and peers. Sociohistorical contexts refer to such matters as social norms in society and how historical conditions may influence the individual's behavior. Biological contexts involve health and physical skills. In regard to all of these contexts, we can speak not only of the contexts influencing the adolescent, but the adolescent influencing the contexts as well. For example, because the sun is hot, an individual either plants trees (alters the context) or moves to a colder climate (changing the context). Alternatively, the adolescent's family might begin making unreasonable demands, and so the adolescent begins to refuse them more often. This might alter the family's subsequent behavior, which in turn alters the adolescent's own behavior, and so forth.

Some developmental psychologists have preferred to describe the contextual world view as **dialectical** in nature. This means the adolescent is continually changing and contexts are changing as well rather than being in equilibrium. For instance, Klaus Riegel (1977) argued that too much of our theorizing about development has consisted of efforts to portray the developing individual as striving for balance or equilibrium.

By constrast, Riegel believed a better understanding of development will take place if we study disequilibrium and change. For Riegel, development is always in a state of flux. Balance and equilibrium, while strived for, are never attained. From the dialectical perspective, developing adolescents are changing beings in a changing world. Riegel said that the moment when completion or equilibrium seems to be reached, new questions and doubts arise in the adolescent and in society. Riegel stressed that contradiction and conflict are an inherent part of development and that no single goal or end point is ever reached.

An overview of key points in the world views is presented in Concept Table 2.1.

Theories of Development: Beyond Rats, Concrete Thought, and Couches

While **theories** are still abstract in nature, they generally are not as broad and abstract as world views. Theories are assumptions made to explain the nature of adolescent development. Some theories fit more precisely with a particular world view while others cut across several world views. As we describe theories of development, we will point out the main points of each of the theories, describe two main variations of each theoretical perspective, and tell about its ties to world views.

Concept Table 2.1

MECHANISTIC, ORGANISMIC, AND CONTEXTUAL WORLD VIEWS

World view	Characteristics/description
Mechanistic	1. Organism viewed as passive, machine-like 2. Social, environmental experiences very important 3. Psychological phenomena are analyzed in fine-grained, molecular fashion
Organismic	1. Organism viewed as active, mindful 2. Strong biological foundation stressed 3. More molar approach to psychological phenomena than mechanistic view
Contextual	1. Organism is neither purely active nor purely passive, but interactive 2. Organism is continually responding to and acting on contexts 3. Important to consider variety of contexts and possibly dialectical nature of development

Behavioral Theories

The behavioral point of view is often talked about as a unified perspective on development, but like most theoretical perspectives, it contains more than one viewpoint. The two main forms of the behavioral viewpoint are the traditional behavioral view of B. F. Skinner and the social learning theory of Albert Bandura. Before we talk about these two prominent variations of the behavioral viewpoint, however, let's look at some commonalities of the behavioral perspective.

The Behavioral Perspective

First, it is important to note that the **behavioral perspective** emphasizes the influence of the environment on the behavior of the adolescent. Second, the adolescent's behavior is viewed as learned. Third, a strong methodological orientation is followed that emphasizes the fine-grained observation of the adolescent's behavior. Fourth, the adolescent's mental events or cognitive processes either are viewed as outside the realm of scientific study or as mediators of environmental experience and behavior, rather than causes of behavior. Now let's look more closely at the traditional, behavioral view of Skinner and the social learning theory of Bandura, then at the world views of these theorists, and finally at the strengths and weaknesses of the behavioral perspective.

Skinner's Behaviorism

Skinner's behaviorism is the protypical example of the mechanistic world view. While much of his research has been with rats and pigeons, Skinner has applied his ideas to human development on numerous occasions (1948, 1971, 1974). In recent years, the book that has stirred the most interest is *Beyond Freedom and Dignity* (1971), the main theme focusing on how individuals are controlled by their external environment. Skinner believes that if we are to unravel the mysteries of adolescent development, we need look no further than the behavior of adolescents. He believes that looking for the internal determinants of behavior inhibits the search for the true causes of the adolescent's behavior that reside in the external environment. Some psychologists believe that Skinner is saying adolescents are empty organisms, but Skinner (1953) objects to looking for these determinants, not because they do not exist, but because they are irrelevant to the relation between stimuli (observable characteristics of the environment) and responses (overt behaviors of the adolescent).

According to Skinner, one of the major ways stimuli and responses are linked together is through the principle of **operant conditioning** (sometimes referred to as **instrumental conditioning**). In this type of learning, the adolescent operates on the environment; that is, the adolescent does something, and, in turn, something happens to him or her. Another way of saying this is that the adolescent's behavior is instrumental in causing some effect in the environment. The lives of adolescents are full of operant conditioning situations. For example, consider the following conversation:

John   Hey, where did you get that new jacket?
Bob   My mother bought it for me.
John   Oh, yeah? Why?
Bob   Because I got mad about something and started yelling at her.
John   You mean if you get mad and throw a fit, your mom buys you a jacket?
Bob   I guess that's the way it works!

At the heart of such occurrences is this principle: behavior is determined by its consequences. According to this principle, behavior followed by a positive stimulus is likely to recur, while behavior followed by a negative stimulus is not as likely to recur. Information about how the consequences for an adolescent's behavior can be used to help the adolescent become better adjusted is described in Perspective on Adolescent Development 2.1.

Social Learning Theory

Cognitive social learning theory is the label that best describes the view of Albert Bandura (1977). From Bandura's perspective, the statement that behavior is determined by its consequences refers to the self-produced consequences of one's own actions as well as to consequences of the actions of others.

Consider the achievement behavior of an adolescent who is required to perform certain duties at his job. Although he cannot ignore his desire for a salary

In return, Billy's father agreed to (1) not yell at Billy, but, if angry about something to ask Billy in a low tone of voice to explain what had happened; (2) not criticize teenagers, particularly Billy's friends; and (3) give Billy a small sum of money each week for gas and dates—but only until Billy obtained a job, at which time Billy would start paying his own expenses.

The counselor encouraged Billy and his father to agree to a point system for each of these three behavioral areas. If they failed to meet the standards they had agreed to, they lost points; if they met the standards, they gained points. The points could be transferred into money at the end of each week. Both Billy and his father agreed that Billy's mother could keep track of the number of points earned each day to assess their progress. If the system began to break down or if disputes about the system needed to be settled, the participants could discuss the problem at the weekly meeting with the counselor. The points of conflict and contingencies might change as the situation improved or worsened. The behavioral therapist would monitor the system and change the contract accordingly.

increase, his own need for excellence will just as likely motivate him to improve and to do a better job on his work assignment. Substandard performance, on the other hand, might lead him to self-criticism. In this sense, the boy's achievement behavior is as much a function of his reaction to himself as to the reactions of others. This concept differs from Skinner's theory, since he argues that behavior is determined only by external consequences.

Bandura emphasizes the concept of **reciprocal determinism.** The adolescent is not completely driven by inner forces or manipulated helplessly by environmental factors; rather, the adolescent's psychological makeup is best understood by analyzing the continuous reciprocal interaction between behavior and its controlling conditions. In other words, behavior partly constructs the environment, and the resulting environment, in turn affects behavior.

Bandura (1971, 1977) also believes that adolescents learn extensively by example. Much of what adolescents learn involves observing the behavior of parents, peers, teachers, and others. This form of social learning is called **imitation, modeling,** or **vicarious learning.** For example, the fourteen-year-old who watches the teacher smile at her friend for turning in her work on time may be motivated to do likewise.

Bandura believes that if learning proceeded in the trial-and-error fashion advocated by Skinner, it would be very laborious and even hazardous. For example, to put a fifteen-year-old girl in an automobile, have her drive down the road, and reward the positive responses she makes would be senseless. Instead, many of the complex educational and cultural practices of individuals are learned through their exposure to competent models who display appropriate ways to solve problems and cope with the world.

We mentioned at the beginning of this section on social learning theory that Bandura's view is best described as a cognitive social learning perspective. What does this label mean? The cognitive revolution in psychology has infiltrated social learning theory. It became apparent to social learning theorists that the adolescent's cognitive interpretation of environmental experiences is important in understanding the adolescent's behavior rather than relying on a careful analysis of environmental stimuli alone. In addition to Bandura, Walter Mischel (1968, 1973, 1984) has been a strong proponent of cognitive social learning theory. It was Mischel (1973) who actually coined the label "cognitive social learning theory." Adding the adjectives "cognitive" and "social" to learning theory changes the character of the view considerably. Even early social learning theorists (e.g., Dollard and Miller, 1950) believed that Skinner's behaviorism provided a view that was too narrow for understanding human social learning. Expanding social learning theory to include cognitive mediation of environmental experiences places the theory even further from the behavioral view of Skinner. Nonetheless, cognitive social learning theorists still view environmental experiences as the primary causes of the adolescent's behavior—cognitive processes are mediators of social experiences that help in the prediction of the adolescent's behavior, but they do not cause the adolescent's behavior.

World Views of Behaviorists and Social Learning Theorists

While Skinner's behavioral view is a mechanistic world view, Bandura's social learning theory has the ingredients of both the mechanistic and the contextual world views.

The Strengths and Weaknesses of the Behavioral and Social Learning Theories

Among the strengths of the behavioral and social learning theories are:

1. The behavioral and social learning approaches have shown us that specific behaviors and environmental stimuli are important determinants of adolescent development.

2. Both views have demonstrated the contribution of the observational method in learning about adolescent development.

3. The rigorous experimental approach of the behavioral and social learning views has fostered a climate of scientific investigation in the field of adolescent development.

4. The social learning perspective has highlighted the tremendous importance of information processing in mediating the relation between behavior and environmental stimuli.

5. The social learning perspective has sensitized us to the importance of adapting to changing environmental circumstances, and both the behavioral and social learning perspectives have stressed how development may vary from one context to another depending upon the nature of the contexts.

Among the weaknesses of the behavioral and/or social learning perspectives are:

1. The behavioral view has been heavily criticized for believing that cognitive processes are irrelevant for understanding development. This criticism does not apply to cognitive social learning theory.

2. Both the behavioral and social learning views are nonchronological views in that the processes that determine development are essentially the same at all ages.

3. The behavioral and social learning approaches have paid too little attention to the biological foundations of development.

4. Both the behavioral and social learning perspectives are too reductionistic. That is, they reduce development to elements that are very fine-grained, possibly missing the gestalt of development (which may only be captured by looking at more global dimensions as well).

5. Critics have said that the behavioral and the social learning views are too mechanical. That is, they describe adolescents as if they were emotionless, mindless machines, helplessly buffeted by their environment. However, this is perhaps not a fair charge against contemporary cognitive social learning theory as developed by Bandura. Bandura's emphasis on social interaction makes his ideas at least partly consistent with a contextual world view.

In our discussion of cognitive social learning, we have seen that cognition plays an important mediating link between environmental experiences and the adolescent's behavior. Next, we focus on a theory that places cognition in a more causative role—the cognitive developmental theory of Jean Piaget.

Cognitive Theories

As indicated in Chapter 1, we are in the midst of a cognitive revolution in psychology. This cognitive revolution has infiltrated developmental psychology and the study of adolescent development. During the 1960s and 1970s in particular, developmental psychologists became enamored with the fascinating insights of the Swiss psychologist, Jean Piaget. Rather than emphasizing the role of environmental experiences as the predominant focus of developmental study, the cognitive approach stresses that mental or cognitive processes are the key ingredients of development.

Cognitive Developmental Theory

Cognitive developmental theory focuses on the rational thinking of the developing individual. It also stresses that cognitive development unfolds in a stage-like sequence, which is ordered and uniform for all individuals. The leading figure in cognitive developmental theory is Jean Piaget. Another is Lawrence Kohlberg, whose views on moral development will appear later in this book. Since we will talk at length about Piaget in Chapter 4, we will provide only a brief presentation of Piaget's ideas here.

Piaget's ideas form one of the most complete theoretical statements about intelligence available in psychology. Piaget believes that the core of development is rationality—that is, logical thinking—and that intelligence develops from the interaction of hereditary and environmental forces. Piaget is more interested in how children think than in what they think. For example, it is more important to Piaget that an adolescent uses a logical series of steps in reasoning about a solution to a problem than whether an adolescent can correctly provide an answer to a problem. Let's look more closely at Piaget's cognitive developmental stages and how they represent qualitatively different ways of thinking.

A brief outline of Piaget's stages of thought follows (Piaget, 1967). As is the case with all such theories, the time periods designated for various stages are only approximate. An individual child may move out of a stage sooner or remain in a stage longer than is indicated by the ages given. The more significant claim is that a child moves through the given stages in the established sequence and that no child violates this sequence. These stages will be discussed in greater detail in Chapter 4.

Stages of Development The **sensorimotor stage** lasts from birth to about two years of age, corresponding to the period known as infancy. During this time, the infant develops the ability to organize and coordinate his or her sensations and perceptions with his or her physical movements and actions. This coordination of sensation with action is the source of the term *sensorimotor*. The stage begins with the newborn, who has little more than reflexes to coordinate his or her senses with actions. The stage ends with the two-year-old, who has complex sensorimotor patterns and is beginning to develop a primitive symbol system. For example, the two-year-old can imagine looking at a toy and manipulating it with his or her hands before he or she actually does so. The child can also use simple sentences—for example, "Mommy, jump"—to represent a sensorimotor event that has just occurred.

The **preoperational stage** lasts from two to seven years of age, cutting across the preschool and early middle school years. During this time, the child's symbol system expands. The use of language and perceptual images moves well beyond the capabilities of a child at the end of the sensorimotor period. The child tends to see things from his own perspective and to confuse this perspective with that of others. He has difficulty manipulating the images and representations of events and is therefore likely to get stuck (centered) in static states and to be unable to reverse situations mentally. For example, if liquid is poured from a short, fat container into a tall, thin one, the child may notice only that the height of the water has changed (centering). If asked to imagine what would happen if the water were returned to the original container, he would have a tough time visualizing the reversal (irreversibility).

The **concrete operational stage** lasts from seven to eleven years of age, cutting across the major portion of the middle school years. During this time, the child's thinking crystallizes into more of a system. The shift to a more perfect system of thinking is brought about by several changes. One of these is the shift from egocentrism to relativism. Relativism is the ability to think about something from different perspectives and to think simultaneously about two or more aspects of a problem. Another change is the child's ability to pose and operate mentally in a series of actions. Performing mental arithmetic, imagining a game of table tennis, and thinking about how to tie a knot are all examples of this change. Children in the sensorimotor and preoperational stages, by contrast, are unable to perform these mental operations.

One limitation of concrete thinking is that the child has to rely on concrete events in order to think in this way. He or she needs to be able to perceive the objects and events that he or she will think about.

The final stage in Piaget's theory is the **formal operational stage,** which appears between the ages of eleven and fifteen years. Piaget believed individuals enter the most advanced form of thought during early adolescence. The most important aspect of this stage is the ability to move beyond a world of actual, concrete experiences and think in abstract and more logical terms. In developing a more abstract system of thought, the adolescent often thinks about ideal circumstances rather than what is concrete and real. He or she may begin to think about what the ideal parent is like and compare his or her parents to that standard. He or she usually begins to entertain many possibilities for his or her future, and is more fascinated with what he or she can become rather than what he or she is right now. The adolescent begins to think in a more systematic way in solving problems, developing hypotheses about why something is happening the way it is. Subsequently, he or she may test these hypotheses in a deductive fashion.

Processes Responsible for Cognitive Changes Piaget believed several processes that are interrelated are responsible for changes in thought: Adaptation, which can be subdivided into assimilation and accommodation, organization, and equilibration. The adaptiveness Piaget emphasizes is subdivided into **assimilation** and **accommodation,** which usually occur together. In assimilation, we try to incorporate new features of the environment into already existing ways of thinking about it. In accommodation, we try to incorporate new features of the environment into our thinking by slightly modifying existing modes of thought. An example may help to clarify these concepts. A young girl is given a hammer and nails to hang a picture on the wall. She has never used a hammer before. From experience and observation, though, she realizes that a hammer is an object to be held, that it is swung by the handle to hit the nail, and that it is usually swung a number of times. Realizing each of these things, she incorporates her behavior into a conceptual framework that already exists (assimilation). However, the hammer is heavy, so she has to hold it near the top. As she swings too hard the nail bends, so she has to adjust the pressure of her strikes. These adjustments reveal her ability to alter the concept slightly (accommodation). Keep in mind that equilibration is not a state of balance to be attained in the sense it has been reached and remains static. Rather, equilibration is a dynamic state representing a desirable state of organization of "goodness of fit" that will fluctuate as it is applied (assimilation) and adjusted (accommodation).

In addition to adaptation, Piaget believes two other properties of thought are important: organization and equilibration. Every level of thought from sensorimotor to formal operational is organized in some manner. Continual refinement of this **organization** is a part of development. Another important aspect of thought focuses on the development of a more lasting balance. This goal is achieved as thought becomes more logical and abstract. But before a new stage of thought can be attained, we must face the inadequacy of our current one. We must experience cognitive conflict or uncertainty. The mechanism by which we resolve cognitive conflict and reach a balance of thought is called **equilibration.** If a child believes that the amount of liquid is changed simply because we pour it into a container of a different shape, he or she might be puzzled by such issues as where the "extra" liquid came from and whether there actually is more liquid to drink. These puzzles eventually will be solved as the child's thought process moves to a higher stage. The adolescent is faced with many such inconsistencies and counterexamples every day.

Piaget's lasting contributions to the field of development are that he identified a broad spectrum of cognitive abilities that develop, he invented many clever tasks that are still used to gauge intellectual change, and he offered many intriguing hypotheses that have been pursued by others in the field. We will discuss his theory in much greater detail in Chapter 4.

The Information Processing Perspective

At about the same time that Piaget's theory was becoming a fixture in developmental psychology, another cognitive approach was gaining favor among American psychologists. The **information processing approach** is concerned with how we process information about our world—how we attend to information, how we store the information for further use, how we reason about the information, and so forth. An important influence on the information processing approach has been the growth of computer science (Siegler, 1983). Computers are essentially high-speed information processing systems that can be programmed. It was thought that computers could provide a logical and concrete, though perhaps overly simplified, version of how information might be processed in the mind (Hunt, 1982).

The information processing approach shares with behaviorism the belief that careful experimentation is crucial to advancing knowledge about development. Although cognitive psychologists are dealing with unobservable processes, like memories and plans, they have been very precise in controlling conditions and developing ingenious experiments to reveal how mental processes work. Much more about the information processing perspective appears in Chapter 5 where we discuss different models of information processing, information processing views of intelligence, and applications of information processing to education. It should be noted that the information processing perspective and cognitive social learning theory share similar views on the adolescent. However, the information processing perspective has devoted more attention to nonsocial aspects of thought and behavior, such as thinking about numbers and words, while cognitive social learning theory has been concerned more with personality and social behavior. Over the next decade, these two perspectives are likely to come closer together in appearance as information processing psychologists become interested in social factors that influence how we process information and cognitive social learning theorists delve more deeply into the processes of thought that determine social behavior and personality.

World Views of the Cognitive Theorists

Both Piaget's theory and the information processing perspective have an organismic flavor in that the adolescent's thoughts are an important aspect of his or her development. The Piagetian view has an added organismic tie due to its emphasis on the biological maturation of cognitive structures. Piaget's theory also has a contextual flavor through an emphasis on hereditary interaction as the determinant of cognitive structures and the belief that environmental settings are important contexts for the unfolding of cognitive structures. However, in Piaget's theory, there has been more of a tendency to emphasize biological processes as stronger causes of development than environmental stimulation. The information processing perspective has ties with another world view as well. Its mechanistic ties stem from a fine-grained, rather mechanical description of mental activity and the attribution of causes of behavior and thought to environmental experiences rather than biological maturation.

The Strengths and Weaknesses of the Cognitive Theories

Among the strengths of the Piagetian and information processing perspectives are the following.

1. Piaget's theory was a breath of fresh air in developmental psychology. It came at a time when thought was viewed as unconscious (psychoanalytic theory), not an important influence on behavior (behaviorism) or highly varied among individuals (psychometric theory). Piaget's theory was the first theory to provide a rich description of children's and adolescents' thought processes.

2. Piaget's theory directed research toward uncovering how the adolescent's thought processes unfold maturationally, and how important biological adaptation is to development.

3. The information processing perspective has provided a very strong research-oriented atmosphere for the study of the adolescent's cognitions.

4. The information processing perspective has demonstrated a precision in conceptualizing how adolescents think. For example, this approach has produced detailed examination of the memory processes of children and adolescents.

The weaknesses of the Piagetian and information processing perspectives include the following.

1. There is skepticism about the pureness of the Piagetian stages.

2. Piaget's concepts are somewhat loosely defined.

3. The information processing model has not yet produced an overall perspective on development.

4. Both the Piagetian and information processing views may have underestimated the importance of environmental experiences, particularly those involving families, and of the unconscious mind in determining behavior.

Psychoanalytic Theories

So far, we have studied behavioral theories that stress environmental influences on development, and cognitive theories that emphasize the importance of conscious cognitive thought in development. The cognitive theory of Jean Piaget also places a premium on the biological adaptation of the adolescent. A third set of prominent theories in development are called psychoanalytic theories. The psychoanalytic theories stress the importance of biology and thought in development but in a manner different from the cognitive theories. You will discover, for example, that Sigmund Freud believed the central core of development consists of the biological unfolding of psychosexual stages rather than the biological adaptation of thought. You also will learn that rather than stressing conscious thought, or thought the adolescent is aware of, the psychoanalytic theorists emphasize the importance of unconscious thought, thought the adolescent is not aware of.

Classical Psychoanalytic Theory

The year is 1904. You are lying on a comfortable couch in an office in Vienna, Austria. A gentleman with a stern look on his face walks in and sits down near you. He asks you to close your eyes. After several minutes of silence, he starts inquiring about what you remember about your childhood. The man asking the questions is Sigmund Freud. Unlike many of the early figures in developmental psychology we have discussed so far, Freud was fascinated by the abnormal aspects of people's lives.

Freud believed that the key to understanding the mind and behavior rested in the unconscious aspects of the mind—that part of an adolescent's mind of which he or she is unaware. Freud compared the human mind to an iceberg, the conscious mind being only the tip of the iceberg, with the bulk being taken up by the unconscious aspects.

It is not surprising that Freud believed biological forces shape our development because he was trained as a medical doctor. He stressed that **instincts,** particularly those related to sex and aggression, control and motivate us to think, feel, and behave in particular ways (Freud, 1924).

Although Freud emphasized that much of the adolescent's existence was biologically determined, he also had some opinions about parenting. Freud saw the first five years of life as the critical years in the adolescent's personality development. That is why he asked you about your early childhood years while you were relaxing on the couch. It was his hope that by getting you to talk about your early family life, you would unconsciously reveal some clues about conflicts that were causing your current psychological problems. During these early years, the development of identification with parents is a central theme. Freud actually saw identification as a defense mechanism in which the child resolves inner conflict and sexual desires for the opposite-sex parent by patterning himself or herself after the same-sex parent. By identifying with the same-sex parent, the child is thought to incorporate the parent's standards and characteristics into his or her own personality.

Freud's view of the nature of human beings is not a very optimistic one. He saw people as being in constant conflict—being pulled between their sexual and aggressive instincts, and contact with reality. Freud's views on instinct and psychosexual development have been moderated by some psychoanalytic theorists, but his views about the importance of unconscious motivation and early family experiences remain as important ingredients in contemporary psychoanalytic theory.

Freud's psychoanalytic theory is often referred to as **classical psychoanalytic theory.** It places heavy emphasis on the unconscious aspects of the mind and the biological unfolding of psychosexual stages. The psychosexual stages are particularly important in developmental psychology since they stress the emergence of certain characteristics at particular points in development. Thus, just as Piaget's theory is a stage theory, so is Freud's, but Piaget emphasized the unfolding of cognitive stages while Freud stressed maturation in the form of psychosexual stages. A summary and overview of Freud's oral, anal, phallic, latency, and genital stages of development are presented in table 2.1.

Table 2.1 The Freudian psychosexual stages of development

*T*he first stage, known as the **oral stage,** centers on the child's pleasure from stimulation of the oral area—mouth, lips, tongue, gums. This stage lasts from birth to around one year of age. The activities of sucking, chewing, and biting provide the chief sources of pleasure. When the oral area is stimulated some instinctual energy is freed and tension is reduced.

The period called the **anal stage,** lasting from two to three years of age, centers on the child's pleasure from eliminative activity. The shift to the anal stage is brought about by maturation of the sphincter muscles and the child's ability to hold back or expel waste material at will. It is assumed that exercise of the anal muscles results in the freeing of instinctual energy and the reduction of tension. This period is not easily forgotten by parents, who typically experience great concern over their initially unsuccessful efforts to toilet train their child. When toilet training has been accomplished, the anal stage has reached its peak—the child has achieved well-regulated control over anal activity. Many debates have arisen about the proper method and time for toilet training (e.g., Anthony, 1957); however, few of the premises offered have much to do with the specific theoretical claims of Freud (e.g., Beloff, 1962).

During the **phallic stage,** which lasts from about four to five or six years of age, instinctual energy is focused on the genital area. Physical changes in the child cause this area to be a pleasurable one when stimulated. It is during this period, Freud thought, that boys and girls become acutely aware of their sexual anatomy and the anatomical differences between sexes. This awareness sets up a number of complex psychological events referred to as the **Oedipus complex** in boys and the **Electra complex** in girls. Each complex consists of the child's alternating feelings of love and hate for each parent as the child competes with one parent for the love and attention of the other parent. Working through these complexes, which are actually highly stressful conflicts about sexual affiliation and identity, takes from eight to ten years and forms the basis for the mature adult's personal and sexual identity.

The troublesome feelings and thoughts experienced while attempting to work out these conflicts are often repressed, driven from consciousness and locked away in the unconscious id. This repression marks the onset of the **latency stage,** the long period of middle childhood from about six to twelve years of age. During the latency stage, the child concentrates on exploring the environment and mastering the vast number of intellectual skills and tricks needed for getting along in society. This activity channels much of the child's psychological energy into "emotionally safe" areas that help the child forget the highly stressful problems of the previous stage.

The **genital stage,** the last of Freud's stages of development, occurs from about thirteen to nineteen years of age. During this period, the repression of Oedipal and Electra conflicts is lifted and teenagers experience a sudden surge of interest in sexual matters. After a number of groping attempts, the adolescent forms a stable sense of personal and sexual identity. The period is brought on by, among other things, the rapid physiological changes occurring in the adolescent at about twelve or thirteen years of age.

Neopsychoanalytic Theories

Although psychoanalytic theory has survived as a major theory of developmental psychology, its form has changed somewhat from the classical manner in which it was set forth by Sigmund Freud.

Many contemporary psychoanalytic theorists downplay the importance of sexual instincts in determining an adolescent's personality, instead placing more emphasis on rational thought processes and cultural influences. Contemporary psychoanalytic theory still stresses the developmental unfolding of personality and the way in which adolescent and adult characteristics are heavily determined by childhood experiences. Unconscious thought processes are still believed to be an important part of the mind. Many contemporary psychoanalytic theorists are called **neopsychoanalytic theorists,** because they accept a number of Freudian ideas, such as unconscious thought and the developmental unfolding of personality, but disagree with Freud about one or more main issues. For example, Sigmund Freud believed that **defense mechanisms** were an important aspect of the adolescent's ability to maintain contact with reality. One such mechanism is **regression,** which occurs when the adolescent reverts to an earlier stage of development. As discussed in Perspective on Adolescent Development 2.2, some important neopsychoanalytic theorists gave defense mechanisms a new life in understanding adolescent development.

THE ROLE OF DEFENSE MECHANISMS IN ADOLESCENT
ADJUSTMENT: THE VIEWS OF PETER BLOS AND
ANNA FREUD

For Peter Blos (1962), one of the most well-accepted contemporary psychoanalytic theorists who studies adolescents, regression during adolescence is not defensive at all, but rather is an integral part of puberty. Such regression, according to Blos, is inevitable and universal. The nature of this regression may vary from one adolescent to the next. It may involve childhood autonomy, compliance, and cleanliness, or it may involve a sudden return to the passiveness that characterized the adolescent's behavior during infancy or early childhood. Blos believes that intrafamilial struggles during adolescence reflect the presence of unresolved conflicts from childhood.

An excellent example of how the psychoanalytic theorist works in tying together adolescent feelings with childhood experiences rests in the work of Joseph Adelson and Margery Doehrman (1980). When their patient, John, was sixteen he entered a group therapy session with other adolescents. At this time he was recovering from severe depression following the break-off of a serious relationship with a girlfriend. The girl's mother actually referred John to the clinic, sensing that John's depression was severe, just as she had earlier detected that his dependency on her daughter was acute. John was a handsome, intelligent, articulate adolescent and a leader at school, hardly the type of person you would think might be deeply and severely depressed.

After a series of sessions with John, it became apparent that he kept most girls at a distance, particularly when they seemed to want to get seriously involved or to "mother" him. On the other hand, he was attracted to girls who were either aloof or tom-boyish. It gradually became clear that John's relationships with girls were characterized by a wish to reestablish a union with his mother and that he had an intense fear of that wish. He was attracted to girls who were standoffish, but once he established a relationship with one of them, he would sink into an uncontrollable dependency upon her, to the point of being enthralled by such dependency.

To some degree, then, John's attachments to girls represented a wish to become reunited with his mother. What was John's relationship with his mother like in adolescence? He was often abusive toward her; he complained that she nagged at him all the time; but in truth he was frightened by his regressive feelings toward her, according to Adelson. The regressive feelings came out clearly in group therapy when his intelligent participation would be replaced by sarcasm and then scorn whenever he seemed to be drawn to the "maternal" females in the group. This was particularly true with the woman therapist, who was seen as the group's "mother."

Although some psychoanalytic writers, like Blos, consider regression a normal part of adolescent development, for individuals like John the reappearance of unresolved conflicts from early childhood requires therapy. For most individuals, however, the conflicts are not so serious that therapy is warranted. Thus, the intensity and persistence of the regression determine whether it is a healthy or unhealthy part of adolescent development.

Anna Freud (1958, 1966) has developed the idea that defense mechanisms are the key to understanding adolescent adjustment. She believes that the problems of adolescence are not to be unlocked by understanding the id, or instinctual forces, but instead are to be discovered in the existence of "love objects" in the adolescent's past, both oedipal and preoedipal. She argues that the attachment to these love objects, usually parents, is carried forward from the infant years and merely toned down or inhibited during the latency years. During adolescence, these pregenital urges may be reawakened, or worse, newly acquired genital (adolescent) urges may combine with the urges that developed in early childhood.

Anna Freud goes on to describe how adolescent defense mechanisms are used to ward off these infantile intrusions. Youth may withdraw from their attachment and identification with their parents and suddenly transfer their love to others—to parent substitutes, to leaders who represent ideals, or to peers. Or, rather than transferring the attachment to someone else, adolescents may reverse their feelings toward the attachment

figure—replacing love with hate or dependence with rebellion. Finally, the instinctual fears may even generate unhealthy defensive solutions—for example, the adolescent may withdraw within himself, which could lead to grandiose ideas of triumph or persecution; or regression could occur. Thus, from Anna Freud's perspective, a number of defense mechanisms are essential to the adolescent's handling of conflicts.

Erik Erikson One well-known contemporary neopsychoanalytic theorist is Erik Erikson. Like Freud, Erikson stresses the importance of early family experiences and unconscious thought. However, he believes Freud shortchanged the importance of culture in determining personality. For example, both Freud and Erikson describe changes that take place during adolescence. For Freud, these changes are primarily sexual in nature, but for Erikson, they involve the development of an identity. Erikson believes it is during adolescence that individuals begin a thorough search for who they are, what they are all about, and where they

are going in life. As part of this search for an identity, the adolescent often experiments with a variety of roles—some sexual, others ideological, and still others vocational.

While Freud described changes in development only through the adolescent years, Erikson's view is truly a life-cycle perspective in that his view of the eight ages of man covers development from birth through the late adulthood years. Each of Erikson's eight ages (or stages) of development centers around a salient and distinct emotional concern stemming from biological pressures from within, and sociocultural expectations

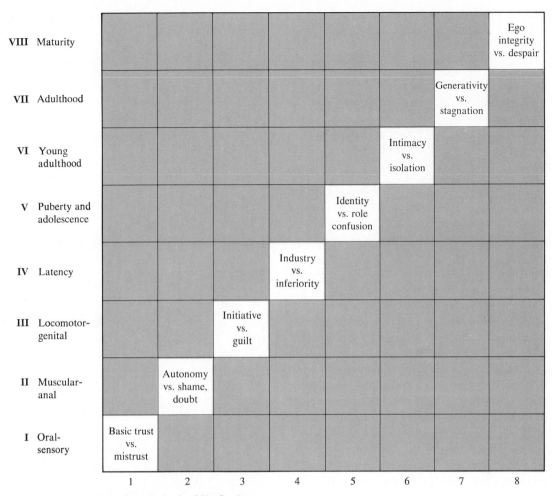

	1	2	3	4	5	6	7	8
VIII Maturity								Ego integrity vs. despair
VII Adulthood							Generativity vs. stagnation	
VI Young adulthood						Intimacy vs. isolation		
V Puberty and adolescence					Identity vs. role confusion			
IV Latency				Industry vs. inferiority				
III Locomotor-genital			Initiative vs. guilt					
II Muscular-anal		Autonomy vs. shame, doubt						
I Oral-sensory	Basic trust vs. mistrust							

Figure 2.1 Erikson's Eight Stages in the Life Cycle

from outside, the person (figure 2.1). Concerns or conflicts may be resolved in a positive and healthy manner or in a pessimistic and unhealthy way (Erikson, 1968).

The first stage, **trust versus mistrust,** corresponds to the oral stage in Freudian theory. An infant is almost entirely dependent upon his or her mother for food, sustenance, and comfort. The mother is the primary representative of society to the child. If she discharges her infant-related duties with warmth, regularity, and affection, the infant will develop a feeling of trust toward the world. The infant's trust is a comfortable feeling that someone will always be around to care for his or her needs even though the mother occasionally disappears. Alternatively, a sense of mistrust or fearful uncertainty can develop if the mother fails to provide for these needs in the role of caretaker. According to Erikson, she is setting up a distrusting attitude that will follow the child through life.

Autonomy versus shame and doubt is the second stage and corresponds to the anal stage in Freudian theory. The infant begins to gain control over the bowels and bladder. Parents begin imposing demands on the child to conform to socially acceptable forms of and occasions for eliminating wastes. The child may develop the healthy attitude of being capable of independent or autonomous control of his or her own actions, or may develop the unhealthy attitude of shame or doubt because he or she is incapable of control.

Erikson's first stage: trust vs. mistrust.

Erikson's second stage: autonomy vs. shame, doubt.

Initiative versus guilt corresponds to the phallic period of Freudian theory. The child is caught in the midst of the Oedipal or Electra conflict, with its alternating love-hate feelings for the parent of the opposite sex and with the fear of fulfilling the sexual fantasies that abound. The child may discover ways to overcome feelings of powerlessness by engaging in various activities. If this is done, then the basic healthy attitude of being the initiator of action will result. Alternatively, the child may fail to discover such outlets and feel guilt at being dominated by the environment.

Industry versus inferiority, coinciding with the Freudian period of latency, covers the years of middle childhood when the child is involved in expansive absorption of knowledge and the development of intellectual and physical skills. As the child is drawn into the social culture of peers, it is natural to evaluate accomplishments by comparing himself or herself with others. If the child views himself or herself as basically competent in these activities, feelings of productiveness and industriousness will result. On the other hand, if the child views himself or herself as incompetent, particularly in comparison with peers, then he or she will feel unproductive and inferior. This unhealthy attitude may negatively color the child's whole approach to life and learning, producing a tendency to withdraw from new and challenging situations rather than meet them with confidence and enthusiasm.

Erikson's third stage: initiative vs. guilt.

Erikson argued that the stage of industry versus inferiority characterizes the elementary school years.

Erikson's sixth stage: intimacy vs. isolation

Erikson's fifth stage: identity vs. identity confusion (diffusion).

Identity versus identity confusion (diffusion) is roughly associated with Freud's genital stage, centering on the establishment of a stable personal identity. For Freud the important part of identity formation resides in the adolescent's resolution of sexual conflicts, whereas for Erikson the central ingredient is the establishment of a clear path toward a vocation—selection of a job or an occupational role to aspire to. This allows the adolescent an objective that he or she and other members of society simultaneously acknowledge. If the adolescent comes through this period with a clearly selected role and the knowledge that others in society can clearly identify this role, feelings of confidence and purposefulness emerge. If not, the child may feel confused and troubled.

Erikson introduced the first of the post-Freudian stages, **intimacy versus isolation.** Early adulthood brings with it a job and the opportunity to form an intimate relationship with a member of the opposite sex. If the young adult forms friendships with others and a significant, intimate relationship with one individual in particular, then a basic feeling of closeness with others will result. On the other hand, a feeling of isolation may result from an inability to form friendships and an intimate relationship.

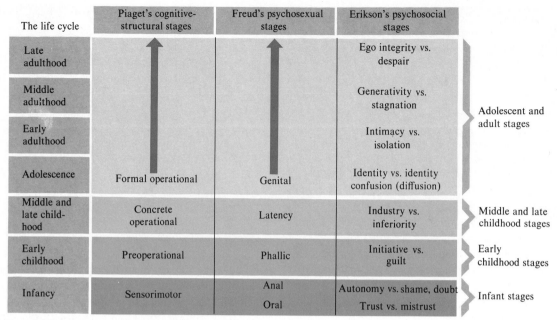

The life cycle	Piaget's cognitive-structural stages	Freud's psychosexual stages	Erikson's psychosocial stages	
Late adulthood			Ego integrity vs. despair	
Middle adulthood			Generativity vs. stagnation	Adolescent and adult stages
Early adulthood			Intimacy vs. isolation	
Adolescence	Formal operational	Genital	Identity vs. identity confusion (diffusion)	
Middle and late childhood	Concrete operational	Latency	Industry vs. inferiority	Middle and late childhood stages
Early childhood	Preoperational	Phallic	Initiative vs. guilt	Early childhood stages
Infancy	Sensorimotor	Anal / Oral	Autonomy vs. shame, doubt / Trust vs. mistrust	Infant stages

Figure 2.2 A comparison of the Piagetian, Freudian, and Eriksonian stages of development.

A chief concern of adults is to assist the younger generation in developing and leading useful lives. **Generativity versus stagnation** centers on successful rearing of children. Childless couples often need to find substitute young people through adoption, guardianship, or a close relationship with the children of friends and relatives. Generativity, or the feeling of helping to shape the next generation, is the positive outcome that may emerge. Stagnation, or the feeling of having done nothing for the next generation, is the negative outcome.

In the later years, we enter the period of **ego integrity versus despair,** a time for looking back at what we have done with our lives. Through many different routes, the older person may have developed a positive outlook in each of the preceding periods of emotional crisis. If so, the retrospective glances will reveal a picture of life well spent, and the person will be satisfied (ego integrity). However, the older person may have resolved one or more of the crises in a negative way. If so, the retrospective glances will yield doubt, gloom,

and despair over the worth of one's life. A summary of Erikson's stages, as well as those of Freud and Piaget, is presented in figure 2.2.

It should be noted that Erikson does not believe the proper solution to a stage crisis is always completely positive in nature. Some exposure and/or commitment to the negative end of the individual's bipolar conflict often is inevitable (for example, the individual cannot trust all people under all circumstances and survive). However, in a healthy solution to a stage crisis, the positive resolution of the conflict is dominant. Much more about Erikson's view is presented in Chapter 10 where we discuss identity development.

The World Views of Psychoanalytic Theorists
Freud's classical psychoanalytic theory has much in common with an organismic world view—the organism's biological heritage, the active nature of the organism, and the emphasis on mind all fit this world view. However, while Erikson's ideas fit with an organismic

view, his strong emphasis on sociocultural and historical conditions stress a contextual world view as well.

We have discussed the views of Freud and Erikson. To conclude our overview of the psychoanalytic perspective, we will describe the strengths and weaknesses of that perspective.

The Strengths and Weaknesses of the Psychoanalytic Theories

Like most grand theories of development, psychoanalytic theory has its strengths and weaknesses. First, we will discuss some of its major contributions and strengths, and second, we will look at some of its possible flaws and weaknesses.

Six strengths of psychoanalytic theory focus on (1) the role of the past, (2) the developmental course of personality, (3) the mental representation of the environment, (4) the role of the unconscious mind, (5) conflict emphasis, and (6) its influence on developmental psychology as a discipline. Today we assume that past experiences influence current thoughts and behavior. The psychoanalytic emphasis on the importance of early experience in influencing thought and behavior at later points in development has remained as an important part of developmental psychology. It is important to note that both classical and psychoanalytic theories emphasize the importance of how children carry forward relationships with people to influence relationships later in development. Thus, relationships with parents during the early years of childhood are seen to be carried forward to influence the nature of peer and dating relationships in adolescence. The idea of how individuals carry forward earlier relationships to construct relationships in development has emerged during the 1980s as an important aspect of understanding the nature of development. We will pursue this point in some detail as we describe the nature of family processes in Chapter 6.

The importance of viewing personality from a developmental stance continues to be an important theme in the field. The psychoanalytic belief that environmental experiences are mentally transformed and represented in the mind also continues to be given considerable attention by psychologists. Psychoanalytic theorists forced psychologists to recognize that the mind is not all consciousness—some of what is in the mind is unconscious as well. Psychoanalytic theory has promoted the belief that conflict is an important ingredient of psychological problems and adjustment. And, psychoanalytic theory has continued to play an important role in forcing developmental psychologists to study the importance of personality and adjustment rather than being interested only in such experimentally oriented topics as sensation, perception, and learning.

However, while psychoanalytic theory has made important contributions to psychology and has a number of strengths, it is not without its flaws and weaknesses. Some of the strengths listed turn out to be some of its weaknesses as well, often because such orientations were stated in such an extreme manner. Five such prominent weaknesses are (1) the difficulty of testing psychoanalytic concepts, (2) the lack of an empirical data base and overreliance on self-reports of the past, (3) overemphasis on the unconscious mind and sexuality, (4) a negative and pessimistic view of human nature, and (5) too much emphasis on early experience.

The main concepts of psychoanalytic theory have been very difficult to test scientifically. Researchers have tried to investigate concepts like repression in the laboratory, but such efforts have generally not met with a great deal of success. Much of the data used to support psychoanalytic theory come from patients' reconstruction of the past, often the distant past (adults' perception of their infant and early childhood years), so the accuracy may be doubtful. Other data called on to support psychoanalytic theory come from the subjective evaluation of clinicians, in which it is very easy for the clinicians to see what they expect to see because of theory they are used to. Freud and many other psychoanalytic theorists (though not Erikson) overemphasized the importance of sexuality in development. Most psychoanalysts also place too much faith in the power of the unconscious mind to control behavior, often to the point of ignoring the role of conscious thought processes.

THEORIES OF ADOLESCENT DEVELOPMENT

Theory	Theorist/example	Themes/processes	World view	Strengths/weaknesses
Behavioral and social learning	Skinner	Behavioral control; external environment; operant conditioning; mind unimportant.	Mechanistic	*Strengths:* 1. Specific behaviors and environmental stimuli are important determinants of development. 2. Observational methods. 3. Rigorous experimental approach. 4. Social learning theories emphasis on cognitive mediation. 5. Adaptation to changing social world and importance of context. *Weaknesses:* 1. Failure to recognize causative role of cognition. 2. Non-chronological view. 3. Too little attention to biological processes. 4. Too reductionistic. 5. Too mechanical.
	Bandura	Cognitive social learning theory; reciprocal determinism; imitation; cognitive processes mediate relation of environment to behavior.	Mechanistic-contextual	
Cognitive	Piaget	Biological adaptation (assimilation, accommodation), organization, and equilibration; cognitive structures; cognitive developmental stages; conscious thought.	Organismic-contextual	*Strengths:* 1. Piaget's rich description of children's thought. 2. Piaget's emphasis on biological maturation and adaptation. 3. Strong research orientation of information processing. 4. Precision of

The psychoanalytic view provides a perspective of the person that is too negative and pessimistic. We clearly are not born into the world with only a bundle of evil instincts and drives. Psychoanalytic theory often places too much emphasis on the first five years of life as determinants of subsequent development. Personality development continues throughout the human life cycle and is influenced by past, present, and anticipated future circumstances, a point accurately captured by Erikson. Later experiences may be just as important as early experiences in determining development in many instances.

We have studied many different aspects of three main theoretical perspectives on adolescent development. A summary of main ideas related to these major perspectives is presented in Concept Table 2.2. Next, we see that an eclectic theoretical orientation may be a wise strategy.

THEORIES OF ADOLESCENT DEVELOPMENT

Theory	Theorist/example	Themes/processes	World view	Strengths/weaknesses
	Information processing	Often calls on comparison of mind to computer; cognitive processes such as attention, memory, speed of processing information and capacity for processing.	Organismic-mechanistic	describing how child's mind works by information processing view. *Weaknesses:* 1. Skepticism about Piagetian stages; 2. Loose definitions of Piaget; 3. No overall developmental perspective in information processing approach; 4. Underestimation of environmental family processes and unconscious thought by cognitive theories.
Psychoanalytic	Freud, classical psychoanalytic theory Erikson, neopsychoanaltyic theory	Biological instincts; unconscious thought; psychosexual stages. Eight stages of development; psychosocial stages; life-cycle perspective; interaction of biology and culture.	Organismic Organismic-contextual	*Strengths:* 1. Concern about past. 2. Developmental emphasis. 3. Mental representation of world. 4. Role of unconscious mind. 5. Emphasis on conflict. 6. Influence on developmental psychology as a discipline. *Weaknesses:* 1. Concepts difficult to test. 2. Lack of empirical data base. 3. Too much emphasis on unconscious mind. 4. Too much emphasis on sexual basis of behavior. 5. Negative, pessimistic view of development. 6. Too much stress on early experience.

An Eclectic Theoretical Orientation

There is no single all-encompassing theory or world view in explaining adolescent development. Each of the theories and world views has made a contribution to our understanding, but none provides a complete description and explanation of adolescent development. For example, the mechanistic perspective provides a thorough account of environmental influences, but has told us little about biological maturation. Cognitive-developmental and information processing theories have provided the best explanation of the workings of the adolescent's conscious mind, but much less information about the unconscious mind and environmental influences. Erikson's life-span developmental view has contributed greatly to our thinking about the location of adolescence in the human life cycle, but it has not provided a detailed examination of the conscious cognitive processes involved in development.

There are many other theories of development that we have not mentioned in this chapter, but which will be woven into discussions of adolescent development throughout the remainder of the book. For example, in our discussion of cultural aspects of adolescence, we will look at sociological and anthropological theories. The humanistic perspective in Chapter 10 emphasizes the development of the self and how the self-concept is important in understanding mind and behavior.

Now that we have seen how pervasive theory construction has been in the scientific study of adolescent development, we turn our attention to the nature of the methods involved.

Methods: Collecting Data and Designing Research

Our discussion of methods focuses on ways of collecting information about adolescent development: the measures we use; the strategies of research design; and the time span of inquiry.

Ways of Collecting Information about Adolescent Development

There are many different ways to conduct systematic observations under controlled conditions. We can watch the behavior of adolescents in a laboratory or in the natural setting in which they live, ask questions of adolescents in interviews or surveys, develop and administer standardized tests, conduct a case study or use the clinical method, and do physiological research with animals.

Systematic Observation

We watch things all the time, but it doesn't usually constitute what we would call scientific observation or research. If we are not trained as an observer and don't practice our skills on a regular basis, we're not quite sure what to look for, may not remember what we have seen, may change what we look for from one moment to the next, and often communicate our observations ineffectively.

For observation to be an effective method, we have to know what we are looking for, whom we are going to observe, when and where we are going to observe, how the observations are going to be made, and in what form they are going to be recorded. That is, our observations have to be made in some systematic way. The most common way of recording what we see is to write it down, using shorthand or symbols. Tape recorders, cameras, special coding sheets, and one-way windows all have been used to make observations more efficient.

When we observe, it is frequently necessary to control certain factors that determine development, but are not the focus of our inquiry. For this reason, some research on adolescent development has been in a laboratory, a controlled setting in which much of the "real world" with its complex factors is removed. However, there are costs involved in conducting laboratory research. First, it is virtually impossible to do research in a laboratory without the participants knowing they are in an experiment. Second, the laboratory setting may be "unnatural" and cause "unnatural" behavior on the part of the participants. Third, there are some aspects of development that are difficult if not impossible to produce in the laboratory. Certain types of stress, for example, might be difficult (and unethical) to investigate in the laboratory; thus, matters pertaining to the impact of marital discord and the use of physical punishment on adolescent development would not be viable candidates for laboratory observation. While

"Would you say you are, 'extremely happy,' 'happy,' 'average' or 'bored stiff'?"

laboratory research remains an extremely valuable tool for developmental psychologists, naturalistic observation or field studies have sometimes been used when information about development in real-world settings is needed. Observations have been made at home, work, schools, parks, shopping malls and other places where adolescents commonly go. Piaget's observations of his children at home were naturalistic observations. Jane Goodall (1963) spent months living in Africa with chimps in the wild to observe their behavior in a natural setting. Roger Barker wrote *One Boy's Day* after he had followed a young boy around for an entire day and observed his behavior in a variety of natural settings (Barker and Wright, 1951).

Though often presented as a dichotomy, laboratory and field research are really two points on a continuum that can be labeled *naturalism* or *control*. For example, we can conduct laboratory studies with a decidedly "natural" character. Thus, instead of studying memory for some unknown combination of letters like *isz, bkd,* and so on, we might investigate the adolescent's memory of autobiographical events. We can also carry out naturalistic studies under controlled conditions. For example, we might observe the behavior of adolescents at school after we had created two decidedly different teaching styles, one a high degree of verbal interaction and question asking with students and the other a low degree of verbal interaction and question asking.

Interviews and Surveys

An **interview** is a set of questions asked of someone and the responses to them. The interview can range from very structured to very unstructured. For example, a very unstructured interview might include questions like "Tell me about some of the things you do with your friends," or "Tell me about yourself," while a very structured interview might question whether the respondent highly approves, moderately approves, moderately disapproves, or highly disapproves of his friends using drugs.

Researchers also are able to question adolescents through surveys or questionnaires. A **questionnaire** is similar to a highly structured interview, except that adolescents read the questions and mark their answers on a sheet of paper rather than giving a verbal response. One major advantage of surveys and questionnaires is that they can easily be given to a very large number of adolescents, sometimes as many as 10,000. Questions on surveys should be concrete, specific, and unambiguous, but often they are not. Some assessment of the authenticity of the replies should also be made, but often is not.

Structured interviews conducted by an experienced psychologist can produce more detailed responses than are possible in a questionnaire and can help eliminate careless responses. A good interviewer can encourage the respondent to open up as well. But interviews are not without problems. Perhaps the most critical of these problems involves the response set of "social desirability," in which the adolescent tells you what he thinks is socially most acceptable or desirable rather than how he truly feels or thinks. When asked about her sexual relationships, for example, a female may not want to admit having had sexual intercourse on a casual basis. Skilled interviewing techniques and built-in questions to eliminate such defenses are critical in getting accurate information from an interview.

Another problem with both interviews and surveys or questionnaires is that some questions may be retrospective in nature; that is, they may require the participant to recall events or feelings that occurred at some point in the past. It is not unusual, for example, to interview adults about experiences they had as adolescents or adolescents about experiences they had as children. Unfortunately, retrospective interviews are seriously affected by distortions in memory. It is exceedingly difficult to glean accurate information about the past from verbal reports. Because of the importance of understanding retrospective verbal reports, 1978 Nobel prizewinner Herbert Simon and others are investigating better ways to gain more accurate verbal assessments of the past (Erickson and Simon, 1978). These people focus on the information-processing aspects of cognition, such as short- and long-term memory and incomplete and inconsistent verbalized information. And as we continue to recognize the importance of carrying forward relationships to understand the adolescent's development, a thorough effort to understand how our memory works becomes even more crucial.

Standardized Tests

Standardized tests actually can be questionnaires, structured interviews, or behavioral in nature. Their distinctive feature is that they are developed to identify an adolescent's characteristics or abilities, in relation to those of a large group of similar adolescents. The score of one adolescent is then compared to those of a large number of adolescents to see how she compares with them. In standardized tests, we usually give individuals a percentile score, such as telling the adolescent he scored in the ninety-second percentile on the verbal section of the SAT test. This tells how much higher or lower he scored than the large group of individuals who initially were given the test. Among the standardized tests widely used are intelligence tests like the Stanford-Binet and Wechsler Scales, and personality tests like the MMPI (Minnesota Multiphasic Personality Inventory).

The main advantage of standardized tests is their ability to provide a comparison of one individual's score with large numbers of other people's scores. That is, they provide information about individual differences among adolescents. However, information obtained on standardized tests doesn't always predict behavior in nontest situations successfully. Standardized tests are based on the belief that an adolescent's behavior is consistent and stable, varying little from one context to the next. But while personality and intelligence, two of the primary targets of standardized tests, have some stability, they sometimes vary depending on the situation in which an adolescent is evaluated. So, an adolescent may perform poorly on a standardized test of intelligence, but when observed in a less anxious context, such as the natural surroundings of his or her home setting, he or she may perform much better. This criticism is particularly relevant to minority group adolescents, some of whom have been inappropriately classified as mentally retarded on the basis of their scores on an intelligence test. Much more about standardized intelligence tests appears in Chapter 5.

Case Study and Clinical Method

A **case study** is an in-depth look at a single adolescent and is used mainly by clinical psychologists. In some instances, the unique aspects of an adolescent's life cannot be duplicated, either for practical or ethical reasons, yet have implications on our understanding of the mind and behavior. Traumatic experiences, emotional and physical, have led to some fascinating case studies in psychology. One example involves a sixteen-year-old who had damage to the right side of his brain that left him with an inability to express himself emotionally. Also, consider the case of Genie, a child who was raised almost in complete isolation from the age of twenty months to the age of thirteen. Genie is proof of human resilience in learning language, although she never learned to ask questions and didn't understand much grammar (Curtiss, 1978).

The clinical method or case study can be viewed as a variation of naturalistic observation. In many cases, we can only look at the unique aspects of a particular adolescent when we use the clinical method or case study whereas when we use naturalistic observation, we may look at large numbers of adolescents in our search for some general principles about the mind and behavior. The **clinical method** involves sophisticated observation and interviewing skills that have been developed through experiences with many people, many of whom have psychological problems. Piaget relied heavily on the clinical method with his three children to discover the structure of their thought. There are disadvantages to the clinical method and case study, however, because the research is based on a single individual, in the case study format, and usually on a small sample in the clinical method. They often involve judgments of unknown **reliability** in the sense that no check is made to see if other psychologists or observers agree with the observations being made. So, how well such observations generalize to large numbers of adolescents can be questioned, as can the accuracy of the judgments.

Physiological Research and Research with Animals

A final example of the kinds of observations developmental psychologists make focuses on physiological research and research with animals. There is no question that much physiological research cannot be carried out with humans, but must be conducted with lower animals. Research with lower animals allows far more control than usually is possible with humans. With lower animals as participants, we can control genetic endowment, diets, experiences during infancy, and countless other factors in experiments that can affect development. In studies with humans, these factors have to be treated as "random variation" or "noise" and may interfere with accurate results. We also can investigate the effects of treatments (brain implants, for example) that would be unethical to attempt with humans. Moreover, it is possible to track the lives of some animals over their entire life course in a short time—laboratory mice have a life span of approximately one year, and monkeys live about twenty years, for example.

The disadvantage of research with lower animals is the existence of differences between lower animals and humans, and the possibility that such research therefore does not generalize to humans. Many aspects of human development simply cannot be studied in animals, such as complex decision making, language, divorce, time perspective, and so forth.

We have looked at a number of different ways observations of development can be made—through systematic observation, interviews and surveys, standardized tests, case study and clinical method, and physiological research with animals. A summary of main ideas related to these measures is presented in Concept Table 2.3.

METHODS USED TO OBTAIN INFORMATION ABOUT ADOLESCENT DEVELOPMENT

Method	Main characteristics	Advantages	Disadvantages
Systematic observation	Controlled conditions in laboratory or naturalistic setting; involves careful watching of behavior.	Precise control over what is being studied.	In laboratory, subject awareness, unnatural aspects; in natural setting, less control.
Interviews and questionnaires	Questions asked of someone and the responses he/she makes. Ranges from structured to unstructured. Interview involves verbal responses to interviewer whereas questionnaire involves paper-and-pencil responses.	Allow person's perceptions to be assessed, which may give important information beyond observed behavior. Questionnaires can be given to very large samples.	Assesses person's perception which may not tell much about his/her behavior. Social desirability.
Standardized tests	Questionnaires, structured interviews, or behavior designed to identify an individual's characteristics relative to those of a large group of similar individuals.	Ability to provide a comparison of one individual's score with those of large numbers of other people.	Based on belief that behavior is stable, yet behavior may be different outside of test situation.
Case study and clinical method	Case study is in-depth look at a single individual and clinical method involves sophisticated observation and interviewing skills developed through many experiences.	Provides a very detailed look at a single individual's mind and behavior.	May not generalize to large numbers of people and their accuracy may be questioned.
Physiological research and research with animals	Research by scientists and physiological psychologists. Involves the biological state of the organism. Work often carried out with lower animals.	Research with lower animals often involves greater control and allows treatments that ethically cannot be carried out with humans.	Generalizability to humans.

Strategies of Research Design

In addition to selecting what measures to use in studying development and behavior, another important methodological decision involves the **strategy** for setting up a research study. There are three main ways a research study can be set up: experimental, quasi experimental, and correlational.

Experimental Strategy

Ideally, we would like for our research in adolescent development to be conducted in an experimental way because more than other strategies, it allows us to more precisely determine whether something is causing an adolescent to act, feel, or think in a particular way. An **experiment** is a carefully controlled context in which the factors that are believed to influence the mind or behavior are controlled. The experimenter manipulates the "influential" factors, called **independent variables,** and measures the **dependent variables,** which are the measures/behaviors examined for any change due to the influence of the independent variables.

In an experiment, we randomly assign adolescents to the treatments or experiences. If the assignment is truly random, then there is only a slim chance that the two groups will differ from one another on some particular characteristic since any extraneous factor will have been randomly distributed in the groups. The following experiment should help you understand the importance of the experiment in the study of adolescents.

The problem to be investigated is how aerobic activity on the part of pregnant adolescent mothers affects the development of the infant. First, in order to clearly define our independent variable, we need to decide the nature and frequency of the aerobic activity. We decide to have the pregnant adolescent mothers perform the aerobic activity four times per week (one hour per session) under the guidance of a trained instructor.

We also give careful consideration to what our dependent variables will be. We choose to use two measures (breathing and sleeping patterns of their offspring). We decide that not only do we need to have a group of pregnant adolescent mothers exercise aerobically, but we need a group of pregnant adolescent mothers who do not. We randomly assign the adolescent mothers to the two treatments, one in which they get the exercise, the other in which they do not. The group that gets the exercise is called the **experimental group,** while the group that gets zero level of the independent variable is referred to as the **control group.** The control group is the comparison or baseline group. After the experimental group has exercised aerobically four times a week during their pregnancy and the other group abstains from aerobic exercise during the same time frame, the two sets of offspring are tested during the first week of life on the dependent variables. When we compare the results of the two groups, we find that the experimental group infants had more regular breathing and more regular sleeping patterns than the control group infants. We conclude that aerobic exercise by pregnant adolescent mothers promotes more regular breathing and sleeping patterns in their newborns.

A final comment about the random assignment of the subjects to the experimental and control groups should be made. By randomly assigning the pregnant adolescent mothers to the two treatments, we greatly reduced the likelihood that the two groups differed on some relevant subject variable, the mother's exercise history, health problems, intelligence, and so forth.

Why? Because every subject with any particular degree of a specific characteristic is equally likely to end up in either the experimental group or the control group. How did we do the random assignment? We consulted a table of random numbers in a statistics book, but we could have accomplished the same result by flipping a coin.

Quasi-Experimental Strategy

Often a technique can be used that resembles the experiment in all important respects except one—the degree of prior control exercised over the independent variable. In such a pseudoexperiment, sometimes called a quasi experiment, we acknowledge that we cannot randomly assign our subjects to experiences or conditions. In such investigations, people determine which group they will be in because of the experiences in their lives. Thus, we might study the self-esteem of adolescents whose mothers work compared to those whose mothers are homemakers or the coping skills of adolescents from divorced versus intact families. Quasi experiments, thus, are useful in getting information about social matters that create tricky problems for exercising tight experimental control, although they are not true experiments since we cannot randomly assign the participants to the categories of the investigation. Therefore, causation cannot be inferred from quasi experiments.

To further understand the principle of **quasi-experimental strategy,** let's consider another investigation involving aerobic exercise. In this study, we decide to study aerobic exercisers as they actually exist in society rather than randomly having one set of subjects exercise and another not. We might decide that to be included in the aerobic exercise group, adolescent mothers will have said they exercise aerobically on a regular basis, defined as three or more forty-five-minute aerobic classes per week. We also believe it is important to have a control group of adolescent mothers who have not exercised aerobically at all during their pregnancy. Since we do not randomly assign subjects to a group in a quasi-experimental strategy, it is very important to match the subjects in the groups on certain characteristics (Cook and Campbell, 1979), such as age, social class (e.g., education and occupation), and sex. We are still interested in finding out the relation of aerobic activity by pregnant adolescent mothers to breathing and sleeping patterns of their newborns.

In the quasi experiment, we find no differences between the infants whose mothers are aerobic exercisers and those whose mothers are nonexercisers. This may have happened due to our failure to match the subjects on certain variables, such as intelligence or health. Or, it may have occurred because the aerobic exercisers did not exercise as regularly as they said they had, while the nonexercisers may have exercised more than they indicated.

Correlational Strategy

Often it is of interest to know how one measured characteristic is associated with another—height with weight, intelligence with motivation, self-esteem with social class, drug use with parental upbringing, and so forth. One measure of such associations is the **correlation coefficient.**

The correlation coefficient ranges from -1.00 to $+1.00$. A negative number indicates an inverse relation. For example, a frequent finding is that individuals with high IQs are reasonably rapid learners, which would indicate a high positive correlation. By contrast, we usually find a negative correlation between permissive parenting and the adolescent's self-control. The higher the number in the index (whether positive or negative), the stronger the association between the variables. An index of 0 indicates that there is no association between the variables.

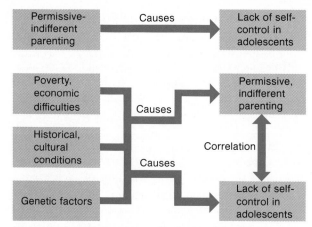

Figure 2.3 Evaluating the correlation between parenting and adolescent behavior.

A correlation alone cannot be used to support the argument that one event causes another. We can't argue, for example, that because height and weight are positively correlated, we grow tall because we gain weight (or vice versa). It is always possible that some unnoticed third factor is the causal agent, linking these two events together. See figure 2.3 for an example of the subtle but critical distinction between correlation and causation.

To further understand the principle of correlation, let's consider another example related to aerobic activity. In this case, we are interested in the correlation between the aerobic activity of adolescent females and whether their best friends and their parents exercise aerobically. We find a positive correlation between the adolescent's frequency of aerobic exercise and that displayed by either parents or peers.

At the beginning of our discussion of the experimental strategy, we indicated that ideally we would like to be able to study adolescents in this fashion because it allows us to infer causation. However, much of our research about adolescent development cannot be conducted in the experimental tradition. Researchers who study adolescents recognize how complexly organized adolescent development is and that simple experimental designs may not account for complex relations among interconnected factors. Thus, not only is there eclecticism in our theorizing about adolescents, but it is important to recognize that different methodological strategies are necessary to fully understand adolescent development.

The Time Span of Inquiry

Discussion of research designs can be complicated, especially when issues of development are involved. Our approach here is to start with the simplest designs, which we actually introduced above. These are the simple cross-sectional and simple longitudinal designs, which are the basis for all developmental research. Then, we describe the sequential designs which are the most complex, although they are actually only further elaborations of simple cross-sectional and simple longitudinal designs.

Cross-Sectional and Longitudinal Designs

Consider two different ways in which we might attempt to examine effects related to age. First, we might perform a cross-sectional study, comparing groups of people in different age ranges. A typical **cross-sectional study** might include a group of eight-year-olds, thirteen-year-olds, and eighteen-year-olds. The different groups could be compared with respect to a variety of dependent variables, such as IQ performance, memory, and group puzzle-solving ability. All of this could be accomplished in a very short time; even a large study can be completed within a month or so.

Second, we might perform a **longitudinal study** to examine effects related to age. In this case, we would take a single group of subjects, all of approximately the same age, and test them today and on one or more occasions in the future. For example, we might decide to examine problem-solving ability at ages ten, thirteen, and sixteen. This longitudinal study would last for approximately seven years, from the time the subjects

were ten until they were sixteen years of age. An advantage of cross-sectional designs, then, is that they are very efficient in terms of time. A major disadvantage of cross-sectional designs is their inability to control for **cohort effects,** that is, effects that are due to a subject's time of birth or generation, but not actually to her or his age. (Recall our discussion of historical time and the role of cohort effects in understanding adolescent development in Chapter 1.) For example, cohorts can differ with respect to years of education, child-rearing practices, health, and attitudes on topics such as sex and religion. These cohort effects are important because they can powerfully affect the dependent measures in a study ostensibly concerned with age. The effects of cohort can look like age effects, but they are not.

Although longitudinal studies are time-consuming, they are valuable in allowing us to track changes in individual subjects over time. If one's concern is with individual differences in the course of development, longitudinal designs are indispensable. Unfortunately, the problems of testing and history are especially troublesome in longitudinal studies.

Sequential Designs

In recent years, a number of life-span developmental researchers (e.g., Baltes, 1973; Baltes, Reese, and Lipsitt, 1980; Schaie, 1965, 1977) have constructed **sequential designs** that combine the features of cross-sectional and longitudinal designs in a search for more effective ways to study development. These designs allow us to see whether the same pattern of development is produced by each of the research strategies. In particular, the sequential designs are adept at providing insight about possible cohort effects that might be responsible for research findings. An example of a sequential design is described in Perspective on Adolescent Development 2.3.

COHORT EFFECTS AND ADOLESCENT PERSONALITY DEVELOPMENT

*W*hile the majority of research on cohort effects has focused on adult development and aging (e.g., Baltes, 1973; Schaie, 1977), one sequential study with adolescents illustrates the importance of considering cohort effects in our understanding of adolescent development. John Nesselroade and Paul Baltes (1974) investigated the personality development of adolescents under the assumption that such development is influenced by cultural change. And, these researchers also assumed that adolescents, in turn, play an important role in shaping cultural change as well. Their focus was on a representative mapping of personality development during adolescence, from the ages of thirteen to eighteen in a given historical period, 1970 to 1972.

Age, sex, and cohort membership were varied according to the strategy of sequential data collection. Longitudinal sequences were used as the data collection strategy and produced the research design shown in table 2.1. Specifically, four short-term longitudinal studies, each involving three times of measurement evenly spaced across a two-year period were conducted. Since only a two-year time period was used, the four longitudinal studies did not cover the same age ranges.

The researchers chose standardized personality tests to assess adolescent personality. The subjects were drawn from thirty-two junior and senior public high schools with approximately two thousand students initially being involved in the study. One of the main findings to come

Table 2.2 Longitudinal sequences design and data collection scheme

Cohort	Sex	1970	1971	1972
1954	M F	16	17	18
1955	M F	15	16	17
1956	M F	14	15	16
1957	M F	13	14	15

Note: Entries are ages of subjects at particular times of measurement. January 1 of each year was the mean testing time (± 2 months). Samples of randomly selected retest control subjects were drawn from cohorts 1954–57 and tested for the first time in 1972. The core longitudinal sample and dropouts were contrasted on 1970 scores to estimate dropout effects.

Source: From Nesselroade, J. R., and P. B. Baltes, in S. A. Mednick, M. Harway, and K. M. Finello, (eds.), Handbook of Longitudinal Research, *1984. New York: Praeger Publishing Company.*

Summary

I. The science of adolescent development is characterized by a set of world views, theories, and methods.

II. Three world views characterize the study of adolescent development: mechanistic, organismic, and contextual, which can be described as reactive, active, and interactive respectively.

A. The mechanistic world view describes the adolescent as passive and machinelike, emphasizes social, environmental experiences, and focuses on fine-grained analyses.

B. The organismic world view stresses that the adolescent is active and mindful, with biological foundations, and a more molar approach than the mechanical view.

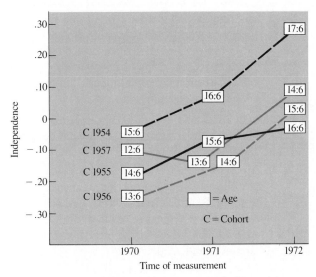

Figure 2.4 Longitudinal sequences for independence showing main effect of time of measurement.

out of this sequential study was the dramatic increase in independence shown by all cohorts (regardless of their age) over the two-year period (figure 2.4). The outcome is one of marked differences between cross-sectional studies and different levels for the same-age groups from different cohorts.

Among the sociohistorical circumstances that likely contributed to this cohort effect observed in adolescent independence are the focus on aggressive behavior displayed by a large segment of society in the United States in conjunction with youth activism and the Vietnam war; the tendency of youth to occupy itself with ethical, moral, and political issues rather than cognitive achievements; and reports by various public polls of gradual decline in respect for public and educational leadership by adults. These are all elements of the cultural context in the time span of personality testing that may have produced the cohort findings.

Nesselroade and Baltes (1984) argue that longitudinal designs by themselves are not the solution to understanding developmental changes in adolescents. They believe that some changes developmental psychologists interpret as age changes in longitudinal studies may indeed be cohort effects. Therefore, Nesselroade and Baltes (1984) stress that multiple groups of cohorts need to be included in our longitudinal study of adolescents to tease apart true developmental change from cohort effects.

C. The contextual world view sees the adolescent as interactive, continuing to respond to and act on contexts; and sees the importance of studying the adolescent in multiple contexts.

III. Three main sets of theoretical perspectives on adolescent development are: behavioral and social learning; cognitive; and psychoanalytic. An eclectic orientation also needs to be considered.

A. The behavioral and social learning perspective consists of the behavioral view of B. F. Skinner and the social learning theory of Albert Bandura.

1. Skinner's view stresses behavioral control, the influence of the external environment, operant conditioning, and the unimportance of cognition. It fits with the mechanistic world view.

2. Bandura's social learning theory is a cognitive social learning theory, emphasizing reciprocal determinism, imitation, and how cognitive processes mediate environment-behavior relations. It fits with a mechanistic-contextual world view.

B. Two major sets of cognitive theories are cognitive developmental theory and information processing.

1. Jean Piaget's cognitive developmental theory has had a profound impact on the study of adolescent development. His view emphasizes biological adaptation (assimilation, accommodation), organization, equilibration, cognitive structures, cognitive developmental stages, and conscious thought. His theory fits with an organismic-contextual world view.

2. The information processing perspective often compares the mind of the adolescent to a computer and focuses on how much adolescents use cognitive processes like attention and memory to process information about the world. It fits with an organismic-mechanistic world view.

C. The psychoanalytic theories include the classic psychoanalytical theory of Sigmund Freud and the neopsychoanalytic views of theorists such as Erik Erikson, Anna Freud, and Peter Blos.

1. Freud's theory focuses on biological instincts, unconscious thought, and psychosexual stages. It fits with an organismic world view.

2. Erikson's theory emphasizes eight psychosocial stages of development and how biology and culture interact to produce those stages. It fits with an organismic-contextual world view.

D. Each of the theories described has a number of strengths and weaknesses, but no single theory or world view is capable of explaining the complexity of adolescent development. For that reason, it may be wise to adopt an eclectic theoretical orientation in studying adolescent development.

IV. Methods used to study adolescent development focus on measures, strategies of research design, and the time span of inquiry.

A. Methods include systematic observation, interviews and questionnaires, standardized tests, case studies, and clinical methods, as well as physiological research and research with animals. Each of these methods has strengths and weaknesses.

B. Three strategies for setting up a study of adolescent development include: experimental, quasi-experimental, and correlational.

C. Three research designs characterize the time span of inquiry in the scientific study of adolescent development: cross-sectional, longitudinal, and sequential.

Key Terms

accommodation *54*

anal stage *58*

assimilation *54*

autonomy versus shame and doubt *63*

behavioral contract *50*

behavioral perspective *49*

case study *71*

classical psychoanalytic theory *57*

clinical method *71*

cognitive developmental theory *53*

Suggested Readings

Achenbach, T. (1978). *Research in developmental psychology: Concepts, strategies, and methods.* New York: Free Press.
A well-written introduction to research in developmental psychology with examples of different strategies and designs.

Adelson, J. and Doehrman, M. J. (1980). *The psychodynamic approach to adolescence.* In *Handbook of adolescent psychology,* ed. J. Adelson. New York: John Wiley.
An up-to-date, authoritative overview of contemporary psychoanalytic views, including those of Blos and Anna Freud.

Cowan, P. A. (1978). *Piaget with feeling: Cognitive, social, and emotional dimensions.* New York: Holt, Rinehart & Winston.
Cowan's book is an excellent interpretation of Piaget, particularly in discussing the relevance of Piaget's ideas about adolescence to the social dimensions of the adolescent's world.

Erikson, Erik. (1968). *Identity: Youth and crisis.* New York: Norton.
This is Erikson's most detailed work on adolescents. Exciting reading, with many insights into the lives of individual adolescents that apply to the lives of all adolescents.

Muuss, R. E. (1982). *Theories of adolescence,* 4th ed. New York: Random House.
This book provides a broad overview of theories of adolescence, including those discussed in this chapter, a number of European theories, as well as others.

Patterson, G. R. (1982). *Coercive family processes.* Eugene, Ore.: Castalia Press.
Patterson, a leading social learning theorist, describes in fine-grained manner the nature of family interaction and how it can become destructive in childhood and adolescence.

Part 2

Biological and Cognitive Processes and Development

Barbara Henson is ten years old and is in the fifth grade at a suburban elementary school. She is four feet, six inches tall and weighs seventy-five pounds. Her mother has to prod her to take care of her appearance at times—she doesn't keep her hair clean and sometimes goes two days without washing her face. Barbara often spends her after school hours playing with several girl friends in her neighborhood. In cognitive terms, she interprets her world in a very concrete manner—her use of imagery has become an effective memory tool, and her attention to tasks has improved in recent years, but she still seems to need objects and events to be present to think and reason about them. Her thought is characterized by what she is experiencing and what is happening to her.

When we look at Barbara at the age of twelve we find that some remarkable changes have gradually taken place over the last two years. She is now a seventh grader and has undergone a growth and weight spurt—she presently is five feet, three inches tall and weighs 110 pounds. She looks at her mother at eye level now, rather than having to look up at her. Within the last six months, Barbara has shown much more concern about her physical appearance. She has started to wash her face daily and washes and brushes her hair frequently. Two months ago, Rodney, a boy in her class at school, called and asked her to go to a school party with him. Barbara not only spends more time thinking about Rodney than she would have at age ten, but finds that boys are gradually starting to take over more and more of her thoughts and play a more important part in her life. Barbara had her first period six months ago, but since then she has experienced it only twice. She recently has started to spend more time in front of the mirror, looking at her body, checking over every inch of it. She has also started to worry more about how others perceive her body—sometimes she feels embarrassed about it, and at other times she feels proud that she is "developing." In the cognitive area, Barbara has just started to engage in more abstract speculation—her thoughts about what other people are thinking about her are a part of this changing cognitive orientation. She has also begun to reason more about things, people, and events that are not immediately present.

At the age of fifteen, Barbara is in the tenth grade, in her first year at the senior high school in her town. She has only grown one inch since she was twelve, and she has been able to keep her weight at 110 lbs. She and her friend Ashley jog two to three miles several times a week. When they go

Puberty: The time of life in which the two sexes begin first to become acquainted.

Samuel Johnson

jogging, Barbara likes to take her St. Bernard dog along—her parents say she does it to get attention from boys, but Barbara swears it's to keep the dog in shape. Barbara spends a lot of time now on her appearance. Her mother says that if she spent as much time studying as brushing her hair she would be making straight A's. Barbara's figure is more shapely now than when she was twelve, and she takes a great deal of pride in keeping her body toned up. Her period is occurring on a more regular basis now. Her interest in boys remains strong and she enjoys the admiring stares she gets from some of them when she walks down the hall at her school, although she could do without some of the "sleazy" comments some make. She has finished first-year algebra, and her problem-solving ability has become more organized—she used to just go ahead and solve a problem without thinking about alternative strategies.

At the age of eighteen, Barbara has just graduated from high school and is getting ready for her first year of college. She hasn't grown any since she was fifteen. Her weight has given her problems on a couple of occasions, but she recently has gotten back into her running schedule and is down to 115 pounds. For a while her body image wasn't very good, but she is starting to feel better about herself again. The biological and hormonal changes in her body during the last four to five years have not been nearly as great as they were during her junior high school years. And, while she still shows a concern about her body and her appearance, the concern doesn't preoccupy her thoughts quite as much as during early adolescence. Something Barbara has noticed is that at certain times of the month she seems to be more moody than at others—often the moodiness increases several days before her period occurs. Nonetheless, her menstrual cycle has become an accepted part of her existence, and most of the time it does not involve much pain or bother for Barbara.

Cognitively, Barbara sometimes engages in more abstract speculation about herself, others, and the world than when she was fifteen. Her thoughts are also even more organized than when she was fifteen—she manages her time better, thinks through problems in more detailed ways, and doesn't jump to conclusions as quickly as she did earlier in her adolescence. Her vocabulary has increased, and her more sophisticated reasoning skills have now taken her to the point where she can often come up with solutions that are just as intelligent or more intelligent than those of her parents, something that she has learned to moderate somewhat so she won't make her parents feel too badly.

Chapter 3

Biological Processes and Physical Development

*I*magine a toddler displaying all the features of *puberty*—a three-year old girl with fully developed breasts, or a boy just slightly older with a deep male voice. That is what we will see by the year 2250 if the age at which puberty arrives keeps decreasing at its current pace.

In Norway, the average girl begins to menstruate at just over 13 years of age, as opposed to 17 years in the 1840s. In the United States—where children mature up to a year earlier than in European countries—the average age at first menstruation has declined from 14.2 in 1900 to about 12.45 today. According to British pediatrician J. M. Tanner, who has compiled statistics on the subject, the age at menarche (first menstruation) has declined an average of four months per decade for the past century.

Fortunately, perhaps, we are unlikely to see pubescent toddlers, since what has happened during this century may be quite special. Tanner has noted that an extrapolation of the recent trend backward to medieval times would have the average woman beginning to menstruate in her early thirties, an age not much younger than the life expectancy in those times. Had this been the case, our species would have become extinct, or at least "endangered," because women's reproductive years would have been comparatively few. Writers from this period make references to menarche typically occurring somewhere between the fifteenth and twentieth year of life: the historian Quarinonium, writing in 1610, said that Austrian peasant girls seldom menstruated before their seventeenth, eighteenth, or even twentieth years.

If teenage puberty was a fact of life even in medieval times, something must have happened more recently to decrease the age of onset. The best guess is that that "something" is a higher level of nutrition and health. The available data show that the age of menarche began to get earlier at about the time of the Industrial Revolution, a period associated with an increasing standard of living and advances in medical science.

Cross-cultural data also suggest that better nutrition is related to earlier maturation. Girls growing up in countries or regions with adequate diets tend to begin menstruating earlier than those with less nutritious diets. Similarly, earlier menarche has been associated with higher social class, fewer children in the family, and living in urban rather than rural areas—all of which may reflect nutritional status.

If improved nutrition and the corresponding decrease in illness and disease are responsible for the trend toward earlier puberty in the past century, the trend should level off when people are nourished at an optimal level. There is some evidence that this is occurring in industrialized countries. The average age of menarche is becoming more similar from country to country. Where major variations exist, there also appear to be large differences in nutrition and the general level of health care. In New Guinea, for example, two highland tribes show average ages at menarche of 17.6 and 18.1 years.

Does this mean that in the future all youth will begin puberty at the same age? It's unlikely. There are other sources of variation that appear to be unrelated to nutrition and health. For example, girls living at lower elevations menstruate earlier than those of similar socioeconomic status living at higher elevations.

Genetic factors also play a role. By comparing identical and fraternal twins, we see the impact of heredity when diet is presumably controlled. Identical twins typically differ in age at menarche by about two months (a minimal difference, attributable to slight differences in birth weight), while fraternal twins differ by about eight months. In addition, girls in countries with differing economic levels sometimes show the reverse of what we would expect if nutrition alone determined the age of menarche. One study found that Chinese girls, even those who were very poor, menstruated earlier than several different groups of much wealthier Europeans. Genetic factors currently account for only about ten to fifteen percent of the variation in age at menarche, a proportion that is increasing as growing uniformity of nutrition and health eliminates other variations.

What initiates the onset of puberty? Rose Frisch and Roger Revelle at Harvard have found that menarche occurs at a relatively constant weight in girls. Similarly, they have found that the adolescent growth spurt begins at relatively constant weights for boys and girls. Though the spurt occurs two years later in boys than in girls, and at a higher weight, it begins at a similar metabolic level for both groups. Frisch and Revelle speculate that attainment of a critical metabolic rate triggers the physiological processes of puberty. New data from Frisch suggest that for menarche to begin, and to continue, fat must make up about 17 percent of body weight. Thus, both teenage anorexics (suffering from loss of appetite) whose weight drops precipitously and female athletes in certain sports may become *amenorrheic* (abnormal absence or suppression of menstrual discharge).

The Frisch and Revelle explanation is intriguing and does fit much of the existing information. Some researchers, however, remain skeptical; they note that causality has not been shown and that alternative explanations are possible.

Defining what puberty is has complicated the search for its "trigger." Puberty is not a single, sudden event, but part of a slowly unfolding process beginning at conception. We know when a young person is going through puberty, but pinpointing the onset and cessation of the process is more difficult. Except for menarche, which occurs relatively late in the process, there is no single event heralding puberty. In boys, the first seminal emission (wet dream) and the first whiskers are events that could be used to mark its arrival. Both may go unnoticed.

Pubertal changes, however, are well defined: there is a spurt in growth as well as clear changes in secondary sex characteristics, endocrine levels and processes, and other physiological factors. But these are all gradual processes. The gradual nature of puberty has made it difficult to study its causes.

Further complicating the study of what initiates puberty is that several different characteristics are changing and they do not all change together. For example, the development of reproductive capacities and the adolescent growth spurt have slightly different hormonal determinants, and may proceed at different rates, but both are components of the pubertal process.

Perhaps the most accurate way of thinking about puberty is that it is a phase in the maturational process over the life span from conception to death. It signals the beginning of reproductive capacity, a capacity that diminishes later in life. In general, reproduction requires a minimal level of nutritional adequacy and general health status; it is the first system to shut down when the body is poorly nourished or diseased.

Our improved health has led to a lengthening of the reproductive years; puberty is coming earlier, and, at the same time, the age when fertility ends is getting later and later. The longer period of reproduction has implications not only for biological processes, but also for social and psychological development.

Information on the social and psychological correlates of puberty is surprisingly meager. In our own research with adolescents, we have begun to examine the impact of pubertal development as a psychological experience, observing the way it affects relationships with peers and parents. When our research is completed, we may know what "growing up faster" really means.

The onset of puberty stimulates many different types of feelings and reactions from adolescents. Some young girls can't wait until their breasts begin to develop and their bodies start to become shapely; other girls are embarrassed about such matters and try to hide and cover up their maturing bodies in every way they can. Many boys eagerly await the day when they can shave for the first time, when their first pubic hair begins to grow, and when their shoulders start to broaden. Others may be embarrassed and guilty about their first wet dream.

We begin this chapter by describing the foundation of the biological basis of adolescent development. This foundation rests in an understanding of the role heredity plays in determining the nature of adolescence. Then, we turn our attention to the general nature of growth processes in adolescence and provide considerable detail on the pubertal process. The chapter concludes with a fascinating look at the manner in which adolescents psychologically adapt to pubertal change.

Genetic Influences on Adolescent Development: Still Important Ten to Twenty Years after Conception

When we observe and talk with adolescents, it is very easy to forget that genetic influences still are very important some ten to twenty years after conception. To understand genetic influences, it is important to know something about genes and some basic genetic principles, and the field known as behavior genetics, which has generated a number of methods to study genetic influences. And, as you read about genetic influences, you repeatedly will be reminded of how both heredity and environment are necessary when interpretation of the adolescent's development is at issue.

Genes and Genetic Principles

What is a gene and what are genotypes and phenotypes? Are genetic influences transmitted by the action of a single gene or mainly by the multiple interaction of genes? How extensively can genetic influences be modified and to what extent is a developmental path programmed in the genes? These are some of the intriguing questions we now pursue.

Genes and the Importance of Distinguishing Genotype and Phenotype

Each adolescent still has with him or her the genetic code inherited from his or her parents. Physically, this code is carried by biochemical agents called genes and chromosomes. The genes and chromosomes all adolescents have inherited are alike in one very important aspect: they all contain human genetic codes. A fertilized human egg cannot develop into a dog, a cat, or an aardvark.

The general hereditary code that all humans share is important. Aside from the obvious physical similarity this code produces among adolescents (for example, in anatomy, brain structure, and organs), this hereditary code also accounts for much of the psychological sameness (or the universality) among us. The particular kind of brain the adolescent inherits, however, is largely responsible for how the adolescent's thought processes develop.

The special arrangement of chromosomes and genes each person has inherited make her unique; this arrangement or configuration is referred to as a person's **genotype.** On the other hand, all the observed and measurable characteristics of the adolescent are referred to as his or her **phenotype.** Phenotypical characteristics may be physical, as in height, weight, eye color, and skin pigment, or they may be psychological, as in intelligence, creativity, identity, and moral character.

Identical phenotypical characteristics may be produced by different genotypes. For example, three unrelated adolescents may each have a measured IQ of 110, but vastly different genes for intelligence; in such a case, the adolescents have different genetic makeups but the same IQ. The opposite also is possible: differences in phenotypical characteristics may be produced by the same genotype. For example, identical twins may have different IQs (a not uncommon finding); thus, different IQs may be produced by identical genetic makeups.

What is the relation between genotype and phenotype? In other words, to what extent does heredity determine what each person becomes in life? Hardly any characteristics of the adolescent are solely the result of a particular genetic code. Virtually all of the adolescent's psychological characteristics are the result of the

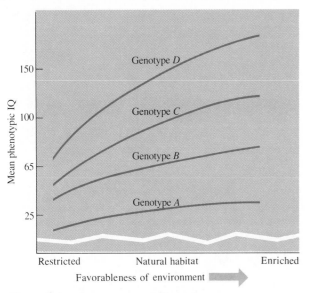

Figure 3.1 Genotypes and Phenotypes

interaction between the adolescent's inherited code and environmental influences. So when someone asks you whether you believe that some trait of an adolescent (for example, aggressiveness, shyness, activity level, intelligence, and so forth) is inherited or the product of environment, a safe answer is both!

Polygenic Inheritance

A very important genetic principle is that of **polygenic inheritance.** Genetic transmission is usually highly complex. Few psychological characteristics are the result of the actions of single gene pairs. Most are actually determined by the interaction of many different genes (remember that there are as many as fifty thousand of these) in the chromosomes. Traits produced by the mixing of genes are said to be polygenically determined.

Reaction Range

Given any individual genotype, there is a range of phenotypes that could be expressed (figure 3.1). Suppose, for example, that we could identify all the genetic loci that can contribute to intelligence in the embryo. Would measured intelligence during adolescence be directly predictable from knowledge about the specific **alleles** (two or more alternative forms of a gene that

can occur at a particular chromosomal locus) at all these loci? That is, would we know, from the genetic codes at each of these loci, precisely how bright the individual will be? No, we would not, because even if we had a good enough genetic model (and, of course, we don't), intelligence is a characteristic that is continuously shaped by the experiences a person has throughout life. Let us suppose, for simplicity, that intelligence is a measure of how efficiently and rapidly individuals learn and store new information. Genetically, adolescents may be predisposed to learn faster or slower, to package certain kinds of information (e.g., sounds) relatively more effectively than other kinds (e.g., sights), to take in information optimally during different lengths of time, and other differences. The learning environment created for the adolescent throughout his or her development will determine how much this individual genotype can maximize opportunities to acquire and store information. Suppose a "visual" learner predisposed to focus on new experiences over short periods of time is exposed mostly to new auditory (sound) experiences over long periods of time during formative periods of childhood. She or he is not being provided optimal stimulation, may learn little, and most importantly, may become an inactive and inefficient visual learner through disuse.

For most characteristics, like intelligence, it is useful to think about a collection of genetic codes that predispose an adolescent to develop in a certain way and environments that are more or less responsive to this development. The environment may be highly supportive of the expression of the characteristic or it may be highly stultifying. It is also useful to think about the genetic codes as setting broad limits on the range of outcomes that might be possible. For example, there may be a number of adolescents whose genotype would predispose them to be geniuses in the right environment, or mentally retarded under extremely impoverished conditions. By contrast, other adolescents in the same range of environmental conditions, might not have the capability of expressing genius, but only moderate brightness, and still others would express only average or slightly retarded status in the same circumstances.

Reaction range suggests that environmental change can mold intelligence, though within certain limits. Sandra Scarr (1984) explains reaction range this way. Each adolescent has a range of potential. For example, an adolescent with "medium-tall" genes for height who grows up in a poor environment may be shorter than average; but in an excellent nutritional environment, the adolescent would grow up taller than average. However, no matter how well fed the adolescent is, an adolescent with "short" genes will never be taller than average. Scarr believes intelligence works in the same manner. That is, there is a range within which environment can modify intelligence, but intelligence is not completely malleable. Reaction range gives us an estimate of how modifiable intelligence is. The idea of reaction range is compatible with the view that intelligence is influenced by genetic–environmental interaction.

Canalization

Some experts argue that genotypes, in addition to yielding a range of phenotypical outcomes, also experience just the opposite phenomenon for many human characteristics. That is to say that many human characteristics seem to be immune to vast changes in environmental events and seem to stay on track, regardless of what assaults are made on their expression by the environment (Waddington, 1962).

Canalization refers, then, to the narrow path or track that marks the development of some characteristic. It is clear that in human development there are a variety of conserving and preserving forces that seem to protect an individual from changing much, even in the face of drastic environmental inputs. Jerome Kagan (1984), for example, has repeatedly reminded us of the Guatemalan children he studied who seemed to experience normal social and cognitive development though many had undergone extreme malnourishment as infants. Also, many children who are exposed to clinically pathological parenting or child abuse do not grow up to be pathological parents or child abusers themselves. However, since the concept of canalization has not been explained with respect to any particular genetic mechanisms, it has led some recent critics to wonder about its scientific usefulness (Gottlieb, 1983).

How can identical twins be used to study the role of genes in development?

Behavior Genetics

A field of inquiry in psychology and biology that has received considerable attention in recent years is called *behavior genetics,* the discipline that is concerned with the degree and nature of hereditary basis of behavior. Workers in this field assume that adolescent development is jointly determined by the interaction of heredity and environment. Behavior geneticists have devised a number of strategies to investigate genetic influences on a number of adolescent characteristics. Among the most widely studied characteristics is intelligence.

Methods of Behavior Geneticists

Of course, we cannot conduct selective breeding and inbreeding experiments with adolescents. So what are we to do? Several strategies are now used more than others by behavior geneticists to investigate the role of genetics in adolescent behavior: the twin study, family of twins design, kinship studies, and adoption studies.

These strategies focus on the genetic relationship of an adolescent to members of his or her family. In the twin study and family of twins design, the focus is on the genetic relationship between twins. In the *twin study,* the comparison is between identical twins (**monozygotic,** meaning they come from the same egg) and fraternal twins (**dizygotic,** meaning they come from two different eggs and are therefore genetically more distant than identical twins). In the *family of twins de-*

Fraternal twins are more distant genetically than identical twins.

sign, monozygotic twins, siblings, half-siblings, and parent and offspring are compared. *Kinship studies* of the role of heredity in behavior include other family members as well, members such as uncles, cousins, grandparents, and so forth.

And, by means of *adoption studies,* we can study adolescents who are genetically more similar or more dissimilar from each other. An adopted adolescent is genetically closer to her biological parents than to the caregivers who have reared her. Investigators look to see if the adolescent's characteristics are more similar to those of biological parents or those of her adopted parents.

Heritability

Estimates often vary widely as to the heritability of a particular characteristic. **Heritability** is a mathematical estimate, which is often computed with a standard heritability quotient. It compares, for a population, the amount of variation in genetic material to the total amount of variation between people. Similarity is measured by use of the correlation coefficient *r*. The highest degree of heritability is 1.00. A heritability quotient of .80 suggests a strong genetic influence, one of .50 suggests a moderate genetic influence, and one of .20 suggests a much weaker, but nonetheless perceptible, genetic influence.

Although heritability values may vary considerably from one study to the next, it is often possible to determine the average magnitude of the quotient for a particular characteristic. For some kinds of physical characteristics and mental retardation, the heritability quotient approaches 1.00. That is, the environment makes almost no contribution to variation in the characteristic. This is not the same as saying the environment has no influence; the characteristic could not be expressed without it.

The heritability index is by no means a flawless technique for assessing the contribution of genetic factors to development. It is only as good as the data to which it is applied and the assumptions the investigator is willing to make about the nature of genetic-environment interactions. As Sandra Scarr and Kenneth Kidd (1983) have explained, there are at least three limitations to be kept in mind. First, there is the issue of how varied the environments are in the sample tested. The narrower the range of environmental differences represented in the sample, the higher the heritability quotients will be. The opposite will be true if a broader range of environmental differences are present. Secondly, there is the question of the reliability and validity of the measures of the underlying characteristic being investigated in the study (e.g., IQ, temperament). The weaker the measure, the less confidence we may place in the heritability quotient, which is likely to be falsely low due to the poor measurement. Finally, the heritability quotient assumes that we can treat inheritance and environmental influences as factors to be quantitatively added together, with each part contributing a distinct amount of influence. In reality, of course, these two factors must interact. The role and nature of the interaction is lost in the heritability computation.

Genetic Factors and Intelligence

What aspects of development are influenced by genetic factors? Quite clearly, they all are. Behavior geneticists have been interested in more precise estimates of the variation in a characteristic accounted for by genetic factors. Most of the conclusions from such research efforts are imprecise. Nonetheless many different aspects of development, including intelligence and personality, have been evaluated with respect to the degree they are related to genetic factors. Let's look more closely at the role of genetic factors in intelligence.

What do we know about the role of genetics in intelligence? The family of twins design has helped to provide a more accurate estimate of the heritability of intelligence. It consists of studies of monozygotic (MZ) twins, siblings, half-siblings, and parent-offspring. In one investigation that used this strategy, estimates of heritability for half-siblings were .40 whereas for parent-offspring they were .56 (Rose, Harris, and Christian, 1979).

Earlier studies of the heritability of intelligence placed the figure at approximately .80 (for example, Loehlin and Nichols, 1976), a figure that is now disputed and thought to be too high. In a recent review of human behavior genetics, Norman Henderson (1982) argues that a figure of .50 seems more appropriate. And in keeping with the trend of providing a range rather than a point estimate of heritability, intelligence is given a range of from .30 to .60. Clearly then, intelligence is not totally malleable. By the same token, although genetic inheritance makes an important contribution to intelligence, environmental factors can modify intelligence substantially.

As we already have seen, there are difficulties inherent in the heritability concept and as we now see, there are other difficulties with predicting the genetic contribution to intelligence as well. First, although there has been a long history of testing for some ability called intelligence, there is by no means agreement on what it is. One provocative proposal is that human beings really have eight or nine highly developed and divergent cognitive skills (Gardner, 1982), very few of which have been sampled on standard intelligence tests. Another view (Sternberg, 1982) is that intelligence consists of a number of basic cognitive operations that manifest themselves in different arrangements, depending upon the problem or task that is confronted. In this latter view, it could also be argued that our existing tests don't do a good job of measuring individual differences in intelligence. Second, intelligence is perhaps the most widely researched topic in all of behavioral genetics, so there is more information available on the question, but less agreement on how to synthesize it or interpret what it means. Third, the question asked about the role of genetics in intelligence, to be a manageable one, must be broken down into more

modest queries. For example, it would be more fruitful to ask about the role of genetics in phenomena that are logical subsets of the larger domain (e.g., spatial reasoning, numerical reasoning, short-term memory) than to focus on the whole domain at once. Fourth, there are separate questions to ask for which our science has progressed to different levels of elegance. The nuts-and-bolts analysis of how particular genetic loci cause certain chemical reactions to occur to produce certain differences in brain and central nervous system development is very far removed from a tractable solution. We haven't the foggiest notion which brain functions might discriminate among different levels of intelligence, let alone which genetic loci, in combination, might contribute to such differences. However, we have a much greater likelihood of success if the question is, What do we know about current factors contributing to individual differences in large populations in society (Santrock and Yussen, 1986)?

Some Conclusions about Genetic-Environmental Interaction and Its Effects on Development

First, a general conclusion about genetic-environmental interaction is provided, followed by a discussion of what we know in a more specific way about this important aspect of adolescent development. Then, we turn to what we need to know about genetic-environmental interaction.

No Genes, No Adolescent; No Environment, No Adolescent

Both genes and an environment are necessary for an adolescent to exist. Sandra Scarr and Richard Weinberg (1980) in an article titled, "Calling All Camps! The War Is Over," summarized this often repeated point: "One cannot assess the relative impact of heredity and environment on intelligence per se, because everyone must have both a viable gene complement and an environment in which the genes can be expressed over development. No genes, no organism; no environment, no organism. Behavioral differences among individuals, on the other hand, can arise in any population from genetic differences, from variation among their environments, or both" (p. 860). Scarr (with Kenneth Kidd) also provided insight about what we know and what we need to know about genetic–environmental interaction.

What We Know about Genetic–Environmental Interaction

Among the facts we know about genetic–environmental interaction are the following:

1. There literally are hundreds of disorders that appear because of miscodings in such genetic material as DNA. Normal development clearly is inhibited by these defects in genetic material.

2. Abnormalities in chromosome number adversely influence the development of physical, intellectual, and behavioral features of individuals, usually in a severe manner.

3. There is no one-to-one relation between genotype and phenotype.

4. It is very difficult to distinguish between genetic and cultural transmission. There usually is a familial concentration of a particular behavioral disorder, but most familial patterns are considerably different than what would be precisely predicted from simple modes of inheritance.

5. When we consider the normal range of variation, the stronger the genetic resemblance, the stronger the behavioral resemblance. This holds more strongly for intelligence than personality or interests. The influence of genes on intelligence is present in early child development and continues through the late adulthood years.

6. Being raised in the same family accounts for some portion of intellectual differences among individuals, but common rearing accounts for little of the variation in personality or interests. One reason for this discrepancy may be that families place similar pressures on their children

for intellectual development in the sense that the push is clearly toward a higher level, while they do not direct their children toward similar personalities or interests, in which extremes are not particularly desirable. That is, virtually all parents would like for their children to have above average intellect, but there is much less agreement about whether a child should be encouraged to be highly extraverted.

What We Need to Know

In answering the question, "What do we need to know?" Scarr and Kidd commented that it is very beneficial to know the pathways by which genetic abnormalities influence development. The PKU success story is but one such example in which scientists discovered the genetic linkage of the disorder and subsequently how the environment could be changed to reduce the damage to development.

Understanding variation in the normal range of development is much more complicated in most instances than revealing the genetic path of a specific disorder. For example, to understand the differences between two brothers, one with an IQ of 95 and the other with an IQ of 125, requires a polygenic perspective. Models of cultural and genetic inheritance, and their complex interactions, are more likely to explain behavioral variation than more molecular models of gene pathways, at least in the foreseeable future.

Developmental models of genetic influence across the entire life cycle are critical to understanding development. While developmental psychologists are very familiar with the species-specific patterns of development described by Piaget and Erikson, few of us attribute these patterns to evolutionary, genetic factors. Rather, developmental psychologists have tended to search for the proximal, immediate causes of these patterns. However, there may be some distal reasons for such patterns of development, namely causes that have evolved over the course of millions of years. For instance, puberty is not an environmentally produced accident of development, rather it is heavily influenced

Concept Table 3.1

GENETIC INFLUENCES ON ADOLESCENT DEVELOPMENT

Concept	Processes/related ideas	Characteristics/description
Genes and genetic principles	Genes and the genotype/phenotype distinction	Genes are the basic building blocks of heredity; they are biochemical agents. The actual combination of genes is genotype; the observed and measureable characteristics of genetic material is phenotype.
	Polygenic inheritance	Few psychological characteristics are the result of single gene action; this principle refers to the determination of phenotype by some mixture of genes.
	Reaction range	Given any individual genotype, there is a range of phenotypes that could be expressed. Suggests an important role for environment in modifying heredity, but argues that such modification has some limitations.
	Canalization	The narrow path or track that marks the development of some characteristic.
Behavior genetics	Methods	With humans, behavior geneticists rely on the twin study, family of twins design, kinship study, and adoption study to investigate heredity.
	Heritability	Refers to the mathematical estimate of the degree a characteristic is inherited. It is by no means flawless and unfortunately the nature of genetic-environment interaction becomes lost in the heritability computation.
	Influence of heredity on adolescent development and intelligence	All behaviors to one degree or another are influenced by heredity. The most widely studied aspect of adolescent development in terms of hereditary influence is intelligence. Early estimates placed the heritability index in the range of .80 for intelligence. More recent estimates range from .30 to .60. It is important to remember that intelligence is a global concept with issues about its measurement still widely debated. Further there likely are many intelligences.

GENETIC INFLUENCES ON ADOLESCENT DEVELOPMENT		
Concept	*Processes/related ideas*	*Characteristics/description*
Genetic–environmental interaction	No genes, no adolescent; No environment, no adolescent	Both genes and environment are necessary even for an adolescent to exist.
	What we know about genetic–environmental interaction	There are literally hundreds of disorders that appear because of miscodings in genetic material. There is no one-to-one correspondence between genotype and phenotype. It is very difficult to distinguish cultural and genetic transmission. In the normal range, the stronger the genetic resemblance the stronger the behavioral resemblance. Being raised in the same family accounts for some portion of intellectual differences among individuals, but common rearing accounts for much less variation in personality or interests.
	What we need to know about genetic–environmental interaction	We need to know the pathways by which genetic abnormalities influence development. We also need to unravel the complicated nature of genetic transmission in normal development. Developmental models of genetic influence across the entire life cycle are needed.

by evolutionary and genetic programming. While puberty can be affected by such environmental influences as nutrition, social interaction, exercise, and the like, the basic evolutionary and genetic program is wired into the species. Neither can it be eliminated, nor should it be ignored. Such an evolutionary perspective is becoming an important facet of developmental psychology and in the process is directing attention to new forms of analysis, raising new questions, and providing a more complete account of the nature of development.

A summary of main ideas in our discussion of genetic influences on adolescent development is presented in Concept Table 3.1. Now that we have considered the importance of genetic influences on adolescent development and the fact that puberty is influenced by heredity, we turn our attention more closely to the nature of the pubertal process.

Biological Processes, Puberty, and Physical Development: More Than the First Whisker and Pubic Hair

Attention given to biological processes during adolescence is focused on the general features of physical growth and development as well as the complex nature of the pubertal process.

General Features of Physical Growth and Development in Adolescence

There are many aspects to the physical growth and development of the adolescent. Among those that have received the most attention are height and weight, skeletal growth, reproductive functions, and hormonal

Source: © 1986, Washington Post Writer's Group, reprinted with permission.

changes. Although the adolescent undergoes many physical changes concurrently, not all aspects of physical development have the same growth rate.

Four Different Developmental Growth Curves

Let's now look at the developmental growth curves of physical development, in general, for the reproductive organs, the brain and head, and the lymphoid glands (figure 3.2).

Most skeletal and muscular components of growth, such as height and weight, follow the general curve, as do organs like the liver and kidneys. This growth curve changes gradually in the beginning, but rises dramatically at about age twelve—which indicates the phenomenon commonly referred to as the adolescent growth spurt.

However, the growth curve for the reproductive organs changes even more dramatically than the general curve for height and weight does. The prepubertal phase of reproductive development is fairly dormant, but the adolescent phase of the curve is even more precipitous than the general height and weight curve. Why is there a difference in the growth curves for height and weight as compared to reproductive functions? The answer lies in an analysis of glandular and hormonal influences. The glands and hormones that control height and weight are not the same ones that regulate reproductive functions. The development of the skeletal and muscular systems, along with that of most organs, is controlled by the pituitary and thyroid glands. On the other hand, the growth of the reproductive organs is regulated by the sex hormones (androgens and estrogens), which show marked increases in activity at the onset of adolescence.

A third growth curve represents the development of the skull, eyes, and ears, which mature sooner than any other parts of the body. At any point during childhood, the head is, in general, more advanced developmentally than any other aspect of the body. And the top parts of the head, the eyes and brain, grow faster than the lower portions, such as the jaw.

Some biologists (Epstein, 1974, 1978) and educators (Toepfer, 1979) argue that the brain does not grow in the relatively smooth, continuous fashion illustrated in figure 3.2. These same individuals argue that just as there is a height, weight, and sexual spurt that characterizes puberty, so too there is a spurt in brain growth. Brain growth spurts are said to occur between two and four, six and eight, ten and twelve, and fourteen and sixteen years of age. During these spurts, the brain is believed to increase from five to ten percent in size. Since cell formation in the brain is essentially complete at birth, these growth spurts are not due to new cells being formed but to growth within the cells that already have been formed.

The scientists who stress brain growth spurts also believe that these growth spurts affect the brain's synapses (the points of contact between axons or sending connectors, and dendrites, or receiving connectors). During the growth spurts, the axons and dendrites

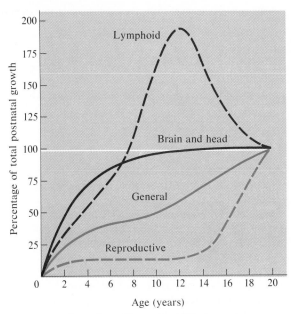

Figure 3.2 Growth and maturity of body systems as a percentage of total postnatal growth.

lengthen. This view of brain development, which emphasizes stages or spurts of brain growth, is called **brain-growth periodization.** For more information about the importance of the brain in adolescent development and the nature of brain spurts read Perspective on Adolescent Development 3.1.

The fourth type of growth pattern is very different from the first three. The lymphoid tissues of the tonsils, adenoids, appendix, and lymph nodes reach a developmental peak before the onset of adolescence, and then decline, presumably under the influence of increases in sex hormones.

Factors That Influence Growth Curves

What are the factors that influence growth curves? Damon (1977) says that we are neophytes as far as knowledge of the mechanisms that regulate physical growth is concerned. At the present time, we know that the following four mechanisms help explain physical growth and development:

Target seeking or self-stabilizing. In cases where growth has been stunted by disease or poor nutrition, the individual's growth often catches up with its original path after the negative conditions have been removed. This regulatory force seems to have a genetic basis, and it is stronger in females than in males.

Maturity gradients. A second principle that regulates physical development is the presence of maturity gradients in different regions of the body. For instance, the head is always more advanced developmentally than the trunk, and the trunk is always more advanced than the limbs.

Feedback regulation. A third regulatory principle entails the adaptation of biological structures to feedback. For example, the secretions of the pituitary hormone influence various other glands, such as the thyroid and sex glands; specifically, the pituitary secretions adjust to the levels of hormones in the other glands. When the secretions of the other glands reach appropriate levels, the pituitary regulates its output to continue the equilibrium that has developed.

Body Mass. A fourth regulatory mechanism that has received increased attention in recent years is the amount of body mass. Rose Frisch and Roger Revelle (1970) believe that the body has built-in sensors that detect when a certain mass is reached. These detectors then trigger the growth spurt that occurs at the onset of adolescence. For young girls, a body weight approximating 106 ± 3 pounds signals menarche (the first menstruation) and the conclusion of the adolescent growth spurt. According to Frisch and Revelle, the age at which menarche occurs in different cultures can be explained by the approximate time female adolescents reach the critical mass of 106 ± 3 pounds.

THE ADOLESCENT'S BRAIN, BRAIN SPURTS, COGNITIVE DEVELOPMENT, AND EDUCATION

"As long as the brain is a mystery, the universe, the reflection of the structure of the brain, will also be a mystery."

Santiago Ramón y Cajal

We are not very knowledgeable about what probably is the most important physical structure in the adolescent's development—the brain. As we discuss the adolescent's cognitive growth and development later in this section, we will discover that the manner in which the adolescent processes information about himself or herself and the world is a hallmark of cognition in adolescence. The underlying hardware or machinery that makes this information processing possible is made up of the brain and nervous system. If you think for one moment that the brain is an unimportant aspect of the adolescent's development, consider the following awesome magnitude and complexity of the brain. There are some ten to twenty billion neurons (nerve cells) in the adolescent's brain. The average nerve cell has been described as being as complex as a small computer, each one having as many as fifteen thousand physical connections with other cells (Kolb and Whishaw, 1980). At times the adolescent's brain may be lit up with as many as a quadrillion connections!

The nerve cells in a canary's brain are exactly the same as those in a frog's brain. The reason frogs croak and canaries sing is that the nerve cells are organized differently in the two brains. The adolescent's own gift of speech is present because human nerve cells are organized in ways that permit language processing.

Given that the adolescent's brain is different than a canary's or a frog's, is it any different than a child's? We know precious little information about this important question, yet neuroscientific research over the course of the next 100 years may well hold some important keys in our ability to understand the maturation of the brain and thought as individuals move from childhood through the adolescent years.

One biologist, Herman Epstein (1974, 1980) proposed a simple hypothesis: When boys and girls move into one of Piaget's cognitive developmental periods, their brains reveal an unusual amount of growth as well. How does Epstein measure brain growth? He has called on two methods—growth of the head, particularly its circumference, which is closely linked to brain size, and evaluation of electrical waves through use of the electroencephalograph (EEG). These brain waves are influenced by cognitive activities like thinking and problem solving.

With regard to the circumference of the head, children appear to experience growth at three points in development: at approximately the time of the onset of Piaget's concrete operational period about six to seven years of age, the onset of the formal operational period (about ten to twelve years of age), and at a second time in the formal operational period (about fourteen to sixteen years of age). With regard to electrical waves, as shown in figure 3.3, spurts in electrical activity of the brain coincided with increases in the circumference of the head.

Do the head circumference and electrical activity data document important changes in Piaget's stages of concrete and formal operational thought? Epstein argued that they did. Not only did Epstein suggest that the brain data indicated underlying changes in Piaget's stages, but he and others (e.g., Toepfer, 1979) argued that the brain data had implications for how children and adolescents should be educated. For example, based primarily on the

Epstein's interpretation of brain growth data regarding early adolescent education were unwarranted.

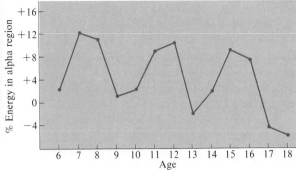

Figure 3.3 Spurts of Electrical Activity in the Brain According to Age.

head circumference and brain wave data, it was publicized that adolescents between the ages of twelve and fourteen are likely to be incapable of learning new skills because this age span reflects little or no growth of the brain. It also was emphasized that adolescents only can consolidate earlier learned skills during this time period, so middle and junior high schools should not attempt to teach new learning skills during this age span.

Did the Epstein data warrant such generalizations and implications for the education of adolescents? Quite clearly they did not! The Epstein data described information about the nature of brain growth and included no measures of cognitive or educational skills. More recent research (e.g., McCall et al., 1983) has revealed that no correlation exists between spurts in head growth and cognitive changes when cognitive skills are actually measured in concert with head growth. Yet another investigation (Lampl and Emde, 1983) focused on whether growth spurts in head circumference, as well as other types of growth, such as height and weight, actually correspond to certain developmental growth periods, like six to seven years of age, ten to twelve years of age, and so

forth. Each boy and girl in the study did show growth spurts, but the growth spurts were not consistently related to developmental time periods.

In sum, there do seem to be some periods of development when brain growth is particularly rapid. The degree to which these brain spurts are closely linked with rapid growth in cognitive skills, such as those associated with the onset of Piagetian stages, has not been fully documented. Also, it clearly has not been discovered that adolescents should only be taught to consolidate skills learned at an earlier time because their brain growth is slow at a particular point in development. It also should be noted that the measures of the brain are extraordinarily crude and global. Many neuroscientists believe the most important changes in the brain occur at a more micro level than was assessed in the Epstein studies. These scientists argue that we only will understand the mysteries of the brain, including the adolescent's brain, by studying neurological development at the biochemical, cellular level. So far our knowledge of such changes at the biochemical level in adolescents is zero because such research has not been conducted. So, while changes in the brains of adolescents represent a frontier of important knowledge about adolescent development, we are very naive about what kind of changes actually goes on in the brains of adolescents.

Now that we have considered some of the basic growth curves that occur during adolescent development, we turn our attention to a more detailed look at the biological process called puberty.

Puberty

As we discussed in the prologue, *puberty,* a rapid change in maturation, has been coming earlier and is influenced heavily by genetic, evolutionary factors. Factors such as nutrition and improved health also contribute to an understanding of pubertal onset. However, it is important to remember that puberty is not a single, sudden event, but part of a slowly unfolding process and it is difficult to pinpoint its onset and termination.

The Pubertal Process and Adolescence

It is important to understand that puberty can be distinguished from the phase of development referred to as adolescence. Generally, puberty has ended long before adolescence has been exited, although puberty often is used as the most important marker for the beginning of adolescence. For the most part, then, puberty coincides with early adolescence rather than late adolescence.

What is puberty? It usually is considered a period of rapid change to physical maturation. Sexual maturation is one of the most prominent aspects of the pubertal process. In figure 3.4, a rough representation of sexual maturation and decline is presented in terms of sex-hormone levels (Petersen and Taylor, 1980).

The Endocrine System

Before we describe the physical changes that characterize puberty, such as sexual maturation and gains in height and weight, it is important to know something about the hormonal system that stimulates these physical changes. Endocrinology, or the study of the endocrine system, is highly complex. Here we will outline several basic ideas that help us understand how the endocrine system works.

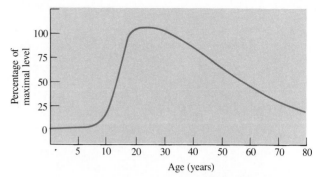

Figure 3.4   Hypothetical representation of sexual development in terms of sex-hormone levels.

The endocrine system is made up of endocrine glands and their secretions. The endocrine glands are often less noticeable than other glands because their secretions are carried in the bloodstream instead of through ducts. Glands with ducts are called exocrine glands and secrete such substances as saliva, sweat, and breast milk. The secretions of endocrine glands are **hormones,** which are powerful chemical substances that regulate organs. These organs are often far from the endocrine glands where the secretions are first emitted.

The aspects of the endocrine system that are most important in puberty involve the **hypothalamic-pituitary-gonadal axis** (Nottelmann et al., 1985; Nottelmann et al., in press). The **hypothalamus** is a structure in the higher portion of the brain and the **pituitary gland** is often referred to as a master gland. It is located at the base of the brain and its reference as a master gland comes from its regulation of a number of other glands. The term **gonadal** refers to the sex glands, the testes in males and the ovaries in females. The hormonal system involving the hypothalamus, pituitary gland, and gonads works like this. While the pituitary monitors endocrine levels, it is regulated by the hypothalamus. The pituitary sends a signal via a **gonadotropin** (a hormone that stimulates the testes or ovaries) to the appropriate gland to manufacture the hormone. Then, the pituitary, through interaction with the hypothalamus detects when the optimal level is reached and responds by maintaining gonadotropin and sex-hormone secretion (Petersen and Taylor, 1980).

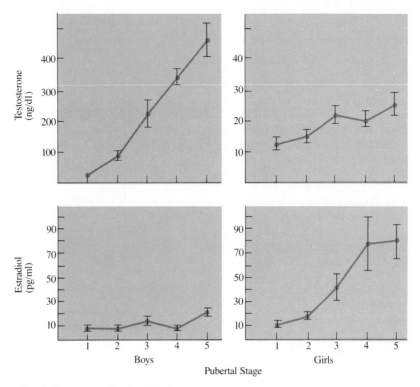

Figure 3.5 Hormone levels by sex and pubertal stage for testosterone and estradiol.

There are two main general classes of sex hormones that are important in understanding pubertal development—androgens and estrogens. **Androgens** mature primarily in males and **estrogens** mature mainly in females. Current research, however, has been able to pinpoint more precisely which androgens and estrogens seem to play the most important roles in pubertal development. For example, **testosterone** appears to assume an important role in the pubertal development of males. Throughout puberty, increasing testosterone levels are clearly linked with a number of physical changes in boys: development of external genitals, increase in height, and voice changes (Fregly and Luttge, 1982). In females, **estradiol** is likely the most important hormone responsible for pubertal development. The level of estradiol increases throughout puberty and then varies in women across their menstrual cycle. As estradiol level rises, breast and uterine development occur

and skeletal changes appear as well (Dillon, 1980; Fregly and Luttge, 1982). As shown in figure 3.5 in one study (Nottelmann et al., 1985) testosterone levels were found to increase eighteen fold in boys, but only twofold in girls across the pubertal period. For girls in the same study, there was an eightfold increase in estradiol, but the increase for this hormone in boys was only twofold. Note that both testosterone and estradiol are present in the hormonal makeup of both boys and girls, but that testosterone is dominant for boys while estradiol is stronger in girls. It should be mentioned that testosterone and estradiol are part of a complex hormonal system and that each hormone is not solely responsible for pubertal change. Nonetheless, their strong association with the physical changes of puberty suggest that they clearly play a very important role in the pubertal process.

HORMONE LEVELS AND ADOLESCENT ADJUSTMENT

*T*he same influx of hormones that put hair on a male's chest and impart curvature to a female's breasts may be linked to psychological adjustment during adolescence as well. As we have seen, it is during puberty that hormone levels increase dramatically, setting in motion physical changes that transform a child's body into an adult's body. In an effort to determine the role of hormones in the adolescent's adjustment, Editha Nottelmann, Elizabeth Susman, and their colleagues (1985, in press) have studied the hormone levels, physical development, and behavioral characteristics of 108 normal adolescent boys and girls, aged nine to fourteen. They focused on three types of hormones—gonadotropins, **sex steroids** (testosterone and estradiol), and **adrenal androgens** (secreted by the adrenal gland).

In addition to creating a hormone "profile" for each adolescent, the adolescents and their parents filled out a variety of questionnaires related to the adolescent's personality traits, moods, self-image, behavior problems, and competence in physical, social, and cognitive activities.

What conclusions have been reached from this research on hormone levels and adolescent adjustment? First, hormone levels were associated with adolescent

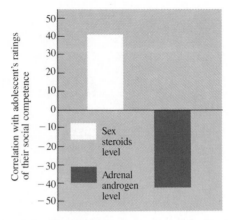

Figure 3.6   Relationship of sex steroid and adrenal androgen levels to adolescent boys' perception of their social competence.

adjustment. The most consistent finding was that higher sex steroid and lower adrenal androgen levels were associated with competent adjustment. For example, higher sex steroid levels in boys were associated with whether boys rated themselves as competent in social matters, while higher adrenal androgen levels were linked with adolescent boys' negative perception of their competence in social affairs (figure 3.6). Further, the mothers

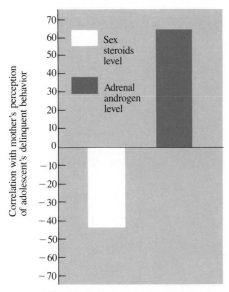

Figure 3.7 **Maternal perceptions of delinquent behavior of adolescent boys related to levels of sex steroids and adrenal androgens.**

of adolescent boys with higher concentrations of adrenal androgens and lower levels of sex steroids, rated the boys as showing more delinquent behavior than their lower adrenal androgen, higher sex steroid counterparts (figure 3.7). Second, the links between hormone levels and adjustment were stronger for boys than girls. This could be due either to biological or environmental factors. It also could be due to the fact that hormonal levels are more difficult to measure accurately in girls, probably because they are cyclical (move up and down). Third, in a number of instances, the timing of changes in hormone levels was more likely to be associated with the adjustment of adolescents than the actual pubertal stage in which the adolescents were classified due to their external physical characteristics. The onset of hormonal changes often precedes changes in external physical characteristics that usually are called on as an index of pubertal maturity (such as breast development in girls and testicular volume in boys). Thus, using only external physical characteristics as pubertal markers may obscure important relations between pubertal change and adjustment. Fourth, it should be remembered that in the investigation by Nottelmann and her colleagues (1985, in press) the adrenal androgens were associated in important ways with the adjustment of adolescent boys. Previously, the adrenal androgens have been thought to play only a minor role in pubertal development, but this research suggests that perhaps they should be studied more closely in future inquiries about the nature of relations between hormones, puberty, and adolescent adjustment.

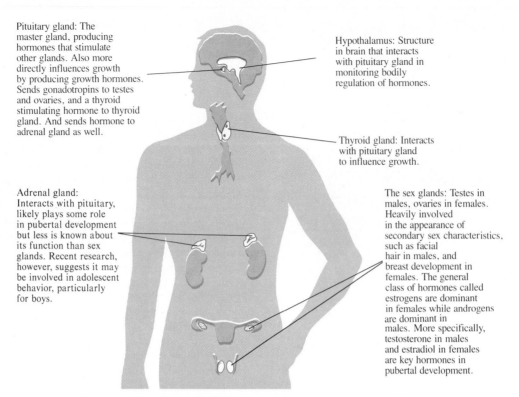

Pituitary gland: The master gland, producing hormones that stimulate other glands. Also more directly influences growth by producing growth hormones. Sends gonadotropins to testes and ovaries, and a thyroid stimulating hormone to thyroid gland. And sends hormone to adrenal gland as well.

Hypothalamus: Structure in brain that interacts with pituitary gland in monitoring bodily regulation of hormones.

Thyroid gland: Interacts with pituitary gland to influence growth.

Adrenal gland: Interacts with pituitary, likely plays some role in pubertal development but less is known about its function than sex glands. Recent research, however, suggests it may be involved in adolescent behavior, particularly for boys.

The sex glands: Testes in males, ovaries in females. Heavily involved in the appearance of secondary sex characteristics, such as facial hair in males, and breast development in females. The general class of hormones called estrogens are dominant in females while androgens are dominant in males. More specifically, testosterone in males and estradiol in females are key hormones in pubertal development.

Figure 3.8　The major endocrine glands involved in pubertal development.

While it has been known for some time that hormones play a very powerful role in the development of puberty, only recently has research been conducted that demonstrates the manner in which hormones might not only be associated with pubertal changes, but with the behavior of adolescents as well. As described in Perspective on Adolescent Development 3.2, hormonal level may turn out to be an important predictor of adolescent behavior and adjustment.

Before we leave the discussion of hormones and puberty, one additional aspect of the pituitary gland's role in development needs to be portrayed. Not only does the pituitary gland release gonadotropins that stimulate the testes and ovaries, but through its interaction with the hypothalamus, it also secretes hormones that either directly lead to growth and skeletal maturation, or produce such growth effects through interaction with the **thyroid gland,** located in the neck region. Remember we earlier commented that the pituitary gland often is viewed as the master gland because of its interconnections with so many other glands. Here we have seen the role of the pituitary gland in sending hormones to the sex glands, the testes and ovaries, and to the thyroid gland.

Note that an overview of the location of the major endocrine glands and their functions is shown in figure 3.8. Now that we have studied the important role of the endocrine system in pubertal development, we turn our attention to the external physical changes that characterize puberty.

Physical Changes
Among the most striking changes during puberty are increases in height and weight, as well as one of the most widely discussed aspects, sexual maturation.

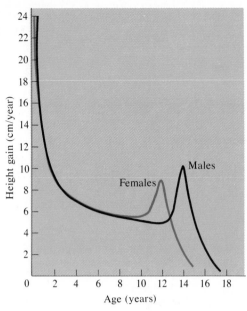

Figure 3.9 Typical individual growth curves for height in boys and girls. These curves represent the height of the typical boy and girl at any given age.

The growth spurt for girls occurs approximately two years earlier than for boys.

Height and Weight

As they undergo the adolescent growth spurt, both boys and girls make rapid gains in height and weight. But as is indicated in figure 3.9, the growth spurt for girls occurs approximately two years earlier than for boys. The growth spurt in girls begins at approximately age ten and one-half and lasts for about two years. During this time period, girls increase in height by about three and one-half inches per year. The growth spurt for boys usually begins at about twelve and one-half years of age and also lasts for approximately two years. Boys usually grow about four inches per year in height during this growth spurt (Faust, 1977; Tanner, 1966, 1970). These averages do not reflect the fairly wide range of time within which the adolescent growth spurt begins. Girls may start the growth spurt as early as age seven and one-half or as late as age eleven and one-half, while boys may begin as early as age ten and one-half or as late as age sixteen (Faust, 1977; Tanner, 1970).

Boys and girls who are shorter or taller than their peers before adolescence are likely to remain so during adolescence (Tanner, 1970). In our society, there is a stigma attached to short boys and tall girls. At the beginning of the adolescent period, girls tend to be as tall or taller than boys their age, but by the end of the junior high years most boys have caught up or, in many cases, even surpassed girls in height. And even though height in the elementary school years is a good predictor of height later in adolescence, there is still room for the individual's height to change in relation to the height of his or her peers. As much as thirty percent of the height of late adolescents is unexplained by height in the elementary school years (Tanner, 1970).

The rate at which adolescents gain weight follows approximately the same developmental timetable as the rate at which they gain height. Marked weight gains coincide with the onset of puberty. During early adolescence, girls tend to outweigh boys, but by about age fourteen, just as with height, boys begin to surpass girls (Faust, 1977; Tanner, 1970).

But although boys do begin to catch up with and surpass girls in weight by midadolescence, looking thin and not being overweight have become obsessions for many adolescent girls. In Chapter 15, which discusses a variety of problems and disturbances of adolescence, various eating disorders in adolescence will be outlined.

It is important to remember that these growth curves represent averages. The wide age range during which the features of the adolescent growth spurt appear suggests the importance of considering both individual and cultural differences in physical development.

Now let's turn our attention to another hallmark of pubertal development—sexual maturation.

Sexual Maturation

Think back to your last few years of childhood and then to your first few years of adolescence. Probably nothing comes to mind more strikingly than the sexual maturation that began to occur during the first two years of adolescence. You also likely recall that during the last several years of childhood, your interest in sexual activity and sexual relationships was nowhere near the level it reached during the first several years of adolescence. Few aspects of development throughout the life cycle attract more curiosity and mystery than the onset of sexual maturation during early adolescence. Let's look at the sexual maturation of boys, and then girls.

Researchers have found that male sexual characteristics develop in the following order: increase in size of testicles and penis, appearance of straight pubic hair,

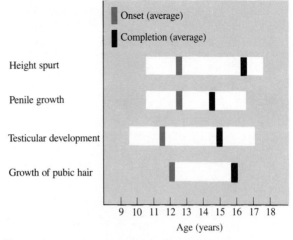

Figure 3.10 **Normal range and average age of development of sexual characteristics in males.**

minor voice changes, first ejaculation (the first ejaculation usually occurs through masturbation or during sleep—the so-called wet dream), appearance of kinky pubic hair, onset of maximum growth, growth of axillary hair (in armpits), more detectable voice changes, and growth of facial hair (Faust, 1977; Garrison, 1968).

Three of the most noticeable areas of sexual maturation in boys are penis elongation, testes development, and the growth of pubic hair. The normal range and average age of development for these sexual characteristics, as well as for the height spurt, is shown in figure 3.10. Figure 3.11 depicts the typical course of male sexual development during the pubertal period.

Adolescent females experience the following sequence of physical changes in puberty. First, either the breasts enlarge, or pubic hair appears. Later some hair

    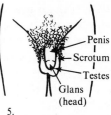

1.
No pubic hair. The testes, scrotum, and penis are about the same size and shape as those of a child.

2.
A little soft, long, lightly colored hair, mostly at the base of the penis. This hair may be straight or a little curly. The testes and scrotum have enlarged, and the skin of the scrotum has changed. The scrotum, the sack holding the testes, has lowered a bit. The penis has grown only a little.

3.
The hair is darker, coarser, and more curled. It has spread to thinly cover a somewhat larger area. The penis has grown mainly in length, the testes and scrotum have grown and dropped lower than in stage 2.

4.
The hair is now as dark, curly, and coarse as that of an adult male. However, the area that the hair covers is not as large as that of an adult male; it has not spread to the thighs. The penis has grown even larger and wider. The glans (the head of the penis) is bigger. The scrotum is darker and bigger because the testes have gotten bigger.

5.
The hair has spread to the thighs and is now like that of an adult male. The penis, scrotum, and testes are the size and shape of those of an adult male.

Figure 3.11 **Different stages of male sexual development: the growth of pubic hair, testes, scrotum, and penis.**

will appear in the armpits. As these changes occur, the female grows in height, and her hips become wider than her shoulders. Fatty tissue in and encircling the breasts, shoulders, and hips creates a more rounded appearance in the adolescent female. Her first menstruation, referred to as menarche, indicates that sexual maturity is near. Initially, her menstrual cycles may be very irregular, and even for the first several years she may not be ovulating in every cycle—in other words, it may only be several years after her period begins that she becomes fertile. There is no exaggerated enlargement of the larynx in females during puberty; hence, no voice change comparable to that occurring in adolescent males (Faust, 1977; Haeberle, 1978).

By the end of puberty, the female adolescent's breasts have become fully rounded and serve as the most obvious external female sexual characteristic. The breasts do not produce milk, though, until after pregnancy.

Two of the most noticeable aspects of the female's sexual maturation are pubic hair and breast development. Figure 3.12 illustrates the normal range and average age of development of these sexual characteristics, as well as information about menarche and height gain. Figure 3.13 depicts the typical course of development for these characteristics.

For the most part, we have described the average ages at which sexual maturation occurs in boys and girls. While we have called attention to the tremendous individual variation in the onset of pubertal events, such variation merits further attention.

Individual Variation in Puberty

The pubertal sequence may begin as early as ten years of age and as late as thirteen and one-half for most boys, at which time there is an acceleration in the growth of the testes. If this sequence terminates at the time of the first ejaculation, the average age of termination is thirteen and one-half to fourteen (although ejaculation could occur much earlier or later depending upon when the process started). However, the average range is wide enough that if we have two boys of the same chronological age, one may complete the pubertal sequence before the other has begun it. And, in girls, the age range of the first menstrual period is even wider—it may occur at age ten or it may not happen until fifteen and one-half (Hill, 1980).

In some cases, puberty may be delayed until very late in adolescence. In the United States, if puberty has not been reached by the age of fifteen or sixteen for boys, it represents a serious lag in the development of sex organs and hormones. Today, there is an increasing

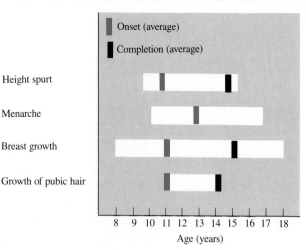

Figure 3.12 Normal range and average age of development of sexual characteristics in females.

tendency to administer sex-hormone treatment to boys and girls who have not reached puberty by age fourteen or fifteen. The effects of such extended pubertal delay in boys are discussed in Perspective on Adolescent Development 3.3, which focuses on the possible physical and social implications such a delay may have. Adolescent boys are so sensitive about their height, the width of their shoulders, their strength, and the size of their penises that even a one-year difference in the onset of puberty can produce strong effects on their psychological makeup. Adolescent girls have similar fears about growing too tall, or having overdeveloped or underdeveloped breasts.

A summary of main ideas related to biological processes and puberty is presented in Concept Table 3.2. In this section, we saw that very late maturation influences the adjustment of boys. In the next section, we explore in greater detail the effects of early and late maturation on the development of both boys and girls.

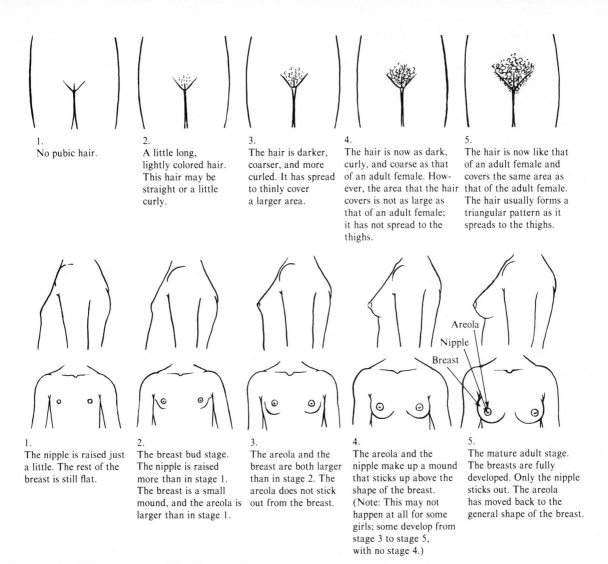

1.
No pubic hair.

2.
A little long, lightly colored hair. This hair may be straight or a little curly.

3.
The hair is darker, coarser, and more curled. It has spread to thinly cover a larger area.

4.
The hair is now as dark, curly, and coarse as that of an adult female. However, the area that the hair covers is not as large as that of an adult female; it has not spread to the thighs.

5.
The hair is now like that of an adult female and covers the same area as that of the adult female. The hair usually forms a triangular pattern as it spreads to the thighs.

1.
The nipple is raised just a little. The rest of the breast is still flat.

2.
The breast bud stage. The nipple is raised more than in stage 1. The breast is a small mound, and the areola is larger than in stage 1.

3.
The areola and the breast are both larger than in stage 2. The areola does not stick out from the breast.

4.
The areola and the nipple make up a mound that sticks up above the shape of the breast. (Note: This may not happen at all for some girls; some develop from stage 3 to stage 5, with no stage 4.)

5.
The mature adult stage. The breasts are fully developed. Only the nipple sticks out. The areola has moved back to the general shape of the breast.

Figure 3.13 **Different stages of female sexual development: pubic hair and breast growth.**

Perspective on Adolescent Development 3.3
EXTENDED PUBERTAL DELAY IN BOYS

John Money and his colleagues at the Johns Hopkins endocrine clinic have studied many different sexual aberrations. In one such investigation (Lewis, Money, and Bobrow, 1977) 150 cases involving delay of puberty were studied long enough that the adult status of the adolescents with sexual abnormalities could be evaluated. In some cases, but not all, pubertal delay includes retardation in the stature of the adolescents. Both types of adolescents were included in this study. Further comparison was made by classifying boys in which the onset of puberty had occurred prior to the age of fifteen (late-normal group) separately from those in which it had not occurred by age fifeen (prolonged-delay group). The data described here reflect the behaviors and growth of twelve of these boys and were collected from one to eighteen years later.

The age of the patients at follow-up ranged from seventeen to thirty-five years of age. All five of the patients with prolonged delay of puberty, and five of the seven with late-normal puberty, had been given sex-hormone treatments at the Hopkins endocrine clinic. The treatment was given from fifteen and one-half to seventeen and one-half years of age for the prolonged-delay group and between the ages of fourteen and one-half and sixteen and one-half for the late-normal group. The treatment was given to "prime" or speed up the early part of the puberty process.

Adult height. The adult heights of the members of the prolonged-delay group were less than the adult heights of their fathers (mean of sixty-seven inches for sons versus sixty-nine inches for fathers). The adult heights of the members of the late-normal group were numerically greater than their fathers' heights (mean of seventy-two inches versus seventy inches). Due to the small sample size, Money did not conduct any statistical tests on these data. The most obvious conclusion, though, is that there actually was very little effect of significant pubertal delay on adult height when hormonal treatment was given to the boys during middle adolescence.

Social behavior. Prior to hormonal treatment, four of the five adolescent males with prolonged pubertal delay had not had a date; the fifth had started dating but subsequently quit, shifting his attention to cars instead. Follow-up data collected after hormonal treatment suggested that only one of the five boys had any confidence in his social interaction and dating skills. He was one of the two males who eventually married and he remained married, while the other male later divorced. Three of the five adolescent males who experienced prolonged pubertal delay still had serious difficulties in their social development during their young adult years.

Of the seven late-normal pubertal-delay boys, two were not given androgen treatment. One of the two had a steady girlfriend at the age of fifteen and reported successful peer relations. The other untreated boy said he would like to be popular with girls, but showed less interest than other males his age. For the most part, he interacted with boys several years younger. The other five late-normal pubertal-delay boys had had little or no dating activity prior to androgen treatment. One of these boys did date some, but he often resorted to a "tough-guy facade" when interacting with his peers. After androgen treatment, the only one of the boys who dated regularly was the untreated male who had dated earlier in adolescence as well. The other untreated male began his puberty spontaneously (i.e., without androgen treatment) and began to show more social interaction with his peers. Two of the five androgenized adolescents married, while none of the other three showed any inclination for dating or marriage.

Based on these results, Money and his colleagues (1977) suggest that an abnormally long delay in sexual maturation probably induces a social disenfranchisement among peers, which may lead to other complications.

BIOLOGICAL PROCESSES AND PUBERTY

Concept	Processes/related ideas	Characteristics/description
General features of physical growth and development	Developmental growth curves	A general growth curve, including most skeletal and muscular aspects, involves gradual changes early in development but rises dramatically during puberty. The growth curve for the reproductive organs changes even more dramatically in this regard during puberty. The growth curve for the brain and head is accelerated much earlier in development than the first two curves. However, some biologists believe there are periodic spurts in brain growth. A fourth growth curve involves the lymphoid tissues, which reach a peak of growth before adolescence and then decline.
	Factors influencing growth curves	These include target-seeking or self-stabilizing factors, maturity gradients, feedback regulation, and body mass.
Puberty	The pubertal process and adolescence	Puberty is a rapid change to maturation. Generally puberty has ended long before adolescence ends and corresponds more to the period of early than late adolescence.
	The endocrine system	The endocrine system is made up of endocrine glands and their secretions. The secretions of these ductless glands are called hormones, which are powerful chemicals that regulate organs. The hypothalamic-pituitary-gonadal axis is an important aspect of the complex hormonal system that contributes to pubertal change. Current knowledge suggests that testosterone, a member of the general class of hormones called androgens, plays a key role in the pubertal development of males, and that estradiol, a member of the estrogen family of hormones, has a key role in the pubertal development of females. Recent research has demonstrated a link between hormonal levels and the adolescent's behavior. The pituitary gland also stimulates growth, either through the thyroid gland, or more directly through growth hormones.

BIOLOGICAL PROCESSES AND PUBERTY		
Concept	*Processes/related ideas*	*Characteristics/description*
	Physical changes	Among the most important physical changes in puberty are those involving height, weight, and sexual maturation. The growth spurt for boys occurs approximately two years later than for girls, with twelve and one-half being the average onset for boys and ten and one-half representing the average onset for girls. Sexual maturation is a predominant aspect of puberty and includes a number of physical developments in both boys and girls. Menarche occurs very late in the pubertal development of girls.
	Individual variation	For normal development in boys, the pubertal sequence may begin as early as ten and one-half and as late as thirteen and one-half. For girls, the age range for average normal development involves menarche occurring as early as ten or as late as fifeen and one-half. When pubertal onset has not occurred toward the end of early adolescence, hormonal treatment generally is called on.

Psychological Adaptation to Changes in Physical Development in Adolescence: A Lot of Mirror Watching

There are a host of psychological and social consequences that accompany changes in the adolescent's physical development. Think once again about your changing body as you began puberty. Not only did you likely begin to think about yourself in different ways, but important individuals, such as peers and parents, likely began acting differently toward you as well. Maybe you were proud of your changing body, even though you probably were perplexed about what was going on. Or possibly you felt embarrassed about the changes that were taking place and experienced a lot of anxiety. Perhaps you looked in the mirror on a daily or even on an hourly basis to see if you were maturing physically and to see if you could detect anything different about your changing body. It is likely that as your body changed, you were no longer treated as a little boy or a little girl, and instead were perceived by peers in terms of your sexual attractiveness. Your parents probably no longer perceived you as someone they could sit in bed and watch television with or as someone who should be kissed goodnight.

Among the most widely studied psychological adaptations to changes in physical development during adolescence are those pertaining to body image; early and late maturation; menarche and the menstrual cycle; cognitive abilities of females and their relation to pubertal change; and on-time, off-time in pubertal development.

Body Image

One thing is certain about the psychological aspects of physical development—adolescents show a great deal of preoccupation with their bodies and develop individual images of what their bodies are like. Surveys of

Table 3.1 The average importance of selected body characteristics for personal physical attractiveness for males and females. Lower numbers indicate *greatest* importance.

Body characteristics	Males' own importance Mean	Females' own importance Mean	Body characteristics	Males' own importance Mean	Females' own importance Mean
Facial complexion	1.8	1.6	Hips	2.8	2.2
Ears	3.5	3.9	Width of shoulders	2.9	3.4
Chest	2.6	2.4	Mouth	2.4	2.4
Profile	2.3	2.5	Neck	2.8	3.2
Distribution of weight	2.0	1.7	Teeth	2.0	1.9
Eyes	2.4	1.9	Nose	2.4	2.4
Height	2.7	2.9	Chin	2.8	3.1
Ankles	4.2	4.1	Hair texture	2.3	2.3
Waist	2.4	2.3	Body build	1.9	1.7
Arms	3.0	3.1	Hair color	3.2	3.2
Shape of legs	2.8	2.2	Thighs	2.9	2.5
General appearance	1.5	1.3	Face	1.5	1.4

Source: From Lerner, R. M., and S. A. Karabenick, "Physical Attractiveness, Body Attitudes, and Self-Concept in Late Adolescence," Journal of Youth and Adolescence, *1974, 3, 307–316. Reprinted with permission of Plenum Publishing Corporation.*

adolescents reveal that young adolescents are more preoccupied and dissatisfied with their bodies than late adolescents (Hamburg, 1974). And in another investigation (Lerner and Karabenick, 1974), girls who were judged as being attractive, and who generally had positive attitudes about their bodies, were found to have higher opinions of themselves in general. Boys with athletic physiques also had more positive self-concepts, but those who were overweight had more negative self-images. Table 3.1 provides an overview of some of the bodily characteristics adolescents rate as important.

Source: LUANN by Greg Evans. © by and permission of News America Syndicate, 1986.

Note that boys and girls did not differ much in their ratings of which parts of their bodies are important to them.

Early and Late Maturation

The effects of early and late maturation may have a number of different effects on adolescents—let's now think about what these effects might be and then study the results of two longitudinal investigations on early and late maturation.

Conceptualization of Early and Late Maturation

Dale Blyth, Richard Bulcroft, and Roberta Simmons (1981) have described three ways in which puberty can influence the social and psychological development of adolescents. First, puberty may have negative consequences mainly because change itself is viewed as essentially stressful. From this perspective, endocrine changes as well as marked changes in physical appearance are viewed as stresses, particularly for girls (Petersen and Taylor, 1980). It may be that the negative impact of puberty will be short-lived and wither away as the adolescent adjusts to his or her new body and self-image. According to the negative-consequences view, the stress, problems, and disturbances of puberty are most likely to begin and end early for early-maturing girls compared to late-maturing girls, although both are likely to show signs of stress when physical change is at its peak.

A second view of how puberty might influence social and psychological development focuses on positive consequences for the adolescent. The basic tenet is that if the adolescent looks more like an adult and is reacted to in more adult ways, the change will be positive (Faust, 1960). As in the negative-consequences model of puberty, the effects are likely to be short-lived since all adolescents will soon be adults. Early maturers are in the most advantageous position from this perspective since they are the first among their peers to reach adult status.

The second line of reasoning in this model of pubertal timing is based on psychoanalytic theory. According to this theory, not having enough time in a life stage may have negative consequences that extend into the next stage (Peskin and Livson, 1972). Early-maturing individuals are thus likely to have problems and disturbances during adolescence because of a shortened latency period. Similarly, late maturers who have a limited amount of time in the adolescent stage are likely to manifest problems in early adulthood.

The third view of the impact of puberty on psychological and social development focuses on the timing of development as a critical factor: from this view, puberty in itself is neither positive nor negative. There are two separate lines of thought in this view. First, puberty possibly has the strongest influence on two deviant groups—early maturers who are changing when few others are, and late maturers who lag behind their peers in physical development. Being a member of a minority or deviant group may prove to be stressful, particularly in peer relations (Gold and Tomlin, 1975; Petersen and Taylor, 1980). From this view, early maturers will show negative characteristics during and just after pubertal change, and late maturers will have negative reactions before they change (that is, when they are in the minority).

The California Longitudinal Study

Many of the data used to support conclusions about the effects of early and late maturation during adolescence have been collected as part of a longitudinal growth study at the University of California (Jones, 1938; Jones, 1965, 1967; Jones and Bayley, 1950; Jones and Mussen, 1958; Mussen and Jones, 1957, 1958). The indicator that has been used to define early and late maturation in most studies is skeletal age. One way in which skeletal age is measured in these investigations is to take X rays of hand and knee bones.

In most instances, early or late maturation has a significant influence on the personality and social behavior of adolescents (e.g., Jones and Bayley, 1950; Mussen and Jones, 1957, 1958). The upshot of the California investigations concerning early and late maturation is that boys who mature early in adolescence (as measured by their skeletal growth) perceive themselves more positively and are more successful in peer relations than their late-maturing counterparts. Both peers and adults rated the early-maturing boys as physically more attractive, more composed, and more socially sophisticated than the late-maturing boys. Most of these investigations focused on the self-perceptions of boys in early and middle adolescence (about twelve to seventeen years of age). Also, the Berkeley longitudinal study found that some of the psychological characteristics associated with early maturation (such as dominance, independence, and self-control) were still apparent even when the individuals were in their thirties (Jones and Mussen, 1958).

In the California study, early maturation generally seemed to have positive psychological benefits for adolescent girls as well (Jones and Mussen, 1958). But the results were not quite as clear-cut as they were for boys. For example, girls who were developmentally advanced in elementary school had less prestige among their age-mates, but in the junior high school years, early physical maturity was an advantage. However, even in the sixth grade, the more physically advanced girls had more prestige with adults and older friends than their less physically mature classmates had (Faust, 1960).

The possibility that early maturation may force premature identity formation has been investigated by Mary Cover Jones (1965) and Harvey Peskin (1967). Peskin found that adolescents who mature early tend to respond in an inhibitory and rigid manner. He, like Jones, believes that early maturers may be pushed into decisions about their identity too early. By contrast, those adolescents who mature late may have more time to handle their physical changes, and therefore may be more flexible in identity formation. Jones (1965) reported that when late maturers were followed into their thirties, they were less likely to have familial, vocational, and marital commitments. However, an alternative interpretation of such findings is that delayed maturers also are having difficulty establishing an identity; while the early maturers may reach a "false" identity that comes too early in their development, the late maturers do not seem to attain an identity, even by the time they are thirty or thirty-five. Since comparisons with individuals who matured "on schedule" during adolescence were not made, a clear interpretation of these data is not possible. Researchers need to include a control group of adolescents who mature on schedule in future studies of early and late maturation.

The Milwaukee Study

Recently another longitudinal investigation of early and late maturation has been conducted by Dale Blyth and his colleagues (Blyth, Bulcroft, and Simmons, 1981). Rather than skeletal development, the presence or absence of menstruation and the relative onset of the menses were used to classify girls as early, middle, or late maturers. For boys, the classification was made on the basis of the peak rate of growth in height. More than 450 individuals were studied for five years, beginning in the sixth grade and continuing through the tenth grade in Milwaukee, Wisconsin from 1974 through 1979. Students were individually interviewed and achievement test scores and grade point averages were obtained.

Somewhat surprisingly, there were fewer significant relationships between pubertal development, and psychological and social development than was anticipated. However, the significant findings that did occur reveal some interesting patterns:

Self-concept. Early-maturing boys had a higher level of self-esteem than middle- or late-maturing boys in the seventh grade, but there were no differences in the ninth and tenth grades.

Body image. One of the most important tasks of adolescence is to incorporate dramatic physical changes into a positive body-image. Students were asked to report how satisfied they were with their height, weight, figure development (for girls) and muscular development (for boys). Early maturers were less satisfied with their bodies than were late maturers, and early maturers were less satisfied with their weights at all grade levels. When weight was controlled, the significant differences between early and late maturers disappeared, suggesting that weight, not early maturation, was the culprit.

For the girls, a complex pattern developed in regard to satisfaction with figure development. In the sixth grade, the more developed, menstruating girls showed greater satisfaction with their figures than late-maturing girls did. But by the ninth and tenth grades, the pattern was reversed. When all the girls had developed, it was the late maturers who were the most satisfied with their figures. Thus, by the ninth and tenth grades early maturers were less satisfied with their heights, weights, and figures than were late maturers (figure 3.14). One possible reason for this pattern of findings is that by the ninth and tenth grades, early maturers are usually shorter and stockier and late maturers are often taller and thinner. Possibly the late-maturing females in the ninth and tenth grades more closely approximate the American ideal of feminine beauty—tall and slim, with a figure.

Maturation seemed to have less influence on the body images of boys, although when differences appeared, they invariably favored early rather than late maturers. These differences seemed to be more pronounced in early adolescence.

Opposite-sex popularity. In the sixth and seventh grades, girls who had reached menarche reported that they were more popular with boys and dated more than girls had who had not reached menarche. In the tenth grade, early-maturing girls said they were dating more than their late-maturing counterparts. Note that opposite-sex behavior is the first category in which early maturing girls seem to have an advantage.

Independence. Early-maturing girls also seem to have more independence than late-maturing girls. Girls who had reached menarche in the sixth or seventh grades reported that they were more likely to be allowed to take the bus home alone, more likely to be left alone when their parents were gone, more likely to babysit, and more often perceived that they are making their own decisions. By the tenth grade, however, such differences seemed to have disappeared.

Academic behavior. In the sixth and seventh grades, early-maturing girls were less likely to have good grades and scored lower on achievement tests than their peers. These effects did not appear in the later adolescent years. Whether they are long-lasting is difficult to determine, though, since a number of the early-maturing girls dropped out of the study.

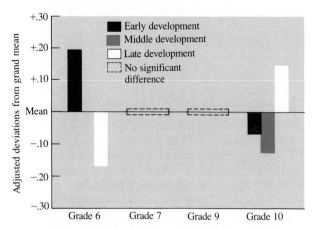

Figure 3.14 **Female pubertal development and satisfaction with figure.**

Problem behavior at school. Early-maturing girls said that they got into trouble more at school than their peers in the sixth and seventh grade. For example, in the seventh grade the early maturers reported that they often skipped school.

Participation in activities. Early-maturing boys participated in fewer school activities and were less often chosen as leaders in the sixth grade. The trend was reversed in the tenth grade, at which time early-maturing boys participated in more activities.

In summary, in the recent longitudinal investigation by Dale Blyth and his colleagues, early maturation for girls seemed to have mixed effects, while early maturation seems to have an overall positive effect for boys. However, it is important to examine the particular dimension of psychological and social development in question. For example, while early maturation seems to be disadvantageous for the girl's body image, school performance, and school behavior, it appears to be an advantage in opposite-sex relationships and independence. Finally, note that many of these findings appeared only during early adolescence; by the beginning of late adolescence, many of the differences between early and late maturers had disappeared.

There likely are many factors that mediate the effects of early and late maturation on the adolescent's development. One such factor is physical attractiveness. To learn more about the role of physical attractiveness and its influence on maturation and self-esteem, read Perspective on Adolescent Development 3.4.

Menarche and the Menstrual Cycle

The onset of puberty and **menarche,** the girl's first period, have often been described as "main events" in most historical accounts of adolescence (e.g., Rousseau, 1762; Hall, 1904; A. Freud, 1958; Erikson, 1968). Basically, these views suggest that such change and events produce a different body that requires considerable change in self-conception, possibly leading to an identity crisis. While there has been conceptual interest in such change for many years, it only has been within recent years that empirical research has addressed such matters as the female adolescent's adaptation to menarche and the menstrual cycle (e.g., Brooks-Gunn and Ruble, 1982; Grief and Ullman, 1982).

In one investigation (Ruble and Brooks-Gunn, 1982) of 639 girls, a wide range of reactions to menarche were unveiled. Most of the reactions, however, were quite mild, as girls described their first period as a little upsetting, a little surprising, or a little exciting and positive. In this study, 120 of the fifth and sixth grade girls were telephoned to obtain more personal, detailed views of their experience with menarche. The most frequent theme of the girls' responses was positive, namely, that menarche was an indicator of their maturity. Other positive aspects to menarche included reports that they now could have children, were experiencing something that made them more like adult women, and now were more like their friends. The most frequent negative aspects of menarche reported by the girls were its hassle, having to carry supplies around, and its messiness. A minority of the girls also indicated that menarche involved physical discomfort, produced behavioral limitations, and created emotional changes.

Questions also were asked about the extent to which the girls communicated with others about the appearance of menarche, the extent to which the girls were prepared for menarche, and how the experience was related to early/late maturation. Virtually all of the girls told their mothers immediately, but most of the girls did not tell anyone else about menarche, with only

PHYSICAL ATTRACTIVENESS, PUBERTAL CHANGES, AND
THE SELF-ESTEEM OF ADOLESCENT GIRLS

How might physical attractiveness mediate the effects of maturation on self-esteem?

*T*he body as a social stimulus has been given increased research attention in recent years (e.g., Berscheid and Walster, 1974; Dion, Berscheid, and Walster, 1972). The possibility exists that individual differences in physical attractiveness may mediate the effects of early and late maturation on adolescent development. As part of the Milwaukee Longitudinal Study focused on early and late maturation, David Zakin, Dale Blyth, and Roberta Simmons (1984) examined the effects of early pubertal development and physical attractiveness on the popularity, body image, and self-esteem of more than two hundred sixth grade girls. Attractiveness was rated by a nurse using two five-point scales, one ranging from fat to skinny, the other from ugly to very good-looking. Attractive girls were defined as those whom observers rated as both above average in looks and average to thin in body build. Unattractive girls were defined as those who observers rated as both chubby in body build and below average in looks. Girls who fell between these categories were labeled as average in attractiveness. With regard to the assessment of self-esteem, girls were asked to answer six questions from the Rosenberg Self-Esteem Scale specifically designed for children and young adolescents. High scores on this scale suggests the girl considers herself to be a person of worth while low scores indicate that she experiences some degree of self-rejection or dissatisfaction.

What were the results of this inquiry? First, regardless of puberty status, unattractive girls perceived themselves as less popular with others and as having a less satisfactory body image than attractive girls; however, in the midst of pubertal change (that is, developing), they exhibited higher self-esteem than their attractive counterparts (figure 3.15). Why might this be so? This finding may be explained by considering the degree of risk or

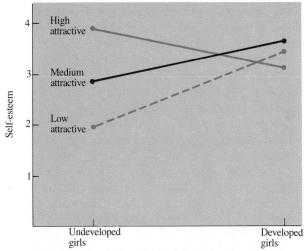

Figure 3.15 **The self-esteem of developed and undeveloped sixth grade girls of varying degrees of attractiveness.**

uncertainty involved in making the transition through early adolescence. The attractive girl, prior to experiencing pubertal change, has been accustomed to preferential treatment because of her looks. Presumably her self-esteem is to some extent tied to her physical appearance; thus, when the attractive girl begins to experience the pubertal transition, the physical changes may be more threatening to her because of the risk involved in possibly losing her attractiveness. She does not know at this point in development what the final outcome will be. By contrast, the unattractive girl may welcome the onset of puberty. From her view, there likely will not be any loss as her body changes—the final version may offer some improvement. The popular myth of the ugly duckling who turns into a beautiful swan may offer her some hope. So, she holds the possibility that puberty will make her body more beautiful. Therefore, she may cope relatively better during the pubertal change process than the girl who initially was more attractive.

An alternative explanation also is possible. Attractive developing girls meet a different arena of social circumstances than unattractive developing girls. The developing girl's bodily changes, including breast development, alter the nature of her interactions with the opposite sex, imbuing them with sexual overtones. For example, in the Milwaukee study, early involvement with boys was linked with lower self-esteem and poor school performance. These young, physically maturing girls may not yet be emotionally mature enough to handle the adult-like pressures of dating and opposite-sex relationships. Physically attractive girls, due to their greater appeal, are especially likely to receive more attention from boys. Because of these reactions, they may become more acutely aware that they face the transition to new roles in life. This realization combined with an increase in emotional demands may lead to a change in self-image, which is reflected in lower self-esteem. However, this alternative interpretation does not account for the unattractive developing girl's higher self-esteem.

In sum, this investigation reveals that puberty may have different meanings for girls differing in physical attractiveness. It is particularly interesting that, at least during the peak of physical changes in puberty, the attractive girl shows more difficult adjustment than the unattractive girl.

one in five informing a friend. However, after two or three periods had occurred, most girls had talked with girlfriends about menstruation. Girls not prepared for menarche indicated more negative feelings about menstruation than those who were more prepared for its onset. Girls who matured early had more negative reactions than average or late maturing girls. In summary, menarche initially may be disruptive particularly for early maturing and unprepared girls, but it typically does not reach the tumultuous, conflicting proportions described by some early theoreticians.

Puberty and the Spatial Abilities of Female Adolescents

Recently there has been a flourish of interest in the possibility that pubertal change in girls may disrupt cognitive abilities, particularly in the area of spatial abilities (e.g., Brooks-Gunn, 1985; Newcombe, Dubas, and Moore, 1985; Peterson, 1985; Rovet, Netley, and Dewan, 1985; Waber, 1985). Among the factors given for possible changes in spatial abilities during adolescence are those related to hormonal changes, hemispheric specialization of the brain, pubertal timing in boys and girls; sex role orientation, genetics, and prenatal hormonal environment. One offshoot of ideas about puberty and spatial abilities is that late maturing adolescents may have superior spatial abilities than early maturing adolescents. This hypothesis, and others relating pubertal change to disruption in spatial abilities, either have been unsupported or met with mixed results. Indeed, one recent longitudinal investigation (Petersen, 1985) involved the administration of a number of cognitive tests (such as those related to spatial ability and formal operational thought) to 335 early adolescents from the sixth through the eighth grades.

The dominant pattern of cognitive growth, both for boys and girls, was one of linear increase rather than disruption from the sixth through the eighth grade.

On-Time and Off-Time in Pubertal Development

In this chapter, we have seen that not all boys and girls move through the pubertal sequence at the same time and that they often are acutely aware of their pubertal status vis-à-vis their peers. Jeanne Brooks-Gunn, Anne Peterson, and Dorothy Eichorn (1985) recently evaluated the timing of maturational events and its implications for pubertal development. Our conclusion to this chapter focuses on their ideas about the importance of understanding asynchronies among the normative events involved in puberty.

Being on-time or off-time in terms of pubertal events is a complex affair. In terms of such timing, it is important to consider not just biological status or pubertal age, but chronological age, grade in school, cognitive functioning, and social maturity as well. Such complexity in the development of the adolescent suggests that it may be inappropriate to categorize the individual on only one dimension of development, such as pubertal age. A seventh grade girl may be on-time for pubertal age (i.e., biological growth) but off-time socially or cognitively in terms of comparison with her peers. Or, the girl may be on-time socially, but off-time cognitively and biologically.

And, variability may occur within a particular domain—such as biological changes. For example, when investigators use different measures to index pubertal events, variability among various characteristics often is considerable. A girl may be on time with regard to breast development, but not pubic hair development. In too many investigations, only one measure is used to index puberty—thus, in such studies, asynchrony in pubertal development may be hidden. One investigation (Brooks-Gunn and Warren, 1985) found that the onset of breast development, but not pubic hair, was linked with the social development of fifth and sixth grade girls.

The discussion of on-time and off-time events regarding puberty fit nicely with the ideas presented in Chapter 1 about life time and social time. Bernice Neugarten (1980) believes social time is just as important in understanding adolescent development as life time or chronological time. She believes that off-time and on-time events can be thought of both in terms of biological and social markers. Neugarten also argues that it is important to consider historical time as well. The findings by Dale Blyth and his colleagues described earlier in the chapter call attention to the importance of historical time as do the data on the earlier occurrence of puberty in recent years. Remember that Blyth's interpretation of the body image differences of early and late maturing girls pertained to the fact that the current model of the ideal female body image involves a very thin figure.

Given that there are a number of different domains we must consider when we are evaluating the nature of pubertal timing, the **goodness-of-fit model** proposed by Richard Lerner (1985) takes on added meaning. He believes that adolescents may be at risk when the demands of a particular social context and the adolescents' physical and behavioral characteristics are mismatched. On-time dancers are one such example (Brooks-Gunn and Warren, 1985). With regard to general peer comparisons, on-time dancers should not show adjustment problems. However, they do not have the ideal characteristics thought to be important in the world of dancers. That is, the ideal characteristics of dancers are those generally associated with late maturity—thin, lithe body build. The dancers, then, are on-time in terms of their peer group in general, but there is an asynchrony to their development in terms of their more focused peer group—dancers. Clearly, as we have seen throughout this chapter, understanding pubertal timing is a complex affair with many different domains and no simple conclusions.

Summary

I. Information about genetic influences on adolescent development includes ideas about the nature of genes and genetic principles, behavior genetics, and genetic–environment interaction.

   A. A discussion of genes and genetic principles focuses on what genes are, the distinction between genotype and phenotype, polygenic inheritance, reaction range, and canalization.

      1. Genes are the basic building blocks of heredity. They are biochemical agents. The actual combination of genetic material is genotype; the observed and measureable characteristics of genetic material is phenotype.

      2. Few psychological characteristics are the result of single gene action; the principle of polygenic inheritance suggests that phenotype is determined by a mixture of genes.

      3. The concept of reaction range suggests that for any given genotype, there is a range of phenotypes that could be expressed. This concept underscores the important role environment plays in modifying heredity, but argues that such modification has some limitations.

      4. Canalization refers to the narrow path or track that marks the development of some characteristic.

   B. Information about behavior genetics focuses on methods, heritability, and the influence of heredity on adolescent development, particularly in the area of intelligence.

1. With human behavior, geneticists rely on the twin study, family of twins design, kinship study, and adoption study to investigate heredity.

2. Heritability refers to the mathematical estimate of the degree a characteristic is inherited. It is by no means flawless and obscures the importance of genetic–environmental interaction.

3. All behaviors to one degree or another are influenced by heredity. The most widely studied aspect of adolescent development in terms of heredity is intelligence. Early estimates placed the heritability index at about .80, but more recent estimates range from .30 to .60. It is important to remember that intelligence is a global concept and that there likely are multiple intelligences that adolescents display.

C. Among the most important ideas housed in genetic–environmental interaction are those related to the concept of no genes, no adolescent; no environment, no adolescent, as well as what we know and what we need to know about genetic–environmental interaction.

II. Understanding biological processes and puberty requires knowledge of general features of physical growth and development, and many different aspects of the pubertal process.

A. Among the most important general features of growth are those pertaining to the nature of developmental growth curves and the factors that influence those curves.

1. Four general growth curves involve: a general growth curve, consisting of most aspects of skeletal and muscular growth; a reproductive curve; a curve for the brain and head; and a curve for the lymphoid tissues. Some biologists also have suggested that brain growth occurs in spurts.

2. Among the most important factors responsible for these different growth curves are: target-seeking or self-stabilizing factors; maturity gradients; feedback regulation; and body mass.

B. Information about puberty includes ideas about puberty and adolescence, the endocrine system, physical changes, and individual variation.

1. Puberty is a rapid change to maturation. Generally, puberty has ended long before adolescence ends and corresponds more to early than late adolescence.

2. The endocrine system is heavily involved in the pubertal process. The endocrine system is made of ductless glands that secrete hormones to various bodily organs. The hypothalamic-pituitary-gonadal axis is an important aspect of the complex hormonal system that contributes to pubertal change. Current knowledge suggests that testosterone, a member of the class of

hormones called androgens, plays a key role in the pubertal development of males, while estradiol, a member of the family of hormones called estrogens, has an important function in the pubertal development of females. Recent research has demonstrated a link between hormone levels and the behavior of adolescents. The pituitary gland also is involved in the adolescent's growth, either through interaction with the thyroid gland in the neck region or, more directly, by producing growth hormones.

3. Among the most impressive physical changes in puberty are those involving height, weight, and sexual maturation. The growth spurt for boys occurs approximately two years later than for girls, with the onset for boys being on the average twelve and one-half years and for girls ten and one-half years of age. Sexual maturation is a predominant aspect of pubertal development and includes a number of physical developments in both boys and girls. Menarche occurs very late in the pubertal process for girls.

4. For normal development in boys, the pubertal sequence may begin as early as ten and one-half and as late as thirteen and one-half. For girls, the age range for normal development involves menarche occurring as early as ten and as late as fifteen and one-half. If pubertal onset has not happened by the end of early adolescence, hormonal treatment usually is started.

III. Consideration of psychological adaptation to changes in physical development during adolescence includes a discussion of body image, early and late maturation, menarche and the menstrual cycle, and the relation of puberty to spatial abilities in girls.

A. During puberty, adolescents show a heightened preoccupation with their body image.

B. Learning about early and late maturation focuses on its conceptualization, as well as the California and Milwaukee longitudinal studies.

1. Three views of early and late maturation include: the belief that puberty has negative consequences regardless of when maturation is occurring; the idea that puberty may have positive consequences, a view that suggests that early maturers may have an advantage; and the argument that the timing of puberty is crucial—from this view, puberty can have either positive or negative consequences.

2. Data from the California Longitudinal Study suggested that early maturation favors boys and girls, being particularly strong for boys. However, one follow-up of the early-maturing adolescents suggested that late maturation was more beneficial in terms of identity development.

3. In the Milwaukee Longitudinal Study, the findings again favored early-maturing boys, while the data for girls was more mixed. With regard to body image, early-maturing girls are at an advantage early in adolescence, but at a disadvantage by late adolescence. During the midst of pubertal change, the self-esteem of attractive girls seems to be lowered more than for their unattractive counterparts.

C. While menarche and the menstrual cycle have been described as main events in many early theories of adolescence, only recently have they been studied empirically. It appears that menarche produces a wide range of reactions in girls.

D. It has been speculated that the pubertal process may be disruptive to the development of spatial abilities in girls, but current research data suggest this likely is not the case.

E. There is considerable complexity to understanding the nature of maturational timing involved in puberty. It is important to recognize that there are a number of biological, cognitive, and social domains to pubertal change. Using only one pubertal marker may hide asynchrony in development. One recently proposed model, developed by Lerner, is called the goodness-of-fit model. It is intriguing because the complexity of maturational timing is considered.

Key Terms

adrenal androgens *100*	heritability *89*
alleles *87*	hormones *98*
androgens *99*	hypothalamic-pituitary-gonadal axis *98*
brain-growth periodization *95*	hypothalamus *98*
canalization *88*	menarche *115*
dizygotic *88*	monozygotic *88*
estradiol *99*	phenotype *86*
estrogens *99*	pituitary gland *98*
genotype *86*	polygenic inheritance *87*
gonadal *98*	sex steroids *100*
gonadotropin *98*	testosterone *99*
goodness-of-fit model *119*	thyroid gland *102*

Brooks-Gunn, J. and Petersen, A., eds. (1983). *Girls at puberty.* New York: Plenum Press.
This book of readings, written by experts in different areas of adolescent development, provides considerable insight into current thinking about the role of puberty in the psychological life of girls.

Damon, A. (1977). *Human biology and ecology.* New York: Norton.
An excellent overview of biological influences on development. Includes detailed information on genetic influences, the interaction of genes and the environment, and the role of ecology in physical development. Moderately difficult reading.

Hyde, J. S. (1979). *Understanding human sexuality.* New York: McGraw-Hill.
A scholarly but entertaining look at the physical aspects of sexual development, including much material focused on understanding our sexuality. Easy to read.

Journal of Youth and Adolescence, 1985, Vol. 14, Nos. 3, 4.
Two issues of this excellent research journal have been devoted to the study of maturational timing in adolescence, including many insights into how puberty is experienced.

Netter, F. H. (1965). "Reproductive system." *The Ciba collection of medical illustrations,* vol. 2. Summit, N.J.: Ciba.
A book filled with what is generally considered the best set of illustrations on sexual anatomy available.

Scarr, S. and Kidd, K. K. (1983). "Developmental behavior genetics." In *Handbook of child psychology,* 4th ed., Vol. 2, edited by P. H. Mussen. New York: Wiley.
This very thorough, up-to-date scholarly treatment of hereditary–environmental interaction is very worthwhile reading for those interested in more detailed information about the role of genetics and environment in adolescent development.

Chapter 4

Cognitive Development and Social Cognition

Prologue

Sandy's Personal Fable

We will discover in this chapter that adolescents spend a great deal of time thinking about social matters. As part of this thinking, particularly in early adolescence, they often begin to show a heightened interest in their personal uniqueness as well as a belief in their indestructibility. As part of this thinking, their ideas often are filled with idealistic notions and hypothetical possibilities. And their thoughts often reveal an increased ability to mentally step outside of one's self and anticipate what the reactions of others will be in imaginative circumstances. To retain their sense of uniqueness and preserve their feeling that they are seen in a positive and powerful way by others, it is not unusual for individuals in early adolescence to construct a personal fable like that put together by Sandy in her description of her relationship with Bob. Later in this chapter, we will study the nature of the personal fable in greater detail.

Bob was important to me before I really knew him at all. It began when my mother invited him to a dance at the end of my ninth grade year. I didn't see much of him at the dance because I was actively pursuing someone else, and my brother's friends from prep school were being very nice to me as little sister. Afterwards, however, he asked me out a couple of times. We didn't get along particularly well or ill, weren't particularly attracted or repelled; but then I went away to school.

At school, I found that everyone else had someone "on the outside" to talk about, and, in most cases, to correspond with or even to visit and have visit them. My problem was that I had never been able to bear any of the boys who had shown a great interest in me, probably because I didn't like myself and thought there had to be something basically wrong with anyone who did. Consequently, I had nothing remotely approaching an outside attachment and little hope of forming a spectacular one at school. Still, I was determined to keep up with the competition, so I made up a relationship with Bob. This had the advantage of being based in fact. I had gone out with him and he was real. Also, he was in school in England, which explained why he never showed up and, to some extent, why he didn't write, since he would have had to ask his parents to find out from my parents where I was. Then, too, his not having shown much interest in me meant that I didn't despise him. This made it easier for me to represent myself as being madly in love with him.

After a few days I had the other girls convinced, and after a few months I believed it myself.

Source: Goethals and Klos, 1970.

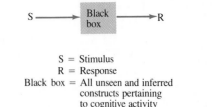

S = Stimulus
R = Response
Black box = All unseen and inferred
constructs pertaining
to cognitive activity

Figure 4.1 **One image of the black box and cognitive activity.**

Preview

*I*n this chapter, we begin the exciting inquiry of the adolescent's mind. Attention is given to what cognitive development is like; to Piaget's views on cognitive development, particularly the stage known as formal operational thought; and to the growing field of social cognition.

The Nature of the Adolescent's Cognitive Development: The Black Box Is Not As Mysterious As Once Thought

In the preceding chapters, the cognitive development of adolescents has been discussed without precisely defining the term. One of the leading cognitive-developmental experts, John Flavell, has grappled with this definitional issue for many years and concluded that the area of inquiry is so broad and complex that it really defies a tidy statement. Flavell put the matter this way:

> The really interesting concepts of this world have the nasty habit of avoiding our most determined attempts to pin them down, to make them say something definite and make them stick to it. Their meanings perversely remain multiple, ambiguous, imprecise, and above all unstable and open—open to argument and disagreement, to sometimes drastic reformulation and redefinition, and to the introduction of new and often unsettling concept instances and examples. It is perhaps not a bad thing that our prize concepts have this kind of complexity and instability (some might call it richness and creativity). . . . So it is with that concept called "cognition" . . . (Flavell, 1985)

Flavell's warning notwithstanding, some images are presented in this chapter to help you understand what the term *cognitive development* means. These images communicate some of the meanings that are agreed on by the experts who study cognitive development.

The simple diagram in figure 4.1 illustrates the most widely shared image of cognitive development. In this view, the world is divided into observable events (stimuli), responses by the adolescent (responses), and covert events that take place in the adolescent's mind (the black box). Each of these categories is distinct and separate from the others, with mental activity occurring between stimuli and responses. In this view, cognition is defined as all of the unobservable events in the black box—all the processes, activities, units, and the like of the human mind (e.g., Ault, 1977; Elkind, 1976). The study of cognitive development, then, is the study of how this mental machinery changes with age, presumably as the result of the complex interaction between mental maturation and experience. The black box conveys a sense of mystery and uncertainty because the mind can be known only indirectly and is never directly seen or observed. However, many facets of the mind and its activities *are* capable of being understood.

What is the mental activity of the adolescent like? Is it possible to be more precise about it than simply to draw a box and label it? The answer is, of course, yes; however, in doing so, a theoretical perspective is immediately assumed. As with other facets of development, any one of a number of theoretical perspectives can be adopted in regard to the adolescent's cognitive development. To describe or define mental activity is to define oneself into or out of a theoretical school of thought.

Some of the cognitive activities psychologists believe mediate or modify incoming stimuli before they connect up with actual behavior are expectancies, insight, attention, memory, plans, imagery, problem solving, decision making, thinking, and the like. So far in our discussion of the nature of cognitive development, we have described cognitive activities in terms of their function as a mediating link between stimuli and responses. However, the initial discussion of Piaget's theory in Chapter 2, showed that the cognitive developmental view gives cognitive activity a more central role in causing behavior. Rather than referring to such activity as only serving a mediating function, Piaget believed that the biological unfolding of cognitive stages is the primary core of development and serves as a primary determinant of the adolescent's behavior.

Piaget's View of Cognitive Development: More Abstract with Wings in Adolescents

To learn about Piaget's view of cognitive development, we review some of the basic ideas discussed in Chapter 2, focusing in greater detail on the two stages of thought most likely to characterize adolescents—concrete operational and formal operational; discuss whether there is a fifth stage beyond formal operational thought; outline the application of Piaget's theory to education, and evaluate the contributions of the theory.

An Overview of Piaget's Theory

Remember that Piaget's theory is one of the most well-known views of adolescent development. Piaget stressed that the most important aspect of understanding adolescent development involves viewing the adolescent in terms of biological adaptation and the cognitive unfolding of stages. Recall that the processes of assimilation, accommodation, organization, and equilibration explain the nature of changes in thought. Also, remember that Piaget emphasized that cognitive development unfolds in terms of four main stages: sensorimotor thought, preoperational thought, concrete operational thought, and formal operational thought. Let's now explore in greater detail the two stages most likely to characterize adolescent thought—concrete and formal operational thought.

Concrete Operational Thought

A better understanding of concrete operational thought comes from knowing about decentering, reversibility, and the nature of a concrete operation, classification, and some constraints of concrete operational thought.

Decentering, Reversibility, and the Nature of a Concrete Operation

For Piaget, concrete operational thought is made up of **operations;** that is, mental actions or representations that are reversible (Piaget, 1967). A critical feature of the concrete operational stage is the child's ability to pass tests such as the conservation of liquid quantity. Other such tests include the conservation of weight (testing knowledge that weight is unaffected by changing the physical shape of material) and number (testing knowledge that number is unaffected by spreading out stimuli or massing them together). For example, a well-known test of reversibility of thought involving the conservation of weight involves two identical balls of clay. The experimenter rolls one ball into a long, thin shape, and the other remains in its original ball shape. The child is then asked if there is more clay in the ball or the long, thin piece of clay. By the time children reach the age of seven or eight, most answer that the amount of clay is the same. In order to answer this problem correctly, children have to be able to imagine that the clay ball is rolled out into a long, thin strip and then returned to its original round shape. Such imagination involves a reversible mental action; thus, a concrete operation is a reversible mental action on real, concrete objects. Such concrete operations allow the child to decenter and to coordinate several characteristics rather than focusing on a single property of an object. In the clay example, the preoperational child likely focuses on height *or* width, and the concrete operational child coordinates information about both dimensions.

Classification

Many of the concrete operations identified by Piaget focus on the way children reason about the properties of objects. One important skill that characterizes the concrete operational thinker is the ability to classify or

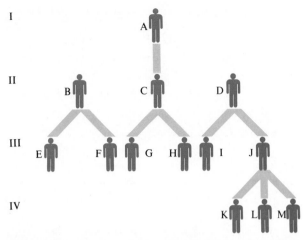

Figure 4.2   A family tree of four generations (I) to (IV).

divide things into different sets and subsets, and to consider their interrelationships. An example of the concrete operational child's classification skills involves a family tree of four generations (figure 4.2; Furth and Wachs, 1975). This family tree suggests that the grandfather (A) has three children (B, C, and D), each of whom has two children (E through J), and finally one of these children (J) has three children (K, L, and M). A child who comprehends the classification system can move up or down a level (vertically), across a given level (horizontally), and up and down and across (obliquely) within the system. He or she understands that person J can at the same time be father, brother, son, and grandson, for example.

Some Constraints of Concrete Operational Thought

Reference to the *concrete* nature of thought in the middle and late childhood years suggests that there is a limitation to concrete operational thought in that the child needs to have clearly available perceptual physical supports. That is, the child needs to have objects and events present in order to think about them. The concrete operational thinker is not capable of imagining the necessary steps to complete an algebraic equation, for example.

Formal Operational Thought

It seems that more research papers have been published on adolescent thought in the past decade than in the six previous decades combined. This impressive growth in interest focused on adolescent thought is due almost entirely to Piaget's theory about formal operational thought (Hill, 1985).

The Characteristics of Formal Operational Thought

According to Piaget, the formal operational stage appears between the ages of eleven and fourteen. What are the characteristics of formal operational thought that make it qualitatively different than concrete operational thought? We discuss the following candidates: abstractness, idealism and extended possibilities, problem solving governed by hypothetical deductive and logical reasoning, advanced understanding of language, and perspective taking.

Abstractness Most significantly, adolescent thought is more abstract than child thought. The adolescent no longer is limited to actual, concrete experience as the anchor of thought. Instead, she or he may conjure up make-believe situations, events that are strictly hypothetical possibilities, or purely abstract propositions, and try to reason logically about them.

The abstract quality of the adolescent's thought at the formal operational level is evident in adolescent's verbal problem-solving ability. While the concrete operational thinker would need to see the concrete elements A, B, and C to be able to make the logical inference that if A = B and B = C, then A = C, the formal operational thinker can solve this problem merely through verbal presentation.

Another indication of the abstract quality of the adolescent's thought is his or her increased tendency to think about thought itself. One adolescent commented, "I began thinking about why I was thinking what I was. Then I began thinking about why I was thinking about why I was thinking about what I was." If this sounds abstract, it is, and it characterizes the adolescent's enhanced focus on thought and its abstract qualities.

Idealism and What Is Possible Accompanying the abstract nature of formal operational thought in adolescence is thought full of idealism and possibilities. While children frequently think in concrete ways, or in terms of what is real and limited, adolescents begin to engage in extended speculation about ideal characteristics—qualities they desire in themselves and in others. During adolescence, such thoughts often lead adolescents to compare themselves and others in regard to such ideal standards. And during adolescence, the thoughts of individuals are often fantasy flights into future possibilities. It is not unusual for the adolescent to become impatient with these newfound ideal standards and become perplexed over which of many ideal standards to adopt.

Hypothetical Deductive and Logical Reasoning Adolescents are more likely than children to think in hypothetical deductive ways and reason in more logical ways about problems. It is sometimes said that the adolescent's thought is more like a scientist's than a child's, meaning that the adolescent often entertains many possibilities and tests many solutions in a planned way when faced with having to solve a problem. This kind of problem solving has been called **hypothetical-deductive reasoning.** Basically this means that in solving a problem, an individual develops hypotheses or hunches about what will be a correct solution to the problem and then in a planned manner, tests one or more of the hypotheses, discarding the ones that do not work. (See table 4.1 for one example of hypothetical-deductive reasoning.) Jerome Bruner and his associates have used a modification of the familiar game, Twenty Questions, in extensive work on cognitive skills (Bruner, 1966). The adolescent is given a set of forty-two colorful pictures displayed in a rectangular array (six rows of seven pictures each) and is asked to determine which picture the experimenter has in mind (that is, which is "correct"). The person is allowed to ask only questions to which the experimenter can reply yes or no. The object of the game is to select the correct picture by asking as few questions as possible. The person who is a de-

Adolescence is full of idealism—thoughts often take wings.

ductive hypothesis tester formulates a plan to propose and test a series of hypotheses, each of which narrows the field of choices considerably. The most effective plan consists of a "halving" strategy. (*Q:* Is it in the right half of the array? *A:* No. *Q:* Okay; is it in the top half? And so on.) Used correctly, the halving strategy guarantees the questioner the correct solution in seven questions or less, no matter where the correct picture is located in the array. Even if he is using a less elegant strategy than the optimal "halving" one, the deductive hypothesis tester understands that when the experimenter answers no to one of his guesses, several possibilities are immediately eliminated.

By contrast, the concrete thinker may persist with questions that continue to test some of the same possibilities that previous questions should have eliminated. For example, the child may have asked whether

Table 4.1 An exemplary task of hypothetical-deductive reasoning

A common task for all of us is to determine what can logically be inferred from a statement made by someone else. Young children are often told by teachers that if they work hard, they will receive good grades. Regardless of the empirical truth of the claim, the children may believe that good grades are the result of hard work, and that if they do not get good grades, they did not work hard enough. (Establishing the direction of the relationship between variables is an important issue.)

Children in late concrete operations, too, are concerned with understanding the relations between their behavior and their teachers' grading practices. However, they are beginning to question the "truths" of their childhood. First, they now know that there are four possible combinations if two variables are dichotomized (work hard—not work hard; good grades—not good grades).

Behavior	*Consequences*
1. Work hard	good grades
2. Work hard	not good grades
3. Not work hard	good grades
4. Not work hard	not good grades

Two combinations are consistent with the hypothesis that [a student's] hard work is necessarily related to good grades: (1) they work hard and get good grades, (4) they do not work hard and do not get good grades. When the presumed "cause" is present, the effect is present; when the cause is absent, the effect is absent. There are also two combinations that do not fit the hypothesis of a direct relation between hard work and good grades: (2) they work hard and do not get good grades, and (3) they get good grades without working hard.

The adolescent's notion of possibility allows her to take this analysis of combinations one important step further. Each of the four basic combinations of binary variables may be true or it may not. If 1, 2, 3, or 4 are true alone or in combination, there are sixteen possible patterns of truth values.

1 or 2 or 3 or 4 is true	4 patterns
1–2 or 1–3 or 1–4 or 2–3 or 2–4 or 3–4 are true	6 patterns
1–2–3 or 1–2–4 or 1–3–4 or 2–3–4 are true	4 patterns
All (1–2–3–4) are true	1 pattern
All are false	1 pattern
Total	16 patterns

The list is critically important because each pattern leads to a different conclusion about the possible relation between two variables.

Source: Excerpted from Piaget With Feeling, *by Philip A. Cowen. Copyright © 1978 by Holt, Rinehart and Winston, CBS College Publishing.*

the correct picture was in row 1 and received the answer no, but he later asks whether the correct picture is *x,* which is in row 1.

David Moshman (1979) analyzed the nature of formal hypothesis-testing ability in a group of seventh graders, tenth graders, and college students. He believes that there are actually three components to this ability. One component is the ability to understand *conditional relationships*. For example, the statement "If a student works hard, he will do well in class" is a conditional statement of the form: If *P,* then *Q*.

Moshman believes that the formal thinker must be able to apply this general conditional statement to all specific cases (that is, all students encountered who work hard). Another component is the ability to apply a *falsification strategy*. This is the realization that to test a hypothesis, a person has to try to find information that could prove it wrong. Conversely, the third component of the ability is *nonverification insight*. This is an appreciation of the fact that even when certain information is consistent with a hypothesis, the hypothesis is not necessarily proven. For example, suppose we hypothesize that because the sun comes up, people will wake up in the morning. To prove this hypothesis, we must seek to falsify it. One way might be to block the sun's appearance for a group of people, and see if they still wake up at the same time (falsification strategy). The hypothesis would not be verified simply by observing many people who wake up just after sunrise (nonverification insight). In Moshman's (1979) research, it was shown that each component undergoes a different pattern of development in the adolescent years and even many college students do not have all three readily under control.

Thus, the formal operational thinker tests her hypotheses with judiciously chosen questions and tests. Often a single question or test will help her to eliminate an untenable hypothesis. By contrast, the concrete thinker often fails to understand the relation between a hypothesis and a well chosen test of it—stubbornly clinging to the idea despite clear, logical disconfirmation of it.

Advanced Understanding of Language Piaget himself did not write extensively about adolescent changes in language development. For example, Piaget (1952) believed that cognition always directed language and that what was most important about understanding changes in development were primary changes in cognition, not secondary changes in language. However, it is important to recognize that debate still exists over whether cognition directs language, language directs cognition, or both possibilities exist (e.g., Jenkins, 1969). Nonetheless, it appears there are more significant changes in language development during adolescence than Piaget believed. Many scholars believe these changes occur within the context of the stage of formal operational thought and its abstract qualities (Bereiter and Scardamalia, 1982; Brown and Smiley, 1977; Fischer and Lazerson, 1984; Gardner, 1983; Labov, 1972; Werner and Kaplan, 1952). Among the significant language changes during adolescence are those pertaining to words and concepts, prose and writing, and pragmatics.

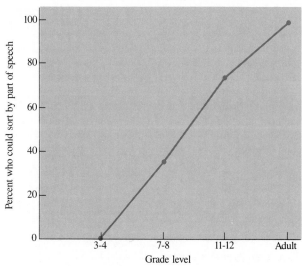

Figure 4.3 **Percentage of subjects by different ages who could sort words by parts of speech.**

Adolescents are more sophisticated in their ability to understand words and their related abstract concepts (Fischer and Lazerson, 1984). The understanding of grammar is a case in point. While children can learn the definition of a part of speech, such as what a noun is, and can become fairly adept at imitating model sentences in English workbooks, it appears that is is not until adolescence that a true understanding of grammar appears. With the increase in abstract thinking, adolescents seem to be far superior to children in analyzing the function a word plays in a sentence.

For instance, in one research study (Anglin, 1970), elementary school children, adolescents, and adults were asked whether they knew what nouns, verbs, adjectives, and prepositions were. Since parts of speech are taught in most schools by the third grade, it was not surprising that most of the people, including the third- and fourth-graders, gave correct definitions. However, when the people were required to sort twenty words (such as during, flower, dead, poor, cry, listen, and white) according to parts of speech, none of the elementary school children could do this task. As shown in figure 4.3, many of the adolescents and adults were successful at this task.

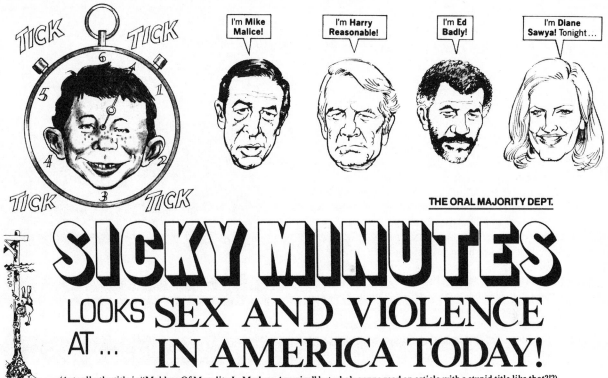

Figure 4.4 Excerpt from *Mad Magazine*.

ARTIST: ANGELO TORRES   WRITER: LOU SILVERSTONE

Another aspect of language that increases during adolescence that is related to words and concepts is **metaphor.** A metaphor is an implied comparison between two ideas that is conveyed by the abstract meaning contained in the words used to make the comparison. A person's faith and a piece of glass may be alike in that both can be shattered easily. A runner's performance and a politician's speech may be alike in that both are predictable. Concrete thinkers have a difficult time understanding such metaphorical relations. Consequently, many elementary school-aged children are puzzled by the meanings of parables and fables (Elkind, 1976).

Yet another aspect of language that reveals an increased understanding during adolescence is satire (Fischer and Lazerson, 1984). **Satire** refers to a literary work in which irony, derision, or wit in any form is used to expose folly or wickedness. Caricatures are an example of such satire. During adolescence, satire often takes on rhythmical qualities. Junior high school students may make up satirical labels for teachers, such as "The walking wilt Wilkie and wilking machine" or "The magnificent Manifred and his manifest morbidity." They also substantially increase their use of nicknames that are satirical and derisive—"Stilt," "the refrigerator," "spaz," are three such examples. The satire of Mad magazine also is more likely to be understood by adolescents than children (figure 4.4). This magazine relies on double meaning, exaggerations, and parody to highlight absurd circumstance and contradictory happenings. Such complexities in the use of language and caricature are lost on children, but begin to find an audience in adolescents.

*T*o comprehend the full meaning of a speaker's message, an adolescent needs to be sensitive to the speaker's belief and purpose (Searle, 1979). In most instances, people say what they believe. However, such conversational sincerity may be broken, and it may be broken for different reasons. Consider a circumstance in which a swimmer, after diving into a pool, comes up to the surface and says, "Come on in. The water is warm." The statement may be sincere or deliberately false. To distinguish between these possibilities, the listener must determine the facts and the speaker's belief about the facts. In addition to whether the statement is sincere or deceptive, the speaker also may try to signal the listener that the statement is false by using sarcasm.

To test the possibility that understanding the sincerity, deception, and sarcasm in a speaker's message follows a developmental sequence, Amy Demorest and her colleagues (1984) studied six-, nine-, and thirteen-year-olds and adults. The subjects were given stories

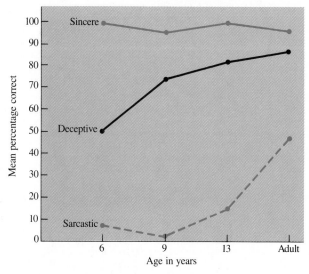

Figure 4.5 Children's, adolescent's, and adult's understanding of whether a conversation involves sincerity, deception, or sarcasm.

The written language of adolescents is often very different from their spoken language (Bereiter and Scardamalia, 1982; Fischer and Lazerson, 1984; Olson, 1977). When adolescents talk with each other they typically are face to face so they can monitor the listener's interest and understanding. When an adolescent writes, however, no other person is present. Therefore, the writer must create an abstract idea of what his or her audience is like. Further spoken communication is usually much shorter before a reply is given by the other person, while in written communication, it may be necessary to write a number of paragraphs without interruption or a response.

As can be seen, writing is a complex aspect of language and communication, and it is not surprising that children are very poor at writing (Hunt, 1970; Scardamalia, Bereiter, and Goelman, 1982). An organization of ideas is very important in writing—logical thought processes help the writer provide a hierarchical organization for the reader, letting him or her know which ideas are more general, which are more specific, as well as those that are more important than others. Not only has it been found that children are very poor at organizing their ideas ahead of time before they write, but they also have considerable difficulty detecting the most salient points in a prose passage as well (Brown and Smiley, 1977).

While many adolescents are not yet Pulitzer Prize winning novelists, they do seem to be more capable of beginning to recognize more general points from more

Versions

Sincere ...... Jay needed to get his hair cut. A new barbershop had just opened in town. Jay went to the new barbershop for a haircut. *Jay got the best haircut he had ever had. It was just the right length.* Jay walked home from the barbershop. He saw Mike walking down the street. Mike noticed Jay's new haircut. He crossed the street to speak to Jay. Mike said to Jay, "That new haircut you got looks terrific."

Deceptive ... *Jay got the worst haircut he had ever had. It was so short that his ears seemed to stick out.* He [Mike] put his arm around Jay's shoulders and smiled at Jay.

Sarcastic .... *Jay got the worst haircut he had ever had. It was so short that his ears seemed to stick out.* He [Mike] laughed and pointed to Jay's head.

Source: From Demorest, A., Meyer, C., Phelps, E., Gardner, H. and E. Winner, "Words Speak Louder Than Actions: Understanding Deliberately False Remarks," Child Development, 55, 152–153. © The Society for Research in Child Development, Inc.

about a conversation between two people containing sincere, deceptive, or sarcastic statements (See table 4.2 for what the conversations between the story characters were like). The subjects' ability to identify speaker belief and communicative purpose in sincere, deceptive, and sarcastic remarks was assessed. As shown in figure 4.5, all of the six-year-old children took remarks as sincere by assuming that a speaker's belief and purpose are in line with his or her statement. By nine years of age though, children are able to appreciate the deliberate deception of the speaker; however, at this age deception and sarcasm are both seen as deceptive. Finally, at some point between thirteen years of age and adulthood, adolescents become capable of better appreciating that a speaker's purpose may also be out of line with his or her statement. That is, it is during adolescence that sarcasm and deception are distinguished. When sarcasm is detected, the listener gives more weight to the speaker's behavior than to his or her statement.

specific points they are making as they write. And, they seem better than children at highlighting important points to be made as they write. With their increased logical thought, the sentences adolescents string together make more sense than those of children. Further, their essays are more likely to include an introduction, several paragraphs that represent a body of the paper, and concluding remarks (Fischer and Lazerson, 1984).

Pragmatics refers to the rules of conversation. There no doubt that most adolescents are much better conversationalists than children. Such rules allow adolescents to convey intended meanings and to "get along" with those they are talking to. The domain of pragmatics is broad. It covers such things as (a) taking turns in discussions, instead of everyone talking at once; (b) using questions to convey commands (Why is it so noisy in here?), (c) using words like "the" and "a" in ways that enhance understanding (He is *the* living end! or He is not just *a* person.), (d) using polite language in appropriate situations (when a guest comes to the house), and even (e) telling stories that are interesting, jokes that are funny, and lies that convince. To learn more about the ability of children and adolescents to detect when someone is lying as well as their sense of when sarcasm is being used read Perspective on Adolescent Development 4.1.

THE NATURE OF COGNITIVE DEVELOPMENT AND THE CHARACTERISTICS OF CONCRETE AND FORMAL OPERATIONAL THOUGHT

Concept	Processes/related ideas	Characteristics/description
The nature of cognitive development	What is cognitive development	It sometimes is referred to as the adolescent's mind, sometimes as all mental activities between stimuli and responses, at other times it is described more as biological, maturational unfolding of mental structures. Sometimes cognition is labeled as the cause of behavior, at other times merely a mediating link between environmental experiences and behavior. In all instances, the black box of mind is not as mysterious as once was thought—we now talk about and empirically study such aspects of cognition as expectancies, insight, attention, memory, plans, imagery, problem solving, decision making, and thinking.
Concrete operational thought	Decentering, reversibility, and the nature of a concrete operation	Concrete operational thought is the third major stage in Piaget's theory of cognitive development, ranging in age from approximately seven to eleven years of age according to Piaget. For Piaget, concrete operational thought is made up of operations—mental actions or representations that are reversible. Concrete operations allow the child or adolescent to decenter and coordinate several characteristics rather than focusing on a single property.
	Classification	One important skill that characterizes concrete operation is the ability to classify or divide things into different sets and to consider their interrelationships.
	Constraints	The individual needs to have clearly available perceptual physical supports present for reasoning to proceed. That is, objects and events need to be present for them to be reasoned about.

Our description of the adolescent's ability to improve in the area of conversational skills is closely aligned with the discussion of the next characteristics of formal operational thought. As we see next, adolescents are better than children at perspective taking.

Perspective Taking Not only do adolescents think about thought, but they also develop an awareness that others often are thinking in different ways than they themselves are. Piaget has shown that young children are basically egocentric in that they often perceive that others have the same view of the world as they do. Young children have considerable difficulty taking the perspective of another individual. It seems that the

Concept Table 4.1 **(Continued)**

THE NATURE OF COGNITIVE DEVELOPMENT AND THE CHARACTERISTICS OF CONCRETE AND FORMAL OPERATIONAL THOUGHT

Concept	Processes/related ideas	Characteristics/description
Formal operational thought	Abstractness	Most significantly, formal operational thought is more abstract than concrete operational thought. Make-believe situations are often crafted, strictly hypothetical possibilities are constructed, and purely abstract propositions are put forth. Verbal problem solving ability improves dramatically.
	Idealism and what is possible	Formal operational thought is full of idealism and possibilities rather than always focusing on what is real and limited as in the case of concrete operational thought. Adolescents often compare themselves with others based on ideal standards. Thoughts often take wings and future fantasies are engaged in.
	Hypothetical deductive and logical reasoning	Formal operational thought involves hypothetical-deductive reasoning, reasoning that is more logical than that of concrete operational thought. Such logical thought is more often planful than that of concrete operational thought.
	Advanced understanding of language	Formal operational thought includes more advanced understanding of language. Adolescents are better than children at understanding the abstract meaning of words, including the parts of speech, metaphor, and satire. Formal operational thinkers, with their more logical reasoning, are much better at writing than concrete operational thinkers, and they also are much better at understanding the key points when reading prose. Adolescent thinkers are better at pragmatics, understanding the rules of conversation, than children.
	Perspective taking	Formal operational thinkers are better than concrete operational thinkers at taking the perspective of another person.

ability to take the perspective of another person and recognize that she or he has different viewpoints than one's own improves during the adolescent years. There has been a considerable amount of research interest in the topics of egocentrism and perspective taking during the adolescent years, and we will describe this interest in greater detail later in the chapter under the topic of social cognition.

We have now considered a number of ideas about what cognitive development is and described a number of characteristics of concrete and formal operational thought. A summary of main ideas related to these aspects of adolescent cognition is presented in Concept Table 4.1.

Early and Late Formal Operational Thought

Early formal operational thought typically comes into play between the ages of twelve and fourteen, and late formal operational thought appears from about fifteen to eighteen years of age. Recall that Piaget's ideas about formal operational thought focus on the development of the adolescent's ability to consider all possible combinations of events and situations when given a problem to solve. In the early formal operational stage, the adolescent begins to see many of the possible combinations necessary to solve a problem, but he is not as likely as the late formal operational thinker to start with a plan and organize his search for a solution. In other words, early formal operational thinkers experiment with many different strategies, but they don't seem to have a systematic strategy from the start, as the late formal operational thinker does.

The changing relation between observations and hypotheses also reveals differences in the way the early formal operational thinker pursues a solution to a problem when compared with the late formal operational thinker. Piaget describes significant changes in the way adolescents deal with the relation between observations and hypotheses when tested with a pendulum problem. A weight is placed at the bottom of a string, which is fastened to the top of a rod. The boys and girls are asked to discover what causes the pendulum to move faster or slower. The subjects may change the length of the string, the weight of the object, the height from which they drop it, or the force with which they push it. Only the length of the string, however, influences the speed of oscillation.

The early formal operational thinker goes beyond providing a summary statement about his observations; he looks for a general hypothesis that will explain what happened. For example, the early formal operational thinker might mention his idea that the length of the string may influence the speed of the pendulum

Early formal operational thought often comes in from twelve to fourteen years of age.

after experimenting with it. But the early formal thinker is hardly ever concerned with trying out ideas that do not influence the pendulum. Consequently, the length of the string usually is not separated from the other variables when the causes of velocity are investigated, and the early formal thinker is left with uncertainty about the validity of his hypothesis. He is unable to systematically test his ideas against his observations.

By the late formal operational stage, the adolescent thinks differently about such matters. Her hypotheses are not always derived from the data, but are sometimes created at the beginning of the experiment to guide her investigation. Also, the late formal operational thinker is not satisfied with just a general statement about cause and effect—she searches for something that tells her what is *necessary* and what is *sufficient* to account for what has happened. In the pendulum problem, this leads her to further separate the weight and length variables to ascertain what the necessary and sufficient causes of velocity are. Is the length of the string acting alone, or is it interacting to produce the effect? The formal operational thinker might design an experiment to test these speculations out (Cowan, 1978).

Individual Variation in Formal Operational Thought

For the most part, Piaget emphasizes universal and consistent patterns of formal operational thought. Piaget's theory does not adequately account for the unique, individual differences that characterize the cognitive development of adolescents. These differences have been documented in a far-ranging set of research studies, meaning that certain modifications in Piaget's theory of formal operational thought need to be pursued (e.g., Bart, 1971; Berzonsky, Weiner, and Raphael, 1975; Higgens-Trenk and Gaite, 1971; Neimark, 1982; Overton and Meehan, 1982; Stone and Day, 1980).

The studies suggest that formal operational thought does develop during early adolescence for many boys and girls, but that this stage of thinking is far from pervasive. Instead, early adolescence is more likely to be characterized by a consolidation of concrete operational thought (Hill, 1983). One limitation of formal reasoning may involve the content of the reasoning; while the fourteen-year-old may reason at the formal operational level when it comes to analyzing algebraic equations, he may not be able to do so with verbal problem-solving tasks or when reasoning about interpersonal relations.

One model of cognitive development that emphasizes the individual variation in formal operational thought is called the **branch model** (Dulit, 1972). The formal operational stage is thought to be intermediate between concrete thinking about common, universal skills and reasoning about specialized talents. In the branch model, the first three stages of Piaget's view (sensorimotor, preoperational, and concrete operational) are virtually universal. But when the individual reaches adolescence, a number of alternative cognitive tracks are possible, one of which is formal operational thought. To be sure, formal operational thought is the path most adolescents follow. The branch model (figure 4.6), however, allows for the inconsistencies in the cognitive abilities of many adolescents. Piaget (1972)

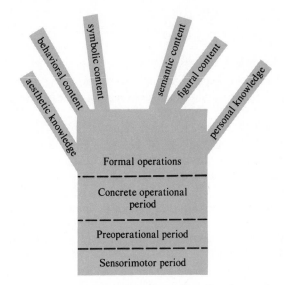

Branch model of cognitive development.

himself has pointed out that while most adolescents have the capability to engage in formal operational thought, whether they actually do so rests on a number of reasonably specific learning experiences. Some cognitive developmentalists believe that, contrary to popular belief, adolescent cognitive development may be shaped more by educational instruction and other environmental experiences than by cognitive development earlier in life (e.g., Case and Fry, 1972; Siegler, Liebert, and Liebert, 1973). In other words, progress through Piaget's first three stages is relatively free of environmental influence, whereas formal operational thought may be more sensitive to differences in the environment (Berzonsky, 1978).

Is There a Fifth Stage beyond Formal Operational Thought?

In the branch model just described, it was mentioned that Piaget's stage of formal operational thought may be an intermediate stage between concrete thinking about common universal skills and reasoning about special talents. Piaget did not believe this was so, however. For Piaget, change to reasoning about a special talent, such as the kind of thinking engaged in by a nuclear physicist or a medical researcher, is no more than window dressing. A nuclear physicist may engage in a kind of thinking that cannot be matched by the adolescent, but the adolescent and the nuclear physicist differ only in their familiarity with an academic field of inquiry—in the content of the thought, not in the operations brought to bear on that content (Piaget, 1970).

One set of theorists who emphasize the specialized nature of adult thought and how it may differ from adolescent thought are the **adult contextual theorists.** Gisela Labouvie-Vief (1980, 1982), indeed, has argued from this perspective that Piaget's theory is an inappropriate model of adult thought. In particular, she and the adult contextualists argue that in most cultures adulthood brings extensive experience with the world of work. In addition, there is increased responsibility for one's self. We expect an adult to be self-sufficient and to earn a living by himself or herself, for example. Because of such experiences, the thought of adults is more likely to be specialized, pragmatic, and reality-oriented than the thought of adolescents.

Even Piaget (1967) detected that formal operational thought may have its hazards:

> With the advent of formal intelligence, thinking takes wings and it is not surprising that at first this unexpected power is both used and abused. . . . Each new mental ability starts off by incorporating the world in a process of egocentric assimilation. Adolescent egocentricity is manifested by a belief in the omnipotence of reflection, as though the world should submit itself to idealistic schemes rather than to systems of reality. (pp. 63–64)

Formal operational thinking, then, may be a faulty choice at times because idealism may insulate the individual from pragmatic orientation to the specialization and reality of the actual world. In this vein, Piaget said that dreams eventually have to be discarded or modified to accommodate reality.

As individuals move through their college-age years, there is some evidence that the absolute nature of adolescent logic begins to diminish. Some psychologists believe that the realization that there are multiple perspectives and alternative solutions to problems accounts for the diminishing use of formal operational thought during the transition from adolescence to adulthood. If we were to assume that buoyant idealism and logical formal thought represent the criteria for cognitive maturity, we would have to admit that the cognitive activity of adults is overly concrete and likely represents a regression to concrete operational thought. However, from the adult contextual view, rather than reflecting regression, the pragmatic, specialized, and realistic thought of adults represents cognitive maturity.

Piaget's Theory and Adolescent Education

Hardly a day passes without the appearance of a new article applying the principles of Piaget's theory of cognitive development to the education of American children. Frank Murray (1978) describes why Americans have moved so swiftly to embrace Piaget. Two social crises, the proliferation of behaviorism and the dominance of the psychometric approach to intelligence (IQ testing) have made the adoption of Piagetian theory inevitable, he says. The first social crisis was the post-Sputnik concern of a country preoccupied with its deteriorating position as the engineering and scientific leader in the world, and the second was the need for compensatory education for minority groups and the poor. Curriculum projects that soon came into being after these social crises include the "new math," Science Curriculum Improvement Study, Project Physics, "discovery learning," and Man: A Course of Study. All of these projects have been based upon Piaget's notion of cognitive-developmental changes in thought structure. Piaget's theory contains a great deal of information about the young person's reasoning in the areas of math, science, and logic—material not found anywhere else in the literature of developmental psychology.

While there have been numerous efforts to apply Piaget's ideas about cognitive development to the education of children, applications to the education of adolescents have been meager. Philip Cowan (1978) reasoned about why the application of Piaget's ideas to the education of adolescents has been neglected:

> First, those adolescents who do arrive at formal operations function at a level similar to their teachers and the authors of textbooks; it no longer seems necessary to pay attention to qualitative differences in intellectual structure. But the fact that the formal operations stage is divided into early and late substages indicates that there are noticeable differences between the first application of formal structures and their completion. Second, the structure of education itself undergoes a marked change between elementary and secondary levels. In preschools, kindergartens, and grades one through six, the basic focus of education is the child in the classroom; children may be involved with, at most, several teachers during the day. In secondary schools and colleges, the focus shifts to subject matter divisions of curriculum. Each teacher sees a student for forty-five to sixty minutes only in connection with a particular content area (English, history, math, philosophy, etc.). Thus, both teachers and texts may become more focused on the development of curriculum and less on the developmental characteristics of the students. And when they are concerned with the developmental level of the students, teachers may pay more attention to individual differences in personality-social-emotional characteristics than to variations in the structure of adolescent thought. . . .
>   In the United States it is the usual practice to divide secondary education into two levels, junior high and high school. Children in grades seven, eight, and sometimes nine (twelve-to-fifteen-year-olds) attend junior high while fifteen-to-eighteen-year-olds are enrolled in high school. This division represents an implicit recognition of the qualitative differences inherent in Piaget's distinction between early and late formal operations.
>   In stage-structural terms, there are both advantages and disadvantages to be gained from attempts to keep children of the same age in one school. Junior high schools, usually larger than elementary schools but smaller than high schools, are meant to serve as a transition between the two—a middle ground between the child-in-the-classroom focus and the independent-student, subject-matter orientation of later education. It is hoped that the narrow age range will reduce the social and intellectual heterogeneity of the student population and facilitate the creation of a more coherent educational program. In fact, within the twelve-to-fifteen-year age span, normal children range from early concrete to late formal structures. Teaching to the "average" in this range is virtually impossible given current classrooms, and so junior high programs usually begin the controversial practice of separating children into as many as nine educational tracks. (Children in elementary schools are also grouped on the basis of reading ability, and sometimes math, but most still spend the rest of the day in a heterogeneous classroom.) Even when the age restriction does reduce heterogeneity, it tends to gather together adolescents who are in the early formal stage—the more egocentric phase of formal operations. . . . There are fewer older students available to provide the social disequilibration which encourages progress to the next cognitive-developmental stage. (Cowan, 1978, pp. 276–77)

Research on whether instruction following traditional methods or Piagetian methods is likely to promote cognitive growth in adolescents is beginning to accumulate. To read more about the application of Piaget's ideas to instruction in science, read Perspective on Adolescent Development 4.2.

Consider a curriculum area that virtually every adolescent is exposed to during the junior high and high school years—science. Most science courses (or at least the majority of the units taught in each of them) follow a reasonably formal, straight-forward lecture format. Classifications of animals and plants are memorized through exposure to the teacher's lecture and the text.

Some educational experts believe that this format is not the best way to teach science, particularly for students who have not yet reached the stage of formal operational thought. Instead, they believe that improved learning and advances in cognitive development are more likely to occur when adolescents observe and collect organisms from their natural habitats and then relate them to various subjects covered in the course. In this manner, the adolescent is forced to restructure his or her concrete way of thinking about the world and logically categorize events and objects in more formal, logical ways.

One investigation was specifically designed to test whether the more formal lecture method or the hands-on experience of student participation was superior at promoting cognitive development (Renner, Stafford, Lawson, McKinnon, Friot, and Kellogg, 1976). Students in junior high school science courses were taught

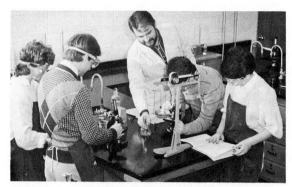

Hands-on, participatory science classes advance formal, operational thought in students.

using either the formal lecture method or the hands-on, participatory method. In the formal classes, the students used standard textbooks, read and recited from the books, and learned concepts about the scientific method. In the experimental, hands-on classes, the junior high science students were given considerable experience in solving laboratory problems and there was extensive open inquiry and student-directed investigations. There also was a considerable amount of structure in the hands-on strategy with precise expectations and careful directions

Evaluation of Piaget's Theory

In the mid-1970s, Piaget's theory was very much the central focus of attention in the field of cognitive development. There were skeptics even then (e.g., Brainerd, 1972, 1976), but the attitude seemed to be one of wait and see. That is, "Piaget's theory has served us well; it seems to be wrong in places, but let's see how we can shore it up." Now in the 1980s, a new feeling has caught up with many cognitive scholars (e.g., Fischer, 1980; Flavell, 1985; Gelman, 1982; Gelman and Baillargeon, 1983; Kuhn, 1980; Mandler, 1983).

The last line in John Flavell's (1980) eulogy to Piaget stated that our main task is to extend and go beyond what Piaget began so well. Let's now consider what Piaget began so well as well as what some of the current misgivings are in regard to Piaget's view.

Piaget's Major Contributions
Four main contributions of Piaget involve: (1) his brilliant observations of children; (2) his ideas of what to look for in development; (3) the qualitative nature of children's mental life; and (4) imaginative ideas about how children's thought changes.

being given. The students in both types of classes were tested on Piaget's concrete and formal operational tasks both before and after participation in the classes. As shown in figure 4.7, junior high students who were taught in the hands-on, participatory way advanced their formal operational thought more than their counterparts who were taught in a more standard format. It is important to note that the use of very concrete materials did not interfere with the transition to formal operational thought, but actually seemed to enhance the move. One primary argument that has come out of the study of applications of Piaget's ideas to the education of adolescents is that too often instruction may be at a formal operational level when the majority of adolescents actually are concrete operational thinkers.

Piaget's ideas even have been applied in this manner at the college level. For example, in one investigation in the area of humanities, curriculum designed to enhance the transition from concrete to formal operational thought with college freshmen was successful, with twenty-one of twenty-two students beginning the year at the concrete level moving to the formal operational level by the end of the term (Wideck, Knefelkamp, and Parker, 1975).

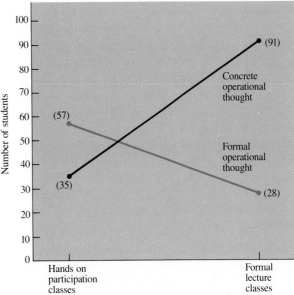

Figure 4.7   The effects of two different forms of instruction and curriculum in junior high school science on concrete and formal operational thought.
Note: Seventy-two of 92 students were at the concrete level at pretest for the hands-on participation classes; ninety-two of the 119 students were at the concrete level in the formal lecture classes. As the graph indicates, in the hands-on participation classes, fifteen of the concrete thinkers became formal thinkers while in the formal lecture classes, only one student moved from concrete to formal thought.

Brilliant Observations of Children To begin with, Piaget was a brilliant observer of children and adolescents. He collected thousands of firsthand observations of what children do and how they seem to think that have withstood the scrutiny of time (in some cases thirty to fifty years). There are many reasons for crediting Piaget with genius, but this accomplishment alone would be sufficient. The more we attempt to verify Piaget's observations with children and those that we encounter professionally, the more impressed we are. The insights are easily and often surprisingly verified. The young infant really does fail to search for an object when it is hidden. The four-year-old who watches a liquid poured from one container into another differently shaped actually says that there is now "more" or "less" liquid

than before. The nine-year-old really does get stuck in hypothetico-deductive problem solving. And the list goes on. There are literally hundreds of such observations, first made by Piaget, that accurately describe how children generally reason in these situations.

Ideas about What to Look for in Development A second contribution is that Piaget has given us many good ideas about what to look for in development. For example, he has shown us that infants are very complex and subtle creatures whose seemingly chaotic patterns of response are actually highly organized and structured. Contemporary experts on infancy have benefited to an extraordinary degree by his suggestions and descriptions of this organization. Or, as another example, he has shown us that the major change from childhood to adolescence involves a shift from the world of concrete and narrow logic to the plane of verbal reasoning and broad generalization. This insight has had a widely felt influence on educators and those who work with adolescents.

Qualitative Changes in Mental Life A third contribution is Piaget's focus on the qualitative nature of mental life. By always directing us to think of what the "mental environment looks like," he has served up a forceful argument for adults to learn how to deal with children and adolescents on their own intellectual terms. This qualitative focus has also been a refreshing antidote to the behavioral psychologist's lack of concern for the subject's mental life and the psychometric expert's preoccupation with attaching numbers to intellectual performance.

Imaginative Ideas about Cognitive Changes A final contribution is the host of imaginative ideas that Piaget has offered about how the child changes. The concepts of *assimilation* and *accommodation,* for example, are now well-rehearsed terms in the vocabulary of most psychologists. The concepts remind us of the double-sided nature of each of our exchanges with the environment. We must make the experience fit our cognitive framework (schemas, operations), yet simultaneously adjust our cognitive framework to the experience. The concept of *equilibration* offers an elegant view of developmental pacing. According to this idea, significant cognitive change comes only when our cognitive frameworks (schemas, operations) are clearly shown to be inconsistent with each other or the environment. And then change will only be likely if the situation is structured to permit gradual movement to the very next higher level of cognition.

The Criticism of Piaget's Theory

Piaget (1970) once remarked that he "always has considered himself one of the chief 'revisionists of Piaget' " (p. 103), but there are quite a few others, and some of them feel his theory is fundamentally wrong. Five sorts of research findings are troublesome for the Piagetian perspective (Gelman and Baillargeon, 1983; Mandler, 1983). These findings focus on: stages, nature of concepts, procedures involving Piagetian problems, training studies, and the timing involved in the emergence of cognitive abilities.

Stages Perhaps the broadest criticism concerns Piaget's claim for stages of development (Brainerd, 1976; Flavell, 1985; Hill, 1985; Keating, 1980). To claim that a child or adolescent is in a particular stage of development is to claim that she possesses a universally characteristic, prototypical system by which she approaches many different tasks. It should be possible to detect many similarities in the quality of thinking in a variety of tasks, and there should be clear links between stages of development such that successful attainment of one conceptual understanding predicts successful attainment of another. For example, we might expect children to learn how to conserve at about the same time that they learn how to cross-classify or seriate items. All three capabilities are supposed to provide evidence of concrete operational thought. As several critics have noted, however, lack of similarity, lack of cross-linkages, and lack of predictability seem to be present everywhere (Fischer, 1980; Flavell, 1985; Keating, 1980; Kuhn, 1980). As Kurt Fischer (1980) puts it, unevenness seems to be the rule in cognitive development, rather than the exception.

Fuzziness of Concepts Another problem is that the most interesting concepts in the theory—assimilation, accommodation, and equilibration—which are used to explain how progress is made in development, are tricky to pin down operationally, despite their theoretical glitter. That is, unlike concepts like reinforcement and imitation, these Piagetian concepts have very loose ties to experimental procedures and manipulations. They sound nice, but it is not always clear to what they refer. Despite work over the years to flesh out these concepts and anchor them in concrete procedures, not much progress has been made (Hill, 1985; Keating, 1980).

Procedural Changes in Piagetian Problems Very small changes in the procedures involving a Piagetian problem have significant effects on child's and adolescent's cognition. To some degree, this is due to the fact that such matters as remembering the various parts of a task can determine the likelihood that it will be completed correctly (Trabasso, 1977). Thus, a child's or adolescent's stage is at best one of several factors involved in solving Piagetian tasks.

Training Studies It has been possible to take a child or adolescent who seems to be at one Piagetian stage, such as concrete operational thought, and train the adolescent to pass tasks at the formal operational level (e.g., Renner et al., 1976; Wideck et al., 1975). Such findings pose problems for Piaget, who argued that such training only works at a superficial level and is ineffective unless the adolescent is at a transitional point from one stage to the next.

Timing of Emerging Cognitive Abilities Recent studies of infants and young children reveal that certain cognitive abilities emerge earlier than Piaget believed and their subsequent development may be more prolonged than Piaget thought (Gelman and Baillargeon, 1983; Mandler, 1983). For example, Piaget claimed that conservation of number does not appear until about seven or eight years of age, yet there is evidence that this ability may emerge as early as three years of age (Gelman, 1979). And, the adolescent may not be able to do as much cognitively as Piaget believed. Piaget was a brilliant person and he may well have projected onto others the intellectual precocity he himself possessed.

For example, at the age of ten, young Jean was offered the job as curator of the Geneva Museum of Natural History because of an article he had published about the rare albino sparrow. The heads of the museum quickly retracted their offer when they discovered Jean was only ten years of age.

To be sure, many adolescents do not engage in hypothetical deductive reasoning or produce propositional logic when it is needed. Of 588 individuals in grades seven through twelve, the percentages of students engaging in formal operational thought ranged from seventeen percent for the seventh graders to thirty-three percent for the twelfth graders (Renner et al., 1976). Other research confirms a minority of adolescents think in formal operational ways when hypothetical deductive reasoning is called for (Elkind, 1961; Nadel and Schoeppe, 1973; Tomlinson-Keasey, 1972; Wheatley, 1971). Depending on the study, it has been found that anywhere from seventeen to sixty-one percent of college students reason in formal operational ways, so formal operational is not the clear choice of thought even for college students.

In considering whether adolescents are viewed as formal operational thinkers or not, remember that there are many different dimensions to formal operational thought. The task that has been used to assess formal operational thought in most studies has been a hypothetico-deductive reasoning task. It likely is the case that if we consider the abstract nature of thought, idealism, advances in understanding words and concepts, and perspective taking as equally important criteria of formal operational thought, then higher percentages of adolescents would appear to be thinking in formal operational ways than the existent studies suggest. Too often a decision about whether an adolescent is a formal operational thinker or not is based on one task—a highly complex, high-level reasoning task. Further research on formal operational thought should consider the multidimensional nature of the concept and include multiple measures of formal operational thought.

In addition to describing the basic characteristics of formal operational thought earlier in this chapter, we have studied a number of other aspects of cognitive development in adolescence related to formal operational thought and Piaget's theory. A summary of these ideas related to formal operational thought and Piaget's theory is presented in Concept Table 4.2. Now we turn our attention to a growing area of interest in the cognitive development of adolescents called social cognition.

Social Cognition: Thinking and Reasoning about Social Matters—From the Personal Fable to Cognitive Monitoring

One of the major changes in the study of cognition in recent years focuses on the increased interest in thoughts about social matters. For too long the majority of theory and research on adolescent cognition emphasized cognition about nonsocial matters only, such as thought about logic, number, words, and the like. Now there is a great deal of lively interest in studying the manner in which adolescents reason about their social world as well.

The Nature of Social Cognition

Let's explore what social cognition is and then study the two main perspectives that have provided the impetus for research on social cognition—cognitive developmental and information processing.

What Is Social Cognition?

The field of **social cognition** is a very broad one. It is interested in how people conceptualize and reason about their social world—the people they watch and interact with, the relationships with those people, and the groups in which they participate. And, the field of social cognition includes how individuals reason about themselves in relation to others as well. Cognitive developmental psychologist John Flavell (1981) described social cognition as:

. . . all intellectual endeavors in which the aim is to think or learn about social or psychological processes in the self, individual, others, or human groups of all sizes and kinds (including social organizations, nations, and "people in general"). Thus, what is thought about during a social-cognitive enterprise could be a perception, feelings, motive, ability, intention, purpose, interest, attitude, thought, belief, personality structure, or another such process or property of self or other(s). It could also be the social interactions and relationships that obtain among individuals, groups, nations, or other social entities. A social-cognitive enterprise can be very brief (e.g., "I sense that my last remark hurt your feelings") or very extended (e.g., "I feel I am still learning new things about the kind of person you are, even after all these years of trying to understand you"). (Flavell, 1981, pp. 1–2)

The Cognitive Developmental View

The cognitive developmental view of social cognition has been promoted primarily by the theories of Jean Piaget (1957) and Lawrence Kohlberg (1969, 1976), as well as the research and thinking of John Flavell (Flavell et al., 1968; Flavell, 1981). The theme of the cognitive developmental perspective on social cognition is that social thoughts can be better understood if we take into account the child's and adolescent's maturational development. Kohlberg, in particular, has promoted the role of cognitive developmental theory in understanding many different facets of social and personality development.

Kohlberg (1969, 1976) is known by many psychologists primarily for his contributions to understanding the development of moral thinking. But Kohlberg has expanded Piaget's ideas on cognitive development to account for many social phenomena, not just the development of morality. For example, Kohlberg also has applied his cognitive-developmental perspective to sex-role development, role-taking abilities, peer relations, attachment-dependency relations, and the development of identity.

Like Piaget, Kohlberg believes that biological maturation and environmental experiences interact to produce the individual's stage of thought. Kohlberg says that adolescents attempt to attain intellectual balance or equilibrium. These attempts are influenced by

Concept Table 4.2

FURTHER ASPECTS OF ADOLESCENT COGNITIVE DEVELOPMENT AND AN EVALUATION OF PIAGET'S THEORY

Concept	Processes/related ideas	Characteristics/description
Further aspects of adolescent cognitive development	Early and late formal operations	Early formal operational thought often comes into play between twelve and fourteen years of age and late formal operational thought between fifteen and eighteen years of age. Planned and organized thought prior to solution of problems is more characteristic of late formal operational thought.
	Individual variation	There is a great deal of individual variation in adolescent thought; Piaget inadequately recognized such variation. The branch model suggests that there is more variation in adolescent thought than childhood thought.
	The fifth stage theory	Some theorists believe Piaget was wrong to think that formal operational thought is the highest, most mature stage of thought. They often believe that adult thought is more specialized than adolescent formal operational thought. The adult contextualists have argued that Piaget's model is an incorrect way to view adult thought. They believe adult thought is much more pragmatic and realistic than formal operational thought.
	Piaget and adolescent education	Piaget's theory has been applied to the education of children more so than to the education of adolescents. For the most part, applications suggest that many adolescents may be taught in a manner that is too formal and does not allow enough hands-on experience. Studies reveal that concrete experiences are more likely to promote formal operational thought than formal lecturing at an abstract level.
Evaluation of Piaget's theory	Contributions	Among the most important contributions are his brilliant observations of children and adolescents, ideas about what to look for in development, view of the qualitative nature of thought, and imaginative ideas about how thought changes.
	Criticisms	The criticisms of Piaget's theory focus on stages, fuzziness of concepts, procedural changes in tasks that produce different results, training studies that speed up the development of cognitive abilities, and the timing of emerging cognitive abilities.

moment-to-moment interactions with people and events in the world. As the individual reaches a new stage of thinking, she is able to balance her own past impressions about the world and herself with currently incoming information. Hence, the adolescent who has achieved a stable sense of identity ("I know who I am and where I am going") can handle ostensible threats to her identity ("You aren't working hard enough—you play around too much") without being intellectually blitzed. Over a reasonably long period of time, the balance that has been achieved in a particular stage of thought is disrupted because the maturing adolescent gains cognitive abilities that enable him to perceive inconsistencies and inadequacies in his thinking. Just as a scientist who is confronted with unexplained events and outcomes must reformulate his theory to explain them, so the individual must shift his former way of thinking to account for new discrepancies. When the individual is able to balance the new information with past impressions, he has reached a new stage in thinking.

Hence, the child in elementary school may categorize the identities of herself and others along a limited number of dimensions—even just one or two, such as "He is a boy, and I am a girl." But as she grows into adolescence, such a child begins to realize that different people are characterized by traits other than just gender. She recognizes, for example, that someone's introverted, quiet style of interaction may shape their personal identity just as much or more than their "maleness" or "femaleness."

Kurt Fischer (1980; Fischer, Hand, and Russell, 1983) refers to this ability of the adolescent to coordinate two or more abstract ideas as the stage of **abstract relations,** and argues that it appears in most adolescents from about fourteen to sixteen years of age. For example, at the age of sixteen, the individual may now be able to coordinate the abstraction of conformity with the abstraction of individualism in thinking about his or her personality or the personality of others. Consider the adolescent girl who sees herself as a conformist at school, where she dresses in conventional ways and behaves according to the rules of the school, but views herself as an individualist in social relationships, choosing unconventional friends and wearing unusual clothes in their company. By piecing together these abstractions, she likely views herself as being a different kind of person in the two contexts and senses that in some ways she is a contradictory person.

Thus, from the cognitive developmental perspective, adolescence involves a great deal of change in how individuals think and reason about themselves and others. Later in our discussion of social cognition, we will describe the nature of egocentrism and perspective taking in adolescence—two topics that also have been part of the cognitive developmental view of social cognition in adolescence. Now, however, we describe a second conceptual perspective on adolescent social cognition, that of social information processing.

Social Information Processing

Two converging conceptual developments have led to the belief that a better understanding of the adolescent's social cognition can come from viewing such cognition in terms of **social information processing.** First, when Walter Mischel (1973) introduced the view called cognitive social learning theory, he included a number of cognitive processes that serve as important mediators between experiences with the social world and the adolescent's behavior. Mischel spoke of the importance of plans, memory, imagery, and other mechanisms as highly significant contributors in how individuals process information about themselves and their social world. At the same time, a perspective that was to become the dominant view in cognitive science was maturing, the view known as information processing, which we initially described in Chapter 2 and will discuss in much greater detail in Chapter 5. Scientists interested in studying social cognition have drawn heavily from the information processing perspective in their focus on social memories, social problem solving, social decision making, and so forth. Keep in mind, however, that the information processing perspective is not a developmental perspective, so nothing is housed in this view that would tell us about how adolescents might process information about themselves and their social world differently than chil-

Egocentric thought is common in adolescence.

dren. Nonetheless, the information processing perspective has been valuable in informing us of the importance of many cognitive factors in the adolescent's processing of social information and will continue to provide an important framework for studying the social cognition of adolescents in the decades ahead.

Now that we have surveyed the domain of social cognition and looked at two important views of social cognition, we turn our attention to some of the specific areas of interest to those who study the social cognition of adolescents.

Egocentrism and Perspective Taking

Two important aspects of thinking about the self and others that develop in adolescence are egocentrism and perspective taking.

Egocentrism

"Oh my gosh! I can't believe it. Help! I can't stand it!" Tracy desperately yells. "What is wrong? What is the matter?" her mother asks. Tracy responds, "Everyone in here is looking at me." The mother queries, "Why?" Tracy says, "Look, this one hair just won't stay in place," as she rushes to the rest room of the restaurant. Five minutes later she returns to the table in the restaurant after she has depleted an entire can of hair spray. During a conversation between two fourteen-year-old girls, the one named Margaret says, "Are you kidding, I won't get pregnant." And, thirteen-year-old Adam describes himself, "No one understands me, particularly my parents. They have no idea of what I am feeling."

These comments of Tracy, Margaret, and Adam represent the emergence of egocentrism in adolescence. David Elkind (1967, 1976, 1978) believes two types of thinking represent the emergence of this unique kind of **egocentrism in adolescence**—the imaginary audience and the personal fable—and that underlying this egocentric thought is the emergence of formal operational thought.

Tracy's comments and behavior reflect the **imaginary audience** phenomenon. The imaginary audience is the belief that others are as preoccupied with the adolescent's behavior as he or she is. Attention-getting behavior, so common in early adolescence, may reflect this interest in an imaginary audience, that is the desire to be noticed, visible, and "on stage." An adolescent may think that others are as aware of a small spot on his trousers as he is, possibly knowing or thinking that he has masturbated. The adolescent girl, walking into her eighth grade classroom, thinks that all eyes are riveted on her complexion. So, particularly during early adolescence, individuals see themselves as constantly on stage, believing they are the main actors and all others are the audience.

The comments of Margaret and Adam reflect a second aspect of adolescent egocentrism called the **personal fable.** This construction refers to the adolescent's sense of personal uniqueness and indestructibility. Their sense of personal uniqueness suggests that no one can understand how they really feel. An adolescent girl thinks that her mother can in no way sense the hurt she feels because her boyfriend broke up with her, for example. In addition to sensing their uniqueness, another aspect of the personal fable involves the belief that one is indestructible. As part of their effort to retain this sense of personal uniqueness, adolescents often craft a story about the self that is not true. Likely tied to an emerging interest in idealism and the ability to think in more abstract and hypothetical ways, young adolescents often get caught up in a mental world far removed from reality, one that may entail the belief that things just can't or won't happen to them and that they are omnipotent and indestructible.

There has been a flourish of research interest in the phenomenon of adolescent egocentrism in recent years (e.g., Adams and Jones, 1981; Damon and Hart, 1982; Elkind, in press; Elkind and Bowen, 1979; Enright, Shukla, and Lapsley, 1980; Gray and Hudson, 1984; Lapsley, in press; Lapsley and Murphy, in press; Selman, 1980; Stephensenson and Wicklund, 1983; Walker, 1980; Wicklund, 1979). Much of the thrust of this research interest has focused on Elkind's conceptualization of egocentrism. Issues focus on such matters as what the components of egocentrism really are, the nature of self-other relationships in adolescence, and why egocentric thought emerges in adolescence. For example, by reading Perspective on Adolescent Development 4.3 you will learn about Elkind's interest in the imaginary audience and the possibility that two aspects of the self are involved in the adolescent's manufacture of an imaginary audience. And, while Elkind (in press) continues to argue that egocentrism and the adolescent's construction of an imaginary audience come about because of the emergence of formal operational thought, others believe that the nature of interpersonal understanding is involved as well (e.g., Lapsley, in press; Lapsley and Murphy, in press). Daniel Lapsley (in press) argues that the imaginary audience is due both to the ability to think hypothetically (formal operations) and the ability to mentally step outside of one's self and anticipate what the reactions of others will be in imaginative circumstances (perspective taking). Lapsley, for example, believes that Robert Selman's view of the development of perspective taking and interpersonal understanding provides an excellent context for understanding egocentric thought. Let's turn our attention more closely now to the development of perspective taking and interpersonal understanding. As part of this discussion, Selman's theory will be outlined.

Perspective Taking

Role taking and **perspective taking** are both terms used to describe an individual's ability to infer and adopt the perspective of another (Shantz, 1983). Often investigators are not only interested in understanding cognitive changes that produce different forms of role taking, but they also want to know how role taking is associated with empathy (showing feeling for another) and moral judgment (Flavell, 1974; Rubin, 1973; Selman, 1976a; Selman and Byrne, 1974; Shantz, 1983).

Robert Selman has developed the most well-known theory of social perspective taking (Selman, 1976 a,b; 1980; Selman and Byrne, 1974). Selman assumes that role-taking skills increase with age, at least into adolescence. In his view, role taking proceeds in a sequence of five stages (Selman, 1980):

THE IMAGINARY AUDIENCE OF THE ADOLESCENT

*P*resumably, younger adolescents are more prone to play to an imaginary audience—that is, to be more self-conscious—than older ones, because they are less experienced at using formal operational thinking. This egocentric self-consciousness should diminish during the adolescent years.

Roberta Simmons and her colleagues (Simmons, Rosenberg, and Rosenberg, 1973) developed a clever device to measure this possibility. They created a self-inventory questionnaire called the Imaginary Audience Scale (IAS). The items pose situations about hypothetical teenagers who must perform in the presence of an audience and ask actual teenagers how willing they might be to do these things. Several items like those in table 4.3 were used in the study.

Working with children and adolescents ranging from eight to eighteen years of age, the authors found that the twelve-year-olds were the most likely to choose the more self-conscious alternatives.

More recently, David Elkind (Elkind and Bowen, 1979) distinguished between two facets of the imaginary audience. One centers on a subject's willingness to reveal characteristics of the self that are believed to be permanent or stable over time. For example, most people view their levels of intelligence or features of personality as relatively constant over time. The other facet centers on the person's willingness to reveal characteristics of the self that are believed to vary considerably over time. For example, showing up dressed inappropriately, saying something inappropriate, or getting a bad haircut are all occasional occurrences, not permanent fixtures of the self. Elkind labeled the first phenomenon the **abiding self** and the latter one the **transient self.** He predicted that adolescent self-consciousness would be more pronounced in regard to the abiding self than for the transient self. Correspondingly, he predicted that only the abiding self is related to the individual's self-esteem.

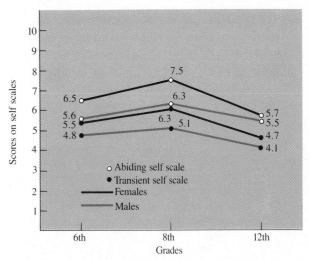

Figure 4.8 Transient self and abiding self scores for males and females in the sixth, eighth, and twelfth grades.

Elkind and Bowen constructed two scales. Items 1 and 2 in table 4.3 both represent the abiding self, while items 3 and 4 represent the transient self. In all, there were 6 items on each scale. Following pilot work, the authors tested 697 boys and girls in the fourth, sixth, eighth, and twelfth grades in a large, middle-class suburban school district. Each child was asked to complete the two scales of imaginary audience along with other scales, including a measure of self-esteem and self-concept.

There were two major findings in the study. The first was that both children and adolescents demonstrate relatively independent transient and abiding concepts of self. This independence was shown by the significant, but low correlation between the TS and AS scales and by the fact that the AS scale was correlated more highly with measures of self-esteem than was the TS scale.

| *Table 4.3* The imaginary audience scale (IAS) | | |

Instructions: Please read the following stories carefully and assume that the events actually happened to you. Place a check next to the answer that best describes what you would do or feel in the real situation.

AS scale

1. Let's say some adult visitors came to your school and you were asked to tell them a little bit about yourself.
   _____ I would like that.
   _____ I would not like that.
   _____ I wouldn't care.

AS scale

2. If you went to a party where you did not know most of the kids, would you wonder what they were thinking about you?
   _____ I wouldn't think about it.
   _____ I would wonder about that a lot.
   _____ I would wonder about that a little.

TS scale

3. You are sitting in class and have discovered that your jeans have a small but noticeable split along the side seam. Your teacher has offered extra credit toward his/her course grade to anyone who can write the correct answer to a question on the blackboard. Would you get up in front of the class and go to the blackboard, or would you remain seated?
   _____ Go to the blackboard as though nothing had happened.
   _____ Go to the blackboard and try to hide the split.
   _____ Remain seated.

TS scale

4. Your class is supposed to have their picture taken, but you fell the day before and scraped your face. You would like to be in the picture but your cheek is red and swollen. Would you have your picture taken anyway or stay out of the picture?
   _____ Get your picture taken even though you'd be embarrassed.
   _____ Stay out of the picture.
   _____ Get your picture taken and not worry about it.

Source: From Elkind, D., and R. Bowen, "Imaginary Audience Behavior in Children and Adolescence," in Developmental Psychology, *15, 38–44. Copyright © 1979 by the American Psychological Association. Reprinted by permission of the author.*

The second major finding was that young adolescents were significantly less willing than children or older adolescents to reveal either the transient or the abiding self to an audience (figure 4.8). This finding provides additional support for the hypothesis of heightened self-consciousness in early adolescence and for the construct of an imaginary audience during this age period. To the extent that the two subscales are comparable, the data also suggests that young adolescents are a little more self-conscious about their abiding than about their transient selves.

Stage 0 The egocentric, undifferentiated stage (approximately ages three to seven)

Stage 1 The differentiated and subjective perspective-taking stage (ages five to nine)

Stage 2 The self-reflective thinking or reciprocal perspective-taking stage (ages six to twelve)

Stage 3 The third person or mutual perspective-taking stage (ages nine to fifteen)

Stage 4 The in-depth and societal perspective-taking stage (age twelve to adulthood)

Recently, Selman (1980) has shown how these stages of perspective taking can be applied to four areas of individual and social development: individual concepts; friendship concepts; peer group concepts; and parent–child concepts. At level 0, the child is capable of recognizing the relation of subjective states of self and other, but frequently they are not distinguished. At level 1, the child comprehends that even in similarly perceived circumstances the self and other's perspective may be either the same or different. But the child shows no concern for the unique psychological lives of people. At level 2, the child can reflect on his own thoughts and feelings from someone else's perspective—that is, he can put himself in another person's shoes and see himself the way the other person sees him. At level 3, the recursive nature of reciprocal perspectives develops, and the individual begins to think "He thinks that I think that she wants. . . ." Also, at this level, the adolescent can move to a third-party position in order to understand the mutuality of various human perspectives. Finally, at level 4, the highest level in Selman's model, perspectives among individuals form a network or system, and generalized concepts of society's viewpoints are developed (legal, moral, and so forth). At this level there is a belief that the mutuality of individuals occurs not only at superficial levels of shared expectations, but at deeper levels of unverbalized feelings and values (Shantz, 1983).

The relationship between the self and another person is a complex topic. We have just reviewed ideas about one aspect of this topic—role taking or perspective taking. Most major developmental theorists (for example, Piaget) believe that developmental changes in self-other relationships are characterized by movement from egocentrism to perspectivism (Shantz, 1983).

A summary of main ideas discussed so far about the nature of social cognition and egocentrism/perspective taking is presented in Concept Table 4.3. Now that we have studied the nature of egocentrism and perspective taking, we turn our attention to another closely related aspect of social cognition—impression formation.

Impression Formation

Three aspects of impression formation have received considerable attention: differentiation, inference, and organization (Hill and Palmquist, 1978). Essentially, **impression formation** is the formation of concepts about one's self, about others, and about relationships with others. Some definitions of cognitive development, particularly the behavioral perspective, emphasize that the more differentiated the individual's concepts are, the more cognitively mature he is. Concept differentiation in regard to one's self and others does not seem to increase as rapidly during adolescence as it does during the elementary school years (Bigner, 1974; Fry, 1974; Peevers and Secord, 1973). In one investigation, seventh graders, twelfth graders, and adults were asked about the different categories they used to describe themselves (Mullener and Laird, 1971). The older individuals tended to use a wider variety of categories to describe themselves.

A second aspect of impression formation that has been investigated extensively is the interpretation of feelings. From middle childhood through adolescence, there is an increase in the youth's ability to interpret or *infer* the feelings of herself and others. And research shows that as her age increases, the adolescent reads feelings and thoughts into the interpretation of stimuli, even when the experimenter's instructions do not suggest it (e.g., Collins, 1977). In one investigation, the

THE NATURE OF SOCIAL COGNITION AND EGOCENTRISM/PERSPECTIVE TAKING

Concept	Processes/related ideas	Characteristics/description
The nature of social cognition	What is social cognition?	It refers to the field that studies the manner in which people conceptualize and reason about their social world, including the relation of their self to that world.
	Cognitive developmental view	While Piaget described some aspects of social cognition, Kohlberg's ideas have covered a broader set of social circumstances. They, along with John Flavell, have argued that social cognitive enterprises need to be studied in terms of the maturational unfolding of development.
	Social information processing	Both cognitive social learning theory and the information processing perspective have contributed to the belief that the adolescent's reasoning and thinking about social matters should be studied in the context of how he or she processes information about the social world. This view has not prescribed how social cognition might unfold developmentally.
Egocentrism/perspective taking	Egocentrism	Elkind proposed that adolescents, particularly in early adolescence, develop a curious sort of egocentrism that includes the construction of both an imaginary audience and a personal fable. While Elkind believes egocentrism comes about because of formal operational thought, some have emphasized that perspective taking and self–other relationships are involved as well.
	Perspective taking	Adolescents become more sophisticated at perspective taking than children. Selman stresses that an in-depth and societal perspective-taking stage emerges during adolescence.

marked increase in such inferential strategies in young adolescents was believed to be associated with the onset of formal operational thought (Gollin, 1958).

In one research strategy, adolescents were asked to infer what another person is thinking about (Barenboim, 1978). A major change in inference was found between twelve-year-olds and fourteen-year-olds. Inferences that other individuals were thinking about concrete actions and objects did not significantly increase until after the age of twelve, and inferences that other persons were thinking about thought did not increase until after the age of fourteen.

In another research strategy focused on impression formation, Andrew Collins (1973) has investigated developmental trends in children's and adolescents' recall, understanding, and evaluation of television programs. When commercial breaks were placed at important junctures in the TV programs the youngsters were watching, Collins found that third graders had more difficulty than sixth and tenth graders in relating character actions to their consequences (that is, they had trouble determining whether the character was rewarded or punished for his actions). When the commercial breaks were taken out, the third graders

One important aspect of impression formation in adolescence is the interpretation of feelings.

were still not able to pinpoint the connection between motivation and consequences, but the sixth and tenth graders were.

So, more differentiated and inferential cognitive strategies are used by adolescents than by elementary school children, but the changes in these strategies do not seem to be as rapid in adolescence as in the elementary school years. The most distinct characteristic of impression formation during adolescence appears to be *organization*. Barenboim (1977) suggests that the products of the concrete-operational period are organized and coordinated into new, more abstract systems of thought during adolescence. Such changes have been investigated by focusing on how the adolescent develops impressions about himself and others; the young adolescent appears to begin to develop a rudimentary, but implicit personality theory.

Developmental psychologists also have been interested in the emergence of implicit personality theory in adolescence. Not only do psychologists and scientists develop theories of personality, but people have ideas about what personality is like as well (what is known as implicit personality theory). Individuals develop ideas about what their own and other people's personalities are like. Carl Barenboim (1977, 1981, 1985) has investigated the developmental unfolding of implicit personality theory in children and adolescents.

Initially, it appears that between the ages of six and nine children increasingly are able to infer personality characteristics in others and to treat them as stable and causative factors that help to account for people's

behavior (Livesley and Bromley, 1973; Rholes and Ruble, 1984; Rotenberg, 1980). Barenboim (1985) argues that the creation of personality constructs are something like a social-cognitive version of concrete operational thought. That is, the concrete attributes of people, including their behaviors, are classified. The resulting personality constructs are much like the beginning of a concrete classification of objects.

Barenboim (1985) also suggests that the emergence of implicit personality theory may represent a formal operational solution to person perception. In this regard, implicit personality theory is a set of abstractions upon personality constructs. That is, in terms of Piaget's ideas about formal operations, a set of operations upon operations is being used when adolescents engage in the construction of an implicit personality theory.

What kinds of changes during adolescence index the individual's development of an implicit personality theory? The development of an implicit personality theory during adolescence seems to consist of several elements that appear to be absent during the elementary school years. First, when the adolescent is given information about another person, she considers previously acquired information as well, not relying solely on the concrete information at hand. Second, the adolescent has more of a tendency than the elementary school child to detect the contextual or situational variability in her and others' behavior, rather than thinking that she and others always behave consistently. Third, rather than merely accepting surface traits as a valid description of another person or herself, the adolescent begins to look for deeper, more complex—even hidden—causes of personality. These factors are not merely considered in isolation, but as interacting forces that determine personality. This complex way of thinking about one's self and others does not appear until adolescence in most individuals. As is the case with formal operational thought, though, these implicit personality theories are not always employed—whether the adolescent uses such a strategy to understand herself and others may depend upon a number of specific factors (as was suggested in the branch model of adolescent cognitive development discussed earlier). It is important to note here, though, that it does not seem

THE ADOLESCENT'S COGNITIVE MONITORING OF THE SOCIAL WORLD

*A*n individual's ability to monitor and make sense of his social thoughts seems to increase during middle childhood and adolescence. An important aspect of social cognition is the individual's development of conscious self-awareness. Flavell (in press) believes that developing differentiated thoughts about oneself is a gradual process. Statements such as "I think I am not easily fooled by others" or "I tend to give people the benefit of the doubt" evidence the development of such self- and social awareness. And although the child may distinguish only between succeeding or failing to learn something he wants to know about someone else, the adolescent may understand the more complex notion that what he has learned may be either accurate or inaccurate. Acquiring this latter distinction can serve as the basis for still further development in monitoring social thought. For example, later in development the individual may recognize that the accuracy of social thought is difficult to assess and that knowledge of certain aspects of the self or of others may actually decrease accuracy. For instance, prejudice, intense emotions, or

Adolescents monitor their social world more extensively and intensely than children do.

mental or physical illness might produce inaccurate perceptions of oneself and others. While some forms of social-cognitive knowledge do not develop until later, other aspects of this awareness may emerge quite early in development, according to Flavell. Thus, a young child may

that the individual is even capable of such thought until the beginnings of the adolescent age period (e.g., Barenboim, 1977, 1978; Livesley and Bromley, 1973; Stricker, Jacobs, and Kogan, 1974).

In the following comments obtained in one developmental investigation of how individuals perceive others (Livesley and Bromley, 1973), we can see how the development of an implicit personality theory proceeds:

Max sits next to me, his eyes are hazel and he is tall. He hasn't got a very big head, he's got a big pointed nose. (p. 213; age seven years, six months)

He smells very much and is very nasty. He has no sense of humor and is very dull. He is always fighting and he is cruel. He does silly things and is very stupid. He has brown hair and cruel eyes. He is sulky and eleven years old and has lots of sisters. I think he is the most horrible boy in the class. He has a croaky voice and always chews his

pencil and picks his teeth and I think he is disgusting. (p. 217; age nine years, eleven months)

Andy is very modest. He is even shyer than I am when near strangers and yet is very talkative with people he knows and likes. He always seems good tempered and I have never seen him in a bad temper. He tends to degrade other people's achievements, and yet never praises his own. He does not seem to voice his opinions to anyone. He easily gets nervous. (p. 221; age fifteen years, eight months)

. . . she is curious about people but naive, and this leads her to ask too many questions so that people become irritated with her and withhold information, although she is not sensitive enough to notice it. (p. 225; young adult)

As part of their increased awareness of others, including what others are doing and what they are thinking, adolescents engage in a great deal of social monitoring, as we see next.

be entirely able to recognize that her friend is not thinking clearly about people because she is upset or in a bad mood.

Individuals also learn to evaluate the social behavior of others and to recognize when this behavior is not accompanied by social thought. Flavell argues that in the early years of development, the child attributes no social cognitions to others. Later on, the child may automatically assume that others' social thoughts always coincide with their social behavior. For example, the child may assume that helpful actions reflect an intent to help and harmful actions the intent to harm. Still later, the child may think that both types of actions portray either no intent at all or an incongruent one, such as a helpful action performed unintentionally for purely selfish reasons, or even with an intent to achieve ultimate harm.

Flavell goes on to talk about the implications of children's and adolescents' ability to monitor their social cognitions as an indicator of their social maturity and competence:

In many real-life situations, the monitoring problem is not to determine how well you understand what a message means but rather to determine how much you ought to believe it or do what it says to do. I am thinking of the persuasive appeals the young receive from all quarters to smoke, drink, commit aggressive or criminal acts, have casual sex without contraceptives, have or not have the casual babies that often result, quit school, and become unthinking followers of this year's flaky cults, sects, and movements. (Feel free to revise this list in accordance with *your* values and prejudices.) Perhaps it is stretching the meanings of . . . cognitive monitoring too far to include the critical appraisal of message source, quality of appeal, and probable consequences needed to cope with these inputs sensibly, but I do not think so. It is at least conceivable that the ideas currently brewing in this area could some day be parlayed into a method of teaching children (and adults) to make wise and thoughtful life decisions as well as to comprehend and learn better in formal educational settings. (Flavell, 1979, p. 910)

Social Monitoring

Bob, a sixteen-year-old, feels that he does not know as much as he wants or needs to know about Sally, another sixteen-year-old. He also wants and needs to know more about Sally's relationship with Brian, a seventeen-year-old. In his effort to learn about Sally, Bob decides that he wants to know more about the groups that Sally belongs to—her student council friends, the clique she belongs to, and so forth. Bob thinks about what he already knows about all these people and groups, and decides he needs to find out how close he is to his goal of understanding them by taking some appropriate, feedback-producing action. What he discovers by taking that action will determine his social-cognitive progress and how difficult his social-cognitive task is. Notice that the immediate aim of this feedback-producing action is not to make progress toward the main goal, but to monitor that progress.

There are a number of cognitive monitoring methods that adolescents engage in on virtually a daily basis. A student may meet someone new and quickly think, "It's going to be hard to really get to know this guy." Another adolescent may check incoming information about an organization (school, club, group of friends) to determine if it is consistent with the adolescent's impressions of the club or the group. Still another adolescent may question someone or paraphrase what that person has just said about her feelings to ensure that he has understood them correctly. Perspective on Adolescent Development 4.4 presents further details of John Flavell's ideas on the importance of cognitive monitoring of social matters during adolescence.

The Link between Social Cognition and Social Behavior

One of the most promising areas of interest in social cognition focuses on the link between social cognition and social behavior. Much of this interest has involved the assessment of social-cognitive skills, how these skills can be taught, and whether such skills and training are associated with changes in the adolescent's behavior.

For example, one approach stresses the importance of viewing the adolescent's mind in terms of an information-processing system (Ford, 1982). To study the manner in which adolescents call on information-processing behavior to perform more competently in social situations, two samples of ninth and twelfth graders were evaluated. Social competence was defined as "the attainment of relevant social goals in specified social contexts, using appropriate means and resulting in positive developmental outcomes. The social goal chosen for this study was being able to behave effectively in challenging social situations involving salient social objects." In summarizing the results of the investigation, Ford concluded:

> Adolescents who are judged as able to behave effectively in challenging social situations involving salient social objects assign relatively high priorities to interpersonal goals such as helping others, getting socially involved, and getting along with parents and friends, and are likely to describe themselves as possessing the intrapersonal resources required to accomplish these goals. They also tend to be more goal-directed than their peers; that is, they like to set goals for themselves and control their own destiny rather than to just "go with the flow". . . (during adolescence) empathy plays a crucial role in regulating behavior so as to promote social welfare and harmony. (Clark, 1980; Hogan, 1973)

> It is noteworthy that adolescents who are judged to be socially competent tend to perceive themselves as having a relatively large social support network surrounding them. One possibility is that they are superior in terms of both personal and environmental resources . . . socially competent adolescents are (also) more cognitively resourceful; that is, they are better able to think of ways to address interpersonal problem situations and to construct coherent plans or strategies for solving them. There is also some evidence that these individuals are more likely to consider the possible consequences of their actions for themselves and others. (pp. 335–36)

Ford believes that certain kinds of social-cognitive skills, such as perspective taking and impression (those involving representation construction) have little impact on behavior, while others, such as empathy, social interest, planning skills, monitoring, and evaluation skills, have a stronger impact on behavior.

Another approach to studying the link between social cognition and social behavior involves conflict relations (Shantz, 1983). Coming into conflict with other people is a part of everyday life. What do adolescents know about solving interpersonal conflict and how do they reason about it? One effort (Spivak, Platt, and Shure, 1976) stresses that the social adjustment of adolescents is strongly influenced by the capacity to think through social problems, in particular: (1) the ability to think of alternative ways of solving problems; (2) knowing the likely response of the other person to certain solutions; and (3) understanding the necessary steps or means to reach a resolution of the conflict. In some cases, but not all, adolescents who have gone through social skills training programs that focus on increasing these three aspects of social cognition are characterized by improved social adjustment (Shantz, 1983).

Discussion of Social Cognition in the Remainder of the Text

As we have indicated, interest in social cognition has blossomed and the approach of social cognition has infiltrated the study of many different aspects of adolescent development. In the next chapter, for instance, we will investigate the topic of social intelligence. In our discussion of families in Chapter 6, information about the emerging cognitive abilities of the adolescent will be discussed in concert with the nature of parent–adolescent conflict and parenting strategies. In the description of peer relations in Chapter 7, considerable information is provided about the importance of social knowledge, the cognitive interpretation of the nature of friendships, and social cognitive skills training in the areas of peer relations. In our overview of the self and identity, we will return to the importance of social cognition in understanding self–other relationships (Chapter 10). And, in Chapter 12, one of the most prominent aspects of social cognition will be charted in some detail—the adolescent's reasoning about moral issues. As can be seen, considerable interest has been generated in how adolescents think about social circumstances.

Summary

I. Cognitive development is sometimes referred to as the study of the developmental unfolding of the mind, giving a maturational flavor to the study of adolescent cognition, while at other times, it is discussed more in terms of all mental activities between stimuli and responses. Sometimes cognition is labeled as the cause of behavior, as in the maturational approaches; while at others, it is described as a mediating factor, linking environmental experiences and behavior. However, one thing is sure, the black box is not as mysterious as once was believed— we now talk about and empirically study such aspects of adolescent cognition as expectancies, insight, attention, memory, plans, imagery, problem solving, decision making, and thinking.

II. Piaget's theory of cognitive development includes information about concrete operational thought and formal operational thought.
   A. Information about concrete operational thought focuses on its stage characteristics, decentering, reversibility, and the nature of a concrete operation, classification, and the constraints of this type of thought.
      1. Concrete operational thought is the third stage in Piaget's theory, ranging in age from approximately seven to eleven according to Piaget.
      2. For Piaget, concrete operational thought is made up of operations—mental actions or representations that are reversible. Concrete operations also allow the child or adolescent to decenter and coordinate several characteristics rather than focusing on a single property.
      3. One important skill that also characterizes concrete operational thought is the ability to classify or divide things into different sets and to consider their interrelationships.
      4. A major constraint of concrete operational thought is that the individual still needs to have perceptual, physical supports available for reasoning to proceed.
   B. Information about the characteristics of formal operational thought include its stage properties, abstractness, idealism and what is possible, hypothetical deductive and logical reasoning, advanced understanding of language, and perspective taking.
      1. For Piaget, formal operational thought is the fourth stage and final stage of cognitive development, emerging at some point between eleven and fourteen years of age.

2. Most significantly, formal operational thought is more abstract than concrete operational thought. Make-believe situations are often imagined, strictly hypothetical possibilities are constructed, and purely abstract propositions are put forth. Verbal problem solving also improves dramatically.

3. Formal operational thought is full of idealism and possibility rather than always focusing on what is real and limited. Adolescents often compare themselves with others on the basis of ideal standards. Thought often takes wings and future fantasies are engaged in.

4. Formal operational thought involves hypothetical deductive reasoning, thought that is more logical than in the concrete operational period. Such logical thought often is more planned than that of concrete operational thought.

5. Formal operational thought includes more advanced language development. Adolescents are better than children at understanding the meaning of words, including parts of speech, metaphor, and satire. Formal operational thinkers, with their advanced logic, are better at writing and also superior at reading prose. Adolescent thinkers are better at pragmatics as well.

6. Formal operational thinkers are better than concrete operational thinkers at taking the perspective of another person.

III. Further aspects of adolescent cognitive development include a consideration of early and late formal operations, individual variation, the fifth stage theory, Piaget and adolescent education, and an evaluation of Piaget's theory.

A. Early formal operational thought often comes into play between twelve and fourteen years, while late formal operational thought emerges between fifteen and eighteen years. Planned and organized thought prior to beginning problem solving characterize late formal operational thought.

B. There is a great deal of individual variation in formal operational thought. The branch model suggests that there is more variation at the formal operational level than at earlier stages.

C. Some theorists believe Piaget was wrong in thinking that formal operational thought is the most mature stage of thought. They argue that formal operational thought may be an inappropriate model to analyze adult thought, arguing that adult thought is more specialized, pragmatic, and realistic.

D. Piaget's theory has been applied to the education of adolescents, but less so than to the education of children. For the most part, the applications suggest that many adolescents may be taught in a manner that is too formal and does not allow enough hands-on experience.

E. Among the most important contributions of Piaget's theory are his brilliant observations—ideas about what to study in development, view of the qualitative nature of thought, and imaginative ideas about how thought changes. His critics believe he was wrong in his views on stages, argue that his concepts are too fuzzy, emphasize that procedural changes in tasks produce different results, stress that training studies often show how thought can be speeded up, and suggest that the timing of emerging cognitive abilities is different than Piaget believed.

IV. The growing field of social cognition involves information about the nature of social cognition, egocentrism/perspective taking, impression formation, social monitoring, and the link between social cognition and social behavior.

A. Social cognition refers to the field that studies the manner in which people conceptualize and reason about their social world, including the relation of their self to the world. Two major views of social cognition are: the cognitive developmental view, particularly Kohlberg's, and social information processing, which includes ideas from cognitive developmental theory and the information processing perspective.

B. There has been increased research interest in egocentrism and in perspective taking.
   1. Elkind proposed that adolescents, particularly those in early adolescence, develop a curious sort of egocentrism that includes the construction of both an imaginary audience and a personal fable. While Elkind believes egocentrism emerges because of formal operational thought some others argue that self–other relationships are involved as well.
   2. Adolescents become more sophisticated at perspective taking than children. Selman argues that an in-depth and societal perspective-taking stage appears in adolescence.

C. The aspects of impression formation that have received the most attention are differentiation, inference, and organization—adolescents improve in their ability to think in these ways about social matters. It also is during adolescence that individuals for the first time construct a personality theory.

D. Adolescents are far superior to children in their ability to monitor their social world, including their "detective like" strategy in getting desired information.

E. It is important to study the link between social cognition and social behavior. Included in this study is adolescents' social knowledge and whether such knowledge enhances mature social behavior.

Key Terms

abiding self *151*	metaphor *133*
abstract relations *148*	operations *128*
adult contextual theorists *140*	personal fable *150*
branch model *139*	perspective taking *150*
egocentrism in adolescence *149*	pragmatics *135*
	satire *133*
hypothetical-deductive reasoning *130*	social cognition *146*
imaginary audience *149*	social information processing *148*
impression formation *153*	transient self *151*

Suggested Readings

Elkind D. (1976). *Child development and education.* New York: Oxford University Press.
An excellent, easy-to-read introduction to the implications of Piaget's ideas for educators. Practical examples are given for approaching classroom teaching from the Piagetian perspective.

Flavell, J. H. (1985). *Cognitive development,* 2d ed. Englewood Cliffs, N.J.: Prentice-Hall.
An outstanding statement of the major contemporary ideas about cognitive development by one of the leading scholars in the field. Although inspired by Piaget's work, Flavell goes well beyond it, offering new insights, critical evaluation, and reflections about his own original research.

Selman, R. L. (1981). What children understand of intrapsychic processes: the child as a budding personality theorist. In *Cognitive and affective growth,* ed. E. K. Shapiro and E. Weber. Hillsdale, N.J.: Erlbaum & Associates.
This article contains Selman's account of how he thinks the adolescent forms a theory of personality. Includes an overview of his ideas about role taking.

Shantz, C. U. (1983). *Social cognition.* In *Handbook of child psychology,* 4th ed. New York: John Wiley.
Carolyn Shantz, one of the pioneers of research on contemporary issues in social cognition, provides a very detailed and critical appraisal of the information on social-cognitive development.

Chapter · 5

Information Processing and Intelligence

Prologue

Brave New Worlds of Intelligence Testing

You probably have heard that there still is a great deal of controversy and turmoil that surround the use of intelligence tests to measure intelligence. Amidst this turmoil and controversy, a number of critics are calling for innovative ways to measure the intelligence of adolescents. The critics want tests that are more relevant to real life than those now being used. The demands of the critics are occurring at a time when there is renewed interest by a number of creative scientists who are conducting research on the nature of intelligence by doing such diverse things as:

> listening to clicks in earphones while electrodes taped to temples of the head send brain impulses to be analyzed by a computer
>
> testing mental abilities that may be influenced by watching television daily
>
> documenting whether individuals can tell which person in a social situation is the boss and which is the employee
>
> observing the cognitive/motoric abilities of professional athletes

Quite clearly this list looks very different than the kind of items you have encountered on a traditional test of your intelligence.

The search for the nature of intelligence and how to measure it has a long history. Psychologists have been trying to learn more about how to measure intelligence more effectively for almost a century. The 1980s is witnessing a flourish of new efforts to define and measure intelligence more effectively. Robert Sternberg believes there are three basic kinds of intelligence: one involving the mental mechanisms we use to plan and carry out tasks, particularly tasks that require us to solve problems; one focusing on the effects of experience; and one emphasizing practical intelligence, such as the ability to pick up nonverbal cues in social interaction that give us insight about understanding people. Sternberg also has developed some provocative thoughts about the importance of insight in gifted adolescents.

Sternberg's efforts to study the mechanisms of thought is part of the information processing revolution that has come to dominate American cognitive psychology in the 1970s and 1980s. The main emphasis in the information processing perspective of cognition is on how the adolescent processes information about his or her world, not on what he or she knows; thus Sternberg's approach includes an effort to evaluate the kinds of processes the adolescent uses to effectively generate knowledge rather than merely assessing the adolescent's

164   Biological and Cognitive Processes and Development

knowledge per se. Much more about Sternberg's ideas on intelligence and giftedness as well as the nature of the information processing perspective appear later in this chapter.

Sternberg also argues that it is important to study practical intelligence, sometimes referred to as social intelligence. For some time now, experts have wondered about the relevance of many traditional measures of intelligence to predict the adolescent's ability to handle the stresses and demands of everyday living. As Sternberg says, social intelligence (he also calls it tacit intelligence) are all of those things they don't teach you in school. Sternberg believes that success in life often depends a great deal on tacit knowledge rather than explicit information. For example, in working on a test of social intelligence that could be given to medical school applicants, the psychologist might want to measure such human dimensions as sensitivity to feelings by using simulated patient interviews and medical history taking. Another situation might call for items that would predict success in business school in which measures would be developed in which the student would respond as "supervisors" to videotaped "employees" who present problems such as requests for raises or promotions. The students' responses might be spoken into a tape recorder. These responses would evaluate their knowledge of what to do and their ability to do it.

Howard Gardner is another psychologist who in the 1980s is influencing the way we think about the intelligence of adolescents and how it should be measured. In a book, *Frames of Mind* (1983), he proposed that we likely have seven intelligences, three conventional kinds—verbal, spatial, and mathematical, as well as four others not commonly found on traditional intelligence tests—musical ability, bodily skills, adroitness in dealing with others, and self-knowledge. For example, Gardner comments about the bodily skills of Boston Celtic Larry Bird. Bird has almost a sixth sense of where to throw a basketball. To do this, he has to know where his teammates are on the court, where the opponents are, where they likely are going to move to, and call on analysis, inference, planning, and problem solving to decide what to do. In Gardner's view, there is reasoning involved in such highly developed situations pertaining to bodily movement.

As can be seen, there is a rich broadening of thinking about the nature of intelligence and how it should be measured. As we explore the concept of intelligence in greater detail later in this chapter, you will learn more about information processing approaches to intelligence and more about the nature of social intelligence as well.

*I*n this chapter, we continue our exploration of the fascinating world of the adolescent's thought. In the last chapter, we studied Piaget's cognitive developmental theory of intelligence, a theory that emphasizes the maturational unfolding of cognitive structures. In this chapter, we study two other approaches to adolescent cognition—the information processing perspective and the psychometric view of intelligence. The word **psychometric** refers to the measurement of a phenomenon, so our discussion of the psychometric approach to intelligence will heavily emphasize the measurement of intelligence. Together with Piaget's cognitive developmental theory, the information processing perspective and the psychometric orientation comprise the three main ways the adolescent's cognition is studied.

What cognitive processes are involved in solving an algebraic equation?

Information Processing: A Human Computer and More

What is meant by taking an information processing approach to adolescent cognition? What kind of research do information processing psychologists conduct when they study adolescent development? And, what are the implications of the information processing perspective for the education of adolescents? Let's explore these three questions in greater detail.

The Information Processing Perspective

When an adolescent is solving an algebraic question he or she is processing information. When the adolescent is using a computer, both the adolescent and the computer are involved in information processing. By thinking about how an algebraic equation is solved and by considering how we use computers and how the computers themselves function, we can learn about the manner in which information processing works.

Some Cognitive Processes Involved in Solving an Algebraic Equation

An event (S) occurs in the environment. Suppose the event is the appearance of the following algebraic equation on the chalkboard in a mathematics class with the accompanying instruction: "$2x + 10 = 34$. Solve for x."

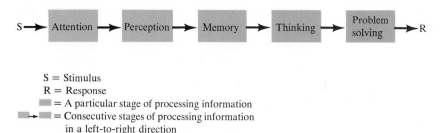

S = Stimulus
R = Response
▉ = A particular stage of processing information
▉→▉ = Consecutive stages of processing information
in a left-to-right direction

Figure 5.1 **Hypothetical series of steps involved in processing information to solve an algebra problem.**

This event contains information that a person can detect and understand. Success in detecting and making sense of it depends on how completely and efficiently the information is processed. Development can be equated with becoming more skillful and efficient at information processing. Once the processing is complete, the person produces an observable response (R). In this model, then, cognitive activity refers to the flow of information through the different steps of processing.

Consider how a well-seasoned algebra student engages cognition. The teacher writes the equation on the board (S). The student looks up and notes that something has been written on the board (*attention*). This "something" is then determined to be a series of numbers, letters, and signs, and—at a higher level of identification—two simple statements: (1) "$2x + 10 = 34$" and (2) "Solve for x" (*perception*). The student must preserve the results of this perceptual analysis over a period of time (*memory*), even if only for the brief interval needed to write the problem on a worksheet.

The student then begins to elaborate on the product of perception and memory (*thinking*). This level of analysis can be described best with an imaginary mental soliloquy (though, of course, the reasoning might take an altogether different track or even a nonverbal form): "Let's see. It's an equation—x is the unknown, and I'm supposed to figure out the value of x. How do I do that?" And the final level of analysis (*problem solving*) addresses the question: "How do I do that?" Problem

solving then takes the following form: "Okay, $2x + 10 = 34$. First, I have to collect the unknown on one side of the equation and the known values on the other side. To do this, I'll leave the $2x$ where it is—on the left. Then I'll subtract 10 from each side to remove the 10 from the left. This leaves $2x = 24$. Now I have to express the equation as '$x =$ something,' and it's solved. How do I do this? I know! Divide each side by 2 and that will leave $1x$, or x, on the left side. Now I have $x = 12$. That's the answer!" A summary of the processes described in solving of the algebraic equation is presented in figure 5.1.

The information processing approach, then, is concerned with the nature of information adolescents pick up from the vast body of environmental stimuli around them, the various steps involved in this pickup, and the mechanisms or processes by which the information is absorbed and transformed. Figure 5.1 is a necessarily oversimplified representation of this process that omits a great deal and does not indicate the many routes that the flow of information may take. For example, each hypothetical step (for example, perception) may overlap with other steps (for example, memory) or be composed of several substeps. However, neither of these features is captured in the diagram, whose purpose is to focus on the basic elements of this process. Indeed, the processing of information usually is simultaneous and dynamic.

Bobby "Hi, how are you?"

Robert "I'm fine thank you. What can I do for you today?"

Bobby "I'm in a big hurry. My math answers are due tomorrow and I don't have time to finish them. Do you think you can help me with them?"

Robert "Yes. Math is no problem for me."

Bobby "O.K. I'll give you the problems and come back for them later."

This conversation was between fourteen-year-old Bobby and his computer he named Robert. Unlikely? Well, human beings have been enthralled by the idea that they might in some way construct lifelike mechanisms in their own image—robots, androids, thinking machines. The plots of various movies often go something like this. The machine at first obeys its creator, then becomes sophisticated and outgrows its maker, becoming more impudent and dangerous, but in the end it is defeated by the wisdom of the human being.

Until recently this scenario was couched in heavy science fiction, but today an electronic network can come precariously close to having power over us. Computer scientists have created programs that mimic human intelligence in a number of ways and even outdo human intellect in certain areas. We know that computers can calculate numbers much faster and more accurately than we could ever hope to (consider Bobby and his math homework dilemma). Some computers can summarize news stories, comprehend spoken sentences, follow orders, and play games. Let's explore in greater detail the similarity of the computer to the adolescent's mind and then suggest several things the adolescent's mind can do that computers cannot.

The Computer Analogy About thirty years ago, a startling idea was introduced to the field of information theory (Broadbent, 1958). Scientists sought for the first time to explain the general nature of information as it is transmitted in humans by comparing human information processing with information transmission in machines. Analogies were drawn between how physical energy is generated, transmitted, and received (for example, through television, radio, and the telephone) and how psychological information is produced, transmitted, and decoded (for example, through seeing, hearing, feeling, and thinking). The infant field of computer science added credibility to the analogy. It was reasoned that if computers (basically high-speed information systems with thoughtlike activity) could be constructed and programmed, then certainly it would be possible to understand the flow of information in the mind as a machinelike system (Newell and Simon, 1972).

For the discussion of adolescent cognitive development, a useful distinction can be borrowed from computer science—the contrast between hardware and software (e.g., Flavell, 1970). Hardware refers to the physical equipment of the computer: the logic unit, the memory registers, the input consoles, the printer—the "nuts and bolts" of the machinery. Software refers to the program devised for the computer's operation; for information storing and retrieving, performing mathematical functions, solving problems, and so forth. Mental activity may also be said to have its hardware and software components. As hardware, the adolescent mind has the brain and the nervous system and their organization. As software, the adolescent mind has the plans, intentions, strategies, and goals that put the mental hardware to work.

With each new generation of computers developed, the hardware and software are made more sophisticated. So it is with the developing mind of the child and the adolescent: cognitive development involves both hardware and software changes (Eichorn, 1970). The fact that an eight-year-old can recall ten items from a list while a fourteen-year-old can recall twenty items is usually interpreted to mean that the fourteen-year-old is more mature in terms of the development of the brain and nervous system—a hardware difference. But the adolescent may also employ some memory strategies that the child does not, which is a software difference.

Adolescents can engage in parallel processing of information.

For both the computer and the adolescent mind, the capacity to process information is limited. Both can handle only a certain amount of input, store only a certain amount of information, compute (or think) at only a certain speed and retrieve only a certain amount of information per unit of time (e.g., Case, 1978; Pascual-Leone, 1977). As the child develops into an adolescent, as the younger adolescent develops into an older adolescent, and as each new generation of computers is invented, the capacity to process information increases. Although physical changes are responsible for some of the improvements, software, or programming, may account for many of them.

What the Adolescent's Mind Can Do That a Computer Cannot Do The computer should, in theory, be able to translate verbal and other symbols into its own kind of symbols, rework them according to its own programmed instructions, and process information in ways that are said to be intelligent and to be called thinking. However, there are some things adolescents' minds can do that computers cannot. First, it is important to recognize that all artificial intelligence works toward known end states, goals defined by their creators, you and me. A machine can learn and improve on its own program, but it doesn't have any means of developing a new goal for itself. Second, computers seem to be better at simulating the logical processes of our mind than the nonlogical, intuitive, and possibly unconscious aspects of our mind. Many of the adolescent's most creative efforts seem to be based on such nonlogical intuitive mental processes. Third, the extraordinary multiple pathways in the brain likely produce thinking that cannot be mimicked by a computer. A computer can be made to look like it is performing parallel processing, as it pursues one line of thought for a millisecond and then switches to another point and considers it for another several milliseconds. But the computer really is not engaging in **parallel processing,** the simultaneous consideration of a number of lines of thought. Adolescents do much of this at a nonconscious level, and these multiple simultaneous considerations seem to be responsible for many of the new ideas adolescents develop. Donald Norman, cognitive psychologist at University of California, San Diego, also points out that we don't have any programs that are self-aware or that even begin to approach the consciousness that adolescents have. The adolescent's mind can create its own ideas and react to them—not just with thoughts about them, but with emotions as well. We are not even close to simulating consciousness on a computer and perhaps never will.

Questions about the Adolescent's Thought Raised by the Information Processing Perspective

The information processing perspective raises some important questions about the adolescent's thought. Three such questions are: Does processing speed increase as children and adolescents develop? Does processing capacity likewise increase as they grow older?

What is the role of knowledge in accounting for developments in cognitive processing by adolescents? (Santrock and Bartlett, 1986).

Processing Speed Implicit in the information processing models is that speed is an important factor. First, many cognitive tasks—both in the laboratory and in real life—are performed under time pressures. For example, when driving, the adolescent must read signs quickly and when taking the SAT exam, he or she has a limited time to finish. Second, speed is an advantage even without time pressure. Consider the adolescent who is memorizing a list of foreign vocabulary words. While the student may have the entire semester to learn the set of words, more time is available to do other things if these words can be learned quickly rather than slowly. The speed of processing information does seem to be related to development with children being slower than adolescents. Still, much needs to be done in charting developmental trends in the speed of information processing and the reasons for these developmental changes might be biological and/or experience and practice.

Processing Capacity Information **processing capacity** can be thought of as a type of "mental energy" needed to perform work. The difficulty an adolescent has in dividing his or her attention between two things at once, or performing a highly complex task, such as mentally working through a verbal reasoning problem, is often attributed to limits on capacity. While capacity is thought to be limited at all ages of people, there is no generally accepted measure of a child's or adolescent's capacity, so findings about capacity often are ambiguous. However, it may be that children spend more time on lower level tasks, such as identifying stimuli, than adolescents, leaving children less time for higher level, more complex tasks, such as performing complex calculations.

Role of Knowledge If an adolescent has knowledge that is relevant to a task, information processing is generally more efficient. It is obvious that adolescents know more than children. Could it be that age differences in information processing are due to age differences in knowledge? This seems unlikely, but the role of knowledge in cognitive development is currently an important research focus (e.g., Flavell, 1985; Hunt, 1982; Sternberg, 1985).

Now that we have considered some of the important issues about adolescent cognition raised by an information processing approach, we turn our attention to an overview of research on information processing during adolescence.

Research on Adolescent Information Processing

While the bulk of research on information processing has been conducted with children and adults, the information processing perspective is an important one for understanding adolescent cognition. As we saw in our discussion of the adolescent solving the algebraic equation, attention and memory are two important processes.

Attention Two ways we can use **attention** are called selective attention and divided attention. In **selective attention,** the adolescent has the problem of ignoring some stimuli while focusing on others more relevant to his or her interests or goals. For example, the adolescent may need to ignore the blaring television while studying for an exam. Research has revealed that adolescents are superior to children at selective attention (Higgins and Turnure, 1984; Sexton and Geffen, 1979).

In other situations, adolescents may be called on to handle two or more information channels at once. This is a problem in **divided attention** for the adolescent. For example, while listening to the teacher the adolescent may also want to hear what a friend in the next row is whispering. Following the content of both messages simultaneously is not an easy task. In an interesting investigation (Schiff and Knopf, 1985), nine- and thirteen-year-olds viewed displays showing a set of visual symbols (e.g., *, &, =, +, $) in the center and some letters (e.g., A, G, M, P, Y) in the corners. The adolescents were much better than children at dividing their attention in that they (a) detected whether the symbols at the center included a certain target symbol, and (b) remembered the letters shown in the corners. Other types of divided attention have shown improvement developmentally as well (Guttentag, 1984).

Memory Perhaps the most widely studied aspect of information processing is **memory,** the retention and retrieval of information over time. How might memory be involved in solving a complex problem, such as an analogy? In a series of experiments focused on analogies, Robert Sternberg (Sternberg, 1977; Sternberg and Nigro, 1980; Sternberg and Rifkin, 1979) studied third-graders, sixth-graders, ninth-graders, and college students. The major differences occurred between the younger students (the third and sixth graders) and the older students (the ninth graders and college students). The older subjects were more likely to complete the information processing required to solve the analogy task. The children, by contrast, often stopped their processing of information before they had considered all of the necessary steps required to solve the problems. Sternberg believes the incomplete information processing on the part of the children occurred because their short-term memory was overloaded. Solving problems such as analogies requires an individual to make continued comparisons between newly encoded information and previously coded information. Sternberg argues that adolescents likely have more storage space in short-term memory, which results in fewer errors on problems like analogies.

One task that has been devised to assess short-term memory is the **memory-span task.** If you have ever taken an IQ test, you likely have taken a memory-span task. You simply hear a short list of stimuli, usually digits, presented at a rapid pace (typically one per second).

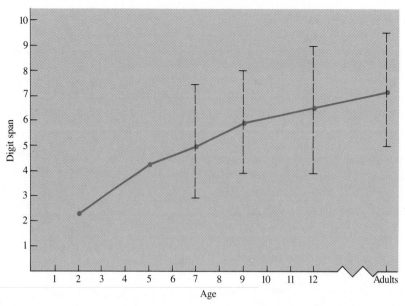

Figure 5.2 Developmental differences (solid line) and individual differences, expressed as ranges (dashed lines), in digit span.

Then you are asked to repeat the digits back. There is good evidence that short-term memory increases during early childhood based on research with the memory-span test. For example, as shown in figure 5.2, memory span increases from about two digits in two- to three-year-old children to about five digits in seven-year-old children. Yet between seven and thirteen years of age, memory span only increases by one-and-one-half digits (Dempster, 1981). Keep in mind though that there are individual differences in memory span, which is why IQ tests and various aptitude tests are used. And, as an indication of the importance of memory span, research with adolescents suggests that performance on a memory-span test is strongly linked to performance on the Scholastic Aptitude Test (SAT), accounting for about fifty percent of the predictability of scores on both the math and verbal sections of this test (Dempster, 1985).

Is it important for us to ask why there are age differences in memory span? It turns out that while there are many factors involved, such as rehearsal of information, what seems to be most important in these age

changes is the speed and efficiency of information processing, particularly the speed with which memory items can be identified.

It is important to ask the question of whether adolescents know more about their memory processes than children do. Knowledge about one's memory processes is called **metamemory.** It includes information about sensing that specific memory strategies are sometimes required for learning and the ability to monitor memory during the course of learning. For example, can the adolescent tell whether he or she has studied adequately to pass an exam tomorrow? The sophistication of metamemory—as assessed through answers to verbal test batteries—improves from the preschool years through adolescence, and beyond (Brown et al., 1983; Flavell, 1985).

Information Processing and Education

We have discussed a number of different issues raised by the information processing perspective and described a number of processes involved in processing information. As we said earlier, one of the issues raised by the information processing perspective is the importance of considering a distinction between knowledge and process in cognition. This issue, in particular, has implications for the education of adolescents. In thinking about the schooling of adolescents, let's also consider intelligence tests. Intelligence tests do a reasonably good job of predicting success at school, but they are not as good at predicting career success or adaptation to real world situations outside of school. One of the reasons that IQ tests likely do a reasonably good job at predicting success in school is that IQ tests basically assess what a person knows, that is, knowledge. And, schools basically have been in the business of imparting knowledge to children and adolescents. Traditional IQ tests likely do not do as good a job at predicting career success or adaptation because they do not focus on assessing information processing skills that might benefit an individual as a life-long learner and they do not assess adaptation to real-world problems. In the prologue, we discussed some ways that intelligence tests currently are being revised to place more emphasis on information processing skills and adaptation to the world, and these issues will be discussed further later in the chapter. By reading Perspective on Adolescent Development 5.1 you can see how the possible interface between the information processing perspective and education might benefit the information processing skills of adolescents and increase the likelihood that adolescents will carry with them into the adult years the ability to process information efficiently.

We have now discussed many different aspects of the impressive perspective on adolescent cognition called information processing. A summary of main ideas pertaining to the information processing perspective is presented in Concept Table 5.1. Now we turn our attention to the topic of intelligence.

Intelligence: IQ and Beyond

Among the important aspects of intelligence are its theories, definition, and measurement, as well as alternatives and supplements to intelligence tests.

Alfred Binet (1857–1911).

Theories, Definition, and Measurement

Ideas about theories, definition, and measurement of intelligence emphasize the early ideas of Binet and the concept of intelligence, the Wechsler scales, the factor analytic approach, the information processing approach, knowledge versus process in intelligence, R. J. Sternberg's componential analysis of intelligence, and a comparison of the psychometric and Piagetian views of intelligence.

Binet and the Concept of Intelligence

Alfred Binet and Theodore Simon devised the first intelligence test in 1905 to determine which students in the schools of Paris would not benefit from regular classes and consequently should be placed in special classes. Binet and Simon did not work from a basic definition of intelligence, but proceeded in a trial-and-error fashion, simply relying on the test's ability to discriminate between youth who were successful in school and those who were not. On this basis they found that "higher" mental abilities (memory, attention, and comprehension) were more important than "lower" mental abilities (reaction time, speed of hand movement in specified amount of space, and the like). The

INFORMATION PROCESSING AND THE EDUCATION OF ADOLESCENTS

When you were in elementary and secondary school, did any teacher at any time work with you on improving your memory strategies? Did any of your teachers work with your reading skills after the first few grades of elementary school? Did any of your teachers work with you on trying to improve your speed of processing information? Did any of your teachers discuss with you ways that imagery can be used to enhance your processing of information? Did any of your teachers work with you in developing your ability to make inferences about information you encounter in the classroom and outside of school? If you are like the students who I query in the classes on adolescent development that I teach and like me, most of you spent little or no time improving these important processes involved in our everyday encounters with our world.

Why is it important to have an educational goal of improving the information processing skills of children and adolescents? Think for a moment about yourself and the skills that likely are necessary for you to be successful in adapting to your environment and improving your chances for getting a good job and having a successful career. To some extent, knowledge itself is important, and more precisely, content knowledge in particular areas also is important. Our schools have done a much better job of imparting knowledge to students, particularly content knowledge about a particular subject (basically, schools have been in the business of pouring knowledge into children's and adolescents' heads) than in instructing individuals in how to process information about their world.

As we have seen in this chapter, the story of adolescent information processing is one of attention, perception, memory (particularly the control processes involved in memory), thinking, and the like. Such information processing skills become even more important in education when we consider that we are now in the midst of a transition from an industrial society to a postindustrial, information processing society, with approximately sixty-five to seventy percent of all workers involved in services. The information revolution in our society has placed stressful demands on workers who are called on daily to process huge amounts of information in a rapid fashion, to have efficient memories, to attend to relevant details, to reason logically about difficult issues, and to make inferences about information that may be fuzzy and unclear. Students graduate from high school, college, or postgraduate education and move into jobs calling for efficient skills at processing information and often have had little or no instruction in improving such skills.

Instruction in information processing skills would have helped you tremendously when you took the SAT or ACT test. Why are there so many SAT cram courses popping up everywhere? Because our schools for the most part have not effectively taught information processing skills. Is speed of processing important on the SAT? Most of you likely felt you did not have as much time as you wanted to handle such difficult questions. Are memory strategies important on the SAT? You had to read paragraphs and hold a considerable amount of information in your mind to answer some of the questions. And, you certainly had to remember some of the ways math problems are solved. Also, didn't you have to remember the definitions of a tremendous number of vocabulary words? And what about problem solving, inferencing, and understanding? Remember the difficult verbal problems you had to answer and the inferences you had to make when reasoning was needed. Also remember how it was necessary for you to read several paragraphs and process what some key points were?

At this time, however, we do not have a specified curriculum of information processing that could be taught in a stepwise, developmental fashion to children and adolescents. And, we do not have the trained personnel to do this instruction either. Further, it should be pointed out that some experts in information processing believe that processes such as attention and memory cannot be trained in a general way. Rather, they argue that information processing often is domain- or content-specific.

They do believe, however, that an infusion of the information processing orientation into all parts of the curriculum in secondary schools would greatly benefit adolescent cognition. Let's now look at one specific domain, geometry, to see how an information processing strategy might lead to more effective instruction.

Robert Glaser (1982) points to the area of geometry to give one example of how instruction in information processing would be very helpful to high school students. Information processing research suggests that solving problems in geometry benefits from three separate types of knowledge: (a) knowledge of different geometric *objects* such as points; (b) knowledge of facts and rules for making inferences and proving theorems (such as the sum of the angles of a triangle equal 180°); and (c) knowledge of strategies for carrying out proofs (such as knowledge that one should set goals, form plans, and organize one's attack on the problem). Interestingly, while the first two types of knowledge are specifically taught in schools, the third is not—it simply is left up to the student to devise the appropriate strategies. And, of course, many students do not develop these strategies.

Research in educational psychology is beginning to look seriously at the importance of information processing in school learning. A recent book by Ellen Gagne (1985), in particular, provides a menu of information processing strategies that need to be given attention when instructing adolescents in specific content areas, such as reading, writing, math, and science. She concluded that research has shown that successful high school students (e.g., those who make better grades, get higher achievement test scores) are better than their unsuccessful counterparts at such information processing components as focusing their attention, elaborating and organizing information, and at monitoring their study strategies. As yet, however, we are not sure of the extent to which these important information processing abilities can be taught. Nonetheless, Gagne (Gagne, Weidemann, Bell, and Ander, in press) recently demonstrated how seventh grade students can be taught effective ways to elaborate information so it can be remembered more efficiently.

Patricia Cross (1984) also has addressed the point of how information processing instruction might benefit individuals for a lifetime of learning. The goal of schools should be to construct a lifetime learner who has the information processing skills to acquire new information efficiently throughout life. Schooling has been shown to improve the information processing skills of children when children who attend schools in rural and isolated communities are compared with children in the same communities who do not attend schools. For example, Harold Stevenson (1982) found that Peruvian children who attended school were better than their nonschool counterparts at many different memory and conceptualization tasks. However, while significant, the effects were small. Perhaps if a concentrated effort were made to begin instructing individuals from kindergarten through the college years in ways to improve their information processing skills, the effects of schooling would be much more pronounced. Several prominent universities, such as Carnegie-Mellon and UCLA, encourage students to take courses in information processing and in some instances try to teach such higher level information processing skills as problem solving. And, Robert Sternberg, whose ideas about intelligence were discussed in the prologue to this chapter, is working on a book to be published soon, *Intelligence Applied,* that describes how to teach intelligence.

Frank Barron (1985) also believes that critical thinking skills can be taught. He is interested in how individuals can be taught to think in less irrational ways. For example, Baron argues that adolescents should be more critical of the first ideas that pop into their heads—they should be instructed to think longer about important things and to search in more organized ways for evidence to support their views. It is exciting, indeed, to think about the possibilities the information processing perspective offers for the education of children and adolescents. In the next several decades, it is hoped, there will be increased commerce between the fields of information processing and education, although there may be limits to how extensively information processing skills can be taught.

THE INFORMATION PROCESSING PERSPECTIVE

Concept	Processes/related ideas	Characteristics/description
Adolescent information processing and computer information processing	Nature of adolescent's information processing	The adolescent experiences an event in the environment. The adolescent detects and trys to make sense out of the event. To do this, cognitive processes such as attention, perception, memory, thinking, and problem solving are needed. Once this processing is complete, the adolescent makes a response. Thus, information processing emphasizes the cognitive mediation of environment-behavior relations through a number of cognitive processes.
	The computer analogy	The field of computer science has added credibility to thinking about the mind as being like a computer. Comparisons between the adolescent mind and a computer involve thinking about the hardware and software of a computer as roughly like the brain and mind of the adolescent. Both adolescent minds and computers have memories and can solve problems. Computers are even better than adolescents at remembering in effortless fashion huge amounts of data and in conducting lightening fast maneuvers with those data.
	The superiority of the adolescent mind	A computer cannot develop a goal for itself; it does not do very well at simulating the nonlogical, intuitive, and possibly unconscious processes of the mind; it cannot engage in parallel processing; and it is not aware of itself. By contrast, the adolescent's mind can do all of these wondrous things.
	Questions raised by the information processing perspective	Three questions raised by information processing focus on the nature and importance of processing speed, processing capacity, and knowledge.
Research on adolescent information processing	Its nature	Most of the research base in the information processing perspective comes from children and adults, not adolescents. Nonetheless, the information processing approach is important in understanding how the adolescent's mind works. During the next several decades there will probably be an increased research effort on information processing skills in adolescence.

THE INFORMATION PROCESSING PERSPECTIVE

Concept	Processes/related ideas	Characteristics/description
	Attention and memory	Two areas where research on information processing have been conducted are attention and memory. Adolescents are better at both selective and divided attention than children. And adolescents are superior at solving problems such as analogies, possibly because of their superior short-term memory. Adolescents also are better at metamemory, knowledge of their own memory processes, than children.
Information processing and education	Schooling, IQ tests, and career development/adaptation	Schooling and IQ testing have been basically in the business of imparting knowledge and assessing knowledge respectively rather than providing instruction in how to effectively process information and assess such information processing skills. This, to some degree, may explain why IQ tests have been superior at predicting success in school than at predicting career success and/or adaptation to real world situations.
	The information revolution, the information processing perspective, and the education of adolescents	We have moved from an industrial society to a postindustrial, information society. However, while adults are called on to perform an extensive amount of information processing as part of this new society, they have not been adequately instructed in the elementary and secondary schools in ways to improve the efficiency of such processing. While there have been tremendous advances in the last two decades in cognitive psychology in detailing the nature of processes involved in processing information, this knowledge has yet to filter into the education of adolescents in any systematic manner. Nonetheless, research on information processing with adolescents has lagged behind similar research with children and adults. Further, some experts believe information processing skills in general are difficult if not impossible to train. The major thrust so far has been to work on improving domain specific information processing skills, as in the subject of geometry. Information processing psychologists do believe adolescent cognition would be improved by an infusion of this perspective into all areas of secondary school curricula.

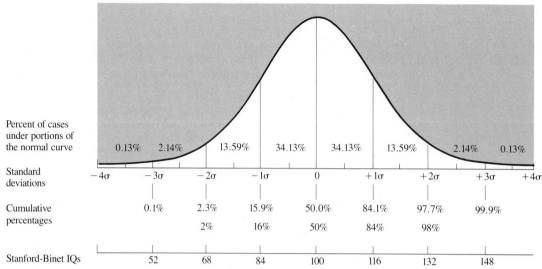

Figure 5.3   Relationship of normal curve to scores on the Stanford-Binet intelligence test.

lower measures had been used by the American psychologist, James McKeen Cattell, as indicators of intelligence, but Binet found that Cattell's tests were not very good predictors of which boys and girls would succeed in French schools.

Although the Binet test was made up of items that tested several different mental capacities (including memory, comprehension, attention, moral judgment, and aesthetic appreciation), Binet was primarily concerned with the student's general intelligence rather than her specific mental abilities. He developed the concept of mental age (MA) to reflect the level of the students' general intellectual functioning. Mental age was determined by measuring the number of items an individual could correctly identify and remember in relation to the number of items that the average individual of a given age could correctly handle. For example, if a thirteen-year-old adolescent has only as many items correct as the average ten-year-old child, that adolescent would have the MA of a ten-year-old. By comparing the adolescent's general level of intellectual functioning with that of the average adolescent at that age, Binet had a means of indicating how dull or how bright the youth would probably be in the classroom.

Over the years, extensive effort has been expended to standardize the Binet test. The test has been given to many thousands of children, adolescents, and adults of different ages, selected at random from different parts of the United States. By administering the test to large numbers of people and recording the results, it has been found that intelligence, as measured by the Binet test, has an almost perfect bell-shaped distribution. As demonstrated by the curve shown in figure 5.3, intelligence is distributed in an almost symmetrical fashion across the population. The revisions of the Binet tests done at Stanford University have resulted in what are now called the Stanford-Binet tests. The Stanford-Binet has a mean IQ score of one-hundred and a standard deviation (or variance) of sixteen. As you can see by looking at figure 5.3, about sixty-eight percent of the scores fall within what is called the average range of eighty-four to one-hundred-sixteen.

Historically, labels have been used to reflect how far away from the mean an adolescent scores on the IQ test. An adolescent who scored one-hundred-two was labeled average; one who scored sixty was labeled mentally retarded; and one who scored one-hundred-fifty-six was labeled genius. The evaluation of intelligence is rapidly moving away from such categorization. Many experts believe that an intelligence quotient based on the results of a single intelligence test should not be the basis for classifying an adolescent as mentally retarded—or, for that matter, as a genius. A label often remains with the youth for many years, even though the testing circumstances may have led to inappropriate measurement of her intelligence.

What is the current Stanford-Binet like? It can be given to individuals from the age of two years through adulthood. It includes many different types of items, some requiring verbal responses and some calling for nonverbal performance. For example, items that a thirteen-year-old might be tested on include the definition of abstract words like *connection,* his memory for long sentences, explanations of facts, and his ability to organize scrambled sentences. Items are standardized for each year through fourteen years of age; then standardization occurs only for the categories of average adult, superior adult I, superior adult II, and superior adult III. Like Piaget, Binet and other psychometric intelligence theorists have not been able to separate the intellectual functions of adolescents of different ages as easily as those of children at earlier stages of development.

The fourth edition of the Stanford-Binet was published in 1985 (Thorndike, Hagan, and Sattler, 1985). One important addition to the latest edition is the analysis of the individual's responses into four separate area scores: verbal reasoning, quantitative reasoning, abstract-visual reasoning, and short-term memory. In addition, a composite score also is completed, just as in earlier versions of the test.

The Wechsler Scales

The most widely used intelligence test, next to the Binet, is the Wechsler. This test, named after psychologist David Wechsler, actually consists of several different intelligence tests. Younger adolescents are usually given the Wechsler Intelligence Scale for Children (WISC-R), while older adolescents are usually administered the Wechsler Adult Intelligence Scale (WAIS). The Wechsler scales, like the Binet, provide a score designed to reflect the adolescent's general level of intellectual functioning. Wechsler originally defined intelligence as "the global capacity of the individual to act purposefully, to think rationally, and to deal effectively with his environment" (1958, p. 7). In 1975, he redefined it as "the capacity of the individual to understand the world about him and his resourcefulness to cope with its challenges" (1975, p. 139). This statement reflects Wechsler's belief in the importance of intelligence as a general capacity of the adolescent.

The components of the Wechsler scales are divided into verbal and performance categories, with the verbal section subdivided into information, comprehension, arithmetic, similarities, vocabulary, and digit span, and the performance section subdivided into picture completion, picture arrangement, block design, object assembly, coding, and mazes. Binet recognized that intelligence actually consists of many different functions, but he did not measure these functions individually. (Note, however, that the 1985 version of the Binet has moved closer to the Wechsler by providing for the analysis of four different kinds of mental abilities). The Wechsler scales, by contrast, have been designed to provide specific scores for overall intelligence as well as for the individual functions through which intelligence is revealed and by which it can be measured. Thus, while retaining the idea of general intelligence, the Wechsler scales approach intelligence as a cluster of many different abilities.

In many places, the WISC-R and WAIS are used more frequently than the Stanford-Binet by school and clinical psychologists. They believe the WISC-R and WAIS provide a better measure than the Binet of the strong and weak components of the adolescent's thought processes. I asked several clinical psychologists regarded as experts on the WISC-R and WAIS how they felt these tests benefit them in assessing adolescents. Some of their comments are presented in Perspective on Adolescent Development 5.2.

Q*uestion* What is the value of the Wechsler scales (WISC-R and WAIS)?

Dr. L. They allow us to pinpoint areas of strength and weakness in an adolescent's mental performance. An adolescent may demonstrate a good vocabulary, for example, but poor visual-motor coordination. Such knowledge is important because it allows us to help her work to improve in areas where she is weak. An overall IQ score hides the peaks and valleys in an adolescent's abilities.

Dr. R. The Binet doesn't permit us to quantify and compare adolescent's subscales.

Dr. B. Many clinical psychologists believe valuable information about other aspects of an adolescent's psychological functioning can be gained from the WISC-R and WAIS as well.

Question Can you give some examples of other aspects of psychological functioning revealed by the WISC-R and WAIS?

Dr. L. The testing situation is approached as a structured interaction between the psychologist and the adolescent. It provides an opportunity to sample an adolescent's behavior and from it to develop inferences about the adolescent's thought processes and emotions.

Dr. B. These inferences are based on observations of the adolescent's behavior in the assessment situation as well as the adolescent's responses to the test items.

Dr. R. During testing, we observe the ease with which rapport is established, the level of energy and enthusiasm the adolescent expresses, and the degree of frustration tolerance and persistence the adolescent shows in performing difficult tasks. Each of these observations contributes information that can help us understand an individual adolescent.

Question Can any of you give an example of an actual case in which you feel the WISC-R or WAIS was extremely helpful in providing clinical information about the adolescent?

Dr. B. Yes. A fourteen-year-old boy, Robert, seemed dissatisfied with his responses while taking the WISC-R—even though later analysis rated his performance as superior. He often asked if his answers were correct, and in the middle of the test he asked whether anyone had ever given correct answers on everything in the test. On the picture arrangement subtest, Robert put the pictures in the correct order, but for each sequence he described how they could be put in another order to tell a different story. Because he was unable to be satisfied with his work, it took him much longer to commit himself to a solution, and so he lost bonus points for fast work.

Dr. L. This behavior does seem unusual for a fourteen-year-old boy in this situation. Most adolescents show anxiety about their test performance, but it usually doesn't interfere with their success. Also, by the middle of the test, most adolescents have responded to reassuring and supporting comments, and are much more relaxed.

Dr. B. Since Robert's teachers had reported that he had trouble completing assignments on time and seemed withdrawn in group discussions, I formed a tentative hypothesis. Perhaps Robert's perfectionistic needs and fear of failure affect his classroom performance in the same way they seemed to be interfering with his performance on the WISC-R. I made a mental note to look for other evidence that would confirm or contradict this hypothesis and to try to learn from further interviews and personality tests the reason for Robert's compulsive need for perfection.

Dr. R. This case example illustrates several processes involved in the clinical use of the WISC-R and WAIS. First, the clinician notes behavior that seems to be affecting the adolescent's adjustment adversely. Next this behavior is compared with a set of internal norms built up over years of testing. One may find that it is very different from the way adolescents typically behave in a test situation. This observation is then used to generate a hypothesis that will guide further observations during the evaluation. If other information appears to contradict the hypothesis, the clinician is prepared to reject the original assumption and pursue another explanation for this sample of the adolescent's behavior. For example, if the adolescent reveals that just prior to testing he was told by another youth that poor performance on the test would result in his being expelled from school, then the clinician's original assumption would have to be modified. Finally, information about the adolescent's psychological processes is related to the original problems for which that adolescent is being evaluated.

Question What about responses to test items? What can these reveal about psychological processes?

Dr. L. I'll answer that question by giving an example—one in which the quality of an incorrect answer on the WISC-R revealed something about an adolescent's psychological difficulties. On the block design task, an adolescent named Sarah constructed several designs that were rotated ninety degrees from the test stimuli. On the coding subtest, she copied many of the symbols in reverse and was unable to work fast enough to achieve an average score. Since the rest of her performance was in the average IQ range, her difficulty on these two subtests raised the possibility of perceptual or visual-motor coordination problems. The psychologist decided to assess this possibility by using additional procedures.

Dr. R. As you can see from this example, specific items are studied in the context of the entire evaluation. The psychologist doesn't approach the WISC-R or WAIS looking for signs that can be translated automatically into an understanding of the adolescent—it's the entire pattern that's studied. The more evidence that points in one direction, the more confident the psychologist can be in drawing conclusions.

Dr. B. When the psychologist needs more data, additional assessment tools are used. An accurate description of the adolescent depends on the psychologist's ability to combine knowledge of cognitive functioning, emotional development, and psychopathology with behavioral observations and test data.

VERBAL REASONING
Choose the correct pair of words to fill the blanks. The first word of the pair goes in the blank space at the beginning of the sentence; the second word of the pair goes in the blank at the end of the sentence.

. . . . . . is to night as breakfast is to . . . . . .

A. supper — corner
B. gentle — morning
C. door — corner
D. flow — enjoy
E. supper — morning

The correct answer is E.

NUMERICAL ABILITY
Choose the correct answer for each problem.

Add 13	A 14		Subtract 30	A 15
12	B 25		20	B 26
	C 16			C 16
	D 59			D 8
	E none of these			E none of these

The correct answer for the first problem is B; for the second, E.

ABSTRACT REASONING
The four "problem figures" in each row make a series. Find the one among the "answer figures" that would be next in the series.

The correct answer is D.

CLERICAL SPEED AND ACCURACY
In each test item, one of the five combinations is underlined. Find the same combination on the answer sheet and mark it.

V. <u>AB</u> AC AD AE AF

W. aA aB BA Ba <u>Bb</u>

X. A7 7A B7 <u>7B</u> AB

Y. Aa Ba <u>bA</u> BA bB

Z. 3A 3B <u>33</u> B3 BB

	AC	AE	AF	AB	AD
V.				∎	

	BA	Ba	Bb	aA	aB
W.			∎		

	7B	B7	AB	7A	A7
X.	∎				

	Aa	bA	bB	Ba	BA
Y.		∎			

	BB	3B	B3	3A	33
Z.					∎

Figure 5.4 **Sample items from the Differential Aptitude Tests, which seek to measure intelligence through analysis of individual factors of intelligence.**

The Factor Analytic Approach

The **factor analytic approach** is similar to the Wechsler in its emphasis on specific components of intelligence. It differs from the Wechsler in that it involves a mathematical analysis of large numbers of responses to test items in an attempt to come up with the basic common factors in intelligence.

A General and a Specific Factor Many years before Wechsler began analyzing intelligence in terms of its general and specific nature, C. E. Spearman (1927) had proposed that intelligence has two factors. His was called a two-factor theory and suggested that intelligence consists of *g*, standing for general intelligence, and *s*, standing for specific factor. Spearman believed that these two factors could explain an individual's performance on an intelligence test. However, some factor approaches abandoned the idea of a general structure for intelligence and instead searched for specific factors only.

Multiple-Factor Theory L. L. Thurstone (1938) developed an elaborate framework for understanding the idea that there are many specific types of intelligence. This view that a number of specific factors rather than one general and one specific factor make up intelligence is called **multiple-factor theory.** Thurstone consistently discovered six to twelve abilities that he called primary mental abilities. The seven that appeared most consistently when Thurstone analyzed people's test responses were (1) verbal comprehension, (2) number ability, (3) word fluency, (4) spatial visualization, (5) associative memory, (6) reasoning, and (7) perceptual speed. Figure 5.4 provides examples of the types of items that are included on tests designed to assess specific factors.

Today, we still believe it is important to look at the different aspects of intelligence rather than general intelligence alone. From time to time, psychologists have attempted to distinguish academic from nonacademic intelligence, social from nonsocial (abstract) intelligence, and so on. (Many people who do very well at verbal reasoning may not be able to replace a fuse. Others can take one look at an automobile engine and tell what is wrong with it, but are not able to make verbal analogies.) The factor analytic approach to intelligence has fostered the belief that we should be searching for different kinds of intelligence rather than one general intelligence.

Fluid and Crystallized Intelligence Yet another entrant in the search for the structure of intelligence is the theory of fluid and crystallized intelligence proposed by Raymond Cattell. Cattell (1963) proposed that two forms of intelligence act to influence the primary mental abilities described by Thurstone. Cattell labeled the two forms, fluid and crystallized. **Fluid intelligence** focuses on the individual's adaptability and capacity to perceive things and integrate them mentally. It appears to be independent of education and experience. For example, some individuals seem to intuitively think through problems with strategies they have never been taught. In comparison, schooling and environment are said to determine **crystallized intelligence,** which involves skills, abilities, and understanding. Instruction and observation are thought to enhance such skills. For example, an individual may learn how to play a particular game only after he or she has seen someone else do it or has been given instructions on how to proceed.

The Structure of Intellect If Thurstone's seven primary mental abilities were not enough, consider that J. P. Guilford (1967) proposed 120 mental abilities, calling his perspective the **structure of intellect.** As shown in figure 5.5, the 120 mental abilities are made up of all the possible combinations of five operations, four contents, and six products ($5 \times 4 \times 6 = 120$).

Operations are intellectual activities or processes, that is, what one does with information. Guilford's five cognitive operations focus on cognition (such as discovery, recognition, and awareness), memory, divergent production (generation of many different ideas), convergent production (finding a single best answer), and evaluation. **Contents** can be figural (such as visual or spatial), symbolic (e.g., letters, numbers, or words), semantic (word meanings), or behavioral (nonverbal

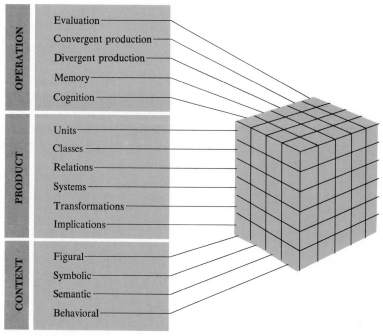

Figure 5.5   **Three-dimensional model of the structure of the intellect.**

performance). **Products** index the form in which information occurs—units, classes, relations, systems, transformations, or implications. The products dimension is hierarchical in that units combine into classes, classes form relations, relations comprise systems, and so on.

The Information Processing Approach to Intelligence

We already have seen earlier in this chapter that the information processing perspective has become prominent in the study of adolescent cognition. Our treatment of information processing here focuses on how this perspective views intelligence.

Knowledge Versus Process in Intelligence The information processing approach raises two very important questions about intelligence: (1) what are the information processing abilities that occur in development, and (2) what are the changes in world knowledge or "expertise" that occur in development (Santrock and Bartlett, 1986).

Few would deny that both changes in processing and changes in knowledge occur in development; however, there is disagreement about which is more fundamental. For example, though there is an accumulation of knowledge in childhood and adolescence, this accumulation might simply be the consequence of a growing reserve of "processing capacity." That is, the adolescent's greater capacity might be what allows him or her to learn more sophisticated knowledge. Alternatively, though processing efficiency clearly goes up as children move into and through adolescence, perhaps this reflects: (a) the adolescent's greater knowledge, and (b) the fact that greater knowledge allows more efficient information processing activities. It has been difficult to decide between these two possibilities, creating what Frank Keil (1984) calls the "structure-process dilemma" of cognitive development. The dilemma concerns the basic issue of what the "mechanisms" of intellectual development (Sternberg, 1984) are. Are such mechanisms those of changing information-processing abilities? Or are they those of changing knowledge and expertise? Or are they both?

To make the structure-process dilemma somewhat more concrete, consider a simple "computer metaphor." Suppose we have two computers, and that each is capable of solving multiplication problems (e.g., 13 × 24, 45 × 21), but one computer works much faster than the other. What could be the explanation? One possibility is that the "faster" computer truly is faster—it has faster subroutines for performing arithmetic computations, or more core (i.e., short-term memory) allowing two or more computations to proceed at once. Alternatively, the faster computer might have a greater store of relevant knowledge—perhaps it has in its data bank (long-term memory) a complete multiplication table going up to 99 × 99. The slower computer might be forced to get by (as do most humans) with a smaller table going up to only 12 × 12. In this case, the faster computer need not be fundamentally faster—its subroutines might be relatively slow—but it is able to perform the multiplication task relying on knowledge instead of computation. The issue we face in the development of intelligence is similar to that of explaining the difference between the fast and slow computers—is it processing or knowledge that is responsible for how intelligence changes with age? Based on some recent research on memory (Zembar and Naus, 1985), it seems likely that the answer might be "both." If so, the essential task for researchers is to determine the ways that processing and knowledge interact in the course of intellectual development.

R. J. Sternberg's Componential Analysis R. J. Sternberg (1982) has proposed that we might better understand intelligence if it were viewed in terms information processing components. His view—called **componential analysis**—attempts to understand the availability, accessibility, and ease of execution of a number of information processing components. The basic concept in this approach is the **component,** an elementary information process that operates on internal representations of objects (Newell and Simon, 1972; Sternberg, 1977). A component may translate sensory input into conceptual representation, transform one conceptual representation into another, or translate conceptual representation into some form of motor output. In Sternberg's perspective we see the model of receiving, processing, and reacting that is used by neuroscientists

R. J. Sternberg has developed an information processing view of intelligence.

to describe how the brain processes information. According to Sternberg, a component can be classified according to function (what it does) and level (whether it has a higher-level function in terms of planning and decision making or a lower-level, more precise function).

Sternberg has identified five such information-processing components, each performing a different function: metacomponents, performance, acquisition (or storage), retention (or retrieval), and transfer components.

1. **Metacomponents** are higher-order control processes used for executive planning and decision making when problem solving is called for. The decisions of which problem to solve and how to solve it are metacomponential decisions.

2. **Performance components** are processes used to carry out a problem-solving strategy. A set of performance components involve the actual working through of a problem.

E arl Hunt and his colleagues (Hunt, 1978; Hunt, Frost, and Lunneborg, 1973; Hunt and Lansman, 1975) have described the mechanics of information processing that underlie performance on tests of verbal ability. Hunt (1978) says that tests of verbal ability reflect two kinds of processes: (1) those related to knowledge acquired through experience, and (2) pure mechanical processes whose operations are independent of the specific information that is processed. One such mechanical process is decoding. Decoding is the process in which an external stimulus activates overlearned information in long-term memory, such as when you have to retrieve the name of a familiar word after you have been given a printed word related to the familiar word.

The measure Hunt used to study decoding was devised by Michael Posner (1970). Two letters are flashed on a screen next to each other. The subject has to indicate as rapidly as possible whether the letters are the same or different. In the Hunt (1978) experiment, one condition involved giving the subjects instructions to respond "same" only if the two letters were physically identical to each other (such as AA). In the second condition, a name identity judgment was required in that the subjects were to respond "same" if the letters had the same name (AA or Aa). The college population that served as the subjects typically took about seventy-five

to eighty milliseconds longer in the name identity than in the physical identity condition. Physical identity can be directly compared, but name identity requires decoding to determine the name of the two symbols.

Using the information processing task of decoding, Hunt (1978) found differences between the name and physical identity reaction times of a number of groups, ranging from high-verbal university students to mentally retarded school children (see table 5.1). Of particular interest are the three university groups. The high-verbal group had scored in the top twenty-five percent of a standardized test of verbal ability, the low-verbal group in the bottom twenty-five percent, and the normal group in between. As can be seen, the low-verbal college students had longer decoding times than the high-verbal students. Hunt argues that the slower decoding times are due to slower activation of long-term memory, more precisely, the slower activation of correct names stored there. Though there is more to verbal ability than decoding, the evidence provided by Hunt suggests that decoding is one important component of verbal ability. Other research indicates that the ability to maintain ordered information in short-term memory for a brief time is also more evident in the way high-verbal students process information than the way low-verbal students do (Hunt, Lunneborg, and Lewis, 1975).

3. **Acquisition (or storage) components** are processes used in learning new information. For example, this might involve rehearsing new information to transfer a trace of it into long-term memory.

4. **Retention (or retrieval) components** index processes involved in accessing previously stored information. For example, you might search through your long-term memory store in an organized manner to find a fact you need at a particular moment.

5. **Transfer components** are processes used in generalization, such as using information learned on one task to help solve another task. For example, having learned how to use a typewriter should expedite your ability to use a computer.

In addition to Sternberg's componential analysis, Earl Hunt (1978) has focused on describing the mechanics of information processing that might undergird performance on tests of verbal ability. More about Hunt's ideas on this matter appears in Perspective on Adolescent Development 5.3.

Table 5.1	Verbal ability and decoding
Group	Difference between name identity and physical identity (msec)
High-verbal university students	64
Normal university students	73–80
Low-verbal university students	89
Young adults not in a university	110
Severe epileptic adults	140
Adults past 60 years of age	170
10-year-old children	190
Mildly retarded schoolchildren	310

Average differences in response time between name identity and physical identity conditions in a letter-matching task for various groups of subjects.

Source: Hunt, 1978.

SAT and IQ tests are two of many different ways theorists measure intelligence.

The shift in interest to information processing and away from products as measured by intelligence tests does not mean that information-processing theorists are uninterested in products (Sternberg, 1982). Rather, these theorists are suggesting that attention should be given to the knowledge base generated by the processes.

Our discussion of the information processing approach to intelligence suggests that traditional standardized IQ tests will require some revision if we truly begin to incorporate information processing components into our assessment of intelligence. As we see next, Piaget's ideas about intelligence also are at odds with the intelligence measurers.

A Comparison of Piagetian and Psychometric Approaches to Adolescent Cognition

By now you probably have guessed that Piaget's views about adolescent intelligence differ from the views of Binet and Wechsler. The approach of the latter two, the **psychometric** approach, emphasizes measurement-based tests. A professional who administers tests is sometimes referred to as a psychometrist, or psychometrician. David Elkind (1969) has described some of the similarities and differences between the psychometric approach and Piaget's theories.

Piaget began his career as a developmental psychologist by working in Binet's laboratory, but he was more intrigued by the errors boys and girls made on the tests than by their correct answers. Piaget and the psychometricians agree that intelligence has a genetic component and that the maturation of thought processes is critical to understanding intelligence. The two types of theorists also agree that the most important aspect of intelligence is reasoning.

The most obvious difference between Piaget and the psychometric theorists lies in their views on the course of mental growth. The psychometric theorists are interested in quantifying mental growth to describe the adolescent's general level of intellectual functioning and to predict intelligence from one age to other ages. The psychometric approach, then, maximizes individual differences and seeks to measure them. The Piagetian approach, in contrast, essentially ignores individual differences and emphasizes the dynamic nature of intelligence and its qualitative changes. Piaget is particularly concerned with how new cognitive structures emerge.

Another difference between the two approaches is evident in a comparison of their views on genetics. While both approaches stress the importance of heredity in determining intelligence, the psychometric theorists are interested in differences among individuals—for example, they are interested in how scores from a random sample of 5,000 adolescents fall into place on a distribution of scores. Piaget, on the other hand, focuses more on changes within the adolescent that shape the organization of intelligence—for example, he is interested in how egocentrism constrains the way the adolescent organizes information about the world.

Finally, the psychometric approach focuses on predicting intelligence at a later point in development. Not only have IQ tests been used to predict IQ at a later point in time, but they also have been used to predict other aspects of the person's life as well—success in school, reading ability, and job success, to name just a few.

In considering the information processing and Piagetian approaches to intelligence, we have studied two alternatives to the use of standardized IQ tests to measure intelligence. Next, we look at other efforts to supplement or replace the standardized IQ tests.

Alternatives and Supplements to Intelligence Tests

Further alternatives and supplements to intelligence tests include testing for competence, culture-fair intelligence tests, and social intelligence.

Testing for Competence

In an article called "Testing for Competence Rather Than for Intelligence," David McClelland (1973) argued that although intelligence tests do a reasonably good job of predicting school performance, they often do not fare as well in predicting occupational success. Most standardized intelligence tests are heavily weighted with verbal items, in particular those requiring verbal reasoning or knowledge. McClelland's argument is that such verbal reasoning and knowledge may not always be efficient at predicting how competent someone will be at a particular job. It has been found, for instance, that intelligence test scores predict performance more reliably for jobs requiring abstract, symbolic thinking than for jobs that are less dependent on these skills (Ghiselli, 1966). For example, they are better at predicting job success as a stockbroker, an occupation that requires the ability to make financial analyses and projections, than success as a police officer, an occupation that calls for extensive person-to-person contact and routine reports. Even for jobs requiring abstract, symbolic thought, however, IQ tests are not as reliable in predicting success as they are in predicting performance in school.

If we do not use intelligence tests to predict competence in an occupation, then what will we use? McClelland (1973) makes three recommendations. First, **criterion sampling** should be called on. If one wants to find out whether a senior graduating from high school can expect to be successful as a police officer, one would start by defining what a police officer does. Certainly one of the criteria would have to be communication skills and the type of vocabulary used by a police officer on the job. In criteria testing, then, the first step is to define the criteria for success at what you are trying to predict. Testers must rely less on paper-and-pencil measures, like IQ tests and abstract word games; instead, they should go out into the real world and watch what successful people do in specific occupations. For example, Jacob Kounin (1971) attempted to define the criteria for good teaching by going into classrooms and videotaping the performance of "good" and "bad" teachers.

The second recommendation McClelland makes is that tests should be designed to reflect changes in what the individual has learned. Intelligence tests have been designed to measure intellectual skills that were thought to be stable. In other words, if a person's scores on tests administered at different times and under approximately the same circumstances vary greatly, the tests are generally thought to be unreliable. McClelland believes that instead of developing tests that measure stability, we should be attempting to measure criteria that reflect areas in which people can improve. For example, if it is found that teaching in elementary school requires a great deal of patience and highly developed communication skills, ways to measure these skills should be designed. It should be expected that individuals who initially do poorly on these criteria can improve and perform better on later tests.

This leads to McClelland's third recommendation for improving assessment: ways to improve the characteristic tested should be made public and explicit. How to do well on important tests has often been viewed as a deep, dark secret. McClelland stresses that we should be as open as possible about the criteria that are evaluated by a test and state in a simple way how to improve on the test. So, if an important test measures reading comprehension and arithmetic skills, an individual should be aware of exactly how he or she is going to be tested, how to best prepare for the test, and how the test will be scored. Some tests follow this procedure, but many do not.

Most experts find merit in McClelland's recommendations, but some do not agree that intelligence testing should be eliminated completely. Intelligence tests are often efficient in predicting such significant outcomes as success in school subjects, different aspects of reading ability, and some aspects of job success. Again, however, it is important to remember that intelligence tests are invariably most effective when used in conjunction with the types of criterion testing McClelland recommends.

To make a long story short, intelligence tests are reasonably good at predicting grades in school (Stevenson, Hale, Klein, and Miller, 1968) and not bad at predicting occupational success (Cronbach, 1970). There is much less evidence that they can predict the ability to get along with people or predict creativity, although intelligence and creativity are positively related (Richards, 1976).

Nonetheless, there have been a number of efforts to replace standardized intelligence tests with other measures and to develop additional tests that supplement the standardized tests.

Culture-Fair Intelligence Tests

A second set of measures designed to replace traditional standardized intelligence tests are called **culture-fair tests.** These tests have been developed in an attempt to eliminate cultural bias. It has been argued that traditional standardized intelligence tests, such as the Binet and Wechsler scales, favor individuals from white, middle-class backgrounds more than individuals from lower-class, minority backgrounds. The argument is that the standardized tests are not culturally fair to the latter individuals because they have not had the same experience and exposure to information that the tests measure as have middle-class whites. For example, individuals with greater exposure to verbal knowledge and verbal reasoning are likely to perform better on such tests.

Two types of culture-fair tests have been developed. In the first, verbal items are removed (e.g., Raven, 1960). Figure 5.6 shows one kind of item on this type of test; however, while tests such as the Raven Progressive Matrices are designed to be culture-fair, there is evidence that individuals with more education do better on them than individuals with less education (Anastasi, 1976). A second type of culture-fair test focuses on the development of items that are familiar to people from all socioeconomic and ethnic backgrounds, or items that are at least familiar to the people who are taking the test. For example, a child might be asked how a bird and a dog are different—on the assumption that virtually all children have had exposure to birds and dogs.

Table 5.2 The Chitling Intelligence Test

1. A "gas head" is a person who has a:
   (a) fast-moving car
   (b) stable of "lace"
   (c) "process"
   (d) habit of stealing cars
   (e) long jail record for arson
2. "Bo Diddley" is a:
   (a) game for children
   (b) down-home cheap wine
   (c) down-home singer
   (d) new dance
   (e) Moejoe call
3. If a pimp is uptight with a woman who gets state aid, what does he mean when he talks about "Mother's day"?
   (a) second Sunday in May
   (b) third Sunday in June
   (c) first of every month
   (d) none of these
   (e) first and fifteenth of every month
4. A "handkerchief head" is:
   (a) a cool cat
   (b) a porter
   (c) an Uncle Tom
   (d) a hoddi
   (e) a preacher
5. If a man is called a "blood," then he is a:
   (a) fighter
   (b) Mexican-American
   (c) Negro
   (d) hungry hemophile
   (e) red man, or Indian
6. Cheap chitlings (not the kind you purchase at a frozen-food counter) will taste rubbery unless they are cooked long enough. How soon can you quit cooking them to eat and enjoy them?
   (a) forty-five minutes
   (b) two hours
   (c) twenty-four hours
   (d) one week (on a low flame)
   (e) one hour

Answers: 1. c   2. c   3. e   4. c   5. c   6. c

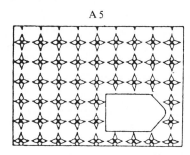

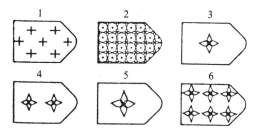

Figure 5.6 Sample items from the Raven Progressive Matrices Test.

In the United States, particular concern has been voiced about the lack of intelligence tests that are culturally fair to blacks. The Dove Counterbalance General Intelligence Test (table 5.2) sometimes referred to as the Chitling Test, was developed by a black sociologist, Adrian Dove, as a sarcastic rejoinder to the middle-class bias of most intelligence tests. Dove's test was not presented as a serious effort to develop a culture-free test for blacks; it was designed to illustrate how the language used by many blacks differs from that of middle-class whites.

A recently developed intelligence test, the Kaufman Assessment Battery for Children (K-ABC), has been promoted as an improvement over past culture-fair tests (Kaufman and Kaufman, 1983). It can be administered to children aged two-and-one-half to twelve-and-one-half. This test has been standardized on a more representative sample than most tests, including more minority and handicapped children. The intelligence portion of the test focuses less on language than the Stanford-Binet, and the test includes an achievement section involving such subtests as arithmetic and reading. Nonetheless, like other culture-fair intelligence tests, the K-ABC test already has found some detractors (Bracken, 1985; Keith, 1985).

Although the development of culture-fair tests has served to remind us that cultural bias exists in intelligence testing, the available culture-fair tests have not provided a satisfactory alternative. Crafting a truly culture-fair test, one that rules out the role of experiences due to socioeconomic and ethnic background, not only has been elusive, but it may be impossible.

Social Intelligence

Life is more than solving verbal and numerical problems. We also need to get along with people and be able to adapt to the social world in which we live. This point was made in the prologue to this chapter, where we introduced the concept of **social intelligence.** So, some psychologists believe intelligence should be construed to involve interpersonal skills as well (e.g., Gardner, 1983; Mercer and Lewis, 1978; Sternberg, 1985). Jane Mercer (e.g., Mercer and Lewis, 1978) has put together a battery of measures she believes provides a more complete assessment of intelligence than a single traditional intelligence test. Her battery of tests is called SOMPA, which stands for System of Multicultural Pluralistic Assessment. It can be given to children from five to eleven years of age. SOMPA was particularly designed for use with children from an impoverished background. Instead of relying on a single test, SOMPA includes information about the child's intellectual functioning in four main areas: (1) verbal and nonverbal intelligence in the traditional intelligence test vein, assessed by the WISC-R; (2) social and economic background of family, obtained via a one-hour parental interview; (3) social adjustment to school, evaluated by an adaptive behavior inventory filled out by parents; and (4) physical health, ascertained by a medical examination. Thus, Mercer hopes to obtain a more complete picture of the experiences and environmental background of the child than would be possible from giving the WISC-R alone. She also shows a concern for assessing the child's health, which might interfere with intellectual performance.

There have been very few comprehensive views of social intelligence developed with regard to adolescents. One promising effort to create a taxonomy of social intelligence during adolescence is presented in

Perspective on Adolescent Development 5.4, where the views of Martin Ford are described.

We have discussed a number of important ideas about intelligence so far. A summary of these ideas is presented in Concept Table 5.2.

Giftedness and Creativity

So far in our discussion of intelligence, we have had little to say about some other aspects that need to be considered in the development and education of adolescents—giftedness and creativity.

Giftedness

Many years ago the label, gifted, had a single meaning, namely high intelligence (White House Conference on Children, 1931). The **gifted child** still is described as an individual with well-above-average intellectual capacity (an IQ of 120 or more, for example), but he or she may also be a child with a superior talent for something (Owen, Froman, and Moscow, 1981). In their selection of children for gifted programs, most school systems still place the heaviest weight on intellectual superiority and academic aptitude and do not look as carefully at such areas of competence as the visual and performing arts, psychomotor abilities, and other specific aptitudes.

R. J. Sternberg (Sternberg, 1984) believes that giftedness can be better understood if it is thought of in terms of the individual's ability to think in novel ways, particularly in terms of insight. He points out that significant and exceptional intellectual accomplishments such as major scientific discoveries, important inventions, and new understandings of literary and philosophical works almost always involve major intellectual insights. As can be seen later in our discussion of creativity, considering giftedness in terms of intellectual insight places it very close to what is meant by creativity as well.

One classic study that dominates our knowledge about gifted children is that of Lewis Terman (1925). In the 1920s, Terman began to study approximately 1,500 children whose Stanford-Binet IQ scores averaged 150. Terman's research was designed to follow these children through their adulthood—it will not be complete until the year 2010.

A TAXONOMY OF SOCIAL INTELLIGENCE DURING ADOLESCENCE

*W*hat makes an adolescent socially intelligent? This question has been addressed by Martin Ford (1986), who has proposed a number of self-assertive and integrative accomplishments of the socially intelligent adolescent. Ford's eight-category scheme is shown in table 5.3, where four defining issues of social intelligence are listed (identity, control, social comparison, and resource distribution) along with corresponding self-assertive and integrative goals. Regarding identity, the self-assertive task is to develop and express one's individuality. Examples of how this type of social intelligence might be developed include a unique behavioral style or an unusual pattern of interests. The self-assertive adolescent also may show that he or she has developed a strongly endorsed system of personal values and a clear, stable set of self-conceptions. The existence of the self-assertive nature of the adolescent would not depend on other individuals or social groups for self-definition. The integrative aspect of identity development is referred to as belongingness. It involves efforts to create, maintain, or enhance the identity of social units of which the adolescent is a part. The units might be small and intimate, as in one's family or close friendships, or large, abstract units such as an ethnic group, profession, or political party. Just as adolescents inherit some characteristics of individuality, they become members of some social groups by accident. Ford believes the emphasis should be on active engagement of the social environment in creating situations that will enhance the self-assertive and belongingness aspects of identity.

Regarding the second issue, control, it is argued that self-determination is the self-assertive goal, while social responsibility is the integrative goal. Adolescents who are making progress in self-determination are beginning to establish and maintain personal control over their life circumstances and regain control when it is lost. Social responsibility is attained by accepting legitimate and necessary types of social control. The control is exercised to some degree through broad rules of society, such as the prohibition of certain immoral or illegal actions (e.g.,

Social comparison is an important aspect of social intelligence.

violence and theft), and through the regulation of conduct in social contexts, such as classrooms, neighborhoods, and the like. Social control, though, is developed through formal obligations to personal roles as well, such as a student, employee, citizen, and so forth. And social control also is accomplished by informal obligations involving social contracts with friends, relatives, and other individuals. As can be seen, social responsibility is shown in situations where duties are upheld, commitments are kept, and roles are fulfilled. And social responsibility is

Table 5.3 A taxonomy of self-assertive and integrative goals

	Type of goal	
Defining issue	Self-assertive goals	Integrative goals
Identity:	Individuality	Belongingness
Control:	Self-determination	Social responsibility
Social comparison:	Superiority	Equity
Resource distribution:	Resource acquisition	Resource provision

Source: From Ford, M., "A Living Systems Conceptualization of Social Intelligence: Outcomes, Processes, and Developmental Change," in R. J. Sternberg (Ed.), Advances in the Psychology of Human Intelligence, Vol. 3, 1986. Hillsdale, N.J.: Lawrence Erlbaum Associates, Inc.

reflected in such characteristics as dependability, trustworthiness, and integrity. The socially responsible adolescent is learning how to take his or her place in a network of expectations and mutual obligations and becomes capable of meeting such expectations and obligations in a reliable way.

In the next two forms of social intelligence, the main issue is the process of social comparison. When an adolescent compares himself or herself to others, the self-assertive consequence is to sense that he or she is better or higher on some relevant dimension than the other person or reference group. Since superiority is relative rather than absolute, self-assertiveness here occurs most often in competitive situations. In these situations, a high social status is attained through active engagement of the social world rather than through social assignment or social accident. Further, superiority is likely to be revealed through commerce with peers, since individuals who are dissimilar, such as adults, are not as likely to provide the best basis for meaningful comparison. Related to this last comment is the integrative aspect of social intelligence defined by social comparison, that of equity. At the same time, equity is an important interest of group leaders such as teachers, parents, and employers, who need to be concerned with adolescents' demands for fair, unbiased treatment. Equity may be manifested in relationships with siblings, peers, and friends of similar status to the adolescent, where powerful norms regarding sharing and fairness are likely to be important in the quality of the social relationships. Equity also may be demonstrated in relationships and interactions involving dissimilar circumstances such as comparisons with disadvantaged others (adolescents with less money, less intelligence, and so forth).

The final two domains in Ford's outcome theory of social intelligence are defined by the issue of resource allocation. To maintain or promote the functioning of the self, the adolescent needs to be competent at resource allocation. And, alternatively, resource provision may be required to enhance the functioning of other individuals and social groups. Such resources may involve goods and possessions, such as food, clothing, or money. And the resources may pertain to such matters as assistance, advice, or cognitive validation. Since social resources often are distributed in friendships and social support networks developed through mutual give-and-take processes, resource acquisition and provision often can be attained in the same contexts. Indeed, the adolescent's unwillingness to provide resources reciprocally to others may make it very difficult for the adolescent to acquire resources for himself or herself.

In summary, Ford (1986) argues that adolescents who can maintain and promote the functioning of themselves as well as that of other individuals and social groups are more socially intelligent than adolescents who are competent in only one category.

INTELLIGENCE

Concept	Processes/related ideas	Characteristics/description
Theories, definition, and measurement	Binet and the concept of intelligence	Binet (with Simon) developed the first intelligence test in 1905. Binet emphasized the assessment of general intelligence and conceived of intelligence as a general ability. The Stanford-Binet is organized along chronological lines, but the most recent revision in 1985 includes an analysis of four areas of thought.
	The Wechsler scales	Wechsler, while assessing intelligence at both the general and specific levels, nonetheless defined intelligence as a global property of a person. The WISC-R can be given to younger adolescents, while older adolescents may need to be given the WAIS.
	The factor analytic approach	Spearman, Thurstone, Cattell, and Guilford all proposed factor analytic views of intelligence, emphasizing the use of statistical analysis to generate the dimensions of intelligence. Spearman argued that intelligence consists of a general and a specific factor. Thurstone emphasized that intelligence is made up of primary mental abilities. Cattell proposed that there are basically two kinds of intelligences—fluid and crystallized. Guilford developed the structure of intellect model, consisting of 120 mental abilities made up of all combinations of operations, contents, and products.
	The information processing approach	The information processing approach calls attention to importance of considering a distinction between knowledge and process in understanding intelligence. R. J. Sternberg believes we might better understand intelligence if we viewed it in terms of components, elementary information processes such as metacomponents, performance components, acquisition components, retention components, and transfer components.

The accomplishments of the 1,500 children in Terman's study are remarkable. Of the 800 males, 78 have obtained Ph.Ds., 48 have earned M.Ds., and 85 have been granted law degrees. Nearly all of these figures are ten to thirty times greater than would have been found among 800 men of the same age chosen randomly (Getzels and Dillon, 1973).

Scrutiny of the gifted 1,500 continues. The most recent investigation focused on whether the gifted individuals had been satisfied with their lives (Sears, 1977). When the average age of the Terman gifted population was sixty-two, four target factors were assessed: life-cycle satisfaction with occupation; satisfaction with family life; degree of work persistence into their sixties; and unbroken marriage versus a history of divorce. The recorded events and expressions of feelings have been obtained at decade intervals since 1922. One of the most interesting findings of the study is that in spite of their autonomy and extensive success in their occupations, these men placed more importance on achieving satisfaction in their family life than in their work. Furthermore, the gifted individuals felt that they

INTELLIGENCE

Concept	Processes/related ideas	Characteristics/description
	A comparison of Piagetian and psychometric approaches	Piaget's views differ substantially from those of psychometricians. Piaget was interested in the universal ways all children and adolescents think, whereas psychometricians are interested in how individuals differ in their thinking. Piaget was interested in qualitative changes in intelligence whereas the psychometricians are interested in the quantification of intelligence.
Alternatives and supplements to intelligence tests	Testing for competence	Tests of competency use criterion sampling to develop items that reflect competence.
	Culture-fair intelligence tests	Culture-fair tests have been designed because it has been argued that many standardized tests are culturally biased. However, it is extremely difficult, if not impossible, to develop a truly culture-fair intelligence test.
	Social intelligence	Social intelligence tests have been devised to supplement standardized intelligence tests by psychologists who believe social matters are important in assessing intelligence just as cognitive matters are. The SOMPA has been devised for use with individuals from impoverished backgrounds. Ford argues that social intelligence is best conceptualized as having both self-assertive and socially integrative domains.

had found such satisfaction. As Terman suggested, they are not only superior intellectually, but are physically, emotionally, morally, and socially more able as well.

Programs for gifted children usually follow one of three paths: enrichment, grouping, or acceleration. Enrichment focuses on special provisions for gifted children, including college-level courses in high school, advanced classes, independent study, and so forth. Grouping occurs when students with similar capacities are placed in a class together. Acceleration refers to any strategy that abbreviates the time required for a student to graduate, such as skipping a grade (Owen, Froman, and Moscow, 1981).

Do such programs work? Julian Stanley (1977), widely known for his study of gifted children, has pointed out that most gifted children enrichment programs are comprised of busywork, are irrelevant, and in many instances are just plain boring. Research directed at assessing the impact of acceleration provides

"Stars" devote tremendous amounts of time to practice and training.

a more favorable picture; a summary of the acceleration studies suggests that, from first grade through college, acceleration seems to have a positive intellectual and emotional effect on gifted children (Laycock, 1979).

In the Terman study, for example, the individuals who had been accelerated in school were more successful in their jobs, education, and marriage, and maintained better physical health than those who had not been accelerated (Terman and Oden, 1959). Grouping has been much more controversial than enrichment or acceleration. Research on grouping children into tracks has produced mixed results (Esposito, 1973), and many critics point out that it is unfair to poor children and ethnic minority groups.

Individuals who turn out to have exceptional talents as adults suggest that there is more to becoming a "star" in their respective fields than gifted programs. In one recent inquiry (Bloom, 1983), 120 individuals who had achieved stardom in six different areas, concert pianists and sculptors (arts), Olympic swimmers and tennis champions (psychomotor), and research mathematicians and research neurologists (cognitive) were interviewed to learn what they felt was responsible for their lofty accomplishments. It seems that exceptional accomplishments require particular kinds of environmental support, special experiences, excellent teaching, and motivational encouragement throughout development. Regardless of the quality of their gifts, each of the individuals experienced many years of special attention under the tutelage and supervision of a remarkable series of teachers and coaches. And they also were given considerable support and attention by their parents. All of the "stars" devoted great amounts of time to practice and training, easily outrivaling the amount of time spent in other activities.

Creativity

Most of us would like to be creative, and parents and teachers would like to be able to develop situations that promote creative thinking in children. Why was Thomas Edison able to invent so many things? Was he simply more intelligent than most people? Did he spend long hours toiling away in private? Somewhat surprisingly, when Edison was a young boy his teacher told him he was too dumb to learn anything! And there are other examples of famous individuals whose creative genius went unnoticed when they were younger (Larson, 1973): Walt Disney was fired from a newspaper because he did not have any good ideas, Enrico Caruso's music teacher informed him that he could not sing and that he didn't have any voice at all, Albert Einstein was four years old before he could speak and seven before he could read, and Winston Churchill failed one year of secondary school. Among the reasons such individuals are overlooked as youngsters is the difficulty we have in defining and measuring creativity.

Definition and Measurement

The prevailing belief of experts who study creativity is that intelligence and creativity are not the same (Wallach, 1973). For example, scores on widely used tests of creativity developed by J. P. Guilford and by Michael Wallach and Nathan Kogan are only weakly related to intelligence scores (Richards, 1976). Yet it is as difficult to define creativity as it is to define intelligence. Just as intelligence consists of many disparate elements, so creativity is a many-faceted phenomenon. An important question is whether measuring general creative functioning is appropriate or even possible.

David Ausubel (1968) emphasized that creativity is one of the most ambiguous and confusing terms in psychology and education. He believes that the term creative should not be applied to as many people as it is, but should be reserved for describing people who make unique and original contributions to society.

The term **creativity** has been used in many ways. Following are the ways that some well-known figures define creativity and attempt to measure it in individuals.

Creative thinking is part of J. P. Guilford's model of intelligence (Guilford, 1967). The aspect of his theory of intelligence that is most closely related to creativity is what he called **divergent thinking,** a type of thinking that produces many different answers to a single question. Divergent thinking is distinguished from **convergent thinking,** a type of thinking that goes toward one correct answer. For example, there is one correct answer to this intellectual problem-solving task: "How many quarters can you get from sixty dimes?" It calls for convergent thinking. But there are many possible answers to this question: "What are some unique things a coat hanger can be used for?" This question requires divergent thinking. Going off in different directions may sometimes lead to more productive answers. Examples of what Guilford means by divergent thinking (his term for creativity) and ways of measuring it follow:

Word fluency: How facile are you with words? For example, name as many words as possible, as fast as possible that contain the letter z.

Ideational fluency: Here you have to name words that belong to a particular class. For example, name as many objects as you can that weigh less than one pound.

Adaptive flexibility: In this type of divergent thinking you must be able to vary your ideas widely. For example, if you are shown a series of match sticks lined up on a table, you may be asked to put them together to form four triangles.

Originality: This time you would be required to name some unique ways to use an object. For example, what are some unusual ways to use hairpins?

Michael Wallach and Nathan Kogan (1965) attempted to refine the ability to separate creativity from intelligence. Their work has included efforts to specify how creative people in the arts and sciences think.

People who are rated as highly creative individuals are asked to probe introspectively into what it is that enables them to produce creative pieces of work. Two major factors evolve from this self-analysis by creative people. First, they have what is called **associative flow.** That is, they can generate large amounts of associative content in their effort to attain novel solutions to problems. Second, they have the freedom to entertain a wide range of possible solutions in a playful manner. These responses led Wallach and Kogan to remove time limits from tests of creativity and to make sure that the tests were given in very relaxed, nonthreatening, informal situations.

Developmental Changes in Creativity

Some commonly held beliefs about developmental changes in creativity are: (1) it begins to weaken around the age of five because of the societal pressure to conform, (2) serious drops in creativity occur at the age of nine and at the age of twelve, (3) adults are less creative than children (Dudek, 1974).

These stereotypes are not supported by good research data. Actually, a drop in creativity probably does not occur at the age of nine; what happens instead is that the child's form of expression changes. At about eight or nine years of age, the child begins to develop a more differentiated view of reality compared to an earlier, more global view. The child is freer from perceptual dominance and clearly into the concrete operations stage. Consider the child's art, for example. The child now paints as he or she sees, not feels. Feeling does not entirely disappear from art, but it now is less important to the child than realistic detail.

According to Steven Dudek (1974) this change represents increased subtlety in thought and increased imagination, not less. Others may interpret the art as less creative and less imaginative because surprise and vividness are missing. It has lost some of its spontaneity, but not its complexity. At this point, the child may require time to master the skills of the concrete operational period before he or she can use them spontaneously and freely.

The drop in creativity reported at about the age of twelve also occurs just after the child has entered a new stage in Piaget's theory. In the formal operations stage, the child is learning how to develop hypotheses, how to combine ideas in complex ways, and how to think in more imaginative and abstract ways. Piaget has pointed out that when children begin to develop new cognitive skills, egocentrism often results and pressures to conform are very strong. An increase in creativity might be expected during adolescence as the child gradually masters the use of these newly acquired cognitive skills. Evidence suggests that if repressive forces are not too strong, creativity does seem to increase in adolescence (Greenacre, 1971). So, neither adolescents nor adults are necessarily less creative than young children.

Encouraging Creativity

Let's look at ways creativity can be encouraged. You are a school teacher. How might you go about fostering creativity on the part of your students? **Brainstorming** is one technique that has been effective in several programs developed to stimulate creativity in children. In brainstorming sessions, a topic is presented for consideration and participants are encouraged to suggest ideas related to it. Criticism of ideas contributed must be withheld initially to prevent stopping the flow of ideas. The more freewheeling the ideas, the better. Participants are also encouraged to combine ideas that have already been suggested. Studies with children in regular classrooms (e.g., Torrance and Torrance, 1972) and in classrooms with educationally handicapped children (e.g., Sharpe, 1976) indicate that brainstorming can be an effective strategy for increasing creative thinking.

More important perhaps than any specific technique, however, is the need to foster a creative atmosphere in the classroom. Children need to feel that they can try out ideas, even if the ideas seem crazy or far-fetched, without being criticized by the teacher. The only way to produce a creative environment on a sustained basis is to do things creatively on a regular basis.

Creative thinking can be encouraged in any type of curriculum and in any kind of classroom situation; neither an open classroom nor progressive education is required. A word of caution is needed here. Although experts believe that creative thinking exercises should be practiced in every classroom, they caution against spending too much time on creative activities at the expense of other equally important learning activities. Michael Wallach (1973), for one, has commented that many children do not need to read more creatively, they just need to learn how to read.

Summary

I. Ideas about the information processing perspective include adolescent information processing and computer information processing, processes involved in processing information, and the interface of information processing and education.

  A. An understanding of adolescent information processing and computer information processing includes an overview of the nature of adolescent information processing, the computer analogy, and questions raised by the information processing perspective.

    1. The adolescent experiences an event in the environment. The adolescent detects and trys to make sense out of the event. To do this, cognitive processes such as attention, perception, memory, thinking, and problem solving are called on. Once this processing is complete, the adolescent makes a response; thus, information processing emphasizes the cognitive mediation of environment-behavior relations through a number of cognitive processes.

    2. The field of computer science has added credibility to thinking about the mind as being like a computer. Comparisons between the adolescent's mind and a computer involve thinking about the hardware and software of a computer as being roughly equivalent to the brain and mind of the adolescent. Both adolescent minds and computers have memories and can solve problems. Computers are even better than adolescent minds at remembering in an effortless fashion huge amounts of data and in conducting lightning fast maneuvers with those data.

    3. A computer, however, cannot develop a goal for itself; it does not do well at simulating the nonlogical, intuitive, and

possibly unconscious processes of the mind; and it is not aware of itself. By contrast, the adolescent's mind can do all of these wondrous things.

4. Three questions raised by information processing focus on the nature and importance of processing speed, processing capacity, and knowledge.

B. Among the most important processes involved in information processing are attention, memory, and thinking.

1. Attention refers to focusing perception to produce increased awareness of a stimulus. Two important types of attention are selective and divided.

2. Memory can be defined as the process by which information is retained over time and retrieved. Distinctions are made between short-term and long-term memory, and there are a number of control processes or strategies that can improve the efficiency of the adolescent's memory—rehearsal, organization, semantic elaboration, imagery, retrieval activities, knowledge (particularly metamemory), and the context of memory.

3. Thinking refers to a number of higher order cognitive processes such as inferencing, problem solving, and understanding. Inferences refer to relations between two events that are not directly stated. Problem solving refers to processing information to attain a goal.

C. Ideas about information processing and education include a discussion of schooling, IQ tests, and career development/adaption, as well as the information revolution, the information processing perspective, and the education of adolescents.

1. Schooling and IQ testing have basically been in the business of imparting knowledge and assessing knowledge respectively rather than providing instruction in how to process information more efficiently and assessing that processing. This, to some degree, may explain why IQ tests have been better at predicting success in school than career success or adaptation to the real world.

2. We have moved from an industrial society to a postindustrial, information society; however, while adults are called on to perform an extensive amount of information processing as part of this new society, they have not adequately been trained in elementary and secondary schools in ways to improve their efficiency of such processing. Research on information processing with adolescents has lagged behind similar efforts with children and adults, so applications to secondary schooling are not easy. Further, some experts believe that information processing skills, in general, are very difficult if not impossible to train. The major thrust thus far has been to work on improving domain-specific information processing skills, as in the subject of geometry. Information-processing psychologists believe adolescent cognition would be improved by an infusion of their perspective into all areas of the secondary school curricula.

II. Ideas about intelligence include information about theories, definition, and measurement, alternatives, and supplements to intelligence tests, as well as giftedness and creativity.

A. An overview of theories, definition, and measurement focuses on Binet and the concept of intelligence, the Wechsler Scales, the factor analytic approach, the information processing approach, and a comparison of Piagetian and psychometric approaches.

1. Binet (with Simon) developed the first intelligence test in 1905. Binet emphasized the assessment of general intelligence and conceived of intelligence as a general ability. The Stanford-Binet is organized along chronological lines, but the most recent revision in 1985 includes an analysis of four areas of thought as well.

2. Wechsler, while assessing intelligence at both the general and specific levels, nonetheless defined intelligence as a global property of the person. The WISC-R can be given to younger adolescents and the WAIS can be administered to older adolescents.

3. Spearman, Thurstone, Cattell, and Guilford all proposed factor analytic views of intelligence, emphasizing the use of statistical analysis to generate the dimensions of intelligence.

4. The information processing approach calls attention to the importance of considering a distinction between process and knowledge in understanding intelligence. R. J. Sternberg believes we might better comprehend intelligence if we viewed it in terms of components, elementary information processes like metacomponents, performance components, acquisition components, retention components, and transfer components.

5. Piaget's views differ from those of psychometricians. Piaget was interested in the universal ways children and adolescents think, whereas psychometricians are interested in how individuals differ in the way they think. And, Piaget was interested in qualitative changes in intelligence, whereas the psychometricians are interested in the quantification of intelligence.

B. A discussion of alternatives and supplements to intelligence tests includes ideas about testing for competence, culture-fair tests, and social intelligence.

1. Tests of competency use criterion sampling to develop items that reflect competence.

2. Culture-fair tests have been crafted because it is believed that standardized tests are culturally biased; however, it is extremely difficult, if not impossible, to devise a completely culture-fair test.

3. Social intelligence tests have been designed to supplement standardized intelligence tests by psychologists who believe social matters are important in assessing intelligence just as cognitive matters are. The SOMPA is one test that has been created to assess the intelligence of individuals from impoverished backgrounds with an eye toward assessing social intelligence. Ford emphasizes that social intelligence includes both self-assertive and socially integrative domains.

C. Other ideas related to a discussion of intelligence include giftedness and creativity.

1. Information about giftedness includes an overview of what giftedness is (which usually has been defined in terms of intelligence but likely should be broadened to describe more diverse talents; Sternberg believes giftedness involves insight), the Terman study of giftedness, programs for the gifted, and an analysis of the lives of "stars" in different talent domains.

2. An overview of creativity focuses on its definition and measurement, both of which have been somewhat elusive, developmental changes in creativity, and programs designed to increase creativity, such as brainstorming.

Key Terms

acquisition (or storage) components *186*

associative flow *197*

attention *171*

brainstorming *198*

component *185*

componential analysis *185*

contents *183*

convergent thinking *197*

creativity *197*

criterion sampling *188*

crystallized intelligence *183*

culture-fair tests *189*

divergent thinking *197*

divided attention *171*

factor analytic approach *183*

fluid intelligence *183*

gifted child *191*

memory *171*

memory-span task *171*

metacomponents *185*

metamemory *172*

multiple factor theory *183*

operations *183*

parallel processing *170*

performance components *185*

processing capacity *170*

products *184*

psychometric *187*

retention (or retrieval) components *186*

selective attention *171*

social intelligence *191*

structure of intellect *183*

transfer components *186*

Suggested Readings

Bransford, J. D., and Stein, B. S. (1984). *The ideal problem solver: a guide to improving thinking, learning, and creativity.* San Francisco: W. H. Freeman.
This paperback provides a guide for ways to improve your ability to solve problems. Bransford, a well-known cognitive psychologist, adds to the list of people who believe problem solving can be taught. Contains numerous enjoyable problem-solving exercises.

Gardner, R. (1983). *Frames of mind.* New York: Basic Books.
Gardner describes what he believes are the seven intelligences of humans.

Hunt, M. (1982). *The universe within.* New York: Simon and Schuster.
Hunt traveled to many universities and talked to top scholars in the cognitive area. This book represents his distillation of their ideas. The outcome is a well-written, informative book about the information processing revolution in psychology. It includes many intriguing ideas about the relation between the human mind and computers.

Matlin, M. (1983). *Cognition.* New York: Holt, Rinehart, and Winston.
This book presents an excellent overview of the field of cognition, written in a logical and interesting way. It includes separate chapters on imagery, problem solving, and reasoning.

Sternberg, R. J. (1985). *Beyond IQ.* Cambridge, England: Cambridge University Press.
Sternberg explains why we should be focusing more on how people process information rather than their IQ.

Part 3

The Contexts of Adolescent Development

Don Mitchell is a ten-year-old black boy. His father works as an officer at a bank and his mother is a teacher. He has two younger sisters—Rena, age five, and Martha, age seven. His parents have worked hard to provide a good life for themselves and their children. They encourage Don and his sisters to work hard in school and to listen carefully to what their teachers say. The Mitchells could be characterized as achievement-oriented, serious parents. They spend considerable time monitoring Don's academic and social world. The Mitchells recently moved to a predominantly white, middle-class neighborhood in a suburb of Houston, Texas. Don's parents believe the schools are better there than in the urban area in the north where they previously lived.

When we look at Don at the age of fourteen, we find that he is in the ninth grade of his junior high school. He is an excellent basketball player and is the leading scorer on his junior high school team. He is one of the most popular boys in his junior high school and over the course of his early adolescence seems to gradually have adapted to living in a predominantely white area. He has three close friends, two who are black and one who is white. The two black friends also play on the basketball team, and the white friend lives next door to him. Don's parents still monitor his academic and social world closely—"sometimes too closely," says

Don. His mother was recently transferred to his school and is teaching eighth-grade English—Don frankly would have preferred it if his mother had stayed at the school where she had been teaching. Conflict between Don and his parents seems to have increased somewhat during the last several years, but most of the conflict is neither prolonged nor intense. Don is pushing to become a more independent individual and his parents are still trying to get him to conform to their high standards.

At age seventeen Don is a junior in high school and has become the leading scorer on his high school basketball team. College coaches are already talking with him about a possible college scholarship. Don's parents are very proud of him—he has successfully managed to juggle the demands of sports and a rather rigorous set of classes in school. He has an A− average. Don's parents have recognized that he is now capable of making more mature decisions, so they feel comfortable in "letting loose" more than they did in the junior high school years. Still, Don has done some things they consider wrong—last summer, he and several of his friends went on a drinking binge one night. It was 3 A.M. and they didn't know where he was. At 3:30 A.M., Don and his friends finally realized they had better go home, even if they weren't sober. Don's parents were not very understanding. He wishes they would realize that you don't become an adult overnight; they don't seem to recognize that going from childhood to adulthood is a very long, gradual process and that adolescents are going to fall on their faces more than once during this time. Still, Don says he doesn't think he is going to stay out drinking until 3:00 or 4:00 in the morning any more, and when he drinks he is going to do it more moderately and be very careful that his parents do not find out.

What about his little sisters? They are now twelve and fourteen years old. The night Don came home from his night of drinking, the commotion woke them up and they listened from the stairway as their parents yelled at Don in the living room. The next day they teased him about it—he didn't think it was very funny, especially since he wasn't feeling too good. Don's sisters are close to each other—Martha, the fourteen year old, is dating someone steadily, and she and her sister talk about boys a lot. Still, their relationship contains a mixture of attachment and conflict. They sometimes fight about wearing each other's clothes or taking things from each other's rooms, but they still share many intimate conversations. They, too, have done well in school, although they have not been as popular as Don. They seem to sense that their father, in particular, caters to Don more than to them.

Conflict between the two girls and their parents, particularly their mother, seems to have escalated in the last year. Both girls show a strong inclination to spend more time on the weekends with their peers than they used to. Last Saturday night, Martha's boyfriend was spending some time with his friends, and Martha couldn't find anything to do. She was mad at her sister and didn't want to spend Saturday night at home. She told her mother: "What a boring place this is— I never have anything to do!" Several minutes later, Don walked by and told everyone what a great time he was looking forward to—after having been grounded for three months for his drinking episode, he had the family car to take his girlfriend out. His fourteen-year-old sister took a swipe at him, but missed, as he walked out the door. If she couldn't have any fun tonight, she didn't want anyone else in the family to have any either.

When we follow Don's sisters into their later adolescent years they are still doing well in school, and are getting ready to go away to college. Their mother says she doesn't think she could stand it if they stayed at home and went to school nearby! The sisters are proud of their older brother now— he is a college basketball star, and they don't have to contend with him on a daily basis, as they did several years ago. Like Don, they seem to conflict with their parents less as they grow older, although they still complain that their mother "sticks her nose" in their business too often.

Chapter 6

Family Processes and Parent–Adolescent Relationships

Prologue

Hal's Adolescent Independence

These humorous comments by Erma Bombeck suggest the importance of autonomy in the lives of adolescents. To be sure adolescent autonomy is an important dimension of adolescent development. However, we will discover in this chapter that autonomy is a complex, multidimensional concept, and that adolescents continue to show a strong connectedness and attachment to parents as they move toward independence.

In my mind, I always dreamed of the day I would have teenagers.

Young boys would pinch me in the swimming pool and exclaim, "Gee, ma'am, I'm sorry, I thought you were your sensuous daughter, Dale."

The entire family would gather around the piano and sing songs from the King Family album. And on Friday nights, we'd have a family council meeting to decide what flavor of ice cream their father, Ozzie, would bring home from the ice cream parlor.

It never worked out that way. Our teenagers withdrew to their bedrooms on their thirteenth birthday and didn't show themselves to us again until it was time to get married. If we spoke to them in public, they threatened to self-destruct within three minutes. And only once a young boy grinned at me, then apologized quickly with "Gee, sir, I'm sorry. I thought you were Eric Sevareid."

Heaven knows, we tried to make contact. One day when I knew our son Hal was in his bedroom, I pounded on the door and demanded, "Open up! I know you are in there staring at your navel."

The door opened a crack and I charged into my son's bedroom shouting, "Look Hal, I'm your mother. I love you. So does your father. We care about you. We haven't seen you in months. All we get is a glimpse of the back of your head as you slam the door, and a blurred profile as the car whizzes by. We're supposed to be communicating. How do you think I feel when the TV set flashes on the message, 'IT'S ELEVEN O'CLOCK. DO YOU KNOW WHERE YOUR CHILDREN ARE?' I can't even remember *who* they are."

"I'm not Hal," said the kid, peeling a banana. "I'm Henny. Hal isn't home from school yet."

Another time I thought I saw Hal race for the bathroom and bolt the door.

"I know this isn't the place to talk," I shouted through the keyhole, "but I thought you should know we're moving next week. I'm sliding the new address under the door and certainly hope you can join us. I wouldn't have brought it up, but I thought you'd become anxious if you came home and the refrigerator and the hot water were gone."

Source: Bombeck, E. and Keane, B. Just Wait Till You Have Children of Your Own. *New York: Fawcett/Crest, 1971.*

A note came slowly under the door. It read, "I'll surely miss you. Yours very truly, Hartley."

Finally, my husband and I figured out the only way to see Hal was to watch him play football. As we shivered in the stands, our eyes eagerly searched the satin-covered backsides on the bench. Then, a pair of familiar shoulders turned and headed toward the showers.

"Hey, Hal," said his father, grabbing his arm. "Son of a gun. Remember me? I'm Father."

"Father who?" asked the boy.

"You're looking great, Hal. I remember the last time I saw you. You were wearing that little suit with the duck on the pocket. Your mother tells me you're going to be joining us when we move."

"You have me confused, sir," said the boy. "I'm not Hal, I'm Harry."

"Aren't you the guy I saw poking around our refrigerator the other night? And didn't you go with us on our vacation last year?"

"No sir, that was Harold. Incidentally, could you give me a lift to your house? I'm spending the night with Hal."

We thought we saw Hal a few times after that. Once when we were attending a movie and they announced a car bearing our license number had left its parking lights on, a rather thin boy raced up the aisle, but we were never sure.

Another time at a father-son banquet, someone noticed a resemblance between my husband and a boy who hung on the phone all night mumbling, "Aw c'mon, Wilma," but that was also indefinite.

One day in the mail I received a package of graduation pictures and a bill for $76. It was worth it. "Look, dear," I said to my husband, "it's Hal." Our eyes misted as we looked at the clear-skinned boy with the angular jaw and the sideburns that grew down to his jugular vein. It made spotting him at graduation a snap.

"Son of a gun," said his father, punching him on the arm, "if you aren't a chip off the old block, Henny."

"Hartley," I corrected.

"Harry," interjected a mother at my elbow.

"Harold," interjected another voice.

"I'm Hal," said the boy graduate, straightening his shoulders and grimacing.

"Hal who?" we all asked in unison.

Preview

The study of family processes in adolescent development has experienced a flourish of research interest in recent years. There are many issues that are brought up when we consider the role of family processes in adolescent development. Parenting strategies and the nature of parent-adolescent conflict need to be considered. Adolescent autonomy is a major concern, as is the nature of separateness-connectedness of adolescents and their families. Sibling relationships also contribute to adolescent development. And adolescents are growing up in a greater hodgepodge of family structures than at any point in history.

The Nature of Family Processes: A Complex World of Changing Minds, Bodies, and Behaviors

Among the important considerations in studying adolescents and their families are those pertaining to reciprocal socialization and the family system, how adolescents construct relationships and how such relationships influence the development of social maturity, and the role of social and historical influences on the family.

Reciprocal Socialization, Mutual Regulation, and the Family as a System

The adolescent's relationships with other family members involve mutual influences. And there are many aspects to studying the family system of the adolescent.

The Nature of Reciprocal Socialization

For many years, the socialization process between parents and adolescents was viewed as a one-way affair. Adolescents were considered the products of their parents. Willard Hartup (1983) negatively refers to such perspectives as **social-mold theories** to describe the way the adolescent is molded by his environment. In such theories (the radical behavioral position of Skinner being the most prominent example), maturational processes have been given little attention. Instead, the child and adolescent are looked upon as infinitely malleable—parents, as well as other adults, can shape children by effectively managing and manipulating their environments.

To get a better feel for how parent–adolescent relationships should be viewed, consider the following two situations. One dramatically illustrates how the adolescent is influenced by and must adapt to parental influences, and the second readily suggests how parents are influenced by and must adapt to the adolescent. This is the process of **reciprocal socialization,** in which adolescents socialize parents, just as parents socialize adolescents.

The first situation emphasizes the impact of growing up in a single-parent home. Fourteen-year-old Robert is the speaker.

> I never have seen my father. He never married my mother, and she had to quit school to help support us. Maybe my mother and I are better off that he didn't marry her because he apparently didn't love her . . . but sometimes I get very depressed about not having a father, particularly when I see a lot of my friends with their fathers at ball games and such. My father still lives around here, but he has married, and I guess he wants to forget about me and my mother. . . . A lot of times I wish my mother would get married and I could at least have a stepfather to talk with about things and do things with me.

In the second situation, consider how the adolescent influences her parents.

> "Mother, my skating coach says that I have a lot of talent, but it is going to take a lot of lessons and travel to fully develop it." Her mother responds, "Kathy, I just don't know. We will have to talk with your father about it tonight when he gets home from work." That evening, Kathy's father tells his wife, "Look, in order to do that for Kathy I will have to get a second job, or you will have to get a job. There is no way we can afford what she wants with what I make."

The Adolescent's Family as a System of Interacting Individuals

As a social system, the family can be thought of as a constellation of subsystems defined in terms of generation, gender, and role (Feiring and Lewis, 1978). Divisions of labor among family members define particular subunits, and attachments define others. Each family member is a participant in several subsystems, some dyadic (two-sided), some polyadic (many-sided).

Since fathers have become recognized as important socialization agents, it has become obvious that researchers should study more than two-party social interactions (Lamb, 1976). Adolescents interact with more than one parent almost every day of their lives, yet we know very little about how parents serve each other as sources of support, as well as sources of dissatisfaction. One subsystem of the family system that merits special attention is the husband–wife support system. Since many mothers now work and are divorced as well, the nature of the husband–wife support system may be substantially altered.

A major function of family relations from early childhood through adolescence seems to be the provision of a basis for environmental exploration. Exploratory activity brings the child or adolescent into contact with many different people. Through interaction with these contacts, the child or adolescent extends his own competencies in communication and role taking. These associations also result in the direct acquisition of a constellation of unique attitudes and affects—each essential to social adaptation.

Jay Belsky (1981) has developed an organizational scheme of the family system that highlights the possible reciprocal influences that marital relations, parenting, and the behavior or development of the adolescent may have on each other. By following the arrows in figure 6.1, you can see that these three aspects of the family system may have both direct and

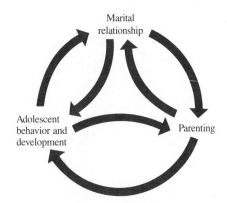

Figure 6.1 Interaction between the adolescent and her parents: Direct and indirect effects.

indirect effects on each other. An example of a direct effect is the influence of the parents' behavior on the adolescent, while an example of an indirect effect is how the relationship between spouses mediates the way a parent acts toward the adolescent.

Third party influences on the nature of dyadic relationships in families have become known as **second-order effects** (Bronfenbrenner and Crouter, 1983). Second-order effects reveal the interconnectedness of parent–adolescent/parent–parent relationships. When a parent–adolescent dyad is embedded in a mother–father–adolescent triad, a parent's role requirements are modified from serving exclusively a parenting function to assuming an additional role as a spouse as well. Thus, the inclusion of the second parent likely transforms the parent–adolescent dyad into a family system made up of marital and parent–adolescent relationships. In one recent investigation (Gjerde, 1985; Gjerde,

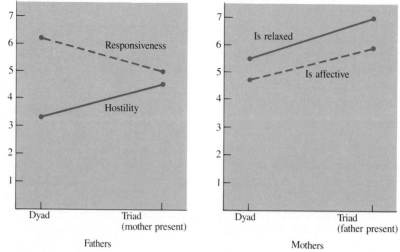

Figure 6.2 Second-order effects: Parent–adolescent relationships in dyadic (without the other parent present) and triadic (with both parents present) situations.

Block, and Block, 1985), forty-four adolescents were observed either separately with their mother and father (dyadic settings) or in the presence of both parents (triadic setting). It was found that the presence of the father seemed to improve mother–son relationships, but the presence of the mother appeared to reduce the quality of father–son relationships (figure 6.2). This may have occurred because the father often takes some of the strain off of the mother in terms of controlling the adolescent (enhances mother–son relationships) and because the mother's presence may reduce father–son interaction (decreases paternal involvement, which often is not high anyway).

The family systems approach to adolescent development has been very popular with therapists who see an adolescent with a serious problem or disturbance. An overview of the family systems approach to therapy is presented in Perspective on Adolescent Development 6.1.

The Construction of Relationships

Very recently a great deal of interest has been generated in understanding how we construct relationships and carry them forward in time. Psychoanalytic theorists always have been interested in understanding how this process occurs in families. However, the current rendition of this process is virtually stripped of psychosexual stage overtones and, further, is not confined to experiences in the first five years of life, as has been the case in classical psychoanalytic theory. The current ideas about the construction of relationships have been influenced by the cognitive revolution in psychology as well as conceptual and research interest in the nature of the attachment process in families. Three aspects of this interest require further examination: continuity and coherence, close relationships and functioning in the wider social world, and carrying forward relationships (Hartup, 1985; Sroufe and Fleeson, 1985).

*P*sychoanalytic theories of development have spawned some unusually creative forms of treatment for children and adolescents with a range of emotional disturbances such as depression, schizophrenia, and phobias. The insight of this perspective was that disturbed behavior is the product of unconscious conflicts that the adolescent cannot release. Even with the shift in focus to culture, as in Erikson's theory, one principle of therapy remained constant: the definition of who "owned" the psychological problem—the adolescent did! The adolescent was typically treated alone, and even when others were known to have contributed to the disturbance (as, for example, an overbearing father), the others were not directly involved in therapy. The adolescent was to work through the problem alone.

Now, a new era of therapists has arrived. Some of them take Freud's notion about the role of the family more seriously, perhaps, than he did. In their view, the family is often the origin of the adolescent's problems. The adolescent doesn't "own" the problems; the whole family does. If the adolescent is disturbed, it is likely the result of other problems in the family. And, whatever their origin, the adolescent's problems must interfere with the lives and interactions of other members of the family. The solution, then, is to treat the whole family, as a unit, during the course of therapy. This perspective, known as the family systems approach, has received critical praise as an important new breakthrough in therapy (e.g., Minuchin, 1974; Napier and Whitaker, 1980).

In a warmly presented narrative account of how one "composite" family weathered this treatment approach, *The Family Crucible,* written by Augustus Napier and Carl Whitaker, offers important insights into this new theory and treatment approach. Here are some of the salient points.

The family is a system. Each member is related to every other member. When one person changes or develops, the whole system changes. Although we may think of one person having a problem in the family, such a perception necessarily oversimplifies what is really going on. Since any change in the system affects the whole system, any problem in it must be viewed as a problem in the way the whole system is working.

The family systems approach to therapy.

There are many levels on which to analyze the family system. There may be dyadic or two-sided relations (for example, mother-father, mother-daughter, father-daughter, brother-sister), triadic or three-sided relations (for example, mother-father-daughter, mother-father-son), or a relation among parts of the whole (for example, mother-father-daughter-son). Each family also learns from and evolves from earlier families—that is, from each set of grandparents, aunts, and uncles. Thus, mothers learn how to "mother" by modeling what their mothers did; likewise, fathers learn to "father" by modeling what their fathers did. (For simplicity, here we are considering the case of a nuclear family that repeats itself over generations. It is easy to generalize the analysis of other family structures as well.)

The process of therapy, then, teaches the members of the family how to analyze their patterns of interaction with one another; how to spot roles they each play, such as "scapegoat"; and how to alter the way they feel about each other when the need to change is great. Thus, the family in Napier and Whitaker's book came to therapy because their adolescent daughter seemed alienated, a bit schizophrenic, and suicidal: "The daughter had a problem." However, the therapy process revealed that the daughter's problems were a reaction to a well-disguised battle between her parents that caught her in the middle.

Close relationships with parents allow the adolescent to function independently in the wider social world.

Continuity and Coherence

Changes in the infant's, child's, and adolescent's behavior do occur, but through all of this change there exists some continuity and systemization as well. There is continuity, for instance, to such close relationships as that involving the mother and the child over time. Some infants, children, and adolescents learn over the course of ten to twenty years that their caregiver will be emotionally available; others come to expect their caregiver to not be very available. What goes on in the close relationships between caregivers and the child/adolescent lead the adolescent to construct a picture of relationships with social objects, as we see next.

Close Relationships and Functioning in the Wider Social World

Our experiences in close relationships, particularly those with parents, serve as bases or resources that allow the child or adolescent to function independently in the wider social world and affect how he or she constructs relationships with others. It has been argued that a secure attachment to parents during infancy likely promotes exploration of the environment by the infant (Ainsworth, 1979; Bowlby, 1969) as well as a positive sense of self (Mahler, 1979). While much less research has been conducted on the nature of the attachment process in adolescence, it would seem that connectedness and attachment to parents serves as an important base for the development of independence and identity (e.g., Cooper and Ayers-Lopez, 1985; Santrock and Sitterle, 1985). A healthy exploration of the widening social world in adolescence likely is enhanced when the adolescent senses that parents are there when needed. And past and current interactions with parents undoubtedly influence the way the adolescent pictures his or her continuing relationship with parents as well as the way the adolescent constructs relationships with peers. More about the coordinated worlds of parents and peers appears later in the chapter as we discuss autonomy, attachment, and separation–connectedness.

Carrying Forward Relationships

Close relationships with parents are important in the development of the adolescent in terms of their function as models or templates that often are carried forward over time to influence the construction of new relationships. Clearly, close relationships do not repeat themselves in an endless fashion over the course of the child's and adolescent's development. And, the quality of any relationship depends to some degree on the specific individual with whom the relationship is formed. However, the nature of earlier relationships that are developed over many years often can be detected in later relationships, both with those same individuals and in the formation of relationships with others at a later point in time. Thus, the nature of parent–adolescent relationships does not just depend on what happens in the relationship during adolescence. Relationships with parents over the long course of childhood are carried forward to influence, at least to some degree, the nature of parent–adolescent relationships. And, the long course of parent–child relationships also could be expected to influence, again at least to some degree, the fabric of the adolescent's peer relationships, friendships, and dating relationships.

In considering the nature of the adolescent's development, it is important not only to evaluate how childhood experiences with parents are carried forward, but it also is valuable to look at the nature of intergenerational relationships as well. As the life-span perspective has taken on greater acceptance among developmental psychologists, researchers have become interested in the transmission of close relationships across generations (Santrock, 1986; Troll, 1985). The middle generation in three generations seems to serve a salient role in the socialization process. For example, the parents of adolescents can be studied in terms of their relationships with their own parents, when they were children and presently, and they can be evaluated in regard to the nature of their relationships with their own adolescents, both when they were children and presently. Life-span theorists argue that the middle-aged parents of adolescents may feel a strong squeeze as they may have to give more help than they receive. Not only are their adolescents reaching the point where they often require considerable financial outputs for college but their parents, whose generation is living longer than past generations, may require financial support from their middle-aged children. In addition to financial help, their aging parents also may need more comfort and affection than earlier in the life cycle.

Now that we have seen the importance of considering the adolescent's family in terms of reciprocal socialization and a system of interacting individuals, as well as the significance of viewing the manner in which the adolescent constructs relationships, we turn our attention to yet another important consideration. As we see next, studying the adolescent and his or her family also involves ideas about the maturation of the adolescent and the maturation of parents.

The Maturation of the Adolescent and the Maturation of Parents

Our overview of biological and cognitive changes suggested that the adolescent is a changing being, particularly in the early adolescent years. Successful parenting requires at least some adaptation to these changes. And, it is important to consider that the parent, as well as the adolescent, is changing as well.

The Adolescent

Let's look at some of the physical, cognitive, and social changes that might call for changes in the way parents relate to the adolescent.

Physical Changes There are universal physical changes in individuals as they move from childhood into the early adolescent years. Pubertal change brings with it dramatic increases in height and weight as well as sexual maturation. By the age of fourteen or fifteen, many adolescents are now as large as or larger than their parents, while some three to five years earlier, they were much shorter and smaller. So, parents now look at eye level or upward as they communicate with the adolescent, no longer being able to look downward and feel a sense of physical power over their offspring. Based on sheer physical size and power, adolescents more so than children are equal to their parents. The sexual maturation of the adolescent also calls for adaptation on the part of the parent. No longer can the son or daughter crawl into bed with an opposite-sex parent and be cuddled. And parents must now deal with questions of sexuality—how much freedom should the adolescent be allowed in dating curfews, if and what kind of sexual information should be given to the adolescent, and how much and how should sexual activity be monitored?

Studies of parent–adolescent relationships are beginning to recognize the importance of following boys and girls through the transition from childhood through puberty and beyond to the later adolescent years. Several recent investigations have revealed that relationships between mothers and sons are most stressful during the apex of pubertal growth, while father–son relationships seem to be less influenced by the son's transition through puberty (Hill, Holmbeck, Marlow, Green, and Lynch, 1985; Steinberg, 1981; Steinberg and Hill, 1978). For example, as shown in figure 6.3, mothers were less satisfied with their sons' participation in family activities during the apex of pubertal change (Hill et al., 1985). And, actual observations of parent–adolescent relationships revealed that the father retains his influence over family decision making throughout the pubertal transition and asserted his dominance by requiring increasing deference by the son. During the pubertal change process, mothers and sons interrupted each other more, explained themselves less, and deferred less to each other. Ultimately though, toward the end of the pubertal change process, as sons have grown much larger and become more powerful,

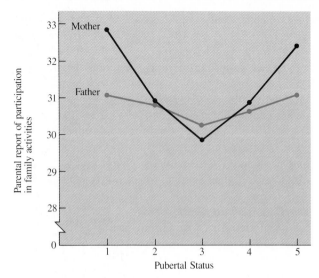

Note: 1 = prepubertal (n=11); 2 = early pubertal (n=34); 3 = apex pubertal (n=33); 4 = postapex pubertal (n = 17); 5 = late pubertal (n=5).

Figure 6.3 **Parents' perception of their son's participation in family activities at five points in puberty.**

Source: Hill, J. P., Holmbeck, G. N., Marlow, L., Green, T. M., & Lynch, M. E. "Pubertal status and parent-child relations in families of seventh-grade boys." Journal of Early Adolescence, 5, 31–44. Reprinted with permission of H.E.L.P. Books, Inc.

mothers were more likely to defer to their sons and less likely to engage in conflict with them than during the apex of pubertal change. Less is known about the pubertal change of girls and the nature of parent–adolescent relationships, although discussion of sex differences in parent–adolescent conflict appears later in the chapter. Clearly, though, it appears that where the adolescent is in the pubertal cycle is to some degree linked with the nature of parent–adolescent relationships.

Cognitive Changes The adolescent, compared to when he or she was a child, can reason in more logical ways with parents. During childhood, a parent may be able to get by with saying, "O.K. That is it. We do it my way or else," and the child conforms. But with increased cognitive skills, the adolescent no longer is likely to accept such a statement as a reason he or she should conform to parental dictates. The adolescent wants to know, often in fine detail, why he or she is being disciplined. And even when the parent gives what to the parent seems to be a logical reason, the adolescent's cognitive sophistication may call attention to a deficiency in the parent's reasoning. Such prolonged bouts of discourse with parents usually do not characterize parent–child relationships, but are a frequent occurrence in parent–adolescent relationships.

In addition to increased logical reasoning skills, the idealistic nature of the adolescent's thought, compared to when he or she was a child, also comes into play in our attempt to understand the nature of parent–adolescent relationships. Parents often are now evaluated vis-a-vis what an ideal parent would be like. The very real interactions with parents, any of which inevitably contain negative interchanges and flaws, are placed next to the schema of what an ideal parent is like in the adolescent's head. Also, as part of their egocentrism, the adolescent's concern with how others view him or her is likely to lead to an overreaction to comments by parents. A mother may comment to her adolescent daughter that she needs a new blouse. The daughter may respond, "What's the matter? You don't think I have good taste? You think I look gross don't you?" The same comment made to the daughter during the late childhood years likely would not have evoked such a response.

Yet another aspect of the changing cognitive world of the adolescent and his or her parents is the expectations they have for each other. Andrew Collins (1985) has described how expectations can influence parent–adolescent relationships. Expectations may be violated because the child is making such rapid changes that lead to the possibility of past behavior of the child being an unreliable predictor of future behavior. For instance, consider the common situation of the preadolescent child who has been compliant and easy to manage. As he or she enters puberty, the child begins to question or seek rationales for parental demands (Maccoby, 1984). Parents often perceive such behavior as resistant and oppositional because it departs from the child's usual compliant behavior and they may respond to the lack of compliance with increased pressure for compliance. In this situation, expectations that were prematurely stabilized in a period of relatively slow developmental change are now lagging behind as behavior of the adolescent is changing more rapidly.

Collins (1985) also gives another example of how violation of expectations can influence parent–adolescent relationships. Consider the situation of the compliant behavior of the child and adolescent. The adolescent may interpret the parent's behavior as unfair or repressive. This sense of unfairness or repression may come about because of experiences in other social settings, such as the peer group or school, where questioning and challenging are more typical forms of communication. Or they may suggest partial, but not fully recognized, ideas about reciprocity and mutuality in parent–adolescent relationships (e.g., Selman, 1980). Thus, the approach by Collins (1985) suggests that parents and adolescents are frequently violating and modifying each other's expectations as they move from childhood to adulthood.

We have discussed several important changes in the adolescent's cognition that may contribute to changes in parent–adolescent relationships—among them, the expanded logical reasoning of the adolescent, the increased idealistic and egocentric thought of the adolescent, and violated expectations (on the part of both the adolescent and parents). Next, we look further at changes in the adolescent, specifically, at social change that may contribute to parent–adolescent relationships.

Social Changes John Hill (1980) has pointed to a number of social changes in the adolescent's world that might contribute to understanding the nature of parent–adolescent relationships. Adolescence usually brings with it new definitions of socially appropriate behavior. In our society, such definitions often are linked with changes in schooling arrangements—transitions to middle or junior high school. The adolescent is required to function in a more anonymous, larger environment with multiple and varying teachers. More work is required and more initiative and responsibility must be in place to pull it off successfully. The social world of adolescents at school is not the only arena likely to influence parent–adolescent relationships. Adolescents, compared to children, spend more time with peers and develop more sophisticated friendships. Further, in the social realm, adolescents begin to push for more autonomy. Parents, then, are called on to adapt to changing worlds of adolescent schooling and peer relations, as well as their movement toward independence in this expanding environment.

The Maturation of Parents

There are some interesting complementarities in the developmental issues confronting both adolescents and their parents (Hill, 1980; Hill, 1985; Steinberg, 1980). The intriguing issues focus on the following beliefs: (a) Marital dissatisfaction is greater when the offspring is an adolescent than a child or an adult, (b) A greater economic burden is placed on parents when they are rearing adolescents, and (c) Reevaluation of occupational achievement often occurs. The parents of adolescents often evaluate whether they have met their youthful aspirations for success they had during earlier years. Further, the parents often look to the future in terms of how much time they have left to accomplish what they want. With regard to career orientation and time perspective, adolescents, however, often look mainly to the future, and do so with unbounded optimism. Adolescents sense that they have an unlimited amount of time to accomplish what they desire. (d) And, health concerns as well as interest in body integrity and sexual attractiveness become prominent themes of the parents of adolescents. Even when their body and sexual attractiveness are not deteriorating, many parents of adolescents perceive that they are. By contrast, adolescents are at or are beginning to reach the peak of their physical attractiveness, strength, and health. Thus, while both the adolescent and his or her parents often show a heightened preoccupation with their bodies, the adolescent's view likely is a more positive one.

It is important to note that the parents of adolescents either are in midlife or are rapidly approaching the middle adulthood years. And, if current trends continue, the parents of adolescents will be even older in the future. As shown in table 6.1, adults are waiting longer to get married, with the median age of marriage changing from 20.8 to 23.0 years for females just in the

Table 6.1 Median age at first marriage

	1970	1984
Men	23.2	25.4
Women	20.8	23.0

1970 to 1984 time frame. And, there currently is a trend for married couples to delay having children so they can stabilize and advance their careers. The upshot of these trends is that the parents of adolescents in the future are likely to be further into the middle adulthood years than in the present. What do we know about how the age of parents influences parent–adolescent relationships? Very little research has been conducted, but several studies reveal some insights. In one set of studies (Nydegger, 1975, 1981; Mitteness and Nydegger, 1982), younger and older fathers were compared. The older fathers seemed to fare better than the younger fathers in some ways—being warmer, communicating better, encouraging more achievement, and showing less rejection. However, the older fathers were less likely to place demands on their children and were less likely to enforce rules.

Sociocultural, Historical Influences on the Family

Family development does not occur in a social vacuum. There are important sociocultural and historical influences that influence the development of the child in the family. Let's look more closely at how the family is embedded in sociocultural and historical contexts.

Changes in the family may be due to great upheavals in a nation such as war, famine, or mass immigration, or it may be due to more subtle transitions in ways of life. The Great Depression in the early 1930s had some negative effects on families. During its height, the depression produced economic deprivation that seemed to heighten adult discontent, depression about living conditions, likelihood of marital conflict, inconsistencies in relations with children, and risk of the father's impairment—heavy drinking, demoralization, and health disabilities (Elder, 1980).

Some more subtle changes in a culture that have significant influences on the family have been described by Margaret Mead (1978). These changes focus on the longevity of the elderly and their role in the family, the urban and the suburban orientation of families and their mobility, television, and a general dissatisfaction and restlessness. Fifty years ago, the older people who survived were usually hearty and still closely linked to the family, often helping to maintain its existence. As more elderly live to an older age, their middle-aged children have been pressed into a caretaking role for their parents or the elderly parents may be placed in a nursing home. Elderly parents may have lost some of their socializing role in the family during the twentieth century as many of their children moved great distances away.

Many of these moves on the part of families were away from farms and small towns to urban and suburban settings. In the small towns and farms, individuals were surrounded by lifelong neighbors, relatives, and friends. Today, neighborhood and extended-family support systems are not nearly as prevalent. Families now move all over the country, often uprooting the child from a school and peer group he or she has known for a considerable length of time. And for many families, it is not unusual for this type of move to occur every year or two, as one or both parents are transferred from job to job.

Television has played a major role in the changing family. Many children who watch television find that parents are too busy working to share this experience with them. Children increasingly have experienced a world their parents are not a part of. Instead of participating in neighborhood peer groups, children have come home after school and plopped down in front of the television set. And television has allowed children and their families to see new ways of life. Lower class families can look into the family lives of the middle-class more readily by simply pushing a button.

Another subtle change in families has been an increase in general dissatisfaction and restlessness. Women became increasingly dissatisfied with their way of life, placing great strain on marriages. With fewer elders and long-term friends close by to help and advise young people during the initial difficult years of marriage and childbearing, marriages began to fracture at the first signs of disagreement. Divorce has become epidemic in our culture. As women moved into the labor market, men simultaneously became restless and looked for stimulation outside of family life. The result of such restlessness and the tendency to divorce and remarry has produced a hodgepodge of family structures with far greater numbers of single parent and stepparent families than ever before in history. Later in the chapter, we will have much more to say about such aspects of the changing social world of the adolescent and the family.

We have considered a number of important aspects of family processes involved in the adolescent's development. A summary of main ideas involved in family processes is presented in Concept Table 6.1. Now we turn our attention to a discussion that virtually every parent of an adolescent is interested in—the nature of parenting techniques and parent–adolescent conflict.

Parenting Techniques and Parent–Adolescent Conflict: It Takes Ten to Fifteen Years to Become an Adult, Not Ten to Fifteen Minutes

We have seen how the expectations of adolescents and their parents often seem to become violated as the adolescent changes dramatically during the course of puberty. Many parents see their child moving from a compliant being to someone who is noncompliant, oppositional, and resistant to parental standards. The tendency on the part of parents often is to clamp down tighter and put more pressure on the adolescent to conform to parental standards. Parents often deal with the

THE NATURE OF FAMILY PROCESSES

Concept	*Processes/related ideas*	*Characteristics/description*
Reciprocal socialization, mutual regulation, and the family as a system	Reciprocal socialization and mutual regulation	Social-mold theories are inaccurate descriptions of adolescent socialization. Rather reciprocal socialization occurs, in which adolescents socialize parents just as parents socialize adolescents. Parents and adolescents engage in a mutual regulation process.
	The family as a system	As a social system, the family can be considered a constellation of subsystems defined in terms of generation, gender, and role. Second-order effects occur when a third party influences dyadic relationships. Recent research reveals that the presence of the father changes mother–adolescent interaction and the presence of the mother modifies father–adolescent interaction. The father seems to serve as an important support in mother–adolescent interaction. The family systems approach has been a popular approach in psychotherapy with adolescents.
The construction of relationships	Development of interest	Influenced by psychoanalytic theory, cognitive theory, and attachment theory.
	Continuity and coherence	While change occurs in development and relationships, there is a continuity and coherence to this development and relationships.
	Close relationships and functioning in the wider social world	Close relationships serve as important bases or resources that allow the child and adolescent to function independently in the complex social world. Close relationships with parents influence how adolescents construct relationships with others, such as with peers.

THE NATURE OF FAMILY PROCESSES

Concept	Processes/related ideas	Characteristics/description
	Carrying forward relationships	Close relationships, particularly those within the family, serve as models or templates that are carried forward in time, often over many years, to influence the construction of new relationships. These relationships can be transmitted intergenerationally as well.
The maturation of the adolescent and the maturation of parents	Maturation of the adolescent	Physical, cognitive, and social changes in the adolescent's development influence parent-adolescent relationships. Physical changes include the rapid maturation of puberty; cognitive changes include the development of logical thought as well as idealism and expectations; and social changes encompass schooling, peers, friendships, and dating as well as independence.
	Maturation of parents	Among the changes in the parents of adolescents that contribute to parent-adolescent relationships are: marital dissatisfaction, economic burdens, career reevaluation and time perspective, and health and bodily concerns.
Sociocultural, historical influences on the family	Great upheavals	Changes in the family may be due to great upheavals such as war, famine, mass immigration, and economic changes, such as the Great Depression.
	More subtle changes	More subtle changes in a culture also influence families. Such changes include the longevity of the elderly and their role in the family, the suburban movement of families and their mobility, television, and a general dissatisfaction and restlessness.

CHEEVERWOOD

by Michael Fry

© 1986 Washington Post Writer's Group, reprinted with permission.

young adolescent as if they expect the adolescent to become a mature being within the next ten to fifteen minutes. Of course, the transition from childhood to adulthood is a long journey with many hills and valleys. Adolescents are not going to conform to adult standards immediately. Parents who recognize that adolescents take a long time "to get it right" may well be able to more competently and calmly deal with adolescent transgressions than parents who demand immediate conformity to parental standards. Yet other parents, rather than placing heavy demands on their adolescents for compliance, do virtually the opposite, letting the adolescent do as he or she pleases in a very permissive manner. As we discuss parent–adolescent relationships, we will discover that neither high intensity demands for compliance, nor an unwillingness to monitor and be involved in the adolescent's development are likely to be wise parenting strategies. Further, we will look at another misperception that parents of adolescents often entertain. Parents often perceive that virtually all conflict with their adolescent is bad. We will discover that a moderate degree of conflict with parents in adolescence is not only virtually inevitable, but may well serve a positive developmental function. Let's now explore some different dimensions of parent–adolescent relationships and parent–adolescent conflict.

Parent–Adolescent Relationships

Parents want their adolescents to grow into socially mature individuals and they often feel a great deal of frustration in their role as parents. Psychologists have long searched for ingredients of parenting that will promote competent social development in their adolescents. For example, in the 1930s the behaviorist John Watson argued that parents were too affectionate with their charges. Early research focused on a distinction between physical and psychological discipline, or between controlling and permissive parenting. More recently, greater precision in unraveling the dimensions of competent parenting has been accomplished. We study four dimensions of parenting styles, evaluating which of these styles seems to promote social competence in adolescents.

Diana Baumrind's (1971) research has revealed that parents should be neither punitive toward their adolescents nor aloof from them, but rather should develop rules and regulations for their adolescents and enforce them. She emphasizes three types of parenting that are associated with different aspects of the child's social behavior: authoritarian, authoritative, and laissez-faire (permissive). More recently, developmental psychologists have argued that permissive parenting comes in two different forms—permissive-indulgent and permissive-indifferent.

Authoritative parenting involves warmth, extensive verbal give-and-take, as well as some control.

	Accepting Responsive Child-centered	Rejecting Unresponsive Parent-centered
Demanding controlling	Authoritative reciprocal High in bidirectional communication	Authoritarian Power assertive
Undemanding low in control attempts	Indulgent	Neglecting, ignoring, indifferent, uninvolved

Figure 6.4   A four-fold scheme of parenting styles.

Authoritarian Parenting

This describes parents who are restrictive, have a punitive orientation, exhort the adolescent to follow their directions, respect work and effort, place limits and controls on the adolescent, with little verbal give and take between the adolescent and the parent. **Authoritarian parenting** is linked with the following social behaviors of the adolescent: an anxiety about social comparison, failure to initiate activity, and ineffective social interaction.

Authoritative Parenting

This form of parenting encourages the adolescent to be independent, but still places limits, demands, and controls on his or her actions. There is extensive verbal give and take, and parents demonstrate a high degree of warmth and nurturance toward the adolescent. **Authoritative parenting** is associated with social competency on the part of the adolescent, particularly self-reliance and social responsibility.

Recently, Eleanor Maccoby and John Martin (1983) revealed a scheme for categorizing parenting styles that involves various combinations of a demanding–undemanding dimension and an accepting–rejecting dimension. As shown in figure 6.4, an authoritarian parent (also called power assertive in the sense that the parent exercises considerable power over the child and/or the child's resources) is demanding and controlling as well as rejecting, unresponsive, and parent-centered. An authoritative parent also is demanding and controlling, but is accepting, responsive, and child-centered. This parenting style is called authoritative-reciprocal by Maccoby and Martin.

Two Forms of Permissive Parenting

Notice that in the fourfold scheme of parenting described by Maccoby and Martin that indulgent parents are undemanding, but accepting and responsive while neglecting parents are also undemanding, but rejecting as well. The **permissive-indulgent pattern** on the whole seems to have more negative than positive effects on adolescents. Consider the parents who are highly involved in their adolescent's life, but allow him or her a great deal of freedom and do not condemn negative behaviors on the part of the adolescent. These adolescents often grow up learning that they get away with just about anything and often show a disregard for rules and regulations. Consider also the **permissive-indifferent parent,** who is very uninvolved in the adolescent's life. This type of parenting consistently has been

Perspective on Adolescent Development 6.2
BETWEEN PARENT AND TEENAGER AND
MAN THE MANIPULATOR

*I*n his best-selling book, *Between Parent and Teenager,* Haim Ginott (1969) details a number of common-sense solutions and strategies for coping with the everyday problems of adolescents. Ginott, in the humanistic tradition, stresses above all else that the key to peaceful coexistence between parents and adolescents is for parents to let go. He says that the adolescent's need is to *not* need parents, and that the parent should resist the need to hold on, even when it seems the most necessary. This attitude, says Ginott, is what parental love for an adolescent is all about.

Relying on catchy phrases like "don't collect thorns" and "don't step on corns," Ginott describes how to let the adolescent become a mature person. Ginott's phrase "don't collect thorns" refers to his belief that parents who constantly detect imperfections in themselves often expect perfection from adolescents. "Don't step on corns" indicates that although all teenagers have a lot of imperfections they are sensitive about (ranging from zits to dimples), they don't need parents to make them acutely aware of such imperfections. Other "Ginottisms" that make sense include the following: "Don't talk in chapters" refers to lecturing rather than sensitive communication; "don't futurize" captures the frequent parental

habit of telling the adolescent he or she won't ever amount to anything in the future; "don't violate his privacy" reminds parents that teens need their own territory to develop their sense of autonomy and identity; "don't emulate his language and conduct" warns parents not to use teenage slang—because most teens resent it; and "accept his restlessness and discontent" reminds parents that adolescence is a period of uncertainty and difficulty. Parents can help by not prying into many of their teenagers' affairs.

Other strategies Ginott recommends for parents of adolescents also focus on the parent's struggle to let go of the adolescent. For example, Ginott advises: "Don't push them into popularity battles," "don't push them into early dating," "consider the feelings of the adolescent," and "don't put down their wishes and fantasies." In regard to the first two suggestions, Ginott describes a young girl whose mother constantly prods her to be the most popular girl in school, and another girl whose mother set up a party for boy–girl pairs of twelve-year-olds. This same mother purchased a padded bra for her daughter when the girl was only eleven.

Ginott talks intelligently and simply about many different situations that result in conflict between parents and teenagers—driving, drinking, drugs, sex, and values are but a few of the many topics for which he suggests coping strategies. His descriptions of conversations between adolescents and parents can provide a useful source

linked to a lack of self-control on the part of adolescents. In sum, a lack of self-control seems to be one of the prominent results of adolescents who experience permissive-indulgent or permissive-indifferent parenting.

There have been many other prescriptions for the parents of adolescents as well. And, you should note that Baumrind (1968) points out that parents likely

need to let go more during adolescence than during childhood. Clearly, there appears to be a belief that competent parenting during adolescence does not involve a punitive orientation with little or no verbal give and take between the parent and the adolescent. And, it may well be that as the individual moves toward the latter part of adolescence, even less directive influence on the part of parents may be helpful in fostering positive parent–adolescent relationships. This does not imply a complete lack of monitoring or connectedness

of information about the real world of parents and teenagers—take a look at some of them and think about whether you would handle them in the way Ginott suggests.

Everett Shostrum, author of *Man, the Manipulator: The Inner Journey from Manipulation to Actualization* (1967), believes that to help teenagers become competent adults, parents have to "let go" when they most want to hold on. Shostrum details conversations between parents and teenagers to illustrate how most parents are not self-actualized in the way they communicate with their teenagers.

Shostrum describes the ways teenagers manipulate their parents and vice versa. Teens say, "You don't love me or you would————," "Everybody else is going," and "I'm going to quit school if you don't————." They play one parent against the other, blackmail, and mope to get what they want from their parents. Parents manipulate by making threats and comparisons: "Bob does better in school than you do," "If you loved me you wouldn't do that," "I'll tell your father when he gets home." Teenagers see interaction with parents as a competition. The game is between the "top dog" (the parent) and the "underdog" (the adolescent). Many encounters with parents end up as minor skirmishes.

Shostrum mentions several specific examples of competitive parent–teen encounters. Steve doesn't want to wear a particular coat his mother tells him he has to wear, and Mary tries to coerce her parents into letting her go out on a date Saturday night. In most cases like these, the parents and the teenagers assume an "I win–you lose" strategy. Shostrum says that the key for parents is to turn such battles into mutual win–win experiences—sharing love and respect for each other's feelings.

The primary goal of the self-actualized parent is to assist rather than inhibit the adolescent in channeling his or her feelings into competent behavior. Parents must recognize that their teenagers are going to try to battle with them and realize that this is the teens' way of trying to adapt to a frustrating world. As part of the actualizing process, parents should create an atmosphere in which teenagers feel comfortable about discussing their true feelings, and in which the parents feel secure about telling the teenager their own feelings as well.

Shostrum goes on to say that teenagers are not as bad as many parents think they are. And, he says, if parents will stay out of the picture, most teenagers will turn into mature, competent young adults. Above all else, Shostrum says, parents must recognize and accept that the teenager is a manipulating individual trying to become a self-actualizing one.

on the part of parents. Rather, as adolescents move closer to adulthood, when the adolescent is showing responsibility and maturity, parents likely need to let go more than they sometimes would like to. The point of being able to let go of the adolescent is made nicely in the comments described in Perspective on Adolescent Development 6.2, where we present the recommendations of several prominent psychologists who have influenced the way counselors deal with adolescents and their parents.

Parent–Adolescent Conflict

Few topics about adolescent development generate as much interest among parents as the nature of conflict with their adolescents. The stereotypical view of such conflict suggests that such conflict is extensive and intense. Let's now see just how pervasive or limited such conflict between parents and adolescents really is.

"I want to talk to you about the way you're frittering away your life."

"Oh, I know what you're going to say: 'You just don't understand.' Well, I understand this, my friend. You're headed down a dead-end street!"

"I'm talking about a sense of purpose. You've got to look for direction to find direction."

Background of Interest and Developmental Course

There appears to be some increase in conflict between parents and adolescents during early adolescence, although this conflict is often not as severe as many parents expect it to be and not as intense and pervasive as the media have sometimes pictured it. Many different reasons have been given as to why there is an increase in parent–adolescent conflict during early adolescence—they include biological changes in levels of aggression (Hall, 1904), the appearance of adult sexuality (Freud, 1905, 1953; Blos, 1962), the push for independence (Ausubel, Montemayor, and Svajian, 1977), and the quest for identity (Erikson, 1968). Other explanations focus on the difficulties parents may have as they enter midlife (Hill, 1980a,b; Steinberg, 1980), and the mother's unwillingness to let her adolescent loose from the family circle. Yet other explanations emphasize the disequilibrium that erupts in the family social system with the onset of adolescence, an upheaval that replaces the relatively smooth-functioning family system that existed during childhood. Further reasons involve the cognitive changes in the adolescent described earlier in the chapter—logical thought, idealism and egocentrism, and violated expectations. In reviewing the existing research on parent–adolescent conflict, Raymond Montemayor (1982a) concluded that conflict increases during early adolescence, is reasonably stable during middle adolescence, and declines when the adolescent moves away from home. But what kinds of conflict are involved?

Kinds of Conflict between Parents and Adolescents

Most arguments between parents and their adolescents focus on normal, everyday events, such as schoolwork, social life, peers and friends, home chores, disobedience, sibling fights, and personal hygiene (Montemayor, 1982b). While many of these conflicts are a result of the adolescent's push for independence, they

"I suppose it's my fault. What kind of example have I been, right? Well, I'm not ashamed of the modest success I've had with my materialistic orientation."

"O.K., so I suppose I'm wrong. Put down that paper and tell me how I've failed."

Drawing by Saxon; © 1970 The New Yorker Magazine, Inc.

also are often a product of the parents' continuing efforts to teach their offspring to delay gratification and conform to a set of societal and family rules and regulations.

In one investigation of parent–adolescent conflict (Montemayor, 1982b), sixty-four high school sophomores were interviewed at their homes on three randomly selected evenings during a three-week period. The youth were asked to tell about the events of the previous day, including any conflicts they had with their parents. Conflict was defined as "either you teased your parent or your parent teased you; you and your parent had a difference of opinion; one of you got mad at the other; you and your parent had a quarrel or an argument; or one of you hit the other." During a period of 192 days of tracking the sixty-four adolescents, an average of sixty-eight arguments with parents was reported representing a rate of .35 arguments with parents per day or about one argument every three days. The average length of these arguments was about eleven minutes. The adolescents reported that most of the disagreements were moderately upsetting. Also, most conflicts were with mothers rather than fathers, and the majority were between girls and their mothers.

There is an increasing consensus that greater conflict characterizes the nature of parent–adolescent relationships than parent–child relationships. The kind of conflicts described by Montemayor, many of which involve interpersonal intrusions, do not reach the proportions suggested by G. Stanley Hall's *sturm und drang*. The increase in conflict described is of a moderate degree, not a tumultuous kind. So, parents should not be alarmed when adolescents do not conform to their standards and push away from such standards; however, as we see next, intensive, prolonged conflict with parents has a negative impact on adolescent development.

Prolonged, Intense Conflict

A high degree of conflict between parents and their adolescents is not healthy for the adolescent's psychological growth. For example, physical abuse of adolescents by parents may be the culmination of intense conflict and turmoil in parent–adolescent relationships (e.g., Garbarino, 1980). High levels of parent–adolescent conflict also have been linked to adolescents moving away from home (Gottlieb and Chafetz, 1977) and joining religious cults (Ullman, 1982). Adolescent girls who report that their relationships with their parents are highly stressful are more likely to marry early (Moss and Gingles, 1959) or become pregnant (McHenry, Walters, and Johnson, 1979) than classmates who report a low degree of conflict with their parents. Adolescents who drop out of school report more conflict with their parents than do those who graduate (Bachman, Green, and Wirtanen, 1971). Many juvenile delinquents report a high degree of conflict with their parents (e.g., Duncan, 1978), and parent–adolescent conflict has been associated with the adolescent's use of a variety of drugs (e.g., Kandel, Dessler, and Margulies, 1978). Thus, high levels of parent–adolescent conflict are linked with a wide-ranging set of problems and disturbances in adolescence. The particular form of problem behavior is likely influenced by a complex set of personal, family, and peer factors.

It is possible that an intense, prolonged degree of parent–adolescent conflict causes these adolescent problems, but it also is possible that many of these problems had their origins before the onset of adolescence. It is the belief of Albert Bandura and Richard Walters (1959) that most serious adolescent problems can be traced to circumstances that existed before adolescence. Simply because the child is much smaller than the parents, the parents may be able to suppress oppositional behavior. But, by adolescence, some individuals have grown as large or larger than their parents—and with increased size and strength comes an increase in indifference to parental dictates. Consider the following case:

Interviewer   What sort of things does your mother object to your doing when you are out with your friends?

Boy   She don't know what I do.

Interviewer   What about staying out late at night?

Boy   She says, "Be home at eleven o'clock." I'll come home at one.

Interviewer   How about using the family car?

Boy   No. I wrecked mine, and my father wrecked his a month before I wrecked mine, and I can't even get near his. And I got a license and everything. I'm going to hot wire it some night and cut out.

Interviewer   How honest do you feel you can be to your mother about where you've been and what things you have done?

Boy   I tell her where I've been, period.

Interviewer   How about what you've done?

Boy   No. I won't tell her what I've done. If we're going to have a beer bust, I'm not going to tell her. I'll tell her I've been to a show or something.

Interviewer   How about your father?

Boy   I'll tell him where I've been, period.

Thus, in a minority of parent–adolescent relationships, conflict becomes prolonged and intense, in some cases being carried forward from childhood. One estimate of the percentage of adolescents who experience prolonged and intense conflict with parents is between fifteen and twenty percent (Montemayor, 1982a). While this figure represents a minority of adolescents, it suggests that between four and five million American families encounter serious, highly stressful parent–adolescent conflict.

How might a moderate increase in parent-adolescent conflict have a positive developmental function?

with your parents more and disagreed with their standards as well on more than one occasion. Was this healthy for your development? While you were arguing and disagreeing with your parents, they likely did not think so. However, such argumentation and disagreement may well serve a positive developmental function that promotes independence and identity on the part of the adolescent. This point has been made by neopsychoanalytic theorists such as Peter Blos (1962), whose views will be aired later when we discuss independence. One recent investigation (Cooper, Grotevant, Moore, and Condon, 1982) also documents the role of a moderate increase in parent-adolescent conflict in terms of identity development. Adolescent identity exploration, the pursuit of alternatives in roles, was positively related to the frequency with which the adolescents expressed disagreement with parents during discussions. Within some normal range, then, conflict with parents seems to be psychologically healthy for the adolescent's development. A virtually conflict-free relationship may signal an adolescent's fear of separation, exploration, and independence.

We have discussed many different ideas about parenting techniques and parent-adolescent conflict. A summary of main ideas about parenting techniques and parent-adolescent conflict is presented in Concept Table 6.2. Next, the adolescent's independence as well as his or her continued connectedness and attachment to parents are described.

The Moderate Increase in Parent-Adolescent Conflict and Its Positive Developmental Function

The majority of you reading this book did not experience parent-adolescent relationships that were steeped in conflict over prolonged periods of time. However, as you think back and try to reconstruct your relationships with parents as you moved from the elementary school years through early adolescence, you likely recall that your relationships with parents seemed to be more abrasive in the seventh to ninth grades than they were in the elementary school years. You likely argued

Autonomy and Attachment/Connectedness: The Coordinated Worlds of Parents and Adolescents

Historically, there has been a much greater interest in autonomy during adolescence than in attachment. Recently, there has been considerable interest in how autonomy and attachment are not isolated from each other: rather adolescents and their parents and peers live in a coordinated social world that not only requires consideration of autonomy and separation, but of connectedness as well.

Concept Table 6.2

PARENTING TECHNIQUES AND PARENT-ADOLESCENT CONFLICT

Concept	Processes/related ideas	Characteristics/description
Parenting techniques	Authoritarian parenting	Describes parents who are restrictive, have a punitive orientation, respect work and effort, and place limits and controls on the adolescent with little verbal give-and-take. Linked with anxiety about social comparison, failure to initiate activity, and ineffective social interaction.
	Authoritative	Encourages the adolescent to be independent, but still places limits on his or her actions. There is extensive verbal give-and-take and warmth. Is associated with social competence on the part of the adolescent, particularly self-reliance and responsibility.
	Two forms of permissive parenting	Permissive-indulgent parents are often highly involved with their adolescents, but rarely place limits on their behavior. Permissive-indifferent parents are very uninvolved with the adolescent and similarly place few or no restrictions on behavior. Both types of permissive parenting are associated with a lack of self-control on the part of the adolescent.
	Other comments	Too often parents handle the adolescent's misbehavior as if he or she will become an adult overnight without thinking about how the transition from childhood to adulthood takes many years. As the individual moves through late adolescence, the wise parent will let go more while still monitoring the adolescent's development and maintaining a strong connectedness with the adolescent.

The Nature of Adolescent Autonomy

The increased independence that typifies adolescence is labeled as rebellious by some parents, but in many instances the adolescent's push for autonomy has little to do with the adolescent's feelings toward her parents. A psychologically healthy family will adjust to the adolescent's push for independence by treating her in more adult ways and including her more in family decision making. A psychologically unhealthy family will often remain locked into power-oriented parent control and move even more heavily toward an authoritarian posture in its relationships with the adolescent.

The adolescent's quest for autonomy and a sense of responsibility creates puzzlement and conflict for many parents. Parents begin to see their teenagers slipping away from their grasp. Often the urge is to take stronger control as the adolescent seeks autonomy and responsibility for himself. Heated emotional exchanges may ensue, with either side calling names, making threats, and doing whatever seems necessary to gain control. Often, parents are frustrated because they expected their teenager to heed their advice, to want to

PARENTING TECHNIQUES AND PARENT-ADOLESCENT CONFLICT

Concept	Processes/related ideas	Characteristics/description
Parent-adolescent conflict	Background of interest and developmental course	Psychologists have been interested in parent-adolescent conflict for many years. Hall and Freud, for example, believed such conflict was highly intense and related to biological change. More recently, many other ideas have been offered to explain parent-adolescent conflict, including various physical, cognitive, and social matters. Parent-adolescent conflict does seem to be greater than conflict between parents and children. Parent-adolescent conflict also seems to be greater in early adolescence than late adolescence.
	Kinds of conflict	Conflict between parents and adolescents can range from minor daily squabbles to intense, prolonged arguments that continue for years. It seems that the kind of conflict most parents and adolescents encounter with each other is of a moderate nature.
	Prolonged, intense conflict	A high degree of conflict with parents over many years is unhealthy for the adolescent's development. Such conflict is associated with a number of adolescent problems. Such conflict often does not emerge just in adolescence, but has a long history with childhood antecedents.
	The positive developmental function of moderate conflict	The moderate increase in parent-adolescent conflict that characterizes early adolescence likely serves the positive developmental function of increasing the adolescent's identity and independence.

spend time with his family, and to grow up to do what is right. To be sure, they anticipated that their teenager would have some difficulty adjusting to the changes adolescence brings, but few parents are able to accurately imagine and predict just how strong the adolescent's desire will be to be with his peers, and how much he will want to show that it is he, not they, who is responsible for his success or failure. As discussed in Perspective on Adolescent Development 6.3, some adolescents show such a strong desire to be away from parents that they leave home.

Trying to define adolescent autonomy is more complex and elusive than it might seem at first. Think about autonomy for a moment. For most people, the term connotes self-direction and independence. But what does it really mean? Is it an internal personality trait that consistently characterizes the adolescent's immunity from parental influence? Is it the ability to make responsible decisions for oneself? Does autonomy imply consistent behavior in all areas of adolescent life, including school, finances, dating, and peer relations? What are the relative contributions of peers and other adults to the development of the adolescent's autonomy?

Perspective on Adolescent Development 6.3
RUNAWAYS—YOUTH WHO FLEE

Her name was Barbara and she came from the hills of West Virginia. She was homely looking, naive, and not very well socialized. A smooth-talking New York pimp told her she was "foxy" and gave her the name "Country Roads." He broke her into a prostitute's life on the streets of New York. One evening she was stabbed to death by a drunk customer who demanded some things of her she didn't want to do.

Sammy was fourteen years old, a handsome, blue-eyed blond. An older man in Chicago became a father figure to him, in many ways replacing the father Sammy had never had. The older man was, in fact, one of the first adult males to show considerable interest in Sammy. But after repeated, abusive homosexual assaults, Sammy was found by the police lying unconscious in an alley.

Both Barbara and Sammy were runaways. While many runaways are not exposed to the worst elements of street life, as Barbara and Sammy were, these two examples nevertheless illustrate dangers runaways may encounter. Why do these adolescents run away from their homes? Mary-Anne Raphael and Jenifer Wolf (1974) suggest several reasons. Generally, runaways are very unhappy at home. The reasons many of them leave seem legitimate by almost anyone's standards. When they run away, they usually don't leave a clue to their whereabouts—they just disappear.

Many runaways are from families in which one of their parents or another adult beats them or sexually exploits them. Their lives may be in danger daily. Their parents may be drug addicts or alcoholics. In some cases, the family may be so poor that the parents are unable to feed and clothe their teenagers adequately. The parents may be so overburdened by their material inadequacies that they fail to give their adolescents the attention and understanding they need. So the teenager hits the streets in search of the emotional and material rewards he is not getting at home.

But runaways are not all from our society's lower class. Teenage lovers, confronted by parental hostility toward their relationship, may decide to run off together and make it on their own. Or the middle-class teenager may decide that he has seen enough of his hypocritical parents—people who try to make him live by one set of moral standards, while they live by a loose, false set of ideals. Another teen may live with parents who constantly bicker. Any of these adolescents may decide that she would be happier away from home.

Running away often is a gradual process, as the adolescent begins to spend less time at home and more time on the streets or with his peer group. His parents may be telling him that they really want to see him, to understand him; but the runaway often feels he isn't understood at home, and that his parents care much more about themselves than about him.

It is clear that adolescent autonomy is *not* a unitary personality dimension that consistently comes out in all behaviors (Hill and Holmbeck, in press). For example, in one investigation (Psathas, 1957), high school students were asked twenty-five questions about their independence from their families. Four distinct patterns of adolescent autonomy emerged from analyses of the high school students' responses to the questions. One dimension was labeled "permissiveness in outside activities," and was represented by questions such as

"Do you have to account to parents for the way you spend your money?" A second dimension was called "permissiveness in age-related activities" and was reflected in questions such as "Do your parents help you buy your clothes?" A third independent aspect of adolescent autonomy was referred to as "parental regard for judgment," indicated by responses to items like "In family discussions, do your parents encourage you to give your opinion?" And a fourth dimension was characterized as "activities with status implications," and was indexed by parental influence on choice of occupation.

Regardless of the causes of the adolescent's decision to run away from home, some provision must be made for his or her physical and psychological well-being. In recent years, nationwide hotlines and temporary shelters for runaways have been established. However, there are still too few of these shelters, and often there is a noted lack of professional psychological help for the runaways at such shelters.

One exception is the temporary shelter in Dallas, Texas, called Casa de los Amigos (house of friends). At the Casa, there is room for thirteen runaways who are provided with the necessities of life as well as medical and legal assistance. In addition, a professional staff of thirteen includes counselors and case managers, assisted by VISTA volunteers and high school and college interns. Each runaway is assigned a counselor, and group discussion sessions are held each day to expose the youth to each other's feelings. Whenever possible, the counselors explore the possibility of working with the runaways' families to see if there are ways that all of the family members can learn to help each other in more competent ways than in the past. It is hoped that more centers like Casa de los Amigos will appear in cities around the United States, so that runaways will not meet the fates that Sammy and Barbara encountered.

Running away from home is often based on a long, gradual set of circumstances developing over many years.

Further support for the importance of considering adolescent autonomy as multidimensional comes from a recent investigation of college freshmen and sophomores between the ages of eighteen and twenty-one (Moore, 1985). At issue was the nature of parent–adolescent separation when adolescents leave home. Eight factors reflected the diversity of how late adolescents viewed leaving home: autonomy (movement toward adult status, making independent decisions), emotional detachment (feelings of not belonging or not being close), financial independence, separate residence (moving to an apartment and not living with parents in the summer), disengagement (parents no longer telling the individual what to do, being physically away), school affiliation, starting a family, and graduation. Adolescent autonomy, then, is not a unitary phenomenon, but a summary label for a variety of adolescent interests, behaviors, thoughts, and feelings.

Parent Attitudes

There have been a number of investigations focused on the relationship between parental attitudes and the adolescent's development of autonomy. Researchers have attempted to obtain information of this sort through various strategies, including having parents fill out surveys, interviewing adolescents and/or parents about the parents' attitudes and the ways the parents deal with adolescent problems, and actually presenting discussion problems to parents in the presence of their adolescents. To obtain valid information about adolescents, it is necessary to use a variety of information-collecting methods. While many individual studies of parental attitudes and behaviors in relation to adolescent autonomy have included only a limited number of methods, there are some very consistent agreements across different studies that have used different data sources. Parents who adopt authoritarian decision-making strategies in dealing with their adolescent sons and daughters have adolescents who show little autonomy. Whether the adolescent's self-perceptions are sampled, whether her confidence in her decision making is evaluated, or whether her initiative in joining her parents in a mutual decision-making process is observed, the same conclusion about the relationship between adolescent autonomy and parenting strategies is evident (Hill and Steinberg, 1976).

For example, in an investigation of value independence by Strodtbeck (1958), male adolescents and their parents were queried separately about their values. While there were few links between adolescent and parental values, there was a strong association between the father's dominance in the family and the son's belief in his ability to control himself and his world (what is now referred to as an internal locus of control). In a cross-cultural study of adolescents and their families, further documentation was obtained for the relation between authoritarian parenting and lack of autonomy in adolescents (Kandel and Lesser, 1969). It was revealed that the structure of the average American family is much more authoritarian than the structure of a typical family in Denmark. This difference in family structure should indicate that Danish adolescents are generally more autonomous than their American counterparts.

While there is agreement that an authoritarian family structure restricts the adolescent's development of autonomy, there is not as much consistency in pinpointing the parenting practices that increase autonomy. Some investigations have found that a permissive parenting strategy allows the adolescent to become more independent (Elder, 1968). Others suggest that a democratic parenting strategy is best (Kandel and Lesser, 1969). While investigators vary in how they define permissive and democratic parenting techniques, in most instances a permissive strategy generally entails little parental involvement and fewer parental standards. By contrast, a democratic strategy usually consists of equal involvement on the part of parents and adolescents, with the parents having the final authority to set limits on their teenagers. When the overall competence and adjustment of the adolescent is evaluated (rather than just autonomy) an even more clearcut advantage can be attributed to democratic over permissive strategies of parenting.

In summary, adolescence is a period of development when the individual pushes for autonomy (or the perception that she has control over her behavior) and gradually develops the ability to take that control. This ability may be acquired through appropriate adult reactions to the adolescent's desire for control. At the onset of adolescence, the average person does not have the knowledge to make appropriate or mature decisions in all areas of his life. As he pushes for autonomy, the wise adult will relinquish control in areas where the adolescent can make mature decisions and help the adolescent to make reasonable decisions in areas where his knowledge is more limited. Gradually, the adolescent will acquire the ability to make mature decisions on his own.

Developmental Views of Autonomy

Two prominent views of adolescent autonomy have been proposed—one by David Ausubel, the other by Peter Blos.

Satellization–Desatellization

David Ausubel's theory of adolescent autonomy (Ausubel, Montemayor, and Svajian, 1977) emphasizes the importance of parent–child relationships in the adolescent's growth toward maturity. Ausubel theorizes that parent–child interactions transform the helpless, submissive infant into an independent adult who monitors his or her own life.

During infancy, parents cater to their children's needs and demands. Later, parents expect children to begin to do things for themselves—for example, use the toilet, pick up their toys, control their tempers, and so forth. However, as they develop cognitively, children begin to realize that they are not completely autonomous from their parents. This perception creates some conflict for the child and may lead to a crisis wherein her self-esteem is threatened. One way the child can resolve this conflict is through what Ausubel calls **satellization.** This simply means that the child gives up her sense of self-power and the perception that she can do everything for herself. The result is that the child accepts her dependence on her parents.

However, Ausubel believes that many parents are not capable of developing or maintaining a satellizing relationship with their children. For satellization to occur, children must perceive that their parents love them unconditionally and entrust their care to their parents' hands. Two parenting styles that do not produce satellization are **overvaluation** and **rejection.** When parents overvaluate, they continually interact with their children as if the children are in control. An example is the parent who lives vicariously through the child and hopes that the child will accomplish things he didn't—such as becoming a baseball player or a doctor. When parents reject, they view the child as an unwanted part of their existence. The child's needs are served unwillingly and only if necessary. Love and acceptance are absent, or at least are perceived as being absent by the child.

As the child approaches adolescence, satellization is eventually replaced by **desatellization**—breaking away and becoming independent from parents. Total self-rule is not achieved in desatellization. Instead, the adolescent achieves a preparatory phase wherein his potential separation from parental rule begins to develop. When final desatellization is reached, an individual has secure feelings about himself and does not demonstrate the need to prove himself. He shows strong exploratory tendencies and focuses his energies on tasks and problem solving rather than self-aggrandizement. The desatellized individual also views failure as a learning situation rather than as a source of frustration.

Other desatellization mechanisms may occur during adolescence that are unlike the competent form of desatellization just described. In many instances, however, the other mechanisms may be preliminary steps in the adolescent's attainment of the final stage of desatellization. One of these preliminary stages is called **resatellization** by Ausubel. In resatellization, the individual's parents are replaced by other individuals or a group. Resatellized individuals abdicate their identities to their spouse's identity, or to the identity of a fraternity, sorority, or other social group. As a permanent solution to self–other relationships, resatellization can be detrimental to the adolescent's development. But as a temporary solution, it can provide a testing ground for the development of a more complete, autonomous form of desatellization (Berzonsky, 1978).

Individuation

Peter Blos (1962), borrowing from Margaret Mahler's ideas about the development of independence during early childhood, introduced the concept of individuation to the study of adolescence. Like Mahler, Blos believes that there is a critical sharpening of the boundaries of the adolescent's self as distinct from others, particularly parents. Sometimes Blos refers to adolescence as the **second individuation crisis,** the first being the striving for independence during the second year of life. During the second individuation, Blos believes it is critical for adolescents to gain difference and distance from parents to transcend infantile ties to them. Individuation during adolescence is defined as a sharpened sense of one's distinctness from others, a heightened awareness of one's self-boundaries. Blos (1967) stresses that individuation in adolescence means that the individual now takes increasing responsibility for what he does and what he is, rather than depositing this responsibility on the shoulders of those under whose influence and tutelage he has grown up. Blos' ideas about individuation are reflected in the comments of Debbie, a girl in late adolescence:

> Up to a certain age, I believed everything my parents said. Then, in college, I saw all these new ideas and I said, "Okay, now I'm going to make a new Debbie which has nothing to do with my mother and father. I'm going to start with a clean slate," and what I started to put on it were all new ideas. These ideas were opposite to what my parents believed. But slowly, what's happening is that I'm adding on a lot of the things which they've told me and I'm taking them as my own and I'm coming more together with them. (Josselson, 1973, p. 37)

Debbie's thinking reflects a now commonly held belief about adolescents and their parents. While many adolescents seem to be rejecting their parents and attempting to pull away from them, most adolescents still retain a fundamentally positive, valuing, close, and warm relationship with their parents (e.g., Douvan and Adelson, 1966; Offer, 1969). Indeed, today many adolescents complain that they do not get to spend enough time with their parents (although they often want to spend the time at their own convenience) and wish they had better relationships with their parents. Our following discussion reveals in greater depth how it is erroneous to view adolescent autonomy apart from a connectedness with parents.

Attachment, the Coordinated Worlds of Parents and Peers, and Connectedness

Adolescents do not simply move away from parental influence into a decision-making process all their own. There is continued connectedness to parents as adolescents move toward autonomy.

Attachment in Adolescence

Attachment theorists (e.g., Ainsworth, 1979; Bowlby, 1969; Sroufe and Fleeson, 1985) have argued that secure attachment is central to the infant's relationship with its caregiver. By **secure attachment** is meant the positive bond that develops between the infant and the caregiver. This bond is believed to promote the healthy exploration of the world because the caregiver provides a secure base to which the infant can return if stressors are encountered. By contrast, **insecure attachment** refers to relationships between parents and infants in which the infant either avoids the caregiver or is ambivalent toward her. This type of anxious attachment to the caregiver is believed to be associated with incompetent behavior on the part of the infant.

It may well be that secure attachment is important in understanding the nature of the adolescent's as well as the infant's development. A secure attachment in infancy and childhood likely is carried forward to influence the adolescent's continuing relationships with parents. And a continuing secure attachment in adolescence likely promotes the healthy exploration of the

Adolescents who are securely attached to their parents are more satisfied with their lives and have higher self-esteem.

environment, including peer, friendship, and dating relationships, as well as identity development. Adolescents who do not sense there is a predictable home base that can be returned to in times of considerable stress are more likely to pursue autonomy in an unhealthy manner and possibly develop a negative rather than a positive identity.

There have been very few investigations of the nature of secure attachment in adolescents and its link to adolescent adjustment. One study (Armsden and Greenberg, 1982), however, did investigate the possibility that secure attachment to parents might be associated with healthy adjustment in late adolescence.

In this study, 179 individuals aged sixteen to twenty years were asked to describe the nature of their relationships with parents by indicating the extent a number of statements characterized such relationships. For example, they were asked the extent to which their parents respect their feelings, the degree to which parents respect the adolescent's judgment, how much the individual can talk to his or her parents about problems, and the likelihood that when parents know something is bothering the adolescent they will ask him or her about it. In particular, the element of trust in relationships between adolescents and parents was weighed heavily in assessing secure attachment. In addition to assessing secure and insecure attachment, the self-esteem and life satisfaction of the adolescents also were evaluated. As predicted, adolescents who were securely attached to their parents had higher self-esteem and life satisfaction than their insecurely attached counterparts. Let's look further at the coordinated worlds of parents and peers as we see further connectedness with parents rather than complete separation.

The Coordinated Worlds of Parents and Peers

In the investigation just described (Armsden and Greenberg, 1982), attachment to peers also was assessed, along with attachment to parents. It was found that adolescents who were securely attached to parents also were more likely to show a secure pattern of attachment to peers. For example, forty-five percent of the adolescents who were securely attached to parents were also securely attached to peers, while only sixteen percent of the securely attached parent group of adolescents showed insecure attachment with peers (note that not all adolescents could be clearly categorized as either securely or insecurely attached to parents or peers).

Both parents and peers have continuing important influences throughout adolescence.

Another investigation (Brittain, 1963) focusing on adolescent autonomy, also revealed the continuing importance of both parents and peers in the adolescent's development. Adolescents were queried about whether they were influenced more by their peers or their parents in a variety of contexts, such as taking different classes at school, selecting different styles of clothing, or choosing to decline or accept a part-time job offer. As you might anticipate, in some situations the adolescents chose to adhere to the wishes of their friends, while in other contexts they chose to rely on their parents' advice. For example, when decisions involved basic values and vocation orientations, they were more likely to listen to their parents; but when peer activities were involved, they were more likely to accede to the influence of their friends.

As can be seen, adolescents and their parents live in separate, but coordinated worlds. As Willard Hartup (1979) concluded,

"Family relations and peer relations constitute similar sociobehavioral contexts in some ways and different ones in others. Children may not conceive of separate normative worlds until early adolescence, because child associates are not used extensively as normative models before that time (Emmerich, Goldman, and Shore, 1971). But the family system and the peer system elicit distinctive socioemotional activity many years before these normative distinctions are made. The complex interrelations between the family and peer systems thus work themselves out over long periods of time." (Hill, 1980; Hartup, 1979, pp. 947–48)

Connectedness of Adolescents and Parents

We have seen that the worlds of parent–adolescent relationships and peer relationships are distinct, but coordinated. A recent review of parent–adolescent and peer relationships by Catherine Cooper and Susan Ayers-Lopez (1985) provides further insight into the connectedness of these worlds. They stress that early models of adolescents and their relationships emphasized the differences and distinctiveness of parent and peer worlds. Traditionally, adolescents have been described as attempting to separate themselves from their parents and, at the same time, engage themselves with peers. The process of separation characteristically has been studied in relation to parents, and engagement and connectedness has been evaluated almost exclusively among peers. Cooper and Ayers-Lopez argue that this is an artificial distinction and an oversimplification of the complex, coordinated relationships of adolescents with parents and peers. They go on to describe the ideas of ethologist Robert Hinde (1983), who emphasized a distinction between interactions, relationships, and groups. Let's look more closely at this distinction and examine further the connectedness of parent and peer worlds.

Hinde believes that **interactions** involve patterns of communications that occur between persons who may or may not be intimates. **Relationships,** by contrast, occur between people with enduring bonds to each other, often marked by histories of past interactions as well as commitments to the future. **Groups** carry with them normative expectations about acceptable and unacceptable aspects of behavior and influence both the interactions and relationships of group members (Hartup, 1985).

For example, one key aspect of adolescent peer relations can be traced to basic decisions by parents at the group level. Parents' choices of neighborhoods, churches, schools, and their own friends influence the pool from which their adolescents might select possible friends. For instance, choice of schools can lead to differences in grouping policies, academic and extracurricular activities, and classroom organization (e.g., open, teacher-centered, and so forth). In turn, such factors affect which students their adolescent is likely to meet, their purpose in interacting, and eventually who become friends. For instance, classrooms in which teachers encourage more cooperative peer interchanges have fewer isolates (Epstein, in press).

At the interaction level, parents may model or coach their adolescents in ways of relating to peers. For instance, in one investigation (Rubin and Sloman, 1984) parents revealed they recommended specific strategies to their children in their relationships with peers. For example, parents told their children how to mediate disputes or how to become less shy with others. They also encouraged them to be tolerant and to resist peer pressure. However, while such strategies may be beneficial with children, there may be times, particularly in early adolescence, when adolescents resist such coaching strategies by parents. Nonetheless, it is quite clear that a connectedness rather than a separateness exists between the world of parent–adolescent relationships and peer relationships. For example, when positive relationships exist between parents and adolescents, parents may coach their offspring, particularly those who are the same sex as they are, in dating relationships. During late adolescence, it is not unusual for mothers and daughters, and fathers and sons to converse about the nature of relationships with the opposite sex. And, such conversations may be cross-sexed as well, with fathers coaching their daughters about the type of guys to watch out for, what to look for in a relationship, and so forth.

John Hill and Grayson Holmbeck (in press) point out that the use of the label *detachment* for processes or outcomes of parent–child relationships during adolescence is misleading. They stress that the use of the label *autonomy* as a label for freedom from attachments with parents is equally misleading. Such labels fail to recognize the importance of continuing close relationships between parents and adolescents, and how such relationships influence the adolescent's development. Moreover, they argue that indices of autonomy are positively related to close ties with parents. And they emphasize that independence striving, described as a drive, need, or motive, has little use in describing parent–adolescent relationships. Autonomy becomes useful as a concept when it ceases to be described negatively in terms of freedom from parental attachments and begins to be defined positively in terms of processes and individual variations in self-governance or self-regulation. These processes do not first appear in adolescence and they do not end there. Further, they do not preclude close relationships or an orientation toward connectedness or attachment with parents.

As can be seen, there is much more connectedness between the family and peer worlds of adolescents than earlier conceptualizations allowed for. We have seen that adolescents do not just move away from parents into a separate world of themselves and peers. Throughout adolescence, the world of parents and peers works in coordinated ways to influence the adolescent's development.

So far in our discussion of families, we have spoken extensively about parent–adolescent relationships, but virtually nothing has been said about another aspect of most adolescents' family lives. Next, we focus on the nature of sibling relationships in adolescence.

Siblings and Sibling Relationships: Experiencing Different Worlds in the Same Family

Sandra describes to her mother what happened in a conflict with her sister:

> We had just come home from the ball game. I sat down on the sofa next to the light so I could read. Sally (the sister) said, "Get up. I was sitting there first. I just got up for a second to get a drink." I told her that I was not going to get up, and that I didn't see her name on the chair. I got mad at her and started pushing her—her drink spilled all over her. Then she got really mad and started shoving me up against the wall and hitting me. I managed to grab her hair.

At this point Sally comes into the room and begins to tell her side of the story. Sandra interrupts, "Mother, you always take her side."

Competition among **siblings**—that is, brothers and/or sisters—along with concern about being treated fairly and equally by parents, are among the most pervasive characteristics of sibling relationships (Santrock, Readdick, and Pollard, 1980).

More than eighty percent of American children have one or more siblings. Because there are so many possible sibling combinations in a family, it is difficult to generalize about sibling influence and conflict.

In studying sibling influences, it is important to consider whether the socialization influences of siblings and parents are different; the extent to which an adolescent's birth order is associated with his or her development; and environmental worlds of siblings within the same family, investigating whether siblings in the same family experience highly differentiated worlds.

Sibling and Parent–Child Relationships

Is sibling interaction different than parent–child interaction? There is some evidence that it is. Linda Baskett (1974; Baskett and Johnson, 1982) observed the members of forty-seven families, each of which had two or three children. The siblings ranged from five to ten years of age. Observations were made for forty-five minutes on five different occasions. The children's observed behaviors included teasing, whining, yelling, commanding, talking, touching, nonverbal interacting, laughing, and complying. The interaction of the children with their parents was far more positive than their interaction with each other. Children and their parents had more varied and positive interchanges—they talked, laughed, and comforted one another more than siblings did. Children also tended to follow the dictates of their parents more than those of their siblings, and they behaved more negatively and punitively during interaction with their siblings than with their parents.

In some instances, siblings are a stronger socializing influence on the child than parents are. Victor Cicirelli (1977) believes, in particular, that older siblings teach their younger siblings. Someone close in age to the child may understand his problems more readily and be able to communicate more effectively with him than his parents can. In areas such as dealing with peers, coping with difficult teachers, and discussing taboo

There is more aggression between siblings than between parents and children.

subjects, siblings often fare better than parents in the socialization process. Older siblings also may serve effectively in teaching younger siblings about identity problems, sexual behavior, and physical appearance—areas in which the parents may be unwilling or incapable of helping an adolescent.

Birth Order

Think about your birth order. Are you the firstborn? The last born? The middle child? Do you think being born in a particular sibling order has influenced your development? Birth order has been studied extensively over many years. To summarize some of the main conclusions from this large body of literature, firstborn children seem to be more achievement oriented (Schachter, 1963; Glass, Neulinger, and Brim, 1974) and more socially responsible than those born later (Sutton-Smith and Rosenberg, 1970). It also seems that firstborns are more affiliative and sociable than later borns (Schachter, 1959). Nonetheless, there are some mixed findings in the sociability-affiliation domain since later-born children often have better peer relationships and in the case of boys, may have fewer behavior problems (Miller and Maruyama, 1976; Lahey, Hammer, Crumrine, and Forehand, 1980). It is important to point

out that birth order findings often account for a small percentage of variance when we are trying to predict the social competence of the child. Birth order, then, is best viewed as one of many variables that influences the child's development. It clearly is erroneous to conclude that because you are a firstborn child, you will be more achievement oriented than your friend who is a later-born child. And remember that when differences between later-born and firstborn children are reported, they represent average differences. There clearly are many later-born children who are highly achievement oriented because their birth order did not produce a rigid social script that their parents followed.

Environmental Differences within the Family and the Socialization of Siblings

If you grew up with a sibling, think how your parents socialized you and your sibling(s). Did they give more attention to you or your sibling? Did your father seem to get along better with one of you more than the other? And was the same likely not true for your mother as well? When we study environmental influences in the family and their effects on the adolescent's development, it now is becoming apparent that two adolescents within the same family often experience very different environments. Too often in the past, we have thought of a family as a homogeneous environment experienced the same by all adolescents in that particular family. Recent investigations suggest that nonadoptive and adoptive adolescent siblings (Daniels and Plomin, 1984) as well as twins (Rowe, 1983) do not perceive their environments in the same way. To learn more about how adolescent siblings do not always experience the same family environment, read Perspective on Adolescent Development 6.4.

We have discussed several important aspects of siblings and their relationships. And earlier, we outlined the nature of autonomy and attachment/connectedness in the adolescent's development. A summary of main ideas related to these aspects of the adolescent's development is presented in Concept Table 6.3. Next, we investigate the fascinating world of changes in families.

THE DIFFERENT FAMILY ENVIRONMENTS OF ADOLESCENT SIBLINGS

*I*n a recent investigation (Daniels, Dunn, Furstenberg, and Plomin, 1985), sibling data from 348 families with adolescents aged eleven to seventeen years were studied. Each sibling was interviewed separately and the mother was asked to describe each sibling independently as well. The investigators were interested in the environmental factors that were recorded separately for each sibling and those reported by both the siblings and the mother. The environmental measures included information about: family cooperation, family stress, parental rule expectations, parental chore expectations, maternal closeness, paternal closeness, adolescent's say in decisions, sibling friendliness, and peer friendliness. Sibling developmental outcomes also were assessed so that differences in the family environments of siblings could be studied in relation to the adolescent's adjustment. Measures of the adolescent's adjustment included emotional distress, delinquency, disobedience, and dissatisfaction as perceived by the parent, adolescent, and teacher.

The results indicated that siblings in the same family do experience different environments—these differences were more likely to be reported by the siblings than the parents, however. It is important to note also that differences in the family environments of siblings were not related to a number of family status variables, such as age, birth order, and sex. That is, it appeared that family environments differed less in terms of whether a sibling was firstborn or last born than in terms of how he or she was socialized and the kinds of experiences he or she had in the family.

The results also confirmed that within family differences in the environments, adolescent siblings' experiences are related to the adjustment and development of the siblings. Both the parent and sibling reports of the

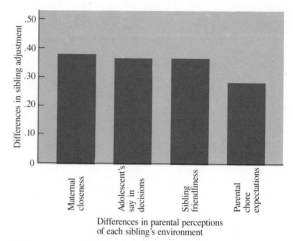

Figure 6.5 Relation of differences in sibling adjustment to differences in perceptions of each sibling's environment.

environment converged to find that the sibling who was more psychologically well adjusted (as reported by parents, siblings, and teachers) experienced more maternal closeness, more sibling friendliness, more say in family decision making, and more parental chore expectations as compared to the other sibling. For example, as shown in figure 6.5, differences in maternal closeness were related to differences in the adolescent's emotional distress, differences in the adolescent's say in decisions were related to delinquent behavior, differences in sibling friendliness were linked to differences in disobedience, and differences in parental chore expectations were associated with differences to delinquency as well.

Concept Table 6.3

AUTONOMY, ATTACHMENT/CONNECTEDNESS, AND SIBLING RELATIONSHIPS

Concept	Processes/related ideas	Characteristics/description
Autonomy	The nature of adolescent autonomy	Many parents have a difficult time handling the adolescent's push for autonomy. This push for independence is one of the hallmarks of adolescent development. Trying to define adolescent autonomy, though, is difficult. Autonomy is a multidimensional concept.
	Parent attitudes	Democratic parenting is associated with adolescent independence while authoritarian parenting restricts such autonomy. Adolescents develop maturity in some areas more so than others. The wise parent relinquishes control in areas where the adolescent makes mature decisions and helps the adolescent make reasonable decisions in areas where the adolescent's knowledge is more limited.
	Developmental views of autonomy	Two important developmental views of autonomy have been proposed by Ausubel and Blos. Ausubel argues that individuals move through a process of satellization and desatellization; while Blos, like many other theorists, such as Erikson, believes that the second year of life and adolescence are two developmental points when independence is a key focus. Blos emphasizes the process of individuation in adolescence, arguing that adolescence represents the second individuation crisis.
Attachment, the coordinated worlds of parents and peers, and connectedness	Attachment	While secure and insecure attachment have been concepts reserved primarily for infancy, they have important implications for adolescence as well. It is likely that a secure attachment to parents during adolescence enhances the likelihood the adolescent will explore and pursue independence in psychologically more healthy ways than insecurely attached adolescents. The attachment process with parents in both the childhood years and in the adolescent years likely are important contributors to adolescent development.
	The coordinated worlds of parents and peers	Adolescents do not just move away from parents into a separate world of peers. Indeed, adolescents who show a secure attachment to parents seem to show a more positive affiliation with peers than those who are insecurely attached. Both peers and parents continue to show coordinated effects on the adolescent's development of autonomy.

AUTONOMY, ATTACHMENT/CONNECTEDNESS, AND SIBLING RELATIONSHIPS

Concept	Processes/related ideas	Characteristics/description
	Connectedness of adolescents and parents	Historically, parent–adolescent relationships have been described in terms of disengagement and conflict, while peer relationships have been discussed in terms of engagement and connectedness. The new look in the study of adolescents and their families suggests a great deal of connectedness between adolescents and their parents. Robert Hinde's ethological view serves as an important framework for analyzing such connectedness. He described the distinctiveness of interactions, relationships, and groups. Group characteristics of families can produce considerable influence over the nature of adolescent school and peer relationships. And, at the interaction level, parents often engage in considerable discussions with adolescents about their peer world. Quite clearly, there is much more connectedness between parents and adolescents, and between parent and peer worlds than earlier theorizing led us to believe.
Siblings and sibling relationships	Sibling and parent-adolescent relationships	Siblings and parents often have different socializing functions. Sibling interchanges often are more negative and less varied than parent–adolescent interchanges, although there is a great deal of attachment to siblings as well. Siblings often discuss topics that are taboo with parents and siblings may feel their brother or sister understands them better than their parents. Older siblings serve as important models and teachers of younger siblings.
	Birth order	Firstborns often are more achievement oriented, more socially responsible, and more affiliative than later-born siblings. However, there is a great deal of individual variation in the domain of birth order and birth order does not account for a large portion of variance when we predict the nature of the adolescent's adjustment and social competence.
	Environmental differences within the family	Siblings within the same family often experience very different environments. These differences have been shown to link up with measures of the adolescent's adjustment.

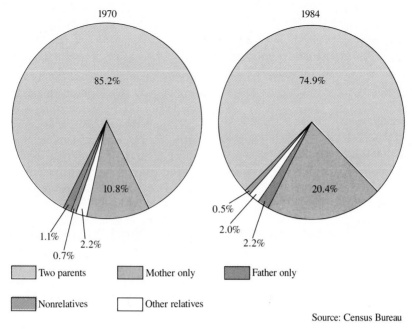

Source: Census Bureau

Figure 6.6   **Where children under eighteen live.**

The Changing Family in a Changing Society: A Hodgepodge of Family Structures

In previous eras, the majority of families consisted of a married mother and father with one or more children living with them. In most of these families, the father was employed outside the home, but the mother was not. No longer are the majority of adolescents exposed to this type of family environment. Adolescents are growing up in increasing numbers in a greater variety of family structures than ever before in history. As shown in figure 6.6, a larger number of children under the age of eighteen lived in single parent families in 1984 than in 1970. Further, a much greater percentage of adolescents are growing up in stepfamilies. The most rapid increase in the divorce rate seems to be in those families with adolescents—in 1982, fourteen million ten- to eighteen-year-olds lived in single parent families, for example (Select Committee on Children, 1983).

And it has been estimated that if present trends continue, by the time we reach the year 2000, some one-fourth to one-third of all children by the time they are eighteen years of age will have lived at least part of their life in a stepfamily. Further changes in the family world of adolescents focus on the dramatic increase of mothers who work outside the home in some full-time career. Less than ten percent of the adolescents in the United States now live in a family in which only one parent (usually the father) is the breadwinner. Let's now explore the effects of this rapidly changing family topography on the adolescent's development, first studying the effects of divorce on adolescents, second looking at the nature of stepfamilies, and third at the lives of adolescents in working mother families. To conclude our discussion of the changing family in a changing society, we will also investigate the lives of adolescents who become parents themselves.

Divorce

Divorce is now being investigated in very different ways than it was in the past. Researchers currently are studying many complex aspects of the adolescent's world in divorced families.

The Old and New Approaches

Early studies of the effects of divorce on children and adolescents were cast in a **father absence tradition** (e.g., Biller, 1970; Hetherington, 1966; Santrock, 1970). In this tradition, children from father-absent and father-present families were compared with differences in their development attributed to the absence of the father, particularly absence in the first five years of the individual's life. This tradition was heavily influenced by psychoanalytic theory, which argued that identification with the father, especially for boys, early in development serves a key role in promoting healthy psychological adjustment. It was reasoned that boys with an absent father would likely experience a disruption in the identification process and thereby would risk problems.

While it became apparent that family structure (such as whether an adolescent grows up in an intact, father-present family, a divorced family, or a widowed family) was one factor in determining the adolescent's adjustment, it clearly was incorrect to assume it was the only factor in determining the adolescent's adjustment. For example, it is all too easy to fall into the trap of generalization and stereotyping by saying that an adolescent is having problems because he or she is from a divorced home. Such an approach, focused on the family structure of the adolescent alone, obscures the critical importance of looking at the postdivorce family functioning that the adolescent is experiencing for possible clues to his or her adjustment. The old father absence tradition is being replaced with an approach that focuses on the effects of divorce in a more fine-grained manner, particularly in terms of pinpointing factors that mediate the effects of divorce on adolescents, such as the nature of postdivorce family functioning (e.g., Hetherington, Cox, and Cox, 1978; Santrock and Warshak, 1979; Santrock and Madison, 1985; Wallerstein and Kelly, 1980). Let's now look more closely at some of the factors that mediate the effects of divorce on adolescents.

Family Conflict

Many separations and divorces are highly emotional affairs that immerse the child in conflict. Conflict is a critical aspect of family functioning that appears to even outweigh the influence of family structure on the child's development. Children in single-parent families function better than those in conflict-ridden, nuclear families (Hetherington, Cox, and Cox, 1978; Rutter, 1983). Although escape from conflict may be a positive benefit of divorce for children, conflict does not decline, but increases in the year immediately following the divorce (Hetherington, Cox, and Cox, 1978).

Parenting and Relationships with Ex-Spouse

The child's relationship with both parents after the divorce influences the ability to cope with stress (Hetherington, Cox, and Cox, 1978). During the first year after the divorce, the quality of parenting that the child experiences is often very poor; parents seem to be preoccupied with their own needs and adjustment, experiencing anger, depression, confusion, and emotional instability that inhibit their ability to respond sensitively to the child's needs. During this period, parents tend to discipline the child inconsistently, be less affectionate, and be ineffective in controlling the child.

Let's consider in more detail one important aspect of parenting behavior, the extent to which parents respond with affection and positive statements when the child complies with the parent's requests or demands. Less than half the time children were given positive reinforcement regardless of whether they were from a divorced or intact family. Second, boys were given less positive reinforcement for compliance than girls. This particularly seemed to be the case for divorced mothers, although it can be seen that divorced mothers more appropriately responded to child compliance from one to two years after the divorce. By contrast, divorced fathers were becoming less reinforcing and attentive to positive behavior by their children in this period. For the most part, however, during the second year after the divorce, parenting was more effective, particularly on the part of the mother. Further, the degree to which a continuous, harmonious relationship between the custodial parent and the ex-spouse existed was an important predictor of the child's adjustment in divorced families (Hetherington, Cox, and Cox, 1978; 1982).

Support Systems

The majority of information we have about divorced families emphasizes the absent father or the relationship between the custodial parent and the child, but child psychologists have become increasingly interested in the role of support systems available to the child and the family. Support systems for divorced families seem more important for low-income than for middle-income families (Colletta, 1978). The extended family and community services may play a critical role in the functioning of low-income families. Competent support systems may be particularly important for divorced parents with infant and preschool children because the majority of these parents must work full-time to make ends meet.

Age of the Child and Carrying Forward Relationships

Another factor involving children of divorce focuses on the developmental level of the child at the time of divorce. Adolescents are less likely to blame themselves for the divorce than children are. Further, adolescents may be able to immerse themselves in peer relationships and friendships more extensively than children, a possible protective buffer for the stress in their family they are experiencing. In a well-known study of divorce (Wallerstein and Kelly, 1974), it was found that the adolescents who distanced themselves from parental conflict seem to be coping more effectively than others. In many instances, these adolescents spend large chunks of time with peers and their parents kept their arguments away from the adolescents as much as possible. At first, these youth seemed to be very insensitive to their interviewers, but over time they were better able than other adolescents to realistically assess their family circumstances.

Yet another issue involved in the lives of adolescents who experience divorce is how such matters will influence their dating relationships. Mavis Hetherington (1972) has demonstrated that the heterosexual behavior of girls from divorced homes is different from that of daughters from widowed and intact families. She studied three groups of twenty-four girls in the early adolescence age range: girls from homes where both parents were present, girls from homes in which their parents were divorced and not remarried, and girls

Adolescent girls from divorced homes often are more uninhibited around males than their intact and widowed family counterparts.

from homes in which their father had died and their mother had not remarried. Girls from the father-absent homes either were very withdrawn, passive, and subdued around males or they were overly active, aggressive, and flirtatious.

The girls who were inhibited, rigid, and restrained around males were more likely to have come from widowed homes. Those who sought the attention of males, showed early heterosexual behavior, and seemed more open and uninhibited were more likely to have come from homes in which the parents were divorced. In addition, early separation from fathers usually was associated with more profound effects, and the mothers' attitudes toward themselves and marriage differed between widows and divorcees. Divorced women were more anxious, unhappy, hostile toward males, and more negative about marriage than were the widows. And perhaps not surprisingly, daughters of divorcees had more negative attitudes about men than did the daughters of widows.

Several examples of the actual behavior of the girls should provide a clearer picture of the study. One technique used to investigate the girls' behavior was to interview them sometimes with a male interviewer and sometimes with a female interviewer. Four chairs were placed in the room, including one for the interviewer.

Table 6.2 Group means for observational variables in the recreational center

Observational variable	Group		
	Father absent		Father present
	Divorce	Death	
S (subject) = physical contact and nearness with male peers	3.08	1.71	1.79
Male areas	7.75	2.25	4.71
Female areas	11.67	17.42	14.42

Source: Hetherington, E. M. "Effects of Father-Absence on Personality Development in Adolescent Daughters." Developmental Psychology 7 (1972):316. Copyright © 1972 by the American Psychological Association.

Daughters of widows most frequently chose the chair farthest from the male interviewer, while daughters of divorcees generally selected the chair closest to him. There were no differences when the interviewer was a female.

The interviewer also observed the girls at a dance and during activities at the recreational center. At the dance, the daughters of widows often refused to dance when asked. One widow's daughter even spent the entire evening in the restroom. The daughters of the divorcees were more likely to accept the boys' invitations to dance. At the recreation center, the daughters of divorcees were more frequently observed where boys were playing, while the daughters of the widows more often engaged in traditional "female" activities, like sewing and cooking (table 6.2).

Hetherington (1977) continued to study these girls, following them into young adulthood to determine their sexual behavior, marital choices, and marital behavior. The daughters of divorcees tended to marry younger (eight of the daughters of widowed mothers still were not married at the time of the report), and tended to select marital partners who more frequently had drug problems and inconsistent work histories. In contrast, daughters of widows tended to marry men with a more puritanical makeup. In addition, both the daughters of the widows and the divorcees reported more sexual adjustment problems than the daughters from intact homes; for example, the daughters from homes where the father is absent generally experienced fewer orgasms than daughters from intact homes. The daughters from intact homes also showed more variation in their sexual role behavior and marital adjustment. They seemed to be more relaxed and dealt more competently with their roles as wives, suggesting that they have worked through their relationships with their fathers and are more psychologically free to deal successfully in their relationships with other males. On the other hand, the daughters of the divorcees and widows appear to be marrying images of their fathers.

The Hetherington (1977) data suggest that adolescents carry forward experiences in a divorced family to influence their relationships with others as they move into late adolescence and early adulthood. Recent research by Judith Wallerstein and Joan Kelly provides further evidence of how children and adolescents carry forward experiences in the divorced family into their adolescent and adult years respectively. For further information about the longitudinal investigation of divorce conducted by Wallerstein and Kelly, read Perspective on Adolescent Development 6.5.

The Sex of the Child and the Sex of the Custodial Parent

One research study has directly compared children living in father-custody and mother-custody families (Santrock and Warshak, 1979; 1986). Children were videotaped during social interaction with their same-sex parent as the parent and child discussed a weekend plan and problems surfaced. The videotapes were rated by two people to ensure a high degree of reliability. On a number of ratings of observed behavior, children living with a same-sex parent were characterized by greater social competence than those living with an opposite-sex parent. For example, as shown in figure 6.7, father-custody boys and mother-custody girls were rated the highest in social maturity, and father-custody girls were rated the lowest. Possible explanations for this focus on the importance of the child's identification with the same-sex parent, the coercive interaction that may characterize mother–son relationships because boys are

Judith Wallerstein and Joan Kelly (Springer and Wallerstein, 1983; Wallerstein, 1982, 1984; Wallerstein and Kelly, 1980) are the only investigators to conduct a longitudinal study of the effects of divorce on children and adolescents of different ages. In their Children of Divorce project, Wallerstein and Kelly interviewed 131 children and adolescents, and their parents, about their reactions to divorce. The participating children were interviewed at the time their parents were taking action for the divorce, at one year following the divorce, and more recently at five and ten years after the divorce. The sample consisted of white, middle-class families who responded to an invitation for free preventive counseling.

The recent reports by Judith Wallerstein (1982, 1984) of adolescents and young adults ten years after they experienced the divorce of their parents provide fascinating insights into the manner in which individuals carry forward experiences in the family over long periods of time. Wallerstein (1984) found that adolescents had few memories of the intact family or of family disruption that existed a decade earlier. However, these same individuals, as children, had shown considerable distress and fear at the time of the divorce. A substantial number of the adolescents, while they had spent most of their lives in either a single-parent divorced family or a stepfamily, perceived that their lives would have been happier if they had grown up in an intact family. More than half of the adolescents showed reconciliation fantasies (wanting their parents to get back together). Wallerstein (1984) concluded that when divorce occurs very early, children are less burdened and may carry fewer bad memories forward. However, other research has shown that divorce in the first two years of life may be more detrimental to later development than divorce at a later time (e.g., Biller, 1970, 1974; Hetherington, 1972; Santrock, 1970, 1972). Disruption in the attachment process during infancy, inclusion of lower-income families in the earlier divorce group (particularly those in which the father has deserted the mother during pregnancy), the length of time spent without a second adult in the home, and the possible harmful effects of stress on the mother and infant are possible candidates for explaining the early onset of divorce findings.

In the ten-year followup of individuals who experienced the divorce of parents in adolescence (Wallerstein, 1982), these adults now report that the divorce of their parents some ten years earlier has had a lasting effect on their lives. Many of the young adults sensed that the divorce of parents during the adolescent years burdened their efforts at growing up and becoming mature adults. As the young adults looked backward, their emotions were filled with sadness and wishes they had grown up in an intact family. They also expressed considerable concern about repeating divorce in their own marriages and were anxious to avoid having their own children grow up in divorced circumstances.

---

more aggressive than girls, and the possibility that the child in an opposite-sex custodial situation may be pushed into adult roles too soon by substituting for the absent spouse.

We have seen how pervasive divorce has become in our society and observed its effects on adolescents. Divorced parents, however, often do not stay divorced very long. Next, we look at the lives of adolescents in stepparent families.

Stepparent Families

When a remarriage occurs, adjustment to the new family is substantial. The mother who remarries not only has to adjust to having another father for her children, but to being a wife again. There may not be much time for the husband–wife relationship to develop in stepfamilies. The children are a part of this new family

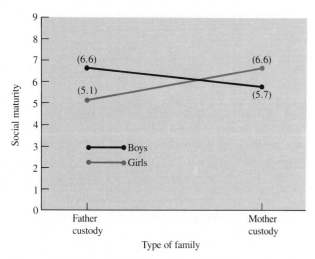

Figure 6.7 **The effects of sex of custodial parent and sex of child on the child's development.**

from the beginning, a situation that leaves little time for the couple to spend time alone and to grow with each other (Visher and Visher, 1978).

We do not have nearly as much research information about stepparent families as divorced families, but recently, attention has been given to the increasing number of children growing up in stepparent families. It has been found that children show more adjustment problems when they are in a complex rather than a simple stepfamily (Hetherington, Cox, and Cox, 1982). A **complex stepfamily** is one in which both the stepparent and the biological parent have brought children to the newly formed stepfamily while a **simple stepfamily** is one in which the stepparent has not brought children from a previous marriage to live in the newly formed stepfamily. In another investigation (Santrock, et al., 1985), children in stepfather, stepmother, and intact families were observed interacting with their parents and both the parents and the children were interviewed about family relationships. When differences appeared, they invariably suggested the family

atmosphere was more positive than in a stepparent family. Within the stepparent families, relationships between the child and the stepfather or stepmother were more strained than between the child and his or her biological parent. The relationship between the child and the stepfather was a very distant, somewhat unpleasant one, while the relationship between the child and the stepmother appeared to involve an extensive, but sometimes abrasive set of interactions. In stepfather families, the remarried mother was performing the bulk of the childrearing duties, while in stepmother families, the stepmother was receiving much more parenting support from the biological father, who undoubtedly gained considerable parenting experience as a single father. The continuity of attachment to a biological, remarried parent was clearly evident in the child's life, as was the difficulty in establishing an attachment to the stepparent. Other information suggested that in both stepfather and stepmother families, when a new child was born to the stepparent and remarried parent (**step-procreation**), it was linked with poorer adjustment on the part of the stepchild. For example, in observations of stepchildren from stepfather families, videotaped observations revealed that stepchildren whose remarried mother and stepfather had a child of their own interacted less competently with their mother and had more adjustment problems with peers than their stepfather counterparts who did not encounter a new child being born in the stepfamily (Santrock, Sitterle, and Warshak, 1986). In this study, it also was found that the more hours the remarried mother worked per week the more likely the child was to report separation anxiety and have more negative interchanges with the stepfather. As can be seen, sorting out the complexities of life in the stepfamily is a difficult task. Relationships with an increasing number of attachment figures occurs and considerable disequilibrium likely is experienced as the child moves from an intact to a divorced to a stepparent family. Next, we look more closely at one of the factors just mentioned in the lives of children from stepparent families, whether or not their mothers have a full-time career outside the home.

Working Mothers

Not only do many stepmother and remarried mothers seek employment to meet economic needs, but many divorced single parents may have an even more urgent need to work full-time to make ends meet. Interestingly, indications are that divorced women with children are more productive and committed to their work than married or single women (Feldman, 1973). Aletha Huston-Stein (Huston-Stein and Higgins-Trenk, 1978) believes that the divorced mother's orientation to the work ethic may be the product of a midlife crisis not unlike that previously attributed only to men. Girls in the United States traditionally have been socialized under the aura of what Huston-Stein refers to as "the Cinderella myth." According to the myth, Prince Charming will sweep her away on his white stallion, and the two will have a few babies and live happily ever after. Of course, life is not this simple and the reality of divorce has brought disillusionment.

While divorce is the most obvious example of the failure of the Cinderella myth, disillusionment also occurs for many married women as well. Mothers who choose to go to school or seek a job after marriage and childbearing, likely do so in a more serious vein and with more long-term commitment than women who believe their highest degree of satisfaction is to be found in the home.

Because household operations have become more efficient and family size has decreased in America, it is not certain that children with mothers who work outside the home actually receive less attention than children in the past whose mothers were not employed. Outside employment, at least for mothers with school-aged children and adolescents, may simply be filling time previously taken up by added household burdens and more children. And it cannot be assumed that if the mother did not go to work, the child or adolescent would benefit from the time freed up by streamlined household operations and smaller families. Lois Hoffman (1979) has studied working mothers for many years:

Maternal employment is a part of modern life. It is not an aberrant aspect of it, but a response to other social changes and as such meets the needs that the previous family ideal of a full-time mother and homemaker cannot. Not only does it meet the parent's needs, but in many ways it is a pattern better suited to socializing the child for the adult roles he or she will occupy. This is particularly true for the daughter, but for the son, too, the broader range of emotions and skills that each parent presents are more consistent with this adult role. Just as his father shares the breadwinning role and the child-rearing role with his mother, so the son, too, will be likely to share these roles. The rigid sex-role stereotyping perpetuated by the divisions of labor in the traditional family is not appropriate for the demands children of either sex will have made on them as adults. Furthermore, the needs of the growing child require the mother to loosen her hold on the child and this task may be easier for the working woman whose job is an additional source of identity and self-esteem.

Latchkey Children

Nonetheless, while Hoffman and others conclude that the working mother is not associated with negative child outcomes, a certain set of children from working-mother families bears further scrutiny—the so-called latchkey children. A very important point to consider when we study the effects of working mothers on children is what is happening to the children when they are away from their parents. During the course of the day, elementary school-aged children and adolescents are at school. Infants are placed in some form of day care and preschool-aged children likely attend nursery school or are in some form of day care. The quality of day care many young children receive is far from optimal; thus, when negative effects of working mothers on young children are found it may not be due to mothers working per se, but rather to the inferior quality of care they are receiving when they are not with their parents.

But more about latchkey children needs to be said. **Latchkey children** typically do not see their parents from the time the children leave for school until sometime late in the evening, about six or seven P.M. These children are called latchkey because they are given the key to their home and take the key with them to school, using it in the evening to let themselves in the home while their parents are still at work. Latchkey children are largely unsupervised for a two to four hour period every evening during the school week. In addition, during the summer months, many children who only spent several hours an evening unsupervised now spend whole days, five days a week unsupervised. We still know very little about possible adverse effects of being a latchkey child, although interviews with latchkey children suggest some of the negative influences.

Thomas and Lynette Long (1983) have conducted interviews with more than 1,500 latchkey children. They concluded that "a slight majority of these children have negative latchkey experiences." For example, some latchkey children may grow up too fast, hurried by the responsibility placed on them. David Elkind (1981) points out that latchkey children are stressed by taking on the psychological trappings of adulthood before they are prepared to deal with them. Still some latchkey children may thrive on such responsibility, developing a mature sense of independence and accountability. One of the major problems for latchkey children is the lack of limits and structure in their lives during their latchkey hours. Without such limits and involvement of parents in their lives, it becomes easier for latchkey children to find their way into trouble—possibly abuse of a sibling, stealing, or vandalism. The Longs point out that ninety percent of the adjudicated juvenile delinquents in Montgomery County, Maryland were latchkey children. All too often, self-care is forced on children because of a divorce or death of a spouse. The custodial parent, now the main breadwinner, must work. Now the child, already having to deal with the stress of divorce or death, must also cope with further loss of time spent with the custodial parent.

Latchkey children—what effects might such experiences have on development?

To investigate variations in the after-school experiences of latchkey adolescents, Laurence Steinberg (1986) recently studied 865 adolescents in grades five through nine. Consistent with the findings of other research (e.g., Rodman, Pratto, and Nelson, 1985), the latchkey adolescents as a whole group were not significantly different from a control group of adolescents whose parents supervised them at home in the after-school hours. However, when the sample of latchkey adolescents was expanded to include greater variation in after-school experiences, adolescents who were more removed from adult supervision were more susceptible to peer pressure than those who were at a friend's house after school. Further, those adolescents who were at a friend's house were, in turn, less susceptible to peer influence than adolescents who described themselves as just "hanging out." And latchkey adolescents whose parents knew their whereabouts and those who had been reared in an authoritative manner were less susceptible to peer pressure than their counterparts whose parents do not know where they are and what they are doing, and who use other parenting strategies such as authoritarian and permissive. Even when the adolescents whose parents knew their whereabouts and had reared them in an authoritative way were in situations in which adult supervision was lax and susceptibility to peer pressure was high, these adolescents showed an ability to resist peer influence.

Joan Lipsitz (1983), in testifying before the House Select Committee on Children, Youth, and Families, called the lack of adult supervision of adolescents in the after-school hours one of the major problems confronting families of adolescents today. Lipsitz referred to this problem as the three o'clock to six o'clock issue because at the Center for Early Adolescence at the University of North Carolina where she is director, it is during this time period that a peak in adolescent referrals and calls for counseling occur. In a survey of 996 parents conducted at the Center for Early Adolescence, the largest group of parents with pressing needs were those from households where no adult was home during the late afternoon to supervise their youth. The parents worried about this lack of supervision, about such possibilities as fires, kitchen accidents, traffic accidents, and muggings. They worried about peer influences, about whether they really knew where their youth were. The most frequently cited reasons for their youth's lack of involvement in the after-school hours were that the costs were too high, the youth cannot get to the locations, and the youth are too busy (this latter reason was given by the high-income parents only). Low-income parents were most likely to cite cost and lack of transportation as the main barriers. One low-income mother said that more community activities need to be offered to all youth since many parents cannot afford private clubs and classes for their youth.

We have discussed a number of different aspects of working mothers and latchkey children. Earlier, we described in some detail the effects of divorce on adolescents and we evaluated some key ideas in the lives of stepparent families. A summary of main points in these aspects of the substantial change going on in families with adolescents is presented in Concept Table 6.4. Next, we look at adolescents as parents themselves.

Adolescent Parents

Among the significant aspects of studying adolescents as parents is determining how many such parents there are and the quality of their parenting. Of particular interest is the role of the adolescent father in these families.

How Many Adolescent Parents Are There?

The teenage childbearing rate has declined. In 1960, the birthrate per 1,000 women aged fifteen to nineteen was 89.1, a figure that dropped to 52.4 by 1978 (Testa and Wulczyn, 1980). However, while the teenage birthrate has been declining, the incidence of out-of-wedlock births among youth has been increasing. In 1978, over one-half of all births to teenagers were out-of-wedlock compared to only seventeen percent in 1960. Also, so powerful is the link between teenage pregnancy and financial matters that each year a woman delays her first birth, the probability she will be in poverty at age twenty-seven is reduced by approximately two percentage points (Testa and Wulczyn, 1980).

The Offspring of Adolescent Parents

Popular wisdom suggests that childbearing should occur between the ages of twenty-two and thirty-one (Rindfuss and Bumpass, 1978). It is believed that parenthood at earlier ages means increased biomedical risks, less positive child behavioral outcomes, and/or less competent maternal attitudes. In some cases, though, research has not supported such beliefs.

DIVORCE, STEPFAMILIES, AND WORKING MOTHERS

Concept	Processes/related ideas	Characteristics/description
Divorce	The old and new view	The old father absence tradition emphasized the importance of family structure in determining development. The new look in divorce research stresses the importance of factors that mediate the effects of divorce on adolescents, particularly postdivorce family functioning.
	Family conflict	Conflict is a key construct in understanding the adolescent's development. Family and marital conflict seem to outweigh family structure in importance.
	Parenting and relationships with the ex-spouse	The child's and adolescent's relationships with both parents after the divorce influence his or her adjustment. Positive relationships with the ex-spouse are important predictors of the adolescent's adjustment. Disruption seems to be greatest in the first year after the divorce, but becomes somewhat less two years after the divorce.
	Support systems	These become particularly important for low-income, divorced families. The extended family and community services may help in this regard.
	Age of the child and carrying forward relationships	Adolescents are less likely to blame themselves for the divorce, can help buffer themselves from the stress of divorce by immersing themselves in the peer group, and have more logical reasoning to help them understand the nature of the divorce process. Divorce, however, is still a highly stressful experience for adolescents. Divorce has been shown to influence the dating behaviors and cross-sexed relationships of adolescent girls. As children who have experienced divorce move through the adolescent years, they look at their adolescent years and contemplate how divorce influenced their life. Similarly, they look back at their childhood years and think about what life in an intact family would have been like. Also, adolescents whose parents divorced look back as adults and think about how divorce influenced their lives then and how it has continued to have an impact on their lives as adults.

Recent reviews of biomedical risks have minimized the risk due to early childbearing (Baldwin and Cain, 1980). Moreover, the neonatal behavior and temperaments of the offspring of adolescent and adult mothers has not been found to differ (Field et al., 1980; Sandler, Vietze, and O'Conner, 1976), although negative effects for the offspring of adolescent mothers have been reported in one investigation (Thompson, Cappleman, and Zietschel, 1979).

However, studies of subsequent child behavior show positive relationships between maternal age and children's intellectual development. Consistent results suggest that children born to adolescent mothers do not perform as well on intelligence tests as those born to mothers in their twenties (Broman, 1981; Maracek, 1979). Teenage mothers also express less desirable child-rearing attitudes and have less realistic expectations for their infants' development than do older

DIVORCE, STEPFAMILIES, AND WORKING MOTHERS

Concept	Processes/related ideas	Characteristics/description
	The sex of the child and the sex of the custodial parent	Adjustment of the child has been shown to be better in same-sex child, custodial arrangements than opposite-sexed ones.
Stepparent families	Simple and complex stepparent families	Simple stepparent families involve those in which only a remarried parent brings a child to live in the stepfamily, while complex stepfamilies are those in which both the remarried parent and the stepparent bring children with them. Adjustment seems better in simple than complex stepfamilies.
	Parenting and attachment	Just as divorce brings with it a great deal of disequilibrium and adjustment so does movement into a stepfamily. The attachment to a biological, remarried parent may be particularly salient in the child's adjustment in stepparent families. Relationships with biological, remarried parents are much better than relationships with stepparents. Relationships of children with stepfathers often are distant and uninvolved. Step-procreation, in which the remarried parent and stepparent have their own child, seems disruptive to the stepchild's development.
Working mothers	Overview	Overall, the research literature on working mothers has not shown adverse effects on children and adolescents.
	Latchkey children	A subset of working-mother children may be especially vulnerable, however, because their lives are often not closely monitored. Latchkey children seem to show a particularly high rate of problems. Recently, the latchkey problem has been referred to as the "three o'clock to six o'clock P.M. issue." Problems also may arise during the summer months when latchkey adolescents live even more unmonitored lives. Variations in latchkey experiences suggest that parental monitoring and authoritative parenting are important in helping the adolescent's adjustment in latchkey situations.

mothers (Field et al., 1980; Epstein, 1980). Other investigations have not found such negative effects during either the infant years (Svedja, Campos, and Emde, 1980) or the preschool years (Philliber and Graham, 1981).

While in many instances the findings regarding the effects of adolescent parenting on offspring are mixed, there are clearly some instances where adolescent parenting has negative effects when compared to adult parenting. It may be that such negative effects of adolescent parenting are better explained in terms of the postnatal environments of the offspring of younger and older mothers than in terms of the biological consequences of adolescent pregnancy (Baldwin and Cain, 1980). The stress associated with adolescent pregnancy and the emotional immaturity or egocentrism of extremely young mothers are likely candidates for explanation (Baldwin and Cain, 1980; Epstein, 1980; Ragozin et al., 1982).

What are adolescents like as parents?

Adolescent Parenting

Not only has there been an increased interest in the role adolescent mothers play in the development of their offspring, but the role of adolescent fathers is receiving increased attention as well. Ross Parke and his colleagues (1980) describe some of their findings. A common misconception is that adolescent fathers have little or no contact with their infants. This myth has two parts: (a) the majority of teenage births occur out-of-wedlock, and (b) unmarried fathers have little to do with the mother or child after the birth. The facts are that although slightly more than half of all births to teenagers are conceived out-of-wedlock, only about thirty-five percent of all *births* to teenagers occurred out-of-wedlock (Alan Guttmacher Institute, 1976). (Nonetheless, between the early 1960s and the early 1970s, the proportion of children born to unwed adolescent mothers doubled [Alan Guttmacher Institute, 1976]). And several investigations of unmarried adolescent fathers revealed a surprising degree of paternal involvement for extended periods following the birth.

For instance, in one investigation (Nettleton and Cline, 1975), fifty percent of the mothers who did not relinquish custody of their infants dated the father during the infant's first year of life. And twenty percent of these girls eventually married their children's fathers.

In presenting these data, Parke and his colleagues emphasize that they are not suggesting that all, or even the majority, of relationships between unmarried adolescent parents are supportive, mutually satisfying, and stable. In fact, there is considerable evidence to the contrary. It is well documented that divorce rates among adolescent parents are much higher than in the general population (Furstenberg, 1976; Lorenzi, Klerman, and Jekel, 1977). And, teenage mothers frequently harbor unrealistic expectations about the father's marriage plans. In one investigation (Lorenzi, Klerman, and Jekel, 1977), of the forty-seven percent of the mothers who expected to marry the father, only thirty-six percent had married him by the second birthday of the baby. However, Parke and his colleagues believe that such figures have been overemphasized in the literature of adolescent parenting and may in part be responsible for the predominantly negative perception of the adolescent father. Parke recommends the development of cultural support systems that recognize the full range of needs of adolescent fathers, both as individuals and as parents. Providing such supportive interventions may produce positive consequences for the father, mother, and child. Parke calls for programs that teach adolescent fathers parenting skills and for school districts to provide infant care services in locations near high school facilities that would permit both the mother and the father to continue their educations (e.g., Card and Wise, 1978).

This concludes our chapter on families. We have covered an extensive number of ideas about adolescents and families, and these ideas call attention to the importance and complexity of the family in the adolescent's development. In the next chapter, we'll focus on the adolescent's development in another context—peer relations and groups.

I. Information about the nature of family processes focuses on reciprocal socialization, mutual regulation, and the family as a system; the construction of relationships; the maturation of the adolescent and the maturation of parents; and sociocultural, historical influences on the family.

   A. Social-mold theories inaccurately pictured adolescent socialization. Rather reciprocal socialization is a more accurate portrayal, in which adolescents socialize parents just as parents socialize adolescents. As a social system, the family can be thought of as a constellation of subsystems. Second-order effects need to be considered as a third party often changes the nature of dyadic relationships.

   B. There currently is a flourish of interest in the construction of relationships—this interest coming about through some meshing of attachment, cognitive, and psychoanalytic theories. Three important aspects of the construction of relationships are continuity and coherence, close relationships and their importance in the adolescent's functioning in the wider social world, and carrying forward relationships.

   C. Parent–adolescent relationships are influenced by the maturation of the adolescent and the maturation of parents.

1. Physical, cognitive, and social changes in the adolescent's development influence parent–adolescent relationships. Among these are the nature of pubertal change, logical thought, idealistic thought, expectations, changes in schooling, peers, friendships, dating, and independence.

2. Parental changes include those involving marital dissatisfaction, economic burdens, career reevaluation, time perspective, and health and bodily concerns.

D. Sociocultural, historical changes also influence the adolescent and his or her family relationships. Some of these changes involve major upheavals, such as war, while others consist of more subtle changes, such as a general restlessness and dissatisfaction.

II. There are many different facets to a discussion of parenting techniques and parent–adolescent conflict.

A. Authoritative parenting seems to be a more effective parenting scheme in promoting the development of social competence in adolescents than authoritarian, permissive–indulgent, or permissive–indifferent styles. Too often parents do not stop to think how long it takes to make the long transition from child to adult. As the individual moves toward the later part of adolescence, the parent may be wise to relinquish more control and monitor the adolescent's life more indirectly while still maintaining a connectiveness with the adolescent.

B. Interest in parent–adolescent conflict has a long history with Hall and Freud believing biological matters induced such conflict in tumultuous portions. More recently other ideas have served to explain why such conflict occurs. Conflict with parents does seem to increase in adolescence but more so in early than late adolescence. Such conflict typically is of the moderate variety rather than the prolonged, intense genre the ancients envisioned. Still, a minority of families experience such intense, prolonged parent–adolescent conflict and this type has been associated with a number of adolescent problems. This type of conflict often has childhood antecedents. The moderate increase in parent–adolescent conflict during early adolescence serves the positive developmental function of promoting independence and identity.

III. Information about autonomy and attachment/connectedness has involved some recent revisions in the way we think about the adolescent's independence and parent–adolescent relationships.

A. Information about autonomy suggests that many parents have a difficult time handling the adolescent's strong push for independence and that this push is one of the hallmarks of adolescent development. Trying to define autonomy is difficult; conceptualizing autonomy as a multidimensional construct is important.

B. Democratic parenting is associated with enhanced independence of adolescents, while authoritarian parenting seems to restrict such independence. The wise parent understands that adolescents develop autonomy in more mature ways in some areas than others. Therefore, it is important to allow more independence in those areas where maturity is shown and monitor the adolescent's life more closely in domains where more immature behavior is shown.

C. Two important developmental views are the satellization–desatellization concept of David Ausubel and the individuation ideas of Peter Blos.

D. There is an increased interest in the connectedness and attachment of adolescents and their parents. Historically, connectedness has been reserved for peer relations while disconnectedness has been used to describe parent–adolescent relationships. Now, there is considerable enthusiasm in looking at parent–adolescent relationships in terms of attachment and connectedness, as well as at the coordinated worlds of parents and peers. It is likely that a secure attachment to parents through the childhood and adolescent years promotes a healthy exploration of independence and identity. Hinde's view that interactions, relationships, and groups can be distinguished has led to further emphasis on the connectiveness of family relationships to the wider social world of the adolescent.

IV. Sibling relationships also are an important facet of the family life of most adolescents. Sibling and parent relationships often have distinctive characteristics, yet both involve attachment and conflict. Some research has shown the association of birth order to adolescent characteristics, but overall birth order contributes only a small portion of the variation in the adolescent's development. Rather the most important aspect of understanding siblings seems to be how they likely experience a world within the same family that is very different for each. These distinctive sibling worlds in the same family are associated with the sibling's adjustment.

V. The adolescent lives in a changing family in a changing world. Among those changes are divorce, stepfamilies, and working mothers.

A. Information about divorce focuses on the old and new views, family conflict, parenting and relationships with the ex-spouse, support systems, age of the child and carrying forward relationships, and sex of the child and sex of the custodial parent. The old father absence tradition has been replaced by a view that emphasizes more strongly the factors that mediate divorce effects. Low family and marital conflict, competent parenting, a harmonious relationship with the ex-spouse, and support systems all help the child in a divorced circumstance cope more effectively with the stress that he or she encounters. While adolescents can reason more logically about divorce, blame themselves less than children do for the occurrence of the divorce, and may insulate themselves in a world of peers, divorce is still a highly stressful experience for them. Divorce experiences in childhood are carried forward to adolescence and such experiences in adolescence are also carried forward to adulthood to influence how individuals construct relationships. Boys seem to fare better in father-custody and girls in mother-custody families.

B. Stepfamilies experience a period of disequilibrium initially. Simple stepfamilies and those in which step-procreation has not occurred seem to involve better adjustment on the part of the stepchild. The continuing attachment to a remarried biological parent likely is an important factor in the child's adjustment. Relationships with remarried parents are much better than with stepparents. Children's relationships with a stepfather seem particularly uninvolved and distant.

C. Overall, working mothers do not seem to have a negative effect on the adolescent's development; however, a subset of working-mother adolescents, known as latchkey children, may be particularly vulnerable. They seem to show an unusually high number of problems and further attention needs to be given to ways their lives can be monitored more effectively, possibly through the development of better community support systems and activities. Variations in latchkey experiences suggest that parental monitoring and authoritative parenting are important in helping the adolescent's adjustment in latchkey situations.

VI. While we have talked extensively about the adolescent's relationships with parents, there also are a number of adolescents who become parents themselves. Their ranks have been decreasing lately, but there has been an increase in the number of out-of-wedlock births. Research on the biological and cognitive development of the offspring of adolescent mothers is somewhat mixed. Some studies do show increased risks, but it may be wise to look carefully at the postnatal environments of the infants for further clues about their development. While many adolescent fathers do not take an active part in the mother's and the baby's life, there is more participation than suggested by the media. While some adolescents are competent parents, they overall are not as competent as adult parents.

Key Terms

Suggested Readings

Journal of Early Adolescence, Spring 1985, vol. 5, no. 1.
The entire issue is devoted to contemporary approaches to the study of families with adolescents. Includes articles by Catherine Cooper and Susan Ayers-Lopez on the connectedness of adolescents and their families, by Raymond Montemayor on parent–adolescent conflict, by John Hill and his colleagues on pubertal status and parent–adolescent relationships, as well as many others.

Maccoby, E. E., & Martin, J. A. (1983). Socialization in the context of the family: parent–child interaction. In P. Mussen (Ed.), *Handbook of child psychology* (4th ed., vol. IV). New York: Wiley.
A very extensive, competent overview of what we know about children's socialization in families. Provides many new ideas about research on children and their families.

Sroufe, L. A., & Fleeson, J. (1985). Attachment and the construction of relationships. In W. Hartup and Z. Rubin (Eds.), *Relationships and development*. Hillsdale, N.J.: Erlbaum.
In this article, the very important idea that to understand family development, we need to study how people construct relationships is presented. Details from research on child development as well as clinical studies across generations are provided.

Steinberg, L. D. (1980). *Understanding families with young adolescents*. Carrboro, N.C.: Center for Early Adolescence.
An easy-to-read overview of the maturation of adolescents and the simultaneous maturation of parents. Ideas for coping with adolescent change in families are included.

Wallerstein, J. S., & Kelly, J. B. (1980). *Surviving the breakup. How children and parents cope with divorce.* New York: Basic Books.
In addition to providing details of their extensive investigation of the effects of divorce on children, many suggestions for how parents should deal with children in a divorced family are provided.

Chapter 7

Peers, Friends, and Group Relations

Prologue

You Jerk!

"Y ou Jerk, what are you trying to do to me," Jess yelled at his teacher. "I got no use for this school and people like you. Leave me alone and quit hassling me."

Jess is ten years old and already has had more than his share of confrontations with society. He has been arrested three times for stealing, been suspended from school twice, and has a great deal of difficulty getting along with people in social circumstances. He particularly has difficulty with authority figures. No longer able to cope with his outbursts in class, his teacher recommended that he be suspended from school once again. The principal was aware of a different kind of school she thought might help Jess.

Jess began attending the Manville School, a clinic in the Judge Baker Guidance Center in Boston for learning disabled and emotionally disturbed seven-to-fifteen-year-old children. Jess, like many other students at the Manville School, has shown considerable difficulty in interpersonal relationships. Since peer relationships become a crucial aspect of development during the elementary school and adolescent years, Robert Selman (Selman, Newberger, and Jacquette, 1977) has designed a peer therapy program at the Manville School to help students like Jess improve their peer relations in classroom settings, group activities, and sports. The staff at the Manville School has been trained to help peers provide support and encouragement to each other in such group settings, a process referred to as **peer sociotherapy.**

Structured programs at the Manville School are designed to help the children assist each other in such areas as cooperation, trust, leadership, and conformity. Four school activities were developed to improve the student's social reasoning skills in these areas.

First, there is a weekly peer problem-solving session in the classroom in which the peers work cooperatively to plan activities and relate problems. At the end of each week the peers evaluate their effectiveness in making improvements in areas like cooperation, conflict resolution, and so forth.

Second, the members of a class, numbering from six to eight students, plan a series of weekly field trips, for example, going to the movies or visiting historical sites. While the counselor provides some assistance, peer decision making dominates. When each activity is completed, the students discuss how things went and what might have been done to improve social relations with each other on the outings.

Third, Selman recognizes that there are times when the student has to get away from a setting where intense frustration occurs. When the student finds himself or herself in a highly frustrating situation (e.g., angry enough to strike out at a classmate), he or she is allowed to leave the room and go to a private "time-out" area of the school to regain composure. In time-out, the student also is given the opportunity to discuss the problems with a counselor who has been trained to help the child or adolescent improve social reasoning skills.

Fourth, during social studies and current events discussion sessions, the students evaluate a number of moral and societal issues that incorporate the thinking of theorists such as Lawrence Kohlberg.

*I*n this chapter, we study the existing world of peer relationships in adolescence. When you think back to your adolescent years, many of your most enjoyable moments were spent with peers—on the telephone, at school activities, in the neighborhood, in cars, on dates, at dances, and just fooling around. Let's look further at many different aspects of peer relations and then at the nature of adolescent friendships. Subsequently, we focus on adolescent groups and finally, on dating relationships and adolescent marriage.

Peer Relations: Bob with No Close Friends and Steve with Three Close Pals

Among important ideas about peer relations are those pertaining to the functions of the peer group, the co-ordinated world of parents and peers, and peer relations and social behavior/thought.

Functions of the Peer Group

What do we mean by the term *peers?* What is the link between peer relations and competent social development? Do peer relations vary across cultures? And, what is the effect of peer relations on perspective taking among adolescents? Let's now explore these questions in some detail.

The Meaning of the Term Peers

Adolescents spend a great deal of time with their peers; many of their greatest frustrations and happiest moments come when they are with their peers. To many adolescents, how they are seen by peers is the most important aspect of their lives. Some adolescents will go along with anything just to be included as a member of the group. To them, being excluded means stress, frustration, and sadness. Think about Bob, who has no close friends to speak of, in contrast to Steve, who has three close buddies he pals around with all of the time. Sally was turned down by the club at school that she was working to get into for six months, in contrast to Sandra, who is a member of the club and who frequently is told by her peers how "super" her personality is.

Some friends of mine have a daughter who is thirteen years old. Last year, she had a number of girl-friends—she spent a lot of time on the phone talking with them and they frequently visited each other's homes. Then her family moved and this thirteen-year-old girl had to attend a school with a lower socioeconomic mix of students than at her previous school. Many of the girls at the new school feel my friends' daughter is "too good" for them, and because of this she is having difficulty making friends this year. One of her most frequent complaints is, "I don't have any friends. . . . None of the kids at school ever call me. And none of them ever ask me over to their houses. What can I do?"

Peers are a very important part of the world of the adolescent, whether the youth is twelve or eighteen years old. The term **peers** usually refers to adolescents who are about the same age, but adolescents often interact with children or other adolescents who are three or four years older or younger. Peers have also been described as adolescents who interact at about the same behavioral level (Lewis and Rosenblum, 1975). Defining peers in terms of behavioral level places more emphasis on the maturity of the adolescents than on their age. For example, consider the precociously developed thirteen-year-old female adolescent who feels very funny around underdeveloped girls her own age. She may well find more satisfaction and want to spend more time with adolescents of seventeen to eighteen years of age than with those thirteen years of age.

The influence of adolescents who are the same age may be quite different from that of peers who are younger or older. For example, mixed-age groups often produce more dominant and altruistic behavior than do groups of adolescents of the same age (Murphy, 1973). Willard Hartup (1976), however, has emphasized that same-age peer interaction serves a unique role in our culture:

> I am convinced that age grading would occur even if our schools were not age graded and children (and adolescents) were left alone to determine the composition of their own societies. After all, one can only learn to be a good fighter among age-mates: the bigger guys will kill you, and the littler ones are no challenge. Sexual experience at pubescence with bigger people is too anxiety-laden and sexual experience with littler ones is really not very interesting (p. 10).

Peers are powerful social agents in the adolescent's life.

Perhaps one of the most important functions of the peer group is to provide a source of information and comparison about the world outside the family. From the peer group, the adolescent receives feedback about her abilities. She evaluates what she does in terms of whether it is better than, as good as, or worse than what other adolescents do. It is hard for her to do this at home, because siblings are usually older or younger. But through interaction with peers, she can find out whether she is popular with boys, whether she is good in sports, or whether she knows how to read well for her age.

The adolescent relies on the peer group for rehearsing roles and testing out ideas and behaviors, including sex-role behavior, dating, information about sex, cooperative and competitive behavior among equals, the expression of aggression, and play. These behaviors or ideas are often inhibited or impossible in the adolescent's interaction with adults, but they occur frequently in the context of peer relations.

Peer Relations and Competent Social Development

Good peer relations may be necessary for normal social development in adolescence. Social isolation, or the inability to "plug in" to a social network, is linked with many different forms of problems and disturbances, ranging from delinquency and problem drinking to depression. Adolescent social isolates, those individuals who during their teenage years are neither accepted nor rejected by their peers, seem to be particularly vulnerable to problems and disturbances in late adolescence and adulthood. This likely happens because they miss out on a considerable amount of socialization that only comes through association with peers (Hill, 1980). In one investigation (Roff, Sells, and Golden, 1972), very poor peer relations in childhood was linked with abnormal development in late adolescence and youth, including a tendency to drop out of school and engage in antisocial behavior.

In the human development literature, there is a classic example of the importance of peers. Anna Freud (Freud and Dann, 1951) studied six children from different families who banded together after their parents were killed in World War II. Intensive peer attachment was observed; the children were a tightly knit group, dependent on one another and aloof with outsiders. Even though deprived of parental care, they became neither delinquent nor psychotic.

Cross-Cultural Comparison of Peers

Peer relations are an important aspect of development in all cultures. One of the most widely cited studies of peers in different cultures is the work of Beatrice and John Whiting (1975). For their observations, the Whitings placed six teams of anthropologists in six different cultures, five of which were primarily farming communities: northern India; the Philippines; Okinawa, Japan; Oaxaca, Mexico; and western Kenya. The sixth setting was a small, nonfarming town in New England. The teams interviewed the mothers and conducted standardized observations of the children in the six cultures. Aggressiveness, prosocial activity, and sociable behavior were the most frequently occurring behaviors in peer relations across the six cultures.

Other cross-cultural comparisons have included information about Russian and American children. For example, it has been argued that children in the United States succumb to peer pressure more than children in other cultures (Bronfenbrenner, 1970). It has been found in comparisons of Russian and American children, for instance, that Russian children resist peer pressure more when peer norms conflict with adult norms (Devereaux, 1970). The reason for these findings becomes clearer when the Soviet socialization process is evaluated. As soon as schooling begins in Russia, the peer group is assigned important duties in assisting the teacher. Conformity to group norms is stressed throughout education, and subordination of the individual to the group is omnipresent. Group competition between grades, schools, rooms, and rows within each room is emphasized. Although these practices are not foreign to schools in the United States, they are not as systematized as they are in the Soviet Union. In the United States, the peer group may undermine the socialization practices of adults; in the Soviet Union, however, peer group norms even in adolescence support adult norms.

Next, we look at the nature of peer relations in different cultures and different cultural settings, looking at the importance of perspective taking in peer relations.

Perspective Taking

A research investigation that took place in Norway and Hungary provides further support for the belief that peer relations serve important developmental functions. In this study (Hollis, 1975), the main interest focused on **perspective taking,** which can be defined as the ability to take someone else's point of view (perspective). The Norwegian and Hungarian children were seven to nine years old and lived in one of three settings in each country—an isolated, dispersed farm community, a village, or a town, which varied in terms of the relative physical isolation of the children from one another. The children were assessed on three measures of perspective taking—visual perspective taking, communication accuracy, and role taking. In the visual perspective-taking task, the children observed a three-dimensional display of buildings and were asked to tell what the view of the buildings would look like if they were seated at different locations around the table on which the buildings were placed. This is a widely used Piagetian task and provides an index of how egocentric a child is. The child who can decenter is able to provide a perspective of how the buildings look from other locations than where he or she is seated. Communication accuracy was assessed by telling each child a story and then having the child repeat the story to another person. Role taking was investigated by showing the child a seven-picture cartoon sequence that told an obvious story. Three pictures were then removed from the sequence and the child was told to tell the story to another person who had not seen all seven pictures. To analyze the results, the researchers combined the scores

Martin Gold and Denise Yanof (1985) investigated the relation between adolescent girls' relationships with their mothers and their relationships with their closest girlfriends. They gave questionnaires to 134 high school girls asking them about mother–daughter affection, democratic treatment by their mothers, and appropriateness of their mothers as models. In addition, they asked the high school girls about the intimacy of their relationships with their closest girlfriends, the mutual influence in these peer relationships, and their identification with their girlfriends.

The results of the study clearly revealed that consideration of their mothers as appropriate models was positively related to not only the girls' identification with their closest girlfriends, but to the intimacy of those friendships. This intimacy involved high levels of affection. A summary of these results is pictured in figure 7.1. As can be seen, the general extent to which the girl identified with her mother was significantly related to her identification with her girlfriend(s). Identification with mothers was assessed by such items as the extent the girl said she "would like to become like" her mother in regard to such characteristics as career attainment, appearance, relationships with people, and the like. Identification with a girlfriend(s) was assessed by asking the girl to rate the general extent she wanted to be like her girlfriend. Note also that the more girls perceived their

Adolescent girls' relationships with their girlfriends are related to mother–daughter relationships.

mothers treated them in a democratic way, the more likely the girls were to report mutual influence in relationships with their girlfriends.

Gold and Yanof (1985) concluded that these data support a developmental rather than a compensatory model of adolescent relationships. A developmental model suggests that parents, through close, positive relationships with adolescents, influence the adolescent's construction of positive relationships with others. A

on these measures to obtain a total perspective-taking score. In both Norway and Hungary, children from the isolated farm regions were much poorer at perspective taking than the children from the villages and towns.

Now that we have studied some of the important functions of the peer group, we return to a theme of the last chapter that deserves further elaboration. While we will study many different aspects of peer relations in this chapter, it is important to keep in mind the connectedness of parent and peer worlds in understanding the adolescent's development.

The Coordinated Worlds of Parents and Peers

As was described in the last chapter, the history of studying adolescents' relationships with their parents and peers has been one filled with references to disengagement and disconnectedness with parents and one consisting of approach and connectedness to peers. Comments have been made about how peers become deeply immersed in peer relations when their relationships with parents are poor; and about how as adolescence unfolds, adolescents distance themselves from their parents and live in a world of peers separated and aloof from their parents. To be sure, adolescents who

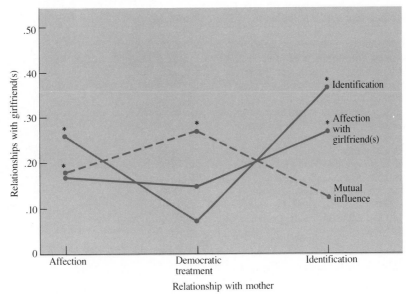

*Significant correlation

Figure 7.1 **Linking mother-daughter relationships with girlfriend relationships of the adolescent female.**

compensatory model indicates that adolescents immerse themselves in relationships with peers when they lack close, positive relationships with parents. Quite clearly, such data support our argument that connectedness and attachment to parents continue as adolescents form relationships outside of their family, and that the positive nature of parent–adolescent relationships contributes to healthy peer relationships.

have problems in their relationships with parents often do try to find a strong identity with the peer group, and adolescents do show a strong motivation to be with peers and develop a sense of independence and identity. However, it is incorrect to assume that movement toward independence and strong peer involvement is not continually linked to parent–adolescent relationships. Even the adolescent who seems to show a complete preoccupation with the world of peers, friendships, and dating cannot be fully understood without knowing the nature of his or her relationships with parents, both in the present and in the past. Parent and peer relations simply are not opposing forces in many instances. And even when parent and peer relations seem to be in conflict, to understand adolescent development, it is important to study how relationships with parents have shaped peer relationships.

One recent investigation revealed how important relationships with parents are in understanding an important aspect of adolescent development, friendship. To learn more about this study, read Perspective on Adolescent Development 7.1, where we discuss mother–daughter relationships and the adolescent girl's relationships with her girlfriends.

Willard Hartup (1983) accurately summarized the importance of secure family relationships in peer relations:

> Secure family relations are the basis for entry into the peer system and success within it. Family breakdown tends to interfere with adaptation to the peer culture and good family relations are needed throughout childhood and adolescence as bases for peer relations. Parent and peer values are mainly concordant, especially on issues "that matter." Normative opposition is probably more acute in early adolescence than before or after, with the most intense oppositional experience surrounding antisocial behavior. Most adolescents remain attuned to parental norms even though much time is spent with other children. Dissonance may be considerable when adolescents are alienated from their parents and associate with age-mates who endorse misconduct, but the majority of adolescents are able to synthesize their understandings and expectations of the family and the peer system . . .

Peer Relations and Social Behavior / Thought

Peer relations connect with many different aspects of the adolescent's behavior and thought. Among these connections are those involving peer pressure and conformity; popularity and social acceptance; reinforcement, modeling, and social comparison; social knowledge and social information processing; and social skills training.

Peer Pressure and Conformity

The pressure to conform to peers becomes very strong during the adolescent years. Consider the comments of Kevin, a seventh grader:

> I feel a lot of pressure from my friends to smoke and steal and things like that. My parents do not allow me to smoke, but my best friends are really pushing me to do it. They call me a pansy and a momma's boy if I don't. I really don't like the idea of smoking, but my good friend Steve told me in front of some of our friends, "Kevin, you are an idiot and a chicken wrapped up in one little body." I couldn't stand it any more, so I smoked with them. I was coughing and humped over, but I still said, "This is really fun—yeah, I like it." I felt like I was part of the group.

Vandalism sometimes is a form of negative conformity behavior in adolescence.

Also, think about the statement by fourteen-year-old Andrea:

> Peer pressure is extremely influential in my life. I have never had very many friends, and I spend quite a bit of time alone. The friends I have are older. . . . The closest friend I have had is a lot like me in that we are both sad and depressed a lot. I began to act even more depressed than before when I was with her. I would call her up and try to act even more depressed than I was because that is what I thought she liked. In that relationship I felt pressure to be like her. . . .

These examples show how peer pressure can influence adolescents to act in ways they don't really want to. *Conformity* refers to the act of agreeing with the expressed group opinion when pressed to do so. It also refers to the act of concurring with the rules and social practices of a culture or subculture. The use of slang or jargon, adherence to a dress code, and many behavioral mannerisms reflect conformity.

In thinking about conformity to peer pressure in adolescence, it is important to remember that such conformity can consist of positive or negative circumstances. Teenagers engage in all sorts of negative conformity behavior—they go places in cars with people they are afraid of, use seedy language, steal, vandalize, and make fun of parents and teachers. However, a great deal of peer conformity is not negative and consists of the desire to be involved in the peer world, such as dressing like friends and wanting to spend huge chunks of time with members of a clique. Such circumstances may involve prosocial activities as well, as when clubs raise money for worthy causes.

In one investigation of peer conformity focused on negative, neutral, and positive aspects of conformity, Thomas Berndt (1979) studied 273 third through twelfth grade students. Hypothetical dilemmas were presented to the students, requiring them to make choices about conformity with friends on prosocial and antisocial behavior and conformity with parents on neutral and prosocial behaviors. For example, one prosocial item questioned whether students relied on their parents' advice in such situations as deciding about helping at the library or instructing another child to swim. An antisocial question asked a boy what he would do if one of his peers wanted him to help steal some candy. A neutral question asked a girl if she would follow peer suggestions to engage in an activity she wasn't interested in—for example, going to a movie she didn't want to see.

Some interesting developmental patterns were found in this investigation. In the third grade, parent and peer influences often directly contradicted each other. Since parent conformity is much greater for third-grade children, children of this age are probably still closely tied to and dependent on their parents. However by the sixth grade, parent and peer influences were found to be no longer in direct opposition. Peer conformity had increased, but parent and peer influences were operating in different situations—parents had more impact in some situations, while peers had more clout in others. For example, it was found that parents were more influential in a discussion of political parties but peers seemed to have more to say when sexual behavior and attitudes were at issue (Hyman, 1959; Vandiver, 1972).

By the ninth grade, parent and peer influences were once again in strong opposition to one another, probably because the increased conformity of adolescents to the social behavior of peers is much stronger at this grade level than at any other. At this time adolescent adoption of antisocial standards endorsed by the peer group inevitably leads to conflict between adolescents and parents. Researchers have also found that the adolescent's attempt to gain independence meets with more parental opposition around the ninth grade than at any other time (Douvan and Adelson, 1966; Kandel and Lesser, 1969).

A stereotypical view of parent–child relationships suggests that parent–peer opposition continues into the late high school and college-age years. But Berndt (1979) found that adolescent conformity to antisocial, peer-endorsed behavior decreases in the late high school years, and greater agreement between parents and peers begins to occur in some areas. In addition, by the eleventh and twelfth grades, students show signs of developing a decision-making style more independent of peer and parent influence. A summary of peer conformity to antisocial, neutral, and prosocial standards found in Berndt's (1979) study is presented in figure 7.2.

Other recent research also has focused on a distinction between different kinds of conformity. For instance, Bradford Brown and his colleagues (Brown, Clasen, and Eicher, in press) have studied peer involvement (the degree of socializing with friends) and misconduct (drug/alcohol use, sexual intercourse, and minor delinquent behavior). Adolescents perceived less peer pressure toward misconduct than peer involvement and also were less willing to follow peers in misconduct. And, males were more likely to accede to antisocial peer pressures than females.

So far, we have looked at how adolescents conform to peer pressure and societal standards. While the majority of adolescents are conformity oriented, some could best be described as independent or rebellious. The truly *independent* or **nonconformist** adolescent knows what the people around him expect, but he doesn't use these expectations to guide his behavior. However, the *rebellious* or **anticonformist** teenager reacts counter to the group's expectations and deliberately moves away from the actions or beliefs they advocate.

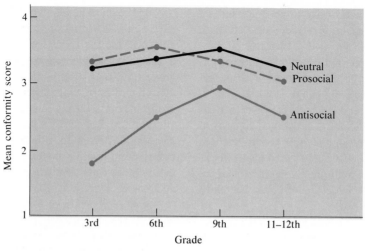

Figure 7.2 Mean scores for peer conformity on different types of behavior. Higher scores indicate greater conformity: The neutral point is 3.5.

There are many ways in which peers influence each other in addition to applying pressure to conform. One motivation affecting most teenagers' behavior is the desire to be popular, as we see next.

Popularity and Social Acceptance

Every adolescent wants to be popular—you probably thought about popularity a lot when you were in junior and senior high school. Teenagers commonly think, "What can I do to have all of the kids at school like me?" "How can I be popular with both girls and guys?" "What's wrong with me? There must be something wrong, or I would be more popular." Sometimes adolescents will go to great lengths to be popular; and in some cases, parents go to even greater lengths to try to insulate their adolescents from rejection and to increase the likelihood that they will be popular. Students show off and cut up because it gets attention and makes their peers laugh. Parents set up elaborate parties, buy cars and clothes for their teens, and drive adolescents and their friends all over in the hope that their sons or daughters will be popular.

What makes an adolescent popular with peers? Adolescents who give the most reinforcements get the most in return (e.g., Hartup, 1970). Coaching sessions designed to help boys and girls gain social acceptance in the peer group (Oden and Asher, 1975) focus on getting students to help their peers have fun, to listen carefully to what peers are saying, and to maintain open lines of communication with peers. Being yourself, being happy, being the "life of the party," conforming to peer group norms, being friendly, showing enthusiasm, indicating concern for others, and showing self-confidence, but not conceit are among the characteristics that lead to popularity in adolescence (Hartup, 1970, 1983). In many instances, the opposites of these characteristics invite rejection from peers. Nobody wants to be around a cocky, conceited adolescent; few adolescents want to be around others who are not enthusiastic, who don't listen to what they have to say, and who fail to take their views and feelings into account (e.g., Hollingshead, 1975).

Certain physical and cultural factors also affect an adolescent's popularity. Youth who are physically attractive are more popular than those who are not and, contrary to what some believe, brighter adolescents are more popular than less intelligent ones. Adolescents growing up in middle-class surroundings tend to be more popular than those growing up in lower-class surroundings, presumably in part because they are more in control of establishing standards for popularity (e.g., Hollingshead, 1975). But remember that findings such as these reflect group averages—there are many physically attractive teenagers who are unpopular, and some physically unattractive ones who are very well liked. James Coleman (1980) points out that for adolescents in the average range, there is little or no relation between physical attractiveness and popularity. It is only in the extremes (very attractive and very ugly) that a link between popularity and attractiveness holds. And, with the increase in concern for equal treatment of minority groups, lower-class and ethnic group adolescents can be expected to gain in popularity. In addition, popularity may fluctuate—even the adolescent who is very popular with peers may have doubts about her ability to maintain her popularity. Being popular with peers is an ongoing concern for almost every adolescent.

In recent years, there also has been considerable interest in making a distinction between two sets of children and adolescents who are not popular with their peers—those who are neglected or rejected (Asher and Dodge, 1986). **Neglected children,** while they may not have friends, are not particularly disliked by their peers. However, **rejected children** are overtly disliked by their peers. Rejected children are much more likely to demonstrate disruptive and aggressive behavior than neglected children. And, rejected children are much more likely to continue to be unaccepted by their peers as they move into a new setting, while neglected children seem to get a new social life in new groups (Coie and Dodge, 1983; Coie and Kupersmidt, 1983; Newcomb and Bukowski, 1984). Also, neglected children differ in the amount of loneliness and social unhappiness they experience, with rejected children reporting more problems in this area (Asher and Wheeler, 1985). Further, rejected children seem to have more serious adjustment problems later in life, both as adolescents and

as adults (Cown et al., 1973; Kupersmidt, 1983; Roff, Sells, and Golden, 1972). In sum, it appears that rejected children are more at risk for adjustment problems in adolescence while the risk status of neglected children is less clear.

So far in our overview of peer relations and social behavior/thought, we have learned about peer conformity and popularity. Now we turn our attention to three processes that are very important in learning about the nature of adolescent behavior in peer contexts.

Reinforcement, Modeling, and Social Comparison

Processes involved in the nature of the adolescent's behavior in peer relations are the nature of reinforcement, modeling, and social comparison.

Peer relations are affected by the extent to which the individuals dispense rewards to each other. The members of a peer group who give out the most reinforcements are the ones most likely to receive the most reinforcements in return (Charlesworth and Hartup, 1973). This indicates the reciprocal nature of peer interaction. In one investigation, it was found that training peers to selectively use reinforcement reduced disruptive activity in the classroom (Solomon and Whalen, 1973).

Peers also are influenced by the model their associates provide. Positive relationships between models and observers tend to enhance the model's effectiveness (Hartup and Coates, 1967) as does the extent to which the individual perceived the model as similar to himself or herself (Rosenkrans, 1967). Models who are more powerful are often more likely to be followed than those who are less powerful (Bandura, 1977). So, the leaders of the school, captains of the football team and drill team, president of the student council, and so forth are more likely to be imitated than those not in school leadership positions. And, in some instances, older adolescents are more likely to be adopted as someone to model behavior after than adolescents the same age as the youth. Because of their age, experience, and knowledge, older adolescents are more likely to come across as more powerful than younger adolescents.

Social comparison is a persuasive process during the adolescent years.

In discussing the functions of the peer group earlier in the chapter, it was mentioned that one of the primary functions of the peer group is to provide a means of **social comparison** about one's abilities, talents, characteristics, and the like. Social comparison seems to heighten as boys and girls move from the elementary school years into early adolescence. On a daily basis, it is not unusual to hear comments such as, "I don't like her hair. It is not as natural as yours and mine." And, "What a yucky looking car he has. Mine is much better. Don't you think?" Or, "I got an A on the biology test. What did you get?" Consider also the following comments of one person describing her girlfriend as a social comparison source:

> "Girlfriends were as essential as mothers . . . girlfriends provided a sense of security, as belonging to any group does . . . (but) a best friend was more complicated: using a friend as a mirror or as a model, expanding your own knowledge through someone else's, painfully acquiring social skills. What little we learned about living with another person in an equal relationship, outside our own families, we learned from our girlfriends" (Toth, 1981, p. 60).

Social comparison, of course, can have either negative or positive effects. As adolescents look around their peer world and compare themselves with others, they likely find some things about themselves they like better than other peers yet others they like less. Adolescents who see themselves more positively than most others likely have higher self-esteem than those who compare themselves more negatively to others. Quite clearly, though, social comparison is a highly motivating aspect of adolescent life, as adolescents strive to find out where they stand vis-a-vis their peers on many different abilities and characteristics.

So far much of what we have discussed about peer relations and social behavior/thought has focused on the nature of peer relations and social behavior. As we see next, currently considerable interest has been generated in learning more about the role of social knowledge and social information processing in understanding peer relations.

Social Knowledge and Social Information Processing
Recall from our discussion of intelligence in Chapter 5 that a distinction can be made between knowledge and process. In studying cognitive aspects of peer relations the same distinction can be made. It is important to learn about the social knowledge an adolescent brings with him/her to peer relations and it also is helpful to study how the adolescent processes information during peer interaction.

Social Knowledge As children move into adolescence, they acquire more social knowledge. And there is considerable individual variation in how much one adolescent knows about what it takes to make friends, to get peers to like him or her, and so forth. For example, does the adolescent know that giving out reinforcements will increase the likelihood that he or she will be popular? That is, does Mary consciously know that by telling Barbara such things as, "I really like that sweater you have on today," and "Gosh, you sure are popular with the guys," will enhance the likelihood Barbara will want her to be her friend? Does the adolescent know that when others perceive he or she is similar to them, he or she will be liked better by the others? Does the adolescent know that friendship involves sharing intimate conversations and that a friendship likely is improved when the adolescent shares private, confidential information with another adolescent? To what extent does the adolescent know that comforting and listening skills will improve friendship relations? To what extent does the adolescent know what it takes to become a leader? Think back to your adolescent years. How sophisticated were you in knowing about such social matters? Were you aware of the role of nice statements and perceived similarity in determining popularity and friendship? While you may not have been aware of these factors, those of you who were popular and maintained close friendships likely were competent at using these strategies.

One investigation (Dooley, Whalen, and Flowers, 1978) revealed information about the social knowledge of individuals from the ages of seven to fifteen. They asked fifth-, sixth-, eighth-, and tenth-grade boys and girls to respond in writing to videotaped, role-played vignettes as though they actually were in contact with the speakers themselves. The videotapes focused on the problems disclosed by males and females aged seven to fifteen years old. The observers were induced to believe that some of the individuals in the videotapes were problem youngsters while others were not. In addition to responding in writing to the videotapes, the boys and girls were asked to rate how often their friends came to talk to them about personal problems.

Compared to younger respondents, the adolescents made more negative statements, gave more advice in general, advised less often to obtain help from a third person, and made fewer disclosures. Female subjects gave more advice, focused on solving problems verbally, and made fewer interpretations than males did. Females shown on the videotapes elicited less advice in general, more advice to change their own thoughts and feelings, and more interpretations than did males. Students portrayed as disturbed on the videotapes were given fewer negatives, more advice to seek third-person help, and more disclosures than students depicted as not disturbed.

Analysis of the advice suggested that the high school students used more instrumental-physical (for example, "Why don't you try distracting your brother by giving him a game to play with?") and cognitive-affective (for example, "Put yourself in your brother's shoes," or "You are just going to have to put up with his anger") advice than younger students did. This supports the belief that high school students have more real and self-perceived competence. They have had more experience in coping with problems, are capable of generating more cognitively complex ideas, and are better at finding direct, active solutions to their problems. The decrease in self-disclosure by high school students may indicate increased concern about self-presentation during the high school years.

With regard to the question "What is the best thing you can do when a friend comes to you to talk about a problem?", the most frequent response at the elementary school level was "Try to solve it." However, this was the third most frequent response at the high school level. "Try to help the person understand the problem" was the most frequent response given by junior high students, while "Understand" and "Find out more about the problem" were most frequently the replies of high school students.

From a social cognitive perspective, children and adolescents who are maladjusted likely do not have adequate social cognitive skills necessary for skillful social interaction (Asarnow and Asarnow, 1982; Asher and Renshaw, 1981; Butler and Meichenbaum, 1981; Spivack, Platt, and Shure, 1976). One recent investigation (Asarnow and Callan, 1985) explored the possibility that social cognitive skill deficits characterize maladjusted children. Boys with and without peer adjustment difficulties were identified and then a number of social cognitive processes or skills were assessed. These included the boy's ability to generate alternative solutions to hypothetical problems, to evaluate these solutions in terms of their effectiveness, to describe self-statements, and to rate the likelihood of self-statements. It was found that boys without peer adjustment problems generated more alternative solutions, proposed more assertive and mature solutions, gave less intense aggressive solutions, showed more adaptive planning, and evaluated physically aggressive responses less positively than the boys with peer adjustment problems. For example, as shown in figure 7.3, negative peer status sixth grade boys were not as likely to generate alternative solutions and much less likely to adaptively plan ahead than their positive peer status counterparts.

While it is becoming clear that social cognitive knowledge is a very important ingredient of peer relations, as yet, we have not developed a precise body of social cognitive knowledge believed to be beneficial to children and adolescents at different developmental levels. However, it seems clear that adolescents who get along better with others, both peers and adults, likely have significantly greater knowledge about social skills than those who are not popular and not well liked.

Social Information Processing In our discussion of information processing, we discovered that a number of processes are involved in our effort to extract and use information about the world—such processes as attention, memory, and problem solving.

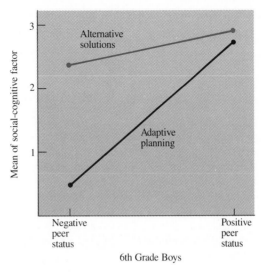

Figure 7.3   Generation of alternative solutions and adaptive planning by negative and positive peer status boys.

Kenneth Dodge (Dodge, 1980, 1983; Dodge, Coie, and Brakke, 1982; Dodge and Frame, 1982) believes children and adolescents go through five steps in processing social information: decoding of social cues, interpretation, response search, selecting an optimal response, and enactment. In one investigation (Dodge, 1980), it was demonstrated that distortions during the early phases of processing social information may lead to aggression among boys. For instance, aggressive boys are more likely than nonaggressive boys to perceive another person's actions as hostile when there actually is considerable ambiguity in a peer's intention. And, when aggressive boys are allowed to search for cues to determine a peer's intention, they respond more rapidly and engage in a less efficient search than their nonaggressive counterparts. Further information about the important social skill in being able to detect intention by a peer is presented in Perspective on Adolescent Development 7.2.

The development of ideas about social knowledge, communication, and information processing has important implications for improving the social skills of adolescents in peer contexts. Next, we look more closely at the nature of these social skills training programs.

Social Skills Training

Remember in the prologue to this chapter the peer-oriented school developed by Robert Selman? Selman's approach to helping children and adolescents who have problems with peers is a social cognitive approach that emphasizes social skills training. Other social cognitive strategies are being tried out in efforts to improve social skills with peers as well (e.g., Asher, 1985; Dodge, 1985; Ladd and Mars, 1985). One recent investigation (Mize, 1985) revealed that teaching children how to ask questions, how to be a leader, how to show support to peers, and how to make appropriate comments to peers was invaluable in getting the children to behave

A peer accidentally trips and knocks the boy's soft drink out of his hand. The boy misinterprets the encounter as hostile, which leads him to retaliate aggressively against the peer. His aggression is viewed as inappropriate by peers who observed the encounter. Through repeated encounters of this nature, peers come to perceive the boy as having a habit of acting inappropriately. In a recent investigation, Kenneth Dodge and his colleagues (Dodge, Murphy, and Buchsbaum, 1984) studied boys like the one just mentioned who misinterpreted social cues on a consistent basis. They developed a measure to assess **intention-cue detection,** investigated whether this skill develops across the elementary school years, examined the relation between intention-cue detection and deviant behavior on the part of children, and described the role of intention-cue detection in developing a model of developmental psychopathology.

The measure of intention-cue detection skill was a discrimination task in which a child was presented with fourteen sets of three short videotaped vignettes, each showing social interaction between two children in which one child provokes the other. In two of the three vignettes, the actor shows the same intention, but in the third he shows a different intention. The subject's task is identify the different vignette. Intentions included those that were hostile, prosocial, accidental, and others.

This measure was given to 176 children in kindergarten, second, and fourth grades who were identified as having a peer status as popular, average, socially rejected, or socially neglected. Scores on the intention cue measure increased with age and normal children (popular and average) had higher scores than deviant children (neglected and rejected). The mistakes made by the deviant children consistently involved erroneously labeling prosocial intentions as hostile (figure 7.4). A hostile intention was represented by a display of obviously purposeful destructive behavior accompanied by corresponding verbalizations and facial expressions. A prosocial intention was reflected in a purposeful destruction of a peer's play object, but in an effort to help someone else (such as destroying a block tower while cleaning up the room).

So, children who are deficient (relative to their age-mates) in intention-cue detection are likely to show behavior viewed as inappropriate by their peers. Since children are capable of identifying hostile intentions at an earlier age than prosocial intentions, children deficient in intention-cue detection are likely to make errors in judging nonhostile actions as hostile. This error is likely to lead some children to act aggressively. Other children who make this attributional error may respond by withdrawing. Either response is likely to be judged by peers as inappropriate to the situation. Those who respond aggressively have a high probability of being rejected by peers, while those who withdraw have a high probability of being neglected by peers (Dodge, 1983).

In sum, Dodge and his colleagues believe that aggressive children show a systematic bias toward attributing hostile intentions to peers, even in situations when they are not warranted. This bias increases the likelihood they will retaliate aggressively toward peers, behavior they sense is appropriate, but behavior their peers view as inappropriate. The peer group likewise eventually comes to display a bias toward expecting the aggressive children will be hostile, justifying their rejection of them. An implication of these findings is that aggressive children perpetuate their deviant status and behavior through their biased patterns of perceiving the social world; thus they may have difficulty changing their behavior.

---

in more socially competent ways during peer interaction. Sophisticated counselor training programs that were designed for adults (e.g., Carkhuff, 1969) now are being used with adolescents and children (e.g., Cooker and Cherchia, 1976; Kloba and Zimpfer, 1976).

It seems that some of the most effective strategies are a conglomerate of processes. For example, in the strategy used by Jacquelyn Mize (1985), not just a single skill or approach was used, but rather a combination of strategies were called on to facilitate peer

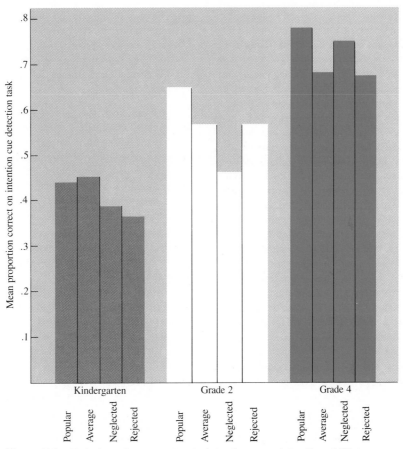

Figure 7.4 **Relation of peer status to intention cue detection ability.**

relations. These conglomerate strategies are often re-ferred to as **coaching.** A conglomerate strategy might consist of demonstration or modeling of appropriate so-cial skills, discussion, and reasoning about the social skills, as well as the use of reinforcement for their en-

actment in actual social situations. In one coaching study, students with few friends were selected and trained in ways to have fun with peers. The "unpop-ular" students were encouraged to participate fully, to show interest in others, to cooperate, and to maintain

A number of strategies for training the social skills of adolescents have been described by Arnold Goldstein and his colleagues in a book, *Skill-Streaming the Adolescent* (Goldstein, Sprafkin, Gershaw, and Klein, 1981). These include such behavior management strategies as reinforcement, including social and group reinforcement, punishment, including time-out procedures, modeling, and role playing. A major focus of the book is how such social skills can be trained in the school setting. One particularly helpful set of strategies involves those pertaining to relationship-based techniques.

Psychologists and educators have known for many years that the better the relationship between a helper and a student, the more positive and productive will be the outcome of their interaction. In many instances, relationship-based techniques require the social skills trainer to become aware of broader aspects of the adolescent's life than just those happenings in the classroom. The helper tries to gain some sense of the adolescent's motivation for behaving in a particular way and attempts to respond to the adolescent's needs. One particular strategy that can be beneficial focuses on empathetic encouragement. In using this strategy, the trainer shows the adolescent that she or he understands his or her difficulty, and encourages the adolescent to participate as instructed. A series of steps then are followed:

1. The adolescent is offered the chance to explain in detail the problems being encountered while the trainer listens nondefensively.
2. The trainer indicates that she or he understands the adolescent's behavior.
3. If it is appropriate, the trainer indicates that the adolescent's view is a reasonable interpretation or alternative.

4. The trainer restates his or her view with supporting reasons and likely outcomes.
5. The trainer expresses the appropriateness of delaying a resolution of the problem.
6. The trainer encourages the adolescent to try to participate.

An example is the case of Rose, a somewhat temperamental, disruptive adolescent who was very negative about getting involved in the social skills training program, responding by laughing and making mocking gestures. After attempting to ignore such behavior, the trainer finally decided to discuss Rose's behavior in an empathetic manner. Rose was asked to explain why she was acting this way (laughing, mocking). Rose said she thought the skill training was stupid. She said in her family, if she wanted permission for anything she had to wait for a week. At home, then, she said she simply took what she wanted.

The trainer then told Rose that it is understandable why this skill won't work at home. It might be a skill she would not want to use there, she was informed. Rose was informed that there might be a lot of situations away from home, such as at school, where the skill could be helpful. She was told that at school there are many times that a student has to ask permission to do certain things, such as leaving the classroom and turning in an assignment late. The trainer indicated that if you just go ahead and do these things without asking permission, you can wind up in a lot of trouble. Rose was told that maybe it would be a good idea to hold off on judging whether this skill involving asking permission was good or bad until she had a chance to try it out. Rose subsequently agreed to try the skill out in a small group and she became reasonably attentive through the remainder of the social skills training session.

communication. A control group of students (who also had few friends) was directed in peer experiences, but was not coached specifically in terms of improved peer strategies. Subsequent assessment revealed that the coaching was effective with the coached group showing more sociability when observed in peer relationships than their noncoached counterparts (Oden and Asher, 1975).

Social skills training can help adolescents engage in more competent peer relations.

Another helpful strategy described by Goldstein and his colleagues (1981) focuses on the elicitation of peer support. To the degree peer group goals are important to the adolescent, peer pressure can be used to the helper's advantage in working with the adolescent. The trainer's task becomes one of structuring the group activity so peer support can be mobilized. The trainer also may elicit specific group support for particular behaviors shown by hesitant or less skilled adolescents in the group.

Consider the following circumstances. The trainer noticed that before and after role-playing strategies, a number of negative comments, jokes, and insults were being hurled around by the adolescents. To deal with these sarcastic rejoinders, the trainer decided to teach the skill called giving a compliment. The trainer made the role-playing task one of giving a true compliment to someone in the class about what they were doing in the class. The adolescents had to think about this for awhile, but eventually were able to compliment each other on their helpfulness, communicating better, and so forth. When the next skill was taught, the trainer gave the adolescents the task of giving a compliment to each adolescent who had role played.

Through strategies such as those described by Goldstein and his associates (1981), skill-deficient adolescents are being helped to live more socially competent lives and function more maturely in school settings.

To learn more about strategies being used with adolescents who have deficient social skills, read Perspective on Adolescent Development 7.3, where we discuss skill-streaming with adolescents. We have evaluated a number of ideas about peer relations. A summary of these ideas is presented in Concept Table 7.1.

Now that we have studied many different aspects of peer relations, we turn our attention in more detailed ways to an aspect of peer relations we already have commented on several times. Next, information about adolescent friendships is provided.

PEER RELATIONS		
Concept	*Processes/related ideas*	*Characteristics/description*
Functions of the peer group	Meaning of the term *peers*	The term *peers* refers to people who are about the same age and/or developmental level. Social comparison and a source of information outside the family represent two important functions of peers.
	Peers and competent social development	Good peer relations represent an important aspect of competent social development. Children and adolescents who have poor peer relations are at risk for psychological problems.
	Cross-cultural comparisons	Peer relations are an important aspect of development in virtually all cultures. It has been argued that adolescents in the United States succumb to peer pressure more than in most cultures.
	Perspective taking	In cultural settings where peer relations are more prominent, perspective taking is enhanced.
Coordinated worlds of parents and peers	Connectedness	Connectedness occurs within families and within peer groups as well as between families and peer groups.
Peer relations and social behavior/thought	Peer pressure and conformity	The pressure to conform to peers becomes very strong during the adolescent years. It seems to be stronger in early adolescence than late adolescence. At about the ninth grade conformity to antisocial peer norms seems to heighten. Most conformity behavior focuses on peer involvement, such as socializing with friends, rather than antisocial conformity. Males are more likely to conform to antisocial standards than females. Rejected children seem to be more at risk than neglected children.

Friendships: My Best Friend is Nice, My Best Friend is a Kite

My best friend is nice. She's honest, and I can trust her. I can tell her my innermost secrets and know that nobody else will find out about them. I have other friends, too, but she is my best friend. We consider each other's feelings and don't want to hurt each other. We help each other out when we have problems. We make up funny names for people and laugh ourselves silly. We make lists of which boys are the sexiest and which are the ugliest, which are the biggest jerks, and so on. Some of these things we share with other friends, but some we don't.

Although all adolescents want to be popular with large segments of their age group, they also want to have one or two best friends. Unfortunately, however, many adolescents do not have a best friend, or even a circle of friends, in whom they can confide. A certain school psychologist always made a practice of asking children and adolescents about their friends. One twelve-year-old boy, when asked who his best friend was, replied, "My kite." Further discussion revealed that his parents had insulated him from the society of neighborhood peers. Similarly, in one investigation of college-age youth, as many as one out of every three

Concept Table 7.1 (Continued)

PEER RELATIONS		
Concept	*Processes/related ideas*	*Characteristics/description*
	Popularity and social acceptance	Among the factors that contribute to popularity are giving out reinforcements, the ability to have fun, listening skills, open communication lines, being yourself, conforming to peer norms, being friendly, showing enthusiasm, showing concern for others, and having self-confidence, but not being conceited.
	Reinforcement, modeling, and social comparison	These three processes represent important ways in which peers interact with each other.
	Social knowledge and social information processing	Adolescents have more social knowledge than children, but there is considerable variation in social knowledge among adolescents. Social knowledge contributes to effective social relationships. One study has shown that boys with more social knowledge are better adjusted than their counterparts with less social knowledge. The manner in which adolescents process information about their social world is an important determinant of their social competence. An example of an important social information processing skill is the ability to detect intention by a peer.
	Social skills training	Various social cognitive strategies are being tried out with adolescents who are deficient in social skills. These strategies usually involve conglomerate skills and often are given the label *coaching*.

students surveyed said that they had not found, or were not sure whether they had found, a close, meaningful relationship with a same-sex peer (Katz, 1968). John Conger (1977) suggests several explanations for why many adolescents have difficulty establishing close friendships. While many adolescents indicate that meaningful friendships are high on their list of needs, they may lack the skills necessary to get and retain friends (for example, the ability to consistently demonstrate active listening and open communication styles). It also may be that adolescents have a more stringent definition of "meaningful" friendship than other age segments in the population. And, while many adolescents stress that they have a strong need for close friends, they may be suspicious of what such a commitment will mean in terms of reciprocation—"Can I really trust her? Does she really like me for me, or is she just using me?" In sum, while friendship is considered a strong need by adolescents, many lack the skills to initiate and maintain friendships, and others are wary of the commitments such friendship brings.

Cognitive Factors

As boys and girls move through the childhood and adolescent years, their cognitive development likely changes the manner in which friendship is characterized. Particularly by the time children have reached the age of ten, they likely have developed a true sensitivity to the feelings of another child (Sullivan, 1953). As children and adolescents are asked to characterize their best friend, with age they are more likely to use more interpersonal constructs, are more flexible in their use of these constructs, provide more complex and organized information about their friends, and understand that particular attributes characterize their friends compared to their acquaintances (Hartup, 1983; Shantz, 1983).

Intimacy in Friendships

Intimacy in friendships has been defined in different ways; for example, it has been broadly defined to include everything in a relationship that makes it seem close or intense (Huston and Burgess, 1979). But in most research studies, **intimacy in friendship** has been defined more narrowly in terms of intimate self-disclosure and the sharing of private thoughts. Another factor in intimacy is private and personal knowledge about a friend (Selman, 1980; Sullivan, 1953).

Most efforts to obtain information about friendships simply involve asking children such questions as "What is a friend?" or "How can you tell that someone is your best friend?" (Berndt, 1982). Researchers find that intimate friendships rarely appear during childhood, but are most likely to first arise during early adolescence. For example, in one investigation (Diaz and Berndt, 1982), fourth- and eighth-graders were asked about external or observable characteristics of their best friends, such as their friends' birthdates, and about more intimate information, such as the friends' preferences and personality characteristics (for example, what the friend worried about the most). To determine the accuracy of the reports, they were compared with their best friends' self-reports. Fourth- and eighth-graders did not differ in their knowledge of external or observable characteristics of their friends, but eighth-graders knew more intimate things about their best friends than fourth-graders did.

While an intimate relationship with a best friend seems to arise often in early adolescence, this period does not appear to be the time when adolescents rate their intimate friendships in the most positive light. Why might early adolescence be a time of less positive intimate relationships in friendship? The decline in positive ratings of friendship that seems to appear around the age of thirteen may be explained by the temporary period of conflict generated by an adolescent's cross-sex interests (Sharabany, Gershoni, and Hofman, 1981), or it may be due to the changes in friendships that accompany the transition to junior high school (Simmons, Rosenberg, and Rosenberg, 1973).

It has been argued that girls have more intimate friendships than boys do (Douvan and Adelson, 1966). The assumption behind this suggested sex role difference is that girls are more oriented toward interpersonal relationships while boys are interested in assertiveness and achievement rather than warmth and empathy. Also, intimacy between boys may be discouraged because of the fear that it may lead to homosexuality. When children are asked to describe their best friends, girls refer more to intimate conversations and intimate knowledge and show more concern about faithfulness and rejection (Berndt, 1981; Bieglow and LaGaipa, 1980; Douvan and Adelson, 1966). While there are some investigations that find no sex differences in the intimate aspects of friendships (e.g., Sharabany, Gershoni, and Hofman, 1981), the weight of the evidence suggests that girls' friendships are characterized by more intimacy than boys' friendships are. For example, more girls than boys are likely to describe their best friend as "sensitive just like me" or "trustworthy just like me" (Duck, 1975).

Does intimate friendship have an effect on personality? There is some evidence that having a close and stable best friend is positively associated with self-esteem (Mannarino, 1978, 1979), but we do not know whether the differences between youth are caused by self-esteem or intimacy in friendship. In other words, children with high self-esteem may be more likely to be able to develop a close, intimate friendship, just as easily as having a close friend could promote self-esteem.

Similarity in Friendships

The extent to which there is similarity between friends on a variety of characteristics has been of interest to psychologists for many years. Throughout the childhood and adolescent years, friends are generally similar in terms of age, sex, and race (Hallinan, 1979; Kandel, 1978; Tuma and Hallinan, 1979). Friends also usually have similar attitudes toward school, similar educational aspirations, and closely aligned achievement orientations (Ball, 1981; Kandel, 1978; Epstein, 1983). Such findings reveal the importance of schooling in children's lives and the tendency toward agreement between friends on its importance. As Thomas Berndt (1982) suggests, if friends have different attitudes about school, one of them may want to play basketball or go shopping rather than doing homework. If one friend insists on completing his homework while the other insists on playing basketball, conflicts are likely to weaken the friendship.

Friends also tend to be similar in their orientations toward teenage or youth culture. Friends generally like the same kinds of music, the same kinds of clothes, and the same kinds of leisure activities (Ball, 1981). But some friendships are based on specific interests, such as horseback riding or playing golf. These types of friends often do not share as many similar ideas and attitudes.

Contemporary Issues in the Study of Adolescent Friendships

Currently there is a great deal of interest in the role of friendships in adolescent development (Serafica and Blyth, 1985). Researchers continue to be interested in such matters as similarity and intimacy in friendship, as well as such factors as age and sex differences (Montemayor and Van Komen, 1985). The importance of social cognition, and whether such thoughts are linked up with the adolescent's social behavior, is being studied (Cairns, Perrin, and Cairns, 1985). The connectedness of adolescents with their families has emerged as an important trend in friendship studies during adolescence (Coates, 1985; Hunter, 1985). The importance of friendships, or the lack of, in the development of problems and disturbances is being investigated (Reisman, 1985). And while theories of the development of friendship have been few in number, one promising approach has been proposed by James Youniss (1980; Youniss and Volpe, 1978). He believes that adolescent development involves discovering social exchanges, conceptualizing them as interpersonal relationships, and continuing to organize these relationships within the constraints of social reality. Peer and friendship relationships are thought to have a central role in this portrayal of adolescent development, although the connectedness of parents, peers, and friends is a noticeable ingredient as well. It is believed that the ability to discover, construct, and conceptualize relationships is part of an advancing social cognitive ability.

Adolescent Groups: From Boy Scouts to Druggies

Our study of adolescent groups focuses initially on the nature of such groups, then at naturalistic observations of how such groups are formed. Then we turn our attention to differences in children's groups and adolescent groups, as well as cultural variations in adolescent groups. To conclude the discussion of adolescent groups, ideas about a very important type of adolescent group—the clique—is explored.

The Nature of Adolescent Groups

Think back to your junior high and high school years and develop an image of the groups you were involved in. You likely were a member of both formal and informal groups. You might have been a member of such formal groups as a basketball team or drill team, Girl Scouts or Boy Scouts, the student council, and so forth.

Similarly, you probably were a member of a more informal group of peers, particularly a clique. An assemblage of adolescents is not necessarily a group or clique. A clique exists when several adolescents interact with each other on an ongoing basis, sharing values and goals. **Norms** and **status positions** also are important to the functioning of the group. Norms are the standards, rules, and guidelines by which the group abides, and status positions are positions of more or less power and control in the group. Stable groups have values or norms that become established and maintained over time. And when leaders and followers become differentiated, the aggregation takes on the distinctive flavor of a group (Hartup, 1970).

Naturalistic Observation of Adolescent Groups

The most extensive work conducted on the formation of children's and adolescent groups is that of Muzafer Sherif and his colleagues (Sherif et al., 1961). The Sherif naturalistic experiments often proceed according to a particular format. Middle-class white Protestant boys are recruited and removed to a campsite during the summer. There they are exposed to an experiment in the natural setting of the camp. The observers are members of the camp staff.

In the first phase of the experiment, in-group formation is established by placing two groups of boys who don't know one another together for a few days. In the second phase, the two groups are brought together for the intergroup conflict phase. This conflict includes win–lose competition and planned frustration that is expected to increase the tension between the groups. In the third phase (e.g., Sherif, 1961), ways to reduce intergroup conflict are explored. The observers use strategies such as experiencing a common enemy, or constructing superordinate goals that the two groups can only achieve together, to reduce conflict.

Some of the important findings to come out of Sherif's naturalistic experiments follow:

1. Hierarchical structures invariably emerge within the groups. The top and bottom status positions are filled first, then the middle positions.

2. Norms develop in all groups. "We-they" talk is a frequent part of the groups' conversations. The groups often adopt nicknames, like the Bulldogs or the Sorcerers.

3. Frustration and competition contribute to hostility between the groups.

4. Intergroup hostility often can be reduced by setting up a superordinate goal that requires the mutual efforts of both groups. For example, Sherif's camp directors deliberately broke a water line so both groups of boys would have to pitch in together to help. Another time, the camp truck taking the boys to a movie in town was driven into a muddy ditch, requiring considerable team effort to get it out.

In addition to recruiting boys for camp to explore the nature of group formation, Sherif has also simply gone out to street corners and hangouts in towns and cities to find out what adolescent groups are like. In one such effort (Sherif and Sherif, 1964), the observers went to a town and began to infiltrate student gathering places. They got to know the adolescents and became their confidants by doing such things as buying them a new basketball when their old ball got a hole in it. After the observers gained the adolescents' acceptance, they began to record information about the conversations and activities of the youth. The strategy was to spend several hours with them and then write down what had transpired.

What do adolescents talk about when they get together regularly on their own volition? The Sherifs (1964) found that in each group of adolescents they studied, much time was spent just "hanging around" together, talking and joking. In addition, many of the groups spent a great deal of time participating in, discussing, or attending athletic events and games. The only exceptions were groups from lower-class neighborhoods.

Cars are a frequent concern of adolescent males when they are observed in peer groups.

Cars occupied the minds of many of the group members. Whether they owned cars or not, the adolescent boys discussed, compared, and admired cars. Those who did not own cars knew what kinds they wanted. The boys also discussed the problem of having access to a car so they could go somewhere or take a girl out. The adolescents who did have cars spent tremendous amounts of time in and around cars with their buddies. On numerous occasions, the adolescent boys just drove around, looking to see what was going on around town or wanting to be seen by others.

Discussions about girls frequently infiltrated the adolescent boys' conversations. As part of this talk, they focused extensively on sexual activities. They planned, reminisced, and compared notes on girls. Particularly in the middle- and upper-income adolescent groups, looking for opportunities to be with girls and making sure they had dates for the weekend were important group activities.

Much time in every group was spent reflecting on past events and planning for games, parties, and so forth. Thus, despite the fact that the boys just "hung around" a lot, there were times when they constructively discussed how they were going to deal or cope with various events.

Adults were depicted in the adolescents' conversations as a way to obtain needed resources (such as cars, money, and athletic equipment); as figures whose authorization was needed; as obstacles to be overcome; and, occasionally, in terms of obligation.

While the particular activities of the adolescent boys differed from group to group, there was a remarkable similarity in the general nature of the activities of all the groups. All the groups were preoccupied with the pleasure of each other's company, the problems of having places to meet with peers apart from adults, relationships with adult authorities, relationships with the opposite sex, and with the appurtenances of being an adult male (including a car).

Also, in every group the Sherifs studied, the members engaged in some form of deviant behavior not sanctioned by adults. The most common behavior of this type involved alcoholic beverages. In one of the highest socioeconomic groups, the boys regularly drank, sometimes engaged in illicit sexual activities, and set up a boy-girl swimming party at a motel by forging the registration. The party included not only illegal drinking, but the destruction of property as well. The boys paid for the property destruction themselves without ever telling their parents what had happened.

During the adolescent years, peer groups become more racially mixed.

Children's Groups Compared to Adolescent Groups

Children's groups differ from adolescent groups in several important ways. The members of children's groups often are friends or neighborhood acquaintances. Their groups are usually not as formalized as many adolescent groups. During the adolescent years, groups tend to include a broader array of members—in other words, adolescents other than friends or neighborhood acquaintances often are members of the adolescent groups. Try to recall the student council, honor society, or football team at your junior high school. If you were a member of any of these junior high organizations, you likely recall that they were comprised of a number of individuals you had not met before, and that they were a more heterogeneous group than your childhood peer groups. Rules and regulations likely were well defined, and captains or leaders were formally elected or appointed. Formalized structure and definition of status positions probably did not characterize many of your childhood peer groups.

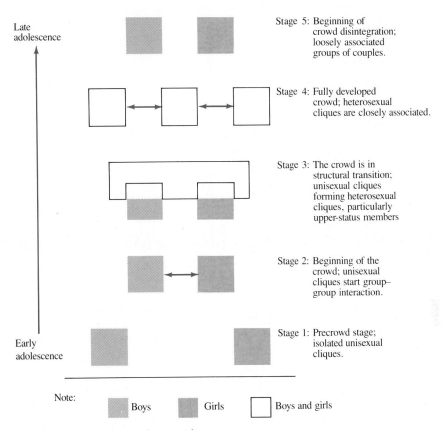

Late
adolescence

Stage 5: Beginning of
crowd disintegration;
loosely associated
groups of couples.

Stage 4: Fully developed
crowd; heterosexual
cliques are closely associated.

Stage 3: The crowd is in
structural transition;
unisexual cliques
forming heterosexual
cliques, particularly
upper-status members

Stage 2: Beginning of the
crowd; unisexual
cliques start group–
group interaction.

Early
adolescence

Stage 1: Precrowd stage;
isolated unisexual
cliques.

Note:

[ ] Boys   [ ] Girls   [ ] Boys and girls

Figure 7.5 **Dunphy's stages of group development in adolescence.**

In addition to more formalized structure and greater heterogeneity of members, adolescent peer groups also are more often cross-sexed than children's peer groups (Dunphy, 1963). The increased frequency of formal groups in junior high, combined with the psychological changes of puberty, explain to some extent why adolescent groups have mixtures of boys and girls more often than children's groups do.

A well-known observational study by Dexter Dunphy (1963) in Australia provides support for the development of opposite-sex group participation during adolescence. In later childhood, boys and girls participate in small, same-sex cliques. As they move into the early adolescent years, the same-sex cliques begin to interact with each other. Gradually the leaders and high-status members form further cliques based on heterosexual relationships. Eventually the newly created heterosexual cliques replace the same-sex cliques. The heterosexual cliques interact with each other in larger crowd activities as well, such as during dances and at athletic events. In late adolescence, Dunphy believed the crowd begins to dissolve as couples begin to develop more serious relationships and make long-range plans that often include engagement and marriage. A summary of Dunphy's ideas is presented in figure 7.5.

Cultural Variations in Adolescent Groups

Whether an adolescent grows up as part of the peer culture in a ghetto or in a middle-class suburban area influences the nature of the groups she belongs to. For example, in a comparison of middle-class and lower class adolescent groups, lower class adolescents displayed more aggression toward the low-status members of the group, but showed less aggression toward the president of the class or group than their middle-class counterparts did (Maas, 1954).

In many schools, peer groups are virtually segregated according to race and social class. Where middle- and lower class students are both included, the middle-class students often assume the leadership roles in formal organizations such as student council, the honor society, fraternity-sorority groups, and so forth. Athletic teams represent one type of adolescent group where blacks and lower class students have been able to gain parity with or surpass middle-class students in achieving status.

Black and white (and lower and middle-class) students have spent more time with each other during the past two decades than in previous eras, but it has been in the schools rather than in the neighborhoods where the greatest mixture of different backgrounds has occurred. Even when schools are mixed in terms of ethnic and social-class background, it still appears that friendships, cliques, and crowds are more likely to follow social-class and ethnic group lines (Hartup, 1970; Kandel, 1978). It is usually in formal groups such as athletic teams and student council that the greatest mixture of social class and ethnicity occurs.

In some cultures, children are placed in peer groups for much greater lengths of time at an earlier age than they are in the United States. For example, in the Murian culture of eastern India, both male and female children live in a dormitory from the age of six until they get married (Barnouw, 1975). The dormitory is seen as a religious haven where members are devoted to work and spiritual harmony. Children work for their parents, and the parents arrange the children's marriages. When the children wed, they must leave the dormitory.

In our discussion of peer groups, we have mentioned adolescent cliques. For example, in describing Dunphy's work, we found the importance of heterosexual relationships in the evolution of adolescent cliques. Now, we turn our attention in greater detail to the nature of adolescent cliques.

Cliques and Crowds

What are adolescent cliques and crowds like? Do you think it makes any difference for the adolescent's self-esteem whether he or she is a member of a clique? What do adolescents do when they get together in groups? Let's explore these and other questions.

Distinguishing Cliques and Crowds

Most peer group relationships in adolescence can be categorized in one of three ways: the **crowd,** the **clique,** or individual friendships (Mussen, Conger, and Kagan, 1974). The largest and least personal of these groups is the crowd. The members of the crowd meet because of their mutual interest in activities, not because they are mutually attracted to each other. By contrast, the members of cliques and friendships are attracted to each other on the basis of similar interests and social ideals. Cliques are smaller in size, involve greater intimacy among members, and have more group cohesion than crowds.

Allegiance to cliques, clubs, organizations, and teams exerts powerful control over the lives of many adolescents. Group identity often overrides personal identity. The leader of a group may place a member in a position of considerable moral conflict asking, in effect, "What's more important, our code or your parents'?" or "Are you looking out for yourself, or for the members of the group?" Labels like "brother" and "sister" sometimes are adopted and used in group members' conversations with one another. These labels symbolize the intensity of the bond between the members and suggest the high status of membership in the group.

Coleman's Study of Leading Adolescent Groups

One of the most widely quoted studies of adolescent cliques and crowds is that of James Coleman (1961). Students in ten different high schools were asked to identify the leading crowds in their schools. They also were asked to name the students who were the most outstanding in athletics, popularity, and different activities in the school. Regardless of the school sampled, the leading crowds were likely to be composed of athletes and popular girls. Much less power in the leading crowd was attributed to the bright student. Coleman's finding that being an athlete contributes to popularity for boys was reconfirmed in a more recent investigation by Eitzen (1975).

The General Nature of Cliques in Adolescence

Think about your high school years—what were the cliques, and which one were you in? While the names of cliques change, we could go to almost any high school in the United States and discover three to six well-defined cliques or crowds. In an investigation of high school cliques, students in one school described six distinct cliques: "Collegiates," "leathers," "the true individuals," "the quiet kids," "the intellectuals" and "the kids going steady" (Riester and Zucker, 1968). One clearly defined group, called the "collegiates," was comprised of establishment-oriented, socially active, "all-American" students. Another group was called the "leathers." They were described as rough and tough— "hoods" was another label applied to them. A third group was called "the true individuals." Their most distinct feature was their clothing; over the years, they have been called "beatniks," "hippies," and "freaks." Three other more or less distinct groups were identified: the "quiet kids," who were independent, did their own thing, and sometimes belonged to more identifiable groups outside of school; the "intellectuals," who studied a lot and were usually very serious about some particular area of academic work; and "the kids going steady," who spent considerable lengths of time with each other and sometimes with other couples. In an in-

vestigation at another high school in the mid-1970s, the cliques were described as "sporties," "workers," "crispies," "musicians," and "debaters" (Hartup, 1983).

The exact nature of cliques and crowds depends on the geographical region of the country where the adolescents live. For instance, in towns and cities in Texas, the "kickers" and the "potheads" often create the most controversy. This dichotomy (as well as the dichotomy between groups in most areas) is due to the mixing of cultures—urban and rural, Northern and Southern. The term *kicker* originates from cowboy boots, which were worn mostly by working cowboys. The term has been modified to either "chip kickers" or "cowboys," depending on the purposes of the adolescent using the label. Observers say the kickers may or may not have anything to do with agriculture, but they usually wear cowboy boots, western shirts and jeans, listen to country-and-western music, often drive pick-ups, and carry around tins of snuff in their hip pockets. The other side of the dichotomy has a wider variety of names, depending on the locale: freaks, potheads, slickers, or thugs. Freaks supposedly prefer rock music, dress in worn-out clothes, and drive hyped-up cars.

Sociologists say that adolescents growing up in America usually must decide on which culture to go with—whether to be a "roper" or a "doper," an "intellectual" or a "going-steady type" (Hawkins, 1979). This decision often reflects some conflict that exists throughout society—in many instances, the students are making a political statement by siding with one clique or crowd rather than another (the kickers and cowboys are on the right, and potheads are on the left). Political statements made during adolescence, though, may not be very strong; sometimes they boil down to nothing more than which radio station you listen to or which clothes you buy. The split is fairly easy to see in most high schools. In many instances, the two extreme groupings, such as the "ropers" and the "dopers" are not well integrated into the school system itself and are easily distinguished from students who are making good grades and who are social leaders.

Cliques, Crowds, and Self-Esteem

Crowds and cliques have been portrayed as playing a pivotal role in the adolescent's maintenance of self-esteem and development of a sense of identity (e.g., Coleman, 1961; Erikson, 1968). Several theoretical perspectives suggest how crowd and clique membership might be linked with the adolescent's self-esteem (Brown and Lohr, in press). In an extension of Erikson's identity development theory, it is argued that virtually all thirteen to seventeen year olds will regard clique and crowd membership as highly salient and that self-esteem will be higher among clique and crowd members than nonmembers (at least those satisfied with the crowd). The peer group is viewed as a "way station" between relinquishing childhood dependence on parents and adult self-definition, achievement, and autonomy. Group affiliation and acceptance by the crowd is seen as important in keeping the adolescent's self-concept positive during this long transition period. Social comparison theory also has implications for understanding crowd attachment and self-esteem. It implies that while group members as a whole may have higher self-esteem than nonmembers, there will be differences among group members according to the position of their crowd in the peer group status hierarchy. This argument is based on the belief that individuals often compare their own attributes with those of significant others to evaluate the adequacy of their ideas or characteristics (Festinger, 1954). A recent investigation evaluated the importance of crowd identification in the adolescent's self-esteem. An overview of this study is presented in Perspective on Adolescent Development 7.4.

We have studied many different aspects of friendships and group behavior. A summary of main ideas related to friendships and group behavior is presented in Concept Table 7.2. Recall in our discussion of Dunphy's portrayal of adolescent cliques that heterosexual relationships played an important role. In the next section, we investigate another very important aspect of heterosexual relationships in adolescence, dating.

Perspective on Adolescent Development 7.4
THE SELF-ESTEEM OF JOCKS, POPULARS, NORMALS, DRUGGIES/TOUGHS, AND NOBODIES

*B*radford Brown and Mary Jane Lohr (in press) examined the self-esteem of 221 seventh through twelfth graders. These adolescents were either associated with one of five major school crowds or were relatively unknown by classmates and not associated with any school crowd. To discover which students were identified with a crowd, adolescents were asked to name, in their own words, the major crowds they perceived existed in their school. They then described the stereotypic traits of each group, rank-ordered the crowds in terms of status, and listed five classmates they considered to be members of each crowd. Listed from highest to lowest in peer status, the crowds were: *jocks* (athletically oriented), *populars* (well-known students who lead social activities), *normals* (middle-of-the-road students who make up the "masses"), *druggies/toughs* (known for illicit drug use and/or delinquent activities) and *nobodies* (low in social skills and/or intellectual abilities). Self-esteem was measured by a ten-item scale developed by Rosenberg (1965).

The results confirmed the belief that the self-esteem of crowd members is higher than that of nonmembers, and that the higher-rated a crowd is, the more likely the adolescent's self-esteem will be higher as well (figure 7.6). The members of the crowds rated the most prestigious by peers (such as jocks) had the highest self-esteem among the various crowds.

Other information collected by Brown and Lohr (in press) provided further elaboration of the link between crowd affiliation and self-esteem. For example, a group of adolescents who were labeled outsiders also were studied. Those who realized that they were outsiders, but placed little importance on group membership (that is, the *independents*), had higher self-esteem than those who perceived themselves as group members when their peers did not (called the *distorters*) or those who recognized they were not part of the group, but rated crowd affiliation as important (called the *envious*). The independents' self-esteem was not significantly lower than any

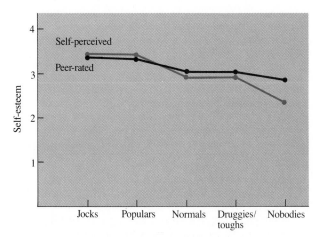

Figure 7.6 The self-esteem of crowd and noncrowd members.

"Jocks" often have high self-esteem in adolescence.

"Independents" may have high self-esteem, particularly if they show little or no interest in clique membership.

of the crowds, while the self-esteem of the distorters and the envious was lower than the two leading crowds.

In considering the linkages between crowd affiliation and self-esteem, it is important to keep several things in mind. First, it is not possible to conclude that crowd affiliation causes enhanced self-esteem. These data are correlational in nature. Indeed, it is likely that self-esteem improves the likelihood that an adolescent will be included in a leading crowd, while at the same time, membership in such a crowd also is likely to engender self-esteem. Second, as seen by the fact that the independents actually had self-esteem that was as high as the leading crowd members, it is important to recognize that while crowd affiliation often is a viable path to increased self-esteem in adolescence, there are other avenues as well.

FRIENDSHIPS AND GROUP BEHAVIOR

Concept	Processes/related ideas	Characteristics/description
Friendships	Importance and incidence	Friendships, like peer relations in general, are an important aspect of social relationships in adolescence. Some adolescents have no close friends and lack the social skills to develop such friendships.
	Cognitive factors	By age ten, children likely have developed a true sensitivity to the feelings of another child. During adolescence, individuals are likely to describe their friends with more interpersonal constructs, provide more complex and organized information about them, and understand the attributes that differentiate them from mere acquaintances.
	Intimacy	Intimacy, usually defined in terms of self-disclosure, is an important aspect of friendship. Intimate relationships usually appear during early adolescence, but they are not always seen in a positive light. Many researchers believe the friendship of girls is more intimate than in the case of boys. Intimacy likely influences personality and vice versa.
	Similarity	Friends are similar on many dimensions.
	Contemporary issues in the study of adolescent friendships	Currently, there is considerable research interest in adolescent friendships, focused on many different issues, such as the role of intimacy and similarity, age and sex differences, social cognition, connectedness with families, importance for mental health, and theory construction. Youniss's social cognitive theory has highlighted a rather weak theoretical base for understanding friendship.
Group behavior	The nature of adolescent groups	In addition to shared values and goals, norms and status positions are important in group functioning. When leaders and followers have been differentiated, an aggregation takes on the flavor of a group.

FRIENDSHIPS AND GROUP BEHAVIOR

Concept	Processes/related ideas	Characteristics/description
	Naturalistic observation of adolescent groups	The Sherifs have studied group formation in natural settings, such as at a camp and on street corners. Hierarchical structures emerge, there is considerable in-group, out-group comparison and talk, frustration and competition contribute to hostility between groups, and superordinate tasks can reduce such hostility. Most adolescent groups engage in some form of behavior that violates adult standards at some point in their existence. Adolescent male groups often involve talk about girls and cars, and there is a great deal of just fooling around that goes on.
	Children and adolescent groups	Children groups are not as formal, are less heterogeneous, and are less cross-sexed than adolescent groups. Dunphy found that the development of adolescent groups moves through five stages to the point at which heterosexual cliques replace same-sex cliques. Well into late adolescence, the crowds begin to dissolve.
	Cultural variations	More aggression often is shown toward low status members in lower class groups. In many schools, groups are segregated according to race and social class. In formal groups, more crossing of racial and social class lines occurs.
	Cliques and crowds	Crowds are less personal. Members of cliques are attracted to each other on the basis of similar interests and social ideals. Allegiance to cliques exerts powerful control over the adolescent's life. In the Coleman study of adolescent groups, the leading crowds were made up of athletes and popular girls. There are usually three to six well-defined cliques in most any high school observed in the United States. Membership in cliques is generally associated with higher self-esteem than not being a member; however, independents, those who place little importance on clique membership, show self-esteem that is as high as the leading clique members.

Dating and Marriage: I Met This Really Neat Guy Named Frank

Dating rarely occurs before the middle school or junior high schools; thus, it represents the emergence of a new aspect of social relationships during the adolescent years. And, in most cultures, marriage represents another aspect of relationships that rarely occurs before the adolescent years.

Dating

> I met this really neat, good-looking guy, Frank—a college senior. He seemed to like me, but why would a college guy be interested in me, a high school junior, anyway? . . . That guy, Frank, asked me out. I think he is pretty nice, but I'm not sure I want the kind of experience he wants to show me! . . . At any rate, I said he could pick me up after school. I thought he might not show up because he would be too embarrassed to be seen at the high school. . . . But he came, and we went out for some pizza and talked. He wanted me to go out with him that night, but I told him I had to study, and he should take me home. He did. He keeps calling all the time, and my mother always is saying to me, "Who is that guy that keeps calling you all the time?" (I don't want her to know I'm going out with somebody as old as Frank is.) . . . Frank sure is persistent. I finally agreed to go out with him again. And then I went out with him again, and again. Now, I think I'm falling in love with him. . . . I'm starting to get jealous when he doesn't call me every evening—I think maybe he is out with some girl who is older and a lot more experienced than I am. I sure hope not. . . . Frank is so neat—he is so much more mature than most of the guys in our high school. He is sensitive to my feelings, and doesn't smart off to get attention. . . . But I'm still not sure why he likes me.

While many adolescent boys and girls have social interchanges through formal and informal peer groups, it is through dating that more serious contacts between the sexes occur. Many agonizing moments are spent by young male adolescents worrying about whether they should call a certain girl and ask her out—"Will she turn me down?" "What if she says yes, what do I say next?" "How am I going to get her to the dance? I don't want my mother to take us!" "I want to kiss her, but what if she pushes me away?" "How can I get to be alone with her?" And, on the other side of the coin: "What if no one asks me to the dance?" "What do I do if he tries to kiss me?"

Or, "I really don't want to go with him. Maybe I should wait two more days and see if Bill will call me." Think about your junior high, high school, and early college years. You probably spent a lot of time thinking about how you were going to get a particular girl or boy to go out with you. And many of your weekend evenings were probably spent on dates, or on envying others who had dates. Some of you went steady, perhaps even during junior high school—others of you may have been engaged to be married by the end of high school.

Functions of Dating

Dating is a relatively recent phenomenon. It wasn't until the 1920s that dating as we know it became a reality, and even then, its primary role was for the purpose of selecting and winning a mate. Prior to this period, mate selection was the sole purpose of dating and "dates" were carefully monitored by parents, who completely controlled the nature of any heterosexual companionship. Often, parents bargained with each other about the merits of their adolescents as potential marriage partners and even chose mates for their children. In recent times, of course, adolescents themselves have gained much more control over the dating process; today's adolescents are not as much at the mercy of their parents in regard to whom they go out with. Furthermore, dating has evolved into something more than just courtship for marriage. Dating today serves four main functions for adolescents (Skipper and Nass, 1966):

1. Dating can be a form of recreation. Adolescents who date seem to have fun and see dating as a source of enjoyment and recreation.

2. Dating is a source of status and achievement. Part of the social comparison process in adolescence involves evaluating the status of people one dates—are they the best looking, the most popular, and so forth.

Dating emerges as an important aspect of close relationships during adolescence.

3. Dating is part of the socialization process in adolescence—it helps the adolescent to learn how to get along with others and assists in learning manners and sociable behavior.

4. Dating can be a means of mate sorting and selection—it retains its original courtship function.

Incidence of Dating and Age Trends

Most girls in the United States begin dating at the age of fourteen, while most boys begin sometime between the ages of fourteen and fifteen (Douvan and Adelson, 1966; Sorenson, 1973). Most adolescents have their first date sometime between the ages of twelve and sixteen. Less than ten percent have a first date before the age of ten and by the age of sixteen, more than ninety percent have had at least one date. More than fifty percent of the tenth, eleventh, and twelfth graders in one study

averaged one or more dates per week (Dickinson, 1975). About fifteen percent of these high school students dated less than once per month, and about three out of every four students had gone steady at least once.

Dating and going steady, then, are standard fare on the menu of most teenagers' social relationships. Adolescents who do not date very much may feel left out of the mainstream in their high school and community. Social skills training has been developed for adolescents who have difficulty in peer relations, and programs have been created to improve the ability of the adolescent to obtain a date and to interact more effectively during social relationships with the opposite sex (e.g., Curran, 1975; Rehm and Marston, 1968; Twentyman and McFall, 1975).

Going Steady At some point in their junior high or high school years, a number of adolescents "go steady" or "go with" each other. Going steady, though, may not mean the same thing to all adolescents. Recently, one of my daughter's thirteen-year-old friends was discussing her history of "going steady." It turned out that in the course of six months she had "gone" with five different boys. In two of those situations, the girl agreed to go steady with the boys over the phone and then broke off the relationships before she ever even had a date with them!

In one investigation of high school juniors and seniors who were going steady (Schneider, 1966), seventy-five percent felt that their relationship involved a commitment to forgo dating other people, and a full twenty-five percent felt they were in love. Forty percent had informally agreed to get married, another forty percent had considered marriage seriously, but had made no commitment, and twenty percent had not considered marriage at all. The longer the couples had gone steady the more likely they were to consider marriage seriously. For those who had only gone steady for two months, for example, only three percent indicated they planned to get married, while for those who had gone steady for one year or longer, fifty percent said they planned to get married. Thus, going steady becomes more serious business during the high school than junior high school years, and the longer a couple goes steady, the more likely they are to consider marriage.

"Going steady" becomes more serious during late adolescence.

What Attracts Adolescents to Each Other

Let's look at several reasons adolescents are attracted to each other in heterosexual relationships, focusing in particular on the role of similarity and physical attraction.

Adolescents are attracted to other adolescents in many instances because those adolescents are similar to themselves. This finding is so common that it is often possible to estimate how much an individual will like another person on the basis of the proportion of issues on which they agree (figure 7.7). This factor comes into play further as adolescents date others who are from a similar social class and parental background. The fact that individuals are attracted to each other on the basis of similar characteristics and attitudes is even reflected in the questions that computer-dating services ask their clients (table 7.1).

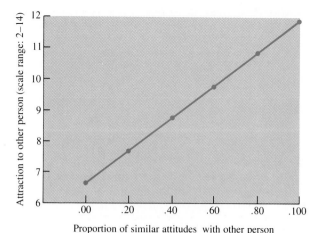

Figure 7.7 **The relation between liking and the similarity of the other person's attitudes.**

Adolescents also are very much attracted to opposite-sex peers who they perceive to be physically attractive (Berscheid and Walster, 1974). Possibly adolescents perceive some of this attractiveness will rub on them and sense that others will think more highly of them if they are seen with someone who is physically attractive. The importance of physical attractiveness in dating was demonstrated in an experiment that supposedly involved computer matching (Walster, Aronson, Abrahams, and Rottman, 1966). When merely asked what they thought was the most important characteristic for a date to have, the respondents said "personality," with looks coming in second. However, when an actual dating situation was created, physical attraction assumed a higher status. Out of a number of personal characteristics, only "looks" was positively associated with how the students rated their date's appeal. The students assumed a computer had determined their date on the basis of similar interests. In actuality, the dates were randomly assigned. The students' social skills, physical appearance, intelligence, and personality were measured. Then a dance was set up for the matched partners. At intermission, the partners were asked individually and in private to rate the attractiveness of

Table 7.1 A sample of items from a computer dating questionnaire

Computer dating is based almost entirely on the idea that people with similar interests and attitudes are compatible. In applying for a date, the person completes a questionnaire, such as the one below, and is then matched with a person of the opposite sex who has similar interests and attitudes.

KEY A—Yes definitely!   B—Yes   C—Maybe   D—No   E—No definitely!

1. Do you sometimes look down at others? — A B C D E
2. Do you enjoy being the center of attention in group activities? — A B C D E
3. Do you think it proper for unmarried couples to go on a trip by themselves? — A B C D E
4. Do you think you would be content married to an unaffectionate mate? — A B C D E
5. Do you believe that our schools should teach evolution? — A B C D E
6. Do you find yourself getting angry easily or often? — A B C D E
7. Do you usually prefer being with groups of people to being alone? — A B C D E
8. Do you think that a theft is ever justifiable? — A B C D E
9. Do you think that sex is over-exploited in advertising? — A B C D E
10. Do you believe some religious instruction is necessary for all children? — A B C D E
11. Do you feel that your life as a child was enjoyable? — A B C D E
12. Do you ever go out of your way to avoid someone? — A B C D E
13. Do you think it proper for a schoolteacher to smoke or drink in public? — A B C D E
14. Do you think college campuses are too sexually liberated? — A B C D E
15. Do you believe you could permit your child to choose a different religion? — A B C D E

Source: Middlebrook, 1974, Knopf, p. 434.

Source: © 1986, Washington Post Writer's Group, reprinted with permission.

their date and to indicate which attributes contributed to that attractiveness. The overwhelming reason that a male or female partner was attractive to the college youth was that he or she was good looking. Of course, the partners did not have the opportunity to get to know each other very well when the ratings were made, so over time, personality and character may assume more importance. However, in other research, physical attractiveness has been linked with the number of dates female college students have in the time span of a year. Physical attractiveness seems to be more important when males rate the appeal of females than when females judge males (Bar-Tal and Saxe, 1976). Let's now explore more about sex differences and similarities in dating relationships.

Sex Differences and Similarities in Dating

It generally has been believed that females are more strongly oriented toward affection in opposite-sex relationships, while males are more interested in sexual matters. With regard to sexual interest, it does appear that during adolescence, males show a stronger sexual interest than females do, although both males and females show a heightened desire for sexual involvement as the relationship deepens. For example, both male and female adolescents who go steady show a stronger desire for sexual involvement than their counterparts who have only had several dates with the same person (McCabe and Collins, 1979).

With regard to affectional and personality aspects of dating, there does seem to be a tendency of females to show more interest in personality exploration and self-disclosure than males (e.g., Douvan and Adelson, 1966; Simon and Gagnon, 1969). However, in one investigation (McCabe and Collins, 1979), both males and females said they begin a dating relationship with an affectional orientation. Further, as with sexual interest, the deeper the relationship becomes, as when adolescents go steady, this affectional orientation increases.

The Construction of Dating Relationships: Family and Peer Factors

We have emphasized that close relationships influence the nature of other relationships. It is likely, for example, that the commerce of adolescents with family members and peers contributes in meaningful ways to how adolescents construct their dating relationships.

Peter Blos (1962) sees adolescent dating as tied to parental relationships. At the beginning of adolescence, Blos says, adolescents attempt to separate themselves from the opposite-sex parent as a love object. As the adolescent separates himself or herself, the adolescent is seen as very narcissistic. Blos believes this narcissism helps give the adolescent a sense of strength about himself or herself as separation from parents develops. Particularly in early adolescence, this narcissistic, self-orientation likely produces self-serving, highly idealized, tenuous, and superficial heterosexual relationships.

Psychoanalytic theorists, such as Blos, also believe that relationships with parents are carried forward to influence the construction of dating relationships. Thus, the adolescent's relationships with his or her opposite-sex parent, as well as the relationships with parents of the person he or she dates likely contribute to the nature of dating relationships. For example, an adolescent male whose mother has been very nurturant, warm, and involved with him, yet not smothering, likely feels that relationships with females in a dating relationship will be rewarding. By contrast, the adolescent male whose mother has been somewhat unloving and aloof may increase the likelihood that he does not trust females and perceives that relationships with females will be unrewarding.

It is also probably true that in addition to the manner in which parents interact with children and adolescents, the adolescent's observation of his or her parents' marital relationship also contributes to his or her dating relationships. Consider an adolescent girl who has come from a divorced family and grew up

Adolescents relationships with their opposite-sex parent often influences their dating relationships.

seeing her parents fight on many occasions. Her dating relationships may take one of two turns. She may immerse herself in dating relationships to insulate herself from the stress she has experienced or she may become aloof and untrusting with males and not wish to become involved heavily in dating relationships. Even when she does date considerably, it may be difficult for her to develop a trusting relationship with males because she has seen promises broken by her parents.

There has been little empirical investigation of the role of parents in influencing the manner in which adolescents construct dating relationships. It may be helpful to recall the investigation of Hetherington (1972, 1977), who found that divorce was associated with a stronger heterosexual orientation of adolescent daughters than was the death of a parent or coming from an intact family. Further, it was suggested that the daughters of divorcees had a more negative opinion of males than did the girls from other family structures. And, it was revealed that girls from divorced and widowed families were more likely to marry images of their fathers than girls from intact families. The argument was made that females from intact families likely have had a greater opportunity to work through relationships with their father and therefore are more psychologically free to date and marry someone different than their father.

It also appears that girls are more likely to have their parents involved or interested in their dating patterns and relationships than males. For example, in one investigation (Knox and Wilson, 1981) college females were much more likely than their male counterparts to say their parents tried to influence who they dated during adolescence. They also indicated that it was not unusual for their parents to try to interfere with their dating choices and relationships.

Birth order and sibling relationships also could be expected to be linked with dating relationships. While a number of studies of birth order and attraction in dating have been conducted (e.g., Altus, 1970; Critelli and Baldwin, 1979; Toman, 1971), sometimes older siblings are attracted to opposite-sex persons who are younger siblings, while in others they like opposite-sex persons who are also older siblings themselves. Thus, it may be necessary to observe the actual nature of sibling relationships rather than birth order alone to find how sibling relationships influence dating relationships. Nonetheless, it is likely that younger siblings learn a great deal from the triumphs and failings of their older sibling's dating practices. It may be that younger siblings date earlier than older siblings, influenced by the model of their older siblings. And it may be that a younger sibling with an opposite-sex older sibling finds the transition to dating easier as they have learned much about the opposite sex during their sibling life while they have grown up. One investigation did reveal that girls often used sibling relationships to their advantage when dealing with parents. Younger siblings pointed to how their older sibling was given dating privileges they had been denied. And, an adolescent would sometimes side with a sibling when the sibling was having an argument with parents in hope that the sibling would do likewise when he or she needed dating privileges parents were denying (Place, 1975).

Peer relationships also are involved in the adolescent's dating relationships. In Dunphy's (1963) research, which was discussed earlier in the chapter, he found that all large peer crowds were heterosexual and that males in these crowds consistently were older than females. Dunphy also noted the dominant role of the group leader in dating relationships. Both the leaders of large crowds and smaller cliques had a high degree of involvement with the opposite sex. Leaders dated more frequently, were more likely to go steady, and achieved these characteristics earlier than other members of the cliques. Also, leaders were ascribed the task of maintaining a certain level of heterosexual involvement in the peer group. They functioned as confidants and advisors in regard to dating and even put partners together for the "slow learners."

Now that we have studied a number of different aspects of dating in adolescence, information about another type of relationship that occurs for some adolescents is considered—adolescent marriage.

Marriage

As indicated earlier in the chapter, individuals are waiting longer to have children. They also are waiting longer to get married. Adolescents are now less likely to foreclose their education and career options by getting married than in the past. For example, in 1960, sixteen percent of teenage girls were married, in 1969, the figure was 7.7 percent, and by 1968 the figure had moved further down to 6.9 percent. The parallel figures for boys were: eight percent, 2.1 percent, and 1.6 percent respectively (Rosenbaum, 1983).

For those adolescents who do get married, the prognostication for marital success is not high. And, the younger adolescents get married, the more likely they are to become divorced (DeLissovoy, 1973). Further, many adolescents who get married look back and say things would have been better if they had waited longer to get married. In one investigation (Burchinal, 1959), more than half of the females who became married in adolescence said that if they could do it over again, they would not get married during high school.

When adolescents do get married, what factors contribute to the likelihood the marriage will be a good one? Lee Burchinal (1965) has summarized the major factors that contribute to whether adolescent marriages have a poor, intermediate, or good chance of being successful. These factors are displayed graphically in table 7.2.

Why do adolescents marry early rather than waiting until they have finished their schooling and achieved a secure financial position? The main reason adolescents marry is pregnancy (e.g., DeLissovoy, 1973). Many adolescents do not foresee the problems an early marriage and childbearing may bring. They may cling to the idealized notion that love will conquer everything, wanting to show everyone that they can make it on their own. A critical moral issue for the pregnant adolescent is whether she should get an abortion. Abortion counseling is now available through hot lines, clinics, and counselors in most communities, and the choice to have an abortion now carries less stigma

than in past times. Still, abortion is considered out of the question for many individuals, particularly those from certain religious backgrounds.

Many adolescents who marry drop out of school, although this is much more prevalent among females than males. As could, perhaps, be expected, pregnant females are the most likely to quit school. At one time, schools barred married and pregnant students from attendance, and these students are still looked at with a jaundiced eye in too many school systems. In 1972, a federal law was passed stating that all married students and pregnant adolescents are entitled to a full education in the public school system.

Even when they are encouraged to attend school, though, many pregnant adolescents feel uneasy and uncomfortable doing so, particularly as their pregnancy progresses. Some progressive school systems have instituted special programs that include counseling sessions for pregnant teenagers (e.g., Heller and Kiralry, 1973; Kappelman, 1974). These programs vary in the ways they try to help the pregnant teenager with her education. In some instances, special schools are set up in which pregnant females from an entire county come to a centralized location to attend classes; in others, more effort is made to mainstream the pregnant females into the regular classes at their high schools. The programs also vary in the extent and nature of the counseling they offer the girls. Most of the programs, though, attempt to help the adolescent deal not only with personal problems, but with the prospect of handling the financial burden of caring for her infant after it is born.

We are at the end of the chapter on peers. As we have seen, peer relations are among the most important experiences adolescents have. In the next chapter, another context in which adolescence takes place is described—the school. Our discussion of schools in the lives of adolescents will include more information about peers as we describe peer relations and social interaction in schools.

Table 7.2
Table 7.2 Hypothesized relationship between selected characteristics and outcomes of young marriages

Characteristic	Forecast of marital competence and satisfaction		
	Poorest	Intermediate	Best
Ages at marriage	Both 17 or younger	Female 17, male 20 or older	Female at least 18, male 20 or older
Educational attainment	Both school dropouts	Female dropout, male high school graduate	Both high school graduates; male, at least, with some post-high school education
Pregnancy	Premarital pregnancy	No premarital pregnancy; pregnancy immediately following marriage	Pregnancy delayed until at least one year following marriage
Acquaintance before marriage	Less than six months; no engagement period, formal or informal	One year, at least, with at least six months understanding or engagement to marry	Several years, with at least six months understanding or engagement to marry
Previous dating patterns	Limited number of dating partners; went steady immediately, or short period between first date and first date with fiance	Some dating experience before dating fiance	Numerous dates, played the field; some previous experience with going steady
Personality dynamics	Generally poor interpersonal skills; lacking maturity; limited interests; poor personal and social adjustment	Mixed	Generally competent in interpersonal relations; flexible, mature; maintaining healthy and pleasurable relations with others

Table 7.2 (Continued)

Forecast of marital competence and satisfaction

Characteristic	Poorest	Intermediate	Best
Motivation for marrying	Drifted into marriage; because of pregnancy; seemed like the thing to do; just wanted to; other impulsive reasons with no strong emphasis on marital and parental roles	Mixed; marriage preferred to career, though had previous post-high school educational aspirations and, for females, perhaps tentative plans to work, etc.	No post-high school educational aspirations; and, for females, marriage, family, and homemaking preferred over working, living independently; positive emphasis upon role as wife and mother
Status of families	Both lower class	Mixed: lower and middle or upper class	Both middle or upper class
Parental attitudes before marriage	Strongly opposed	Mildly opposed or resigned acceptance	Supportive, once the decision was clear
Wedding	Elopement and civil ceremony	— — —	Conventional, hometown, church-sanctioned
Economic basis	Virtually completely dependent upon relatives	Low dependence upon relatives; mostly independent income, even if near hardship level	At least assured income above self-perceived hardship level
Residence	Always lived with in-laws or other relatives	Doubled up with relatives some of the time, independent other times	Always maintained own independent place of residence
Postmarriage parental views	Rejecting or punitive, assistance provided as a method of controlling the marriage	Cool	Psychologically supportive, sincerely want to help, assistance provided with no strings attached

Source: From Burchinal, L. G., "Trends and Prospects for Young Marriages in the United States," Journal of Marriage and Family, *May 1965, p. 251. Copyright © 1965 by the National Council on Family Relations, 1219 University Avenue Southeast, Minneapolis, Minnesota 55414.*

Summary

I. An understanding of peer relations focuses on the functions of the peer group, the coordinated worlds of parents and peers, as well as peer relations and social behavior/thought.

   A. Information about the functions of the peer group involves the meaning of the terms *peers,* peers and competent social development, cross-cultural comparisons and perspective taking.

   1. The term *peers* refers to people who are about the same age and/or developmental level. Social comparison and a source of information outside the family are two important functions of peers.

   2. Good peer relations represent an important aspect of competent social development. Children and adolescents who have poor peer relations are at risk for psychological problems.

   3. Peer relations are an important aspect of development in virtually every culture. It has been argued that adolescents in the United States succumb to peer pressure more than in most cultures.

   4. In cultural settings where peer relations are more prominent, perspective taking is enhanced.

   B. Connectedness occurs within families and within peer groups as well as between families and peers.

   C. Among the important aspects of peer relations and social behavior/thought are peer pressure and conformity, popularity and social acceptance, reinforcement, modeling, social comparison, social knowledge, social information processing, and social skills training.

   1. The pressure to conform to peers becomes very strong during the adolescent years. It seems to be stronger in early adolescence than late adolescence. At about the ninth grade, conformity to antisocial peer norms seems to heighten. Boys show more conformity to antisocial peer standards than girls. Most conformity focuses on peer involvement, such as socializing with friends, rather than antisocial standards.

   2. Among the most important factors that contribute to popularity are giving out reinforcements, the ability to have fun, listening skills, open communication lines, being yourself, conforming to peer norms, being friendly, showing enthusiasm, showing concern for others and having self-confidence, but not being conceited. Rejected children seem to be more at risk than neglected children.

   3. Adolescents have more social knowledge than children, but there is considerable variation in social knowledge among adolescents. Social knowledge contributes to effective social relationships. One study showed that boys with more social knowledge were better adjusted than their counterparts with low social knowledge. The manner in which adolescents process

information about their social world is an important determinant of their social competence. An example of an important social information processing skill is the ability to detect intention by a peer.

4. Various social cognitive strategies are being tried out with adolescents who are deficient in social skills. These strategies usually involve conglomerate skills and often are given the label *coaching*.

D. Currently, there is considerable research interest in adolescent friendships, focusing on different issues, such as the role of similarity and intimacy, sex and age differences, social cognition, connectedness with families, importance for mental health, and theory construction. Youniss's social cognitive theory of friendships highlights the theoretical views.

II. Information about friendships involves its importance and incidence, cognitive factors, intimacy, and similarity.

A. Friendships, like peer relations in general, are an important aspect of social relationships in adolescence. Some adolescents have no close friendships and lack the social skills to develop such friendships.

B. By age ten, children have likely developed a true sensitivity to the feelings for another child. During adolescence, individuals are likely to describe their friends with more interpersonal constructs, provide more complex and organized information about them, and understand their attributes that differentiate them from mere acquaintances.

C. Intimacy, usually defined in terms of self-disclosure, is an important aspect of friendships. Intimate relationships usually appear during early adolescence, but they are not always in a positive light. Many researchers believe the friendship of girls is more intimate than is the case for boys. Intimacy likely influences personality and vice versa.

D. Friends are similar on many dimensions.

E. Currently, there is considerable research interest in adolescent friendships, focused on many different issues, such as the role of intimacy and similarity, age and sex differences, social cognition, connectedness with families, importance for mental health, and theory construction.

III. Among the most important aspects of group behavior are the nature of adolescent groups, naturalistic observation of groups, children and adolescent groups, cultural variations, and cliques and crowds.

A. In addition to shared values and goals, norms and status positions are important in group functioning. When leaders and followers have been differentiated, an aggregation takes on the flavor of the group.

B. The Sherifs have studied group formation in naturalistic settings, such as at a camp and on street corners. Hierarchical structures emerge, there is considerable in-group, out-group comparison; talk, frustration, and competition contribute to hostility between groups, and superordinate tasks can reduce such hostility. Most adolescent groups engage in some form of behavior that violates adult standards at some point in their existence. Adolescent male groups often involve talk about girls and cars, and there is a great deal of just fooling around that goes on.

C. Children groups are not as formal, less heterogeneous, and less heterosexual than adolescent groups. Dunphy found that the development of adolescent groups moves through five stages to the point at which heterosexual cliques replace same-sex cliques. Well into late adolescence, the crowds begin to dissolve.

D. More aggression often is shown toward low status members in lower class groups. In many schools, groups are segregated according to race and social class. In formal groups, more crossing of racial and social class lines occurs.

E. Crowds are less personal than cliques. Members of cliques are attracted to each other on the basis of similar interests and social ideals. Allegiance to cliques exerts powerful influence over the adolescent's life. In the Coleman study of leading crowds, athletes and popular girls were most often involved. There are usually from three to six well-defined cliques in most high schools observed. Membership in cliques is generally associated with higher self-esteem than not being a member. However, independents, those who place little importance on clique membership show self-esteem that is as high as the leading clique members.

IV. Ideas about dating and marriage represent other aspects of close social relationships in adolescence.

A. Information about dating focuses on its functions, incidence of dating, age trends, what attracts adolescents to each other, sex differences and similarities in dating, and the construction of dating relationships.

1. Dating can be a form of recreation, is a source of status and achievement, is part of the socialization process, and can be a means of mate sorting and selection.

2. Most adolescents are involved in dating. Most girls begin dating at about fourteen, while boys begin at about fourteen to fifteen years of age. Going steady is another important consideration of adolescent dating.

3. Similarity of interests and physical attraction are very important in the attraction of adolescents to each other in heterosexual relationships.

4. It appears that females are more likely to be interested in the affectional aspects of dating, while males are more motivated by its sexual aspects.

5. Relationships with parents, siblings, and peers influence the manner in which adolescents construct dating relationships. Dunphy's study found that group leaders were important in the development of dating.

B. There has been a slowing in the rate at which adolescents get married. For those who do get married, the prognostication for marital success is not high. The earlier the marriage, the greater likelihood it will end in a divorce. The main reason adolescents get married is the pregnancy of the female. There are many factors involved in predicting whether an adolescent marriage will succeed.

Key Terms

anticonformist *269*

clique *288*

coaching *277*

crowd *288*

intention-cue detection *276*

intimacy in friendship *282*

neglected children *271*

nonconformist *269*

norms *284*

peers *263*

peer sociotherapy *262*

perspective taking *265*

rejected children *271*

social comparison *272*

status positions *284*

Suggested Readings

Goldstein, A. P., Sprafkin, R. P., Gershaw, N. J., & Klein, P. (1981). *Skill-streaming the adolescent.* Champaign, Ill.: Research Press.
An excellent set of exercises that can be used to improve social skills of adolescents.

Hartup, W. W. (1983). The peer system. In P. H. Mussen (Ed.), *Handbook of child psychology,* 4th ed., Vol. IV. New York: Wiley.
A detailed look at the development of peer relations from infancy through adolescence by one of the leading researchers on peer relations.

Hartup, W. W., & Rubin, Z. (Eds.). (1984). *Relationships and development.* Hillsdale, N.J.: Erlbaum.
Very recent thinking about how we construct relationships and how they develop in childhood. Includes articles by many leading researchers.

Journal of Early Adolescence 5 (1985).
The entire issue is devoted to friendships in early adolescence.

Rice, F. P. (1979). *Marriage and parenthood.* Boston: Allyn and Bacon.
A number of references are made to adolescent marriages in this book on marriage and parenting.

Sherif, M., & Sherif, C. W. (1964). *Reference groups.* New York: Harper & Row.
An entire book is devoted to the Sherifs' study of adolescent groups. It is an excellent source of information about everyday happenings in adolescent male cliques.

Chapter 8

Schools

Prologue

These excerpts from a variety of middle schools in different areas of the United States reveal the great diversity among schools for adolescents. They also tell us that despite the inefficiency of many schools for adolescents, others are very effective. One of the themes of this chapter is that schools can be breeding grounds for competent academic and social development. As part of our discussion of schools, you will read in greater detail about the qualities that make middle schools effective.

A teacher sits in the back of the room, her legs up on her desk, asking students questions from a textbook. The students, bored and listless, sit in straight rows facing no one in the front of the room, answering laconically to a blank blackboard. When the principal enters the room, the teacher lowers her legs to the floor. Nothing else changes.

A teacher drills students for a seemingly endless amount of time on prime numbers. After the lesson, not one of them can say why it is important to learn prime numbers.

A visitor asks a teacher if hers is an eighth grade class. "It's called eighth grade," she answers archly, "but we know it's really kindergarten, right class?"

In a predominantly Hispanic school, only the one adult hired as a bilingual teacher speaks Spanish.

In a biracial school, the principal and the guidance counselor cite test scores with pride. They are asked if the difference between the test scores of

Humane environments in middle schools translate into student growth.

black and white students is narrowing: "Oh, that's an interesting question!" says the guidance counselor with surprise. The principal agrees. It has never been asked by or of them before.

A teacher in a social studies class squelches several imaginative questions exclaiming, "You're always asking 'what if' questions. Stop asking 'what if'!" When a visitor asks who will become president if the president-elect dies before the electoral college meets, the teacher explodes, "You're as bad as they are! That's another 'what if' question!"

These vignettes are from middle schools where life seems to be difficult and unhappy for students. By contrast, consider the following circumstances in effective middle schools:

Everything is peaceful. There are open cubbies instead of locked lockers. There is no theft. Students walk quietly in the corridors. "Why?" they are asked. "So as not to disturb the media center," they answer, which is self-evident to them, but not the visitor who is left wondering. . . . When asked, "Do you like this school?" (They) answer, "No, we don't like it. We love it!"

When asked how the school feels, one student answered, "It feels smart. We're smart. Look at our test scores." Comments from one of the parents of a student at the school are revealing. "My child would have been a dropout." In elementary school, his teacher said to me, "That child isn't going to give you anything but heartaches." He had perfect attendance here. He didn't want to miss a day. Summer vacation was too long and boring. Now he's majoring in communications at the University of Texas. He got here and all of a sudden, someone cared for him. I had been getting notes about Roger every other day, with threats about exclusion. Here, the first note said, "It's just a joy to have him in the classroom."

The humane environment that encourages teachers' growth . . . is translated by the teachers . . . into a humane environment that encourages students' growth. The school feels cold when one first enters. It has the institutional feeling of any large school building with metal lockers and impersonal halls. Then one opens the door to a team area and it is filled with energy, movement, productivity, doing. There is a lot of informal relating among students and between students and teachers. Visible from one vantage point are students working on written projects, putting the last touches on posters, watching a film, and working independently from reading kits. . . . Most know what they are doing, can say why it is important, and go back to work immediately after being interrupted.

Authors' Week is yet another special activity built into the school's curriculum that entices students to consider themselves in relation to the rich variety of making and doing in people's lives. Based on student interest, availability, and diversity, authors are invited . . . to discuss their craft. Students sign up to meet with individual authors. They must have read one individual book by the author . . . Students prepare questions for their sessions with the authors . . . Sometimes an author stays several days to work with a group of students on his or her manuscript.

Source: J. Lipsitz, Successful Schools for Young Adolescents, *New Brunswick, N.J., Transaction Books, pp. 27, 84, 109, 141, 169-70.*

Our evaluation of schools initially emphasizes the nature of the adolescent's schooling. Then, many different aspects of school organization, the classroom, and teachers are examined. Next, ideas about patterns of social interaction with peers in the school context are presented. Finally, information about social class and ethnicity in schools is discussed.

The Nature of the Adolescent's Schooling: Ten Thousand Hours in the Classroom

To learn more about the nature of the adolescent's schooling, the impact of schools on adolescents is evaluated as we ask the questions, Do schools make a difference? and What is the function of schools? Then, the importance of considering the child's and adolescent's developmental level is portrayed as we briefly look at the nature of the social context at schools. Next, we look at criteria for effective schools, and some examples of middle schools that seem to meet these criteria.

The Impact and Function of Schools

It is justifiable to be concerned about the impact of schools on children because of the degree of influence schools have in their lives. By the time an individual has graduated from high school, she or he will have spent ten thousand hours in the classroom. School influences are more important today than in past generations because more children are in school longer. For example, in 1900, 11.4 percent of fourteen- to seventeen-year-olds were in school; today, ninety-four percent of the same age group are in school (Smith and Orlosky, 1975).

Children and adolescents spend many years in schools as members of a small society in which there are tasks to be accomplished; people to be socialized and to be socialized by; and rules that define and limit behavior, feelings, and attitudes. The experiences children and adolescents have in this society are likely to have a strong influence in areas such as identity development, belief in one's competence, images of life and career possibilities, social relationships, standards of right and wrong, and conceptions of how a social system beyond the family functions.

It may seem odd to even question whether school has any effect, given the previous statements about the incredible number of hours adolescents spend at school and the diversity of socialization activities taking place in secondary school. But the issue has been raised and has been evaluated from two points of view: (1) Is there a difference between the cognitive performances of those who have gone to school and those who have not? (2) Can schools override the negative effects of poverty? Concerning the first question, there is evidence that schooled children and adolescents do perform differently than the unschooled on a variety of cognitive tasks (Greenfield, 1966; Wagner and Stevenson, 1982). However, we do not yet have a very complete picture of how schooling affects adolescent social development. Research on the second question, regarding poverty, has been extraordinarily controversial. The disagreement is rooted in the work of James Coleman and Christopher Jencks (e.g., Coleman et al., 1966; Jencks et al., 1972). In such investigations, characteristics of schools are compared with family and economic factors as predictors of school achievement and success. Both Coleman and Jencks argue that the evidence supports their belief that schools have little impact on the cognitive development of poverty-stricken students.

But Coleman and Jencks are not without their critics, who fault them on a variety of issues, including the methods they used for collecting their data. One of the most serious criticisms leveled at them is that their analysis is too global, that it was conducted at the level of the school as a whole rather than at the more fine-grained level of everyday happenings in classrooms. In their study of achievement in school and after, the dissenters have compared the effectiveness of schools and classrooms and arrived at the exact opposite conclusion from Coleman and Jencks's (e.g., Brookover et al., 1979;

Edmonds, 1979; Klitgaard and Hall, 1975; Rutter et al., 1979). These researchers identify an important idea that we will carry through the remainder of this chapter; namely, that academic and social patterns are intricately interwoven. Schools that produced high achievement in lower income students were identified not only by particular types of curriculum and time involved in teaching, but by many features of the climate of the school, such as the nature of the teachers' expectations and the patterns of interaction between teachers and students. In other words, various aspects of the school as a social system contributed to the achievement of students in the school.

Additional research focusing on whether schools make a difference in a student's achievement suggests that this question cannot be appropriately addressed unless the extensive variation in schooling is considered. Schools vary even in similar neighborhoods serving similar populations. And they may differ on such dimensions as whether they are integrated or segregated, coed or single sex, parochial or secular, rural or urban, and large or small. Schools are also different in terms of their social climates, educational ideologies, and their concepts of what constitutes the best way to promote the adolescent's development.

Schools seem to be wrapped in controversy regardless of the time period in history we investigate. Historically, questions have been asked about whether adolescents should be treated more like children or more like adults (Stipek, 1981). For the most part, in the United States, we have kept adolescents in school as long as possible. This policy has had practical applications because it has delayed the entry of youth into the labor force. Further, high schools have been perceived as the most competent environment for adolescents to gain the maturity and skills they need to function in the adult world. For more than 150 years, there has been a consistent trend in compulsory school attendance.

However, in the 1960s, the distress over alienated and rebellious youth brought up the issue of whether secondary schools were actually beneficial to adolescents. During the early 1970s, three independent panels agreed that high schools contributed to adolescent alienation and actually restricted the transition to adulthood (Brown, 1973; Coleman et al., 1974; Martin, 1976). These prestigious panels argued that adolescents should be given educational alternatives to the comprehensive high school, such as on-the-job community work, to increase their exposure to adult roles and decrease their sense of isolation from the adult world. To some degree in response to these reports, a number of states lowered the age at which adolescents could leave school from sixteen to fourteen.

Now in the 1980s, the back to basics movement has gained momentum, arguing that the main function of schools should be rigorous training of intellectual skills through subjects like English, math, and science. Proponents of the back to basics movement emphasize that there is too much fluff in the secondary school curricula with students being allowed to select from many alternatives that will not give them a basic education in intellectual subjects. Some critics of schools also argue that too much emphasis is placed on extracurricular activities. Such arguments suggest that schools should be in the business of imparting knowledge to adolescents and little or no concern for the social and emotional development of adolescents should be evidenced. And, related to the issue of the function of schools is the proverbial dilemma of whether schools should include a vocational curriculum in addition to training in basic subjects such as English, math, science, and history. Critics of the fluff in secondary schools also may argue that the school day should be longer and the school year should be extended into the summer months as well. Clearly, such arguments continue to be made by those who feel that the main function of schools should be the training of intellectual skills. Little concern is evident in such arguments for the developmental unfoldings that characterize adolescents in other domains, such as social and emotional development.

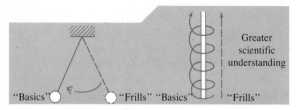

Figure 8.1 **The swinging pendulum solution.**

Should the main and perhaps only major goal of schooling for adolescents be the development of an intellectually mature person? Or should schools also show a strong concern for the development of maturity in social and emotional matters as well? And, should schools be very comprehensive and provide a multifaceted curriculum that includes many elective and alternative subjects to a basic set of core subjects? These are provocative questions and they continue to be heatedly debated in educational and community circles (Cross, 1984; Goodlad, 1983; Sizer, 1984).

There may always be tension between the various functions of schooling thought to be important by educators, psychologists, and parents. Is true cognitive development the main function? Should cognitive development be only one of the functions, with preparation for work, social and emotional development, and the development of a life-long learner also assuming important functions as well? Patricia Cross (1984) argues that this tension produces shifts of emphasis much like a swinging pendulum. It is hoped, though, that we might be able to achieve something like a spiral staircase rather than a pendulum just swinging back and forth (e.g., between something like back to basics and comprehensive training for life) (figure 8.1). That is, we might continually be developing more sophisticated ways of fulfilling the varied and changing functions of schooling. Now that we have considered the impact and function of secondary schools, we turn our attention to the nature of the school as a social context.

Development and the Social Context at School

The social context differs at the preschool, elementary, and secondary level.

The Preschool Setting

The preschool setting is a protected environment, whose boundary is the classroom. In this limited social setting, preschool children interact with one or two teachers, almost always female, who are very powerful figures in the young child's life. The preschool child also interacts with peers in a dyadic relationship or in small groups. It appears that preschool children have little concept of the classroom as an organized social system, although they are learning how to make and maintain social contacts and communicate their needs. The preschool serves to modify some patterns of behavior developed through family experiences. Greater self-control may be required in the preschool and, in many instances, social patterns are mutually developed.

The Elementary School Setting

The classroom is still the major context for the elementary school child, although it is more likely to be experienced as a social unit than in the preschool. Further, the network of social expression is more complex now. Teachers and peers have a prominent influence on the child during the middle childhood years, with teachers symbolizing authority establishing the climate of the classroom, conditions of interaction with students, and the nature of group functioning. The peer group takes on a very prominent status in the lives of elementary school children. Not only is there interest in friendship, belonging, and status in peer groups at school, but the peer group also is a learning community in which social roles and standards related to work and achievement are formed.

The Secondary School Setting

As children move into the junior high school years, the school environment increases in scope and complexity. The school as a whole is the social field rather than the classroom. Adolescent students socially interact with

As children move into the junior high school setting, the school as a whole becomes their social context rather than the classroom.

many different teachers and peers from a range of social backgrounds. Students are often exposed to a greater mix of male and female teachers as well. And social behavior is heavily weighted toward peers, extracurricular events, activities, clubs, and the community. The student in secondary schools is frequently aware of the school as a social organization and may be motivated to conform and adapt to the system or challenge it.

Effective Schools

Joan Lipsitz (1984), Director of the Center for Early Adolescence at the University of North Carolina, in a book called *Effective Schools for Young Adolescents,* has tried to answer the question of what an effective school is for adolescents and looked for examples of such effective schools. Letters were sent to leading researchers and practitioners in diverse fields related to early adolescence and education. Each respondent was asked to recommend schools for visitation and answer the question, "What are five characteristics of effective

schools for young adolescents?" Respondents, interestingly, focused primarily on the developmental appropriateness of the schools with only one or two of the five answers being devoted to academic matters. They emphasized such characteristics as the development of self-discipline, industriousness, respect for authority, persistence, patience, honesty, ability to work toward goals, a sense of respect for self and others, assertiveness, enthusiasm and interest in learning, confidence, ability to function in the peer group, individuality, communication skills, knowledge, and the like. From the respondents' recommendations of schools that were able to produce such characteristics in young adolescents, twelve schools were selected for two-day visits. After these initial two-day visits, four schools were selected for more detailed observations, which were conducted for seven days. Nine categories of observation and discussion were focused on:

1. *Purposes, Goals, Definitions:* Investigated was the underlying rationale or purpose of the school.
2. *School Climate:* Evaluated were the norms, beliefs, responsiveness to developmental needs, academic purpose, learning, socialization for discipline, working conditions, and the school's physical setting.
3. *Organization:* Studied were staff organization, graded or multiaged organization, scheduling, grouping, open or contained classroom structure, and responsiveness to the school's clientele.
4. *Curriculum:* Investigated were issues of balance in the curriculum, interface with elementary and senior high schools, and consideration of adaptation to the nature of the school population.
5. *Instructional Practices:* Studied were the work process, how objectives were identified and accepted, student participation in decisions, allocation of time, rewards, and the assessment process.
6. *Leadership:* Evaluated were the principal's leadership, how authority was created and norms were established, as well as the principal's role as interpreter of the school for the community.

7. *The Community Context:* Monitored were the external pressures that impinge on the school, its history, the role of parents in the schools, and the school's response to the community, as perceived by the principal, superintendent, school board members, community leaders, and parents.
8. *Public Policy Questions:* Assessed were the school's response to desegregation, the education of handicapped students, and the equal treatment of boys and girls.
9. *Self-Evaluation:* Studied was the school's motivation to scrutinize its own practices and hold itself accountable for the effectiveness of the school.

With these guidelines in mind as they observed the effective schools, what did Lipsitz and her observational team find when they visited the recommended schools? The most striking feature of the four best middle schools was their willingness and ability to adapt all school practices to the individual differences in intellectual, biological, and social development of their students. The schools took seriously what is known about early adolescent development. This seriousness was reflected in decisions about many different aspects of school life. For example, one middle school fought to keep a schedule of mini-courses on Friday so that every student could have responsible choices, be with friends, and pursue personal interests. Two other middle schools expended considerable energy on a complex school organization so small groups of students were known by small groups of teachers who could vary the tone and pace of the school day depending on the students' needs. Another middle school developed an advisory scheme so each student had daily contact with an adult who was willing to listen, explain, comfort, and prod the adolescent. Such school policies reflect thoughtfulness and personal concern about individuals whose developmental needs are compelling.

Another aspect of the effective middle schools observed was that very early in their existence (the first year in three of the schools and the second year in the fourth school) they emphasized the importance of creating an environment that is positive for the adolescent's social and personality development. This goal was set forth, not only because such environments contribute to academic excellence, but because social and personality development are intrinsically valued as important in themselves in the schooling of adolescents. To learn more about the nature of the four effective middle schools read Perspective on Adolescent Development 8.1.

In our discussion of effective schools, we have described ideas about school organization, the classroom, and teachers. Now we turn our attention in greater detail to these important aspects of the adolescent's schooling.

School Organization, the Classroom, and Teachers: One Never Smiled, Another Was Happy and Vibrant

In this section, we first study the overall manner in which schools are organized, giving particular attention to middle school and junior high school arrangements. Then, information about the classroom itself is presented, followed by a description of the role teachers play in the adolescent's development.

School Organization

Let's now look at the nature of how schools are organized and see if this organization is linked with the adolescent's development. In particular, we highlight the importance of the transition from the elementary school to the middle or junior high school. Then, we consider the relation of school and class size to the adolescent's development.

The Organization of Secondary Schools

The organization of junior high schools, and more recently, middle schools, has been justified on the basis of the physical, cognitive, and social changes that characterize early adolescence. As John Hill (1980) points out, the growth spurt and the onset of puberty were the basis for removing seventh-and eighth-grade students from elementary schools. And, because puberty has been occurring earlier in recent decades, the same kind

Joan Lipsitz (1984) commented about the nature of leadership, school climate, curriculum, school organization, and the school in the community in her protrayal of effective schools for young adolescents:

Leadership: The principal served as an important leader in each of the effective middle schools. She or he often was an independent and resourceful person. From motley sources often came dinners, trips, extra supplies, and other perks for outstanding teachers. Students, teachers, and parents were made to feel their school was a very special place. These principals recognized the important principle that when people are made to feel special and they are in a special situation, they usually will respond and perform competently.

School Climate: Many young adolescents are impulsive, self-absorbed, antagonistic toward adult authority, alternately energetic and enervated, and so on. When teachers complain about young adolescents, animal imagery is extensive: "That school is a zoo," "Those students are like animals," and "It's a jungle in that classroom." How did the successful schools get their young adolescents to behave in more humane ways? They insisted on the common humanity of their inhabitants. They emphasized the school context as a community in which there is a great deal of caring. Hours upon hours of time were spent in and outside of school on the students' personal welfare—on canoeing expeditions, at baseball games, and in promoting rock concerts. This level of caring is important at any age group, but it is particularly valuable for an age where individuals feel so fragile about their development of independence and identity. These schools recognized that young adolescents

Successful schools offer a climate of caring.

The school board can be an influential force in determining the success or failure of schools for adolescents.

are not ready for the strong independence foisted on them by secondary school organization. The schools granted more independence than elementary schools do, but established strong support groups (houses, teams, wings, advisory groups) to help them in their transition from childhood to more mature status.

Curriculum: The curriculum at each of the four effective middle schools was diverse and it was exciting. They placed emphasis on creating numerous opportunities for competence and achievement, self-exploration and definition, social interaction, and effective school participation. There were spectacular instances of curricular success, such as a camping trip, a Fifties Week, Authors' Week, and the like. These schools recognized the importance of flamboyance in educating young adolescents. An awards ceremony for campers, Black History Week, and WNOE (a simulated rock music station) all represent the school as theatre. Such brilliant moments in these schools gave variety to what otherwise would be regarded as a rather dull, uninspired curriculum.

School Organization: None of the four effective middle schools used the same method of grouping students. A particular practice distinguishes each school, such as a full period for advisory at one school, multiaging in core subjects at another school, and a variety of teaming options at yet another school. Each principal was creative in fashioning the school organization and school day to enhance communication, personalization, and continuity in relationships. Each school's organization evolved over a number of years. Each school has had at least one major overhaul in organization and many minor tune-ups. Each of the schools adopted a house and team structure so that groups of students live together for several hours each school day, sometimes for two to three years.

The School in the Community: Schools often thrive or fail depending on their particular community context. The public makes tremendous demands on schools. While each of the four effective middle schools functioned in different contexts, all four schools were responsive to the particular social and political milieu in those communities. One school survives because of its strict discipline and substantial curricular predictability; another because it has turned inward, away from a contentious district; another because it has developed strong math and science programs and prepares students for success on the SAT. The distinctiveness of each effective school is the result of interplay between a coherent concept of schooling for the age group, particular personalities, and the constraints and demands of the community context.

of thinking has lead to the creation of middle schools that house sixth-graders and sometimes fifth-graders with seventh- and eighth-graders.

Many educators and psychologists believe that junior high schools have merely become watered-down versions of high schools, simply mimicking their curricular and extracurricular schedules. These critics argue that unique curricular and extracurricular activities reflecting the wide range of individual differences in biological and psychological development in early adolescence should be incorporated into our junior high schools. It also has been argued that most secondary schools foster passivity rather than autonomy, and that schools should develop a variety of pathways for junior high and high school students to achieve an identity. But there is little evidence that schools have made much headway in accomplishing these difficult tasks (Hill, 1980).

There are many ways the secondary school years can be packaged. As we entered the 1980s, there were at least thirty-four different grade combinations that encompassed the middle grades (Lipsitz, 1984). Several examples include: seven through nine, seven through twelve, six through eight, five through eight, and kindergarten through eight. In particular, there has been considerable interest in the transition to middle or junior high school.

The Transition to Middle or Junior High School
The transition to middle school or junior high school from an elementary school is of interest to developmental psychologists because even though it is a normative experience for virtually all children in our society, this transition can be stressful. The transition may be stressful because of the point in development at which the transition takes place (Hawkins and Berndt, 1985; Nottlemann, 1982). Transition to middle or junior high school occurs at a time in the development of children when a number of simultaneous changes are occurring, including changes in the individual, the family, and the school. These changes include the occurrence of puberty and related concerns about body image; the emergence of at least some aspects of formal operational thought, including accompanying changes in social cognition, increased responsibility and independence in association with decreased dependency on parents; change from a small, contained classroom structure to a larger, more impersonal school structure; change from one teacher to many teachers and a small, homogeneous set of peers to a larger, more heterogeneous group of peers; and increased focus on achievement and performance (and assessment of such achievement and performance). While this list includes a number of negative features of the transition to middle school or junior high school, there are positive aspects to the change as well. Students are more likely to feel grown up, have more subjects to select from, have more opportunities to spend time with peers and more chances to locate compatible friends, enjoy increased independence from direct parental monitoring and teacher monitoring, and may be more challenged intellectually by academic work (Hawkins and Berndt, 1985).

A number of research inquiries are beginning to appear that chart children's development as they move from an elementary school into a middle or junior high school (e.g., Blyth, Simmons, and Bush, 1978; Douvan and Adelson, 1966; Simmons, Rosenberg, and Rosenberg, 1973; Felner, Ginter, and Primavera, 1982; Goodlad, 1983; Gump, 1983; Hawkins and Berndt, 1985). The upshot of these investigations is that the first year of a middle school or a junior high school can be very difficult for many students. This is not surprising given the large number of changes that accompany movement into the middle or junior high school years. One major reason for the difficulty students in middle or junior high school encounter is what is referred to as the **top-dog phenomenon** (Blyth, Simmons, and Carleton-Ford, 1983). Moving from the top position (in elementary school, as the oldest, biggest, and most powerful students in the school) to the bottom or lowest position (in middle or junior high school, the youngest, smallest, and least powerful group of students) may create a number of difficulties for students.

What are the many adjustments involved in the transitions from elementary to middles or junior high school?

However, there is increased interest in the nature of schooling experiences that might produce better adjustment for children as they move from elementary school to middle or junior high schools. It has been found that schools providing more supportiveness, less anonymity, more stability, and less complexity have a salutary effect on student adjustment in middle and junior high school transition.

And, adjustment to the transition to middle or junior high school may be somewhat different for boys than girls and for early maturing students compared with late maturing students. With regard to social matters, boys may be at a disadvantage compared to girls as they enter middle or junior high school. As we said in our discussion of physical development in Chapter 3, girls enter puberty on the average about two years earlier than boys; thus, a much larger percentage of girls in the first year of middle or junior high school have entered puberty than is the case for boys. Their

sexual maturation and growth spurt may put them more on par with the older girls and boys in middle and junior high schools. And, since it is in middle and junior high school that pressures for dating begin to emerge, girls, many of whom already are moving well along the path to physical maturity, are likely to fare better. It also is helpful to consider whether children making the transition to middle or junior high school are maturing early, on time, or late. Recall from our discussion of early and late maturation in Chapter 3 that early maturing girls, while they seemed to get along better with male adolescents, nonetheless seemed to have more difficulty in achievement and academic related matters. To learn more about the transition to the junior high school years, read Perspective on Adolescent Development 8.2, where information about a recent research study is presented.

As can be seen, school organization is related to the adolescent's development. Next, we focus on other aspects of school organization—school and class size.

THE ROLE OF TYPE OF SCHOOL AND FRIENDSHIP
IN THE TRANSITION FROM ELEMENTARY SCHOOL
TO JUNIOR HIGH SCHOOL

To provide more information about the nature of research on transition to middle or junior high school, we describe a recent investigation by Jacquelyn Hawkins and Thomas Berndt (1985). In this research inquiry, the investigators were interested in the transition from elementary to junior high school, in particular what the role of friendships might be in this transition. They studied 101 students at three points in time: the spring of the sixth grade (pretransition), and twice in the seventh grade (early and late posttransition). The sample consisted of students in two different kinds of schools, one being a traditional junior high school, the other a school in which the students were grouped into small teams (one hundred students, four teachers). A number of different measures were called on to assess the students' adjustment, including self-reports, peer ratings, and teacher ratings. The results indicated that adjustment dropped during posttransition, that is, during the seventh grade. For example, the self-esteem of students in both schools dropped in the seventh grade; however, the influence of the nature of the school environment appeared in the results. For instance, in the traditional junior high school, students reported they received less teacher support than in the sixth grade, but in the junior high with smaller student classes, more teacher support was reported during

Smaller classes with teacher support help ease the transition of middle or junior high school.

posttransition (table 8.1). Also, friendship (as measured by the quality of relationship and contact with friends) improved by late posttransition and influenced adjustment to junior high school. Students with higher scores on friendship measures had a more positive perception of themselves and more positive attitudes toward school in junior high school. These data show how a supportive, more intimate school environment and friendship formation and maintenance can ease the transition for students as they move from the elementary to middle or junior high school years.

Table 8.1   Classroom environment in the transition from elementary school to junior high school

		Sixth Grade (Spring)	Seventh Grade (Fall)	Seventh Grade (Spring)
Total sample	Involvement	.57	.55	.51
	Affiliation	.71	.66	.67
	Support	.48	.44	.41
Traditional junior high school	Involvement	.50	.47	.45
	Affiliation	.71	.68	.68
	Support	.47	.38	.35
Team-organized junior high school	Involvement	.66	.65	.57
	Affiliation	.75	.71	.70
	Support	.49	.53	.49

Note: Numbers are mean scores on Classroom Environment Scale; scores range from 0–1 with higher scores being more positive.
Source: Hawkins and Berndt, 1985, p. 18.

School and Class Size

High school students no longer spend the day in a self-contained room. They are exposed to the school as a whole much more than was true during the elementary school years, when the majority of a school day was spent in one or two rooms. While there have not been any consistent relationships discovered between most aspects of the school as a physical context and student development (Rutter et al., 1979), researchers have gathered more systematic findings on school size.

According to Patricia Minuchin and Edna Shapiro (1983), a combination of factors has led to the increased number of large secondary schools. There are an increasing number of students in urban areas, decreasing budgets in most regions, and an educational rationale that stresses the possibilities for academic stimulation in consolidated institutions (Conant, 1959; Garbarino, 1980). While no systematic relation has been found between school size and academic behavior (e.g., Coleman et al., 1966; Rutter et al., 1979), there is evidence that more prosocial and possibly less antisocial behavior occurs in small schools. Five hundred has been suggested as an optimal threshold size, though experts have set the optimal size at different points under one thousand (Garbarino, 1980; Paskal and Miller, 1973; Rosenberg, 1970; Turner and Thrasher, 1970). However, beyond a certain point, school size seems to make little difference in regard to the occurrence of antisocial behavior by students; that is, small reductions in very large schools would likely result in few social benefits.

While some investigators have not found a relation between school size and antisocial behavior (e.g., Rutter et al., 1979), a number of researchers have been able to document that negative behavior is more prevalent in larger than in small schools (Duke and Perry, 1978; McPartland and McDill, 1977; Reynolds et al., 1980). Why would large schools be more likely to promote antisocial behavior? Large schools may not create enough of a personalized climate or develop an effective system of social control, so students may feel alienated and not responsible for their conduct. This explanation may be particularly appropriate for the behavior of unsuccessful students who do not identify academically with their schools and who become members of oppositional peer groups (Garbarino, 1978; Wynne, 1977).

The responsiveness of the school may also be a mediating factor. For example, in one investigation, responsiveness was defined in terms of rewards for desirable behavior, punishments for misbehavior, and student accessibility to decision making. In low-responsive schools, the crime rate was higher (McPartland and McDill, 1976). Small schools may be generally more flexible and responsive to change than larger schools, a factor that may mediate the incidence of negative behavior.

Research focused on the relation between school size and prosocial behavior has consistently indicated that small schools provide a greater opportunity for participating in school activities, and that in small schools more students are active in and identified with such activities (Barker and Gump, 1964). In small schools, even marginal students may become mobilized to become a member of one or more social groups and as a consequence feel more responsibility to and identity with the school (Wicker, 1968; Willems, 1967).

Although researchers have found some correlation between school size and student behavior, there is little consistency in how classroom size affects adolescent development. Traditional schools in the United States usually have about thirty students per class, give or take ten. Although most teachers insist they do a better job with smaller groups, empirical evidence to support this belief has not yet been developed. The most comprehensive investigation of class size has been conducted with elementary school children in which 163 classrooms were evaluated (U.S. Office of Education, 1974). The results were contradictory—at some grade levels, small classes seemed to improve academic performance, while at others it did not. Thus, while there is every intuitive reason to argue for smaller classes, there is little empirical evidence to back up this argument.

Raoul Schmiedeck (1979) raises the serious question of what large student populations, at both the school and classroom levels, do to the adolescent's need for personal attachment and group formation:

> The situation is . . . complicated by the mobility within the school populations. Students individually select different subjects every year or even semester, and find themselves with a different group of peers in almost every course. As a result there are no classes in the traditional sense, no small, coherent communities of children who go through high school together.
>
> There is, of course, grouping, but it exists mostly in the form of cliques. Athletes, outstanding students, or children with special interests tend to flock together. For the majority of students the group in a grade is too large for lasting contact, and the clique too homogeneous or small for new and varied attachments.
>
> What is missing are groups of a size and mixture which permit unification on the one side, and definition by contrast on the other. There is reliable evidence that such groups should contain no more than twenty to forty people. In a psychological test on interpersonal relationships, the number of people "who have been important in your life" centers around fifteen, and in no case exceeds forty. . . .
>
> In a "traditional" class of about thirty, children can get to know one another. They can become familiar with each other's strengths and weaknesses. For example, a student will be known as good in English but poor in science, or as a nice guy, or as vain or sensitive. It does not matter so much what he is, but that he is known in all his facets and not only in the one or the other. In any case, he will be reacted to as a whole person, and can be admired and accepted, and also criticized and rejected.
>
> This totality of reaction, the coexistence of positive and negative characteristics, makes for a variety of bonds, and for their confluence and continuity. One needs these bonds in order to define oneself, and to define others. Only if they exist can one develop an accurate sense of self and belonging. . . .
>
> I have described aspects of the size and the organizational structure of high schools which reduce human contact and have a negative influence on the sense of community, the development of relationships, and the formation

of personal identity. They are part of the progress and the malaise of our time, and it seems unlikely that we could modify them substantially. But we should try to remain aware of their potential effect during a growing phase which is already marked by confusions, uncertainty, and vulnerability.

> In his book *Young Radicals,* Kenneth Keniston states, "In the life histories of alienated college students . . . [we could find] . . . no mention of overt alienation and midadolescence, about the age of sixteen. At this age we hear accounts of growing feelings of cynicism, distance, estrangement and scorn—initially for classmates, later for parents and teachers, finally for all of society. . . . As our society becomes more technological, more specialized, more highly organized . . . the most talented and sensitive . . . of our youth will be repelled . . . and will experience transient, and, in many cases, enduring phases of alienation." (Keniston, 1968)
>
> In a recent article in the *New York Times* the following was said about the members of a graduating class in one of the nation's most prestigious public high schools: "The seniors seem to care less . . . about politics, about each other . . . than their older brothers and sisters. . . . They reflect passivity, conformity, and materialism. . . . They are part of a national trend. . . . They worry about the future in starkly practical terms—grades, college admissions and jobs. . . . They did not know each other well." (*New York Times Magazine,* 1977) (Schmiedeck, 1979, pp. 191–196)

So far in our discussion of schools, we have described many different aspects of the nature of the adolescent's schooling and school organization. To help you remember the main points of this discussion, a summary is provided in Concept Table 8.1. Now we turn our attention to an evaluation of classroom structure and climate.

Classroom Structure and Climate

Classroom environments also influence the adolescent's development. Certain structures and climates have dominated the classroom of the adolescent in the United States.

Concept Table 8.1

THE NATURE OF THE ADOLESCENT'S SCHOOLING AND SCHOOL ORGANIZATION

Concept	Processes/related ideas	Characteristics/description
Nature of the adolescent's schooling	The impact and function of schools	By the time an individual has graduated from high school he or she has spent more than 10,000 hours in the classroom. Schools are contexts where individuals are members of a small society. Some sociologists have argued that schools have little impact on the adolescent's development; however, when researchers have conducted more precise, observational studies of what goes on in schools and classrooms, the effects of schooling on the adolescent's development become much more prominent. Controversy surrounds the functions of secondary schools. Arguments have been made that the function of secondary schools should be the intellectual development of the adolescent, while other statements suggest that secondary schools should have more comprehensive functions, such as social and emotional development, preparation for work, and the creation of a life-long learner.
	Development and the social context at school	The social context differs at the preschool, elementary, and secondary levels. At the secondary school level, the entire school assumes a more important role in the individual's development.
	Effective schools	Joan Lipsitz has expended considerable time discovering the characteristics of effective schools for young adolescents. Among the criteria developed to evaluate the effectiveness of such schools are purposes, goals, definitions, school climate, organization, curriculum, instructional practices, leadership, the community context, public policy questions, and self-evaluation. Effective schools take seriously individual differences in physical, cognitive, and social development and reveal a deep concern for what is known about early adolescence—such schools are not just watered-down high schools or stepped up elementary schools. These effective schools also emphasize social development as well as academic development

THE NATURE OF THE ADOLESCENT'S SCHOOLING AND SCHOOL ORGANIZATION

Concept	Processes/related ideas	Characteristics/description
School organization	The organization of secondary schools	The organization of junior high schools and more recently middle schools has been justified on the basis of physical, cognitive, and social changes in the adolescent. The earlier onset of puberty has had a strong impact on the appearance of middle schools. There are many ways secondary schools can be organized, such as seven through nine, seven through twelve, six through eight, five through eight, kindergarten through eight, and so forth.
	The transition to middle or junior high school	This transition coincides with a number of individual, familial, and social changes. The transition is associated with adjustment difficulties for many children, although supportive, more intimate school settings, as well as friendships, seem to make the adjustment less taxing. Sex differences and early-late maturation likely are other factors influencing adjustment during this transition.
	School and class size	More prosocial and possibly less antisocial behavior occurs in small schools than in large schools. Five hundred has been stressed as an optimal threshold size by some experts, while others emphasize that one thousand is a more reasonable number. While little consistency has been found in research attempting to link class size with adolescent development, at an intuitive level there is every reason to believe that small classes increase the adolescent's sense of belongingness and connectiveness in the school and decrease his or her alienation and sense of anonymity. Responsiveness of schools and teachers to students clearly mediates the effects of school and class size on the adolescent's development.

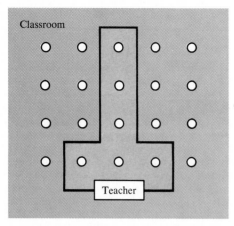

Classroom

Teacher

Figure 8.2 Typical pattern of teacher–student interaction in a classroom with traditional seating arrangement.

Structure

The typical American schoolroom has seats fixed in rows facing the front of the room, where the teacher's desk is located. In recent years, however, many schools have developed less structured physical arrangements in the classroom. Some education experts have even commented that the most significant event in education in the last one hundred years has been removing the bolts that attach seats to the floor, allowing adolescents to move around the classroom (e.g., Smock, 1975).

An interesting study of the traditional seating arrangement indicates that in such an arrangement, the teacher interacts with some students more than others because of seat location (Adams and Biddle, 1970). Adolescents who sit in the front and in the center are more likely to interact with the teacher than are students sitting on the fringes (figure 8.2). This pattern of interaction occurred in both sixth- and eleventh-grade classrooms, with both male and female teachers, and in both social studies and mathematics classes. (It should be noted that the student's selection of a classroom seat may reflect his or her willingness to participate in classroom exchanges.)

Climate

Perhaps the most widely debated aspect of classroom climate in recent years has focused on open versus traditional classrooms. The **open classroom** (or open education) **concept** has referred to many different dimensions of schools (Marshall, 1981; Giaconia and Hedges, 1982):

> free choice by students of activities they will participate in
>
> space flexibility
>
> varied, enriched learning materials
>
> emphasis on individual and small group instruction
>
> the teacher is more of a facilitator rather than a director of learning
>
> students learn to assume responsibility for their learning
>
> multiage grouping of children
>
> team teaching
>
> classrooms without walls in which the physical nature of the school is more open

Some open classroom programs have more of these features than others. Thus, research that compares open with traditional classrooms is difficult to interpret because there are so many variations of open classrooms. Part of the problem with studies of open and traditional classrooms also is that these terms are not always measured directly in the classroom. As a result, in some classrooms defined as open, the teachers may be using a teaching style more characteristic of traditional classrooms. One inadequate strategy that has been used too often is simply to ask teachers or school officials (who may have varying definitions of what constitutes open and traditional classrooms) to rate classroom climate.

In many instances, the measures that have been used to assess the effects of classroom climate have been standardized tests of intelligence and achievement. However, Rudolf Moos (Trickett and Moos, 1974; Moos and Moos, 1978) believes that it may be wise to assess educational effects other than those evaluated by standardized tests. Cognitive preferences, school satisfaction, and persistent motivation to learn are several factors that adolescents should be measured on as well.

Furthermore, experts believe that not only should different measures be used to assess the effects of classroom climate, but better instruments to evaluate classroom climate are needed. One such measure is the **Classroom Environment Scale (CES)** developed by Trickett and Moos (1974). The CES attempts to evaluate the social climate of both junior high and high school classrooms. Teacher–student and peer relationships, as well as the organization of the classroom, are assessed. Students are asked to respond to a number of questions concerning nine different categories: teacher support, affiliation, task orientation, competition, order and organization, rule clarity, involvement, teacher control, and innovation.

Because open classrooms have been defined in so many different ways, some researchers have recommended that the open classroom concept be evaluated in terms of its components, or in some combination of the components, rather than as a whole. One such evaluation of the components of open classrooms has been conducted (Giaconia and Hedges, 1982). They performed a **meta-analysis** of approximately 150 studies. A meta-analysis involves the application of statistical techniques to already existing research studies. The investigator sorts through the research literature looking for common results of many different studies to discover some consistent themes. These results indicated that open classrooms:

lowered language achievement, but by a very small amount

had little effect on math, reading, and other types of academic achievement

enhanced achievement motivation, cooperativeness, creativity, and independence a moderate amount

had no effect on adjustment, anxiety, locus of control, or self-concept

slightly improved student attitudes toward school, the teacher, curiosity, and general mental ability.

However, these results tell us nothing about the particular dimensions of the open classrooms. To investigate these more precise effects, the following characteristics were investigated:

role of the child (the degree of activity in learning)

diagnostic evaluation (use of work samples, observations, but rare use of tests to guide instruction)

materials to manipulate

individualized instruction (adjusting rate, methods, materials; calling on small group methods)

multiage grouping of students (two or more grades in the same area)

open space (flexible use of areas, activity centers, no interior walls, flexible seating)

team teaching (two or more teachers combining to plan and instruct the same students; use of parents as teaching aides)

The results of the analysis by Giaconia and Hedges (1982) revealed that when the open classroom concept was associated with the child's positive self-concept, the role of the child invariably was a key dimension of how "open classroom" was defined. Diagnostic evaluation, materials to manipulate, and individualized instruction also were important ingredients when the open classroom was positively linked to the adolescent's self-concept. When nonachievement outcomes were considered, all dimensions of open classrooms were important except team teaching and open space. For achievement outcomes, materials to manipulate and team teaching were the dimensions of open classrooms most likely to have a positive effect, while multiage grouping appeared to be the least important dimension.

Open classrooms have been defined along many different dimensions.

Teachers

Virtually everyone's life is affected in one way or another by teachers: you have probably been influenced by teachers as you grew up; you may become a teacher yourself or work with teachers through counseling or psychological services; and you may one day have adolescents whose education will be guided by many different teachers through the years. How much influence do teachers really have on adolescents? Try to think of some characteristics of the teachers you have liked or disliked, particularly their communication and social interaction styles. You can probably remember several of your teachers vividly: perhaps one never smiled, another required you to memorize everything in sight, and yet another always appeared happy and vibrant, and encouraged verbal interaction.

To learn more about teachers and their role in the adolescent's development, we study the characteristics and styles of teachers, aptitude-treatment interaction, and sex roles in schools.

Teacher Characteristics and Styles

The following list of rules for teachers was found pasted in the back of a general history textbook published in 1872:

1. Teachers every day will fill lamps, clean chimneys, and trim wicks.
2. Make your pens carefully. You may whittle nibs to the individual taste of the pupil.
3. Men teachers take one evening each week for courting purposes, or two evenings each week if they go to church regularly.
4. After ten hours in school, the teachers spend their remaining time reading the Bible or other good books.
5. Women teachers who marry or engage in unseemly conduct will be dismissed.
6. Every teacher should lay aside from each pay a goodly sum of his earnings for his benefit during his declining years so he will not be a burden on society.
7. Any teacher who smokes, uses liquor in any form, frequents pool or public halls, or gets shaved in the barbershop will give reason to suspect his worth, integrity, and honesty.
8. The teacher who performs his labors faithfully and without fault for five years will be given an increase of 25 cents per week, if the board of education approves.

Teachers do abide by certain codes or sets of rules even today—a few of the restrictions of 1872 exist in some form more than a full century later. Parents have certain expectations for teachers, and they believe particular rules should apply to teachers' behavior. To learn more about the characteristics of good teachers, information is presented about Erik Erikson's criteria for a good teacher, research on personality traits of competent teachers, as well as some desirable characteristics of junior high school teachers.

Erikson's Criteria for a Good Teacher

Erik Erikson (1968) believes that good teachers are able to produce a sense of industry rather than inferiority in their students. Good teachers are trusted and respected by the community and know how to alternate play and work, games and study. They know how to recognize special efforts and encourage special abilities. They also know how to give an adolescent time and how to handle those adolescents to whom school is not important.

Good teachers, in Erikson's view, allow a student to engage in peer interaction when academic work is getting to him and his interaction with the teacher seems to be deteriorating. At stake is the adolescent's development of identification with those who know things and know how to do things. Time after time in interviews with talented and creative people, spontaneous comments reveal that one teacher helped to spark hidden talent. Without such teachers, many adolescents never develop their abilities.

Erikson believes that many teachers emphasize self-restraint and a strict allegiance to duty, as opposed to encouraging adolescents to make discoveries on their own. Erikson remarks that either method may work well with some adolescents but not with others. He also stresses that if the first method is carried to the extreme, adolescents may develop too much self-restraint and sense of duty in conforming to what others do. If the opposite method is used in the extreme, Erikson believes that adolescents should be "mildly but firmly coerced into the adventure of finding out that one can learn to accomplish things which one would never have thought of by oneself." (1968, p. 127)

There is another possible hazard in the adolescent's development that Erikson feels teachers need to watch for. When the adolescent conforms too much, he may view work as the only worthwhile activity in his life. This type of adolescent probably will not engage in imaginative activities and games to the extent that an individual with better identity development would. There are times when the grind of hard work should be left behind, and teachers can encourage students to do so.

The Personality Traits of Good Teachers

For many years, psychologists and educators have been trying to create a profile of the personality traits of a good teacher. A definitive answer is still not and, perhaps, will never be available, but several studies suggest that some traits are better than others. Teacher traits that relate positively to the student's intellectual development are enthusiasm, the ability to plan, poise, adaptability, and awareness of individual differences (Gage, 1965). Teachers who are impulsive tend to have students who become more impulsive and less reflective in solving school tasks (e.g., Yando and Kagan, 1968). And teachers who are warm and flexible and who encourage responsibility have students who respond constructively to failure and who tend to engage willingly in class activities (Thompson, 1944).

Diana Baumrind (1972) indicates that the three styles of discipline she has discovered in parent–youth interaction generalize to teacher–student relations as well. The authoritarian teacher is dominant and controlling. The authoritative teacher is directive but rational, encourages verbal give-and-take, and values independence but still admires disciplined conformity. The laissez-faire teacher provides little or no direction and behaves passively. Baumrind argues that the authoritative teaching style fosters the development of competence in adolescents. More about the teacher's discipline orientation and a number of other aspects of a competent teacher of junior high school students is presented in Perspective on Adolescent Development 8.3.

Not all adolescents respond equally well to a particular teacher style or personality trait. In one investigation, for example, achievement by low-anxiety adolescents was greater in informal classes that emphasized active student participation, while achievement by high-anxiety students was greater in formal, teacher-centered classes. Let's look more closely at the idea that some teaching styles are better with some students than others. In doing so, we will look not only at the concept of matching teaching styles and characteristics with students' abilities and characteristics, but at the climate and structure of the classroom as well.

Aptitude–Treatment Interaction

Some children may benefit from structure more than others, and some teachers may be able to handle a flexible curriculum better than others. As a result, a whole field of educational research has sprung up, referred to

as **aptitude x treatment interaction,** or (ATI). The term **aptitude** refers to academic potential and personality dimensions in which students differ; **treatment** refers to the educational technique (e.g., structured class or flexible class) adopted in the classroom. Lee Cronbach and Richard Snow (1977), as well as other education experts, argue that ATI is the best way to study teaching effectiveness.

Recent research has shown that a child's achievement level (aptitude) may interact directly with classroom structure (treatment) to produce the best learning and the most enjoyable learning environment (Peterson, 1977; Porteus, 1976). That is, students with high-achievement orientation often do well in a flexible classroom and enjoy it; students with low-achievement orientation do not usually do as well and dislike the flexibility. The reverse is true in a structured classroom. There are many other ATI factors operating in the classroom. Education experts are just beginning to pin some of these down; further clarification of aptitude x treatment interaction should lead to useful information about how children can be taught more effectively. Richard Snow (1977) points out that individual differences (aptitudes) were ignored for many years in the design of instruction and curriculum. Now individual differences in student aptitudes, learning styles, cultural backgrounds, and so forth are forcing curriculum teams to consider more specific instructional situations and more specific groups of children.

Two ways that the teacher's orientation can be classified are as challenging and demanding, or as encouraging good performance. Jere Brophy (1979) reviewed several studies focused on these types of teacher orientations. Teachers who work with high-socioeconomic status/high-ability students usually are more successful if they move at a quick pace, frequently communicating high expectations and enforcing high standards. These teachers try to keep students challenged, will not accept inferior work, and occasionally criticize the students' work when it does not meet their standards. Teachers who generally are successful with low-socioeconomic status/low-ability students also are interested in getting the most out of their students, but they usually do so by being warm and encouraging rather than demanding. They are friendly with their students, take more time out from academic subject matter to motivate the youth, praise and encourage more often, rarely criticize poor work, and move the curriculum along at a slower pace. When they call on individual students, they allow more time for the student to respond; they may provide hints to help the student get the correct answer (Brophy and Evertson, 1974, 1976). As can be readily seen by this example,

"You'll find 'Teaching Methods That Never Fail' under fiction."

Reprinted by permission of Ford Button.

successful teaching varies according to the type of student being taught—one teaching strategy is superior with lower class students, another with higher socioeconomic status students.

Now that we have considered some of the important characteristics of teachers who work with adolescents and seen that some characteristics may enhance the learning of some students more than others, we turn our attention to another aspect of teachers and their adolescent students. In recent years, the interest in changing sex roles has touched teachers and the classrooms.

Teachers, Sex Roles, and Schools

The sex of the teacher and of the adolescent may affect the nature of adolescent–teacher interaction. Imagine teaching twenty-five to thirty-five adolescents in junior high school. Orderliness and allegiance to rules might become an overriding concern. Boys tend to show more out-of-control and aggressive behavior than girls do (e.g., Maccoby and Jacklin, 1974). Might you react in a more authoritarian manner to the students trying to get your attention in negative ways?

There is some empirical evidence that girls react more favorably to authoritarian discipline than boys do (e.g., Douvan and Adelson, 1966). And, both male and female teachers seem to scold boys more than girls (Etaugh and Marlow, 1973). Thus, the belief that teachers of young adolescents like female students better than males is not surprising. However, the relationship between secondary school teachers and female adolescents does not always encourage these students to pursue achievement-oriented careers. In the past, female students were often even discouraged from pursuing careers.

Aletha Huston-Stein and Ann Higgins-Trenk (1978) discuss other aspects of the adolescent female's difficulty in pursuing a career. The educational aspirations of adolescent females seem to be affected more by teachers' expectations than the aspirations of males are, probably because the girls have been provided with less clear-cut prescriptions of the type of education and work roles their parents expect them to pursue after they get out of high school (Williams, 1972).

The evidence is very strong that innovative programs in high schools can exert a powerful influence on the adolescent female's achievement aspirations. In Minneapolis, Minnesota, high school courses and other experiences were developed to encourage the cognitive and personality development of adolescent females. After a one-semester course, females scored at higher levels on Lawrence Kohlberg's moral development scale and Jane Loevinger's ego development scale. And from the beginning to the end of the course, the adolescent females' attitudes shifted from stereotypic sex-role thinking to more introspective and differentiated thinking about sex roles (Erickson, 1977).

But there is a curious paradox when all of the information about the sex of the adolescent, the sex of the teacher, and the sex-role orientation of the school is pieced together (Minuchin and Shapiro, 1983).

Schools are generally perceived to be "feminine institutions," and teachers tend to prefer students with "feminine" characteristics (that is, conforming, quiet, and nonagressive). But although boys are reprimanded more by teachers than girls, they are more confident and persistent in academic situations. Further, while girls do well in school during childhood, by the end of high school boys often have academically surpassed girls. How can we explain this?

One suggestion rests in the ideas developed by Carol Dweck and her associates (e.g., Dweck and Eliot, 1983; Dweck and Bush, 1976; Dweck et al., 1978). According to Dweck, girls tend to attribute their failures in achievement situations to lack of ability rather than to lack of effort, and teachers may reinforce their beliefs. For example, although equal amounts of feedback were given by teachers to boys and girls in the fourth- and fifth-grade classrooms studied, the teachers emphasized that the intellectual quality of the boys' work was superior. In other words, the teachers told the boys they were doing higher quality work than the girls. Other findings suggested teachers were more likely to attribute the cause of boys' failures to lack of motivation, but more often felt that girls were not doing well because of lack of ability. The work of Carol Dweck and her associates makes a strong argument that the *pattern* rather than the sheer amount of feedback influences children's and adolescents' achievement orientations in school. To learn more about possible sex bias in schools, read Perspective on Adolescent Development 8.4, where sex roles in curricula and the school hierarchy are portrayed.

We have considered many different aspects of the adolescent's relationships and interactions with adults in the school setting. As we see next, the adolescent's relationships with peers in the school setting also are an important aspect of the adolescent's development.

Perspective on Adolescent Development 8.4

SEX ROLES IN CURRICULA AND IN THE
SCHOOL HIERARCHY

Gender-related stereotyping in learning materials was more or less unsuspected until the late 1960s, but subsequent documentation has been startling in its scope and consistency, demonstrating bias in readers, curriculum materials, the items on standardized tests, and textbooks across a wide range of topics from social studies to math (e.g., Child, Potter and Levine, 1946; Frazier and Sadker, 1973; Jay and Schminke, 1975; Kingston and Lovelace, 1977–78; Oliver, 1974; Pottker and Fishel, 1977; Saario et al., 1973; Scott and Feldman-Summers, 1979; Shirreffs, 1975; Stockard et al., 1980; U'ren, 1971; Weitzman and Rizzo, 1974; Women on Words and Images, 1972). The language, illustrations, and depictions of roles as well as the ratio of male to female figures reflect conventional assumptions and, in the opinion of many, a clear bias against females. The generic "he" is consistently used to refer to girls as well as boys. These attitudes run deep. Even the Bank Street Readers, specifically designed to provide a realistic, ethnically mixed urban context for beginning readers, portrayed girls and boys in stereotyped ways (Saario et al., 1973; Women on Words and Images, 1972).

Little nurturance of social and emotional complexity is associated with men and boys in these materials, and little strength, skill, or capacity for making decisions with women and girls. Occupational roles are more evident and varied for men than women, who are usually shown as housewives or as engaged in a limited and conventional set of occupations. Women are seldom portrayed as both working and raising families. Since a significant proportion of women are currently carrying both roles, such portrayals indicate, at the least, a lag between educational materials and social reality (Saario et al., 1973).

In addition, the content of history and social studies have typically bypassed the activities of women. Trecker's (1977) detailed analysis of U.S. history texts shows that women are inadequately discussed in all periods, and the length of skirts may receive more attention than the contribution of female intellectuals or those who worked against slavery, for the labor movement, or for other social and legal reforms.

The distribution of males and females in the educational system is well known: most teachers are women, most administrators are men. There are more male teachers in secondary schools than in the early grades, but many teach science and math, while female teachers more often teach English and foreign languages (Stockard et al., 1980). Issues about gender imbalance in administration or the rights of pregnant teachers filter through the system, but are not directly experienced by the children. On the other hand, distinctions in status between male principals and female teachers, and the clustering of female and male teachers in certain subjects are part of the immediate school context. They may have a direct impact on children's identification with teaching adults and on what they learn about the distribution of power in the adult world. We do not know of any research that examines children's perceptions of these phenomena.

Since American education has not been uniform, it would be interesting to know if these biases have been as characteristic of alternative settings as traditional schools. Comparative research reported earlier indicates that sex-role behavior is less stereotyped in open settings, but alternative environments have not been systematically examined from this point of view. A close

How are sex roles involved in curricula and the school hierarchy?

look at teacher interaction with boys and girls, and at curriculum materials in nontraditional settings might well uncover some conventional patterns. Detailed analysis of equity and bias in alternative settings offers an interesting arena for investigation.

In considering the research on bias in the schools, it is important to regard the children themselves as part of a self-perpetuating system, since they have internalized the same assumptions as those appearing in school material and held by school personnel. Children have clear images of gender-associated occupations, reinforce each other for sex-typed behavior, and may resist possibilities for new directions and nonstereotyped careers (e.g.,

Coleman et al., 1966; Garrett, Ein, and Tremaine, 1977; Guttentag and Bray, 1976; Mitchell, 1978; Papalia and Tennent, 1975; Pottker and Fishel, 1977; Stockard et al., 1980; Weinraub and Brown, in press; Williams, Bennett, and Best, 1975). Efforts to change materials, opportunities, and relationships in the school setting are essential if equity is desired, but it is simplistic to postulate immediate modifications in children's behavior and development.

Source: Minuchin, P. P., and Shapiro, E. K., "The School as a Context for Social Development," in P. H. Mussen (Ed.), *Handbook of Child Psychology,* 4th ed., Vol. 4. Copyright © 1983 John Wiley and Sons, Inc.

Patterns of Social Interaction with Peers in Schools: The School Provides the Locus for Many Adolescent Peer Activities

As was indicated earlier in the chapter, in secondary schools the entire school is more likely to serve as a social context than in elementary schools, where students are usually confined to one or two classrooms for most of the school day. In secondary schools, adolescents come in contact with a variety of teachers and peers and are given the choice of a number of different activities outside the classroom. Social behavior often involves peers, extracurricular activities, and community events. In adolescence, the individual becomes more aware of the school as a social system and an organization than in the elementary school years. He may either adapt to and participate in this social system or attempt to challenge it (Minuchin and Shapiro, 1983).

There are few times in life when friendships and bonds between peers are stronger than in adolescence. Adolescence is a transitional period bridging the life of the child and the young adult. Since the adolescent is gaining independence from the family of her childhood, but has not yet become a part of the family she will be in as an adult, her peers have an especially strong impact on her life. James Coleman (1961) believes that high schools are partly responsible for such strong peer ties. At school, adolescents are with each other for at least six hours every day. The school also provides the locus for many of the adolescents' activities after school and on weekends.

In studying the association patterns of students, Coleman (1961) found that social structures vary from school to school. In some schools, the association patterns of students are very intense, while in others they are more casual. In small schools, more students are members of various cliques than in large schools, where simple pair relationships occur more frequently. There are even differences between group structures among the large schools. In one suburban school that Coleman studied, the social structure was far more complete and fully developed than in another. Probably because of greater community solidarity, middle-class status, and greater parental interest in the schooling process, many more community functions were carried out in and after school in the first school. Clustering social activities around a school helps to strengthen the social system of the students.

Coleman (1961) analyzed the peer associations of boys and girls separately in small schools. Boys achieved status within their schools in a variety of ways. In some schools, the "all-around boy"—athlete, ladies' man, and to some extent, scholar—achieved status, while in other schools, being either an athlete or a scholar was enough to assure high status.

There was a considerable amount of variation in the association patterns of the girls in small schools as well. Elmtown had the largest number of girl cliques, the largest percentage of girls in cliques, and the smallest average clique size. Marketville was the opposite in each of these respects. In Marketville and Maple Grove, middle-class girls from well-educated families formed cliques that dominated social activities, school activities, and adolescent attention. Teachers perceived these cliques as being in control of the student body and as the girls most encouraged by the adults in the community.

Athletic achievement played an important role in the status systems of boys in all ten schools Coleman (1961) studied. Why are athletics so important in the status systems of American high schools? Adolescents identify strongly with their schools and communities. The identification, in part at least, is due to the fact that the school and the community of adolescents are virtually synonymous. They compete as a school against other schools in athletic contests. So the heroes of the system, those with high status, are the boys who win for the school and the community of adolescents. When they win, the entire school and the entire community of adolescents feel better about themselves.

Athletics are an important part of school life.

Because boys have had greater opportunity to participate in interscholastic athletics than girls have, they have been more likely to attain high-status positions in schools. However, in the 1970s the federal government took a big step toward reducing this form of discrimination against female adolescents. Title IX of the 1972 Educational Amendments Act prohibits any educational program from receiving federal funds if sex discrimination is practiced. So far this act has not produced parity for girls and boys in interscholastic athletics, but girls have made greater strides than ever before in participating in interscholastic events. Also since the passage of Title IX, female enrollments in previously male-dominated fields such as engineering, medicine, law, and business have more than doubled, and reams have been written about sexism in the language, policies, and practices of education (Lockheed, 1978).

But even though some progress has been made for adolescent females in regard to their participation in athletics, differential access to sports activities still is widely practiced. Sports for boys are more varied and extensive and have much larger budgets than athletic programs for girls. Girls still do not have the same opportunities for physical training, for developing competitive skills, or for the experience of team camaraderie. However, many adolescent boys may suffer from excessive emphasis on competition rather than the pleasures of participation and mastery (Minuchin and Shapiro, 1983; Stockard et al., 1980).

Participation in school activities is likely to be an important ingredient in the adolescent's identity with the school, and in the development of her own identity. As was mentioned earlier, adolescents have a greater chance of participating in school activities in smaller schools, so that even marginal students (those not usually thought of as socially facile) have a greater opportunity to participate in activities and may develop a stronger sense of identity with the school. In large schools the same students may be considered as "tribe members" rather than "citizens"—that is, they are inactive and alienated rather than involved in and satisfied with the school (Todd, 1979).

We have discussed many different aspects of school structure and climate, teachers, and peers at school. A summary of main ideas related to these aspects of schools and the adolescent's development is presented in Concept Table 8.2. In most schools sampled by James Coleman (1961), students from middle- to high-income families held more high-status positions in school than students from low-income families. Let's explore the adolescent's socioeconomic background, as well as his ethnic background, in the context of the school.

Concept Table 8.2

CLASSROOM STRUCTURE AND CLIMATE, TEACHERS, AND PEERS AT SCHOOL

Concept	Processes/related ideas	Characteristics/description
Classroom structure and climate	Structure	Most classrooms have their seats fixed in rows facing the front of the room. In recent years, more flexible classroom structures have been developed. One of the most significant events in classroom history was the act of removing the bolts that attached seats to the floor.
	Climate	The most widely discussed aspect of classroom climate in recent years has been the issue of open versus traditional classrooms. The open classroom concept is multidimensional and the criteria for its evaluation often have differed from one study to the next. The Classroom Environment Scale has been a helpful addition to better assessment of classroom climate. Through a meta-analysis, it has been found that open classrooms seem to lower language achievement by a very small amount, but have little effect on other types of academic achievement, including reading; enhance achievement motivation; and slightly improve attitudes toward school. Perhaps the most important research question here is how specific dimensions of open classrooms link up with particular aspects of the adolescent's development, a more fine-grained investigation of the open classroom concept. Through further meta-analysis, it has been found that a number of features of open classrooms seem to improve certain aspects of academic and nonacademic performance, but others do not seem as beneficial. For example, features such as individualized instruction and emphasizing the role of the child are associated with strong effects on positive self-evaluation, while open space and multiage grouping do not have such strong effects.
Teachers	Teacher characteristics and styles, Erikson's criteria for a good teacher, and the personality traits of good teachers	Teacher characteristics vary a great deal. Erikson believes that good teachers are able to create a sense of industry rather than inferiority in their students. He also stresses that good teachers are sensitive to the social as well as academic aspects of the student's development. Teacher traits that relate to positive student outcomes are enthusiasm, the ability to plan, poise, adaptability, and awareness of individual differences. An authoritative style also seems advantageous and adults who work with young adolescents would do well to have some of the characteristics of individuals who work with preschool children. Competent teachers of young adolescents are knowledgeable about the nature of adolescent development.

Concept Table 8.2 (Continued)

CLASSROOM STRUCTURE AND CLIMATE, TEACHERS, AND PEERS AT SCHOOL		
Concept	*Processes/related ideas*	*Characteristics/description*
	Aptitude–treatment interaction	Also called ATI, this refers to the belief that there is no one educational setting, set of teacher characteristics, or classroom climate that is right for all adolescents. Rather, such aspects of the educational setting need to be considered in concert with the aptitudes of the adolescent. In this regard, Brophy has found that low-ability students may need more time, be criticized less, and praised more often than their high-ability counterparts, who need to be moved along at a quicker pace, experience high expectations, and be given occasional criticism if their work does not meet high standards.
	Teachers, sex roles, schools	The sex of the adolescent and the sex of the teacher may affect teacher–adolescent interaction. There has been a particular interest in recent years focused on the achievement orientation of the adolescent female. Curiously, while schools have been basically feminine institutions, females have shown lower achievement orientation than males. However, this may be changing as a consequence of sociohistorical modifications in the female's role in society. Further, it is important to look at many different aspects of the curricula and school hierarchy to see how the roles of males and females often operate differently.
Patterns of social interaction among peers in secondary schools	The locus of the school	At school, adolescents are with each other for at least six hours per day. The school provides the locus for many peer group activities after school and on weekends as well.

Social Class and Ethnicity: Beyond White, Middle-Class Schools

It has seemed at times that one of the major functions of schools in this country during the twentieth century has been to train adolescents to function in and has contributed to a white, middle-class society—legislators and community leaders who vote on school funding are often white and middle class, and principals and teachers often have been white and middle class as well. Some critics believe that schools have done a much better job of educating white, middle-class adolescents to function in a white, middle-class society, but they have not done a competent job of educating lower class and/or black youth to overcome the barriers to advancement they may encounter. This theme characterized the educational protest literature in the 1960s and early 1970s. Let's look more closely at different aspects of social class and ethnicity in schools.

Social Class

To learn more about social class and schools, we focus initially on some general findings and comments about students from lower class backgrounds, then we turn our attention to educational aspirations, teacher attitudes, and school textbooks.

Students from Lower Class Backgrounds

Several years ago, I visited a family who lived in an urban ghetto. Although it was dark outside, there were no lights on in the house. The father opened the door and invited me in. He removed a lightbulb from a drawer and screwed it into one of the light sockets, commenting that this was the only light they ever used. There were eight boys and girls in the family—how could any of them study in the evening? Middle-class adolescents take much for granted; they know they can go to their rooms well-fed and warm, switch on a light, and concentrate on their studies in peace and quiet. This often is not the case for the adolescent from a lower class family.

In *Dark Ghetto,* Kenneth Clark (1965) described some of the ways lower and middle-class youth are treated differently in school. According to Clark's study, teachers in middle-class schools spent more time teaching their students and evaluated their work more than twice as often as teachers did in low-income schools. And teachers in the low-income schools made three times as many negative comments to students as teachers did in the middle-class schools; the latter made more positive than negative comments to their students.

Christine Bennett (1979) vividly describes a school comprised of lower class students in a large urban slum area:

> It is 2 P.M., beginning of the sixth-period class, and Warren Benson, a young teacher, looks around the room. Eight students are present out of thirty. "Where is everybody?" he demands. "They don't like your class," a girl volunteers. Three girls saunter in. Cora, who is playing a cassette recorder, bumps over to her desk in time with the music. She lowers the volume. "Don't mark us down late," she shouts. "We was right here, you mother f———."
>
> . . . Here you find students from poverty homes, students who can't read, students with drug problems, students wanting to drop out . . .

Schools like this are described in Charles Silberman's *Crisis in the Classroom* (1970) and John Holt's *How Children Fail* (1964).

Educational Aspirations

Perhaps the most interesting information about adolescents' educational aspirations is the relation between what they would like to do and what they expect to do. The discrepancy between job aspirations and job expectations is greater for lower class adolescents than for middle-class adolescents (Gribbons and Lohnes, 1964). The aspirations of lower class students are as high as those of middle-class students; however, when asked which occupations they actually expected to enter, lower class adolescents mentioned occupations no more prestigious than those of their parents.

Lower class parents can have a significant impact on their adolescents' aspirations. Lower class high school boys whose parents encouraged them to advance their educational and occupational levels reached higher aspirations than boys whose parents did not (Kandel and Lesser, 1969).

Teacher Attitudes

Teachers have lower expectancies for adolescents from low-income families than for adolescents from middle-income families. A teacher who knows that an adolescent comes from a lower class background may spend less time trying to help him solve a problem and may anticipate that he will frequently get into trouble. The teacher may also perceive a gap between his or her own middle-class position and the lower class status of the adolescent's parents; as a result, the teacher may believe that the parents are not interested in helping the youth and may make fewer efforts to communicate with them.

The growing-up experiences of teachers with middle-class backgrounds are quite different from those of adolescents or teachers with lower class backgrounds. A teacher from the middle class has probably not gone hungry for weeks at a time or experienced such conditions as an overcrowded apartment, perhaps without electricity or plumbing, where several boys and girls may sleep with one or two adults in one small room.

There is evidence from at least one study that teachers with lower class origins may have different attitudes toward lower class students than middle-class teachers have (Gottlieb, 1966). Perhaps because they have experienced many inequities themselves, they tend to be empathetic to the problems that lower class students encounter. In Gottlieb's study, teachers were asked to indicate the most outstanding characteristics of their lower class students. The middle-class teachers checked adjectives like "lazy," "rebellious," and "fun-loving," while the lower class teachers checked such adjectives as "happy," "cooperative," "energetic," and "ambitious." The teachers with lower class backgrounds perceived the behaviors of the lower class adolescents as adaptive, whereas the middle-class teachers viewed the same behaviors as falling short of their standards.

School Textbooks

By the time a boy or girl reaches adolescence, he or she has been heavily indoctrinated into the middle-class life through the books adopted for classroom use by school administrators. The books that children read in school are usually oriented to the experiences and life settings of middle-class rather than lower class children. The typical reading text for the early elementary grades depicts children growing up in white, middle-class suburbia. The father leaves for work in a business suit, waving goodbye to his smiling family. The story characters experience few (if any) frustrations—life is easy and pleasant. This world is not the world of the lower class child (Blom, Waite, and Zimet, 1970).

Although there has been a healthy trend toward establishing a more realistic balance in the stories and pictures of school textbooks, the depiction of the lower class family in the readers is an idealized one (Waite, 1968). The low-income family is integrated successfully into the dominant white, middle-class culture, with few accompanying tensions and frustrations. A more realistic textbook would include more of the problems and frustrations of lower class families as well as of middle-class children. The stories would also demonstrate various coping mechanisms to help children deal

with the frustrations of the imperfect world we live in. Such books would present a far more realistic world than those currently in use do and might well serve to increase students' interest in reading, and encourage them to think and reason more as they read.

Ethnicity

Not only do students from lower class backgrounds often experience discrimination in our schools; adolescents from many different ethnic backgrounds do as well. In most American schools, blacks, Mexican-Americans, Puerto Ricans, native Americans, Japanese, and Asian Indians are minorities. Teachers have often been ignorant of different cultural meanings that non-Anglo adolescents have learned in their communities. The problems that boys and girls from non-Anglo backgrounds have had in conventional schools are well-documented (e.g., Casteñada et al., 1971; Fuchs and Havighurst, 1973; Minuchin and Shapiro, 1983).

The social and academic development of adolescents from minority groups depends on such factors as teacher expectations; the teacher's preparation for working with adolescents from different backgrounds; the nature of the curriculum; the presence of role models in the school for minority students; the quality of relations between school personnel and parents from different ethnic, economic, and educational backgrounds; and the relations between the school and the community (Minuchin and Shapiro, 1983).

By far the largest effort to study the role of ethnicity in schools has dealt with desegregation (e.g., Bell, 1980; Hughes, Gordon, and Hillman, 1980; Stephan and Feagin, 1980). The focus of desegregation has been on improving the proportions of black and white student populations in schools. Efforts to improve this ratio have typically involved busing students, usually the minority-group members, from their home neighborhoods to more distant schools. The underlying belief in such efforts is that bringing different groups together reduces stereotyped attitudes and improves intergroup relationships. But busing tells us nothing about what is going on inside the school. Black adolescents bused to a predominantly white school are usually resegregated

in the classroom. Segregation is frequently reinstituted by seating patterns, ability grouping, and tracking systems (e.g., Epstein, 1980; Rist, 1979).

In one comprehensive national study that focused on factors that contribute to positive interracial relations (Forehand, Ragosta, and Rock, 1976), over five thousand fifth-grade students in more than ninety elementary schools and over four hundred tenth graders in seventy-two high schools were evaluated. It was concluded that multiethnic curricula, projects focused on racial issues, and mixed work groups lead to positive changes, and that improved relationships are enhanced by the presence of supportive principals and teachers.

Overall, however, the findings pertaining to desegregation have not been encouraging (Minuchin and Shapiro, 1983). Desegregation in itself does not necessarily improve race relations—positive consequences

depend on what goes on in the classroom once adolescents get there. School personnel who support the advancement of minority students, curricula that acknowledge ethnic pluralism, and the participation of students in cooperative activities and learning situations are likely to improve the minority student's development.

In this chapter, we have seen that school is a very important part of the culture the adolescent grows up in, and that many aspects of the adolescent's culture are centered around school functions. In the next chapter we'll focus on the culture and social class of the adolescent and on cross-cultural comparisons of adolescents. Chapter 15 will discuss school-related problems and disturbances, including underachievement, school phobia, and school dropouts, which are often related to cultural concerns.

Summary

I. Among the important aspects of the nature of the adolescent's schooling are investigating the impact of schools, development and the social context at school, and determining which schools are effective.

    A. By the time an individual has graduated, he or she has spent more than ten thousand hours in the classroom. Schools are contexts where individuals are members of a small society. Some sociologists have argued that schools have little impact on the adolescent's development; however, when researchers have conducted more precise, observational studies of what goes on in schools and classrooms, the effects of schooling become more apparent. Controversy surrounds the functions of secondary schools. Arguments have been made that the function of secondary schools should be the intellectual development of the adolescent. Other statements suggest secondary schools should have more comprehensive functions—in addition to intellectual development, they should be promoting social and emotional development, and preparing the adolescent for adult work and existence as a life-long learner.

    B. The social context differs at the preschool, elementary, and secondary levels. At the secondary school level, the entire school assumes a more important role in the individual's development.

    C. Joan Lipsitz has expended considerable effort to discover the characteristics of effective schools for young adolescents. Among the criteria developed to evaluate the effectiveness of middle schools are: purposes, goals, and definitions; school climate; organization; curriculum; instructional practices; leadership; the community context; public policy questions; and self-evaluation. Effective schools take seriously individual differences in the physical, cognitive, and social development of adolescents and show a deep concern for what is known about early adolescence— such schools are not just watered down versions of high schools or stepped up copies of elementary schools. These effective middle schools also emphasize social development as well as academic development.

II. Information about the effects of school organization on the adolescent's development focuses on the organization of secondary schools, the transition to middle or junior high school, and school/class size.

    A. The organization of junior high schools and, more recently, middle schools has been justified on the basis of physical, cognitive, and social changes in the adolescent. The earlier onset of puberty has had a strong impact on the appearance of middle schools. There are many different ways secondary schools are organized, such as seven through nine, seven through twelve, six through eight, five through eight, kindergarten through eight, and so forth.

    B. The transition from elementary school to middle or junior high school coincides with a number of individual, familial, and societal changes. The transition is associated with adjustment difficulties for many children, although supportive, intimate school environments and friendships seem to make such adjustment less taxing. Sex differences and the timing of maturation likely are other factors that mediate the nature of this transition.

C. More prosocial and possibly less antisocial behavior occurs in small schools than in large schools. Five hundred has been stressed as an optimal threshold size by some experts, while others put the figure as high as one thousand. While little consistency has been found in research attempting to link class size and the adolescent's development, intuitively there is every reason to believe that small classes increase the adolescent's sense of belongingness and decreases his or her feeling of anonymity.

III. There are many aspects to the classroom and teachers that influence the adolescent's development.

A. Information about classrooms includes ideas about structure and climate.

1. Most classrooms have their seats in fixed rows facing the front of the room where the teacher's desk is located. In recent years, more flexible classroom structures have been created. One of the most significant events in the history of the classroom was the act of removing the bolts that attach seats to the floor.

2. The widely discussed aspect of classroom climate in recent years has focused on the debate of whether open classrooms are superior to traditional classrooms. The open classroom concept is multidimensional and the criteria for its evaluation often have differed from one study to the next, making generalization difficult. The Classroom Environment Scale is a needed addition in this research because it more precisely defines and maps out the dimensions of open and traditional classrooms. Through a meta-analysis, it has been found that open classrooms seem to lower language achievement by a very small amount, but have little effect on other types of achievement, such as reading. The open classroom strategy appears to improve achievement, motivation, and creativity, as well as slightly improve attitudes toward school. Perhaps the most important research question here is how specific dimensions of open classrooms link up with particular aspects of the adolescent's development. Through further meta-analysis, it has been discovered that a number of features of open classrooms seem to improve different dimensions of the adolescent's academic and nonacademic development, but other features do not seem as beneficial. For example, features such as individualized instruction and consideration of the child's role are consistently linked with positive self-evaluation, while open space and multiage grouping seem to have weaker effects.

B. Among the many important aspects of studying the teacher's role in adolescent development are teacher characteristics and styles, aptitude–treatment interaction, and sex roles.

1. Teacher characteristics involve many different dimensions and vary a great deal. Erikson believes that a good teacher is able to create a sense of industry rather than inferiority in students. He also stresses that good teachers are sensitive to factors that promote the student's social as well as academic development. Teacher traits that relate to positive student outcomes are enthusiasm, the ability to plan, poise, adaptability, and awareness of individual differences. An authoritative style also seems advantageous and adults who work with young adolescents would do well to have some of the characteristics of adults who work with preschool children. Competent teachers of young adolescents are knowledgeable about the nature of adolescent development.

2. Aptitude–treatment interaction (ATI) refers to the belief that there is no one educational setting, set of teacher characteristics, or classroom climate that is right for all adolescents. Rather, such aspects of the educational setting need to be considered in concert with the aptitudes of the adolescent. In this regard, Brophy has found that low-ability students may need more time, be criticized less, and be praised more often than their high-ability counterparts who need to be moved along at a faster pace, experience higher expectations, and be given occasional criticism if their work falls below certain standards.

3. The sex of the adolescent and the sex of the teacher may affect teacher–adolescent interaction. There has been a particular interest in recent years focused on the achievement orientation in the adolescent female. Curiously, while schools basically are feminine institutions, females have shown lower achievement orientation than males. However, this may be changing as the female's role in society changes. Further, it is important to look at many different dimensions of the curricula and the school hierarchy for clues about the nature of sex roles in schools.

IV. At school, adolescents are with each other for at least six hours per day. The school provides a locus for many peer group activities after school and on weekends as well.

V. Schools have had a stronger white, middle-class orientation than a lower class, ethnic minority orientation. Teachers from lower class backgrounds perceive students differently than teachers from middle-class backgrounds. The major investigation of ethnicity and schooling has involved busing for racial integration, a procedure that by itself has not led to improved adolescent development. Researchers believe it is important to focus on what goes on at the school after adolescents get there, rather than busing per se.

Key Terms

aptitude *330*

aptitude-treatment interaction *330*

Classroom Environment Scale (CES) *327*

meta-analysis *327*

open classroom concept *326*

top-dog phenomenon *319*

treatment *330*

Suggested Readings

Coleman, J. C. (1961). *The adolescent society.* New York: MacMillan.
This book represents a study of the adolescent peer culture in schools. Full of detailed descriptions of the social interaction of students at different kinds of high schools.

Cross, K. P. (Nov. 1984). "The rising tide of school reform reports." *Phi Delta Kappan,* pp. 167–72.
Cross surveys the controversy surrounding educational reform and provides insight into the functions of schools.

Feeney, S. (1980). *Schools for young adolescents.* Carrboro, N.C.: Center for Early Adolescence.
An excellent, easy-to-read overview of what makes a good junior high school teacher.

Harvard Educational Review.
Go to the library and leaf through the issues of the last three to four years. You'll find a number of articles that address the issues raised in this chapter.

Lipsitz, J. (1984). *Successful schools for young adolescents.* New Brunswick, NJ: Transaction Books.
Must reading for anyone interested in better schools for young adolescents. Filled with rich examples of successful schools and the many factors that contribute to success in the education of young adolescents.

Minuchin, P. P., & Shapiro, E. K. (1983). "The school as a context for social development." In P. H. Mussen (Ed.), *Handbook of child psychology,* 4th ed, vol. 4. New York: John Wiley.
An authoritative, up-to-date review of the role of the school in the adolescent's development by two leading educators. Covers most of the topics in this chapter.

Review of Educational Research.
This journal publishes reviews of educational research. By leafing through the issues of the last several years in your library, you will come across research summaries with references to many of the topics in this chapter.

Chapter 9

Culture

Trans Ams and Telephones

Clothes play a major role in the adolescent's need system.

As soon as the last bell rings at West High School, Rob rushes out to the parking lot, hops into his Trans Am, flips the knob on the radio to a high pitch, and peels out ot the school lot, leaving a trail of rubber. Rob heads for McDonald's, where he works twenty-five hours a week so that he can have his own money to spend. He is saving to buy a tape deck for his car. Not all high school students drive their own cars, and not all of them are as possession-oriented as Rob. In general, however, money and cars are highly desirable commodities for adolescents.

It isn't possible to gain a true feeling for what the adolescent culture in the United States is like without considering the material aspects of the culture. Money, cars, and clothes, to name a few items, play a big part in the adolescent need system. They contribute to the adolescent's sense of self-esteem and identity. The adolescent with his or her own car or motorcycle achieves a status level in the youth culture beyond that of the adolescent who does not have these material goods.

Social scientists have commented that material goods often reflect the adolescent's personality. For example, an adolescent who dresses casually, lets his hair grow long, and buys a motorcycle probably has a very different personality from that of the adolescent who dresses conservatively, trims and neatly parts his hair, and drives his mother's car when it is available. In addition, the appearances of the two adolescents are likely to elicit very different expectations from their peers and other individuals in their environment.

Think about your own adolescent years—about the material aspects of the culture . . . wishing for the day you could get your driver's license . . . trying to convince your parents you needed a car, or at least needed ready access to their car . . .

or if all else failed, at least having a good friend who owned a car so you could cruise around and get to where you wanted to go. Think about how much time you spent looking at and trying on different clothes. In a *Seventeen* magazine back-to-school study in 1979, adolescent girls in the United States spent $7,913,893,000 in preparation for going back to school (table 9.1).

When we think about the American youth culture, other aspects also come to mind . . . for one, the telephone. Adolescents spend much more time talking on the telephone than children do. The telephone plays a particularly important part in culture of the early adolescent, who is not yet old enough to drive. At the time I wrote the first edition of this book, my oldest daughter was thirteen. Her telephone use drastically increased at about this age. One night I came home about 11 P.M. and asked my wife how her evening had gone. She replied, "Your daughter was on the phone from 7:30 to 10:00—either she was calling her friends or they were calling her." Many young adolescents spend long hours talking with each other on the phone about school, about members of the opposite sex, about parents, clothes, and friends. And the telephone comes in handy when the moment comes to ask someone out for a first date—adolescents use the telephone as a "long distance" communication system to avoid the anxiety of asking in person.

Another of the peculiarities of the adolescent culture is the development of special language to describe themselves, their friends, their activities, and their world. For example, we might overhear two adolescents saying: "O.K., Frank, let's get it on, let's burn, light the tires," when they are talking about racing their cars, or, "Adrian, that dress is the absolute max," when talking about how great a dress looks.

Table 9.1 Back-to-school spending by adolescent girls in the United States during 1979

Outerwear	
coats, jackets, suits,	
dresses, skirts, shirts /	
blouses, sweaters, tops,	
pants	$4,395,081,000
Footwear	1,004,756,000
Underwear	
hosiery, foundations, bras,	
lingerie, sleepwear / loungewear	637,720,000
Accessories	739,276,000
Miscellaneous	1,137,060,000
Total	$7,913,893,000

Before we conclude this prologue, however, it is important to point out that not all adolescents are part of the same culture. In a country like the United States, there are many variations in the youth culture. While money, cars, and clothes are the pervasive interests of most adolescent groups in the United States, some adolescents have more ready access to such items than others. One of the major themes of this chapter will be to explore socioeconomic and ethnic variations in the cultures adolescents grow up in.

Preview

*A*s you read this chapter, you will find that the word *culture* is a very broad label. In fact, it is so broad that we already have spent three chapters describing some of the most important aspects of culture—families, peers, and schools. We can define **culture** as the behavioral patterns, beliefs, values, and other products of humans that are learned and shared by a particular group of people and passed on from one generation to the next. This chapter focuses on the nature of the cultural process, including the youth culture and its place in the larger culture, cross-cultural comparisons of adolescents, social class and ethnicity, as well as the powerful role of the media in adolescents' lives.

The Cultural Process: From Microsystems to Exosystems

Think about the community you grew up in. What was it like? Was it rural or urban? Were the schools traditional or progressive? What kind of community organizations for youth existed? How much did the townspeople support the school and its athletic teams? What values were emphasized in the community? Were community leaders oriented toward conservative or liberal political philosophy? What kinds of goals were promoted for adolescents—was going to college standard fare, or was the orientation more toward finishing high school and working in town or on the family farm? What were the people like? Were most of them white- or blue-collar workers? Did most people have two cars, take expensive vacations, and send their adolescents off to summer camp? By thinking about and responding to questions such as these, you can get a feel for what a community subculture is like.

Ideas about the nature of adolescence and the techniques used to raise adolescents differ from culture to culture and within the same culture over different time periods. The cultural beliefs about adolescents that leaders within a society share have important implications for how adolescents are dealt with.

Governments and political bodies can exert strong influences on the lives of adolescents through decision making based on these beliefs. Consider the different experiences adolescents will have if the leaders of a country decide to wage war against another country (as in the case of Vietnam) and many adolescents are forced to make critical decisions about whether to follow or confront and resist the adult decision makers. Further, consider the experiences of those youth who do go to war compared with youth who grow up in an era when there is a nonaggressive political orientation. In ways such as these, government and political structures can exert a strong influence on youth.

There are many other aspects of the cultural milieu to consider in addition to political structure. We already have analyzed the effects of several important aspects of the cultural milieu—namely, the institutions of family and school, as well as the structure and function of peer groups. Further components of culture that are important to evaluate are the nature of the communities and neighborhoods an adolescent grows up in, as well as the strength of the church within those communities. Other significant cultural forces include television and the other media, which have gained influence over adolescents in recent years. Movies, records, magazines, books, and television provide insight into the lives of adolescents.

Bronfenbrenner's Ecological Model of Development

Urie Bronfenbrenner (1979; Bronfenbrenner and Crouter, 1983) argues that systematic analyses of cultural influences on the adolescent's development have been relatively few in number. He points out that many studies have focused on cultural influences on the adolescent, but careful, empirical analyses of community influences; cohesiveness and values in neighborhoods; and interactions among the subcultural components of church, community, neighborhood, and family have not

School boards and local governments represent aspects of the adolescent's exosystem.

The Mesosystem

The **mesosystem** refers to linkages between microsystems or connectiveness between contexts. Examples include the relation of family experiences to school experiences, school experiences to church experiences, or family experiences to peer experiences. In the discussion in Chapter 6 on families, we described the importance of how close relationships influence the nature of how relationships with others are constructed. Bronfenbrenner's ideas about the mesosystem are much like our comments about the construction of relationships based on relationships with meaningful others in our lives. As Bronfenbrenner points out, too often our observations are focused on only one setting such as the family, rather than on multiple settings such as family, school, and peer contexts.

The Exosystem

The **exosystem** refers to settings in which the adolescent does not participate although important decisions that affect the adolescent's life are made in these settings. Examples include the work world of the adolescent's parents, the school board, and the local government. A very important question pertaining to the exosystem involves asking whether decisions are made with the adolescent's best interests in mind.

At the level of the exosystem, important decisions are made about whether legitimate opportunities are available for adolescents in the community. For instance, in one investigation (Cloward and Ohlin, 1960), a community was found to be a positive influence on the adolescent's development to the extent that legitimate opportunities for activity were available. The degree to which illegitimate opportunities are unavailable may also influence the adolescent's development, but the provision of legitimate activities may be even more important. These researchers argued that juvenile delinquency increased because of a lack of legitimate, socially approved activities in the community.

been fully explored. Bronfenbrenner believes that we need to understand cultural influences on the adolescent in terms of these systems: microsystem, mesosystem, and exosystem.

The Microsystem

The adolescent's **microsystem** refers to contexts in which the adolescent has face-to-face interactions with others who are influential in his or her life. Examples include the face-to-face encounters adolescents have with parents, siblings, teachers, and friends, many of the topics we have covered in Chapters 6, 7, and 8. In this regard, most of our information about the adolescent's microsystem focuses on the adolescent's interaction with one other person, for example, the adolescent and his or her mother or the adolescent with his or her teacher. We know much less about three person social interactions, although many of the adolescent's interactions involve these types of encounters such as the adolescent's relationship with the mother when the father is present in a context compared to when he is away on business, for example. As we discussed in Chapter 6 on families, the nature of the adolescent's interaction with a parent often is very different depending on whether the other parent is present in the immediate context.

Joan Lipsitz (1983) obtained funding from a foundation and spent one year trying to identify the after-school needs of adolescents. She found that no network of professionals or volunteers to help youth in the after-school hours exists. Youth workers who are not part of a specific national organization, like Boy or Girl Scouts, have no one to turn to for new ideas, mutual support, and information about what works and why. Parents seem even more isolated, not having printed materials telling them what exists in their community and what criteria they should be using to guide them in selecting after-school programs. She did find that adolescents often spend such hours in places like community centers, libraries, schools, churches and synagogues, Boys Clubs, Girls Clubs, 4-H, and such. They go to these places mainly because there is an adult present who knows and understands them. While a particular activity may be the "hook" that gets the adolescent to the community setting, their loyalty to the program seems to be linked to the sensitivity and caring of an adult who has time to listen and provide advice.

Lipsitz found that such community settings have been and could continue to serve as providers of safe, supervised recreation, academic and cultural enrichment, and counseling. However, inflation, cutbacks in funding, and taxpayer revolts are not encouraging. For example, given cutbacks in Title XX funds, day care programs have been forced to institute increased fee schedules. Parents have been forced to decide which of their children they will send to after-school programs. Understandably, they usually choose to pay for younger children and withdraw older siblings, who typically become latchkey children. And, libraries are finding that more and more young adolescents are dropping in during the after-school hours. Parents approve of their adolescents going to libraries because a library is perceived as a warm, safe environment where there is supervision and it is believed nothing disastrous will happen to the adolescent there. Ideally, libraries would increase the number of adults who specialize in understanding young adolescents. However, with budget cuts, libraries often have had to cut back in hours and acquisitions. At the same time, municipal recreation departments have had to cut back the number of their youth worker positions at exactly the time when more such positions are needed.

The provision of legitimate, socially approved activities by communities likely serve as important support systems for the families of adolescents. Such activities likely will become increasingly important in the future as we witness an increase in the number of working mother and single parent families. This point was made in Chapter 6 on families when the increasing number of latchkey children in our society were described. Elaboration of the role the community places in the adolescent's after-school hours and vacations is revealing, as described in Perspective on Adolescent Development 9.1.

The Settings in Which Adolescents Spend Their Time

What do adolescents do during a typical week in their lives? This was the question posed by Mihaly Csikszentmihalyi and Reed Larson (1984) in a fascinating look into the daily goings on of adolescents. They wanted to know what an observer likely would see if he or she were privileged to follow adolescents around in their environment. How much time do they spend in educational settings compared to recreational settings? How much time do they spend with friends rather than adults? These are examples of questions that were interesting to the researchers.

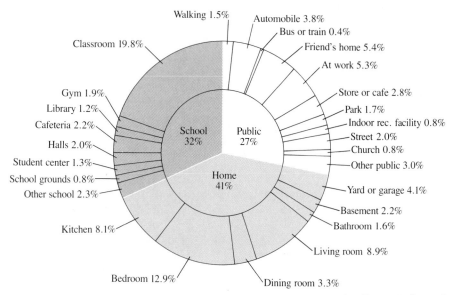

Figure 9.1 **Where adolescents spend their time. Graph shows the percentage of self-reports in each location (N=2734). In this and the following figures, one percentage point is equivalent to approximately one hour per week spent in the given location or activity.**

The data that provide the basis for this look into the lives of adolescents were collected in a novel way. Self-reports were made by the adolescents at random times during their lives. All of the subjects carried electronic pagers for one week, and a transmitter sent the adolescents signals to fill out reports on their experiences from early morning until late at night. This method provided several thousand samples of what adolescents do and where they spend their time. The researchers call their procedure the **experience sampling method.** It is a method of obtaining the thoughts, activities, and feelings of the individual at approximately forty to fifty randomly chosen moments in their daily lives.

The community chosen to be studied, of course, cannot be perfectly representative of adolescents everywhere. The community selected for the research, however, did provide a heterogeneous population of adolescents from urban and suburban backgrounds near Chicago. Seventy-five students, with approximately equal numbers of boys and girls, were selected from

four school grades, nine through twelve. Approximately equal numbers came from a lower middle-class background and an upper middle-class sector of the community.

The adolescents' social worlds were studied in terms of where they were, what they were doing, and who they were with at the time of the signals. The paths of adolescents' lives seem to pass through three main locations—home, school, and public places such as parks, buses, supermarkets, and friends' houses. Figure 9.1 reveals where adolescents were when they were beeped. The most prominent location in their lives is their home, although almost one-third of the time they were at school, and more than one-fourth of the time they were in public places. When at home, adolescents spent more time in their bedroom than at any other location in their house. At school, about two-thirds of the time was spent in formal classrooms, but the remainder involved time in fringe areas of classrooms, such as the cafeteria, hallways, and a student center.

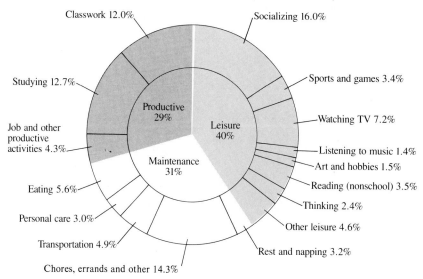

Figure 9.2   **What adolescents spend their time doing.**

What were adolescents doing when they were beeped? Figure 9.2 reveals that twenty-nine percent of their time was taken up by productive activities, mainly those related to school work. An additional thirty-one percent involved various maintenance activities such as eating, resting, bathing, and dressing. The rest of the time adolescents were engaging in other activities, such as talk, sport, and reading, which can be classified primarily as leisure. By far, the largest amount of time spent in a single productive activity was individual studying, which took up thirteen percent of the adolescent's waking hours. The time spent studying by the Chicago adolescents, however, is considerably less than is spent by some technologically strong cultures, such as Japan. In the Chicago sample, combined school and home studying added up to about eleven hours less than the Japanese. And the Japanese spend sixty-nine more days in school each year than their American counterparts. With regard to work, forty-one percent of the adolescents in the Chicago study were employed, with most jobs being in food services, retail sales, and other unskilled areas. The adolescents averaged working eighteen hours per week at their jobs.

Within leisure, the main activity was socializing, which took up approximately one sixth of waking time. It also was found that adolescents spend about three times as much of their day talking with friends and peers as they do with parents or other adults. And, thirteen percent of talking occurred by phone! The Chicago adolescents were spending far more time socializing and talking than their counterparts in Japan, Germany, or the Soviet Union. Adolescents watched television as a main activity about one hour per day, but also watched an additional 1.5 hours per day as a secondary activity. About 1.25 hours per day were spent in more active, structured activities such as sports, games, hobbies, reading, and listening to music together.

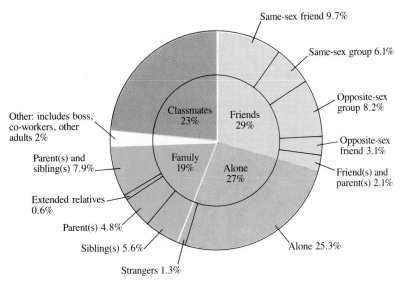

Figure 9.3 **People with whom adolescents spend their time.**

Concerning time spent with companions, according to figure 9.3, adolescents are not often in the company of adults. During one fifth of their waking hours, adolescents were with the family and only a portion of this was with parents. One fourth of the day was passed as solitude. A full fifty percent of the week's waking hours was spent with peers, partly in the classroom and partly outside of class with friends. As adolescents moved from the ninth to the twelfth grades, they increasingly spent even more time with peers, away from home and family, often in the company of friends.

Now that we have obtained a glimpse of the overall nature of the cultural process and looked at many different settings and their linkages in the lives of adolescents, we turn our attention to another aspect of culture, the culture of adolescents themselves.

The Adolescent Culture: Slang and More

We already have talked about the youth culture from time to time in this book. In Chapter 1, we discussed the nature of the youth culture at different points in history and how easy it is to stereotype the youth culture based on a visible minority of youth. In Chapter 7, we talked about adolescent cliques and crowds, and in the prologue to this chapter, we talked about the material aspects of the youth culture. And, we discussed the environmental settings in which adolescents spend their time. Here we will explore further the nature of the youth culture as we investigate adolescent interests, expand on ideas about the language of the youth culture, and cover information about youth movements.

Reprinted by permission: Tribune Media Services.

Adolescent Interests

We have already seen that money, cars, and clothes are important to adolescents. So, too, are relationships with the opposite sex. Table 9.2 presents a comparison of ninth-grade students' interests in 1970 and 1977, broken down separately for boys and girls. Note the similarity in the interests of adolescent girls and boys, although boys not surprisingly rated sex and cars of much greater interest than girls did, and girls, in contrast, showed more interest in love.

Another aspect of adolescent culture focuses on the values of youth. Thornburg and Thornburg (1979) investigated the importance of different values to high school sophomores. Freedom, true friendship, and happiness were very high in the value hierarchies of both boys and girls. A comfortable life was much more important to boys, while family security was much more valuable to girls. Achieving inner harmony was also more important to girls than to boys.

Attitudes and values likely vary according to an adolescent's socioeconomic and ethnic background. In one investigation (Eisenberg-Berg, 1979), for example, it was found that the sociopolitical attitudes of adolescents from middle-class backgrounds were better defined, more liberal, and more democratic than those of adolescents from lower class backgrounds.

The Youth Culture and Language

Insights into the culture of the adolescent can be gained by looking closely at one important aspect of behavior—language. Slang expressions characterize the communication patterns of many adolescent peer groups. Consider the following communication pattern between two adolescent boys:

> "Hey man, let's go check out some chicks and see if we can get a bender going."
> "How? We don't have any wheels!"
> "Hey, a dude like me don't need no wheels to get chicks!"

This style of conversation is not typical among young children and adults—it is, however, a common communication style among many teenagers. The use of slang makes the adolescent feel that she is a part of her group. Sometimes it also serves as a time-saving method, so that longer, more elaborate explanations do not have to be given. For example, an adolescent girl may say, "He's a hunk," in less time than it takes to say, "He is a really good looking, sexually attractive guy."

In one investigation of adolescent language, there was an amorphous group with no apparent distinct lifestyle and no **argots** (a label used by linguists for the language style of a subculture). There were also three distinct large cliques in the three-thousand-student high school studied—the "jocks," the "motorheads," and the "fleabags," each of which used its own distinct slang.

Table 9.2 Ninth-grade students' interests, 1970 and 1977

	Girls			Boys		
	1970 Study	1977 Study			1970 Study	1977 Study
Variable	Rank	Rank		Variable	Rank	Rank
Boys	4	1		Girls	1	1
Love	1.5*	2		Sex	3.5*	2
Life	1.5*	3		Life	7	3
People	6	4		Love	5.5*	4
Peace	3	5		Cars	5.5*	5.5*
Animals	11	6		Sports	2	5.5*
Sex	8	7		Movies	13	7
Sports	13	8		Animals	8	8
Pop music	9	9		People	10	9
God	5	10		Travel	14	10
Cooking	14	11		Motorcycles	12	11
Generation gap	10	12		God	9	12
School	18	13		Pop music	3.5*	13
Drugs	7	14		Countries	17	14
Death	15	15		Generation gap	20	15
Hippies	12	16		School	23	16
War	16	17		Wild West	24	17
Communism	17	18		Voting age	11	18
				Teachers	21	19
				Death	17	20
				Vietnam	17	21
				War	22	22
				Hippies	15	23
				Drugs	19	24

*Represents tie in rank

Source: From "A Comparison of Ninth-Grade Students' Interests Over Seven Years," by N. T. Gill, High School Journal, 1978, 61, 26–33. Copyright 1978 by The University of North Carolina Press.

The slang of the "jocks" reflected their interest in sports. Calisthenics were dubbed "cals," somebody who made a mistake was a "flake," and an uncoordinated person was a "spaz." The jocks frequently talked about getting "psyched up" or "pumped up" for a game, and getting drunk was referred to as being "buzzed."

The "motorheads" generally were enrolled in vocational training programs and often had grease stains on their clothes and hands. They often chose the argot "cool" to describe themselves, as did others: "The 'motorheads' think they are 'cool.'" Like the slang of the jocks, the motorheads' language reflected their interests: "getting it on," "burning," and "lighting the tires" were terms used when they talked about racing their cars.

The third large clique in the school, the "fleabags," were a group of male and female drug users. The major reason many of these individuals came to school was to see their friends and take drugs. Much of their clique language focused on drugs. Words like "wasted," "spaced," and "roaches" frequently infiltrated their conversations.

In 1982, a phenomenon known as the "Valley Girl," complete with her own style and language, evolved in California's San Fernando Valley and spread across the United States. Perspective on Adolescent Development 9.2 surveys the adolescent culture of the Valley Girls

"It's so awesome." "It's, like, tubular, y'know." "Grody to the max." "Like, barf out." These are phrases from one of the most popular songs in the adolescent culture of 1982. The "Valley Girls" who used such phrases originally were girls who lived in the suburbs of California's San Fernando Valley. Was a whole new culture of adolescent girls developing? Not likely, since the development of a special language has characterized different groups of adolescents for many generations. As popular columnist Bob Greene stated:

In this, the summer of the "Valley Girl," it is tempting to forget that teenage girls have acted and spoken oddly in places and times other than California's San Fernando Valley in 1982. "Valley Girl" has become such a huge hit record that some people are deluding themselves that girls like the one on the record are a new phenomenon.

We know better. Fifteen- and sixteen-year-old girls have always acted funny, wherever and whenever they have lived. As proof, today we offer excerpts from notes saved and kept in a box by a woman who grew up in Indianapolis during the sixties. The notes— passed to her by her female classmates at Bishop Chatard High School—are a stirring historic document that proves teen-age girls have always been wacky—but no one used to write songs about the wackiness.

Here are the excerpts. By the way, this is not some dim attempt at satire on my part; the notes are real, and are quoted here verbatim.

"You wouldn't believe this queer study hall! That Marshall is such a fruit! He gave Helen a detention for saying about two words. She goes up to him and says, 'I'm not going to serve it!' It was funny. We were talking to Mike Carr, and some boy from North Central is going to ask Fink out. He saw her at the dance on Friday, but I forget his name. I wonder if he's cool. If Fink gets the car today and she picks you up, you have to make her pick me up. Bowers said that Steve Binham was real conceited, but I suppose I would be if I was that cool and was in one of the best bands."

***

"Kevin said he was all mixed up because he didn't know who to like, either Joyce, Ryan, Quinn, or Reese. He thinks he can get anybody. I don't think he'll like Ryan now, 'cause Sunday they were walking home from the Huddle and she was saying that he felt sorry for himself and that she wasn't going to. Then somebody came and gave her a ride and she left Kevin. I guess he was a little mad."

"God, we are only going to have the biggest RIOT. I can't wait, it is going to be so much fun. Listen, if Bissel gets us some stuff [beer], then maybe I won't have to take Billy's stuff. Tim just asked me if he could come to my party and I said yes. He is so cute. I can't wait, it will be so much damn FUN. You can go to the lake with us, nobody will find out. Maybe you can have a little 'fun' with Doug. I really want him to bring Johnny McDowl instead of Tim.

"I know, I can't wait much longer either. I wish the days would hurry and go by. I really told Joey that you had another date Saturday, and it was really funny. I just keep thinking about Saturday, we are going to be bombed on our BUTTS, BIGGEST RIOT. Yes, Doug is quite nice-looking, and I don't think he can wait either. I asked him if he liked Donna Shaw and he said no. Donna asked my sister in gym to ask me to ask Doug if he liked her. If I went up to him and said 'she likes ya' maybe he wouldn't come over to see ya Saturday night. But I still think he would come over to 'see' you. Because he likes ya.

"That Nicholson in study hall just smiled at me. Have you told anybody about Saturday night? I hope not. I just hope Doug doesn't tell anybody about it, because I'll get killed. I'm pretty sure Barb is getting that COOL car. I had to sit in the back of the room in Religion because I was talking. Don't let anybody read or see this note. Nothing else to say except I CAN'T WAIT for three days."

***

"If you don't want to go to the lake I bet you could stay at our house if your DAD would let you. He probably would because last time you couldn't because you had to read those books. It was so funny in study hall, me and Sheila and Howard were looking at this

The valley girls of 1982

book called the epic of man, it was so funny cause it showed all these ladies with nothing on the top and a couple feeding their baby. We were laughing real hard and Sheila lets out this big snort!!"

***

"You know about Marty liking Sheila—I sincerely doubt it, he didn't even act like it yesterday. You know when you were in N.Y., I just sorta (beating around the bush—you know what I mean) asked him why he's never asked you out and why doesn't he because you get along so much better than you used to and he sounded like he wants to and I know he will. You know last fall when you liked Dwyer, Marty liked you. He never came right out and said it but he wanted you and Dwyer to break up so he could move in. I used to kid him about it and he would give me that 'INNOCENT' smile of his. He loved (loves) your bod. I want you to come down and see my dress soon. Not much, I'll tell ya, it's way too big on top though, but that's normal."

Source: Greene, B., "Valley Girls," *Charleston Daily Mail,* Charleston, West Virginia, Wednesday, July 21, 1982.

and compares this phenomenon with the Indianapolis girls of 1962. As indicated, adolescents have been using their own special type of language for many years.

Youth Movements

The media have focused a great deal of attention on adolescent rebellion against prevailing cultural norms and standards. Sometimes such movements are even referred to as countercultures. By far the most attention has been given to youth movements that involve activist, rebellious, and socially alienated youth. While such youth have been given extensive coverage by the media, in virtually every era of United States history, they have represented only a small minority, albeit a very vocal minority, of youth.

As indicated in table 9.3, youth movements, particularly those that are activist in nature, are often associated with political issues. In recent years, the most well-known and active youth movements were those that rebelled in the late 1960s. As that decade drew to an end, the goals and objectives—but not necessarily the tactics—of the youth movement spread to a much larger segment of the adolescent population (President's Commission on Campus Unrest, 1970; Peterson and Bilorusky, 1971). These young people wanted to change the adult political and value systems that the country operated under. While many nonviolent youth sympathized with the causes and political stands of the rebellious adolescents of the 1960s, estimates of the hardcore membership in all radical youth groups rarely exceeded five percent of the total student body of this country at any one time (Block, Haan, and Smith, 1968). Much of the unrest caused by both radical youth and their sympathizers involved their vehement disagreement with political powers over the Vietnam war.

Today, campuses seem relatively calm, but it may be an uneasy calm. Numerous social problems continue to disturb some members of the youth culture—human rights, energy, and ecology are still high on the list of issues on which there is considerable disagreement with the dominant adult political power figures (Braungart, 1979).

As we have seen there are similarities and differences in youth cultures at different points in history. As we see next, there are similarities and differences among the adolescents from different cultures around the world as well.

Cross-Cultural Comparisons: Iks and Mangaians

Much of the interest in cross-cultural studies of adolescents has come from anthropologists. Let's look more closely at the anthropological view of adolescence and then consider a number of cross-cultural comparisons of adolescence.

The Anthropological View

The **anthropological view** stresses the scientific study of the origin of human beings and cultural influences on their development. Anthropologists believe that the adolescent's behavior may vary from one culture to another in ways the individual would have difficulty recognizing. Anthropologists also suggest that many cultural variations survive from one generation to the next—that they are not merely passing thoughts, behaviors, and feelings.

The anthropologist, like the sociologist, is interested in charting culturally patterned experiences. Anthropologists have significantly influenced thinking about the socialization of adolescents. One of the major contributions of the anthropological view has been to show similarities and differences between the more industrialized North American and Western European cultures and primitive, less developed cultures. Such studies are useful in confirming or disconfirming whether theories and data about adolescents are culture-specific or universal in nature.

Also like the sociologist, the anthropologist believes that it is important to recognize that a culture like that of the United States is not homogeneous—it has subcultures of social class, ethnicity, religion, and region (for example, Southerners). Let's look more closely at the adolescent from a cross-cultural and ethnic perspective.

Table 9.3 Temporal locations and decisive political events in relation to youth movements

Temporal location	Decisive political events	Youth movements
1900–1929	Economic growth and cultural liberalism Industrialization; United States·develops favorable balance of trade and becomes world industrial power World War I Isolationism Prohibition Women's suffrage "Roaring Twenties"	Youth culture challenges Victorian social and sexual mores

1930–1940	The Great Depression
	    Poverty
	    Election of Franklin Roosevelt; "New Deal"
	    Government economic programs
	    Growth of national socialism in Germany
		Youth join antiwar movement
		Sign Oxford Pledge
		Campus strikes

1941–1949	World War II
	    Truman administration
	    Atomic bomb
	    Returning GIs
	    Global reconstruction, United Nations
		Little youth movement activity

1950–1959	The Cold War—Eisenhower years
	    Growth of "military-industrial complex"
	    Dulles foreign policy
	    Recession
	    McCarthyism
	    1954 Supreme Court desegregation decision
	    House Un-American Activities Committee
		"The silent generation"

1960–1968	Kennedy-Johnson years
	    "New Frontier"
	    Civil rights demonstrations
	    Peace Corps, poverty programs
	    Vietnam escalation
	    Assassinations of Kennedy brothers and Martin Luther King
	    "Great Society" programs
	    Ghetto riots and campus disruption
		New Left
		New Right
		Civil rights and Black Power
		Protest demonstrations, strikes, violence

1969–1976	Nixon-Ford Years
	    Emphasis on "law and order"
	    Voting Rights Act
	    Vietnam War ends
	    Kissinger foreign policy
	    Inflation, job squeeze
	    Growth of multinational corporations
	    Watergate
	    OPEC and Middle East oil embargo
		Women's rights
		Ecology movement
		Charismatic religious movements
		Quiet seventies

1977–1979	Early Carter administration
	    Conciliatory, practical, informal mood in White House
	    Emphasis on government reorganization
	    National energy crisis
	    Inflation, job squeeze continues
		"No-Nuke" movement
		Gay liberation

From Braungart, R. G., "Reference Groups, Social Judgements and Student Politics," Adolescence, *1979, 14, (53), 135–137. Reprinted by permission of Libra Publishers.*

Robert Havighurst (1976) believes that earlier in this century there was an overgeneralization about the universal aspects of adolescence based on data and experience in a single culture. It was believed that all adolescents everywhere went through a period of "storm and stress," characterized by plaguing self-doubts and conflicts. Further, it was thought that adolescents everywhere experience extensive conflict with the adults in their society. However, when Margaret Mead (1928) visited the island of Samoa, she found that not only were the adolescents in the Samoan culture not encountering much stress, they were not generally in conflict with the adults in their world.

Anthropologist Colin Turnbull (1972) studied the culture of the Ik in Uganda. For about 2,000 years the Ik lived as nomadic hunters. But some forty years ago, their livelihood was destroyed when the government of Uganda turned their hunting grounds into a national park. Hunting was forbidden in the park, so the Ik were forced to try to farm the steep, barren mountain areas of the park.

Turnbull lived among the Ik for a one-and-one-half-year period. He described the disastrous results of the displaced Ik in a book called *The Mountain People* (1972). Famine, crowding, and drought led to tremendous upheavals in family orientation and moral values. Children and adolescents were sent out on their own with no life supports supplied by the parents. The youth often banded together in pairs and triplets to fend off adults and other youth who vied with them for food and water.

By the time the boys and girls reached adolescence, they had learned that to exist in their world, they had to look out for themselves and show little respect or concern for others. Interestingly, when they had children of their own, they, in turn, put them out on their own at a very early age, even as young as three years old.

The principle of individual survival became far and away the most important motive in the life of the adolescent Ik. Turnbull described the Ik as having no love at all. Positive virtues such as kindness, affection, and consideration for others simply did not exist in the Ik youth. Imagine yourself on a barren mountainside away

The culture in which an adolescent grows up plays a powerful role in his or her development.

from civilization in the country of Uganda. Your way of life has been disrupted. You no longer have food. Would you act as the adolescents of the Ik culture did?

When anthropologists and psychologists study cultures in different parts of the world, important information can be gleaned from a single culture, such as in Turnbull's study of the Ik. But it is also very important to compare the beliefs, values, and experiences of adolescents in different cultures by collecting data simultaneously in several cultures.

Cross-Cultural Comparisons of Adolescent Development

There have been many comparisons of adolescent development in one culture with adolescent development in another culture. These include evaluations in achievement orientation, morality, and sexual behavior.

Achievement Orientation

The United States, as we have observed, is an achievement-oriented country. Many anthropologists believe that the socioeconomic conditions and values in a culture are transmitted to adolescents through the child-rearing techniques of parents.

Barry, Child, and Bacon (1959) followed this line of thought. They wanted to find out whether the child-rearing practices of parents in industrialized countries differed from those of parents in nonindustrialized countries. It was their guess that parents in nonindustrialized countries would place a lower value on socializing their youth for achievement and independence and a higher value on obedience and responsibility. In their evaluation of 104 societies, Barry, Child, and Bacon found support for their hypothesis.

Direct observation of youth from different cultures also lends support to the belief that the United States is an achievement-oriented culture. Millard Madsen and his colleagues (Kagan and Madsen, 1971, 1972; Madsen and Shapira, 1970; Shapira and Madsen, 1969) have compared the competitive and cooperative behavior of boys and girls from urban Afro-American,

Anglo-American, Mexican-American, village Mexican, kibbutz Israeli, and urban Israeli cultures. In direct comparisons of village Mexican and Anglo-American youth, Mexican youth generally were more cooperative and American youth more competitive. In one set of observations, Anglo-American students were more likely to reduce gains for other students when they could not obtain them for themselves (Kagan and Madsen, 1972).

Wayne Holtzman and his colleagues (Holtzman, 1982; Holtzman, Diaz-Guerrero, and Schwarz, 1975) have found that Mexican boys and girls are more cooperative in interpersonal activities, whereas their American counterparts are more competitive. In their comprehensive evaluation of the lives of Mexican and American youth, they found that the Mexicans were more pessimistic and fatalistic in their outlooks than the Americans were. Furthermore, the Mexicans were more family-centered and the Americans more individual-centered. Although some of the cross-cultural comparisons of American adolescents and adolescents from other cultures are encouraging, some results lead anthropologists to suggest that our culture is too achievement-oriented for optimal mental health during adolescence.

Morality

Except for the incest taboo, which is virtually universal, most theorists believe that the substance of moral prohibition varies greatly across cultures and is deeply embedded in the values of each individual culture (Benedict, 1934, 1958; Murdock, 1949). However, Lawrence Kohlberg (1976) believes there are basic abstract moral principles shared by cultures with different moral systems. Still, many experts feel that Kohlberg has not adequately accounted for the cultural variation addressed by Benedict and Murdock.

James Garbarino and Urie Bronfenbrenner (1976) stress that cultural experiences can advance the youth's moral development by exposing her to a variety of settings and social agents that represent different expectations and moral sanctions. Such differences produce conflict in the adolescent and motivate her to reassess her own moral convictions. A single setting, by contrast, usually exposes the adolescent to only one set of rules. The pluralistic theory can be applied to families (two parents mean two moral systems instead of one), peers, schools, neighborhoods, communities, employment, and civic and political organizations.

Garbarino and Bronfenbrenner (1976) created a model for understanding the link between developmental period, socialization experiences, and the extent to which individuals are exposed to different social agents and sociopolitical views. A summary of the model is presented in table 9.4. The main theme of Garbarino and Bronfenbrenner's argument is that increased exposure to multiple social agents and multiple sociopolitical views produces advances in the individual's moral development. Their research suggests that individuals who grow up in a culture that is more sociopolitically plural (United States, West Germany) are less likely to be authority oriented and have more plural ideas about moral dilemmas than their counterparts who grow up in less sociopolitical cultures (Poland, Hungary). Bronfenbrenner and Garbarino further commented about the kinds of families children are likely to be exposed to in Eastern countries, that are less sociopolitically plural, and Western countries, that are more sociopolitically plural. In the East, the family is expected to support the governmental regime—family styles there are likely to be more monolithic. In Western cultures, where more individual freedom is allowed, more diverse family styles are common, and children are exposed to more varied cultural experiences.

Sexual Behavior

A third aspect of adolescent development that has been given considerable attention in cross-cultural studies is sexual behavior. Cross-cultural studies of adolescent sexual behavior indicate that culture and learning play a major role in shaping sexual conduct. Such studies indicate that sexual behavior is not totally under the control of biological influences. For example, women who live in the Ines Beag culture off the coast of Ireland never have orgasms. But every woman who lives in the Mangaia culture in the South Pacific achieves an orgasm. The two sets of women have similar constructed vaginas and clitorides that are approximately the same size and that have virtually the same nerve supply. The reason for the difference, then, must be learned. Let's look more closely to see if the experience of adolescents in the two cultures has anything to do with the differences in sexual behavior (Hyde, 1979).

John Messinger (1971) describes life in Ines Beag. The inhabitants of Ines Beag are among the most sexually repressed in the world. They know nothing about French kissing, breast kissing, or hand stimulation of the penis. Sex education is nonexistent. They believe that after marriage, nature will take its course.

The men believe that intercourse is bad for their health. And they detest nudity—only babies can bathe nude. Adults wash only the parts of their bodies that extend beyond their clothing. Premarital sex is totally taboo, and after marriage, the sexual partners keep their underwear on during intercourse. It is not too difficult to understand why females in the Ines Beag culture never achieve orgasm.

By contrast, consider the Mangaian culture. Boys learn about masturbation as early as age six or seven; by age eight or nine, they usually have started to masturbate. When a boy is thirteen, he undergoes a ritual in which a long incision is made in his penis, a custom designed to introduce him into manhood. The person who conducts the ritual provides him with information about sexual strategies—such as how to help his partner achieve orgasm before he does. Two weeks after the incision ceremony, the thirteen-year-old boy has intercourse with an experienced woman, which causes the scab from his penis to be removed. The woman trains the boy in various sexual techniques and helps him to learn how to hold back ejaculation so she can achieve orgasm with him. Soon after, the boy looks for girls to try out his techniques—or they search for him, knowing that he is now a "man." Adolescent girls expect him to have intercourse with them—if he does not, it is a sign

Table 9.4 A model for studying the relationship between sociopolitical pluralism and moral development

Developmental level	Moral socialization outcome	Critical pluralistic variables
Infancy	Establishment of attachment, i.e., primary socialization.	Care-giving patterns, both behavioral and normative, contribute to progressively more complex systems of infant–adult interaction.
Early childhood	Expansion of primary attachment relationships into ever-widening circles.	Progressive expansion of patterns of attachment from primary caregiver to larger social systems. Initial pluralistic social settings, with several different persons serving as objects for the child's attention and affiliation and as sources of demands. Initial ability to respond to differential influences.
Later childhood	Development of relationships with social groups, particularly peer groups and children's institutions.	Development of multiple associations rather than complete immersion in one group.
Adolescence	Resolution of conflicting relationships to social groups so as to achieve both objective-principled moral orientation and social identity.	Integration of individual into adult roles and experiences. Relative congruence between goals and values of peer groups and adult institutions: neither "cultural warfare" of peer group against adult social structures nor domination of peer groups by adult authority. Pathways to adult activities consonant with previous socialization experiences.
Adulthood	Maintenance of creative tension between social identity and objective-principled moral orientation.	Systems of social support for alternative patterns of access to economic and social resources. Feedback to parental child rearing that supports encouragement of identity and diversity (i.e., neither authoritarian nor permissive, but authoritative child rearing). Pluralism in adults to encourage pluralism in children.

From Garbarino, J., and U. Bronfenbrenner, "The Socialization of Moral Judgement and Behavior in Cross-Cultural Perspective," in T. Lickona (Ed.), Moral Development and Behavior. Copyright © 1976 Holt, Rinehart and Winston, New York.

that he does not like them. By late adolescence, Mangaian boys and girls have sex every night and average three orgasms per night. It is easy to see how cultural experiences influence the Mangaian woman's ability to achieve orgasm.

In some primitive cultures, elaborate ceremonies signify the adolescent's movement to adult sexual maturity. Perspective on Adolescent Development 9.3 discusses such rites of passage. Thus, we see that findings from cross-cultural studies of adolescence are useful in confirming or disconfirming ideas about generalized principles that have been based primarily on observations in only one culture. Both variation and congruence have been noted across cultures in adolescent development.

We have discussed many different aspects of the cultural process, the adolescent culture, and cross-cultural comparisons. Some of the key concepts in these aspects of adolescent development are in Concept Table 9.1.

*B*arbara Sommer (1978) has studied a variety of ceremonies and activities associated with **rites of passage** in a number of primitive cultures. Sometimes the ceremonies are referred to as puberty rites and are defined as the avenue through which adolescents gain access to sacred adult practices, to knowledge, and to sexuality (Eliade, 1958). These rites often involve very dramatic practices intended to facilitate the separation of the adolescent from the immediate family, particularly his mother. The transformation usually is characterized by some form of ritual death and rebirth, or by means of contact with the spiritual world. And, bonds are forged between the adolescent and his adult instructors by means of shared rituals, hazards, and secrets to allow the adolescent to enter into the adult world. Such rituals stimulate a forceful and discontinuous entry into the adult world at a time when the youth is ready for change.

According to Sommer, rites of transition are more directly related to the specific events of puberty for females than for males. The fact that there is a more direct link for females is likely a consequence of the single marker of menarche; there is no such clear signal of the onset of puberty in males. Also, for boys, the rites of passage reflect an introduction to the more ethereal world of spirit and culture, whereas for girls they emphasize natural phenomena such as menstruation and childbirth.

Africa has been the location of many rites of passage for adolescents, particularly the area of Africa known as Sub-Saharan Africa. Under the influence of Western culture, many of the rites are disappearing today, although some vestiges still remain. In locations where formal education is not readily available, rites of passage during early adolescence are still prevalent. Let's look at the rites of passage of boys and girls in several different primitive cultures.

Boys' initiation rites. Themes of death and rebirth are prevalent in the initiation ceremonies of males. Boys frequently are violently removed from their mothers and families by evil-looking masked figures. In the Congo and Loange coastal regions of Africa, boys between the ages of ten and twelve years are given a potion that makes them lose consciousness. They are then taken into the jungle, circumcised, and ritually buried. When they awake, it is assumed that they have forgotten their past lives (Eliade, 1958).

Circumcision is a prominent practice in rites of passage and has both sexual and spiritual meanings. Circumcision may be done at the onset of puberty for hygienic reasons, to test the endurance of the youth, to reflect symbolic sacrifice, to sanctify procreation, to symbolize incorporation into the community, to represent symbolic castration by a father figure, or to express male envy of women's menstruation (Allen, 1967).

Girls' initiation rites. According to Barbara Sommer (1978), the reproductive capabilities of the female and the onset of menstruation are often the central focus of female rites of passage. As was true for male rites, such ceremonies serve sexual, spiritual, and communal functions. Female rites similar to male rites have been reported in a number of primitive cultures. In such rites, it is not unusual for the girl's clitoris to be removed. In some rites, girls are tortured or scared, while in others they are admired and celebrated (Opler, 1972).

Two frequent themes characterize female initiation rites: a childbirth scenario that is supposed to guarantee fertility and ease of childbirth, and procedures that are designed to ensure the further achievement of cultural standards of beauty and sexual desirability. Information about modes of dress and sexual matters may be passed on during the ceremony, and spirituality is often included by associating femininity with the powers of the moon.

It's clear that adolescents' responses to puberty are largely determined by culture. In the culture of the United States, adolescents don't go through such elaborate initiation rites, and passage into adolescence and adulthood is much more continuous. Separation, transition, and incorporation seem to be three themes that characterize puberty initiation rites. An underlying belief in such rites of passage is that puberty brings changes in sexual maturation and intellectual prowess.

Concept Table 9.1

THE CULTURAL PROCESS, THE ADOLESCENT CULTURE, AND CROSS-CULTURAL COMPARISONS

Concept	*Processes/related ideas*	*Characteristics/description*
The cultural process	Its nature	Culture is a very broad concept, referring to the behavior patterns, beliefs, values, and other products of humans that are learned and shared by a particular group of people and passed on from one generation to the next.
	Bronfenbrenner's ecological model	Bronfenbrenner argues that systematic analyses of culture have been too few in number. He proposes that the culture of adolescents can be understood better if it is divided into these parts: microsystem, mesosystem, and exosystem. The community context often becomes an important part of the adolescent's exosystem.
	The settings in which adolescents spend their time	The "beeper" study by Csikszentmihalyi and Larson focused on the locations where adolescents spend their time, what they do, and with whom they associate. Adolescents spent more time at home than in other settings, but they also spent about one-third of their time at school, and more than one-fourth of their time in public places. About twenty-nine percent of their time involved productive activities, particularly school work. They also spent considerable time socializing. They were much more likely to be interacting with peers than with parents or other adults.
The adolescent culture	Adolescent interests	The opposite sex, sex, and love are high on the interest lists of adolescent males and females. Freedom, true friendship, and happiness rank very high on adolescents' lists of values.
	The youth culture and language	The adolescent culture is often characterized by the use of slang expressions—cliques often take on their own special language.
	Youth movements	Activitist, rebellious youth movements have often captured a great deal of media attention in the history of looking at adolescents. In reality, such youth usually represent a vocal, visible minority of adolescents. Youth movements are frequently associated with political issues.
Cross-cultural comparisons	The anthropological view	The anthropological view stresses the scientific study of the origin of human beings and cultural influences on their development. Anthropologists believe many cultural variations survive from one generation to the next.
	Cross-cultural comparisons of adolescents	Adolescents in the United States, compared to adolescents in other cultures, are very achievement oriented. The substance of moral prohibition may vary from one culture to another. Garbarino and Bronfenbrenner believe exposure to multiple social agents and sociopolitical views promotes moral development. There is considerable variation in sexual behavior among adolescents across cultures. In some primitive societies, rites de passage signal the sexual maturity of the adolescent.

Not only do we learn more about adolescent development by comparing adolescents in the United States with adolescents in other cultures, but a culture like that of the United States is very complex and consists of many subcultures. These subcultures include social class, ethnicity, religion, and region. Let's look more closely at adolescents from different social classes and ethnic backgrounds.

Social Class and Ethnicity: Social Stratification and Ancestry

The cultural settings in which the adolescent develops can be described in terms of their social class and ethnic characteristics. Far too often when we think about and study adolescents, only middle-class, white individuals are involved. Here we are sensitized to the socioeconomic and ethnic plurality of our culture.

Social Class

What is social class? How is it categorized and measured? How do families, schools, and neighborhoods vary in their socioeconomic makeup? What is the adolescent's life like in the subculture of the poor? How is social class related to the adolescent's personality and the way he or she is socialized by parents? What kinds of cautions should be exercised when interpreting social-class research? Let's explore these questions.

What Is Social Class?

What do we mean when we refer to **social class?** We talk about it all the time: "He's from a lower class family." "She comes from a middle-class family." In general, we are speaking about an adolescent's socioeconomic status and lifestyle when we refer to his or her social class. Along with the labels, however, often come certain connotations.

Social stratification in the United States carries with it certain inequalities. It is generally acknowledged that members of society (1) have occupations that vary in prestige, (2) have different levels of power to influence the institutions of a community, (3) have different economic resources, and (4) have different educational and occupational opportunities. These differences in ability to control resources and to participate in the rewards of society produce unequal opportunities for adolescents (Hess, 1970). Social class, or socioeconomic status (SES), thus influences the adolescent's socialization.

Categorization and Measurement

There is by no means total agreement on what the categories of social class should be and how they should be measured. Robert Hess (1970), for instance, has described six ways to analyze social class (table 9.5). Perhaps the greatest common denominator in categorizing social class is occupation. In one classification, **upper class** individuals have professional and managerial positions, **middle-class** individuals work at lower level blue-collar and skilled blue-collar jobs, and **lower class** individuals are semiskilled and unskilled workers. But this is only one classification; other experts disagree on how to measure social stratification. How can information about education, occupation, and income be combined to arrive at an accurate system of categorization? How many groups should be included in the classification system—two, three, or six?

For convenience, this discussion will focus on the lower class and the middle class; these two classes include the majority of people in most social-class scales, and experts know the most about them. The following occupations help to define these classes: (1) lower class—factory workers, manual laborers, welfare recipients, maintenance workers; (2) middle class—salespeople, managers, professionals (doctors, lawyers, teachers, accountants, and so on).

Table 9.5 Different ways to analyze social class

Number of social class (SES) groups indexed	Method of categorization used	Number of social class (SES) groups indexed	Method of categorization used
5	(1) Professional, (2) semiprofessional and large business, (3) skilled workers, (4) semiskilled workers, (5) unskilled workers.	4	(1) Professional and technical workers, (2) clerical workers, (3) skilled workers, (4) semiskilled and unskilled workers.
10	Index based on occupational prestige in a town; grouped into ten different strata.	3	(1) Upper: professional and managerial, (2) middle: lower-level white collar and skilled blue-collar; (3) lower: semiskilled and unskilled workers.
2	(1) Middle class: subjects whose parents were salespeople, office workers, owners, managers, and professionals; (2) working class: subjects whose fathers were service and maintenance workers, factory workers, and manual laborers.	3	(1) Professional, managerial; (2) wage earner with semiskilled clerical or sales job, education ranging from about ninth grade to high school graduate; (3) wage earner unemployed or in an unskilled or semiskilled job, education through eighth grade or less.

Based on data from Hess, 1970. Used by permission of John Wiley and Sons, Inc.

Socioeconomic Variations in Families, Schools, and Neighborhoods

The families, schools, and neighborhoods of adolescents have socioeconomic characteristics. Some adolescents have parents who have a great deal of money, work in prestigious occupations, live in attractive houses and neighborhoods, and attend schools where the mix of students is primarily from such middle and upper class backgrounds. Other adolescents have parents who do not have very much money, work in less prestigious occupations, do not live in very attractive houses and neighborhoods, and attend schools where the mix of students is mainly from lower class backgrounds.

Let's look at one important aspect of the adolescent's intellectual background and see how social class differences in families are involved. Most school tasks require students to use and process language. As part of this language orientation, students often are called on to read efficiently, write effectively, and give competent oral reports. While there is considerable variation within a particular social class, middle-class students are more likely to make use of verbal skills, especially reading, and to enjoy their use more than lower class students (also called working-class students). As shown in figure 9.4, working-class students tend to read less, but watch television more than middle-class students. While television involves some verbal activity, it is primarily a visual medium; and the working-class adolescents' preference for this medium suggests that they are more interested in visual than verbal experiences unlike middle-class adolescents.

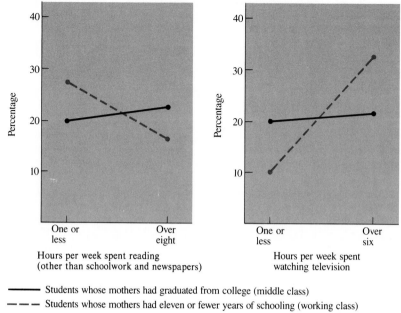

Students whose mothers had graduated from college (middle class)

Students whose mothers had eleven or fewer years of schooling (working class)

Figure 9.4 The reading and television habits of high school students from working-class and middle-class families.

The parents of middle-class adolescents likely direct their offspring from very early in the child's development more toward verbal experiences than their lower class counterparts. For example, Steven Tulkin and Jerome Kagan (1971) observed thirty middle-class and twenty-six lower class Caucasian mothers at home with their first-born, 10-month-old daughters. As shown in table 9.6, social class differences were minimal in areas of physical contact, prohibitions, and nonverbal interactions. By contrast, *every* verbal behavior observed was more frequent among middle-class mothers. They concluded that lower class mothers less frequently believed their infants were capable of communicating with other people and, therefore, felt it was futile to interact with them verbally.

A sizeable portion of adolescent students from lower social class backgrounds, however, do perform well in school; in many cases, better than some middle-class students. In the family background of adolescents from lower class settings, it is not unusual to find a parent or parents making special efforts and sacrifices to provide the necessary living conditions and support that contribute to enhanced school success.

Turning our attention to schools themselves, schools in low-income neighborhoods often have fewer resources than schools in high-income neighborhoods. The schools in the low-income areas also are likely to have more students with lower achievement test scores, lower rates of graduation, and fewer percentages of students going to college (Garbarino and Asp, 1981). There are some instances, however, where federal aid to schools has provided a context for enhanced learning in low-income areas. The school personnel in the schools set in lower class neighborhoods often is different than in middle-class settings. Younger, less experienced teachers often are the ones who end up with jobs in schools in lower class neighborhoods while older, more experienced teachers are more often found in schools in middle-class neighborhoods.

Table 9.6 Maternal behaviors with infants in working-class and middle-class families

Variable	Working class Mean	Middle class Mean
Interaction:		
Interaction episodes	36.08	65.97
Total interaction	132.50	251.83
Location:		
Over 2 ft from child	1,402.73	1,243.27
Within 2 ft	1,424.50	1,525.60
Face to face	53.19	110.77
Physical contact:		
Kiss	4.00	5.73
Total holding	210.73	265.17
Active physical contact	21.42	31.37
Prohibitions:		
Verbal only	15.50	18.33
Physical only	12.19	11.00
Prohibitions ÷ time on floor	36.19	33.93
Prohibitions ÷ walk and crawl	19.04	16.50
Responses to nonverbal behaviors:		
Positive response (%), child touches mother	56.36	63.89
Positive response (%), child offers object to mother	90.65	86.40
Maternal vocalization:		
Over 2 ft away	17.65	40.57
Within 2 ft	148.77	329.37
Face to face	19.00	38.20
Total maternal vocalization	192.00	422.40
Reciprocal vocalization (%)	11.27	20.70
Keeping infant busy:		
Entertainment	54.65	99.13
Give objects	26.23	38.53
Response to spontaneous frets:		
Frets (%) to which mother responded	38.36	58.41
Latency to respond (no. of 5-sec intervals)	1.98	1.62

From Tulkin, S. R., and J. Kagan, "Mother–Child Interaction in the First Year of Life," Child Development, 43, 31–41, 1971. © The Society for Research in Child Development, Inc.

The neighborhoods of lower and middle-class adolescents also may be very different. Middle-class adolescents typically live in settings where buildings and houses are newer, parks and recreational facilities are more readily available, library facilities are more plentiful and fully stocked, and crime and delinquency are less likely to occur.

As can be seen, the social-class backgrounds of adolescents often differ on many dimensions. Next, we focus on a particular subset of adolescents from lower class backgrounds—those classified as poor.

The subculture of the poor is of particular concern to educators who work with adolescents.

The Subculture of the Poor

Of particular concern to psychologists and educators who work with adolescents is the subculture of the poor—those adolescents from the lower strata of working-class families. While the most noticeable aspect of this subculture is economic poverty, there are many other psychological and social characteristics as well (Hess, 1970).

First, the poor are often powerless. In occupational circles, they do not participate in decision-making processes; rules and regulations are usually handed down to them in an authoritarian way. They frequently feel that they cannot change their own plight; they believe that even if they wanted to, they would not be able to deal more effectively with their world. Lower class individuals may sometimes succumb to relying on luck—playing the numbers games or betting on horses—because of these feelings of helplessness.

Second, the poor are vulnerable to disaster. This vulnerability is closely related to their lack of power. People of this subculture are often not given advance notice when laid off from work; they usually do not have financial resources such as savings accounts to fall back on when problems arise; and they usually have difficulty getting loans and credit.

Third, the range of alternatives for the poor is restricted. They do not have much mobility in terms of housing, and a limited range of job opportunities is open to them. They have little freedom in choosing medical services and are often at the mercy of governmental agencies who control welfare and health payments. Even when alternatives are available, the poor may not know about them or may not be able to decide wisely between them because of inadequate education and the inability to read well.

Fourth, poor members of the working class lack prestige. The adolescent can detect her own lack of prestige by observing other adolescents who wear nicer clothes and live in more attractive homes. Others frequently communicate information to the adolescent about her relative position in the community; for example, lower class adolescents are rarely asked to visit the homes of middle-class adolescents.

Finally, the experiences of the lower class in general do not overlap with those of the dominant middle class. Their working conditions within the same companies and their lives within the same communities differ from those of middle-class persons.

In particular, social support may be an important factor in whether adolescents who come from such impoverished backgrounds develop competently. In one investigation (Cauce, Felner, and Primavera, 1982), 250 ninth and eleventh graders from inner city, predominantly low-income, minority group backgrounds were studied. Information was obtained about their school performance (grade point average and absences), self-concept, and social support. With regard to the measurement of social support, students were asked how helpful a number of different people, such as parents, teachers, friends, and the clergy, were to them. The researchers divided this help into the categories of family support (parents and other relatives); formal support (counselors, teachers, and clergy); and informal support (friends and other adults). The results indicated that family support as well as formal support were unrelated to the student's school performance. However, informal support was related to the adolescent's school performance, but in a negative way. That is, adolescents with higher informal support had lower grades and were absent from school more than adolescents with less informal support. How can this finding be explained? In this impoverished inner city neighborhood, high degrees of contact with the peer group and other adults may not always be of a positive nature. Indeed, in this investigation, the adolescents with strong informal support systems had a positive perception of their relationship with peers. Many of these adolescents likely were not adopting peers' standards that were related to achievement and school, as evidenced by their lower grades and frequent absences from school. While we usually think of support groups as positive influences on the adolescent's development, this research calls attention to the importance of considering the nature of the support and the degree to which it coincides with values in the larger culture.

Now that we have discussed the subculture of the poor, we return to an overview of social class comparisons in regard to other important aspects of adolescent development—personality and parenting strategies.

Social Class, Personality, and Parenting Strategies

The social class an adolescent grows up in can have a significant effect on how highly he values himself. In a stratified society like that of the United States, an individual's ranking and prestige influence his self-perception. For example, in one study of 5,024 high school juniors and seniors, students from higher social classes revealed higher self-esteem than students from lower social classes did (Rosenberg, 1965).

Earlier in our discussion of social class, we found that lower class mothers engage in considerably less verbal interaction with their offspring than their middle-class counterparts. Other social-class differences focus on independence training and discipline. Several studies suggest that lower class parents do not provide as much systemized independence training for adolescents as middle-class parents do (e.g., Elder, 1968; Jacob, 1974). Further, lower class parents discipline adolescents in an authoritarian manner more often than middle-class parents do (Jacob, 1974). As stated in Chapter 6 in the discussion on families, consistent linkages between authoritarian parenting and restrictions on independence have been documented (e.g., Kandel and Lesser, 1972).

Some Cautions about Interpreting Social-Class Research

Stereotypes often develop about adolescents from both lower and middle-class backgrounds. In many studies of social class, the differences between lower and middle-class adolescents may actually be very small even though they are statistically significant. For example, fifty percent of the lower class adolescents in one sample reported that they have a low opinion of themselves, compared to only thirty-five percent of the middle-class adolescents sampled. Although this difference may well be significant, it obviously does not mean that all lower class adolescents have negative views of themselves nor does it mean that all middle-class adolescents have positive self-images. It is important to keep in mind that generalizations are never completely accurate. It is also wise to remember that many aspects of an adolescent—for example, feelings of self-esteem—can fluctuate from situation to situation. More middle-class than lower class adolescents may have high self-esteem in English class, but more lower class than middle-class adolescents may have high self-esteem in an auto mechanics or physical education class.

Social class is not as easy to define as it might at first appear. No clear differentiation can be made between a lower class adolescent and a middle-class adolescent. Furthermore, it is all too easy to stereotype an adolescent from a lower class background as having specific personality traits she does not actually have. We have emphasized the differences between lower and middle-class adolescents, but there are many similarities between them as well. For example, when personality is evaluated in terms of self-concept, achievement, and aggression, there is often a great deal of overlap in the scores of lower and middle-class adolescents. Such similarities are sometimes overlooked or excluded in comparisons of adolescents from different social classes.

Ethnicity

Think about your ethnic background and how it influenced your life when you were an adolescent. Were you a member of the predominant ethnic group or a minority ethnic group? How well did adolescents from different ethnic backgrounds get along in the secondary school(s) you attended? Let's now look closer at the nature of ethnic influences in adolescence.

The Nature of Ethnicity and Ethnic Groups in the United States

Ethnicity refers to the condition of belonging to a particular ethnic group. Each of you is a member of one or more ethnic groups and so is every adolescent. Membership in an ethnic group is based on racial, religious, national, and ancestral background. As shown in table 9.7 adolescents in the United States come from many different ethnic backgrounds. Note that black and Hispanic adolescents make up the largest portion of minority group adolescents in the United States.

Table 9.7 Percentages of adolescents aged ten to nineteen from different ethnic backgrounds

Ethnic group	Percent of adolescent population
Caucasian	
(Age 10–19)	76.5
Age 10–14	35.2
Age 15–19	41.3
Black	
(Age 10–19)	13.7
Age 10–14	6.5
Age 15–19	7.2
Hispanic origin	
(Age 10–19)	7.5
Age 10–14	3.6
Age 15–19	3.9
Asian and Pacific islander	
(Age 10–19)	1.5
Age 10–14	.7
Age 15–19	.8
American Indian, Eskimo, and Aleut	
(Age 10–19)	.8
Age 10–14	.4
Age 15–19	.4

Source: United States Bureau of the Census, 1980, Detailed Population Characteristics of the United States, Table 253.

It should also be pointed out that there has been an increase in the number of ethnic minority group adolescents in recent decades. In 1970, 11.8 percent of adolescents were black, while in 1980, the figure reached 13.7 percent. In 1970, 4.7 percent of adolescents were of Hispanic origin, while in 1980, 7.5 percent were from a Spanish background. In 1970, eighty-seven percent of adolescents were Caucasian, but by 1980, that figure decreased to 76.5 percent. Let's now look more closely at adolescents from different ethnic minority backgrounds.

Black Adolescents

To learn more about black adolescents, we describe Erik Erikson's ideas about the identity of black adolescents, then turn to discussions of self-concept and poverty.

Erikson's Ideas on Black Adolescents

> The concept, or at least the term, *identity* seems to pervade much of the literature on the Negro revolution in this country and to have come to represent in other countries as well something in the psychological core of the revolution of the colored races and nations who seek emancipation from the remnants of colonial patterns of thought . . .

Erik Erikson has written extensively on the problem of identity development in *Identity: Youth and Culture* (1968). Although he is especially sensitive to the problems of black youth in the United States, Erikson points out that throughout the world, minority groups have struggled to maintain their cultural identities while blending with the dominant culture. Erikson believes that this struggle for inclusive identity, or identity within the larger culture, has been the driving force in the founding of churches, empires, and revolutions throughout history. He quotes Robert Penn Warren (1965), who described in his book, *Who Speaks for the Negro?* the developing sense of identity in adolescent blacks:

> The auditorium had been packed—mostly Negroes, but with a scattering of white people. A young girl with pale skin, dressed like any coed anywhere, in the clothes for a public occasion, is on the rostrum. She is leaning forward a little on her high heels, speaking with a peculiar vibrance in a strange, irregular rhythm, out of some inner excitement, some furious, taut elan, saying: "And I tell you I have discovered a great truth. I have discovered a great joy. I have discovered that I am black. I am black! You out there—oh yes, you may have black faces, but your hearts are white, your minds are white, you have been white-washed!" (Warren, 1965, p. 17).

Many American blacks look to their African heritage to develop a sense of racial and cultural identity. But Erikson warns that this positive sense of identity must be integrated into the larger culture in which American blacks participate—a culture dominated by nonblack elements. Robert Penn Warren also refers to the problem of inclusive identity:

> I seize the word *identity*. It is a key word. You hear it over and over again. On this word will focus, around this word will coagulate, a dozen issues, shifting, shading into each other. Alienated from the world to which he is born and from the country of which he is a citizen, yet surrounded by the successful values of that new world and country, how can the Negro define himself? (Warren, 1965, p. 17)

Erikson believes that for young blacks to achieve a positive, healthy integration into American culture, they must avoid antisocial, angry behavior and work toward what he calls vocational competence and moral commitment. Through these means, black adolescents can earn their rightful place in American society while maintaining their cultural and racial identity. It is important to point out that Erikson's ideas about black adolescents may well apply to adolescents from any minority group within a culture. Further, Erikson's ideas are based mainly on clinical evidence rather than scientific inquiries.

The Black Adolescent's Self-Concept In the 1960s, it was reported that the self-concept of black adolescents was lower than that of white adolescents (e.g., Coopersmith, 1967). However, more recent investigations have not found this to be true (e.g., Simmons et al., 1978).

Black Adolescents in Poverty One of the major difficulties many minority groups face is lower income than the majority group. While in recent years, the prospects for increased income for black families have improved, the percentage of black adolescents growing up in poverty and lower class circumstances far outdistanced the percentage of white adolescents in such circumstances (U.S. Bureau of the Census, 1980). Black adolescents experience more poverty in the South than in other regions of the United States. Being in the minority in terms of both ethnicity and income is particularly difficult for an adolescent. Unfortunately, most adolescents from minority backgrounds experience a lifetime of having much less money than many of their white counterparts.

Hispanic, Mexican-American, and Puerto Rican Adolescents

Hispanic Americans are the second largest minority group in the United States, following blacks. The term *Hispanic* refers to anyone of Spanish descent. This includes Mexican-Americans, Puerto Ricans, and Cubans. The majority of Hispanics in the United States are Mexican-American (about sixty percent) and approximately half live either in Texas or California. Hispanic Americans often have the poorest educational backgrounds of all minority groups in the United States, with higher dropout rates and the fewest numbers attending college. Approximately one of five Hispanics drops out of school between the ages of fourteen and nineteen.

Native American Adolescents

Another minority group, the **native Americans** (American Indians), has experienced an extraordinary amount of discrimination. While virtually any minority group experiences some discrimination in being a member of a larger, majority-group culture, in the early years of our country, native Americans were the victims of terrible physical abuse and punishment. Injustices that these 800,000 people have experienced are reflected in the lowest standard of living of any ethnic group, the highest teen-age pregnancy rate, the highest teen-age suicide rate, and the highest high school dropout rate of any ethnic group (Thornburg, 1982).

It is not unusual for relationships between ethnic groups to conflict. Next, we look at ways to improve the relationships of adolescents from different ethnic backgrounds.

Improving Ethnic Relationships

In the last chapter we discussed school desegregation. While desegregation through busing was intended to improve the educational opportunities of black adolescents and improve race relations, there is no evidence that desegregation in itself has been successful. For example, in a survey of more than 120 studies of the effects of desegregation on the academic achievement of elementary and secondary school blacks, there was no evidence that there was improvement among the blacks, and there was no indication that the achievement-orientation of either black or white adolescents was lowered. However, as we have reported, specific classroom and school practices have been shown to promote educational opportunity and improve race relations (Minuchin and Shapiro, 1983). One attempt to improve intergroup relations between black and white adolescents involves the development of structured cooperative-learning situations (e.g., Aronson, Bridgeman, and Geffner, 1978; Sharan, 1980).

Eliot Aronson's "jigsaw classroom" approach to improving ethnic relations is discussed in the Perspective on Adolescent Development 9.4. In this box, we will discuss some analyses of ethnic relations by social psychologist Roger Brown.

In support of the use of structured cooperative-learning situations to reduce ethnic conflict, Slavin (1980) summarized the results of twelve studies—there was improvement in ethnic relations in ten of the studies with no differences in the remaining two. In one investigation (Weigel, Wiser, and Cook, 1975), mixed groups of white, black, and Mexican-American students in

Perspective on Adolescent Development 9.4

THE JIGSAW CLASSROOM AND ETHNIC GROUPS

When the schools of Austin, Texas, were desegregated through extensive busing, the outcome was increased racial tension among blacks, Mexican-Americans, and Anglos, which produced violence in the schools. The superintendent of schools consulted with Eliot Aronson, a prominent social psychologist who then was at the University of Texas in Austin. Aronson thought it was more important to attempt to prevent racial hostility than to control it. This led him to observe a number of elementary school classrooms in Austin. What he saw was intense competition between persons of unequal status.

Aronson stressed that the reward structure of the elementary school classrooms needed to be changed from a setting of unequal competition to a setting of cooperation among equals without making any curriculum changes. Roger Brown (1986) describes an example of how the **jigsaw classroom** that emphasizes cooperation among equals might work. Consider a class of thirty students, some Anglos, some black, and Hispanics. The lesson to be learned focuses on the life of Joseph Pulitzer. The class could be broken up into five groups of six students each, with the groups being as equal as possible in terms of ethnic composition and academic achievement level. The lesson about Pulitzer's life could be divided into six parts, with one part being given to each member of the six-person groups. The parts might be paragraphs from Pulitzer's biography, such as how the Pulitzer family came to the United States, Joseph's childhood and education, Joseph's early work, and so forth. The components are like parts of a jigsaw puzzle in that they have to be put together to form the complete picture.

Each student in the group would be alotted time to study his or her part of the biography. Then, the group would meet together and each member would try to teach his or her part to the group. Subsequently, after an hour or so, each person would be tested on the entire life of Pulitzer, and each person would be given an individual score, not a group score. Each student must, therefore,

What does the jigsaw classroom concept involve?

learn the entire lesson, not just his or her part, and would depend on the five others to help him or her. They, in turn, would depend on him or her to help learn about Pulitzer's life. Aronson believed this type of task increases the interdependence of the students. The jigsaw classroom, thus, emphasizes cooperation in trying to reach a common superordinate goal. Recall from our discussion in Chapter 7 how Sherif and his colleagues were able to reduce intergroup hostilities by setting up an overarching superordinate goal that required the contributions of competing groups to achieve.

A number of research studies were conducted to determine the effectiveness of the jigsaw classroom. Summaries of the research (e.g., Aronson et al., 1978; Blaney et al., 1977) suggest that the interdependent learning strategy is associated with increased self-esteem, academic performance, liking of classmates, and some interethnic and intraethnic perceptions. However, it is important to note that the improvements often were not dramatic and in many cases were very small. And, in one of the assessments, Hispanic students who participated in traditional classrooms liked school better at the end of six weeks than their Hispanic counterparts who participated in the jigsaw classrooms. Consider the problem of Carlos, who stammers and hesitates in presenting his part of a lesson because of language problems. The other members of the group ridicule and tease him. Mary says something like, "Carlos, you dummy, you don't know what you are doing." The inventors of the jigsaw classroom envisioned that students like Carlos eventually would benefit from having their language problems repeatedly exposed. But the students placed in each interethnic group had very different skills. There invariably are differences in a student's ability to present information to others so it can be learned effectively. The jigsaw classroom did not adequately account for such individual variation in skills.

Roger Brown (1986) calls attention to another difficulty with the jigsaw classroom. Academic achievement is necessarily not a team sport, but a game of individual competition. It is individuals who enter college, jobs, and careers, not groups. Aronson recognized the importance of the individual by emphasizing that grades would be assigned to individuals not groups. However, imagine an academically advantaged Anglo student bringing home lower grades than he or she normally has in the past. His father asks him why he is getting lower grades. He tells his father that maybe it's the new way the classes in his school are being taught. He says, "The teacher is getting us to teach each other. In my group, we have this kid named Carlos who can barely speak English." His father says, "Are you kidding? What are we paying these teachers for? I'm calling the principal right now and we are going to get this changed in a hurry!"

Roger Brown (1986) argues that the principles on which the jigsaw classroom are based basically are sound. He comments, "I find . . . that the idea of the jigsaw classroom seems so right and the metaphor so powerful that I resist reading the qualifications, let alone the numbers in the tables of the original articles, because I feel that the jigsaw classroom must work. Besides I want it to (p. 617)." However, Brown worries that the interdependence which is at the heart of the jigsaw classroom may have a built-in, self-destructive feature. When the self-esteem of an individual is lowered, as in the case of the academically advantaged child who brought home lower grades, the tendency is to blame external factors. In the case of Carlos, the academically advantaged child and his father may develop increased ethnic hostility due to such procedures as the jigsaw classroom. In sum, procedures like the jigsaw classroom may benefit some students, but not others, and it does not seem to be a panacea for reducing ethnic hostility.

newly integrated secondary schools were placed in co-operative-learning programs. The members of each group divided their labor and helped each other achieve common goals and rewards as they competed against other groups. The results suggested that harmonious relationships within each group developed across racial lines, as evidenced by more cross-racial helping and less interracial conflict.

Cross-ethnic attitudes also improved in such structured cooperative-learning environments in secondary schools, although the change was not as great as for interracial helping. For example, following cooperative-learning situations in one investigation (Weigel, Wiser, and Cook, 1975), white students said that they liked Mexican-American classmates more, but their feelings toward black classmates did not improve. And there was no increased affinity toward white students on the part of either black or Mexican-American students.

Of course, there are factors outside of the school that influence interracial relationships. Most research on desegregation treats the school as an environmental vacuum in the sense that community and family influences are rarely studied in combination with what is going on within the school (Minuchin and Shapiro, 1983). One relevant investigation (Stephan and Rosenfield, 1978 a, b) focused on the relation between family influences and the attitudes of children and adolescents in a multiethnic school situation. A questionnaire was given to mothers of fifth- and sixth-grade students, eliciting information about authoritarianism, punitiveness, and attitudes toward integration. Two years later, the researchers continued to evaluate a number of students who had been in either segregated schools or triethnic schools. Increased ethnic contact was positively related to the self-esteem of the adolescents, and both of these factors were found to be negatively related to parental punitiveness and authoritarian parenting. Such investigations that attempt to link school and family settings over time have been far too rare in our attempts to understand adolescent development.

As Patricia Minuchin and Edna Shapiro (1983) concluded, it has been assumed that desegregating schools will result in unmitigated good. But contact between different ethnic groups can produce hostility and intensify stereotypes unless such contact is long-term, institutionally sanctioned, and organized between groups of equal status striving for shared goals. Such conditions are very difficult to meet. For many minority students, the school may be the first social institution where they experience the values of a dominant white society. Black students in desegregated schools frequently experience racial prejudice, conflicting values, and difficult academic competition (Rosenberg and Simmons, 1971).

In this section, we have discussed many ideas about social stratification and ethnicity. These ideas are reviewed in Concept Table 9.2. While we already have covered many topics in our exploration of culture, there remain several further concepts that require attention. Next, we investigate the powerful role of the media, particularly television, in the adolescent's development.

The Media and Television: Eighteen Thousand Murders in Twenty-two Thousand Hours

Few developments in the last twenty-five years have had greater impact on children and adolescents than television. Many youth spend more time in front of the television set than they do with their parents. Although television is only one of the vehicles of mass media, it is undoubtedly the most influential. Other influential media include radio, records, and music video.

Television

Think about your experiences with television when you were an adolescent. Was it a positive or negative influence in your life? How much time did you and your friends spend watching television? Did you ever watch any special television programs specifically designed for adolescents?

Concept Table 9.2

SOCIAL CLASS AND ETHNICITY

Concept	Processes/related ideas	Characteristics/description
Social class	What is social class?	Social class refers to social stratification involving socioeconomic status and lifestyle.
	Categorization and measurement	Complete agreement does not exist on the categories of social class. Occupation, education, and income are the most widely used indicators, with occupation often viewed as the most important. While as many as six or more classes have been described, the most common distinction is between middle class and lower or working class.
	Socioeconomic variations in families, schools, and neighborhoods	The families, schools, and neighborhoods of adolescents have socioeconomic characteristics.
	The subculture of the poor	The subculture of the poor is characterized not only by economic poverty, but also by powerlessness, vulnerability to disaster, a limited range of alternatives, low prestige, and few overlapping experiences with the middle class. Social support systems likely are very important in promoting healthy adolescent development in the subculture of the poor.
	Social class, personality, and parenting styles	Lower class adolescents are more likely to have lower self-esteem than their middle-class counterparts. Lower class mothers engage in less verbal interaction with their offspring than middle-class mothers, and lower class parents do not provide as much systematic independence training. However, they often discipline in an authoritarian manner.
	Cautions about interpreting social class research	When we say there are differences between lower class and middle-class adolescents, it does not mean for all adolescents. Remember that there is considerable individual variation within a social class.
Ethnicity	Nature of ethnicity and ethnic groups in the United States	Ethnicity refers to the condition of belonging to a particular ethnic group, membership being based on racial, religious, national, and ancestral background. Blacks and those of Spanish origin are the largest ethnic minority groups in the United States.
	Black adolescents	Erikson's ideas about identity development are important in understanding black adolescents. Currently, there is no evidence that black adolescents have lower self-concepts than white adolescents. The percentage of black adolescents growing up in poverty far outdistances white adolescents.
	Hispanic, Mexican–American, and Puerto Rican adolescents	Hispanic adolescents often have the poorest educational backgrounds of all adolescents.

SOCIAL CLASS AND ETHNICITY

Concept	Processes/related ideas	Characteristics/description
	Native American adolescents	These adolescents have experienced a great deal of discrimination and have had a high suicide, pregnancy, and school dropout rate.
	Improving ethnic relationships	Recall that busing per se has not been demonstrated to have a positive effect on the development of adolescents. Research suggests that structured cooperative-learning situations in some instances can reduce ethnic conflict. The jigsaw classroom is one example of a structured cooperative-learning situation. While the jigsaw classroom concept intuitively seems right, it does not seem to be a panacea for reducing ethnic conflict. The individual differences that students bring to the classroom and factors outside the classroom need to be considered in implementing such structured cooperative-learning circumstances.

The Functions of Television

Television has been called a lot of things, not all of them good; depending upon one's point of view, it is a "window on the world," "a one-eyed monster," or the "boob tube." The functions of television are to entertain and to communicate information. There has been little concern, however, for using television to promote the healthy development of youth. Television is a business, and like all businesses, it is intended to make money. Making money generally takes precedence over public concern when television programming for youth is concerned.

Television has been attacked as one of the reasons that scores on national achievement tests in reading and mathematics are lower now than they have been in the past. Television, it is claimed, distracts adolescents away from books and schoolwork. Furthermore, it is argued, television trains the adolescent to become a passive learner; rarely, if ever, does television call for active responses from the adolescent.

To determine how strong the influence of television is on youth, John Murray and Susan Kippax (1978) evaluated the social behavior of boys and girls in late childhood and early adolescence in three towns located in Australia. The towns were similar in size and social structure, but differed in the frequency, duration, and content of television exposure. Television had been available for five years in the form of both public and commercial stations in the high-TV town. Only one channel, a public TV station, was available in the low-TV town, and it had only existed for a year. No television signals had ever been received in the no-TV town.

The eight-to-twelve-year-old boys and girls and their parents were interviewed individually in their homes. The parent interviews focused on information about the social roles of family members and the parents' perceptions of the influence of television. The interviews with the boys and girls elicited comments about the use and functions of television and other media, why they watched, and their daily life patterns.

Murray and Kippax evaluated the degree to which the boys and girls used six different media sources (radio, records, books, comics, newspapers, and television). There were no differences in media use by the youth in the high- and low-TV towns. In both communities, over sixty percent of the children were likely to watch TV three hours a day or more. However, there

How does television influence the lives of adolescents?

were significant differences when the TV towns were compared with the no-TV town on the five other media. Youth in the no-TV town were much more likely to read comics and to listen to the radio and records than were youth in the TV towns. Newspaper reading by youth was low in all three communities.

Murray and Kippax also investigated the influence of the availability of television on the amount of time youth devote to other leisure and social activities. Youth in the no-TV town spent much more time in leisure activities than did those in the two TV towns. The leisure activities that contributed to these differences included playing and watching sports and other outdoor pastimes.

In addition to taking young people away from other activities, television is also accused of deception; that is, some critics feel that television teaches the adolescent that problems are easily resolved and that everything always comes out right in the end. For example,

on television, it usually takes only thirty to ninety minutes for detectives to sort through a complex array of clues and discover who the killer is—and they always find the killer.

Violence is pictured as a way of life in many television shows. Police often use violence in their fights against evildoers. And the lasting results of violence are rarely made apparent to the adolescent; a person who is injured suffers on the screen for only a few seconds.

Just how much violence is pictured on television? As adolescents move from the ninth through the twelfth grade, they will have seen eighteen thousand murders in twenty-two thousand hours of television—twice the time they spend in twelve years of school. This extensive portrayal of violence on television shows contemporary life as more dangerous than it really is.

The Federal Communications Commission (FCC), a federal agency responsible for monitoring the media, has been reluctant to intervene by requiring networks to air more programs directed toward educating youth (Leifer, Gordon, and Graves, 1974). To its credit, the FCC has developed parent report groups in different areas of the United States to keep track of the number of educational programs compared to the number that merely attempt to entertain. In one year, thirty-two weekend programs supplied to stations by the three major networks followed a straight entertainment format eighty-seven percent of the time. Information on history, science, drama, music, fine arts, human relations, other cultures, language, reading, math, sex roles, and age roles appeared only thirteen percent of the time.

Adolescent Exposure to Television

Children and adolescents watch a lot of television. American adolescents between ages ten and fifteen, for example, watch approximately twenty-three hours of television per week (Schwarz, 1982). As further evidence of how pervasive television is in the United States, on a typical evening between 8:00 and 9:00 P.M., approximately ninety-eight million people are watching their television sets. The Super Bowl alone draws about seventy-five to eighty million viewers each year (Nielson, 1976).

But children's and adolescents' viewing patterns are more complex than just the sheer volume of viewing indicates. Programming preferences change as the adolescent develops. For example, sixth graders choose both situation comedies and adventure programs as their favorites (Lyle, 1972). And, in one investigation (Rubin, 1977), older teenagers liked musical variety shows more than younger teenagers and children did. Any interest in public affairs programs, even in the form of television news, tends to occur late in adolescence if at all. Similarly, educational programs are not generally watched by adolescents.

Older adolescents (seventeen to eighteen years old) do not seem to have as strong an affinity toward television as younger adolescents (thirteen to fourteen years old) do. The older adolescents more readily perceive that television does not adequately reflect reality (Rubin, 1977). The preferences of some adolescents do shift from adventure and comedy shows to variety and public affairs presentations, but most members of the older group simply view slightly less of the same programming they watched in childhood and early adolescence. Changing social needs, increased social demands, and peer and dating activities likely play a role in the reduced TV viewing habits of older adolescents.

Television as a Socialization Agent

George Comstock (1978) argues that television is such a strong socialization force it should be given status as a social agent—competing with parents, teachers, and other agents in providing models for emulation and furnishing information that influences the adolescent's beliefs, values, and expectations. Social scientists are not sure whether this influence is positive or negative. Although a number of negative effects have been observed, there are some possible positive aspects to television's influence on teenagers, as well. For one, television presents to the adolescent worlds that are different from the one he lives in. This means that through television the adolescent is exposed to a wider variety of views, attitudes, and ideas than he would be if he were socialized only by his parents, teachers, and peers. For example, black adolescents report that they use television as a source for ideas about dating (Gerson, 1966).

There is evidence that the level or intensity of certain types of adolescent behavior can be increased through television. For example, erotic and violent sequences (Zillman, 1971), humor (Tannenbaum, 1972), and unresolved dramatic climax (Zillman, Johnson, and Hanrahan, 1973) have been demonstrated to physiologically excite or arouse the adolescent.

Television is also a medium through which the adolescent can acquire new behaviors via the process of observational learning (e.g., Bandura, 1977). The modeling theory of Albert Bandura has served as a theoretical source for a number of inquiries about the effects of television on youth. The results from a number of studies indicate that television violence contributes to the adolescent's aggressive behavior, although there is no evidence that the aggression will be antisocial in nature (e.g., Comstock, 1972; Liebert, Neale, and Davidson, 1973). In one investigation, the amount of television violence observed during the elementary school years was linked with the aggressive tendencies of adolescents at the age of nineteen (Lefkowitz et al., 1972).

But television viewing may influence the prosocial behavior of adolescents as well. In an intriguing laboratory and field investigation of antisocial and prosocial television content, Ann McCabe and Richard Moriarity (1977) were able to demonstrate that prosocial activities portrayed in television sports were significantly related to the incidence of prosocial behavior adolescents engaged in when they played hockey, baseball, and lacrosse. In the study, television sports events were shown to ten-to-thirteen year olds and fourteen-to-seventeen year olds. The sports shows were edited so the focus was on a high incidence of either prosocial or aggressive content. A control group of adolescents viewed sports shows with neutral content. Prosocial behavior was defined as any verbal or nonverbal act that appears to encourage, console, or otherwise enhance the well-being of another person or group.

The effects of exposure to prosocial incidents in TV sports shows were relatively long-lasting. In the hockey group, an increased incidence of prosocial behavior lasted as long as twenty-four hours following the sports shows; for the baseball group prosocial behavior lasted as long as a week; and for the lacrosse group, prosocial behavior continued for one to three weeks. In this particular study, viewing the antisocial, aggressive TV sports shows did not influence the adolescents' incidence of aggressive behavior.

Television, then, influences the adolescent, just as input from parents, teachers, and peers does. It is important to evaluate television viewing patterns in the context of parental and peer influences. For example,

one survey indicated that parents rarely discuss the content of TV shows with their adolescents (e.g., Leifer, Gordon, and Graves, 1974). Clearly, those interested in understanding the development of the adolescent can no longer ignore the powerful influence of the mass media, particularly television.

Special Television Programs for Early Adolescents

For many years, early adolescents were ignored by the television networks. They were too old for Saturday morning cartoons and too young for the adult fare of evening television. However, as Squire Rushnell (1982) reports, in the early 1970s, ABC television began a series of bimonthly specials designed for early adolescents. These programs, called the "ABC Afterschool Specials," were aired after school hours in the afternoons. In one of the first specials, a young girl attempted to break through existing sex barriers to play on a baseball team.

These afterschool specials have attracted a significant audience. For example, in 1979 and 1980, twenty-three percent of the TV audience was tuned in to the early-adolescent specials. The specials tackle such topics as teenage alcoholism, the effects of marijuana, unwed pregnancy, runaways, divorce, and parenting styles, with each topic explored from the adolescent's point of view. In 1977, one afterschool special, "My Mom's Having a Baby," was the highest-rated daytime special in network history. And, in 1979, a sequel called "Where Do Teenagers Come From?" explained to adolescents the complexities of puberty.

In addition to the ABC Afterschool Specials, NBC began a similar type of program called "NBC Special Treats," and CBS soon produced the "CBS Library Series," both of which are late-afternoon shows designed for an adolescent audience. These programs were developed to enhance the adolescent's understanding of herself and her world. They seem to be a very effective learning tool, and it is hoped that television networks will continue and expand such programming targeted for adolescent audiences.

BLOOM COUNTY

by Berke Breathed

Radio, Records, and Other Media

Anyone who has been around teenagers very often knows that many of them spend huge chunks of time listening to music on the radio and playing records or tapes of their favorite music. For example, sixty-four percent of all records and tapes in 1984 were purchased by listeners aged ten to twenty-four years old. And one-third of the nation's 8,200 radio stations broadcast rock music aimed at a pool of adolescent listeners.

The music that adolescents enjoy on records, tapes, and the radio is an important aspect of their culture. Rock music does not seem to be a passing fad—it has now been around for more than thirty years. The themes of many rock songs are geared to adolescent problems and dreams. Such songs no longer contain lyrics that reflect protest as much as they did in the 1960s and early 1970s—instead, songs oriented toward youth now tend to stress love and the development of relationships (Seltzer, 1976). The positive role rock stations can play in adolescents' lives is described in Perspective on Adolescent Development 9.5.

Record playing and radio listening increase dramatically during adolescence. When adolescents want to relax, to entertain themselves, or to avoid loneliness, listening to music is one of the activities that will help them (Avery, 1979). In one investigation, listening to music was rated second only to going away alone as a way to cope with anger and hurt feelings. There actually has been a decrease in radio listening by adolescents in recent years, but this is probably due to the increased availability of record and tape systems (Avery, 1979).

In recent years, music video has become a prominent part of the media world adolescents experience. Adolescents often push parents to pay the cable fee required to obtain access to MTV, the cable music video station. And parents, in return, often question the degree to which violence and sexuality are portrayed in the music videos. Thus, music videos may be involved in the confrontation between adolescents and their parents in terms of what the adolescent should be allowed to do and whether exposure to sexuality and violence is basically bad for the adolescent. Further, music videos may assume a role in the friendship network of the adolescent and the life of latchkey adolescents. Adolescents who have access to music video may increase their popularity by inviting others to come to their home to watch and listen to the videos. And, in the case of latchkey adolescents, less monitoring of the music videos is likely.

Adolescent females are evidently more likely to listen to music on the radio than adolescent males. Some broadcasting researchers point out, however, that "top forty" listeners are not always teenagers (Lull, Johnson,

RADIO, ROCK, AND RESPONSIBILITY

For "Moose"
A song just played on my radio.
Yes, I know, an innocent mistake.
Some unknowing DJ just didn't realize.
But I heard it in my ears and can see it in my eyes.
That haunting memory
Ripping my insides; lighting a fire
I extinguished many years before.
I guess you never believed
Everything I told you then.
The night was cruel and gave no comfort
To our tears.
It's over now, I know, but
That song just played on my radio.
(Karyn Chater, Camden-Rockport High School, 1982)

Radio stations, through the songs they play, tell adolescents, "tonight's the night," "good girls don't, but I do," and "my Sharonna should feel it growin' down my thigh." Michael Hirsch (1982) believes it would be wrong to tell rock stations not to play such songs, but that rock radio stations should be doing a better job of airing helpful information about adolescent issues and problems. For example, in Chicago, WLS, a station so powerful that on clear nights it often reaches adolescent audiences in as many as forty-three states, has begun to air a twenty-five-minute program called "Express." This program has dealt with an array of adolescent concerns, including venereal disease, pregnancy, parent–adolescent conflict, peer relations, and dating. One Express show presented the best entries in an essay contest entitled, "The hardest thing about being a teenager is . . ." The entries read on the air focused on such varied matters as problems with parents, not having enough freedom, and not being allowed to stay out late enough.

Public service radio spots that are read by famous individuals that adolescents identify with may serve an important function as well. An example of how such radio spots were used to provide adolescents with information about responsible parenthood follows:

LINDA RONSTADT

I had a roommate, this girl had a kid and she stayed with me, and I really got a first-hand experience at caring for a kid. I know exactly how much responsibility is involved. It's more than anybody dreams of that doesn't have a kid and I know that sometime I'll have time for it. I don't think anything should stop people, like "Oh, this is a terrible world" to have children or any of that stuff, but what should stop them is whether they really think they're ready to handle it.

and Sweeney, 1978). Young adults, who apparently became hooked on rock music during their adolescent years, choose a top forty music station as their favorite more than teenagers do. Such data point to the pervasive influence of the youth culture on other age segments.

Moviegoing among adolescents seems to vary greatly from town to town, depending on the availability of theaters and competing recreational activities. Most adolescents see moviegoing as simply a source of entertainment; but in some cases, moviegoing facilities provide a locale for dating and a source of discussion topics for peer groups (McLeod and O'Keefe, 1972).

Adolescents also begin to read the newspaper more than when they were children. In one investigation, almost all tenth graders interviewed said they had ready access to a newspaper in their homes. While children usually are drawn to the newspaper because they are interested in reading the comics, adolescents become more interested in local news, sports, personal advice columns (particularly girls), and entertainment sections (Avery, 1979).

JANIS IAN

Ian: I know people who have had babies 'cause they wanted their old man to marry them. To have a kid in order to leave home is out of the frying pan into the fire. To have a kid to get married: it's a *huge* step; it's a life-long commitment.

Announcer: The Rock Project asks you to think about having a child before you make a baby.

CHIC

Announcer: We asked Nile Rogers of Chic about who *is* responsible for birth control.

Rogers: That's another thing that really bothers me is the lack of responsibility on both parts. In other words, it has to be a mutual thing. If she's not prepared and you're not prepared, oh well, then you just, you know, kiss and shake hands or something. You know, like, accidents, man, are a drag.

Announcer: For information about birth control call The Answer line at 942–6006. That number again is 942–6006.

MUHAMMAD ALI

Announcer: Muhammed Ali, do you think being a teenage father would have affected your career?

Ali: I think it would have affected my life. I wasn't making no money at the time. I would have had to get out and work to support the child and take care of it. At the age of seventeen or eighteen I don't think I could have put my mind fully to boxing like I did.

Announcer: Nobody wins with an unwanted pregnancy.

Text of public service radio spots on responsible parenthood, courtesy of the Center for Population Options.

Magazine reading also increases during adolescence (Avery, 1979). Teenagers are more likely to read weekly news magazines than children are. There do not seem to be any sex differences in the amount of magazine reading during adolescence, but as would be anticipated, boys prefer men's and sports magazines (such as *Playboy* and *Sports Illustrated*), while girls choose young people's, women's, and fashion magazines (for example, *Seventeen, Redbook,* and *McCall's*).

Interesting comparisons between pictorial and printed media have been made by Greenberg and Dominick (1969). Television, movies, and comic strips are examples of pictorial media; the youth who uses any one of these pictorial media tends to use the others also. But youth who frequently use pictorial media are not high consumers of newspapers and magazines. Use of pictorial media increases until children are about twelve, after which it declines.

And as we learned in the section of this chapter on social class, adolescents from middle-class families are more likely to read frequently and watch television less than their working-class counterparts.

Summary

I. Information about culture includes ideas on the cultural process, the adolescent culture, and cross-cultural comparisons.

   A. The cultural process is broad and complex, and is difficult to systematize.

      1. Culture refers to the behavior patterns, beliefs, values, and other products of humans that are learned and shared by a particular group of people and passed on from one generation to the next.

      2. Bronfenbrenner argues that systematic analyses of culture have been too few in number. He proposes that the culture of adolescents can be better understood if it is divided into these parts: microsystem, mesosystem, and exosystem. The community context often becomes an important part of the adolescent's exosystem.

      3. The "beeper" study of Csikszentmihalyi and Larson focused on the locations where adolescents spend their time, what they do, and with whom they associate. Adolescents spent more time at home than in any other location, although they spent considerable time at school and in public places as well. About twenty-nine percent of time was spent in productive activities, primarily school work. Adolescents also spent considerable time socializing and they were much more likely to interact with their peers than their parents or other adults.

   B. The adolescent's culture includes information about adolescent interests and values, language, and youth movements.

      1. The opposite sex, sex, and love are high on the interest lists of adolescents. Freedom, true friendship, and happiness rank very high on adolescents' lists of values.

      2. The adolescent culture often is characterized by the use of slang expressions. Cliques often take on their own distinctive language style.

      3. While activist, rebellious youth movements have often captured a great deal of media attention in the history of studying adolescents, in reality, such youth usually represent only a visible, vocal minority of adolescents. Youth movements frequently are associated with political issues.

   C. Information about cross-cultural comparisons focuses on the anthropological view and a number of cross-cultural evaluations.

      1. The anthropological view stresses the scientific study of the origin of human beings and cultural influences on their development. Anthropologists believe that many cultural variations survive from one generation to the next.

      2. Adolescents in the United States are more achievement oriented than those in many other cultures. The substance of moral prohibition may vary from one culture to another. Garbarino and

Bronfenbrenner believe that exposure to multiple social agents and sociopolitical ideas promotes moral development. There is considerable variation in sexual behavior when adolescents from different cultures are observed. In some primitive societies, rites of passage signal the sexual maturity of the adolescent.

II. Social class and ethnicity represent two important variations in a culture.

A. Information about social class involves what the concept is, categorization and measurement, socioeconomic variations in families, schools, and neighborhoods, the subculture of the poor, personality and parenting styles, and cautions about interpreting social-class research.

   1. Social class refers to social stratification involving socioeconomic matters and lifestyle.

   2. Complete agreement does not exist on the categorizations of social class. Occupation, education, and income are the three most widely used markers, with occupation often the main characteristic. While as many as six or more classifications have been proposed, the most common distinction is between middle and lower or working class.

   3. The families, schools, and neighborhoods of adolescents have socioeconomic characteristics.

   4. The subculture of the poor is characterized not only by economic poverty, but also by powerlessness, vulnerability to disaster, a limited range of alternatives, low prestige, and few overlapping experiences with the middle class. Social support systems likely are very important in promoting healthy adolescent development in the subculture of the poor.

   5. Lower class adolescents are more likely to have lower self-esteem than middle-class adolescents. Lower class mothers engaged in less verbal interaction with their offspring than their middle-class counterparts. And lower class parents are more likely to be authoritarian in their discipline and provide less systematic training for independence than middle-class parents.

   6. When we say there are differences between lower and middle-class adolescents, it does not mean for all adolescents. There is considerable variation among adolescents within a particular social class.

B. Ideas about ethnicity involve the nature of ethnicity and ethnic groups in the United States, black adolescents, Hispanic, Mexican-American, and Puerto Rican adolescents, native American adolescents, and improving ethnic relationships.

1. Ethnicity refers to the condition of belonging to a particular ethnic group, membership being based on racial, religious, national, and ancestral background. Blacks and those of Spanish origin are the largest ethnic minority groups in the United States.

2. Erikson's ideas about identity development are important in understanding black adolescents. There is no evidence that black adolescents have a lower self-concept than white adolescents. The percentage of black adolescents in poverty contexts far outdistances white adolescents.

3. Hispanic adolescents often have the poorest educational backgrounds of all adolescents in the United States.

4. Native American adolescents have experienced a great deal of discrimination and have high suicide, pregnancy, and drop-out rates.

5. Recall that busing per se has not been demonstrated to have a positive effect on adolescent development. Research suggests that structured cooperative-learning situations in some instances can reduce ethnic conflict. The jigsaw classroom is one example of a structured cooperative-learning context. While the jigsaw classroom seems intuitively right, it does not appear to be a panacea for reducing ethnic conflict. The individual differences that students bring to the classroom and factors outside the classroom, such as community and parental attitudes, need to be considered in implementing such cooperative-learning contexts.

III. Information about the media, particularly television, provides further insight about the culture that adolescents experience.

A. To learn more about television ideas that need to be studied, we need to include the functions of television, adolescent exposure to television, television as a social agent, and special television programs for adolescents.

1. Few developments in the cultural milieu have had a greater impact on adolescents in the last three decades than television. The functions of television are to communicate and to entertain. There has been little concern about the use of television to help promote the healthy development of adolescents.

2. Children and adolescents watch a lot of television. From the ninth through twelfth grades, adolescents are exposed to eighteen thousand murders in twenty-two thousand hours of television viewing. Older adolescents do not seem to have as strong an affinity for television as younger adolescents.

3. Some experts believe television should be given status as a socialization agent. Television influences both the antisocial and prosocial behaviors of adolescents.

4. For many years, early adolescents have been virtually ignored by the television networks, with TV fare being mainly directed at young children and adults. In recents years, some networks have developed afterschool specials for adolescents.

B. Adolescents spend huge chunks of time listening to music on the radio or playing records/tapes of their favorite music. Rock music does not seem to be a passing fad. In recent years, music videos have gained considerable popularity among adolescents. Popular music designed for adolescents today contains more reflections of love and relationships than it did in the late 1960s and early 1970s, and less political overtones. Youth who frequently use pictorial media are often low users of printed media.

Key Terms

Suggested Readings

"Action for children's television." (1982). In *TV and Teens,* ed. M. Schwarz. Reading, Mass.: Addison-Wesley.
A very easy-to-read, exciting overview of what is being done and what should be done in television and radio programming for adolescents.

Bronfenbrenner, U. and Crouter, A. C. (1983). "The evolution of environmental models in developmental research." In P. H. Mussen (Ed.), *Handbook of Child Psychology,* 4th ed., vol. 1. New York: Wiley.
A thorough presentation of Bronfenbrenner's ideas about micro-, meso-, and exosystems is made.

Csikszentmihalyi, M. and Larson, R. (1984). *Being adolescent.* New York: Basic Books, 1984.
This book describes in considerable detail the lives of seventy-five adolescents—where they spend their time, what they do, and with whom they associate.

Havighurst, R. J. (1976). "A cross-cultural view." In J. F. Adams (Ed.), *Understanding Adolescence.* Boston: Allyn and Bacon.
Presents ideas that are important in the sociological and anthropological views of adolescence. Series of data about national characteristics of adolescents in different countries and in subcultures of countries.

Hess, R. D. (1970). "Social class and ethnic influences on socialization." In P. H. Mussen (Ed.), *Carmichael's Manual of Child Psychology,* 3rd ed., vol. 2. New York: John Wiley.
A comprehensive and critical survey of the effects of social class on the social development of youth. Discusses a wide variety of theoretical and research issues pertaining to social class.

Sommer, B. B. (1978). *Puberty and adolescence.* New York: Oxford.
An easy-to-read overview of many aspects of puberty, including extensive information about rites of passage.

Part 4

Social, Emotional, and Personality Processes and Development

Angela Bliss is ten years old. When asked to describe herself as a person, she replies that she has blonde hair and blue eyes and that she will be eleven in December. She also says she is a girl, that she likes to play soccer, and that she likes school. Angela hasn't shown much interest in boys yet, although she is in a school system that includes some sex education in the late elementary grades. She goes to church with her parents every Sunday, yet she is rather naive about religion and spiritual matters. Her moral development has progressed to the point where she believes that when people do something wrong they should be punished for it.

Angela is achievement oriented, but is more motivated in English class than in math. She is a somewhat feminine young girl, not much of a tomboy. Her father is the single breadwinner in their family, and her parents have reared her to follow rather traditional sex roles. Angela really hasn't thought much about a future career, but she says she wouldn't mind being a beauty queen.

Frank Martin is also ten years old. When asked to describe himself as a person, he responds, "I am strong, big for my age, and I have lots of friends. I love sports, and I want to be a professional football player when I grow up." Frank hasn't shown much interest in girls yet, preferring to spend most of his spare time with his male buddies in sports activities or just fooling around the neighborhood. Frank is just an average student and is not very achievement oriented—his father has rewarded him mostly for his accomplishments in sports.

When we reenter Angela Bliss's life at the age of fourteen we find that she is now able to describe herself as "a truthful person, reasonably pretty, and well liked by both boys and girls." Her sexual maturation has changed dramatically since we last saw her at the age of ten—she has almost fully matured physically, and she shows a much stronger interest in boys. She still sees herself as being very feminine, and acts accordingly. She has begun to think about religious and spiritual matters and has thought about joining the church she attends. Angela's moral system could best be described as conventional—she believes rules and regulations should be abided by and that it is morally wrong to violate those rules. She continues to like school, but she is still doing better in English than in math. Angela has started thinking more about a career—she is taking a career education class at her school, and she is considering four or five possible vocations.

When we look at Frank's life at the age of fourteen and ask him to once again describe himself as a person, he says, "I am a good football player and I am popular at school. A lot of girls like me, and I have a lot of male buddies as well. We hang around a lot together. Me and my friend, Mark, are a lot alike—he's good in athletics, neither one of us studies very much, and we usually have a good time." Frank likes girls, and they seem to like him. Almost every night, he says, a girl calls him. Frank sees himself as very masculine—"macho," he says. His moral orientation at age fourteen is based on expedience—it's all right to do some things that are not accepted by parents or the police as long as you don't get burned. Frank hasn't thought much about a possible career—he says he is too busy having fun and will think more about a career when the time comes to go to work. Church has never played much part in Frank's life, since neither of his parents go. Last year he did go to a church youth group with one of his buddies, but he went more for social than spiritual reasons.

At age nineteen, Angela Bliss has just finished her first year of college. She still hasn't decided on an occupation or work she would like to pursue in life. She has given some thought to getting married and raising a family, letting a husband support her. Angela is not exactly sure what she wants from life, but over the last couple of years she has spent a lot of time thinking about it. Her identity has not yet crystalized, but she doesn't sense any need to hurry out into the world and commit herself to a husband or to some type of work at this point. Angela is still very feminine and doesn't really like to be pushed into more ''masculine'' sex roles— she feels secure in her feminine role.

Angela is still a virgin, but she has been tempted to have intercourse on more than one occasion with the guy she has been dating for eight months. She still shows a conventional orientation toward rules and regulations and believes they should be abided by—it bothered her last month when her roommate cheated on a test. She also believes that moral values are important in relationships. Indeed, for Angela probably the most important aspect of morality is the interdependence that two people develop and the commitment they give to each other. When asked if her personality has changed much during her adolescent years, she responds that she basically is the same old Angela, but that in some ways her personality has gradually changed. She feels more mature now than when she was in junior high—she thinks more before she does something impulsive, and she is more conscientious about her study habits. She also says she is a little more outgoing now than when she was in junior high, but she realizes that how extraverted she is often depends on the situation and whom she is with at the time.

At age nineteen, Frank Martin has completed high school but elected not to go to college. He has worked for a year in an automobile repair shop—during his last two years of high school he worked part-time there, and worked close to full-time during the summer. Frank is still recognized around town as the guy who intercepted a pass and scored a touchdown to win the state championship in football when he was a junior in high school, and Frank still thinks a lot about his last several years of high school and his football stardom. Unfortunately, he injured his knee during his senior year—and this, combined with his deteriorating high school grades, made Frank a rather unattractive candidate for college football. Frank still sees himself as ''macho.'' He lost his virginity when he was sixteen. In the last six months he has had sex with his steady girlfriend about three or four times a week, and he is unofficially engaged to be married to her. But Frank isn't sure that marriage is what he wants— he says that his fiancée and her parents want the marriage more than he does but that he will probably go along.

Chapter 10

The Self and Identity

Prologue

Family experiences likely play an important role in the adolescent's development of identity. When involved in a family planning activity, Carol's father said, "I think probably what we all ought to do is decide the things that we want to do, each one of us individually. And, then maybe we'll be able to reconcile from that point . . . Let's go ahead and take a few minutes to decide where we'd like to go and what we would like to do. And, maybe we'll be able to work in everything everybody wants to do in these fourteen days. Okay?" In this planning of a two-week vacation, Carol, her mother, and her father all were active and involved, displaying humor, candor, spontaneity, and vulnerability. For example, Carol's mother commented, "I think we all have good imaginations," while the father said, "I think that's kind of nice. I think we ought to be a rich gang."

Carol seemed to be aware of her role in the family and of the boundary between the adolescent and parent generations. During her identity interview, she said, "I have a say, but not a deciding vote in family decisions." Carol's identity exploration rating . . . was very high. A distinctive quality of her identity exploration was that she experienced her parents as providing room for her to explore beyond their own experiences or needs.

For example, she reported that both parents felt that religion had been forced on them as children, so they decided not to force it on her. Consequently, she had been able to explore several religions as possible alternatives with her friends. In the domain of friendship, Carol had maintained a relationship with a girl who had been a close friend, but who later became involved with drugs and turned against her parents. Carol had been able to maintain this relationship and see how it differed from her other close friendships without compromising her own standards. Her parents were concerned about this friendship, but they trusted Carol and permitted her to work through this situation. In a comparable pattern, Carol's score of fifteen on the Role-Taking Task was also very high. She achieved the highest reciprocal level score by clearly coordinating the perspective of two characters in her story and by elaborating both their external and psychological states.

In contrast, the family of Janet, the firstborn of two, reflected nonindividuated spousal and parent–child relationships with few disagreements, self-assertions that largely coincided with the family's point of view, and frequent expressions of connectedness. The ratio of agreements to disagreements between mother and father (sixteen) was unusually high, suggesting a marked imbalance between expression of individuality and connectedness. In addition, Janet disagreed with her father only once, and he never disagreed with her, whereas she was responsive to him twenty-nine times, and he was responsive to her ten times. Enmeshment in this family's interaction was illustrated in the first five utterances on the Family Interaction Task:

Mother: Where shall we go?
Father: Back to Spain.
Mother: Back to Spain.
Janet: Back to Spain.
Sister: Back to Spain.

When Janet's father later asked for more suggestions, she said, "And then, I don't . . . I mean, you go on, Dad, 'cause I don't know . . . what else."

Janet's low identity exploration rating of thirteen may reflect a lack of exploration of issues outside the consensual family beliefs. In this family, in which signs of individuated spousal and parent–child relationships were less evident, the necessity for agreement and connectedness among family members and the family members' excessive involvement in each other's identity appeared to hinder the adolescent's development of individual ideas regarding career, dating, and other issues. With regard to career choice, Janet commented, "I'm having a hard time deciding what to do. It would be easier if they would tell me what to do, but of course I don't want that."

Janet's low role-taking score of nine suggests a lack of ability to express both separate and reciprocal points of view. While telling her story, Janet commented, "I don't know what the others are thinking, because I'm thinking of it only as if I'm the girl." Perhaps the nonindividuated communication patterns that Janet observed in her parents' relationship and that she participated in with her father inhibited her ability both to engage in identity exploration and to coordinate different perspectives (Cooper, Grotevant, and Condon, 1983, pp. 54–55).

In these excerpts from the lives of two adolescent girls, we have seen the importance of family interaction in the development of identity. Later in the chapter, we explore in greater detail the role of family experiences in the adolescent's quest for identity.

Preview

*E*rik Erikson's ideas about identity development continue to represent one of the most powerful and provocative views of adolescence. Many experts consider Erikson's ideas to be the single most influential theory of adolescent development. For this reason, it is impossible to confine his work to a single chapter. Erikson's ideas have been interwoven throughout this book, but it is in this chapter that we devote the most attention to his work. The theme of identity development in adolescence is closely aligned with the study of the self. In the first part of this chapter, we explore many facets of the self in adolescence and then turn our attention to identity in the second part.

The Self: "There Is No One Quite Like Me"

Adolescents carry within them a sense of who they are and what makes them different from everyone else. They cling to this identity and begin to feel secure in the knowledge that this identity is becoming more stable. "I am male, bright, an athlete, a political liberal, an extravert, and a compassionate person," thinks one eighteen year old. And he takes comfort in his uniqueness: "There is no one quite like me. I am 5'9" tall and weigh 140 pounds. I grew up on a farm and attend the state university, where I take courses in secondary education. I am not married, but some of my friends are. I want to be a Home Economics teacher, I am expert at building canoes, and when I am not studying for exams, I write science-fiction stories that I hope to publish some day." Real or imagined, an adolescent's developing sense of identity and uniqueness is a strong motivating force in his life.

"I" and "Me": The Self As Knower and As Object

Most scholars who have devoted thoughtful attention to understanding the self have concluded that two distinct, but closely intertwined, aspects of self exist (Harter, 1983): the **self as knower** and the **self as object.** Such a distinction was made very early in psychology by William James (1890–1963), who described the "I" as knower in contrast to the "Me" as aggregate of things objectively known. More recently, Ruth Wylie (1979) has continued the distinction between I and Me in understanding the self. She contrasts the self as active agent or process with the self as the object of one's knowledge and evaluation. The I, then, is the active observer, while the Me is the observed (that is, the product of the observing process when attention to the self occurs). However, most research attention has been given to the self as an object of one's knowledge and evaluation as indicated by the many studies of children's self-concept and self-esteem (Wylie, 1979). Self-concept and self-esteem are viewed as objects of one's knowledge in this categorization of the self. First, we focus on the topics of self-concept and self-esteem, and then turn to the recent emphasis on the self as knower.

Self-Concept

Early in the history of psychology William James showed a strong interest in the self. During the twentieth century, the psychologists most interested in the self are humanists. These psychologists follow the tradition of **humanism,** which places a strong emphasis on the role of the self and self-concept as central to understanding the child's development (Rogers, 1961; Maslow, 1971; Gordon, 1975). The humanistic approaches have little scientific credibility. Indeed, the humanists believe scientific approaches keep the investigator from learning the most important facts about the child's existence—his or her uniqueness as a person and creative potential for instance. In this regard, the humanists believe that science is too concerned with general principles that are common to all adolescents rather than discovering the unique nature of each adolescent. Humanists also believe that to understand the adolescent, it is necessary to evaluate the adolescent's global self. In particular, the adolescent's **global self-concept,** how he or she generally perceives himself or herself, is seen as the key organizing principle of personality.

Theorists, like the humanists, who advocate the importance of such global self-perceptions, are taking a **phenomenological approach** to the study of adolescence. That is, the adolescent's perception of himself or herself is more important in understanding what he or she is like than his or her actual behavior. From this view, reality exists in adolescents' perceptions rather than in their actual behavior. As you can readily imagine, this view contrasts with the view of behaviorists, who argue that reality exists in behavior, not perceptions.

Carl Rogers (1961,1969) is one of the humanistic architects of self-concept theory. Rogers has argued that the adolescent needs to find congruence between the self that he or she perceives and real world experiences. From Rogers' view, when the adolescent finds this congruence between the self that he or she perceives and real world experiences, the adolescent is likely to be better adjusted than when there is a lack of congruence.

In our discussion of the cognitive development of the adolescent, we have seen that adolescents often portray a strong idealistic orientation. Rogers has emphasized the importance of distinguishing between the **ideal self** and the **real self.** The real self is the self as it really is, whereas the ideal self is the self the adolescent would like to be. While Rogers generally believes that the greater the discrepancy between the ideal and real selves, the more maladjusted an individual will be, this prediction may not always hold true during adolescence as the adolescent's thoughts often take wings. Thus, particularly in early adolescence, there is nothing unusual about an adolescent having a strong discrepancy between the ideal self and the real self. By the end of adolescence and the beginning of early adulthood, it is likely that the ideal and real self are more closely aligned as the individual is forced into more pragmatic roles.

One recent study of parenting practices and self-esteem of preschool children revealed the importance of the consistency in parenting and the sensitivity of parents to the young child's signals (Burkett, 1985). In particular, the parents' respect for their children as individuals separate from them and as having their own needs were the best predictors of the preschool child's self-esteem. And, in another investigation, Jack Block (1985) reported information from a longitudinal inquiry about the self. He found that parent–child relationships in the early childhood years are related to the adolescent's self-esteem. In general, when young children experienced family environments that were supportive, active, nonconflicted, and articulated (e.g., complex and sophisticated), they were likely to show high self-esteem during the adolescent years. These results characterized both boys and girls, but were stronger for boys.

Another investigation (Coopersmith, 1967) provides further evidence of the importance of parenting strategies in determining the adolescent's self-esteem. The following parental characteristics were significantly linked with the boys' self-esteem: expression of affection, concern about the child's problems, harmony in the home, participation in friendly joint activities, availability to give competent, organized help when needed, setting clear and fair rules, abiding by these rules, and allowing the child freedom within well-prescribed limits.

Many studies indicate a positive correlation between the youth's concept of himself and different measures of achievement and school performance (e.g., Taylor, Winne, and Marx, 1975). These studies seem to show that a student who thinks well of himself excels in school. But what is the nature of this relationship? Does the adolescent do well in school because he has a positive self-concept? Or does he have a positive self-concept because he does well in school? There is evidence that the latter is closer to the truth. A teacher or counselor will apparently be more successful in changing a student's behavior (elevating his achievement level) and thereby improving the student's self-image than in changing the self-image and, as a result, improving achievement (Bandura, 1969).

The Self As Knower

A number of contemporary researchers are beginning to develop insight into the self as knower (Greenwald and Pratkanis, in press; Lewis and Brooks-Gunn, 1979; Dickstein, 1977; Broughton, 1981; Lapsley and Quintana, 1985; Harter, 1983; Gergen, in press). The interest is in crafting an account of the self that not only encompasses the self as object of knowledge, attention, and evaluation, but one that also includes the self as an active observing process. Thus, there is interest in combining I and Me into a common theoretical account of the self. One of the first steps is to establish the domain of the self as knower. The approach in contemporary psychology offering the most help in such a project is information processing (Lapsley and Quintana, 1985). Some researchers call on a computer metaphor to distinguish between self-concept and the self as knower (Greenwald and Pratkanis, in press). That is, the self-concept is analogous to computer content (what is stored in memory) and the self as knower is much like a computer program.

One area of interest that is emerging in the investigation of the self as knower is memory development. Two aspects of memory thought to reflect the self as knower are self-generation and self-reference. Self-generation describes instances when information that is self-generated is more easily retrieved and recalled than information that is passively encountered (Bobrow and Bower, 1969; Jacoby, 1978). For instance, individuals are more likely to recall their own contributions to discussion of a controversial topic than the inputs of others (Greenwald and Albert, 1968). Self-reference refers to the efficient retrieval of information encoded in terms of the self as opposed to information not self encoded.

There is a clear indication in a number of memory studies that individuals are more likely to remember information that is encoded about the self than information that is not self-referenced (Rogers, 1981; Markus, 1977; Greenwald, 1981). For example, in one investigation (Rogers, Kuiper, and Kirker, 1977), individuals were given either physical, acoustic, or semantic-meaning kinds of tasks. Another group of people were asked whether a particular word could be related to themselves. As suggested by figure 10.1, self-reference was the most effective strategy. For example, if the word *win* were on the list, you might think of the time you won a bicycle race, and if the word *cook* appeared, you might image the last time you cooked dinner.

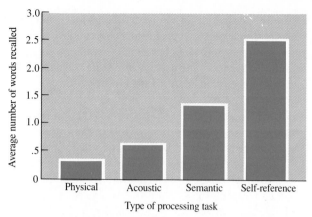

Figure 10.1   **Number of words recalled as a function of level of processing.**

The future is likely to see more investigations of the self as knower and how such processing of information about the self is linked with self-concept. However, as indicated earlier, by far the greatest amount of research has been directed at understanding the self as object, in particular self-concept. Next, we look at some problems in measuring self-concept and then turn to some developmental characteristics of self-conceptions.

Measuring Self-Concept

Although it generally is accepted that every adolescent has a self-concept and that self-evaluation is an important aspect of personality, measuring self-concept has not been an easy task.

The Traditional Approach

A widely used measure of self-concept is the Piers–Harris Scale (Piers and Harris, 1964). It reflects a traditional approach to evaluating self-concept by obtaining a score that reveals an overall estimation of the adolescent's self-worth. By responding yes or no to such items as "I have good ideas," adolescents reveal how they view themselves. The Piers–Harris as well as

Information about social skills provides one index of perceived competence on the Harter Scale.

Physical skills are evaluated as an important dimension on the Harter Scale.

other traditional self-concept and self-esteem scales (e.g., the Coopersmith Self-Esteem Inventory), include items that range across many different areas of the individual's life. It is hoped that by sampling the adolescent's self-perceptions across many different domains of his or her life, a more accurate assessment of general self-worth can be attained. Also, in addition to asking the adolescent about how he or she feels about himself or herself in certain domains (how do you usually feel about yourself when you are with your peers and friends?), such tests usually include some global self-worth items (I like myself very much).

Some Contemporary Measures of Self-Concept

One of the major problems with the traditional measures of self-concept is their inability to assess situational variability in self-concept. Indeed, this has been a problem of most measures of personality and intelligence in general. The adolescent's self-perceptions may not be the same in all domains of life. For example, the adolescent may have a positive self-perception in regard to academic matters but a negative self-perception in reference to social activities. The traditional measures of self-concept provided an overall indication of self-concept, but did not break such perceptions down into different domains to determine how self-perceptions might possibly vary. Let's look at two measures that have been developed recently that provide measurement of general self-worth as well as self-perceptions in different domains.

A promising measure of self-concept, called the Perceived Competence Scale for Children, was recently developed by Susan Harter (1982). While Harter's scale has not yet been standardized for adolescents, it has important implications for the study of self-concept during adolescence. Harter emphasizes the individual's sense of competence across different domains rather than viewing perceived competence as a unitary concept. Three types of skills are assessed on separate subscales: cognitive (academic abilities, memory skills); social (relationships with friends, feelings about self as viewed by others); and physical (athletic abilities and sportsmanship). A fourth subscale, evaluating general self-worth (self-confidence, feelings toward self), and independent of any particular skill domain, is also included.

Table 10.1 Scales and sample items from SIQYA

Scale (item example)

1. Impulse Control
   (I keep an even temper most of the time)

2. Emotional Tone
   (I feel nervous most of the time)

3. Body Image
   (I feel proud of my body)

4. Peer Relationships
   (I think that other people just do not like me)

5. Family Relationships
   (My parents are usually patient with me)

6. Mastery and Coping
   (I am fearful of growing up)

7. Vocational-Educational Goals
   (I enjoy learning new things)

8. Psychopathology
   (I fear something constantly)

9. Superior Adjustment
   (I am a leader in school)

From Peterson, A. C., Schulenberg, J. E., Abramowitz, R. H., Offer, D., and H. D. Jarcho, "A Self-Image Questionnaire for Young Adolescents (SIQYA): Reliability and Validity Studies," Journal of Youth and Adolescence, 13, 1984. Copyright © 1984 by Plenum Publishing Corporation.

Another recent measure of self-concept, one specifically designed for young adolescents, is called the Self-Image Questionnaire for Young Adolescents (SIQYA) (Peterson et al., 1984). It is a downward extension of the Offer Self-Image Questionnaire and uses nine scales: emotional tone, impulse control, body image, peer relationships, family relationships, mastery and coping, vocational-educational goals, psychopathology, and superior adjustment (table 10.1). The adolescent chooses the extent to which each of the ninety-eight items describes him or her—from "very well" to "not me at all."

Multimethod Assessment

Some assessment experts believe that a combination of several methods should be used in measuring self-concept and other personality traits. In addition to self-reporting, rating of an adolescent's self-concept by others and careful observation of the adolescent's behavior in various settings could give a more complete, and hence more accurate, picture of her self-concept. Peers, teachers, parents, and even others who do not know the adolescent should be asked for their perceptions of her. Peers are particularly good at rating each other, so it may be helpful to listen carefully to what adolescents have to say about each other. The adolescent's facial expressions and the extent to which she congratulates or condemns herself are also good indicators of how she views herself. (Adolescents who never smile or act happy, for example, are revealing something about their self-concepts.) One recent example of an investigation that used behavioral observations in the assessment of self-concept (Savin-Williams and Demo, 1983) provides insight into some of the positive as well as negative behaviors that may provide clues to the nature of the adolescent's self-concept (table 10.2). By using a variety of measures to obtain information about the adolescent's concept (such as self-report and behavioral observations) and obtaining information from multiple sources (such as the adolescent, parents, friends, and teacher), a more accurate construction of the adolescent's self-concept likely is possible.

Developmental Changes in Self-Conceptions during Adolescence

In our discussion of cognitive development in Chapter 4, we pointed to a number of cognitive changes about adolescents that have important implications for understanding changes in the self during adolescence. Some of these changes focus on the increase in abstract thought, idealism, organization, language sophistication, logical reasoning, perspective taking, and personality assessments that often characterize adolescent

Table 10.2 Behavioral indicators of self-concept

Positive Indicators
1. Gives others directives or commands
2. Voice quality is appropriate for situation
3. Expresses opinions
4. Sits with others during social activities
5. Works cooperatively in a group
6. Faces others when speaking or being spoken to
7. Maintains eye contact during conversation
8. Initiates friendly contact with others
9. Maintains comfortable space between self and others
10. Little hesitation in speech, speaks fluently

Negative Indicators
1. Puts down others by teasing, name calling or gossiping
2. Gestures are dramatic or out of context
3. Inappropriate touching or avoids physical contact
4. Gives excuses for failures
5. Glances around to monitor others
6. Brags excessively about achievements, skills, appearance
7. Verbally puts self down; self depreciation
8. Speaks too loudly, abruptly or in a dogmatic tone
9. Does not express views or opinions, especially when asked
10. Assumes a submissive stance

Source: Savin-Williams, R. C. & Demo, D. H., "Conceiving or misconceiving the self: Issues in adolescent self-esteem." Journal of Early Adolescence, 3, 121–140. Reprinted with permission of H.E.L.P. Books, Inc.

development. It would be helpful for you to think about those ideas now, either by reviewing the main concepts in Chapter 4 or by going over them in your head. We will review some of these ideas here and expand on these cognitive changes by also discussing Robert Selman's view on the development of the self and perspective taking.

Some Changes in the Adolescent's Self-Conceptions

The adolescent begins to think in more abstract and ideal ways about the self—about what the self is capable of being. Such thoughts often are very elaborate, idealistic, and organized. Adolescents also have a more differentiated view of themselves than they did as children. As children, they may simply have perceived themselves as "good" or "bad." As adolescents, they are likely to perceive themselves in more detailed ways such as, "I am a good person most of the time, except when my older sister bugs me, when my father won't let me have the car, and when I have to study for a biology test." Adolescents also have a more individuated view of themselves than children do. This indicates that adolescents have a more distinct view of themselves as unique persons and more readily differentiate themselves from others than they did as children. Young children tend to label themselves in terms of how similar they are to other children, but as they approach adolescence, they begin to describe themselves more in terms of differences. Adolescents also may have a more stable self-concept than children, but in an extreme form, stability can produce rigidity and unrealistic self-appraisals. Even though it is said that adolescents have a more stable self-concept than children, this does not imply that such self-conceptions do not change. These self-conceptions clearly do change, but as adolescents mature cognitively, they become more capable of integrating information into a stable sense of who they are. While adolescents perceive that change is occurring, they are more adept than children at detecting continuity and stability in themselves (Chandler et al., 1985). Adolescents also evidence a stronger interest than children in understanding the self, sometimes searching for hidden reasons as to why they are a particular way.

We indicated that the adolescent's self-perception becomes more abstract and idealistic during the adolescent years. To see this increase in abstractness and idealism, consider the comments of the following three individuals:

9-year-old boy (concrete descriptions) My name is Bruce C. I have brown eyes. I have brown hair. I have brown eyebrows. I'm nine years old. I love! sports. I have seven people in my

Self-awareness in the form of self-consciousness becomes more acute during adolescence.

family. I have great! eye site. I have lots! of friends. I live on 1923 Pinecrest Drive. I'm going on ten in September. I'm a boy. I have an uncle that is almost seven feet tall. My school is Pinecrest. My teacher is Mrs. V. I play hockey! I'm almost the smartest boy in the class. I love food! I love fresh air. I love school.

11½-year-old girl (increase in interpersonal descriptions) My name is A. I'm a human being. I'm a girl. I'm a truthful person. I'm not pretty. I do so-so in my studies. I'm a very good cellist. I'm a very good pianist. I'm a little bit tall for my age. I like several boys. I like several girls. I'm old-fashioned. I play tennis. I am a very good musician. I try to be helpful. I'm always ready to be friends with anybody. Mostly I'm good, but I lose my temper. I'm not well liked by some girls and boys. I don't know if boys like me or not.

17-year-old girl (increase in interpersonal descriptions, characteristic mood states, and ideological and belief statements) I am a human being. I am a girl. I am an individual. I don't know who I am. I am Pisces. I am a moody person. I am an indecisive person. I am an ambitious person. I am a big curious person. I am not an individual. I am lonely. I am an American (God help me). I am a Democrat. I am a liberal person. I am a radical. I am conservative. I am a pseudoliberal. I am an atheist. I am not a classifiable person (i.e., I don't want to be). (Montemayor and Eisen, 1977, pp. 317–18)

Self-awareness in the form of self-consciousness becomes particularly acute during adolescence, in contrast with late childhood, when self-concept seems to be more stable (Rosenberg, 1979). It is sometimes argued that unreflective self-acceptance begins to disappear during early adolescence, and the self becomes more volatile and evanescent. What were once unquestioned self-truths become problematic self-hypotheses and search for the truth about one's self is on.

Erikson also points out the adolescent's tortuous self-consciousness. He believes that in the effort to find a coherent, unified self, adolescents are often preoccupied with what they appear to be in the eyes of other people and with the question of how to connect earlier roles and skills with their new, idealized views of themselves and others. Most theorists believe that preoccupation with the self begins to dissipate toward the end of adolescence and the beginning of early adulthood.

According to both Rosenberg and Erikson, then, it is necessary to pay particular attention to adolescents with low self-esteem since they are likely to experience considerable anxiety and have difficulty in interpersonal relationships. In Rosenberg's (1965) view, low self-esteem is linked with internal distress in several ways. Putting on a front is anxiety-producing. An adolescent with low self-esteem has a less stable idea of her identity and does not have an adequate frame of reference for herself or others. Such an adolescent is often lonely and vulnerable, is likely to be sensitive to criticism, and often becomes upset when she senses that she is inadequate in some way. Adolescents with low self-esteem are often awkward in social relationships, frequently assume that others do not like them, and infrequently participate in extracurricular activities, class discussions, and informal conversations. The linkage of attitudes towards one's self and others emphasized in Erikson's theory is portrayed as well in the ideas of Morris Rosenberg (Hill, 1980).

Self-Conception, Piaget's Theory, and Selman's Theory of the Self and Interpersonal Understanding

Two important cognitive theories of self development in adolescence are Piaget's and Selman's.

Self-Conception and Piaget's Theory Morris Okun and Joseph Sasfy (1977) have analyzed the relation between self-concept theory and Piaget's views on adolescent cognitive growth. Okun and Sasfy point out that it is not until adolescence that individuals begin to develop formal theories about the self. At this time, their self-theory begins to take on the air of a scientific search for the answer to a difficult question.

David Elkind pointed out the emerging characteristics of a self-theory:

> During adolescence the young person develops a true sense of self. While children are aware of themselves, they are not able to put themselves in other people's shoes and to look at themselves from that perspective. Adolescents can do this and do engage in such self-watching to a considerable extent. Indeed, the characteristic "self-consciousness" of the adolescent results from the very fact that the young person is now very much concerned with how others react to him. This is a concern that is largely absent in childhood. (Elkind, 1971, p. 111)

In early adolescence, the individual's self-theory is somewhat tenuous. This is reflected in the self-consciousness and apprehension young adolescents express in regard to how others view them. Like a new scientific theory, the young adolescent's self-theory is particularly open to disconfirming data. However, adolescents are continually searching for new data that will help them generate support for their self-theory. As Okun and Sasfy (1977) point out, such adolescent events as getting a driver's license and going on a first date provide critical data for important components of this self-theory. After such events take place, an adolescent may think to herself, "I am competent," or "Boys like me."

It is true, however, that many adolescents have idealized images of themselves. The onset of formal-operational thought allows them to step outside the concrete aspects of their experience and literally "trip off" on a number of thought excursions about what they might be like and what they are capable of becoming. That is, adolescent self-theory begins to hinge more on idealized self-images than on actual concrete experiences. As teenagers mature into later adolescence, they accumulate experiences (often painful ones) that tell them whether their idealized self-images are accurate or not. Gradually, older adolescents begin to modify their self-theories to be less grandiose, more realistic, and more specific. Older adolescents place boundary lines on their self-theories so that they can function more competently and not be saddled with unnecessary disillusionments.

Robert Selman's View of the Self and Interpersonal Understanding Robert Selman (1976; 1980) has proposed a developmental sequence of the self and perspective taking. He believes perspective taking moves through a series of five stages, ranging from three years of age through the adolescent years. As shown in table 10.3, these stages span the egocentric viewpoint of the preschool child to the in-depth societal perspective taking

---

Table 10.3 Selman's stages of perspective taking

Social role-taking stage

Stage 0—Egocentric viewpoint (age range 3-6)[a]

Child has a sense of differentiation of self and other, but fails to distinguish between the social perspective (thoughts, feelings) of other and self. Child can label other's overt feelings, but does not see the cause and effect relation of reasons to social actions.

Stage 1—Social-informational role taking (age range 6-8)

Child is aware that other has a social perspective based on other's own reasoning, which may or may not be similar to child's. However, child tends to focus on one perspective rather than coordinating viewpoints.

Stage 2—Self-reflective role taking (age range 8-10)

Child is conscious that each individual is aware of the other's perspective and that this awareness influences self and other's view of each other. Putting self in other's place is a way of judging his intentions, purposes, and actions. Child can form a coordinated chain of perspectives, but cannot yet abstract from this process to the level of simultaneous mutuality.

Stage 3—Mutual role taking (age range 10-12)

Child realizes that both self and other can view each other mutually and simultaneously as subjects. Child can step outside the two-person dyad and view the interaction from a third-person perspective.

Stage 4—Social and conventional system role taking (age range 12-15+)

Person realizes mutual perspective taking does not always lead to complete understanding. Social conventions are seen as necessary because they are understood by all members of the group (the generalized other) regardless of their position, role, or experience.

[a]*Age ranges for all stages represent only an average approximation based on our studies to date.*

---

view of the adolescent. Recently, Selman (1980) has shown how these stages of perspective taking can be applied to four dimensions of individual and social development: concepts of individuals; concepts of friendships; concepts of peers; and concepts of parent–child relationships. We consider the child's developing conception of individuals in greater detail. These concepts

Psychologist Robert Selman of Harvard University.

have often been assessed by Selman through individual interviews with the child based on the following dilemma:

> Eight-year-old Tom is trying to decide what to buy his best friend, Mike, for his birthday party. By chance, he meets Mike on the street and learns that Mike is extremely upset because his dog, Pepper, has been lost for 2 weeks. In fact, Mike is so upset he tells Tom, "I miss Pepper so much I never want to look at another dog again." Tom goes off, only to pass a store with a sale on puppies; only two are left and these soon will be gone. (Selman, 1980, p. 94)

The dilemma is whether to buy the puppy and how this will influence Mike psychologically.

To explore the issue of self-awareness, the interviewer now begins with a general question such as, "Mike said he never wants to see another puppy again. Why did he say that?" Depending in part on the child's response, the interviewer subsequently would choose from a range of questions related to stages. Let's now look further at the stages of the child's conception of individual development. As shown in table 10.4, issues of interpersonal understanding related to concepts of the individual involve such matters as subjectivity, self-awareness, personality, and personality change. A description of the child's reasoning at different levels about the self and perspective taking is presented in Perspective on Adolescent Development 10.1.

We have touched on many different aspects of the self during adolescent development. To help you remember the important concepts involved in the study of the self, read Concept Table 10.1. Now we turn our attention to the hallmark of self-development in adolescence: identity.

Level 0: Physicalistic Concepts of Self-Awareness
Two aspects of children's responses characterize the earliest reflective concept of self-awareness. First, when asked about the inner self, the child does not seem to view the nature of inner or psychological experiences as different from the material nature of outer experience. And, second, while very young children can describe a sense of being aware of a self, the nature of the self itself appears to have a quasi-physical air. Thus, a three-year-old child was asked the following:

> WHERE DOES THE RAIN COME FROM?
> I think from the clouds.
> HOW DO YOU KNOW THAT?
> I just told myself. That's how I knew.
> WHAT DO YOU MEAN YOU TOLD
> YOURSELF?
> My words told me.
> WHEN YOU THINK, WHERE DO YOU THINK?
> In my mouth.
> HOW DO YOU THINK?
> My words tell me.

And, in another comment by a three-year-old child, we see how the psychological self does not seem to be differentiated from the physical self in the early years of development:

> I am the boss of myself.
> HOW DO YOU KNOW?
> My mouth told my arm and my arm does what my mouth tells it to do.

Level 1: Awareness of Distinctions between Actions and Intentions
There are three intriguing aspects to the kind of thinking about self-awareness that characterizes level 1 thinking. First, young children are not aware that people can hide their inner or true feelings. For example, consider the following comments of a nine-year-old child:

> MIKE SAYS HE NEVER WANTS TO SEE
> ANOTHER PUPPY AGAIN. WHY DID HE SAY
> THAT?

> Because he lost his dog, Pepper.
> DID HE MEAN WHAT HE SAID?
> Yes
> HOW DO YOU KNOW?
> Because he said it.
> IS IT POSSIBLE THAT MIKE DOESN'T
> REALLY KNOW HOW HE FEELS?
> He said he was sad.

A second and related aspect of self-awareness at level 1 is that while covert attitudes and their overt actions are seen as separate, children using this level of reasoning seem to believe that the person's overt actions are the same as the inner attitudes. For example, consider the comments of this eight-year-old child:

> HOW DOES MIKE FEEL INSIDE?
> Sad.
> HOW DO YOU KNOW?
> Because of the way he looks.
> COULD HE LOOK SAD AND BE HAPPY
> INSIDE?
> He could, but you would be able to tell if you
> watched him long enough, he'd show you he
> was happy.

And, third, the young child's conception of fooling oneself or "awareness of unawareness" is different from that of older children and adults. Because level 1 perspective taking is yet actually self-reflective on the inner self, the young child seems to perceive fooling oneself as changing one's subjective beliefs and feelings rather than being unaware of such beliefs and feelings. For instance, an eight-year-old child was asked the following:

> WHAT DOES IT MEAN TO FOOL THE SELF?
> You do something and then you disagree with
> it. You find out you didn't want to do it.

Level 2: The Emergence of an Introspective Self and the Second-Person Perspective
Concepts at level 2 suggest a further understanding that the individual can take a clear perspective on the inner life that was separated from outer experiences at level

1. In social perspective-taking language, the self is now able to put itself in the place of the second person and look back toward the self's inner states. There are four aspects to this change in perspective taking and self development. First, the ability to take a second-person perspective permits the adolescent to rethink the relative significance of outer appearance and inner reality. There now appears to be a sense of greater importance attributed to inner experience and how one truly feels about social interactions beyond outward appearances. For instance, consider this ten year old's comments:

> HOW IS IT YOU CAN HIDE THE WAY YOU FEEL?
>> If he felt real sad and stuff, you put a smile on your face and you go with everyone else and try to be regular, but sometimes you can really be sad.
>
> IS THERE A KIND OF INSIDE AND OUTSIDE TO A PERSON?
>> Yes.
>
> WHAT WOULD THAT MEAN?
>> If there was a brother and a sister, like the brother always says I can't stand you, but really inside, he really likes her.

Second, at level 2, perspective taking now involves a working belief in the self's ability to closely monitor the self's thoughts and actions. Consider the following excerpts from a twelve year old:

> IS IT POSSIBLE TO FOOL YOURSELF?
>> Yes, sometimes.
>
> HOW CAN YOU FOOL YOURSELF?
>> You can say to yourself, I didn't really care and keep on saying you didn't care, and when someone brings up the subject, you say I didn't really care and sometimes it works and you don't really care about it.

Also at level 2, a third dimension arises. The adolescent becomes reflectively aware that the individual, the self as well, can consciously and often deceptively put on a facade that is meant to mislead others with regard to what he or she thinks is going on internally. The concept of putting on a front is understood by the adolescent as a useful strategy in covering up feelings. For instance, consider a 12 year old's comments:

> DO YOU THINK THERE IS A DIFFERENCE BETWEEN FOOLING YOURSELF AND FOOLING SOMEBODY ELSE?
>> Yes.
>
> WHAT IS THE DIFFERENCE?
>> It is easier to fool them because they don't have your mind.

And, a final, fourth dimension to level 2 thinking about perspective taking and self-development is the individual's belief that one can attain an inner strength by gaining confidence in one's abilities. Self-awareness now can be related to the content of self-esteem. Inner awareness itself is now viewed as a confidence builder. For example, an eight year old's comments:

> DO YOU THINK THERE ARE ANY OTHER REASONS THAT KEITH MIGHT HAVE HAD FOR LETTING JERRY WIN?
>> Well, because he didn't want him to go off and start being a poor sport about it.
>
> HOW WOULD LETTING JERRY WIN STOP HIM FROM BEING A POOR SPORT?
>> Because it would let him think that Jerry did it by himself and so he is improving in playing Ping-Pong, so he will start playing a lot.
>
> WHY WOULD HE START PLAYING A LOT IF HE THOUGHT HE HAD WON THE GAME?
>> Because if he won the game he would think he would start getting better and play ping-pong more.
>
> DO YOU THINK HE MIGHT BE TRYING TO BUILD UP JERRY'S CONFIDENCE?
>> Yah, he lets him win so he can make him think, "I am really better now. I can play better and sometimes win with Keith. . . ."

Level 3: Concepts of the Self as Observed and Observer, and Taking a Third-Person Perspective.

George Herbert Mead (1934) believed that a mature concept of self comes from the adolescent's cognitive capacity to take the perspective of another one's own actions (Selman's level 2). Out of this self-as-action view emerges a self as entity phase that requires the ability to observe the self simultaneously as observed and observer. In Mead's terms, there evolves a concept of "mind," or what Selman calls a third-person perspective on the self—this is the hallmark of Selman's level 3 thinking. Three aspects appear at level 3: the concept of the mind as the observer of a self-aware self, the idea of fooling the self through an act of will, and the notion that thoughts and feelings can appear even when opposed by mind and will. In the following comments of a twelve year old, we can see the depth to the young adolescent's thinking about the mind:

> IS IT POSSIBLE TO HIDE YOUR FEELINGS FROM YOURSELF?
> Yes, you just don't tell it to anybody. You put it out of your mind.
> IS IT POSSIBLE TO REALLY SUCCEED IN HIDING IT FROM YOURSELF?
> Yah, you just put it out of your mind. You don't want to know about it.
> DO YOU THEN NOT KNOW ABOUT IT, OR INSIDE, DO YOU STILL KNOW ABOUT IT?
> You still know about it, but you don't think about it or talk about it.

Level 4: The Discovery of the True Self-Deception and the Unconscious as a Natural Explanatory Concept

The key theme of level 4 thinking is that no matter how vigilant the conscious mind is, and no matter how hard it works, there still are inner experiences that are not readily available to awareness. At this level, the adolescent sees that individuals can and do have thoughts, feelings, and motivations that are resistant to self-analysis

by even the most introspective, probing thinker. Consider the thoughts of a 16 year old:

> IF MIKE SAYS HE NEVER WANTS TO SEE ANOTHER PUPPY AGAIN, WHY DOES HE SAY THAT?
> Because he doesn't think that any puppy could take the place of Pepper.
> DOES HE REALLY MEAN THAT, THAT HE NEVER WANTS TO SEE ANOTHER PUPPY AGAIN?
> No.
> CAN YOU SAY SOMETHING AND NOT MEAN IT?
> That is something right off the top of his head, like when you are really upset, you might say, "Get out of here. I never want to see you again." But you are really going to see them tomorrow and you are not going to be mad at them.
> SO MIKE MAYBE DOESN'T KNOW HOW HE FEELS?
> He is just talking out of emotions. He may think that at that instant he doesn't want to see another puppy, but he will grow over the initial loss.
> IF MIKE THINKS ABOUT WHAT HE SAID, WILL HE REALIZE THAT HE REALLY WOULD LIKE ANOTHER DOG?
> Maybe, but maybe not. He might not be aware of his deeper feelings.
> HOW IS THAT POSSIBLE?
> He may not want to admit to himself that another dog could take Pepper's place. He might feel at some level that it would be disloyal to Pepper to just go out and replace the dog. He may feel guilty about it. He doesn't want to face these feelings, so he says, no new dog.
> IS HE AWARE OF THIS?
> Probably not.

From Selman, R. L., "Social-Cognitive Understanding," in T. Lickona (Ed.), *Moral Development and Behavior.* Copyright © 1976 Holt, Rinehart and Winston, New York.

THE SELF

Concept	Processes/related ideas	Characteristics/description
Self as knower and as object	Basic distinction	Self as knower is "I" and self as object is "me." Self as knower emphasizes active processing of information about self, while self as object stresses product of observing process, usually measured as self-concept.
	Self-concept	The humanistic view has argued that self-concept is the central, organizing part of personality. Self-perceptions are viewed as very important determinants of behavior, referred to as a phenomenological approach. Rogers argued that a distinction between the ideal self and real self is important to understanding development. Relations between self-concept, and parenting and school behavior have been found.
	Self as knower	The information processing perspective is being called on to develop ideas about the self as knower. One strategy is to view the self as social memory. Research has shown that adolescents remember information more efficiently when it relates to themselves.
Measuring self-concept	The traditional approach	Emphasizes the global nature of self-concept; combines perceptions of self into overall self-concept rather than providing global perception plus breakdown into different dimensions.
	Some contemporary measures	The Harter Perceived Competence Scale for Children provides information about general self-worth as well as cognitive, social, and physical competence. The SIQYA (Self-Image Questionnaire for Young Adolescents) also provides information about specific aspects of the self.
	Multimethod assessment	A combination of methods may provide a more complete analysis of self-concept rather than relying on a single self-concept scale.
Developmental changes in self-conceptions during adolescence	Cognitive changes and Piaget	Among the cognitive changes in the self during adolescence are those involving increased abstractness, idealism, organization, sophisticated use of language to describe the self, logical reasoning, perspective taking, and personality assessment. The adolescent's thoughts are more differentiated, individuated, and stable than the child's thoughts. According to Elkind, it is during adolescence that a person develops a true self theory.
	Selman's view of levels of thinking about the self and interpersonal understanding	Selman proposed five stages of perspective taking: egocentric viewpoint, social-informational role taking, self-reflective role taking, mutual role taking, and social and conventional system role taking. These stages are believed to unfold sequentially with the latter two characterizing adolescence.

Identity: Who Am I? What Am I All About?

Who am I? What am I all about? What am I going to do with my life? What is different about me? How can I make it on my own? These questions are not usually considered during the childhood years, but during adolescence, they become common concerns. Adolescents clamor for solutions to these questions that revolve around the concept of identity.

Erikson's Ideas on Identity

By far the most comprehensive and provocative story of identity development was proposed by Erik Erikson.

Revisiting the Eight Stages of the Life Cycle

The description of identity development can be traced directly to the thinking and writing of the famous psychoanalyst Erik Erikson (1963; 1968). As you may recall from Chapter 2, identity versus identity diffusion (confusion) represents the fifth stage in Erikson's eight stages of the life cycle, occurring at about the same time as adolescence. Please either return to Chapter 2 and review Erikson's eight stages of development or go over them in your head to provide a developmental setting for understanding identity development. The following passage from *Identity: Youth and Crisis,* Erikson's most detailed work on identity, should give you some sense of Erikson's ideas on adolescent development:

> The youth of today is not the youth of twenty years ago. This much an elderly person would say, at any point in history, and think it was both new and true. But here we mean something very specifically related to our theories. For whereas twenty years ago we gingerly suggested that some young people might be suffering from a more or less unconscious identity conflict, a certain type today tells us in no uncertain terms, and with the dramatic outer display of what we once

considered to be inner secrets, that yes, indeed, they have an identity conflict—and they wear it on their sleeves, Edwardian or leather. Sexual identity confusion? Yes, indeed; sometimes when we see them walking down the street it is impossible for us to tell without indelicate scrutiny who is a boy and who is a girl. Negative identity? Oh, yes; they want to be everything which "society" tells them not to be: in this, at least, they "conform." And for such fancy terms as psychosocial moratorium, they will certainly take their time, and take it with vengeance, until they are sure whether or not they want any of the identity offered in a conformist world. (1968, p. 26)

Also from *Identity: Youth and Crisis* is this commentary about the adolescent's search for truth, virtue, and fidelity:

> The evidence in young lives of the search for something and somebody to be true to can be seen in a variety of pursuits more or less sanctioned by society. It is often hidden in a bewildering combination of shifting devotion and sudden perversity, sometimes more devotedly perverse, sometimes more perversely devoted. Yet in all youth's seeming shiftiness, a seeking after some durability in change can be detected, whether in the accuracy of scientific and technical method or in the sincerity of obedience; in the veracity of historical and fictional accounts or in the fairness of the rules of the game; in the authenticity of artistic production, and the high fidelity of reproduction, or in the genuineness of convictions and the reliability of commitments. This search is easily misunderstood, and often it is only dimly perceived by the individual himself, because youth, always set to grasp both diversity in principle and principle in diversity, must often test extremes before setting on a considered course. These extremes, particularly in times of ideological confusion and widespread marginality of identity, may include not only rebellious but also deviant, delinquent, and self-destructive tendencies. However, all of this can be in the nature of a moratorium, a period of delay in which to test the rock bottom of some truth before committing the powers of the mind and body to a segment of the existing (or a coming) order. (1968, pp. 235–36)

DOONESBURY

During adolescence, world views become important to an individual, who enters what Erikson terms a "psychological moratorium"—a gap between the security of childhood and the new autonomy of approaching adulthood. Numerous identities can be drawn from the surrounding culture. Adolescents can experiment with different roles, trying them out and seeing which ones they like. The youth who successfully cope with these conflicting identities during adolescence emerge with a new sense of self that is both refreshing and acceptable. The adolescent who is not successful in resolving this identity crisis becomes confused, suffering what Erikson refers to as identity confusion. This confusion may take one of two courses: the individual may withdraw, isolating herself from peers and family, or she may lose her own identity in that of the crowd.

Adolescents want to be able to decide freely for themselves such matters as what careers they will pursue, whether they will go to college or into military service, and whether or not they will marry. In other words, they want to free themselves from the shackles of their parents and other adults and make their own choices. At the same time, however, many adolescents have a deep fear of making the wrong decisions and of failing.

The choice of an occupation is particularly important in identity development. Erikson (1968) remarks that in a highly technological society like that of the United States, students who have been well trained to enter a work force that offers the potential of reasonably high self-esteem will experience the least stress during the development of identity. Some students have rejected jobs offering good pay and traditionally high social status, choosing instead to work in situations that allow them to be more genuinely helpful to their fellow humans, such as in the Peace Corps, in mental health clinics, or in schools for children from low-income backgrounds. Some adolescents prefer unemployment to the prospect of working at a job they would be unable to perform well or at which they would feel useless. To Erikson, this attitude reflects the desire to achieve a meaningful identity through being true to oneself (rather than burying one's identity in that of society at large).

Identity confusion may account for the large number of adolescents who run away from home, drop out of school, quit their jobs, stay out all night, or assume bizarre moods. Before Erikson's ideas became popular, these adolescents were often labeled delinquents and looked at with a disapproving eye. As a result of Erikson's writings and analyses, the problems these youth encounter are now viewed in a more positive light. Not only do runaways, school dropouts, and job quitters struggle with identity—virtually all adolescents go through an identity crisis, and some are simply able to resolve the crisis more easily than others.

Certainly the idea of the **identity crisis** has permeated our society. The term is applied to practically anyone of any age who feels a loss of identification or self-image—teenagers who cannot "find" themselves; teachers who have lost their jobs; the newly divorced; business executives who are questioning their values. The term has even been applied to companies and institutions. For example, the federal government might be undergoing an "identity crisis" when it has been rocked by scandal, or a school system may be having an identity crisis when it must choose between a traditional and an innovative curriculum. In fact, the use of the term *identity crisis* has become so pervasive that defining it is difficult.

These general applications have gone far beyond Erikson's original use of the term; for Erikson (1968), identity is primarily the property of an individual person, not a group or an institution. According to Erikson, although identity is important throughout a person's life, it is only in adolescence that identity development reaches crisis proportions. A positive or negative identity is being developed throughout childhood as a result of the way various crises have been handled. The positive resolution of earlier crises, such as trust versus mistrust and industry versus inferiority, helps the individual cope positively with the identity crisis that, Erikson believes, occurs in adolescence.

Because Erikson's ideas about identity are so prevalent in today's social and educational systems, and because they reveal such rich insight into the thoughts and feelings of adolescents, I will again strongly recommend that you read one or more of his original writings. A good starting point is *Childhood and Society* (1963) or *Identity: Youth and Crisis* (1968). Other works that portray identity crises successfully resolved include *Young Man Luther* (1962) and *Gandhi's Truth* (1969)—the latter won a Pulitzer Prize. A sampling of Erikson's writings from these books is presented in Perspective on Adolescent Development 10.2.

Perspective on Adolescent Development 10.2
THE YOUTHS OF TOM SAWYER, ADOLF HITLER, MARTIN LUTHER, AND MAHATMA GANDHI

*E*rik Erikson is a master at using the psychoanalytic method to uncover historical clues about identity formation. Erikson has used the psychoanalytic method both with the youths he treats in psychotherapy sessions and in the analysis of the lives of famous individuals. Erikson (1963) believes that the psychoanalytic technique sheds light on human psychological evolution. He also believes that the history of the world is a composite of individual life cycles.

In the following excerpts from Erikson's writings, the psychoanalytic method is used to analyze the youths of Tom Sawyer, Adolf Hitler, Martin Luther, and Mahatma Gandhi.

Hitler in elementary school. He is in the center of the top row.

The occasion, while not pathological, is nevertheless a tragic one: a boy named Tom Sawyer, by verdict of his aunt, must whitewash a fence on an otherwise faultless spring morning. His predicament is intensified by the appearance of an age mate named Ben Rogers, who indulges in a game. It is Ben, the man of leisure, whom we want to observe with the eyes of Tom, the working man.

"He took up his brush and went tranquilly to work. Ben Rogers hove in sight presently—the very boy, of all boys, whose ridicule he had been dreading. Ben was impersonating the *Big Missouri,* and considered himself to be drawing nine feet of water. He was boat and captain and engine-bells combined. Tom went on whitewashing—paid no attention to the steamboat. Ben stared a moment, and then said: 'Hiyi! You're a stump, ain't you! You got to work, hey?' " (Erikson, quoting Twain, 1963, pp. 209–10)

Erikson presented this conversation between Tom and Ben to a class of psychiatric social work students and asked them to interpret Ben's behavior. They indicated that Ben must have been a frustrated boy to take so much trouble to play so strenuously. They went on to say that the frustrations likely emerged as a consequence of having a tyrannical father. But Erikson provided them with a more positive analysis—namely, that Ben was a growing boy, and growing means that he has to gradually master his gangling body and divided mind. Flexible and happy might be better labels to place on Tom's friend Ben.

In other passages, Erikson (1962) describes the youth of Adolf Hitler:

I will not go into the symbolism of Hitler's urge to build except to say that his shiftless and brutal father had consistently denied the mother a steady residence; one must read how Adolf took care of his mother when she wasted away from breast cancer to get an inkling of this young man's desperate urge to cure. But it would take a very extensive analysis, indeed, to indicate in what way a single boy can daydream his way into history and emerge a sinister genius, and how a whole nation becomes ready to accept the emotive power of that genius as a hope of fulfillment for its national aspirations and as a warrant for national criminality. . . .

The memoirs of young Hitler's friend indicate an almost pitiful fear on the part of the future dictator that he might be nothing. He had to challenge this possibility by being deliberately and totally anonymous; and only out of this self-chosen nothingness could he become everything. (Erikson, 1962, pp. 108–9)

But while the identity crisis of Adolf Hitler led him to turn toward politics in a pathological effort to create a world order, the identity crisis of Martin Luther in a different era led him to turn toward theology in an attempt to deal systematically with human nothingness or lack of identity:

In confession, for example, he was so meticulous in the attempt to be truthful that he spelled out every intention as well as every deed; he splintered relatively acceptable purities into smaller and smaller impurities; he reported temptations in historical sequence, starting back in childhood; and after having confessed for hours, would ask for special appointments in order to correct previous statements.

In doing this he was obviously both exceedingly compulsive and, at least unconsciously, rebellious. . . .

At this point we must note a characteristic of great young rebels: their inner split between the temptation to surrender and the need to dominate. A great young rebel is torn between, on the one hand, tendencies to give in and fantasies of defeat (Luther used to resign himself to an early death at times of impending success), and the absolute need, on the other hand, to take the lead, not only over himself but over all the forces and people who impinge on him. (Erikson, 1968, pp. 155–57)

And in his Pulitzer Prize winning novel on Mahatma Gandhi's life, Erikson (1969) describes the personality formation of Gandhi during his youth:

Straight and yet not stiff; shy and yet not withdrawn; intelligent and yet not bookish; willful and yet not stubborn; sensual and yet not soft . . . We must try to reflect on the relation of such a youth to his father, because the Mahatma places service to the father and the crushing guilt of failing in such service in the center of his adolescent turbulence. Some historians and political scientists seem to find it easy to interpret this account in psychoanalytic terms; I do not. For the question is not how a particular version of the Oedipal Complex "causes" a man to be both great and neurotic in a particular way, but rather how such a young person . . . manages the complexes which constrict other men. (Erikson, 1969, p. 113)

In these passages, the workings of an insightful, sensitive mind is shown looking for a historical perspective on personality development. Through analysis of the lives of famous individuals such as Hitler, Luther, and Gandhi, and through the thousands of youth he has talked with in person, Erikson has pieced together a descriptive picture of identity development.

kdown in the adolescent's time perspective, initia-
and ability to coordinate present behavior toward
re goals. This kind of breakdown implies a struc-
l deficit. The dynamic aspects of identity devel-
ent are reflected in Erikson's view:

Identity formation begins where the usefulness of
identification ends. It arises from the selective
repudiation and mutual assimilation of childhood
identifications, and their absorption in a new
configuration . . . which, in turn, is dependent
upon the process by which a society . . . identifies
the young individual. (Erikson, 1968)

en the subjective aspects of identity are mentioned,
eans that the individual senses an inner feeling of
esiveness or lack of coherence. This subjective
ing may produce a great deal of confidence in the
lescent or a lack of assuredness. Concerning reci-
city, identity development implies a mutual rela-
ship of the adolescent with his or her social world
community. Thus, identity development is not just
ntrapsychic self-representation, but rather also ines a particular relationship with people, commu-
, and society. Finally, the existential aspect of
tity development is seen in Erikson's belief that
ntity is a way of "being in the world." In the exis-
ialist mold, the adolescent seeks the meaning to his
er life as well as the meaning of life in general, much
an existential philosopher. As can be seen, the con-
t of identity as developed by Erikson includes many
plex components.

ontemporary View of Identity Development

expert on identity development, James Marcia
80) has described some ideas that provide insight
ut the role of identity in contemporary life that seem
nake sense:

The identity process neither begins nor ends with
adolescence. It begins with the self-object
differentiation at infancy and reaches its final
phase with the self-humankind integration at old
age. What is important about identity in
adolescence, particularly late adolescence, is that
this is the first time that physical development,
cognitive skills, and social expectations coincide to

enable young persons to sort through and
synthesize their childhood identifications in order
to construct a viable pathway toward their
adulthood. Resolution of the identity issue at
adolescence guarantees only that one will be
faced with subsequent identity "crises." A well-
developed identity structure, like a well-developed
superego, is flexible. It is open to changes in
society and to changes in relationships. This
openness assures numerous reorganizations of
identity *contents* throughout the "identity-
achieved" person's life, although the essential
identity *process* remains the same, growing
stronger through each crisis.

Identity formation does not happen neatly. At
the bare minimum, it involves commitment to a
sexual orientation, an ideological stance, and a
vocational direction. Synthesizing the identity
components is as much a process of negation as
affirmation. One must relinquish one's parents as
psychosexual objects, relinquish childhood
ideology based on one's position as a "taker," and
relinquish the fantasized possibilities of multiple,
glamorous life styles. In the ongoing construction
of an identity, that which one negates is known;
what one affirms and chooses contains an element
of the unknown. That is one of the reasons why
some young people either do not form an identity
or form only a partial one. They cannot risk
saying "no" to elements of their past of which
they are certain and make the affirmative leap
into an uncertain future.

Although some identity crises are cataclysmic
and totally preoccupying, identity formation
usually proceeds in a much more gradual and
nonconscious way. It gets done by bits and pieces.
Decisions are not made once and for all, but have
to be made again and again. And the decisions
may seem trivial at the time: whom to date,
whether or not to break up, having intercourse,
taking drugs, going to college or working, which
college, what major, studying or playing, being
politically active, and so on. Each of these
decisions has identity-forming implications. The
decisions and the bases on which one decides
begin to form themselves into a more or less
consistent core or structure. Of course, there are
ways in which one can circumvent the decision-
making process: one can let previously
incorporated, parentally based values determine
one's actions; one can permit oneself to be pushed
one way or the other by external pressures; or one
can become mired in indecision. (pp. 60–61)

Personality and Role Experimentation

Two ingredients at the core of the adolescent's developing identity are personality and role experimentation. As was previously stated, Erikson believes that adolescents are faced by an overwhelming number of choices and at some point during their youth enter a period of "psychological moratorium." During this moratorium, they try out different roles and personalities before they reach a stable sense of self. They may be argumentive one moment and pleasant the next, they may dress neatly one day and look sloppy the next, and they may like a friend or acquaintance one week and hate them the next. Such personality experimentation is a deliberate effort on the part of adolescents to find out where they fit in the world.

As they begin to realize that they will be responsible for themselves and their own lives, adolescents search for what those lives are going to be. Many parents and other adults, accustomed to having their children go along with what they say, fail to change their methods of interaction as the children become adolescents. Adults are often bewildered or incensed by the wise cracks, the rebelliousness, and the rapid mood changes that accompany adolescence. They must learn to give young adolescents the time and opportunity to explore different roles and personalities. In turn, adolescents will often eventually discard undesirable roles.

There are literally hundreds of roles for the adolescent to try out, and probably as many ways to pursue each role. Erikson believes that by late adolescence, occupational choices are central to the development of identity. Other important role choices involve sexuality (including decisions on dating, marriage, and sexual behavior), politics, religion, and moral values. For example, many adolescents have been indoctrinated in the religious beliefs of their parents. By late adolescence, youth come to understand that they can make their own decisions about religion. The same can be said of political identity—most children report that they adopt their parents' political choices. But by late adolescence, youth make their own decisions. Unfortunately, some adolescents consistently and deliberately adopt choices that are opposite those of their parents as a means of attaining "independence." Such behavior does

not meet the criteria for successful develop tonomy or identity, but represents a negati

At the same time adolescents are st come to grips with occupational, political, a identities, they also are trying to achieve a s identity. As indicated in the chapter on se: opment, one means of exploring sex roles tion, or living with a member of the opposit of marriage. Other issues involve the adopt culine" and "feminine" roles.

Thus, the development of an integra identity is a complex and difficult task. Ad expected to master many different roles in It is the rare, perhaps even nonexistent, ad doesn't experience serious doubts about hi in handling at least some of these roles c

Before we leave Erikson's theory of and move on to contemporary research an identity, it is helpful to think about the c Erikson's development theory.

The Complexity of Erikson's Theory

Edmund Bourne (1978) analyzed the c Erikson's developmental view and propos ponents to Erikson's definition of identi clude the following components: gene structural, dynamic, subjective or experie social reciprocity, and existential status.

With regard to what Bourne refers t component, identity development is ofte a developmental product or outcome inc individual's experiences over the first fiv life cycle stages. Identity development re the adolescent has resolved prior stages vs. mistrust," and "industry vs. infe cerning the adaptive dimension of identi cent's identity development can be adaptive accomplishment or achievemen aptation of the adolescent's special skills, strengths to the society in which he or sh also described identity in structural wa possibility of identity confusion or diffu

Table 10.5 The four statuses of identity

Position on occupation and ideology		Identity status			
		Psychological moratorium	Identity foreclosure	Identity confusion	Identity achievement
	Crisis	Present	Absent	Absent	Present
	Commitment	Absent	Present	Absent	Present

Note in these comments by Marcia his view that emphasizing identity as a *crisis* in adolescence may be too strong a label. His view that identity proceeds in a more gradual fashion and is a life-long process seems intuitively correct. Nonetheless, remember that it is during adolescence that physical, cognitive, and social skills are sufficiently advanced to allow a questioning and synthesis of who one is and what one is all about as a person. Next, we see that Marcia also believes that adolescents can wear four different faces in their effort to achieve identity.

The Four Statuses of Identity

James Marcia (1966; 1980) analyzed Erikson's identity theory of adolescence and concluded that four identity statuses, or *modes of resolution,* appear in the theory—identity diffusion, foreclosure, moratorium, and identity achievement. The extent of an adolescent's commitment and crisis is used to classify him as having one of the four identity statuses. Marcia (1966) defines crisis as a period during which the adolescent is choosing among meaningful alternatives. He defines commitment as the extent to which an adolescent shows a personal investment in what he is doing or is going to do. Most researchers now use the term *exploration* rather than crisis, although in the spirit of Marcia's original formulation, we will refer to crisis. Crisis essentially refers to exploration here.

Adolescents classifed as **identity diffused** (or **confused**) have not experienced any crisis (that is, they haven't explored meaningful alternatives) or made any

commitments. Not only are they undecided upon occupational or ideological choices, they also are likely to show little or no interest in such matters.

The adolescent experiencing **identity foreclosure** has made a commitment, but has not experienced a crisis. This occurs most often when parents simply hand down commitments to their adolescents, more often than not in an authoritarian manner. In such circumstances, adolescents may not have had enough opportunities to explore different approaches, ideologies, and vocations on their own. Some experts on adolescence, such as Kenneth Kenniston (1971), believe that experiencing a crisis is necessary for the development of a mature and self-integrated identity.

Marcia (1966) states that adolescents in the **identity moratorium** status are in the midst of a crisis, but that their commitments are either absent or only vaguely defined. Such adolescents are searching for commitments by actively questioning alternatives.

Adolescents who have undergone a crisis and made a commitment are referred to as **identity achieved.** In other words, to reach the identity achievement status, it is necessary to first experience a psychological moratorium, exploring different roles and experimenting with different personalities, then make an enduring commitment.

An overview of Marcia's four identity statuses is provided in table 10.5. Now we turn our attention to research on identity development, studying developmental changes in identity, sex differences, and sociocultural influences, particularly the family. You will see that Marcia's four statuses of identity have figured prominently in research on identity development.

Developmental Changes

Research on identity development has focused primarily on college students and to some extent high school students with little attention given to early adolescence (Adams and Montemayor, 1983). Several investigations do reveal that early adolescents primarily are in the identity diffusion and moratorium states.

In one recent investigation of the lower age boundaries of identity development, Sally Archer (1982) interviewed early and mid-adolescent males and females in the sixth, eighth, tenth, and twelfth grades in regard to such aspects of identity development as vocational choice, religious beliefs, political philosophies, and sex-role preferences. She found that the frequency of identity achievement went up with an increase in grade level. The diffusion and foreclosure statuses were most apparent at all grade levels. Similar patterns were found for both girls and boys.

Another investigation of Marcia's four identity statuses (Meilman, 1979) focused on five age groups of males: twelve, fifteen, eighteen, twenty-one, and twenty-four years of age. Most of the subjects studied were found to be in identity diffusion or foreclosure. The most significant changes in identity status occurred between the ages of eighteen and twenty-one. The most prominent shifts at this time were from identity diffusion and foreclosure to identity achievement.

James Marcia (1983) believes that three aspects of the adolescent's life are important in the development of identity during early adolescence. He argues that young adolescents must establish confidence in parental support, develop a sense of industry, and gain a self-reflective perspective into their future. These are viewed by Marcia as early adolescent precursors to the achievement of an identity in late adolescence.

Note that in Meilman's (1979) study the most significant changes in identity status occurred between the ages of eighteen and twenty-one. The upshot of most studies focused on age changes in identity find that it is in the post-high school years that the main changes in identity status take place. Over time during the college years, individuals are likely to move in the direction of identity achievement (Marcia, 1976; Waterman, Geary, and Waterman, 1974). One investigation (Adams and Fitch, 1982) studied 148 freshmen, sophomore, and junior college students. While half of the students remained stable in their identity status from 1976 to 1977, the other half either regressed or advanced. Few who were judged as having an identity diffusion status in 1976 remained at the same point in 1977. Moratorium-status students also advanced toward identity achievement. Identity-achieved students either remained that way, or in some cases regressed to a moratorium status. In view of the research discussed here, then, identity achievement is more common in post-high school youth, whereas early adolescents are more likely to be identity diffused.

Some experts on adolescence argue that college experiences increase the likelihood that adolescents will enter a status of moratorium. The theory is that professors and peers stimulate older adolescents to rethink their vocational and ideological orientations (e.g., Waterman and Waterman, 1971). In one investigation, as many as four out of every five adolescents in a moratorium status switched their occupational orientation during their college years (Waterman and Waterman, 1972). As a rule, the incidence of successful resolution to the identity crisis and successful development of an identity commitment increases from the first year to the final year of college (Constantinople, 1969).

Sex Differences in Identity

Is the identity development of the adolescent male the same as that of the adolescent female? In the 1960s through the mid-1970s, researchers were finding sex differences in the development of identity during both the high school and college years. For example, Joe La Voie (1976) has found that vocational identity is central to the identity formation of mid-adolescent males, while affiliative needs are more important to their female counterparts. Similarly, in college-aged adolescents, ideological choices and vocational orientations provide the core for the identity development of males, while intimacy and interpersonal relationships play a more important role in the identity development of females (Constantinople, 1969; Toder and Marcia, 1973). This information blends with the findings reported earlier in this chapter regarding the sex differences apparent in adolescent self-concepts; the self-concept of

the adolescent male was linked more with competency and independence while that of the adolescent female was tied more to dependence. Furthermore, it has been found that by the end of the college years, males have been able to resolve an identity crisis more readily than females (Constantinople, 1969).

However, in considering the nature of sex differences in identity, it is important to consider the domain of identity being evaluated and the historical time period in which identity is being assessed. A review of the identity development literature by Alan Waterman (1982) suggested that there are actually fewer sex differences in identity than some of the earlier studies indicated. Because so much emphasis has been placed on vocational commitment in the assessment of identity, it likely is the case that as adolescent females have assumed a stronger vocational orientation in the late 1970s and in the 1980s, they no longer differ from males in substantial ways in regard to identity development. Among the domains of identity development sampled in Waterman's review were vocational choice, religious beliefs, political ideology, and sex role attitudes.

Sociocultural Influences

Erikson's theory of identity development emphasizes the importance of sociocultural conditions in determining the ease or difficulty the adolescent has in developing an integrated identity.

Culture

Erikson believes that a richer identity can be achieved when the adolescent grows up in a culture that allows a longer period of time for moratorium. In the following comments, Erikson suggests the important role the ideology of a culture plays in the adolescent's development of identity.

> Industrial democracy poses special problems in that it insists on self-made identities ready to grasp many chances and ready to adjust to the changing necessities of booms and busts, of peace and war, of migration and determined sedentary life. Democracy, therefore, must present its adolescents with ideals which can be shared by young people of many backgrounds, and which emphasize autonomy in the form of independence and initiative in the form of constructive work. These promises, however, are not easy to fulfill in increasingly complex and centralized systems of industrial, economic, and political organization, systems which increasingly neglect the "self-made" ideology still flaunted in oratory. This is hard on many Americans because their whole upbringing has made the development of a self-reliant personality dependent on a certain degree of choice, a sustained hope for an individual's chances, and a firm commitment to the freedom of self-realization. (Erikson, 1968, p. 133)

The development of adolescent identity, then, is wrapped up in the sociopolitical structure of the culture—the components and course of identity development are different in totalitarian countries like Russia and China from those in democracies like the United States. In China and Russia, adolescents likely have not been given opportunities to make vocational and ideological choices to the extent their counterparts in the United States have. And in rural villages and remote areas, adolescents usually are not as concerned with ideological and vocational decisions as are their counterparts in more industrialized areas, where more diverse occupational choices are available.

Social class and race are other factors that contribute to the adolescent's identity development. According to Erik Erikson, being a member of a minority group can easily lead to the development of a negative identity. Identity may be developed out of hatred and anger directed toward a dominant majority rather than out of the positive elements of an individual's ethnic background and current situation. (It should be mentioned that we have little empirical information about the development of identity in lower class American adolescents—the majority of information, both Erikson's data and the data described in this chapter, come from middle-class American college students.)

Schools and teachers also can influence the adolescent's identity development. In Chapter 8, Erikson discussed how most talented individuals can remember a special teacher who challenged their talents, but was sensitive to their needs and emotions. Although Erikson's ideas have not been applied as systematically to the education of adolescents as Kohlberg's have, several ways to include Erikson's ideas in educational curricula are discussed in Perspective on Adolescent Development 10.3.

Family and Peer Influences

Parents and peers represent important figures in the adolescent's development of identity. By the time individuals have reached adolescence, they have been exposed to a long history of parental interaction and have learned numerous expectations for their conduct. Have their parents, over the course of fifteen to twenty years

ERIKSON'S IDEAS ABOUT ADOLESCENT IDENTITY DEVELOPMENT APPLIED TO EDUCATIONAL CURRICULA

John Miller (1978) recently explored the possibility of applying Erikson's ideas to the educational system. Miller points out that it is difficult for adolescents to develop a sense of occupational identity since long periods of training are needed for most careers in our industrialized society. Some occupations (for example, physician or college professor) more or less require that individuals be in their middle to late twenties before they finish their schooling. Because they spend such long periods as students, it may be difficult for individuals in such fields to achieve a stable sense of identity.

Erikson believes that active role experimentation is essential to identity achievement. He suggests that the adolescent obtain experience in a variety of occupational settings. Working in the community can be particularly exciting for an adolescent searching for her place in the world. The Parkway program for disadvantaged youth in Philadelphia is one program that provides this kind of opportunity. For example, in the Parkway program, students are encouraged to work in and explore the city through various businesses and agencies, including the police department, the district attorney's office, a drug manufacturer, and an insurance company. The temporary commitment the students make to these agencies provides valuable experience in forming later, more permanent commitments.

One educational curriculum that embodies many of Erikson's ideas has been developed by Ralph Mosher and Norman Sprinthall (1970). Mosher and Sprinthall want to develop in the adolescents

> . . . a more complex and more integrated understanding of oneself; the formation of personal identity; greater personal autonomy; a greater ability to relate to and communicate with other people (for example, peers and the opposite sex); the growth of more complex ethical reasoning; and the development

of more complex skills and competencies—in part by trying prevocational and "adult" roles. (Mosher and Sprinthall, 1970, p. 915)

As part of the educational program, eleventh and twelfth graders take a course in human development focused on stages of development. Emphasis is placed on the maturation of a personal identity and on self-understanding. Discussion focuses on such questions as "Who was I as a child?" "What am I like now?" "Where am I headed, and what will I be like as a person five years from now?" The high school students read some of Erikson's writings and discuss them in class. They also read literature on adolescence, such as *The Way It Is* and *The Graduate*. And they read about case studies of adolescents, such as those described in Kenneth Kenniston's book, *The Uncommitted*.

Students also engage in a number of laboratory activities designed to encourage them to think more deeply about identity development. These activities include filmmaking sessions that focus on adolescence, teaching in settlement houses and in elementary and preschool programs, volunteer work in hospitals and community action programs, student-initiated action projects, group discussion focused on developing communication skills, and the development of counseling knowledge through the study of counseling theories and actual counseling experience.

More programs directed toward developing adolescent identity are badly needed in our schools. Mosher and Sprinthall's efforts provide one base from which such programs can be constructed.

Other ideas on the role of education in identity development come from a recent investigation by Robert Enright and his colleagues (Enright et al., 1983). They have developed a number of cognitive strategies tied to social perspective taking that can be used to induce advances in identity.

of interaction with them, provided opportunities for them to explore alternative solutions to problems? Or have the parents handed down decisions in an authoritarian manner? Have they been actively interested and involved with the adolescent, or uninterested, uninvolved, and aloof? Have they encouraged their adolescents to go to college or have they pushed them into low-income jobs and deemphasized college? What were your parents like? Which paths did they follow in socializing you? Parental influence on identity development is tremendous—extending to sex roles, vocational choices, and moral, political, and religious ideology.

In particular, the work of Harold Grotevant and Catherine Cooper (e.g., Cooper, Grotevant, and Condon, 1983; Grotevant, 1984; Grotevant and Cooper, 1983) has highlighted the importance of a number of family processes in the development of identity. In the prologue to this chapter, you read about the communication patterns in two families, one of which promoted the development of individuation in the adolescent and one which did not. It is the belief of Grotevant and Cooper that both connectedness to parents and the presence of a family context that promotes individuation are likely to promote identity achievement. **Individuation** is viewed as having two main parts—separateness and self-assertion. Separateness is seen in the expressions of how distinctive the self is from others. Self-assertion is involved in the adolescent's expression of his or her own point of view and in taking responsibility for communicating this clearly. **Connectedness** is reflected in mutuality and permeability. Mutuality refers to the adolescent's sensitivity to and respect for the views of others. Permeability indexes openness and responsiveness to the views of others. Mutuality can provide adolescents with support, acknowledgement, and respect for their own beliefs, while permeability allows the adolescent to sense how to manage the boundaries between the self and others. More about Grotevant and Cooper's research and the family processes involved in identity development is described in Perspective on Adolescent Development 10.4.

Perspective on Adolescent Development 10.4
INDIVIDUATION AND CONNECTEDNESS IN THE FAMILY CONTEXT: THE ENHANCEMENT OF IDENTITY DEVELOPMENT

*I*n a recent research study, Harold Grotevant and Catherine Cooper (1985) studied eighty-four white, middle-class, two-parent families, each with an adolescent and one or two siblings present. They were observed in a family interaction situation designed to elicit the expression and coordination of different points of view. The mean age of the adolescents was 15.2 years. The Family Interaction Task involved the family in developing plans together for a fictional two-week vacation for which they had unlimited money. Twenty minutes were allowed for discussion, during which the family members were asked to plan a day-by-day itinerary. The family interaction was audiotaped and then coded according to separation, self-assertion, mutuality, and permeability—the factors Grotevant and Cooper believe are important in identity development. An overview of the conceptual dimensions of individuation and connectedness is shown in table 10.6, along with family communication patterns that reflect each of the dimensions.

In addition to the Family Interaction Task, the adolescents were given an extension of the Ego Identity Interview developed by Marcia (1966). This extension focuses on six domains of identity: occupational choice, religion, politics, friendship, dating, and sex roles.

The data suggested somewhat different family interaction patterns for male and female adolescents in terms of their identity exploration. The fathers of adolescent

Individuation and connectedness in families promote the adolescent's identity development.

males who were exploring identity seemed to be encouraging or at least tolerant of their sons' assertiveness and directedness. By contrast, the picture of fathers in the families with daughters who were exploring identity was one in which the fathers seemed to comment on others' suggestions rather than express their own and these fathers also disagreed with both their wives and their daughters. For the daughters who were exploring identity, their mothers were not just mirroring their husbands' views. Rather, the mothers tended to express their own ideas directly and had a strong role in coordinating family discussion. In sum, then, sons' relationships with their father and daughters' relationships with each parent appeared to provide the context for individuality and connectedness important in identity exploration.

Table 10.6 Dimensions of individuation and connectedness in the family context

Individuation

Separateness: Expresses distinctiveness of self from others

1. Requests action
   a. Write that down there.
   b. Wait a minute.
   c. Let's vote on it.
2. Disagrees/challenges other's idea directly
   a. I don't want to go on a train.
   b. No.
3. Disagrees/challenges other's idea indirectly
   a. But, two or three months.
   b. We don't have time to do all that.
   c. Why do you want to go there?
4. Irrelevant comment
   a. I'd like some more tea.
   b. You know, we're missing my favorite show.

Self-assertion: Displays awareness of own point of view and responsibility for communicating it clearly

1. Suggests action or location directly
   a. Something I've always wanted to do—to go up to the northwest part of the country.
   b. I'd like to go to Italy.

Connectedness

Mutuality: Shows sensitivity and respect for other's views

1. Suggests action or location indirectly
   a. Let's go to Canada.
   b. Would either of you like to go back to Italy?
2. Initiates compromise
   a. While Mom's in the antique shop, we can hike for a while.
   b. We can take Cindy to the Bahamas, and then we can go wherever you want to go.

From Grotevant, H. D., and C. R. Cooper, "Patterns of Interaction in Family Relationships and the Development of Identity Exploration in Adolescence," in Child Development, 56, 415–428, 1985. © The Society for Research in Child Development, Inc.

Table 10.6 (Continued)

	3. States other's feelings
	a. The kids will love to see Disneyworld.
	b. Your mother has always wanted to go to England.
	4. Answers request for information/validation
	a. A rail you go by train.
	b. It's about 400 miles.
Permeability:	Expresses responsiveness to the views of others
	1. Acknowledgement
	a. You said go to Canada.
	b. Oh.
	c. Uh huh.
	d. Okay.
	2. Requests information/validation
	a. In what perspective?
	b. What is a rail?
	c. How far is it from Rome to Athens?
	3. Agrees with/incorporates other's ideas
	a. I'd like to go there, too.
	b. Yeah, Yellowstone.
	c. Let's use Jim's idea of Spain and go to Madrid.
	4. Relevant comment
	a. So, we have two weeks and unlimited funds.
	b. Spain is next to France.
	c. Rail express. (elaborates response)
	5. Complies with request for action
	a. I'll write that down right now.
	b. Okay.

Peers, too, make critical contributions to the development of identity during adolescence. Peer discussion provides a particularly important opportunity for exploring alternatives that adolescents feel their parents won't approve of or are afraid to discuss. Adolescents' expectations of their peers and the feedback peers give are important elements of identity development. Are the standards of the peer group counter to those of the larger society? Or are they more prosocial? To what extent have adolescents had the opportunity to participate in decision making among peers? Do adolescents rely on peers for advice and help? Peer relationships increase the adolescent's sense of belonging and self-esteem, and contribute to individual identity achievement.

In our discussion of the research by Grotevant and Cooper, we mentioned their extension of the identity interview developed by James Marcia. Next, we explore how identity is measured in greater detail.

The Measurement of Identity

How do researchers investigate the development of identity status? Many researchers use either a semistructured individual interview procedure, a survey (questionnaire), or a sentence-completion test. For example, Marcia (1966) has developed a fifteen-to-thirty-minute structured interview technique that focuses on crisis and commitment in occupation, religion, and politics. His sentence-completion test is comprised of twenty-three incomplete sentence stems that are to be completed truthfully and honestly by the adolescent. The sentences are usually scored to indicate to what degree the adolescent has reached identity achievement (e.g., Kacerguis and Adams, 1980). An extension of Marcia's identity-status interview into interpersonal situations is presented in table 10.7.

Constantinople (1969) has developed a questionnaire that asks the adolescent to respond to a number of items, each of which reflects some aspect of one of Erikson's bipolar conflicts. In Constantinople's scale, trust versus mistrust, autonomy versus shame and doubt, and so on can be assessed along with identity. Adolescents simply check whether each of the items are very much like them, somewhat like them, neutral, usually not like them, or definitely not like them.

Such measures represent means of assessing identity that are very different from the psychoanalytic inquiry Erickson has used so ingeniously. Erikson's procedure is more individualized and requires considerable lengths of time—he conducts repeated interviews that probe deeply into the adolescent's life or extensively peruses an individual's life through writings and historical documents. Some of the problems involved in assessing identity, as well as in the nature of the construct itself, follow.

If you want to find out about an adolescent's identity development, where do you start? You might follow Erikson's pattern of probing the depths of an individual's personality by conducting a number of extensive open-ended interviews. Or you might decide to develop a questionnaire or survey to give to the adolescent that asks how he really feels about himself. But are either of these methods adequate for fully and accurately evaluating the adolescent's development of identity? The problem becomes particularly acute when you are faced with the necessity of having to investigate identity development for a large number of adolescents. In most cases, even ten to fifteen hours of in-depth interviewing and analysis of eighty to one hundred adolescents may be too time-consuming. Researchers who use a survey or questionnaire hope their instrument will validly and reliably assess the adolescent's identity. However, many experts on adolescent development, such as David Ausubel (1979), as well as experts on

Table 10.7 An extension of Marcia's identity-status interview into the interpersonal domain

*H*arold Grotevant and his colleagues (Grotevant, Thorbecke, and Meyer, 1982) extended Marcia's identity interview so it would include several important areas of interpersonal relationships. As noted in our discussion of Grotevant and Cooper's research, this extension allows identity to be assessed in six different domains: occupational choice, religion, politics, friendships, dating, and sex roles. The latter three categories provide more information about the adolescent's social relationships.

The interview includes eleven questions on occupation, ten on religion, nine on politics, fifteen on friendship, seventeen on dating, and thirteen on sex roles. Several questions also have probe cues indicated in the interview protocol. Examples of key questions in the three interpersonal areas follow:

Friendship. Would you say that your close friends are similar to you or different from you? In what ways? (Probe: How about the rest of your friends and acquaintances?) If your closest friend changed in some way that you didn't, would you still be friends? (for example . . .) What kinds of friends do your parents think you should have? Have you ever begun a friendship or maintained a

friendship with someone of whom your parents disapproved? Was this disagreement resolved in some way? How?

Dating. What are you looking for in the people you date? Has that idea changed since you started dating? How? How does that compare to what you look for in a friend? What standards or unwritten rules do you follow on a date? How do your rules compare to those of your friends? Have you changed your rules or standards since you started dating? If yes, what brought about those changes?

Sex roles. Now I'm interested in finding out how you think married couples should deal with the many tasks involved in the family. Who should take care of the young children (infants or preschoolers)? How should major decisions, such as buying a car or house, be made? What if only one person makes the money? How do your parents handle each of the family responsibilities we have been discussing? Do you expect that your ideas about men's and women's roles will stay the same or change over the next few years? Have your ideas changed over the last few years? (pp. 41–42)

From Grotevant, H. D., Thorbecke, W., and M. L. Meyer, "An Extension of Marcia's Identity Status Interview Into the Interpersonal Domain," Journal of Youth and Adolescence, *11, 33–47. Copyright © 1982 by Plenum Publishing Corporation.*

personality, such as Walter Mischel (1976), have criticized the use of the survey or questionnaire as a means of getting information about detailed, complex constructs like identity. Such experts believe that multiple assessments of the adolescent's identity development are necessary, and that if possible these assessments should include information not only from the adolescent herself, but from others as well.

We have discussed many different aspects of identity development in this chapter, including Erikson's ideas, the four statuses of identity, developmental changes, sex differences, sociocultural influences, and the measurement of identity. A summary of main ideas

related to these aspects of identity development is presented in Concept Table 10.2. Now we turn our attention to one final important aspect of identity, its relation to intimacy.

Identity and Intimacy

Erikson believes there are important links between identity and intimacy. And others, including Orlofsky, have described the nature of intimacy.

Concept Table 10.2

IDENTITY

Concept	Process/related ideas	Characteristics/description
Erikson's ideas on identity	Revisiting the eight stages of the life cycle	Identity versus identity confusion (diffusion) is the fifth stage in Erikson's theory, coming approximately at the time of adolescence. Identity involves the adolescent's search for who he or she is as a person.
	Personality and role experimentation	An important aspect of identity development is the opportunity to try out different personalities and roles.
	Complexity	Erikson's concept of identity is complex, involving the following components: genetic, adaptive, structural, dynamic, subjective or experiential, psychosocial reciprocity, and existential status.
	A contemporary view of identity development	Identity development is a life-long process, although it is during adolescence that for the first time in development physical, cognitive, and social skills are sufficiently advanced for the individual to seriously inquire and investigate who she or he is as a person. Although some identity crises are cataclysmic, the majority involve gradual development over many years.
The four statuses of identity	Crisis and commitment	Crisis refers to the exploration of alternatives, while commitment is the extent to which the individual shows a personal investment in what he or she is doing.
	Diffusion, foreclosure, moratorium, and achievement	The adolescent who is diffused has not undergone a crisis or made a commitment; one who is foreclosed has made a commitment, but not undergone a crisis; one who is in moratorium is in the midst of a crisis, but has not yet made a commitment; and one who is achieved has both undergone a crisis and made a commitment.
Developmental changes	Early adolescence	Most young adolescents are identity diffused or foreclosed, with the majority being diffused. Confidence in parental support, a self-reflective perspective about the future, and a sense of industry are important early adolescent characteristics that pave the way for the development of more mature identity later in adolescence and early adulthood.

Erikson's View of Identity and Intimacy

Erikson (1968) has written extensively about intimacy as well as identity. He believes that intimacy should come after adolescents are well on their way to achieving a stable and successful identity. The development of intimacy, in Erikson's view, is another life crisis—if intimacy is not developed in young adulthood, the person may be left with what Erikson refers to as isolation. Erikson described intimacy versus isolation as the sixth stage in the human life cycle, coming after the identity versus identity confusion issue has been explored.

IDENTITY

Concept	Process/related ideas	Characteristics/description
	Late adolescence	It is during the post-high school years that the greatest shifts in identity are thought to occur, as many individuals move closer to identity achievement at this time. Some experts believe that college experiences promote identity exploration.
Sex differences	Vocational and interpersonal identity	Early research has indicated that a theme of vocational achievement is more characteristic of the identity of males, while interpersonal interests occupy the identity of females more, but more recent research in the late seventies and eighties suggests little, if any, sex differences.
Sociocultural influences	Culture	Erikson believes that cultural influences are very important in the development of identity. Sociopolitical climate, race, and social class are cultural factors that contribute to identity development. There have been few applications of Erikson's ideas to educational curricula, although some educational strategies reveal increases in identity exploration.
	Family and peer influences	Both family and peers influence identity development. In particular, a family context involving individuation and connectedness seems to enhance identity exploration.
Measuring Identity	Problems and prospects	Identity is a very global construct, and like many such broad ideas, is very difficult to measure. The same problems associated with evaluation of self-concept apply to identity assessment as well. Nonetheless, a number of researchers are actively working on better assessments of identity—one such measure expands its measurement to interpersonal dimensions.

Erikson refers to intimacy in terms of both sexual relationships and friendships. He comments:

As the young individual seeks at least tentative forms of playful intimacy in friendship and competition, in sex play and love, in argument and gossip, he is apt to experience a peculiar strain, as if such tentative engagement might turn into an interpersonal fusion amounting to a loss of identity and requiring, therefore, a tense inner reservation, a caution in commitment. Where a youth does not resolve such a commitment, he may isolate himself and enter, at best, only stereotyped and formalized interpersonal relations; or he may, in repeated hectic attempts and dismal failures, seek intimacy with the most improbable of partners. For where an assured sense of identity is missing, even friendships and affairs become desperate attempts at delineating the fuzzy outlines of identity by mutual narcissistic mirroring; to fall in love means to fall in love with one's mirror image, hurting oneself and damaging the mirror. (1968, p. 167)

An inability to develop meaningful relationships with others during adolescence and young adulthood can be harmful to an individual's personality. It may lead him to repudiate, ignore, or attack those who appear frustrating to him. Erikson (1968) asserts that such situations can account for the shallow, almost pathetic attempts of adolescents to merge themselves with a "leader." Many adolescents want to be apprentices or disciples of leaders and adults who will shelter them from the harm of an "out-group" world. If this fails, and Erikson believes that it must, then sooner or later the adolescent will recoil into a self-search to discover where she went wrong. Such introspection sometimes leads to painful feelings of isolation and depression, and may contribute to mistrust of others and restrict the adolescent's willingness to act on her own initiative.

The Five Statuses of Intimacy

Just as Marcia has classified the development of identity into four different statuses, he and his colleagues have also divided the development of intimacy into different levels characterized by intimate, preintimate, stereotyped, pseudointimate, and isolated styles of interaction. (Orlofsky, Marcia, and Lesser, 1973). The **intimate** individual forms and maintains one or more deep and long-lasting love relationships. The **preintimate** individual has mixed emotions about commitment—this ambivalence is reflected in his strategy of offering love without any obligations or long-lasting bonds. In most instances, the **stereotyped** individual has superficial relationships that tend to be dominated by friendship ties with same-sex rather than opposite-sex individuals. The **pseudointimate** individual appears to

One type of intimacy status called "isolated" is one in which the adolescent withdraws from social encounters.

be maintaining a long-lasting heterosexual attachment, but the relationship has little or no depth or closeness. Finally, the **isolated** individual withdraws from social encounters and has little or no intimate attachment to same- or opposite-sex individuals. Occasionally the isolate shows signs of developing interpersonal relations, but usually such interactions are anxiety provoking. One investigation indicated that intimate and preintimate individuals are more sensitive to their partners' needs, as well as more open in their friendships, than individuals characterized by the other three intimacy statuses (Orlofsky, 1976).

Research on Intimacy

Research on intimacy has attempted to establish the importance of identity development as a precursor for intimacy. For example, in one investigation (Kacerguis and Adams, 1980), college males and females who indicated they had a stable sense of identity were more likely to attain intimacy status based on Orlofsky's classification than their counterparts who were less identity achieved. By contrast, students who were foreclosed, in moratorium, or diffused were more likely to have one of the other four intimacy statuses. This work supports Erikson's belief that identity development is closely linked (and perhaps is even an important precursor) to intimacy.

Other recent research (e.g., Levitz-Jones and Orlofsky, 1985) also supports the belief that individuation is an important precursor for mature intimacy. For example, low-intimacy women had a lower capacity for individuation and self-reliance and a higher degree of insecure attachment. And, as we see next, the lack of establishing a mature identity may be involved in the failure of many adolescent marriages.

Sally Archer (1985) interviewed divorced women about their expressions of identity and intimacy at the points of high school, marriage, divorce, and the present. Foreclosed identity and romantic intimacy were highest at high school and marriage. Identity moratorium was highest at divorce, while identity achievement and friendship intimacy were highest at the time the divorced women were interviewed in their adult years. (See figure 10.2 for a portrayal of the identity statuses of the divorced women at different points in their lives.)

Complexity in the Path of Identity and Intimacy

We have emphasized that Erikson's belief about identity coming before intimacy seems intuitively correct if optimal development is to occur. However, there are other possibilities, according to John Meacham and Nicholas Santilli (1982). One issue they raise is, What happens when identity foreclosure occurs? One possibility is that the individual progresses to the point of experiencing, but not necessarily resolving, the crisis of intimacy versus isolation. Any of several resolutions is then possible. For example, this new crisis may be irresolvable until the individual returns to and successfully resolves the identity crisis. Such a sequence is

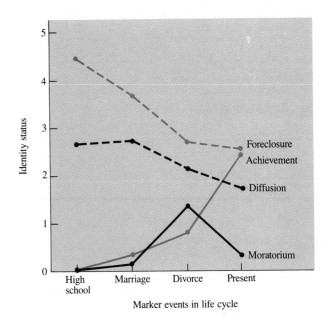

Figure 10.2 Identity statuses of divorced women during high school, at the time of marriage, at the time of divorce, and at present.

compatible with Erikson's belief that the crises may be experienced out of order, but must be resolved in a universal order. A second possibility is that the individual may resolve the intimacy crisis and then move forward to the generativity versus stagnation crisis. Finally, a third possibility is that, after resolving the intimacy crisis, the individual may return to the identity crisis. The three possible paths (which at present have not been researched) would then be, respectively: intimacy (unresolved), identity, intimacy and generativity; intimacy and generativity; or intimacy, identity, and generativity. Other sequences are possible, but these three provide some indication of the variability in which individuals may experience and/or resolve the identity and intimacy crises. For example, there is some evidence that women experience the crisis of intimacy before identity (e.g., Douvan and Adelson, 1966; Fischer, 1981).

Summary

I. Information about the self focuses on the self as knower and as object, the measurement of self-concept, and developmental changes in self-conceptions during adolescence.

  A. The self as knower, or I, refers to the active processing of information about the self, while the self as object, or Me, emphasizes the product of observing the self, usually evaluated in terms of self-concept.

    1. The humanistic view argues that self-concept is the central, organizing part of personality. Self-perceptions are viewed as very important determinants of behavior—this emphasizes a phenomenological approach. Rogers argued that a distinction between the ideal and real self is important in understanding adjustment. Relations between self-concept and parenting as well as academic behavior have been documented.

    2. The information processing perspective is being called on to develop ideas about the self as knower. One strategy is to view the self as social memory. Research has shown that adolescents remember information more efficiently when it relates to themselves.

  B. Ideas about measuring self-concept involve the traditional approach, some contemporary measures, and multimethod assessment.

    1. The traditional approach focuses on the global nature of the self—information about many dimensions of the self is combined into one overall self-concept score that is viewed as positive or negative.

    2. Contemporary measures of self-concept are more likely to evaluate general self-worth as well as self-perceptions about different dimensions of the self. The Harter Perceived Competence Scale for Children provides information about general self-worth plus self-perceptions of cognitive competence, social competence, and physical competence. The SIQYA, Self-Image Questionnaire for Young Adolescents, also provides information about specific dimensions of the self.

    3. A combination of methods may provide a more complete analysis of self-concept than relying on a single paper-and-pencil measure.

  C. Ideas about developmental changes in the self involve cognitive changes and Piaget's theory as well as Selman's view of levels of thinking about the self and interpersonal understanding.

    1. Among the cognitive changes in the self during adolescence are those involving increasing abstractness, idealism, organization, sophisticated use of language, logical reasoning, perspective taking, and personality assessment. The adolescent's thoughts are more differentiated, individuated, and stable than the child's thoughts. According to Elkind, it is during adolescence that an individual develops a true self theory.

    2. Selman proposed five stages of perspective taking that provide information about self-development: egocentric viewpoint, social-informational role taking, self-reflective role taking, mutual role taking, and social and conventional system role taking. These stages are believed to unfold sequentially with the latter two characterizing adolescence.

II. Information about identity involves Erik Erikson's theory, the four statuses of identity, developmental changes, sex differences, sociocultural influences, measuring identity, and the relation of identity to intimacy.

A. To learn more about Erikson's ideas, it is necessary to revisit the eight stages of the life cycle, consider personality and role experimentation, and look at a contemporary view of identity development.

1. Identity versus identity confusion (diffusion) is the fifth stage in Erikson's theory, coming approximately at the time of adolescence. Identity involves the adolescent's search for who he or she is as a person.

2. An important aspect of identity development is the opportunity to try out different personalities and roles.

3. Erikson's concept of identity is complex, involving such components as genetic, adaptive, structural, dynamic, subjective or experiential, psychosocial reciprocity and existential status.

4. Identity development is a life-long process, although it is during the adolescent years that for the first time in development physical, cognitive, and social skills are sufficiently advanced for the individual to seriously inquire and investigate who she or he is as a person. Although some identity crises may be cataclysmic, the majority involve gradual development over many years.

B. Information about the four statuses of identity focuses on crisis and commitment as well as diffusion, foreclosure, moratorium, and achievement.

1. Crisis refers to the exploration of alternatives, while commitment is the extent to which the individual shows personal investment in what he or she is doing.

2. The adolescent who is diffused or confused has not undergone a crisis or made a commitment; one who is foreclosed has made a commitment, but not undergone a crisis; one who is in moratorium is in the midst of a crisis, but has not yet made a commitment; and one who is achieved has both undergone a crisis and made a commitment.

C. Ideas about developmental changes in identity involve early and late adolescence.

1. Most young adolescents are identity diffused or foreclosed, with the majority being diffused. Confidence in parental support, a self-reflective perspective about the future, and a sense of industry are important early adolescent characteristics that pave the way for the development of more mature identity exploration in late adolescence and early adulthood.

2. It is during the post-high school years that the greatest changes in identity exploration occur with many individuals moving closer to identity achievement. Some experts believe college experiences promote identity exploration.

D. Early research revealed that the identity development of males was more likely to involve vocational achievement, while the identity development of females was more heavily focused on interpersonal relationships. More recent research has revealed few, if any, sex differences in identity development.

E. Sociocultural influences on identity include different aspects of culture as well as the important contributions of family and peers.

1. Erikson believes that cultural influences are very important in identity development. Sociopolitical climate, race, and social class are cultural factors that influence identity development. There have been few applications of Erikson's ideas to educational curricula, although some educational strategies reveal increases in identity exploration.

2. Both family and peers influence identity development. In particular, a family context involving individuation and connectedness seems to enhance identity development.

F. Identity is a global construct, and like many such broad ideas, it is very difficult to measure. The same problems associated with the measurement of self-concept apply to identity as well. Nonetheless, a number of researchers are working on better assessments of identity—one such measure expands its assessment to include interpersonal dimensions of identity.

G. Ideas about the relation of identity to intimacy focus on Erikson's ideas, the five statuses of intimacy, research on intimacy, and the complexity of identity–intimacy pathways.

1. Erikson describes intimacy versus isolation as the sixth state in his life-cycle theory, coming after the crisis of identity versus identity confusion has been explored.

2. Orlofsky describes five statuses of intimacy—intimate, preintimate, stereotyped, pseudointimate, and isolated.

3. There is some indication that identity exploration, prior to the kind of intimacy involved in a deep love relationship, is a psychologically healthy developmental path.

4. Keep in mind, though, that the link between identity and intimacy is complex, and there often are different pathways to developmental maturity.

Key Terms

connectedness *424*

global self-concept *398*

humanism *398*

ideal self *398*

identity achieved *419*

identity crisis *414*

identity diffused (confused) *419*

identity foreclosure *419*

identity moratorium *419*

individuation *424*

intimate *432*

isolated *432*

phenomenological approach *398*

preintimate *432*

pseudointimate *432*

real self *398*

self as knower *398*

self as object *398*

stereotyped *432*

Coles, R. (1970). *Erik H. Erikson: The growth of his work*. Boston: Little, Brown.
Robert Coles is famous for his psychoanalytic interpretations of the life histories of different American cultures. In this biography of Erikson, he writes about Erikson's personal life and interprets Erikson's identity theory.

Erikson, E. H. (1963). *Childhood and society,* 2d ed. New York: Norton.
This is Erikson's first book. It includes his initial writings about identity development. Many examples of identity crisis are discussed, including those in the lives of Adolf Hitler, the Yurok Indians, and Maxim Gorky.

Erikson, E. H., ed. (1965). *The challenge of youth*. New York: Doubleday.
This excellent book of readings on youth includes articles by Erikson on the fidelity and diversity of youth, by Bruno Bettelheim on the problem of generations, and by Kenneth Kenniston on social change and youth in America. The focus of the articles is the adolescent's development of identity.

Harter, S. (1983). Developmental perspectives on the self-system. In P. H. Mussen (Ed.), *Handbook of child psychology,* 4th ed., vol. 4. New York: Wiley.
A thorough overview of the development of the self, particularly in terms of its development during childhood. Provides extensive information about self-concept and self-esteem.

Journal of Early Adolescence, Special Issue on Identity Development, 3 (1983).
This special issue of the Journal of Early Adolescence *is devoted to identity development with particular attention given to the neglected topic of identity formation in early adolescence. Includes articles by leading thinkers and researchers such as Marcia, Grotevant and Cooper, Adams and Montemayor, and Archer and Waterman.*

Selman, R. L. (1980). *The growth of interpersonal understanding*. New York: Academic Press.
Considerable detail is given about Selman's developmental theory of perspective taking and self development. Includes information about clinical implications for helping.

Chapter · 11

Sex Roles and Sexuality

Prologue

Her Daughter Knew More about Chickens Than Any Girl Has a Right to Know

There is no need for you to be embarrassed about S-E-X," I told my daughter. "Sit down and I will tell you all I know about it. First, Lassie is a girl. Second, I lied. Sensuous lips do not mean fever blisters. Third, I did not conceive you by drinking the blood of an owl and spitting three times at a full moon. Here is the bra and girdle section from the Sears catalogue. If you have any questions, keep them to yourself."

I don't suppose that was too technical, but a friend of mine overdid it. She bought books and charts depicting the reproduction cycles of chickens. Together they studied mating, fertilization, and a racy chapter on chromosomes. Her daughter knew more about chickens than any young girl has a right to know.

One day, her mother walked out on the front porch and saw a rooster perched on the porch swing and liked to have had a heart attack.

Anyway, two weeks after my "talk" with my daughter she brought home Leroy.

Leroy was big for his brain. I couldn't look at him without remembering why the dinosaurs disappeared from the earth.

During the two years he was to live with us I can remember only one expression he used. He would come into the house and say, "You look like a drowned rat." (I always looked up and smiled only to discover he was talking to the dog.)

The first time my husband noticed Leroy, he was polishing off a loaf of toast, and a half gallon of milk.

"Who's that?" asked my husband.

"It's Leroy," I answered.

"He's a sex maniac," he said.

"Don't worry about it," I said.

"What do you mean, 'Don't worry about it'?"

"You haven't lost a daughter. You've only gained a disposal with teeth."

We saw a lot of Leroy, which is the greatest understatement since Noah called the weather bureau and got a recording predicting light showers and drizzle.

He arrived in time for breakfast, returning after school, spent entire evenings, plus weekends, holidays, and summers.

They never seemed to do anything together except eat and drink. One day I was passing through the kitchen when Leroy leaned over close to my daughter's ear. I held my breath. This was it. Was he going to nibble on it? Blow into it? Proposition it? I leaned closer, straining to pick up a few words. He spoke. "You got anything to settle my stomach?"

I know enough about sex to know that when bicarbonate enters the room . . . love flies out of the window.

Source: Bombeck, E., and Keane, B. Just wait till you have children of your own! *New York: Fawcett/Crest, 1971.*

*E*ach of us is curious about our sex, and how we behave and think as males and females. This curiosity includes our biological makeup as male and female, but it goes far beyond these biological underpinnings as well. Culture has played a prominent role in shaping the thoughts and behaviors of males and females. In this chapter, we begin by exploring the burgeoning interest in the roles of adolescents as males and females. Then, in the second part of the chapter, considerable time is spent evaluating the nature of adolescent sexuality.

Sex Roles: Images of Boys and Girls

The roles of adolescents as males and females have become a highly stimulating field of research as these roles have become revised considerably in recent years. We begin by describing the nature of masculinity, femininity, and androgyny, the latter term being the most controversial and provocative aspect of roles pertaining to males and females in the 1970s and 1980s. Next, we turn to the biological and cognitive factors involved, then environmental contributions, and conclude with information about stereotypes and differences between males and females.

Masculinity, Femininity, and Adrogyny

When conducting research on sex roles in the mid-1960s, we classified individuals as being either masculine or feminine. In recent years, though, there has been a tremendous amount of interest in looking at people in terms of combinations of masculine and feminine characteristics. Let's now look at the masculinity-femininity tradition and, subsequently, at the more recently developed idea of androgyny.

Masculinity and Femininity

For many years, it was believed that the well-adjusted adolescent was an individual who behaved in a sex-appropriate way, that is, a male adolescent was supposed to be masculine and a female adolescent was supposed to be feminine. A variety of characteristics have been described as "masculine" and many others have been referred to as "feminine." Basically, these character-istics are those that are stereotypically masculine or feminine in a particular culture; thus, in the United States, it has been masculine to be independent and aggressive and it has been feminine to be dependent and unaggressive. It has been masculine to be oriented toward math and feminine to be interested in verbal skills. And, it has been masculine to become power-oriented and feminine to not be power-oriented.

Androgyny

By the mid-1970s, the landscape of sex roles had changed considerably. It had become obvious that increased numbers of females in our culture were unhappy with being labeled "feminine," and stigmatized with adjectives such as passive, dependent, and unassertive. And there were a number of males, who likewise were unhappy with being described as "masculine," and labeled with such characteristics as rugged, aggressive, and power-oriented. It seemed apparent to a number of lay people and scientists that traditional concepts of "masculinity" and "femininity" no longer were as useful as they once were because the sex roles of society were changing so rapidly. The byword in sex–gender roles in the 1970s became **androgyny,** which refers to a combination of masculine and feminine characteristics in the same individual. The androgynous adolescent is referred to as an individual who has both positive features of masculinity and femininity, rather than only having strong masculine or strong feminine characteristics.

Among the measures that are used to assess androgyny are the Bem Sex-Role Inventory, the BSRI, (Bem, 1974); the Personal Attributes Questionnaire, the PAQ, (Spence, Helmreich, and Stapp, 1974); the masculinity and femininity scales of the Adjective Check List, the ACL, (Heilbrun, 1976); the masculinity and femininity scales of the California Psychological Inventory, the CPI, (Baucom, 1976); and the Personality Research Form ANDRO scale, the PRF ANDRO, (Berzins et al., 1978); as well as the children's versions of the PAQ, the CPAQ, (Hall and Halberstadt, 1980) and the BSRI, the CSRI, (Trupin, 1979).

Being dominant and forceful are among the masculine characteristics of sex role measures.

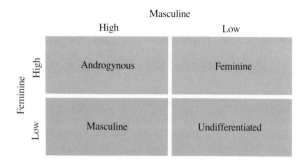

Figure 11.1 The categories used on androgyny scales.

The core dimensions of these measures appear to be related to self-assertion and integration (Ford, 1986). For example, the masculinity items on the BSRI and the PRF ANDRO tend to be similar and reflect self-assertion. They include acts as leader, has leadership qualities, dominant, willing to take a stand, willing to take risks, independent, forceful, competitive, strong personality, and individualistic. The items for femininity on the BSRI and the PRF ANDRO also are similar and reflect integration: sympathetic, loves children, eager to soothe hurt feelings, sensitive to the needs of others, tender, compassionate, affectionate, gentle, warm, and understanding.

Thus, it is important to recognize that new items and new characteristics have not been developed to characterize the individual with an androgynous orientation. Rather, the androgynous adolescent is simply either a male or female who has a high degree of both masculine and feminine characteristics. That is, there is no third set of items on the sex roles measures that tap androgyny—categorizing the adolescent as androgynous comes from his or her responses that are masculine as well as feminine. On most androgyny scales, a fourth category also is possible. The adolescent who says that neither the masculine nor the feminine characteristics portray him or her is often referred to as **undifferentiated.** Figure 11.1 shows the four categories used on most androgyny scales—masculine, feminine, androgynous, and undifferentiated, as well as the kind of responses to the items required to be placed in one of the categories.

Masculinity, Femininity, Androgyny, and Competence
Which adolescents are the most competent—those who are masculine, feminine, or androgynous? The answer to this question is difficult for several reasons. There has been a failure to untangle the multiple meanings of sex–gender roles and masculinity–femininity and androgyny. Second, there has not been a clear specification of why and when masculinity, femininity, and androgyny should be linked with greater personal and social competence. There have been far too many research studies about androgyny that lack any theoretical foundation (Worrell, 1978). In the area of androgyny, researchers have developed a rash of new scales and have related androgyny to anything and everything! The anything and everything includes variables as diverse as self-esteem, achievement, health, sexual maturity, hypnotic suggestibility, fantasy content, personal space, menstrual distress, appreciation of sexual humor, arousal, and so on.

An important task for masculinity–femininity and androgyny research is the specification of dimensions involved. Some researchers (e.g., Block, 1973; Ford, 1986) argue that when we limit our discussion of androgyny to the dimensions of self-assertion and integration, we have gone further in specifying the nature of the androgyny concept than frequently has been the case in research on the topic. As Jeanne Block (1973) has argued, the competent male should temper his self-assertion with mutuality in social encounters and the competent female should modify her integrative tendencies with a stronger sense of self-assertion.

However, it is important to recognize that competence criteria are often governed by more than just self-assertion and integration. The idea that androgynous individuals should be better at everything is very simplistic and will not hold water. For example, androgyny likely is not closely linked with factors that are heavily cognitive or biological in nature such as intelligence, physical health, and creativity. These factors are likely dependent on other powerful forces such as genetic potential, quality of schooling, nutrition, life stress, and many other variables. Even outcomes focusing on social and personality development are likely to be related to many factors unrelated to self-assertive and integrative qualities of the individual. This seems to occur in particular under two types of conditions: first, when distinct gender-related criteria are used as outcome variables (such as attitudes toward women, sexual orientation, vocational choice) (Helmreich et al., 1979; Storms, 1980; Wolfe and Betz, 1981; Zeldow, 1976), and second, when the outcome variables involve attitudes, perceptions, or beliefs (such as expectancies or attributions) rather than performance, adjustment, or development (Baumcom and Danker-Brown, 1979; Bem, 1977; Crimmings, 1978; Cummings, 1979; Pritscher, 1980).

Further refinement of when androgyny may or may not be an advantageous sex-role makeup involves consideration of the relevant contexts in a culture that promotes and values self-assertive and integrative behaviors. Some behaviors that are adaptive in one setting may not be adaptive in another setting. For example, in achievement-oriented settings, self-assertion usually is promoted and valued. And for that matter,

"Feminine" or "integrative" individuals may show better adaptation in religious contexts than "masculine" or "androgynous" individuals.

in our entire American culture, self-assertion tends to be valued more than integration. Along this line of thinking, such self-assertive qualities as initiative and competitiveness are adaptive, but in other contexts, they may not be as adaptive. For example, most religious contexts emphasize fellowship and interdependence rather than self-reliance or self-interest. In such contexts, androgynous adolescents may not be judged as competent as feminine or integratively oriented individuals.

The implications of our discussion on androgyny suggest that androgynous adolescents will not be more competent than other adolescents in all circumstances. If the criteria for competence primarily involve self-assertion *and* integration, then we would expect the androgynous adolescent to fare better than adolescents of other sex-role makeups. However, for criteria that primarily involve self-assertion, we would anticipate both masculine and androgynous adolescents to perform effectively, but for criteria focusing on integration, we would expect feminine and androgynous adolescents to do well. And, for criteria unrelated to self-assertion and integration, we would anticipate that androgynous adolescents would not perform more competently than nonandrogynous adolescents.

Yet another important point to be made about the androgyny research literature is that the self-assertive dimension has been valued as more important than the integrative dimension. Thus, just as our culture has been biased toward the masculine, self-assertive dimension, so have the criteria used to assess competence been oriented in this direction as well. For example, an analysis of the criteria used to assess social competence when it is linked to androgyny suggests that self-assertive dimensions outnumber integrative dimensions by about a two-to-one margin (Ford, 1986). A disturbing outcome of this tendency is that overgeneralizations about the desirability of masculine, self-assertive characteristics are sometimes made along with comments about the undesirability of feminine or integrative characteristics when social competence is at issue (e.g., Antill and Cunningham, 1979; Deutsch and Gilbert, 1976; Hansoon et al., 1980; Jones et al., 1978; Kelly and Worrell, 1977; Kenworthy, 1979; Olds and Shaver, 1980; Silvern and Ryan, 1979; Williams, 1979).

An example of research pertaining to the link between sex roles and social competence in adolescence focuses on adolescents' abilities to handle challenging situations. To learn more about this investigation, read Perspective on Adolescent Development 11.1.

Now that we have studied some of the important dimensions of sex roles, such as masculinity, femininity, and androgyny, we turn our attention to the factors that contribute to the development of sex roles.

Biological and Cognitive Factors in Sex-Role Development

There has been an increased interest in the developmental aspects of sex roles in recent years, as witnessed by the number of theoretical views on sex roles that contain developmental components. Most developmental views of sex roles rely heavily on biological and cognitive processes.

Biological Factors

Biological factors in sex roles are represented in the psychoanalytic views of Freud and Erikson, the role of hormones, and the interaction of biology and culture.

Freud and Erikson: Anatomy Is Destiny

One of Freud's basic assumptions is that human behavior and history are directly related to reproductive processes. From this assumption arises the belief that sexuality is essentially unlearned and instinctual. Erik Erikson (1968) has extended this argument, claiming that psychological differences in males and females stem from anatomical differences between the two groups. Erikson argues that because of genital structure, males are more intrusive and aggressive, while females are more inclusive and passive. Erikson's belief is sometimes referred to as the **anatomy is destiny** doctrine.

To support his ideas, Erikson (1951) designed and observed the play-building activities of eleven- through thirteen-year-old boys and girls. He found that girls tended to construct low edifices that almost always were enclosed, while boys were more likely to build taller, elongated towers. According to Paula Caplan (1978), Erikson's conclusion that play configuration differences are due to sexual anatomy is unwarranted. She argues that when Erikson's data are closely inspected, of a total of 468 play configurations only thirty-nine, or eight percent, included any sort of tower structure. And boys actually constructed about three to four times as many enclosures as towers.

Some psychoanalytic thinkers, however, believe that Caplan's interpretation of Erikson is naive, representing a misunderstanding of Erikson's view. Erikson does not say, they protest, that anatomy is destiny in an absolute sense; he simply argues that imagery is partly a function of body structure and that imagery provides a person with a unique perspective. Erikson also points out that women are transcending that perspective to correct our society's overemphasis on male intrusiveness and to arrive at a truly androgynous sexual orientation.

Hormones

Additional support for the importance of biological forces comes from the fact that the sexes differ genetically and biochemically. Much of the research used to support this belief has been conducted with animals,

ANDROGYNY AND SOCIAL COMPETENCE DURING
ADOLESCENCE—THE IMPORTANCE OF SELF-ASSERTION
AND INTEGRATION

*O*ne of the most direct assessments of the link between androgyny and social competence in adolescence involved judgments made in six hypothetical
situations (Ford and Tisak, 1981). The study focused on
304 ninth graders and 316 twelfth graders in two different schools. Ratings were made of the degree to which
integrative and self-assertive skills were required to meet
the challenge described in each situation. Social competence was assessed by the Social Competence Nomination Form as well as during an interview. The
nomination form was obtained from the adolescents
themselves, their peers, and their teachers. A summary
of the social competence ratings in relation to the sex-
role status of the adolescents is presented in table 11.1.
As can be seen, the androgynous adolescents were superior overall when compared with other adolescents, although it was found that self-assertive and integrative
adolescents did quite well in circumstances related to
their particular skills. Disengaged adolescents (those not
classified as self-assertive, integrative, or androgynous)
were socially ineffective, scoring the lowest regardless of
the sample, the judge, or the situation.

No developmental changes in self-assertion and integration were found in the investigation. However, it is
possible that when adolescents themselves are allowed
to define criteria for success, they are less likely than
adults to evaluate androgyny as desirable, at least for
males. These comparisons of adolescents and adults, and
their developmental differences on androgyny have been
found in several studies (Massad, 1981; Mussen, 1962).
For example, in one investigation (Massad, 1981), integration was linked with peer acceptance in females,

*Kindness and consideration of others are important
aspects of integration.*

but not males, while self-assertion was related to peer
acceptance for both sexes. Such results indicate that developmental and individual variation in the desirability
of androgyny may occur when the criteria used to judge
social competence are varied.

The results described here in terms of the Ford and
Tisak (1981) study suggest that when specific criteria
for androgyny are outlined and these correspond to the
dimensions used to define social competence, we can expect androgyny and social competence to be related.
However, when self-assertion and integration are used
as the referents for androgyny and other unrelated criteria are used to index social competence, we would expect far less congruence between androgyny and social
competence.

since experimental manipulation of hormones is unethical with humans. Sex-related hormone levels in children are low and appear to be about the same for boys
and girls, so it is unlikely that behavioral differences in
boys and girls could be due to hormonal levels. However, with the onset of puberty, both boys' and girls'

bodies are flooded with sex-related hormones. One review of the literature on sex hormones concluded that
testosterone (male hormone) levels are related to
aggression in adolescent males, but environmental influences can change hormonal levels drastically (Hoyenga and Hoyenga, 1979; Reinisch and Karow, 1977).

Table 11.1 Adolescent androgyny and social competence

Social competence	Sex-role categorization			
	Androgynous (balanced)	Masculine (self-assertive)	Feminine (integrative)	Undifferentiated (disengaged)
Self ratings (1 = high; 5 = low)				
School 1	2.03	2.52	2.55	3.01
School 2	2.24	2.48	2.51	2.82
Teacher ratings (1 = high; 5 = low)				
School 1	2.62	2.94	3.00	3.51
School 2	2.81	2.89	2.92	2.94
Peer nominations (number of actual nominations)				
School 1	36	22	18	11
School 2	27	19	23	14
Interview rating (1 = high; 5 = low)				
School 1	1.94	2.44	2.51	3.13

Note: In this particular aspect of the investigation, the self ratings are based on 216 and 347 for schools one and two respectively. The Ns for the teacher and peer ratings are 218 and 356; and the N for interview ratings was 204. (N refers to number of subjects.)

Source: From Ford, M. E., and S. M. Tisak (April 1981). "Adolescent Androgeny and its Relationship to Social Competence, Identity Status, and Academic Achievement." Paper presented at the biennial meeting of the Society for Research in Child Development, Boston.

In addition to the adolescent years, the period before birth is another time during which sex hormones are produced extensively. Anna Ehrhardt has extensively studied the influence of prenatal hormonal changes on sex-role development (Ehrhardt and Baker, 1973). In the 1950s, a number of expectant mothers were given doses of androgen (a male sex hormone); these women had a history of miscarriage, and the hormone was believed to ameliorate conditions that cause this problem. Six offspring of these mothers were studied, ranging from four to twenty-six years of age. They were compared with siblings of the same sex who were unaffected by the hormonal treatment because their mothers had not been treated with androgen during the prenatal period. Results indicate that hormones are an important factor in sex-role development. The fetally androgenized girls expended comparatively more energy in their play and seemed to prefer boys over girls as playmates. Instead of dolls they chose male sex-typed toys for play. They displayed little interest in future marriage and did not enjoy taking care of babies. They also preferred functional over attractive clothes and were generally unconcerned with their appearance. The boys whose mothers received androgen engaged in rough-and-tumble play and outdoor sports to a greater extent than their unaffected brothers did.

Ehrhardt's work has been criticized for a number of reasons, two of which follow. First, the inflated androgen levels require that these individuals be treated with cortisone for the remainder of their lives. One of the side effects of cortisone is a high activity level. The high energy and activity levels of the androgenized girls and boys, then, may be due to the cortisone treatment rather than to high levels of androgen (Quadagno, Briscoe, and Quadagno, 1977). Second, "masculinized" girls may be perceived as deviant by their parents, siblings, and peers. Those around them may have thought of them as "tomboyish" and treated them accordingly.

No one argues about the existence of genetic, biochemical, and anatomical differences between the sexes. Even strongly environmentally oriented psychologists acknowledge that boys and girls will be treated differently because of their physical differences and their different roles in reproduction. Consequently, the importance of biological factors is not at issue; what is at issue is the directness or indirectness of the effect of biological factors on social behavior. If a high androgen level directly influences the central nervous system, which in turn produces a higher activity level, then the effect is reasonably direct. By contrast, if a high level of androgen produces strong muscle development, which in turn causes others to expect the adolescent to be a good athlete and in turn leads her to participate in sports, then the biological effect is more indirect.

John Money is a well-known theorist and researcher who sees sex-role development as affected by both biology and culture (Money, 1973). His ideas are based on the notion of what he calls "critical periods," or brief times in the individual's life when biological changes combine with environmental events to produce a virtually irreversible sex-role patterning. These critical periods are crucial in the formation of the adolescent's sex role (Money, 1965).

In Money's view, there are two critical periods for sex-role development in youth: the first three years of life and puberty. During each of these periods, the young child or adolescent is confronted with rapid changes that influence his or her sex-role concept. One of several outcomes is possible: (1) the individual may form an adaptive concept of "maleness" or "femaleness" to fit his or her own physical category; (2) the individual may be confused about the psychological characteristics associated with his or her physical category; or (3) the individual may settle on some mixed sex role (that is, female role-male body, or male role-female body).

During the early critical period, from ages one to three, the child exercises his newly formed ability to discriminate anatomical sex differences and simple sex-role conventions (for example, hair style, clothing) and to associate these with social attitudes about what boys and girls are like. During the critical adolescent period, sex-role identity once again is transformed, this time for different reasons. The adolescent experiences rapid physiological and anatomical changes, and becomes able to deal with abstract social possibilities (for example, what the ideal woman or man is like). These changes cause conflict and force the adolescent to reconsider his or her ideas about sex roles.

Quite clearly, biological processes play an important role in sex-role development. And, as we see next, cognitive factors need to be considered as well if we are to fully understand sex roles.

Cognitive Factors

The role of cognition in sex roles has involved study of the importance of self-categorization and language. The ideas of Lawrence Kohlberg and others suggest that a stable gender indentity must be reached before a sense of masculinity or femininity is achieved.

Self-Categorization and Stable Gender Identity

Lawrence Kohlberg (1966) argued that to have an idea of what is masculine or feminine, a child must be able to categorize objects into these two groups—masculine or feminine. According to Kohlberg, the categories become relatively stable for a child by the age of six. That is, by the age of six, children have a fairly definite idea of which category they belong to. Further, they understand what is entailed by belonging to one category or the other, and seldom fluctuate in their category judgments. This self-categorization is seen as the impetus for the unfolding of sex-role development according to Kohlberg.

Kohlberg reasons that sex-role development proceeds in this sequence: "I am a boy, I want to do boy things, therefore, the opportunity to do boy things is rewarding" (1966, p. 89). The child, having acquired the ability to categorize, strives toward consistency between the use of the categories and actual behavior. This striving for consistency forms the basis for the development of sex typing.

Others have expanded on Kohlberg's cognitive developmental theme (e.g. Block, 1973; Pleck, 1975; Rebecca, Hefner, and Oleshansky, 1976). For example, one proposal suggests that initially there is a stage of undifferentiated sex-role concepts among very young children, then in the next stage (about the time of the preschool years) children adopt very rigid, conventional sex roles (Pleck, 1975). It is believed that this rigidity often peaks during the early adolescent years. Then, at some point later in development, often not until the adult years, a stronger androgyny orientation emerges (e.g., Block, 1973; Pleck, 1975).

To investigate the cognitive developmental concepts of Kohlberg and others, Eileen O'Keefe and Janet Hyde (1983) studied the relation of cognitive developmental level to occupational choice and stereotyping. Two types of occupational attitudes were assessed: personal aspirations and ideas about jobs men and women do. Preschool, third-grade, and sixth-grade children were studied. Children chose stereotyped occupations for themselves even before they had developed a concept of gender stability. Boys' personal aspirations were more stereotyped than girls'. Gender stable preschoolers gave more stereotyped responses

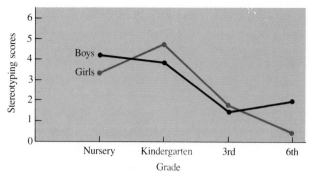

Note: 0 = no stereotyping; 10 = high stereotyping

Figure 11.2   Stereotyping of adult occupations by children of different ages.

than those not yet gender stable. And, stereotyping decreased among the third and sixth graders (figure 11.2). The results concerning the gender stable preschoolers support Kohlberg's ideas about self-categorization; however, the early stereotyped responses of the nursery school children does not. The fact that young children already have stereotypes before they have developed a stable gender identity is more compatible with the belief that environmental experiences contribute to sex-role development. We will discuss such environmental contributions shortly, but first further information about the role of cognitive factors is explored as we study language and sex roles.

Language, Cognition, and Sex Roles

There has been considerable interest generated in understanding the nature of sexism in language—the notion that the English language contains sex bias, particularly in terms of usages such as "he" and "man" referring to everyone. To learn more about sexism in language, read Perspective on Adolescent Development 11.2. Intriguing research on children's, adolescents', and adults' interpretation of various sex-related aspects of language is presented along with a discussion of whether sexist language produces sexist thought or vice versa.

Cognitive capacities are extremely important in the development of sex roles, but as we see next, they do not explain entirely the wide variation in behavior observed in members of the same sex. Such individual variation undoubtedly is strongly influenced by environmental experiences.

HOW GOOD ARE GIRLS AT WUDGEMAKING IF THE WUDGEMAKER IS "HE"?

*O*ne manner in which the role of language in sex-role development can be investigated is by studying children's interpretation of the gender neutral use of *he* and *his*. Janet Hyde (1984) investigated this issue by presenting cue sentences to first, third, and fifth graders, as well as college students. The individuals, then, told stories in response to a cue sentence containing *he, he or she,* or *they.* The individuals also supplied pronouns in a fill-in task and were questioned about their knowledge of the gender-neutral use of "he." It was found that 12, 18, and 42 percent of the stories were about females when "he," "she," and "he or she" were used, respectively. Children, even first graders, supplied "he" in gender-neutral, fill-in sentences. Only twenty-eight percent of the first graders, but eighty-four percent of the college students seemed to understand the grammatical rule for the gender use of "he."

In a second experiment, Hyde (1984) replicated some aspects of the first experiment and expanded the design to include third and fifth graders. "She" was included as a fourth pronoun condition in the storytelling and produced seventy-seven percent female stories. The following description of a fictitious, gender-neutral occupation, wudgemaker, was read to the children, with repeated references either to *he, they, he or she,* or *she:*

> Few people have heard of a job in factories, being a wudgemaker. Wudges are made of plastic, oddly shaped, and are an important part of video games. The wudgemaker works from a plan or pattern posted at eye level as *he or she* puts together the pieces at a table while *he or she* is sitting down. Eleven plastic pieces must be snapped together. Some of the pieces are tiny, so that *he or she* must have good coordination in *his or her* fingers. Once all eleven pieces are put together, *he or she* must test out the wudge to make sure that all of the moving pieces move properly. The wudgemaker is well paid and must be a high school graduate, but *he or she* does not have to have gone to college to get the job. (Hyde 1984, p. 702)

One-fourth of the children were given *he* for the pronoun; one-fourth, *they;* one-fourth, *he or she* (as shown above); and one-fourth, *she.* They were asked to rate how

How sexist are our thoughts and language?

well women could do the job on a three-point scale and how well men could do the job. As shown in figure 11.3, subject ratings of how well women could make wudges was influenced by pronoun, with ratings being lowest for *he,* intermediate for *they* and *he or she,* and highest for *she.* These data indicate that the use of gender-neutral *he,* compared to other pronouns, influences the formation of gender schema in children.

The research conducted by Janet Hyde (1984) touches on the important classic issue in developmental psychology—to what extent does language influence thought or vice versa? In Hyde's research, the question becomes whether sexist language is primary and influences thought, or whether sexist thought is primary and produces sexist language. Stated in the language of schema theory, does sexist language produce the schema, or does the schema produce the sexist language? Hyde

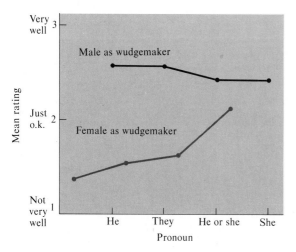

Note: Mean ratings of how well women and men would do as wudgemakers, according to pronoun used in the description.

Figure 11.3 Ratings of how well women and men would do as wudgemakers according to pronoun usage.

presented further data that address this issue. When the cue pronoun was *he,* the percentage of female stories was very low (twelve percent in one experiment and seventeen percent in another.) However, when the truly neutral pronoun *they* was used, the percentage of female stories still was significantly below fifty percent (eighteen percent and thirty-one percent in the two experiments). Such results lead Hyde to the conclusion that sexism in thought might be primary since an overwhelming majority think of males even when presented with a neutral pronoun—*they.* However, it is important to note that even the youngest subjects had been exposed to sexist language for six or more years of their lives, including hearing *he* and *they* used interchangeably in sentences. So, sexist thought may be the product of years of exposure to sexist language or other factors.

Environmental Influences

Although the child may have developed a clear idea of "male" and "female," the motivation for enacting appropriate behavior may be lacking. For example, consider a 13-year-old boy who knows he is a boy and readily labels appropriate objects as male or female; however, he has parents who support the women's liberation movement and stress equality between the sexes. We would expect his sex-role orientation to be less stereotyped along masculine lines than that of boys reared in more traditional homes.

One considerable change in the role of environmental influences on sex-role development in recent years has resulted in a de-emphasis on parents as the critical socialization agents. There has been a corresponding increase in the belief that schools, peers, the media, and other family members should be given more attention when the adolescent's sex-role development is at issue. Parents clearly are only one of many sources through which adolescents learn about sex-role development. Yet it is important to guard against swinging too far in this direction, because particularly in the early years of life, parents do play a very important role in sex-role development.

Parent-Child Relationships

Fathers and mothers both seem to be psychologically important for children even during infancy. Mothers are consistently given the responsibility for nurturance and physical child care, while fathers are more likely to engage in playful interaction with the child and be responsible for seeing that the child conforms to existing cultural norms. Fathers are more exacting and demanding with children than mothers; and whether or not they have more influence on them, fathers are more involved in socializing their sons than daughters (Lamb, 1981).

Fathers seem to play an important role in the sex-typing of both boys and girls. Reviews of sex-typing research indicate that fathers are more likely to act differently toward sons and daughters than mothers are (e.g., Huston, 1983). And most reviews of the father-absence literature (e.g., Lamb, 1981) conclude that boys show a more feminine patterning of behavior in father-absent than in father-present homes; however, close inspection of those studies suggests that this conclusion is more appropriate for young children, while the findings for elementary and secondary school children are mixed. For example, Hetherington, Cox, and Cox (1978) found that children's sex-typed behavior reflected more than the unavailability of a consistent adult male model. While many single-parent mothers were overprotective and apprehensive about their son's independence, when single parents encouraged masculine and exploratory behavior and did not have a negative attitude toward the absent father, disruption in the son's sex-typed behavior did not occur.

Many parents encourage boys and girls to engage in different types of play activities even during infancy. In particular, many parents emphasize that doll play is for girls only, while boys are more likely to be rewarded for engaging in gross motor activities. And often, parents play more actively with male babies and respond more positively to physical activity by boys. There also is some evidence that parents encourage girls to be more dependent, more affectionate, and more emotional than boys; but there is no indication that parents show different reactions to aggression according to their child's sex. And with increasing age, boys are permitted more freedom by parents who allow them to be away from home without supervision more than girls (Huston, 1983).

Thus, we can see that parents, by action and example, influence their child's sex-role development. In the psychoanalytic view, this influence stems principally from the child's identification with the parent of the same sex. The child develops a sense of likeness to the parent of the same sex and strives to emulate that parent. In social learning theory, the child acquires a motive to imitate the actions of the parent of the same sex.

Peer Relations

Children already have acquired a preference for sex-typed toys and activities before most of them are exposed to school. During the preschool and elementary school years, teachers and peers usually maintain these preferences through feedback to the boy or girl.

Children who play in sex-appropriate activities tend to be rewarded for doing so by their peers, while those who play in cross-sex activities tend to be criticized by their peers or left to play alone. Indeed, children seem to differentiate their peers very early on the basis of sex, with such patterns reflecting the preschool child's increasing awareness of culturally prescribed expectancies for males and females.

One of the most frequent observations of elementary school children's play groups is their gender segregation—boys tend to play with boys, and girls are much more likely to play with girls. In one recent investigation (Luria and Herzog 1985), children's free play was observed in several contexts—during lunch, on a museum trip and at public or private schools, for example—and with different ages of children, three to four year olds and fourth through sixth graders. All female, all male, and cross-sexed groups of children were observed in all settings and at all ages. Interestingly, public school fourth through sixth graders showed much less cross-sex peer groupings than their private school counterparts. And, it only was in the public school groupings that an overt ideology of cross-sex exclusion was ever heard. Overall, however, there appears to be an acceptance of cross-sex play in most children's peer groups, even though the majority of elementary school children express a same-sex play group preference.

Teachers

Female teachers are more likely to reward "feminine" behavior than "masculine" behavior. Beverly Fagot (1975) reasoned that teachers would most probably support student behaviors that were a part of their own behavioral system. Since most preschool and elementary school teachers are females, they would be expected to reward behaviors consistent with the feminine, or "good girl," stereotype. As expected, she found that teachers reinforced both boys' and girls' feminine behaviors eighty-three percent of the time. In a similar study Boyd McCandless (1973) found that female teachers rewarded feminine behaviors fifty-one percent of the time and masculine behaviors forty-nine

It is not unusual for young adolescent girls to develop "crushes" on their male teachers.

percent of the time. Perhaps if more male adults were involved in early education, there would be more support of masculine behavior and activity.

It appears that by the time children have entered junior high school, they will have developed the expectancy that teachers are more likely to reward feminine than masculine behaviors. However, in the junior high school years a change in the mix of teachers that young adolescents are exposed to occurs: during the junior high school years, they are exposed to more equal numbers of male and female teachers. Unfortunately, few studies focus on how male and female teachers interact with male and female students during the adolescent years. A good guess is that some important cross-sex effects begin to emerge with the onset of puberty. For example, many young adolescent girls develop "crushes" on their male teachers. Also, some strong same-sex effects may result, one example being the adolescent male's identification with a male coach or teacher.

One study of junior high school students did reveal that teachers have reasonably strong stereotypes about male and female students (Buxton, 1973). "Good" male students were described by the junior high school teachers as active, adventurous, aggressive, assertive, curious, energetic, enterprising, frank, independent, and inventive. By contrast, "good" female students were depicted as appreciative, calm, conscientious, considerate, cooperative, mannerly, poised, sensitive, dependable, efficient, mature, obliging, and thorough. Such stereotypes may guide the way the teacher interacts with boys and girls, and may influence the way boys and girls view their own sex role.

In sum, during the early years of schooling, teachers react more negatively to boys than to girls, but do not necessarily give them less positive reinforcement or reward them differently for sex-typed behavior. However, teachers do have stereotypes about "good" masculine and "good" feminine behavior, and are more likely to reward "feminine" behaviors in boys and girls. Teachers, then, do exert a strong influence on children's sex typing, as do peers.

Media Influence

As we saw in the chapter on culture, there are many different media effects on adolescent development, such as television, records, newspapers, and so forth. The media that adolescents are exposed to present males and females in certain ways. Children and adolescents watch an average of three to five hours of television every day of their lives. The programs they watch portray distinct male and female roles, and these portrayals can influence their concepts of sex roles. Leading feminists argue that television teaches stereotyped values and does particular damage to girls (e.g., Deckhard, 1979; Hennessee and Nicholson, 1972). The evidence suggests that adolescents see very different images of males and females on television. Males and females appear with different frequencies on television, occupational stereotypes are rampant, and these stereotypes appear not just on television, but in movies, magazines, and books as well (Perloff, Brown, and Miller, 1978).

In one recent investigation of the achievement scripts in television commercials (Geis et al., 1984), the belief that sex stereotypes implicitly enacted, but never explicitly articulated, may inhibit the female's achievement aspirations was studied. College students viewed either replicas of four current television commercials or four replicas that were identical, but had the sex roles reversed. For example, one traditional commercial involved a husband and wife being interviewed at the dinner table about which food he prefers with chicken. After she guesses the vegetable, he is given a taste test, and she is dismayed to hear him choose the advertised product. Quickly recovering, she resolves to serve his preference in the future. In the role reversal commercial, the female and male actors switched roles in the scenario. For example, in the commercial, it was the wife who was asked her food preference and the husband who was embarrassed, then promised to honor her choice when he served chicken for dinner in the future. Then the students wrote an essay imagining their lives ten years from the present. The essays were coded for achievement and homemaking themes. The female students who saw the traditional commercials deemphasized achievement in favor of homemaking compared to males and to female students who had seen the role reversal commercials. The reversed role commercials eliminated the sex difference in achievement (figure 11.4). Examples of typical female students' responses follow (Geis et al., 1984, p. 520):

After reversed-role commercials: Ten years from now I hope to be in a job I like and the one I'm training for now [+2]. I guess I want to be married [−1], perhaps starting a family [−1], although that isn't one of my first priorities. Hopefully, I'll have a good bank account [+2] and maybe even own my own home [+1]. I'm kind of worried about the future. [Net achievement score = +3].

After traditional commercials: In ten years I plan to be married [−2] with children [−2], but I intend to work as a physical therapist for as long as possible, both before [+2] and after [+2] having children. My family will be my main concern [−2]; my occupation of slightly less importance. I will like the responsibility of a home and family [−2], but I may dislike getting into a routine way of life. I prefer changes in a routine. [Net achievement score = −4].

In addition to communicating different roles related to males and females, there is substantial evidence that just in terms of sheer numbers, males significantly outnumber females in their exposure on television. About seventy percent of the characters on prime-time shows are male (e.g., Miller and Reeves, 1976; Tedesco, 1974).

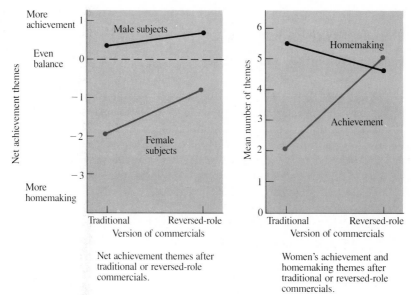

Net achievement themes after traditional or reversed-role commercials.

Women's achievement and homemaking themes after traditional or reversed-role commercials.

Figure 11.4 Achievement aspirations and sex role portrayal in commercials.

In recent years the television networks have become more sensitive to how males and females are portrayed on television shows. Many programs now focus on divorced families, cohabitation, and women in high-status roles. But even with the onset of this type of programming, the overwhelming conclusion is that adolescents are exposed to a sex-role stereotype that features males in dominant, assertive, high-status positions and females in submissive, nurturant, low-status positions.

Sex-role stereotypes appear in the print media as well. In magazine advertising, females are generally portrayed as homemakers who are dependent on men for protection (Courtney and Lockeretz, 1971). Females usually appear in advertisements for beauty products, cleaning products, and home appliances, while males are usually in advertisements for cars, liquor, and travel.

Even in comic strips, there is perpetuation of inequality between the sexes. A recent analysis of randomly selected comic strips that included Andy Capp, B.C., Broom Hilda, Dennis the Menace, Peanuts,

Wizard of Id, and Ziggy revealed males were present in far greater numbers than females and, further, that females more frequently were portrayed in derogatory ways (Chavez, 1985).

We have seen how many different aspects of the culture in which the child and adolescent live present males and females in different ways. Next, we look at another aspect of environmental influences on sex roles, interventions aimed at changing sex roles.

Changing Sex-Typed Behavior

Efforts to change children's sex-typed behavior have taken two directions (Huston, 1983): "gender-deviant" children are trained to show more appropriate sex-typed behavior and attempts are made to free normal children from rigidly sex-typed patterns. Both types of intervention create ethical concerns; yet both produce valuable information about sex typing, that is, psychological aspects of being male or female.

Most studies of gender deviance have included only boys who are diagnosed as gender deviant when they play mostly with feminine sex-typed toys, dress up in female clothes, choose girls rather than boys as play-

The increased number of females engaging in athletics and changing sex roles complicates a diagnosis of gender deviance.

mates, engage in female role playing, fantasize about being a girl, and express themselves with feminine gestures (Green, 1974; Rekers, 1979). In one investigation based on detailed observations, girls used very different gestural patterns than boys, such as hanging their wrists, limply holding books with their arms folded toward their body, and so forth (Rekers, 1979). Gender-deviant boys not only displayed these female sex-typed characteristics, but also preferred participating in female activities and purposely avoided masculine activities. The gender-deviant boys indicated that rough and tumble play either disinterested or frightened them (Green, 1974).

Gender deviance among girls has received less attention, possibly because our society allows girls more flexibility in their dress, play activities, and sex-typed interest than it does boys. For example, in one study, a majority of junior high girls described themselves as "sort of tomboyish" and a majority of adult women indicated that they were tomboys during childhood (Hyde, Rosenberg, and Behrman, 1977). The characteristics used to describe gender-deviant girls are similar to those used for boys—preferring masculine activities and boys as playmates, taking male roles in fantasy, fantasizing about being a boy, and dressing in male clothes. While masculine clothing and interests are commonplace among girls, gender-deviant girls also are characterized by strong avoidance of feminine clothing, activities, and playmates.

Both behavioral and psychoanalytic treatment procedures have been used in attempts to alter the sex-typed behavior of gender-deviant children. These treatment procedures have led to changes in children's play patterns, but usually only in the situation where the treatment occurred. Consequently, clinical treatment has been augmented by direct interventions at home and at school. Parents and teachers have been taught behavior modification techniques, and young male adults have visited the children at home or at school, attempting to teach the gender-deviant boys athletic skills because feminine boys tend to perform very poorly in athletic skills. Indications are that such programs have led to more normal sex-typed behavior in boys, lasting for as long as one to three years after the intervention (Rekers, 1979).

While diagnosis and treatment of gender deviance have occurred we have little knowledge of the origins of such patterns. One possibility is that many parents are indifferent to the occurrence of gender-deviant patterns of behavior in young children. Some parents think it is cute when little boys continue to dress up as females and play with dolls. Such children often are referred for treatment only after someone outside the family points out the child's effeminate characteristics. Other factors that show up in the case histories of some gender-deviant boys are maternal overprotection of boys and restrictions on rough and tumble play, absence of an adult male, weak father-son relationship, physical beauty on the part of the small boy that led to his being treated as a girl, absence of male playmates, and maternal dominance.

In addition to attempts at changing the sex-typed behavior of gender-deviant children, another effort focused at changing sex roles has involved the teaching of androgynous concepts, particularly in schools. To learn about such educational efforts to enhance an androgynous sex-role orientation, read Perspective on Adolescent Development 11.3.

So far, we have discussed many different aspects of sex roles. A summary of main ideas related to our description of sex roles so far is presented in Concept Table 11.1. Next, we look in more detail at several aspects of sex roles that we already have touched on briefly—sex-role stereotypes and sex differences.

Perspective on Adolescent Development 11.3
CAN AND SHOULD ANDROGYNY BE TAUGHT TO CHILDREN AND ADOLESCENTS IN SCHOOL?

*B*elieving that rigid sex roles may be detrimental to both males and females, a number of educators and social scientists have developed materials and created courses involving the teaching of androgyny to students. Among the curricula developed have been resource guides and examples of materials that can be used to study sex roles (Nickerson, 1975; Hahn, 1975; Biemer, 1975; Holman, 1975) as well as courses with outlines and lesson plans (Stein, 1972; Emma Willard Task Force on Education, 1971; Gaskell and Knapp, 1976; National Education Association, 1974; van Manen et al., 1975).

In one recent study (Kahn and Richardson, 1983), tenth through twelfth grade students from three high schools in British Columbia were exposed to a twenty-unit course in sex roles. Students analyzed the history and modern development of male and female gender roles and evaluated the utility of traditionally accepted stereotypes of males and females. The course centered on student discussion, supplemented by films, videotapes, and guest speakers. The materials included exercises to heighten awareness of one's own attitudes and beliefs, role reversal of typical sex-typed behaviors, role play of difficult work and family conflict circumstances, and assertiveness training for direct, honest communication.

A total of sixty-nine students participated in the sex-role course. To determine whether the sex-role course changed the participant's sex-role orientation, these students were compared with fifty-nine students from the same schools who did not take the sex-role class. Prior to the start of the course, all students were given the Bem Sex Role Inventory. No differences were found at this time on the sex-role measure when students who were going to take the sex-role course were compared with those who were not. After the students completed the course, they and the control group were given the Attitudes Toward Women Scale (Spence and Helmreich, 1972) in an effort to determine their attitudes, either liberal or traditional, toward the changing roles of women in society. Scores on this measure can range from twenty-five (highly traditional) to one hundred (highly liberal). As shown in table 11.2, in schools one and two, the students who took the sex-role class had more liberal attitudes about the female's role in society than students who did not take the course. In these schools, the students primarily were girls who chose to take the class as an elective. In school three, students who took the sex-role class actually had more conservative attitudes toward the female's role in society than those who did not. The sex-role class in school three was a required course and it was comprised almost equally of females and males.

Another attempt to induce a more androgynous sex-role orientation in students also met with mixed results when all students were considered (Guttentag and Bray, 1976). The curriculum lasted for one year and was implemented in the kindergarten, fifth-, and ninth-grade classes. It involved books, discussion materials, and classroom exercises. The antisex-role stereotype program was most successful with the fifth-graders and was the least successful with the ninth-graders (who actually displayed a "boomerang effect" that produced even more rigid sex-typed behavior). The program's success varied from class to class, seeming to be most effective when the teacher produced sympathetic reaction in the peer group; however, some classes ridiculed and rejected the curriculum.

Table 11.2 Sex role attitudes related to the woman's role in society following a high school course on sex roles that emphasized androgyny

Schools	Groups	
	Experimental (took sex role course)	Control (did not take course)
1	83.3	75.6
2	85.3	73.9
3	68.8	76.2

Source: Based on data presented by Kahn, S. E., and A. Richardson, "Evaluation of a Course in Sex Roles for Secondary School Students," Sex Roles: A Journal of Research, 9, 431–440. Copyright © 1983 by Plenum Publishing Corporation.

Ethical concerns are also aroused when the issue is one of teaching children to depart from socially approved behavior patterns, particularly when there is no evidence of extreme sex typing in the groups of children to whom the interventions are applied. The advocates of the androgyny programs believe that traditional sex typing is psychologically harmful for all children and that it has prevented many girls and women from experiencing equal opportunity. Aletha Huston (1983) concluded that while some people believe androgyny is more adaptive than either a traditional masculine or feminine pattern, it is not possible to ignore the imbalance within our culture which values masculinity more than femininity.

Concept Table 11.1

SEX ROLES

Concept	Processes/related ideas	Characteristics/description
Masculinity, femininity, and androgyny	Masculinity/femininity	For many years, the male- and female-related aspects of sex roles were categorized as either masculine or feminine. The competent male adolescent was described as masculine, for example being independent and aggressive, while the competent female adolescent was characterized as feminine, for instance being dependent and unaggressive.
	Androgyny	Androgyny became an important part of sex-role research in the 1970s. Androgyny refers to the combination of both masculine and feminine characteristics in the same person. Most androgyny scales allow an individual to be categorized as masculine, feminine, androgynous, or undifferentiated. Note that such scales do not develop new items for the androgyny classification, rather an individual saying that both a number of masculine and feminine items are like him or her is described as androgynous. Two of the most widely used androgyny scales are those devised by Spence and Bem.
	Masculinity, femininity, androgyny, and competence	Considerable interest has been generated in whether individuals with a particular sex-role makeup are more competent. In instances where the criteria for competence involve both self-assertion and integration, androgynous adolescents often are more competent. However, it is very important to specify the contexts in which androgyny is being evaluated. In contexts in which feminine characteristics are valued, then an adolescent with a feminine sex-role makeup will likely perform more competently. It is very important not only to specify the dimensions of social competence being assessed, but also the dimensions of sex roles. There has been a tendency to value masculinity and self-assertion more than femininity and integration. And the criteria for competence have tended to follow this pattern as well.
Biological and cognitive factors in sex roles	Biological factors	The psychoanalytic theorists, Erikson and Freud, argue that anatomy is destiny, meaning that psychological aspects of sex roles are wedded to the physical structure of males and females, with males being more intrusive and females more inclusive. There is no research evidence to support this view. Hormones are important aspects of the biological contribution to sex roles. Research has included the study of individuals with abnormally high levels of sex hormones, such as girls exposed to high doses of the male sex hormone androgen. The results of these studies are inconclusive. John Money commented that while there are two time periods when sex hormones likely are prominent in influencing children's sex-role behavior and attitudes—the first three years and puberty—sex roles are always determined by the interplay of biology and culture.

SEX ROLES

Concept	Processes/related ideas	Characteristics/description
	Cognitive factors	The cognitive developmental theory of Lawrence Kohlberg suggests that self-categorization and the development of a stable gender identity are precursors for sex-typed behavior. Others who have expanded on Kohlberg's cognitive theory seem to feel that a rigidity of sex roles often occurs during early adolescence, although research suggests this rigidity is much stronger for boys than girls. Language also is involved in sex roles. Researchers have explored sexism in language. A particularly salient issue here focuses on whether sexist language produces sexist thought or vice versa.
Environmental factors	Overview	While biological and cognitive factors are important in sex roles, they do not explain entirely the wide individual variation in sex roles. Such variation undoubtedly is influenced by environmental factors. In recent years, there has been a widening of interest to include many cultural factors outside the family as influences on sex roles. However, it is important not to go too far in the direction of thinking that family influences are unimportant in sex-role development.
	Parent–child relationships	Fathers and mothers are psychologically important in both the adolescent male's and female's sex-role orientation. Parents, by action and example, influence sex roles.
	Peer relations	By the time they have reached adolescence, individuals have been exposed to huge numbers of hours of social interaction with both parents and peers who have provided feedback about the nature of sex roles. In elementary school, peer groups are often heavily segregated according to gender, but as we move through the adolescent years, these groups become increasingly heterosexual.
	Teachers	Teachers also can influence sex roles. Female teachers are more likely to reward feminine than masculine behaviors, and the majority of teachers are females. Many junior high school teachers seem to have stereotypes about male and female sex roles.
	Media influences	Adolescents see very different images of males and females on television, in magazines, in commercials, and even in comic strips. Generally, these images are highly stereotyped in terms of traditional sex roles and, in some instances, they are derogatory to females.
	Changing sex-typed behavior	Efforts to change sex-typed behavior have taken two directions: ''gender-deviant'' children are trained to show more appropriate sex-typed behavior and attempts are made to free normal children from rigid sex roles. Gender deviance among boys has received more attention than among girls. Programs to teach androgyny in the schools have met with mixed success, with girls often changing much more than boys. Early adolescent boys sometimes even show more rigid sex-role stereotypes when exposed to androgyny programs. Ethical issues are involved in changing sex-typed behavior.

Sex Differences and Stereotypes

What is the nature of sex-role stereotypes? And what sex differences truly exist?

Sex-Role Stereotypes

Stereotypes are defined as broad categories that reflect our impressions about people, events, and ourselves (Mischel, 1970). The world is extremely complex; every day we are confronted with thousands of different stimuli. The use of stereotypes is one way we simplify this complexity. If we simply assign a label (for example, the qualities of "softness" or "aggressiveness") to someone, we then have much less to consider when we think about the person. However, once these labels have been assigned, we find it remarkably difficult to abandon them, even in the face of contradictory evidence. Do you have a repertory of sex-role stereotypes? Record your answers to the questions in table 11.3 on a separate sheet of paper so you can check them later when they are discussed.

Many stereotypes are so general that they are extremely ambiguous. Take, for example, the stereotypes "masculine" and "feminine." Very diverse behaviors may be called up to support the stereotype, such as scoring a touchdown or growing facial hair. The stereotype, of course, may also be modified in the face of cultural change; whereas at one time muscular development might be thought masculine, at another time masculinity may be typified by a lithe, slender physique. The behaviors popularly agreed upon as reflecting the stereotype may fluctuate according to subculture.

Walter Mischel (1970) comments that even though the behaviors that are supposed to fit the stereotype often do not, the label itself may have significant consequences for the individual. Labeling a person *homosexual, queer,* or *sissy* can produce dire social consequences in terms of status and acceptance in

Table 11.3	Knowing the sexes

How well do you know the sexes? For each of the adjectives listed below, indicate whether you think it *best* describes women or men—or neither—in our society. Be honest with yourself, and follow your first impulse in responding.

After recording your answers, continue reading the chapter for an interpretation of your responses.

a.	verbal	g.	mathematical
b.	sensitive	h.	suggestible
c.	active	i.	analytic
d.	competitive	j.	social
e.	compliant	k.	aggressive
f.	dominant		

groups, even when the person so labeled is not a homosexual, queer, or sissy. Regardless of their accuracy, stereotypes can cause tremendous emotional upheaval in an individual and undermine his or her own opinions about himself or herself and his or her status.

What about sex-role stereotypes in adolescence? Are they more likely to be stronger at this point in development than at other points? There seems to be some indication that sex-role stereotypes are particularly strong during the adolescent years (Galambos et al., 1985; Urberg, 1979). And, while males and females across the life span have different attitudes about sex equity with males being more sexist than females, this discrepancy is particularly acute during the adolescent years (Benson and Vincent, 1980). Remember in our discussion of changing sex-role attitudes how androgynous sex-role programs in secondary schools seem to be much more effective with females than males.

To further study the nature of sex-role stereotypes in adolescence, Nancy Galambos, Anne Peterson, Maryse Richards, and Idy Gitelson (1985) constructed the Attitudes Toward Women Scale for Adolescents (AWSA). As shown in table 11.4, this scale consists of twelve items. It is based on the Attitudes Toward Women Scale (Spence, Helmreich, and Stapp, 1973), the content of which is more suitable for older age

Table 11.4 The Attitudes Toward Women Scale for Adolescents (AWSA)

1. Swearing is worse for a girl than for a boy.
2. On a date, the boy should be expected to pay all expenses.
3. On the average, girls are as smart as boys.
4. More encouragement in a family should be given to sons than daughters to go to college.
5. It is all right for a girl to want to play rough sports like football.
6. In general, the father should have greater authority than the mother in making family decisions.
7. It is all right for a girl to ask a boy out on a date.
8. It is more important for boys than girls to do well in school.
9. If both husband and wife have jobs, the husband should do a share of the housework such as washing dishes and doing the laundry.
10. Boys are better leaders than girls.
11. Girls should be more concerned with becoming good wives and mothers than desiring a professional or business career.
12. Girls should have the same freedoms as boys.

Each item represents an attitude to which the subject responds on a 4-point Likert-type scale ranging from 1 = "agree strongly" to 4 = "disagree strongly." Items 3, 5, 7, 9, and 12 were reverse scored. All scores are then summed (and divided by 12 in order to retain the item metric), producing a global score of attitudes toward women, with a higher score indicating less traditional attitudes.

Source: From Galambos, N. L., Peterson, A. C., Richards, M., and I. B. Getelson, "The Attitudes Toward Women Scale for Adolescents (AWSA): A Study of Reliability and Validity," Sex Roles: A Journal of Research, 13m 343–356. Copyright © 1985 by Plenum Publishing Corporation.

groups. In four different samples of adolescents, ranging from the sixth through the twelfth grades, males were much more likely to have traditional attitudes toward women than females were. Further, girls who had more egalitarian attitudes toward women had higher self-esteem, as measured by the Rosenberg Self-Esteem Scale (Rosenberg, 1965). According to Galambos and her colleagues, the girl who has more traditional sex-role attitudes may limit her occupational and educational opportunities in favor of more stereotyped occupations and roles. The young adolescent girl who has more egalitarian attitudes and a more positive self-image, by contrast, may pursue vocational and family paths that are less stereotyped and characterized by more flexible opportunities.

Now that we have considered information about sex-role stereotypes, we turn our attention to actual sex differences.

Adolescent males seem to have particularly strong sexist feelings.

Sex Differences

How did you answer the items in table 11.3? According to a well-known review by Eleanor Maccoby and Carl Jacklin (1974), females are more verbal, less mathematical, and less aggressive than males—the others are not more characteristic of one sex or the other.

With regard to verbal ability, girls tend to understand and produce language more competently than boys do. Girls are superior to boys in higher-order verbal tasks, such as making analogies, understanding difficult written material, and writing creatively, as well as on lower-order verbal tasks, such as spelling. Maccoby and Jacklin speculated that girls probably get an early start on boys in the use of language, but studies indicate that differences in the verbal abilities of boys and girls are not consistent until about the age of eleven. A similar developmental trend can be seen for mathematical skills, but this time in favor of boys. Boys' superiority in math skills does not usually appear until the age of twelve or thirteen and does not seem to be entirely influenced by the fact that boys take more math courses. Likewise, male superiority on visual-spatial tasks does not consistently appear until adolescence. However, sex differences in aggression appear early, by the age of two or three, and continue through adolescence. The differences are not confined to physical aggression—boys also show more verbal aggression as well as more fantasy aggression (imagining harm to someone or to some object rather than actually performing an aggressive act).

Closely related to ideas about math and visual spatial abilities is whether there are differences in computer use, interest, and ability. Recent information suggests we as a society already are beginning to define computers as predominantly male machines. Is this a stereotype or are there sex differences related to computers? To learn about the research done on this important topic in contemporary society, read Perspective on Adolescent Development 11.4.

Perspective on Adolescent Development 11.4
GIRLS AND COMPUTERS

Marlaine Lockheed (1985) recently reviewed what we know about girls and computers. While girls and boys seem to show similar appreciation of the importance computers have for their personal futures, boys are more likely to take computer courses in school than girls, to report using computers in extracurricular settings more than girls, to indicate more frequent home use of computers than girls, and to have more positive attitudes toward computers. For example, in computer courses offered in schools, male to female ratios range from 2:1 to 5:1 (Hess and Miura, 1985; Revelle et al., 1984). And boys have outnumbered girls at computer camps by approximately 3:1 (Hess and Miura, 1985). Further, a survey of home computer use found that seventy percent of the main users were male (USA Today, 1984). Several investigators also have found that males have more positive attitudes toward computers than females (Fetler, 1985; Chen, 1985; Collis, 1985).

While computers can be studied from the perspective of their function (such as object of study, recreation, tool), most research focused on sex differences has not made this distinction. It appears, though, that sex differences in computer usage emerge for some uses and not others. Males use computers more than females for programming and game playing, but not more for other computer applications, such as word processing. Further, sex differences seem to depend on the context in which the computer is used. For instance, computers in computer centers and arcades, which are often male "game preserves," are more frequently used by males (Lockheed et al., 1983; Kiesler et al., 1983), while computers in mixed-sex classrooms and offices are used equally by both sexes (Becker, 1985; Gutek and Bikson, 1985).

Let's look in greater detail at the use of computers for programming and why males outdistance females in this regard. Lockheed (1985) describes six reasons this may occur. First, both boys and girls are socialized to associate programming with math, mainly because programming courses are offered in conjunction with math courses or because math courses are prerequisites for programming courses. Math is perceived more as a masculine than a feminine domain (Fennema, 1984). Second,

What sex differences are emerging in the computer area?

the cognitive skills needed for programming, as noted in our emphasis on sex differences in math abilities. However, on many cognitive skills there are no sex differences (Linn and Peterson, in press). Fourth, the content and depth of introductory programming as taught in secondary schools are seen as irrelevant by girls to their academic objectives (Lockheed and Frakt, 1984). Fifth, parental economic and personal support for computer programming is less positive for girls than boys—note the difference in sex enrollments in computer camps mentioned earlier. And, sixth, teachers may unknowingly discriminate against girls in computer classes, providing a more positive climate for male use (McKelvey, 1984).

Undergirding much of the concern about sex differences in computers is that if girls fail to become involved with computers, they will become left behind males in an increasingly technological society. In two recent books, *Turing's Man* (Bolter, 1984) and *The Second Self* (Turkle, 1984), technology is portrayed as overwhelming humanity. In both books, females are not pictured in this technological, computer culture. One comment notes, "There are few women hackers. This is a male world" (Turkle, 1984, p. 210). As Marlaine Lockheed (1985) concludes, Turkle's computer hacker as a male should not serve as the model of computer users in the future.

the demands of programming, which emphasize rules and winning, are more compatible with male than female values (which emphasize relational ethics—Gilligan, 1985). Third, boys are more likely than girls to possess

cathy®   **by Cathy Guisewite**

Some further comments should be made about the conclusions reached by Maccoby and Jacklin (1974). The review is now more than a decade old. In the late 1970s and 1980s, sex roles have continued to change, particularly in the area of achievement with greater numbers of females showing stronger occupational interests and achievement motivation than at any time in history. As sociohistorical changes continue to take place in the 1980s and 1990s, there well may be a greater blurring of sex differences. Further, soon after the Maccoby and Jacklin (1974) review came out, there were dissidents. For example, Jeanne Block (1976) acknowledged that Maccoby and Jacklin (1974) made an important contribution to information about sex roles, but she also believes that some of their conclusions, and some of the data on which the conclusions are based, are shakier than Maccoby and Jacklin lead readers to believe. She argues that Maccoby and Jacklin did not differentiate between those studies that were methodologically sound and those that were not. She further criticizes the decisions they made about what kinds of studies should go into a particular category. For example, Maccoby and Jacklin lumped together many measures in their assessment of parental pressure on achievement motivation, including the following: amount of praise or criticism for intellectual performance; parental standards for intellectual performance as expressed on a questionnaire item; expectations of household help from the youth; the ages at which parents feel it is appropriate to teach a boy or girl more mature behaviors; number of anxious intrusions in the youth's task performance; and pressure for success on memory tasks. While many of the measures are clearly linked with the achievement dimension, others may be more peripheral. More about sex differences in achievement will appear in Chapter 13.

Although Block does commend Maccoby and Jacklin for their completion of the long, difficult task of organizing a sprawling, unruly body of information, she also suggests that such data are open to error and reasonable argument at virtually every step of the analysis. In other words, anyone attempting to impose structure and meaning on some 1,600 disparate studies

of sex role is bound to make a few questionable decisions. For those of you interested in reading more about sex differences in adolescence, both Maccoby and Jacklin's book and Block's critique are highly recommended.

Another critic of Maccoby and Jacklin (Tieger, 1980) argues that sex differences in aggression are not biologically based, but are instead learned. Tieger argues that consistent sex differences do not emerge until about the age of six and that there are ample conditions in the first six years of the child's life for aggression to be learned. In a rejoinder to Tieger, Maccoby and Jacklin (1980) reviewed their data and conducted some further analyses. The reassessment supported their earlier claim that greater aggression in boys occurs well before the age of six, is present in studies of nonhuman primates, and appears in cross-cultural studies of children and adolescents.

In the first part of this chapter, we have looked at the many complex dimensions of the adolescent's sex role. We have seen that sex roles are influenced by the interaction of biology and culture. And we have seen that there is much disagreement about what constitutes an appropriate sex role for the adolescent—masculine, feminine, or androgynous. Finally, we have studied the actual sex differences between adolescent females and males.

A summary of main ideas related to sex-role stereotypes and sex differences is presented in Concept Table 11.2. As we see next, our discussion of adolescent sex roles would be incomplete, however, without evaluating the important dimension of sexuality.

Sexuality: More Interest Than Leroy

The prologue to this chapter introduced Leroy. The mother of the girl he was dating overreacted to his behavior, perceiving him to be more sexually motivated and active than he really was. As we will see in this section, most adolescents have a much greater interest in sexual matters than Leroy. Sexual barriers in adolescents are being broken down, and adolescents today are not as inhibited as they once were in terms of both sexual practices and sexual discussion. While sexual

SEX-ROLE STEREOTYPES AND SEX DIFFERENCES

Concept	Processes/related ideas	Characteristics/description
Sex-role stereotypes	Nature of stereotypes	Stereotypes are broad categories that reflect our impressions of people, events, and ourselves. We often use stereotypes to simplify the complexity of information in our lives. Once the broad labels are assigned, they often are difficult to remove, even though they are inappropriate.
	Stereotypes in early adolescence	Sex-role stereotypes seem to be particularly strong during early adolescence, with males being more sexist than females. Young adolescent girls with more egalatarian sex-role conceptions seem to have more positive self-images.
Sex differences	The Maccoby and Jacklin conclusions	Maccoby and Jacklin, in 1974, reviewed a large number of research studies on sex differences, concluding that overall, boys are more aggressive, better at math, and better at visuospatial relations; but girls are superior in verbal ability. A recent corollary of the Maccoby and Jacklin conclusions focuses on possible sex differences in computer interest and competency.
	The criticisms of Maccoby and Jacklin's work	The conclusions of Maccoby and Jacklin did not go unscathed. The review is now more than a decade old and sex roles have continued to change in the late 1970s and 1980s. Also, they lumped together many studies of different quality to come up with general conclusions.

behavior among adolescents is more liberal than earlier in history, keep in mind that it still is more conservative than in some cultures. In the discussion of sexuality in Chapter 9, we saw how virtually all adolescents in the Mangaian culture are sexually active from puberty on. In this chapter, our overview of sexuality focuses on the nature of adolescent sexuality, contemporary sexual attitudes and behavior, contraceptives and sexually transmitted disease, and sex education.

The Nature of Adolescent Sexuality

In Chapter 3, we studied the biological basis of sexual maturation, discovering the important role hormones play in this important aspect of adolescent development. Here we focus on the sexual experiences of adolescents rather than the biological basis of sexual development. Adolescence is a time when exploratory

and experimental sex play turns into more purposeful behavior; however, many adolescents, because of social and religious standards, stop short of sexual intercourse. Even when they find a partner they sincerely would like to have intercourse with, they often restrict themselves to petting. And for many young adolescents, masturbation may be their only sexual outlet. And, as a rule in our society, adolescent girls often are more sexually inhibited than males, not being encouraged to acknowledge their sexual needs. While they usually are taught to make themselves attractive, their own sexual needs often go undiscussed. As a consequence, the sexual drives of adolescent girls often tend to be oriented toward fantasies about the future, such as becoming a bride. By contrast, the sexual fantasies of adolescent boys frequently focus more specifically on sexual activity itself.

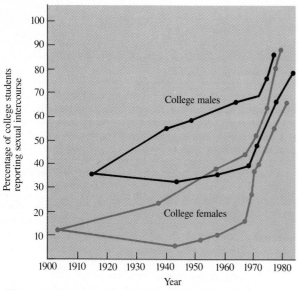

Figure 11.5 Percentage of college youth reporting having sexual intercourse at different points in the twentieth century.

Contemporary Sexual Attitudes and Behavior in Adolescence

What are the contemporary sexual attitudes and behavior of adolescents like? Let's look at some trends in such attitudes and behavior during the twentieth century, then turn to an overview of research on heterosexual attitudes and behavior, followed by information about homosexual behavior and self-stimulation.

Trends in Sexuality during the Twentieth Century

In a review of sexual practices and attitudes involving college females and males from 1900 to 1980 (Darling, Kallen, and VanDusen, 1984), two major trends were apparent. First, there has been a major increase in the proportion of young people reporting intercourse and second, the proportion of females reporting coital involvement has increased more rapidly than the proportion of males, although the initial basis for males is greater (figure 11.5). Previous to 1970, about twice as many college males as females reported coital involvement, but since 1970, the proportions of males and females are almost equal. Such changes are viewed as supporting major shifts in the standards governing

sexual behavior. That is, there has been a move away from a double standard in which it was more appropriate for males to have intercourse, but not females. As we soon will see, however, certain aspects of a double standard for adolescent males and females still operate.

Heterosexual Attitudes and Behavior

While the majority of early inquiries about sexual attitudes and behavior focused on adults and college students, more recently a number of efforts have been made to chart the nature of such attitudes and behavior among adolescents (e.g., Chilman, 1979; Cvetkovich and Grote, 1975; DeLamater and MacCorquodale, 1979; Hass, 1979; Kantner and Zelnick, 1973; Sorenson, 1973; Vener and Stewart, 1974; Zelnick and Kantner, 1978 a,b; 1980).

While there seems to be a great deal of pressure on male adolescents to have sexual intercourse, it appears that sexual attitudes are at least somewhat more liberal than actual behavior. For example, in one investigation (Haas, 1979), ninety-five percent of the boys and eighty-three percent of the girls approved of genital touching, while only fifty-five percent of the boys and forty-three percent of the teenagers sampled had experienced this kind of heavy petting. The same trend was true of oral sex as well: ninety percent of the boys and seventy percent of the girls approved, but only one-third had actually engaged in oral sex. Data from other research (e.g., DeLamater and MacCorquodale, 1979), however, suggest that genital touching is greater than indicated by the Haas research, although the subjects were slightly older (sixteen to eighteen years of age). In this investigation with older adolescents, the incidence of genital touching was approximately eighty percent.

At the behavioral level, there also seems to be an increase in sexual behavior among adolescents, and such behavior is engaged at an earlier age than in the past. Many adolescents point out that mid- to late adolescence is the best time to first have sexual intercourse. In one investigation (Hass, 1979), at age sixteen slightly over forty percent of the males had engaged in sexual intercourse, while approximately thirty to forty percent of the females had (table 11.5). Also note in table

The sexual fantasies of adolescent boys focus specifically on sexual activity.

Table 11.5	Age at first intercourse by age group			
	Females (percent)		Males (percent)	
Present age	15-16	17-18	15-16	17-18
Age of first intercourse				
13	7	3	18	7
16	31	41	43	42

Source: After data presented by Hass, A., Teenage Sexuality: A Survey of Teenage Sexual Behavior. New York: MacMillan, 1979.

11.5, that at age thirteen almost twice as many males as females had engaged in sexual intercourse. This finding has been discovered by other researchers as well, namely that male adolescents engage in sexual intercourse at an earlier age than females. Such results are curious in light of the fact the females reach puberty on the average two years earlier than males. The curious findings undoubtedly are related to the different standards we have in our culture for males and females, and the distinctive way we socialize children and adolescents because of their sex.

One well-known study of adolescent sexuality (Sorensen, 1973) provides further support for some of the conclusions we have reached so far. For example, in regard to sex differences in sexuality, it was found that forty-four percent of the boys and thirty percent of the girls had sexual intercourse prior to age sixteen. This and other interesting information about adolescents' sexual behavior is presented in table 11.6. You will read about different subclasses of nonvirgins and virgins, and their heterosexual activity at ages thirteen to fifteen and sixteen to nineteen.

The Sorensen data, however, may give a more conservative picture of adolescent sexuality than currently exists. Those data were based on a national sample and they were collected in the early 1970s. More recent data suggest that sexual activity may be greater among adolescents, particularly in certain communities. For example, in an investigation of sexual intercourse in a Baltimore inner-city school in the early 1980s, eighty-one percent of the males and forty-seven percent of the females had experienced sexual intercourse by the time they were in the seventh and eighth grade. By the senior year in high school, ninety-one percent of the males and seventy-two percent of the females had engaged in intercourse and twenty-three percent of the sexually experienced females had become pregnant. Other recent data on sexual activity among black urban male adolescents indicates a high incidence of sexual intercourse at very early ages (table 11.7) (Clark, Zabin, and Hardy, 1984).

Relationships, Affection, and Exploitation

Some researchers, such as Philip Dreyer (1982), argue that the new norm of adolescent sexuality suggests sexual intercourse is acceptable, but mainly in the boundary of a loving and affectionate relationship. By contrast, Dreyer (1982) believes that promiscuity, exploitation, and unprotected sexual intercourse are often perceived as unacceptable by adolescents. Other researchers (e.g., Darling et. al., 1984) emphasize that while intercourse is acceptable in a nonlove relationship during adolescence, physical or emotional exploitation of the partner is not. While these standards vary

Table 11.6 The heterosexual activity of American adolescents

Group	Total	Boys	Girls	Ages 13–15	Ages 16–19	White	Non-white
1. Virgins (adolescents who have not had sexual intercourse)	48%	41%	55%	63%	36%	55%	49%
Sexually inexperienced (virgins with no experience in any type of sexual activity)	22%	20%	25%	39%	9%	25%	23%
Sexual beginners (virgins who have actively or passively experienced some type of sexual activity)	17%	14%	19%	12%	21%	20%	9%
Unclassified virgins (virgins who could not be classified in the above groups)	9%	7%	11%	12%	6%	9%	17%
2. Nonvirgins (adolescents who have had sexual intercourse one or more times)	52%	59%	45%	37%	64%	45%	51%
Serial monogamists (nonvirgins having a sexual relationship with only one person)	21%	15%	28%	9%	31%	19%	14%
Sexual adventurers (nonvirgins freely moving from one sexual partner to another)	15%	24%	6%	10%	18%	11%	18%
Inactive nonvirgins (nonvirgins who have not had sexual intercourse for more than one year)	12%	13%	10%	15%	10%	11%	14%
Unclassified nonvirgins (nonvirgins who could not be classified in the above groups)	4%	7%	1%	3%	5%	4%	5%
Currently intercourse-experienced (nonvirgins who have had sexual intercourse during the preceding month)	31%	30%	33%	15%	45%	24%	31%
Noncurrent intercourse-experienced (nonvirgins who have not had sexual intercourse during the preceding month)	21%	29%	12%	22%	19%	21%	20%

Source: Sorensen, 1973

Table 11.7 Sexual experience of urban black male adolescents

Behavior	Subgroup of study	Total	Age fourteen	Ages fifteen to nineteen
Ever had coitus	Yes	87%	81%	92%
	No	13	19	8
Age at first coitus	9	23	28	20
	10	11	16	8
	11	10	14	7
	12	20	26	16
	13	18	12	23
	14	12	4	17
	15	3	(Not asked)	6
	16–17	2	(Not asked)	3

Note: figures in percentages
Source: After data presented by Clark, S. D., Zabin, L. S., and J. B. Hardy, "Sex, Contraception, and Parenthood: Experience and Attitudes Among Urban Black Young Men," Family Planning Perspectives, *16, 77–82. Copyright © 1984 Alan Guttmacher Institute.*

as to whether sexual intercourse should involve a relationship or not, both stress that the double standard, which once existed, does not operate like it once did. That is, they believe the physical and emotional exploitation of adolescent females by males is not as strong in the 1980s.

However, other researchers disagree. For example, Diane Morrison (1985) argues that remnants of the double standard in which our society promotes and accepts sexual activity for males, but not for females still exist. As one adolescent male recently remarked, "Look, I feel a lot of pressure from my buddies to go for the score." Some adolescents perceive they will be viewed as having homosexual tendencies if they have not had sexual intercourse.

Further, evidence that physical and emotional exploitation of the female adolescent was found in a survey of 432 fourteen to eighteen year olds (Goodchilds and Zellman, 1984). Both male and female adolescents accepted the right of the male adolescent to be sexually aggressive, but left matters up to the female to set the limits for the male's sexual overtures. Yet another attitude related to the double standard for boys and girls focuses on the belief that girls should not plan ahead

to have sexual intercourse, but it is somewhat permissible for them to be swept away by the passion of the moment, more permissible than taking contraceptive precautions (Morrison, 1985). While there are some instances when double standards are not taking place in regard to sexual behavior in adolescence, the evidence suggests that some aspects of the double standard still operate, particularly in regard to the exploitation of females by males.

Now that we have studied heterosexual attitudes and behavior, we turn our attention to homosexual behavior and self-stimulation.

Homosexual Attitudes and Behavior
Homosexual behavior is not very widespread during the adolescent years. Only three percent of boys and two percent of girls report participating in an ongoing homosexual relationship (Chilman, 1979; Haas, 1979). And less than fifteen percent of boys and ten percent of girls report ever having even one homosexual encounter.

However, while homosexual behavior is not widely practiced in adolescence, attitudes about homosexual behavior are somewhat more liberal than the actual behavior. In one investigation (Haas, 1979), nearly seventy percent of sixteen to nineteen year olds accepted sexual relationships among two girls and only slightly fewer adolescents accepted such contacts among boys. But male adolescents were much less likely to accept homosexual behavior among boys than among girls. Indeed, many male adolescents actually added harsh, condemning words, saying that such behavior was sick or perverted. These responses may be an attempt to deny their own homosexual feelings and/or assert their sense of masculinity.

One point needs to be made about the acceptance and incidence of homosexual behavior. Data collected after the recent AIDS epidemic are likely to show reduced acceptance of homosexual behavior.

Self-Stimulation
The most extensive data collected about adolescent sexual behavior are those reported by Alfred Kinsey (1948). According to Kinsey (1948), there is a rapid increase in the incidence of masturbation for boys between the ages of thirteen and fifteen. By age fifteen,

for example, eighty-two percent of all boys interviewed had masturbated. Girls tend to begin masturbating later, and do not do so as often as boys. For example, by the age of fifteen, only twenty-five percent of all girls had masturbated to orgasm.

A recent investigation (Hass, 1979) reveals that masturbation is very common among adolescents. For example, among sixteen- to nineteen-year-olds more than two-thirds of the boys and half of the girls masturbate once a week or more. Sexually active adolescents tended to masturbate more than those who were less sexually active. Although boys involved in sexual relationships tended not to masturbate as much, the opposite was found to be true for girls, apparently because sexually active girls felt the need to release sexual tensions that resulted from failure to achieve orgasm during intercourse.

Male adolescents today do not seem to feel as guilty about masturbating as they once did, although interview data collected in the 1970s suggest that they still feel embarrassed and defensive about it (Sorensen, 1973). Consider the following comments, though, taken from a popular handbook in 1913 entitled *What a Boy Should Know*. These comments reveal the stigma attached to masturbation in another era:

> Whenever unnatural emissions are produced . . .
> he will be more easily tired. . . . He will
> probably look pale and pasty, and he is lucky if he
> escapes indigestion and getting his bowels
> confined, both of which will probably give him
> spots and pimples on his face. . . . The results on
> the mind are the more severe and more easily
> recognized. . . . His wits are not so sharp. . . .
> A boy like this is a poor thing to look at. . . .
> . . . The effect of self-abuse on a boy's
> character always tends to weaken it, and in fact,
> to make him untrustworthy, unreliable,
> untruthful, and probably dishonest. (Schofield
> and Vaughan-Jackson, 1913, pp. 30–42)

As Janet Hyde (1979) points out, masturbation was thought in past eras to cause everything from warts to insanity. Today, as few as fifteen percent of adolescents believe that masturbation is wrong.

Not only do adolescents (particularly males) masturbate, they also are prone to engage in frequent flights of sexual fantasy. As we said, the sexual fantasies of adolescent males usually involve actual sexual activity, while the sexual fantasies of adolescent females are more socially oriented. The adolescent boy may fantasize about having an orgy with a number of girls. He may daydream about having sex with a teacher. Such daydreaming does not mean there is anything sick or wrong with the teenager—he also has flights of fantasy about being a millionaire, a sports hero, and so forth. David Elkind states that such daydreaming and egocentrism are typical of the adolescent, particularly the young adolescent.

Now that we have studied many different aspects of heterosexual activity, we turn our attention to some related, often controversial topics.

Contraceptives and Sexually Transmitted Disease

Two major issues wrapped up in adolescent sexuality focus on knowledge about and use of contraceptives, and the incidence and type of sexually transmitted diseases that may accompany sexual intercourse.

Contraceptives

Premarital intercourse can be meaningful and educational for mature adolescents, usually those in late adolescence; however, possibly because of the generally poor quality of sex education in the United States, many adoelscents are ill-equipped to handle the psychological ramifications of such experiences. Adolescents may attempt intercourse without knowing exactly what to do or how to satisfy their partners, leading to frustration and fears of sexual inadequacy. In addition, many adolescents are not well-informed about contraceptives. Only about one out of five unmarried female adolescents who have sexual intercourse uses birth control pills, and many sexually active adolescents never use any contraceptives whatsoever (Jessor and Jessor, 1975). Even by late adolescence, only sixty percent of all females use any contraceptive method (Zelnik and Kantner, 1977). Perhaps more surprising, a majority of

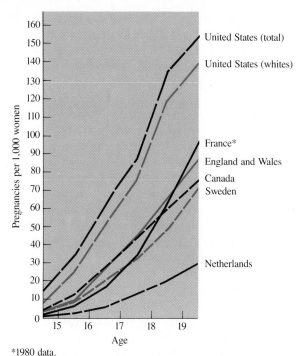

*1980 data.

Note: pregnancies are defined here as births plus
abortions; age is the age at outcome.

Figure 11.6 **Pregnancy rates per 1,000 women by
women's age, 1981.**

adolescent females are under a complete misconception about when during the menstrual cycle they are most likely to become pregnant. Amazingly, most of them believe that the risk of pregnancy is greatest during menstruation (Zelnick and Kantner, 1977)!

Pregnancy in adolescence is a major national problem. The adolescent pregnancy rate is increasing even though the birth rate is decreasing. If current trends continue, four in ten young women will become pregnant at least once while they are in adolescence (Alan Guttmacher Institute, 1981). Indeed, teenage fertility and abortion rates are higher in the United States than in other developed countries (Jones et al., 1985). For example, as shown in figure 11.6, adolescents from the United States have the highest pregnancy rate at all ages when compared with adolescents from England, France, Canada, Sweden, and the Netherlands. And, the pregnancy rate of black adolescent females in the United States is particularly high.

Table 11.8 **Types of contraceptives used by urban adolescents**

Method	Method first used		Method last used	
	1976	1979	1976	1979
Pill	33%	19%	48%	41%
IUD	2	1	3	2
Diaphragm	0	1	1	4
Condom	36	34	23	23
Douche	3	1	3	2
Withdrawal	18	36	15	19
Rhythm	5	5	4	6

*Source: From Zelnik, M., and J. F. Kantner, "Sexual Activity,
Contraceptive Use and Pregnancy Among Metropolitan-Area
Teenagers: 1971–1979," Family Planning Perspectives, 12,
230–237. Copyright © 1980 Alan Guttmacher Institute.*

Table 11.9 **The increased use of contraceptives by adolescents**

Contraceptive use status	1976	1979
Always used	29%	34%
Used at first intercourse, but not always	10	15
Not used at first intercourse, but used at some time	26	25
Never used	36	27

*Source: From Zelnik, M., and J. F. Kantner, "Sexual Activity,
Contraceptive Use and Pregnancy Among Metropolitan-Area
Teenagers: 1971–1979," Family Planning Perspectives, 12,
230–237. Copyright © 1980 Alan Guttmacher Institute.*

Further data about the type of contraceptive use by adolescents comes from a research study among urban boys and girls aged fifteen through nineteen (Zelnick and Kantner, 1980). As shown in table 11.8, the pill and condoms were the most widely used contraceptive devices. Note that the use of the pill has declined and seems to have been replaced by more ineffective measures, such as withdrawal. In this research, it was reported that adolescents are increasing their use of contraceptive methods (table 11.9), but as we just have seen, their choice of methods seems to not be as intelligent as in the past.

Investigations of social characteristics reveal that the factors most related to poor, inconsistent, or nonuse of contraceptives among adolescents are being under the age of eighteen; being single and not involved in a steady, committed, dating relationship; having intercourse sporadically; being from a lower socioeconomic status family; desiring a pregnancy; being black or Hispanic; not being a college student; and not having had a previous pregnancy experience (Chilman, 1979). Personality and attitudinal factors that are associated with sexually active adolescents' failure to adequately use contraceptives include viewing oneself as not sexually active, being poorly socialized, having a poor sense of personal efficacy (feeling incompetent), having poor cognitive skills (poor coping skills), having no future orientation, being neurotic or anxious, having poor social adjustment, and having negative attitudes about contraceptives (Oskamp and Mindick, 1981).

The following conversation between a boy and girl reveals a communication pattern that far too often characterizes the situation in which an adolescent girl becomes pregnant:

Susan: Come in.

Skip: I'm sorry I'm late Susan. I had to go to the U store and the library and run around and, you know, all kinds of things and I'm sorry . . .

Susan: Yeah, well I'm glad you came. I called because I want to talk to you.

Skip: Yeah. How was your day today?

Susan: Oh, all right. Did you get much studying done?

Skip: No, I was running around and uh, you know just thinking, sitting around.

Susan: Yeah. I've been thinking a lot also. I really want to talk with you about last night. (pause)

Skip: Are you sorry or anything?

Susan: No, I'm not sorry. I'm just really worried.

Skip: (surprise) About what?

Susan: You know I'm not using any birth control.

Skip: (shock) You're not using any birth control? (pause) No, I didn't know you weren't using any birth control. How was I supposed to. . . . How could you do that?

Susan: My mother always told me the man would take care of it.

Skip: The man *can* take care of it, but I *wasn't* taking care of it, obviously. It's the woman's responsibility to take care of it, you know that. All women use the pill nowadays.

Susan: Not all women use the pill and why is it my responsibility if we're both involved? Besides we never really talked about it and when was I supposed to bring it up, in the middle of . . . I didn't know you were planning to go to bed.

Skip: I didn't plan it. Aw, come on, Susan, You don't plan things like that, they just happen.

Susan: We both must have been thinking about it . . . why didn't we say anything? Aren't we supposed to trust each other?

Skip: Sure we trust each other. Aw, come on it's not that, it's just not the kind of things you talk about. Susan, could you see me going up to you and saying, "Susan are you using any. . . ." I can't say that. I can't say it.

Susan: Skip, I'm really scared. I could be pregnant. What are we going to do? (Looking at each other scared and questioningly)

Source: Gordon, Karen A., "Great Expectations," 1976: Unprotected Intercourse Scenario. Princeton University, McCosh Health Center.

Sexually Transmitted Disease (STD)

Formerly called venereal disease (or VD), sexually transmitted disease is primarily transmitted through sexual intercourse, although it can be transmitted orally. Sexually transmitted disease is fairly common among adolescents today. The most common sexually transmitted diseases that adolescents are likely to encounter are chlamydia, gonorrhea, venereal warts, and herpes.

Chlamydia affects as many as ten percent of all college students. The disease, which is named for the tiny bacterium that causes it, appears in both males and females. Males experience a burning sensation during urination and a mucoid discharge, and females often encounter painful urination or a vaginal discharge. These signs often mimic gonorrhea; however, while penicillin is prescribed for the gonorrhea-like symptoms, the problem does not go away, as it would if gonorrhea were the culprit. If left untreated, the disease can infect the entire reproductive tract. In particular, this can lead to problems left by scar tissue that prevent the female from becoming pregnant. Drugs have been developed to treat this very common sexually transmitted disease and they are very effective.

Another major sexual problem in recent years has focused on a virus called genital herpes. While this sexual disease is more common among young adults (estimates range to as high as one in five sexually active adults), as many as one in thirty-five adolescents has been estimated to have genital herpes (Oppenheimer, 1982). The first herpes symptom is a vague itching or burning sensation in or near the genital area. Two or three days later, the burning usually turns into a more painful feeling. Shallow, fluid-filled blisters appear on the shaft or tip of the penis in males and on the outer genitalia, vagina, or cervix in females. The first attack is usually the most painful, often accompanied by flu-like symptoms. The severity of the attacks and whether they recur vary extensively from one individual to another, although approximately seventy percent experience a repeat attack within nine months of the first.

Usually when you catch a virus like measles or chicken pox, your body produces antibodies that try to destroy the invading virus. The antibodies remain in your bloodstream for the rest of your life and instantly attack the virus if it reappears. This is the reason why we only get the measles once. Unfortunately, herpes antibodies do not work this way. They help victims recover when the virus attacks, but they do not completely kill it. Instead, the virus retreats to the nerve cells at the base of the spine, where it can remain dormant anywhere from several weeks to a lifetime. During new attacks, the virus travels down the nerve fibers to the genitalia and produces another crop of painful blisters.

Girls and women with herpes need to be especially cautious, since there is some indication that it is linked with cervical cancer. It has been reported that women with genital herpes are five to eight times more likely to develop this form of cancer than those not infected. Women with herpes should have a Pap smear every six months—fortunately, this type of cancer develops slowly and can easily be detected in an early form. While many doctors and researchers are working on a cure for genital herpes, none has yet been found. Before a cure for herpes is found, several questions will have to be answered: How is the virus able to persist in the body? Why does it become dormant? What happens when it reactivates? And how does the body finally suppress the recurrences?

We have discussed a number of aspects of contemporary attitudes and behaviors related to sexuality. A summary of main ideas related to sexuality described so far is presented in Concept Table 11.3. Our discussion of contraceptives and sexually transmitted disease brings up the important question of how competent the sex education is that adolescents receive. Next we explore this sex education in greater detail.

Sex Education

Although the task of teaching adolescents about the physical and psychological aspects of human sexual development should probably fall to the adolescent's parents, many parents are either insufficiently knowledgeable or are unwilling to discuss sexual issues with their adolescents. Think about your adolescent years. Did one or both of your parents sit down and talk with you about "the facts of life?" If so, how valuable do you feel the information was? Our discussion of sex education begins by focusing on sources of sex information, then turns to sex education in the schools. Next, we study the fascinating topic of cognitive development and sex education.

Concept Table 11.3

ADOLESCENT SEXUALITY

Concept	Processes/related ideas	Characteristics/description
Adolescent sexuality	Its general nature	Adolescence is a time when exploratory and experimental sex play turns into more purposeful sexual behavior. During early adolescence, many individuals restrict themselves to petting and the main sexual outlet is masturbation. Adolescent females overall seem to be more sexually inhibited than adolescent males. In late adolescence, sexual intercourse becomes a more prominent aspect of sexual activity. The sexual fantasies of males are more explicit than those of females.
Contemporary sexual attitudes and behavior in adolescence	Trends in the twentieth century	There has been a major increase in the number of young people reporting intercourse and the proportion of females engaging in intercourse has increased more rapidly than in the case of males, although males had a higher plateau to begin with.
	Heterosexual attitudes and behavior	There often is more acceptance of sexual behavior at the attitudinal level than incidence of actual sexual behavior. There seems to have been increased acceptance of sexuality by adolescents in recent years, particularly on the part of girls. At the behavioral level, increases seem to be occurring as well and at younger ages. Curiously, while male adolescents mature on the average two years later than females, they engage in sexual intercourse earlier. Many adolescents feel that middle to late adolescence is the best time to first have intercourse, although some adolescents have intercourse at earlier ages. National data indicate that at age 16, roughly one-fourth to one-half of adolescents report having had sexual intercourse, but urban data suggest that certain areas reveal a much higher incidence by this age.
	Relationships, affection, and exploitation	Some researchers argue that the standard of the 1980s involves sex within an affectionate relationship while others emphasize the standard is sex in a nonloving, but nonexploitative relationship. Other researchers stress that physical and emotional exploitation of females by males during adolescent still is rampant. The research evidence indicates that in a number of instances certain aspects of the double standard still operate.

ADOLESCENT SEXUALITY

Concept	Processes/related ideas	Characteristics/description
	Homosexual behavior	Homosexual behavior is not very widespread during the adolescent years. Only about three percent of boys and two percent of girls report an ongoing homosexual relationship. Acceptance of homosexual behavior is much more widespread, although boys are much less likely to accept such behavior by their own sex than among girls. The AIDS epidemic may reduce the acceptance of homosexual behavior.
	Self-stimulation	Masturbation is very common among adolescents, particularly boys. Adolescents feel much less guilty about masturbating now than in earlier eras. During masturbation, there often are flights of fantasy.
Contraceptives and sexually transmitted disease	Contraceptives	Possibly due to the poor sex education they receive, many adolescents do not have good information about sexual matters and often are not very good sexual partners. There has been an increase in the use of contraceptives by adolescents in recent years, but large numbers of adolescents still do not use contraceptives even though they are sexually active on a regular basis. Even though the birth rate is decreasing, the adolescent pregnancy rate is increasing. While adolescents are increasing their use of contraceptives, their choice of contraceptives does not seem to be as intelligent as it was once. Birth control pills are being used less and the withdrawal method is used more.
	Sexually Transmitted Disease (STD)	Just as in adulthood, there are a number of diseases that may accompany sexual intercourse. The four most common among adolescents are chlamydia, gonorrhea, venereal warts, and herpes.

Table 11.10 Initial sources of sex information

	Abortion	Conception	Contraception	Ejaculation	Homosexuality	Intercourse	Masturbation	Menstruation	Petting	Prostitution	Seminal emissions	Venereal disease	Totals
Peers	20.0	27.4	42.8	38.9	50.6	39.7	36.3	21.5	59.7	49.7	35.2	28.2	37.1
Literature	32.0	3.2	23.8	22.1	19.4	15.2	25.0	11.2	10.0	26.8	37.4	21.2	21.9
Mother	21.5	49.4	13.1	8.9	7.5	23.8	11.1	41.5	4.5	7.5	4.2	9.4	17.4
Schools	23.7	16.4	16.7	20.7	16.1	7.6	17.5	15.7	9.0	11.7	21.1	36.8	15.2
Experience	.5	.8	1.0	5.2	2.1	7.5	8.0	7.6	14.0	2.0	.7	1.1	5.4
Father	1.0	1.2	2.4	2.6	4.3	3.9	1.3	1.1	2.2	1.0	1.4	2.1	2.2
Minister	1.0	.9	.0	.7	.0	1.0	.0	.7	.2	1.0	.0	.0	.5
Physician	.3	.7	.2	.9	.0	1.3	.8	.7	.4	.3	.0	1.2	.3
Totals	100.0	100.0	100.0	100.0	100.0	100.0	100.0	100.0	100.0	100.0	100.0	100.0	

N = 1152

"Don't know" responses were eliminated from the table. Percentages are on all terms listed as known.

Source: From Thornberg, H. D., "Sources of Sex Education Among Early Adolescents," Journal of Early Adolescence, 1981, 1, p. 174.

Sources of Sex Information

One fourteen-year-old adolescent recently was asked where he learned about sex. He responded, "In the street." When asked if that was the only place, he said, "Well, I learn some more from Playboy and the other sex magazines." What about school, he was asked. He responded, "No, they talk about hygiene, but not anything that could help you out that much." And, when asked about his parents contributions to his sex education, he said, "They haven't told me anything."

Hershel Thornburg has been surveying adolescents' sources of sex information for a number of years (e.g., Thornburg, 1968, 1981). He recently asked all of the students in a midwestern high school (1,152 in all) where they first learned about a number of aspects of sex, including venereal disease, seminal emissions, prostitution, petting, menstruation, masturbation, intercourse, homosexuality, ejaculation, contraception, conception, and abortion. They were also asked from which of the following sources they obtained their information: mother, father, peers, literature (including the media), schools, physician, minister, or experience. As in other investigations, peers were the most cited source of information (more than thirty-seven percent of sex information came from peers), followed by literature, mothers, and the schools. Experience was the adolescent's teacher more often than fathers, physicians, or ministers. Table 11.10 presents the most common sources of specific types of sex information (Thornburg, 1981). Note that while schools are often thought of as the primary source of sex information for adolescents, in the recent survey by Thornburg (1981), the school was not the main source of sex information. Other surveys have also found that peers are usually the main source of adolescents' sex information.

In another investigation, only nine percent of adolescent males and sixteen percent of adolescent females listed parents as the main sources of their sexual information (Hunt, 1974). By contrast, seventy-nine percent of the females and sixty-eight percent of the males indicated that friends and books were their main sources of information on sex. (Interestingly, when I went to a university library to check out some source books as background for writing this section, I had a difficult time getting three or four books. The librarian told me that a number of junior high school boys had been hiding the books in different areas of the library, so they could come in and read them.) A variety of social problems—for example, teenage promiscuity, unwanted pregnancy, and prostitution—suggest that adolescents are not receiving adequate sex education. Since many parents seem to feel either unwilling or inadequate as sex educators, the information has to come from other sources.

Since sexuality is wrapped up in individual values, it seems logical to look for sexual guidance from various religious organizations. But religious organizations typically do not reach the adolescents who could benefit the most from instruction (and this is not necessarily because of a lack of effort on the organizations' part).

Although schools may not be the most appropriate or logical alternative, in the long run, they may be the most effective and best equipped to handle sex education. Schools reach the greatest number of adolescents of all ages, and the teachers responsible for sex education are usually knowledgeable in many different aspects of adolescent development, family studies, biological development, and psychology.

Most public opinion polls suggest that parents approve of sex education in schools. For example, in a nationwide poll conducted by NBC in 1981, seventy-five percent of adults in the United States approved of sex education classes in schools while only twelve percent believed such instruction would encourage sexual activity. Eighty percent of parents supported sex education, while only nine percent said it would increase sexual behavior.

Sex Education in the Schools

Whether sex education should be a part of the curriculum of secondary schools has been one of the most heated issues in education in recent years. While the issue of whether sex education should be provided in school has still not been settled, one point is clear: adolescents are not presently obtaining a very large percentage of their sex education from schools. In Thornburg's surveys, adolescents consistently obtained only sixteen percent of their sex information from schools.

One recent survey of ninety-nine secondary schools in the United States explored the curricula of sex education classes in the ninth, tenth, eleventh, and twelfth grades (Newton, 1982). As is shown in table 11.11, sex education is most likely to be taught in the tenth grade, and sex education programs are much more likely to appear in grades nine through twelve than in grades seven and eight. The emphasis in sex education classes is on biological topics such as anatomy and physiology, reproduction, pregnancy, childbirth, and venereal disease. These topics are twice as likely to be discussed as social topics like homosexuality, variations in sexuality, and prostitution. However, exceptions to this rule are topics such as love, marriage, and sex roles, all of which receive relatively high attention in grades nine through twelve.

Sex education programs vary extensively from school to school. Many schools have no sex education programs at all. Among those that do, a sex education program can refer to a well-developed, full-semester course on human sexuality or to a two-week unit on anatomy and physiology in a biology course. Indeed, biology at the tenth-grade level is the most common place for adolescents to be exposed to at least a small dose of sex education.

Another concern for a quality sex education program is the teacher—the qualifications and talents of the person who handles the curriculum. Most instructors have majored in biology, health education, home economics, or physical education. Few have majored in

Table 11.11 Topics and grade levels for the most popular topics in sex education programs

Topic / grade level	Number of classes*
Anatomy and physiology (10)	41/20 = 61
Reproduction (10)	32/26 = 58
Venereal disease (10)	28/28 = 56
Pregnancy and childbirth (10)	36/19 = 55
Contraception (10)	13/36 = 49
Sex roles (10)	22/25 = 47
Anatomy and physiology (10)	30/16 = 46
Pregnancy and childbirth (12)	32/14 = 46
Love (10)	23/33 = 46
Abortion (12)	14/30 = 44
Reproduction (9)	20/25 = 45
Sex roles (12)	27/17 = 44
Love (12)	26/18 = 44

Other topics mentioned by more than 40 respondents: sexual intercourse (10); anatomy and physiology (11); marriage and nonmarriage (11 and 12); venereal disease (10, 11, 12); reproduction (12); contraception (12); and pregnancy and childbirth (9).

*Shown are the numbers reporting "heavy" and "moderate" emphasis and then the total of these two. That is, for anatomy and physiology, grade 10, 41 respondents report "heavy" emphasis on this topic, and 20 a "moderate" emphasis, for a total of 61 respondents on this topic and grade level.

Source: From Newton, D. E., "The Status of Programs in Human Sexuality: A Preliminary Study," The High School Journal, Vol. 6, 1982. Copyright 1982 The University of North Carolina Press.

human sexuality per se (Newton, 1982). But while the teacher doesn't have to have a Ph.D. in human sexuality to impart adequate and useful information about sexual matters to adolescents, he or she should be reasonably well-trained and knowledgeable about sexuality.

Among other characteristics that may help the sex education instructor in secondary schools is the willingness to admit it when he or she doesn't know an answer and to look things up in reference books for or

with students. The sex education teacher also should be skilled in handling adolescent emotions. In a class of twenty or thirty junior high school students, at least half of them will probably be embarrassed or uncomfortable discussing sex-related topics. The teacher's ability to make the students feel at ease in discussing sexual matters can be a key ingredient in helping adolescents learn about sexuality in a competent and healthy manner.

A discussion of a recently developed sex education program is described in Perspective on Adolescent Development 11.5. You will note that the program, called the Postponing Sexual Involvement Series, is designed to strengthen the ability of adolescents to say no to sex by improving their communication about sex.

Cognitive Development and Sex Education in Early Adolescence

Joan Lipsitz (1980) commented about the importance of cognitive development in sex education. She points out that having information about contraceptives is not enough. Whether adolescents will use contraceptives or not seems to depend on their acceptance of themselves and their sexuality. Such acceptance likely requires cognitive as well as emotional maturity.

Most discussions of adolescent pregnancy and its prevention assume the adolescent has the ability to anticipate consequences, to weigh the probable outcome of behavior, or to project into the future what will happen in his or her life if certain acts, such as sexual intercourse, are practiced. That is, prevention is based on the belief that the adolescent has the formal operational ability to approach problem solving in a planned, organized, and analytical manner. However, many young adolescents are just beginning to develop such capacities and others have not yet developed these cognitive abilities. We discussed the personal fable when we described adolescent egocentrism in Chapter 4. We will discuss how the young adolescent's personal fable and cognitive development may be linked to adolescent pregnancy in Perspective on Adolescent Development 11.6.

Perspective on Adolescent Development 11.5
POSTPONING SEXUAL INVOLVEMENT

*P*ostponing Sexual Involvement is an approach designed for use with thirteen- through fifteen-year-old adolescents. It is aimed at reducing pregnancy by decreasing the number of adolescents who become sexually involved. It was developed in Atlanta, Georgia (Howard, 1983).

This program does not offer factual information about sexual reproduction and it does not discuss family planning. Rather the program concentrates on social and peer pressures that often lead an adolescent into early sexual behavior. Particular emphasis is placed on building social skills to help adolescents communicate better with each other when faced with sexual pressures.

One main difference between this curriculum and most sex education programs is that it starts with a given value—that is, you should not be having sex at such a young age. Everything in the curriculum is designed to support this argument. Traditional sex education programs invariably have the implicit goal of reducing teenage pregnancy, but they usually include information on birth control and reproduction so that if young adolescents choose to have sex, they can behave in a responsible manner. This curriculum avoids the double message implied in such traditional programs.

The series is divided into four sessions, each one and a half hours long. The first three sessions occur fairly close together, while the fourth session is used as a reinforcement some three to six months later. The first session focuses on social pressure, with students given opportunities to explore why they feel adolescents engage in sex at an early age. The reasons they usually give involve various needs, such as to be popular, to hang onto a boyfriend, and so forth. The leaders then help the adolescents to understand that sexual intercourse will not necessarily fulfill these needs.

The second session presents further information about peer pressure, both in group sessions and in one-on-one sessions. Adolescents are provided with opportunities to become familiar with common pressure statements and after responses are modeled for them, they practice responding in their own words. Session three involves information and exercises about problem solving. It encourages an understanding of limiting physical expression of affection and through developing and practicing skits, provides help in handling difficult sexual situations. As indicated earlier, the fourth session occurs a number of months later and is used to reinforce the ideas in the first three sessions by applying them to new situations.

This series on "how to say no" was designed to provide young adolescents with the ability to bridge the gap between their physical development and their cognitive ability to handle the implications for such development. It was not developed to replace the provision of actual factual information about sexuality and family planning.

It should be pointed out that as part of the Postponing Sexual Involvement Series, some adolescents' parents also are participating. The goal of the parental involvement is to determine the acceptance level both by the community (parents) and the young adolescents themselves, as well as to learn which delivery styles are most effective. For instance, some of the series are being delivered by peers several years older than the adolescents, while others have adult leaders.

Perspective on Adolescent Development 11.6
PERSONAL FABLES AND PREGNANCIES

*J*oan Lipsitz (1980), in addressing the American Association of Sex Educators, Counselors, and Therapists, described the personal fable and how it may be linked to adolescent pregnancy. The young adolescent often says, "Heh, it won't happen to me." If the adolescent is locked into this personal fable, he or she may not respond well to a course on sex education that preaches prevention. She points out that the best of what we know about prevention is not appropriate for early adolescents. A developmental perspective on cognition may provide some insight into what should be taught in sex education courses to early adolescents.

Late adolescents (e.g., eighteen to nineteen years of age) are at least to some degree realistic and future-oriented about sexual experiences, just as they are about careers and marriage. Middle adolescents (e.g., fifteen to seventeen years of age) often romanticize sexuality. However, young adolescents, those ten to fifteen years of age, appear to experience sex in a depersonalized way that is filled with anxiety and denial. At the same time, it also is known that even college students who are anxious and guilty about sex are more likely to risk pregnancy than their less uptight counterparts. Thus, it seems that the somewhat depersonalized way that young adolescents experience sexuality is not very likely to lead to preventive behavior.

Now consider what the outcome will be if the following are combined: the nature of early adolescent cognition, the personal fable, anxiety about sex, sex-role definitions about what is masculine and what is feminine, the sexual themes of music in the adolescent culture, as well as the sexual overtones that are rampant on television and in magazines, and a societal standard that says sex is appropriate for adults, but is promiscuous for adolescents. That is, as Lipsitz (1980) says, "Sex is fun, harmless, adult—and forbidden . . . the combination of early physical maturation, risk-taking behavior, egocentrism, the inability to think futuristically, and this ambivalent contradictory culture is more than most of us

Older adolescents are at least to some degree realistic and future oriented about sexual experiences.

want to face up to. Add to that the growing need young adolescents have, as they mature, for meaningful social commitment in a society which puts its young people on 'hold' in order to reduce the strain on the glutted job market. To be a young adolescent with a newly forming sense of destiny facing a thirty-five percent youth unemployment rate is to be turned away from the future, intensively toward the present. . . . Put together early adolescent development, America's sexual ambivalence, and adolescents' vulnerability to economic forces, and I think you have social dynamite" (p. 31).

Summary

I. Information about sex roles focuses on the nature of masculinity, femininity, and androgyny; biological and cognitive factors in development; environmental influences; and sex differences as well as sex-role stereotypes.

A. Ideas about masculinity, femininity, and androgyny focus on the nature of the terms and whether one type of sex-role makeup is associated with more competence.

1. For many years, the male- and female-related aspects of sex/gender roles were categorized as either masculine or feminine. The competent male adolescent was described as masculine (for example, being independent and aggressive), while the competent female adolescent was characterized as feminine (for instance, being dependent and unaggressive).

2. Androgyny became an important part of sex-role research in the 1970s. Androgyny refers to the combination of both masculine and feminine characteristics in the same person. Most androgyny scales allow the individual to be categorized as masculine, feminine, androgynous, or undifferentiated. Note that such scales do not develop new items for the androgyny classification, rather an individual saying that both a number of masculine and feminine items are like him or her is described as androgynous. Two of the most widely used androgyny scales are those devised by Spence and Bem.

3. Considerable interest has been generated about whether individuals with a particular sex-role makeup are more competent. In instances where the criteria for competence involve both self-assertion and integration, androgynous adolescents often are more competent. However, it is very important to specify the contexts in which androgyny is being evaluated. In contexts where feminine characteristics are valued, then an adolescent with a feminine sex-role makeup will likely perform more competently. It is very important not only to specify the dimensions of social competence being assessed, but also the dimensions of sex/gender roles. There has been a tendency to value the masculine role and self-assertion more than the feminine role or integration in our culture. And the criteria for competence have tended to follow this pattern as well.

B. Both biological and cognitive factors are important in understanding sex roles.

1. The psychoanalytic theorists, Erikson and Freud, argue that anatomy is destiny, that is psychological aspects of sex roles are wedded to the physical anatomy of males and females with males being more intrusive and females more inclusive. Research has not verified this belief. Hormones are important aspects of biological influences on sex roles. Research has included the study of individuals with unusually high levels of sex hormones, such as girls exposed to high levels of androgen, a male-linked sex hormone. The results have been inconclusive. Keep in mind John Money's belief that while there are two time periods when sex hormones are likely to be prominent in influencing sex roles (the first three years and puberty), sex roles inevitably are influenced by the interplay of biology and culture.

2. The cognitive developmental theory of Lawrence Kohlberg suggests that self-categorization and the development of a stable gender identity are precursors of sex-typed behavior. Others have expanded Kohlberg's ideas and seem to feel that early adolescence is a time of sex-role rigidity. The research suggests this may be more true for males than females. Language also is involved in sex roles. Researchers who explore sexism in language point to the important issue of whether sexist language produces sexist thought or vice versa.

C. While biological and cognitive factors are important in sex roles, they do not explain entirely the wide individual variation in sex roles. Such variation is undoubtedly tied up in environmental experiences. In recent years, there has been a widening view of the environmental factors that contribute to sex roles, including peers, teachers, and the media, although it would be unwise to think that parental influences are unimportant.

1. Fathers and mothers are psychologically important in both the adolescent male's and female's sex-role development. Parents, by action and example, influence sex roles.

2. By the time they have reached adolescence, individuals have been exposed to huge numbers of hours with peers and parents who have provided extensive feedback about sex roles, either implicitly or explicitly. In elementary schools, peer groups usually are sex segregated, but as we move through the adolescent years, they become increasingly integrated in terms of sex.

3. Teachers also can influence sex roles. Female teachers are likely to reward feminine behaviors and the majority of teachers are female. Many junior high teachers have stereotyped views of male and female roles.

4. Adolescents see very different images of males and females on television, in magazines, in commercials, and even in comic strips. Generally, these images present traditional sex roles, some of which are derogatory to females.

5. Efforts to change sex-typed behavior have included attempts to get gender-deviant children to become more normal in their sex-typed behavior and normal children to become more flexible in their sex-role orientation, in particular to develop a more androgynous sex-role orientation. The results of school interventions involving androgyny have been mixed, leading to greater change toward androgyny in females, but not in males. In some cases, early adolescent males exposed to androgynous sex-role programs become more masculine.

D. Ideas about sex-role stereotypes and sex differences focus on the nature of stereotypes, stereotypes in early adolescence, the Maccoby and Jacklin conclusions on sex differences, and criticisms of their work.

1. Stereotypes are broad categories that reflect our impressions of people, events, and ourselves. These stereotypes usually do not take into consideration individual variation. We often use stereotypes to simplify complex information. Once the broad labels are assigned, they are difficult to change.

2. Sex-role stereotypes seem to be particularly strong in early adolescence, more so for boys than girls. Young adolescent girls with egalitarian sex roles seem to have more positive self-images than their more traditional counterparts.

3. Maccoby and Jacklin concluded that, overall, boys are more aggressive, better at math, superior at visuospatial relations, but girls are better at verbal matters. A recent corollary of Maccoby and Jacklin's conclusions relates to computers, as males seem to show a greater interest in their use.

4. The conclusions of Maccoby and Jacklin have not gone unscathed. The review is now more than a decade old, and during this time, sex roles have continued to change rather dramatically. Further, they lumped together studies of very different qualities to arrive at their conclusions.

II. Information about adolescent sexuality focuses on the general nature of sexual matters, contemporary sexual attitudes and behavior, contraceptives and sexually transmitted disease, as well as sex education.

A. Adolescence is a time when exploratory and experimental sex play turn into more purposive sexual behavior. During early adolescence, many individuals restrict themselves to petting and the main sexual outlet is masturbation. Adolescent females overall seem to be more inhibited sexually than males. In late adolescence, sexual intercourse becomes a more prominent aspect of sexual activity. The sexual fantasies of male adolescents are more explicit than those of females.

B. To learn more about contemporary sexual attitudes and behavior, it is important to study trends in the twentieth century, the nature of heterosexual attitudes and behavior, relationships, affection, and exploitation, homosexual behavior, and self-stimulation.

1. There has been a major increase in the number of young people reporting intercourse and the proportion of females engaging in intercourse has increased more rapidly than in the case of males, although males had a higher plateau to begin with.

2. There often is more acceptance of sexual behavior at the attitudinal level than incidence of actual sexual behavior. There seems to have been increased acceptance of sexual behavior by adolescents, particularly girls, in recent years, and at the behavioral level, increases seem to be occurring as well and at earlier ages. Curiously, while male adolescents mature on the average two years later than females, they engage in sexual intercourse at an earlier age. Many adolescents feel that middle to late adolescence is the best time to first have sexual intercourse, although some adolescents have intercourse at a much younger age. National data indicate that at age sixteen, roughly one-fourth to one-half of adolescents report having had sexual intercourse, but urban data suggest that certain areas reveal a much higher incidence by this age.

3. Some researchers argue that the standard of the 1980s involves sex within an affectionate relationship, while others emphasize the standard is sex within a nonloving relationship. Yet other researchers stress that physical and emotional exploitation of females by males during adolescence is still rampant. The research evidence indicates that in a number of instances certain aspects of the double standard still operate.

4. Homosexual behavior is not very widespread during the adolescent years. Only about three percent of boys and two percent of girls report an ongoing homosexual relationship. Acceptance of homosexual behavior is much more widespread than its incidence, although boys are much less likely to accept this type of behavior in their own sex than among girls. The AIDS epidemic may reduce the acceptance and incidence of homosexual behavior.

5. Masturbation is very common among adolescents, particularly boys. Adolescents feel much less guilty about masturbating than in earlier eras. During masturbation, there often are flights of fantasy.

C. Contraceptives and sexually transmitted diseases represented two important aspects of adolescent sexuality.

1. Possibly due to the poor sex education they receive, many adolescents do not have good information about sexual matters and often are not very good sexual partners. There has been an increase in the use of contraceptives by adolescents in recent years, but large numbers of sexually active adolescents still do not use a contraceptive. Even though the birth rate is decreasing, teenage pregnancy is increasing. While adolescents are increasing their use of contraceptives, their choice of contraceptives often is not very wise. Birth control pills are used less than in the past, while the withdrawal method is used more.

2. Just as in adulthood, there are a number of sexually transmitted diseases that can accompany sexual intercourse. The four most common among adolescents are chlamydia, gonorrhea, venereal warts, and herpes.

D. Peers are the most common source of sex information. Little information about sex is obtained from parents and only about sixteen percent comes from schools. A survey of sex education classes suggests that the biological aspects of sex are more likely to be taught than the social side. Exceptions are love, marriage, and sex roles. Sex education classes vary considerably, ranging from none to a full semester course on human sexuality. The most likely place and time an adolescent will be exposed to sex education is in biology class in the tenth grade. Most studies suggest that the adolescent's knowledge about sex is very inadequate. An understanding of cognitive development provides some clues as to why many sex education programs with early adolescents do not work very well.

Key Terms

Suggested Readings

Chilman, C. S. (1979). *Adolescent sexuality in a changing American society: Social and psychological perspectives.* Washington, D.C.: Public Health Service, National Institute of Mental Health.
This book presents extensive data about adolescent sexuality, some of which were touched on in this chapter. An invaluable source of detailed information about adolescent sexuality.

Dreyer, P. H. (1982). Sexuality during adolescence. In B. J. Wolman (Ed.), *Handbook of developmental psychology.* Englewood Cliffs, N.J.: Prentice-Hall.
A thorough, comprehensive review of what is currently known about adolescent sexual attitudes and behaviors.

Family Planning Perspectives
This bimonthly publication contains many informative articles about adolescent sexuality.

Huston, A. C. (1983). Sex-typing. In P. H. Mussen (Ed.), *Handbook of child psychology,* 4th ed., vol. 4. New York: Wiley.
A lengthy, up-to-date version of what is known about androgyny and biological/environmental influences on sex roles.

Hyde, J. S. (1985). *Half the human experience,* 3rd ed. Lexington, Mass.: D. C. Heath.
An excellent overview of what is known about sex-role development in females by one of the leading researchers in this field.

Meikle, S., Peitchinis, J. A., and Pearce, K. (1985). *Teenage sexuality.* San Diego: College Hill Press.
An up-to-date, authoritative report on the nature of adolescent sexual attitudes and behavior is provided.

Sex Roles
A number of articles in this chapter were taken from this journal. For example, you might want to take a look at the 1985, vol. 13, nos. 3/4 Issue, which is focused exclusively on girls, women, and computers.

Chapter 12

Moral Development, Values, and Religion

Prologue

Opera Glasses, the Nomadic Tribe, and a Lifeboat

While it seems probable that such rules and reasoning about the rules is embedded in the fabric of social relationships and cultural experiences, we will discover in this chapter that considerable controversy exists about the degree to which moral development is generated by societal and cultural experiences. Indeed, while virtually all theories accept the fact that social relationships are involved in moral development, the views vary in how much emphasis is placed on individualism and internalization of moral standards. We will discover that some social scientists believe morality is never completely internalized, always being wedded to the commerce of social relationships, while others argue that the most advanced level of moral development occurs when the individual has constructed his or her own individualistic standards that will guide moral behavior.

In a theater in a small city in the English Midlands, attached to the backs of many of the seats is a small rack that once contained opera glasses. The racks were coin-operated: the insertion of a shilling released the opera glasses from their holder. At the end of a performance, the user would return the glasses to the rack, which locked automatically. The glasses would then be ready for a member of the next audience. The glasses were small, and in the darkness a user could easily slip them under a coat or in a pocket and carry them out of the theater without being seen. But for many years almost no one took them. The rate of theft was so low that the intake of shillings covered the losses and yielded a profit to the management. In the 1960s the rate of theft began to rise and reached the point where the management could no longer afford to replace the stolen glasses. So the system fell into disuse; only the empty racks remained to remind the theater-goer of a convenience made possible by the honesty of an earlier generation.

We may speculate about social changes in the Midlands (and elsewhere in the industrialized world) in the late 1960s. But more important for our present concerns is the fact that many social arrangements depend on the willing compliance of large numbers of people with social rules or customs that run counter to their immediate self-interest. The sight of the empty racks forcibly draws attention to the fragility of social arrangements fostering well-being or convenience. We can no longer take it for granted that these arrangements will be maintained.

In a sense the example of the opera glasses is trivial—a mere convenience that is easily dispensed with. But other arrangements can be vital to the survival of a group and its way of life, and these practices are less likely to be abandoned in a drift toward noncompliance. In a culture that depends upon both corn and cattle for its food supply, all members of the society must close the gate that keeps the cattle out of the corn patch. And in a nomadic desert tribe every member must cooperate in conserving and protecting the precious water supply. No child can be allowed in a playful moment to pull the corks from the goatskins that carry the water. Social arrangements differ, then, in how vital they are to the survival and optimal functioning of the group and in the degree of compliance the society expects. A group adrift in a lifeboat cannot tolerate one single deviant who proposes to bore a hole in the bottom of the boat. A modern nation can tolerate a certain number of thieves or murderers, but it must keep theft and murder at a low rate or the social fabric will disintegrate.

Efforts by social scientists to examine human societies and to identify universal themes have a long and honorable history. Some problems seem to arise in all societies, and societies solve these problems in ways suited to their ecological niche. . . All or nearly all societies have developed rules and norms to deal with these problems, applying socialization pressures as they teach them to their children. . .

Such rules exist because human beings are social animals and each person's capacity to act—and indeed, each person's welfare and safety—depends upon the actions of other people. Each individual's behavior, then, must be integrated into a network of social arrangements. (Maccoby, 1980, pp. 296, 297, 299)

*I*n this chapter, we spend considerable time exploring the nature of moral development in adolescence. We also will discuss adolescent values, religion, and cults.

Moral Development: Thoughts, Feelings, and Behaviors about Standards of Right and Wrong

Our interest in moral development focuses on what moral development, moral reasoning, moral behavior, moral feelings and guilt, and altruism mean.

What Is Moral Development?

In one sense, the study of **moral development** is one of the oldest topics of interest to those who are curious about human nature. In prescientific periods, philosophers and theologians heatedly debated the child's moral status at birth, which they felt had important implications for how the child was to be reared. Today, people are hardly neutral about moral development; most have very strong opinions about acceptable and unacceptable behavior, ethical and unethical conduct, and the ways that acceptable and ethical behaviors are to be fostered in children. We will discuss three important facets of moral development—thought, action, and feeling.

Moral development concerns rules and conventions about what people should do in their interactions with other people. In studying these rules, psychologists examine three different domains of moral development. First, how do individuals reason or think about rules for ethical conduct? For example, cheating is generally considered unacceptable. An individual can be presented with a story in which someone has a conflict about whether or not to cheat in a specific situation. The individual is asked to decide what is appropriate for the character to do, and why. The focus is thereby placed on the rationale, the type of reasoning the individual uses to justify his moral decision. A second domain concerns how people actually behave in the face of rules for ethical conduct. Here, for example, the concern is whether the individual himself actually cheats in different situations and what factors influence this behavior. A third domain concerns how the individual feels after making a moral decision. There has been more interest in an individual's feelings after he has done something wrong than after he has done something right. Here the concern is whether a person feels guilty as the result of having cheated. We now devote considerable attention to moral thought, moral action, and moral feeling.

Moral Reasoning

First we look at Piaget's cognitive developmental view of moral development, then we study Kohlberg's cognitive developmental perspective, and finally we focus on social conventional reasoning.

Piaget's View

Piaget is best known for his ideas about the development of morality in childhood. We initially discuss these ideas, but also describe a cognitive disequilibrium view that emphasizes some basic ideas about the importance of formal operational thought in moral development.

Moral Reasoning in Childhood Piaget's work (1932) has stimulated an interest in how the child thinks about ethical issues. He conducted extensive observations and interviews with children from four to twelve years of age. He watched them in natural play with marbles, trying to understand the manner in which they used and thought about the rules of the game. Later he asked them several questions about ethical concepts (e.g., theft, lies, punishment, justice) in order to arrive at a similar understanding of how children think about ethical rules. He concluded that there are two different modes (or stages) of moral thought. The more primitive one, **moral realism,** is associated with younger children (from four to seven years old); the more advanced one, **moral autonomy,** is associated with older children (ten years old and older). Children from seven to ten years old are in a transition period between the two stages, showing some features of both.

What are some of the characteristics of these two stages? The moral realist judges the rightness or goodness of behavior by considering the consequences of the behavior, not the intentions of the actor. For example, a realist would say that breaking twelve cups accidentally is worse than breaking one cup intentionally. For the moral autonomist, the reverse is true; the intention of the actor becomes more important.

The moral realist believes that all rules are unchangeable and are handed down by all-powerful authorities. When Piaget suggested that new rules be introduced into the game of marbles, the young children became troubled; they insisted that the rules had always existed as they were and could not be changed. The moral autonomist, by contrast, accepts change and recognizes that rules are merely convenient, socially agreed upon conventions, subject to change by consensus.

A third characteristic is the moral realist's belief in **immanent justice**—if a rule is broken, punishment will be meted out immediately. The realist believes that the violation is connected in some mechanical or reflexlike way to the punishment. Thus, young children often look around worriedly after committing a transgression, expecting inevitable punishment. The moral autonomist recognizes that punishment is a socially mediated event that occurs only if a relevant person witnesses the wrongdoing, but that even then punishment is not inevitable. Recent research (e.g, Jose, 1985) verifies that immanent justice responses declines during the latter part of the elementary school years.

Piaget's theory of moral judgment was crafted as a counterargument to the sociologist Emile Durkheim's view that the socialization process should instill respect in each individual for the social group. In Durkheim's view, each member of the group should accept its constraints and rules. Piaget's main thrust was to reveal the limitations of Durkheim's view (which was basically heteronomous in nature) by arguing that as the child develops, she or he becomes more sophisticated in thinking about social matters, particularly about the possibilities and conditions of cooperation. Piaget believed this social understanding comes about through the mutual give-and-take of peer relations. In the peer group where others have status and power similar to the individual, plans are negotiated and coordinated and disagreements are reasoned about and

eventually settled. It is in the peer group that the child learns of the possibilities for cooperation not based on unilateral respect (as is typically the case in parent-child relationships, relationships in which the child simply acquiesces to the demands of more powerful social agents). In peer relationships, the child learns about cooperation through collaboration and commerce with others. Through such relationships, the fundamental nature of the child's moral development changes.

Cognitive Disequilibrium and Formal Operational Thought Piaget believes that adolescents usually become formal-operational thinkers. Thus, they are no longer tied to immediate and concrete phenomena, but are more logical, abstract and deductive reasoners. Formal-operational thinkers frequently compare the real to the ideal, create contrary-to-fact propositions, are cognitively capable of relating the distant past to the present, understand their roles in society, in history, and in the universe, and can conceptualize their own thoughts and think about their mental constructs as objects. For example, it usually is not until about the age of eleven or twelve that boys and girls spontaneously introduce concepts of belief, intelligence, and faith into their definitions of their religious identities. Thus, many of Piaget's tenets of cognitive-developmental theory have significant implications for the moral development of the adolescent.

When children move from the relatively homogeneous grade school neighborhood to the more heterogeneous high school and college environments, they are faced with contradictions between the moral concepts they have accepted and the happenings in the world outside their family and neighborhood. Adolescents are ripe for recognizing that their beliefs are only one of many and that there often is a great deal of debate about right and wrong in ethical matters. Consequently, many adolescents may start to question and sometimes reject their former beliefs, and in the process may develop their own moral system. Martin Hoffman (1980) refers to this Piagetian-related view of moral development as **cognitive-disequilibrium theory.**

Kohlberg's Theory

The most provocative view of moral development was crafted by Lawrence Kohlberg (1958; 1976). Initially, we provide an overview of the theory, then turn to research that is related to the theory, and conclude with a number of criticisms of Kohlberg's work.

Overview of Kohlberg's Work Kohlberg believes that moral development is primarily based on moral reasoning and unfolds in a stagelike manner. Kohlberg arrived at this view after some twenty years of using a unique procedure in interviewing children, adolescents, and adults. In an interview, the individual is presented with a series of stories in which characters face moral dilemmas. The following is one of the more popular Kohlberg dilemmas (Kohlberg, 1969):

> In Europe a woman was near death from a special kind of cancer. There was one drug that the doctors thought might save her. It was a form of radium that a druggist in the same town had recently discovered. The drug was expensive to make, but the druggist was charging ten times what the drug cost him to make. He paid $200 for the radium and charged $2,000 for a small dose of the drug. The sick woman's husband, Heinz, went to everyone he knew to borrow the money, but he could only get together $1,000 which is half of what it cost. He told the druggist that his wife was dying and asked him to sell it cheaper or let him pay later. But the druggist said, "No, I discovered the drug, and I am going to make money from it." So Heinz got desperate and broke into the man's store to steal the drug for his wife. (p. 379)

The interviewee is then asked a series of questions about each dilemma. For the Heinz dilemma, Kohlberg asks such questions as these: Should Heinz have done that? Was it actually wrong or right? Why? Is it a husband's duty to steal the drug for his wife if he can get it no other way? Would a good husband do it? Did the druggist have the right to charge that much when there was no law actually setting a limit on the price? Why?

Based on the types of reasons individuals have given to this and other moral dilemmas, Kohlberg arrived at three levels of moral development, each of which is characterized by two stages:

1. The **Preconventional Level.** At this low level, the child shows no internalization of moral values— his or her moral thinking is based on the punishments (stage 1) and rewards (stage 2) he or she experiences in the environment.

2. The **Conventional Level.** At this level of morality the child's internalization of moral values is intermediate. He or she abides by certain standards of other people, such as parents (stage 3) or the rules of society (stage 4). Internalization is intermediate because even though the individual is adopting the standards of others, she or he does not abide by those standards.

3. The **Postconventional Level.** At the highest level, morality is completely internalized and not based on the standards of others. The individual recognizes alternative moral courses, explores the options and then develops a moral code of his own. The code may be among the principles generally accepted by the community (stage 5) or it may be more individualized (stage 6).

For a more detailed look at Kohlberg's three levels and six stages of moral development, see table 12.1.

For an individual at the postconventional level, the rules of the society must mesh with underlying moral principles. In cases where the rules of the society conflict with the individual's principles, the individual will follow his or her own principles rather than the conventions of the society. Some specific responses to the Heinz and the druggist dilemma are presented in table 12.2, which should provide you with a better sense of moral reasoning at the six stages in Kohlberg's theory.

Table 12.1 Kohlberg's three levels and six stages of moral development

Level and stage	What is right	Reasons for doing right	Social perspective of stage
Level I: Preconventional			
Stage 1: Heteronomous morality	To avoid breaking rules backed by punishment, obedience for its own sake, and avoiding physical damage to persons and property.	Avoidance of punishment, and the superior power of authorities.	*Egocentric point of view.* Doesn't consider the interests of others or recognize that they differ from the actor's; doesn't relate two points of view. Actions are considered physically rather than in terms of psychological interests of others. Confusion of authority's perspective with one's own.
Stage 2: Individualism, instrumental purpose, and exchange	Following rules only when it is to someone's immediate interest; acting to meet one's own interests and needs and letting others do the same. Right is also what's fair, what's an equal exchange, a deal, an agreement.	To serve one's own needs or interests in a world where you have to recognize that other people have their interests, too.	*Concrete individualistic perspective.* Aware that everybody has his own interest to pursue and that these interests conflict, so that right is relative (in the concrete individualistic sense).
Level II: Conventional			
Stage 3: Mutual interpersonal expectations, relationships, and interpersonal conformity	Living up to what is expected by people close to you or what people generally expect of your role as son, brother, friend, etc. "Being good" is important and means having good motives, showing concern about others. It also means keeping mutual relationships, such as trust, loyalty, respect, and gratitude.	The need to be a good person in your own eyes and those of others. Your caring for others. Belief in the Golden Rule. Desire to maintain rules and authority which support stereotypical good behavior.	*Perspective of the individual in relationships with other individuals.* Aware of shared feelings, agreements, and expectations, which take primacy over individual interests. Relates points of view through the concrete Golden Rule, putting oneself in the other guy's shoes. Does not yet consider generalized system perspective.
Stage 4: Social system and conscience	Fulfilling the actual duties to which you have agreed. Laws are to be upheld except in extreme cases where they conflict with other fixed social duties. Right is also contributing to society, the group, or institution.	To keep the institution going as a whole, to avoid the breakdown in the system "if everyone did it," or the imperative of conscience to meet one's defined obligations (easily confused with stage 3 belief in rules and authority.)	*Differentiates societal point of view from interpersonal agreement or motives.* Takes the point of view of the system that defines roles and rules. Considers individual relations in terms of place in the system.

Level and stage	What is right	Reasons for doing right	Social perspective of stage
Level III: Postconventional, or principled			
Stage 5: Social contract or utility and individual rights	Being aware that people hold a variety of values and opinions, that most values and rules are relative to your group. These relative rules should usually be upheld, however, in the interest of impartiality and because they are the social contract. Some nonrelative values and rights like *life* and *liberty,* however, must be upheld in any society and regardless of majority opinion.	A sense of obligation to law because of one's social contract to make and abide by laws for the welfare of all and for the protection of all people's rights. A feeling of contractual commitment, freely entered upon, to family, friendship, trust, and work obligations. Concern that laws and duties be based on rational calculation of overall utility, "the greatest good for the greatest number."	*Prior-to-society perspective.* Perspective of a rational individual aware of values and rights prior to social attachments and contracts. Integrates perspectives by formal mechanisms of agreement, contract, objective impartiality, and due process. Considers moral and legal points of view; recognizes that they sometimes conflict and finds it difficult to integrate them.
Stage 6: Universal ethical principles	Following self-chosen ethical principles. Particular laws or social agreements are usually valid because they rest on such principles. When laws violate these principles, one acts in accordance with the principle. Principles are universal principles of justice; the equality of human rights and respect for the dignity of human beings as individual persons.	The belief as a rational person in the validity of universal moral principles, and a sense of personal commitment to them.	*Perspective of a moral point of view from which social arrangements derive.* Perspective is that of any rational individual recognizing the nature of morality or the fact that persons are ends in themselves and must be treated as such.

Source: Kohlberg, L., "Moral Stages and Moralization," in T. Lickona (Ed.), Moral Development and Behavior, *New York, Holt, Rinehart and Winston, 1976, pp. 34-35.*

Moral Development, Values, and Religion   **493**

Table 12.2 Examples of Kohlberg's six stages of moral development

Stage	Pro	Con
1	He should steal the drug. It is not really bad to take it. It is not like he did not ask to pay for it first. The drug he would take is only worth $200; he is not really taking a $2,000 drug.	He should not steal the drug; it is a big crime. He did not get permission; he used force and broke and entered. He did a lot of damage stealing a very expensive drug and breaking up the store, too.
2	It is all right to steal the drug, because she needs it and he wants her to live. It is not that he wants to steal, but it is the way he has to use to get the drug to save her.	He should not steal it. The druggist is not wrong or bad, he just wants to make a profit. That is what you are in business for, to make money.
3	He should steal the drug. He was only doing something that was natural for a good husband to do. You cannot blame him for doing something out of love for his wife, you would blame him if he did not love his wife enough to save her.	He should not steal. If his wife dies, he cannot be blamed. It is not because he is heartless or that he does not love her enough to do everything that he legally can. The druggist is the selfish or heartless one.
4	You should steal it. If you did nothing you would be letting your wife die. It is your responsibility if she dies. You have to take it with the idea of paying the druggist.	It is a natural thing for Heinz to want to save his wife but it is still always wrong to steal. He still knows he is stealing and taking a valuable drug from the man who made it.
5	The law was not set up for these circumstances. Taking the drug in this situation is not really right, but it is justified to do it.	You cannot completely blame someone for stealing, but extreme circumstances do not really justify taking the law in your own hands. You cannot have everyone stealing whenever they get desperate. The end may be good, but the ends do not justify the means.
6	This is a situation which forces him to choose between stealing and letting his wife die. In a situation where the choice must be made, it is morally right to steal. He has to act in terms of the principle of preserving and respecting life.	Heinz is faced with the decision of whether to consider the other people who need the drug just as badly as his wife. Heinz ought to act not according to his particular feelings toward his wife, but considering the value of all the lives involved.

Source: Rest, as quoted in Kohlberg, 1969, pp. 379–80.

Research on Kohlberg's Stages and Influences on the Stages First, we review information about Kohlberg's own research, and then turn to an overview of influences that move children through the moral stages—cognitive development, modeling and cognitive conflict, and peer interaction and role/perspective taking opportunities.

In his original work, Kohlberg (1958) found that as the age of the child increased, his moral judgments became more advanced. He also reported (1969) that age changes in children's responses to moral judgment items have been found in most industrialized Western countries, such as the United States, France, and Great Britain. And these changes occur regardless of the

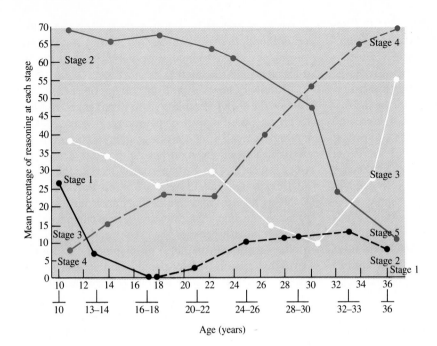

child's sex or social class. The stages are also significantly related to intelligence (Kohlberg, 1969). Kohlberg (1958) also found support for his belief that social participation in groups is one way to advance the moral judgment of children. While Kohlberg's original research was conducted in 1958, he recently has charted moral development in a longitudinal study (Colby, et al., 1980). This twenty-year longitudinal investigation traces moral development from late childhood through the early adulthood years. The mean percentage of individuals reasoning at each of Kohlberg's stages at a given age is shown in figure 12.1.

The data show a clear relation between age and moral judgment. Over the twenty-year period, the use of stages 1 and 2 decreased. Stage 4, which did not appear at all in the moral reasoning of the ten-year-old children, was reflected in sixty-two percent of the moral thinking of the thirty-six-year-old adults. Stage 5 did not appear until the age of twenty or twenty-two and never characterized more than about ten percent of the

individuals interviewed. Thus, just as formal operational thought does not always emerge in adolescence, neither do the higher stages of Kohlberg's theory of moral development. Reasoning about moral dilemmas does seem to change in adulthood—adults in their thirties reason at more advanced levels than adolescents or children.

Kohlberg believes that moral development unfolds as a consequence of cognitive development. As we discussed, cognitive development depends on the interaction of genetic and social experiences. Kohlberg believes the individual is capable of moving through six stages in an invariant sequence, from less to more advanced. The individual acts constructively on the world as he or she proceeds from one stage to the next, rather than passively accepting a cultural norm of morality.

Several investigators have attempted to advance an individual's level of moral development by providing arguments that reflect moral thinking one stage above the individual's established level. These studies are based on the cognitive-developmental concepts of equilibrium and conflict. By finding the correct environmental match slightly beyond the child's cognitive level, a disequilibrium is created that motivates him to restructure his moral thought. The resolution of the disequilibrium and conflict should be toward increased competence, but the data are mixed on this question. In one of the pioneer studies on this topic, Eliot Turiel (1966) discovered that children preferred a response one stage above their current level over a response two stages above it. However, they actually chose a response one stage below their level more often than a response one stage above it. Apparently the children were motivated more by security needs than by the need to reorganize thought to a higher level. Other studies indicate that children do prefer a more advanced stage over a less advanced stage (e.g., Rest, Turiel, and Kohlberg, 1969).

Since the early studies of stage modeling, a flourish of investigations have attempted to more precisely determine the effectiveness of various forms of stage modeling and arguments (Lapsley and Quintana, in press). The upshot of these studies is that virtually any plus-stage discussion format, for any length of time, seems to promote more advanced moral reasoning. For example, in one investigation (Walker, 1982), exposure to plus-two stage reasoning (arguments two stages above the child's current stage of moral thought) was just as effective in advancing moral thought as plus-one reasoning. Plus-two stage reasoning did not produce more plus-two stage reasoning but rather, like plus-one stage reasoning, increased the likelihood the child would reason one stage above his or her current stage. And in other recent research it has been found that reasoning only one-third of a stage higher than the individual's current level of moral thought will advance moral thought (Berkowitz and Gibbs, 1983). In sum,

current research on modeling and cognitive conflict reveals moral thought can be moved to a higher level through exposure to models or discussion that is more advanced than the child's.

Kohlberg believes that peer interaction is a critical part of the social stimulation that challenges children to change their moral orientations. Whereas adults characteristically impose rules and regulations on children, the mutual give-and-take in peer interaction provides the child with an opportunity to take the role of another person and to generate rules democratically. Kohlberg stresses that role-taking opportunities can, in principle, be engendered by any peer group encounter. While Kohlberg believes that such role-taking opportunities are ideal for moral development, he also believes that certain types of parent-child experiences can induce the children to think at more advanced levels of moral thinking. In particular, parents who allow or encourage conversation about value-laden issues promote more advanced moral thought in their children. Unfortunately, many parents do not systematically provide their children with such role-taking opportunities. More about this importance of peer relations, particularly the nature of discussion, is presented in Perspective on Adolescent Development 12.1.

The Critics of Kohlberg Kohlberg's theory has not gone unchallenged. Among the criticisms are those involving the link between moral thought, moral behavior, and moral feelings; the quality of the research; sex differences and the care perspective; and societal contributions. We consider each of these criticisms in turn.

Moral reasons can always be a shelter for immoral behavior. That is, some critics believe Kohlberg has placed too much emphasis on moral thought and not paid enough attention to what children morally do or morally feel (Gibbs and Schnell, 1985). No one wants a nation of individuals who can reason at stages 5 and 6 of Kohlberg's stages, but who are liars, cheaters, and stealers lacking empathy. Thus, the critics stress that Kohlberg's view is too cognitive and too cold. Elizabeth Simpson (1976) captured this point nicely:

> Reasons can be a shelter, as we all know, especially when they are developed after the fact and are applied to our own behavior or to that of someone in whom we have an ego investment. In any case, reasons are inseparable from the personality of the reasoner, whether they apply to his own behavior or that of others. They are grounded not in the situation in which decisions are made, but in the reasoner's psychic definition of past experience, and that psychic definition frequently crosses all boundaries of rationality. Passionate irrationality in the name of impassioned reason occurs in the market, the classroom, and in science, as well as elsewhere, and often unconsciously. (pp. 162–63)

James Rest (1976; 1977; 1983) believes that more attention should be paid to the way moral judgment is assessed. Rest (1976) points out that alternative methods should be used to collect information about moral thinking rather than relying on a single method that requires individuals to reason about hypothetical moral dilemmas. Rest further points out that the Kohlberg stories are exceedingly difficult to score. To help remedy this problem, Rest (1976; 1977; 1983) has devised his own measure of moral development, called the Defining Issue Test, or the DIT.

In the DIT, an attempt is made to determine which moral issues individuals feel are most crucial in a given situation by presenting them with a series of dilemmas and a list of definitions of the major issues involved (Kohlberg's procedure does not make use of such a list). In the dilemma of Heinz and the druggist, individuals might be asked whether a community's laws should be upheld or whether Heinz should be willing to risk being injured or caught as a burglar; they might also be asked to list the most important values that govern human interaction. They are given six stories and asked to rate the importance of each issue involved in deciding what ought to be done. Then the subjects are asked to list what they believe are the four most important issues.

Table 12.3 Actual moral dilemmas generated by adolescents

Story subject	Grade 7	Grade 9	Grade 12
		Percentage	
Alcohol	2	0	5
Civil rights	0	6	7
Drugs	7	10	5
Interpersonal relations	38	24	35
Physical safety	22	8	3
Sexual relations	2	20	10
Smoking	7	2	0
Stealing	9	2	0
Working	2	2	15
Other	11	26	20

Source: From Yussen, S. R., "Characteristics of Moral Dilemmas Written by Adolescents," Developmental Psychology, 13, 162-163. Copyright © 1977 by the American Psychological Association.

Rest believes that this method provides a more consistent and accurate measurement of moral thinking than Kohlberg's system.

One research investigation provides further criticism of the nature of the Kohlberg stories (Yussen, 1977). Most of the Kohlberg stories focus on the family and authority. However, when adolescents were invited to write stories about their own moral dilemmas, adolescents generated dilemmas that were broader in scope, focusing on such matters as friends, acquaintances, and other issues, as well as family and authority. The moral dilemmas also were analyzed in terms of the issues that concerned the adolescents the most. As shown in table 12.3, the moral issue that concerned adolescents more than any other was interpersonal relationships. As can be seen, there is reason to be concerned about the manner in which Kohlberg's data on moral development were collected.

*R*ecall how researchers have found that modeling and discussion of moral matters above the child's moral stage often advance the child's moral reasoning. Recent research suggests that an important factor in whether discussion of moral stages will advance children's moral reasoning is the quality of peer interaction and discussion involved (Berkowitz, 1981; Berkowitz, Gibbs, and Broughton, 1980; Berkowitz and Gibbs, 1983). For example, in one investigation (Berkowitz and Gibbs, 1983), thirty dyads were observed and the nature of their discourse about moral issues assessed. The nature of the discourse focused on solutions to moral dilemmas in Kohlberg's moral judgment interview. Of the thirty dyads, sixteen showed stage change in moral development, while fourteen of the dyads did not change. The researchers concluded that moral advances were made by certain dyads and not others because of the style of reasoning of both members of the dyad. Such reasoning was labeled **transactive discussion,** meaning reasoning that operates on the reasoning of another individual.

In the investigation of transactive discussion, it was found that such discussion can follow one of two forms: representation of another's reasoning (such as feedback request, paraphrase, justification request, dyad paraphrase, and the like) or operation upon another's reasoning (such as clarification, contradiction, competitive extension, common ground/integration, comparative critique, and so on). Operational transactions are presumed to reflect more sophisticated discussion patterns than representation transactions. In this research effort, operational transaction was observed to advance moral reasoning more than representation transaction (Berkowitz and Gibbs, 1983) (table 12.4).

This investigation was conducted with college students, but it is likely that the transactional strategy would benefit younger adolescents as well. The lesson to be learned here is the importance of communication in peer discussion. In particular, it appears that the language and listening skills of the peer discussants would be important factors in whether the peer discussion would promote advances in moral judgment. Many children have substandard vocabularies, a fact that likely contributes to their lack of ability to engage in transactive discussion. Indeed, children and adolescents have been found to have difficulty conducting competent discussions in general (Danner, 1984).

In another recent study, Ann Kruger and Michael Tomasello (1985) investigated whether the use of transactions occurs more often in peer discussion or parent-child discussion. Seven and eleven year olds were paired either with a female agemate or their mother. Their consensus-seeking discussions about several moral dilemmas were coded for the presence of transactions. Individuals of both ages used transactions more in their conversational turns with an agemate than with their mother. And, more significant debate occurred with agemates than with mothers.

In sum, it appears that an important new avenue of inquiry in moral development has been unveiled, one that emphasizes the importance of children's communication skills in peer discussion aimed at advancing moral development (Lapsley, Enright, and Serlin, 1986).

How can peer group discussion contribute to moral development?

Table 12.4 Percentages of total statements in each transact category for pre- to posttest moral stage changers and nonchangers

Group	Transact Type			
	All transacts	Representational transacts	Operational transacts	N
Nonchangers	19.9	7.2	12.9	14
Changers	26.6	8.8	17.8	16

Source: From Berkowitz, M., and J. Gibbs, "Measuring the Developmental Features of Moral Discussion," Merrill-Palmer Quarterly, *29, 399–410. Copyright © 1983 Merrill-Palmer Institute, Wayne State University Press.*

Table 12.5 Kohlberg's versus Gilligan's understanding of moral development

Kohlberg's levels and stages	Kohlberg's definition	Gilligan's levels
Level I. Preconventional morality Stage 1: Punishment orientation	Obey rules to avoid punishment	**Level I. Preconventional morality** Concern for the self and survival
Stage 2: Naive reward orientation	Obey rules to get rewards, share in order to get returns	
Level II. Conventional morality Stage 3: Good-boy/good-girl orientation	Conform to rules that are defined by others' approval/disapproval	**Level II. Conventional morality** Concern for being responsible, caring for others
Stage 4: Authority orientation	Rigid conformity to society's rules, law-and-order mentality, avoid censure for rule-breaking	
Level III. Postconventional morality Stage 5: Social-contract orientation	More flexible understanding that we obey rules because they are necessary for social order, but the rules could be changed if there were better alternatives	**Level III. Postconventional morality** Concern for self and others as interdependent
Stage 6: Morality of individual principles and conscience	Behavior conforms to internal principles (justice, equality) to avoid self-condemnation, and sometimes may violate society's rules	

Source: From Hyde, J. S., Half the Human Experience. Lexington, MA: D. C. Health, 1985.

No other aspect of Kohlberg's theory has generated as much controversy recently as the extent to which Kohlberg's stages are more characteristic of the moral development of males than females. Carol Gilligan (1982), writing in her book *In a Different Voice,* argues that Kohlberg's theory and research are heavily sex-biased. She argues that females, because of their unique perspectives and concerns, should be included in the study of moral development. She reasons that their inclusion might produce a different perspective on moral development. Gilligan thinks that individuals move from a level of selfishness focused on personal survival and practical needs to a level involving sacrificing one's own wishes for what other people want, and then finally to the third and highest level in which moral equality is sought between one's self and others (see table 12.5, for a comparison of Gilligan's and Kohlberg's levels). Woven through Gilligan's concerns is her belief that Kohlberg has grossly underestimated the importance of interpersonal relationships and caring in moral development, regardless of whether males or females are under consideration. More details about Gilligan's view on the construction of moral thought is described in Perspective on Adolescent Development 12.2.

Carol Gilligan (1982) describes how the main character in Kohlberg's dilemma is Heinz, a male. Possibly females have a difficult time identifying with him. While some of the other Kohlberg dilemmas are gender neutral, one also is about the captain of a company of Marines. Gilligan also points out that the subjects in Kohlberg's original research, those he has followed for twenty years, were all males. And, Gilligan believes Kohlberg's interpretations are flawed—the findings that females often only reach stage 3 is described as a deficiency by Kohlberg, yet it easily could be analyzed as a deficiency in Kohlberg's theory.

Going beyond her critique of Kohlberg's failure to consider females in the construction of his theory and the conduct of his researcher, Gilligan has provided a reformulation of Kohlberg's theory based on the premise that an important voice is not present in his view. Following are two excerpts from her book, one from eleven-year-old Jake and a second one from eleven-year-old Amy that reflect the importance of this voice. First, Jake's comments:

> For one thing, human life is worth more than money, and if the druggist only makes $1,000, he is still going to live, but if Heinz doesn't steal the drug, his wife is going to die. *(Why is life worth more than money?)* Because the druggist can get a thousand dollars later from rich people with cancer, but Heinz can't get his wife again. (Gilligan, 1982, p. 26)

Now, the comments of 11-year-old Amy:

> Well, I don't think so. I think there might be other ways besides stealing it, like if he could borrow the money or make a loan or something, but he really shouldn't steal the drug—but his wife shouldn't die either. *(Why shouldn't he steal the drug?)* If he stole the drug, he might save his wife then, but if he did, he might have to go to jail, and then his wife might get sicker again, and he couldn't get more of the drug, and it might not be so good. So, they should really just talk it out and find some other way to make the money. (Gilligan, 1982, p. 28)

Jake's comments would likely be scored as a mixture of stages 3 and 4, but also including some of the components of a mature Level III moral thinker. Amy, by contrast, doesn't fit into the scoring system as well. Jake, like Kohlberg, sees the problem as one of rules and balancing the rights of persons. However, Amy views the problem as one involving relationships—the druggist fails to live up to his relationship to the needy woman, the need to maintain the relationship between Heinz and his wife, and the hope that a bad relationship between Heinz and the druggist can be avoided. Her solution also does not seem to focus on rules but rather relationships as well. Amy concludes that the characters should talk it out and try to repair their relationships.

Gilligan (1982; 1985a, b) concludes that there are two basic approaches to moral reasoning. In the **justice perspective,** people are differentiated and seen as standing alone—the focus is on the rights of the individual, that is justice. In the **care perspective,** people are viewed in terms of their connectedness with other people and the focus is on their communication with others. From Gilligan's view, Kohlberg has greatly underplayed the importance of the care perspective in the moral development of both females and males.

Are there sex differences in moral development? A recent review of a larger number of studies of sex differences in moral development by Lawrence Walker (1984) concluded that the overall pattern is one of non-significance. Of the one hundred eight studies reviewed, only eight revealed sex differences favoring males. Walker argues that rather than debating whether sex bias is inherent in Kohlberg's theory, it might be more fruitful to ask why the myth that males are more advanced in moral development than females persists in light of so little evidence. Gilligan (1985a, b) believes Walker has missed her main point. She states that her orientation focuses on the difference between two moral orientations, one a justice perspective, the other a care perspective. She now is quick to argue that her perspective does not stress whether males and females will differ on Kohlberg's stages of justice reasoning, that is, a feminine "voice" is not necessarily spoken more often by girls than boys (in a statistical sense). Rather the feminine "voice" is associated with a feminine stereotype of caring and relationships. Gilligan fears that because so much empirical attention has been focused on sex differences in the expression of the feminine "voice," her view that a concern for caring and relationships as a key ingredient of the moral development of both females and males will be lost (Gilligan, 1985b).

A final criticism of Kohlberg's work is that moral development is more culture specific than Kohlberg believes. For example, when children around the world are observed, moral standards are not always consistent with those that children abide by in the United States (Bronfenbrenner and Garbarino, 1976).

Social Conventional Reasoning

In recent years considerable interest has been generated in whether reasoning about social matters is distinct from reasoning about moral matters (Nucci, 1982; Turiel, 1977, 1978; Smetana, 1983, 1985). Adherents of the belief that social reasoning is distinct from moral reasoning cast their thoughts within a cognitive-developmental framework (Enright, Lapsley, and Olson, 1984).

The architects of the social reasoning approach argue that conventional rules focus on behavioral irregularities. To control such behavioral improprieties, conventional rules are created. In this manner, the actions of individuals can be controlled and the existing social system maintained. Such conventional rules are thought to be arbitrary with no prescription necessary. For example, not eating food with our fingers is a conventional rule, and so is not addressing a teacher by his or her first name. Chewing gum in class and talking without raising one's hand in class are other social conventional rules individuals learn to adhere to.

By contrast, it is argued that moral rules are not arbitrary and certainly do involve prescription. Further, moral rules are not created through any social consensus, but rather are obligatory, virtually universally applicable, and somewhat impersonal (Turiel, 1978). Thus, rules pertaining to lying, stealing, cheating, and physically harming another person are moral rules because violation of these rules confronts ethical standards that exist apart from social consensus and convention. In sum, moral judgments are constructed as concepts of justice whereas social conventional judgments are structured as concepts of social organization (Lapsley, Enright, and Serlin, 1986).

A review of research on **social conventional reasoning** suggests the major thrust has been to demonstrate the independence of this form of reasoning apart from moral reasoning and to reveal how even young children make this distinction (Lapsley, Enright, and Serlin, 1986). For example, in two studies children were queried about spontaneously occurring moral and social conventional transgressions (Nucci and Turiel, 1978; Nucci and Nucci, 1982). Children were asked, "What if there was no rule in the school about (the observed event), would it be all right to do it then?" Approximately eighty percent of the children at each grade level believed the social conventional act would be appropriate if no rule existed to prohibit it. By contrast, more than eighty-five percent of the children at each grade level said that moral transgressions would not be appropriate even if there were no rules related to the transgressions. Other research suggests that

What is social conventional reasoning?

children are more likely to evaluate actions in the moral domain on the basis of their intrinsic features (such as justice or harm), while social conventional actions are more likely to be interpreted in terms of their regulatory status in a social context (Nucci, 1982). Thus, it seems that actions in the social conventional area are judged wrong only if a social rule exists prohibiting the action. By contrast, moral transgressions appear to be judged as universally wrong even in the absence of social consensus.

Researchers also have revealed that children's understanding of social rules unfolds in a stage-like fashion. The development of social conventional concepts seems to involve the progressive understanding that conventions involve shared knowledge of uniformities in the social system and further that such uniformities function to coordinate social interaction (Nucci, 1982).

An important contribution of research and thinking about social conventional reasoning is the recognition that complex social issues consist not only of moral components, but issues of social convention as well. While early research suggests that even young children distinguish moral and social conventional reasoning and that a cognitive developmental sequence of reasoning about social rules occurs, much further research is required to spell out the empirical basis of this sequence as well as the environmental experiences that might promote more advanced social conventional reasoning (Lapsley, Enright, and Serlin, 1986).

We have considered many different aspects of moral development and thought. To help you remember the main ideas related to the nature of moral development, moral reasoning, and social conventional reasoning, see Concept Table 12.1.

Moral Behavior

The study of moral behavior has been influenced primarily by social-learning theory. The familiar processes of reinforcement, punishment, and imitation have been invoked to explain how and why adolescents learn certain responses and why their responses differ from one another. When adolescents are reinforced for behavior that is consistent with laws and social conventions, they are likely to repeat those behaviors. When models are provided who behave "morally," adolescents are likely to adopt their actions. Finally, when adolescents are punished for "immoral" or unacceptable behaviors, these behaviors can be eliminated; but only at the expense of sanctioning punishment and of causing emotional side effects for the adolescent.

To these general conclusions, the usual qualifiers are added. The effectiveness of rewards and punishments depends on the consistency with which they are administered and the schedule (for example, continuous or partial) that is adopted. The effectiveness of modeling depends on the characteristics of the model (for example, warmth and power) and the retention of

THE NATURE OF MORAL DEVELOPMENT AND MORAL THOUGHT

Concept	Processes/related ideas	Characteristics/description
The nature of moral development	Rules/regulations	Moral development concerns rules and conventions about what people should do in their interaction with other people.
	Components	There are three main domains of moral development: thought, behavior, and feelings.
Moral reasoning	Piaget's view	Piaget argued that children from four to seven years of age are in the stage of moral realism and from about ten years on, move into the stage of moral autonomy. Formal operational thought may undergird changes in the moral reasoning of adolescents.
	Kohlberg's theory	Kohlberg proposed a provocative theory of moral development with three levels and six stages. As the individual develops through the levels, increased internalization is shown.
	Kohlberg's research and influences on the stages	Kohlberg's original research documented age changes in moral thought. His more recent longitudinal data continue to show a relation to age and that the higher stages often do not emerge in adolescence. Among the most important influences on the stages are cognitive development, imitation, peer relations, and opportunities for role/perspective taking.
	The critics of Kohlberg	Kohlberg's views have been criticized on a number of grounds including the overemphasis on cognition and the underemphasis on behavior and feeling, the quality of the research, failure to consider females and the underevaluation of a care perspective and relationships, and too much individualistic emphasis with too little attention given to cultural and societal matters.
Social conventional reasoning	Distinction of moral and social conventional reasoning	Social conventional reasoning refers to thoughts about social consensus and convention whereas moral reasoning pertains more to ethical matters. Social conventional reasoning is more arbitrary while moral reasoning is more prescriptive. Social conventional reasoning focuses more on social regulation and the control of behavioral irregularities so the social system can be maintained while moral reasoning places more emphasis on consideration of justice.

the modeled behavior. From the viewpoint of the social-learning theorist, the study of moral behavior is a matter of describing how these principles operate within different moral behavior systems.

Cognitive Social Learning Theory

Combining elements of the cognitive development process with elements of the behavioral learning process highlights the cognitive social learning view of Walter and Harriet Mischel (1976). They distinguish between the child's **moral competence,** or ability to produce moral behaviors, and his **moral performance** of those behaviors in specific situations. In their view, competence or acquisition depend primarily on cognitive-sensory processes; it is an outgrowth of these processes. The competencies include what he is able to do, what he knows, his skills, his awareness of moral rules and regulations, and his cognitive ability to construct behaviors. His moral performance or behavior, however, is determined by his motivation, and the rewards and incentives to act in a specific moral way.

In general, social learning theorists have been critical of Kohlberg's view. Among other reasons, they believe he places too little emphasis on moral behavior and the situational determinants of morality. However, while Kohlberg argues that moral judgment is an important determinant of moral behavior, he, like the Mischels, stresses that the individual's interpretation of both the moral and factual aspects of a situation lead him to a moral decision (Kohlberg and Candee, 1979). For example, Kohlberg mentions that "extramoral" factors, such as the desire to avoid embarrassment, may cause the child to avoid doing what he believes morally right. In summary, both the Mischels and Kohlberg believe that moral action is influenced by a complex of factors.

Both the moral thought and the moral behavior of an individual are important components of moral development. Although psychoanalytic theory has always placed strong faith in the role of feelings in personality development, the emotional aspects of moral development were virtually ignored for many years. Now there seems to be a reemergence of interest in the affective aspects of moral development (Hoffman, 1979). In the next two sections, we will explore this renewed interest in the emotional aspects of morality, discussing first the role of guilt and then the concept of altruism.

Moral Feelings

An emphasis on moral feelings has come primarily from psychoanalytic theory. Recently, however, considerable interest outside of psychoanalytic theory has focused on an aspect of moral feelings—empathy. **Empathy** is the ability to participate in the feelings or ideas of another person. Placing emphasis on empathy calls attention to the positive side of moral development, while an emphasis on guilt stresses the negative side more. Historically, there has been more interest in the negative side of moral development than the positive side; although in recent years, as researchers have investigated empathy and altruism, more positive aspects are being considered. More comments about empathy will be made as we discuss altruism later. For now, let's look more closely at the psychoanalytic views of guilt, first focusing on the traditional, classical psychoanalytic account, and then turning to Erik Erikson's perspective.

The Traditional, Classical Psychoanalytic View of Guilt

In psychoanalytic accounts, **guilt** develops when a child identifies with her parents and then undergoes the withdrawal of their love for disciplinary purposes. The child turns her hostility inward and experiences guilt. This guilt is primarily unconscious and reflects the personality structure known as the *superego* (see Chapter 2). It is believed that guilt-prone individuals avoid transgressing in order to avoid anxiety; on the other hand, the person with little guilt has little reason to resist temptation. Thus, in this view, guilt is responsible for harnessing the evil drives of the *id* and for maintaining the world as a safe place in which to live. In particular, it is believed that the family processes mainly responsible for guilt are: identification with parents and the use of love withdrawal discipline techniques.

Erikson's Perspective

As we discussed in Chapters 2 and 10, Erik Erikson is a psychoanalytic theorist. Erikson's (1970) views are thus an example of a psychoanalytic view of the development of morality. Erikson believes there are three stages of moral development: specific moral learning in childhood, ideologies in adolescence, and ethical consolidation in adulthood. As we have seen, Erikson's main focus is on the adolescent's search for identity, which requires a sense of purpose. If the adolescent becomes disillusioned with the moral and religious beliefs that she acquired during childhood, she is likely to, at least temporarily, lose her sense of purpose and experience a vacuum in her life. This may lead to a search for an ideology that will give some purpose to the adolescent's life. For the ideology to be acceptable, it must fit both the "evidence" and the adolescent's relatively high level of logical reasoning ability. If others share in this ideology, it promotes a sense of community in the adolescent as well. For Erikson, then, ideology emerges as the "guardian" of identity during adolescence because it provides a sense of purpose, assists in tying the present to the future, and contributes meaning to behavior (Hoffman, 1980).

In studying guilt, the negative side of moral development is being investigated. And, when social learning theorists have studied moral behavior, they often have focused on such negative behaviors as cheating, lying, and stealing in trying to demonstrate how socialization practices can inhibit these behaviors. Next we see that it is important to study the positive side of moral development as well.

Altruism

Let's now look at the general nature of altruism, family influences on altruism, and a developmental perspective on altruism.

What is Altruism?

The positive side of moral development can be evaluated by examining a trait such as **altruism,** or selfless concern for the welfare of others. Altruistic behaviors include sharing possessions, contributing to worthy causes, and helping people in distress. In some studies, adolescents play games with the opportunity to share their winnings or prizes with others, either their friends or with a charity, such as children from an orphanage. In other studies, situations are created in which someone (actually a confederate of the experimenter) acts as if he or she is in need of help. The extent to which the youth assists the person provides the index of altruistic or helping behavior.

Family Influences

Family experiences play a critical part in the development of altruistic behavior in youth (e.g., Yarrow and Waxler, 1975). Parents who model altruistic behaviors have boys and girls who display an altruistic orientation. Parental nurturance, particularly in the context of parental modeling of altruism, is also an important factor in whether boys and girls develop altruistic motives. Assignment of responsibility, maturity demands, and inductive discipline are other parental practices that promote altruism in boys and girls. And cultural factors outside the family, peer relations, and cognitive factors also have to be taken into account when the youth's altruistic orientation is evaluated (Mussen and Eisenberg-Berg, 1977).

A Developmental View of Altruism

How do adolescents become altruistic? Martin Hoffman (1975; 1979; 1980) believes that we must look at the individual's infancy, childhood, and adolescence to get a complete picture of the development of altruism.

Soon after birth, children feel distressed about certain events associated with primary discomfort (hunger, thirst, pain, and so on). Soon, the reaction of another—such as a concerned or alarmed mother or father—becomes associated with the feelings that cause primary discomfort. Because infants cannot distinguish between "self" and "other," they may soon start to show distress when another person is distressed, as if something bad was happening to them. Children also recognize noxious events they themselves have felt, and when they see others experiencing such events, they are likely to react with distress. This reaction is one type of empathy.

With the basic response of empathy to build on, the child later develops altruistic motives. The development of altruism is guided by the child's social and cognitive growth. This growth is marked by three significant landmarks: first, by the end of infancy, children develop a sense of person permanence—the sense that people exist independently of themselves. At this point, children convert their empathy into efforts to help the other person in distress. But they are still egocentric and often confuse their own inner thoughts and feelings with those of others.

A second step in the development of altruism is the development of role-taking skills—the understanding that other people have feelings and perceptions different from one's own. By seven or eight years of age, the average child has mastered complex role-taking skills (e.g., Flavell et al., 1968; Selman, 1971a, b). Some children, however, master simple role-taking skills at an age as early as two or three (Flavell, 1977).

Finally, adolescents develop a sense of personal identity somewhat akin to Erikson's stage of ego identity. They recognize that despite variation in thought and mood, they have a stable personality or basic nature, and they recognize the same trait in others, too. With this new awareness in early adolescence, empathy is channeled to help others overcome causes of chronic distress. Chronic distress (for example, melancholia over a lost parent) is a stable, enduring disturbance that may be observed by transitory events that cause distress (for example, an argument with a good friend).

Young adolescents are fully aware not only that others feel pleasure and pain, but that these feelings occur in the context of a longer pattern of life experience. That is, they are aware that others have inner states that transcend the situation, and this awareness enables them to respond not only to transitory distress, but also to a general condition of distress.

With continued cognitive growth, adolescents are able not only to understand the plight of an individual, but also of an entire group of individuals, or a class of people—such as the poor, the politically oppressed, the socially outcast, victims of war, and the mentally retarded.

The path through our overview of moral development has been not only a fairly long one, but a fairly complex one as well. We have seen the cognitive revolution in socialization theory and research and its effect on the study of moral development. We have studied the positive side of moral development (altruism) as well as its negative side (yielding to temptation and cheating, for example). We have also examined the idea that moral thought, action, and feeling are all important components of moral development. Before we leave the field of moral development, however, there is one last aspect of moral development that bears exploration. This society has been acutely concerned about moral values and how they should be transmitted to our children and adolescents. In 1975, a Gallup poll indicated that seventy-nine percent of the adults in the United States were in favor of letting schools handle at least some of the moral training of children and adolescents. In the last ten years, there has been an increase in the number of moral education programs in our schools.

Moral Education

To learn more about moral education, we study its historical background, Kohlberg's ideas, as well as alternatives to Kohlberg's approach.

Historical Background

Some years ago, John Dewey (1933) argued that the most important values taught in school focus on how the school is organized and governed. Educational experts sometimes refer to this as the "hidden curriculum." In the hidden curriculum, students learn about obedience and defiance of authority rather than about democratic principles. As Dewey suggested, schools were in the business of moral education long before the current "new morality" programs came on the scene. In the 1800s, youth who were exposed to McGuffey's Readers were taught how to behave as well as how to read.

Dewey was correct in arguing that the school is a moral system. Schools, like families, are settings for moral development. Teachers serve as models of ethical behavior. Classroom rules and peer relations transmit attitudes about cheating, lying, stealing, and consideration of others. And the school administration, through its rules and regulations, represents a specific value system to adolescents.

Kohlberg's Ideas

Kohlberg stresses that it is the moral reasoning skills of adolescents that require educational attention, not adherence to a particular value system. While moral education programs embodying Kohlberg's philosophy vary from school to school, most have emphasized the role of the teacher as a facilitator rather than a lecturer, the importance of discussing moral dilemmas, and the importance of give-and-take peer-group discussion. However, Kohlberg himself established "the Just Community" (actually called the Cluster School), a small school for black and white students from different socioeconomic backgrounds, in 1974. In the Just Community, Kohlberg emphasized realistic issues that arise in school, the nature of moral behavior as well as moral thought, and active roles for teachers as moral advocates. The Just Community shared with other alternative schools a belief in self-governance, mutual caring, and group solidarity. The goal for moral development was geared toward increasing students' responsibility to the community (stage 4 in Kohlberg's theory) rather than toward self-principled reasoning. In a recent investigation of the effectiveness of the Just Community (Power, 1979), it was found that students did develop a more positive orientation toward the community and that they were likely to adhere to the rules they themselves had established. However, in a comparison of Just Community students and students who simply participated in moral discussion programs, both groups advanced in moral reasoning at about an equal rate.

By the late 1970s and into the 1980s, Kohlberg had embarked on a revision of ideas on moral education. For information about this revision, read Perspective on Adolescent Development 12.3.

Alternatives to Kohlberg's Ideas

There are a number of alternatives available to educators who wish to introduce a curriculum involving moral matters—among these are the direct tuition of moral values, social learning approaches that emphasize altruism, values clarification, and recently social conventional reasoning.

A Bag of Virtues Some experts believe that, while it is difficult to specify the appropriate moral virtues to instill in adolescents, it is possible to identify generally accepted moral virtues and didactically inform students about them. For example, Cornell Hamm (1977) pointed out that the moral education of adolescents should emphasize honesty, loyalty, and fairness.

Hamm (1977) goes on to say that parents, teachers, and peers "teach" moral values by establishing rules and regulations, and by rewarding and punishing behavior. Parents and teachers have not always effectively taught moral values to their youth, but Hamm believes they are capable of doing so. There are some socialization techniques that are better than others for developing moral values in youth. Sensible youth who have a feeling for fairness and respect for others usually come from social environments in which adult social agents show a warm acceptance towards them, combined with a firm and consistent enforcement of rules.

Perspective on Adolescent Development 12.3
KOHLBERG'S REVISIONIST THINKING ON MORAL EDUCATION

Although moral education programs embodying Kohlberg's beliefs vary from school to school, most have emphasized the role of the teacher as a facilitator rather than a lecturer, the importance of discussing moral dilemmas, and the belief that moral advancement comes through give-and-take peer group discussion. However, in somewhat of an about-face, in 1974 Kohlberg established the "Just Community," a small school for black and white students from different socioeconomic backgrounds. The Just Community emphasis was placed on considering realistic issues that arise in school, the nature of moral behavior as well as moral thought, and an active role for teachers as moral advocates.

The Just Community shared with other alternative schools a belief in self-governance, mutual caring, and group solidarity. The goal for moral development was geared toward increasing students' responsibility to the community (stage 4 in Kohlberg's theory) rather than self-principled reasoning. In a recent investigation of the effectiveness of the Just Community—actually named the Cluster School—(Power, 1984), it was found that a more positive orientation toward the community did develop and that students were likely to adhere to the rules they had established. However, although the moral reasoning of the students at the Cluster School did advance, students who simply participated in moral discussion programs advanced their moral reasoning just as much as the students in the Cluster School.

The manner in which Kohlberg set up the Cluster School brings him closer to educators who are concerned with the moral "givens" in life. However, as indicated before, most programs that have included Kohlberg's

The whole atmosphere of the school is involved in the adolescent's moral reasoning.

ideas emphasize the process of moral reasoning rather than a scientific moral content. The effectiveness of the programs often varies from school to school and from student to student. Success is usually better at the lower stages (2, 3, and 4) than at postconventional levels (5, 6) (Minuchin and Shapiro, 1983), and in open schools rather than traditional schools (Sullivan, 1975). There is also some question about the persistence of the effects—how long lasting are the effects of such moral education programs? Usually, assessment takes place immediately after the semester in which moral education is taught, and rarely are there long-term follow-ups.

With the development of the Cluster School in the middle 1970s, Kohlberg himself seemed to change his ideas about moral education. Kohlberg (1980) reported that he was not satisfied with the discussion approach to moral education. He realized that attempts to instill principled reasoning about morality in adolescents may be unrealistic because most people do not reach this level of cognitive maturity even in adulthood. And he began to believe that the moral climate of the country was shifting to an emphasis on the self and away from a concern for others in the 1970s. As a consequence, Kohlberg began to show a stronger interest in the school as a social system and in creating moral school communities (Minuchin and Shapiro, 1983).

As a further indication of Kohlberg's belief in the importance of the moral atmosphere of the school, he has developed the Moral Atmosphere Interview. This interview poses dilemmas that deal with typically occurring problems in high schools, problems that are likely to involve social responsibility. In a recent investigation (Higgins, Power, and Kohlberg, 1983), the Moral Atmosphere Interview was administered to samples of approximately twenty students from three democratic alternative high schools and three more traditional, authoritarian high schools. Students in the democratic schools perceived the rules of their schools to be more collective and described themselves and their peers as more willing to act responsibly than did students from the traditional schools.

Hamm (1977) also believes that youth need to be reminded consistently of *why* actions *a* and *b* and *c* are required and *x* and *y* and *z* are prohibited. This allows the adolescents to call these reasons and rules to mind when moral decisions have to be made.

Hamm (1977) believes that through social experience with parents, teachers, peers, and other social agents, moral virtues can be learned. But exactly what virtues should be taught? At a general level, most people agree that we should teach adolescents to be just, fair, and impartial; to consider other people's interests; to avoid interfering with another's freedom; to respect their fellow human beings; to refrain from killing or injuring others; to be honest; to keep promises and abide by contracts; to avoid cheating, lying, and stealing; and to make no discriminations against others on the basis of irrelevant differences such as color, sex, or ethnic origin. Some of Hamm's critics believe that these moral virtues are too heavily laden with middle-class values, but Hamm (1977) insists that most people would agree that they are universal values rather than old-fashioned middle-class standards.

Social Learning, Altruism, Values Clarification, and Social Conventional Reasoning A number of other approaches to moral education also are being tried out. In many of these approaches, an understanding that both moral thought and moral behavior need to be considered is evidenced. Further, it seems to be understood that the positive as well as the negative side of moral development should be stressed.

In contrast to Kohlberg's moral-reasoning approach to moral education, social-learning or behavioral approaches to moral education emphasize the control of unacceptable behavior (e.g., Mischel and Mischel, 1976). Many social-learning programs include the familiar elements of rewarding pro-social behavior and providing negative consequences for antisocial behavior. Such programs often fall under the label of behavior modification programs. The current orientation of most social-learning oriented moral-education programs emphasizes prosocial behavior, especially helping, altruism, and cooperation (e.g., Yarrow and Zahn-Waxler, 1983). One of the few curricula based on social-learning theory that was developed for use in schools, Skills for Ethical Action, is oriented toward increasing ethical behavior in daily life (Chapman and Davis, 1978). This program consists of thirty-eight sequenced lessons for junior high school students. Six strategies are followed: identifying value problems, thinking up action ideas, considering self and others, judging, acting, and evaluating effects.

The Skills for Ethical Action program has some components of what have been called *values-clarification* programs. Adolescents have all kinds of questions and ponder a wide variety of issues. They may think about whether they should smoke marijuana or cigarettes even though their parents think they should not. Most of their friends drink—should they? Should they keep going to church even though they have doubts about religion? Is it ever morally right to fight a war? How far should they go with sex? Should people who live on welfare be required to get jobs and work? What kind of individuals do they want to be? By stimulating discussion about such questions and issues, teachers encourage students to find their own answers by values clarification.

Recall that there has been increased interest recently in investigating the domain of social conventional reasoning to obtain a more complete picture of how children interpret complex social issues rather than relying only on their moral reasoning alone. Along this line of thinking, it has been argued that contemporary values education is limited due to a failure in coordinating the teaching of social values with students' conceptions of morality. For example, it would seem inappropriate to discuss the morality of a particular dress code at a school because the issue of dress codes falls into the domain of social rather than moral convention (Nucci, in press). The implication is that students not only should be moved to a higher level of moral understanding, but to a higher level of social conventional understanding as well.

One recent investigation reveals the importance of social conventional reasoning in education (Geiger and Turiel, 1983). The relation between disruptive school behavior (such as violations of classroom rules and defiance of school authorities) and social conventional reasoning was evaluated in a group of young adolescents. It was predicted that disruptive behavior by junior high school students would be related to the level of their social conventional reasoning. The findings revealed that virtually all of the nondisruptive students were at a higher level of social reasoning (an understanding that social convention is mediated by the social system), while three-fourths of the disruptive students reasoned at a lower level about social conventional matters. Thus, it may be possible to better understand the dynamics of school misbehavior when we investigate social conventional domains as well as moral domains (Lapsley, Enright, and Serlin, 1986).

Since our overview of moral reasoning, we have discussed many additional, important dimensions of moral development. A summary of these further ideas is presented in Concept Table 12.2. In our discussion of moral education, we observed that one approach focuses on getting adolescents to clarify their values. Next, we look more closely at the nature of adolescent values.

Values, Religion, and Cults: A Heightened Interest in Adolescence

In this section, we'll discuss several topics that invariably carry moral overtones—values, religious beliefs, and cults. In Chapter 9, we discussed adolescent interests and the values of adolescents. It was found that freedom, true friendship, and happiness were important in the value hierarchies of adolescents. We also pointed out that a comfortable life was more important to boys, while family security was more salient for girls. Further, achieving an inner harmony was more important to girls than boys. Now, let's look further at the values of adolescents, as we discuss adolescent values in different cultures.

Values

Each of us carries a set of values that influence our thoughts, feelings, and behavior. Think for a moment: what are your values? Not everyone agrees on how to define values, although one expert has merely referred to them as general beliefs (Rokeach, 1973). While the label *values* has been used very broadly, we'll define **values** as the adolescent's abstract beliefs. It is during

Concept Table 12.2

Moral Behavior, Moral Feelings, Altruism, and Moral Education

Concept	Processes/related ideas	Characteristics/description
Moral behavior	Basic ideas	The study of moral behavior has been influenced primarily by social learning theory. The focus is on learned moral behavior, learned through interaction with people.
	Cognitive social learning theory	This view argues that cognitive processes mediate the influence of the environment on moral conduct. Moral competence and moral performance also are distinguished, suggesting that what an adolescent knows does not always relate to what he or she morally does.
Moral feelings	Basic ideas	Emphasizes that moral feelings are one of the most important contributors to moral development. Most interest here has been generated by psychoanalytic theory, although recently cognitive psychologists interested in empathy have made contributions.
	Psychoanalytic theory	Classical psychoanalytic theory emphasizes that guilt inhibits immoral behavior and that guilt is developed primarily through identification with parents and the use of love withdrawal discipline. Erikson's theory stresses that moral development moves through three stages—specific moral learning in childhood; ideologies in adolescence; and ethical consolidation in adulthood.
Altruism	What is altruism?	Altruism reflects the positive side of moral development, referring to a selfless concern about the welfare of others.
	Family influences	Parenting modeling of altruism and nurturance are important family influences. Inductive discipline also is important (mainly involving reasoning, particularly consequences of one's actions for others).
	A developmental view of altruism	Martin Hoffman believes that altruism develops through empathy, person permanence, role-taking skills, and identity.
Moral education	Historical background	John Dewey described the hidden curriculum of moral education years ago, as he talked about the moral atmosphere that exists in every school.
	Kohlberg's ideas	Kohlberg emphasizes that moral education should involve working to improve the adolescent's moral reasoning skills rather than transmitting a set of moral virtues. Much of the Kohlberg effort involves peer discussion of moral dilemmas. One example of Kohlberg's moral education program is called the Just Community. More recently, Kohlberg has revised his philosophy of moral education, recognizing the importance of the entire school as a social, moral context.
	Other moral education orientations	Some moral education programs believe a bag of virtues can be identified and taught, other programs stress social learning concepts and the reinforcement of altruistic behavior, other programs emphasize values clarification, and yet others place a premium on social conventional reasoning.

Table 12.6 The four most important and four least important values in five groups of male students

	Rank of value	United States	Canada	Australia	Israel	Papua New Guinea
		Terminal values			Terminal values	
Highest	1	Freedom	Freedom	Wisdom	A world at peace	A world at peace
	2	Happiness	Happiness	True friendship	National security	Equality
	3	Wisdom	Mature love	Freedom	Happiness	Freedom
	4	Self-respect	Self-respect	A sense of accomplishment	Freedom	True friendship
	15	Pleasure	A world of beauty	A world of beauty	A comfortable life	A sense of accomplishment
	16	Salvation	Social recognition	Social recognition	Social recognition	Pleasure
Lowest	17	National security	National security	National security	A world of beauty	Mature love
	18	A world of beauty	Salvation	Salvation	Salvation	A world of beauty
		Instrumental values			Instrumental values	
Highest	1	Honest	Honest	Honest	Honest	Honest
	2	Responsible	Responsible	Broad-minded	Responsible	Helpful
	3	Ambitious	Loving	Responsible	Logical	Responsible
	4	Broad-minded	Broad-minded	Loving	Capable	Ambitious
	15	Cheerful	Imaginative	Imaginative	Clean	Independent
	16	Polite	Polite	Polite	Imaginative	Clean
Lowest	17	Clean	Clean	Clean	Obedient	Logical
	18	Obedient	Obedient	Obedient	Forgiving	Imaginative

Source: From Feather, N. T., "Values in Adolescence," in J. Adelson (Ed.), Handbook of Adolescent Psychology. *Copyright © 1980 by John Wiley and Sons, Inc. Reprinted by permission.*

adolescence that individuals begin to develop abstract belief systems. These abstract belief systems include concepts like freedom, salvation, pleasure, true friendship, wisdom, peace, effort, and so forth.

In one of the most far-ranging studies of adolescent values, Norman Feather (1975; 1980) collected information from college males in five different countries in the late 1960s and early 1970s—the United States, Canada, Australia, Israel, and Papua New Guinea. The four most important and four least important adolescent values in each country are presented in table 12.6. The values are listed as either *terminal* or *instrumental*—which means they are either abstract or action-oriented, respectively.

The similarities in value priorities between the three affluent countries—the United States, Canada, and Australia—are obvious. However, note that the American youth were more materialistic, more achievement-oriented, and more traditionally religious

(salvation-minded) than their Australian counterparts. The Australian youth placed more importance on peace of mind, an active life, and a cheerful approach to life. Also, they were more interested in values that involved close interpersonal relationships. These differences reflect the emphasis on achievement in our American culture as compared with a higher interest in community, or "mateship," as it is called, in Australia. In contrast, Israeli youth demonstrated a relatively high concern for competence, peace, and national security, reflecting the stress of political instability in the Mideast. And finally, the Papua New Guinea youth ranked world peace and national security as very important values, which is not surprising in a nation that was very new at the time the adolescents were surveyed.

As table 12.6 shows, the abstract values of adolescents often differ according to the culture the adolescents grow up in. Further, adolescent values may change

Table 12.7 Priorities in life (class of 1982)

	Males	Females
A good marriage and family life	69%	83%
Finding steady work	73	70
Being successful in my work	61	60
Strong friendships	62	66
Finding purpose and meaning in my life	51	71

Source: Bachman, 1982.

with age and life circumstances—the youth in Feather's comparisons were attending college, and noncollege youth in these cultures may have different values. As was pointed out in Chapter 9, even social class has an effect: in the United States, middle-class adolescents seem to have more democratic values. Finally, it is likely that male and female adolescents have different values. We know in particular that girls often show a stronger interest in interpersonal relations than boys (e.g., Block, 1973). Based on a more recent survey (1982) of American high school seniors asked to rate the priorities in their lives, males said that finding steady work was the most important, while a good marriage and family life was the highest on the females' list (table 12.7). Compared to a similar group of seniors in 1976, the 1982 high school seniors rated advancement, money, and prestige as more important (Bachman, 1982).

Now that we have considered values in general and seen that adolescents begin to show a greater interest in the abstract nature of values than children, we turn our attention to a particular set of values, those that are religious in nature.

Religious Beliefs and the Church

Not only do adolescents show a stronger interest in values in general than children, but they also show a much keener interest in religious matters as well. Let's explore the development of religious concepts and then evaluate the role of the church in the adolescent's development.

The Development of Religious Concepts

Two important cognitive developmental approaches to religious concepts are those of David Elkind and James Fowler.

Elkind's View David Elkind (1978) is a well-known expert on Piaget's theory of cognitive development. He has conducted numerous research investigations to document the wide-ranging impact of Piagetian stages on boys' and girls' conceptions of their social world. Recently, he summarized some of his work aimed at uncovering what youth know about their religious identities:

> Every child who is exposed to religious teaching eventually arrives at an understanding of what it means to belong to a particular religious group, i.e., a conception of his or her religious denomination or identity. The question arises, however, as to whether this conception of religious identity is entirely due to the effects of religious instruction or whether its formation is determined, at least in part, by developmental factors. According to Jean Piaget, for example, conceptions develop in a necessary sequence of stages that are related to age. (Elkind, 1978, pp. 5–6)

In a series of studies, Elkind tested several hundred Jewish, Catholic, and Congregational Protestant boys and girls from about five to fourteen years of age. He asked questions such as "Are you a Catholic?" "Is your family Jewish?" "Are all boys and girls in the world Christians?" The answers the children gave reflected their ideas about membership in a religious group. Elkind also asked questions like, "What is a Jew?" "How do you become a Catholic?" to elicit comments about external and internal explanations of religious membership. Finally, Elkind asked the question, "Can you be an American and a Protestant (or Jew, or Catholic) at the same time?" to assess the children's understanding that a person can belong to different groups at the same time.

Distinctions were drawn between those boys and girls who were concrete-operational and formal-operational thinkers. The formal-operational thinkers, those just entering early adolescence, showed a different way of thinking about religious concepts than concrete-operational boys and girls. The older youth were much more *reflective* than their younger counterparts. They no longer looked for manifestations of religious identity in a person's outward behavior but rather sought it in the evidence of his or her innermost beliefs and convictions. For example, one concrete-operational thinker said that the way you can tell that a person is a Catholic is by whether he goes to church or not. By contrast, one formal-operational thinker pointed out that you can tell a person is a Protestant because such a person is free to repent and to pray to God in their own way.

Fowler's Perspective James Fowler (1976) stresses that late adolescence is a particularly important time in the development of religious identity. Beginning at about age eighteen, adolescents enter a stage characterized by *individuating-reflexive faith.*

Fowler indicates that there is a close relationship between the adolescent's development of moral values and religious values, and that the individuating-reflexive faith stage is much like Kohlberg's self-principled level of moral thinking. In both instances, for example, the adolescent makes the transition from a conventional perspective on values to an individualized perspective. And both of these theorists note that many adolescents and young adults never make the transition from conventional to individualized thinking about values.

As part of developing an individualized perspective on religious identity, Fowler believes that for the first time in their lives late adolescents have to take full responsibility for their beliefs and ideas about religion—as opposed to earlier in adolescence, when they could rely heavily on their parents' commitments. During late adolescence, individuals come face to face with personal decisions such as "Do I consider myself first, or should I act in the service of others?" and "Are the doctrines I have been taught absolute, or are they more relative than I have been led to believe?" Adolescents who have grown up in strongly religious families may go away to college and live with roommates

How do one's religious beliefs change during adolescence?

who call into question their unwavering faith. Philosophy and religion classes expose the adolescent to varying points of view about religion, expanding the options the youth can follow.

During late adolescence, it is easy to lose one's self in the religious beliefs of others rather than thinking autonomously. In Chapter 6, we discussed David Ausubel's theory of independence. Ausubel believes that many late adolescents develop a pseudoautonomy from the family by replacing the family with some other group, such as a fraternity or religious group. The same idea can be found in Erik Erikson's descriptions of the false identities of late adolescents who adopt the standards of groups rather than thinking for themselves.

In our discussion of religion, we see that while adolescents show a strong religious interest, they believe the church has not fulfilled their needs. As we see next, this spiritual interest sometimes becomes fulfilled through membership in a cult.

Cults

> Barb is seventeen years old. She grew up in an affluent family and was given all of the material things she wanted. When she was fifteen, her parents paid her way to Europe and for the last three years, she had been attending a private boarding school. Her parents attended a Protestant church on a regular basis, and when Barb was home they took her with them. Six months ago, Barb joined the "Moonies."

According to George Gallup and David Poling (1980) there are currently six unorthodox religious movements that have attracted considerable attention from the youth of America: Transcendental Meditation (TM), yoga, the charismatic movement, mysticism, faith healing, and various Eastern religions. More than 27 million Americans have been touched by these religions, either superficially or deeply. For adolescents and young adults, involvement in and exploration of such religious movements is greater than for children or older adults. There are more than 2,500 cults in the United States. Two to three million adolescents and young adults are members of these cults (Swope, 1980).

Among the more specific religious groups that have commanded the attention of adolescents are the Unification Church of Sun Myung Moon (the Moonies), the Divine Light Mission of Maharaj Ji, the Institute of Krishna Consciousness, the Children of God, and the Church of Scientology.

Some criticisms of cults have included the beliefs that cult leaders are hypocritical and exploit members to gain wealth, and that they brainwash adolescents, developing a hypnotic control over their lives. In some instances, cults have been accused of kidnapping youth and placing them in deprived circumstances in order to gain control over their minds. Most cults have elaborate training programs in which the preachings of the church must be memorized. And cult members usually are required to turn over their wealth to the cult leaders. Usually, cult members are told that they can associate with and/or marry only other members of the religion.

It has not been unusual for the parents of adolescents who become cult members to try to persuade their children to leave the cults and come home. Parents who successfully get their youth to leave cults sometimes place them in deprogramming sessions because they believe the adolescents were brainwashed as part of cult procedures.

Religious Beliefs and Church Interest

The sociocultural conditions in which adolescents grow up combine with their developing cognitive capacities to influence their religious identities. Some writers have emphasized that it is important to consider whether adolescents see the teen years as a time of gradual religious awakening or a time when a precipitous, catastrophic change occurs. For example, it has been pointed out that adolescents who grow up in lower socioeconomic conditions, particularly in the "Bible belt" of the rural South, are more likely to be exposed to a doctrine that emphasizes immediate, catastrophic conversion. By contrast, adolescents growing up in a middle-class culture may be more likely to view the development of religious identity as the culmination of a more gradual socialization process (Hurlock, 1967).

With some exceptions, such as pockets of fundamental religion, the role of the church in imparting values to youth does not seem as strong as it once was. Traditionally, the church has relied on somewhat dogmatic policy in teaching values to boys and girls. Rather than providing youth with positive, alternative solutions to issues, the church (particularly those with strong fundamentalist doctrines) often tends to emphasize what *not* to do. Adolescents may develop strong guilt feelings through constant exposure to this type of doctrine. Specific taboos often include drinking, dancing, smoking, and premarital sex.

While in other eras, adolescents frequently accepted the doctrines of the church, many youth now question or even openly reject them. Some church leaders are beginning to attempt to create an atmosphere in which autonomous moral thinking is possible, but the specifics of how to accomplish this have not been mapped out and the efforts are few in number. The decline in church attendance indicates the failure of church leaders to recognize that an authoritarian approach is not the best way to create more advanced moral thinking in adolescents.

The role of the church in imparting values to youth does not seem as strong as it once was.

In a poll conducted by George Gallup and David Poling (1980), adolescents showed a very strong interest in spiritual questions and a high level of personal involvement in spiritual matters. For example, almost nine of ten adolescents pray, an extraordinarily high proportion believe in God or a universal spirit, and only one out of one hundred says that she does not have some kind of religious preference or affiliation.

But at the same time, adolescents report that organized religion has little meaning for them, that they feel frustrated about the church's role in society, and that they generally have a negative attitude toward churchgoers and church members. In the 1980 poll, only twenty-five percent said they had a high degree of confidence in organized religion. About forty percent of the youth said that honesty and the personal ethical standards of the clergy are "only average," "low," or "very low."

While it has been argued that today's adolescents are very self-centered, Gallup believes that adolescents are extremely interested in the helping professions. His data suggest that twenty-five percent of adolescents fourteen years and older volunteer time for nonprofit organizations. Gallup also finds that adolescents attend church with as high, if not higher, a regularity than adults. More than seventy percent of the adolescents said they were church members and, again, only one percent said they had no religious affiliation at all.

Why do some adolescents leave home and become members of cults? According to some experts (e.g., Gallup and Poling, 1980), the reason may be the failure of organized religion and churches to meet the strong spiritual needs of adolescents, as well as a weakening of family life.

In one effort to determine the type of youth who are most vulnerable to the appeal of cults, Swope (1980) identified six characteristics:

1. *Idealistic.* Due to the teachings and example of family, religious leaders, peers, educators, and others, there has developed within young people a desire to help others, to improve society, and often to know God better. The cults manipulate this idealism, convincing (their) members that only within their specialized groups can such inclinations be actualized.

2. *Innocent.* Because relationships with religious leaders in the past have been wholesome, the potential recruit naively believes that all who claim to speak in the name of God are sincere and trustworthy. Elmer Gantry and Jim Jones notwithstanding, the trappings of religion are a powerful lure here.

"We were hoping you'd be home for vacation, or whatever Moonies call it when they're not doing what they do."

Drawing by Saxon; © 1967 The New Yorker Magazine, Inc.

Why do some adolescents leave home and become the members of cults?

3. *Inquisitive.* On college and high school campuses around the country, intelligent young people, looking for interesting groups to join, are approached by enthusiastic, "together" recruiters who invite them to meetings where, they are told, they will meet other fine young people. It sounds exciting. Discussion, they are assured, will focus on ecology, world problems, religion, ethics, education—anything in which the recruit has shown some interest.

4. *Independent.* Many young people are recruited into cults when they are away from home— independent for the first time. Parents of such students are not always aware of how their children spend evenings and weekends, and often do not learn that they have left college until several weeks or months after they drop out. Backpackers are particular targets for cult recruiters. These young people are often lonely and susceptible to invitations for free meals and fellowship.

5. *Identity-seeking.* Young adults in every generation experience identity crises as they seek to determine their own strengths and weaknesses, their value systems, goals, religious and social beliefs.

6. *Insecure.* Inquisitive young people—looking for new experiences, seeking to clarify their own identities, away from the influence of family, friends, and mentors—develop uneasy feelings of insecurity. Lacking trusted counselors to whom they can turn when upset or disturbed, they are especially vulnerable to smiling, friendly people who show great interest in them and manipulate them through what one cult calls "love bombing." (1980, pp. 20–21)

We have seen in this chapter that moral and religious values are an important aspect of the adolescent's search for an identity. In the next chapter, other important aspects of adolescent identity development are discussed—achievement orientation and career development.

Summary

I. Learning about moral development emphasizes what moral development is, as well as the meaning of moral reasoning, moral behavior, moral feelings, altruism, and moral education.

A. Moral development concerns rules and regulations about what people should do in their interaction with others. There are three main domains of moral development: thought, behavior, and feelings.

B. Information about moral reasoning focuses on Piaget's ideas, on Kohlberg's theory, Kohlberg's research and influences on the stages, the critics of Kohlberg, and a distinction between moral and social conventional reasoning.

1. Piaget argued that children from four to seven years of age are in the stage of moral realism and from about ten years on move into the stage of moral autonomy. Formal operational thought may undergird some of the changes in the moral reasoning of adolescents.

2. Kohlberg proposed a provocative theory of moral development, emphasizing moral reasoning. He argued that there are three levels of moral thinking with two stages at each level. As the individual moves through the levels, there is increased internalization.

3. Kohlberg's original research documented age changes in moral reasoning. His more recent longitudinal data continue to show a relation to age and that higher stages (5 and 6) do not emerge during adolescence. Among the most important influences on the stages are cognitive development, imitation, peer relations (including mutual give-and-take opportunities and transactive discussion), and opportunities for role/perspective taking.

4. Kohlberg is not without his critics, having been attacked on a number of grounds. The critics say he has overemphasized cognition and underemphasized behavior and feeling. The quality of his research has been questioned. Gilligan, in particular, believes his view is more characteristic of males than females and that a care perspective should be included more in understanding the moral development of both males and females. Kohlberg's view is said to be too individualistic and does not give adequate attention to societal and cultural matters.

5. Social conventional reasoning refers to thoughts about social consensus and convention whereas moral reasoning stresses ethical matters. Social conventional reasoning is more arbitrary while moral reasoning is more prescriptive. Social conventional

reasoning focuses more on social regulation and control of behavioral irregularities so the social system can be maintained while moral reasoning places more emphasis on consideration of justice.

C. The study of moral behavior has been influenced primarily by social learning theory. The focus is on learned moral behavior, learned through interaction with people. The cognitive social learning theory argues that cognitive processes mediate the effect of the environment on moral behavior. Moral competence and moral performance also are distinguished in cognitive social learning theory, suggesting that what a moral adolescent knows does not always predict what he or she morally does.

D. Moral feelings also are an important aspect of moral development. The greatest interest in moral feeling has been generated by psychoanalytic theorists; although in recent years, cognitive psychologists interested in empathy also have made important contributions. Classical psychoanalytic theory emphasizes that guilt inhibits immoral behavior, guilt being generated primarily through the family processes of parental identification and love withdrawal discipline. Erikson's theory stresses that moral development moves through three stages—specific moral learning in childhood, ideologies in adolescence, and ethical consolidation in adulthood.

E. Altruism reflects the positive side of moral development, referring to a selfless concern for the welfare of others. Among family influences on altruism are parental modeling of altruism, nurturance, and inductive discipline. Hoffman crafted a developmental view of altruism emphasizing empathy, person permanence, role-taking skills, and identity.

F. An understanding of moral education focuses on its historical background, Kohlberg's ideas, and other moral education philosophies.

1. John Dewey described the hidden curriculum of moral education years ago, as he talked about the moral atmosphere that exists in every school.

2. Kohlberg's ideas stress that moral education should involve working to improve the adolescent's moral reasoning skills rather than transmitting a set of moral virtues. Much of the Kohlberg approach involves peer discussion of moral dilemmas. One example of Kohlberg's program is called the Just Community. More recently, Kohlberg has revised his philosophy on moral education, recognizing the importance of the entire school as a sociomoral context.

3. Some moral education programs stress that a bag of virtues can be defined and taught. Other programs emphasize social learning concepts and the reinforcement of altruism, others highlight values clarification, and yet others place a premium on social conventional reasoning.

II. Values, religion, and cults represent other areas that sometimes carry moral overtones.

A. Values are abstract beliefs and adolescents show a greater interest in values than children do. Peace, freedom, and happiness seem to be important values among the youth of most cultures. However, American youth seem to be more materialistic and achievement-oriented in their values than the youth of many other cultures. Advancement, prestige, and money seemed to have increased in the value hierarchy of adolescents in recent years when American adolescents are surveyed across a number of years.

B. Not only do adolescents show a stronger interest in values in general than children, but they also exhibit a stronger religious interest as well.

   1. Elkind argues that when adolescents are compared to children, even young adolescents show more reflection about religion. Further, he points out that adolescents show more interest in innermost beliefs and convictions.

   2. Fowler argues that during late adolescence, at about age eighteen, individuals enter a stage called individuating-reflexive faith, a time when they begin to switch from a conventional orientation toward a religious identity that is more internalized.

   3. While adolescents show a very strong interest in spiritual and religious matters, a majority indicate that the church has not been adequate in fulfilling their spiritual needs.

C. As many as two to three million adolescents and young adults are members of cults, which are often described as unorthodox religious movements. Some of the reasons that cults appeal to adolescents are young people's lack of confidence in organized churches and the weakening of family life.

Key Terms

altruism *506*	moral development *489*
care perspective *501*	moral performance *505*
cognitive-disequilibrium theory *490*	moral realism *489*
conventional level *491*	postconventional level *491*
empathy *505*	preconventional level *491*
guilt *505*	social conventional reasoning *502*
immanent justice *490*	transactive discussion *498*
justice perspective *501*	values *511*
moral autonomy *489*	
moral competence *505*	

Suggested Readings

Fowler, J. W. (1976). Stages in faith: The structural-developmental approach. In T. Hennessy (Ed.), *Values and moral development*. New York: Paulist Press.
Fowler's theory of the development of religious concepts is fully described. Details the difficult transition from adopting others' religious views to creating one's own.

Gallup, G., and Poling, D. (1980). *Search for America's faith*. New York: Abington.
A detailed look at the Gallup poll focused on the gap between religious interest and involvement in organized churches. Includes interesting information about cults.

Gilligan, C. (1982). *In a different voice*. Cambridge, Mass.: Harvard U. Press.
Gilligan's provocative book details her views on the care perspective in moral development.

Lapsley, D. K., Enright, R. D., and Serlin, R. C. (1986). Moral and social education. In J. Worrell and F. Danner (Eds.), *Adolescent development: Issues for education*. New York: Academic Press.
A thorough overview of what is known about moral education and the more recently developed field of social education. Includes thoughtful, detailed comments about the nature of moral and social conventional reasoning.

Lickona, T. (Ed.). (1976). *Moral development and behavior*. New York: Holt, Rinehart and Winston.
Contemporary essays outlining the major theories, research findings, and educational implications of moral development. Included are essays by Kohlberg, Hoffman, Mischel, Aronfreed, Bronfenbrenner, and Rest.

Lofland, J. (1977). Becoming a world-saver revisited. *American Behavioral Scientist, 20*, 805–18.
Provides a fascinating look at world of adolescents who join a cult.

Chapter 13

Achievement, Careers, and Work

Prologue

Bobby and Cleveland—Their Achievement and Career Orientations

Bobby Hardwicke, whose parents are professionals, attends a private school in the suburbs of Hartford, Connecticut. His home is luxurious, his future prospects (as his parents would say) limitless, and his manner charming. He is seventeen years old. Ask Bobby a question and he will first demur, claiming he doesn't have much to say. If you can get him to open up, however, he will go on at length.

No one recognizes what people like me have to go through. I'm sure if you asked most people they'd say the life of a teenager is all fun. Everyone I talk to seems to want to be young again—which is one of the sicknesses of our culture. But no one sees teenagers for what we are. First off, teenagers, or whatever you want to call us, are people. Real, live people. I know that sounds strange, but you can't believe how many times I'm treated like I'm a thing. In stores, or the post office, I'm this one's son, that one's classmate, that one's student.

I'll go to college, although I think now the best thing for me would be to take a year out and work somewhere. I've never really worked—at something real, I mean. Something that would make the slightest difference to anybody. I've studied Latin for two years. I get A's. I get A's in history, European history. Okay, so I've done well, although I think anybody could do well at this place if they were halfway verbal. All the classes are small and we don't have that many exams, so all you have to do, like we always kid each other, is "talk good." "I talk good, Mrs. Arnold, so can I get a good grade now?"

So with all the studying and talking good, you know what I'd really like to do? Carpentry. I'd like to build a house, or fix someone's stairs or porch. Something real.

You know what it is? You go to a good school like this, it costs a lot of money, a whole lot, in fact, and all you think about is doing well so you can get into a good college, and because just going to college these days doesn't mean a thing, you ask yourself "What am I doing? What does any of this matter?" And the answer is, it doesn't matter at all. One course is only meant to get you to the next one, and then the one after that, and none of it makes the slightest bit of difference until you're all done. So you can look back and say, "Well I did it, I passed; so now what?" All school is, you know, is the great time passer. It's all a big invention to keep kids from becoming anything. What can you become in this society, until you're thirty? You can't do anything real or worthwhile, no matter how many A's you get or how good you talk. Say I learned carpentry, like I learn all the other dilettante things I learn. Where would I get a job? Where do I get any worthwhile job for that matter, regardless of what I know or how well I do in school? And why should I get a job just to get a job? For the experience. That's what people say, for the experience. What experience? So you can learn how boring it is to park cars at a summer carnival place? Or take tickets at a movie theater? Is that supposed to get you anything?

There isn't anything people my age can do that matters in the slightest to anybody in this country unless you're a sensational athlete, and, even then, you have to

524 Social, Emotional, and Personality Processes and Development

be a gymnast or a swimmer. This country doesn't have the time or the place or the interest in young people. We're a waste to them, that's all. There isn't a single responsibility I could get at my age which the person giving it could honestly call worthwhile. Anything I could get to do could be done by a billion people; smarter people, dumber people, older, younger, it wouldn't make the slightest bit of difference.

When I'm twenty-five or thirty, I'll probably get jobs. And the jobs I get will be the exact same jobs I could do right now. No difference, except for one thing. When I'm thirty they'll say, "Well, you've worked hard for this, Mr. Hardwicke" or "Dr. Hardwicke, you've earned this, so here's your nice big adult job." But it's a fake. You know what they're really saying? They're really saying, you made it to twenty-five or thirty, so now you get the job and the status or whatever else you're supposed to get. But it's all a lie.

All it is, is a big age thing. From zero to twenty-five, you get the big runaround, the big zilch. From twenty-five on, or thirty—maybe it's getting later and later, for all I know—they let you in. You still don't have any great skills, but you got a few wrinkles. That's what they're looking for—wrinkles, signs of old age. Hey, if I suddenly went bald they'd let me in. I swear they would!

Cleveland Wilkes's family in Providence, Rhode Island, has never had much money; he and his parents know what unemployment can do to a family. Nevertheless, Cleveland, who is seventeen, is referred to by his friends as "the Dresser" because of his penchant for flamboyant clothes—especially shoes. What little money Cleveland manages to scrape together is all channeled into maintaining his wardrobe. In conversation, Cleveland may grow quite animated, but he always has time to check the press of his trousers or smooth the wrinkles in his sleeve.

I don't go around talking about what young people can go do or not; ain't my business to care one way or the other. Dudes like you gotta come up with those answers. What are the big problems facing kids like me? How the hell am I supposed to know?

Take the kids around here; they ain't all alike. This one worries about this, another one, he'd like to bust the hell out of this place. I got a sister talking about going to college. She may do it, too, man. You can't tell. I seen stranger things going on.

Saw a man get knifed once . . . person stuck him so many times doctor came and couldn't figure out which hole to stop him up with first. Tell you, man, the dude was lying on the street, wasn't an inch of him didn't have blood coming out of him. Bunch of cats, we was watching the whole thing, ten feet away. I heard and saw most everything they did. Finally, you know, doctor told him, "Hey, listen to me, man, I don't know what to do for you first." And I'm telling you, man, the dude is bleeding from all over the place. Doctor, he didn't know where to go. So the dude gets up and walks into the ambulance.

Whole world floats by around here. This here's the whole world, only in miniature, like they call it. There ain't nothin' you can't see on these streets. See more in a month here than a lifetime where the rich folks live, all protected from the big bad world. I ain't saying it's so great over here, ain't saying this would be my first choice for children growing up in this city. I'm only saying where we ain't rich with money we are rich, man, with things happening every second. Only thing we don't have is the thing we need the most of: jobs. Ain't no jobs for us over here. Not a one, man, and I know too, because I been looking for three years, and I ain't all that old. Act old, but I ain't old. Seen things old people seen, but I ain't old. Next week I may be old; next year I sure am fixin' on being old if I don't find no work.

I'd take anything, too, man anything they got for me. That surprise you? Don't surprise me none. You sit in the middle of all this, you ain't got no choice. Like they say, beggars can't be choosy. I ain't about to go begging, except that seems like all I do, specially in the summer. Man, we go to these fat cats sitting there in their offices, you know. "Hey, mister, you got a job?" "We'll call you. We'll call you." Tell me that or they'll say, "Got your name, Mr. Cleveland, on the top of my list!"

I say to the cat, "Hey, that's cool. You got the only list I ever heard of with my name right at the top. But if you're thinking about me so special, how come you call me Mr. Cleveland when Cleveland's my first name?"

Country got no use for me, folks around here neither. Ain't nobody care too much what happens to us. Tell us, "Ain't you boys got nothing better to do than stand around all day? What you find to talk about all these hours? And ain't you supposed to be in school? Ain't you supposed to be doing this or doing that?" I tell them, "Hey, listen to me, turkey. I ain't supposed to be doing nothin' if I don't want to. You hear me? Ain't supposed to be nowhere, helping no one!"

If you want to know what the teenagers on this side of town are doing to pass the time of day, now you got it. We got so many folks here out of work it's enough to blow your mind. I can hear my brain rotting it's been so long I ain't done nothin'. How they let this happen in a country like this, having all these kids walking around the streets, got their hands jammed down in their pockets, head down, like their necks was bent in half? What do folks think these kids gonna do, when they go month after month, year after year without nothing that even smells like a job? Not even no part-time affair. Hell, they might get to the point to where they'll waste some kid working for the cleaners, waste the kid and take his job. Folks do it when they ain't got enough food, and they'll start doing it for jobs, too. (*Psychology Today*, February 1979)

*I*n this chapter, we look at three important aspects of the adolescent's world. First, we explore the fascinating topic of achievement. Next, the topic of careers and vocational choice is outlined. Then, we conclude with an overview of one of the major changes in the adolescent's world in recent years, the increasing number of adolescents who work.

Achievement: The Achievement-Oriented Culture of the United States

Adolescents in the United States live in an achievement-oriented culture. This cultural standard suggests that success is important in life and that such success involves a competitive spirit, a desire to win, a motivation to do well, and the wherewithal to cope with adversity and persist until obstacles are overcome. Quite clearly, some adolescents have such talents, while others do not. Some psychologists believe that our culture places such a high premium on achievement and success that our adolescents too often have a strong fear of failure and an anxiety about comparing themselves with others. In this section, we look at the concept of motivation itself, then turn to an overview of achievement and different theories of achievement motivation. Sociocultural influence on achievement is explored and, finally, the topic of sex differences in achievement, which we discussed in other chapters, is investigated in greater detail.

Motivation and Its Importance in the Adolescent's Development

Some adolescents are bored, others highly enthusiastic. And some adolescents seem to work relentlessly, struggling through incredibly difficult matters, while others may take one look at a difficult or time consuming problem and not lift a finger to solve it. What accounts for these wide individual differences in the adolescents just described? This topic in psychology is known as motivation.

Motivation involves the question of *why* people behave, think, and feel the way they do. When the adolescent is motivated, his or her behavior is energized and directed. For example, if the adolescent is sexually motivated, he or she may want to stay at a dance long after it is over so someone whose affection is desired can be pursued. Similarly, if the adolescent is hungry, the book being studied likely will be put down and a trip to the refrigerator will transpire. And, likewise, if the adolescent is motivated to achieve, long hours may be spent studying for an exam. The adolescent's motivation pushes him or her into action.

In our discussion of Piaget's cognitive developmental theory and information processing, we touched on the *why* question. Both of these cognitive perspectives believe that motivation rests with the individual's desire for information and knowledge and that this desire is wired into the nature of the adolescent's mind. From the cognitive developmental perspective, the adolescent's mind is viewed as motivated to function at a higher, more efficient level. Therefore, it is argued that providing the adolescent with information that is slightly above where the adolescent is mentally should stimulate the adolescent to think at a higher level and thus motivate the adolescent. From the information processing perspective, the implication is that an analysis of the cognitive processes that make up the adolescent's cognitive system should help. Then, by providing environmental stimulation aimed at improving such processes as attention, memory, and problem solving, the adolescent's motivation should improve as his or her information processing abilities work more efficiently. As we said in our discussion of information processing and education in Chapter 5, schools need to work more on ways to improve the information processing skills of adolescents. However, there seems to be much more to motivation than these basic points about cognition and its inherent motivating capacity made by the major cognitive theorists. Such grand views simply do not tell the whole story about why some adolescents show a great deal of boredom while others are so enthusiastic. And they do not tell us all there is to know about why some adolescents persist with considerable effort while others don't try very hard.

Behavioral views of motivation also have been set forth. From the perspective of such behaviorists as Skinner, the issue of motivation is one of arranging the environment of the adolescent so it is rewarding. Cognitive processes are unimportant in this view of motivation; rather motivation is seen as external to the adolescent. And the psychoanalytic theorists also have commented about motivation. From the traditional psychoanalytic view of Freud, motivation is primarily unconscious, with such important matters as achievement motivation being wedded to biological processes housed in the id, particularly sexual motivation. Freud, for example, saw even great works as those crafted by Michelangelo as basically a sublimation, or repressing of sexual, instinctual forces in order to engage in socially accepted and desirable conduct. Thus, from some of the major theoretical perspectives in psychology, we find that motivation is seen primarily as a biological, internal force that is either cognitive (cognitive developmental, information processing); instinctual and unconscious (psychoanalytic theory); or behavioral, environmental (behaviorism) in nature.

The view taken in this text is that biological and environmental factors contribute to the adolescent's motivation; that both internal and external factors need to be examined; and that there are cognitive, affective, and behavioral aspects to the adolescent's motivation. Next, we focus in greater detail on a very important aspect of the adolescent's motivation, his or her achievement motivation.

Theories of Achievement and Achievement-Related Factors

In addition to the grand theories of psychology and developmental psychology, some theories have been constructed that are specifically focused on achievement motivation.

The Achievement Motivation Views of McClelland and Atkinson

David McClelland argued that achievement motivation is a property of the individual's psychological makeup and need system. Borrowing from the personality theory of Henry Murray (1938), McClelland stressed that individuals vary in how much achievement motivation they have and further that such motivation can be measured. Achievement motivation was referred to as *n* **achievement** (standing for need for achievement) and meant the individual's internal striving for success. This need for achievement was viewed as a general property of the individual, one that should be reasonably consistent across a number of different domains and across time. It was believed to develop primarily through the child's and adolescent's interactions with parents and the cultural standards in which the individual lives. Two frequently mentioned factors by McClelland that were believed to be influential in promoting achievement motivation were independence training by parents and living in a democratic culture that emphasizes achievement orientation and individuality (McClelland et al., 1953; Winterbottem, 1958).

The concept of need for achievement has been criticized because research suggests that it is not as stable as McClelland predicted (e.g., Mischel, 1976). For example, adolescents identified as high in need for achievement do not always behave in accordance with this trait in all situations. The same can be said about students low in need for achievement. Adolescents usually do show consistent achievement behavior in different school subjects, but grades and standardized achievement test scores in those subjects are not always linked up with behavior outside the classroom (e.g., Hollands and Richards, 1965). In such criticisms, we find the behaviorist argument that concepts such as achievement motivation are too global and do not adequately pay attention to situational variation in behavior and, further, may ignore important environmental determinants of behavior. Therefore, in analyzing the adolescent's achievement orientation, it is important to conduct a thorough observation of different achievement domains, both those related to academic and nonacademic functioning. This same point was made in our discussion of evaluating self-concept in Chapter 10, where we discovered that in addition to measuring the adolescent's general self-worth, self-conceptions of cognitive, social, and physical skills should be assessed as well.

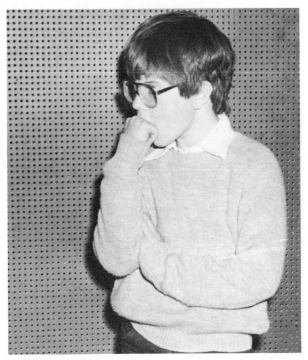

Anxiety can impede or enhance learning and school achievement.

John Atkinson (Atkinson and Feather, 1966; Atkinson and Raynor, 1974) described further some of the important aspects of achievement motivation. He believes that the extent to which adolescents believe they will succeed and the degree they feel they are likely to fail are important components of achievement motivation. **Hope for success** is the equivalent of achievement motivation—the adolescent's underlying drive for success. **Fear of failure** refers to the adolescent's anxiety about not doing well. Motivation is believed to be a function of expectancy for success and the incentive value of success or failure. Thus, if adolescents think they will do well on a math test, and if this outcome is very rewarding, then their achievement motivation for the math test is likely to be high. On the other hand, if their anxiety about the test is also high, it can counteract their motivation to do well.

How do hope for success and fear of failure combine to produce or inhibit the desire to achieve? Atkinson believes that motivation should be behaviorally measured by assessing adolescents' aspiration levels and/or their persistence at a task. An adolescent's aspiration level is how well the adolescent expects or hopes to perform. (In the example of the math test, the girl who threw away her paper in disgust may have hoped to get an A on the test; the girl who was pleased with her test score may have hoped or expected to get a C.) Persistence is measured by how long adolescents maintain effort. For instance, students may be given a difficult science project and be evaluated on how long they work at solving it.

Researchers generally believe that moderate levels of aspiration and persistence are signs of healthy achievement orientation. It has been found that adolescents whose hope for success is greater than their fear of failure develop moderate levels of aspiration and show lengthy persistence on problem-solving tasks (Atkinson and Feather, 1966). Thus, the adolescent's achievement motivation can be increased if her hopes for success are encouraged.

In Atkinson's conceptualization of achievement, high levels of anxiety can have a debilitating effect on achievement behavior. Even though anxiety is a difficult concept to pin down, it is one of the most widely used terms in psychology. Most psychologists agree that anxiety is an unpleasant state, that it is linked to the physiological arousal of the adolescent, and that it involves anticipation of something uncomfortable or painful (Sarason and Spielberger, 1975).

Anxiety can have an adaptive, or positive, influence as well as a maladaptive, or negative, influence; therefore, the removal of all achievement anxiety from the adolescent's experiences is not a desirable goal. A moderate level of anxiety can motivate the adolescent to do better on an examination, for example. The act of overcoming anxiety can also enhance development; mastery and competence in dealing with the world may be positive outcomes of such anxiety. You yourself have probably experienced the exhilaration that follows the completion of a task that made you extremely nervous. Some philosophers have even argued that anxiety is one of the necessary engines for social progress.

Anxiety can impede or enhance learning and school achievement. An extensive amount of work has been conducted to determine the relation between anxiety

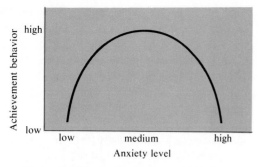

Figure 13.1 Anxiety and achievement level.

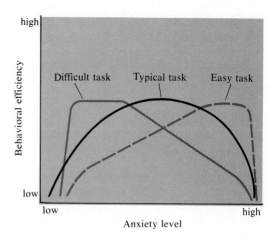

Figure 13.2 Achievement, anxiety, and task difficulty.

and school performance. Charles Spielberger and his colleagues (e.g., Spielberger, Gorsuch, and Lushene, 1970) have developed an anxiety measure that distinguishes between trait anxiety and state anxiety. **Trait anxiety** is the more or less stable and permanent tendency to experience a certain level of anxiety across time and circumstances; by contrast, **state anxiety** comes and goes depending upon particular experiences. Spielberger and his fellow researchers developed the State-Trait Anxiety Inventory to measure these two different types of anxiety. Trait anxiety is measured by asking adolescents how they generally feel about specific situations. State anxiety is evaluated by asking "How do you feel right now?" about specific situations. Examples of answers on the state-trait anxiety scale are "I feel pleasant," "I feel regretful," "I find myself worrying," and "I am calm." It is possible for an adolescent to have a high state anxiety but a low trait anxiety. Such youth are generally calm and easygoing, but once in a while they become intensely upset for some reason that may be difficult for other people to understand.

Trait anxiety is not consistently linked to the student's learning or school performance, but state anxiety is (e.g., Spielberger, 1966). The relation between state anxiety and performance is a curvilinear one for most tasks—that is, achievement behavior is maximized by moderate levels of anxiety (figure 13.1). Either high or low levels of anxiety result in less than maximum efficiency. At the low end of the anxiety continuum, the adolescent may be too lethargic to attend to the cues necessary to efficiently perform the task. At

extremely high levels of anxiety, irrelevant responses often appear to compete with task-oriented behavior. At high levels of anxiety, discrimination between appropriate and inappropriate cues also breaks down, resulting in behavioral inefficiency.

While the curvilinear relation between anxiety and achievement behavior is presumed to hold for most tasks, the exact nature of the relation may depend on the difficulty of the task for the adolescent. For well-learned or simple tasks (signing one's name, pushing a button on request), the optimal level of anxiety is quite high, as shown in figure 13.2. On the other hand, when the adolescent is just learning a task (learning to drive a car or to play tennis) or when the task is extremely complex (solving an algebraic equation), the optimal level of anxiety is much lower. For these tasks, achievement is enhanced by the ability to relax yet be alert and attentive.

Atkinson's work helped pave the way for a more detailed look at the components that comprise achievement motivation. However, as we see next, it has been the attribution theory that has provided the impetus for increased research on achievement.

Attribution Theory

Attribution theory argues that individuals are cognitive beings who want to know why they and others are behaving the way they are because it will help them cope more effectively with situations that confront them.

Further, when we do not know the causes of our own or others' behavior, such behavior may not make sense to us. Thus, attribution theorists interested in achievement motivation want to know how adolescents infer causes that underlie achievement behavior and their attempts to make sense out of that behavior.

The Internal–External Factor We can classify the reasons we and others behave in a number of ways, but we make one basic distinction more than any other—between internal causes (such as personality traits or motives) and external causes (environmental, situational factors such as rewards or how difficult a task is). If the adolescent does not do well on a test, does he or she attribute it to the fact that the teacher plotted against him or her and made the test too difficult (external cause) or to the fact that he or she didn't study hard enough (internal cause)? The answer to such a question influences how the adolescent feels about himself or herself—if the adolescent believes his or her performance was the teacher's fault, the adolescent likely does not feel as bad as when the student doesn't spend enough time studying.

The Stability Factor Many attribution theorists make another distinction as well. The cause of achievement behavior may be due either to a stable factor (something that remains almost constant, such as the adolescent's ability) or some unstable factor (such as luck or effort). In particular, the distinction of stability–instability has been helpful in charting adolescent's expectations following success or failure experiences.

One research study with college freshmen shows how an attributional perspective can influence achievement behavior (Wilson and Linville, 1982). The research study began by selecting college freshmen who were not doing well in school and showed a great deal of anxiety about their grades. Half of the freshmen were told that their scholastic problems were merely caused by temporary factors, and they were given information showing how students' grades invariably improve between their freshman and senior years. Further, these students watched videotapes of interviews with college upperclassmen who talked about how their grades were poor during their freshman year but improved substantially over the next few years. On the other hand,

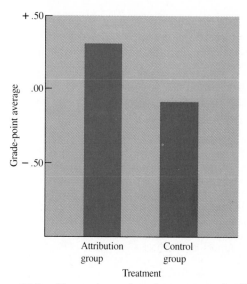

Figure 13.3 Change in grade-point average of college freshmen over one year following causal attribution treatment.

a control group of college freshmen experienced no information of this kind. On a test of academic performance (with items from the Graduate Record Exam), the first group, the attribution group, did significantly better when the test was administered just after the session and one week later. During the course of the next year, students in the attribution group also had significantly higher grades than those in the control group and were less likely to drop out of school. The grade-point results are shown in figure 13.3. Just by getting students to attribute the causes of their academic problems to temporary conditions and to observe others giving information that suggests grades and academic performance are likely to improve during the college years, positive changes in the behavior of the college students occurred.

Weiner's View: Attribution and Emotion Bernard Weiner (Weiner 1979, 1984; Weiner, Kun, and Benesh-Weiner, 1981) believes we tend to attribute the causes of success and failure to four elements described by Fritz Heider (1958): ability, effort, task difficulty, and luck. Weiner's work focuses on the relation of these causal attributions to our feelings. For example, we tend to feel pleased, happy, satisfied, good, and so on after success, and unpleasant, sad, dissatisfied, and bad after failure. The following examples represent the reasoning college students may go through when they are asked to interpret the causes and feelings experienced in an achievement circumstance:

> "I just received an A on this exam. That's a very high grade" (generating happiness). "I received this grade because I worked hard during the entire school year" (producing contentment and relaxation). "I really do have some positive qualities that will persist in the future" (followed by high self-esteem, feelings of self-worth, and optimism).
> "I just received a D on the exam. That's a very low grade" (generating feelings of unhappiness, frustration, and upset). "I received this grade because I just am not smart enough" (followed by feelings of incompetence). "There is really something lacking in me and it is likely to remain that way" (leading to feelings of low self-esteem and hopelessness) (Weiner, Kun, and Benesh-Weiner, 1980, p. 112).

These comments suggest that emotional reactions differ considerably, depending on the cognitive interpretations adolescents make, such as attributes about themselves and others in the situation. As we saw earlier, attribution theorists believe it is important to distinguish external and internal causes of behavior. Next, we explore the concept of internal locus of control, a closely related idea.

Locus of Control Attribution theory stresses that the causes that adolescents ascribe success and failure to are important determinants of achievement behavior. Closely linked to the way an adolescent views achievement is the adolescent's sense of personal responsibility. Adolescents who have strong beliefs that they are in control of their world, that they can cause things to happen if they choose, and that they command their own rewards, have an **internal locus of control.** Adolescents who perceive that others have more control over them than they do over themselves have an **external locus of control.** The perceived locus of control, internal or external, has important implications for how the adolescent can be expected to behave in a variety of situations. The adolescent who is more internally than externally controlled is generally considered more socially competent.

The type of subculture in which boys and girls live is a significant determinant of their locus of control. Youth who grow up in lower-class environments demonstrate a less internal locus of control than those from middle-class backgrounds do (Stephens and Delys, 1973). Important to the development of an internal locus of control is the quality of an adolescent's social interactions with important people in his life. Brenda Bryant (1974) has discovered that boys and girls with an external locus of control attribute more negative attributes to themselves and to their teachers than those with an internal locus of control do.

Adolescents with an internal locus of control seem to process information about themselves and their environments differently. Jerry Phares (1976) has conducted a number of research projects with late adolescents focusing on the relation between their locus-of-control orientations and their use of psychological defenses. In one investigation, externally oriented individuals actually preferred a task with a built-in reason for failure, while those internally oriented did not (Phares and Lamiell, 1975). In general, externally oriented adolescents tend to be threatened by possible failure but still believe that failure is not their fault.

At the same time Bernard Weiner and others have argued for the importance of understanding the attributions adolescents make about achievement-related matters, an equally important aspect of achievement has been emphasized by another leading psychologist. As we see next, Walter Mischel believes that the ability to delay gratification is a key ingredient in evaluating the adolescent's achievement orientation.

Delay of Gratification

Walter Mischel has intensively studied delay of gratification, a process he believes is a fundamental aspect of the adolescent's personality, including his or her achievement orientation. **Delay of gratification** refers to the quality of purposefully deferring immediate gratification for delayed, but more desired future gratification. For instance, delay of gratification is at work when the adolescent turns off his or her stereo each evening to study for two hours so that the likelihood he or she will get better grades at the end of the semester will be enhanced. The entire educational enterprise is built around the belief that if the adolescent works hard now and puts considerable effort and work into study and school while denying some alluring, immediate pleasures, at various points in the future, there will be rewarding consequences. Thus, the adolescent who works hard in school and denies many immediately pleasurable things is believed to increase the likelihood that years into the future the individual will be more likely to get into college and obtain a better job than those adolescents who give in to immediate pleasures and do not delay gratification.

Mischel's research has focused on the mechanisms that are involved in self-control, both in terms of the person and the situational influences on the person (Mischel, 1974; 1984). An enduring concern of the research is how children and adolescents can overcome stimulus control—the power of situations—and attain an ever increasing volitional control over their own behavior when faced with tempting situations.

Mischel's investigations have helped to specify how mental representations influence delay of gratification regardless of the power of the situation facing the person at the moment. In a typical experiment, children are given the opportunity to have a desired goal object now or wait until a later time to get an even more preferred object. For example, children may be told that they can have one marshmallow now or two marshmallows if they wait a specified amount of time (such as until the experimenter returns). The results of one experiment involving such delay of gratification is shown in figure 13.4. The data reported in this figure reflect how long the child was willing to wait by himself or herself for a preferred, but delayed gratification (e.g., two marshmallows rather than one). When the rewards were unavailable for attention (obscured from view during the delay period), children waited more than ten times longer than when the rewards were exposed and could

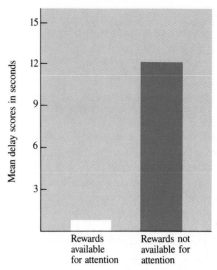

Figure 13.4 **Delay of gratification as a function of the desired goal object being available for attention.**

be observed. This suggests that individuals can gain control over their ability to delay gratification by keeping desired objects out of sight.

Further exploration of how individuals can control the situation involves their use of cognitive strategies to represent the environment. For example, Mischel's research has revealed that if individuals represent rewards mentally in consummatory or "hot" ways (such as focusing on their taste, as thinking about how yummy, crunchy, and tasty pretzels are), they cannot delay gratification very long (Mischel and Baker, 1975). However, if they focus on their nonconsummatory or "cool" features, thinking of pretzels as if they were sticks or tiny logs, they can wait for them easily. How people mentally represent the outcomes of a situation is very important in determining their ability to delay gratification.

Recently, Mischel has studied the extent to which the ability to delay gratification in childhood is a good predictor of adjustment during the adolescent years. To learn more about Mischel's recent research, read Perspective on Adolescent Development 13.1.

*T*he research concerning how attention and cognitive strategies can modify delay of gratification is process-oriented research. It focuses on how personality or some aspect of personality (in this case, delay of gratification) can be changed. An equally important aspect of research on personality and achievement is the study of the individual, including differences between one adolescent and another. Recently, Mischel has turned his attention to the stability of individual differences in delay of gratification from childhood through the adolescent years.

Mischel's research on the stability of individual differences (e.g., Mischel, 1983; Mischel, Peake, and Zeiss, 1984) reveals impressive contiguity between a preschool child's delay of gratification (for pretzels and marshmallows) and independent ratings of the adolescent's cognitive and social competence by parents some twelve years later. Mischel (1984) points out that while his research has shown that the preschool child who delays behavior in one situation may not do so in even slightly different contexts, he is now finding significant links between the preschool child's delay of gratification and cognitive and social competence in adolescence. As shown in table 13.1, the correlations between delay of gratification in early childhood and cognitive/social competence in adolescence reveal a picture of a child who delayed gratification in the childhood years as developing into an adolescent who is seen as attentive and

Table 13.1 The relation between delay of gratification in early childhood and rated cognitive and social competence during adolescence

Items	Correlation	Items	Correlation
Positive		Negative	
Is attentive and able to concentrate	.49	Tends to go to pieces under stress, becomes rattled	−.49
Is verbally fluent, can express ideas well	.40	Reverts to more immature behavior under stress	−.39
Uses and responds to reason	.38	Appears to feel unworthy, thinks of himself as bad	−.33
Is competent, skillful	.38	Is restless and fidgety	−.32
Is planful, thinks ahead	.35	Is shy and reserved, makes social contacts slowly	−.31
Is self-reliant, confident, trusts own judgment	.33	Tends to withdraw and disengage himself under stress	−.30
Is curious and exploring, eager to learn, open	.32	Shows specific mannerisms or behavioral rituals	−.27
Is resourceful in initiating activities	.29	Is stubborn	−.25
Is self-assertive	.29	Turns anxious when his environment is unpredictable	−.25
Appears to have high intellectual capacity	.28	Is unable to delay gratification	−.25
Has high standards of performance for self	.27	Attempts to transfer blame to others	−.24
Can be trusted, is dependable	.25	Teases other children	−.22
Becomes strongly involved in what he does	.25	Tends to be indecisive and vacillating	−.22
Is creative in perception, thought, work, or play	.24		
Is persistent in his activities	.23		

able to concentrate, able to express ideas well, responsive to reason, competent, skillful, able to plan ahead and think ahead, and able to cope with stress in a mature way.

Mischel (1984) argues that taken together, the results of the process-oriented experimental laboratory studies in conjunction with the investigations of individual differences across the childhood and adolescent years portray personality as both adaptive to situations and consistent across time. They also suggest that the development of delay of gratification skills during the childhood years is linked with achievement-related matters in adolescence such as the ability to plan ahead, to be persistent in work efforts, to have high achievement standards, and to be competent and skillful.

Development of delay of gratification in the childhood years is associated with competence in adolescence.

So far in our discussion of achievement, we have described many aspects of motivation, achievement motivation, attribution theory, and delay of gratification. A summary of main ideas related to these aspects of achievement is presented in Concept Table 13.1. When we discussed locus of control, we found that lower class adolescents seem to have a stronger external locus than an internal locus. As we see next, social class is one of a number of important sociocultural factors to consider in evaluating the achievement of adolescents.

Sociocultural Influences

Among the most important aspects of the environment that influence the adolescent's achievement are cultural standards of achievement, parental and peer influences, and school and teacher influences.

Cultural Standards of Achievement

We saw in Chapter 9 that compared to virtually all other cultures, the United States is a very achievement-oriented culture. It may be helpful for you to review that part of Chapter 9 at this time or go over the main ideas in your head. Within our culture, though, achievement standards often vary depending on the adolescent's social class background. Middle-class and lower class parents differ in the way they socialize their youth in achievement situations. Middle-class parents tend to emphasize the future more than lower class parents do (Strodtbeck, 1958). An important part of this orientation toward the future is the ability to delay gratification until a later time when rewards will be greater than they are at present—middle-class youth are more likely to delay gratification than lower class youth are (Mischel, 1976). Lower class youth are motivated more by rewards external to a learning task than to the intrinsic rewards built in to the task. Further, they show less achievement motivation when they are asked to tell stories about achievement-related situations (Rosen, 1959). And lower class youth support values that promote family loyalty more than independent striving for achievement (e.g., Rosen, 1956; Strodtbeck, 1958).

ACHIEVEMENT MOTIVATION AND RELATED ACHIEVEMENT FACTORS

Concept	Processes/related ideas	Characteristics/description
Motivation	Its nature	Motivation involves the question of why people behave, think, and feel the way they do. Motivated behavior is energized and directed.
	The grand theories	Both the cognitive developmental and information processing perspectives do not deal heavily with motivation. In their views, it is evident that motivation rests within the individual's desire for knowledge and information. For behaviorists, motivation rests in making the environment of the individual more rewarding. For psychoanalytic theorists like Freud, motivation is unconscious and biologically based with instincts like sex dominating achievement-related matters.
Theories of achievement and achievement-related factors	The achievement motivation views of McClelland and Atkinson	McClelland argued that achievement motivation is a property of the individual's psychological makeup and need system. He described n Achievement as the individual's internal striving for success. Atkinson elaborated on McClelland's ideas, specifying more clearly the importance of such processes as hope for success and fear of failure. In this regard, he believed expectations for success should outweigh anxiety about failing. In many instances it has been found that moderate anxiety is optimal for achievement, but there are exceptions.
	Attribution theory	There has been considerable interest in attribution theory in recent years. Attribution theory argues that individuals are cognitive beings who want to know why they and others are behaving in a particular way. In particular the attribution theorists have analyzed achievement circumstances in terms of the individual's perception of internal/external factors involved in achievement, as well as also being interested in a stability factor. In general, they argue that when individuals perceive their achievement is internally determined, especially effort based, then achievement behavior will be enhanced. Weiner believes that it is important to understand emotional reactions to attributions. Locus of control is a concept linked to internal/external aspects of achievement.
	Delay of gratification	In addition to achievement motivation and attributions, delay of gratification is another important process in understanding achievement. Mischel argues that delay of gratification can be influenced by situational factors but also often can be predicted in adolescence from information about delay of gratification behavior in childhood. Such a view suggests that personality is both adaptive to situations and consistent across time.

Elkind believes too many adolescents are being hurried into adult roles too soon in their development.

Parental and Peer Influences

As we just saw, middle-class and lower class parents have different achievement expectations for their adolescents and often socialize them differently in terms of achievement orientation. While early studies of achievement motivation suggested that independence training was an important factor, subsequent research seemed to indicate that parental standards for achievement are even more important than independence training (e.g., Crandall and Battle, 1970).

Indeed, the standards against which adolescents judge their performance are key ingredients of achievement. Some adolescents have very low standards of success and are exposed to models, including parents, who have low standards of success. Other adolescents have high standards of success and are exposed to models who have high standards of success. Albert Bandura (1977) has demonstrated that boys and girls who are exposed to models who adopt lenient standards (for example, parents who reward themselves for mediocre work) also tend to adopt lenient standards of achievement. By contrast, adolescents who are around models who adopt stringent standards (e.g., parents who reward themselves only for a high level of performance) are likely to adopt high standards themselves. Adolescents, of course, are exposed to the achievement standards peers bring to the peer group and that teachers and school administrators bring to schools as well.

However, it is important to consider just how high the standards are that parents set in relation to such matters as the adolescent's abilities, the amount of involvement and support parents are willing to give the adolescent, and so forth. David Elkind (1979), for example, believes that many adolescents are being hurried to achieve too much too soon in their development. As described in Perspective on Adolescent Development 13.2, he points to some important relationships between parents and adolescents that have to be worked out for the adolescent to develop a healthy achievement orientation.

Children who were called "spoiled" a generation ago took longer to grow up and had more freedom and power than they knew how to handle. Today's adolescents are pressured to achieve more, earlier—academically, socially, sexually. These "hurried children," as psychologist David Elkind calls them, must contend with a fear of failure—and a feeling that society's promises to them are being broken.

Unlike the spoiled children who remain children too long, hurried children grow up too fast, pushed in their early years toward many different types of achievement.

In adolescence, the symptoms of hurried children become most evident, often taking the form of severe anxiety about academic success. Among the teenagers I have treated, drug use is often associated with school failure. Even young people who are doing well academically may be tempted to fall into drug use because of the great personal toll that their effort to succeed exacts. Many teenage girls get pregnant because [through this] they can accomplish something. . . .

Today's pressures on middle-class children to grow up fast begin in early childhood. . . . Several decades ago . . . trying to accelerate children's acquisition of academic skills was seen as bad parenting. But attitudes toward precocity changed markedly during the 1960s, when parents were bombarded with professional dicta on the importance of learning for the early years. . . .

An important set of familial bonds that interconnect social values, parents, and children are parent-child contracts—implicit agreements about mutual obligation. While those contracts are present through life, the terms of each are constantly rewritten as young people—and their parents—mature. At each point there is often a healthy equilibrium between what parents demand and

what they give in return. When the balance of a particular contract is disturbed by certain social dynamics, however, the result is a particular variety of a "problem child," and a generational conflict that takes the contractual imbalance as its rallying theme.

There are three basic contracts. One involves **freedom and responsibility.** Parents generally grant children freedom insofar as the children demonstrate that they can handle the requisite responsibilities. . . . In adolescence, new types of responsibility are demanded when young people begin to date, drive cars, and want to experiment with drugs. Parents have less control during adolescence than they did earlier, because adolescents can take certain freedoms regardless of parental consent. Yet parents can still set limits and make clear that some freedoms (such as the use of the family car) will be withdrawn if young people transgress.

A second type of parent-child contract has to do with **loyalty and commitment.** Generally, parents take it for granted that their children will be loyal to them, in the sense of preferring them to other adults. In return, parents show commitment to their children in the time they spend with them and in their concern for their children's present and future well-being. In adolescence, when friendships become more important, parents no longer expect the loyal affection they received when children were young. They do expect, however, that their children will be loyal to the values and beliefs that they themselves hold dear. Young people, in return, demand that parents eschew hyprocrisy and show commitment to the values they espouse.

A third kind of contract involves **achievement and support.** From young infants, parents demand little in the way of achievement other than that children sit up, crawl, and walk at appropriate ages. . . . As children grow to school age, the achievement-support contract is . . . rewritten. In middle-class families, the expected achievements are academic, extracurricular (in sports, music, art, and the like), and social (having acceptable friends). Parents reciprocate with affection for good grades; with material support for lessons, instruments, and uniforms; and often, with transportation to and from friends' homes and various social activities. In adolescence, parental demands for achievement become more imperative, as young people prepare for independence.

Social conditions determine, in part, at least, what parents will demand of children in the way of responsibility, loyalty, and achievement. Given a society that puts emphasis on early achievement, when parents do not couple demands for that achievement with a comparable level of support, there is disequilibrium in a parent-child contract. When the disequilibrium persists, the result is the hurried child, achieving ever earlier in adult ways, but acquiring as well the tensions born of the pressure to achieve. As adolescents, these children, in effect, pay their parents back for what they experienced as childhood inequities. Such children come to bitterly resent parents who, say, pushed them to excel in school but who never bothered to look at their work, attend parent conferences, or participate in school functions. They often experience a sense of failure, if not in their school performance, then in their ability to impress their parents.

Some young people direct their anger outward and engage in activities that hurt them and that are designed to hurt the parents as well. They may begin to do poorly in school, and may drop out entirely. Others may become delinquent; some girls may become pregnant in a misguided effort to "pay their parents back." Still other young people turn their anger inward and blame themselves for not measuring up, and may seek escape in drugs or in religious movements. Indeed, the great appeal of many of the charismatic religious groups is that when young people join, they are assured that support is *not* contingent upon achievement.

. . . Toward their future work role, it seems to me that many young people have taken on what Kenneth Keniston has called a "protean" attitude. It is not so much that their goals are diffuse as that they do not know what they want to do. Rather, they are willing to commit themselves to a variety of available job opportunities and career courses depending on which open up. Their willingness to delay commitments is the most adaptive solution to the imbalance between the push to achieve and the available supports.

My guess about the future is that the next emphasis in parent-child contracts will be a return to themes of freedom and responsibility. Parental reaction to the symptoms of hurried children—already evident in the back-to-basics movement in education—could result in a new parenting style that would highlight freedom in exchange for responsible behavior. And as a reaction to the achievement pressure that they experienced as children, some parents may be encouraged to give their own children excessive freedom and too little responsibility. If that happens, we will again have to talk about children growing up too slowly rather than too fast.

Source: Reprinted by permission. Elkind, D. "Growing Up Faster." *Psychology Today,* February 1979, pp. 38–43.

In addition to standards of achievement that adolescents are exposed to, particularly those of parents and peers, other processes that often are at work in peer relations that need to be considered are social comparison and competitiveness. While it has been commonly believed that social comparison, and particularly competitiveness, enhance achievement motivation, a spate of recent studies suggest that this may not be the case (e.g., Ames, 1984; Cooper and Tom, 1984; Covington, 1984; Maehr, 1984; Nicholls, 1984). The argument of these researchers is that competition may be debilitating because it puts the adolescent in an ego-involved, threatening, self-focused state rather than a task-involved, effort- or strategy-focused state. These debilitating effects are most clearly seen as negative self-esteem and corresponding low-effort behavior that produce ineffective performance (Ames and Ames, 1984).

Quite clearly, whether adolescents performing alongside each other hold similar or dissimilar interpersonal perceptions of ability and worthiness is likely to influence achievement behavior (Ames, 1984). Such social comparison may produce avoidance of achievement or reduced achievement behavior if one perceives that one's abilities are less than a peer's or may generate self-aggrandizement if one perceives that one's abilities are superior to those of peer competitors. John Nichols (1979), for example, stresses that such inequalities are a part of academic settings and invariably evolve in competitive circumstances probably because of perceived differences in abilities.

Thus, while cooperative classroom settings are important considerations, particularly in the case of low-ability students, recall from our discussion of ethnic relations in Chapter 7 how Eliot Aronson's Jigsaw Classroom seemed intuitively right but in reality did not always work. The parents of high-ability students may undermine the efforts of teachers to develop cooperative achievement settings. In such circumstances, we see how the achievement standards of a culture, transmitted through family relationships, are brought to the classroom setting and influence the nature of students' achievement orientation.

An example of how social comparison information in addition to goal-setting can promote achievement behavior is reflected in the research of Dale Schunk (1983). Low-achieving boys and girls in math classes were given instruction in math skills. One group was given social comparative information indicating the number of problems solved by their classmates. A second group worked under conditions involving a goal of completing a given number of problems. A third group received both treatments. A fourth group was given no treatment. The boys' and girls' self-efficacy judgments were assessed before and after the conditions, as were their math skills on a test, and how long they persisted at working math problems. Self-efficacy is concerned with judgments about how well one can execute courses of action required in situations (e.g., Bandura, 1981). In addition, their training progress was assessed in terms of how many math problems they worked. As shown in table 13.2, in most instances, those who experienced both the social comparison and the goal conditions showed superior performance to their counterparts in other conditions.

As can be seen, the culture, family experiences, and peers are important contributors to the adolescent's achievement orientation. As we see next, schools and teachers are also important in influencing the adolescent's achievement orientation.

Schools and Teachers

In thinking about factors that motivate students in school settings, it may be helpful to remember the descriptions of effective schools for young adolescents made by Joan Lipsitz in Chapter 8. Recall that while the nature of effective schools varied, some themes did seem to run through those schools where adolescents were highly motivated to achieve. She concluded that schools likely to be successful at motivating adolescents are those that take seriously individual differences in physical, cognitive, and social development, and reveal a deep concern for what is known about adolescent development. Also, in effective schools that are able to motivate students, there often is a strong sense of caring and commitment on the part of the administrators and teachers—principals and teachers willing to spend long hours beyond the beginning and end of class

Table 13.2 The effects of a combined treatment of social comparison and individual goal setting on achievement-related performance

Measure	Phase	Experimental condition			
		Information only	Goals only	Information and goals	Training control
Skill[a]	Pretest	3.4	3.4	4.4	4.0
	Posttest	5.2	4.0	9.5	6.2
Persistence[b]	Pretest	43.1	40.8	64.8	58.0
	Posttest	65.5	81.2	68.3	94.1
Self-efficacy[c]	Pretest	45.6	54.1	54.5	53.6
	Posttest	59.0	74.2	79.4	65.5
Training progress[d]	Total	37.4	36.2	44.0	33.9

[a] Number of correct solutions on 14 problems.

[b] Average number of seconds per problem.

[c] Average judgment per problem; range of scale, 10 (low)–100.

[d] Number of problems worked.

Source: After data presented by Schunk, 1983, p. 81.

hours coming up with ingenious ways to make school both an enjoyable and a challenging learning experience. The development of author's week at one school, Black History Week, and the simulated rock music station—WNOE, were ideas that required considerable effort on the part of their architects, but that were highly effective in influencing student motivation. It may be helpful to review Lipsitz's work in Chapter 8 and keep in mind while thinking about ways that schools and teachers can motivate students, as well as other comments in that chapter about schools and teachers.

Our further investigation of achievement motivation in schools focuses on some of the matters we already have discussed in the area of achievement—we will see how they work in the school setting.

Attribution in the School Setting We found earlier that college students' grades improved when they changed their attributions. Can the same strategy work with younger adolescents as well? More precisely, can students learn to attribute failure to lack of effort and success to appropriate effort? If they can, then it would be predicted from attribution theory that these students would begin to persist longer at difficult tasks.

Several investigations have shown that students can learn to modify their achievement attributions and that corresponding changes in persistence also transpire (e.g., Andrews and Debus, 1978; Chapin and Dyck, 1976; Dweck, 1975). In one investigation (Andrews and Debus, 1978), forty-two sixth grade boys were identified who were below average in attributing their failure to lack of effort. A training program was developed for two-thirds of these students. In this program, they were allowed to experience success half of the time. When the students experienced success and attributed it to effort or when they experienced failure and attributed it to a lack of effort, they were rewarded by being told such things as, "That's good!" or "Very good!" If the students attributed success or failure to something besides effort, then no reinforcement was given and the instructor simply went on to the next task. The students were trained until they made effort evaluations eighty percent of the time or for sixty trials, whichever came first. After this attribution training, they were given block design and anagram tasks as well as a third unsolvable task. The students who received attribution training were much more likely than the control group (the one-third who did not get attribution training) to attribute both success and failure to effort and to persist at the unsolvable task. Another testing one week later produced similar results.

Ellen Gagne (1985) warns that teachers who try to change students' attributions need to be careful and patient. Such attributions, which sometimes are tied to self-conceptions of low ability (Ames, Ames, and Garrison, 1977; Ames and Ames, 1984), usually have been built up over a long number of years through many experiences. Thus, a quick fix that will be maintained over many years without careful monitoring is not likely. Care needs to be given to the selection of tasks at which the student can succeed with effort. Using the behavioral principle of shaping, it may be best to start with tasks that require only a small amount of effort and then as the student shows a greater willingness to work, increase the amount required for success. It also seems likely that students showing low amounts of effort should be encouraged to be more ability-focused and set individualistic goals rather than to be competitively oriented and interested in social comparison (Ames and Ames, 1984). Such strategies on the part of the teacher require a great deal of planning, organization, and classroom management abilities.

Observational Learning A tremendous amount of achievement-related learning goes on during the course of a school year simply by being in proximity to other people. Adolescents watch and listen to what other people are like—in the classroom, teachers and peers— and may be motivated to model their behavior after that of these individuals (Bandura, 1977).

For students to be motivated by a teacher, it generally is very important that the students like the teacher. Very early in the school year, students form impressions of the teacher. Some research has shown that the first two weeks of the semester are very important in setting the achievement tone for the entire semester and are critical in the development of a student's achievement orientation (e.g., Emmer, Evertson, and Anderson, 1980). Effective teachers who know how to motivate students seem to know how to get things off with a good start. As shown in table 13.3,

Table 13.3 Differences between effective and ineffective teachers during the first three weeks of the semester

Variable	More effective teachers	Less effective teachers
Variety of rewards	4.3	3.1
Signals appropriate behavior	5.4	3.8
Eye contact	6.1	4.9
States desired attitudes	5.5	3.9
Stops if disruptive behavior occurs	4.9	3.5
Ignores disruptive behavior	2.9	3.6

Source: After data presented by Emmer, E. T., Evertson, C. M., and L. M. Anderson, "Effective Classroom Management at the Beginning of the School Year," Elementary School Journal, 80, 219-231. Copyright © 1980 University of Chicago Press.

observations of teacher behavior during the first three weeks of the school year revealed that effective teachers were more likely to use a variety of rewards, to signal appropriate behavior, to maintain eye contact, and to state desired attitudes. The effectiveness was measured by more on-task behavior throughout the semester and by improvements on achievement tests at the end of the semester. These effective teachers also were more organized on the very first day of school than their ineffective counterparts—the competent teachers were providing an important achievement-related model for their students to imitate, one who is organized, who values achievement, work, and effort, and who is self-disciplined. Students pick up on such characteristics of models very quickly and see the expectations of these important people in their lives. It also is important while setting an achievement-oriented tone early in the semester for the teacher to establish a classroom climate of warmth and mutual respect.

The most imitated person in many classrooms is not the teacher, but the most popular student(s). If the most popular students are not very achievement oriented, this likely will influence some other students in the class to follow suit. In such circumstances, teachers may determine early in the school year which students are the most popular and seek to get them academically oriented.

In sum, both the teacher and classmates serve as achievement-oriented or nonachievement-oriented models for students. When students sit down to solve a difficult problem and are faced with possibly giving up, the influence of these models likely will influence the student's decision to persist or quit. Through memories and continued observation of such models, including parents, the adolescent's achievement orientation is strongly influenced.

Reinforcement In our discussion of observation and the kind of model teachers present to students, it was pointed out that effective teachers seem to give out a variety of rewards. One choice that is faced by many teachers is the dilemma of whether to emphasize the intrinsic motivation of the adolescent and not give external rewards for work and effort, or to emphasize the extrinsic motivation of the adolescent and be sure to give external rewards. Psychologists define **intrinsic motivation** as behavior that is motivated by an underlying need for competence and self-determination (mastery and competence motivation are two other terms commonly used in this regard). By contrast, **extrinsic motivation** refers to behavior that is influenced by external rewards. If an adolescent works hard at school because he or she knows that it will bring him or her a higher paying job after school is completed, then extrinsic motivation is at work. If the adolescent works hard at school because a personal standard of excellence is important to him or her, then intrinsic motivation is involved.

Incentives are external cues that stimulate motivation. They can be positive in the sense of a teacher telling the class that students who do a specified level of work will get certain privileges or they can be negative in the sense of the teacher taking away privileges if certain levels of work are not reached. Though it often is difficult to decide on whether to introduce incentives to motivate an adolescent, several guidelines are available. If the adolescent is not doing competent work,

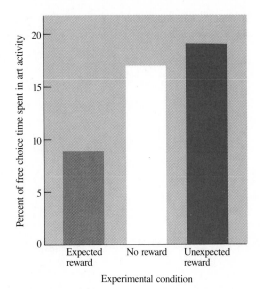

Figure 13.5 Extrinsic and intrinsic motivation: its effects on student art activity.

seems bored with what he or she is doing, and has a negative attitude, then it may be an appropriate time for a teacher to think about introducing incentives to improve performance. However, there are times when extrinsic rewards can get in the way of intrinsic rewards, particularly if the adolescent already is showing competent achievement motivation. One investigation is instructive (Lepper, Greene, and Nisbett, 1973). Baseline observations of initial intrinsic interest in artistic activity were conducted. Students with a high interest in the artistic work were exposed to one of three conditions. In the expected-reward condition, students agreed to engage in the art activity to obtain a reward. In the unexpected-reward condition, they had no knowledge of the reward until they had finished the art work. And in the no-reward condition, the students neither expected nor received a reward. As shown in figure 13.5, the students in the expected-reward condition showed less subsequent intrinsic interest in the art activity than students in either of the other two conditions, presumably because their intrinsic motivation was lessened by the extrinsic motives.

How are incentives related to achievement motivation?

A key point to be made about when extrinsic rewards will likely enhance or diminish motivation involves a distinction between the information and controlling functions of the rewards (Deci, 1975). It may be that when an adolescent receives extrinsic rewards for engaging in intrinsically motivated activities, there may be a change in beliefs on the part of the adolescent about why he or she is performing the activity. If the controlling aspect of external rewards is made salient, then the adolescent may think that external factors are causing his or her behavior. But if informational aspects of external rewards are prominent, then the adolescent may develop feelings of competence and self-determination. Thus, external rewards that indicate to the adolescent that he or she is performing competently would be expected to enhance, rather than diminish, intrinsic motivation. Thus, a trophy for the best performance as an indication of superiority should not undermine motivation. In general, when external rewards are not related to good performance, but rather are linked to simply performing a task, this could be expected to decrease motivation. In such circumstances, the adolescent may just whiz through the task as fast as possible to obtain the external reward.

In our discussion of achievement motivation, the issue of internal and external factors continues to crop up. Now that we have studied a number of views of motivation, achievement motivation, the factors involved in achievement behavior, and sociocultural influences, we will evaluate the internal and external factors in achievement.

Revisiting Internal and External Factors in Achievement

While attribution theorists emphasize the importance of studying both internal and external causes of achievement, it became apparent in our discussion of attribution theory that these theorists favor the encouragement of internal factors. Recall the recent work by attribution theorists documenting that an emphasis on social comparison and competition seems to be detrimental to achievement. However, we pointed out that this finding likely holds for comparison and competitiveness with peers having more ability and being more successful than the student in question rather than peers with less ability and less success. We also just saw that external rewards sometimes get in the way of intrinsic motivation and that this may be particularly true for a student who already is highly motivated. We concluded that incentives may be more helpful to students with low-achievement motivation who are showing little effort. And we also indicated that the most effective teachers, those whose students show the most achievement gains, are those who give out a variety of rewards early in the semester. Continuing on through other aspects of external reasons for achievement behavior, we found that cultural standards, parent and peer influences, and the school context were important environmental contributors to the adolescent's achievement orientation.

It seems likely, then, that there are both internal and external causes of achievement behavior and there are a variety of internal and external factors related to achievement behavior as well. It is instructive to point out that the issue of internal and external causes of behavior is one of the oldest dilemmas faced by psychologists. This issue is so prevalent it already has come up on a number of occasions earlier in the text. It came up in our discussion of moral development, where we found that Kohlberg argues that moral development becomes more internalized as development progresses. However, as we said earlier, Gilligan disagrees with Kohlberg, believing that the highest form of moral development consists of a connectedness with others and emphasizes relationships. Also, as we discussed in our evaluation of family processes in Chapter 6 and identity in Chapter 10, contemporary research has found that autonomy, often conceived of as a personality variable and therefore a property of the person (that is, an internal variable), is closely tied to the enhancement of individuation and connectedness during family interaction. So, on closer inspection, presumably internal variables often have continued ties to external factors.

It seems that too often internal and external factors are pitted against each other as opposites in studies of achievement attribution and achievement orientation. In reality, the adolescent's achievement orientation likely is influenced by a composite of internal and external factors, and even when internal factors are strong, they are not entirely divorced from the sociocultural context. It is important to recognize that some very competent adolescents who show a strong internal motivation for success with very lofty personal standards may be highly competitive persons who also are very motivated to outperform their peers.

We have discussed many different aspects of achievement, but our discussion would not be complete without considering one additional topic. As we see next, perhaps the greatest interest in achievement during recent years has been generated about the achievement orientation of females.

Achievement Orientation in Females

Few topics during the last decade have engendered more controversy than the degree to which females are less achievement oriented than males. Are females less achievement oriented and less competent than males in our society? How do parents socialize boys and girls in terms of achievement-related matters? Might girls develop a sense of learned helplessness about self-assertive, achievement-oriented circumstances? And in considering the achievement and competence of adolescent females, to what extent have conclusions been made that are culturally biased and have viewed success too narrowly in terms of occupations?

Baumrind's Description of Culturally Induced Social Incompetence

Diana Baumrind (1972) has distinguished between instrumental competence and incompetence. Boys, she says, are trained to become instrumentally competent, while girls learn how to become instrumentally incompetent. By instrumental competence, Baumrind means behavior that is socially responsible and purposive. Instrumental incompetence is more aimless behavior.

The following evidence is offered by Baumrind (1972) in support of her argument: (1) few women obtain jobs in science, and of those who do, few achieve high positions; (2) being a female is devalued by society; (3) being independent and achieving intellectual status causes the female to lose her "femininity" in society's eyes—both men and women devalue such behaviors in women; (4) parents usually have lower achievement aspirations for girls than boys (for example, parents expect their boys to become doctors and their girls to become nurses); and (5) girls and women are more oriented toward expressive behavior than boys and men.

Parenting Orientation and Developmental Precursors

There is reason to believe that differences in the achievement orientations of adolescent boys and girls are learned—not innately determined by sex. Aletha Stein and Margaret Bailey (1973) have listed several parental characteristics or attributes that are associated with the development of achievement orientation in girls. For example, achievement orientation can be encouraged through the modeling of a mother who has a career. In some instances, particularly when the mother assumes a traditional female role, the social interaction of the father takes on greater importance. Stein and Bailey also point out that socialization practices fostering so-called femininity in girls are often counter to those practices producing achievement orientation. Moderate parental permissiveness, coupled with attempts to accelerate achievement, is related to achievement orientation in girls. This kind of parenting is not compatible with what is usually prescribed for rearing a young woman.

In their review of the achievement orientation of females, Stein and Bailey (1973) concluded that females have lower expectancies for success across many different tasks than males do, lower levels of aspiration, more anxiety about failure, less willingness to risk failure, and more feelings of personal responsibility when failure occurs. It is important that these differences are more pronounced during the adolescent years than during the middle or early childhood years. In one set of investigations, late adolescent females and males attributed male success to ability and female success to effort and luck (Feldman-Summers and Kiesler, 1974; Frieze, 1975).

Aletha Huston-Stein and Ann Higgens-Trenk (1978) have discussed the developmental precursors of sex differences in achievement orientation. Women who as adults are career and achievement oriented usually showed the signs of this orientation early in their childhood years. Adult women who are attracted to traditionally feminine activities were likely attracted to such activities during middle childhood and adolescence (Crandall and Battle, 1970; Kagan and Moss, 1962). Achievement behavior was more consistent over the childhood, adolescent, and young adult years than any other personality attribute studied in these longitudinal investigations. Interest in "masculine" play activities in childhood (Crandall and Battle, 1970) and in "masculine" subject matter (Sears and Barbee, 1975) is linked with achievement orientation in females during adolescence and young adulthood. In sum, childhood socialization experiences seem to be critical in influencing the achievement orientation of females during adolescence and even into young adulthood. Next, we'll look at another view of why female adolescents may not do as well as their male counterparts in achievement-related circumstances.

Learned Helplessness

A state of learned helplessness develops when a child or adolescent believes that the rewards she or he receives are beyond personal control (Seligman, 1975; Dweck and Eliot, 1983). Two major factors in learned helplessness are a lack of motivation and negative affect. If the adolescent in a failure situation sees her behavior as irrelevant to the outcome, she is displaying learned helplessness. Such perceptions lead the individual to attribute failure to incontrollable or unchangeable circumstances, such as lack of ability, difficulty of the task, or presumably fixed attitudes of other people. In addition, attributions of failure to these factors are often linked with deterioration of performance in the face of failure. Individuals who attribute their failures to controllable or changeable factors, such as effort or luck, are more likely to show improvement in their performance (Dweck, 1975; Dweck and Reppucci, 1973; Weiner, 1974).

A number of investigations of achievement behavior suggest that girls are more likely to attribute failure to uncontrollable factors, such as lack of ability (Dweck and Reppucci, 1973; Nicholls, 1975); to display disrupted performance or decreased effort under the pressure of impending failure or evaluation (Dweck and Gilliard, 1975); and to avoid situations in which failure is likely (Crandall and Rabson, 1960).

These sex differences in the effects of failure feedback on achievement behavior generally are attributed to girls' greater dependency on external social evaluation. However, some investigators believe that different evaluations of boys and girls by adults and peers may influence such sex differences. For example, one investigation found that when failure feedback for girls came from adults, little change resulted in the girls' achievement behavior; but when the feedback came from peers, the girls' achievement behavior increased substantially (Dweck and Bush, 1976).

Conclusions about the Achievement Orientation and Competence of Adolescent Females

From the discussion so far, we might conclude that females are less achievement oriented and less competent than males in our society. While that is just what has happened in some instances, this conclusion is not justified. It may be helpful to remember the discussion of androgyny and sex roles presented in Chapter 11. Social competence was described in terms of many different dimensions. In particular, two dimensions believed to be particularly important in interpreting competence are self-assertion and integration (Ford, 1981). In our culture, self-assertion has been emphasized to a greater degree than integration. And measures of social competence have included far more self-assertive than integrative items. The conclusions about lower achievement and social competence too often are made in terms of self-assertive dimensions. In particular, achievement and competence have been described frequently in terms of occupational success. It may be more instructive to think of achievement and competence in terms of success in many different roles, not just the occupational role. Females and males quite clearly have been socialized into different roles—males often showing a stronger motivation in self-assertive roles, while females reveal a stronger motivation in integrative roles. Females also seem to show a stronger interest in balancing multiple roles than males do (e.g., Fassinger, 1985). Thus, it is inaccurate to conclude that females are less achievement and competence oriented than males—it depends on the domain of achievement and competence being evaluated and the cultural prescriptions for success.

We have discussed a number of aspects of sociocultural influences on achievement and achievement orientation in female adolescents. A summary of main ideas related to these aspects of achievement are presented in Concept Table 13.2. Now we turn our attention to the career development of adolescents.

SOCIOCULTURAL INFLUENCES ON ACHIEVEMENT AND THE ACHIEVEMENT ORIENTATION OF FEMALE ADOLESCENTS

Concept	Processes/related ideas	Characteristics/description
Sociocultural influences	Cultural standards	Adolescents in the United States characteristically are more achievement oriented than adolescents from other cultures. The ingredients for achievement orientation are often much stronger in middle-class than lower class contexts.
	Parental and peer influences	The models of achievement orientation parents present to adolescents is an important contributor to the adolescent's achievement. Parents who model stringent standards for achievement are more likely to have achievement-oriented adolescents. Some parents, however, push too strongly and too early for achievement. This circumstance, according to Elkind, is particularly hazardous when such parents do not provide adequate support for their lofty expectations. Social comparison and competitiveness often are in operation between adolescents and their peers. Adolescents who compare themselves favorably with their peers in regard to their peers are more likely to feel good about themselves than those who compare themselves unfavorably. Some educational strategists argue that competitiveness and social comparison should be discouraged and cooperativeness and internal striving for a personal standard be emphasized. Trying to implement this strategy, however, is not very easy.
	Schools and teachers	The descriptions of effective schools by Lipsitz in Chapter 8 are relevant here in our attempt to understand the role of schools in achievement. She found that a serious orientation toward individual differences, a deep concern for what is known about adolescent development, and a strong sense of caring and commitment on the part of administrators and teachers were evident in schools able to promote a strong achievement orientation in their students. Getting students to attribute their successes and failures to effort rather than external factors has improved the achievement orientation of adolescents. Changing attributions of students, though, can be a very lengthy process. Observational learning is very important in the school setting as well as at home. Adolescents often are motivated to behave like a teacher or a peer. The most popular peer at school is often imitated. With regard to reinforcement, it seems that intrinsic motivation is best when students already show a strong achievement orientation, but that some form of extrinsic motivation, or use of external rewards, may benefit students showing low motivation.

SOCIOCULTURAL INFLUENCES ON ACHIEVEMENT AND THE ACHIEVEMENT ORIENTATION OF FEMALE ADOLESCENTS

Concept	Processes/related ideas	Characteristics/description
	Revisiting internal/external factors in achievement	The implication from attribution theory that internal factors should be promoted when getting the adolescent to analyze the causes of his or her achievement-related behavior is at issue. However, it is important to recognize that achievement behavior is motivated by both internal and external factors and that the adolescent is never divorced from commerce with the social world. Thus, it is somewhat of an artificial distinction when internal and external factors are pitted against each other in research studies. The issue of internal and external causes of behavior has been around since the early beginnings of psychology and it continues to be widely debated. It does seem wise to emphasize that the adolescent learn to attribute causes of failure and success to internal factors, such as effort, but also that achievement behavior is determined by multiple external and internal factors. Further, some of the most achievement-oriented and competent adolescents are those who both have a high personal standard of achievement and are very competitive as well.
Achievement orientation in female adolescents	Cultural standards and instrumental competence/incompetence	Baumrind argued that female adolescents have been socialized into roles of instrumental incompetence, while males have been socialized to be instrumentally competent.
	Parenting orientation and developmental precursors	Childhood and adolescent socialization experiences seem to be very important in the development of achievement in adolescent females. Parents with high demands for success in their daughters are more likely to have achievement-oriented daughters.
	Learned helplessness	Dweck argues that adolescent females have developed a sense of learned helplessness in achievement situations; that is, they perceive that regardless of how much effort they put forth, they will not be able to control the rewards they receive.
	Conclusions about sex differences in achievement and competence	It is inaccurate to conclude that females are less achievement- and competence-oriented than males—the domain of achievement and competence being evaluated and the cultural prescriptions for success need to be considered.

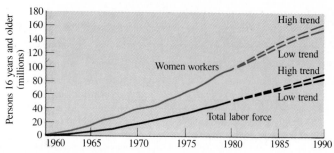

Figure 13.6   Total labor force growth in comparison with the increase in the number of working women. *Source:* From Occupational Outlook Handbook 1982–83 Edition, *U.S. Department of Labor, Bureau of Labor Statistics.*

Careers: More Serious Business in Adolescence

To learn more about career development in adolescence, we begin by surveying the occupations adolescents will be entering, then turn to an overview of theories of vocational choice that has been constructed. Next, cognitive factors that likely play an important role in career development are investigated, followed by a discussion of important sociocultural factors in career development. Last, further information about the achievement orientation of the adolescent female is given as we explore the nature of career development in females.

The Nature of Careers

What is the history of women and men in the labor force? Which occupations will adolescents be entering in the future?

Men and Women in the Labor Force

There still is a large imbalance in the number of males and females employed in different vocations. In the mid-1970s, few women were employed as managers and administrators, while very few males worked in clerical positions. Most craftspeople were men, as were most laborers. The next decade should see these imbalances

evening out—the increase of women in the work force and the predicted increase of females in previously male jobs have important implications for youth who currently are in junior high and high school. (Figure 13.6 shows the increasing proportion of women in the work force.)

Today's Adolescents and Their Future Occupations

Figure 13.7 shows that some of the predicted shifts in occupational structures already are apparent. These figures, drawn up in the late 1970s, involve projections of job availability through the middle 1990s. A large increase in service occupations is predicted while a significant decrease in jobs related to farming will continue to occur. More jobs in trade, manufacturing, government, finance, real estate, insurance, and contract construction are predicted.

Figure 13.8 suggests that there will be a diminishing need for unskilled laborers—jobs requiring nonfarm labor will be at a virtual standstill when compared with mid-1970s figures. Few new openings for farmworkers, transport equipment operatives, and salesworkers will appear either. With regard to private household workers, employment decline will actually more than offset the number of openings created by death and retirement. In figure 13.9, employment predictions drawn up by the U.S. Bureau of Labor Statistics suggest that by far the greatest increase in jobs will be in computer-related areas.

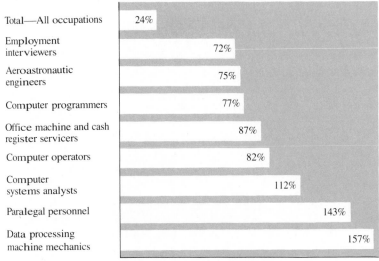

Where the Jobs Will Be–1990

Total—All occupations	24%
Employment interviewers	72%
Aeroastronautic engineers	75%
Computer programmers	77%
Office machine and cash register servicers	87%
Computer operators	82%
Computer systems analysts	112%
Paralegal personnel	143%
Data processing machine mechanics	157%

Percentage of Growth 1978–1990

Projected growth in specific occupations, 1978–90. *Source:* From Occupational Outlook Handbook dition, *U.S. Department of Labor, Bureau of Labor Statistics.*

figures clearly point out that junior high and ol students will need more education and find jobs than in past eras. And because oc- needs are changing so rapidly, it also is clear scents will need to adopt a flexible attitude t jobs they will take and what careers they Counselors need to encourage high school ot to think about a highly stable, static oc- plan that focuses on entering a single, spe- -instead students should be encouraged to nd seriously consider a number of alternative al plans.

hat we have studied the future occupations ents, we turn our attention to the manner in lescents develop ideas about careers and oc-

Theories of Occupational Choice

Three main theories of occupational choice have been offered—Ginzberg's developmental view, Super's vo- cational self-concept perspective, and Holland's per- sonality type theory.

Ginzberg's Developmental Theory

Eli Ginzberg believes that children and adolescents move through three distinct stages in terms of occu- pational choice—fantasy, tentative, and realistic stages. When asked what they want to be when they grow up, young children may answer, "a doctor," "a superhero," "a teacher," "a movie star," or any of a number of other occupations. During the elementary school years, the future seems to contain almost unlimited opportunity. Eli Ginzberg's theory of vocational choice (1951; 1972) emphasizes that the fantasies children entertain about

Projected range of employment growth, 1980–90 (millions)

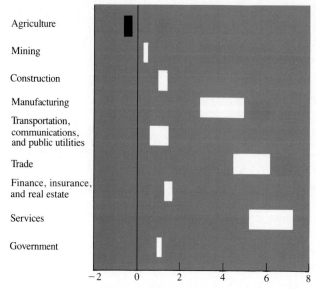

Figure 13.7 **Projected growth and decline in various industries.** *Source:* From Occupation 1982–83 Edition, *U.S. Department of Labor, Bureau of Labor Statistics.*

Figure 1
1974–7

The
high sc
training
cupatio
that ad
about w
will ent
students
cupatio
cific job
evaluate
occupat
No
of adole
which a
cupatio

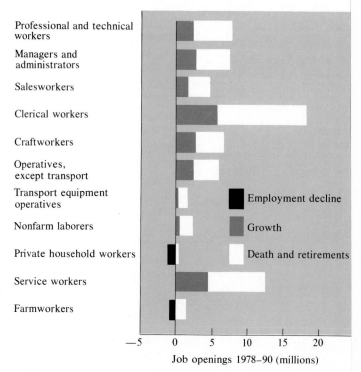

Job openings 1978–90 (millions)

Figure 13.8 **Job openings resulting from employment growth, deaths, and retirements.** *So*
Outlook Handbook 1980–81 Edition, *U.S. Department of Labor, Bureau of Labor Statistics.*

Achievement, C

Source: MISS PEACH by Mell Lazarus. Courtesy of Mell Lazarus and News America Syndicate.

future occupations are an important aspect of career development. Ginzberg believes that until about age eleven, children are in the **fantasy stage** of occupational choice. At this stage, children imagine what they want to be with little or no concern for their abilities, training, or the demands of reality.

From the ages of eleven to seventeen, boys and girls are in what Ginzberg calls the **tentative stage** of vocational choice. It is during the adolescent years that a transition from the fantasy orientation of childhood to the realistic decision making of young adulthood occurs. Ginzberg believes that adolescents progress from evaluating their interests (ages eleven to twelve), to evaluating their capacities (thirteen to fourteen) and their values (fifteen to sixteen). At around the ages of seventeen and eighteen, thinking shifts from a less subjective to a more realistic orientation.

The age period from seventeen or eighteen through the early twenties is called the **realistic stage** of vocational choice by Ginzberg. During this stage, the late adolescent conducts an extensive search of available occupations (called the period of exploration), zeros in on a particular occupation or a set of occupations (called crystallization), and then chooses a specific job within the occupation decided upon (such as family practitioner or orthopedic surgeon from the more general category of doctor).

Ginzberg's theory has been subjected to criticism on a number of grounds. For one, the initial data were collected from middle-class youth, who may well have

had more career options open to them. Also, just as with other developmental theories (such as Piaget's and Freud's), some critics feel that the time frames are too rigid. Moreover, Ginzberg's theory does not adequately account for individual differences—some adolescents make mature decisions about careers (and stick with them) at a much earlier age than Ginzberg suggests, and not all children engage in extensive fantasies about careers during childhood. In a revision of his view, Ginzberg (1972) has conceded that lower class youth do not have as many options available to them as middle-class youth do when career decisions are at issue. Ginzberg's general point, though—that during adolescence boys and girls become more realistic in their appraisal of career matters—is probably correct.

While at one time Ginzberg's theory dominated thinking about career choice, in recent years, the career choice theories of Donald Super and John Holland have been given considerably more attention.

Super's Vocational Self-Concept Theory

Donald Super's theory of vocational choice (e.g., Super, 1967; 1976) emphasizes the importance of the adolescent's self-concept. Super believes that it is during adolescence that boys and girls first construct a vocational self-concept. Other aspects of the adolescent's self-concept undoubtedly appear earlier than adolescence (such as perception of the self as good or bad, perception of maleness and femaleness, and so on), but it is not until adolescence that vocational identity begins to appear.

Super argues that individuals go through five different phases of vocational development. First, at about fourteen to eighteen years of age, adolescents develop ideas about work that mesh with their already existing global self-concept—this phase is called crystallization. Next, between eighteen and twenty years of age, they narrow their vocational choices and initiate behavior that will enable them to engage in some type of career—this phase is referred to as specification. Between twenty-one and twenty-four years of age, young adults complete their education and/or training and enter the work world. Super calls this stage implementation. The decision on a specific, appropriate career is made between the ages of twenty-five and thirty-five—this phase is labeled stabilization. Finally, after the age of thirty-five, middle-aged adults seek to advance their careers and reach higher-status positions. Super calls this consolidation. The age ranges Super suggests should not be thought of as rigid, but rather as approximations of when a large portion of individuals pass through the different phases.

Super believes that adolescence is a period in which the individual engages in extensive exploration of career alternatives. The adolescent finds out about adult roles and tries them on, either in real life or in fantasy. During adolescence, maturing capabilities interact with environmental experiences to influence career development. Super believes that although some individuals are endowed with skills in certain areas, there usually are many vocations that individuals can succeed in that coordinate with their talents. Clearly, exposure to alternative careers is one aspect of the environment that promotes career development during adolescence. Many social agents can aid the adolescent in this respect— parents, teachers, peers, counselors, and so forth.

Super's commitment to the idea that career exploration is a critical component of the adolescent's vocational development has led him to develop a Career Development Inventory (1970) that includes extensive information about career exploration. Many counselors use Super's inventory in vocational guidance.

Holland's Personality Type Theory

Another theory of occupational choice that also has received a great deal of attention during recent years is John Holland's. Holland (1973) emphasizes that individuals select careers that match their personalities. Once an individual finds an occupation that fits with her personality, she is more likely to enjoy that particular occupation and stay in the job for a longer period of time than an individual who works at a job that is not suitable for his personality. Holland believes there are six basic personality types to be considered when matching the adolescent's psychological makeup to an occupation:

Realistic. These individuals show characteristically "masculine" traits. They are physically strong, deal in practical ways with problems, and have very little social know-how. They are best oriented toward practical careers such as labor, farming, truck driving, and construction.

Intellectual. These individuals are conceptually and theoretically oriented. They are thinkers rather than doers. Often they avoid interpersonal relations, and are best suited to careers in math and science.

Social. These individuals often show characteristically "feminine" traits, particularly those associated with verbal skills and interpersonal relations. They are likely to be best equipped to enter "people" professions such as teaching, social work, counseling, and the like.

Conventional. These youth show a distaste for unstructured activities. They are best suited for jobs as subordinates, such as bank tellers, secretaries, and file clerks.

Enterprising. These boys and girls energize their verbal abilities toward leading others, dominating individuals, and selling people on issues or products. They are best counseled to enter careers such as sales, politics, and management.

Artistic. These boys and girls prefer to interact with their world through artistic expression, avoiding conventional and interpersonal situations in many instances. These youth should be oriented toward careers such as art and writing.

If all adolescents fell conveniently into Holland's personality types, vocational counselors would be obsolete. But adolescents are more varied and complex than Holland suggests. Even Holland now admits that his categorization of individuals into six basic types probably is too simplistic, and that most individuals are not "pure" types anyway. Still, the basic idea of matching the abilities and attitudes of the adolescent to a particular occupation that meshes with those abilities and attitudes is an important contribution to the vocational field.

Overall Evaluation of Vocational Choice Theories

The process of determining a career choice is very complex and it seems as if the major career choice theories may have oversimplified some of this complexity. Two of the theories—Ginzberg's and Super's—have developmental components. However, these views, as well as Holland's view, focus primarily on developing characteristics of the person and pay little attention to the role of social contexts in career choice. Indeed, it seems that each of the three major vocational choice theories has underestimated the importance of sociocultural influences on career development.

In addition to underestimating the importance of sociocultural influences, the major theories of vocational choice have virtually ignored another set of important factors in constructing their theories—those related to achievement motivation. Much of what we said during the first part of this chapter about the nature of achievement motivation should be considered in understanding the adolescent's career choice. Such factors as achievement motivation itself, fear of failure, hope for success, attribution, fear of success, achievement anxiety, and the important process of delay of gratification all are likely important candidates for a thorough account of the adolescent's vocational choice.

"Your son has made a career choice, Mildred. He's going to win the lottery and travel a lot."

Source: © 1985; Reprinted courtesy of Bill Hoest and Parade Magazine.

Thus, while the career choice theories have mapped out some general important themes in career choice, two additional aspects of the adolescent's development need to be considered in understanding his or her career choice: sociocultural influences and the many related aspects of achievement motivation. To explore further the nature of career development in adolescents, we turn to a discussion of exploration and cognitive factors and then to sociocultural influences.

Exploration and Cognitive Factors in Career Development

We already have seen in the view of Ginzberg that decision making about careers seems to become more realistic in late adolescence. Thus, the cognitive orientation of the late adolescent, from Ginzberg's view, is less idealistic and more realistic. Further, Super argued that a great deal of cognitive and behavioral exploration needs to take place for career development to be optimal. Let's now look more closely at the factor of exploration, and then at planning and decision making about careers.

Exploration

Donald Super and Douglas Hall (1978) believe that in countries where equal employment opportunities have developed—such as the United States, Great Britain, and France—exploration of various career paths is critical for the adolescent's career development. The role of the school is especially important in career exploration, since families and friends tend to be from the same social class and often know little about educational opportunities and occupations other than their own (e.g., Reynolds, 1949).

Students often approach career exploration and decision making with a great deal of ambiguity, uncertainty, and stress (e.g., Jordaan, 1963; Jordaan and Heyde, 1978). In one investigation, Donald Super and his colleagues (Super, Kowalski, and Gotkin, 1967) studied late adolescents and young adults after they left high school. In their career pattern study, they found that over half the position changes (such as student to student, student to job, job to job) made between leaving school and the age of twenty-five involved floundering and unplanned changes. In other words, the young adults were neither systematic nor intentional in their exploration and decision making about careers.

Several recent efforts have been made to increase career exploration among high school students. In one investigation (Hamdani, 1974), a career education and guidance course was developed for disadvantaged inner-city high school students. A regular teacher, who was not especially motivated or competent, was the instructor, with Hamdani acting as a consultant. The semester-long course did produce an increase in the disadvantaged students' career planning, as well as their use of resources for exploration and decision making.

The nature of the career exploration is important in determining whether a positive effect on adolescents will accrue. Some counseling programs that have been self-oriented (that is, students are left to their own devices more so than in the more directive environmental approach of Hamdani) do not show positive effects on students' career exploration and decision making (Corbin, 1974; Hammer, 1974). In many cases, these programs fail to involve the students in enough exploration for changes to occur. When self-directed student programs are instituted, some instruction, monitoring, and discussion with a counselor seem necessary for the student to benefit from the program. It is just not enough for the high school or college student to engage in career exploration without any guidance.

Most high school students have not explored the world of work adequately on their own, and receive very little direction from high school guidance counselors about how to do this. According to the National Assessment of Educational Progress report (1976), high school students not only do not know what information to seek about careers, they do not know how to seek it. Just as discouraging is the fact that, on the average, high school students spend less than three hours per year with the guidance counselors at their schools (Super and Hall, 1978).

Planning and Decision Making

The first step in making a decision about a career, according to Super and Hall (1978), is to recognize that a problem actually exists. After adolescents become aware that a vocational problem exists, they can seek and weigh various pieces of information about the problem, make and test various plans, and then, if necessary, revise the plans.

In one study of career decision making developed by Super and Overstreet (1960), a large number of ninth-grade boys were asked about their career decision making. Vocational maturity was evident in terms of the adolescents' ability to engage in planning for short- and long-term career goals. The ability of vocationally mature adolescents to develop a structured time perspective about their future careers emerged also in the work of Jepsen (1974 a,b) with high school juniors.

Among the important aspects of planning in career development is an awareness of the educational requirements for a particular career. To learn more about adolescents' career planning and their awareness of educational requirements, read Perspective on Adolescent Development 13.3.

Sociocultural Influences on Careers

Not every child born into the world can grow up to become a nuclear physicist or a doctor—there is a genetic limitation that keeps some adolescents from performing at the very high intellectual levels necessary to enter such occupations. Similarly, there are genetic limitations that keep some adolescents from becoming professional tennis players or golfers. But there are usually a wide range of vocations available to us that are compatible with the abilities we inherited from our parents. The sociocultural experiences of individual adolescents exert a strong influence on career choice from among that wide range (Grotevant, 1979).

In the prologue to this chapter, we read about the lives of Bobby Hardwicke and Cleveland Wilkes, individuals from very different socioeconomic backgrounds. Coming through the description of their lives was the sense that the kind of socioeconomic and family background they came from was going to have strong influences on their career development.

Social Class

Most sociologists believe that social class is a powerful force in career development (e.g., Little, 1969). They point out that the adolescent growing up in a New York ghetto family on welfare has much less chance of entering a middle-class occupation than the adolescent whose parents live in an affluent suburb. In one widely cited study of four thousand male high school seniors (Little, 1969), students who aspired to higher status occupations came from higher socioeconomic backgrounds, usually had a father who had gone to college and who held a white-collar job, were more likely to go to high school in an urban area, had above-average achievement test scores, and planned on going to college. By contrast, high school seniors who aspired to lower status occupations more often came from a lower socioeconomic background, had a father who had not gone to high school and who worked as an unskilled laborer, had below-average achievement test scores, and planned on no education beyond high school.

How might the adolescent's socioeconomic background be related to his or her career choices?

Other research supports Little's conclusions. For example, in one investigation (Blau, 1965), over forty percent of the sons of self-employed professionals entered a profession and thirty percent entered some other white-collar job. By contrast, only about five percent of the sons of laborers entered a profession and only fifteen percent entered other white-collar jobs. The vast majority ended up in lower class blue-collar or service jobs. The chances of attaining true economic security in an upper white-collar professional or business career appear to steadily decrease as socioeconomic background goes toward the lower classes.

The channels of upward mobility open to lower class youth today are largely educational in nature. The school hierarchy from grade school through high school, as well as through college and graduate school, is programmed to orient youth toward some sort of career.

Less than a hundred years ago, only eight years of education were believed to be necessary for vocational competence and anything beyond that qualified the individual for advanced placement in higher status occupations. By the middle of the twentieth century, the high school diploma had already lost ground as a ticket to occupational success. College rapidly became a prerequisite for entering a higher status occupation. Employers simply reason that an individual with a college

CAREER PLANNING AND KNOWLEDGE OF
EDUCATIONAL REQUIREMENTS

*H*arold Grotevant and Mary Ellen Durrett (1980) studied the degree to which late adolescents choose educational requirements that relate to their stated educational goals and the extent to which students' vocational interests are compatible with their occupational choices. A sample of 6,029 high school seniors from fifty-seven different public school districts in Texas were studied.

The results of this investigation suggested that the occupational knowledge of high school students is limited, which corresponds to other research (e.g., DeFleur and Menke, 1975). Students seemed to lack two areas of knowledge about careers: (1) accurate knowledge about the educational requirements of careers they wished to enter, and (2) knowledge of the vocational interests predominantly associated with their occupational choices. Students in this study were asked their first, second, and third choice of occupations. In general, students felt most knowledgeable about the first choice,

less so about the second choice, and least about the third choice (figure 13.10). If our point about the importance of having flexibility in career decision making and the ability to pursue several alternative careers is to be taken seriously, then late adolescents have woefully inadequate knowledge about what it takes to get into even one career, much less two or three career possibilities.

In the investigation by Grotevant and Durrett (1980), even among the high school seniors who said they had considerable knowledge of the careers they wanted to pursue, about one-fifth of them planned on getting too little education and almost one-third too much education for these careers. (table 13.4).

It seems clear that by the time they graduate from high school, students do not have good information about the educational background required to make important decisions about future occupations, particularly a range of occupations.

Table 13.4 Late adolescents claiming to have considerable understanding of occupational choices: their perception of the amount of education required for these occupations

	Undereducated	Appropriately educated	Overeducated	Total N*
		Males		
First choice	21.5	47.4	31.1	1402
Second choice	23.0	43.4	33.6	1147
Third choice	24.1	39.8	36.1	1034
		Females		
First choice	18.7	55.3	26.0	1392
Second choice	20.4	51.0	28.6	1161
Third choice	23.2	49.1	27.7	997

*The total N (number of subjects) is based only on those adolescents who claimed to have at least a considerable understanding of occupational choices.

Source: Based on Grotevant, H. D., and M. E. Durrett, "Occupational Knowledge and Career Development in Adolescence," Journal of Vocational Behavior, 17, 171–182. Copyright © 1980 Academic Press.

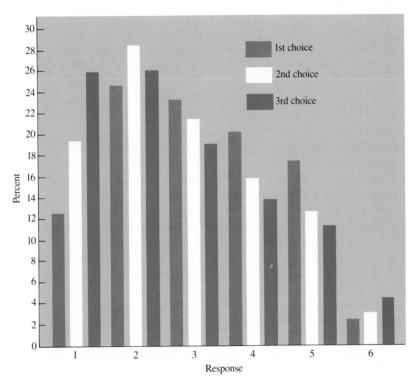

Figure 13.10 **Percentage of students responding to
level of understanding categories for first, second, and
third choice occupations. (Males and females combined:**
$N = 6029$.) Response 1 = very limited understanding;
Response 2 = moderate but general understanding;
Response 3 = considerable but not firsthand
experience; Response 4 = based on firsthand
experience; Response 5 = based on courses taken in
this field; Response 6 = subject did not answer this
item.

degree is a better risk than a high school graduate or a high school dropout. Hence, students keep entering college at reasonably high rates in hope that an education will ensure occupational success.

There is increasing evidence, though, that higher education does not do a very good job of training youth to think more critically or to hone their particular abilities and skills for the vocational world. The integration of work and education may be a more effective strategy of career development for adolescents and young adults.

Parents and Peers

Parents, in particular, and peers exert strong influences on career development. Recall our discussion of David Elkind's views on hurried adolescents and how too many parents are pushing their adolescents into adult roles too early, with the circumstance being particularly harmful when such parents do not provide adequate support and involvement with their youth. In some cases, however, adolescents do not get challenged enough by their parents when achievement and careers are at issue. Consider the twenty-five-year-old female who vividly described the details of her youth that later prevented her from seeking a career. From very early in her adolescent years, both of her parents encouraged her to finish high school, but at the same time, emphasized that she needed to get a job to help them pay the family bills. She was never told she couldn't go to college, but both her parents encouraged her to find someone to marry who would support her. This very bright girl is now divorced and feels intellectually cheated by her parents, who socialized her in the direction of marriage and away from a college education.

From a very early age, boys and girls see and hear about what kinds of jobs their parents engage in. In some cases, parents even take their children to work with them on jobs. Recently, while we were building our house, the bricklayer brought two of his adolescent sons with him to help. They were only fourteen and fifteen years old, yet were already engaging in apprenticeship work with their father.

Unfortunately, a number of parents seem to want to live vicariously through their sons' or daughters' occupational achievements. The mother who didn't get into medical school and the father who didn't make it as a professional athlete may pressure their youth to achieve occupational status that may be beyond the youths' reach or desires.

Some researchers have found that mothers and fathers have different effects on adolescents depending on the adolescents' ages. In one investigation, the work values of parents and youth in grades six, nine, ten, and twelve were compared (Wijting, Arnold, and Conrad, 1978). Work values assessed included social status of the job, activity (desire to keep busy at a job), job involvement (taking an interest in one's job), upward striving (seeking high-level jobs), earnings, and pride in work. The work values of the boys and girls were more similar to their same-sexed parents through the tenth grade, but during the twelfth grade, both boys and girls adopted work values more like those of their fathers than those of their mothers.

However, there are many complex factors that mediate these effects. For one, mothers who work regularly outside of the home and model effort and pride in their work may have strong influences on their daughters and sons throughout adolescence. A reasonable conclusion is that when both parents work and seem to enjoy it, boys and girls learn work values from both parents.

A recent investigation of the factors that contribute to adolescents' career decisions (Noeth, Engen, and Noeth, 1984) underscored the importance of parents. Among many possible factors, family influences (along with interesting classes) were rated the most helpful in making career decisions. Other research also has verified that adolescents are strongly influenced by their parents when career decisions are made (Abernathy and Davis, 1978; Basow and Howe, 1979).

In one study (Simpson, 1962), various combinations of parental and peer influences on occupational ambitions were investigated. When adolescents had friends and parents who had high occupational standards, they were more likely to be influenced by parents and peers than when both sets of social agents showed lower status occupational aspirations. When parents' and peers' standards varied, their occupational aspirations had an intermediate effect on adolescents. For lower class youth, when both parents and peers had high standards for occupational aspiration,

What are the most important factors influencing career decisions by adolescents?

Table 13.5 Some elements and outcomes of a school-based career education model

Element	Outcome
Career awareness	Career identity
Self-awareness	Self-identity
Appreciation, attitudes	Self- and social fulfillment
Decision-making skills	Career decisions
Economic awareness	Economic understanding
Skill awareness and beginning competence	Employment skills
Employability skills	Career placement
Educational awareness	Educational identity

almost three of every four students also showed high occupational aspirations, while less than one of every four students showed such aspirations when both their peers and parents had low standards.

School Influences

Teachers and counselors can have a strong influence on the adolescent's career development. Perhaps you can remember a teacher or a counselor who influenced your career decision making. In addition to thinking about a special teacher who might influence the adolescent's career development, a number of career education models have been established and they provide insight into the type of information adolescents obtain about careers.

Career Education Models Different types of career education models have been given a great deal of attention by vocational experts in recent years. In the 1970s, the U.S. Office of Education funded four different career education models: the school-based model, the employer-based model, the home-based model, and the rural-residential model. Many experts believe that the school is a critical influence on the adolescent's career

development. School is the primary setting where youth first encounter the world of work, and it provides an atmosphere for continuing self-development in relation to achievement and work. Further, it is the only institution in our society presently capable of providing the several delivery systems necessary for career education, such as instruction, guidance, placement, and community interaction. The elements of career education toward which the school-based model is directed, as well as the outcomes sought by the model, are detailed in table 13.5 (Herr, 1974).

Among other aspects of school-based career development models is the belief that the career implications of every school subject should be detailed to motivate students to gain a good education. School systems and state departments of education have developed brochures that describe occupations linked with social studies, math, foreign languages, business, science, and so forth. These brochures are distributed to students to encourage their awareness of the relation between educational curricula and career development (e.g., Stone and Shertzer, 1975).

National Survey of Career Information Systems in Secondary Schools Two national surveys provide further insight into the nature of career information adolescents have available to them (Chapman and Katz, 1983). In the first study, ten percent of all public secondary schools were queried and in the second study, 147 of these schools were asked further questions about their career education programs. Among the findings were that the most common single resource was the *Occupational Outlook Handbook* (OOH), with ninety-two percent of the schools having one or more copies. The second major resource was the *Dictionary of Occupational Titles* (DOT), with eighty-two percent having this book available for students. Of particular interest was the finding that about one-third of the schools had no one serving as head of career guidance and less than thirty percent of the schools had no established committee to review occupational information resources. When students talk to counselors, it usually is about high school courses, not about occupations. There were some differences between students coming from high-poverty areas when they were compared with students from low-poverty areas (both metropolitan, center city areas). Students in the high-poverty areas were more likely to rely on reports from former students and talk with counselors about where to get a job than their counterparts from low-poverty areas. Also, students in the low-poverty areas had more access to computers, more awareness of the computer's availability and use of it, and less participation in any category of experiential activity. Such findings support conclusions that were voiced earlier in the chapter on schools when we commented that schools often vary considerably in terms of their sociocultural characteristics and that schools in lower class neighborhoods often do not have resources that are as competent as schools in more affluent areas.

In our overview of career development, we have studied many different areas, such as the nature of occupations, cognitive factors, and sociocultural influences. Now we turn our attention to one final aspect of careers, the nature of career development in females.

Career Development in Females

We already have reviewed information about the achievement orientation of female adolescents. Here we focus on the related topic of career development in females.

Sociohistorical Context of Career Development in Females

No greater change has taken place in the working world than the increase in the number of females entering occupations that previously were thought to be appropriate only for males. More women than ever before are working outside the home. From 1900 until about 1940, about twenty percent of women fourteen years old and older worked. Since 1940, there has been a steady, marked increase in the number of women who work.

However, although some women are entering previously all-male occupations, the majority of women still have not achieved parity with men in the occupational marketplace. The difference between the average salaries for women and men is still huge. For example, in 1980 women in professional jobs earned only seventy-one percent of what their male counterparts made, and in clerical and sales jobs women earned only sixty-four percent and fifty-one percent of male earnings (Bureau of Labor Statistics, 1980). And while women have entered the work force in greater numbers than ever before, many of the jobs they have taken have been low-paying, low-status positions such as clerical jobs (Knudson, 1966).

In recent years, the ratio of females to males entering college has increased—in a recent five-year period, there was a thirty percent increase in female enrollment but only a twelve percent increase in male enrollment (VanDusen and Sheldon, 1976). More women are entering law school and medical school. Thus, greater numbers of late adolescent females are choosing education and a career over the traditional pattern of marriage, children, and homemaking.

Aletha Huston-Stein and Ann Higgens-Trenk (1978) have discussed some of the sociocultural factors that have affected the increasing numbers of women in colleges and jobs outside the home. The demand for female employees increased significantly after World War II because the number of job openings in traditionally female occupations (for example, nurse, teacher, clerical worker) increased at a more rapid pace than job availability in male occupations. Many married women were induced to enter the labor market for the first time. More recently, the number of traditionally female professional jobs, particularly in teaching,

Table 13.6 Expectations of High-, Average-, and Low-Achieving Boys and Girls

Group	Initial expectation		
	Grade 1	Grade 3	Total
Girls			
High achievers	6.2	2.6	4.4
Average achievers	6.6	7.8	7.2
Low achievers	6.6	8.2	7.4
Boys			
High achievers	7.6	6.6	7.1
Average achievers	8.8	6.4	7.6
Low achievers	4.6	4.8	4.7

Source: Stipek, D. J., and J. M. Hoffman, pp. 861–65.

has declined, so the greatest demand for female employment is in low-status positions (VanDusen and Sheldon, 1976).

A Model of Factors That Influence Career Choice in Females

In a recent study of factors that influence college women's career choices, Ruth Fassinger (1985) found that such career choices are influenced by an orientation toward both career and family, which are, in turn, affected by a combination of ability, achievement orientation, and feminist orientation. More precisely, high-ability feminist college females who show a strong achievement orientation seem to be both strongly career oriented and strongly family oriented as well. This career-family orientation appears to lead to career choices that tend to be high in prestige and often nontraditional for women. Much of the research effort aimed at identifying factors in the career choice of women has focused strongly on the career versus family distinction with examination of such variables as career salience being viewed as important in this inquiry. The present investigation suggests that both career *and* family plans are important in the career choice of college females. This orientation of females toward both family and career has been called the "new cultural imperative" for women (Rand and Miller, 1972). As an overall model of career choice for females, the information given here should be evaluated in the context of the sample selected—the females were juniors and seniors in college and selected a somewhat homogeneous set of careers—business/management/merchandising and allied medical professions (e.g., dental hygiene and nursing). Data from more varied samples, such as noncollege and/or lower socioeconomic status females as well as females with more varied occupational choices might reveal other predictive factors. Nonetheless, such research as that conducted by Fassinger (1985) calls clear attention to the fact that females are showing a strong interest in combining both family and career interests in their occupational choice.

The Career Development of Bright, Gifted Adolescent Girls

It appears that sometimes it is the brightest and most gifted adolescent girls who do not have achievement aspirations and career orientations that match their talents. For example, in one investigation (Stipek and Hoffman, 1980), the highest achieving girls actually had lower expectancies for success than the average or low achieving girls (for boys, the anticipated results were obtained, that is, higher achieving boys generated higher expectations for success) (table 13.6). And, in the gifted research at Johns Hopkins University (Fox, Brody, and Tobin, 1979), while many female junior high school students identified through a talent search for mathematically precocious youth did aspire to scientific and medical careers, only forty-six percent of these girls aspired to have a full-time career (compared to ninety-eight percent of the boys in the study). Gifted girls, perceiving a conflict between family and career, may decide against an occupation that requires an extensive personal commitment, precisely those careers that offer the highest status and salary. This decision to drop out of education or a career to marry and raise a family has been found to be detrimental to career advancement and income, with such females rarely ever catching up with their male counterparts (Card, Steele, and Abeles, 1980).

To counter such developmental sequences in females, several career education programs have been drafted and in some instances their effectiveness evaluated. An overview of such career development programs for gifted females is provided in Perspective on Adolescent Development 13.4.

REDIRECTING THE CAREER PATHS OF TALENTED ADOLESCENT FEMALES

*O*ne example of a career development program designed to change the career attitudes of gifted girls is called Project CHOICE (Creating Her Options in Career Education) and was developed by Case Western University (1979) to encourage gifted females to expand their career options by detecting barriers to reaching their potential. Eleventh-grade gifted female students were given prescriptive, individualized counseling that included interviews with female role models, referral to appropriate occupational groups, and information about career workshops.

Another career development program (Fox, 1976) was designed to change the career attitudes of junior high school females in regard to science and math, as well as to modify their course taking strategies. The girls were exposed to a three-month course taught by women that emphasized how math could be called on to solve social problems. In addition, individual and family counseling was given to the girls—counseling oriented toward increasing the girls' perceived competence. In comparison to a control group of junior high school girls who did not get these experiences, the participants subsequently were more likely to enroll in accelerated math classes. And over a two-year assessment period, the participants evidenced stronger interest in math careers than the control group girls. However, by the time the talented girls reached the tenth grade (the intervention program occurred in the seventh grade), the gains they had made in developing a stronger math and science orientation began to fade. Thus, as time passed and when further encouragement and support was not forthcoming, apparently the talented girls lost interest in such careers.

A third intervention program with gifted females was developed by Barbara Kerr (1983). The participants were twenty-three gifted girls and twenty-five gifted boys, all in the eleventh grade, who voluntarily attended the Guidance Laboratory at the University of Nebraska.

They initially were given career interest tests and then were allowed to select any part of the university to visit, such as the library or computer center, and were accompanied there by a university student host. Next, they were asked to select and attend a university class related to their career interest area, and arrangements were made for them to sit in on the class. After class visitation, the students lunched with the guidance center staff and university faculty members, discussing such matters as the morning's activities, school activities, and future career plans. In the afternoon, the students participated in individual and group counseling sessions. In the individual sessions, the counselors interpreted test results and discussed career interests. Counselors then helped the talented students set tentative career goals. The counselor attempted to raise the student's career aspirations if such aspirations (1) were clearly below the student's abilities as evidenced by grade-point average and achievement test scores; (2) were a sex-role stereotyped response by a female that was based on a lack of awareness; and (3) were a low-paying, low-status occupation. The counseling session ended with the discussion and completion of three forms: Personal Map of the Future, a goal-setting exercise; Suggestions for Parents, in which participants list three ways parents could help them achieve their career goals; and a similar exercise, Suggestions to a Significant Teacher or Counselor.

After individual counseling, all students participated in a life-planning group. In this exercise, the talented students were led on a guided fantasy into a "Perfect Future Day." The students shared fantasies with each other and then were moved toward a discussion of possible barriers that might impede their fantasies. The counselors focused on both internal and external constraints to career success. Sex-role stereotypes were discussed and high aspirations were encouraged. Counselors then distributed a Fact Sheet for Gifted Women and

How can the career paths of talented adolescent girls be helped?

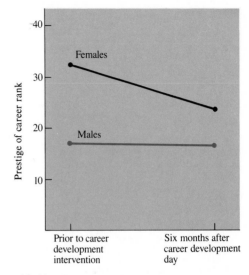

Figure 13.11 **The prestigiousness of careers selected by gifted eleventh grade boys and girls before and six months after an intensive, day-long career orientation at a university.** *(Note: Lower scores = more prestigious career.)*

Men, briefly describing the importance of high aspirations and the possibilities of combining both a family and a career. The afternoon ended with an evaluation of the workshop and an invitation to come to the guidance facility in the future and continue to use its resources.

Approximately six months after the one-day career development orientation, the gifted students responded to the question, "What occupation have you most recently considered?" The response to this question was compared to the gifted student's earlier response to his or her main career interest, assessed prior to the day-long career orientation. The results suggested that the girls increased their choices of prestigious careers over the six-month period, while the boys did not (figure 13.11). It is encouraging that the gifted girls raised their achievement aspirations after the intensive career development experience. It is not surprising that the prestige of the boys' aspirations did not change because they initially were very high. While other experiences in the six months besides the intensive career guidance seminar may account for the increase that was found, it seems likely that the day-long program is at least to some degree responsible. Still, it is important to be cautious about the long-term benefits of such programs because, as shown in the study by Fox (1976), there is a tendency for such effects to fade when intervention is discontinued.

Concept Table 13.3

CAREERS

Concept	Processes/related ideas	Characteristics/description
The nature of careers	Men and women in the labor force	There still is a large imbalance in the number of males and females employed in different vocations with far more males in managerial positions and far more females in clerical positions. Clearly a major change, though, has been the tremendous increase in the number of females in the labor force.
	The future occupations of today's adolescents	There will be a diminishing need for unskilled laborers and a continuing increase in jobs involving services. Education is still an important factor in the nature of the job obtained. Quite clearly a major increase in jobs related to computers will occur.
Theories of occupational choice	Ginzberg's developmental theory	This view argues that individuals move through three stages of occupational choice—fantasy, tentative, and realistic.
	Super's vocational self-concept theory	This perspective emphasizes that during adolescence a vocational self-concept is formed. Super says there are five stages of developing a vocational self-concept, ranging from crystallization at fourteen to eighteen years to consolidation after the age of thirty-five. Super emphasizes the importance of extensive exploration of careers during adolescence.
	Holland's personality type theory	This theory emphasizes the importance of the adolescent selecting a career that is compatible with his or her personality. Six personality types are described—realistic, intellectual, social, conventional, enterprising, and artistic.
	Evaluation of the vocational choice theories	The process of determining career choice is highly complex and while each of the theories described offers some helpful ideas for understanding career choice, there are some problems germane to each of the theories, such as the rather rigid age ranges in Ginzberg's and Super's views and the fact that adolescents cannot be neatly packaged into six categories as is the case in Holland's views. And, in terms of the vocational theories in general, they fail to emphasize two very important aspects of career choice: sociocultural influences and the nature of achievement-oriented processes.
Exploration and cognitive factors in career development	Exploration	Wide exploration of a variety of career paths during adolescence is one of the most consistent themes of those interested in enhancing the adolescent's career development. Too much of this exploration has been unsystematic. Instruction, guidance, and monitoring is usually helpful in developing more systematic exploration.

CAREERS

Concept	Processes/related ideas	Characteristics/description
	Planning and decision making	The first step in making a decision about a career is to recognize that a problem exists and then develop and possibly revise plans about future careers. Research suggests that even adolescents who say they know a great deal about a particular career often are wrong in their understanding of how much education is required for the career.
Sociocultural influences on careers	Social class	Social class is a powerful force in career development. Adolescents from lower class backgrounds often do not have achievement aspirations that match those of their middle-class counterparts.
	Parents and peers	Parents, in particular, and peers exert strong influences on career development. Parents serve as important career models for adolescents. Adolescents often indicate that their parents are the most important influence on their career choice. And, adolescents whose parents and peers have high occupational standards also are likely to have high standards themselves.
	School influences	Teachers and counselors can have a strong impact on the adolescent's career choice. A number of career education models have been developed. A national survey of career information systems in secondary schools revealed that the greatest resources available were the *Occupational Outlook Handbook* and the *Dictionary of Occupational Titles*. Adolescents from poverty areas have far fewer career resources than those from more affluent areas.
Career development in females	Sociohistorical context	No greater change has taken place in the working world than the increase in females entering occupations previously thought to be only accessible by males. In recent years, the ratio of females to males entering college also has increased and more women are entering such fields as law and medicine. The demand for female employees increased after WW II, but these primarily were low status jobs.
	A model of factors that influence career choice in females	It has been found that a female's career choice is related to an orientation toward both career and family, which are, in turn, affected by a combination of ability, achievement orientation, and feminist orientation. The fact that both a career and family orientation is present has sometimes been called the ''new cultural imperative.''
	Bright, gifted adolescent girls	It often has been the case that gifted, bright adolescent girls have not had achievement aspirations and career orientations that match their talents. Several career intervention programs have been devised to enhance the career aspirations of these talented females.

We have considered many different aspects of careers. A summary of main ideas related to career development in adolescence is presented in Concept Table 13.3. Now we evaluate a final aspect of the adolescent's achievement-oriented world, the nature of work in adolescence.

Work: The Tremendous Increase in Part-Time Work While Going to School

There have been few greater changes in the adolescent's life in recent years than the increased number of adolescents who work at least in some part-time capacity on a regular basis during the school year. First, we study the sociohistorical context of work during adolescence, then describe the types of jobs adolescents have as well as sex differences in those jobs. Next information about the interface of school and work is evaluated, followed by an overview of youth unemployment and career education programs and training programs designed to help out-of-work adolescents get jobs.

Sociohistorical Context of Adolescent Work

In 1974, the government Panel on Youth, headed by James Coleman, concluded that work has a positive impact on adolescents. According to Coleman and his colleagues, a job during adolescence creates a positive attitude toward work, allows students to learn from adults other than teachers or parents, and may help keep them out of trouble. The Panel on Youth recommended that more youth should be included in the work force of our country. To accomplish this goal, the Panel suggested that more work–study programs be developed, that the minimum wage be lowered, and that more flexible school–work schedules be allowed.

Over the past hundred years, the percentage of youth who work full-time as opposed to those who are in school has decreased dramatically. During the last half of the 1800s, less than one of every twenty high school-aged adolescents was in school, while more than

nine of every ten adolescents receive high school diplomas today. In the nineteenth century, many adolescents learned a trade from their father or some other adult member of the community. Now there is a much more prolonged period of educational training that has kept most adolescents out of the work force.

However, while such prolonged education has kept many contemporary youth from holding full-time jobs, it has in no way kept them from working on a part-time basis while going to school. Most high school seniors already have had some experience in the world of work. In a recent national survey of seventeen thousand high school seniors (Bachman, 1982), three of four reported that they have some job income during the average school week. And, for forty-one percent of the males and thirty percent of the females, this income exceeds fifty dollars a week. The typical part-time job for high school seniors involves sixteen to twenty hours a week, although ten percent work thirty hours a week or more.

Clearly, more adolescents are working at part-time jobs today than in past years. For example, in 1940, only one out of twenty-five tenth-grade males attended school and simultaneously worked part-time; in 1970, the number had increased to more than one out of every four. And again, as was just indicated, a full seventy-five percent of the students surveyed by Bachman said they had some kind of job income on a weekly basis. Current estimates also suggest that approximately one of every three ninth and tenth graders combine school and work (Cole, 1981).

Adolescents also are working longer hours now than in the past. For instance, the number of fourteen- and fifteen-year-olds who work more than fourteen hours per week has increased substantially in the last twenty years. A similar picture emerges for sixteen-year-olds. In 1960, forty-four percent of the sixteen-year-old males who attended school worked more than fourteen hours a week, but by 1970, the figure had increased to fifty-six percent.

What kinds of jobs are adolescents working at today? About seventeen percent of adolescents who work do so in restaurants, such as McDonald's, Burger King, and the like, waiting on customers, cleaning up, and such. Other adolescents work in retail stores as cashiers or salespeople (about twenty percent), in offices as clerical assistants (about ten percent), or as unskilled laborers (about ten percent) (Lewin-Epstein, 1981).

Are the jobs that male and female adolescents take the same and are they paid the same for their work? It seems that some jobs are almost always held by male adolescents (such as busboys—compared to busgirls, gardeners, manual laborers, and newspaper carriers) while other jobs are invariably filled by female adolescents (such as food counter workers, waitresses—compared to waiters, maids, and babysitters) (Greenberger and Steinberg, 1983). Further, it appears that male adolescents work longer hours than their female counterparts and they also are paid more (Greenberger and Steinberg, 1983). Thus, it seems that males and females are exposed to sex differences in the world of work before they enter the mature world of adult work, and that some of these differences may be inequitable.

Part-Time Work, School, and the Advantages/Disadvantages of Work during Adolescence

Does the increase in work seem to have benefits for adolescent development? In some cases yes, in others no. Ellen Greenberger and Lawrence Steinberg (1980, 1981) gave a questionnaire focusing on work experiences to students in four California high schools. Their findings disproved some common myths. For example, it generally is assumed that youth get extensive on-the-job training when they are hired for work—the reality is that they get little training at all, according to the researchers. Also, it is assumed that youth, through work experiences, learn to get along better with adults. However, adolescents reported that they rarely feel close to the adults they work with. The work experiences of the adolescents did help them understand how the business world works, how to get and keep a job, and how to manage money. Working also helped the youth to learn to budget their time, to take pride in their accomplishments, and to evaluate their goals.

Working adolescents often have to give up sports, social affairs with peers, and sometimes sleep. And the youth have to balance the demands of work, school, and family.

In their investigation, Greenberger and Steinberg asked adolescents about their grade point averages, school attendance, satisfaction from school, and the number of hours spent studying and in extracurricular activities since they began working. The findings: working adolescents had lower grade point averages than nonworkers. More than one of every four students reported that their grades dropped when they began working, while only one of nine said their grades improved. But it wasn't just working that affected the adolescents' grades—more importantly, it was the number of hours worked. Tenth graders who worked more than fourteen hours a week suffered a drop in grades, while eleventh graders worked up to twenty hours a week before their grades began to drop. When adolescents are spending more than twenty hours a week working, there is little time to study for tests and do homework assignments.

In addition to the effect of work on grades, working adolescents also felt less involved in school, were absent more, and said they didn't enjoy school as much (compared to their nonworking peers). Adolescents who worked also spent less time with their families—but just as much time with their peers—as their nonworking counterparts.

In weighing the benefits and pitfalls of work during adolescence, Sheila Cole (1980) concluded:

> Working is a part of growing up. Like other aspects of growing up, it brings young people independence and freedom. And, like growing up, it introduces teenagers to the limitations of their own lives.
>
> Adolescents do not like to have to ask for money each time they want to go somewhere or buy something. Having their own money makes them free to act and brings a wonderful, powerful feeling that, at least initially, outweighs all but the most serious annoyances of work.

What are the positive and negative features of part-time work coupled with full-time schooling during adolescence?

It is natural for young people to grow impatient with the sheltered circle of family, school, and friends and to want to test themselves in the wider world. Work gives adolescents an opportunity to do just that. It also requires them to get along with others and to adjust their behavior so that a job gets done. And it gives them a chance to learn about money and the general aspects of working that they will need to know as adults.

Families also benefit, at least financially, when a teenager works. Many families can no longer afford to give their children enough pocket money to go out with their friends, to learn skills such as playing the guitar or skiing, to buy the materials for hobbies and projects, or to run a car—the only means of access to social life in some parts of the country. Few would argue that activities of this sort are unnecessary. But having to pay for them is a strain that may cause resentment.

Adolescents who take some of the burden on themselves earn parental respect and often reduce household tensions.

The benefits to society also seem apparent. Working teenagers participate in society and contribute to it by being productive. High schoolers working part-time do not take jobs away from adults; students work in the service and retail sectors of the economy at jobs that adults cannot generally afford to take because the pay is too low and fringe benefits and job protection are lacking. Many companies that employ teenagers would not survive without a ready supply of part-time labor willing to work under such conditions. Adolescent workers also contribute to the economy as consumers. On the average, working high school students in the Greenberger-Steinberg study earned more than two hundred dollars a month.

But there are negative aspects of work that make me a cautious advocate—especially for those who have a choice. While working helps a high school student pay for social activities, it also takes time away from these activities. Teenage jobholders often complain about how little time they have left just to daydream and fool around. Yet daydreaming and fooling around without responsibility to anyone or anything are essential to exploring oneself and one's interests and relations to others. Adolescence is one of the few times in our lives when we have the freedom to make these explorations. Do we really want a society of teenagers who only work and go to school and go to school and work, who are closed in by organized activity and commitments?

Most of the work that young people are paid to do is not very interesting, enriching, or worthwhile in a broad social sense. Adolescent workers learn that sorry fact early, so money becomes the motivating force in their work. This is natural enough, but is it desirable? Do we want money to assume that kind of importance so early?

Cynicism and apathy are some of the inevitable by-products of jobs that exploit and abuse. Such attitudes cloak feelings of powerlessness and helplessness, but do not assuage them. Do we want our kids to be "broken in" to these attitudes at an early age?

All these are questions of values. In some families, teenage work is a necessity. But for many families, there is a choice. Few American households are so affluent that a little extra income would not be welcome, or so poor that full-time adolescent labor is necessary. For such families there is no formula that will yield a "correct" decision in all cases.

Perhaps the most useful contribution of recent research is the estimate it gives us of how many hours a young person can profitably work. It is helpful to know that, on the average, the benefits of work can be acquired in about fourteen hours of work a week, and that after twenty hours negative consequences begin to outweigh the positive ones. Those ball-park figures, plus common sense, represent our best resources for making decisions about kids and work. (Cole, 1980, p. 68)

Unemployment among Adolescents and Career Education Programs and Training Programs

How widespread is unemployment for adolescents? How effective are career education programs and training programs to combat such unemployment?

Unemployment

There has been a considerable amount of media attention directed at unemployment among teenagers in recent years. However, overall it appears that such unemployment is not as widespread as the media stereotype suggests. For example, based on data collected by the U.S. Department of Labor, one study revealed that more than nine of ten adolescent boys either were in school, working at a job, or both, with only five percent out of school, without a job, and looking for full-time employment (Feldstein and Ellwood, 1982). And, most of the adolescents who did not have a job were not unemployed for prolonged periods of time. For instance, almost one-half of the unemployed adolescents had been out of work for one month or less, and only ten percent had been without a job for six months or more. It is important to note that the major portion of adolescents who are unemployed are individuals who have dropped out of school.

Table 13.7 Percentages of unemployed youths and adults

	Whites	Blacks and other minorities
Men twenty years and older	5.1	8.3
Women twenty years and older	3.5	10.2
Men sixteen to nineteen years old	14.1	34.8
Women sixteen to nineteen years old	13.9	35.9

Source: U.S. Department of Labor, Special Labor Force Report No. 218 (Washington, D.C.: U.S. Government Printing Office, 1979), p. 9.

However, while it appears that the media have exaggerated the extent of unemployment among adolescents, a disproportionate number of unemployed adolescents are black. As indicated in table 13.7, the unemployment situation is particularly acute for blacks and other minorities between the ages of sixteen and nineteen. One survey revealed that in 1979 only fifty percent of Hispanic adolescents held jobs (Rosenbaum, 1983). Since 1960, though, the job situation has improved for black adolescents, particularly black males. For example, in 1960, forty-four percent of black male adolescents were unemployed, but by 1979, the figure had been reduced to thirty percent (Rosenbaum, 1983).

Thus, while the world of adolescent unemployment is not as bleak as the media stereotype suggests, there is every reason to be concerned about the disproportionate number of blacks and other minority adolescents, particularly those from low socioeconomic backgrounds, in the unemployed adolescent pool. Let's look now at the nature of programs that have been developed to help unemployed adolescents get jobs.

Career Education and Training Programs

Lawrence Steinberg (1982) has described how career education and youth training programs have not been as successful as their architects had hoped. He points out how in the early 1970s career education was introduced as a means of solving the problems youth encounter in finding jobs and developing careers. Career education was designed to develop competence in basic academic skills, awareness of continuing education opportunities, good work habits, meaningful work values and a desire to work, entry-level occupational skills, competence in making career choices, incorporation of work values into personal values, and successful job placement (Herr, 1977).

In reviewing the success of career education programs, Steinberg (1982) concluded that in many ways the programs have not lived up to their promises. Most career education programs seem to have little or no impact on the acquisition of basic skills or on school retention, and they are not likely to have a dramatic effect on employability. However, there is some evidence that career education does promote the learning of work-related skills and information and does instill healthy values toward work, although such effects are often short-lived and frequently disappear after program termination.

While career education programs are designed to alleviate the transition of all adolescents from school to the workplace, youth employment programs usually have been targeted for those adolescents whose transition is the most difficult—those who are from lower class families and those who are nonwhite. For example, in 1977, the Youth Employment and Demonstration Projects Act (YEDPA), set up by the federal government, was authorized to spend approximately three billion dollars over three years. In summarizing the results of the most massive federal program ever undertaken to improve the occupational development of disadvantaged, minority-group youth, Steinberg (1982) concluded that there is little convincing evidence that such youth employment and training programs have had much of an impact on adolescent education, socialization, and subsequent employment. While such programs do seem to lead to increased rates of school retention and graduation, there are no supporting data on the socialization outcomes of such programs. And, for the most part, the evidence concerning subsequent employment and earnings is disappointing. After a period of years, youth who have participated in the training programs have not fared any better than their counterparts who have not participated.

In examining why such federal youth employment programs have not been as successful as hoped for with disadvantaged and minority-group youth, Swinton (1980) found three problems: (1) structural problems in the labor market (a failure of the labor market to effectively match youth with job demands for youth); (2) low demand for young workers; and (3) difficulties in the supply characteristics of youth (employability problems). A summary of Swinton's thoughts about unemployed youth follows:

> The programmatic implication of our analysis for manpower policies, [i.e., policies designed to affect the supply characteristics, or employability, of youth] as a class is clear. Namely, the youth/adult differential, the overall high level of youth unemployment, and the racial differential can be affected only marginally by policies which operate on the supply characteristics of youth. . . . The characteristics of youth which account for these [employment] gaps are nonpathological and are related to stage of life and thus cannot be reached by [personnel development] programs since the characteristics of youth that can be reached by these programs such as education, skills, motivation, do not account for much of the gap. . . . Our analysis indicates that the principal need is for policies that either increase the market demand for youth or supplement it with nonlabor market activities if either the high levels of youth unemployment, the youth/adult differential, or the problems of the disadvantaged is to be seriously dealt with. (Swinton, 1980, pp. 35–36)

This concludes our discussion of achievement, careers, and the role of work in adolescence. In this chapter, we have seen that achievement, careers, and work are often associated in some ways with the schools adolescents attend. In the next section on problems and disturbances in adolescence, we will see that many of the difficulties adolescents experience often seem to be school-related as well.

Summary

I. Information about achievement focuses on a variety of topics, processes, and issues, which include motivation, theories of achievement and achievement-related factors, sociocultural influences, and achievement orientation in female adolescents.

 A. Motivation involves the question of why people do what they do. Motivated behavior is energized and directed. The grand views of cognitive developmental theory and information processing emphasize the motivation of the adolescent for knowledge and information; psychoanalytic theories, particularly Freud's, stress that achievement behavior is subservient to instinctual forces; and the behavioral views emphasize the rewarding aspects of the environment.

 B. Among the important theories of achievement and achievement-related factors are achievement motivation, attribution theory, and delay of gratification.

  1. McClelland argued that achievement motivation is a property of the individual and is part of the person's need system. He described *n* achievement as the individual's internal striving for success. Atkinson expanded McClelland's ideas, specifying more precisely the importance of such factors as hope for success and fear of failure. In this regard, he believed that expectations for success should outweigh anxiety about failing. In many instances, an optimal level of anxiety is moderate rather than high or low, although there are exceptions.

  2. There has been considerable interest in attribution theory in recent years. Attribution theory argues that individuals are cognitive beings who want to know why they and others are behaving in a particular way. In particular, attribution theorists have analyzed achievement situations in terms of internal and external factors as well as in terms of stability factors. In general, they argue that when individuals perceive their achievement is internally determined, especially effort based, then achievement will be enhanced. Weiner believes emotional reactions to attributions about success and failure are important. Locus of control is a concept closely linked to internal and external aspects of achievement.

  3. In addition to achievement motivation and attribution, it is important to consider the process of delay of gratification, which is an important aspect of success in school and achievement-related situations. Mischel argues that delay of gratification can be influenced by situational factors, particularly the nature of the individual's cognition, but also that information about delay of gratification in childhood can predict adolescent adjustment.

 C. Among the important sociocultural influences on achievement are cultural standards, parental and peer influences, and school and teachers. A consideration of these important sociocultural influences suggests that the issue of internal and external factors involved in achievement is an important one and deserves further attention.

  1. Adolescents in the United States characteristically have been more achievement oriented than most of their

counterparts from other cultures. The ingredients for achievement orientation are often much stronger in middle-class than lower class contexts.

2. Modeling of the achievement orientations of parents and peers is an important part of achievement, as is social comparison with peers. While having parents who model achievement is important, some parents do not provide adequate support for the development of the adolescent's achievement. Some educational strategists recommend that there should be an emphasis on cooperation and internal standards for success rather than competition or social comparison, although the implementation of this strategy is difficult.

3. The descriptions of effective schools by Lipsitz in Chapter 8 need to be considered when evaluating the role of schools in the adolescent's achievement—she found that being serious about individual variation, showing a deep concern for what is known about adolescent development, and a caring and commitment orientation were important. Getting students to attribute their achievement to internal factors, particularly effort, is often a lengthy, difficult process. Observational learning is important in school contexts with the teacher and the most popular peer sometimes imitated. Intrinsic motivation seems best when students are doing well and showing a strong achievement orientation, but extrinsic motivation may be important to call on in low-achieving adolescents.

4. The implication from attribution theory is that internal factors should be promoted when getting the adolescent to analyze the causes of his or her

behavior is at issue. However, it is important to recognize that achievement involves both internal and external causes, and further that teasing these apart is not easy. Too often these factors have been pitted against each other, when actually some of the most highly achievement-oriented adolescents are those who have both a high standard of excellence and are competitive.

5. Information about achievement orientation in females focuses on cultural standards, ideas about instrumental competence or incompetence, parenting orientation and developmental precursors, learned helplessness, and conclusions about sex differences in achievement and competence. It is inaccurate to conclude that female adolescents are less achievement and competence oriented in general—such conclusions must be described in terms of specific domains of achievement and competence, and take into consideration sociohistorical prescriptions for success.

II. Information about career development in adolescence focuses on the nature of careers, theories of occupational choice, exploration and cognitive factors, sociocultural factors, and career development in females.

A. There still is a large imbalance in the labor force in terms of the percentage of males and females in particular occupations. For example, there are far more male managers and far more female clerical workers. Clearly, a major change though has been the tremendous influx of females into the labor pool. There will be a diminishing need for unskilled workers in the future and a continuing increase in need for service jobs. Computer-related careers are expected to be a particularly salient area in the future job market.

B. Three well-known theories of occupational choice are those of Ginzberg, Super, and Holland.

1. Ginzberg argues that individuals move through three stages of career choice from fantasy in childhood, through a tentative stage, and then onto a realistic stage in adolescence.

2. Super says that during adolescence a vocational self-concept is formed and that there are five stages involved in its development. He stresses the importance of career exploration.

3. Holland argues that the adolescent needs to select a career that matches his or her personality.

4. Each of the theories has its own individual problems and as a group, they do not pay nearly enough attention to sociocultural factors and achievement-related processes.

C. Wide exploration of a variety of career paths is one of the most consistently emphasized aspects of career development in adolescence. Planning and decision making are important cognitive factors involved in career development.

D. Among the important sociocultural influences on careers are those involving social class, parents and peers, and schools.

1. Lower class adolescents often do not have achievement aspirations that match those of their middle-class counterparts.

2. Parents, in particular, and peers exert powerful influences on career development.

3. Teachers and counselors can have strong influences on the adolescent's career development as well. A number of career education models have been developed. It has been found that adolescents from poverty areas have far fewer career resources than those from more affluent areas.

E. No greater sociohistorical change in adolescents has occurred in recent years than in the number of females entering occupations that previously were reserved only for males. The adolescent female's career choice often is linked to both career and family roles, rather than one or the other alone, and is influenced by the achievement orientation, ability, and feminist orientation of the girl. It often has been the case that gifted, bright adolescent girls have not had achievement and career aspirations that match their talents. Several career intervention programs have been developed for these talented females.

III. Information about work during adolescence focuses on its sociohistorical context, part-time work, school, and the advantages or disadvantages of work, as well as unemployment and career education and training programs for adolescents.

A. Adolescents are not as likely today to hold full-time jobs as their adolescent counterparts from the nineteenth century. However, while prolonged education has meant a decrease in the number of adolescents holding down full-time jobs, there has been a tremendous increase in the number of adolescents who have part-time jobs and continue to go to school. Adolescents often do not have jobs that pay well or are very meaningful in a direct way for their subsequent careers in adulthood. Female adolescents often have different kinds of jobs than male adolescents and are paid less, mirroring the findings with adults.

B. The adolescents' jobs seem to have advantages and disadvantages. The advantages include learning how the business world works, how to get and keep a job, how to manage money, to learn to budget time, to take pride in their accomplishments, and to evaluate their goals. The disadvantages include the likelihood that they often have to give up sports, social affairs with peers, and sometimes sleep, and they have to balance the demands of work, school, and family. Working more than fourteen hours a week is associated with lower grades in the tenth grade and working more than twenty hours a week similarly is linked with lower grades in eleventh graders. Adolescents who work feel less integrated into the school, are absent from school more, and say they don't enjoy school as much as their nonworking peers.

C. While there has been widespread media attention on youth unemployment, the fact is that such unemployment in general is not that widespread. The major portion of adolescents who are unemployed are school dropouts. The most acute problem of unemployment resides with black and other minority group adolescents, as well as youth from the lower socioeconomic class. While career education and training programs have been developed for unemployed adolescents, they have not met with very much success.

Key Terms

achievement and support *538*

attribution theory *530*

delay of gratification *532*

external locus of control *532*

extrinsic motivation *543*

fantasy stage *553*

fear of failure *529*

freedom and responsibility *538*

hope for success *529*

incentives *543*

internal locus of control *532*

intrinsic motivation *543*

loyalty and commitment *538*

motivation *527*

n achievement *528*

realistic stage *553*

state anxiety *530*

tentative stage *553*

trait anxiety *530*

Suggested Readings

Ames, R. E., and Ames, C. (Eds.). (1984). *Motivation in education.* New York: Academic Press.
This book includes many ideas by leading scholars on the topic of achievement orientation. A number of chapters are devoted to ideas on attributions.

Dweck, C., and Eliot, E. S. (1983). Achievement motivation. In P. H. Mussen (Ed.), *Handbook of Child Psychology,* 4th ed., vol. 4. New York: Wiley.
This detailed chapter provides a contemporary overview of attribution theory and achievement along with considerable information about achievement orientation in female adolescents.

Journal of Occupational Behavior
This research journal has many articles that pertain to career development in adolescence. Go to your library and look through the issues of the last several years to get a feel for the kinds of issues that are interesting to researchers who study the nature of career development.

Lewin-Epstein, N. (1981). *Youth employment during high school.* Washington, D.C.: National Center for Education Statistics.
To learn more about adolescent work experiences read Lewin-Epstein's material. Included is interesting information about many aspects of part-time work and schooling described in this chapter as well as other aspects of adolescent work.

Vocational Guidance Quarterly
This research journal includes many articles pertaining to counseling strategies with adolescents in regard to their career development. Go to your library and look through the issues of the 1980s to get a sense for what kind of career guidance is available for adolescents.

Chapter 14

Drugs, Alcohol, and Delinquency

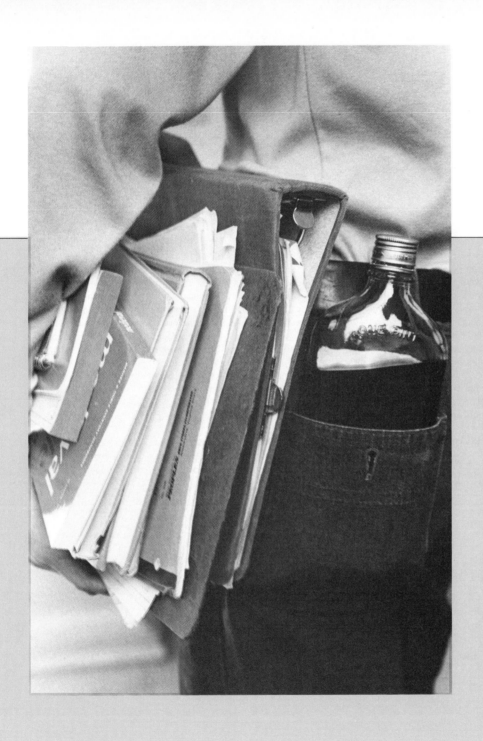

Prologue

Annie, Cheerleader with a Drinking Problem

Some mornings Annie, a fifteen-year-old cheerleader, was too drunk to go to school. Other days, she'd stop for a couple of beers or a screwdriver on the way to school. She was tall and blonde and good looking, and no one who sold her liquor, even at 8:00 in the morning, questioned her age. Where did she get her money? From babysitting and what her mother gave her to buy lunch. She no longer is a cheerleader—she was kicked off the squad for missing practice so frequently . . . and, eventually, her supervisor found out about her drinking problem. Soon she and several of her peers were drinking almost every morning, and often during and after school. Sometimes they even skipped school and went to the woods to drink. Annie's whole life began to revolve around her drinking. It went on for two years, and during the last summer, anytime anybody saw her she was drunk.

Unfortunately, there are hundreds of thousands of adolescents just like this young girl. They live in both wealthy suburbs and inner-city housing projects. The cheerleader grew up in a Chicago suburb, and said she started drinking when she was ten because her older brothers always looked like they were having fun when they were doing it. She said it made her feel good and peaceful, and commented that drinking made her feel more sociable, more confident and open. After a while, her parents began to suspect her problem. But even when they punished her, it didn't stop her drinking. . . . Finally, this year, she started dating a boy she really likes and who wouldn't put up with her drinking. She agreed to go to Alcoholics Anonymous and has just successfully completed treatment. She has stopped drinking for four months now, and hopefully her abstinence will continue. Alcohol abuse often leads to many problems for adolescents, just as it did for the cheerleader.

*T*his is the first of two chapters that focus on problems and disturbances in adolescence. From time to time in our discussion of adolescence, we have touched on problems that adolescents encounter and mentioned some possible ways these problems could be alleviated. For example, Chapter 2 provided examples of how behavioral and psychoanalytic perspectives could be called on to help adolescents with problems. Chapter 6 described the family systems approach to therapy and the humanistic approaches of Haim Ginnott and Everett Shostrum. Chapter 7 portrayed the peer sociotherapy approach of Robert Selman. Chapter 10 discussed problems related to identity development and Chapter 11 evaluated sexual disturbances. However, in the two chapters you are about to read, we will focus exclusively on problems and disturbances in adolescence. This first chapter explores three major problems that affect the lives of many adolescents—drugs, alcohol, and delinquency.

Drugs: Starting to Decline but Still Too Pervasive

Let's explore three questions about drug use in adolescence. What is the range of drugs used by adolescents? What is the actual use of specific drugs by adolescents? And, what is the nature of school involvement in drug use?

The Range of Drugs

Drug abuse has become pervasive among adolescents. The common types of drugs adolescents take are listed in table 14.1. Notice that alcohol and tobacco (which contains the stimulant nicotine) are included on the list. Also noted in the table is the slang name of each drug, its source, general classification of drugs it belongs to, how it is taken, kinds of effects sought, long-term symptoms, physical and mental dependence potential, and whether the drug has the potential to cause organic damage. Note in the table that researchers now believe that marijuana may have damaging organic effects.

The most extensive data about the use of drugs by adolescents comes from ongoing research by Lloyd Johnston, Jerald Bachman, and Patrick O'Malley at the Institute of Social Research, University of Michigan. For a number of years they have been charting the drug habits of very large numbers of randomly selected adolescents across the United States. Among their recent findings for 1984 high school seniors are the following (Johnston, Bachman, and O'Malley, 1985):

> Almost two-thirds of all seniors reported illicit drug use at some point in their lives. However, a substantial proportion have used only marijuana.
>
> Marijuana is by far the most widely used illicit drug with 54.9 percent saying they have used this drug at some point in their lives.
>
> The most widely used class of other drugs is stimulants with 27.9 percent having used these at some point in their lives.
>
> The most widely used licit (legal) drug is alcohol (92.6% ever used in lifetime) with nicotine second in this category (69.7% having smoked cigarettes at some point in their lives).

A summary of these findings for 1984 high school seniors is presented in table 14.2, along with drug information pertaining to use in the past month, past year, not past month, not in the past year, and never used.

Trends in Drug Use

The Institute of Social Research at the University of Michigan has been charting drug use of high school seniors since 1975. In this section, we will study the trends in drug use from 1975 through 1984 (Johnston, Bachman, and O'Malley, 1985).

Table 14.1 Facts about drugs

Name	Slang name	Source	Classification	How taken
Heroin	H., Horse, Scat, Junk, Smack, Scag, Stuff, Dope	Semisynthetic (from morphine)	Narcotic	Injected or sniffed
Morphine	White stuff, M.	Natural (from opium)	Narcotic	Swallowed or injected
Methadone	Dolly	Synthetic	Narcotic	Swallowed or injected
Cocaine	Coke, Corrine, Gold dust, Bernice, Flake, Star dust, Snow	Natural (from coca, not cocoa)	Stimulant, local anesthesia	Sniffed, injected, or swallowed
Marijuana	Pot, Grass, Hash, Tea, Dope, Joints, Reefers	Natural	Relaxant, euphoriant; in high doses, hallucinogen	Smoked, swallowed, or sniffed
Barbiturates	Barbs, Blue devils, Reds, Yellow jackets, Phennies, Downers, Blue heavens	Synthetic	Sedative-hypnotic	Swallowed or injected
Amphetamines	Bennies, Dexies, Speed, Wake-ups, Hearts, Pep pills, Uppers	Synthetic	Sympatho-mimetic	Swallowed or injected
LSD	Acid, Sugar, Big D, Cubes, Trips	Semisynthetic (from ergot alkaloids)	Hallucinogen	Swallowed
Mescaline	Mesc	Natural (from peyote)	Hallucinogen	Swallowed
Psilocybin	Magic mushroom	Natural (from psilocybe)	Hallucinogen	Swallowed
Alcohol	Booze, Juice, etc.	Natural (from grapes, grains via fermentation)	Sedative-hypnotic	Swallowed
Tobacco	Cancer tube, Coffin nail, etc.	Natural	Stimulant-sedative	Smoked, sniffed, chewed

Persons who inject drugs under nonsterile conditions run a high risk of contracting hepatitis, abscesses, or circulatory disorders.

Note: Question marks indicate conflict of opinion.

Source: Adapted from Today's Education: NEA Journal *(February 1971).*

Table 14.1 Continued

Effects sought	Long-term symptoms	Physical dependence potential	Mental dependence potential	Organic damage potential
Euphoria, prevent withdrawal discomfort	Addiction, constipation, loss of appetite	Yes	Yes	No*
Euphoria, prevent withdrawal discomfort	Addiction, constipation, loss of appetite	Yes	Yes	No*
Prevent withdrawal discomfort	Addiction, constipation, loss of appetite	Yes	Yes	No
Excitation, talkativeness	Depression, convulsions	No	Yes	Yes?
Relaxation; increased euphoria, perceptions, sociability	Usually none	No	Yes?	Yes?
Anxiety reduction, euphoria	Addiction with severe withdrawal symptoms, possible convulsions, toxic psychosis	Yes	Yes	Yes
Alertness, activeness	Loss of appetite, delusions, hallucinations, toxic psychosis	Yes?	Yes	Yes
Insightful experiences, exhilaration, distortion of senses	May intensify existing psychosis, panic reactions	No	No?	No?
Insightful experiences, exhilaration, distortion of senses	?	No	No?	No?
Insightful experiences, exhilaration, distortion of senses	?	No	No?	No?
Sense alteration, anxiety reduction, sociability	Cirrhosis, toxic psychosis, neurologic damage, addiction	Yes	Yes	Yes
Calmness, sociability	Emphysema, lung cancer, mouth and throat cancer, cardiovascular damage, loss of appetite	Yes?	Yes	Yes

	Ever used	Past month	Past year, not past month	Not past year	Never used
Marijuana/Hashish	54.9	25.2	14.8	14.9	45.1
Inhalants	*19.0*	*2.7*	*5.2*	*11.1*	*81.0*
Amyl and Butyl Nitrites	8.1	1.4	2.6	4.1	91.9
Hallucinogens	*13.3*	*3.6*	*4.3*	*5.4*	*86.7*
LSD	8.0	1.5	3.2	3.3	92.0
PCP	5.0	1.0	1.3	2.7	95.0
Cocaine	16.1	5.8	5.8	4.5	83.9
Heroin	1.3	0.3	0.2	0.8	98.7
Other opiates	9.7	1.8	3.4	4.5	90.3
Stimulants	*27.9*	*8.3*	*9.4*	*10.2*	*72.1*
Sedatives	13.3	2.3	1.5	9.5	86.7
Barbiturates	9.9	1.7	3.2	5.0	90.1
Methaqualone	8.3	1.1	2.7	4.5	91.7
Tranquilizers	12.4	2.1	4.0	6.3	87.6
Alcohol	92.6	67.2	18.8	6.6	7.4
Cigarettes	69.7	29.3	40.4		30.3

Note: Based on national sample of 15,900 high school seniors.
Source: After Johnston, L. D., Bachman, J. G., and P. M. O'Malley, News and Information Services Release, *Institute of Social Research, University of Michigan, Ann Arbor. January 4, 1985.*

It appears that at some point near the end of the 1970s and the beginning of the 1980s, a turning point in adolescents' use of illicit drugs occurred. Since that time, illicit drug use by adolescents overall has gradually declined. Table 14.3 shows the percentage of high school seniors who used a particular drug in the last thirty days. Note that marijuana use peaked in 1978 and has continued to decline every year thereafter. Also notice that hallucinogen use peaked in 1979 and has declined each year since that time. With regard to licit drugs, alcohol use peaked in 1980 and has gradually declined thereafter. Cigarette smoking peaked in 1976 and has dropped considerably since that time.

Sex Differences

Overall adolescent males are more involved in drug use than their female counterparts (table 14.4). In the national survey by Johnston, Bachman, and O'Malley (1981), marijuana use at any point in the last thirty days was slightly higher for males, but for daily use, males used marijuana about twice as much as females (9.6 versus 4.2 percent). Adolescent males also take most other illicit drugs more often than females—inhalants, hallucinogens, heroin, cocaine, and barbiturates. For the 1981 data, females were more likely to take stimulants than males at any time during the last thirty days. More recent data reveal how it is important to evaluate stimulants in terms of different classes, such as diet pills vs. stay-awake pills. In this regard, females were much more likely than males to take diet pills (43.1 vs. 14.8 percent) while males were somewhat more likely to take stay-awake pills in the thirty-day period (Johnston, Bachman, and O'Malley, 1985). Note also that female adolescents were more likely to smoke cigarettes than their male counterparts at some point in the last thirty days.

Now that we have studied the overall use of a number of drugs, trends in use, and sex differences, we turn our attention in more detail to some of the specific drugs most often taken by adolescents.

Drug	Class of 1975	Class of 1976	Class of 1977	Class of 1978	Class of 1979	Class of 1980	Class of 1981	Class of 1982	Class of 1983	Class of 1984	1983 to 1984 change
Approx. N =	(9400)	(15400)	(17100)	(17800)	(15500)	(15900)	(17500)	(17700)	(16300)	(15900)	
Marijuana/Hashish	27.1%	32.2%	35.4%	37.1%	36.5%	33.7%	31.6%	28.5%	27.0%	25.2%	−1.8%
Inhalants	NA	0.9	1.3	1.5	1.7	1.4	1.5	1.5	1.7	1.9	+0.2
Inhalants Adjusted[a]	NA	NA	NA	NA	3.1	2.7	2.3	2.5	2.7	2.7	0.0
Amyl and Butyl Nitrites[b]	NA	NA	NA	NA	2.4	1.8	1.4	1.1	1.4	1.4	0.0
Hallucinogens	4.7	3.4	4.1	3.9	4.0	3.7	3.7	3.4	2.8	2.6	−0.2
LSD	2.3	1.9	2.1	2.1	2.4	2.3	2.5	2.4	1.9	1.5	−0.4
PCP	NA	NA	NA	NA	2.4	1.4	1.4	1.0	1.3	1.0	−0.3
Cocaine	1.9	2.0	2.9	3.9	5.7	5.2	5.8	5.0	4.9	5.8	+0.9
Heroin	0.4	0.2	0.3	0.3	0.2	0.2	0.2	0.2	0.2	0.3	+0.1
Stimulants[c]	8.5	7.7	8.8	8.7	9.9	12.1	15.8	13.7	12.4	NA	NA
Stimulants Adjusted[b,c]	NA	NA	NA	NA	NA	NA	NA	10.7	8.9	8.3	−0.6
Sedatives[c]	5.4	4.5	5.1	4.2	4.4	4.8	4.6	3.4	3.0	2.3	−0.7
Barbiturates[c]	4.7	3.9	4.3	3.2	3.2	2.9	2.6	2.0	2.1	1.7	−0.4
Methaqualone[c]	2.1	1.6	2.3	1.9	2.3	3.3	3.1	2.4	1.8	1.1	−0.7
Tranquilizers[c]	4.1	4.0	4.6	3.4	3.7	3.1	2.7	2.4	2.5	2.1	−0.4
Alcohol	68.2	68.3	71.2	72.1	71.8	72.0	70.7	69.7	69.4	67.2	−2.2
Cigarettes	36.7	38.8	38.4	36.7	34.4	30.5	29.4	30.0	30.3	29.3	−1.0

[a]*Adjusted for underreporting of amyl and butyl nitrites.*

[b]*Adjusted for overreporting of the nonprescription stimulants.*

[c]*Only drug use which was not under a doctor's orders is included here.*

Source: After Johnston, L. D., Bachman, J. G., and P. M. O'Malley, News and Information Services Release, *Institute of Social Research, University of Michigan, Ann Arbor, January 4, 1985.*

Specific Drugs Taken by Adolescents

Adolescents have sampled a variety of drugs, including marijuana, nicotine, stimulants, depressants, hallucinogens, cocaine, heroin, and inhalants.

Marijuana

What is marijuana? What are its psychological and physical effects? Why do adolescents use marijuana? What are parent–peer influences on marijuana use? What is the nature of marijuana laws? And, what are some further trends in marijuana use?

What Is Marijuana? Marijuana comes from the hemp plant, *Cannabis sativa,* which originated in central Asia, but now is grown in most parts of the world. Marijuana is composed of the hemp plant's dried leaves; its dried resin is known as hashish. Both marijuana and hashish can be taken orally, but are usually smoked. Although the resin is about six times as powerful as the leaf, the marijuana smoked today is more powerful than in past years. More sophisticated cultivation and higher quality seed stock have produced marijuana with six to ten times as much THC, the active chemical ingredient in marijuana (Russell, 1980).

Table 14.4 Thirty-day prevalence of use of sixteen types of drugs by sex (1981)

Drug	Male	Female
Marijuana	35.3	27.3
Inhalants*	1.9	1.1
Amyl/Butyl Nitrites	2.2	0.6
Hallucinogens*	4.6	2.6
LSD	3.4	1.4
PCP	1.7	1.0
Cocaine	6.3	5.0
Heroin	0.3	0.1
Other Opiates	2.4	1.8
Stimulants	14.7	16.7
Sedatives	5.2	3.9
Barbiturates	2.9	2.4
Methaqualone	3.7	2.4
Tranquilizers	2.7	2.6
Alcohol	75.7	65.7
Cigarettes	26.5	31.6

*Unadjusted despite known underreporting of certain drugs.

Psychological and Physical Effects The psychological effects of marijuana use are substantial—relaxation, intensified perception of stimuli, increased self-confidence, a sense of enhanced awareness and creativity, impaired motor coordination, reduced short-term memory, and distorted judgments. Piecing together this menu of psychological effects suggests that safe driving may be impaired when the adolescent is under the influence of marijuana. The active chemical ingredient in marijuana is delta-9-tetrahydrocannabinol (**THC**). The effects of THC may last for four to eight hours after the time the user feels "high"; by contrast, alcohol becomes metabolized more quickly.

As was just indicated, marijuana use impairs short-term memory. Such effects are particularly relevant for adolescents because marijuana use often takes place in a school setting. Let's look at one research investigation focused on the effects of marijuana use on memory. In this study (Miller et al., 1978), the subjects were randomly assigned to a drug condition or a placebo condition (a placebo is an inert substance used in place of an active drug). Before smoking the real marijuana or the fake marijuana, the subjects were given a list of words and then asked to recall them. Their performance was noted, and no differences were revealed between the two groups. Then they smoked. About an hour later, when the effects of marijuana should have been at their peak, the subjects were tested again on the words they had seen before they smoked. The marijuana users did not recall as many of the words as the nonmarijuana users. Most psychologists now concur that marijuana impairs memory, although the precise nature of its effects is still being worked out. For example, some psychologists argue that the influence is greater on short-term memory, or on the transfer of information from short-term to long-term memory, than on long-term memory.

In a massive report issued in 1980, the National Institute on Drug Abuse initiated a campaign to discourage the use of marijuana on a regular basis. This report was not just based on the psychological effects of marijuana. As long ago as 1893, the Indian Hemp Commission found a link between marijuana use and lung disease. Today, researchers have concluded that when marijuana is used daily in heavy amounts, it also may impair the reproductive system. A significant decline in sperm count may result from marijuana use, as well as greater abnormalities in sperm produced. Women using marijuana run the risk of decreased fertility. Although there have been no human studies on the subject, animal studies link marijuana use with an increase in birth defects.

Because of such research conclusions, in 1980, the National Institute of Drug Abuse and in 1982, the National Academy of Sciences issued reports strongly recommending that anyone under the age of eighteen should not use marijuana on a regular basis. Occasional use by healthy adults seems to have negligible health effects, although we still have unanswered questions about the long-term health effects of marijuana.

Reasons Adolescents Use Marijuana Why do adolescents use marijuana? In one survey of 26,000 college students (Mizner, Barter, and Werme, 1970), more than two of every three individuals said that smoking pot is fun and enjoyable. More than one of every two said the

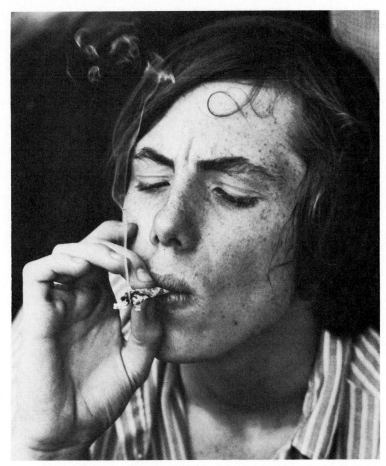

reason they smoked marijuana the first time was because they were curious. Only a very small percentage of the college students said they smoked marijuana to give them greater insight into their personality. Many adolescents see marijuana as a pleasant alternative to harder drugs and alcohol. Usually, only very heavy users of marijuana progress to the use of hard drugs. Adolescents who smoke marijuana infrequently or moderately are unlikely to take hard drugs (e.g., Single, Kandel, and Faust, 1974). Many youths take marijuana simply because it produces a pleasurable experience—a type of experience that is not a part of many of their other dealings with the world.

Parent-Peer Influences To what extent do parents and peers influence adolescents to use marijuana? A host of studies have indicated that there are positive correlations between parental drug use (such as using tranquilizers, amphetamines, alcohol, and tobacco) and the use of marijuana by youth (e.g., Shafer et al., 1973). And adolescents whose peers smoke marijuana are also more likely to smoke marijuana than adolescents whose friends do not (e.g., Tec, 1972).

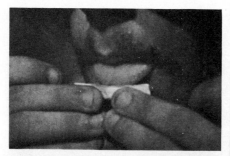

Makeshift marijuana pipes.

Manicured marijuana cigarettes and seeds.

Retail forms of marijuana.

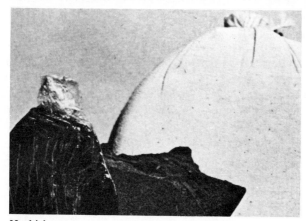

Hashish.

Drug-using adolescents tend to associate with older peers.

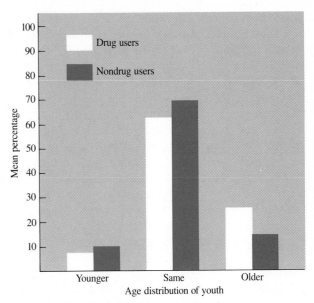

Figure 14.1 **Younger, same, and older age youth in the lives of adolescents using and not using drugs.**

In one investigation of parental and peer influences on marijuana use by adolescents, Denise Kandel (1974) interviewed adolescents, their friends, and their parents about various factors associated with the use of marijuana. Kandel found that associating with friends who use marijuana is more likely to influence an adolescent than parental drug use is. Kandel found that only fifteen percent of the adolescents whose friends did not smoke pot smoked marijuana themselves. By contrast, seventy-nine percent of the youth whose peers smoked pot also smoked it themselves. The highest usage of marijuana occurred when an adolescent's friends smoked marijuana and his parents took drugs (barbiturates, alcohol, and so on).

Another recent study (Blyth, Durant, and Moosbrugger, 1985) investigated more than 2400 seventh through tenth graders. Drug-using adolescents reported a larger number of older peers and greater frequency of contact and intimacy with them than nondrug using adolescents (figure 14.1). This suggests differences in the age appropriateness of particularly intimate peers. Also, drug-using adolescents reported

having a higher percentage of older friends and being even more peer-oriented than adult-oriented than nondrug using adolescents. Finally, parental intimacy was negatively related to drug use.

Marijuana Laws Many adolescents, and adults as well, believe that many of the laws associated with marijuana are antiquated. In 1972, the National Commission on Marijuana and Drug Abuse recommended that possession of marijuana for personal use should no longer be a criminal offense in the United States. However, as late as 1977, of the 18,197 adolescents under the age of nineteen arrested on drug-related charges in the state of Texas, ninety percent were arrested for possession or use of marijuana. In Texas, being convicted of marijuana possession can mean a fifteen-year jail sentence! Other states, such as Florida, have taken a more liberal stance on possession of marijuana. In Florida, possession of small amounts of marijuana is a civil rather than a criminal offense, punished with a small fine.

Trends in Marijuana Use We noted earlier that the use of marijuana during the past thirty days has decreased from a high point in 1978, being about one-third lower in 1984 than 1978. Quite clearly, marijuana use has increasingly been viewed as risky and unacceptable. In the University of Michigan study, the proportion of seniors who disapprove of regular marijuana use has risen from about sixty-five percent in 1977 to eighty-five percent in 1984. Peer acceptance of marijuana use also has been falling since the late 1970s. The adolescents do not view experimental or occasional use of marijuana as negatively as regular use—about one-half to two-thirds disapprove of these behaviors. Overall, it appears that reduced demand, not availability or price, is the key reason marijuana use is declining.

Nicotine

To learn more about cigarette smoking in adolescence, we investigate its incidence, parent and peer influences, and preventive health efforts.

Incidence Cigarette smoking, which had fallen by nearly one-third between 1977 and 1980, leveled off in the early 1980s. However, in 1984, the number of adolescents who smoke daily fell off once again, this time from 21.2 to 18.7 percent. Still, given the strong links between cancer and cigarette smoking, most scientists feel further effort needs to be expended to reduce adolescent smoking. Also, as we discussed, cigarette smoking is one area where females have equaled or surpassed males in drug usage. And, it is important to mention that preadolescent smoking has become an increasing problem. In some areas, such as Los Angeles, as many as one in twenty children smokes by age eleven, and by age twelve, the figure jumps to one in five.

Parent-Peer Influences Recent research inquiries have documented that both parent and peer influences are prominent in predicting whether an adolescent will smoke cigarettes (Chassin, Presson, and Sherman, 1984; Chassin et al., 1985). For example, adolescents with greater smoking involvement were far more likely to have parents who smoked, and adolescents who became regular smokers had more friends who smoked than their nonsmoking counterparts.

Table 14.5 Thirty-day prevalence of stimulant use by high school seniors in 1982 and 1984

	Diet pills		Stay-awake pills		Look-alikes	
	1982	1984	1982	1984	1982	1984
Males	5.0%	4.8%	6.0%	6.2%	4.9%	4.5%
Females	14.0	14.2	4.7	5.5	5.2	3.8

Note: Figures in percentages.
Source: After Johnston, L. D., Bachman, J. G., and P. M. O'Malley, News and Information Services Release, Institute of Social Research, University of Michigan, Ann Arbor, January 4, 1985.

Preventive Health Efforts Because of the negative consequences of smoking on health, health psychologists are interested in ways to continue the decline in smoking among adolescents. One prevention program designed to help junior high students resist the urge to smoke focused on pressure from parents and peers (Evans, 1982; 1983). The junior high school students were shown videotapes of individuals the same age as the students. Actors were shown in situations where they resisted the temptation to smoke when offered a cigarette by a friend. Other tapes dealt with parents who smoke and with the subtle influence of cigarette advertising. Classroom posters also were displayed at the school as reminders, and group discussions continued the negative information about smoking. When compared to a group of control students who did not participate in these experiences, the adolescents in the anticigarette program were less likely to smoke in the seventh grade. To learn more about preventive health efforts in regard to cigarette smoking, read Perspective on Adolescent Development 14.1, where we explore substance abuse in terms of agent, environment, and host.

Stimulants

Many adolescents take synthetic stimulants, or **amphetamines.** The use of stimulants peaked in 1981 and has slightly decreased since that time. The three main types of stimulants currently taken by adolescents are: diet pills, stay-awake pills, and look-alikes. Table 14.5 reveals the use of these stimulants by adolescents at

Perspective on Adolescent Development 14.1

AGENT, ENVIRONMENT, AND HOST IN SUBSTANCE ABUSE

*I*t may be helpful to think of preventing substance abuse with adolescents in terms of agent, environment, and host (Schinke and Gilchrist, 1985). **Agent interventions** focus on abused substances per se, such as tobacco and alcohol. **Environment interventions** emphasize the settings where substance abuse originates and where it can be prevented—schools, homes, and communities. And **host interventions** stress those who will use substances—the adolescents themselves.

Emphasizing the target substance itself, agent interventions approach prevention through legal, technological, and social controls (e.g., Gordon and McAlister, 1982; Wallack, 1984). Thus, agent prevention might control tobacco through licensing, minimum-age laws, and noncompliance.

Preventive interventions in schools, homes, and communities are designed to modify everyday influences on adolescents' substance use (e.g., Bloom, 1983; Perry, 1982). One of the most powerful conduits of intervention is television.

One recent study calling on television to prevent adolescent cigarette smoking (Flay, in press) provided positive results. Smoking prevention segments were aired on television to a selected sample of families with young adolescents. Compared to a control group who did not see the periodic anticigarette smoking campaign on television, the early adolescents reported one year later that they were less likely to have ever smoked cigarettes.

Host interventions build adolescents' cognitive and behavioral skills so they will be able to resist substance abuse (e.g., Murray and Perry, 1984; Wills, 1985). One recent host intervention study (Schinke and Gilchrest, 1985) included a number of strategies to improve the ability of young adolescents to resist smoking cigarettes.

Substance abuse can be analyzed in terms of agent, environment, and host.

The middle school students were shown smoking health-related films, were exposed to peer testimonials on the advantages of nonsmoking, and were shown slides on media glamorization of cigarettes. Also, problem-solving situations were set up in which the adolescents practiced generating, choosing, and applying plans for when the temptation to smoke might arise. The group of young adolescents experiencing this skills intervention were less likely to smoke cigarettes at several later measurement dates, one of which was two years later, than a control group of young adolescents who only were given attention.

some point in the last thirty days—note the significantly greater use of diet pills by female adolescents, as mentioned earlier. Stimulants frequently are used by students to maintain high levels of performance for short periods of time. However, an amphetamine high is often followed by mental depression and fatigue. And because the drug rapidly produces tolerance, before very long, the adolescent will have to swallow a handful of pills to get the same effect that one or two pills produced at an earlier time.

Amphetamines can only be taken legally if they are issued by prescription, but as with many other drugs, they are manufactured illegally in huge quantities. The most damaging form of amphetamine use is engaged in by individuals who inject large doses of amphetamines into their veins several times a day. Prolonged use of amphetamines in this manner leads to loss of appetite and possible psychotic reactions. Amphetamines also are psychologically addictive for many youths, and there is some evidence that their prolonged use may be physically addictive.

Depressants

Many adolescents take depressants as well as stimulants. The depressants most commonly taken by adolescents are barbiturates and Quaaludes. There are more than 2,500 different synthetic barbiturates, divided into two main categories—the "long-acting" barbiturates, dispensed for nighttime use as a sedative or sleep inducer, and the short-acting barbiturates, used in the daytime as tranquilizers to relax highly anxious adolescents. The long-term barbiturates appear to be only moderately addictive, but the short-term ones are very addictive. Taken in large enough doses, the short-term barbiturates produce a sensation similar to alcohol, removing the adolescent's inhibitions and relaxing him or her at the same time. These drugs are particularly dangerous when taken with alcohol. Another dangerous combination is the alternation of depressants and stimulants.

Quaaludes (or methaqualone) are hypnotic sedatives that have been used by adolescents in recent years. They often are used along with cocaine, presumably to bring the user "down."

There has been a downturn in the use of nonmedical stimulants in recent years (table 14.3). In the cases of sedatives and tranquilizers, the percentages of seniors who reported use in the prior month was only about half the peak rates recorded in the 1970s.

Hallucinogens

Hallucinogens are so named because they produce hallucinations or distortions of reality. There are various drugs that have hallucinogenic properties, and the drug the user acquires may in some cases not be the drug she thought she was getting—LSD and PCP, for example, may be passed off to unsuspecting customers as THC, peyote, or mescaline. Marijuana sometimes produces hallucinations, but not nearly as consistently or as powerfully as LSD and PCP. Reactions to hallucinogens vary from one adolescent to the next and are highly unpredictable in intensity and duration. PCP and LSD are easily synthesized and sometimes are manufactured in garages and basements. Consequently, the quality of such a drug may be poor or inconsistent and the effects difficult to predict (Office of Drug Abuse Policy, 1978).

The use of LSD continued to decline in 1984, a decline that had begun at the beginning of the 1980s. PCP use has remained at a low level after a precipitous drop in use between 1979 and 1983, undoubtedly because the drug developed a well-earned reputation for being unpredictable and dangerous.

Cocaine

Did you know that **cocaine,** often referred to as coke, used to be an ingredient of Coca-Cola? Of course, it has long since been removed from that soft drink. Cocaine comes from the coca plant, which is native to Bolivia and Peru. For many years, Bolivians and Peruvians chewed on the plant to increase their stamina. Today, cocaine is taken in the form of either crystals or powder. A stimulant, cocaine provides increased feelings of stamina, enhanced mental capabilities, excitability, and, occasionally, hallucinations. The use of cocaine by adolescents, which has received widespread media coverage, has remained at about the same level among adolescents since 1979 (table 14.3). Useage levels still are too high: lifetime, annual, and monthly prevalence rates among high school seniors in 1984 were sixteen, twelve, and six percent respectively. One bright spot in the University of Michigan survey is that an increasing number of students now see cocaine as dangerous and are disapproving of its use.

Heroin

Heroin, a derivative of opium, is a dangerous drug—if taken in sufficient quantities, it can be toxic. Even after just one month of use, an adolescent can become physiologically addicted to heroin. This means that the youth must continue taking the drug to avoid painful withdrawal symptoms.

Heroin is widely perceived by high school students as having the greatest risk of harm for the user, and so it receives the greatest disapproval from adolescents (Johnston, Bachman, and O'Malley, 1981). Fortunately, heroin is the least widely used of the illicit drugs we have discussed, with only one in ninety adolescents admitting to ever having used it, and only one in two hundred reporting use in the last year.

Inhalants

Inhalants include any aerosol or gaseous fumes, other than smoke, that are inhaled to make the user feel good, high, or intoxicated. The recency of their popularity is suggested by the fact that it was not until 1976 that the Insititute of Social Research at the University of Michigan added inhalants to its list of drugs. The two classes of inhalants that have been used most by adolescents are called amyl nitrites, also known as "poppers" and "snappers," and butyl nitrites, known sometimes as "locker room" or "rush." Adolescents usually cannot remember what happened to them while they were intoxicated with the inhalant. Some deaths have been attributed to the use of inhalants, but for the most part, these deaths actually resulted from the youth placing a plastic bag over her head to enhance the effects of the inhalant rather than from the inhalant itself.

Among the 1984 high school seniors surveyed by the University of Michigan, inhalants were the only classification of drugs showing an overall increase from 1983 to 1984. Prior year use rose from seven percent in 1983 to eight percent in 1984.

Drugs often are taken in a school setting. Or, they may be taken just before coming to school and their effects may still influence the adolescent's behavior while at school. The role of schools in adolescent drug use is discussed next.

Drugs and Schools

Schools are involved in drug use because they are often the location where peers initiate and maintain drug use. Schools could play an important part in preventing or curbing and controlling drug use. There are few other places where the target population is congregated on such a frequent basis.

The teacher may be a critical factor in the cooperative effort of parents, physicians, and others who are trying to help adolescents with drug problems. A teacher's observations may be helpful in monitoring the behavior of any adolescent with a serious problem or disturbance. Surveys of classroom teachers, however, indicate that most teachers know very little about the effects of drugs on adolescent behavior and have received little or no formal education about drug use (e.g., Bosco and Robin, 1976). Because the teacher is a key member of the therapeutic team that can help the disturbed and/or drug abusive adolescent, experts believe more attention should be given to preparing teachers for this role. Some colleges and universities have recently developed special courses in response to this need.

Many schools have developed or housed drug prevention and intervention programs. An overview of some of these programs is provided in Perspective on Adolescent Development 14.2.

As was indicated earlier, alcohol is a drug. However, because its use has become so widespread among adolescents, we'll give separate attention to it in the next section.

We have discussed many different aspects of drugs and adolescents. For a review, the important ideas described so far are in Concept Table 14.1.

Perspective on Adolescent Development 14.2

SCHOOL POLICY AND DRUG USE

*P*atricia Minuchin and Edna Shapiro (1983) recently reviewed the nature of drug prevention and intervention programs in schools. Although most schools have established policies about substance use on the school premises, some have gone further and developed or housed drug prevention and intervention programs. During the 1970s, the nature of these programs changed. Earlier programs emphasized detection, discipline, and scare tactics—and like similar approaches to venereal disease or smoking, they were ineffective (Brecher, 1972; Nowlis, 1976; Randall and Wong, 1976). Subsequent programs have focused on providing relevant information and frequently have dealt with psychological issues, such as self-awareness, values clarification, communication skills, decision making, and peer relationships. Such programs have included effective experiential techniques, using medical and psychological experts, ex-addicts, school counselors, teachers, and fellow students as leaders of small groups. Most of the programs have been relatively short-term, ranging from one or two days to a semester (e.g., Randall and Wong, 1976; Shalom, Inc., 1980; Volpe, 1977).

It is hard to evaluate the effectiveness of most programs described in the literature, since a majority have no associated research. In one review (Randall and Wong, 1976), over two hundred published accounts were scanned. It was found that only twenty-three included any systematic evaluation. From the studies available, though, it is evident that some programs increase student knowledge without demonstrable positive effects on attitudes or substance use (e.g., Randall and Wong, 1976; Swisher, Warner, and Herr, 1972). In one study (Swisher, Warner and Herr, 1972), ninth and eleventh graders experienced four six-week drug education programs—three involving counseling groups (emphasizing relationships, reward by a role model, and verbal reward of positive student statements, respectively) and one that was simply a standard health unit on drugs (the control group). The study included several positive research methods—random assignment; pre- and posttesting for knowledge, attitudes, and self-reported drug use; and training and rotation of counselors, to name a few. All approaches were equally effective in increasing knowledge about drugs but none led to a change in attitudes or drug use. In fact, increases in knowledge after drug education programs have sometimes been linked with effects contrary to intent (Randall and Wong, 1976). For instance, in one investigation (Stuart, 1973), it was found that increased drug use occurred as greater knowledge was accompanied by a decrease in worry.

Some studies have shown positive program effects. A program for sixth and eighth graders, in which teachers were trained in group skills, values clarification, moral development theory and decision-making strategies, led to significant differences between experimental and control groups on attitudes about the self and about drug use and drinking (Rose and Duer, 1978). Some experts have suggested that programs are more effective with elementary school students than those in high school (Warner, Swisher, and Horan, 1973) but there are contrary findings as well.

It has been argued that people seek pleasure and that pleasure-producing substances will continue to be available to adolescents (Brecher, 1972; Randall and Wong, 1976). Given the likelihood that schools will continue to prohibit the use of drugs on the premises, and that the "generation gap" in attitudes will persist (Johnston et al., 1981), many secondary school students probably will continue to view the use of alcohol and drugs as a source of pleasure and a means of challenging authority. School programs designed to prevent or intervene in the use of illicit drugs have, by and large, been only marginally successful. The most promising programs have involved a comprehensive, long-term approach, not only providing specific information and services, but dealing with the social organization of the school as a whole, as well. (Minuchin and Shapiro, 1983).

Concept Table 14.1

DRUGS

Concept	Processes/related ideas	Characteristics/description
The range of drugs and actual drug use by adolescents	The range of drugs	Adolescents take a wide range of drugs from licit drugs such as nicotine to highly illicit drugs like heroin.
	Actual incidence of drug use	The most extensive data about drug use come from the Institute of Social Research at the University of Michigan through studies conducted by Johnston, Bachman, and O'Malley. They have been surveying high school seniors on a national basis for a number of years. Almost two-thirds of adolescents take an illicit drug at some point in their lives. The most widely used illicit drug is marijuana, while the most widely taken licit drug is alcohol. At some point about the end of the 1970s and the beginning of the 1980s, a downward trend in illicit drug use by adolescence occurred. For the most part, males are more involved in drug use than females, although females take one type of stimulant much more often—diet pills.
Specific drugs taken by adolescents	Marijuana	Learning about marijuana requires information about what it is, psychological and physical effects, reasons adolescents use marijuana, parent-peer influences, laws, and trends in use (which have been declining).
	Nicotine	Knowledge about nicotine focuses on its incidence (which is declining), parent-peer influences (they both are important), and preventive health efforts (which can be studied in terms of agent, environment, and host).
	Stimulants	Many adolescents take synthetic stimulants, or amphetamines. Females are more likely to take diet pills while males are somewhat more likely to take stay-awake and look-alike pills.
	Depressants	The most common depressants taken by adolescents are barbiturates and quaaludes. There has been a downward turn in the nonmedical use of depressants by adolescents in recent years.
	Hallucinogens	These drugs produce hallucinations or distortions of reality. They include LSD and PCP. Their use has declined in recent years.
	Cocaine	Cocaine at one time was used in Coca-Cola. It is a stimulant that has received widespread media coverage and its use has remained about the same in recent years.
	Heroin	A derivative of opium, this drug is highly dangerous. It is rarely used by adolescents.
	Inhalants	This category includes any aerosol or gaseous fumes, other than smoke, that are inhaled to make the user feel high. This is the only classification of drugs that increased in use from 1983 to 1984 in the University of Michigan study.
Drugs and schools	The school setting	Schools are often locations for drug use and they can play an important role in prevention or intervention. Teachers are particularly important in detecting drug use.
	School policy, drug use, and research assessment	Effective drug programs do not involve detection, discipline, and scare tactics, but rather provide relevant information and deal with important psychological effects. While there has been a considerable amount of money spent on drug prevention and intervention in schools, there have been few research assessments of the positive or negative effects of these programs.

Alcohol: Heavy Drinking Remains Alarmingly High

To learn more about the effects of alcohol on adolescents, we focus on the prevalence of drinking among adolescents, the physical and psychological effects of drinking, factors associated with the use of alcohol by adolescents, prevention and intervention programs with drinking adolescents, and drinking and deviant behavior.

The Prevalence of Drinking among Adolescents

Alcohol is the most widely used of all drugs by adolescents, according to the national surveys conducted by the Institute of Social Research at Michigan (Johnston, Bachman, and O'Malley, 1981; 1985). There has been concern that as illicit drug use declines, alcohol use by adolescents would increase. However, since 1979, a slight decrease in alcohol use has been noted. For example, the proportion of seniors reporting alcohol use in the prior thirty-day period was seventy-two percent in 1979 and sixty-seven percent in 1984 (table 14.3). More importantly, the number of seniors drinking daily, or almost daily, fell from seven percent to five percent over the same time interval. The number of seniors reporting any occasions of recent "heavy drinking" (defined as five or more drinks in a row during the prior two weeks) still remains alarmingly high, although the percentage did drop from forty-one to thirty-nine percent from 1983 to 1984, the first decline since the surveys began.

Physical, Psychological, and Behavioral Effects of Drinking

Alochol is a depressant that primarily affects the adolescent's central nervous system. It is popularly believed that alcohol increases arousal and excitement, but in reality it slows down or depresses many of the brain's activities. After a certain level of alcohol accumulates in the adolescent's bloodstream, the familiar pattern of drunkenness ensues, usually involving

What trends in alcohol use during adolescence have occurred in the 1980s?

a loss of mental and physical alertness and coordination. After prolonged consumption, unconsciousness may result.

The use of alcohol in large quantities can have a variety of negative consequences for the physical development of the adolescent. For one, he may develop a chronic irritation of the stomach lining, leading to an ulcer. In addition, fat may accumulate in the liver and impair its functioning. And irreparable damage to the central nervous system may eventuate after excessive, prolonged use of alcohol.

The most dramatic consequences of alcohol use pertain to mood and behavior. Alterations of feelings and conduct are due to the action of alcohol on the central nervous system, specifically the brain, and are in direct proportion to the blood-alcohol level or blood-alcohol concentration, sometimes called the **BAC.** Most drinkers who have a relatively low BAC (from .01 to .03 percent), which occurs after one or two servings of an alcoholic beverage, experience only mild effects. Definite impairment begins in the range from .03 percent to just below .10 percent. As the BAC increases, mental efficiency decreases. The drinker experiences feelings of relaxation and sedation, and muscle coordination becomes difficult as a consequence of the progressive depressant action on the brain. After blood-

Number of Drinks* (over a two-hour period)

Weight												
100	1	2	3	4	5	6	7	8	9	10	11	12
120	1	2	3	4	5	6	7	8	9	10	11	12
140	1	2	3	4	5	6	7	8	9	10	11	12
160	1	2	3	4	5	6	7	8	9	10	11	12
180	1	2	3	4	5	6	7	8	9	10	11	12
200	1	2	3	4	5	6	7	8	9	10	11	12
220	1	2	3	4	5	6	7	8	9	10	11	12
240	1	2	3	4	5	6	7	8	9	10	11	12

Be Careful
BAC to .05

Driving Impaired
.05–.09

Do Not Drive
.10 and up

*One drink = 1.5 ounces of 86 proof liquor or 12 ounces of beer.

Source: National Highway Traffic Safety Administration.

Figure 14.2   Know your limits—drinking and driving. *Source: National Highway Traffic Safety Administration.*

alcohol concentration reaches .10 percent, the adolescent's behavior takes one or more of several familiar forms: decreased inhibition, less efficient vision and hearing, slurring of speech, difficulty in performing gross motor skills (for example, driving a car), deterioration of judgment, and a general feeling of euphoria. When the BAC reaches .20 percent, nearly all drinkers show profound and obvious signs of intoxication—difficulty in simply walking or speaking, for example.

A major concern about drinking focuses on those who drive while the alcoholic content of their blood is still high. In recent years, police departments have increasingly relied on tests that are based on constant alcohol concentrations in the blood and in the breath to determine whether an individual is too drunk to drive safely. These devices include the familiar breathalyzer. Figure 14.2 outlines how much alcohol is enough to impair driving skills. Note that the more the drinker weighs, the more he or she can drink before the blood concentration of alcohol reaches a dangerous level.

The startling statistics that in the last two weeks approximately four of every ten high school seniors had five or more drinks on at least one occasion, combined with the increased number of adolescents who drive, leads to only one conclusion—too many alcohol-related adolescent driving accidents and deaths.

Factors Associated with the Use of Alcohol by Adolescents

As with most aspects of adolescent development, biological/genetic factors and psychosocial factors are given as reasons adolescents drink.

Biological and Genetic Factors

There is some evidence for a genetic explanation of alcoholism. For example, in one investigation (Goodwin et al., 1973) the children of alcoholic parents who had been adopted by foster parents still had almost twice the number of alcohol problems by their late twenties as a control group of adopted children whose real parents did not have a history of alcoholism. And, in another study (Goodwin et al., 1974), the sons of alcoholic parents who were adopted in infancy by nonalcoholic parents were compared with those raised by their alcoholic parents. Both adopted and nonadopted sons subsequently showed high rates of alcoholism—twenty-five and seventeen percent respectively.

By contrast, the large majority of children with alcoholic parents do not become alcoholics themselves. Thus, we do not know the precise way that genetic factors work in the development of alcoholism. And, a physical predisposition to alcoholism could be acquired as well as inherited. This might occur through endocrine or enzyme imbalances that could increase the adolescent's vulnerability to alcohol.

Psychosocial Factors

Among the psychosocial factors possibly related to alcohol use by adolescents are personality/adjustment characteristics, family and peer influences, and cultural factors.

Personality/Adjustment Factors Is there a "drinking personality" that characterizes adolescents who drink? That is, is there a type of personality organization that predisposes an adolescent to drink more than others? Most research on the topic of personality/adjustment factors involved in drinking have been carried out with adults and the results are inconclusive. The only characteristic that shows up consistently in the makeup of adult alcoholics is personal maladjustment, yet most maladjusted people do not become alcoholics. The personality of individuals who drink may result from dependence on alcohol rather than being a contributing factor in drinking.

In one recent study with adolescents (McLaughlin and Chassin, 1985), it was found that adolescents at risk for alcohol abuse have stronger expectancies that alcohol will produce "personal effects" such as increased cognitive and motor capabilities as well as tension reduction. Such findings have been revealed with adults as well (Sher and Levensen, 1982). Adolescents at risk for alcohol abuse may actually experience greater tension reduction benefits and therefore come to anticipate that alcohol will bring about this tension reduction. For adolescent males, a strong motive for power also was more evident among the high risk than low risk alcohol group.

Family and Peer Influences Grace Barnes has reviewed a number of studies on family relationships and concluded that family socialization is an important factor in adolescent drinking behavior (Barnes, 1977; 1984). A National Institute on Alcohol Abuse and Alcoholism survey of over thirteen thousand adolescents nationwide (1975) found that heavy adolescent drinkers were more likely to say their parents sanctioned drinking and had favorable attitudes toward adolescent use of alcohol than those adolescents who were not heavy drinkers. In fact, the survey showed a stronger relation between parental sanctioning of drinking than between peer pressure and drinking. However, there still is a link between adolescent drinking and peer relations (National Institute on Alcohol Abuse and Alcoholism, 1975; Forslund and Gustafson, 1970). It may be, as Barnes (1977) suggests, that the peer group provides the social context for drinking and reinforces adolescent behavior learned as part of the family socialization process. Other research on adolescent drinking patterns indicates that adolescents who drink heavily often come from unhappy homes in which there is a great deal of tension (e.g., Prendergast, 1974). And in Barnes's (1984) recent research, she has found parental nurturance and the ability of the parents to function as a support system for the adolescent to be important factors in preventing heavy drinking by adolescents.

Cultural Factors Cultural factors, including the values and customs of the community, also influence the adolescent's drinking behavior. Rates of alcoholism vary considerably from one culture to the next—northern France, the United States, Italy and northern Russia have high incidences of alcoholism, for example. But low rates of alcoholism are not necessarily due to abstinence. Moslems do not drink because of their religious beliefs, and their alcoholism rates are low; by contrast, a large percentage of Jews do drink, but their alcoholism rates are low also. Customs, values, and sanctions in various cultures influence the degree to which alcoholism is a problem within those cultures. The National Institute on Alcohol Abuse and Alcoholism (1974) concluded that among groups who use alcohol extensively, the lowest rate of alcoholism is linked with the following factors:

1. Youths are exposed to alcohol at an early point in their lives within a strong family or religious group. The alcohol is served in diluted form and in small quantities.
2. The beverage served is usually thought of as food and is taken with meals.
3. Parents show an example of moderate rather than excessive drinking.

4. No moral significance is placed on drinking—it is neither considered right, nor wrong.
5. Drinking is not viewed as proof of adulthood or virility.
6. Abstinence is viewed as socially acceptable—it is no more inconsiderate to turn down a drink than to turn down a helping of green beans.
7. Excessive drinking or being intoxicated is not approved of—it is not stylish, in vogue, or "cool" to drink heavily or get drunk.

Prevention and Intervention Programs with Drinking Adolescents

Just as in our discussion of cigarette smoking, it is helpful to think of alcohol prevention efforts with adolescents in terms of agent, environment, and host. With regard to agent, one research study (Wagenaar, 1983) investigated the relation of minimum drinking age law changes to adolescents' alcohol-related traffic accidents. Increases in automobile crashes were in the ten to thirty percent range immediately following reductions in legal age, but when the drinking age was raised there was a corresponding ten to thirty percent reduction in such crashes. Despite such findings, agent interventions (such as raising the age at which adolescents can legally drink) alone seem inadequate to curb alcohol abuse.

With regard to environmental prevention, one study (Wodarski and Offman, 1984) developed a school-based program to help students discuss alcohol-related issues in their peer group. It was believed that such peer discussion would help students become aware of their own drinking problems as well as those of others and be more likely to seek help for themselves or others once this awareness occurred. At a one-year follow-up, students in the intervention schools reported less alcohol abuse and had more often discouraged one another's drinking than did students in test-only control schools. Host interventions also have modified adolescents' attitudes about alcohol abuse (e.g., Stainback and Rogers, 1983).

Attempts to help the adolescent with a drinking problem vary greatly, as do most intervention efforts to assist adolescents with various disturbances. Therapy may include working with other family members, peer group discussion sessions, and specific behavioral techniques. Unfortunately, there has been little or no concern for identifying different types of alcohol abusers in adolescence and then attempting to match appropriate treatment programs to the particular problems of the adolescent drinker. Most efforts simply assume that adolescents with drinking problems are a homogeneous group and do not take into account the varying developmental patterns and social histories of different adolescents. Some adolescents with drinking problems may be helped more through family therapy, others through peer counseling, and yet others through intensive behavioral strategies, depending on the type of drinking problem and the social agents who have the most influence on the adolescent (Finney and Moos, 1979).

Drinking and Deviant Behavior

Heavy drinking in adolescence has a number of negative effects on the adolescent's social and cognitive development. Several investigators have found that adolescents who have drinking problems are more likely to engage in deviant actions and condone transgressions more than those who are not problem drinkers (Jessor et al., 1968; National Institute on Alcohol Abuse and Alcoholism, 1975). These researchers do not, however, have evidence that problem drinking in adolescence actually causes deviant behavior. While problem drinking and deviant behavior are related to each other, the relation is very complex. Assuming that problem drinking causes deviant behavior hinders the search for the sociocultural influences that may be the underlying causes of both deviant behavior and problem drinking.

In studies of delinquency, there is evidence that excessive drinking is fairly common among delinquents. Drinking to excess, even to the point of passing out, is common among approximately four out of ten delinquents, but in less than one out of ten nondelinquents (e.g., Pearce and Garrett, 1970; MacKay, Phillips, and Bryce, 1967). According to the same investigations, approximately one out of every three delinquents had been arrested for drinking, while less than one out of twenty nondelinquents had been arrested for the same offense. And in one investigation of adolescent girls seen at the Massachusetts Youth Reception-Detention Center in Boston, more than one of every two girls drank on a weekly basis, and about four out of every ten girls had passed out while drinking.

Delinquents may drink for reasons different from those of nondelinquents. Grace Barnes (1977) points out that delinquents may drink more for the effect than nondelinquents, who are more likely to drink to help them socialize, celebrate, or simply "to have fun." At any rate, the relation between drinking and delinquency merits further study.

We have discussed a number of different aspects of alcohol use and abuse in adolescence. A summary of main ideas related to alcohol and adolescence is presented in Concept Table 14.2

Next, we'll look in greater detail at the prevalent problem of juvenile delinquency in our society.

Juvenile Delinquency: No Easy Solutions

Some important questions to ask about juvenile delinquency follow: What is it and what is its nature? Are there developmental changes involved? What are intervention programs designed to help delinquents like?

What is Juvenile Delinquency?

The label "juvenile delinquent" is applied to an adolescent who breaks the law or engages in behavior that is considered illegal. Like other categories of disturbance, juvenile delinquency is a broad concept; legal infractions may range from littering to murder. Because the youth technically becomes a juvenile delinquent only after judged guilty of a crime by a court of law, official records do not accurately reflect the number of illegal acts committed. Nevertheless, there is still every indication that in the last ten or fifteen years, juvenile delinquency has increased in relation to the number of crimes committed by adults.

Estimates regarding the number of juvenile delinquents in the United States are sketchy, although FBI statistics suggest that at least two percent of all youths are involved in juvenile court cases. The number of girls found guilty of juvenile delinquency has increased significantly in recent years. Delinquency rates among blacks, other minority groups, and the lower class are particularly high in relation to the overall populations of these groups. However, such groups have less influence than others over the judicial decision-making process in the United States and thus may be judged delinquent more readily than their white, middle-class counterparts.

Some experts on delinquency believe that in defining delinquency, it is misleading to refer only to delinquency rates based on arrests. For example, one recently devised definition of delinquency is "behavior by a juvenile that is a deliberate violation of the law and is believed by the juvenile to make him or her liable to adjudication if it comes to the attention of a law-enforcement agency" (Gold and Petronio, 1980). This definition clearly does not take into account whether the adolescent's behavior actually comes to the attention of legal authorities or not.

Measuring the pervasiveness of delinquency in adolescence is not as easy as it might seem. First, delinquency must be defined to delineate what constitutes a delinquent act. Not everyone would agree with the definition we have chosen, for example. Some might argue that the individual is not delinquent until proven so in a court of law. Delinquent behavior has usually been measured through self-reports by adolescents (Hardt and Bodine, 1965). In most cases care is taken to inform adolescents that their reports are completely confidential—this is clearly important because an adolescent is not going to report that he has recently committed a delinquent act if he thinks his parents, school, or the legal authorities will find out.

The Nature of Delinquency

Many reasons have been given as to why juvenile delinquency occurs—let's explore some of these reasons.

A Wide Range of Explanations for Delinquency

We have seen that it is difficult to define and measure delinquency; there is also a lack of agreement about the nature of delinquency, or how it should be viewed, what causes it, and what factors are associated with it. The causes that have been considered in attempts to explain why adolescents become delinquent include that

Concept Table 14.2

ALCOHOL

Concept	Processes/related ideas	Characteristics/description
Prevalence of drinking among adolescents	Overall incidence	The most widely used drug by adolescents.
	Trends in use	There has been a slight decrease in use since 1979. Heavy drinking, while dropping slightly, remains alarmingly high.
Physical, psychological, and behavioral effects	Physical effects	Influences the central nervous system, depressing many of the brain's activities. After a certain level of alcohol accumulates in the adolescent's blood stream, the familiar pattern of drunkeness ensues. After prolonged consumption, unconsciousness may result. Extensive, prolonged use can produce ulcers and damage to the central nervous system.
	Psychological and behavioral effects	As blood alcoholic content (BAC) increases, there is a loss of mental efficiency, a relaxed, sedated feeling occurs, and muscle coordination becomes difficult. Feelings of euphoria, slurred speech, decreased inhibition, less efficient vision and hearing, deterioration of judgment, and problems with gross motor skills occur when BAC reaches .10 percent. When BAC reaches .20, nearly all drinkers show obvious signs of intoxication, such as serious problems even walking or talking.
	Factors associated with alcohol use by adolescents	Biological/genetic factors and psychosocial factors are involved. There is some evidence for a genetic factor in alcoholism, but the precise way this works is not known. Personality adjustment, family–peer, and cultural factors are important to consider in understanding the adolescent's drinking patterns. No specific personality profile has been linked to drinking although alcoholic individuals do show a pattern of personal maladjustment. Some linkages between parent–peer drinking and adolescent drinking have been found. Rates of drinking vary considerably from one culture to the next.
Prevention and intervention programs with drinking adolescents	Prevention	As with cigarette smoking, it is helpful to think of prevention in terms of agent, environment, and host. Prevention efforts aimed at each of these three domains have shown success.
	Intervention	Intervention efforts run the gamut of therapeutic strategies in psychology, ranging from family therapy to behavioral techniques. Keep in mind that adolescents with drinking problems are not a homogeneous lot and that intervention often has to be tailored to the individual adolescent.
Drinking and deviant behavior	Cause or correlation?	Heavy drinking in adolescence is associated with adjustment problems, but it is not known whether drinking produces deviant behavior or vice versa.
	Drinking and delinquency	Delinquents are more likely to drink for the effect than nondelinquents, who are more likely to drink for socializing purposes.

delinquency is: rooted in biological instincts and delinquents are virtually "animals in captivity" (Hall, 1904); based on an increased biological drive, not necessarily sexual in nature (McCandless, 1970); triggered by the onset of sexual urges that require the adolescent to break away from parents and reestablish bonds with peers, a circumstance that increases the likelihood of acting-out behavior (Blos, 1962); one manifestation of the search for identity (Erikson, 1968); caused by blocked opportunities in a culture (Bloch and Niederhoffer, 1958).

Erikson's View on Delinquency

Recall from our description of Erik Erikson's theory of development that adolescence is the stage when the crisis of identity versus identity diffusion should be resolved. Not surprisingly, Erikson's ideas about delinquency are linked to the ability of the adolescent to positively resolve this crisis. Erikson believes that at the time the biological changes of puberty are occurring, there are concomitant changes in social expectations placed on adolescents by family, peers, and schools. These biological and social changes allow for two kinds of integration to occur in the adolescent's personality—one, the establishment of a sense of consistency in life, and the second, the resolution of role identity, a sort of joining of the adolescent's motivation, values, abilities, and styles with the role demands placed on the adolescent.

Erikson believes that delinquency is characterized more by a failure of the adolescent to achieve the second kind of integration, involving the role aspects of identity. He comments that adolescents whose infant, childhood, or adolescent experiences have somehow restricted them from acceptable social roles or made them feel that they can't measure up to the demands placed on them may choose a negative course of identity development. Erikson describes this as "an identity perversely based on all those identifications and roles, which, at critical stages of development, had been presented to them as most undesirable or dangerous and yet also as most real" (1968, p. 197). Some of these adolescents may take on the role of the delinquent, enmeshing themselves in the most negative currents of the youth culture available to them. By organizing their

How does Erikson explain delinquency?

lives around such a negative identity, they establish a continuity of self from one relationship and situation to another, so that they can imagine how they might behave, think, or feel even in encounters that never occur. Not only does their own behavior become predictable to themselves, but they become capable of predicting how others will act toward them. In this manner the delinquent's self-image and his perception of himself in the peer group begin to fuse. As the adolescent finds support for such a delinquent image among peers, who themselves seek reciprocal support, the image is reinforced. Thus, for Erikson, delinquency is an attempt to establish an identity (Gold and Petronio, 1980).

Delinquency As a Failure in Self-Control

Alan Ross (1979) describes juvenile delinquency as the failure to develop sufficient behavioral control. Some children fail to develop the essential controls that others have acquired during the process of growing up. Most youth have learned the difference between acceptable and unacceptable behavior, but the juvenile delinquent has not. He may fail to distinguish between acceptable and unacceptable behavior, or he may have learned this distinction, but failed to develop adequate control in using the distinction to guide his behavior. To understand the problem of delinquency, it is thus necessary to study different aspects of the development of self-control—for example, delay of gratification and self-imposed standards of conduct. Studies have found that failure to delay gratification is related to cheating and to a general lack of social responsibility often revealed in delinquent behavior (e.g., Mischel, 1961; Mischel and Gilligan, 1964).

Delinquents also may have developed inadequate standards of conduct. An adolescent about to commit an antisocial act must invoke self-critical thoughts to inhibit her tendency to commit the illegal action. These self-critical standards are strongly influenced by the models the youth experiences. Thus, adolescents whose parents, teachers, and peers exhibit self-critical standards can be expected to develop the self-control needed to refrain from an illegal or antisocial act. Others, however, may be exposed to models who praise antisocial acts. For example, an adolescent whose peer models praise or engage in antisocial deeds may follow their example, especially if she also lacks family models who are both strong and positive in terms of standards of conduct.

The expected consequences of negative actions also influence the youth's decision to engage in or refrain from delinquent behavior. When the youth expects some sort of reward for delinquent behavior, he is more likely to perform the antisocial act than if he expects punishment. The expected rewards can take many different forms—the acquisition of stolen goods, for example, or high status in the gang or in neighborhood peer groups.

Whether or not the adolescent engages in juvenile delinquency may also be affected by the competence she has achieved in different aspects of life. Consider a youth who does well in academic subjects at school, who actively participates in socially desirable clubs, or who develops athletic skills. This youth is likely to develop a positive view of herself and receive reinforcement from others for prosocial behavior. Most delinquents, however, have achieved few ego-enhancing competencies; antisocial behavior is one way they can demonstrate self-competence and receive reinforcement from the delinquent subculture.

Sociocultural Influences

Among the most important sociocultural influences that have been studied as contributors to juvenile delinquency are those involving social class, community families, and peers.

Social Class and Community Although juvenile delinquency is less exclusively a lower class problem than it was in the past, some characteristics of the lower class culture are likely to promote delinquency. The norms of many lower class peer groups and gangs are antisocial, or counterproductive to the goals and norms of society at large. Getting into and staying out of trouble in some instances becomes a prominent feature of the lives of some adolescents from lower class backgrounds (Miller, 1958). Status in the peer group may be gauged by how often the adolescent can engage in antisocial conduct, yet manage to stay out of jail. Since lower class adolescents have less opportunity to develop skills that are socially desirable, they may sense that they can gain attention and status by performing antisocial actions. Being "tough" and "masculine" are high-status traits for lower class boys, and these traits are often gauged by the adolescent's success in performing delinquent acts and getting away with them.

The nature of a community may contribute to delinquency. A community with a high crime rate allows the adolescent to observe many models who engage in criminal activities. And adolescents may see these models rewarded for their criminal accomplishments. Such communities often are characterized by poverty, unemployment, and feelings of alienation toward the middle class. The quality of schools, funding for education, and organized neighborhood activities are other community factors that may be related to delinquency. Are there caring adults in the schools and neighborhood who can convince the adolescent with delinquent tendencies that education is the best route to success? When family support becomes inadequate, then such community supports take on added importance in preventing delinquency. Let's look more closely now at peer and family influences on delinquency.

Family and Peer Influences Even if an adolescent grows up in a high crime community, his or her peer relationships may influence whether he or she becomes a delinquent. In one investigation of five hundred delinquents and five hundred nondelinquents in Boston, Massachusetts, a much higher percentage of the delinquents had regular associations with delinquent peers

(Glueck and Glueck, 1950). But even more than peers, it has been family processes that have stimulated the most thinking about why delinquency comes about.

While there has been a long history of interest in defining the family factors that are associated with delinquency (Glueck and Glueck, 1950; McCord, McCord, and Gudeman, 1960; Rutter, 1971), the most recent focus has been on the nature of family management practices. Disruptions or omissions in the parents' applications of family management practices consistently are linked with antisocial behavior on the part of children and adolescents (e.g., Rutter, Tizard, and Whitmore, 1970; Forgatch, Chamberlin, and Gabrielson, 1982; Patterson et al., 1975; Patterson and Stouthamer-Loeber, 1984). The family management skills in question involve such matters as monitoring the adolescents' whereabouts, using effective discipline for antisocial behavior, calling on effective problem-solving skills, and supporting the development of prosocial skills.

In one recent study (Patterson and Stouthamer-Loeber, 1984), family management practices were related to the delinquency of seventh and tenth grade boys. Delinquency was measured both by police contacts and self-report. The measures of family management skills involved monitoring, discipline, problem solving, and reinforcement. Monitoring was assessed through a series of interviews with the parents and the adolescents, basically trying to obtain an accurate account of parental supervision and knowledge of the adolescents' whereabouts. Discipline was assessed in terms of whether the mother followed up on her commands, the father's consistency in discipline style, and the mother's consistency in discipline style. Problem solving was based on videotaped observations of the quality of family interaction and problem resolution. Reinforcement was assessed through observation of parent–child interaction, a child interview, and interviewers' ratings filled out at the end of sessions with the family. In particular, the parents' reinforcement of prosocial behavior was of interest. As shown in table 14.6, parental monitoring was much more strongly related to delinquency than discipline, problem solving, or reinforcement, although discipline, and to a lesser degree,

Table 14.6 Relation of family management practices to delinquency in grades seven and ten

Family management practice	Police contacts	Self-reported delinquent life-style
Monitoring	.55	.54
Discipline	.30	.35
Problem solving	−.03	.04
Reinforcement	−.09	−.24

Source: After data presented by Patterson, G. R., and M. Stouthamer, "The Correlation of Family Management Practices and Delinquency," Child Development, 55, 1299–1307, 1984. © The Society for Research in Child Development, Inc.

reinforcement also showed significant associations with delinquency. Further, it is important to note that parental monitoring also differentiated moderate offenders from persistent offenders. It seems that parents of delinquents are indifferent trackers of their sons' whereabouts, the type of companions they keep, or the kind of activities they engage in. When rule-breaking behavior occurs, such parents are less likely to provide punishment, such as loss of a privilege, work detail, or loss of allowance. If they react to such information at all, it often is in the form of lecturing, scolding, or barking out a threat, abrasive overtures usually not backed up by effective consequences. The significant association of discipline and delinquency suggested that consistent application of effective punishment such as time out, loss of privileges, and the like is necessary for long-term reduction in adolescents' antisocial behavior. Thus, from Patterson's perspective, both parental monitoring and discipline are key ingredients in determining whether an adolescent will engage in delinquent behavior.

An important question arises when we consider the role family processes play in delinquency. Do family processes cause delinquency? Or, are they just correlated with delinquency? And, possibly, are family processes the consequence of delinquency? These intriguing questions are explored further in Perspective on Adolescent Development 14.3.

FAMILY PROCESSES AND DELINQUENCY: CAUSE, CORRELATE, OR CONSEQUENCE?

Michael Rutter and Norman Garmezy (1983) raise the important question of whether research revealing an association of family experiences with delinquency involves family experiences as a cause, a correlate, or a consequence of delinquency. The associations may simply reflect some third factor, such as genetic influences; they may be a result of the disturbing effect of the child's behavior on family interaction; or they may indicate that family stress may lead to delinquency through some type of environmental effect.

The first possibility, whether some third factor is involved, can be examined by determining whether the association between family experiences and delinquency hold up when other significant variables are controlled for. It has been found that even when social class and social atmosphere in the neighborhood are controlled for, a link between family experiences and delinquency still holds (McCord, 1980; West and Farrington, 1977; Wilson, 1980). It also seems that early family stresses have long term effects mainly because they lead to forms of disturbance in the child that seem to persist rather than because a delayed or sleeper effect has occurred (Robins, 1978; West and Farrington, 1977). Further research also reveals that changes for the better in family relationships are linked with reduced conduct disturbances later in development (Rutter, 1971). With regard to the possibility that genetic mechanisms are involved in the association between family experience and delinquency, little research is available. However, several studies do suggest that genetic vulnerabilities on the part of the child might render the child more susceptible to environmental stress (Hutchings and Mednick, 1974; Crowe, 1984).

Not only is it difficult to test the influence of genetic mechanisms, but it also is not an easy task to test the effects the child might have on the association between family processes and delinquency. Clearly, as we have argued throughout this book, socialization is a reciprocal process and one involving mutual regulation. And there is evidence that parental childrearing practices that seem to be effective with most children are not efficient in controlling delinquents (Patterson, 1982). Nonetheless, while causal influences are likely bidirectional, there likely are a number of circumstances where the predominant influence is from parent to child.

Rutter and Garmezy (1983) conclude that family influences do have some kind of environmental influence on the development of delinquency or other conduct disturbances. The key family factors that seem to be involved in the emergence of conduct disturbances are family discord, deviant parental (and sibling) models, weak parent–child relationships, and poor discipline and monitoring of the child's activities. An example of research suggesting the importance of such family variables in the emergence of conduct disturbances is the work of Gerald Patterson (1982; Patterson and Stouthamer-Loeber, 1985). As we saw earlier, through careful and systematic observations of children and their families, Patterson concluded the following two factors were most likely to describe the social world of families with delinquents: (1) inadequate parental supervision and monitoring; (2) inconsistent and inappropriate discipline.

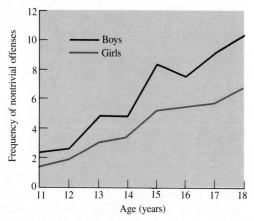

Figure 14.3 Mean frequency of nontrivial incidents committed by boys and girls eleven to eighteen years old.

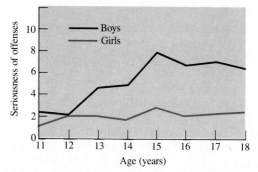

Figure 14.4 Mean seriousness of delinquent offenses for boys and girls eleven to eighteen years old.

Now that we have considered what juvenile delinquency is and its nature, we turn our attention to another important part of understanding delinquency—its developmental course.

The Developmental Course of Delinquency

Let's explore the course of trivial and nontrivial delinquent acts and then whether individuals who are delinquents grow up to become criminals in adulthood.

Age-Related Trivial and Nontrivial Delinquent Acts

The National Survey of Youth (Gold and Reimer, 1975) asked 1,395 adolescents about their delinquent behavior. As is indicated in figure 14.3, the incidence of nontrivial delinquent acts rose from the early part of adolescence to the later stages (from the eleven- to eighteen-year age range); the eighteen-year-old boys and girls confessed to about five times more nontrivial delinquent behavior than the eleven-year-olds did. Note that there is an acceleration of delinquent acts around the age of fifteen. And notice in figure 14.4, which portrays the seriousness of delinquent acts, that there is also a very obvious increase in seriousness for boys around the age of fifteen. Also note that when the seriousness of delinquent acts is considered, there appears to be no increase from age eleven to eighteen for girls, but there is a considerable increase over this age span for boys.

Other information collected by the Institute of Social Research Youth in Transition Study (O'Malley, Bachman, and Johnston, 1977) allows us to see whether delinquent trends continue in late adolescence and young adulthood. In this investigation, delinquent behavior was tracked for boys from the tenth grade through their twenty-third year of life. Like the National Survey of Youth, acts such as vandalism, theft, assault and threatened assault, shoplifting, armed robbery and joyriding were viewed as delinquent. Such behaviors declined from age sixteen to eighteen, rose at nineteen, then declined through age twenty-three. In sum, it appears that serious delinquent acts seem to peak around the age of fifteen and then, in general, decline through late adolescence and early adulthood.

Delinquency in Adolescence and Criminal Activity in Adulthood

We have seen that serious delinquent acts decrease during the latter part of adolescence and during the beginning of early adulthood. But it is also important to assess whether the adolescents who commit serious delinquent acts continue to engage in antisocial behavior as adults. We do not have much actual data related to this important issue, but the information collected as part of the Youth in Transition project at the University of Michigan does shed some light on this matter (Johnston, 1973; Johnston, O'Malley, and Eveland, 1978; O'Malley, Bachman, and Johnston, 1977). For example, the relations of delinquent behavior in adolescence to criminal behavior in young adulthood was investigated. While the correlations are significant—

To what extent is delinquency in adolescence associated with criminal activity in adulthood?

that is, the individual engaged in delinquent behavior in adolescence was more likely to engage in criminal behavior in young adulthood—the relation is not a particularly strong one. In addition to criminal behavior, this investigation also evaluated the illicit use of drugs and the extent of formal education achieved in young adulthood. Piecing all of the findings together, we find that the more heavily an adolescent is engaged in delinquency (which is determined by the seriousness of the offenses and how frequent and prolonged the behaviors are), the less education he will pursue and the more likely he will be involved in criminal activity and in the illicit use of drugs in young adulthood. However, many of the adolescents who engage in serious delinquent acts do not become criminals as adults. And among those who commit less serious delinquent acts, there is virtually no relation to behavior in young adulthood. In sum, for most adolescents, their involvement in delinquent behavior does not predict their behavior in young adulthood very accurately.

Next, let's consider a final, very important aspect of delinquency. What is the best way to intervene and help adolescents who frequently commit delinquent acts?

Intervention Programs Designed to Help Delinquents

Just as many explanations have been given as to why delinquency occurs, so have there been many intervention programs designed to help delinquents.

The Overall Scope of Delinquency Intervention Programs

A large book likely could be filled with just brief descriptions of the varied attempts to reduce delinquency. These attempts include forms of individual and group psychotherapy, family therapy, behavior modification, recreation, vocational training, alternative schools, survival camping and wilderness canoeing, incarceration and probation, "big brothers" and "big sisters," community organizations, and Bible reading to name some of the more popular suggestions (Gold and Petronio, 1980). However, we actually know surprisingly little about what actually does help reduce delinquency and, for the most part, interventions have not been very successful. If they were successful, we would be seeing reduced delinquency rates, but we are not.

The Juvenile Justice System

In a review of intervention programs designed to help delinquents (Gold and Petronio, 1980), it was concluded that the major treatment of delinquency has been housed in the juvenile justice system. Since about 1900, juveniles have been treated differently than adults by the court system. The underlying belief is that children and adolescents, still in their formative years, are not as fully responsible for their actions as adults are. In this way, delinquency is viewed more as a mental illness than as criminality, and the guilt for the offense is not placed on the individual adolescent. Treatment for delinquents is generally designed to be more curative than punitive.

Nonetheless, in recent years, the juvenile justice system has gradually begun to move away from the developmental distinction that was made at the turn of the century. The Supreme Court's landmark decision in 1967 in the Gault case held that juveniles should be punished for their antisocial behavior, just as adults are punished for theirs (U.S. Supreme Court, 1967). Since that time, the juvenile justice system has begun to resemble the adult system more closely in such areas as right to counsel, rules of evidence, and self-incrimination. And, at the same time, there has been a movement to change the definition of juvenile delinquency so that it matches that for adult crime. If this definition were to become law, then running away from home, truancy from school, or frequenting immoral places, for example, would no longer be matters under the jurisdiction of the judicial system.

Arguments for change in the juvenile-delinquency system are rooted in the belief that the system was created to promote child and adolescent development. These arguments state that the freedom of too many adolescents has been restricted based on insufficient evidence and for insufficient reasons, that treatment has been more punitive than curative, and that the overall effect of the judicial system has been to increase rather than decrease juvenile delinquency (Gold and Petronio, 1980). There is actually good reason to believe that the juvenile judicial system does need to be overhauled, although there is little or no agreement on what should be done. For example, investigations usually show either that the judicial system is ineffective (e.g., Gold and Williams, 1969; Gold, 1970; Farrington and West, 1977) or at best, neutral in effect (Gold and Petronio, 1980).

Several Programs That Work in Reducing Delinquency

As was mentioned at the beginning of this section, there are many other programs besides the judicial system that are designed to curb delinquent behavior. While most programs do not seem to work very effectively, some of the programs seem to be better than others at reducing delinquency. Let's look at some of the more successful ones.

One intervention program that was effective in reducing the delinquency rate consisted of an alternative school in Quincy, Illinois (Bowman, 1959). Sixty boys in the eighth grade who were below average in ability and who were not doing well in school were selected for the study and randomly assigned to one of two groups. Forty of the boys were exposed to a curriculum different than the conventional one at the school, while the remaining twenty boys continued to attend conventional classes as a control group. The teachers of the two experimental classes were chosen because they seemed to have an interest in and sympathy for adolescents who get in trouble. The classes were small and the delinquents were given considerable individual attention. Student-teacher interaction was informal and friendly. Formal grading was abandoned, and each student was instead evaluated on the basis of his own progress. Discipline was firm but not punitive, and focused on problem solving. At the end of the school term, the students were given the opportunity to return to conventional classrooms. Only two chose to do so.

When compared with the control group of delinquents who remained in a conventional classroom, those in the experimental classrooms showed marked improvement. While they did not do better on standardized achievement tests, they perceived that they were doing better academically and said they now liked school better. Their attendance improved, while those in the control group attended school even less. School and police records documented that the antisocial and delinquency behavior of the experimental-group delinquents decreased by one-third, while the record for the control group tripled. And finally, a follow-up study suggested that the experimental boys made a better transition to the world of work than their control-group counterparts.

Martin Gold and Richard Petronio (1980) describe why they think the Quincy program was so successful:

> We find features in the Quincy program that we believe were essential to its success because they addressed peculiarly adolescent needs for autonomy and potency. We suspect that adolescent scholastic failures are under exceptional stress. Their failure not only reflects on their current competence, but it also foretells an oppressive future. Education is the gateway to a respectable adult status, and the importance of scholastic competence is impressed on youngsters as they make the transition from elementary to secondary school. Furthermore, the response of teachers and staff to the students' poor performance as well as to the often negative reactions of the students to these responses and to failure generate even heavier demands for docility and dependency on the poor students than the adequate ones. There is great potential in this situation for a deepening cycle of poor performance; poor student-teacher/student-staff relationships; feelings of derogated selves; disruptive behavior, and so on. This cycle runs counter to the social and psychological forces that impel adolescents to develop a self-image as autonomous and effective adults-to-be.
>
> The Quincy program may have been effective because it interrupted this cycle. The alternative program offered its students special opportunities to be autonomous by permitting individual and group decision making to direct classrom activity, and it raised students' feelings of effectiveness by avoiding deprecating comparisons with universalistic norms. Meanwhile, the informal and sympathetic interpersonal relationships with their teachers probably gave students the emotional support they needed to make the transition to the new educational mode without threatening their independence. (Gold and Petronio, 1980)

In another attempt to reduce delinquency (Gold and Mattick, 1974), the focus was on street gangs in Chicago. Boys Clubs assigned street workers and community organizers to specific inner-city locations, while nearby neighborhoods were studied as controls. While there was little reduction in the delinquency rate of the adolescents in the targeted neighborhoods, the workers were able to help boys find jobs or return to school.

In addition to attempts to intervene in schools and community systems, a number of remedial efforts have attempted to change the family systems of delinquent adolescents (e.g., Klein, Alexander, and Parsons, 1977). As family members learn to help rather than to harm one another, the delinquent may feel better understood and may learn to cope more adaptively with his or her world.

But in some cases, particularly as the child grows into adolescence, the family's influence may no longer be dominant. As family influence wanes, teachers, other esteemed adults, and peers become significant socializing influences. As has been mentioned, an understanding teacher or school counselor can make the difference for a troubled youth, influencing her to behave in a more socially competent and desirable fashion. A juvenile delinquent often feels that everyone in the world is against him; he needs someone to show an interest in what he is doing. If a teacher or counselor shows faith in his ability to act in socially responsible ways and develops specific academic and nonacademic programs for him to follow in this belief, the result can be changed behavior in the adolescent.

So far in our description of programs designed to help delinquents, we have had little to say about behavior modification. In some cases, behavior modification has been successful in reducing delinquency; in others, it has not. In Perspective on Adolescent Development 14.4, we explore further the use of behavior modification in reducing delinquency, highlighting a well-known program called Achievement Place.

Achievement Place is a program that was started by Ellery and Elaine Phillips in 1967 (Phillips, 1968). A number of replicas of Achievement Place are now in use around the United States. The basic theme of Achievement Place is to take groups of six to eight boys, usually between the ages of twelve and sixteen, who have been in legal trouble and assign them to a house in the community. There their activities are supervised on a twenty-four-hour basis by "teaching parents," who work with the youths in the house and also interact with parents and teachers to help solve problems.

The main focus of the behavior modification program at Achievement Place involves a token economy. A **token economy** is a system, based on operant conditioning, in which an individual in a clinical setting is given artificial rewards such as poker chips for socially constructive behavior. The tokens themselves can be exchanged for desirable items and privileges. An entering youth is familiarized with the token point system, and tokens can be used to obtain use of the telephone and the playground; snacks; television watching; and home time—weekend passes to his natural home. Other privileges involve one- to three-dollar allowances and a savings bond program.

An important aspect of Achievement Place is that the youths continue to attend the same schools they went to before they entered the program. Their behavior in school is monitored by the teacher, and feedback is provided to the youth as well as the Achievement Place "parents" through weekly or daily report cards. The boys interact with one another at Achievement Place, attend daily conferences, calculate the points they earn, and engage in leisure activities. They are also instructed in study skills to improve their grades at school.

As shown in figure 14.5 by most of the criteria used to evaluate the success of such programs, the Achievement Place experiment has been a success (Fixsen, et al., 1976). For example, the recidivism rates at twelve and twenty-four months after treatment had been completed were much less than for two control groups of boys, one of which attended a traditional boys' training school and one consisting of boys who were placed on probation, but received no special training. Further, ninety percent of the boys who attended Achievement Place were still in school after three semesters of treatment compared to nine percent of the boys' school youth and thirty-seven percent of the boys on probation.

Although these results indicate the success of Achievement Place, the long-term failures of other operant behavior modification programs in institutions (Cohen and Filipczak, 1971; Jeness, 1974) suggest that any final conclusion about such programs should be made with caution. One of the crucial differences may be in the nature of an institution versus a community-based center (Kalish, 1981). The changes that take place in a community-based program like Achievement Place happen in the context of stimuli that originally controlled the undesirable behavior (peers, environment, status seeking, and so on). An institution removed from the community, such as a traditional juvenile home, is a setting that does not contain many of the stimuli that originally controlled the undesirable behavior. Thus, even though operant conditioning may be implemented in such institutional settings, the fact that they are so far removed from the context in which the behavior was learned may be a key factor in their failure.

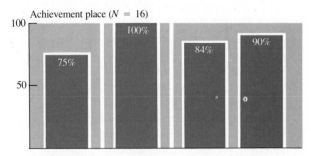

Achievement place (N = 16)

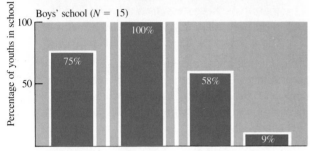

Boys' school (N = 15)

Percentage of youths in school

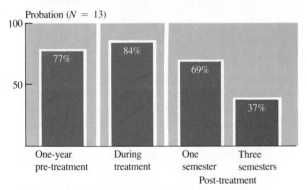

Probation (N = 13)

| One-year pre-treatment | During treatment | One semester | Three semesters |

Post-treatment

Figure 14.5 **The percentage of youths still in school at four points in time at Achievement Place, a traditional boys' training school, and while on probation.**

Conclusions about Intervention Programs with Delinquents

In their review of intervention programs for delinquents, Gold and Petronio (1980) concluded that while the sources and styles of successful programs often vary, two themes seem to be dominant: (1) the support of warm, accepting relationships with adults, and (2) the enhancement of the adolescent's self-image as an autonomous and effective individual.

This concludes our discussion of drugs, alcohol, and delinquency. In the next chapter, we'll look at a number of other problems and disturbances in adolescence, and we'll consider further how to help adolescents with problems and disturbances.

Summary

I. Information about drugs focuses on the range of drugs and actual drug use by adolescents, specific drugs taken by adolescents, and drugs and schools.

   A. Adolescents take a wide range of drugs from licit drugs such as nicotine to highly illicit drugs like heroin.

   B. The most extensive data about drug use come from the Institute of Social Research at the University of Michigan through studies conducted by Johnston, Bachman, and O'Malley. They have been surveying high school seniors on a national basis for a number of years. Almost two-thirds of adolescents take an illicit drug at some point in their lives. The most widely used illicit drug is marijuana, while the most widely taken licit drug is alcohol. At some point about the end of the 1970s and the beginning of the 1980s, a downward trend in illicit drug use by adolescents took place. For the most part, males are more involved in drug use than females, although females take one stimulant far more often—diet pills.

C. Among the specific drugs taken by adolescents are marijuana, nicotine, stimulants, depressants, hallucinogens, cocaine, heroin, and inhalants.

1. Learning about marijuana focuses on what it is, psychological and physical effects (which can be substantial), reasons adolescents take marijuana, parent–peer influences, laws, and trends in use (which has been declining).

2. Knowledge about nicotine emphasizes its incidence (which has been decreasing) parent–peer influences (they both are important), and preventive health efforts (which can be studied in terms of agent, environment, and host).

3. Many adolescents take synthetic stimulants, or amphetamines. Females are more likely to take diet pills, while males are somewhat more likely to take stay-awake and look-alike pills.

4. The most common depressants taken by adolescents are barbiturates and Quaaludes. There has been a downward trend in the nonmedical use of depressants by adolescents in recent years.

5. Hallucinogens produce hallucinations or distortions of reality. They include LSD and PCP. Their use has declined in recent years.

6. Cocaine at one time was used in Coca-Cola. It is a stimulant that has been given considerable media exposure and its use has remained about the same in recent years.

7. Heroin, a derivative of opium, is a very dangerous drug that is rarely used by adolescents.

8. Inhalants include any aerosol or gaseous fumes, other than smoke, that are inhaled to make the user feel high. This is the only classification of drugs that increased in use from 1983 to 1984 in the University of Michigan study.

D. Schools often are locations for drug use and they can play an important role in prevention or intervention. Teachers are particularly important in detecting drug use. Effective drug programs do not involve detection, discipline, and scare tactics, but rather provide relevant information and deal with important psychological effects. While there have been numerous school related drug programs, few research assessments of those programs have been conducted.

II. Information about alcohol emphasizes prevalence of drinking among adolescents; physical, psychological, and behavioral effects; prevention and intervention efforts; and deviant behavior.

A. Alcohol is the most widely used drug by adolescents. There has been a slight decrease in drinking since 1979, but heavy drinking remains alarmingly high.

B. The physical effects of alcohol include a depression of many of the brain's activities, the familiar pattern of drunkenness, and, after prolonged exposure, possibly unconsciousness. Ulcers and damage to the brain can result from prolonged, extensive use. As blood alcoholic content (BAC) increases, there is a loss of mental efficiency, more sedated feelings ensue, and muscle coordination becomes difficult. Feelings of euphoria, slurred speech, decreased inhibition, less efficient vision and hearing, deterioration of judgment, and problems with gross motor skills occur when BAC reaches .10 percent. When BAC reaches .20 percent, nearly all drinkers show obvious signs of intoxication.

C. Biological/genetic and psychosocial factors are associated with adolescent drinking patterns.
1. There is some evidence for a genetic factor in alcoholism, but the precise way this works is unknown.
2. Personality/adjustment, family/peer, and cultural factors are possible psychosocial factors related to adolescent drinking.

D. As with cigarette smoking, it is helpful to think of prevention in terms of agent, environment, and host. Prevention efforts aimed at each of these three domains have shown some success. Intervention efforts are greatly varied and it should be kept in mind that adolescents with drinking problems are not a homogeneous group.

E. Heavy drinking in adolescence is associated with adjustment problems, but it is not known whether drinking causes deviant behavior or vice versa. Delinquents often drink for the effect, while nondelinquents are more likely to drink for social reasons.

III. Our study of juvenile delinquency focused on what juvenile delinquency is, the nature of juvenile delinquency, developmental changes, and intervention programs.

A. A "juvenile delinquent" is an adolescent who breaks the law or engages in behavior that is considered illegal. It is a broad concept ranging from littering to murder. Estimates regarding the incidence of delinquency are sketchy, but at least two percent of youth are involved in court cases. Measuring delinquency is not an easy task.

B. Many different explanations for delinquency have been given, ranging from biological instincts to independence and peer orientation. Erikson's ideas on identity development provide a framework for understanding delinquency as does a view that describes delinquency in terms of a lack of self-control. Sociocultural factors that are important to consider are those involving social class and community as well as family/peer influences.
1. The norms of many lower class peer groups and gangs are antisocial. Getting into and staying out of trouble sometimes becomes a prominent feature of adolescent life in some lower class settings. A community with a high crime rate exposes adolescents to criminal models whose behavior often may be rewarded.
2. A considerable amount of attention has been directed at family influences on delinquency. In particular, Patterson's recent work is important in documenting the importance of parental monitoring and discipline in promoting delinquency. The question has been raised as to whether family processes cause delinquency, are merely correlated with delinquency, or are a consequence of delinquency. While the evidence is not crystal clear, it seems that family processes do play at least some causative role. And, delinquents tend to associate with delinquent peers.

C. The incidence of nontrivial delinquent acts rises as we move from the early to the later part of adolescence. With regard to serious delinquent acts, they peak at about age fifteen for boys and then decrease slightly. For girls, there is a lower, more consistent rate of delinquency in terms of serious acts throughout adolescence. While there is a positive correlation between incidence of delinquency in adolescence and criminal activity in adulthood, the relation is not a very strong one. Many adolescents who engage in serious delinquent acts do not grow up to become criminals.

D. A large book could be filled with brief descriptions of the varied attempts to reduce delinquency. The juvenile justice system clearly has not been effective in reducing delinquency or delinquency rates would be going down, which they are not. Effective programs with delinquents seem to involve (1) support of warm, accepting relationships with adults, (2) enhancement of the adolescent's self-image as an autonomous and effective individual.

Key Terms

agent interventions *591*

amphetamines *590*

BAC *596*

cocaine *592*

environment interventions *591*

hallucinogens *592*

heroin *593*

host interventions *591*

inhalants *593*

Quaaludes (methaqualone) *592*

THC *586*

token economy *610*

Suggested Readings

Coleman, J. C., Butcher, J. N., and Carson, R. C. (1984). *Abnormal psychology and modern life.* Glenview, Ill: Scott, Foresman.
This book provides an interesting overview of the nature of abnormal development and contains an excellent chapter on substance-use problems.

Engs, R. C. (1979). *Responsible drug and alcohol use.* New York: MacMillan.
Contains valuable information about intelligent, responsible choices related to drug and alcohol use. Includes many studies about the effects of various drugs on the human body, including possible harmful effects.

Gold, M., and Petronio, R. J. (1980). Delinquent behavior in adolescence. In *Handbook of adolescent psychology,* ed. J. Adelson. New York: John Wiley. *An excellent overview of the nature of delinquency, developmental factors involved in delinquency, and intervention programs.*

Monitoring The Future (1975–1985).
Each year now the Institute of Social Research at the University of Michigan publishes the national results of their survey on drug use by high school seniors. The volumes are edited by Bachman, Johnston, and O'Malley, the order of editorship varying according to the year published.

Chapter 15

Problems and Disturbances in Adolescence and the Nature of Abnormality

Prologue

Elizabeth—Twelve Year Old with School-Related Problems

Elizabeth, a pretty, twelve-year-old black girl, was brought to the hospital by her mother following an incident in which she had thrown a book at the school principal. The principal had been trying to find out the reason Elizabeth was crying in the classroom. Elizabeth was restless and confused and could not concentrate for more than a few minutes. She said that people didn't like her, that everybody thought she was ugly. She believed that she had been justified in throwing the book at the principal: "He was bugging me; I was nervous." While Elizabeth's mother was interviewed in another room at the hospital, Elizabeth began to pace up and down, saying that she was feeling hot. She showed someone her clammy, perspiring hands, and began to cry, saying, "I'm dying. Something in my throat doesn't let me breathe. My stomach isn't pumping. People are trying to kill me. I'll die if I stay here. I was normal before I came. Now I am dying. . . ." During the next three days, Elizabeth had one or two severe anxiety attacks a day. Between the attacks, she was anxious, restless, and depressed. She did not show any sign of psychosis, clinically or on psychological testings.

The background history obtained on Elizabeth revealed that she had been an insecure, timid, and friendless child since entering school. When Elizabeth was seven years old, her father had been charged with attempting to seduce a thirteen-year-old female neighbor, and though the charges had been dismissed, the family was alienated and ostracized from the neighborhood. Elizabeth's father had then deserted the family, leaving Elizabeth, her thirteen-year-old brother, and her mother with no source of income. Elizabeth's mother was a tense, depressed woman who felt harassed by the responsibilities of finding a job and caring for her children. Six months before Elizabeth's admission to the hospital, her mother had found a job that kept her away from home from 8:00 A.M. to 6:00 P.M. She had not had time to go over to school when Elizabeth brought a letter from her teacher reporting that Elizabeth seemed very unhappy, that her schoolwork had deteriorated, and that she was frequently absent. Elizabeth's mother was now extremely angry at Elizabeth. She explained, "I knew she was sad and hypersensitive, but it was not causing anybody else any problem. Now she has become violent and I can't take that."

In this chapter, we will see that school-related problems are one of the major reasons adolescents are referred for psychological help.

Source: Chess, S. & Hassibi, M. Principles and practice of child psychiatry. New York: Plenum, 1978.

*I*n this chapter, we continue our discussion of problems and disturbances in adolescence. In the first part of the chapter, a number of specific problems and disturbances are evaluated. In the second part, we focus on the nature of abnormality, the science of developmental psychopathology, and continuity–discontinuity in disorders.

Disturbances in Adolescence: A Wide Range of Problems

In the last chapter, we considered the major problems of drug and alcohol abuse as well as delinquency. Here we study other disturbances, but first we consider whether there is an increase in problems during adolescence and the wide range of problems that occur. The specific problems of school-related problems, depression, suicide, eating disorders, and schizophrenia are covered.

The Wide Spectrum of Problems in Adolescence

It is important to evaluate whether there is an increase in problems in adolescence.

Is There an Increase in Problems during Adolescence?

Recall from our discussion in Chapter 1 that a number of prominent adolescent researchers believe too much attention has been given to problems and disturbances in adolescence while ignoring the normal course of adolescent development (e.g., Adelson, 1979; Hill, 1976). They argue that most adolescents do not experience intense turmoil or deep emotional disturbances as the traditional stereotype of storm and stress suggests. Are Joseph Adelson and John Hill correct in arguing that there has been a tendency to overemphasize the degree to which adolescents experience emotional disturbances? Probably so, although there is no overall grand set of data that we can call on to document the point that adolescents do not experience more emotional problems than children. One investigation by Thomas

Drawing by Chas. Addams; © 1974 The New Yorker Magazine, Inc.

Achenbach and Craig Edelbrock (1981), though, provides at least some support for the position of Adelson and Hill. They investigated 1300 children and adolescents who were referred to psychological clinics for professional help. As indicated in figure 15.1 the boys and girls ranged in age from four to sixteen and the adolescents who were referred for help did not have a larger number of problems overall than the younger children. Thirteen hundred children and adolescents who were not referred for clinical help also were evaluated. As indicated in figure 15.1, the adolescents in the nonclinical sample, just as in the clinical sample, did not show a greater number of problems than the children. The measure used to assess the children's and adolescents' problems was the Child Behavior Checklist (CBCL) and consists of 118 problems—in this study, parents filled the checklist out by checking off

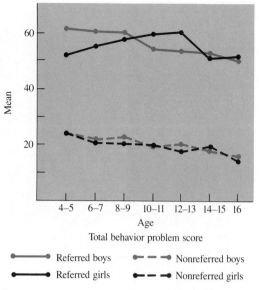

Total behavior problem score

● ———— ● Referred boys   ● – – – ● Nonreferred boys

● ———— ● Referred girls   ● – – – ● Nonreferred girls

Percentage of referred and nonreferred children of each gender for whom each behavior problem was reported, and total behavior problem score for each group.

Figure 15.1 **The total number of problems of clinically and nonclinically referred children and adolescents ages 4–16.**

Adolescent female problems are more internalized than those of males.

which problems their children had. While studies such as Achenbach and Edelbrock's (1981) do not evaluate the intensity or duration of the problems and it was not based on a national sample (it was conducted in the Washington, D.C. area), it casts some gloom over conclusions suggesting there is a dramatic increase in emotional disturbances during the adolescent years. Indeed, as noted in figure 15.1 there actually was a tendency for behavior problems to decline with age.

The Wide Spectrum of Problems

In the study by Achenbach and Edelbrock (1981), the behavior problems that most likely were associated with whether the adolescent was referred for psychological help were: unhappy, sad, or depressed and poor school work (figure 15.2). Certain problems that have been the subject of considerable interest by clinical psychologists, such as fears and bed-wetting, showed very small differences between clinically referred and nonreferred adolescents (figure 15.3). Also, note that fears and bed-wetting were two problems that were more prominent in childhood than adolescence. Other problems that were less likely to occur in adolescence than

childhood were those pertaining to crying, demanding attention (figure 15.4), disobedient at home, poor peer relations, showing off, and talking too much. Problems that were more prevalent in adolescence than childhood were those pertaining to being overly tired, being secretive (figure 15.5), sexual preoccupation, truancy, hanging around children who get in trouble, and alcohol and drugs.

Sex and Social Class Differences in Disturbances

In the investigation by Achenbach and Edelbrock (1981), parents of adolescents from lower class backgrounds reported more problems and fewer competencies than parents of middle socioeconomic status, although there was no overall tendency for more problems to be reported for one gender than the other. Most of the problems reported for lower socioeconomic male adolescents were undercontrolled, externalizing behaviors (such as destroying others' things, or fighting), while the problems reported for girls tended to be either overcontrolled, internalizing behaviors (such as unhappy, sad, or depressed, or not clearly classifiable as undercontrolled). Racial differences were few and small in number.

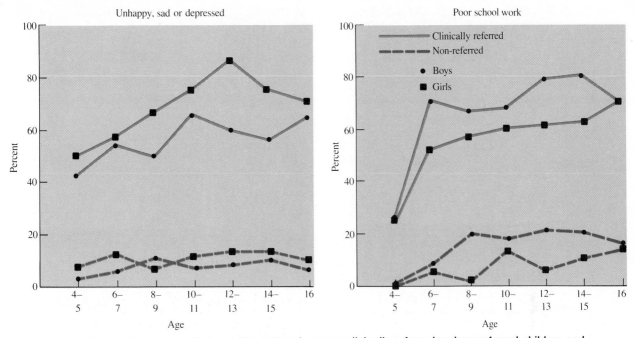

Figure 15.2   The two items most likely to differentiate between clinically referred and nonreferred children and adolescents.

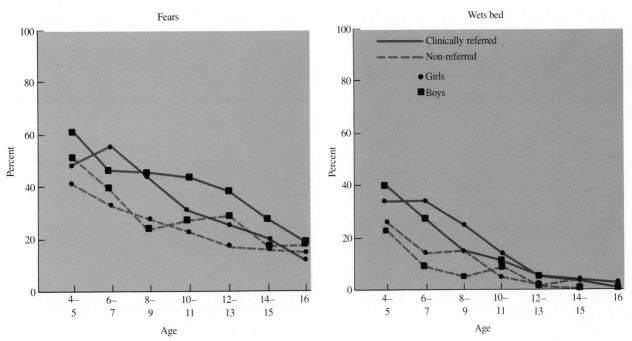

Figure 15.3   Two items that were less likely to characterize adolescents than children and were unable to distinguish clinically referred and nonreferred children and adolescents.

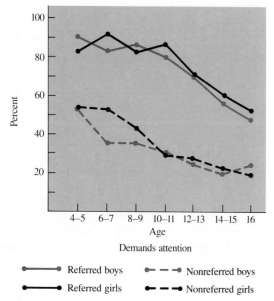

Referred boys   ●– – –● Nonreferred boys
Referred girls   ●– – –● Nonreferred girls

Figure 15.4   **Age decline in demanding attention.**

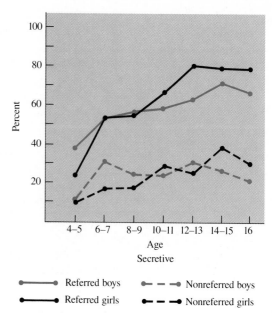

Referred boys   ●– – –● Nonreferred boys
Referred girls   ●– – –● Nonreferred girls

Figure 15.5   **Increase in problems of secretiveness during adolescence.**

Now that we have considered disturbances in adolescence in general, we turn our attention to the two disturbances that were most likely to distinguish clinically referred and nonreferred children and adolescents—school-related problems and depression.

School-Related Problems

Difficulties in school achievement, whether secondary to other kinds of disturbances or primary problems in themselves, seem to account for more adolescent referrals for clinical treatment than any other problem (Weiner, 1980). This fact alone demonstrates the importance our society places on academic achievement, as was discussed in Chapter 13. Because underachievement is so frequently associated with adolescent problems and disturbances, we'll describe it further here, along with the problems of school phobia and dropping out of school.

Underachievement

Underachievement in school refers to the failure to receive grades commensurate with the adolescent's intellectual abilities. Unexpected poor school performance

has been estimated to occur in twenty-five percent of school children. And it appears that approximately one-third of adolescents seen in psychiatric clinics are referred because of learning problems (Gardner and Speery, 1974; Schecter, 1974; Zigmond, 1969). Further, more than fifty percent of college students who request counseling and psychotherapy do so because of worries about studying and grades (Blaine and McArthur, 1971).

According to Irving Weiner (1980), school underachievement may occur because of sociocultural factors such as family and neighborhood value systems that minimize the importance of education and peer group attitudes that stamp academic success as unmanly for boys and unfeminine for girls. From Weiner's perspective, this type of underachievement does not constitute a psychological disturbance. Rather, school problems that do involve psychological disturbances can be traced to two circumstances. First, attention, concentration, and specific learning handicaps, often associated with neurological problems, usually are detected in the elementary school years (Torgesen, 1975). Second, neurotic patterns of family interaction may produce a pattern of what is referred to as **passive–aggressive** underachievement. It is the second pattern of underachievement that is more characteristic of adolescents with achievement problems; this is the pattern we will focus on here.

From Weiner's perspective, there are three factors that usually contribute to the development of passive–aggressive underachievement:

1. Extensive hostility, usually toward parents, that cannot be expressed directly
2. Worry about rivalry with parents and siblings that produces fear of failure or fear of success
3. Adopting a passive–aggressive pattern of behavior in coping with difficult, stressful situations

Investigations of underachieving adolescents frequently reveal that they are more likely than their achieving counterparts to feel hostility that they cannot express directly (e.g., Davids and Hainsworth, 1967). When parental demands include extraordinarily high standards for academic achievement, they are likely to trigger poor school performance (which may be an indirect retaliation toward the achievement-oriented parents).

Passive–aggressive underachieving adolescents often feel either a fear of failure or a fear of success that restricts their achievement. Adolescents who fear failure usually have negative perceptions of their abilities and feel that they will never be able to equal the achievements of their parents or siblings. Such adolescents usually have a very low tolerance for criticism; the more parents or teachers tell them they should be earning better grades, the more they withdraw from trying to compete in school. Adolescents who fear failure often set unrealistically high goals but rarely work hard in trying to achieve them. They usually are unwilling to risk making a mistake, and they often pride themselves on being able to accomplish something with a minimum of effort. This pattern of underachievement is likely to appear at certain transition points in adolescence—during the transition from junior high to high school, high school to college, or from a less to a more competitive school. In such situations, adolescents usually are confronted with more difficult coursework and more demanding academic standards than in the past. Sometimes this has been called "big-league shock" (e.g., McArthur, 1971).

Another group of underachieving adolescents is more concerned with fear of success. In this kind of underachieving pattern, the adolescent worries about doing well in school because she doesn't want to make other family members envious or resentful. In such circumstances, the adolescent often does not compete to avoid the negative comments she fears may follow. When fear-of-failure and fear-of-success adolescents are compared, fear-of-success adolescents are more likely to deprecate their abilities publicly. These adolescents also frequently set goals that can be attained with little effort. When they reach these easy goals, they usually don't push on for higher accomplishments; in fact, they sometimes say they were lucky to do as well as they did (e.g., Romer, 1975). In particular, fear-of-success adolescents may begin to underachieve when they see they are about to surpass the academic accomplishments of their parents. Sometimes this becomes acute during the senior year of high school ("senior neurosis"); students whose parents never attended college begin to do poorly in school, thus reducing their chances to go to college.

According to Weiner (1980), the underlying anger of passive–aggressive underachieving adolescents and their anxiety about rivalry may not be obvious. Such feelings often go undetected until the adolescent undergoes therapy. However, such behavior is often easy to detect from the adolescent's passive–aggressive style of coping with academic problems. What does it mean when we say the achievement behavior of adolescents is *passive–aggressive?* It means that they are purposely inactive. They work hard at making sure nothing happens that will raise their grades up to par. Passive–aggressive underachieving adolescents may turn their energy to extracurricular activities or outside work to the point where they have little time for studying.

These adolescents are just as energetic and hardworking as their achieving peers, but they do not expend their energy on academic concerns (e.g., Morrow and Wilson, 1961).

Think about your own secondary school years, or about adolescents you know today. Chances are you will be able to pick out a number of people you knew or know now whose behavior reflected the underachieving patterns we have described here. Next, let's look at another important aspect of school-related problems in adolescence—dropping out of school.

School Dropouts

Students with learning disabilities and behavioral disorders sometimes quit school, but there are many other adolescents who become alienated from school and simply don't want to attend classes any longer. Approximately twenty-two of every one hundred students who enter the fifth grade this year will not graduate from high school for reasons other than a physical or mental handicap (Jones, 1977). Approximately fifteen percent of these future dropouts are not from low-income families—these students will either grow bored, lack ambition, want to start working, or, for some other personal reason, will choose not to continue their schooling. The remaining eighty-five percent of the dropouts are from lower class families of various racial backgrounds. About 800,000 of these adolescents leave school each year to try to find employment; many of them are unsuccessful. The frustrations of poverty and boredom may lead to any of a number of criminal activities—pushing dope, vandalization, robbery, assault.

Youth who become alienated from school often react in one of two ways—they either retreat into the world of drugs, or they become part of a counterculture. Counterculture groups usually adopt slang and antisocial conduct as a standard of behavior, building their lives around the peer group ties of the gang.

James Mackey (1977) points to three facets of the dropout's life that can help us understand him better—personal incapacity (the feeling that one doesn't have the ability and skills needed to succeed), guidelessness (the rejection of conventional rules and regulations as a means of success), and cultural estrangement (a rejection of the predominant standards for success).

Adolescents who drop out of school often feel incompetent or incapable of dealing with their world—in other words, they have a sense of **personal incapacity.** All adolescents feel some degree of inadequacy in terms of being able to make positive things happen in their social and academic worlds, but the feeling is more intense and more prevalent in the adolescent who drops out of school. Intervention to help the adolescent about to drop out (or the adolescent who has dropped out and returned to school) might focus on establishing a curriculum including interrelated learning situations that make the adolescent feel she can positively deal with her school surroundings. Community programs may be used to make the adolescent feel she can make a positive contribution to her world—day-care centers and homes for the elderly are sorely in need of volunteers and can serve as one place where potential school dropouts might be strategically placed.

When the adolescent senses that the rules in his world have faltered, he is feeling **guidelessness.** To remedy this feeling, the following ingredients are necessary: the adolescent must develop knowledge about social rules; he must be assisted in building goals that he is willing and able to commit himself to; and he must have opportunities for testing these goals out in the real world.

When the adolescent develops a sense of **cultural estrangement,** she feels a lack of commitment to the values of her culture. Many American adolescents feel that schools are dehumanizing places that exert authoritarian control over youth. The culturally estranged adolescent who drops out of school is saying that she doesn't want to live within the boundaries of this dehumanizing setting—that she feels that virtually any experiences outside of school are preferable.

*E*zra Staples (1977) provides the following account of how the Philadelphia school district has been able to keep many adolescents from dropping out of school.

Left to his or her own devices, the disaffected student continues to drift, atrophies intellectually, is apathetic toward almost everything except the gratification of the senses, and is indifferent toward the value of self-discipline and good work habits. Rarely does the disaffection result in any kind of positive accomplishment. If there is any awareness of the external world, it is often as an oppressive, uncaring, hypocritical, and exploitative society—an adversary to be outwitted and "ripped off"; or, if this takes too much effort, one that should be ignored.

In attempting to help students fettered by such anomie, the Philadelphia public schools have initiated many programs featuring guidance, redirection, reinforcement, and encouragement. These are provided in settings that involve the students' peers, school personnel, parents, and many sectors of the community, including business and industry. Work is done in small groups, using practical approaches to the problem. The emphasis is on showing that there is light at the end of the tunnel, that the individual is able through education to shape his or her own destiny and live the good life. . . .

Recognizing that different students learn better in different types of schools, the alternatives stress variety rather than uniformity. In order to be considered an alternative, a program must provide diverse approaches to teaching and learning in core subjects and develop an approach that is significantly different from that of conventional programs. These alternative formats represent a restructuring of a student's learning experience and incorporate components of academic remediation, career education, work-study internships, open classrooms, programs for the academically talented, and special interest programs. . . .

On the secondary level (junior and senior high school), the school district of Philadelphia conducts over sixty alternative programs. The most famous of these is the Parkway Program, which actually consists of four different schools or "communities." Each of these separately housed units exploits the city's educational, cultural, and scientific institutions as part of its extended campus, using the many resources found there. A core faculty provides instruction in basic skills, offers courses in their fields of expertise, and supervises tutorials. Community volunteers with special skills offer on-site programs, classes, and internships in academic, commercial, and vocational subjects (Staples, 1977, pp. 423–24).

Additional programs in the Philadelphia school district involve ninth and tenth graders in an attempt to work with potential school dropouts even earlier. At one such school, the Penn Treaty Junior High School, a motivation and career preparation program has been established for girls who are not doing well in school. One teacher works with the adolescent girls throughout the school day to establish a close teacher-student relationship. Strong emphasis is placed on the development of

---

A number of social activities can be promoted in conjunction with other school curricula to help reduce cultural estrangement. For example, it may be desirable to allow certain youth to participate in social action projects. By working within a local government agency, the adolescent may be forced to more carefully evaluate her simplistic view of the American system. More coordination between the community and the school is critical to reducing the number of culturally estranged youth dropping out of school.

How one large city school system has succeeded in decreasing its dropout rate is detailed in Perspective on Adolescent Development 15.1.

More programs are needed that focus on ways to keep adolescents from dropping out of school.

reading skills while the girls are at school. The career education component of the program allows the girls to pursue work experience at either hospitals or elementary schools. The girls in the hospital career program spend three days a week at school and two days a week working as apprentices at the hospital, while the girls in the elementary school program help with elementary school tutoring three days a week and spend two days a week at their school.

In ways such as these, adolescents who are likely to drop out of school may be induced to continue their secondary school education. Community-based education, work-school coordination, more extensive decision-making roles for students, and more flexibility in curricula are among the factors that seem to keep such youth in school.

School Phobia

School phobia refers to the reluctance or refusal of the child or adolescent to attend school because of the intense anxiety he experiences about being there. While school phobia often is considered to be a problem associated more with elementary schools than secondary schools, it appears that school phobia is far from uncommon among junior and senior high school students, and in some cases, college students (Hodgman and Braiman, 1965; Weiner, 1970). Many clinicians report that adolescents who develop somatic (physical) symptoms that are psychological rather than physical in origin often have a great deal of anxiety about going to school. In one investigation, school phobia peaked around eleven to twelve years of age, and occurred in two to eight percent of the individuals referred to a number of guidance clinics (Kahn and Nursten, 1962).

In Irving Weiner's (1980) review of school phobia, he points out that for the most part, the characteristics of school-phobic adolescents do not differ from those of children with school phobia. School-phobic adolescents try to convince their parents to let them stay home because of some physical problem—headache or nausea—or some school circumstance—such as a teacher who is overly critical. When the adolescent is permitted to stay home, the physical complaints subside, but they reappear when the adolescent is forced to return to school. School-phobic adolescents often have overprotective parents who foster their dependence, so that staying home is reinforced as a way of coping with stress in the outside world (Malmquist, 1965). Weiner believes there are two ways adolescents with school phobia differ from school-phobic children: in adolescence, the condition is more likely to appear because of distressing circumstances at school rather than within the family, and it is more likely to signal a long-lasting style of dealing with school rather than a short-term one.

This concludes our discussion of school-related problems in adolescence. The main ideas about school-related problems as well as the wide spectrum of problems in adolescence are reviewed in Concept Table 15.1. Next, we study another prominent disturbance in adolescence—depression.

THE WIDE SPECTRUM OF PROBLEMS AND SCHOOL-RELATED PROBLEMS

Concept	Processes/related ideas	Characteristics/description
The wide spectrum of problems and disturbances	Number of problems in adolescence compared to childhood	Research data suggest that there is no increase in the number of problems in adolescence compared to childhood, although such matters as the intensity and length of the problems are not taken into account in such studies. It does seem that a stereotype overestimating the abnormality of adolescence has existed.
	The wide spectrum of problems	The behavior problems most likely to differentiate adolescent referrals for psychological help from nonreferrals in the Achenbach and Edelbrock study were: unhappy, sad, depressed and school-related problems. A number of other problems increased in adolescence while others decreased.
	Sex and social class differences	Lower class adolescents had more problems than middle-class adolescents. Girls and middle-class adolescents were more likely to have internalized problems, while boys and lower-class adolescents more often had externalized problems.
School-related problems	Underachievement	Unexpected poor school performance has been estimated to occur in twenty-five percent of children and adolescents. More than fifty percent of college students who request counseling and psychotherapy do so because of worries about studying and grades. Weiner believes underachievement may occur because of sociocultural factors, such as community, family, and peer values that minimize education. However, he believes this kind of underachievement should not be classified as a disturbance; rather, those pertaining to attentional, learning handicaps and neurotic patterns of family interaction that proclude passive–aggressive underachievement should be classed as disturbances.
	School dropouts	Approximately twenty-two of every one hundred students entering the fifth grade do not graduate from high school. The majority of the dropouts are from lower class backgrounds. Frustration and boredom may lead to problems for these youth as their failure to complete their education makes it difficult to obtain meaningful employment.
	School phobia	This problem is more common with young children; however, one study indicated school phobia appeared in two to eight percent of individuals referred to guidance clinics. These individuals often have overprotective parents, although with adolescents the problem is more likely to be school related than family related than in the case of younger children.

Depression

Barbara contacted a college counseling center because she had been depressed for several months. Her situation had deteriorated to the point where she was crying for long periods of time at increasingly frequent intervals. Two months earlier, the boy she had wanted to marry decided marriage wasn't for him. At the time she contacted the counseling center, Barbara said she felt as though just getting out of bed in the morning was a huge effort. She had trouble starting conversations with peers and felt constantly exhausted. Barbara told her counselor she wanted to be by herself more and more of the time. What is the nature of depression in adolescents like Barbara?

Incidence

There is good evidence that depression becomes more prevalent in adolescence than in childhood and that it is more characteristic of females than males (e.g., Achenbach and Edelbrock, 1981; Sroufe and Rutter, 1984). And, in a national survey of depression (Levitt and Lubin, 1975), it was found that females show higher incidences of depression than males, that black females show markedly high depressive traits, and that depression is more common in lower than higher income families.

Loss of Attachment Figure

Adolescents who show strong indications of depression are often responding to the loss of someone they love—a parent, sibling, friend, or fiancé. Depression may also involve anxiety focused on school or a career. The pattern depression follows is usually marked by protest, involving crying, agitation, or denial of the problem; depression–withdrawal, consisting of apathetic and unresponsive behavior; and recovery, or a slow return to optimism and interest in life (Martin, 1977). Depression becomes a severe problem when the youth gets stuck in the depression–withdrawal phase of the cycle. That is what happened to Barbara when her friend decided he didn't want to marry her.

Cognitive and Biological Factors and Learned Helplessness

A well-known cognitive view of depression suggests that depressed individuals interpret environmental events in terms of their own personal inadequacies. Such individuals, it is said, also have a negative perception of themselves because of their personal inadequacies (Beck, 1967). From this view, depressed adolescents exaggerate their inadequacies.

From the genetic studies of depression, it appears that a genetic factor may be implicated only in more severe, long-term depression. In the search for biological factors in depression, two neurotransmitters have been proposed as culprits—norepinephrine (Goodwin and Athanasious, 1979) and serotonin (Asberg, et al., 1976).

Yet another prominent view of depression, one that ties in with loss of an attachment figure and environmental influences, is called **learned helplessness** (Seligman, 1975). According to this perspective, adolescents who are exposed to stress, prolonged pain, or loss over which they have no control, learn to become helpless. Stated another way, the depressed adolescent shows a great deal of apathy because he or she cannot reinstate the rewards that previously were experienced (for example, Barbara cannot make her fiancé come back to her). It should also be pointed out that behaviorists simply argue that adolescents become depressed because they do not have enough rewards in their lives (Carson and Adams, 1981).

Developmental Changes

As we saw earlier, depression occurs much more frequently in adolescence than in childhood. Some psychologists, such as Irving Weiner (1980), believe it also is fruitful to distinguish between depression occurring prior to the age of sixteen or seventeen years of age and depression occurring in the very late part of adolescence. Prior to sixteen or seventeen years of age, adolescents are not likely to show traditional adult symptoms of depression for two main reasons. First, the developmental tasks young adolescents are faced with, such as adjusting to puberty, seeking independence, and developing heterosexual relationships, present serious threats to their self-esteem. Consequently, young adolescents find it very difficult to admit to themselves or to other people any self-critical attitudes they may have about their competence. As a result, young adolescents are not likely to experience or show the gloom, self-deprecation, and feelings of helplessness and hoplessness that usually typify depression in late adolescence or adulthood. Second, young adolescents are still at a point in development where they tend to *do* more things than to *think* about them. Thus, younger adolescents who experience loss and disappointment are more likely than older adolescents to express their depression through various overt behaviors instead of through introspective preoccupation. More specifically, young adolescents are likely to behave in ways that indirectly reflect the psychological pressure of depression, the motivation to ward off depression, or an appeal for help. For example, young adolescents who are constantly worn out may be expressing indirectly the fatigue of toiling with depression. Efforts to ward off depression in early adolescence sometimes take the form of restlessness and a flight to or from people. And, in some early adolescents, appeals for help with depression may appear in the form of such problem behaviors as running away, stealing, and truancy (Anthony, 1968).

Childhood and Family Processes

The famous attachment theorist John Bowlby has developed a view of depression that emphasizes how certain childhood experiences are implicated in depression. Bowlby (1980) argued that insecure attachment, especially with the mother, a lack of love and affection in childrearing, or the actual loss of a parent in childhood often produce a negative cognitive set. This schema that is built up during the childhood years causes the child to interpret later losses as yet other failures to create an enduring close positive relationship. From Bowlby's perspective, then, childhood experiences produce cognitive schemata that are carried forward to influence the way the adolescent interprets new experiences. When these experiences involve further loss, the loss serves as the immediate precipitant of depression. While Bowlby's theory is intriguing, we still have few empirical data to verify it. Nonethelesss,

there are recent data suggesting the importance of childhood experiences in adolescent depression, as indicated in Perspective on Adolescent Development 15.2.

Now that we have considered a number of important ideas about depression, we turn our attention to another significant problem in adolescence—suicide.

Suicide

Is adolescent suicide increasing? What causes adolescent suicide? Can adolescent suicide be prevented?

Incidence

The suicide rate for adolescents has tripled since 1950. Suicide has become the second leading cause of death among adolescents, falling behind only accidents. It has been argued that approximately one of every one thousand adolescents attempts suicide and that about one of every fifty-one hundred attempts is successful (Smith, 1980). An indication of the prevalence of adolescent suicide is presented in figure 15.6, where the number of suicides per 100,000 ten- to nineteen-year-old adolescents in major cities in the United States is given. Also, males are approximately three times more likely to commit suicide than females. The reason for this sex difference is attributed to the fact that males are more likely to use active methods for attempting suicide, such as shooting themselves, that do not allow the adolescent's life to be saved. By contrast, adolescent girls are more likely to use more passive strategies, such as sleeping pills, that do not produce death (Resnick, 1980).

Causes

It may be helpful to think of suicide in terms of long-term experiences and situational, short-term circumstances. In many adolescent suicides, there is often a long-term history of family processes that are involved. Indeed, a number of experts who study suicide feel that depression is involved in suicide (e.g., Jacobs, 1971; Resnick, 1980; Smith, 1980; Weiner, 1980). As we discussed, the role that childhood experiences and family processes play in depression, a combination of early

Perspective on Adolescent Development 15.2
THE CONTINUITY OF DEVELOPMENT—CHILDHOOD EXPERIENCES AND ADOLESCENT DEPRESSION

*R*ecently Per Gjerde (1985) reported on data collected as part of an ongoing longitudinal investigation (Block and Block, 1980) that are germane to understanding childhood experiences in adolescent depression. Family functioning was assessed on numerous occasions between the ages of three and thirteen and focused on fifty-four girls and fifty-two boys. Relations between parental socialization practices and depression in adolescence emerged primarily for girls. It may be that this sex difference is due to girls' socialization history since girls are socialized more toward compliance, passivity, and reliance on others (e.g., Block, 1983). Or it may be that by promoting personality characteristics such as dependency and helplessness parents are unwittingly encouraging a greater likelihood of depression. Or, it also may be that by producing interpersonal orientations in girls, characterized by a greater reliance on others, parents may be raising daughters who are more vulnerable to the lack of affection and deprivation that characterize the parenting style of depressed adolescents.

While both parenting practices of mothers and fathers are related to depression in adolescent girls, the link seems stronger for fathers than mothers (see table 15.1 to read about some of the paternal child orientations when the child was three that were related to adolescent depression at age fourteen). As indicated in the table, the paternal child-rearing practices that are implicated were lack of spontaneity and emotional support, emphasis on impulse control, absence of affection and

Table 15.1 Paternal child-rearing orientations at age three predicting depression at age fourteen

Girls	Boys	
.46**	.05	Feels that the child is a bit disappointing to me
.35*	.25	Children of different sex should not see each other naked
.34*	.06	Teaches child always to control feelings
.38*	−.08	Too much 'TLC' can harm, weaken child
.60***	−.09	Give sex information only when child can understand
−.21	.34*	Long periods with child are interesting and educational
.06	.41*	Does not want child to be seen different from others
−.35*	−.16	Put wishes of mate before those of child
−.43**	−.10	Shows affection by hugging, kissing child
−.44**	.19	Praising good is better than punishing bad
−.37*	.08	Lets child know attempts/accomplishments are appreciated
−.32*	−.05	Lets child know when angry with him/her
−.02	−.42*	Many duties, family chores given to child

* p<.05, ** p<.01, *** p<.001

Source: From Gjerde, P., "Adolescent Depression and Parental Socialization Patterns: A Perspective Study." (April 1985). Paper presented at the biennial meeting of the Society for Research in Child Development, Toronto.

positive reinforcement, concern about sexual matters, disappointment with the daughter, and failure to communicate both negative and positive feelings and opinions.

Maternal socialization practices were observed in a teaching situation at age four. Among the maternal teaching behaviors at age four that were related to depression in girls at age fourteen were authoritarian control, a strong achievement orientation, and absence of emotional support.

Parental socialization practices and quality of the home environment also were observed during early adolescence (ages twelve and thirteen). Relations, again, with depression were stronger for girls than boys. The aspect of the home environment at age twelve most likely to predict depression in girls two years later was the presence of a mother who was overcontrolled and unable to enjoy her relationship with her daughter. Observations of fathers with their daughters revealed a picture of conflict between the father and daughter in the case of depressed adolescent girls. When observed at age thirteen, the mothers of the depressed daughters were not very affiliative and the fathers were disregarding and ambivalent.

In sum, significant sex differences emerged in this research with girls' patterns of depression more closely linked to parental socialization than those of boys. The adolescent depression of the girls was related to parental socialization practices extending all the way back to the preschool years. The fathers of the depressed girls were seen as controlling, withdrawn, and unexpressive individuals. In particular, they emphasized early attainment of self-control, deemphasized father–daughter communication, and avoided expression of affect. Mothers of subsequently depressed adolescent girls were authoritarian, achievement oriented, and low in emotional support when the girls were four years old. Almost a decade later, the mothers were observed to be overcontrolled and unaffectionate. Overall, then, a socialization pattern of early impulse control, achievement, and lack of affection and emotional support was linked with depression in adolescent girls.

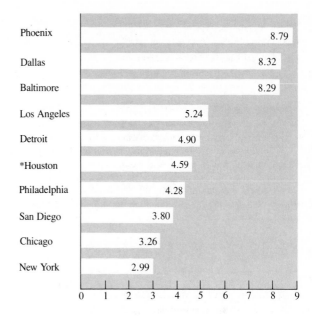

*Houston's rate is estimated

Figure 15.6   Number of suicides per 100,000 ten- to nineteen-year-old adolescents in major U.S. cities.

push for impulse control, achievement emphasis, and a lack of affection and emotional support was implicated. Other research on suicide has found that adolescents who commit suicide have a long history of family instability and unhappiness (e.g., Jacobs, 1971; Weiner, 1980). However, these long-standing family relationships, in themselves, do not alone seem to cause suicide. Rather some more immediate, precipitating factors that occur during adolescence serve as a more proximal trigger for suicide. Such highly stressful circumstances as the loss of a boyfriend or girlfriend, failure in school, and getting pregnant or fear of getting pregnant are circumstances, which, for some adolescents who come from unstable, unhappy family backgrounds may be sufficient to precipitate a suicide attempt.

And, there may be a cognitive explanation of why suicide increases dramatically in adolescence (Elkind, 1980; Lipsitz, 1983). The discussion of cognitive development in Chapter 4 shows how adolescents often construct a personal fable about themselves. The personal fable refers to a story the adolescent tells himself or herself that she or he is somehow unique, immune,

Table 15.2 The early warning signs of suicide among adolescents

1. The adolescent makes suicide threats such as "I wish I were dead." "My family would be better off without me." "I don't have anything to live for."
2. A prior suicide attempt, no matter how minor. Four out of five people who commit suicide have made at least one previous attempt.
3. Preoccupation with death in music, art, and personal writing.
4. Loss of a family member, pet, or boyfriend/girlfriend through death, abandonment, break-up.
5. Family disruptions such as unemployment, serious illness, relocation, divorce.
6. Disturbances in sleeping and eating habits, and in personal hygiene.
7. Declining grades and lack of interest in school or activities that previously were important.
8. Dramatic changes in behavior patterns, such as a very gregarious adolescent becoming very shy and withdrawn.
9. Pervasive sense of gloom, helplessness, and hopelessness.
10. Withdrawal from family members and friends; feelings of alienation from significant others.
11. Giving away prized possessions and otherwise getting affairs in order.
12. Series of accidents or impulsive, risk-taking behaviors. Drug or alcohol abuse, disregard for personal safety, taking dangerous dares. (With regard to drug or alcohol abuse, there has been a dramatic increase in the number of adolescent suicides that are committed while the adolescent is under the influence of alcohol or drugs in recent years).

Source: After information presented in Living with Ten to Fifteen Year Olds, A Planning Guide For A One-Day Conference. *Early Adolescence, Carrboro, N.C., 1982.*

What proximal and distal factors are involved in adolescent suicide?

and even immortal. It is not unusual for adolescents to become locked into their personal fable and feel that something like death cannot happen to them. Further, as part of the personal fable, the adolescent may think that the stress and pain he or she feels in life are unique and that no one else can possibly understand how dreadful things are.

In sum, piecing together the puzzle as to why adolescents are likely to commit suicide requires an understanding of whether there has been a long history of family relationships that are similar to those promoting depression, precipitating events in adolescence that trigger a sense of inadequacy, worthlessness, and despair, as well as the tendency to lock oneself in a personal fable.

Prevention of Suicide

The tendency to overdifferentiate oneself in adolescence, which occurs as part of the personal fable, makes prevention difficult. According to Joan Lipsitz (1983), prevention programs with adolescents are more likely to be successful if an adolescent believes that "it can happen to me" rather than "it can't happen to me. I am unique." If the adolescent cannot make the cognitive leap from immunity to vulnerability then prevention is very difficult.

Table 15.3 What to do and what not to do when you suspect an adolescent is likely to attempt suicide

What To Do

1. Ask direct, straightforward questions in a calm manner. "Are you thinking about hurting yourself?"
2. Assess the seriousness of the suicidal intent by asking questions about feelings, important relationships, who else the person has talked with, and the amount of thought given to the means to be used. If a gun, pills, rope, or other means have been obtained and a precise plan developed, clearly the situation is dangerous. Stay with the person until some type of help arrives.
3. Be a good listener and be very supportive without being falsely reassuring.
4. Try to persuade the adolescent to obtain professional help and assist him or her in getting this help.

What Not To Do

1. Do not ignore the warning signs.
2. Do not refuse to talk about suicide if an adolescent approaches you about the topic.
3. Do not react with horror, disapproval, or repulsion.
4. Do not give false reassurances by saying things like, "Everything is going to be okay." Also don't give out simple answers or platitudes like "You have everything to be thankful for."
5. Do not abandon the adolescent after the crisis has gone by or after professional help has commenced.

Source: After information presented in Living with 10–15 Year Olds, A Planning Guide For a One-Day Conference. *Center for Early Adolescence, Carrboro, NC, 1982.*

The fact that adolescent suicide rates have been increasing suggests that prevention efforts have not been very successful. One strategy has been to focus on the precipitating events by setting up telephone hotlines in various communities. While such steps are a positive trend in helping adolescents with suicidal tendencies, there is some indication that they are not highly effective—one investigation found that ninety-eight percent of individuals who commit suicide never call a hotline center (Wilkins, 1970). While we do not have the answers for detecting when an individual is going to attempt suicide and how to prevent it, the advice offered by the Center of Early Adolescence presented in tables 15.2 and 15.3 is helpful.

We have considered a number of different dimensions of adolescent depression and suicide. A summary of main ideas that will help you remember these dimensions is presented in Concept Table 15.2. Now we turn our attention to another prevalent problem in adolescence—eating disorders.

Eating Disorders

Let's study eating disorders in adolescence, and then turn our attention to three specific disorders: anorexia nervosa, bulimia, and obesity.

Incidence

Two recent Gallup polls (1985) revealed the prevalence of eating disorders among adolescents, particularly adolescent girls. The national poll sampled 502 boys and girls aged thirteen to eighteen and was the first national look at such eating disorders as anorexia (self-starvation) and bulimia (binge-and-purge syndrome). The poll revealed that twelve percent of the adolescent girls suffered symptoms of eating disorders while only four percent of the boys had such problems. Forty percent of the boys and thirty-four percent of the girls reported periodic food binges. Clearly, eating problems have become a prevalent aspect of a number of adolescents' lives.

Anorexia Nervosa

To learn more about anorexia nervosa, let's consider the cultural standards involving ideal figures and the characteristics of anorexic adolescents.

The Ideal Cultural Body Build The ideal female in our culture today is slender and lithe, particularly in comparison to prior eras when a more shapely, robust body was the ideal. Because of this standard, many girls constantly worry about their weight. Kim Chernin (1981) described how two facts make this current obsession

Concept Table 15.2

DEPRESSION AND SUICIDE IN ADOLESCENCE

Concept	Processes/related ideas	Characteristics/description
Depression	Incidence	Becomes more prevalent in adolescence than childhood and is more characteristic of females than males.
	Loss of attachment figure	Depressed adolescents often are responding to the loss of someone they love.
	Cognitive and biological factors and learned helplessness	Beck's ideas suggest that depression occurs because of a negative perception of personal inadequacies. Genetic factors are implicated in the more severe, long-term forms of depression and neurotransmitters also are involved. Seligman's view of learned helplessness argues that adolescents become depressed because they lost control of important rewards in their life and do not have the ability to reinstate those rewards, such as a lost attachment figure.
	Developmental changes	As indicated earlier, depression is more common in adolescence than childhood possibly because of the increased abstractness of thought, increased reasoning capabilities, and the like. Weiner distinguished the onset of depression prior to sixteen to seventeen years of age, which is difficult to detect because it is associated with many other symptoms that often mask it, and depression that occurs in the very late part of adolescence, which is more like adult depression.
	Childhood and family processes	Bowlby's view of depression suggests that childhood experiences are carried forward to adolescence, particularly those pertaining to insecure attachment, loss of a parent, and a lack of love. Then, precipitating experiences in adolescence, such as further losses, trigger depression. Gjerde's research reveals how relationships with parents seem to be more likely to be associated with adolescent girls' depression than boys'. In particular, a pattern of early impulse control, achievement, and lack of affection and emotional support is implicated.
Suicide	Incidence	The suicide rate has tripled since 1950 and suicide has become the second leading cause of death among adolescents. Boys are more likely to use active means in suicide attempts and girls, passive means, possibly explaining why boys are more successful in committing suicide.
	Causes	Suicide is often closely linked to depression so that some of the same childhood and family experiences we found to be important in understanding depression are often implicated in suicide as well. Long-standing family relationships may combine with immediate events in adolescence to trigger a suicide attempt—these events usually involve some loss or failure on the part of the adolescent. The increase in suicide during adolescence likely is linked to cognitive changes and possibly to the adolescent's personal fable.
	Prevention	The personal fable makes prevention difficult. Prevention efforts have not been very successful as witnessed by the increased rate of suicide. Early warning signs of suicide tendencies and what to do when adolescents appear to be ready to attempt suicide have been developed.

The ideal female in American culture is slender and lithe, which may contribute to the incidence of anorexia nervosa.

strual periods as a result of a decrease in body fat). Often anorexic adolescents show an obsession with activity, which they feel will peel off fat. Although anorexic adolescents avoid eating, they have an intense interest in food, cook for others, talk about food, and insist on watching others eat. Usually when they begin dieting, they are average in weight. However, many anorexic adolescents do not feel useful or in control of their lives. They perceive their bodies as something extra—not part of themselves, not their own property. Anorexics complain of feeling full after a few bites of food, which symbolizes a sense of control (by contrast, the obese adolescent feels empty after a full meal and does not feel in control of food). The anorexic adolescent also is excessively preoccupied with body size. A close look at the anorexic adolescent's family often reveals serious problems. The case study presented in Perspective on Adolescent Development 15.3 describes some of the family dynamics often experienced by the adolescent with anorexia nervosa.

Bulimia

Bulimia refers to a binge-and-purge syndrome, that is, periods of very heavy eating are followed by self-induced vomiting—like anorexia nervosa it too is almost exclusively a female disorder. Not only is bulimia a symptom of anorexia nervosa in its final stages, it is also an eating disorder in its own right. Bulimia has been described as the gorging-purging syndrome, typifying the "thin-fat person." This type of adolescent frequently repeats a sequence of compulsive dieting, binging, and purging; in other words, she lives her life dieting, eating, and throwing up. Like anorexics, bulimics do not feel in control of their lives. Most bulimics are not extremely overweight; they usually weigh between ten and thirty pounds above average. But even when they reach their desired weight, bulimics feel anxious and out of control (Deutsch, 1982).

Obesity

While weight gain in adolescence is associated with the skeletal change in height, many other factors also influence weight. An increase in weight can be due to an increase in the fat content of the adolescent's body. Only about five percent of all young adolescents are obese,

with weight loss unusual. One is the scope of the trend. Throughout history there have been dieters, including Roman matrons who willingly starved themselves, but there never has been a period when such large numbers of adolescents and adults have spent so much money, time, and energy on their weight. The second unusual aspect of the current concern about weight loss is the degree to which it involves females rather than males. Females make up more than ninety percent of those who are suffering from anorexia nervosa, for example.

Characteristics of Adolescents with Anorexia Nervosa
There are several physical and psychosocial features that characterize **anorexia nervosa** in adolescence (Bruch, 1973). Severe malnutrition and emaciation are accompanied by amenorrhea (the absence of men-

Problems and Disturbances in Adolescence and the Nature of Abnormality   635

JANE, A SIXTEEN-YEAR-OLD ANOREXIC

Sixteen-year-old Jane is the second of three children in a warm, middle-class Irish Catholic family. She was an "easy" baby who never demanded cuddling. She was also a helpful toddler who learned how to fold clothes at two, a modest child who felt her active siblings deserved more attention than herself, and who, in family snapshots, often stood off to the side as if she were a spectator observing the rest of the family. Her parents are affectionate, but often preoccupied with their own troubles—Mr. Denton has just started a new business and Mrs. Denton is trying to cope with the death of her father. The Denton household has always been well stocked with food, but both parents have broadcast clear messages that thinness is desirable. When Jane was fifteen, she felt very threatened by both academic and social aspects of school. She felt she had an ugly face, a dull personality, and too much fat (at 5'8", she weighed 135 pounds). She didn't know how to change her looks or personality, but she felt she could lose weight. Jane went from 135 pounds to 110 pounds and then stopped menstruating. Gradually she began eliminating more foods; she subsisted by eating *only* applesauce and eggnog. Jane spent many hours observing her body. She often would wrap her fingers around her wrist to see if it was getting thinner. At the same time she fantasized that she was going to become a beautiful fashion model who would wear designer bathing suits. But even when she reached 90 pounds, Jane felt she was still too fat. She had disowned her body, and even spoke in a whisper so she would be inaudible as well as invisible. The thought of meeting a boy terrified her. Feelings of incompetence and loss of control overwhelmed Jane. Her parents begged her, and then nagged at her, to eat. They didn't seek clinical help, however, until she totally isolated and emaciated herself.

In Jane's case, there were three areas of disordered psychological functions that often characterize anorexic adolescents. First, Jane experienced a disturbance of delusional proportion in her body concept; second, she showed a disturbance in the accuracy of cognitive interpretation of stimuli arising in her body, including failure to recognize hunger and nutritional needs; and third, she demonstrated a paralyzing sense of ineffectiveness that pervaded virtually all her thinking and activities (Deutsch, 1982).

Anorexia nervosa has become an increasingly frequent problem among adolescent females.

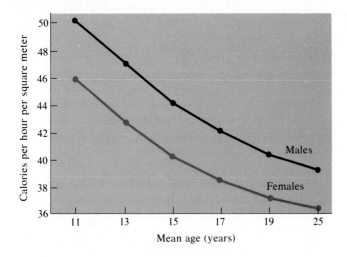

Figure 15.7 Basal metabolism rate (BMR) for adolescent females and males.

but by the time they fully reach adolescence, the number increases to fifteen percent (Nutrition National Canada Survey, 1973). **Obesity** may be defined as weighing more than twenty percent over normal skeletal and physical requirements. For the most part, this is indicated by an excess of fat content in the body. Obesity is influenced by many different factors, among them biological factors and psychological/environmental factors.

Biological Factors To understand biological factors in obesity, it is important to know about genetic influences, set point theory, and basal metabolism rate. Adolescents may have inherited a tendency to be overweight. In addition, it has been argued that the hypothalamus in the brain acts as a set point for the amount of body weight (Kessey, et al., 1976). The adolescent's **set point** is the weight that he or she maintains when no effort to gain or lose weight is expended. If the adolescent is overweight and loses weight, then body weight goes below the set point. And, if the adolescent is underweight and gains weight, the body weight goes above its set point. Biologists argue that this set point in the hypothalamus is to some degree genetically transmitted, but can be influenced by eating patterns.

An additional biological factor involved in obesity is **basal metabolism rate (BMR).** The basal metabolism rate is defined as the minimum amount of energy a

person uses in a state of rest. To considerable extent, BMR is genetically determined (although it can be regulated, within limits, through exercise or drugs). Adolescents with a high basal metabolism rate can eat almost anything and not get fat, while adolescents with a low BMR must constantly monitor their food intake to keep from gaining weight.

As is indicated in figure 15.7, an individual's BMR continuously drops from age eleven to age twenty (from then until old age, it begins to level out). Male adolescents generally have a slightly higher BMR than females. As a young adolescent grows older, then, his basal metabolism rate drops, but his food intake does not usually decrease. This explains why there are fewer fat young teenagers than fat older teenagers. But even though BMR exerts powerful control over weight gain and weight loss, energy intake and output still have strong influences on weight.

Environmental and Psychological Factors Diet, exercise, and family socialization experiences seem to be among the most important environmental factors involved in adolescent obesity.

One of the most obvious characteristics of obese adolescents is a distorted body image. As in other eating disorders, many obese adolescents do not feel in charge of their lives. Obese adolescents become preoccupied with food—thinking about it and eating it. Even though obese adolescents may eat large quantities of food, they often sense a continuous feeling of emptiness and low self-esteem. Many obese adolescents feel that if they only could lose weight everything would be great in their lives. Losing weight "would make my parents happy, and the kids at school would like me; then I could concentrate on other things."

A typical example is Debby, age seventeen, who has been obese since she was twelve. She comes from a middle-class family in which her parents have pressured her to lose weight, repeatedly sending her to reducing centers and taking her to physicians. One summer, Debby was sent to a diet camp, where she went from 200 to 150 pounds. On returning home, she was terribly disappointed that her parents pressured her to reduce more. With increased tension and parental preoccupation with her weight, she gave up all efforts at dieting and her weight rose rapidly. Debby isolated herself and continued her preoccupation with food. Later, clinical help was sought. Fortunately, Debby was able to work through her hostility toward her parents and understand her self-destructive behavior. Eventually she became willing to reduce for herself and not her parents or peers.

To learn more about intervention programs with overweight and obese adolescents, such as Debby, read Perspective on Adolescent Development 15.4.

Schizophrenia

What is schizophrenia and how widespread is it in adolescence?

Incidence and Nature

Schizophrenia, a form of psychosis characterized by illogical thought, hallucinations, and erratic behavior, is one of the most severe forms of disturbance in adolescence. Fortunately, a very small percentage of adolescents are schizophrenic. Although approximately one percent of the adult population is considered schizophrenic, only about four percent of this group (or 0.04 percent of the total adult population) became schizophrenic during childhood. The majority of schizophrenic adults first showed signs of schizophrenia in late adolescence or young adulthood (Erickson, 1978).

The clinical picture of the adolescent schizophrenic includes withdrawal, a decrease in energy, variable moods, and obsessive preoccupations. Other characteristics include hostile and impulsive behavior, depersonalization, hallucinations, and distortions of thought. The most pronounced aspect of adolescent schizophrenia is that the symptoms may be episodic, transitory, and fragmented, except for withdrawal and decreases in energy. Withdrawal may first show up in a reluctance to go to school and be with peers. The adolescent may rationalize her lack of interest in peers by saying that they no longer have common interests. Her decrease in energy may be justified by saying she doesn't want to conform to society or that school is boring. It is not an easy task to differentiate such characteristics from those of the normal adolescent—at one time or another, every adolescent says he is bored with school and that he doesn't like his peers. The problem of differentiating schizophrenic from nonschizophrenic adolescent thought is particularly difficult because adolescents are often trying out new, different, and sometimes bizarre philosophies of life and death. However, nonschizophrenic adolescents are not prohibited by such ideas from carrying out the schedules of their daily lives. By contrast, schizophrenics replace realistic orientations with such obsessions and allow these thoughts to keep them from functioning in the real world.

Biological and Environmental Influences

Kinship studies of schizophrenia suggest that the closer a relative is in the kinship network the more likely she or he is at risk for schizophrenia (Gottesman and Shields, 1982). For monozygotic twins, for example, the risk is 45.6 percent, while for dyzgotic twins it is only 13.7 percent. In addition to genetic factors, scientists also believe there is a biochemical basis to schizophrenia. Tiny neurotransmitters in the brain carry chemicals through the nervous system. One neurotransmitter, **dopamine,** plays an important role in emotion and attention. It is believed by some scientists that individuals who become schizophrenic have brains with neurons that are particularly sensitive to dopamine. The fact that biochemical matters likely are involved in schizophrenia suggests that drugs might be effective in treating schizophrenia. Indeed, drug therapy

INTERVENTION PROGRAMS WITH OVERWEIGHT AND OBESE ADOLESCENTS

*B*ehavior modification programs have been developed for overweight adolescents. A typical behavior modification program consists of having the adolescent keep a daily chart of her or his eating patterns, become aware of circumstances that stimulate eating, change the conditions that promote overeating, give himself or herself a reward for good eating habits, and engage in an exercise program. Being involved in such a program for several months often is not that difficult for many individuals, but developing the self-control to maintain the program for one year or longer is very difficult.

One investigation at a Massachusetts girls' camp vividly showed why some people who exercise do not lose weight (Mayer, 1968). The obese girls actually were eating less than the girls of normal weight, but when they exercised, the obese girls exerted far less physical energy than the girls of normal weight. Activity charts suggested that the obese girls were just as likely to participate in sports and other physical activities at the camp as girls of normal weight were. But a critical difference between the physical activity levels of the two groups was that the obese girls did not exercise as vigorously as the normal weight girls did. The fat girls played tennis, went swimming, and played volleyball, but they moved very lethargically. When a special camera was set up to provide details about their movements, the films indicated that more than fifty percent of the time in all physical activities, the obese girls were motionless.

Exercise can be very beneficial in reducing the weight of obese girls.

Feedback was given to the obese girls about their inactivity, and they were admonished to "work harder, exercise vigorously, and raise a sweat." The results were encouraging. Not only did the camp counselors get the obese girls to exercise more vigorously, but they did not increase their food intake either. Consequently, by creating a negative caloric balance between energy input and energy output, the girls began to lose weight.

---

has been effective in treating schizophrenia in some instances (Alexander and Malouf, 1983). The most widely used drug in treating schizophrenia involves the **phenothiazines** (Hogarty et al., in press). Questions still remain though about the long-term effectiveness of such drugs as well as their side effects.

Among the developmental precursors of schizophrenia are those involving family and interpersonal relationships, neurodevelopmental maturity, and attention. With regard to family relations, for many years, clinical psychologists have been interested in the **schizophrenogenic mother.** Clinicians report that

schizophrenic individuals often have mothers with a high anxiety level who easily become upset. However, efforts to isolate the mother's behavior as the main cause of schizophrenia have not been very fruitful (e.g., Block et al., 1958). Nonetheless, some clinicians believe that schizophrenia is linked with growing up in a "bad" family. For instance, in one investigation of one hundred families with schizophrenic children, seventy-five of the families were rated as pathological with either the mother or the father (and in some cases both) being disturbed (Bender, 1974).

In addition to this maternal relationship, another social precursor of schizophrenia involves odd and vacillating social interaction rather than shyness or timidity (Hanson, Gottesman, and Heston, 1976). These social difficulties may be accompanied by antisocial behavior in boys that is often more solitary and more confined to the home than in the case of juvenile delinquents.

Schizophrenia also is associated with clumsiness and other indications of neurodevelopmental maturity in childhood (Quitkin, Rifkin, and Klein, 1976). Also, there may be an attentional deficit that involves poor signal/noise discrimination (Garmezy, 1978). These findings point to the possibility of cognitive and attentional deficits in the genesis of schizophrenia.

In sum, we have seen there are biogenetic, cognitive, and social contributions to understanding schizophrenia. Now we focus more closely on the developmental pattern of schizophrenia during adolescence.

The Onset of Schizophrenia in Adolescence

There seem to be three characteristics that distinguish the onset of schizophrenia in adolescence from its onset in adulthood (Weiner, 1980):

1. Schizophrenia that begins in adolescence is more likely to present a mixed disturbance in which identifying features of the schizophrenia are obscured by other symptoms. For example, the schizophrenic adolescent initially may complain primarily about depressive symptoms or show sociopathic tendencies, such as running away and truancy. The initial onset of schizophrenia, therefore, is often more difficult to detect in adolescence than in adulthood. Sometimes only the persistence of schizophrenic characteristics, such as incoherent thinking, inaccurate perceptions, and inappropriate affect, after the other symptoms have lessened, allow the disorder to be diagnosed as schizophrenia.
2. Certain aspects of social and personality development during childhood and adolescence can be identified as relatively high-risk factors for the subsequent appearance of schizophrenia. Poor peer group relationships, very few friends and/or infrequent interaction with friends, and

sociopathic behavior within the home itself all make children and adolescents more likely candidates for schizophrenia.
3. The long-term prognosis for the successful treatment of adolescents who develop schizophrenia is not as good as when the disorder first appears in adulthood.

We have considered many different problems and disturbances in adolescence. Now we turn our attention to the nature of abnormality in adolescence.

The Nature of Abnormality and Continuity–Discontinuity in Disorders: Malevolent Demons to the Evils of Masturbation

To conclude our discussion of problems and disturbances in adolescence, we evaluate different views on what makes an adolescent abnormal rather than normal and then we return to an issue discussed earlier in the book, continuity–discontinuity, discussing here its implications for disorders in adolescence.

The Nature of Abnormality in Adolescence

Malevolent gods, demons, witches, vampires, and even the moon and planets have been called responsible for adolescents' abnormal behavior. During the Middle Ages, Satan or Lucifer, as the devil was known, was seen as a major provoker of madness in adolescents. In such supernatural characterizations of abnormality, the adolescents who engaged in such behavior were thought to be not only crazy, but evil as well. Such interpretations have sometimes been referred to as the **religious** or **supernatural model** of abnormality. The causes of the abnormal behavior are traced to sinfulness, demonic possession, or temptation by the devil. Some religious sects in the United States still hold to these beliefs. In the religious model, intervention to try to remove or reduce the abnormal behavior comes in the form of exorcism, repentance, or confession. The goal is to save the adolescent from eternal damnation.

Psychologists do not view the religious or supernatural model as a viable way to explain and understand abnormal behavior. Next, we look at several models that have been given serious consideration by scientists interested in the nature of abnormality—the statistical model, the medical and disease model, the psychological and sociocultural model, and finally the interactionist model.

The Statistical Model

The **statistical model** of abnormality emphasizes that an adolescent is abnormal when he or she deviates from the average. But there are some problems with describing adolescents in this way. Shirley Temple, the famous child actress, would have been considered deviant according to this definition because she was far from the average in terms of her acting ability. But we certainly wouldn't consider Shirley Temple as a deviant actress or person. And all adolescents are deviant from one another on certain dimensions. The fact that one adolescent may like classical music, but none of his friends do does not make the musically inclined adolescent deviant. It is primarily in the areas of social behavior and thought that we look for differences between adolescents that might suggest abnormality. But even in these areas, averages often change from one time to another and from one culture to another. For example, in the Mangaian culture, young male adolescents are trained in sexual techniques and then seek out or are sought out by young girls so the techniques can be practiced. In the United States, even though we have become a more sexually permissive culture, such behavior would be considered deviant for the young adolescent as well as the women.

Similarly, behaviors that were considered abnormal early in the twentieth century are now viewed as normal. Think once again about the following comments on masturbation taken from the popular handbook in 1913 called *What A Boy Should Know:*

> Whenever unnatural emissions are produced . . . he will be more easily tired. . He will probably look pale and pasty, and he is lucky if he escapes indigestion and getting his bowels confined, both of which will probably give him spots and pimples on his face. . . . The results on the mind are the more severe and more easily recognized. . . . His wits are not so sharp. . . . A boy like this is a poor thing to look at. (Schofield and Vaughan-Jackson, 1913, pp. 30–42)

In the past, masturbation was thought to cause everything from warts to insanity. But today, less than fifteen percent of adolescents view masturbation as wrong (Hyde, 1979).

The Medical or Disease Model

Another model of abnormality is the **medical** or **disease model.** According to this view, the adolescent is abnormal when there is some physical malfunctioning in his or her body. Thus psychological abnormality is believed to be some type of disease or illness precipitated by internal factors. Adolescent abnormalities are called "illnesses," and the adolescents become "patients" in hospitals, where they are "treated" by doctors. The form of intervention in the medical model is usually some type of drug therapy or, in rare instances, removal of a portion of the brain. The goal of this treatment is to cure the illness.

There is clear evidence that biological factors play an important role in a number of forms of abnormality, and genetic inheritance has been linked to such debilitating psychological disorders as schizophrenia. Nonetheless, the medical model has underplayed the role of sociocultural factors and overemphasized the analogy between physical and mental disorders. If you break your leg or contract pneumonia, there is general agreement on the symptoms and treatments of the illness or disease. But psychologists and psychiatrists sometimes have a difficult time agreeing on the symptoms of a number of psychological abnormalities, such as anxiety and schizophrenia, much less on their treatments. For such reasons, the medical model has been subjected to strong attacks by some critics. Thomas Szasz (1961; 1977), one of the most vocal critics, goes so far as to say that the medical model of mental illness (which most psychiatrists, but not psychologists, follow) is a pseudoscience that should be placed in the same category as alchemy and astrology. Although the analogy to disease and physical illness may not always be the best way to think of psychological abnormality, it is important that we recognize the significant role that biological and genetic factors seem to play in a number of forms of abnormality.

Psychological and Sociocultural Approaches

Distorted views of reality and unusual behavior are two of the most common characteristics of serious mental disorders. In Chapter 2, one of the prominent theories discussed was the behavioral, social learning view. This perspective emphasizes that abnormality is heavily influenced by the sociocultural experiences we have and how these experiences influence our thoughts and behavior.

The behavioral, social learning perspective has much in common with the **sociocultural model** of abnormality. It seeks to determine the environmental factors that cause adolescents to display unusual behavior and to understand why people in a society call such adolescents sick, mentally ill, crazy, and so on. Thomas Scheff (1966) argues that mentally disturbed adolescents are simply special representatives of social deviance. He points out that all cultures have norms, and if we violate those norms, we will be labeled *deviant*. If adolescents steal, they are delinquents. Scheff says there are certain residual norms that are so widely adopted they are sometimes taken for granted as a part of nature. So, normal adolescents repeatedly steal things. Scheff feels that factors are an important aspect of abnormality. He acknowledges that mental disorders do exist, but feels they are not illnesses but rather problems in living. From Szasz's perspective, mental disorders reflect defective strategies that adolescents have adopted in trying to cope with difficult, stressful situations. Such ideas have much in common with Richard Lazarus's (Lazarus and DeLongis, 1983) belief that to understand stress, we need to look at how adolescents cognitively interpret their self and their world.

The Interactionist Approach

We have looked at a number of ways to view abnormality. We can rule out the supernatural view, and the idea of abnormality as an illness or a disease may not be a very accurate course to follow either. But it would be wrong to go too far in the direction of the sociocultural model when we attempt to understand abnormality because we know that biological factors interact with sociocultural conditions to determine a child's behavior, thoughts, and feelings. Thus an **interactionist approach** to understanding abnormality seems to be the wisest choice. From this view, both biological factors and sociocultural conditions may produce a mental disturbance, and in most instances, these factors interact with each other to produce the problem. We will call on our statement made earlier in the book to support this interpretation of abnormality: no genes, no organism; no environment, no organism. This orientation holds for both abnormal and normal behavior. As part of the environmental contribution, we need to consider what is acceptable and unacceptable behavior in a particular society.

We now have discussed a number of ideas about eating disorders, schizophrenia, and the nature of problems and disturbances. A summary of these ideas is presented in Concept Table 15.3. Next, we study one final important aspect of abnormality in adolescence—the issue of continuity–discontinuity in disorders.

Continuity–Discontinuity in Adolescent Disorders

We conclude our discussion of problems and disturbances by considering some important aspects of continuity–discontinuity and how they are involved in the story of the adolescent's development of disorders.

Reasons for Continuity in Adolescent Disorders

Three reasons child disorders or experiences might be linked with adolescent disturbances focus on biological processes, the continuing influence of early experience, and early experience plus consistent later experience.

Biological Processes and Prenatal Development First, with regard to biological processes, an adolescent may inherit certain disorders or tendencies that increase the likelihood of developing a disorder, and during prenatal development, there are a number of environmental experiences that may lead to the development of abnormality. For example, there are a number of forms of mental retardation that involve a genetic defect or damage to a chromosome, leading to biochemical

EATING DISORDERS, SCHIZOPHRENIA, AND THE NATURE OF ABNORMALITY IN ADOLESCENCE

Concept	Processes/related ideas	Characteristics/description
Eating disorders	Incidence	A recent national poll revealed that twelve percent of adolescent girls suffered symptoms of eating disorders, but only four percent of boys were affected.
	Anorexia nervosa	This increasing disorder in adolescence refers to a pattern of self-starvation. A better understanding of anorexia nervosa involves the ideal body build in our culture, delusional body image, cognitive interpretation of bodily needs, lack of control over such matters as achievement and the sense that controlling food intake is one aspect of the adolescent girl's life that can be controlled.
	Bulimia	This disorder refers to a binge-purge sequence. Like anorexia nervosa, it primarily occurs in adolescent females.
	Obesity	Refers to weighing twenty percent over normal skeletal and physical requirements. Biological factors such as genetic inheritance, a set point in the hypothalamus, and basal metabolism rate (BMR) are involved. Diet, exercise, and family socialization experiences are among the environmental contributors to obesity. Intervention programs have been diverse, but adolescents have trouble developing self-control of weight loss over an extended period of time.
Schizophrenia	Incidence and nature	This disorder involves illogical thought, hallucinations, and erratic behavior—fortunately this very severe disorder characterizes only a very small percentage of adolescents.
	Biological and environmental factors	Kinship studies suggest a genetic factor is involved and the neurotransmitter dopamine is implicated as well. Drug therapy has been helpful in treating schizophrenics, particularly the phenothiazines. Among the developmental precursors of schizophrenia are family and interpersonal relationships, neurodevelopmental maturity, and attention. While a schizophrenogenic mother has been described as a factor, research studies have not been able to document this effectively.
	Onset of schizophrenia in adolescence	Schizophrenia in adolescence often presents a mixed picture in which identifying symptoms are obscured by other symptoms, just as in depression. Poor peer relations, few friends, and bizarre behavior at home are often precursors. The long-term prognosis for successful treatment of adolescents with schizophrenia has not been as good as when the disorder first appears in adulthood.
Models of abnormality	Religious and supernatural model	The adolescent is viewed as abnormal because of sinfulness, demonic possession, or temptation by the devil.
	Statistical model	The adolescent is perceived as abnormal because he or she deviates too far from the average.
	Medical or disease model	The adolescent is seen as abnormal because of some physical malfunction of the body.
	Psychological or sociocultural models	The adolescent is said to be abnormal because he or she has defective strategies in coping with stressful circumstances and/or sociocultural conditions.
	Interactionist model	The adolescent is believed to be abnormal because of an interaction of biogenetic and environmental conditions.

problems in the brain. Also, in recent years, there has been considerable interest generated in discovering harmful agents that disturb prenatal development. These so-called **teratogens** range from the mother's diet to drugs and chemicals to the mother's emotional state. In their effort to identify as early as possible individuals who have or will have psychological disorders, developmental psychologists and biological researchers have coined the terms *at risk* and *perinatal stress.*

In one of the most comprehensive studies of children at risk, a variety of biological, social, and developmental characteristics were identified as predictors of serious coping problems at the age of eighteen (Werner and Smith, 1982). Among the factors were moderate to severe perinatal (at or near birth) stress and congenital defects. Also among the predictors were low socioeconomic status at two and ten years of age, level of maternal education below eight years, low family stability between two and eight years, very high or very low infant responsiveness at age one year, low social responsiveness and a Cattell score below eighty at two years (the Cattell is one of the early measures of infant intelligence—it was developed in 1940), and the need for long-term mental health services or placement in a learning disability class at age ten. When four or more of these variables were present the stage was set for serious coping problems in the second decade of life.

Early Experience and Consistent Later Experiences
Michael Rutter (1980) has listed a number of ways that earlier experience might be connected to later disorders.

1. Experience produces the disorder at the time, and the disorder persists;
2. Experience creates bodily changes that affect later functioning;
3. Experience alters patterns of behavior at the time, which later take the form of a disorder;
4. Early experiences can change family relationships and circumstances, which over time lead to a disorder;
5. Sensitivities to stress or coping strategies are changes, which then later predispose the person to disorder, or buffer the person from stress;

Low socioeconomic status in infancy and late childhood is among the predictors of coping with problems during adolescence.

6. Experiences change the child's self-concept or attitudes, which in turn influence behavior in later circumstances; and
7. Experience influences behavior by affecting the selection of environments or the coping or closing of opportunities.

One of the best-known longitudinal studies of development is the New York Longitudinal Study (Chess and Thomas, 1977). The following is a description of an individual named David whose experiences in childhood reflect the continuity argument being made here:

In early childhood, David was one of the most active boys Chess and Thomas studied. He was always in motion and came across with a friendly and cheerful manner. Unfortunately, however, a considerable number of parental problems surfaced during David's childhood, including a growing sense of competitiveness in his parents. They continually bragged to others about what a superior child David was, although he did not have a superior IQ; any problems David had in school, they attributed to poor teaching. As he developed in his elementary and secondary school years, his school performance and interest in other activities went downhill. The parents totally blamed the school and its teachers. Picking up on his parents' cues that his failures were not his fault, David never developed a critical, evaluative approach to himself: when problems surfaced, he always put the blame—just as his parents did—on someone else. As David moved into the college years, apathy began to dominate his daily life, and, unfortunately, the attitudes of his parents as well as his own self-insulation and reluctance to take responsibility for his actions led to complete resistance to counseling that might have helped him out of his dilemma.

Reasons for Discontinuity in Adolescent Disorders

Reasons there might be discontinuity in disorders include changes in specific life experiences of the adolescent, regular changes in developmental tasks at different points in development, and changes in society at different points in development.

Changes in Specific Life Circumstances Changes in specific life circumstances can diminish earlier disorders or they can produce disorders that were not present earlier in development. Consider Carl, one of Chess's and Thomas's subjects:

> He requested a discussion with Dr. Chess at the end of his first year in college because he felt depressed and was not coping very well with academic or social matters. He had few friends and said that he had difficulty studying, that he was unable to remember what he had read. By contrast, Carl had been a good student in high school, where he had had a number of friends and many interests. During his interview he did not appear depressed, but expressed bewilderment at his situation, saying that it just wasn't like him to be doing so poorly socially and academically.
>
> The background data indicated that during childhood Carl had been one of the most extreme "difficult child" types: he was intense, had negative reactions to new situations, and was slow to adapt to situations even after many exposures to them. This was true whether it was his first bath, his first day at elementary school, or his first shopping trip. Each of these experiences prompted Carl to stormy behavior, such as temper tantrums and shouting. The parents realized that Carl's reactions to his world were not due to their "bad parenting" but instead were part of his temperament. They were patient with him and often gave him considerable time and many opportunities to adapt to new situations that were frustrating to him. As a result, he did not become

a behavior "problem," even though the "difficult group" has a higher risk for disturbed development (e.g., Thomas, Chess, and Birch, 1970).

> Later on in his elementary and secondary school years, Carl met up with few new situations and in the process was able to develop a positive view of himself. College, however, meant a lot of changes in his life. He now was away from home in unfamiliar situations, with new teachers who placed more complex demands on him, with new peers who were harder to get to know, and with a girl with whom he started living. According to Chess and Thomas, the radically different college experiences reawakened the "difficult child" behavioral reactions and brought Carl in for help.
>
> After only one session, Carl began to get back on a more positive track. He discussed his temperamental pattern with Dr. Chess, including coping mechanisms that he might employ to help him out in social and academic situations. By the end of the academic year, his grades had improved, he broke off the living arrangement with the girl, and he started forcing himself to get more involved in peer group activities.

Regular Changes in Life Tasks at Different Ages While adolescence sometimes has been incorrectly stereotyped as a time of stress for all adolescents, the developmental changes that characterize adolescence can trigger problems and disturbances in some individuals. We have seen that independence and identity are important themes of adolescent development. As the adolescent pushes for autonomy and searches for an identity, parents may adopt more stringent controls or become highly permissive in response to the changes going on with their adolescent. Such changes during adolescent development may precipitate problems and disturbances during adolescence that did not appear earlier in development.

Changes in Society at Different Points in the Individual's Development A child may have developed a serious obesity problem, but when we look at the individual in adolescence, we see that he no longer evidences any indication of the earlier serious problem. One reason this positive development may have occurred is through changes in society over the years as he moved from childhood through adulthood. For example, the child with the serious obesity problem has been strongly influenced by the wave of media attention given to health and nutrition in recent years. Always made to clean his plate up as a child, never involved in exercise, and filling his arteries full of sugar for a number of years, he looked in the mirror in adolescence and made the decision to do something about his life. For two years now, he has eaten well-balanced, but reduced calorie meals, exercised regularly, and removed processed sugar from his meals. His psychological well-being has improved along with his physical fitness.

Conclusions about Continuity–Discontinuity and the Development of Disorders

For decades, we assumed considerable individual consistency in the development of disorders. More recently, this view has been questioned by the adult contextualists. The results of major studies, such as the New York Longitudinal Study and the California Longitudinal Study that trace the lives of individuals across the childhood years and into the adult years, suggest that either extreme in the continuity–discontinuity controversy is unsupported, although they give comfort to both. We conclude, then, that the infant and childhood years are far from meaningless in predicting disorders in adolescence in many instances, but later experiences are important as well. Thus, in trying to understand disorders in adolescence, it would be a mistake only to look at the adolescent's life in the present tense, ignoring the unfolding of experience and development. So, too, would it be an error if we only searched through an adolescent's childhood experiences in trying to predict why he or she has the disturbance. The truth about disorders in adolescence, then, lies somewhere between an early experience view and a contextualist perspective that ignores the developmental unfolding of disorders completely.

Summary

I. There is a wide spectrum of problems and disturbances in adolescence.

   A. Research data suggest that there is no increase in the total number of problems adolescents encounter when compared with children, although this conclusion does not consider the intensity and length of the disturbance. It appears that the abnormality of adolescence has been overestimated.

   B. The behavior problems most likely to differentiate adolescent referrals for psychological help from nonreferrals in the Achenbach and Edelbrock study were unhappy, sad, depressed and school-related problems. A number of other problems increased in adolescence, while many others decreased.

   C. Lower class adolescents had more problems than middle-class adolescents in the Achenbach and Edelbrock study. Girls and middle-class adolescents were more likely to have internalized problems, while boys and lower class adolescents were more likely to be characterized by externalized problems.

II. Information about school-related problems focuses on underachievement, school dropouts, and school phobia.

   A. Unexpected poor school performance has been estimated to occur in twenty-five percent of children and adolescents. More than fifty percent of college students who request counseling and psychotherapy do so because of worries about studying and grades. Weiner believes that underachievement may occur because of such sociocultural factors as an underemphasis on achievement by parents and peers, but that this does not constitute a disturbance. Rather underachievement disturbances involve either attentional and learning handicaps, or neurotic family patterns that produce passive–aggressive behavior.

B. Approximately twenty-two of every one hundred students entering the fifth grade do not graduate from high school. The majority of the dropouts are from lower class backgrounds. Frustration and boredom may lead to problems for these youth as their failure to complete their education makes it difficult to obtain meaningful employment.

C. School phobia is more common with young children, but one study indicated that between two and eight percent of individuals referred to guidance clinics had school phobia. Overprotective parents often are involved, although school-related matters themselves may be the culprit for adolescents.

III. Depression is also a common problem in adolescence and it often is involved when an adolescent attempts suicide.

A. Information about depression focuses on its incidence; loss of attachment figure; cognitive and biological factors, and learned helplessness; developmental changes; and childhood and family processes.

1. Depression is more prevalent in adolescents and in girls.

2. Beck's ideas suggest that depression occurs because of a negative perception of personal inadequacies, which often are overexaggerated. Genetic factors are implicated in the more severe, long-term forms of depression and neurotransmitters also are involved. Seligman's view of learned helplessness suggests that adolescents become depressed because they lose the ability to reinstate rewards, such as loss of an attachment figure.

3. Depression likely is more common in adolescence than in childhood because of advances in cognitive development. Weiner distinguished between depression occurring prior to sixteen or seventeen years of age, which is difficult to detect because symptoms are often masked, and depression in very late adolescence, which is more like adult depression.

4. Bowlby's view suggests that insecure attachment, loss of a parent, and a lack of love are carried forward to adolescence. Then, during adolescence, further losses trigger depression. Gjerde's research revealed that a pattern of early impulse control, achievement, and lack of affection and emotional support are implicated in adolescent depression.

B. Information about suicide focuses on its incidence, causes, and prevention.

1. The suicide rate has tripled since 1950 and suicide now has become the second leading cause of death in adolescence. Boys are more likely to use active means to attempt suicide, while girls more often use passive strategies, which may account for the greater success rate boys have in actually committing suicide.

2. Suicide often is closely related to depression so the developmental precursors we discussed pertaining to depression have implications for understanding suicide as well. Just as with depression, long-standing family socialization patterns likely interact with precipitating events in adolescence to produce a suicide attempt. The increase in suicide during adolescence likely is tied to cognitive changes, particularly the adolescent's personal fable.

3. The personal fable makes prevention difficult. Prevention efforts have not been very successful as witnessed by the increase in suicide. Early warning signs and what to do when a suicide attempt is imminent have been developed.

IV. Eating disorders and schizophrenia are two other disturbances in adolescence.

A. Information about eating disorders suggests that they have become prevalent problems in adolescence, particularly for girls. Anorexia nervosa, bulimia, and obesity are the three main eating disorders of adolescence. Information about anorexia nervosa focuses on the ideal body build in the culture, cognitive interpretation, a sense that weight is one of the few things in the adolescent's life that can be controlled, and family processes. Both biological factors such as genes, set point, and basal metabolism rate and environmental factors such as diet and exercise are involved in understanding obesity.

B. Information about schizophrenia focuses on its incidence and nature, biological and environmental factors, and developmental onset.

1. Schizophrenia is a very severe disturbance that does not occur very frequently—it involves bizarre thought patterns, odd behavior, hallucinations, and erratic life styles.

2. Kinship studies suggest a genetic factor is involved and the neurotransmitter dopamine is implicated as well. Drug therapy has been helpful in treating schizophrenia, particularly in the form of the class of drugs known as phenothiazines. Among the developmental precursors are family and interpersonal relationships, neurodevelopmental maturity, and attention. A schizophrenogenic mother has been implicated as well, but firm documentation of her role has not been forthcoming.

3. Just as with depression, the onset of schizophrenia in adolescence often presents a mixture of symptoms that often masks its identification. The onset of schizophrenia in adolescence seems to be more refractory to treatment than when its onset occurs in adulthood.

V. To further understand the nature of abnormality, it is important to consider models of abnormality and continuity–discontinuity.

A. The main models of abnormality that have been proposed include religious and supernatural; statistical; medical and disease; psychological and sociocultural; and interactionist.

1. The religious and supernatural model, no longer viewed as viable, argues that the adolescent is abnormal because he or she is sinful, possessed by demons, or tempted by demons.

2. The statistical model says the adolescent is abnormal because she or he is too far from the average.

3. The medical or disease model argues that the adolescent is abnormal because of some physical malfunction in the body.

4. The psychological and sociocultural models emphasize that the adolescent is abnormal because of the way he or she copes with stressful situations and sociocultural conditions.

5. The interactionist position stresses that abnormality is caused by an interplay of biogenetic and environmental conditions.

B. An important issue in understanding adolescent abnormality is continuity–discontinuity.
   1. Reasons for continuity include biological processes and prenatal development, as well as early experience and later consistent experience.
   2. Reasons for discontinuity involve changes in specific life circumstances, regular changes in life tasks at different ages, and changes in society at different points in development.
   3. Conclusions about continuity–discontinuity suggest that both are likely to characterize the nature of adolescent disorders.

Key Terms

anorexia nervosa *635*

basal metabolism rate (BMR) *637*

bulimia *635*

cultural estrangement *624*

dopamine *638*

guidelessness *624*

interactionist approach *642*

learned helplessness *628*

medical or disease model *641*

obesity *637*

passive–aggressive *623*

personal incapacity *624*

phenothiazines *639*

religious or supernatural model *640*

schizophrenia *638*

schizophrenogenic mother *639*

school phobia *626*

set point *637*

sociocultural model *642*

statistical model *641*

teratogens *644*

Suggested Readings

Achenbach, T. M., and Edelbrock, C. S. Behavioral problems and competencies reported by parents of normal and disturbed children aged four through sixteen. *Monographs of the Society for Research in Child Development*, Serial No. 188, vol. 46, no. 1. *The complete set of data collected by Achenbach and Edelbrock, including graphs of all 118 items on the Child Behavioral Checklist. Tells how to differentiate between adolescents that should be referred for clinical treatment from those who should not.*

Alloy, L. B. (Ed.). (1986). *Cognitive processes in depression.* New York: Guilford Press. *This book of edited readings contains very up-to-date thinking about the role of cognitive processes in depression.*

Bruch, H. (1973). *Eating disorders.* New York: Basic Books. *An excellent source of information about obese, bulimic, and anorexic adolescents.*

Weiner, I. B. (1980). Psychopathology in adolescence. In *Handbook of adolescent psychology*, ed. J. Adelson. New York: John Wiley. *Weiner's chapter represents an excellent analysis of some of the major disturbances in adolescence. Included is information about school-related problems, schizophrenia, depression, and suicide.*

Glossary

A

abiding self
One of two facets of the imaginary audience as defined by Elkind; the abiding self centers on a subject's willingness to reveal characteristics of the self that are believed to be permanent or stable over time. Closely related to self-esteem. p. 151

abstract relations
The ability of the adolescent to coordinate two or more abstract ideas. p. 148

acceleration
Refers to any strategy that abbreviates the time required for a student to graduate, such as skipping a grade.

accommodation
In Piaget's theory of cognitive development, the act of modifying a current mode or structure of thought to deal with new features of the environment. p. 54

achievement and support
One of three implicit agreements about mutual obligation between parent and child. In adolescence, parental support for achievement becomes more imperative in preparation for independence. p. 538

acquisition (storage) components
Processes used in learning new information. For example, rehearsing new information to transfer a trace of it into long-term memory. p. 186

adolescence
The period of transition between childhood and adulthood consisting of biological/physical, cognitive, and social/emotional/personality changes. p. 33

adolescent generalization gap
The development of widespread generalizations based on information about a limited set of adolescents due to a weak research base. p. 20

adoption studies
An examination and comparison of the biological and adopted parents of adopted children to determine the importance of heredity on behavior.

adrenal androgens
Hormone secreted by the adrenal gland associated with the adjustment of adolescent boys. p. 100

adrenal gland
Endocrine gland located near the kidneys that secretes epinephrine and norepinephrine, which are involved in arousal.

adult contextual theorists
Theorists who emphasize the specialized nature of adult thought and how it may differ from adolescent thought. p. 140

age
A concept synonymous with time: In itself unable to affect living function, behavior or otherwise. p. 28

agent interventions
Method of substance abuse prevention that focuses on the target substance itself, through legal, technological, and social controls. p. 591

alleles
Two or more alternative forms of a gene that can occur at a particular chromosomal locus. p. 87

altruism
Selfless concern for the welfare of others. Altruistic behavior includes sharing, contributing to worthy causes, and helping others. p. 506

amphetamines
Synthetic stimulants that are usually available in the form of pills. Amphetamines are often used by students to maintain high levels of performance for short periods of time. p. 590

anal stage
In Freud's theory, the period during which the child seeks pleasure through exercising the anus and eliminating waste, occurring during the second year of life; the second Freudian stage. p. 58

anatomy is destiny
Belief proposed by Erikson claiming that psychological differences in males and females stem from anatomical differences between the two groups. p. 444

androgens
Hormones produced by the sex glands, which mature primarily in males. p. 99

androgyny
A sex-role orientation in which the person incorporates both masculine and feminine aspects into his or her behavior. p. 441

anorexia nervosa
An eating disorder that leads to self-starvation; primarily in females. p. 635

anthropological view
Stresses the scientific study of the origin of human beings and cultural influences on their development. Anthropologists believe that the adolescent's behavior may vary from one culture to another in ways the individual would have difficulty recognizing. p. 360

anticonformist
Adolescent who reacts counter to the group's expectations and deliberately moves away from the actions or beliefs they advocate; rebellious. p. 269

aptitude
The academic potential and personality dimensions in which students differ. p. 330

aptitude-treatment interaction
A field of educational research that determines the best learning conditions for a particular student by considering the interaction between the student's abilities and various teaching methods. p. 330

archival data
Historical data used for comparison purposes in research.

argots
A label used by linguists for the language style of a subculture. p. 356

assimilation
In Piaget's theory, the act of incorporating a feature of the environment into an existing mode or structure of thought. p. 54

associative flow
Ability to generate large amounts of associative content in an effort to attain novel solutions to problems and the freedom to entertain a wide range of possible solutions in a playful manner. p. 197

attention
The focusing of perception to produce an increased awareness of a stimulus. The point at which a stimulus is noticed. p. 171

attribution theory
Theory that views individuals as cognitive beings who attempt to understand the causes of their own and others' behavior. p. 530

authoritarian parenting
A style of parenting having a restrictive, punitive orientation and placing limits and controls on the child with little verbal give and take between the child and the parent. This form of parenting is linked with the following social behaviors of the child: an anxiety about social comparison, failure to initiate activity, and ineffective social interaction. p. 221

authoritative parenting
A form of parenting that encourages the child to be independent, but still places limits, demands, and controls on his or her actions. There is extensive verbal give and take, and parents demonstrate a high degree of warmth and nurturance toward the child. This form of parenting is associated with social competency on the part of the child, particularly self-reliance and social responsibility. p. 221

autonomy versus shame and doubt

The second stage in Erikson's eight-stage theory of development in which children may develop the healthy attitude that they are capable of independent control of their actions, or the unhealthy attitude of shame because they are incapable or doubt that they are capable of such control. p. 63

BAC

Blood alcohol concentration that is responsible for the alteration of feelings and conduct due to the action of alcohol on the central nervous system, specifically the brain. p. 596

basal metabolism rate (BMR)

The minimum amount of energy a person uses in a state of rest. p. 637

behavior genetics

The discipline concerned with the degree and nature of the heredity basis of behavior.

behavioral contract

A signed agreement that spells out what involved parties need to do to help to facilitate behavior modification. p. 50

behavioral perspective

Views of development that emphasize the influence of the environment on the behavior of the adolescent; behavior is seen as learned in this perspective and a methodological orientation is followed that emphasizes the fine-grained observation of behavior. Mental events or cognitive processes either are viewed as outside the realm of scientific study or as mediators of environmental experience. p. 49

brain-growth periodization

View of brain development emphasizing stages or spurts of brain growth. p. 95

brainstorming

Effective technique used to stimulate creativity in which a topic is suggested, ideas are freewheeling, criticism is withheld, and combination of ideas that are suggested is encouraged. p. 198

branch model

A model of cognitive development that emphasizes the individual variation in formal operational thought. p. 139

bulimia

A binge-and-purge syndrome that is marked by periods of very heavy eating followed by self-induced vomiting; occurs primarily in females. p. 635

canalization

The narrow track or path that marks the development of some characteristics in genetic development. p. 88

care perspective

An approach to moral development proposed by Gilligan in which people are viewed in terms of their connectedness with other people and the focus is on their communication with others. p. 501

case study

An in-depth assessment of a particular individual. It is used mainly by clinical psychologists. p. 71

chlamydia

A sexually transmitted disease. The symptoms mimic gonorrhea and can infect the entire reproductive tract if left untreated. p. 473

classical psychoanalytic theory

A form of therapy in which a psychoanalyst encourages his or her patient to talk about the past; places heavy emphasis on the unconscious aspects of the mind and the biological unfolding of psychosexual stages. p. 57

Classroom Environment Scale (CES)

Measure that attempts to evaluate the social climate of both junior high and high school classrooms through assessment of teacher–student and peer relationships, as well as the organization of the classroom. p. 327

clinical method

A variation of naturalistic observation that involves sophisticated observation and interviewing skills, which have been developed through experiences with numerous people, many of whom have psychological problems. p. 71

clique

Peer groups that are smaller in size than a crowd, involve greater intimacy among members, and have more group cohesion. Members of a clique are attracted to one another on the basis of similar interests and social ideals. p. 288

coaching

A conglomerate of strategies used to facilitate peer relations; may consist of demonstration or modeling, discussion and reasoning, as well as reinforcement of appropriate social skills. p. 277

cocaine

A stimulant, taken in the form of either crystals or powder, which provides increased feelings of stamina, enhanced mental capabilities, excitability, and occasionally hallucinations. p. 592

cognitive development

Changes that occur in mental activity, some of which are age-related, such as thought, memory, attention, perception, language, problem solving, intelligence, creativity, and decision making. p. 34

cognitive developmental theory

Theory that focuses on the rational thinking of the developing individual and stresses that cognitive development unfolds in a stage-like sequence, which is ordered and uniform for all individuals. p. 53

cognitive–disequilibrium theory

A Piagetian-related view of moral development in which individuals may start to question and sometimes reject their former beliefs and, in the process, may develop their own moral system. p. 490

cognitive social learning theory

Theory most associated with Bandura and Mischel, which stresses that environment–behavior relations are mediated by cognitive factors. p. 50

cohort effects

In research, effects that are due to a subject's time of birth or generation, but not actually to her or his age. pp. 29 and 45

complex stepfamily

A family in which both the stepparent and the biological parent have brought children to the newly formed stepfamily. p. 248

component

An elementary information process that operates on internal representation of objects. p. 185

componential analysis

View of intelligence involving information processing components; attempts to understand the availability, accessibility, and ease of execution of a number of information processing components. p. 185

concrete operational stage

The third stage in Piagetian theory (seven to eleven years old) during which children acquire mental operations that allow for abstractions of some attributes of reality, such as number and substance, but these operations can only be applied to concrete events. p. 54

conformity

The act of agreeing with the expressed group opinion when pressed to do so; also, the act of concurring with the rules and social practices of a culture or subculture.

connectedness

Method of identity achievement reflected in mutuality and permeability in which the adolescent is sensitive to and respects the views of others, and is open and responsive to the views of others. p. 424

contents

In Guilford's view, the dimension of cognition that is figural (e.g., visual or spatial), symbolic (e.g., letters, numbers, or words), semantic (word meaning), or behavioral (nonverbal performance). p. 183

contextual world view

An interactive perspective of adolescence that views the adolescent as continuously responding to and acting on the contexts in which he or she lives. p. 47

continuity-discontinuity

A controversial issue involving several arguments, the most widely discussed one being the extent to which earlier experiences and/or development is tied to later development or characteristics. There is both continuity and discontinuity in development. p. 24

control group

In experimental research, the group that receives zero level of the independent variable. The comparison or base line group. p. 73

conventional level

The second level in Kohlberg's theory of moral development in which the child's internalization of moral values is intermediate; he or she abides by certain standards of other people, such as parents (stage three) or the rules of society (stage four). p. 491

convergent thinking

A type of thought wherein attention is directed toward finding a single solution to a problem; contrasts with divergent thinking. p. 197

correlation coefficient

A measure of the degree of the relationship between two distributions (samples) which ranges from $+1.00$ to -1.00. A positive coefficient means that the distribution increases together; a negative coefficient means that as one increases the other decreases; and a zero coefficient means no correlation exists. p. 74

creativity

The term used to describe an act or contribution to society that is unique or original. p. 197

criterion sampling

A method of selecting a sample by first defining specific criteria for success at what the researcher wants to predict. p. 188

cross-sectional study

A method of study used to examine effects related to age by testing independent groups of people of different ages. p. 75

crowd

The largest and least personal of peer group relationships. The members of the crowd meet because of their mutual interest in activities, not because of mutual attraction to each other. p. 288

crystallized intelligence

The type of intelligence that involves skills, abilities, and understanding and is determined by schooling and environment. p. 183

cult

An unorthodox religious system with beliefs that are usually centered around the teachings of a leader and whose customs are associated with an object or a person.

cultural estrangement

Development of a lack of commitment to the values of an individual's culture. The adolescent rejects the predominant standards for success. p. 624

culture

The behavioral patterns, beliefs, values, and other products of humans that are learned and shared by a particular group of people and passed on from one generation to the next. p. 350

culture-fair tests

Intelligence tests developed in an attempt to eliminate cultural bias. p. 189

D

defense mechanisms

In psychoanalytic theory, a mental operation designed to prevent the emergence of anxiety-provoking thoughts into consciousness. p. 61

delay of gratification

Refers to the quality of purposefully deferring immediate gratification for delayed but more desired future gratification. p. 532

dependent variables

Those aspects of one's behavior that are measured in an experiment and presumed to be under the control of one or more of the manipulated factors (independent variables). p. 73

desatellization

Process in which the adolescent begins breaking away and becomes independent from parents. Final desatellization results in secure feelings about the self, strong exploratory tendencies, and the focusing of energies on tasks and problem solving. (In Ausubel's theory.) p. 233

development

Refers to a pattern of change or movement that begins at conception and continues through the entire life span. p. 22

dialectical

A term sometimes used to describe the contextual world view; assumes that both the individual and the contexts presented to him or her are continuously changing rather than being in equilibrium. p. 48

divergent thinking
A kind of creative thought process exercised when a person's imagination provides many different answers to a single question; contrast with convergent thinking. p. 197

divided attention
The type of attention required to process several relevant sources of information simultaneously. p. 171

dizygotic
Fraternal twins or coming from two different eggs and therefore genetically more distant than identical twins. p. 88

dopamine
A neurotransmitter that plays an important role in emotion and attention. p. 638

E

early adolescence
Corresponds to the period that encompasses the greatest pubertal change and the middle school or junior high school years. p. 33

early adulthood
Begins in the late teens or early twenties and lasts through the thirties. It is a time of establishing personal and economic independence. p. 33

early childhood
Period of development extending from the end of infancy to about five or six years, roughly corresponds to the period in which the child prepares for formal schooling. p. 31

egocentrism in adolescence
In adolescence, two types of thinking represent the emergence of this thinking style—the imaginary audience and the personal fable. Adolescent egocentrism involves belief that others are as interested in himself/herself as much as he/she is, personal uniqueness, and a sense of indestructability. p. 149

ego integrity versus despair
The final conflict in Erikson's theory of development. This stage involves retrospective glances at and evaluations of life. p. 64

Electra complex
A Freudian conflict involving young girls that is parallel to the Oedipus complex in boys; the girl experiences sexual desire for her father accompanied by hostility toward her mother. p. 59

emotional processes and development
Contains some of the same components as social development but more emphasis is placed on the adolescent's feelings and affective responses. p. 35

empathy
The ability to participate in the feelings or ideas of another person. p. 505

enrichment
Focuses on special provisions for gifted children, including college-level courses in high school.

environment interventions
Method of substance abuse prevention that focuses on the settings where substance abuse originates and where it can be prevented, such as at school, at home, and in the community. p. 591

equilibration
In Piaget's theory, the mechanism by which the child resolves cognitive conflict and reaches a balance of thought. p. 55

estradiol
Important hormone responsible for pubertal development in females; one hormone in a complex hormonal system associated with the physical changes of puberty in females. p. 99

estrogens
Hormones produced by the sex glands, which mature mainly in females. p. 99

ethnicity
The condition of belonging to a particular ethnic group, membership being based on racial, religious, national, and ancestral background. p. 374

exosystem
Refers to settings in which the adolescent does not participate although important decisions that affect the adolescent's life are made in these settings. (Bronfenbrenner's view.) p. 351

experience sampling technique
A method of obtaining the thoughts, activities, and feelings of the individual through approximately forty to fifty randomly chosen moments in their daily lives. p. 353

experiment
A carefully controlled method of investigation in which the experimenter manipulates factors believed to be influential on a subject's mind or behavior (independent variable) and measures any changes in the subject's behavior (dependent variable) that are presumably due to the influence of the independent variables. p. 72

experimental group
The group of subjects in an experiment who receive some treatment that is controlled; the group which is exposed to the manipulation of the independent variables. p. 73

external locus of control
Perception that others have more control over an individual than the individual has over himself or herself. p. 532

extrinsic motivation
Behavior that is influenced by external rewards. p. 543

F

factor analytic approach
A type of intelligence testing that involves a mathematical analysis of large numbers of responses to test items in an attempt to come up with the basic common factors in intelligence. p. 183

family-of-twin studies
A strategy used by behavior geneticists to investigate the role of genetics in human behavior by comparing monozygotic twins, siblings, half-siblings, and parent and offspring.

fantasy stage
In Ginzberg's theory of vocational choice, the period lasting until about age eleven in which children imagine what they want to be with little or no concern for their abilities, training, or the demands for reality. p. 553

father absence tradition
Method of studying the effect of divorce on children and adolescents that compares children from father absent and father present families, and attributes differences in development to the absence of the father, especially in the first five years of the child's life. p. 243

fear of failure
Refers to the adolescent's anxiety about not doing well, which can affect achievement motivation. p. 529

fear of success
Type of underachievement behavior in which the adolescent worries about doing well in school because he or she doesn't want to make other family members envious or resentful.

fluid intelligence
The type of intelligence that involves the individual's adaptability and capacity to perceive things and integrate them mentally. This kind of intelligence appears to be intuitive or independent of education and experience. p. 183

formal operational stage
In Piaget's model, this appears between eleven and fifteen years of age when the individual is believed to achieve the most advanced form of thought possible; the most important feature characterizing this stage is the development of abstract thought. p. 54

freedom and responsibility
One of the three implicit agreements about mutual obligation between parent and child proposed by Elkind. In the freedom and responsibility contract, the parents generally grant children freedom insofar as the children demonstrate that they can handle the requisite responsibility. p. 538

G

generativity versus stagnation
The seventh conflict in Erikson's theory of development. This stage is positively resolved if an adult assists the younger generation in developing and leading useful lives. p. 63

genital stage
The last psychosexual stage in Freud's theory of development, lasting from the beginning of puberty through the rest of the life cycle. The period during which sexual energy is focused on others and work and love become important themes. p. 59

genotype
The special arrangement of chromosomes and genes each person has inherited that make him or her unique. p. 86

gifted child
An individual with well above average intellectual capacity (an I.Q. of 120 or more, for example) or an individual with superior talent for something. p. 191

global self-concept
The sum total of an individual's feelings and perceptions about himself or herself, including his or her feelings about areas of competence, interests, uniqueness, etc.; this self-knowledge is a key organizing principle of personality according to humanistic theorists. p. 398

gonadal
Refers to the sex glands. p. 98

gonadotropin
A hormone released by the pituitary gland, which stimulates the gonads (ovaries or testes). p. 98

goodness-of-fit model
Theory of evaluation of the nature of pubertal timing, which believes that the adolescent may be at risk when the demands of a particular social context and the adolescents' physical and behavioral characteristics are mismatched. p. 119

grouping
Occurs when students with similar capacities are placed in a class together; one of three paths in programs for gifted children.

groups
Social structure that carries with it normative expectations about acceptable and unacceptable aspects of behavior and influences both the interactions and relationships of group members. p. 237

guidelessness
A feeling that the rules in an individual's world have faltered. The adolescent rejects the conventional rules and regulations as a means of success. p. 624

guilt
The affective state of psychological discomfort arising from a person's feeling of having done something morally wrong. p. 505

H

hallucinogens
Drugs that produce hallucinations or distortions of reality. p. 592

heritability
A mathematical estimate of the degree to which a particular characteristic is genetically determined. p. 89

heroin
A derivative of opium, heroin is highly addictive and can be toxic. Perceived by adolescents as having the greatest risk of harm for the user. p. 593

Hispanic
Refers to anyone of Spanish descent, including Mexican-Americans, Puerto Ricans, and Cubans. p. 376

historical time
Dimension of time focusing on the timing of major historical events in the life of the individual. p. 28

hope for success
The equivalent of achievement motivation; the adolescents underlying drive for success. p. 529

hormones
The secretions of endocrine glands, which are powerful chemical substances that regulate bodily organs. p. 98

host intervention
Method of substance abuse prevention that focuses on who will use the substance. This method builds cognitive and behavioral skills so the adolescent will be able to resist substance abuse. p. 591

humanism
Psychological tradition that places a strong emphasis on the role of the self and self-concept as central to understanding development. p. 398

hypothalamic-pituitary-gonadal axis
Aspect of the endocrine system that is important in puberty and involves the interaction of the hypothalamus, the pituitary gland, and the sex glands. p. 98

hypothalamus
A structure in the higher portion of the brain believed to be important in the regulation of hunger, temperature, emotional control, and other visceral functions. p. 98

hypothetical-deductive reasoning
Ability to entertain many possibilities and test many solutions in a planful way when faced with having to solve a problem. (An important aspect of logical thought in the formal operational stage.) p. 130

I

ideal self
The self as the adolescent would like to be. p. 398

identity achieved
Adolescents who have undergone a crisis and made a commitment. To reach the identity achieved status, it is necessary for the adolescent to first experience a crisis, then make an enduring commitment. p. 419

identity crisis
Term applied to practically anyone of any age who feels a loss of identification or self-image. In Erikson's theory, it is the stage that must be resolved during adolescence in order to form a sense of self. p. 419

identity diffused (confused)
Adolescents who have not experienced any crisis (explored any meaningful alternatives) or made any commitments. p. 419

identity foreclosure
Adolescents who have made a commitment, but have not experienced a crisis. p. 419

identity moratorium
Adolescents in the midst of a crisis, but their commitments are either absent or only vaguely defined. p. 419

identity versus identity confusion (diffusion)
Erikson's fifth crisis of psychological development; the adolescent may become confident and purposeful, or may develop an ill-defined identity. p. 63

imaginary audience
The egocentric belief that others are as preoccupied with the adolescent's behavior as he or she is with himself or herself. p. 149

imitation (modeling, vicarious learning)
A form of learning in which new behaviors are acquired by observing others performing the behavior. p. 51

immanent justice
In Piaget's theory of moral development, the naive belief that punishment inevitably follows wrongdoing; part of the early stage of moral realism. p. 490

impression formation
The formation of concepts about one's self, about others, and about relationships with others. p. 153

incentives
External cues that stimulate motivation. Incentives can be positive or negative. p. 543

independent variables
The factors in an experiment that are manipulated or controlled by the experimenter to determine their impact on the subject's behavior. p. 72

individual differences
The consistent, stable ways adolescents differ from each other. p. 27

individuating-reflexive faith
Stage in the development of religious beliefs proposed by Fowler, during which the late adolescent makes the transition from a conventional perspective on values to an individualized perspective.

individuation
The formation of the individual's personal identity, which includes the development of one's sense of self and the forging of a special place for oneself within the social order. Adolescents develop a more distinct view of themselves as unique persons and more readily differentiate themselves from others than they did as children. p. 426

industry versus inferiority
Erikson's fourth crisis of psychological development; the school-aged child may develop a capacity for work and task-directedness, or may view himself/herself as inadequate. p. 63

infancy
Period of development extending from birth to eighteen or twenty-four months; a time of extreme dependence upon adults. p. 31

information processing approach
Theory of cognition that is concerned with the processing of information. Involves such processes as attention, perception, memory, thinking, and problem solving. p. 55

inhalants
Any aerosol or gaseous fumes, other than smoke, that are inhaled to make the user feel good, high, or intoxicated. Use of inhalants by adolescents seems to be on the rise. p. 593

initiative versus guilt
Erikson's third crisis of psychological development, occurring during the preschool years; the child may develop a desire for achievement or he or she may be held back by self-criticism. p. 63

insecure attachment
Refers to the relationship between parents and infants in which the infant either avoids the caregiver or is ambivalent toward her. This type of anxious attachment to the caregiver is believed to be associated with incompetent behavior on the part of the infant. p. 234

instincts
An innate tendency toward particular desires or behavior patterns and responses to the environment. p. 57

instrumental values
A set of values that are action-oriented.

intention-cue detection
The cognitive ability to interpret another's behavior by detecting the intentions of the actor. p. 276

interactionist approach
View of abnormalities that considers both biological factors and sociocultural conditions as causative factors that interact with each other to produce the problem. p. 642

interactions
Patterns of communication that occur between persons who may or may not be intimates. p. 237

internal locus of control
Perception that individuals are in control of their world, that they can cause things to happen if they choose, and that they command their own rewards. p. 532

interview
A set of questions asked of someone and the responses to them; used in psychological research, the interview can be very structured or very unstructured. p. 69

intimacy in friendship
Intimate self-disclosure and the sharing of private thoughts; private and personal knowledge. p. 282

intimacy versus isolation
Erikson's sixth stage of psychosocial development; the young adult may achieve a capacity for honesty and close relationships, or be unable to form these ties and a feeling of isolation may result. p. 63

intimate
An individual who has been able to form and maintain one or more deep and longlasting love relationship(s). p. 432

intraindividual change
Aspect of individual differences studying change and stability within children and adolescents as they develop. p. 27

intrinsic motivation
Refers to behavior that is motivated by an underlying need for competence and self-determination. Also referred to as mastery and competence motivation. p. 543

isolated
A person who withdraws from social encounters and who fails to form an intimate relationship with members of the same or opposite sex. p. 432

J

Jigsaw classroom
Classroom structure that emphasizes cooperation among equals; children are divided into groups with equal ethnic composition and academic achievement levels, and lessons are divided among these groups with one part being given to each member of the group. The components are like parts of a jigsaw puzzle in that they have to be put together to form the complete picture. p. 377

justice perspective
An approach to moral development proposed by Gilligan in which people are differentiated and seen as standing alone; the focus is on the rights of the individual, that is, justice. p. 501

K

kinship studies
A strategy of research used to assess the role of heredity in behavior by comparing the genetic relationship between family members, including uncles, cousins, grandparents, and other more distant relatives.

L

latchkey children
Children of working parents who are given the key to their home and take the key with them to school, using it in the evening to let themselves in the home while the parents are still at work. p. 250

late adolescence
Refers to the latter half of the second decade of life, roughly the ages of sixteen through eighteen to twenty-two years of age. p. 33

latency stage
The fourth psychosexual stage in Freud's theory of development lasts from about six to twelve years of age (the elementary school years). During this stage, the child concentrates on such activities as school and getting along in society. Stressful problems of the previous phallic stage are repressed. p. 59

learned helplessness
View of depression proposing that adolescents who are exposed to stress, prolonged pain, or loss over which they have no control learn to become helpless. p. 628

life time
Perspective of time in the life cycle that is based heavily on the biological timetable governing the sequence of changes in the process of growing up. p. 28

longitudinal study
A method of research in which the same subject or group of subjects is repeatedly tested over a lengthy period of time. p. 75

lower class
A label used to describe the members of society who have less money, education, power, and status than most other members of society. p. 368

loyalty and commitment
One of the three implicit agreements about mutual obligation between parent and children proposed by Elkind. In the loyalty and commitment contract, it is assumed that children will be loyal to the parents in return for the parents concern and commitment. p. 538

M

maturation
Describes a pattern of change or movement which, like the term development, has been associated more with changes dictated by the genetic blueprint rather than environmental experiences. p. 22

mechanistic world view
Views the adolescent as a passive machine that reacts to events in the environment, but does not actively anticipate events, does not formulate its own goals, and does not engage in complex internal mental activity of any kind. p. 47

medical or disease model
View of abnormality that sites some physical malfunctioning as the cause of the problem. p. 641

memory
The maintenance of information over time. p. 171

memory-span task
A task used to assess short-term memory in which the individual hears a short list of stimuli, usually digits, presented at a rapid pace and then is asked to repeat the digits back. p. 171

menarche
The first menstruation in pubertal females. p. 115

mesosystem
Refers to linkages between microsystems or connectiveness between contexts; e.g., relation of family experiences to school experiences. p. 351

meta-analysis
Application of statistical techniques to already existing research studies to obtain an overall picture of results. p. 327

metacomponents
Higher order control processes used for executive planning and decision making when problem solving is called for. p. 185

metamemory
Knowledge of and awareness of how memory processes work. p. 172

metaphor
An implied comparison between two ideas that is conveyed by the abstract meaning contained in the words used to make the comparison. p. 133

microsystem
Refers to contexts in which the adolescent has face to face interactions with others who are influential in his or her life. p. 351

middle adulthood
Period of development entered into at about thirty-five to forty-five years and exited at some point between fifty-five to sixty-five years of age. p. 34

middle and late childhood
Period extending from about six to ten years of age, roughly corresponding to the elementary school years. p. 31

middle class
A label used to describe the members of society who are in the intermediate ranges of income, status, power, and educational opportunity. In democratic societies, the middle class is often the dominant force in government. p. 368

monozygotic
A term referring to identical twins meaning that they come from the same egg. p. 88

moral autonomy
The second stage of moral development in Piaget's theory. The child becomes aware that rules and laws are created by people relative to social systems, and that in judging an action, one should consider the actor's intentions as well as the act's consequences. p. 489

moral competence
Knowledge of moral rules indicating that the person is capable of acting in appropriate moral ways. p. 505

moral development
The acquisition of rules and conventions about what people should do in their interactions with others. p. 489

moral performance
The performance of a particular moral behavior, dependent on factors of motivation as well as of moral understanding. p. 505

moral realism
The first stage of moral development in Piaget's theory. Justice and rules are conceived of as unchangeable properties of the world, removed from the control of people. p. 489

most efficient design
The most elaborate of the sequential designs having both cross-sectional and longitudinal sequences. At each time of measurement, a new sample of subjects in each age group is selected and tested, and subjects who have been tested before are tested again.

motivation
The desires, needs, and interests that energize the organism and direct it toward a goal. p. 527

multiple-factor theory
The view that a number of specific factors rather than one general and one specific factor make up intelligence. p. 183

N

n achievement
Refers to the need and motivation to achieve and the individuals striving for success; viewed as a general property of the individual, remaining consistent across different domains and time. p. 528

Native Americans
American Indians; a minority group with the lowest standard of living, the highest teenage pregnancy rate, the highest teenage suicide rate, and the highest high school drop-out rate of any ethnic group. p. 376

neglected children
Children who are not necessarily disliked by their peers even though they often do not have many friends. p. 271

neonate
Term referring to an infant for the first few days after birth. p. 31

neopsychoanalytic theorists
These are contemporary psychoanalytic theorists who accept a number of Freudian ideas, such as unconscious thought and the developmental unfolding of personality, but place less emphasis on sexuality in development and more emphasis on the importance of culture in determining personality. p. 60

nonconformist
Adolescent who knows what people around him expect, but does not use these expectations to guide his behavior; independent. p. 269

norms
The standards, rules, and guidelines by which the group abides. p. 284

O

obesity
Weighing more than twenty percent over normal skeletal and physical requirements. p. 637

Oedipus complex
A Freudian conflict beginning in early childhood in which the boy exhibits sexual desire for the mother, and hostility and fear of the father. p. 59

open classroom concept
Classroom climate that offers free choice of activities, space flexibility, varied learning materials, individual instruction, self-responsibility by students, multiage grouping of children, team teaching, and classrooms without walls; opposite of traditional classroom setting. p. 326

operant conditioning (instrumental conditioning)
A type of learning described by Skinner in which the individual operates or acts on his environment, and what happens to him, in turn, controls his behavior: the individual's behavior is determined by its consequences. Behavior followed by a positive stimulus is likely to recur, while behavior followed by a negative stimulus is not as likely to recur. p. 49

operations
Intellectual activities or processes; that is, what one does with information. In Piaget's theory, mental actions or representations that are reversible. pp. 128 and 183

oral stage
The first psychosexual stage in Freud's theory of development lasting from birth to around one year; this stage centers on the child's pleasure from stimulation of the oral area—mouth, lips, tongue, and gums. p. 58

organismic world view
A view that assumes the individual is an active, mindful person with goals and plans who uses complex strategies to attain ends; this world view also assumes a strong biological foundation of development, with the social world functioning primarily to provide the setting for the unfolding of development rather than being the cause of development. p. 47

organization
The continuous process of refining and integrating every level of thought from sensorimotor to formal operation (Piagetian theory). p. 55

overvaluation
Parenting style in which the parent continually interacts with their child as if the child was in control. p. 233

P

parallel processing
The simultaneous consideration of a number of lines of thought. p. 170

passive-aggressive
Pattern of underachievement characterized by indirectly expressed hostility, fear of failure or fear of success, and inadequate coping strategies in stressful situations. p. 623

peers
Refers to adolescents who are about the same age or the same behavioral level. p. 263

peer sociotherapy
A process in which peers are trained to provide support and encouragement to each other in group settings. p. 262

performance components
Processes used to carry out a problem-solving strategy. p. 185

permissive-indifferent parenting
A style of parenting in which the parents are very uninvolved in their children's lives, giving them considerable freedom to regulate their own behavior and taking a nonpunitive stance. These parents are rejecting as well as undemanding, and the result is usually a lack of self-control on the part of the child. p. 221

permissive-indulgent parenting
A style of parenting in which the parents are highly involved in their children's lives, but allow them considerable freedom and do not control their negative behaviors. This type of parenting is associated with children's impulsivity, aggressiveness, lack of independence, and inability to take responsibility. p. 221

personal fable
Type of adolescent egocentrism that refers to the adolescent's sense of personal uniqueness and indestructibility. p. 150

personal incapacity
The feeling that one doesn't have the ability and skills needed to succeed; a feeling of incompetence or incapability of dealing with the world. p. 624

personality processes and development
Process of development referring more to a property of the individual adolescent than to his or her commerce with the social world. p. 35

perspective taking

The ability to understand that other people have feelings and perceptions that are different from one's own. pp. 150, 265

phallic stage

The third psychosexual stage in Freud's theory of development lasting from about four to six years of age. The period during which the child's genital area is the chief source of pleasure. p. 58

phenomenological approach

A theoretical view that places greater emphasis on understanding the individual's perception of an event than on the behavioral account of the event. p. 398

phenothiazines

The most widely used drug in treating schizophrenia. p. 639

phenotype

The observed and measurable characteristics of individuals including physical characteristics such as height, weight, eye color, and skin pigmentation; also includes psychological characteristics such as intelligence, creativity, and social tendencies. p. 86

pituitary gland

A small endocrine gland located at the base of the skull which is responsible for the secretion of hormones that directly affect the activity of glands elsewhere in the body. p. 98

polygenic inheritance

A complex form of genetic transmission involving the interaction of many different genes to produce certain traits. p. 87

postconventional level

The highest level of morality in Kohlberg's theory of moral development in which moral values are completely internalized and not based on the standards of others. The moral code that is adopted may be among the principles generally accepted by the community (stage five) or it may be more individualized (stage six). p. 491

pragmatics

Rules of language pertaining to the social context and how people use language in conversation. p. 135

preconventional level

The first and lowest level in Kohlberg's theory; no internalization of morality occurs here. Moral thought follows the belief that morality is determined by the external environment, particularly rewarding and punishing circumstances. p. 491

preintimate

An individual who has mixed emotions about commitment; reflected in the tendency to offer love without any obligations or longlasting bonds. p. 432

prenatal period

The time of development represented from the time of conception to birth. It is a time of tremendous growth. p. 31

preoperational stage

In Piagetian theory, the stage of thought that lasts from about two to seven years of age, and follows the sensorimotor period. Although logical thought is present, there are several "flaws," such as egocentrism, that limit the individual. p. 54

processing capacity

A type of mental energy needed to perform work or to process information. p. 170

products

A cognitive operation that indexes the form in which information occurs—units, classes, relations, systems, transformations, or implications. p. 184

pseudointimate

An individual who appears to be maintaining a longlasting heterosexual attachment, while the relationship actually has little depth or closeness. p. 434

psychometric approach

Approach to intelligence which emphasizes measurement-based tests.

psychometric

The use of measurement to assess a concept of psychology. p. 187

puberty

The stage of development at which the individual becomes capable of reproduction; this stage is usually linked with the onset of adolescence; a period of rapid change to maturation.

Q

Quaaludes (methaqualone)
Hypnotic sedatives that are chemically synthesized; sometimes used in conjunction with cocaine to bring the user down. p. 592

qualitative change
Piagetian claim that an adolescent's intelligence is more abstract than a child's and therefore qualitatively different, not just quantitatively different. p. 23

quasi-experimental
An approximation to an experiment in which there is some loss of control over the independent variables due to the real-life manner in which they are defined. p. 73

questionnaire
A method of study that is similar to a highly structured interview, except the subject reads the questions and marks the answers on a sheet of paper rather than verbally responding to the interviewer. p. 69

R

reaction range
The limits within which the environment can modify genetic inheritance.

realistic stage
In Ginzberg's theory of vocational choice, the age period lasting from seventeen or eighteen through the early twenties during which the individual explores available occupations and decides on a specific job. p. 553

real self
The self as it really is; as opposed to the ideal self. p. 398

reciprocal determinism
The belief that a person's psychological makeup is shaped by the continuous reciprocal interaction between behavior and its controlling conditions; in other words, behavior partly constructs the environment and the resulting environment, in turn, shapes behavior. p. 51

reciprocal socialization
A view of the socialization process as a mutual interaction between parents and the adolescent; the adolescent socializes the parent just as the parent socializes the adolescent. p. 208

regression
Freudian defense mechanism that occurs when the adolescent reverts to an earlier stage of development. p. 61

rejected children
Children who are overtly disliked by their peers and who often have more long-term maladjustment than neglected children. p. 271

rejection
Parental view of the child as an unwanted part of their existence wherein the child's needs are served unwillingly and only if necessary, and love and acceptance are absent or at least are perceived as being absent by the child. p. 233

relationships
Pattern of communication occurring between people with enduring bonds to each other, often marked by histories of past interactions as well as commitments to the future. p. 237

reliability
The degree to which statistical measurements are consistent on repeated trials. p. 7

religious or supernatural model
View of abnormality in which the malevolent gods, demons, witches, vampires, and even the moon and planets are responsible for abnormal behavior in adolescents. p. 640

resatellization
A preliminary step in the adolescent's attainment of the final stage of desatellization in which the individual's parents are replaced by other individuals or a group. p. 233

retention (retrieval) components
Processes involved in accessing previously stored information. p. 186

rites of passage
Pubertal rites that are the avenue through which adolescents gain access to sacred adult practices, to knowledge, and to sexuality. The formal initiation ceremony associated with entry into adolescence in some cultures. p. 366

S

satellization

Process by which the child gives up his or her sense of self-power and the perception that he or she can do everything for himself or herself and accepts dependence on his or her parents. p. 233

satire

A literary work in which irony, derision, or wit in any form is used to expose folly or wickedness. p. 133

schizophrenia

A form of psychosis characterized by illogical thought, hallucinations, and erratic behavior; one of the most severe forms of disturbances in adolescence. p. 638

schizophrenogenic mother

Mothers with a high anxiety level who easily become upset and, as a result, may facilitate the development of schizophrenia in the adolescent. p. 639

school phobia

The reluctance or refusal of the child or adolescent to attend school because of the intense anxiety he or she experiences about being there. p. 626

science

Any discipline or field of study characterized by a systematic body of theories that can be verified or proved false on the basis of actual evidence collected about people. p. 47

second individuation crisis

The critical sharpening of boundaries of the adolescent's self as distinct from others, particularly parents, in an attempt to transcend infantile ties to them and develop self-responsibility. p. 234

second-order effects

Third party influences on the nature of dyadic relationships in families. p. 209

secure attachment

A positive bond that develops between the infant and the caregiver, which promotes the healthy exploration of the world because the caregiver provides a secure base to which the infant can return if stressors are encountered. p. 234

selective attention

What happens when people focus on processing relevant information by ignoring the presence of irrelevant information. p. 171

self as knower

A component of self awareness that actively organizes and determines the quality of the person's experiences (the "I"). p. 398

self as object

A component of self-awareness that consists of everything that can be known about the self (the "me"). p. 400

self-esteem

A term used interchangeably with self-concept by some theorists, which refers to the positive or negative value the individual places on the self. For other theorists, it refers only to the positive aspects of self-concept.

sensorimotor stage

The earliest stage of thought in Piaget's model of cognitive development lasting from birth to about two years of age. This stage extends from simple reflexes through the use of primitive symbols as the means of coordinating sensation and action. p. 54

sequential designs

Those that combine the features of cross-sectional and longitudinal designs in a search for more effective ways to study development. p. 75

set point

The weight an individual can maintain when no effort to gain or lose is expended. p. 637

sex steroids

Hormones including testosterone and estradiol, the levels of which are associated with perception of social competence in adolescent boys. p. 100

siblings

Brothers and/or sisters. p. 238

simple stepfamily

A family in which the stepparent has not brought children from a previous marriage to live in the newly formed stepfamily. p. 248

social

Refers to the adolescent's interactions with other individual's in the environment. p. 35

social class

Categorization of people based on similarities in economic resources, power, prestige, education, and style of life; socioeconomic status. (SES.) p. 368

social cognition

Field of thinking and reasoning that focuses on how people conceptualize and reason about their social world—the people they watch and interact with, the relationships with those people, and the groups in which they participate. Also includes how individuals reason about themselves in relation to others. p. 146

social comparison

The seeking out of others within a peer group to evaluate our reactions, abilities, talents, and characteristics. p. 272

social conventional reasoning

Refers to thoughts about social consensus and convention (as opposed to moral reasoning, which stresses ethical matters). p. 502

social information processing

A nondevelopmental perspective of social cognition that focuses on the processing of social memories, social problem solving, and social decision making. Valuable in examining how the adolescent processes social information. p. 148

social intelligence

Also called tacit intelligence; practical intelligence such as the ability to pick up nonverbal cues in social interactions thus giving us insight into understanding people. p. 191

social-mold theories

Perspectives in which the adolescent is looked upon as infinitely malleable and is molded by his or her environment, particularly within the family. Such theories give little attention to the maturational process. p. 208

social time

Refers to the dimension of time in the life cycle that underlies the age–grade system of a particular society. Characterized in some societies by rites of passage. p. 28

sociocultural model

A view of abnormality that focuses on environmental factors as a cause of unusual behavior and why certain behaviors are viewed by society as "sick," "crazy," or "mentally ill". p. 642

stages

A concept emphasizing that qualitative changes in development occur in sequential phases that are age-related. p. 23

standardized tests

Tests used to assess human characteristics and individual differences. The tests are developed using large samples and have established norms, reliability, and evidence of validity. p. 70

state anxiety

Type of anxiety that comes and goes depending upon particular experiences; opposed to trait anxiety. p. 530

statistical model

View of abnormality that emphasizes that an adolescent is abnormal when he or she deviates from the average. p. 641

status positions

Positions of more or less power and control in a group. p. 284

step-procreation

Stepfather and stepmother families in which a new child is born to the stepparent and the remarried parent; linked with poorer adjustment on the part of the stepchild. p. 248

stereotype

A broad category that reflects our impressions about people, including ourselves. pp. 19, 460

stereotyped

An individual who has superficial relationships that tend to be dominated by friendship ties with same-sex rather than opposite-sex individuals. p. 432

storm and stress view

View of adolescence proposed by Hall that sees adolescence as a turbulent time charged with conflict, and full of contradiction and wide swings in mood and emotion. p. 14

strategy

Methods of setting up a research study: three main ways are experimental, quasi-experimental, and correlational. p. 72

structure of intellect

A concept referring to Guilford's perspective of intelligence which proposes that an individual's intellect is composed of 120 mental abilities formed by all the possible combinations of five operations, four contents, and six products ($5 \times 4 \times 6 = 120$). p. 183

T

tentative stage
In Ginzberg's theory of vocational choice, the transition between the fantasy stage of childhood and the realistic stage of young adulthood; this stage occurs between ages eleven and seventeen, when thinking about careers is still subjective. p. 553

teratogens
Harmful agents that disturb prenatal development. p. 644

terminal values
A set of values that are abstract-oriented.

testosterone
A male sex hormone important in the development of sexual characteristics and behavior. p. 99

THC (delta-9-tetrahydrocannabinol)
The active chemical ingredient in marijuana that produces a "high." p. 586

theories
Broad abstract assumptions constructed to explain the nature of adolescent development; not as broad or abstract as world views. p. 48

thyroid gland
The gland that interacts with the pituitary to influence growth. p. 102

token economy
A system, based on operant conditioning, in which an individual in a clinical setting is given artificial rewards for socially constructive behavior. The tokens can be exchanged for desirable items and privileges. p. 610

top-dog phenomenon
Moving from the top position (in elementary school, as the oldest, biggest, and most powerful students in the school) to the lowest position (in middle or junior high school, the youngest, smallest, and least powerful group of students). p. 319

trait anxiety
The more or less stable and permanent tendency to experience a certain level of anxiety across time and circumstances. p. 530

transactive discussion
Reasoning that operates on the reasoning of another individual; it is of interest to researchers who study the role of communication among peers in moral development. p. 498

transfer components
Processes used in generalization, such as using information learned on one task to help solve another task. p. 186

transient self
Characteristics of the individual that vary over a period of time; not permanent fixtures of the self. p. 151

treatment
Refers to the educational technique (e.g., structured class or flexible class) adopted in the classroom. p. 330

trust versus mistrust
The first stage in Erikson's eight-stage theory of development in which the infant develops either the comfortable feeling that those around him or her care for his or her needs, or the worry that his or her needs will not be taken care of. p. 63

twin studies
An examination of particular behavior patterns or characteristics between monozygotic and dizygotic twins to determine the relative importance of heredity and environment.

U

undifferentiated
Refers to adolescents who perceive themselves as neither masculine nor feminine in gender role orientation. p. 442

upper class
In categorizations of social class, the highest class. In a three-way classification of social class, the upper class includes those who have managerial and professional positions. Describes members of a society who have the most money, education, power, and status of members in the society. p. 368

V

validity
The extent to which a test evaluates what it purports to evaluate.

values
The adolescent's abstract beliefs. p. 511

values clarification programs
A component in the The Skills for Ethical Action program in which teachers stimulate discussion of critical questions and issues by adolescents and encourage the students to find their own answers by value clarification.

world views
Highly abstract perspectives containing ideas that cannot be directly proved or disproved scientifically, but which serve as grand models, stimulating ideas, issues, and questions that can be tested. Three prominent world views that characterize the study of adolescents are: mechanistic, organismic, and contextual. p. 47

youth
Period of development entered as early as seventeen to eighteen years of age or as late as twenty-one to twenty-four years of age: a time of extended sense of economic and personal "temporariness." p. 33

References

Abernathy, T., & Davis, W. (1978). Student perceptions of influences on career and educational decision-making. *Canadian Counselor, 12,* 162–166.

Achenbach, T. M., & Edelbrock, C. S. (1981). Behavioral problems and competencies reported by parents of normal and disturbed children aged four through sixteen. *Monographs of the Society for Research in Child Development, 46*(1, Serial No. 188).

Adams, G., & Jones, R. (1981). Imaginary audience behavior: A validation study. *Journal of Early Adolescence, 1,* 1–10.

Adams, G. R., & Fitch, S. A. (1982). Ego stage and identity status development: A cross-sequential analysis. *Journal of Personality and Social Psychology, 43,* 574–583.

Adams, R. S., & Biddle, B. J. (1970). *Realities of teaching.* New York: Holt, Rinehart, & Winston.

Adelson, J. (1979, January). Adolescence and the generalization gap. *Psychology Today,* pp. 33–37.

Adelson, J., & Doehrman, M. J. (1980). The psychodynamic approach to adolescence. In J. Adelson (Ed.), *Handbook of adolescent psychology.* New York: John Wiley.

Adolescent voices. (1979, February). *Psychology Today,* pp. 43–44.

Ainsworth, M. D. S. (1979). Infant-mother attachment. *American Psychologist, 34,* 932–937.

Alan Guttmacher Institute. (1976). *Eleven million teenagers: What can be done about the epidemic of adolescent pregnancies in the United States?* New York: Planned Parenthood Federation of America.

Alan Guttmacher Institute. (1981). *Teenage pregnancy: The problem that hasn't gone away.* New York: Author.

Alexander, J. F., & Malouf, R. E. (1983). Intervention with children experiencing problems in personality and social development. In P. H. Mussen (Ed.), *Handbook of child psychology* (Vol. 4, 4th ed.). New York: Wiley.

Allen, M. R. (1967). *Male cults and secret initiations in Melanesia.* London and New York: Cambridge University Press.

Altus, W. D. (1970). Marriage and order of birth. *Proceedings of the 78th Annual Convention of the American Psychological Association, 5,* 361–362.

Ames, C. (1984). Competitive, cooperative, and individualistic goal structures: A cognitive-motivational analysis. In R. E. Ames & C. Ames (Eds.), *Motivation in education.* New York: Academic Press.

Ames, R. E., Ames, C., & Garrison, W. (1977). Children's causal ascriptions for positive and negative interpersonal outcomes. *Psychological Reports, 41,* 595–602.

Anastasi, A. (1976). *Psychological testing* (2nd ed.). New York: Macmillan.

Andrews, G. R., & Debus, R. L. (1978). Persistence and causal perception of failure: Modifying cognitive attributions. *Journal of Educational Psychology, 70,* 154–166.

Anglin, J. M. (1970). *The growth of word meaning.* Cambridge, MA: MIT Press.

Anthony, E. J. (1957). An experimental approach to the psychopathology of childhood: Encopresis. *British Journal of Medical Psychology, 30,* 146–175.

Anthony, H. S. (1968). The association of violence and depression in a sample of young offenders. *British Journal of Criminology, 3,* 346–365.

Antill, J. K., & Cunningham, J. D. (1979). Self-esteem as a function of masculinity in both sexes. *Journal of Consulting and Clinical Psychology, 47,* 783–785.

Archer, S. L. (1982). The lower age boundaries of identity development. *Child Development, 53,* 1551–1556.

Archer, S. L. (1985, April). *Reflections on earlier life decisions: Implications for adult functioning.* Paper presented at the biennial meeting of the Society for Research in Child Development, Toronto.

Aristotle. (1941). [Rhetorica] (W. R. Roberts, Trans.). In R. McKeon (Ed.), *The basic works of Aristotle.* New York: Random House.

Armsden, G. G., & Greenburg, M. T. (1984). *The inventory of parent and peer attachment: Individual differences and their relationship to psychological well-being in adolescence.* Unpublished manuscript, University of Washington.

Aronson, E., Bridgeman, D. L., & Geffner, R. (1978). The effects of a cooperative classroom structure on student behavior and attitudes. In D. Bar-Tal & L. Saxe (Eds.), *Social psychology of education, theory and research*. Washington, DC: Hemisphere Publishing.

Aronson, E., Stephan, C., Sikes, J., Blaney, N., & Snapp, M. (1978). *The jigsaw classroom*. Beverly Hills, CA: Sage Publications.

Asarnow, J. R., & Callan, J. W. (1985). Boys with peer adjustment problems: Social cognitive processes. *Journal of Consulting and Clinical Psychology, 53*, 80–87.

Asarnow, R. F., & Asarnow, J. R. (1982). Attention-information processing dysfunction and vulnerability to schizophrenia: Implications for prevention. In M. Goldstein & E. Rodnick (Eds.), *Preventive intervention in schizophrenia*. Washington, DC: U.S. Government Printing Office.

Asberg, M., Thoren, P., Traskman, L., Bertilsson, L., & Ringberger, V. (1976). Serotonin depression, a biochemical subgroup within the affective disorders. *Science, 191*, 478–480.

Asher, S. R. (April, 1985). *Identification of socially rejected children*. Paper presented at the biennial meeting of the Society for Research in Child Development, Toronto.

Asher, S. R., & Dodge, K. A. (1986). Identifying children who are rejected by their peers. *Developmental Psychology, 22*, 444–449.

Asher, S. R., Oden, S., & Gottman, J. M. (1976). Children's friendships in social settings. *Quarterly Review of Early Childhood Education, 1*, 25–42.

Asher, S. R., & Renshaw, P. D. (1981). Children without friends: Social knowledge and social skill training. In S. R. Asher & J. M. Gottman (Eds.), *The development of children's friendships*. New York: Cambridge University Press.

Asher, S. R., & Wheeler, V. A. (1985). Children's loneliness: A comparison of rejected and neglected peer status. *Journal of Consulting and Clinical Psychology, 53*, 500–505.

Atkinson, J. W., & Feather, N. T. (Eds.). (1966). *A theory of achievement motivation*. New York: John Wiley.

Atkinson, J. W., & Raynor, I. O. (1974). *Motivation and achievement*. Washington, DC: V. H. Winston & Sons.

Ausubel, D. P. (1968). *Educational psychology*. New York: Holt, Rinehart, & Winston.

Ausubel, D. P., Montemayor, R., & Svajian, P. (1977). *Theories and problems of adolescent development*. New York: Grune & Stratton.

Ausubel, D. P., Sullivan, E. V., & Ives, S. W. (1979). *Theory and problems of child development* (3rd ed.). New York: Grune & Stratton.

Avery, R. K. (1979). Adolescents' use of the mass media. *American Behavioral Scientist, 23*, 53–70.

Bachman, J. G. (1982, June 28). *The American high school student: A profile based on national survey data*. Paper presented at a conference entitled, "The American High School Today and Tomorrow," Berkeley, CA.

Bachman, J. G., Green, S., & Wirtanen, I. D. (1971). *Youth in transition: Dropping out—problem or symptom?* Ann Arbor, MI.: Survey Research Center, Institute for Social Research.

Baldwin, W., & Cain, V. S. (1980). The children of teenage parents. *Family Planning Perspectives, 12*, 34–43.

Ball, S. J. (1981). *Beachside comprehensive*. Cambridge: Cambridge University Press.

Baltes, P. B. (1973). Prototypical paradigms and questions in life-span research on development and aging. *The Gerontologist, 113*, 458–467.

Baltes, P. B., Reese, H. W., & Lipsett, L. P. (1980). Life-span developmental psychology. *Annual Review of Psychology, 31*, 65–110.

Bandura, A. (1969). *Principles of behavior modification*. New York: Holt, Rinehart, & Winston.

Bandura, A. (1977). *Social learning theory*. Englewood Cliffs, NJ: Prentice-Hall.

Bandura, A. (1981). Self-referent thought: A developmental analysis of self-efficacy. In J. H. Flavell & L. Ross (Eds.), *Social cognitive development*. Cambridge: Cambridge University Press.

Bandura, A., & Walters, R. M. (1959). *Adolescent aggression*. New York: Ronald.

Bar-Tal, D., & Saxe, L. (1976). Perceptions of similarly and dissimilarly attractive couples and individuals. *Journal of Personality and Social Psychology, 33*, 772–781.

Barenboim, C. (1977). Developmental changes in the interpersonal cognitive system from middle childhood to adolescence. *Child Development, 48*, 1467–1474.

Barenboim, C. (1978). The development of recursive and nonrecursive thinking about persons. *Developmental Psychology, 14*, 419–420.

Barenboim, C. (1981). The development of person perception in childhood and adolescence: From behavioral comparisons to psychological constructs to psychological comparisons. *Child Development, 52*, 129–144.

Barenboim, C. (1985, April). *Person perception and interpersonal behavior*. Paper presented at the biennial meeting of the Society for Research in Child Development, Toronto.

Barker, R., & Wright, H. F. (1951). *One boy's day*. New York: Harper.

Barker, R. G., & Gump, P. V. (1964). *Big school, small school: High school size and student behavior*. Stanford, CA: Stanford University Press.

Barnes, G. M. (1977). The development of adolescent drinking behavior: An evaluative review of the impact of the socialization process within the family. *Adolescence, 13*, 571–591.

Barnes, G. M. (1984). Adolescent alcohol abuse and other problem behaviors: Their relationships and common parental influences. *Journal of Youth and Adolescence, 13*.

Barnouw, V. (1975). *An introduction to anthropology: Vol. 2. Ethnology*. Homewood, IL.: Dorsey Press.

Barron, F. (1985). *Rationality and intelligence.* Cambridge, England: Cambridge University Press.

Barry, H., Child, I. L., & Bacon, M. K. (1959). Relation of child training to subsistence economy. *American Anthropologist, 61,* 51–63.

Bart, W. M. (1971). The factor structure of formal operations. *The British Journal of Educational Psychology, 41,* 40–77.

Baskett, L. (1974). *The young child's interactions with parents and siblings: A behavioral analysis.* Unpublished doctoral dissertation, University of Oregon.

Baskett, L., & Johnson, S. M. (1982). The young child's interaction with parents versus siblings. *Child Development, 53,* 643–650.

Basow, S. A., & Howe, K. G. (1979). Model influence on career choices of college students. *Vocational Guidance Quarterly, 27,* 239–249.

Baucom, D. H. (1976). Independent masculinity and femininity scales on the California Psychological Inventory. *Journal of Consulting and Clinical Psychology, 44,* 876.

Baucom, D. H., & Danker-Brown, P. (1979). Influence of sex roles on the development of learned helplessness. *Journal of Consulting and Clinical Psychology, 47,* 928–936.

Baumrind, D. (1968). Authoritarian vs. authoritative parental control. *Adolescence, 3,* 255–272.

Baumrind, D. (1971). Current patterns of parental authority. *Developmental Psychology Monographs, 4*(1, Pt. 2).

Baumrind, D. (1972). From each according to her ability. *School Review, 80,* 161–197.

Baumrind, D. (1982). Are androgynous individuals more effective persons and parents? *Child Development, 53,* 44–75.

Beck, A. T. (1967). *Depression.* New York: Harper & Row.

Becker, H. J. (1985). Men and women as computer-using teachers. *Sex Roles, 13,* 137–148.

Bell, D. (Ed.). (1980). *Shades of Brown: New perspectives on school desegregation.* New York: Teachers College Press.

Beloff, H. (1962). The structure and origin of the anal character. *Genetic Psychology Monographs, 55,* 275–278.

Belsky, J. (1981). Early human experience: A family perspective. *Developmental Psychology, 17,* 3–23.

Bem, S. L. (1974). The measurement of psychological androgyny. *Journal of Consulting and Clinical Psychology, 42,* 155–162.

Bem, S. L. (1977). On the utility of alternative procedures for assessing psychological androgyny. *Journal of Consulting and Clinical Psychology, 45,* 196–205.

Bender, L. (1974). The family patterns of 100 schizophrenic children observed at Bellevue, 1935–1952. *Journal of Autism and Childhood Schizophrenia, 4,* 279–292.

Benedict, R. (1958). *Patterns of culture.* New York: New American Library. (Original work published 1934)

Bennett, C. (1979). Teaching students as they would be taught: The importance of cultural perspective. *Educational Leadership, 36,* 259–260.

Benson, P. L., & Vincent, S. M. (1980). Development and validation of the Sexist Attitudes Towards Women Scale (SATWS). *Psychology of Women Quarterly, 5,* 276–291.

Bereiter, C., & Scardamalia, M. (1982). From conversation to composition: The role of instruction in a developmental process. In R. Glaser (Ed.), *Advances in instructional psychology.* Hillsdale, NJ: Erlbaum.

Berkowitz, M. (1981). A critical appraisal of the educational and psychological perspectives on moral discussion. *Journal of Educational Thought, 15,* 20–33.

Berkowitz, M., & Gibbs, J. (1983). Measuring the developmental features of moral discussion. *Merrill-Palmer Quarterly, 29,* 399–410.

Berkowitz, M., Gibbs, J., & Broughton, J. (1980). The relation of moral judgment stage disparity to development effects of peer dialogues. *Merrill-Palmer Quarterly, 26,* 341–357.

Berndt, T. J. (1979). Developmental changes in conformity to peers and parents. *Developmental Psychology, 15,* 608–616.

Berndt, T. J. (1981). Relations between social cognition, nonsocial cognition, and social behavior: The case of friendship. In J. H. Flavell & L. D. Ross (Eds.), *Social cognitive development.* Cambridge: Cambridge University Press.

Berndt, T. J. (1982). The features and effects of friendship in early adolescence. *Child Development, 53,* 1447–1460.

Berscheid, E., & Walster, E. (1974). Physical attractiveness. In L. Berkowitz (Ed.), *Advances in experimental social psychology* (Vol. 7). New York: Academic Press.

Berzins, J. I., Wellings, M. A., & Wetter, R. E. (1978). A new measure of psychological androgyny based on the Personality Research Form. *Journal of Consulting and Clinical Psychology, 46,* 126–138.

Berzonsky, M. D. (1978). Formal reasoning in adolescence: An alternative view. *Adolescence, 13,* 279–290.

Berzonsky, M. D., Weiner, A. S., & Raphael, D. (1975). Interdependence of formal reasoning. *Developmental Psychology, 11,* 258.

Bieglow, B. J., & LaGaipa, J. J. (1980). The development of friendship values and choices. In H. C. Foot, A. J. Chapman, & J. R. Smith (Eds.), *Friendship and social relations in children.* New York: Wiley.

Biemer, L. (1975). Female studies: The elective approach. *Social Science Record, 12,* 7–11.

Bigner, J. J. (1974). A Wernerian developmental analysis of children's descriptions of siblings. *Child Development, 45,* 317–323.

Biller, H. B. (1970). Father-absence and the personality development of the male child. *Developmental Psychology, 2,* 181–201.

Biller, H. B. (1974). Parental and sex-role factors in cognitive and academic functioning. In J. K. Cole & R. Dienstbier (Eds.), *Nebraska Symposium on Motivation.* Lincoln: University of Nebraska Press.

Blaine, G. B., & McArthur, C. C. (1971). Problems connected with studying. In G. B. Blaine & C. C. McArthur (Eds.), *Emotional problems of the student* (2nd ed.). New York: Appleton-Century-Crofts.

Blaney, N. T., Stephan, C., Rosenfield, D., Aronson, E., & Sikes, J. (1977). Interdependence in the classroom: A field study. *Journal of Educational Psychology, 69,* 121–128.

Blau, P. (1965). The flow of occupational supply and recruitment. *American Sociological Review, 30,* 475–490.

Bloch, H. A., & Niederhoffer, A. (1958). *The gang: A study in adolescent behavior.* New York: Philosophical Library.

Block, J. (1985, October). *Some relationships regarding the self emanating from the Block and Block longitudinal study.* Paper presented at the SSRC conference on selfhood, Center for the Advanced Study in the Behavioral Sciences, Stanford, CA.

Block, J., Haan, N., & Smith, M. B. (1968). Activism and apathy in contemporary adolescents. In J. F. Adams (Ed.), *Understanding adolescence.* Boston: Allyn-Bacon.

Block, J., Patterson, V., Block, J., & Jackson, D. D. (1958). A study of the parents of schizophrenic and neurotic children. *Psychiatry, 21,* 387–397.

Block, J. H. (1973). Conception of sex role: Some cross-cultural and longitudinal perspectives. *American Psychologist, 28,* 512–516.

Block, J. H. (1983). Differential premises arising from differential socialization patterns: Some conjectures. *Child Development, 54,* 1335–1354.

Block, J. H., & Block, J. (1980). The role of ego-control and ego-resiliency in the organization of behavior. In W. A. Collins (Ed.), *Minnesota Symposium on Child Psychology* (Vol. 13). Hillsdale, NJ: Erlbaum.

Block, J. M. (1976). Issues, problems, and pitfalls in assessing sex differences: A critical review of *The psychology of sex differences. Merrill-Palmer Quarterly, 22,* 283–308.

Block, M. H. (1973). Conceptions of sex role: Some cross-cultural and longitudinal perspectives. *American Psychologist, 28,* 512–526.

Blom, G. E., Waite, R. R., & Zimet, S. G. (1970). A motivational content analysis of children's printers. In P. M. Mussen, J. J. Conger, and J. Kagan (Eds.), *Readings in child development and personality.* New York: Harper.

Bloom, B. S. (1983, April). *The development of exceptional talent.* Paper presented at the biennial meeting of the Society for Research in Child Development, Detroit.

Bloom, M. (1983). Prevention/promotion with minorities. *Journal of Primary Prevention, 3,* 224–234.

Blos, P. (1962). *On adolescence.* New York: Free Press.

Blos, P. (1967). The second individuation process of adolescence. In R. S. Eissley (Ed.), *Psychoanalytic study of the child* (Vol. 15). New York: International Universities Press.

Blyth, D. A., Bulcroft, R., & Simmons, R. G. (1981, August). *The impact of puberty on adolescents: A longitudinal study.* Paper presented at the annual meeting of the American Psychological Association, Los Angeles.

Blyth, D. A., Durant, D., & Moosbrugger, L. (1985, April). *Perceived intimacy in the social relationships of drug and non-drug using adolescents.* Paper presented at biennial meeting of the Society for Research in Child Development, Toronto.

Blyth, D. A., Simmons, R. G., & Bush, D. (1978). The transitions into early adolescence: A longitudinal comparison of youth in two educational contexts. *Sociology of Education, 51,* 149–162.

Blyth, D. A., Simmons, R. G., & Carlton-Ford, S. (1983). The adjustment of early adolescents to school transitions. *Journal of Early Adolescence, 3,* 105–120.

Bobrow, S., & Bower, G. (1969). Comprehension and recall of sentences. *Journal of Experimental Psychology, 80,* 455–461.

Bolter, J. D. (1984). *Turing's man.* Chapel Hill: University of North Carolina Press.

Bombeck, E., & Keane, B. (1971). *Just wait till you have children of your own!* New York: Fawcett/Crest.

Bosco, J. J., & Robin, S. S. (1976). Ritalin usage: A challenge to teacher education. *Peabody Journal of Education, 53,* 187–193.

Bourne, E. (1978). The state of research on ego identity: A review and appraisal. Part I. *Journal of Youth and Adolescence, 7,* 223–251.

Bowlby, J. (1969). *Attachment and loss* (Vol. 1). New York: Basic Books.

Bowlby, J. (1980). *Loss: Sadness and depression.* New York: Basic Books.

Bowman, P. H. (1959). Effects of a revised school program on potential delinquents. *Annals, 322,* 53–62.

Bracken, B. A. A. (1985). A critical review of the Kaufman assessment battery for children (K-ABC). *School Psychology Review, 14,* 21–36.

Brainerd, C. J. (1976). "Stage," "structure," and developmental theory. In G. Steiner (Ed.), *The psychology of the twentieth century.* Munich: Kindler.

Braungart, R. G. (1979). Reference groups, social judgments, and student politics. *Adolescence, 14*(53), 135–157.

Brecher, M. (1972). *Licit and illicit drugs: The Consumers' Union report on narcotics, stimulants, depressants, inhalants, hallucinogens, and marijuana—including caffeine, nicotine, and alcohol.* Boston: Little, Brown.

Brim, O. G., & Kagan, J. (Eds.). (1980). *Constancy and change in human development.* Cambridge, MA: Harvard University Press.

Brittain, C. V. (1963). Adolescent choices and parent-peer cross pressures. *American Sociological Review, 13,* 59–68.

Broadbent, D. E. (1958). *Perception and communication.* Elmsford, NY: Pergamon Press.

Broman, S. (1981). Long-term development of children born to teenagers. In K. G. Scott, T. Field, & E. Robertson (Eds.), *Teenage parents and their offspring.* New York: Grune & Stratton.

Bronfenbrenner, U. (1977). *The ecology of human development*. Cambridge, MA: Harvard University Press.

Bronfenbrenner, U., & Crouter, A. C. (1983). The evolution of environmental models in developmental research. In P. H. Mussen (Ed.), *Handbook of child psychology* (Vol. 1, 4th ed.). New York: Wiley.

Bronfenbrenner, U., & Garbarino, J. (1976). The socialization of moral judgment and behavior in cross-sectional perspective. In T. Lickona (Ed.), *Moral development and behavior*. New York: Holt, Rinehart, & Winston.

Bronfenbrenner, U. (1970). *Two worlds of childhood: U.S. and U.S.S.R.* New York: Russel Sage.

Brookover, W., Beady, C., Flood, P., Schweitzer, J., & Wisenbaker, J. (1979). *School social systems and student achievement: Schools can make a difference*. New York: Praeger.

Brooks-Gunn, J. (1985, April). *Changes in spatial ability as a function of age and physical maturation*. Paper presented at the biennial meeting of the Society for Research in Child Development, Toronto.

Brooks-Gunn, J., Petersen, A. C., & Eichorn, D. (1985). The study of maturational timing effects in adolescence. *Journal of Youth and Adolescence, 14*, 149–161.

Brooks-Gunn, J., & Ruble, D. N. (1982). The development of menstrual-related beliefs and behaviors during early adolescence. *Child Development, 53*, 1567–1577.

Brophy, J. (1979). Teacher behavior and its effects. *Journal of Educational Psychology, 71*, 733–750.

Brophy, J., & Evertson, C. (1974). *The Texas teacher effectiveness project: Presentation of nonlinear relationships and summary discussion* (Report No. 74–6). Austin: University of Texas Research and Development Center for Teacher Education.

Brophy, J., & Evertson, C. (1976). *Learning from teaching: A developmental perspective*. Boston: Allyn and Bacon.

Broughton, J. (1981). Piaget's structural developmental psychology: IV. Knowledge without a self and without history. *Human Development, 24*, 320–346.

Brown, A. L., Bransford, J. D., Ferrara, R. A., & Campione, J. C. (1983). Learning, remembering, and understanding. In P. H. Mussen (Ed.), *Handbook of child psychology* (Vol. 3, 4th ed.). New York: Wiley.

Brown, A. L., & Smiley, S. S. (1977). Rating the importance of structural units of prose passages: A problem of metacognitive development. *Child Development, 48*, 1–8.

Brown, B. B., Clasen, D. R., & Eicher, S. A. (in press). Perceptions of peer pressure, peer conformity dispositions and self-reported behavior among adolescents. *Developmental Psychology*.

Brown, B. B., & Lohr, M. J. (in press). Peer group affiliation and adolescent self-esteem: An integration of ego identity and symbolic interaction theories. *Journal of Personality and Social Psychology*.

Brown, R. (1986). *Social psychology* (2nd ed.). New York: Free Press.

Bruch, H. (1973). *Eating disorders: Obesity, anorexia nervosa, and the person within*. New York: Basic Books.

Bruner, J. (1966). *Toward a theory of instruction*. Cambridge, MA: Harvard University Press.

Bryant, B. (1974). Locus of control related to teacher-child interperceptual experiences. *Child Development, 45*, 157–174.

Burchinal, L. G. (1959). How successful are school-age marriages? *Iowa Farm Science, 13*, 7–10.

Burchinal, L. G. (1965). Trends and prospects for young marriages in the U.S. *Journal of Marriage and the Family, 27*, 243–254.

Bureau of Labor Statistics. (1980). *Occupational outlook handbook*. (1974–75 ed.). Washington, DC: United States Department of Labor.

Bureau of Labor Statistics. (1980). *Occupational outlook handbook*. (1980–81 ed.). Washington, DC: United States Government Printing Office.

Bureau of Labor Statistics. (1974). *Occupational outlook handbook*. (1980–81 ed.). Washington, DC: United States Government Printing Office.

Burkett, C. L. (1985, April). *Child-rearing behaviors and the self-esteem of preschool aged children*. Paper presented at the biennial meeting of the Society for Research in Child Development, Toronto.

Butler, L., & Meichenbaum, D. (1981). The assessment of interpersonal problem-solving skills. In P. C. Kendall & S. D. Hollon (Eds.), *Assessment strategies for cognitive-behavioral interventions*. New York: Academic Press.

Buxton, C. (1973). *Adolescents in schools*. New Haven, CT: Yale University Press.

Cairns, R. B., Perrin, J. E., & Cairns, B. D. (1985). Social structure and social cognition in early adolescence: Affiliative patterns. *Journal of Early Adolescence, 5*, 339–356.

Callahan, R. (1962). *Education and the cult of efficiency*. Chicago: University of Chicago Press.

Campbell, D. P., Crichton, L., Hansen, J. I., & Webber, P. (1974). A new edition of the SVIB: The Strong-Campbell interest inventory. *Measurement and Evaluation in Guidance, 7*, 92–95.

Caplan, P. (1978, August). *Erickson's concept of inner space: A data-based reevaluation*. Paper presented at the American Psychological Association Convention, Toronto.

Card, J. J., Steele, L., & Abeles, R. P. (1980). Sex differences in realization of potential for achievement. *Journal of Vocational Behavior, 17*, 1–21.

Card, J. J., & Wise, L. L. (1978). Teenage mothers and teenage fathers: The impact of early childbearing on the parents' personal and professional lives. *Family Planning Perspectives, 10*, 199–205.

Carkhuff, R. (1969). *Helping and human relations* (Vols. 1 & 2). New York: Holt, Rinehart, & Winston.

Carson, T. P., & Adams, H. E. (1981). Affective disorders: Behavioral perspectives. In S. M. Turner, K. S. Calhoun, & H. E. Adams (Eds.), *Handbook of clinical behavioral therapy*. New York: Wiley.

Case, R. (1978). Intellectual development from birth to adulthood: A neo-Piagetian interpretation. In R. Siegler (Ed.), *Children's thinking: What develops?* Hillsdale, NJ: Erlbaum.

Case, R., & Fry, C. (1972). Evaluation of an attempt to teach scientific inquiry and criticism in a working-class high school. *Journal of Research in Science Teaching,* 135–142.

Case Western Reserve University. (1979). *Project Choice: Creating her options in career education.* Cleveland: Author.

Casteñada, A., Ramirez, M., Cortes, C. E., & Barrera, M. (Eds.). (1971). *Mexican-Americans and educational change.* Unpublished manuscript, University of California, Riverside, CA.

Cattell, R. B. (1963). Theory of fluid and crystallized intelligence: A critical experiment. *Journal of Educational Psychology, 54,* 1–22.

Cauce, A. M., Felner, R. D., & Primavera, J. (1982). Social support in high-risk adolescents: Structural components and adaptive impact. *American Journal of Community Psychology, 10,* 417–428.

Center for Early Adolescence. (1982). *Living with 10–15 Year Olds, A Planning Guide for a One-Day Conference.* Carrboro, NC: Author.

Chandler, M., Boyes, M., Ball, L., & Hala, S. (1985, April). *A developmental analysis of children's conceptions of personal identity.* Paper presented at the biennial meeting of the Society for Research in Child Development, Toronto.

Chapin, M., & Dyck, D. G. (1976). Persistence in children's reading behavior as a function of N length and attribution retraining. *Journal of Abnormal Psychology, 85,* 97–111.

Chapman, M. L., & Davis, F. V. (1978). Skills for ethical action: A process approach to judgment and action. *Educational Leadership, 35,* 457–458, 460–461.

Chapman, W., & Katz, M. R. (1983). Career information systems in secondary schools: A survey and assessment. *Vocational Guidance Quarterly, 31,* 165–177.

Charlesworth, R., & Hartup, W. W. (1973). Positive social reinforcement in the nursery school peer group. *Child Development, 38,* 993–1002.

Chassin, L., Presson, C. C., & Sherman, S. J. (n.d.) Cigarette smoking and adolescent psychosocial development. *Basic and Applied Psychology, 5,* 295–315.

Chassin, L., Presson, C. C., Sherman, S. J., Montello, D., & McGrew, J. (1985). *Changes in peer and parent influences during adolescence: Longitudinal vs. cross-sectional perspectives on smoking initiation.* Unpublished manuscript, Arizona State University, Tempe, AZ.

Chavez, D. (1985). Perpetuation of gender inequality: A content analysis of comic strips. *Sex Roles, 13,* 93–102.

Chen, M. (1985). Gender differences in adolescents' uses of and attitudes toward computers. In M. McLaughlin (Ed.), *Communication Yearbook 10.* Beverly Hills, CA: Sage Publications.

Chernin, K. (1981, November 22). Women and weight consciousness. *New York Times News Service.*

Chess, S., & Hassibi, M. (1978). *Principles and practice of child psychiatry.* New York: Plenum.

Chess, S., & Thomas, A. (1977). Temperamental individuality from childhood to adolescence. *Journal of Child Psychiatry, 16,* 218–226.

Chess, S., & Thomas, A. (1984). *Origins and evolution of behavior disorders.* New York: Brunner/Mazel.

Child, I., Potter, E., & Levine, E. (1946). Children's textbooks and personality development: An exploration in the social psychology of education. *Psychological Monographs, 60*(3, Whole No. 279).

Chilman, C. (1979). *Adolescent sexuality in a changing American society: Social and psychological perspectives.* Washington, DC: Public Health Service, National Institute of Mental Health.

Cicirelli, V. (1977). Family structure and socialization: Sibling effects on socialization. In M. McMillan & M. Sergio (Eds.), *Child psychiatry: Treatment and research.* New York: Brunner/Mazel.

Clark, K. (1965). *Dark ghetto.* New York: Harper.

Clark, K. B. (1980). Empathy: A neglected topic in psychological research. *American Psychologist, 35,* 187–190.

Clark, S. D., Zabin, L. S., & Hardy, J. B. (1984). Sex, contraception and parenthood: Experience and attitudes among urban black young men. *Family Planning Perspectives, 16,* 77–82.

Cloward, R., & Ohlen, L. (1960). *Delinquency and opportunity.* New York: Free Press of Glencoe.

Coates, D. L. (1985). Relationship between self-concept measures and social network characteristics for black adolescents. *Journal of Early Adolescence, 5,* 31903338.

Cohen, H. L., & Filipczak, J. A. (1968). *A new learning experience.* San Francisco: Jossey-Bass.

Coie, J. D., & Dodge, K. A. (1983). Continuities and changes in children's social status: A five-year longitudinal study. *Merrill-Palmer Quarterly, 29,* 261–281.

Coie, J. D., & Kupersmidt, J. (1983). A behavioral analysis of emerging social status in boys' groups. *Child Development, 54,* 1400–1416.

Colby, A., Kohlberg, L., Gibbs, J., & Lieberman, M. (1980). *A longitudinal study of moral judgment.* Unpublished manuscript, Harvard University.

Cole, S. (1980, July). Send our children to work? *Psychology Today,* pp. 44–68.

Cole, S. (1981). *Working kids on working.* New York: Lothrop, Lee, & Shephard.

Coleman, J. S. (1961). *The adolescent society.* New York: Free Press.

Coleman, J. S. (1980). The peer group. In J. Adelson (Ed.), *Handbook of adolescent psychology.* New York: Wiley.

Coleman, J. S., Campbell, E. Q., Hobson, C. J., McPartland, J., Mood, A. M., Weinfeld, F. D., & York, R. L. (1966). *Equality of educational opportunity.* Washington, DC: U.S. Government Printing Office.

Coleman, J. S., et al. (1974). *Youth: Transition to adulthood.* Report of the Panel on Youth of the President's Science Advisory Committee. Chicago: University of Chicago Press.

Coles, R. (1970). *Erik H. Erikson: The growth of his work.* Boston: Little, Brown.

Coletta, N. D. (1978). *Divorced mothers at two income levels: Stress, support, and child-rearing practices.* Unpublished thesis, Cornell University.

Collins, W. A. (1977, March). Temporal integration and inferences about televised social behavior. In *Cognitive processing of television content: Perspective on the effects of television on children.* Symposium conducted at the meeting of the Society for Research in Child Development, New Orleans.

Collins, W. A. (1985, April). *Cognition, affect, and development in parent-child relationships.* Paper presented at the biennial meeting of the Society for Research in Child Development, Toronto, Canada.

Collis, B. A. (1984). *The development of an instrument to measure attitudes of secondary school males.* Unpublished doctoral dissertation: University of Victoria, British Columbia.

Comstock, G. A. (1972). *Television violence: Where the surgeon general's study leads.* Santa Monica, CA: Rand Corp.

Comstock, G. A. (1978, Spring). The impact of television on American institutions. *Journal of Communication,* 12–28.

Conant, J. B. (1959). *The American high school today.* New York: McGraw-Hill.

Conger, J. J. (1977). *Adolescence and youth* (3rd ed.). New York: Harper & Row.

Constantinople, A. (1969). An Eriksonian measure of personality development in college students. *Developmental Psychology, 1,* 357–372.

Cook, T. D., & Campbell, D. T. (1979). *Quasi experimentation.* Chicago: Rand McNally.

Cooker, P. G., & Cherchai, P. J. (1976). Effects of communication skill training on high school students' ability to function as peer group facilitators. *Journal of Counseling Psychology, 23,* 464–467.

Cooper, C. R., & Ayers-Lopez, S. (1985). Family and peer systems in early adolescence: New models of the role of relationships in development. *Journal of Early Adolescence, 5,* 9–22.

Cooper, C. R., Grotevant, H. D., & Condon, S. M. (1983). Individuality and connectedness in the family as a context for adolescent identity formation and role-taking skill (pp. 54–55). In H. D. Grotevant & C. R. Cooper (Eds.), *Adolescent development in the family.* San Francisco: Jossey-Bass.

Cooper, H., & Tom, D. Y. H. (1984). Socioeconomic status and ethnic group differences in achievement motivation. In R. E. Ames & C. Ames (Eds.), *Motivation in education.* New York: Academic Press.

Cooper, R., Grotevant, H. D., Moore, M. S., & Condon, S. M. (1982, August). *Family support and conflict: Both foster adolescent identity and role taking.* Paper presented at the meeting of the American Psychological Association, Washington, DC.

Coopersmith, S. (1967). *The antecedents of self-esteem.* San Francisco: Freeman.

Corbin, J. N. (1974). *The effects of counselor-assisted exploratory activity on career development.* Unpublished doctoral dissertation, Columbia University.

Courtney, A. E., & Lockeretz, S. W. (1971). Woman's place: An analysis of the roles portrayed by women in magazine advertisements. *Journal of Marketing Research, 8,* 92–95.

Covington, M. V. (1984). The motive for self-worth. In R. E. Ames & C. Ames (Eds.), *Motivation in education.* New York: Academic Press.

Cowan, P. (1978). *Piaget with feeling.* New York: Holt, Rinehart, & Winston.

Cowen, E. L., Pederson, A., Babigian, H., Izzo, L. D., & Trost, M. A. (1973). Long-term follow-up of early detected vulnerable children. *Journal of Consulting and Clinical Psychology, 41,* 438–446.

Crandall, V. C., & Battle, E. S. (1970). The antecedents and adult correlates of academic and intellectual achievement effort. In J. P. Hill (Ed.), *Minnesota Symposium on Child Psychology* (Vol. 4). Minneapolis: University of Minnesota Press.

Crandall, V. J., & Rabson, A. (1960). Children's repetition choices in an intellectual achievement situation following success and failure. *Journal of Genetic Psychology, 97,* 161–168.

Cremin, L. (1961). *The transformation of the school.* New York: Knopf.

Crimmings, A. M. (1978). *Female causal attribution for success and failure outcomes as a function of sex role identity and degree of competitiveness in the achievement situation.* Unpublished doctoral dissertation, Ohio State University. (University Microfilms No. 7902104)

Critelli, J. W., & Baldwin, A. (1979). Birth order complementarity versus homogamy as determinants of attraction in dating relationships. *Perceptual and Motor Skills, 49,* 467–471.

Cronbach, L. J. (1970). *Essentials of psychological testing.* New York: Harper & Row.

Cronbach, L. J., & Snow, R. E. (1977). *Aptitudes and instructional methods.* New York: Irvington Books.

Cross, K. P. (1984, November). The rising tide of school reform reports. *Phi Delta Kappan,* pp. 167–172.

Crowe, R. R. (1974). An adoption study of antisocial personality. *Archives of General Psychiatry, 31,* 785–791.

Csikszentmihalyi, M., & Larson, R. (1984). *Being adolescent.* New York: Basic Books.

Cummings, C. M. (1979). *Psychological androgyny in new fathers and their expectations of the fathering role.* Unpublished doctoral dissertation, Columbia University. (University Microfilms No. 8006796)

Curran, J. P. (1975). Social skills training and systematic desensitization in reducing dating anxiety. *Behavior Research and Therapy, 13,* 65–68.

Curtiss, S. (1978). *Genie.* New York: Academic Press.

Cvetkovich, G., & Grote, B. (1975, May). *Psychological factors associated with adolescent premarital coitus.* Paper presented at the National Institute of Child Health and Human Development, Bethesda, MD.

Damon, A. (1977). *Human biology and ecology.* New York: Norton.

Damon, W., & Hart, D. (1982). The development of self-understanding from infancy through adolescence. *Child Development, 53,* 841–864.

Daniels, D., Dunn, J., Furstenberg, F. F., & Plomin, R. (1985). Environmental differences within the family and adjustment differences within pairs of adolescent siblings. *Child Development, 56,* 764–774.

Daniels, D., & Plomin, R. (1984). *Differential experiences of siblings in the same family.* Unpublished manuscript, University of Colorado, Boulder.

Danner, F. Personal Communication. Quoted in Lapsley, D. K., Enright, R., & Serlin, R. C. (in press). Moral and social education. In J. Worrell & F. Danner (Eds.), *Adolescent development: Issues in education.* New York: Academic Press.

Darling, C. A., Kallen, D. J., & VanDusen, J. E. (1984). Sex in transition, 1900–1984. *Journal of Youth and Adolescence, 13,* 385–399.

Davids, A., & Hainsworth, P. K. (1967). Maternal attitudes about family life and child rearing as avowed by mothers and perceived by their underachieving and high-achieving sons. *Journal of Consulting Psychology, 31,* 29–37.

Deci, E. L. (1975). *Intrinsic motivation.* New York: Plenum.

Deckhard, B. S. (1979). *The women's movement.* New York: Harper & Row.

DeFleur, L. B., & Menke, B. A. (1975). Learning about the labor force: Occupational knowledge among high school males. *Sociology of Education, 48,* 324–345.

DeLissovoy, V. (1973). High school marriage: A longitudinal study. *Journal of Marriage and the Family, 35,* 245–255.

Demorest, A., Meyer, C., Phelps, E., Gardner, H., & Winner, E. (1984). Words speak louder than actions: Understanding deliberately false remarks. *Child Development, 55,* 152–1534.

Dempster, F. N. (1981). Memory span: Sources of individual and developmental differences. *Psychological Bulletin, 89,* 63–100.

Dempster, F. N. (1985). Short-term memory development in childhood and adolescence. In C. J. Brainerd & M. Pressley (Eds.), *Basic processes in memory development: Progress in cognitive development research.* New York: Springer-Verlag.

Deutsch, C. J., & Gilbert, L. A. (1976). Sex role stereotypes: Effect of perceptions of self and others on personal adjustment. *Journal of Counseling Psychology, 23,* 373–379.

Deutsch, G. (1982). *Eating disorders in adolescence.* Unpublished manuscript, University of Texas at Dallas.

Devereaux, E. C. (1970). The role of peer-group experience in moral development. In J. P. Hill (Ed.), *Minnesota Symposium on Child Psychology* (Vol. 4). Minneapolis: University of Minnesota Press.

Dewey, J. (1933). *How we think: A restatement of the relation of reflective thinking to the educative process* (rev. ed.). New York: D. C. Heath.

Diaz, R. M., & Berndt, T. J. (1982). Children's knowledge of a best friend: Fact or fancy? *Developmental Psychology, 18,* 787–794.

Dickenson, G. E. (1975). Dating behavior of black and white adolescents before and after desegregation. *Journal of Marriage and the Family, 37,* 602–608.

Dickstein, E. (1977). Self and self-esteem: Theoretical functions and their implications for research. *Human Development, 20,* 219–140.

Dillon, R. S. (1980). *Diagnosis and management of endocrine and metabolic disorders* (2nd ed.). Philadelphia: Lea & Febiger.

Dion, K., Berscheid, E., & Walster, E. (1972). What is beautiful is good. *Journal of Personality and Social Psychology, 24,* 285–290.

Dodge, K. A. (1980). Social cognition and children's aggressive behavior. *Child Development, 51,* 162–170.

Dodge, K. A. (1983). Behavioral antecedents of peer social status. *Child Development, 54,* 1386–1399.

Dodge, K. A. (1985, April). *Assessment and training of social skills.* Paper presented at the biennial meeting of the Society for Research in Child Development, Toronto.

Dodge, K. A., Coie, J. D., & Brakke, N. P. (1982). Behavior patterns of socially rejected and neglected preadolescents: The roles of social approach and aggression. *Journal of Abnormal Child Psychology, 10,* 389–409.

Dodge, K. A., & Frame, C. L. (1982). Social cognitive issues and deficits in aggressive boys. *Child Development, 53,* 620–635.

Dodge, K. A., Murphy, R. R., & Buchsbaum, K. (1984). The assessment of intention-cue detection skills: Implications for developmental psychopathology. *Child Development, 55,* 163–173.

Dollard, J., & Miller, N. E. (1950). *Personality and psychotherapy.* New York: McGraw-Hill.

Dooley, D., Whalen, C. K., & Flowers, J. V. (1978). Verbal response styles of children and adolescents in a counseling analog setting: Effects of age, sex, and labeling. *Journal of Counseling Psychology, 25,* 85–95.

Douvan, E., & Adelson, J. (1966). *The adolescent experience.* New York: John Wiley.

Dreyer, P. H. (1982). Sexuality during adolescence. In B. J. Wolman (Ed.), *Handbook of developmental psychology.* Englewood Cliffs, NJ: Prentice-Hall.

Duck, S. W. (1975). Personality similarity and friendship choices by adolescents. *European Journal of Social Psychology, 5,* 351–365.

Dudek, S. Z. (1974). Creativity in young children—Attitude or ability? *Journal of Creative Behavior, 8,* 282–292.

Duke, D. L., & Perry, C. (1978). Can alternative schools succeed where Benjamin Spock, Spiro Agnew and B. F. Skinner have failed? *Adolescence, 13,* 375–392.

Dulit, E. (1972). Adolescent thinking à la Piaget: The formal stage. *Journal of Youth and Adolescence, 1,* 281–301.

Duncan, D. F. (1978). Attitudes toward parents and delinquency in suburban adolescent males. *Adolescence, 13,* 365–369.

Dunphy, D. C. (1963). The social structure of urban adolescent peer groups. *Society, 26,* 230–246.

Dweck, C. S. (1975). The role of expectations and attributions in the alleviation of learned helplessness. *Journal of Personality and Social Psychology, 31,* 674–685.

Dweck, C. S., & Bush, E. S. (1976). Sex differences in learned helplessness: I. Differential debilitation with peer and adult evaluators. *Developmental Psychology, 12,* 147–156.

Dweck, C. S., Davidson, W., Nelson, S., & Enna, B. (1978). Sex differences in learned helplessness: II. The contingencies of evaluative feedback in the classroom; and III. An experimental analysis. *Developmental Psychology, 14,* 268–276.

Dweck, C. S., & Eliot, E. S. (1983). Achievement motivation. In P. H. Mussen (Ed.), *Handbook of child psychology* (Vol. 4, 4th ed.). New York: Wiley.

Dweck, C. S., & Gilliard, D. (1975). Expectancy statements as determinants of reactions to failure: Sex differences in persistence and expectancy change. *Journal of Personality and Social Psychology, 32,* 1077–1088.

Dweck, C. S., & Reppucci, N. D. (1973). Learned helplessness and reinforcement responsibility in children. *Journal of Personality and Social Psychology, 25,* 109–116.

Edmonds, R. (1979). Some schools work and more can. *Social Policy, 9,* 28–32.

Ehrhardt, A., & Baker, S. W. (1973, March). *Hormonal aberrations and their implications for the understanding of normal sex differentiation.* Paper presented at the meeting of the Society for Research in Child Development, Philadelphia.

Eichorn, D. (1970). Physiological development. In P. H. Mussen (Ed.), *Handbook of child psychology* (Vol. 1, 3rd ed.). New York: Wiley.

Eisenberg-Berg, N. (1979). Development of children's prosocial moral judgment. *Developmental Psychology, 15,* 168–175.

Eitzen, D. S. (1975). Athletics in the status system of male adolescents: A replication of Coleman's *The adolescent society. Adolescence, 10,* 267–276.

Elder, G. (1980). *Family structure and socialization.* New York: Arno Press.

Elder, G. H. (1968). Democratic parent-youth relations in cross-national perspective. *Social Science Quarterly, 49,* 216–228.

Elder, G. H. (1975). Adolescence in the life cycle. In S. E. Dragastin & G. H. Elder (Eds.), *Adolescence in the life cycle: Psychological change and social context.* New York: Wiley.

Elder, G. H. (1980). Adolescence in historical perspective. In J. Adelson (Ed.), *Handbook of adolescent psychology.* New York: Wiley.

Eliade, M. (1958). *Birth and rebirth: The religious meaning of initiation in human culture.* New York: Harper & Brothers.

Elkind, D. (1961). Quantity conceptions in junior high and senior high school students. *Child Development, 32,* 551–560.

Elkind, D. (1967). Egocentrism in adolescence. *Child Development, 38,* 1025–1034.

Elkind, D. (1969). Piagetian and psychometric conceptions of intelligence. *Harvard Educational Review, 39,* 319–337.

Elkind, D. (1971). *Sympathetic understanding of the child six to sixteen.* Boston: Allyn & Bacon.

Elkind, D. (1976). *Child development and education: A Piagetian perspective.* New York: Oxford University Press.

Elkind, D. (1978). *A sympathetic understanding of the child: Birth to sixteen* (2nd ed.). Boston: Allyn & Bacon.

Elkind, D. (1978). Understanding the young adolescent. *Adolescence, 13,* 127–134.

Elkind, D. (1979, February). Growing up faster. *Psychology Today,* pp. 38–43.

Elkind, D. (1981). *The hurried child.* Reading, MA: Addison-Wesley.

Elkind, D. (in press). Reply to D. Lapsley and M. Murphy's *Developmental Review* paper. *Developmental Review, 5,* 218–226.

Elkind, D., & Bowen, R. (1979). Imaginary audience behavior in children and adolescents. *Developmental Psychology, 15,* 38–44.

Emma Willard Task Force on Education. (1971). *Sexism in education.* Minneapolis: Author.

Emmer, E. T., Evertson, C. M., & Anderson, L. M. (1980). Effective classroom management at the beginning of the school year. *Elementary School Journal, 80,* 219–231.

Emmerich, W. Goldman, K. S., & Shore, R. E. Differentiation and development of social norms. Journal of Personality and Social Psychology, 1971, 18, 323–353.

Enright, R., Ganiere, Buss, Lapsley, & Olson, (1983). Journal of Early Adolescence, 3,

Enright, R., Lapsley, D., & Olson, L. (1984). Moral judgment and the social cognitive developmental research program. In S. Modgil & C. Modgil (Eds.), *Lawrence Kohlberg: Consensus and controversy.* Slough: NFER Press.

Enright, R., Shukla, D., & Lapsley, D. (1980). Adolescent egocentrism in early and late adolescence. *Journal of Youth and Adolescence, 9,* 101–11k.

Epstein, A. S. (1980). *Assessing the child development information needed by adolescent parents with very young children* (Final Report). Ypsilanti, MI: High-Scope Educational Research Foundation.

Epstein, H. T. (1974). Phrenoblysis: Special brain and mind growth periods. *Developmental Psychobiology, 7,* 217–224.

Epstein, H. T. (1978). Growth spurts during brain development: Implications for educational policy and practice. In J. S. Chall & A. F. Mirsky (Eds.), *Education and the brain.* Chicago: University of Chicago Press.

Epstein, H. T. (1980). EEG developmental stages. *Developmental Psychobiology, 13,* 629–631.

Epstein, J. L. (1980). *After the bus arrives: Resegregation in desegregated schools.* Paper presented at the meeting of the American Educational Research Association, Boston.

Epstein, J. L. (1983). Selecting friends in contrasting secondary school environments. In J. L. Epstein & N. L. Karweit (Eds.), *Friends in school.* New York: Academic Press.

Epstein, J. L. (in press). Choice of friends over the life span: Developmental and environmental influences. In E. C. Mueller & C. R. Cooper (Eds.), *Process and outcome in peer relations.* New York: Academic Press.

Erickson, K. A., & Simon, H. A. (1978). *Retrospective verbal reports as data.* Unpublished manuscript, Carnegie-Mellon University, Pittsburgh.

Erickson, M. T. (1978). *Child psychopathology.* Englewood Cliffs, NJ: Prentice-Hall.

Erickson, V. L. (1977). Beyond Cinderella: Ego maturity and attitudes toward the rights and roles of women. *Counseling Psychologist, 7,* 83–88.

Erikson, E. H. (1951). Sex differences in the play configurations of preadolescents. *American Journal of Orthopsychiatry, 21,* 667–692.

Erikson, E. H. (1962). *Young man Luther.* New York: Norton.

Erikson, E. H. (1963). *Childhood and society.* New York: Norton.

Erikson, E. H. (1968). *Identity: Youth and crisis.* New York: Norton.

Erikson, E. H. (1969). *Gandhi's truth.* New York: Norton.

Erikson, E. H. (1970). Reflections on the dissent of contemporary youth. *International Journal of Psychoanalysis, 51,* 11–22.

Erlick, A. C., & Starry, A. R. (1973, June). *Sources of information for career decisions.* Report of Poll No. 98, Purdue Opinion Panel.

Esposito, D. (1973). Homogeneous and heterogeneous ability grouping: Principal findings and implications for evaluating and designing more effective educational environments. *Review of Educational Research, 43,* 163–179.

Etaugh, C., & Marlow, M. (1975). Behavior of male and female teachers as related to behaviors and attitudes of elementary schoolchildren. *Journal of Genetic Psychology, 127,* 163–170.

Evans, R. I. (1982). Training social psychologists in behavioral medicine research. In J. R. Eiser (Ed.), *Social psychology and behavioral medicine.* New York: Wiley.

Evans, R. I. (1983). Deterring smoking in adolescents: Evolution of an applied research program in social psychology. *International Review of Applied Psychology, 32,* 71–83.

Fagot, B. I. (1975, April). *Teacher reinforcement of feminine-preferred behavior revisited.* Paper presented at the biennial meeting of the Society for Research in Child Development, Denver.

Fassinger, R. E. (1985). A causal model of college women's career choice. *Journal of Vocational Behavior, 27,* 123–153.

Faust, M. S. (1960). Developmental maturity as a determinant in prestige of adolescent girls. *Child Development, 31,* 173–184.

Faust, M. S. (1977). Somatic development of adolescent girls. *Monographs of the Society for Research in Child Development, 42*(1, Serial No. 169).

Feather, N. T. (1975). *Values in education and society.* New York: Free Press.

Feather, N. T. (1980). Values in adolescence. In J. Adelson (Ed.), *Handbook of adolescent psychology.* New York: John Wiley.

Feeney, S. (1980). *Schools for young adolescents: Adapting the early childhood model.* Carrboro, NC: Center for Early Adolescence.

Feiring, C., & Lewis, M. (1978). The child as a member of a family system. *Behavioral Science, 23,* 225–233.

Feldman, S. D. (1973). Impediment or stimulant? Marital status and graduate education. In J. Huber (Ed.), *Changing women in a changing society.* Chicago: University of Chicago Press.

Feldman-Summers, S., & Kiesler, S. B. (1974). Those who are number two try harder: The effect of sex on attributions of causality. *Journal of Personality and Social Psychology, 30,* 846–855.

Feldstein, M., & Ellwood, D. (1982). Teenage unemployment: What is the problem? In R. Freeman & D. Wise (Eds.), *The youth labor market problem: Its nature, causes, and consequences.* Chicago: University of Chicago Press.

Felner, R. D., Ginter, M., & Primavera, J. (1982). Primary prevention during school transitions: Social support and environmental structure. *American Journal of Community Psychology.* New York: Plenum.

Fennema, E. (1984). Girls, women and mathematics. In E. Fennema & M. J. Ayer (Eds.), *Women and education* (pp. 137–164). Berkeley: McCutchen.

Festinger, L. (1954). A theory of social comparison processes. *Human Relations, 7,* 117–150.

Field, J. (1981). Whither quantitative history? A review of some recent work in the economic and social history of education. *Historical Methods, 14,* 85–95.

Field, T. M., Widmayer, S. M., Stringer, S., & Ignatoff, E. (1980). Teenager, lower-class, black mothers and their pre-term infants: An intervention and developmental follow-up. *Child Development, 51,* 426–436.

Finley, M. I. (1985, February 3). [Review of D. B. Davis, *Slavery and human progress.*] *New York Times Book Review,* p. 26.

Finney, J. W., & Moos, R. H. (1979). Treatment and outcome for empirical subtypes of alcoholic patients. *Journal of Consulting and Clinical Psychology, 47,* 25–38.

Fischer, J. L. (1981). Transitions in relationship style from adolescence to young adulthood. *Journal of Youth and Adolescence, 10,* 11–24.

Fischer, K. W. (1980). A theory of cognitive development: The control and construction of hierarchies of skills. *Psychological Review, 87,* 477–531.

Fischer, K. W., Hand, H. H., & Russell, S. (1983). The development of abstractions in adolescence and adulthood. In M. L. Commons, F. A. Richards, & C. Armon (Eds.), *Beyond formal operations.* New York: Praeger.

Fischer, K. W., & Lazerson, A. (1984). *Human development.* San Francisco: W. H. Freeman.

Fixsen, D. L., Phillips, E. L., Phillips, E. A., & Wolf, M. M. (1976). The teaching family model group home treatment. In W. E. Craighead, A. E. Kazdin, & M. J. Mahoney (Eds.), *Behavior modification.* Boston: Houghton-Mifflin.

Flavell, J. H. (1970). Cognitive development. In P. H. Mussen (Ed.), *Handbook of child psychology,* (Vol. 1, 3rd. ed.). New York: Wiley.

Flavell, J. H. (1974). The development of inferences about others. In T. Mischel (Ed.), *Understanding other persons.* Oxford, England: Blackwell, Basil, Mott.

Flavell, J. H. (1979). Metacognition and cognitive monitoring: A new area of psychological inquiry. *American Psychologist, 34,* 906–911.

Flavell, J. H. (1980, Fall). A tribute to Piaget. *Society for Research in Child Development Newsletter.*

Flavell, J. H. (1981). Monitoring social-cognitive enterprises: Something else that may develop in the area of social cognition. In J. H. Flavell & L. Ross (Eds.), *Social cognitive development: Frontiers and possible futures.* New York: Cambridge University Press.

Flavell, J. H. (1982). Structures, stages, and sequences in cognitive development. In W. A. Collins (Ed.), *The concept of development: The Minnesota symposia on child psychology.* Hillsdale, NJ: Erlbaum.

Flavell, J. H. (1985). *Cognitive development* (2nd ed.). Englewood Cliffs, NJ: Prentice-Hall.

Flavell, J. H., Botkin, P. T., Fry, C. L., Wright, J. W., & Jarvis, P. E. (1968). *The development of role-taking and communication skills in children.* New York: Wiley.

Flay, B. R. (in press). What do we know about the social influences approach to smoking prevention? In P. McGrath & P. Firestone (Eds.), *Pediatric and adolescent behavioral medicine.* New York: Springer-Verlag.

Ford, M. E. (1982). Social cognition and social competence in adolescence. *Developmental Psychology, 18,* 323–340.

Ford, M. E. (1986). *Androgyny as self-assertion and integration: Implications for psychological and social competence.* Unpublished manuscript, Stanford University, School of Education, Stanford, CA.

Ford, M. E. (1986). A living systems conceptualization of social intelligence: Outcomes, processes, and developmental change. In R. J. Sternberg (Ed.), *Advances in the psychology of human intelligence* (Vol. 3). Hillsdale, NJ: Erlbaum.

Ford, M. E., & Tisak, S. M. (1981, April). *Adolescent androgyny and its relationship to social competence, identity status, and academic achievement.* Paper presented at the biennial meeting of the Society for Research in Child Development, Boston.

Forgatch, M. S., Chamberlain, P., & Gabrielson, P. (1982). *Time-out: A video training tape.* Eugene, OR: Castalia.

Forslund, M. A., & Gustafson, T. J. (1970). Influence of peers and parents and sex differences in drinking by high school students. *Quarterly Journal of Studies on Alcohol, 31,* 868–875.

Foster, S., & Ritchey, W. (1979). Issues in the assessment of social competence in children. *Journal of Applied Behavior Analysis, 12,* 625–638.

Fowler, J. W. (1976). Stages in faith: The structural-developmental approach. In T. Hennessy (Ed.), *Values and moral development.* New York: Paulist Press.

Fowler, J. W. (1980). Faith and the structuring of meaning. In *Toward moral and religious maturity, The First International Conference on Moral and Religious Development.* Morristown, NJ: Silver Burdett.

Fox, L. H. (1976, September). *Changing behaviors and attitudes of gifted girls.* Paper presented at the meeting of the American Psychological Association, Washington, DC.

Fox, L. H., Brody, L., & Tobin, D. (1979). *Women and mathematics: The impact of early intervention programs on course-taking and attitudes in high school.* Baltimore: Intellectually Gifted Study Group, Johns Hopkins University.

Frazier, N., & Sadker, M. (1973). *Sexism in school and society.* New York: Harper & Row.

Fregly, M. J., & Luttge, W. G. (1982). *Human endocrinology: An interactive text.* New York: Elsevier Science.

Freud, A. (1958). *The ego and the mechanisms of defense.* New York: International Universities Press.

Freud, A. (1958). Adolescence. *Psychoanalytic Study of The Child, 13,* 255–278.

Freud, A. (1966). Instinctual anxiety during puberty. In *The writings of Anna Freud: The ego and the mechanisms of defense.* New York: International Universities Press.

Freud, A., & Dann, S. (1933). An experiment in group upbringing. In R. S. Eisler, A. Freud, H. Hartmann, & E. Kris (Eds.), *The psychoanalytic study of the child* (Vol. 6). New York: Norton.

Freud, S. (1924). *A general introduction to psychoanalysis.* New York: Boni & Liveright.

Freud, S. (1953). Three essays on sexuality. In *Standard edition* (Vol. VII). London: Hogarth Press. (Original work published 1905)

Frieze, I. H. (1975). Women's expectations for and causal attributions of success and failure. In M. T. S. Mednick, S. S. Tangri, & L. W. Hoffman (Eds.), *Women and achievement.* New York: John Wiley.

Frisch, R., & Revelle, R. (1970). Height and weight at menarche and a hypothesis of critical body weights and adolescent events. *Science, 169,* 397–399.

Fry, P. S. (1974). The developmental study. *Journal of Psychology, 87,* 193–202.

Fuchs, E., & Havighurst, R. J. (1973). *To live on this Earth.* New York: Anchor Press.

Furstenberg, F. F. (1976). *Unplanned parenthood: The social consequences of teenage childbearing.* New York: Free Press.

Furth, H. G., & Wachs, H. (1975). *Thinking goes to school.* New York: Oxford.

Gage, N. L. (1965). Desirable behaviors of teachers. *Urban Education, 1,* 85–95.

Gagne, E. D. (1985). *The cognitive psychology of school learning.* Boston: Little Brown.

Gagne, E. D., Weidemann, C., Bell, M. S., & Ander, T. D. (in press). Training thirteen-year-olds to elaborate while studying text. *Journal of Human Learning.*

Galambos, N. L., Petersen, A. C., Richards, M., & Getelson, I. B. (1985). The Attitudes Toward Women Scale for Adolescents (AWSA): A study of reliability and validity. *Sex Roles, 13,* 343–356.

Gallup, G. (1985, November 8). Poll of adolescent eating disorders. *USA Today.*

Gallup, G., & Poling, D. (1980). *The search for America's faith.* New York: Abington.

Garbarino, J. (1978). The human ecology of school crime: A case for small schools. In *School crime and disruption: Prevention models.* Washington, DC: National Institute of Education, U.S. Department of Health, Education, and Welfare.

Garbarino, J. (1980). Meeting the needs of mistreated youths. *Social Work,* 122–126.

Garbarino, J. (1980). Some thoughts on school size and its effects on adolescent development. *Journal of Youth and Adolescence, 9,* 19–31.

Garbarino, J., & Asp, C. E. (1981). *Successful schools and competent students.* Lexington, MA: Lexington Books.

Garbarino, J., & Bronfenbrenner, U. (1976). The socialization of moral judgment and behavior in cross-cultural perspective. In T. Lickona (Ed.), *Moral development and behavior.* New York: Holt, Rinehart, & Winston.

Gardner, G. E., & Speery, B. M. (1974). School problems: Learning disabilities and school phobia. In S. Arieti (Ed.), *American handbook of psychiatry* (Vol. 2). New York: Basic Books.

Gardner, H. (1983). *Frames of mind.* New York: Basic Books.

Garmezy, N. (1978). Attentional processes in adult schizophrenia and in children at risk. *Journal of Psychiatric Research, 14,* 3–34.

Garrett, C., Ein, P., & Tremaine, L. (1977). The development of gender stereotyping of adult occupations in elementary school children. *Child Development, 48,* 507–512.

Garrison, K. C. (1968). Physiological changes in adolescence. In J. F. Adams (Ed.), *Understanding adolescence.* Boston: Allyn & Bacon.

Gaskell, J., & Knapp, H. (1976). *Resource guide for women's studies for high school students.* Victoria, B.C.: Department of Education.

Gazzaniga, M. (1983). Right hemisphere language following brain bisection: A 20-year perspective. *American Psychologist, 38,* 525–537.

Geiger, K., & Turiel, E. (1983). Disruptive school behavior and concepts of social convention in early adolescence. *Journal of Educational Psychology, 75,* 677–685.

Geis, F. L., Brown, V., Jennings (Walstedt), J., & Porter, N. (1984). TV commercials as achievement scripts for women. *Sex Roles, 10,* 513–525.

Gelman, R. (1979). Preschool thought. *American Psychologist, 34,* 900–904.

Gelman, R. (1982). Accessing one-to-one correspondence: Still another paper on conservation. *British Journal of Psychology, 73,* 209–220.

Gelman, R., & Baillargeon, R. (1983). A review of some Piagetian concepts. In P. H. Mussen (Ed.), *Handbook of child psychology.* New York: Wiley.

Gergen, K. J. (in press). Theory of the self: Impasse and evolution. In L. Berkowitz (Ed.), *Advances in experimental social psychology.* New York: Academic Press.

Gerson, W. M. (1966). Mass media socialization behavior: Negro-white differences. *Social Forces, 45,* 40–50.

Getzels, J. W., & Dillon, T. J. (1973). The nature of giftedness and the education of the gifted. In R. M. W. Travers (Ed.), *Second handbook of research on teaching.* Chicago: Rand McNally.

Ghiselli, E. E. (1966). *The validity of occupational aptitude tests.* New York: John Wiley.

Giaconia, R. M., & Hedges, L. V. (1982). Identifying features of effective open education. *Review of Educational Research, 52,* 579–602.

Gibbs, J., & Schnell, S. V. (1985, April). *Moral development "versus" socialization: A critique of the controversy.* Paper presented at the biennial meeting of the Society for Research in Child Development, Toronto.

Gill, N. T. (1978). A comparison of ninth-grade students' interests over seven years. *High School Journal, 61,* 26–33.

Gilligan, C. (1982). *In a different voice: Psychological theory and women's development.* Cambridge, MA: Harvard University Press.

Gilligan, C. (1985, April). *Response to critics.* Paper presented at the biennial meeting of the Society for Research in Child Development, Toronto.

Gilligan, C. (1985a). *Responses to critics.* Unpublished manuscript, Harvard University.

Gilligan, C. (1985b, April). *Remapping development.* Paper presented at the biennial meeting of the Society for Research in Child Development, Toronto.

Ginott, H. (1969). *Between parent and teenager.* New York: Avon Books.

Ginzberg, E. (1972). Toward a theory of occupational choice: A restatement. *Vocational Guidance Quarterly, 20,* 169–176.

Ginzberg, E., Ginzberg, S. W., Axelrad, S., & Herman, J. L. (1951). *Occupational choice.* New York: Columbia University.

Gjerde, P. (1985, April). *Adolescent depression and parental socialization patterns: A prospective study.* Paper presented at the biennial meeting of the Society for Research in Child Development, Toronto.

Gjerde, P. F. (1985). *A family systems perspective on parent-adolescent interaction: Second-order effects and sex differences in family interaction.* Unpublished manuscript, University of California, Berkeley.

Gjerde, P. F., Block, J., & Block, J. E. (1985). *Parental interactive patterns in dyads and triads: Prospective relationships to adolescent personality characteristics.* Unpublished manuscript, University of California, Berkeley.

Glaser, R. (1982). Instructional psychology: Past, present and future. *American Psychologist, 37,* 292–305.

Glass, D. C., Neulinger, J., & Brim, O. G. (1974). Birth order, verbal intelligence, and educational aspiration. *Child Development, 45,* 807–811.

Glueck, S., & Glueck, E. (1950). *Unraveling juvenile delinquency.* Cambridge, MA: Harvard University Press.

Goethals, G. W., & Klos, D. S. (1970). *Experiencing youth.* Boston: Little Brown.

Gold, M. (1970). *Delinquent behavior in an American city.* Belmont, CA: Brooks/Cole.

Gold, M., & Mattick, H. W. (1974). *Experiment in the streets: The Chicago Youth Development Project.* Ann Arbor, MI: Institute for Social Research at the University of Michigan.

Gold, M., & Petronio, R. J. (1980). Delinquent behavior in adolescence. In J. Adelson (Ed.), *Handbook of adolescent psychology.* New York: John Wiley.

Gold, M., & Reimer, D. J. (1975). Changing patterns of delinquent behavior among Americans 13–16 years old, 1967–72. *Crime and Delinquency Literature, 7,* 483–517.

Gold, M., & Tomlin, P. (1975). *Skeletal and chronological age in adolescent development.* Unpublished manuscript, University of Michigan, 1975.

Gold, M., & Williams, J. R. (1969). The effect of "getting caught;" Apprehension of the juvenile offender as a cause of subsequent delinquencies. *Prospectus, 3,* 1–12.

Gold, M., & Yanof, D. S. (1985). Mothers, daughters, and girlfriends. *Journal of Personality and Social Psychology, 49,* (3), 654–659.

Goldstein, A. P., Sprafkin, R. P., Gershaw, N.J., & Klein, P. (1981). *Skill-streaming the adolescent.* Champaign, IL: Research Press.

Gollin, E. S. (1958). Organizational characteristics of social judgment: A developmental investigation. *Journal of Personality, 26,* 139–154.

Goodall, J. V. L. (1962). *In the shadow of man.* New York: Dell.

Goodchilds, J. D., & Zellman, G. L. (1984). Sexual signaling and sexual aggression in adolescent relationships. In N. M. Malamuth & E. D. Donnerstein (Eds.), *Pornography and sexual aggression.* New York: Academic Press.

Goodlad, J. (1983). *A place called school.* New York: McGraw-Hill.

Goodwin, D. W., Schulsinger, F., Hermansen, L., Guze, S. B., & Winokur, G. (1973). Alcohol problems in adoptees raised apart from alcoholic biological parents. *Archives of General Psychiatry, 28,* 238–243.

Goodwin, D. W., Schulsinger, F., Moller, N., Hermansen, L., Winokur, G., & Guze, S. B. (1974). Drinking problems in adopted and nonadopted sons of alcoholic parents. *Archives of General Psychiatry, 31,* 164–169.

Goodwin, F. K., & Athanasious, P. Z. (1979). Lithium in the treatment of mania. *Archives of General Psychiatry, 36,* 840–844.

Gordon, N. P., & McAlister, A. L. (1982). Adolescent drinking. In T. J. Coates, A. C. Petersen, & C. Perry (Eds.), *Promoting adolescent health.* New York: Academic Press.

Gordon, T. (1970). *Parent effectiveness training.* New York: New American Library.

Gottesman, I. I. (1963). Genetic aspects of intelligent behavior. In N. Ellis (Ed.), *Handbook of mental deficiency.* New York: McGraw-Hill.

Gottesman, I. I., & Shields, J. (1982). *The schizophrenic puzzle.* New York: Cambridge University Press.

Gottlieb, D. (1966). Teaching and students: The views of negro and white teachers. *Sociology of Education, 37,* 345–353.

Gottlieb, D., & Chafetz, J. S. (1977). Dynamics of familial, generational conflict and reconciliation. *Youth and Society, 9,* 213–224.

Gottlieb, G. (1983). The psychobiological approach to developmental issues. In P. H. Mussen (Ed.), *Handbook of child psychology* (Vol. 2, 4th ed.). New York: Wiley.

Gottman, J. M., Ganso, J., & Rasmussen, B. (1975). Social interaction, social competence, and friendship in children. *Child Development, 46,* 709–718.

Gray, W. M., & Hudson, L. M. (1984). Formal operations and the imaginary audience. *Developmental Psychology, 20,* 619–627.

Green, R. (1974). One-hundred-ten feminine and masculine boys: Behavioral contrasts and demographic similarities. *Archives of Sexual Behavior, 5,* 425–446.

Greenacre, P. (1971). The childhood of the artist. In P. Greenacre (Ed.), *Emotional growth.* New York: International Universities Press.

Greenberger, E., & Steinberg, L. (1980). Part-time employment of in-school youth: A preliminary assessment of costs and benefits. In B. Linder & R. Taggart (Eds.), *A review of youth employment problems, programs, and policies: Vol. I. The youth employment problem: Causes and dimensions.* Washington, DC: Vice-President's Task Force on Youth Employment.

Greenberger, E., & Steinberg, L. (1981). *Project for the study of adolescent work: Final report.* Report prepared for the National Institute of Education, U.S. Department of Education, Washington, DC.

Greenberger, E., & Steinberg, L. (1983). Sex differences in early work experience: Harbinger of things to come? *Social Forces, 62,* 467–486.

Greenburg, B. S., & Dominick, J. R. (1969). *Television behavior among disadvantaged children.* Unpublished manuscript, Michigan State University, East Lansing, MI.

Greene, B. (1982, July 21). Valley girls. *Charleston Daily Mail,* Charleston, WV.

Greenfield, P. M. (1966). On culture and conservation. In J. S. Bruner, R. R. Oliver, & P. M. Greenfield (Eds.), *Studies in cognitive growth.* New York: Wiley.

Greenwald, A., & Albert, R. (1968). Acceptance and recall of improvised arguments. *Journal of Personality and Social Psychology, 8,* 31–34.

Greenwald, A., & Pratkanis, A. (in press). The self. In R. Wyer & T. Srull (Eds.), *Handbook of social cognition.* Hillsdale, NJ: Erlbaum.

Gribbons, W. D., & Lohnes, P. R. (1964). Relationships among measures of readiness for vocational planning. *Journal of Counseling Psychology, 11,* 13–19.

Grief, E. B., & Ullman, K. J. (1982). The psychological impact of menarche on early adolescent females: A review of the literature. *Child Development, 53,* 1413–1430.

Grotevant, H. D. (1984, February). *Exploration and negotiation of differences within families during adolescence.* Paper presented at the biennial conference on adolescence, Tucson.

Grotevant, H. D., & Cooper, C. R. (1985). Patterns of interaction in family relationships and the development of identity exploration in adolescence. *Child Development, 56,* 415–428.

Grotevant, H. D., & Durrett, M. E. (1980). Occupational knowledge and career development in adolescence. *Journal of Vocational Behavior, 17,* 171–182.

Grotevant, H. D., Thorbecke, W., & Meyer, M. L. (1982). An extension of Marcia's identity status interview into the interpersonal domain. *Journal of Youth and Adolescence, 11,* 33–47.

Guilford, J. P. (1967). *The nature of human intelligence.* New York: McGraw-Hill.

Gump, P. V. (1980). The school as a social situation. In M. R. Rosenzweig & L. V. Porter (Eds.), *Annual Review of Psychology* (Vol. 31).

Gutek, B. A., & Bikson, T. K. (1985). Differential experiences of men and women in computerized offices. *Sex Roles, 13,* 123–136.

Guttentag, M. and Bray, H. (1976). *Undoing sex stereotypes: Research and resources for educators.* New York: McGraw-Hill.

Guttentag, R. E. (1984). The mental effort requirement of cumulative rehearsal: A developmental study. *Journal of Experimental Child Psychology, 37,* 92–106.

Haas, A. (1979). *Teenage sexuality: A survey of teenage sexual behavior.* New York: MacMillan.

Haeberle, E. J. (1978). *The sex atlas.* New York: The Seabury Press.

Hahn, C. L. (1975). Eliminating sexism from the schools: Implementing change. *Social Education, 39,* 140–143.

Hall, G. S. (1904). *Adolescence* (Vols. I & II). Englewood Cliffs, NJ: Prentice-Hall.

Hall, J. A., & Halberstadt, A. G. (1980). Masculinity and femininity in children: Development of the Children's Personal Attributes Questionnaire. *Developmental Psychology, 16,* 270–280.

Hamburg, B. (1974). Early adolescence: A specific and stressful stage of the life cycle. In G. Coelho, D. A. Hamburg, & J. E. Adams (Eds.), *Coping and adaptation.* New York: Basic Books.

Hamdani, R. J. (1974). *Exploratory behavior and vocational development among disadvantaged inner-city adolescents.* Unpublished doctoral dissertation, Columbia University.

Hamm, C. M. (1977). The content of moral education, or in defense of the "bag of virtues." *School Review, 85,* 218–228.

Hammer, B. G. (1974). *The effects of two treatments designed to foster vocational development in disadvantaged inner-city adolescents.* Unpublished doctoral dissertation, Columbia University, New York.

Hanson, D. R., Gottesman, I. I., & Heston, L. L. (1976). Some possible childhood indicators of adult schizophrenia inferred from children of schizophrenics. *British Journal of Psychiatry, 129,* 142–154.

Hanson, P. L., & Vincent, S. M. (1980). Development and validation of the Sexist Attitudes Towards Women Scale (SATWS). *Psychology of Women Quarterly, 5,* 276–291.

Hansson, R. O., O'Conner, M. E., Jones, W. H., & Mihelich, M. H. (1980). Role relevant sex typing and opportunity in agentic and communal domains. *Journal of Personality, 48,* 419–434.

Hardt, R. H., & Bodine, G. E. (1965). *Development of self-report instruments in delinquency research.* Syracuse, NY: Youth Development Center, Syracuse University.

Harter, S. (1982). The perceived competence scale for children. *Child Development, 53,* 87–97.

Harter, S. (1983). Developmental perspectives on the self system. In P. H. Mussen (Ed.), *Handbook of child psychology* (Vol. 4, 4th ed.). New York: Wiley.

Hartup, W. W. (1970). Peer interaction and social organization. In P. H. Mussen (Ed.), *Carmichael's manual of child psychology* (Vol. 2, 3rd ed.). New York: John Wiley.

Hartup, W. W. (1976). Peer interaction and the behavioral development of the individual child. In E. Schopler & R. J. Reichler (Eds.), *Psychopathology and child development.* New York: Plenum.

Hartup, W. W. (1979). The social worlds of childhood. *American Psychologist, 34,* 944–950.

Hartup, W. W. (1983). Peer relations. In P. H. Mussen (Ed.), *Handbook of child psychology* (Vol. 4, 4th ed.). New York: Wiley.

Hartup, W. W. (1985). On relationships and development. In W. W. Hartup & Z. Rubin (Eds.), *Relationships and development.* Hillsdale, NJ: Erlbaum.

Hauinan, M. T. (1979). Structural effects on children's friendships and cliques. *Social Psychology Quarterly, 42,* 43–54.

Havighurst, R. J. (1972). *Developmental tasks and education* (3rd ed.). New York: McKay.

Havighurst, R. J. (1976). A cross-cultural view. In J. F. Adams (Ed.), *Understanding adolescence.* Boston: Allyn & Bacon.

Hawkins, J. A., & Berndt, T. J. (1985, April). *Adjustment following the transition to junior high school.* Paper presented at the biennial meeting of the Society for Research in Child Development, Toronto.

Hawkins, R. (1979, October 29). "Ropers" and "dopers." *Dallas Morning News,* p. 1.

Heider, F. (1958). *The psychology of interpersonal relations.* New York: John Wiley.

Heilbrun, A. B. (1976). Measurement of masculine and feminine sex role identities as independent dimensions. *Journal of Consulting and Clinical Psychology, 44,* 183–190.

Heller, J., & Kiralry, J. (1973). An educational program for pregnant school-age girls. *Clearing House, 47,* 476–482.

Helmreich, R. L., Spence, J. T., & Holahan, C. K. (1979). Psychological androgyny and sex role flexibility: A test of two hypotheses. *Journal of Personality and Social Psychology, 37,* 1631–1644.

Henderson, N. D. (1982). Human behavior genetics. *Annual Review of Psychology, 33,* 403–440.

Hennessee, J. A., & Nicholson, J. (1972, May 28). NOW says: TV commercials insult women. *New York Times Magazine.*

Herr, E. (1977). *Research in career education: The state of the art.* Columbus, OH: Center for Vocational Education.

Herr, E. L. (1974). Manpower policies, vocational guidance, and career development. In E. L. Herr (Ed.), *Vocational guidance and human development.* Boston: Houghton Mifflin.

Hertzog, C., Lerner, J. V., & Hooker, K. A. (1985, April). *A structural equations analysis of negative emotional/behavioral states and adjustment.* Paper presented at the biennial meeting of the Society for Research in Child Development, Toronto.

Hess, R. D. (1970). Social class and ethnic influences on socialization. In P. H. Mussen (Ed.), *Carmichael's manual of child psychology* (Vol. 2, 3rd ed.). New York: John Wiley.

Hess, R. D., & Miura, I. T. (1985). Gender differences in enrollment in computer camps and classes. *Sex Roles, 13,* 193–203.

Hetherington, E. M. (1972). Effects of father-absence on personality development in adolescent daughters. *Developmental Psychology, 7,* 313–326.

Hetherington, E. M. (1977). *My heart belongs to daddy: A study of the remarriages of daughters of divorcees and widows.* Unpublished manuscript, University of Virginia.

Hetherington, E. M., Cox, M., & Cox, R. (1978). The aftermath of divorce. In J. H. Stevens & M. Mathews (Eds.), *Mother-child/father-child relations.* Washington, DC: National Association for the Education of Young Children.

Hetherington, E. M., Cox, M., & Cox, R. (1982). The effects of divorce on parents and children. In M. E. Lamb (Ed.), *Nontraditional families.* Hillsdale, NJ: Erlbaum.

Higgins, A., Power, C., & Kohlberg, L. (1983, April). *Moral atmosphere and moral judgment.* Paper presented at the biennial meeting of the Society for Research in Child Development, Detroit.

Higgins, A. T., & Turnure, J. E. (1984). Distractibility and concentration of attention in children's development. *Child Development, 44,* 1799–1810.

Higgens-Trenk, A., & Gaite, A. J. H. (1971). *Elusiveness of formal-operational thought in adolescents.* Paper presented at the meeting of the American Psychological Association.

Hill, J. P. (1980a). *Understanding early adolescence: A framework.* Carrboro, NC: Center for Early Adolescence.

Hill, J. P. (1980b). The family. In M. Johnson (Ed.), *Toward adolescence: The middle-school years. The seventy-ninth yearbook of the National Society for the Study of Education.* Chicago: The University of Chicago Press.

Hill, J. P. (1980c). The early adolescent and the family. In *The seventy-ninth yearbook of the National Society for the Study of Education.*

Hill, J. P. (1983, April). *Adolescent development.* Paper presented at the biennial meeting of the Society for Research in Child Development, Detroit.

Hill, J. P. (1985). Early adolescence: A research agenda. *Journal of Early Adolescence.*

Hill, J. P., & Holmbeck, G. N. (in press). Attachment and autonomy during adolescence. *Annals of Child Development.*

Hill, J. P., Holmbeck, G. N., Marlow, L., Green, T. M., & Lynch, M. E. (1985). Pubertal status and parent-child relations in families of seventh-grade boys. *Journal of Early Adolescence, 5,* 31–44.

Hill, J. P., & Palmquist, W. J. (1978). Social cognition and social relations in early adolescence. *International Journal of Behavioral Development, 1,* 1–36.

Hill, J. P., & Steinberg, L. D. (1976, April 26–30). *The development of autonomy in adolescence.* Paper presented at the Symposium on Research on Youth Problems, Fundacion Orbegoza Eizaquirre, Madrid, Spain.

Hinde, R. A. (1983). Ethology and child development. In P. H. Mussen (Ed.), *Handbook of child psychology* (Vol. 2, 4th ed.). New York: Wiley.

Hirsch, M. (1982). Rock, radio, and responsibility. In M. Schwarz (Ed.), *TV and teens.* Reading, MA: Addison-Wesley.

Hodgman, C. H., & Braiman, A. (1965). "College phobia": School refusal in university students. *American Journal of Psychiatry, 121,* 801–805.

Hoffman, L. W. (1979). Maternal employment: 1979. *American Psychologist, 34,* 859–865.

Hoffman, M. L. (1975). Developmental synthesis of affect and cognition and its implications for altruistic motivation. *Developmental Psychology, 11,* 607–622.

Hoffman, M. L. (1979). Development of moral thought, feeling, and behavior. *American Psychologist, 34,* 958–966.

Hoffman, M. L. (1980). Moral development in adolescence. In J. Adelson (Ed.), *Handbook of adolescent psychology.* New York: John Wiley.

Hogan, R. (1973). Moral conduct and moral character: A psychological perspective. *Psychological Bulletin, 79,* 2; –232.

Holland, J. L. (1973). *Making vocational choices: A theory of careers.* Englewood Cliffs, NJ: Prentice-Hall.

Holland, J. L., & Richards, J. M. (1965). Academic and nonacademic accomplishments: Correlated or uncorrelated? *Journal of Educational Psychology, 56,* 165–174.

Hollingshead, A. B. (1975). *Elmtown's youth and Elmtown revisited.* New York: John Wiley.

Hollis, M. (1975). Logical operations and role-taking abilities in two cultures: Norway and Hungary. *Child Development, 46,* 638–649.

Holman, D. R. (1975). Teaching about women in secondary schools: Springboard for inquiry. *Social Education, 39,* 140–143.

Holt, J. (1964). *How children fail.* Belmont, CA: Pitman.

Holtzmann, W. (1982). Cross-cultural comparisons of personality development in Mexico and the United States. In D. Wagner & H. W. Stevenson (Eds.), *Cultural perspectives on child development.* San Francisco: W. H. Freeman.

Holtzman, W. H., Diaz-Guerrero, R., & Schwarz, J. D. (1975). *Personality development in two cultures: Cross-cultural and longitudinal study of school children in Mexico and the United States.* Austin: University of Texas Press.

Horner, M. S. (1970). Femininity and successful achievement: A basic inconsistency. In J. Bardwick, E. Douvan, M. Horner, & D. Gutmann (Eds.), *Feminine personality and conflict.* Belmont, CA: Brooks/Cole.

Horner, M. S. (1972). Toward an understanding of achievement-related conflicts in women. *Journal of Social Issues, 28,* 157–175.

Howard, M. (1983, March). Postponing sexual involvement: A new approach. *Siecus Report,* pp. 5–6,8.

Hoyenga, K. B., & Hoyenga, K. T. (1979). *The question of sex differences.* Boston: Little, Brown.

Hunt, E. (1978). Mechanics of verbal ability. *Psychological Review, 85,* 109–130.

Hunt, E., & Cansman, M. (1975). Cognitive theory applied to individual differences. In W. K. Estes (Ed.), *Handbook of learning and cognitive processes* (Vol. 1). Hillsdale, NJ: Erlbaum.

Hunt, E., Frost, & Lunneborg, C. (1973). Individual differences in cognition: A new approach to intelligence. In G. M. Bower (Ed.), *The psychology of learning and motivation* (Vol. 7). New York: Academic Press.

Hunt, E., Lunneborg, C., & Lewis, J. (1975). What does it mean to be high verbal? *Cognitive Psychology, 7,* 194–227.

Hunt, K. W. (1970). Syntactic maturity in school children and adults. *Monographs of the Society for Research in Child Development, 35*(1, Serial No. 134).

Hunt, M. (1982). *The universe within.* New York: Simon & Schuster.

Hunt, M. (1974). *Sexual behavior in the 1970s.* Chicago: Playboy Press.

Hunter, F. T. (1985). Individual adolescents' perceptions of interactions with friends and parents. *Journal of Early Adolescence, 5,* 295–306.

Hurlock, E. (1967). *Adolescent development* (3rd ed.). New York: McGraw-Hill.

Huston, A. C. (1983). Sex-typing. In P. H. Mussen (Ed.), *Handbook of child psychology* (Vol. 4, 4th ed.). New York: Wiley.

Huston, T. L., & Burgess, R. L. (1980). Social exchange in developing relationships: An overview. In T. L. Huston & R. L. Burgess (Eds.), *Social exchange in developing relationships.* New York: Academic Press.

Huston-Stein, A., & Higgins-Trenk, A. (1978). Development of females from childhood through adulthood: Career and feminine role orientations. In P. Baltes (Ed.), *Life-span development and behavior* (Vol. 1). New York: Academic Press.

Hutchings, B., & Mednick, S. A. (1974). Registered criminality in the adoptive and biological parents of registered male adoptees. In S. A. Mednick, F. Schulsinger, J. Higgins, & B. Bell (Eds.), *Genetics, environment, and psychopathology.* Amsterdam: North-Holland.

Hyde, J. S. (1979). *Understanding human sexuality.* New York: McGraw-Hill.

Hyde, J. S. (1984). Children's understanding of sexist language. *Developmental Psychology, 20,* 697–706.

Hyde, J. S. (1985). *Half the human experience.* Lexington, MA: D. C. Heath.

Hyde, J. S., Rosenberg, B. G., & Behrman, J. A. (1977). Tomboyism. *Psychology of Women Quarterly, 2,* 73–75.

Hyman, H. M. (1959). *Political socialization.* New York: Free Press.

Jacob, T. (1974). Patterns of family conflict and dominance as a function of child age and social class. *Developmental Psychology, 10,* 1–12.

Jacobs, J. (1971). *Adolescent suicide.* New York: John Wiley.

Jacoby, L. (1978). On interpreting the effects of repetition: Solving a problem versus remembering a solution. *Journal of Verbal Learning and Verbal Behavior, 17,* 649–667.

James, W. (1963). *Psychology.* New York: Fawcett. (Original work published 1890)

Jay, W., & Schminke, C. (1975). Sex bias in elementary school mathematics texts. *Arithmetic Teacher, 22,* 242–246.

Jencks, C. S., Smith, M., Acland, H., Bane, M. J., Cohen, D., Gintis, H., Heyns, B., & Michelson, S. (1972). *Inequality: A reassessment of the effects of family and schooling in America.* New York: Basic Books.

Jeness, C. F. (1974). *Comparative effectiveness of behavior analysis and transactional analysis programs for delinquents.* Unpublished manuscript, California Youth Authority, Sacramento, CA.

Jenkins, J. J. (1969). Language and thought. In J. F. Voss (Ed.), *Approaches to thought.* Columbus: Merrill.

Jepsen, D. A. (1974a). Vocational decision-making strategy types. *Vocational Guidance Quarterly, 23,* 12–23.

Jepsen, D. A. (1974b). Vocational decision-making patterns among non-college aspiring adolescents. *Journal of Vocational Behavior, 4,* 283–296.

Jessor, R., Graves, T. D., Hanson, R. C., & Jessor, S. L. (1968). *Society, personality, and deviant behavior: A study of a tri-ethnic community.* New York: Holt, Rinehart, & Winston.

Jessor, S. L., & Jessor, R. (1975). Transition from virginity to nonvirginity among youth: A social-psychological study over time. *Developmental Psychology, 11,* 473–484.

Johnson, L. (1983). *Biology.* Dubuque, IA: William C. Brown Publishers.

Johnston, L. D. (1973). *Drugs and American youth*. Ann Arbor, MI: Institute for Social Research at the University of Michigan.

Johnston, L. D., Bachman, J. G., & O'Malley, P. M. (1981). *Student drug use in America, 1975–1981*. Rockville, MD: National Institute of Drug Abuse.

Johnston, L. D., Bachman, J. G., & O'Malley, P. M. (1985, January 4). News and Information Services Release, Institute of Social Research, University of Michigan, Ann Arbor.

Johnston, L. D., O'Malley, P. M., & Eveland, L. K. (1978). Drugs and delinquency: A search for causal connections. In D. G. Kandel (Ed.), *Longitudinal research on drug use: Empirical findings and methodological issues*. Washington, DC: Hemisphere.

Jones, E. F., Forrest, J. D., Goldman, N., Henshaw, S. K., Lincoln, R., Rosoff, J. I., Westoff, C. F., & Wulf, D. (1985). Teenage pregnancy in developed countries: Determinants and policy implications. *Family Planning Perspectives, 17*, 53–63.

Jones, H. E. (1938). The California adolescent growth study. *Journal of Educational Research, 31*, 561–567.

Jones, M. C. (1957). The later careers of boys who were early or late maturing. *Child Development, 28*, 113–128.

Jones, M. C. (1965). Psychological correlates of somatic development. *Child Development, 36*, 899–911.

Jones, M. C., & Bayley, N. (1950). Physical maturing among boys as related to behavior. *Journal of Educational Psychology, 41*, 129–148.

Jones, M. C., & Mussen, P. H. (1958). Self-conceptions, motivations, and interpersonal attitudes of early- and late-maturing girls. *Child Development, 29*, 491–501.

Jones, W. H., Chernovetz, M. E., & Hansson, R. O. (1978). The enigma of androgyny: Differential implications for males and females? *Journal of Consulting and Clinical Psychology, 46*, 298–313.

Jones, W. M. (1977). *Educational Leadership, 34*, 413–416.

Jordaan, J. P. (1963). Exploratory behavior. In D. E. Super, R. Statishersky, N. Mattin, & J. P. Jordaan (Eds.), *Career development: Self-concept theory*. New York: College Entrance Examination Board.

Jordaan, J. P., & Heyde, M. B. (1978). *Vocational development during the high school years*. New York: Teachers College Press.

Jose, P. E. (1985, April). *Development of the immanent justice judgment in moral evaluation*. Paper presented at the biennial meeting of the Society for Research in Child Development, Toronto.

Josselson, R. (1973). Psychodynamic aspects of identity formation in college women. *Journal of Youth and Adolescence, 2*, 3–52.

Kacerguis, M. A., & Adams, G. R. (1980). Erikson stage resolution: The relationship between identity and intimacy. *Journal of Youth and Adolescence, 9*, 117–126.

Kagan, J., & Moss, H. A. (1962). *Birth to maturity*. New York: John Wiley.

Kagan, S., & Madsen, M. C. (1971). Cooperation and competition of Mexican, Mexican-American, and Anglo-American children of two ages under four instructional sets. *Developmental Psychology, 5*, 32–39.

Kagan, S., & Madsen, M. C. (1972). Experimental analysis of cooperation and competition of Anglo-American and Mexican children. *Developmental Psychology, 6*, 49–59.

Kahn, J. H., & Nursten, J. P. (1962). School refusal: A comprehensive view of school phobia and other failures of school attendance. *American Journal of Orthopsychiatry, 22*, 707–718.

Kahn, S. E., & Richardson, A. (1983). Evaluation of a course in sex roles for secondary school students. *Sex Roles, 9*, 431–440.

Kalish, H. I. (1981). *From behavioral science to behavior modification*. New York: McGraw-Hill.

Kandel, D., & Lesser, G. S. (1969). Parent-adolescent relationships and adolescence independence in the United States and Denmark. *Journal of Marriage and the Family, 31*, 348–358.

Kandel, D., & Lesser, G. S. (1972). *Youth in two worlds*. San Francisco: Jossey-Bass.

Kandel, D. B. (1974). The role of parents and peers in adolescent marijuana use. *Journal of Social Issues, 30*, 107–135.

Kandel, D. B. (1978). Similarity in real-life adolescent friendship pairs. *Journal of Personality and Social Psychology, 36*, 306–312.

Kandel, D. B., Dessler, R. C., & Margulies, R. Z. (1978). Antecedents of adolescent initiation into stages of drug use: A developmental analysis. In D. B. Kandel (Ed.), *Longitudinal research on drug use*. New York: John Wiley.

Kantner, J., & Zelnick, M. (1973). Contraception and pregnancy: Experience of young unmarried women in the United States. *Family Planning Perspectives, 5*, 21–35.

Kappelman, M. (1974). A unique school health program in a school for pregnant teenagers. *Journal of School Health, 44*, 303–306.

Katz, J. (1968). *No time for youth*. San Francisco: Jossey-Bass.

Kaufman, A. S., & Kaufman, N. L. (1983). *Kaufman assessment battery for children: Interpretive manual*. Circle Pines, MN: American Guidance Service.

Keating, D. P. (1980). Thinking processes in adolescence. In J. Adelson (Ed.), *Handbook of adolescent psychology*. New York: Wiley.

Kelly, J. A., & Worrell, J. (1977). New formulations of sex roles and androgyny: A critical review. *Journal of Consulting and Clinical Psychology, 45*, 1101–1115.

Keniston, K. (1968). *Young radicals: Notes on committed youth*. New York: Harcourt Brace Jovanovich.

Keniston, K. (1970). Youth: A "new" stage of life. *The American Scholar, 39*, 631–654.

Kenworthy, J. A. (1979). Androgyny in psychotherapy: But will it sell in Peoria? *Psychology of Women Quarterly, 3*, 231–240.

Kerr, B. A. (1983). Raising the career aspirations of gifted girls. *Vocational Guidance Quarterly, 32*, 37–43.

Kessey, R. E., Boyle, P. C., Kemnitz, J. W., & Mitchell, J. S. (1976). The role of the lateral hypothalamus in determining the body weight set point. In D. Novin (Ed.), *Hunger.* New York: Raven Press.

Kiesler, S., Sproull, I., & Eccles, J. S. (1983, March). Second-class citizens? *Psychology Today*, pp. 41–48.

Kieth, T. Z. (1985). Questioning the K-ABC. What does it measure? *School Psychology Review, 14*, 9–20.

Kingston, A., & Lovelace, T. (1977–1978). Sexism and reading: A critical review of the literature. *Reading Research Quarterly, 13*, 133–161.

Kinsey, A. C., Pomeroy, W. B., & Martin, C. E. (1948). *Sexual behavior in the human male.* Philadelphia: Saunders.

Klein, N. C., Alexander, J. F., & Parsons, B. V. (1977). Impact of family-systems intervention on recidivism and sibling delinquency: A model of primary prevention and program evaluation. *Journal of Consulting and Clinical Psychology, 45*, 469–474.

Klitgaard, R. E., & Hall, G. R. (1975). Are there unusually effective schools? *Journal of Human Resources, 10*, 90–106.

Kloba, J. A., & Zimpfer, D. G. (1976). Status and independence as variables in microcounseling training with adolescents. *Journal of Counseling Psychology, 23*, 458–463.

Knox, D., & Wilson, K. (1981). Dating behaviors of university students. *Family Relations, 30*, 255–258.

Knudson, D. D. (1966). The declining status of women: Popular myths and the failure of functionalist thought. *Social Forces, 48*, 183–193.

Kohlberg, L. (1958). *The development of modes of moral thinking and choice in the years 10 to 16.* Unpublished doctoral dissertation, University of Chicago.

Kohlberg, L. (1966). A cognitive-developmental analysis of children's sex-role concepts and attitudes. In E. E. Maccoby (Ed.), *The development of sex differences.* Palo Alto, CA: Stanford University Press.

Kohlberg, L. (1969). Stage and sequence: The cognitive developmental approach to socialization. In D. A. Goslin (Ed.), *Handbook of socialization theory and research. Chicago:* Rand McNally.

Kohlberg, L. (1976). Moral stages of moralization. The cognitive developmental approach. In T. Lickona (Ed.), *Moral development and behavior.* New York: Holt, Rinehart, & Winston.

Kohlberg, L. (1981). *The philosophy of moral development: Moral stages and the idea of justice.* New York: Harper & Row.

Kohlberg, L. (Ed.). (1980). *Recent research in moral development.* New York: Holt, Rinehart, & Winston.

Kohlberg, L., & Candee, D. (1979). *Relationships between moral judgment and moral action.* Unpublished manuscript, Harvard University.

Kounin, J. (1971). *Discipline and group management in classrooms.* New York: Holt, Rinehart, & Winston.

Kruger, A. C., & Tomasello, M. (1985, April). *Moral reasoning with peers and parents.* Paper presented at the biennial meeting of the Society for Research in Child Development, Toronto.

Kuhn, D. (1980). *On the development of developmental psychology.* Unpublished manuscript, Harvard University.

Kupersmidt, J. B. (1983, April). *Assessment and training of isolated children's social skills.* Paper presented at the biennial meeting of the Society for Research in Child Development, Detroit.

Labouvie-Vief, G. (1980). Beyond formal operations: Uses and limits of pure logic in life-span development. *Human Development, 23*, 141–161.

Labouvie-Vief, G. (1982). Dynamic development and mature autonomy: A theoretical prologue. *Human Development, 25*, 161–191.

Labov, W. (1972). *Language in the inner city.* Philadelphia: University of Pennsylvania Press.

Ladd, G. W., & Mars, K. T. (1985, April). *Reliability and validity of preschoolers's perceptions of peer behavior.* Paper presented at the biennial meeting of the Society for Research in Child Development, Toronto.

Lahey, B. B., Hammer, D., Crumine, P. L., & Forehand, R. L. (1980). Birth order x sex interactions in child behavior problems. *Developmental Psychology, 16*, 608–615.

Lamb, M. E. (1976). *The role of the father in the child's development.* New York: Wiley.

Lamb, M. E. (1981). Fathers and child development: An integrative overview. In M. E. Lamb (Ed.), *The father's role in child development.* New York: John Wiley.

Lampl, M., & Emde, R. N. (1983). Episodic growth in infancy: A preliminary report on length, head circumference, and behavior. *New directions for child development.* San Francisco: Jossey-Bass.

Lapsley, D., & Quintana, S. (in press). Recent approaches in children's elementary moral and social education. *Elementary School Guidance and Counseling Journal.*

Lapsley, D. K. (1985). Elkind on egocentrism. *Developmental Review, 5*, 227–236.

Lapsley, D. K., Enright, R. D., & Serlin, R. C. (1985). Toward a theoretical perspective on the legislation of adolescence. *Journal of Early Adolescence, 5*, 441–466.

Lapsley, D. K., Enright, R. D., & Serlin, R. C. (1986). Moral and social education. In J. Worrell & F. Danner (Eds.), *Adolescent development: Issues for education.* New York: Academic Press.

Lapsley, D. K., & Murphy, M. N. (1985). Another look at the theoretical assumptions of adolescent egocentrism. *Developmental Review, 5.*

Lapsley, D. K., & Quintana, S. M. (1985). Integrative themes in social and developmental theories of self. In J. B. Pryor & J. Day (Eds.), *Social and developmental perspectives of social cognition.* New York: Springer-Verlag.

Larson, M. E. (1973). Humbling cases for career counselors. *Phi Delta Kappan, 54*, 374.

LaVoie, J. (1976). Ego identity formation in middle adolescence. *Journal of Youth and Adolescence, 5,* 371–385.

Laycock, F. (1979). *Gifted children.* Glenview, IL: Scott, Foresman.

Lee, C. B. T. (1970). *The campus scene: 1900–1970.* New York: McKay.

Leifer, A. D., Gordon, N. J., & Graves, S. B. (1974). Children's television: More than entertainment. *Harvard Educational Review, 44,* 213–245.

Lepper, M., Greene, D., & Nisbett, R. E. (1973). Undermining children's intrinsic interest with extrinsic rewards. *Journal of Personality and Social Psychology, 28,* 129–137.

Lerner, R. M., & Karabenick, S. A. (1974). Physical attractiveness, body attitudes, and self-concept in late adolescence. *Journal of Youth and Adolescence, 3,* 307–316.

Levine, R. A. (1973). *Culture, behavior, and personality.* Chicago: Aldine.

Levitt, E. E., & Lubin, B. (1975). *Depression: Concepts, controversies, and some new facts.* New York: Springer.

Levitz-Jones, E. M., & Orolofsky, J. L. Separation-individuation and intimacy capacity in college women. (1985). *Journal of Personality and Social Psychology, 49,* 156–169.

Lewin-Epstein, N. (1981). *Youth employment during high school.* Washington, DC: National Center for Education Statistics.

Lewis, M., & Brooks-Gunn, J. (1979). *Social cognition and the acquisition of self.* New York: Plenum.

Lewis, M., & Rosenblum, L. A. (Eds.). (1975). *Friendship and peer relations* (Vol. 4). New York: John Wiley.

Lewis, V. G., Money, J., & Bobrow, N. A. (1977). Idiopathic pubertal delay beyond the age of fifteen: Psychologic study of twelve boys. *Adolescence, 12,* 1–11.

Lewis, Z., & Herzog, E. (1985, April). *Gender segregation across and within settings.* Paper presented at the biennial meeting of the Society for Research in Child Development, Toronto.

Liebert, R. M., Neale, J. M., & Davidson, E. S. (1973). *The early window: Effects of television on children and youth.* Elmsford, N.Y.: Pergamon Press.

Linn, M., & Peterson, A. C. (in press). A meta-analysis of gender differences in spatial ability: Implications for mathematics and science achievement. In J. Hyde & M. C. Linn (Eds.), *The psychology of gender: Advances through meta-analysis.* Baltimore: John Hopkins University Press.

Lipsitz, J. (1980, March). *Sexual development in young adolescents.* Invited speech given at the American Association of Sex Educators, Counselors, and Therapists.

Lipsitz, J. (1983, October). *Making it the hard way: Adolescents in the 1980s.* Testimony presented at the Crisis Intervention Task Force, House Select Committee on Children, Youth, and Families, Washington, DC.

Lipsitz, J. (1984). *Successful schools for young adolescents.* New Brunswick, NJ: Transaction Books.

Little, J. K. (1969). The occupations of non-college youth. In R. E. Grinder (Ed.), *Studies in adolescence: A book of readings in adolescent development* (2nd ed.). New York: MacMillan.

Livesley, W. J., & Bromley, D. B. (1973). *Person perception in childhood and adolescence.* London: Wiley.

Lockheed, M. E. (1978). [Book review.] *American Educational Research Journal, 15,* 586–589.

Lockheed, M. E. (1985). Women, girls, and computers: A first look at the evidence. *Sex Roles, 13,* 115–122.

Lockheed, M. E., & Frakt, S. B. (1984). Sex equity: Increasing girls' use of computers. *Computing Teacher, 11*(8), 16–18.

Lockheed, M. E., Nielsen, A., & Stone, M. K. (1983). *Sex differences in microcomputer literacy.* Paper presented at the National Educational Computer Conference, Baltimore.

Loehlin, J. C., & Nichols, R. C. (1976). Heredity, environment, and personality: A study of 850 sets of twins. Austin, TX: University of Texas Press.

Long, T., & Long, L. (1983). *Latchkey children.* New York: Penguin.

Lorenzi, M. E., Klerman, L. V., & Jekel, J. F. (1977). School-age parents: How permanent a relationship? *Adolescence, 45,* 13–22.

Lull, J. T., Johnson, L. M., & Sweeny, C. E. (1978). Audience for contemporary radio formats. *Journal of Broadcasting, 22,* 439–453.

Lyle, J. (1972). Television and daily life: Patterns of use (overview). In *Television and social behavior* (Vol. 4). Washington, DC: U.S. Government Printing Office.

Maas, H. S. (1954). The role of members in clubs of lower-class and middle-class adolescents. *Child Development, 25,* 241–251.

Maccoby, E. E. (1980). *Social development.* New York: Harcourt, Brace, and Jovanovich.

Maccoby, E. E., & Jacklin, C. N. (1974). *The psychology of sex differences.* Stanford, CA: Stanford University Press.

Maccoby, E. E., & Jacklin, C. N. (1980). Sex differences in aggression. A rejoinder and reprise. *Child Development, 51,* 964–980.

Maccoby, E. E., & Martin, J. A. (1983). Socialization in the context of the family. In P. H. Mussen (Ed.), *Handbook of child psychology* (Vol. 4, 4th ed.). New York: Wiley.

MacKay, J. R., Phillips, D. L., & Bryce, O. B. (1967). Drinking behavior among teenagers: A comparison of institutionalized and noninstitutionalized youth. *Journal of Health and Social Behavior, 8,* 46–54.

Mackey, J. (1977). Strategies for reducing adolescent alienation. *Educational Leadership, 34,* 449–452.

Madsen, M. C., & Shapira, A. (1970). Cooperative and competitive behavior of urban Afro-American, Anglo-American, Mexican-American, American, and Mexican village children. *Developmental Psychology, 3,* 16–20.

Maeher, M. L. (1984). Meaning and motivation: Toward a theory of personal investment. In R. E. Ames & C. Ames (Eds.), *Motivation in education.* New York: Academic Press.

Mahler, M. (1979). *Separation-individuation.* London: Jason Aronson.

Malmquist, C. P. (1965). School phobia: A problem in family neurosis. *Journal of the American Academy of Child Psychiatry, 4,* 293–319.

Mandler, J. M. (1983). Representation. In P. H. Mussen (Ed.), *Handbook of child psychology* (Vol. 3, 4th ed.). New York: John Wiley.

Mannarino, A. P. (1978). Friendship patterns and self-concept in preadolescent males. *Journal of Genetic Psychology, 133,* 105–110.

Mannarino, A. P. (1979). The relationship between friendship and altruism in preadolescent girls. *Psychiatry, 42,* 280–284.

Maracek, J. (1979, September). *Psychological and behavioral status of children born to adolescent mothers.* Paper presented at the meeting of the American Psychological Association, New York City.

Marcia, J. (1966). Development and validation of ego-identity status. *Journal of Personality and Social Psychology, 3,* 551–558.

Marcia, J. (1976). Identity six years after: A follow-up study. *Journal of Youth and Adolescence, 5,* 145–160.

Marcia, J. (1980). Ego identity development. In J. Adelson (Ed.), *Handbook of adolescent psychology.* New York: John Wiley.

Marcia, J. (1983). *Journal of Early Adolescence, 3.*

Markus, H. (1977). Self-schemata and processing information about the self. *Journal of Personality and Social Psychology, 35,* 63–78.

Marshall, H. (1981). Open classroom: Has the term outlived its usefulness? *Review of Educational Research, 51,* 181–192.

Martin, B. (1977). *Abnormal psychology.* New York: Holt, Rinehart, & Winston.

Maslow, A. H. (1971). *The further reaches of human nature.* New York: Harper & Row.

Massad, C. M. (1981). Sex-role identity and adjustment during adolescence. *Child Development, 52,* 1290–1298.

Matousek, M., & Petersen, J. (1973). Frequency analysis of the EEG in normal children and adolescents. In P. Kellaway & I. Peterson (Eds.), *Automation of clinical electroencephalographs.* New York: Raven Press.

Mayer, J. (1968). *Overweight: Causes, cost, and control.* Englewood Cliffs, NJ: Prentice-Hall.

McArthur, C. C. (1971). Distinguishing patterns of student neuroses. In G. R. Blaine & C. C. McArthur (Eds.), *Emotional problems of the student* (2nd ed.). New York: Appleton-Century-Crofts.

McCabe, A. E., & Moriarity, R. J. (1977, March). *A laboratory/field study of television violence and aggression in children's sports.* Paper presented at the biennial meeting of the Society for Research in Child Development, New Orleans.

McCabe, M. P., & Collins, J. K. (1979). Sex role and dating orientation. *Journal of Youth and Adolescence, 8,* 407–425.

McCall, R. B., Meyers, E. D., Hartman, J., & Roche, A. F. (1983). Developmental changes in head circumference and mental performance growth rates: A test of Epstein's phrenoblysis hypothesis. *Developmental Psychobiology, 16,* 457–468.

McCandless, B. R. (1970). *Adolescents: Behavior and development.* Hinsdale, IL: Dryden Press.

McCandless, B. R. (1973). *Male caregivers in day care: Demonstration project.* Atlanta, GA: Emory University.

McClelland, D. C. (1973). Testing for competence rather than for "intelligence." *American Psychologist, 28,* 1–14.

McClelland, D. C., Atkinson, J. R., Clark, R. A., & Lowell, E. O. (1953). *The achievement motive.* New York: Appleton-Century-Crofts.

McCord, J. (1980). Antecedents and correlates of vulnerability and resistance to psychopathology. In R. Zucker & A. Rabin (Eds.), *Further explorations in personality.* New York: Wiley.

McCord, W., McCord, J., & Gudeman, J. (1960). *Origins of alcoholism.* Palo Alto, CA: Stanford University Press.

McHenry, P. C., Walters, L. H., & Johnson, C. (1979). Adolescent pregnancy: A review of the literature. *The Family Coordinator, 28,* 17–28.

McKelvey, B. (1984, January 25). Cited in *Education Daily,* p. 6.

McLaughlin, L., & Chassin, L. (1985, April). *Adolescents at risk for future alcohol abuse.* Paper presented at the biennial meeting of the Society for Research in Child Development, Toronto.

McLeod, J. M., & O'Keefe, J. (1972). The socialization perspective and communication behavior. In G. Kline & P. Tichenor (Eds.), *Current perspectives in mass communication research* (pp. 121–168). Beverly Hills: Sage.

McPartland, J. M., & McDill, E. L. (1976). The unique role of schools in the causes of youthful crime. Baltimore: Johns Hopkins University.

McPartland, J. M., & McDill, E. L. (1977). Research on crime in schools. In J. M. McPartland & E. L. McDill (Eds.), *Violence in schools.* Lexington, MA: Lexington Books.

Meacham, J. A., & Santilli, N. R. (1982). Interstage relationships in Erikson's theory: Identity and intimacy. *Child Development, 53,* 1461–1467.

Mead, G. H. (1934). *Mind, self, and society.* Chicago: University of Chicago Press.

Mead, M. (1928). *Coming of age in Samoa.* New York: William Morrow.

Mead, M. (1978, Dec. 30–Jan. 5). The American family: An endangered species. *TV Guide.*

Meilman, P. W. (1979). Cross-sectional age changes in ego identity status during adolescence. *Developmental Psychology, 15,* 230–231.

Mercer, J. R., & Lewis, J. F. (1978). *System of multicultural pluralistic assessment.* New York: Psychological Corporation.

Messinger, J. C. (1971). Sex and repression in an Irish folk community. In D. S. Marshall & R. C. Suggs (Eds.), *Human sexual behavior: Variations in the ethnographic spectrum* (pp. 3–37). New York: Basic Books.

Miller, J. P. (1978). Piaget, Kohlberg, and Erikson: Developmental implications for secondary education. *Adolescence, 13,* 237–250.

Miller, L. L. et al. (1978). Marijuana: An analysis of storage and retrieval deficits in memory and the technique of restricted reminding. *Pharmacology, Biochemistry and Behavior, 8,* 327–332.

Miller, M. M., & Reeves, B. B. (1976). Children's occupational sex-role stereotypes: The linkage between television content and perception. *Journal of Broadcasting, 20,* 35–50.

Miller, N., & Maruyama, G. (1976). Ordinal position and peer popularity. *Journal of Personality and Social Psychology, 33,* 123–131.

Miller, W. B. (1958). Lower-class culture as a generating milieu of gang delinquency. *Journal of Social Issues, 14,* 5–19.

Mina, M., & Peterson, A. C. (in press). A meta-analysis of gender differences in spatial ability: Implications for mathematics and science achievement. In J. Hyde & M. C. Linn (Eds.), *The psychology of gender: Advances through meta-analysis.* Baltimore: John Hopkins University Press.

Minuchin, P. P., & Shapiro, E. K. (1983). The school as a context for social development. In P. H. Mussen (Ed.), *Handbook of child psychology* (Vol. 4, 4th ed.). New York: Wiley.

Minuchin, S. (1974). *Family and family therapy.* Cambridge, MA: Harvard University Press.

Mischel, W. (1961). Preference for delayed reinforcement and social responsibility. *Journal of Abnormal and Social Psychology, 62,* 1–7.

Mischel, W. (1968). *Personality and assessment.* New York: Wiley.

Mischel, W. (1970). Sex-typing and socialization. In P. H. Mussen (Ed.), *Carmichael's manual of child psychology* (Vol. 2). New York: John Wiley.

Mischel, W. (1973). Toward a cognitive social learning reconceptualization of personality. *Psychological Review, 80,* 252–283.

Mischel, W. (1974). Processes in delay of gratification. In L. Berkowitz (Ed.), *Advances in experimental social psychology* (Vol. 7). New York: Academic Press.

Mischel, W. (1976). *Introduction to personality* (2nd ed.). New York: Holt, Rinehart & Winston.

Mischel, W. (1983, August). *Convergences and challenges in the search for the person.* Invited address at the meeting of the American Psychological Association, Los Angeles.

Mischel, W. (1984). Convergences and challenges in the search for consistency. *American Psychologist, 39,* 351–364.

Mischel, W., & Baker, N. (1975). Cognitive transformations of reward objects through instructions. *Journal of Personality and Social Psychology, 31,* 254–261.

Mischel, W., Ebbesen, E. B., & Zeiss, A. R. (1972). Cognitive and attentional mechanisms in delay of gratification. *Journal of Personality and Social Psychology, 21,* 204–218.

Mischel, W., & Gilligan, C. (1964). Delay of gratification, motivation for the prohibited gratification, and responses to temptation. *Journal of Abnormal and Social Psychology, 69,* 411–417.

Mischel, W., & Mischel, H. (1976). A cognitive-social learning approach to morality and self-regulation. In T. Lickona (Ed.), *Moral development and behavior: Theory, research and social issues.* New York: Holt, Rinehart, & Winston.

Mischel, W., Peake, P. K., & Zeiss, A. R. (1984). *Longitudinal studies of delay behavior.* Unpublished manuscript, Stanford University.

Mitchell, M. H. (1978, January). Attitudes of adolescent girls toward vocational education: Final report. *Research in Education,* pp. 31–34.

Mitteness, L. S., & Nydegger, C. N. (1982, October). *Dimensions of parent-child relations in adulthood.* Paper presented at the meeting of the American Gerontological Association.

Mize, J. (1985, April). *Social skill training with preschool children: The effects of a cognitive-social learning approach.* Paper presented at the biennial meeting of the Society for Research in Child Development, Toronto.

Mizner, G. L., Barter, J. T., & Werme, P. H. (1970). Patterns of drug use among college students. *American Journal of Psychiatry, 127,* 15–24.

Money, J. (1965). Psychosexual differentiation. In J. Money (Ed.), *Sex research, new developments.* New York: Holt, Rinehart, & Winston.

Money, J. (1973). Biology = male/female destiny: A woman's view. *Contemporary Psychology, 18,* 603–604.

Montemayor, R. (1982a, October). *Parent-adolescent conflict: A critical review of the literature.* Paper presented at the first biennial conference on adolescent research, Tucson, AZ.

Montemayor, R. (1982b). The relationship between parent-adolescent conflict and the amount of time adolescents spend with parents, peers, and alone. *Child Development, 53,* 1512–1519.

Montemayor, R., & Eisen, M. (1977). The development of self-conceptions from childhood to adolescence. *Developmental Psychology, 13,* 314–319.

Montemayor, R., & Van Komen, R. (1985). The development of sex differences in friendships and peer group structure during adolescence. *Journal of Early Adolescence, 5,* 285–294.

Moore, D. (1985, April). *Parent-adolescent separation: The construction of adulthood by late adolescents.* Paper presented at the biennial meeting of the Society for Research in Child Development, Toronto.

Moos, R. H., & Moos, B. S. (1978). Classroom social climate and student absences and grades. *Journal of Educational Psychology, 70,* 263–269.

Morrison, D. M. (1985). Adolescent contraceptive behavior: a review. *Psychological Bulletin, 98,* 538–568.

Morrow, W. R., & Wilson, R. C. (1961). Family relations of bright, high-achieving and underachieving high school boys. *Child Development, 32,* 501–510.

Mosher, R., & Sprinthall, N. (1970). Psychological education in the secondary schools. *American Psychologist, 25,* 911–924.

Moshman, D. (1979). Development of formal hypothesis testing ability. *Developmental Psychology, 15,* 104–112.

Moss, J. J., & Gingles, R. (1959). The relationship of personality to the incidence of early marriage. *Marriage and Family Living, 21,* 372–377.

Murdock, G. (1949). *Social structure.* New York: MacMillan.

Murphy, L. B. (1973). *Social behavior and child personality.* New York: Columbia University Press.

Murray, D. M., & Perry, C. L. (1984, August). *The functional meaning of adolescent drug use.* Paper presented at the meeting of the American Psychological Association, Toronto.

Murray, F. B. (1978, August 31). *Generation of educational practice from developmental theory.* Invited address to the meeting of the American Psychological Association, Toronto.

Murray, H. A. (1938). *Explorations in personality.* New York: Oxford.

Murray, J. P., & Kippax, S. (1978, Winter). Children's social behavior in three towns with differing television experience. *Journal of Communication, 19*–29.

Musgrove, F. (1964). *Youth and social order.* Bloomington, IN: Indiana University Press.

Mussen, P. H. (1962). Some antecedents and consequences of masculine sex-typing in adolescent boys. *Psychological Monographs, 75*(1, Whole No. 506).

Mussen, P. H., Conger, J. J., & Kagan, J. (1974). *Child development and personality* (4th ed.). New York: Harper & Row.

Mussen, P. H., & Eisenberg-Berg, N. (1977). *Roots of caring, sharing, and helping.* San Francisco: W. H. Freeman.

Muuss, R. E. (1975). *Theories of adolescence* (2nd ed.). New York: Random House.

Nadel, C., & Schoeppe, A. (1973). Conservation of mass weight and volume as evidenced by adolescent girls in the eighth grade. *Journal of Genetic Psychology, 122,* 309–313.

Napier, A., & Whitaker, C. (1980). *The family crucible.* New York: Harper & Row.

National Assessment of Educational Progress. (1976). *Adult work skills and knowledge* (Report No. 35–COD–01). Denver, CO: Author.

National Education Association. (1974). *Today's changing roles: An approach to non-sexist teaching.* Minneapolis: Author.

National Highway Traffic Safety Administration. (1971). *The Alcohol Safety Countermeasures Program* (p. 2). Washington, DC: United States Government Printing Office.

National Institute of Alcohol Abuse and Alcoholism. (1974). *Facts about alcohol and alcoholism* (Department of Health, Education, and Welfare Publication No. [ADM] 75–31). Washington, DC: Department of Health, Education, and Welfare.

National Institute on Alcohol Abuse and Alcoholism. (1975). *A national study of adolescent drinking behavior, attitudes, and correlates.* Final report prepared by Research Triangle Institute, Research Triangle Park, North Carolina.

National Institute on Drug Abuse. (1980). *Review of the evidence on effects of marijuana use.* Washington, DC: United States Government Printing Office.

Neimark, E. D. (1982). Adolescent thought: Transition to formal operations. In B. B. Wolman (Ed.), *Handbook of developmental psychology.* Englewood Cliffs, NJ: Prentice-Hall.

Nesselroade, J. R., & Baltes, P. B. (1974). Adolescent personality development and historical change: 1970–1972. *Monographs of the Society for Research in Child Development, 39*(1, Serial No. 154).

Nesselroade, J. R., & Baltes, P. B. (1984). Sequential strategies and the role of cohort effects in behavioral development: Adolescent personality (1970–1972) as a sample case. In S. A. Mednick, M. Harway, & K. M. Finello (Eds.), *Handbook of longitudinal research.* New York: Praeger.

Nettleton, C. A., & Cline, D. W. (1975). Dating patterns, sexual relationships, and use of contraceptives of 700 unwed mothers during a two-year period following delivery. *Adolescence, 37,* 45–57.

Neugarten, B. L. (1980, February). Must everything be a mid-life crisis? *Prime Time.*

Neugarten, B. L., & Datan, N. (1973). Sociological perspectives on the life cycle. In P. B. Baltes & K. W. Schaie (Eds.), *Life-span developmental psychology.* New York: Academic Press.

Newcomb, A. F., & Bukowski, W. M. (1984). A longitudinal study of the utility of social preference and social impact sociometric classification schemes. *Child Development, 55,* 1434–1447.

Newcombe, N., Dubas, J. S., & Moore, M. A. (1985, April). *Associations of timing of puberty with spatial ability, lateralization and personality.* Paper presented at the biennial meeting of the Society for Research in Child Development, Toronto.

Newell, A., & Simon, H. A. (1972). *Human problem solving.* Englewood Cliffs, NJ: Prentice-Hall.

Newton, D. E. (1982). The status of programs in human sexuality: A preliminary study. *The High School Journal, 6,* 232–239.

Nichols, J. G. (1975). Causal attributions and other achievement-related cognitions: Effects of task outcomes, attainment values, and sex. *Journal of Personality and Social Psychology, 31,* 379–389.

Nichols, J. G. (1979). Quality and equality in intellectual development: The role of motivation in education. *American Psychologist, 34,* 1071–1084.

Nichols, J. G. (1984). Conceptions of ability and achievement motivation. In R. E. Ames & C. Ames (Eds.), *Motivation in education.* New York: Academic Press.

Nickerson, E. T. (1975). *Intervention strategies for modifying sex stereotypes.* Paper presented at the annual convention of school psychologists, Atlanta.

Nielson, A. C. (1976, November). *Nielson television index: National audience demographics report.* Northbrook, IL: A. C. Nielsen Co.

Noeth, R. J., Engen, H. B., & Noeth, P. E. (1984). Making career decisions: A self-report of factors that help high school students. *Vocational Guidance Quarterly, 32,* 240–248.

Nottelman, E. D. (1982). *The interaction of physical maturity and school transition*. Paper presented at the meeting of the American Educational Research Association, New York, NY.

Nottelmann, E. D., Susman, E. J., Blue, J. H., Inoff-Germain, G., Dorn, L. D., Loriaux, D. L., Cutler, G. B., & Chrousos, G. P. (in press). Gonadal and adrenal hormone correlates of adjustment in early adolescence. In R. M. Lerner & T. T. Foch (Eds.), *Biological-psychosocial interactions in early adolescence: A life-span perspective*. Hillsdale, NJ: Erlbaum.

Nottelmann, E. D., Susman, E. J., Inoff, G. E., Dorn, L. D., Cutler, G. B., Loriaux, D. L., & Chrousos, G. P. (1985, May). *Hormone level and adjustment and behavior during early adolescence*. Paper presented at the annual meeting of the American Association for the Advancement of Science, Los Angeles, CA.

Nowlis, H. H. (1976). Strategies for prevention. *Contemporary Drug Problems, 5,* 5–20.

Nucci, L. (1982). Conceptual development in the moral and conventional domains: Implications for values education. *Review of Educational Research, 52,* 93–122.

Nucci, L. (in press). Teaching children right from wrong: Education and the development of children's moral and conventional concepts. *Teacher Education Quarterly.*

Nucci, L., & Nucci, M. (1982). Children's responses to moral and social conventional transgressions in free-play settings. *Child Development, 53,* 1337–1342.

Nucci, L., & Turiel, E. (1978). Social interactions and the development of social concepts in preschool children. *Child Development, 49,* 400–407.

Nutrition National Canada Survey. (1973). Toronto, Canada: Canadian Goverment Publications.

Nydegger, C. N. (1975, October). *Age and parental behavior.* Paper presented at the meeting of the Gerontological Society of America, Louisville, KY.

Nydegger, C. N. (1981, October). *The ripple effect of parental timing.* Paper presented at the meeting of the American Gerontological Association.

O'Keefe, E. S. C., & Hyde, J. S. (1983). The development of occupational sex-role stereotypes: The effects of gender stability and age. *Sex Roles, 9,* 481–492.

O'Malley, P. M., Bachman, J. G., & Johnston, J. (1977). Youth in transition. Final report of *Five years beyond high school: Causes and consequences of educational attainment.* Ann Arbor, MI: Institute for Social Research at the University of Michigan.

Oden, S. L., & Asher, S. R. (1975, April). *Coaching children in social skills for friendship making.* Paper presented at the biennial meeting of the Society for Research in Child Development, Denver, CO.

Offer, D. (1969). *The psychological world of the teenager.* New York: Basic Books.

Office of Drug Abuse Policy. (1978). Report prepared by the White House Committee on Drug Abuse for the President.

Okun, M. A., & Sasfy, J. H. (1977). Adolescence, the self-concept, and formal operations. *Adolescence, 12,* 373–379.

Olds, D. E., & Shaver, P. (1980). Masculinity, femininity, academic performance, and health: Further evidence concerning the androgyny controversy. *Journal of Personality, 48,* 323–341.

Oliver, L. (1974). Women in aprons. The female stereotype in children's readers. *Elementary School Journal, 74,* 253–259.

Olson, D. R. (1977). From utterance to text: The bias of language in speech and writing. *Harvard Educational Review, 47,* 257–281.

Opler, M. E. (1972). Cause and effect in Apachean agriculture division of labor, residence patterns, and girls' puberty rites. *American Anthropologist, 74,* 1133–1146.

Oppenheimer, M. (1982, October). What you should know about herpes. *Seventeen Magazine,* pp. 154–155, 170.

Orlofsky, J. (1976). Intimacy status: Relationship to interpersonal perception. *Journal of Youth and Adolescence, 5,* 73–88.

Orlofsky, J., Marcia, J., & Lesser, I. (1973). Ego identity status and the intimacy vs. isolation crisis of young adulthood. *Journal of Personality and Social Psychology, 27,* 211–219.

Oskamp, S., & Mindick, B. (1981). Personality and attitudinal barriers to contraception. In D. Byrne & W. A. Fisher (Eds.), *Adolescents, sex, and contraception.* New York: McGraw-Hill.

Overton, W. F., & Meehan, A. M. (1982). Individual differences in formal-operational thought: Sex roles and learned helplessness. *Child Development, 53,* 1536–1543.

Owen, S. V., Froman, R. D., & Moscow, H. (1981). *Educational psychology.* Boston: Little, Brown.

Papalia, D. E., & Tennett, S. S. (1975). Vocational aspirations in preschoolers: A manifestation of early sex-role stereotyping. *Sex Roles, 1,* 197–199.

Parke, R. D., Power, T. G., & Fisher, T. (1980). The adolescent father's impact on the mother and child. *Journal of Social Issues, 36,* 88–106.

Pascual-Leone, J. (1977). *Constructive cognition and substance conservation: Toward adequate structural models of the human subject.* Unpublished manuscript, University of Toronto.

Paskal, D., & Miller, W. C. (1973). Can options work in smaller school districts? *NASSP Bulletin, 57,* 47–54.

Patterson, G. R. (1982). *Coercive family process.* Eugene, OR: Castalia.

Patterson, G. R., Reid, J. B., Jones, R. R., & Conger, R. (1975). *A social learning approach to family intervention: Parent training* (Vol. 1). Eugene, OR: Castalia.

Patterson, G. R., & Stouthamer-Loeber, M. (1984). The correlation of family management practices and delinquency. *Child Development, 55,* 1299–1307.

Pearce, J., & Garrett, H. D. (1970). A comparison of the drinking behavior of delinquent youth versus nondelinquent youth in the states of Idaho and Utah. *Journal of School Health, 40,* 131–135.

Peevers, B. H., & Secord, P. F. (1973). Developmental changes in attribution of descriptive concepts to persons. *Journal of Personality and Social Psychology, 27,* 120–128.

Perloff, R. M., Brown, J. D., & Miller, M. M. (1972, August). *Mass media and sex-typing: Research perspectives and policy implications.* Paper presented at the meeting of the American Psychological Association, Toronto.

Perry, C. (1982). Adolescent health: An educational-ecological perspective. In T. J. Coates, A. C. Peterson, & C. Perry (Eds.), *Promoting adolescent health* (pp. 73–86). New York: Academic Press.

Peskin, H. (1967). Pubertal onset and ego functioning. *Journal of Abnormal Psychology, 72,* 1–15.

Peskin, H., & Livson, M. (1972). Pre- and postpubertal personality and adult psychological functioning. *Seminars in Psychiatry, 4,* 343–353.

Peterson, A. C. (1979, January). Can puberty come any faster? *Psychology Today,* pp. 45–56.

Peterson, A. C. (1985, April). *Change in cognition during early adolescence.* Paper presented at the biennial meeting of the Society for Research in Child Development, Toronto.

Peterson, A. C., Schulenberg, J. E., Abramowitz, R. H., Offer, D., & Jarcho, H. D. (1984). A self-image questionnaire for young adolescents (SIQYA): Reliability and validity studies. *Journal of Youth and Adolescence, 13.*

Peterson, A. C., & Taylor, B. (1980). The biological approach to adolescence: Biological change and psychological adaptation. In J. Adelson (Ed.), *Handbook of adolescent psychology.* New York: John Wiley.

Peterson, P. L. (1977). Interactive effects of student anxiety, achievement orientation, and teacher behavior on student achievement and attitude. *Journal of Educational Psychology, 69,* 779–792.

Peterson, R. E., & Bilorusky, J. A. (1971). *May, 1970: The campus aftermath of Cambodia and Kent State.* Berkeley, CA: Carnegie Commission on Higher Education.

Phares, E. J. (1976). *Locus of control in personality.* Morristown, NJ: General Learning Press.

Phares, E. J., & Lamiell, J. T. (1975). Internal-external control, interpersonal judgments of others in need, and attribution of responsibility. *Journal of Personality, 43,* 23–28.

Philliber, S. G., & Graham, E. H. (1981). The impact of age of mother on mother-child interaction patterns. *Journal of Marriage and the Family, 43,* 109–115.

Phillips, E. L. (1968). Achievement place: Token reinforcement procedures in a home-style rehabilitation setting for predelinquent boys. *Journal of Applied Behavioral Analysis, 1,* 213–223.

Piaget, J. (1932). *The moral judgment of the child.* New York: Harcourt.

Piaget, J. (1952). Jean Piaget. In C. A. Murchison (Ed.), *A history of psychology in autobiography* (Vol. 4). Worcester, MA: Clark University Press.

Piaget, J. (1952). *The origins of intelligence in children.* New York: International Universities Press.

Piaget, J. (1954). *The construction of reality in the child.* New York: Basic Books.

Piaget, J. (1967). The mental development of the child. In D. Elkind (Ed.), *Six psychological studies by Piaget.* New York: Random House.

Piaget, J. (1970). Piaget's theory. In P. H. Mussen (Ed.), *Carmichael's manual of child psychology* (Vol. 1, 3rd ed.). New York: John Wiley.

Piaget, J. (1972). Intellectual evolution from adolescence to adulthood. *Human Development, 15,* 1–12.

Piers, E. V., & Harris, D. B. (1964). Age and other correlates of self-concept in children. *Journal of Educational Psychology, 55,* 91–95.

Plato. (1968). [Plato's republic] (B. Jowett, Trans.). Bridgeport, CT: Airmont.

Pleck, J. (1975). Masculinity-femininity: Current and alternative paradigms. *Sex Roles, 1,* 161–178.

Porteus, A. (1976). *Teacher-centered vs. student-centered instruction: Interactions with cognitive and motivational aptitudes.* Unpublished doctoral dissertation, Stanford University.

Posner, M. (1970). Abstraction and the process of recognition. In J. T. Spence & G. M. Bower (Eds.), *The psychology of learning and motivation* (Vol. 3). New York: Academic Press.

Pottker, J., & Fishel, A. (1977). *Sex bias in the schools: the research evidence.* Cranbury, NJ: Associated University Presses.

Power, C. (1979). *The moral atmosphere of a just community high school: A four-year longitudinal study.* Unpublished doctoral dissertation, Harvard University.

Power, C. (1984). *Moral atmosphere.* Paper presented at the meeting of the American Educational Research Association, New Orleans.

Prendergast, T. J., & Schaefer, E. S. (1974). Correlates of drinking and drunkenness among high school students. *Quarterly Journal of Studies on Alcohol, 35,* 232–242.

President's Commission on Campus Unrest. (1970). *The report of the president's commission on campus unrest.* Washington, DC: U.S. Government Printing Office.

Pritscher, C. M. G. (1980). *A study of choices, expectancy and attribution patterns of psychologically androgynous and sex role congruent females and males.* Unpublished doctoral dissertation, University of Toledo. (University Microfilms No. 8110598).

Psathas, G. (1957). Ethnicity, social class, and adolescent independence. *Sociological Review, 22,* 415–523.

Quadagno, D. M., Briscoe, R., & Quadagno, J. S. (1977). Effect of perinatal gonadal hormones on selected nonsexual behavioral patterns: A critical assessment of the nonhuman and human literature. *Psychological Bulletin, 84,* 62–80.

Ragozin, A. S., Basham, R. B., Crnic, K. A., Greenberg, M. T., & Robinson, N. M. (1982). Effects of maternal age on parenting role. *Developmental Psychology, 18,* 627–634.

Rand, L. M., & Miller, A. L. (1972). A developmental cross-sectioning of women's careers and marriage attitudes and life plans. *Journal of Vocational Behavior, 2,* 317–331.

Randall, D., & Wong, M. R. (1976). Drug education to date: A review. *Journal of Drug Education, 60,* 1–21.

Raven, J. C. (1960). *Guide to using the Standard Progressive Matrices.* London: Lewis.

Rebecca, M., Hefner, R., & Oleshansky, B. (1976). A model of sex role transcendence. *Journal of Social Issues, 32,* 197–206.

Rehm, L., & Marston, R. (1968). Reduction of anxiety through modification of self-reinforcement: An instigation therapy technique. *Journal of Consulting and Clinical Psychology,* 556–574.

Reinisch, J. M., & Karow, W. G. (1977). Prenatal exposure to synthetic progestins and estrogens: Effects on human development. *Archives of Sexual Behavior, 6,* 257–288.

Rekers, G. A. (1979). Psychosexual and gender problems. In E. J. Mach & L. G. Terdal (Eds.), *Behavioral assessment of childhood disorders.* New York: Guilford Press.

Renner, J. W., Stafford, D., Lawson, A., McKinnon, J., Friot, F., & Kellog, D. (1976). *Research, teaching, and learning with the Piaget model.* Norman, OK: University of Oklahoma Press.

Resnick, H. L. P. (1980). Suicide. In H. I. Kaplan, A. M. Freedman, & B. J. Sadock (Eds.), *Comprehensive textbook of psychiatry* (Vol. 2). Baltimore: Williams and Wilkins.

Rest, J. R. (1976). New approaches in the assessment of moral judgment. In T. Lickona (Ed.), *Moral development and behavior.* New York: Holt, Rinehart, & Winston.

Rest, J. R. (1977, March). *Development in judging moral issues—a summary of research using the defining issues test.* Paper presented at the biennial meeting of the Society for Research in Child Development, New Orleans.

Rest, J. R. (1983). Morality. In P. H. Mussen (Ed.), *Handbook of child psychology* (Vol. 3, 4th ed.). New York: Wiley.

Rest, J., Turiel, E., & Kohlberg, L. (1969). Relations between level of moral judgment and preference and comprehension of the moral judgments of others. *Journal of Personality, 37,* 225–252.

Revelle, Honey, M., Amsel, E., Schauble, & Levine, G. (1984). *Sex differences in the use of computers.* Paper presented at the annual meeting of the American Educational Research Association, New Orleans.

Reynolds, D., Jones, D., St. Leger, S., & Murgatroyd, S. (1980). School factors and truancy. In L. Hersov & I. Berg (Eds.), *Out of school: Modern perspectives in truancy and school refusal.* New York: John Wiley.

Reynolds, L. G., & Shister, J. (1949). *Job horizons.* New York: Harper.

Rholes, W. S., & Ruble, D. N. (1984). Children's understanding of dispositional characteristics of others. *Child Development, 55,* 550–560.

Richards, R. A. (1976). A comparison of selected Guilford and Wallach-Kogan creativity thinking tests in conjunction with measures of intelligence. *Journal of Creative Behavior, 10,* 154–164.

Riester, A. E., & Zucker, R. H. (1968). Adolescent social structure and drinking behavior. *Personnel and Guidance Journal, 46,* 304–312.

Rindfuss, R. R., & Bumpass, L. L. (1978). Age and the sociology of fertility: How old is too old? In K. E. Taeuber, L. L. Bumpass, & J. A. Sweet (Eds.), *Social demography.* New York: Academic Press.

Rist, R. C. (Ed.). (1979). *Desegregated schools: Appraisals of an American experiment.* New York: Academic Press.

Robins, L. (1972). Follow-up studies of behavior disorders in children. In H. Quay & J. Werry (Eds.), *Psychopathological disorders of childhood.* New York: Wiley.

Robins, L. N. (1978). Sturdy childhood predictors of adult antisocial behavior: Replications from longitudinal studies. *Psychological Medicine, 8,* 611–622.

Rodman, H., Pratto, D., & Nelson, R. (1985). Child care arrangements and children's functioning. A comparison of self-care and adult-care children. *Developmental Psychology, 21,* 413–418.

Roff, M., Sells, S. B., & Golden, M. (1972). *Social adjustment and personality development in children.* Minneapolis, MN: University of Minnesota Press.

Rogers, C. (1969). *Client-centered therapy* (2nd ed.). Boston: Houghton Mifflin.

Rogers, C. R. (1961). *On becoming a person.* Boston: Houghton Mifflin.

Rogers, T. (1981). A model of the self as an aspect of the human information processing system. In N. Cantor & J. Kihlstrom (Eds.), *Cognition, social interaction, and personality.* Hillsdale, NJ: Erlbaum.

Rogers, T., Kuiper, N., & Kirker, W. (1977). Self-reference and the encoding of personal information. *Journal of Personality and Social Psychology, 35,* 677–688.

Rokeach, M. (1973). *The nature of human values.* New York: Free Press.

Romer, N. (1975). The motive to avoid success has its effects on performance in school-aged males and females. *Developmental Psychology, 11,* 689–699.

Rose, S. E., & Duer, W. F. (1978). Drug/alcohol education: A new approach for schools. *Education, 99,* 198–202.

Rosen, B. C. (1959). Race, ethnicity, and the achievement syndrome. *American Sociological Review, 24,* 47–60.

Rosenbaum, A. (1983). *The young people's yellow pages: A national sourcebook for youth.* New York: Putnam.

Rosenberg, M. (1965). *Society and the adolescent self-image.* Princeton, NJ: Princeton University Press.

Rosenberg, M., & Simmons, R. G. (1971). *Black and white self-esteem: The urban school child.* Washington, DC: Rose Monograph Series, American Sociological Association.

Rosenkrans, M. A. (1967). Imitation in children as a function of perceived similarity to a social model and vicarious reinforcement. *Journal of Personality and Social Psychology, 7,* 307–315.

Ross, A. O. (1979). *Psychological disorders of children* (2nd ed.). New York: McGraw-Hill.

Ross, D. G. (1972). *G. Stanley Hall: The psychologist as prophet.* Chicago: University of Chicago Press.

Rotenberg, K. J. (1980). Children's use of intentionality in judgments of character and disposition. *Child Development, 51,* 282–284.

Rousseau, J. J. (1962). *The Emile of Jean Jacques Rousseau* (W. Boyd, Ed. and Trans.) New York: Teachers College Press, Columbia University. (Original work published 1762)

Rousseau, J. J. (1969). *Emile.* London: Dent-Everyman's.

Rovet, J., Netley, C., & Dewan, V. (1985, April). *Atypical pubertal onset and spatial cognitive functioning.* Paper presented at the biennial meeting of the Society for Research in Child Development, Toronto.

Rowe, D. C. (1981). A biometrical analysis of perceptions of family environment: A study of twin and singleton sibling kinships. *Child Development, 54,* 416–423.

Rubin, A. M. (1977). Television usage, attitudes, and viewing behaviors of children and adolescents. *Journal of Communication, 21,* 355–369.

Rubin, K. H. (1973). Egocentrism in childhood: A unitary construct? *Child Development, 44,* 102–110.

Rubin, Z., & Sloman, J. (1984). How parents influence their children's friendships. In M. Lewis (Ed.), *Beyond the dyad.* New York: Plenum.

Rushnell, S. (1982). Specials and miniseries. In M. Schwarz (Ed.), *TV and teens.* Reading, MA: Addison-Wesley.

Russell, C. (1980, March 27). Marijuana: New abuses, new uses. *Washington Star,* pp. A–1, A–6.

Rutter, M. (1971). Parent-child separation: Psychological effects on the children. *Journal of Child Psychology and Psychiatry, 12,* 233–256.

Rutter, M. (1980). *Scientific foundations of developmental psychiatry.* London: Heinemann.

Rutter, M. (1983, April). *Influences from family and school.* Invited address presented at the biennial meeting of the Society for Research in Child Development, Detroit.

Rutter, M., & Garmezy, N. (1983). Developmental psychopathology. In P. H. Mussen (Ed.), *Handbook of child psychology* (Vol. 4, 4th ed.). New York: Wiley.

Rutter, M., Maughan, B., Mortimore, P., & Ouston, J. (1979). *Fifteen thousand hours: Secondary schools and their effects on children.* Cambridge, MA: Harvard University Press.

Rutter, M., Tizrd, J., & Whitmore, K. (1970). *Education, health, and behavior.* New York: Wiley.

Saario, T. N., Jacklin, C. N., Tittle, C. K. (1973). Sex-role stereotyping in the public schools. *Harvard Educational Review, 43,* 386–416.

Sandler, H. M., Vietze, P. M., & O'Conner, S. (1976). *Obstetric and neonatal outcomes following intervention with pregnant teenagers.* Unpublished manuscript, Vanderbilt University.

Santrock, J. W. (1970). Paternal absence, sex-typing, and identification. *Developmental Psychology, 2,* 262–274.

Santrock, J. W. (1972). The relation of onset and type of father absence to cognitive development. *Child Development, 43,* 455–469.

Santrock, J. W. (1986). *Psychology: The science of mind and behavior.* Dubuque, IA: William C. Brown Publishers.

Santrock, J. W., & Bartlett, J. C. (1986). *Developmental psychology.* Dubuque, IA: William C. Brown Publishers.

Santrock, J. W., Carson, D., & Madison, T. (1986). *The effects of family relationships on the adolescent's development.* Unpublished manuscript, University of Texas at Dallas, Richardson, TX.

Santrock, J. W., & Madison, T. D. (1985). Three research traditions in the study of adolescents in divorced families: Quasi-experimental, developmental; clinical; and family sociological. *Journal of Early Adolescence, 5,* 115–128.

Santrock, J. W., Readdick, C. R., & Pollard, L. (1980). Social comparison processes in sibling and peer relations. *Journal of Genetic Psychology, 137,* 91–107.

Santrock, J. W., & Sitterle, K. (1985). The developmental world of children in divorced families: Research findings and clinical implications. In D. C. Goldberg (Ed.), *Contemporary marriage.* Homewood, IL: Dorsey Press.

Santrock, J. W., Sitterle, K. A., & Warshak, R. A. (1986). Parent-child relationships in stepfather families. In P. Bronstein & C. P. Cowan (Eds.), *Fatherhood today: Men's changing role in the family.* New York: Wiley.

Santrock, J. W., & Warshak, R. A. (1979). Father custody and social development in boys and girls. *Journal of Social Issues, 35,* 112–135.

Santrock, J. W., & Warshak, R. A. (1986). Development, relationships, and legal/clinical considerations in father-custody families. In M. E. Lamb (Ed.), *The father's role: Applied perspectives.* New York: Wiley.

Santrock, J. W., Warshak, R. A., Sitterle, K. A., Dozier, C., & Stephens, M. (1985, August). *The social development of children in stepparent families.* Paper presented at the meeting of the American Psychological Association, Los Angeles.

Santrock, J. W., & Yussen, S. R. (1987). *Child development* (3rd ed.). Dubuque, IA: William C. Brown Publishers.

Sarason, I., & Spielberger, C. D. (Eds.). (1975). *Stress and anxiety.* Washington, DC: Hemisphere.

Savin-Williams, R. C., & Demo, D. H. (1983). Conceiving or misconceiving the self: Issues in adolescent self-esteem. *Journal of Early Adolescence, 3,* 121–140.

Scardamalia, M., Bereiter, C., & Goelman, H. (1982). The role of production factors in writing ability. In M. Nystrand (Ed.), *What writers know: The language, process, and structure of written discourse.* New York: Academic Press.

Scarr, S. (1984, May). [Interview]. *Psychology Today,* pp. 59–63.

Scarr, S., & Kidd, K. K. (1983). Developmental behavior genetics. In P. H. Mussen (Ed.), *Handbook of child psychology* (Vol. 4, 4th ed.). New York: Wiley.

Scarr, S., & Weinberg, R. A. (1980). Calling all camps! The war is over. *American Sociological Review, 45,* 859–865.

Schachter, S. (1959.) *The psychology of affiliation.* Stanford, CA: Stanford University Press.

Schachter, S. (1963). Birth order, emminence, and higher education. *American Sociological Review, 28,* 757–767.

Schaie, K. W. (1965). A general model for the study of developmental problems. *Psychological Bulletin, 64,* 92–107.

Schaie, K. W. (1977). Quasi-experimental research designs in the psychology of aging. In J. E. Birren & K. W. Schaie (Eds.), *Handbook of the psychology of aging.* New York: Van Nostrand, Reinhold.

Schechter, M. D. (1974). Psychiatric aspects of learning disabilities. *Child Psychiatry and Human Development, 5,* 67–77.

Scheff, T. J. (1966). *Being mentally ill: A sociological theory.* Chicago: Aldine.

Schiff, A. R., & Knopf, I. J. (1985). The effects of task demands on attention allocation in children of different ages. *Child Development, 56,* 621–630.

Schinke, S. P., & Gilchrist, L. D. (1985). Preventive substance abuse with children and adolescents. *Journal of Consulting and Clinical Psychology, 53,* 596–602.

Schmiedeck, R. A. (1979). Adolescent identity formation and the organizational structure of high schools. *Adolescence, 14,* 191–196.

Schneider, A. J. (1966). *Measurement of courtship progress of high school upperclassmen currently going steady.* Unpublished dissertation, Pennsylvania State University.

Schofield, A. T., & Vaughan-Jackson, P. (1913). *What a boy should know.* New York: Cassell.

Schunk, D. H. (1983). Developing children's self-efficacy and skills: The roles of social comparative information and goal setting. *Contemporary Educational Psychology, 8,* 76–86.

Scott, K. P., & Feldman-Summers, S. (1979). Children's reactions to textbook stories in which females are portrayed in traditionally male roles. *Journal of Educational Psychology, 71,* 396–402.

Sears, P. S., & Barbee, A. H. (1975, November). *Career and life satisfaction among Terman's gifted women.* Paper presented at the Terman Memorial Symposium on Intellectual Talent, Johns Hopkins University, Baltimore.

Sears, R. R. (1977). Sources of life satisfactions of the Terman gifted men. *American Psychologist, 32,* 119–128.

Select Committee on Children, U.S. House of Representatives. (1983). *U.S. Children and Their Families,* 98th Congress, 1st session. Washington, DC: Author.

Seligman, M. E. P. (1975). *Helplessness: On depression, development, and death.* San Francisco: W. H. Freeman.

Selman, L. (1980). *The growth of interpersonal understanding.* New York: Academic Press.

Selman, R. L. (1971a). The relation of role-taking ability to the development of moral judgment in children. *Child Development, 42,* 79–91.

Selman, R. L. (1971b). Taking another's perspective: Role-taking development in early childhood. *Child Development, 42,* 1721–1732.

Selman, R. L. (1976). Social-cognitive understanding. In T. Lickona (Ed.), *Moral development and behavior.* New York: Holt, Rinehart, & Winston.

Selman, R. L. (1976a). The development of social-cognitive understanding: A guide to educational and clinical practice. In T. Lickona (Ed.) *Morality: Theory, research, and social issues.* New York: Holt, Rinehart, & Winston.

Selman, R. L. (1976b). Toward a structural analysis of developing interpersonal relations concepts: Research with normal and disturbed preadolescent boys. In A. D. Pick (Ed.), *Minnesota Symposium on Child Psychology* (Vol. 10, pp. 156–200). Minneapolis: University of Minnesota Press.

Selman, R. L. (1980). *The growth of interpersonal understanding.* New York: Academic Press.

Selman, R. L., & Byrne, D. F. (1974). *A structural-development analysis of levels of role taking in middle childhood. Child Development, 45,* 803–806.

Selman, R. L., Newberger, C. M., & Jaquette, D. (1977, April). *Observing interpersonal reasoning in a clinic/educational setting: Toward the integration of developmental and clinical child psychology.* Paper presented at the meeting of the Society for Research in Child Development, New Orleans.

Seltzer, S. (1976). Changing adolescent values as the lyrics of popular music. *Adolescence, 11,* 419–429.

Serafica, F. C., & Blyth, D. A. (1985). Continuities and changes in the study of friendship and peer groups during early adolescence. *Journal of Early Adolescence, 3,* 267–283.

Sexton, M. A., & Feffen, G. (1979). Development of three strategies of attention in dichotic listening. *Developmental Psychology, 15,* 299–310.

Shafer, R. P., et al. (1973). *Drug use in America: Problem in perspective* (Second report of the National Commission on Marijuana and Drug Abuse, No. 5266–00003). Washington, DC: U.S. Government Printing Office.

Shalom, Inc. (1980). *Manual of primary prevention and early intervention programs.* Philadelphia: Shalom.

Shantz, C. (1983). The development of social cognition. In P. H. Mussen (Ed.), *Handbook of child psychology* (Vol. 3., 4th ed.). New York: Wiley.

Shantz, C. (1983). Social cognition. In P. H. Mussen (Ed.), *Handbook of child psychology* (Vol. 3, 4th ed.). New York: Wiley.

Shapira, A., & Madsen, M. C. (1969). Cooperative and competitive behavior of kibbutz and urban children of Israel. *Child Development, 40,* 605–619.

Sharabany, R., Gershoni, R., & Hofman, J. E. (1981). Girlfriend, boyfriend: Age and sex differences in intimate friendship. *Developmental Psychology, 17,* 800–808.

Sharan, S. (1980). Cooperative learning in small groups: Recent methods and effects on achievement, attitudes, and ethnic relations. *Review of Educational Research, 50,* 241–271.

Sharpe, L. W. (1976). The effects of a creative thinking program on intermediate-grade educationally handicapped children. *Journal of Creative Behavior, 10*(2), 138–145.

Sher, K. J., & Levenson, R. W. (1982). Risk for alcoholism and individual differences in the stress-response-dampening effect of alcohol. *Journal of Abnormal Psychology, 91,* 350–367.

Sherif, M., Harvey, O. J., White, B. J., Hood, W. R., & Sherif, C. W. (1961). *Intergroup conflict and cooperation: The Robber's Cave experiment.* Norman, OK: Institute of Group Relations, University of Oklahoma.

Sherif, M., & Sherif, C. W. (1964). *Reference groups: Exploration into conformity and deviation of adolescents.* New York: Harper.

Shirreffs, J. (1975). Sex-role stereotyping in elementary school health education textbooks. *Journal of School Health, 45,* 519–529.

Shostrum, E. (1967). *Man, the manipulator.* New York: Bantam Books.

Siegler, R. (1983). Information processing approaches to development. In P. H. Mussen (Ed.), *Handbook of child psychology* (Vol. 3, 4th ed.). New York: Wiley.

Siegler, R. S., Liebert, D. C., & Liebert, R. M. (1973). Inhelder and Piaget's pendulum problem: Teaching preadolescents to act as scientists. *Developmental Psychology, 9,* 97–101.

Silberman, C. E. (1970). *Crisis in the classroom: The remaking of American education.* New York: Random House.

Silvern, L. E., & Ryan, V. L. (1979). Self-rated adjustment and sex-typing on the Bem Sex-Role Inventory: Is masculinity the primary indicator of adjustment? *Sex Roles, 5,* 739–763.

Simmons, R. G., Brown, L., Bush, D. M., & Blyth, D. A. (1978). Self-esteem and achievement of black and white adolescents. *Social Problems, 26,* 86–96.

Simmons, R. G., Rosenberg, F., & Rosenberg, M. (1973). Disturbance in the self-image at adolescence. *American Sociological Review, 38,* 553–568.

Simon, W., & Gagnon, J. H. (1969). On psychosexual development. In D. Goslin (Ed.), *Handbook of socialization theory and research.* Chicago: Rand McNally.

Simpson, E. (1976). A holistic approach to moral development and behavior. In T. Lickona (Ed.), *Moral development and behavior.* New York: Holt, Rinehart, & Winston.

Simpson, R. L. (1962). Parental influence, anticipatory socialization, and social mobility. *American Sociological Review, 27,* 517–522.

Single, E., Kandel, D., & Faust, R. (1974). Patterns of multiple drug use in high school. *Journal of Health and Social Behavior, 15,* 344–357.

Sizer, T. R. (1984). *Horace's compromise: The dilemma of the American high school today.* Boston: Houghton-Mifflin.

Skinner, B. F. (1948). *Walden two.* New York: MacMillan.

Skinner, B. F. (1953). *Science and human behavior.* New York: MacMillan.

Skinner, B. F. (1967). B. F. Skinner. In E. G. Boring & G. Lindzey (Eds.), *A history of psychology in autobiography.* New York: Appleton-Century-Crofts.

Skinner, B. F. (1971). *Beyond freedom and dignity.* New York: Knopf.

Skinner, B. F. (1974). *About behaviorism.* New York: Knopf.

Skipper, J. K., & Nass, G. (1966). Dating behavior. A framework for analysis and an illustration. *Journal of Marriage and the Family, 28,* 412–420.

Slavin, R. E. (1980). Cooperative learning. *Review of Educational Research, 50,* 315–342.

Smetana, J. (1983). Social-cognitive development: Domain distinctions and coordinations. *Developmental Review, 3,* 131–147.

Smetana, J. (1985). Preschool children's conceptions of transgressions: Effects of varying moral and conventional domain-related attributes. *Developmental Psychology, 21,* 18–29.

Smith, B. O., & Orlosky, D. E. (1975). *Socialization and schooling (basics of reform).* Bloomington, IN: Phi Delta Kappa.

Smith, D. F. (1980). Adolescent suicide. In R. E. Muuss (Ed.), *Adolescent behavior and society* (3rd ed.). New York: Random House.

Smock, C. D. (1975). *Piaget and project follow through.* Lecture given at the University of Georgia.

Snow, R. E. (1977). Individual differences and instructional theory. *Educational Researcher, 6,* 11–15.

Solomon, R. W., & Wahler, R. G. (1973). Peer reinforcement control of classroom problem behavior. *Journal of Applied Behavior Analysis, 6,* 49–56.

Sommer, B. B. (1978). *Puberty and adolescence.* New York: Oxford University Press.

Sorensen, R. C. (1973). *Adolescent sexuality in contemporary America.* New York: World.

Spearman, C. E. (1927). *The abilities of man.* New York: MacMillan.

Spence, J. T., & Helmreich, R. (1972). The Attitudes toward Women Scale: An objective instrument to measure attitudes toward the rights and roles of women in contemporary society. *JSAS Catalog of Selected Documents in Psychology, 2,* 66.

Spence, J. T., Helmreich, R., & Stapp, J. (1973). A short version of the Attitudes toward Women Scale (AWS). *Bulletin of the Psychonomic Society, 2,* 219–220.

Spence, J. T., Helmreich, R., & Stapp, J. (1974). The Personal Attributes Questionnaire: A measure of sex-role stereotypes and masculinity-femininity. *JSAS Catalog of Selected Documents in Psychology, 4,* 127.

Spielberger, C. D. (1966). The effects of anxiety on complex learning and academic achievement. In C. D. Spielberger (Ed.), *Anxiety and behavior.* New York: Academic Press.

Spielberger, C. D., Gorsuch, R. L., & Lushene, R. E. (1970). *Manual for the state-trait anxiety inventory.* Palo Alto, CA: Consulting Psychologists Press.

Spivack, G., Platt, J. J., & Shure, M. B. (1976). *The problem-solving approach to adjustment.* San Francisco: Jossey-Bass.

Springer, C., & Wallerstein, J. S. (1983). Young adolescents' responses to their parents' divorce. *New directions for child development.* San Francisco: Jossey-Bass.

Sroufe, L. A., & Fleeson, J. (1985). Attachment and the construction of relationships. In W. W. Hartup & Z. Rubin (Eds.), *Relationships and development.* Hillsdale, NJ: Erlbaum.

Sroufe, A. L., & Rutter, M. (1984). The domain of developmental psychopathology. *Child Development, 55,* 17–29.

Stainback, R. D., & Rogers, R. W. (1983). Identifying effective components of alcohol abuse prevention programs. *International Journal of the Addictions, 18,* 393–405.

Stanley, J. C. (1977). Rationale of the study of mathematically precocious youth (SMPY) during its first five years of promoting educational acceleration. In J. C. Stanley, W. C. George, & C. H. Solano, (Eds.), *The gifted and creative: A fifty-year perspective.* Baltimore: The Johns Hopkins University Press.

Staples, I. E. (1977). Affecting disaffected students: The Philadelphia story. *Educational Leadership, 34,* 422–428.

Stedman, L., & Smith, M. (1983). Recent reform proposals for American education. *Contemporary Education Review, 2,* 85–104.

Stein, A. H., & Bailey, M. M. (1973). The socialization of achievement orientation in females. *Psychological Bulletin, 80,* 345–365.

Stein, M. (Ed.). (1972). *Changing sexist practices in the classroom.* Washington, DC: American Federation of Teachers.

Steinberg, L. (1986). Latchkey children and susceptibility to peer pressure: An ecological analysis. *Developmental Psychology, 22,* 433–439.

Steinberg, L. D. (1980). *Understanding families with young adolescents.* Carrboro, NC: Center for Early Adolescence.

Steinberg, L. D. (1981). Transformations in family relations at puberty. *Developmental Psychology, 17,* 833–840.

Steinberg, L. D. (1982). Jumping off the work experience bandwagon. *Journal of Youth and Adolescence, 11,* 183–205.

Steinberg, L. D., & Hill, J. P. (1978). Patterns of family interaction as a function of age, the onset of puberty, and formal thinking. *Developmental Psychology, 14,* 683–684.

Stephan, W. G., & Feagin, J. R. (1980). *School desegregation: Past, present, and future.* New York: Plenum.

Stephan, W. G., & Rosenfield, D. (1978a). Effects of desegregation on racial attitudes. *Journal of Personality and Social Psychology, 36,* 795–804.

Stephan, W. G., & Rosenfield, D. (1978b). Effects of desegregation on race relations and self-esteem. *Journal of Educational Psychology, 70,* 670–679.

Stephens, M. W., & Delys, P. (1973). External control expectancies among disadvantaged children at preschool age. *Child Development, 44,* 670–674.

Stephenson, B., & Wicklund, R. (1983). Self-directed attention and taking the other's perspective. *Journal of Experimental Social Psychology, 19,* 58–77.

Sternberg, R. J. (1977). *Intelligence, information processing, and analogical reasoning: The componential analyses of human abilities.* Hillsdale, NJ: Erlbaum.

Sternberg, R. J. (1984). Mechanisms of cognitive development: A componential approach. In R. J. Sternberg (Ed.), *Mechanisms of cognitive development.* New York: W. H. Freeman.

Sternberg, R. J. (1985). *Beyond IQ.* Cambridge, England: Cambridge University Press.

Sternberg, R. J. (in press). *Intelligence applied.* San Diego: Harcourt, Brace.

Sternberg, R. J. (Ed.). (1982). *Advances in the psychology of human intelligence.* Hillsdale, NJ: Erlbaum.

Sternberg, R. J., & Nigro, C. (1980). Developmental patterns in the solution of verbal analogies. *Child Development, 51,* 27–38.

Sternberg, R. J., & Rifkin, B. (1979). The development of analogical reasoning processes. *Journal of Experimental Child Psychology, 27,* 195–232.

Stevenson, H. W. (1982). Influences of schooling on cognitive development. In D. A. Wagner & H. W. Stevenson (Eds.). *Cultural perspectives on child development.* San Francisco: W. H. Freeman.

Stevenson, H. W., Hale, G. A., Klein, R. E., & Miller, L. K. (1968). Interrelations and correlates in children's learning and problem solving. *Monographs of the Society for Research in Child Development, 33*(Serial No. 123).

Stipek, D. J. (1981). Adolescents—Too young to earn, too old to learn? Compulsory school attendance and intellectual development. *Journal of Youth and Adolescence, 10,* 113–139.

Stipek, D. J., & Hoffman, J. M. (1980). Children's achievement-related expectancies as a function of academic performance histories and sex. *Journal of Educational Psychology, 72,* 861–865.

Stockard, J. et al. (1980). *Sex equity in education.* New York: Academic Press.

Stone, C. A., & Day, M. C. (1980). Competence and performance models and the characterization of formal-operational skills. *Human Development, 23,* 323–353.

Stone, S. C., & Shertzer, B. (Eds.). (1975). *Career education and the curriculum.* Boston: Houghton Mifflin.

Storms, M. D. (1980). Theories of sexual orientation. *Journal of Personality and Social Psychology, 38,* 783–792.

Stricker, L. J., Jacobs, P. I., & Kogan, N. (1974). Trait interrelations in implicit personality theories and questionnaire data. *Journal of Personality and Social Psychology, 29,* 198–297.

Strodtbeck, F. L. (1958). Family interaction, values, and achievement. In D.C. McClelland, A. L. Baldwin, U. Bronfenbrenner, & F. L. Strodtbeck (Eds.), *Talent and society.* Princeton, NJ: Van Nostrand.

Stuart, R. B. (1973). Teaching facts about drugs: Pushing or preventing. *Journal of Educational Psychology, 66,* 189–201.

Sullivan, E. V. (1975). *Moral learning: Findings, issues and questions.* Paramus, NJ: Paulist/Newman Press.

Sullivan, H. S. (1953). *The interpersonal theory of psychiatry.* New York: Norton.

Super, D. E. (1967). *The psychology of careers.* New York: Harper & Row.

Super, D. E. (1976). *Career education and the meanings of work.* Washington, DC: U.S. Office of Education.

Super, D. E., & Bohn, M. J. (1970). *Occupational psychology.* Monterey, CA: Brooks/Cole.

Super, D. E., & Hall, D. T. (1978). Career development: Exploration and planning. *Annual Review of Psychology, 29,* 333–372.

Super, D. E., Kowalski, R., & Gotkin, E. (1967). *Floundering and trial after high school.* Unpublished manuscript, Columbia University.

Super, D. E., & Overstreet, P. (1960). *Vocational maturity of ninth-grade boys.* New York: Teachers College Press.

Sutton-Smith, B., & Rosenberg, B. G. (1970). *The sibling.* New York: Holt, Rinehart, & Winston.

Svedja, M. J., Campos, J. J., & Emde, R. N. (1980). Mother-infant "bonding": Failure to generalize. *Child Development, 51,* 75–779.

Swinton, D. (1980). Towards defining the universe of need for youth employment policy. In B. Linder & R. Taggart (Eds.), *A review of youth employment problems, programs, and policies: Vol. I. The youth employment problem: Causes and dimensions.* Washington, DC: Vice-President's Task Force on Youth Employment.

Swisher, J. D., Warner, R., & Herr, E. (1972). An experiment comparison of four approaches to drug education. *Journal of Counseling Psychology, 19,* 328–332.

Swope, G. W. (1980). Kids and cults: Who joins and why? *Media and Methods, 16,* 18–21.

Szasz, T. S. (1961). *The myth of mental illness.* New York: Harper & Row.

Szasz, T. S. (1977). *Psychiatric slavery: When confinement and coercion masquerade as cure.* New York: Free Press.

Tanner, J. M. (1966). Growth and physique in different populations of mankind. In P. T. Baker & J. S. Weiner (Eds.), *The biology of human adaptability.* Oxford: Clarendon.

Tanner, J. M. (1968). Growth of bone, muscle, and fat during childhood and adolescence. In G. A. Lodge (Ed.), *Growth and development of mammals.* London: Butterworth.

Tanner J. M. (1970). Physical growth. In P. H. Mussen (Ed.), *Carmichael's manual of child psychology* (Vol. 1). New York: John Wiley.

Tanner, J. M. (1973). Growing up. *Scientific American, 229,* 35–42.

Taylor, T. D., Winne, P. H., & Marx, R. W. (1975, April). *Sample specificity of self-concept instruments.* Paper presented at the meeting of the Society for Research in Child Development, Denver, CO.

Tec, N. (1972). Some aspects of high school status and differential involvement with marijuana. *Adolescence, 7,* 1–28.

Tedesco, N. S. (1974). Patterns in prime time. *Journal of Communication, 24,* 119–124.

Terman, L. M. (1925). *Genetic studies of genius: Mental and physical traits of a thousand gifted children* (Vol. 1). Stanford, CA: Stanford University Press.

Terman, L. M., & Oden, M. H. (1959). *Genetic studies of genius. The gifted at mid-life: Thirty-five years' follow-up of the superior child* (Vol. 5). Stanford, CA: Stanford University Press.

Testa, M., & Wulczyn, F. (1980). *The state of the child.* Chicago, IL: University of Chicago Press.

Thomas, A., & Chess, S. (1977). *Temperament and development.* New York: Brunner/Mazel.

Thomas, A., Chess, S., & Birch, H. G. (1968). *Temperament and behavior disorders in children.* New York: New York University Press.

Thompson, G. G. (1944). The social and emotional development of preschool children under two types of education programs. *Psychological Monographs, 56*(258), 5.

Thompson, R. J., Cappleman, M. W., & Zeitschel, K. A. (1979). Neonatal behavior of infants of adolescent mothers. *Developmental Medicine and Child Neurology, 21,* 474–482.

Thornburg, H. D. (1968). Evaluating the sex education program. *Arizona Teacher, 57,* 18–20.

Thornburg, H. D. (1981). Sources of sex education among early adolescents. *Journal of Early Adolescence, 1,* 171–184.

Thornburg, H. D. (1982). *Development in adolescence* (2nd ed.). Monterey, CA: Brooks/Cole.

Thornburg, H. D., & Thornburg, E. E. (1979). *Value choices among high school students.* Paper presented at the annual meeting of the Rocky Mountain Psychological Association.

Thorndike, R. L., Hagen, E. P., & Sattler, J. M. (1985). *Stanford-Binet* (4th ed.). Chicago: Riverside Publishing.

Thurstone, L. L. (1938). Primary mental abilities. *Psychometric Monographs,* No. 1.

Tieger, T. (1980). On the biological basis of sex differences in aggression. *Child Development, 51,* 943–963.

Todd, D. M. (1979). Contrasting adaptations to the social environment of a high school: Implications of a case study of helping behavior in two adolescent subcultures. In J. G. Kelly (Ed.), *Adolescent boys in high school.* Hillsdale, NJ: Lawrence Erlbaum.

Toder, N., & Marcia, J. (1973). Ego identity status and response to conformity pressure in college women. *Journal of Personality and Social Psychology, 26,* 287–294.

Toepfer, C. F. (1979). Brain growth periodization: A new dogma for education. *Middle School Journal, 10,* 20.

Toman, W. (1971). The duplication theorem of social relationships as tested in the general population. *Psychological Review, 79,* 380–390.

Tomlinson-Keasey, C. (1972). Formal operations in females from eleven to fifty-four years of age. *Developmental Psychology, 6,* 364.

Torgesen, J. (1975). Problems and prospects in the study of learning disabilities. In E. M. Hetherington (Ed.), *Review of child development research* (Vol. 5). Chicago: University of Chicago Press.

Torrance, E. P., & Torrance, P. (1972). Combining creative problem solving with creative expressive activities in the education of disadvantaged young people. *Journal of Creative Behavior, 6*(1), 1–10.

Toth, S. A. (1981). *Blooming.* Boston: Little, Brown.

Trecker, J. L. (1977). Women in U.S. history high-school textbooks. In J. Pottker & A. Fishel (Eds.), *Sex bias in the schools: The research evidence.* Cranbury, NJ: Associated University Presses.

Trickett, E., & Moos, R. (1974). Personal correlates of contrasting environments: Student satisfaction in high school classrooms. *American Journal of Community Psychology, 2,* 1–12.

Trupin, T. (1979). *The measurement of psychological androgyny in children.* Unpublished doctoral dissertation, University of Washington. (University Microfilms No. 7917653)

Tulkin, S. R., & Kagan, J. (1971). Mother-child interaction in the first year of life. *Child Development, 43,* 31–41.

Tuma, N. B., & Hallinan, M. T. (1979). The effects of sex, race, and achievement on schoolchildren's friendships. *Social Forces, 57,* 1265–1285.

Turiel, E. (1966). An experimental test of the sequentiality of developmental stages in the child's moral judgments. *Journal of Personality and Social Psychology, 3,* 611–618.

Turiel, E. (1977). A critical analysis of Kohlberg's contributions to the study of moral thought. *Journal of Theory of Social Behavior, 7,* 41–63.

Turiel, E. (1978). Social regulations and domains of social concepts. In W. Damon (Ed.), *New directions for child development: Vol. 1. Social cognition.* San Francisco: Jossey-Bass.

Turkle, S. (1984). *The second self.* Cambridge, MA: Harvard University Press.

Turnbull, C. M. (1972). *The mountain people.* New York: Simon & Schuster.

Turner, C., & Thrasher, M. (1970). *School size does make a difference.* San Diego: Institute for Educational Management.

Twentyman, C. T., & McFall, R. M. (1975). Behavioral training of social skills in shy males. *Journal of Consulting and Clinical Psychology, 43,* 384–395.

Tyack, D. (1976). Ways of seeing: An essay on the history of compulsory schooling. *Harvard Educational Review, 46,* 355–389.

USA Today, October 16, 1984.

U.S. Bureau of the Census. (1970). *Census of population: General social and economic characteristics.* Washington, DC: U.S. Department of Commerce.

U.S. Bureau of the Census. (1980). *Social indicators III.* Washington, DC: U.S. Department of Commerce.

U.S. Bureau of Labor Statistics, Department of Labor. (1981). *Where the jobs will be in 1990.* Washington, DC: U.S. Government Printing Office.

U.S. Department of Labor. (1979). *Special Report No. 218.* Washington, DC: U.S. Government Printing Office.

U.S. Supreme Court, *In re Gault,* 387 U.S. 1, 1967.

U'ren, M. (1971). The image of women in textbooks. In V. Gornick & G. B. Morgan (Eds.), *Women in sexist society: Studies in power and powerlessness.* New York: Basic Books.

Ullman, C. (1982). Cognitive and emotional antecedents of religious conversion. *Journal of Personality and Social Psychology, 43,* 183–192.

Urberg, K. A. (1979). Sex role conceptualization in adolescents and adults. *Developmental Psychology, 15,* 90–92.

Van Gennep, A. (1969). *The rites of passage.* Chicago: University of Chicago Press.

van Manen, M., Fagan, I. P., Evans, C., Breithaupt, A., & Wayne, D. A. (1975). Content and form of a curriculum for women's studies: The women's kit. *History and Social Science Teacher, 10,* 12–19.

Vandiver, R. (1972). *Sources and interrelation of premarital sexual standards and general liberality and conservatism.* Unpublished doctoral dissertation, Southern Illinois University.

VanDusen, R. A., & Sheldon, E. B. (1976). The changing status of American women: A life cycle perspective. *American Psychologist, 31,* 106–116.

Visher, E. B., & Visher, J. S. (1970). *Stepfamilies.* New York: Bruner/Mazel.

Volpe, R. (1977). Feedback-facilitated relaxation training as primary prevention of drug abuse in early adolescence. *Journal of Drug Education, 7,* 179–194.

Waber, D. (1985, April). *Maturational timing and spatial ability: A possible integration of disparate findings.* Paper presented at the biennial meeting of the Society for Research in Child Development, Toronto.

Waddington, C. H. (1962). *New patterns in genetics and development.* New York: Columbia University Press.

Wagenaar, A. C. (1983). *Alcohol, young drivers, and traffic accidents.* Lexington, MA: Heath.

Wagner, D. A., & Stevenson, H. W. (1982). *Cultural perspectives on child development.* San Francisco: W. H. Freeman.

Waite, R. R. (1968). Further attempts to integrate and urbanize first-grade reading textbooks: A research study. *Journal of Negro Education, 37,* 62–69.

Walker, L. (1980). Cognitive and perspective taking prerequisites for moral development. *Child Development, 51,* 131–139.

Walker, L. (1982). The sequentiality of Kohlberg's stages of moral development. *Child Development, 53,* 1330–1336.

Walker, L. (1984). Sex differences in the development of moral reasoning: A critical review. *Child Development, 55,* 677–691.

Wallach, M. A. (1973). Ideology, evidence, and creative research. *Contemporary Psychology, 18,* 162–164.

Wallach, M. A., & Kogan, N. (1965). *Modes of thinking in young children.* New York: Holt, Rinehart, & Winston.

Wallack, L. M. (1984). Practical issues, ethical concerns and future directions in the prevention of alcohol-related problems. *Journal of Primary Prevention, 4,* 199–224.

Wallerstein, J. S. (1982, July). *Children of divorce: Preliminary report of a ten-year follow-up.* Paper presented at the 10th International Congress of the International Association for Child and Adolescent Psychiatry and Allied Professions, Dublin, Ireland.

Wallerstein, J. S. (1984, April). *Children of divorce: Preliminary report of a ten-year follow-up of young children.* Paper presented at the annual meeting of the American Orthopsychiatric Association, Toronto.

Wallerstein, J. S., & Kelly, J. B. (1974). The effects of parental divorce: The adolescent experience. In E. J. Anthony & C. Koupernik (Eds.), *The child in his family: Children of psychiatric risk.* (Vol. 3). New York: Wiley.

Wallerstein, J. S., & Kelly, J. B. (1980). *Surviving the break-up: How children and parents cope with divorce.* New York: Basic Books.

Walster, E., Aronson, V., Abrahams, D., & Rottman, L. (1966). In attractiveness in dating behavior. *Journal of Personality and Social Psychology, 4,* 508–516.

Warner, R. W., Swisher, J. D., & Moran, J. J. (1973). Drug abuse prevention: A behavioral approach. *The Bulletin of National Association of Secondary School Principals, 57,* 372.

Warren, R. P. (1965). *Who speaks for the negro?* New York: Random House.

Waterman, A. S. (1982). Identity development from adolescence to adulthood: An extension of theory and a review of research. *Developmental Psychology, 3,* 341–358.

Waterman, A. S., Geary, P. S., & Waterman, C. K. (1974). A longitudinal study of changes in ego identity status from the freshman to the senior at college. *Developmental Psychology, 10,* 387–392.

Waterman, A. S., & Waterman, C. K. (1971). A longitudinal study of changes in ego identity status during the freshman year of college. *Developmental Psychology, 5,* 167–173.

Waterman, A. S., & Waterman, C. K. (1972). Relationship between ego identity status and subsequent academic behavior: A test of the predictive validity of Marcia's categorization for identity status. *Developmental Psychology, 6,* 179.

Wechsler, D. (1958). *The measurement and appraisal of adult intelligence* (4th ed.). Baltimore: Williams & Wilkins.

Wechsler, D. (1975). Intelligence defined and undefined: A relativistic appraisal. *American Psychologist, 30,* 135–139.

Weigel, R. H., Wiser, P. L., & Cook, S. W. (1975). The impact of cooperative-learning experiences on cross-ethnic relations and attitudes. *Journal of Social Issues, 31,* 219–245.

Weiner, B. (1974). *Achievement motivation and attribution theory.* Morristown, NJ: General Learning Press.

Weiner, B. (1984). Principles for a theory of student motivation and their application within an attributional framework. In R. E. Ames & C. Ames (Eds.), *Motivation in education.* New York: Academic Press.

Weiner, B., Kun, A., & Benesh-Weiner, M. (1980). The development of mastery, emotion, and morality from an attributional perspective. In W. A. Collins (Ed.), *Minnesota Symposium on Child Psychology* (Vol. 13). Hillsdale, NJ: Erlbaum.

Weiner, I. B. (1970). *Psychological disturbance in adolescence.* New York: John Wiley.

Weiner, I. B. (1980). Psychopathology in adolescence. In J. Adelson (Ed.), *Handbook of adolescent psychology.* New York: John Wiley.

Weinraub, M., & Brown, L. M. (in press). The development of sex-role stereotypes in children: Crushing realities. In V. Franks & E. Rothblum (Eds.), *Sex-role stereotypes and clinical issues: Lessons from the past and implications for the future.* New York: Springer.

Weitzman, L., & Rizzo, D. (1974). *Biased textbooks: Images of males and females in elementary school textbooks in five subject areas.* Washington, DC: National Foundation for Improvement of Education.

Werner, E. E., & Smith, R. S. (1982). *Vulnerable but invincible: A longitudinal study of resilient children and youth.* New York: McGraw-Hill.

Werner, H., & Kaplan, E. (1952). The acquisition of word meanings: A developmental study. *Monographs of the Society for Research in Child Development, 15*(1, Serial No. 51).

West, D. J., & Farrington, D. P. (1977). *The delinquent way of life.* London: Heinemann Educational, 1973.

Wheatley, G. H. (1975). A motion picture test of Piagetian concepts. *Psychology in the Schools, 12,* 21–25.

White House Conference on Children. (1931). Report of the committee on special classes. Gifted children. In *Special Education: The handicapped and the gifted. Education and training. Section 3* (pp. 537–550). New York: Century.

White, S. H. (1985, April). *Risings and fallings of developmental psychology.* Paper presented at the biennial meeting of the Society for Research in Child Development, Toronto.

Whiting, B. B., & Whiting, J. W. M. (1975). *Children of six cultures: A psychocultural analysis.* Cambridge, MA: Harvard University Press.

Wicker, A. W. (1968). Undermanning, performances, and students' subjective experiences in behavior settings of large and small high schools. *Journal of Personality and Social Psychology, 10,* 255–261.

Wicklund, R. (1979). The influence of self-awareness on human behavior. *American Scientist, 67,* 187–193.

Wideck, C., Knefelkamp, L., & Parker, C. (1975). The counselor as a developmental instructor. *Counselor Education and Supervision, 14,* 286–295.

Wijting, J. P., Arnold, C. R., & Conrad, K. A. (1978). Generational differences in work values between parents and children and between boys and girls across grade levels 6, 9, 10, and 12. *Journal of Vocational Behavior, 12,* 245–260.

Wilkins, J. (1970). A follow-up study of those who called a suicide prevention center. *American Journal of Psychiatry, 127,* 155–161.

Willems, E. P. (1967). Sense of obligation to high school activities as related to school size and marginality of student. *Child Development, 38,* 1247–1260.

Williams, J. A. (1979). Psychological androgyny and mental health. In O. Hartnet, G. Boden, & M. Fuller (Eds.), *Sex-role stereotyping.* London: Tavistock.

Williams, J., Bennett, S., & Best, D. (1975). Awareness and expression of sex stereotypes in young children. *Developmental Psychology, 11,* 635–642.

Williams, T. H. (1972). Educational aspirations: Longitudinal evidence on their development in Canadian youth. *Sociology of Education, 45,* 107–133.

Wills, T. A., & Shiffman, S. (1985). Coping and substance use: A conceptual framework. In S. Shiffman & T. A. Wills (Eds.), *Coping and substance use* (pp. 3–24). New York: Academic Press.

Wilson, H. (1980). Parental supervision: A neglected aspect of delinquency. *British Journal of Criminology, 20,* 203–235.

Wilson, T. D., & Linville, P. W. (1982). Improving the academic performance of college freshmen: Attribution theory revisited. *Journal of Personality and Social Psychology, 42,* 367–376.

Winterbottom, M. R. (1958). The relation of need for achievement to learning experiences in independence and mastery. In J. W. Atkinson (Ed.), *Motives in fantasy, action, and society.* New York: D. Van Nostrand.

Wodarski, J. S., & Hoffman, S. D. (1984). Alcohol education for adolescents. *Social Work in Education, 6,* 69–92.

Wohlwill, J. (1973). *The study of behavioral development.* New York: Academic Press.

Wolfe, L. K., & Betz, N. E. (1981). Traditionality of choice and sex-role identification as moderators of the congruence of occupational choice in college women. *Journal of Vocational Behavior, 18,* 43–55.

Women on Words and Images. (1972). *Dick and Jane as victims: Sex stereotyping in children's readers.* Princeton, NJ: Author.

Worrell, J. (1978). Sex roles and psychological well-being. Perspectives on methodology. *Journal of Consulting and Clinical Psychology, 46,* 777–791.

Wylie, R. (1974). *The self concept.* Lincoln, NE: University of Nebraska Press.

Wylie, R. (1979). *The self-concept* (Vol. 2). Lincoln, NE: University of Nebraska Press.

Wynne, E. (1977). *Growing up suburban.* Austin: University of Texas Press.

Yando, R. M., & Kagan, J. J. (1968). The effect of teacher tempo on the child. *Child Development, 39,* 27–34.

Yankelovich, D. (1974). *The new morality: A profile of American youth in the 1970s.* New York: McGraw-Hill.

Yarrow, M. K., & Waxler, C. (1975, April). *The emergence and functions of prosocial behaviors in young children.* Paper presented at the meeting of the Society for Research in Child Development, Denver.

Yarrow, M. K., & Zahn-Waxler, C. (1983). Development of prosocial behavior. In P. H. Mussen (Ed.), *Carmichael's manual of child psychology* (4th ed.). New York: John Wiley.

Youniss, J. (1980). *Parents and peers in social development.* Chicago: University of Chicago Press.

Youniss, J., & Volpe, J. A. (1978). A relational analysis of children's friendships. In W. Damon (Ed.), *New directions for child development: Social cognition.* San Francisco: W. H. Freeman.

Yussen, S. R. (1977). Characteristics of moral dilemmas written by adolescents. *Developmental Psychology, 13,* 162–163.

Zakin, D. F., Blyth, D. A., & Simmons, R. G. (1984). Physical attractiveness as a mediator of the impact of early pubertal changes for girls. *Journal of Youth and Adolescence, 13,* 439–450.

Zeldow, P. B. (1976). Psychological androgyny and attitudes toward feminism. *Journal of Consulting and Clinical Psychology, 44,* 150.

Zelnick, M., & Kantner, J. F. (1977). Sexual and contraceptive experiences of young unmarried women in the United States, 1976 and 1971. *Family Planning Perspectives, 9,* 55–71.

Zelnick, M., & Kantner, J. F. (1978a). First pregnancies to women ages fifteen to nineteen: 1976 and 1971. *Family Planning Perspectives, 10,* 11–20.

Zelnick, M., & Kantner, J. F. (1978b). Contraceptive patterns and premarital pregnancy among women aged fifteen to nineteen in 1976. *Family Planning Perspectives, 10,* 135–142.

Zelnick, M., & Kantner, J. F. (1980). Sexual activity, contraceptive use and pregnancy among metropolitan-area teenagers: 1971–1979. *Family Planning Perspectives, 12,* 230–237.

Zember, M. J., & Naus, M. J. (1985, April). *The combined effects of knowledge base and mnemonic strategies on children's memory.* Paper presented at the meeting of the Society for Research in Child Development, Toronto.

Zigmond, N. K. (1969). Learning patterns in children with learning disabilities. *Seminars in Psychiatry, 1,* 344–353.

Zillman, D. (1971). Excitation transfer in communication-mediated aggressive behavior. *Journal of Experimental Social Psychology, 7,* 419–434.

Zillman, D., Johnson, R. C., & Hanrahan, J. (1973). Pacifying effects of happy ending communications involving aggression. *Psychological Reports, 32,* 967–970.

Credits

Illustrations

Chapter 1

Prologue, pp. 6–7: "Why Don't You Grow Up," from *Just Wait Till You Have Children of Your Own,* by Erma Bombeck and Bil Keane. Copyright © 1971 by Erma Bombeck and Bil Keane. Reprinted by permission of Doubleday and Company, Inc. **Figure 1.1:** From Elder, G. H., "Adolescence in Historical perspective," in J. Adelson (Ed.), *Handbook of Adolescent Psychology.* Copyright © 1980 John Wiley and Sons, Inc.

Chapter 2

Figure 2.1: Reproduced from *Childhood and Society,* 2nd Edition, by Erik Erikson. Copyright 1950, © 1963 by W. W. Norton and Company, Inc. **Figure 2.4:** From Nesselroade, J. R., and P. B. Baltes (1984). In Mednick, S. A., Harway, M., and K. M. Finello (Eds.), *Handbook of Longitudinal Research,* p. 82. New York: Praeger Publishers.

Chapter 3

Figure 3.1: From Gottesman, I., "Genetic Aspects of Intellectual Behavior," in *Handbook of Mental Deficiency,* by Norman R. Ellis, (Ed.). Copyright © 1983 McGraw-Hill Book Company. **Figure 3.2:** Reproduced from *Human Biology and Ecology,* by Albert Damon. Copyright © 1977 by W. W. Norton and Company, Inc. **Figure 3.3:** From Matousek, M., and J. Petersen, "Frequency Analysis of the EEG in Normal Children and Adolescents," in P. Kellaway and I. Petersen (Eds.), *Automation of Clinical Electroencephalographs.* Copyright © 1973 Raven Press, New York. **Figure 3.4:** From Petersen, A. C., and B. Taylor, "The Biological Approach to Adolescence: Biological Change and Psychological Adaptation." In J. Adelson (Ed.), *Handbook of Adolescent Psychology.* New York: John Wiley and Sons, 1980. Reprinted by permission. **Figures 3.5, 3.6, 3.7:** From Nottelman, E. D., Susman, E. J., Inoff, G. E. Dorn, L. D., Cutler, G. B.,

Loriaux. D. L., and G. P. Chrousos, "Hormone Level and Adjustment and Behavior During Early Adolescence," May 1985, p. 38. Paper presented at the annual meeting of the American Association for the Advancement of Science, Los Angeles, CA. **Figures 3.10, 3.12:** From "Growing Up," by J. M. Tanner, September 1973. Copyright © 1973 by Scientific American, Inc. All Rights Reserved. **Figures 3.11, 3.13:** From Morris, M. N., and J. R. Udry, "Validation of a Self-Administered Instrument to Assess Stage of Adolescence Development," *Journal of Youth and Adolescence,* 1980, 9, 271–280. Reprinted by permission of Plenum Publishing Corporation. **Figure 3.14:** Courtesy of Simmons, R. G., Blythe, D. A., and K. L. McKinney, in *Girls at Puberty: Biological and Psychosocial Perspectives,* (Eds. Jeanne Brooks-Gunn and Anne C. Petersen), New York: Plenum Publishing Corporation, 1983. **Figure 3.15:** After data presented by Zakin, D. F., Blyth, D. A., and R. G. Simmons, "Physical Attractiveness as a mediator of the Impact of Early Pubertal Changes for Girls," in *Journal of Youth and Adolescence,* 13, 439–450. Copyright © 1984 Plenum Publishing Corporation, New York.

Chapter 4

Figure 4.3: From J. M. Anglin, 1970. *The Growth of Word Meaning.* Cambridge, MA: MIT Press. **Figure 4.4:** Reprinted by permission from MAD MAGAZINE, © 1985 E. C. Publications, Inc. **Figure 4.5:** From Demorest, A., Meyer, C., Phelps, E., Gardner, H., and E. Winner, "Words Speak Louder Than Actions: Understanding Deliberately False Remarks," in *Child Development,* 55, 152–153, 1984. © The Society for Research in Child Development, Inc. **Figure 4.7:** After data presented by Renner, J. W., Stafford, D., Lawson, A., McKinnon, J., Friot, F., and D. Kellog, *Research, Teaching, and Learning With the Piaget Model,* 1976. Norman, OK: University of Oklahoma Press. **Figure 4.8:** After data presented by Elkind, D., and R. Bowen, "Imaginary Audience Behavior in Children and Adolescents," in *Developmental Psychology,* 15, 38–44. Copyright © 1979 by the American Psychological Association.

Chapter 5

Figure 5.1: From Yussen, Steven R., and John W. Santrock, *Child Development: An Introduction,* 2nd ed. © 1978, 1982 Wm. C. Brown Publishers, Dubuque, Iowa. All Rights Reserved. Reprinted by permission. **Figure 5.2:** From Dempster, F. N., "Memory Span: Sources of Individual and Developmental Differences," *Psychological Bulletin,* 89, 63–100. Copyright © 1981 by the American Psychological Association. **Figure 5.3:** Adapted from Jerome M. Sattler, *Assessment of Children's Intelligence and Special Abilities,* Second Edition. Copyright © 1982 by Allyn and Bacon, Inc. **Figure 5.4:** Sample items reproduced from the *Differential Aptitude Tests.* Copyright 1972 by The Psychological Corporation, New York, NY. All rights reserved. **Figure 5.5:** From *The Nature of Human Intelligence,* by J. P. Guilford. Copyright © 1967 by McGraw-Hill Book Company. **Figure 5.6:** Reproduced from *The Raven Standard Progressive Matrices* by permission of J. C. Raven Limited.

Chapter 6

Prologue, p. 206: "Hal's Adolescent Independence," from *Just Wait Till You Have Children of Your Own,* by Erma Bombeck and Bil Keane. Copyright © 1971 by Erma Bombeck and Bil Keane. Reprinted by permission of Doubleday and Company, Inc. **Figure 6.2:** From Gjerde, P. F., "A Family Systems Perspective on Parent-Adolescent Interaction: Second-Order Effects and Sex Differences in Family Interaction," 1985. Unpublished manuscript, University of California, Berkeley. **Figure 6.3:** After data presented by Hill, J. P., Holmbeck, G. N., Marlow, L., Green, T. M., and M. E. Lynch, "Pubertal Status and Parent-Child Relations in Families of Seventh-Grade Boys," *Journal of Early Adolescence,* 5, 31–44. Copyright © 1985 H.E.L.P. Books, Tucson, AZ. **Figure 6.4:** Source: After Maccoby, 1983, p. 39. **Figure 6.5:** After data presented by Daniels, D., Dunn, J., Furstenburg, F. F., and R. Plomin, "Environmental Differences Within the Family and Adjustment Differences Within Pairs of Adolescent Siblings," *Child Development,* 56, 764–774, 1985. © The Society for Research in Child Development, Inc. **Figure 6.7:** From Santrock, J. W., and R. A. Warshak, "Father Custody and Social Development in Boys and Girls," *Journal of Social Issues,* 35, 112–135. Copyright © 1979 by Plenum Publishing Corporation.

Chapter 7

Figure 7.1: From Gold, M., and D. S. Yanof, "Mothers, Daughters, and Girlfriends," *Journal of Personality and Social Psychology,* 49, 3, 654–659. Copyright © 1985 by the American Psychological Association. **Figure 7.3:** From Asarnow, J. R., and J. W. Callan, "Boys With Peer Adjustment Problems: Social Cognitive Processes," *Journal of Consulting and Clinical Psychology,* 53, 80–87. Copyright © 1985 by the American Psychological Association. **Figure 7.4:** From Dodge, K. A.,

Murphy, R. R., and K. Buchsbaum, "The Assessment of Intention-Cue Detection Skills: Implications for Developmental Psychopathology," *Child Development,* 55, 163–173, 1984. © The Society for Research in Child Development, Inc. **Figure 7.5:** From Dunphy, D. C., "The Social Structure of Urban Adolescent Peer Groups," *Society,* 1963, 26, 230–246. Copyright © 1963 Transaction Periodicals Consortium, New Brunswick, NJ. **Figure 7.6:** After data presented by Brown and Lohr, in press. **Figure 7.7:** From Byrne and Nelson, "Attraction as a Linear Function of Proportion of Positive Reinforcement," *Journal of Personality and Social Psychology,* pp. 659–663. Copyright © by the American Psychological Association.

Chapter 8

Prologue, pp. 310–11: Source of excerpts: Lipitz, 1984. **Figure 8.2:** From Yussen, Stephen R., and John W. Santrock, *Child Development: An Introduction,* 2nd ed. © 1978, 1982 Wm. C. Brown Publishers, Dubuque, Iowa. All Rights Reserved. Reprinted by permission.

Chapter 9

Figures 9.1, 9.2, 9.3: From Csikszentmihalyi, M., and R. Larson, *Being Adolescent.* New York: Basic Books, 1984. **Figure 9.4:** After data presented by Erlick, A. C., and A. R. Starry, (June 1973). Sources of information for career decisions. Report of Poll. No. 98, Purdue Opinion Panel.

Chapter 10

Prologue, pp. 392–93: From Cooper, C. R., Grotevant, H. D., and S. M. Condon, "Individuality and Connectedness in the Family as a Context for Adolescent Identity Formation and Role-Taking Skill." In H. D. Grotevant and C. R. Cooper (Eds.), *Adolescent Development in the Family.* San Francisco: Jossey-Bass, 1983: 54–55. **Figure 10.1:** From Rogers, Kuiper, and Kirker, "Self Reference and the Encoding of Personal Information," in *Journal of Personality and Social Psychology,* 35, pp. 677–688. Copyright 1977 by the American psychological Association. **Excerpt, p. 416:** Excerpt from J. Marcia, "Ego Identity Development," in J. Adelson (Ed.), *Handbook of Adolescent Psychology.* Copyright © 1980 by John Wiley and Sons, Inc. Reprinted by permission. **Figure 10.2:** From Archer, S. L., (April 1985). Reflections on Earlier Life Decisions: Implications for Adult Functioning. Paper presented at the biennial meeting of the Society for Research in Child Development, Inc.

Chapter 11

Prologue, pp. 440–41: From *Just Wait Till You Have Children of Your Own,* by Erma Bombeck and Bil Keane. Copyright © 1971 by Erma Bombeck and Bil Keane. Reprinted by permission of

Doubleday and Company, Inc. **Figure 11.2:** From O'Keefe, E. S. C., and J. S. Hyde, "The Development of Occupational Sex-Role Stereotypes: The Effects of Gender Stability and Age," *Sex Roles: A Journal of Research,* 9, 481–492. Copyright © 1983 by Plenum Publishing Corporation. **Figure 11.3:** From Hyde, J. S., "Children's Understanding of Sexist Language," *Developmental Psychology,* 20, 697–706. Copyright © 1984 by the American Psychological Association. **Figure 11.4:** From Geis, F. L., Brown, V., Jennings, J., (Walstedt), and N. Porter, "TV Commercials as Achievement Scripts for Women," *Sex Roles: A Journal of Research,* 10, 513–525. Copyright © 1984 by Plenum Publishing Corporation. **Figure 11.5:** From Darling, C. A., Kallen, D. J., and J. E. VanDusen, "Sex in Transition, 1900–1984," *Journal of Youth and Adolescence,* 13, 385–399. Copyright © 1984 by Plenum Publishing Corporation. **Figure 11.6:** From Jones, E. F., Forrest, J. D., Goldman, N., Henshaw, S. K., Lincoln, R., Rosoff, J. I., Westoff, C. F., and D. Wulf, "Teenage Pregnancy in Developed Countries: Determinants and Policy Implications," *Family Planning Perspectives,* 17, 53–63. Copyright © 1985 Alan Guttmacher Institute.

Chapter 12

Figure 12.1: From Colby, A., et al., "A Longitudinal Study of Moral Judgement," *Monographs of Society for Research in Child Development.* © The Society for Research in Child Development, Inc. **Excerpt, pp. 488–89:** From Swope, G. W., "Kids and Cults: Who Joins and Why?," *Media and Methods,* Vol. 16, pp. 18–21. Copyright © 1980 by the American Society of Educators. Reprinted by permission.

Chapter 13

Prologue, pp. 524–26: Reprinted from *Psychology Today Magazine.* Copyright © 1979 American psychological Association. **Figure 13.3:** From Wilson, T. D., and P. W. Linville, "Improving the Academic Performance of College Freshmen," *Journal of Personality and Social Psychology,* 42, 367–376. Copyright 1982 by the American psychological Association. **Figure 13.4:** After data presented by Mischel, W., Ebbersen, E. B., and A. R. Zeiss, "Cognitive and Attentional mechanisms in Delay of Gratification," *Journal of Personality and Social psychology,* 21, 204–218. Copyright 1972 by the American Psychological Association. **Perspective on Adolescent Dev. 13.2:** Reprinted from *Psychology Today Magazine.* Copyright © 1979 American Psychological Association. **Figure 13.5:** From Lepper, M., Greene, D., and R. E. Nisbett, "Undermining Children's Intrinsic Interests With Extrinsic Rewards," *Journal of Personality and Social*

Psychology, 28, 129–137. Copyright 1973 by the American Psychological Association. **Figure 13.10:** From Grotevant, H. D., and M. E. Durrett, "Occupational Knowledge and Career Development in Adolescence," *Journal of Vocational Behavior,* 17, 171–182. Copyright © 1980 Academic Press. **Figure 13.11:** After data presented by Kerr, B. A., "Raising the Career Aspirations of Gifted Girls," *Vocational Guidance Quarterly,* 32, 37–43, 1983. National Vocational Guidance Association, American Association for Counseling and Development. **Excerpt, pp. 569–71:** Reprinted from *Psychology Today Magazine.* Copyright © 1980 American Psychological Association.

Chapter 14

Figure 14.1: After data presented by Blyth, D. A., Durant, D., and L. Moosbrugger (April 1985). "Perceived Intimacy in the Social Relationships of Drug and Non-Drug Using Adolescents." Paper presented at the biennial meeting of the Society for Research in Child Development, Toronto. **Figures 14.3, 14.4:** From Gold, M., and R. J. Petronio, "Delinquent Behavior in Adolescence," in J. Adelson (Ed.), *Handbook of Adolescent Psychology.* Copyright © 1980 by John Wiley and Sons. **Figure 14.5:** From Fixsen, D. L., Phillips, E. L., Phillips, E. A., and M. M. Wolf. In Craighead, W. E., Kazdin, A. E., and M. J. Mahoney (Eds.), *Behavior Modification, Principles, Issues and Applications.* Copyright © 1976 by Houghton-Mifflin. Originally presented as a report to the American Psychological Association Convention in Honolulu, Hawaii, September 1972.

Chapter 15

Prologue, p. 618: From Chess, S., and M. Hassiki, "Acute Anxiety," in *Principles and Practice of Child Psychiatry.* Copyright © 1978 Plenum Publishing Corporation. **Figures 15.1, 15.2, 15.3, 15.4, 15.5:** From Achenbach, T., and C. S. Edelbrock, "Behavioral Problems and Competencies Reported by Parents of Normal and Disturbed Children Aged Four Through Sixteen," in *Monographs of the Society for Research in Child Development,* 46, no. 1. Copyright © 1981 by the Society for Research in Child Development, Inc. **Figure 15.7:** Reprinted from Langley, L. L., *Physiology of Man.* New York: Van Nostrand Reinhold, 1971. Courtesy of Dr. Lee L. Langley. **Excerpt, pp. 644–45:** Reprinted with permission from Chess, S., and A. Thomas, "Temperamental Individuality from Childhood to Adolescence," *Journal of Child Psychiatry,* Vol. 16, Copyright © 1977, Pergamon Press, Ltd.

Photos

Chapter 1

Opener: © Jean-Claude Lejeune; **page 13:** Historical Pictures Service; **page 16:** The Bettman Archive; **page 17, 18:** © Jean-Claude Lejeune; **page 26:** © David Grossman; **page 27:** © James Shaffer; **page 32a–h:** © Landrum Shettles, © Mark Antman/The Image Works, © Alan Carey/The Image Works, © Jean-Claude Lejeune, © Ron Meyer/White Eyes Design, © Jean-Claude Lejeune, © Carolyn A. McKeone, © Michael E. Crawford.

Chapter 2

Opener: © Jean-Claude Lejeune; **page 44:** courtesy B. F. Skinner; **page 45:** UPI/Bettman News Photos; **page 46:** The Bettman Archives; **page 51, 60:** © James Shaffer; **page 62a–c:** © Mark Antman/The Image Works, © Suzanne Arms/Jeroboam, Inc., © Michael E. Crawford; **page 63d–f:** © James Shaffer, © Steve Takatsuno, © Ron Meyer/White Eyes Design.

Chapter 3

Opener: © James Shaffer; **page 88:** © Bob Coyle; **page 89:** © Alan Carey/The Image Works; **page 97, 103:** © James Shaffer; **page 111:** © Jill Cannefax/EKM-Nepenthe; **page 116:** © Ron Meyer/White Eyes Design.

Chapter 4

Opener: © James Shaffer; **page 130:** © Carolyn A. McKeone; **page 138:** © Jean-Claude Lejeune; **page 142:** © James Shaffer; **page 149:** © Alan Carey/The Image Works; **page 155:** © James Shaffer; **page 156:** © Carolyn A. McKeone.

Chapter 5

Opener: © McDonald Photography; **page 166:** © Alan Carey/The Image Works; **page 169:** © Carolyn A. McKeone; **page 173:** Culver Pictures; **page 185:** courtesy Robert J. Sternberg; **page 187:** © Alan Carey/The Image Works; **page 192:** © Allen Ruid; **page 196:** © Jean-Claude Lejeune.

Chapter 6

Opener: © Jean-Claude Lejeune; **page 211:** © Carolyn A. McKeone; **page 212:** © Harriet Gans/The Image Works; **page 221:** © Jean-Claude Lejeune; **page 227:** © Dave Schaefer/Jeroboam; **page 231:** © Michael Siluk; **page 235:** © Ron Meyer/White Eyes Design; **page 236, 239:** © Carolyn A. McKeone; **page 245:** © Steve Takatsuno; **page 250:** © Michael Siluk; **page 254:** © Richard Bermack/Jeroboam Inc.

Chapter 7

Opener, page 264: © Carolyn A. McKeone; **page 266:** © James Shaffer; **page 268:** © Carolyn A. McKeone; **page 272:** © Robert Kalman/The Image Works; **page 279:** © Carolyn A. McKeone; **page 285:** © James Shaffer; **page 286:** © Steve Takatsuno; **page 291:** © James Shaffer; **page 295, 296:** © Carolyn A. McKeone; **page 299:** © Frank Siteman/Jeroboam Inc.

Chapter 8

Opener: © McDonald Photography; **page 310:** © James Shaffer; **page 315:** © Steve Takatsuno; **page 317:** © James Shaffer; **page 318:** © Steve Takatsuno; **page 320:** © Jean-Claude Lejeune; **page 321, 328, 334:** © James Shaffer; **page 336:** © Allen Ruid; **page 341:** © James Shaffer.

Chapter 9

Opener: © Jean-Claude Lejeune; **page 348, 351:** © Carolyn A. McKeone; **page 359, 362:** © Jean-Claude Lejeune; **page 372:** © Paul Conklin; **page 377:** © Steve Takatsuno; **page 382:** © Allen Ruid.

Chapter 10

Opener: © Bob Coyle; **page 401a, b:** © Steve Malone; Jeroboam Inc., © James Shaffer; **page 404:** © Carolyn A. McKeone; **page 407:** courtesy Robert L. Selman; **page 414:** Historical Pictures Service; **page 415:** The Bettman Archives; **page 421:** © Michael E. Crawford; **page 425:** © Carolyn A. McKeone; **page 432:** © Alan Carey/The Image Works.

Chapter 11

Opener: © James Shaffer; **page 442, 443:** © Carolyn A. McKeone; **page 445:** © Jean-Claude Lejeune; **page 449:** © Carolyn A. McKeone; **page 452:** © Laima E. Druskis/Jeroboam Inc.; **page 455:** © Steve Takatsuno; **page 461:** © David Strickler/Strix Pix; **page 463:** © Raymond Lopez; **page 467:** © Tom Ballard/EKM-Nepenthe; **page 480:** © Bob Coyle.

Chapter 12

Opener: © James Shaffer; **page 499:** © Ron Meyer/White Eyes Design; **page 503:** © James Shaffer; **page 509:** © Jane Scherr/Jeroboam Inc.; **page 515:** © Jean-Claude Lejeune; **page 517:** © Bob Coyle; **page 518:** © Chuck Isaacs.

Chapter 13

Opener: © Charles Gatewood/The Image Works; **page 529, 535, 537:** © James Shaffer; **page 544:** © Robert Kalman/The Image Works; **page 557:** © Steve Takatsuno; **page 561, 565:** © James Shaffer; **page 570:** © Alan Carey/ The Image Works.

Chapter 14

Opener: © Paul Conklin; **page 587, 588:** U.S. Department of Justice, Drug Enforcement Administration; **page 589:** © Carolyn A. McKeone; **page 591:** © Michelle Vignes/Jeroboam Inc.; **page 596:** © Carolyn A. McKeone; **page 602:** © Alan Carey/The Image Works; **page 607:** © James Shaffer.

Chapter 15

Opener: © James Shaffer; **page 620:** © Ron Meyer/White Eyes Design; **page 626:** © Bob Combs/Free Vision Photography; **page 632:** © Carolyn A. McKeone; **page 635:** © White Coyote Enterprises; **page 636:** © Susan Rosenberg/Photo Researchers, Inc.; **page 639:** © Steve Takatsuno; **page 644:** © Michael Siluk.

Name Index

Eliade, M., 366
Eliot, E. S., 332, 547
Elkind, D., 127, 133, 145, 149, 150, 151–52, 187, 250, 405, 514–15, 537–39, 560, 631
Ellwood, D., 571
Emde, R. N., 97, 253
Emmer, E. T., 542
Engen, H. B., 560
Enright, R., 150, 423, 502
Enright, R. D., 14, 15, 498, 502, 503, 511
Epstein, A. S., 253, 341
Epstein, H. T., 94, 96–97
Epstein, J. L., 237, 283
Erickson, K. A., 70
Erickson, M. T., 638
Erickson, V. L., 332
Erikson, E. H., 24, 45, 61–64, 67, 115, 224, 290, 328, 329, 375, 398, 412–17, 418, 422, 423, 428, 429, 430–33, 444, 506, 515, 602
Esposito, D., 196
Etaugh, C., 332
Evans, R. I., 590
Eveland, L. K., 606
Evertson, C., 331
Evertson, C. M., 542

F

Fagot, B. I., 451
Farrington, D. P., 605, 608
Fassinger, R. E., 547, 563
Faust, M. S., 103, 104, 105, 112, 113
Faust, R., 587
Feagin, J. R., 340
Feather, N. T., 513, 529
Feeney, S., 330
Feffen, G., 171
Feiring, C., 209
Feldman, S. D., 249
Feldman-Summers, S., 333, 546
Feldstein, M., 571
Felner, R. D., 319, 373
Fennema, E., 462
Ferrara, R. A., 172
Festinger, L., 290
Field, J., 14
Field, T. M., 252, 253

Filipczak, J. A., 610
Finley, M. I., 14
Finney, J. W., 659
Fischer, J. L., 433
Fischer, K. W., 132, 133, 134, 135, 142, 144, 148
Fishel, A., 333, 334
Fitch, S. A., 420
Fixsen, D. L., 610
Flavell, J. H., 24, 127, 142, 144, 146, 150, 156–57, 168, 171, 172, 507
Flay, B. R., 591
Fleeson, J., 210, 234
Flowers, J. V., 273
Ford, M., 191, 192–93, 442, 443, 444, 547
Ford, M. E., 158
Forehand, R. L., 239, 341
Forgatch, M. S., 604
Forslund, M. A., 598
Foster, S., 27
Fowler, J. W., 515
Fox, L. H., 563, 564, 565
Frakt, S. B., 463
Frame, C. L., 275
Frazier, N., 333
Fregly, M. J., 99
Freud, A., 61, 115, 265
Freud, S., 24, 25, 57–59, 60–61, 64, 67, 224, 229, 444
Frieze, I. H., 546
Friot, F., 142
Frisch, R., 85, 95
Froman, R. D., 191, 195
Fry, C., 139
Fry, P. S., 153
Fuchs, E., 340
Furstenberg, F. F., 30, 240, 255
Furth, H. G., 129

G

Gabrielson, P., 604
Gage, N. L., 329
Gagne, E. D., 175, 542
Gagnon, J. H., 298
Gaite, A. J. H., 139
Galambos, N. L., 460, 461
Gallup, G., 516, 517, 633
Gandhi, M., 416
Ganso, J., 27
Garbarino, J., 226, 322, 363–64, 365, 367, 502

Gardner, G. E., 622
Gardner, H., 132, 165, 191
Gardner, H., 90
Garmezy, N., 605, 640
Garrett, C., 334
Garrett, H. D., 599
Garrison, K. C., 104
Garrison, W., 542
Gaskell, J., 456
Gazzaniga, M., 22
Geary, P. S., 420
Geffner, R., 376
Geiger, K., 511
Geis, F. L., 453
Gelman, R., 142, 144
Gergen, K. J., 399
Gershaw, N. J., 278
Gershoni, R., 282
Gerson, W. M., 383
Getelson, I. B., 460
Getzels, J. W., 194
Ghiselli, E. E., 188
Giaconia, R. M., 326, 327, 328
Gibbs, J., 496, 498, 499
Gilbert, L. A., 444
Gilchrist, L. D., 591
Gill, N. T., 357
Gilliard, D., 547
Gilligan, C., 463, 500, 501, 502, 545, 603
Gingles, R., 226
Ginott, H., 222–23
Ginter, M., 319
Ginzberg, E., 552–53, 555
Gjerde, P., 209–10, 630–31
Glaser, R., 175
Glass, D. C., 239
Glueck, E., 604
Glueck, S., 604
Goelman, H., 134
Gold, M., 113, 266, 600, 602, 606, 607, 608, 609, 611
Golden, M. W., 264, 271
Goldstein, A. P., 278, 279
Gollin, E. S., 154
Goodall, J. V. L., 69
Goodchilds, J. D., 469
Goodlad, J. I., 314, 319
Goodwin, D. W., 597
Goodwin, F. K., 628
Gordon, K. A., 472
Gordon, N. J., 383, 384, 591
Gordon, T., 398
Gorsuch, R. L., 530

Gotkin, E., 556
Gottesman, I. I., 638, 640
Gottlieb, D., 226, 340
Gottman, J. M., 26, 27
Graham, E. H., 253
Graves, S. B., 383, 384
Gray, W. M., 150
Green, R., 455
Green, S., 226
Green, T. M., 214
Greenacre, P., 198
Greenberg, M. T., 235
Greenberger, E., 569
Greenburg, B. S., 387
Greene, B., 358–59
Greene, D., 543
Greenfield, P. M., 312
Greenwald, A., 399, 400
Gribbons, W. D., 339
Grief, E. B., 115
Grote, B., 466
Grotevant, H. D., 227, 397, 424–27, 429, 557, 558
Gudeman, J., 604
Guilford, J. P., 183, 194, 197
Gump, P. V., 319, 322
Gustafson, T. J., 598
Gutek, B. A., 462
Guttentag, M., 334, 457
Guttentag, R. E., 171

H

Haan, N., 360
Haas, A., 466, 467, 469, 470
Haeberle, E. J., 105
Hagen, E. P., 179
Hahn, C. L., 456
Hainsworth, P. K., 623
Halberstadt, A. G., 441
Hall, D. T., 555, 556
Hall, G. R., 313
Hall, G. S., 11–14, 21, 115, 224, 225, 229, 602
Hall, J. A., 441
Hallinan, M. T., 283
Hamburg, B., 111
Hamdani, R. J., 556
Hamm, C. M., 508, 510
Hammer, B. G., 556
Hammer, D., 239
Hand, H. H., 148
Hanrahan, J., 383
Hanson, D. R., 640
Hansoon, R. O., 444

P

Palmquist, W. J., 153
Papalia, D. E., 334
Parke, R. D., 254, 255
Parker, C., 143
Parsons, B. V., 609
Pascual-Leone, J., 169
Paskal, D., 322
Patterson, G. R., 604, 605
Peake, P. K., 534
Pearce, J., 599
Peevers, B. H., 153
Perloff, R. M., 453
Perrin, J. E., 283
Perry, C., 322, 591
Perry, T., 11
Peskin, H., 112, 113
Petersen, A. C., 78, 85, 112,
    113, 118, 402, 460
Peterson, P. L., 331
Peterson, R. E., 360
Petronio, R. J., 600, 602, 607,
    608, 609, 611
Phares, E. J., 532
Philliber, S. G., 253
Phillips, D. L., 599
Phillips, E. L., 610
Piaget, J., 23–24, 25, 35, 46,
    53–56, 57, 64, 66, 69, 71,
    96, 128–45, 146, 147,
    154, 187–88, 195,
    197–98, 405, 489–90
Piers, E. V., 400
Plato, 9, 21
Platt, J. J., 158, 274
Pleck, J., 448
Plomin, R., 239, 240
Poling, D., 516, 517
Pollard, L., 238
Porteus, A., 331
Posner, M., 186
Potter, E., 333
Pottker, J., 333, 334
Power, C., 508, 509, 510
Pratkanis, A., 399, 400
Pratto, D., 250
Presson, C. C., 590
Primavera, J., 319, 373
Pritscher, C. M. G., 443
Psathas, G., 230
Pulitzer, J., 377–78

Q

Quadagno, D. M., 447
Quadagno, J. S., 447
Quarinonium, 84
Quintana, S., 399, 400, 496
Quitkin, F., 640

R

Rabson, A., 547
Ragosta, J., 341
Ragozin, A. S., 253
Ramon y Cajal, S., 96
Rand, L. M., 563
Randall, D., 594
Raphael, D., 139
Raphael, M., 230
Rasmussen, B., 27
Raven, J. C., 189
Raynor, I. O., 529
Readdick, C. R., 238
Rebecca, M., 448
Reese, H. W., 75
Reeves, B. B., 453
Rehm, L., 295
Reid, J. B., 604
Reimer, D. J., 606
Reinisch, J. M., 445
Rekers, G. A., 455, 456
Renner, J. W., 145
Renshaw, P. D., 274
Reppucci, N. D., 547
Resnick, H. L. P., 629
Rest, J. R., 497
Revelle, H. M., 462
Revelle, R., 85, 95
Reynolds, D., 322
Reynolds, L. G., 556
Rholes, W. S., 155
Richards, J. M., 529, 554–55
Richards, M., 460
Richards, R. A., 189, 196
Riegel, K., 48
Riester, A. E., 289
Rifkin, A., 640
Rifkin, B., 171
Rindfuss, R. R., 251
Rist, R. C., 341
Ritchey, W., 27
Rizzo, D., 333
Robbins, L., 27
Robin, S. S., 593
Robins, L. N., 605

Rock, D., 341
Rodman, H., 250
Roff, M., 264, 271
Rogers, C. R., 398, 399
Rogers, R. W., 599
Rogers, T., 400
Rokeach, M., 511
Romer, N., 623
Ronstadt, L., 384
Rose, R., 90
Rose, S. E., 594
Rosen, B. C., 535
Rosenbaum, A., 301, 572
Rosenberg, B. G., 239, 455
Rosenberg, F., 151, 282, 319
Rosenberg, M., 151, 282, 290,
    319, 322, 373, 379, 405,
    461
Rosenblum, L. A., 263
Rosenfield, D., 379
Rosenkrans, M. A., 271
Ross, A. O., 602
Ross, D. G., 14
Rotenberg, K. J., 155
Rottman, L., 296
Rousseau, J. J., 9–10, 21, 115
Rovet, J., 118
Rowe, D. C., 239
Rubin, A. M., 382
Rubin, K. H., 150
Rubin, Z., 237
Ruble, D. N., 115, 155
Rushnell, S., 384
Russell, C., 586
Russell, S., 148
Rutter, M., 244, 313, 322, 604,
    605, 628, 644
Ryan, V. L., 444
Ryder, N., 29

S

Saario, T. N., 333
Sadker, M., 333
Sandler, H. M., 252
Santilli, N. R., 433
Santrock, J. W., 34, 90, 170,
    184, 213, 238, 243, 244,
    246, 247, 248
Sarason, I., 529
Sasfy, J. H., 405, 406
Sattler, J. M., 179
Savin-Williams, R. C., 402,
    403

Saxe, L., 298
Scardamalia, M., 132, 134
Scarr, S., 23, 88, 89, 90, 91
Schachter, S., 239
Schaie, K. W., 75, 76
Schechter, M. D., 622
Scheff, T. J., 642
Schiff, A. R., 171
Schinke, S. P., 591
Schmiedeck, R. A., 323
Schminke, C., 333
Schneider, A. J., 295
Schnell, S. V., 496
Schoeppe, A., 145
Schofield, A. T., 470, 641
Schumer, H., 329
Schunk, D. H., 540, 541
Schwarz, J. D., 363
Schwarz, M., 383
Scott, K. P., 333
Sears, P. S., 546
Sears, R. R., 194
Secord, P. F., 153
Seligman, M. E. P., 547, 628
Sells, S. B., 264, 271
Selman, L., 150, 153
Selman, R. L., 150, 215, 262,
    275, 282, 406–7, 410, 507
Seltzer, S., 385
Serafica, F. C., 283
Serlin, R. C., 14, 15, 498, 502,
    503, 511
Sexton, M. A., 171
Shafer, R. P., 587
Shantz, C. V., 150, 153, 158,
    282
Shapira, A., 363
Shapiro, E. K., 322, 332, 334,
    335, 336, 340, 341, 376,
    379, 510, 594
Sharabany, R., 282
Sharan, S., 376
Sharpe, L. W., 198
Shaver, P., 444
Sheldon, E. B., 562, 563
Sher, K. J., 598
Sherif, C., 284
Sherif, M., 284, 378
Sherman, S. J., 590
Shertzer, B., 561
Shields, J., 638
Shirreffs, J., 333
Shister, J., 556

Willems, E. P., 322
Williams, J., 334
Williams, J. R., 608
Williams, T. H., 332
Wills, T. A., 591
Wilson, H., 605
Wilson, K., 300
Wilson, R. C., 624
Wilson, T. D., 531
Winne, P. H., 399
Winterbottom, M. R., 528
Wirtanen, I. D., 226
Wise, L. L., 255
Wiser, P. L., 376, 379
Wodarski, J. S., 599
Wohlwill, J., 24
Wolf, J., 230
Wolf, M. M., 610
Wolfe, L. K., 443
Wong, M. R., 594
Worrell, J., 442, 444
Wright, H. F., 69
Wulczyn, F., 251
Wylie, R., 398
Wynne, E., 322

Y

Yando, R. M., 329
Yankelovich, D., 20
Yanof, D. S., 266
Yarrow, M. K., 506, 510
Youniss, J., 283
Yussen, S. R., 90, 497

Z

Zabin, L. S., 467, 469
Zahn-Waxler, C., 506, 510
Zakin, D. F., 116
Zeiss, A. R., 534
Zeitschel, K. A., 252
Zeldow, P. B., 443
Zellman, G. L., 469
Zelnick, M., 466, 470–71
Zembar, M., 185
Zigmond, N. K., 622
Zillman, D., 383
Zimet, S. G., 340
Zimpfer, D. G., 276
Zucker, R. H., 289

Subject Index

brainstorming, 198
branch model, 139
bulimia, 635
busing, 340–41

C

California Psychological
  Inventory (CPI), 441
canalization, 88
career(s), 550–68. *See also*
  work
  females and, 550, 562–65
  nature of, 550–52
  parents and, 560–61
  peers and, 560–61
  school and, 561–62
  social class and, 557, 560
  theories of career choices,
    552–55
career education programs, 572
career exploration, 555–56,
  558–59
care perspective, 501, 502
case study, 71
Cattell score, 644
cervical cancer, 473
Child Behavior Checklist
  (CBCL), 619–20
child custody, 247–48
childhood
  as developmental period, 31
  moral reasoning in, 489–90,
    491, 494–96
children's groups, versus
  adolescent groups, 286–87
Chitling Test, 190
chlamydia, 473
class. *See* social class
classical psychoanalytic theory,
  57–59
classroom. *See also* school
  climate of, 326–28
  jigsaw, 377–78
  open, 326–28
  size of, 322–23
  structure of, 326
Classroom Environment Scale
  (CES), 327
clinical method, 71
cliques, 288, 289–90
Cluster School, 508, 509–10
coaching, 277–78

cocaine, 582–83, 584, 585, 586,
  592–93
cognitive development, 34–35,
  126–46, 147. *See also*
  information processing;
  intelligence
  brain growth and, 96–97
  education and, 140–41,
    142–43
  family relationships and,
    214–15
  nature of, 127–28
  Piaget's view of, 128–46
  puberty and, 96–97, 118
  sex education and, 478
  sex roles and, 447–50
cognitive-disequilibrium theory,
  490
cognitive social-learning theory,
  50–53, 505
cognitive theories of
  development, 53–56
cohort effects, 29–31
  personality development and,
    76–77
  pregnancy and, 30
comic strips, 454
commercials, 453
commitment, 538
competence
  androgyny and, 442–44,
    445–46
  culture and, 546, 547
competence testing, 188–89
complex stepfamily, 248
component, 185
componential analysis, 185–87
computer(s)
  information processing by,
    168–69
  sex differences and, 462–63
computer dating questionnaire,
  297
concrete-operational thought,
  54, 128–29
conditional relationships, 131
conflict
  divorce and, 244
  parent-adolescent, 223–27
conformity, and peer pressure,
  268–70
connectedness, 237–38, 424–27
contextual world view, 47–48,
  49

continuity vs. discontinuity
  in adolescence, 24–26
  in adolescent disorders,
    642–46
contraceptives, 470–72
convergent thinking, 197
Coopersmith Self-Esteem
  Inventory, 401
correlation coefficient, 74
creativity, 196–98
crime, 600–11
"critical periods," 447
cross-sectional study, 75
crowds, 288, 289, 290–91
crystallized intelligence, 183
cults, 516–19, 539
cultural estrangement, 624–25
culture, 348–87
  achievement and, 363,
    535–44
  adolescent development and,
    350–52, 363–68
  adolescent groups and, 288
  alcohol abuse and, 598–99
  ecological model of
    development and, 350–52
  ethnicity and, 374–79
  family relationships and,
    216–17
  free time and, 352–55
  identity and, 422
  interests and, 356
  language and, 355–60
  media, 379–87
  morality and, 363–64
  music and, 384–87
  peers and, 265–66
  rites of passage and, 364–66
  sexual behavior and, 364–65
  social class and, 368–74
  subculture of poverty, 371–73
  television and, 379–84
culture-fair intelligence tests,
  189–90

D

dating, 294–300
  age and, 295
  family and, 298, 300
  functions of, 294
  going steady, 295
  identity and, 429
  incidence of, 295

peers and, 300
sex differences and
  similarities, 298
deception, 134–35
deductive reasoning, 130–32
defense mechanisms, 60–61
Defining Issue Test (DIT), 497
delay of gratification, 532–35
delinquency, 600–11
  defined, 600
  developmental course of,
    606–7
  Erikson's view on, 602
  explanations for, 600–2
  family and, 604–5
  intervention programs for,
    607–11
  peers and, 603
  self-control and, 602–3
  social class and, 603
dependent variables, 73
depressants, 582–83, 585, 586,
  592
depression, 628–29, 630–31
desatellization, 233
desegregation, 340–41
despair, 64
development. *See also specific*
  types of development
  age and, 28
  defined, 22
  individual differences in,
    26–28
developmental periods, 31–34
  adolescent, 33
  adulthood, 33–34
  childhood, 31
  infancy, 31
  prenatal, 31
  youth, 33
developmental processes, 34–35
developmental stages, 23–24
  Erikson's, 61–64
  Freud's, 57–59
  Piaget's, 53–55
developmental tasks, 24
developmental theories, 48–68
  behavioral, 49–53
  cognitive, 53–56
  psychoanalytic, 57–66
dieting, 633–38, 639
Differential Aptitude Tests, 182
diffusion, 63

middle, 368
neighborhoods and, 370
personality and, 373
reading and, 369
school and, 338–40, 369
subculture of poverty, 371–73
television and, 369
upper, 368
social cognition, 146–59
egocentrism, 149–50,
151–52, 154
family changes and, 215–16
impression formation, 153–56
nature of, 146–49
perspective taking, 137, 150,
153, 154
social behavior and, 158
social monitoring and,
156–57
social comparison, 272–73
social competence
androgyny and, 442–44,
445–46
culture and, 546, 547
social conventional reasoning,
502–3, 510–11
social development, and peer
relations, 264–65
social information processing,
148–49, 273, 274–75
social intelligence, 191, 192–93
social interaction, in school,
335–36. See also
adolescent groups; peer(s)
socialization
reciprocal, 208
television and, 383–84
social knowledge, 273–74
social-learning theory, 50–53
social-mold theories, 208
social monitoring, 156–57
social skills, 275–79
social time, 28
sociocultural model of
abnormality, 642

SOMPA (System of
Multicultural Pluralistic
Assessment), 191
spatial abilities, and puberty,
118
stagnation, 63
standardized tests, 70
Stanford-Binet tests, 178–79
state anxiety, 530
State-Trait Anxiety Inventory,
530
statistical model of
abnormality, 641
status position, 284
STDs (sexually transmitted
diseases), 472–73
stepfamilies, 248
step-procreation, 248
stereotype, 19–20
sex-role, 460–61
stereotyped individual, 432
stimulants, 582–83, 584, 585,
586, 590, 592
storm and stress view of
adolescence, 14, 225
strategy
correlational, 74–75
experimental, 72–73
quasi-experimental, 73–74
subculture of poverty, 371–73
success, hope of, 529. See also
achievement
suicide, 629–33
supernatural model of
abnormality, 640–41
support, 538–39
surveys, 69–70
systematic observation, 68–69

T

teachers, 328–32
achievement and, 540–44
attitudes of, 329, 339–40
authoritarian, 329, 331–32

authoritative, 329
career development and,
561–62
characteristics of, 328–30
laissez-faire, 329
sex education and, 477–78
sex roles and, 331–32,
451–53
social class and, 339–40
television, 379–84
adolescent exposure to, 383
for early adolescents, 384
family relationship and, 217
functions of, 381–83
sex roles and, 453–54
social class and, 369
as socialization agent,
383–84
violence on, 382, 383
teratogens, 644
test, standardized, 70. See also
intelligence testing
testes, 98, 102
testosterone, 99, 445
textbooks, 340
THC, 586
therapy, family systems
approach to, 211
thinking, 167. See also
cognitive development;
information processing
convergent, 197
divergent, 197
thyroid gland, 102
time, 28–29
tobacco, 582–83, 584, 585,
586, 590
top-dog phenomenon, 319
trait anxiety, 530
transactive discussion, 498
treatment, defined, 330
trust versus mistrust, 63
twin studies, 88–89, 90
two-factor theory, 183

U

underachievement, 622–24
undifferentiated category, 442
unemployment, 571
upper class, 368. See also
social class

V

"Valley Girl" language,
357–60
values, 356, 511–14. See also
moral development
values-clarification programs,
510–11
variables
dependent, 73
independent, 72
vicarious learning, 51
violence, on television, 382, 383
vocational choice theories,
552–55

W

Wechsler Adult Intelligence
Scale (WAIS), 179–81
Wechsler Intelligence Scale for
Children (WISC-R),
179–81, 191
weight control, 633–38, 639
work, 568–72
school and, 569–71
unemployment, 571
working mothers, 249–51
world views, 47–48, 49

Y

youth, as developmental period,
33
youth culture, 356–60
Youth Employment and
Demonstration Projects
Act (YEDPA), 572
youth movements, 360, 361